MAUDSLEY & BURN'S
LAND LAW: CASES & MATERIALS

MAUDSLEY & BURN'S
LAND LAW

CASES & MATERIALS

Ninth Edition

E H BURN BCL, MA

Barrister and Honorary Bencher of Lincoln's Inn
Emeritus Student of Christ Church, Oxford
Formerly Professor of Law in the City University

J CARTWRIGHT BCL, MA

Solicitor
Student and Tutor in Law, Christ Church, Oxford
Professor of the Law of Contract, University of Oxford
Professor of Anglo-American Private Law, University of Leiden

OXFORD
UNIVERSITY PRESS

OXFORD
UNIVERSITY PRESS

Great Clarendon Street, Oxford OX2 6DP

Oxford University Press is a department of the University of Oxford.
It furthers the University's objective of excellence in research, scholarship,
and education by publishing worldwide in

Oxford New York

Auckland Cape Town Dar es Salaam Hong Kong Karachi
Kuala Lumpur Madrid Melbourne Mexico City Nairobi
New Delhi Shanghai Taipei Toronto

With offices in

Argentina Austria Brazil Chile Czech Republic France Greece
Guatemala Hungary Italy Japan Poland Portugal Singapore
South Korea Switzerland Thailand Turkey Ukraine Vietnam

Oxford is a registered trade mark of Oxford University Press
in the UK and in certain other countries

Published in the United States
by Oxford University Press Inc., New York

British Library Cataloguing in Publication Data

Data available

Library of Congress Cataloging in Publication Data
Burn, Edward Hector.
    Maudsley and Burn's land law : cases and materials / E.H. Burn, J. Cartwright.—9th ed.
        p. cm.
    Includes index.
    ISBN 978-0-19-922617-7
    1. Real property—Great Britain—Cases.   I. Cartwright, John, MA.
II. Title.   III. Title: Land law.
    KD829.B868 2009
    346.4104'3—dc22   2009018049

Typeset by Newgen Imaging Systems (P) Ltd., Chennai, India
Printed in Great Britain
on acid-free paper by
Ashford Colour Press Ltd., Gosport, Hampshire

ISBN 978-0-19-922617-7

10 9 8 7 6 5 4 3 2 1

PREFACE

It is some 40 years since Ronald Maudsley and I wrote *Land Law: Cases and Materials* together. Maudsley died in 1981, and the time has now come for me to hand the book on. Fortunately, I have been able to persuade John Cartwright, Student of Christ Church and Professor of the Law of Contract in the University of Oxford, to take on this ninth edition. He is a long-standing friend of mine, my old pupil and successor as law tutor at Christ Church. We have worked together on this edition and have made use of the 17th edition of *Cheshire and Burn's Modern Law of Real Property* with which John Cartwright is also now associated.

EHB

The object of *Land Law: Cases and Materials* remains the same as in the first edition in 1967, the preface to which included the following paragraphs:

This book is intended to provide the most important readings in Land Law which cannot, in the nature of things, be included in textbooks. It contains a selection of cases and statutes, extracts from books, articles and other materials, linked by passages of explanation and comment—and asks some questions. ...

Our experience as teachers has been that Land Law is a subject which students find difficult. It is a subject in which the study of authoritative sources is especially important, yet one in which students seem reluctant to leave the comforting orderliness of the textbook. It is a subject which must be understood and not merely memorized. We have selected for this book materials which we hope will help students to understand the principles and doctrines of Land Law, and will make their introduction to the sources less forbidding and more interesting. In our selection of cases, we have not always chosen the most recent ones on the point, but have preferred those which provide the best statement of the principles. We have, however, attempted to refer to all relevant material available ...

Over the years which have followed the publication of the first edition, however, this book has changed as Land Law itself has developed, and as the scope of university courses in Land Law have changed. In 1967 registered land was a short final chapter: universal compulsory registration of title was still 23 years away, and the Land Registry's 'strategic objective' of a complete register and the introduction of electronic conveyancing were not even on the horizon. The Law Commission was in its infancy and had not yet opened the floodgates of reform proposals in the field of land law. Human rights were not discussed in the context of land law. On the other hand, much space was devoted in the book to settlements and perpetuities, which were still studied in detail as part of the fundamental building blocks of the law of real property. By contrast, the House of Lords had not yet begun to explore the possibilities of the constructive trust in the context of the family home; and proprietary estoppel was still relatively undeveloped and could be discussed in fewer than 10 pages (using just two cases). Of course, there have been significant changes in the scope and structure of the book in successive editions. In the second edition registered land acquired its proper, prominent place in the presentation of the modern land law; and the treatment of all areas has been developed on the basis of developments in legislation and case law, taking fully into account the direction in which land law doctrines are moving in the light both of reform proposals and of the lead given by the courts.

For this edition we have undertaken a significant reassessment of the structure of the book. The chapters are now re-ordered so as to take the reader through an introduction to basic concepts of land law, the system of registration of title and the significance of (adverse) possession in the modern law, before exploring in detail the freehold and leasehold estates in land; equitable beneficial interests in land; and other legal and equitable interests in land. In devising this structure we have drawn on our work for the 17th edition of *Cheshire and Burn*, to which this book constitutes a companion volume. Throughout, however, we provide cross-reference also to other standard textbooks.

In the course of this restructuring we have had to lose some old friends. Strict Settlements and Perpetuities no longer have their own chapters, although we have still included sufficient reference to them to ensure that the reader sees their significance. We have also reduced the discussion of (and extracts from) the Land Registration Act 1925, except where it is necessary to understand the current law under the 2002 Act. On the other hand, this has allowed us to include more materials on, or give more prominence to, topics such as constructive trusts and proprietary estoppel, commonhold, and human rights, together with extracts from the Law Commission's most significant current proposals. We have also expanded some of our introductions and comments within the chapters, which are designed not to substitute for a textbook but to highlight the basic points in a topic to assist the reader who is starting upon a subject.

The development of land law continues. Since the last edition, Parliament has reformed the law of commons, and of consumer credit; has abolished the landlord's common law remedy of distress (but has put in place an equivalent procedure for the benefit of commercial landlords); and has extended 'home rights' to civil partners. Further steps have also been taken towards the introduction of electronic conveyancing. And (of particular relevance in the current difficult economic situation) a new pre-action protocol has been introduced into the Civil Procedure Rules to discourage hasty repossessions of mortgaged homes. The Law Commission has proposed reforms of the rental sector of the housing market; of the landlord's rights of termination of tenancies (effectively to abolish forfeiture); and of the consequences of breakdown of cohabitation; and has—at long last—published its consultation paper on the reform of easements, covenants and profits à prendre.

There have been significant developments in judge-made law. The House of Lords has set down guidelines to determine the beneficial interests in jointly-held land; twice given guidance on the scope of operation of proprietary estoppel; clarified the nature of a '*Bruton* tenancy'; interpreted the anti-avoidance provisions under the

Landlord and Tenant (Covenants) Act 1995; reassessed the circumstances in which there can be an easement of parking; and considered the law on town and village greens.

The Court of Appeal has considered the creation and nature of the parties' interests under a common-intention constructive trust, and the relationship between the constructive trust and proprietary estoppel (although the answers given to both questions are not entirely consistent with the approaches taken or dicta expressed in the House of Lords in the same period); the scope of the rule in *Wheeldon v Burrows* and its relationship with section 62 of the Law of Property Act 1925; the appropriate remedies for infringement of an easement; and the circumstances in which a breach is capable of remedy in section 146 of the Law of Property Act 1925 (disapproving its own narrow approach in *Scala House & District Property Co Ltd v Forbes*).

In addition, the courts at all levels, from the Grand Chamber of the European Court of Human Rights through all levels of our national courts, have considered the impact of the European Convention on Human Rights, and our own Human Rights Act, on many areas of land law, including adverse possession, the landlord's right to possession, the interpretation of the 'exceptional circumstances' test in *Re Citro* in balancing the claims of the creditors and the bankrupt's family under a trust of land, and the exercise of the mortgagee's power of sale.

We would particularly like to thank Marilyn Kennedy-McGregor, Barrister of Gray's Inn and Lincoln's Inn, for her valuable comments and advice. We would also like to thank our new publishers for undertaking the compilation of the various tables and for their ready and expert help at all times.

This edition purports to state the law as it was on 31 January 2009, but more recent developments have been incorporated where space permitted.

E.H.B.

J.C.

CONTENTS

PART I. BASIC CONCEPTS

PART II. FREEHOLD AND LEASEHOLD ESTATES IN LAND

PART III. EQUITABLE BENEFICIAL INTERESTS IN LAND

PART IV. OTHER LEGAL AND EQUITABLE
INTERESTS IN LAND

9. COVENANTS BETWEEN FREEHOLDERS

10. MORTGAGES

ACKNOWLEDGEMENTS

Grateful acknowledgement is made to all the authors and publishers of copyright material that appears in this book, and in particular to the following for permission to reprint material from the sources indicated:

Extracts from unreported case reports, Law Commission Reports, Consultation papers and documents; Working Papers; Court of Appeal case reports; National Statistics Reports; Ministry of Justice website; Home Office reports and statistics are Crown copyright material and are reproduced under Class Licence Number C2006010631 with the permission of the Controller of OPSI and the Queen's Printer. Land Registry forms and register of title are Crown copyright and are reproduced with kind permission of the Land Registry.

Estates Gazette for extracts from *Estates Gazette* (EG), *Estates Gazette Law Reports* (EGLR) *and Estates Gazette Digest of Cases* (EGD)

Incorporated Council of Law Reporting for extracts from *Appeal Cases* (AC), *Chancery Appeal Cases* (Ch App Cas), *Chancery Division* (Ch), *Family Division* (Fam), *King's Bench Division* (KB), *Queen's Bench Division* (QB) and *Weekly Law Reports* (WLR)

Jordan Publishing for extracts from *Family Law Reports* (FLR)

Reed Elsevier (UK) Ltd trading as Lexis Nexis Butterworths for extracts from *Family Court Reports* (FCR) and *All England Law Reports* (All ER), *New Law Journal*, S. Bridge (2007) 157 NLJ 54 and H. W. Wilkinson (1979) 129 NLJ 523

Oxford University Press for extracts from *Cheshire and Burn's Modern Law of Real Property*, 17th edition by E.H. Burn and J. Cartwright (2006), *Maudsley & Burn's Trusts and Trustees: Cases & Materials*, 7th edition by G.Virgo and E.H. Burn (2008) and *Real Property Law* by G.R.Y. Radcliffe (1933)

Sweet & Maxwell Ltd for extracts from *Conveyancer and Property Lawyer*, M. Friend and J. Newton [1982] Conv 213, M.Dixon [2007] Conv 456, *Law Quarterly Review*, R.E. Megarry (1965) 81 LQR, P.V. Baker (1968) 84 LQR 22; *Restrictive Covenants Affecting Land* (9th edn), C.H.S. Preston and G. Newsom, 1998; *Snell's Equity* (30th edn), J. McGhee, 2000; *European Human Rights Reports* (EHRR) and *Property, Planning and Compensation Reports* (P & CR)

Thomson Reuters Australia for extracts from *Commonwealth Law Reports* (CLR)

News International Syndication Ltd for extracts from *The Times*, *Times Law Reports*

Willan Publishing for extracts from *Land Law Issues, Debates, Policy*, 2002, Editor L. Tee, Author S. Bridge

Every effort has been made to trace and contact copyright holders prior to publication but this has not been possible in every case. If notified, the publisher will undertake to rectify any errors or omissions at the earliest opportunity.

Parliamentary copyright material is reproduced with the permission of the Controller of Her Majesty's Stationery Office on behalf of Parliament. Other Crown copyright material is reproduced under Class Licence Number C01P0000148 with the permission of the Controller of HMSO and the Queen's Printer.

LIST OF ABBREVIATIONS

Statutes and Rules

AEA	Administration of Estates Act
CA	Companies Act
CLRA	Commonhold and Leasehold Reform Act
CPR	Civil Procedure Rules
ECHR	European Convention on Human Rights (Convention for the Protection of Human Rights and Fundamental Freedoms)
FA	Finance Act
HA	Housing Act
HRA	Human Rights Act
IHTA	Inheritance Tax Act
L & T(C)A	Landlord and Tenant (Covenants) Act
LCA	Land Charges Act
LLCA	Local Land Charges Act
LP(MP)A	Law of Property (Miscellaneous Provisions) Act
LPA	Law of Property Act
LRA	Land Registration Act
LRR	Land Registration Rules
LTA	Landlord and Tenant Act
P & AA	Perpetuities and Accumulations Act
SLA	Settled Land Act
TA	Trustee Act
TCPA	Town and Country Planning Act
TLATA	Trusts of Land and Appointment of Trustees Act

Books

Anson	*Anson's Law of Contract* (28th edn, 2002)
Barnsley	*Barnsley's Conveyancing Law and Practice* (4th edn, 1996)
C & B	Cheshire and Burn's *Modern Law of Real Property* (17th edn, 2006)
CFF	Cheshire, Fifoot and Furmston's *Law of Contract* (15th edn, 2006)
Cousins	Cousins and Clarke, *The Law of Mortgages* (2nd edn, 2001)
Emmet	*Emmet and Farrand on Title* (looseleaf)
Farrand	*Contract and Conveyance* (2nd edn, 1973; 4th edn, 1983)
Fisher and Lightwood	Fisher and Lightwood's *Law of Mortgage* (12th edn, 2008)

Gale   *Gale on Easements* (18th edn, 2008)
Gray   Gray and Gray, *Elements of Land Law* (5th edn, 2008)
H & B   Harpum and Bignell, *Registered Land
                             Law and Practice under the Land Registration
                             Act 2002* (2004)
H & M   Hanbury and Martin, *Modern Equity* (17th edn, 2005)
Holdsworth   *A History of English Law* (1903–1972)
M & W   Megarry & Wade, *The Law of Real Property*
                             (7th edn, 2008)
MM   *Megarry's Manual of the Law of Real Property*
                             (8th edn, 2002)
Preston & Newsom   *Restrictive Covenants Affecting Freehold Land*
                             (9th edn, 1998)
R & R   Ruoff and Roper, *The Law and Practice of
                             Registered Conveyancing* (looseleaf)
R & R (1991)   Ruoff and Roper, *The Law and Practice of
                             Registered Conveyancing* (1991 edn)
Smith   *Property Law* (6th edn, 2008)
Snell   *Snell's Equity* (31st edn, 2005)
Treitel   Treitel, *The Law of Contract* (12th edn, 2007)
W & C   Wolstenholme and Cherry, *Conveyancing
                             Statutes* (13th edn, 1972)
W & H   Whitehouse and Hassall, *Trusts of Land, Trustee
                             Delegation and the Trustee Act 2000* (2nd edn, 2001)
Waldock   *Law of Mortgage* (2nd edn, 1950)

TABLE OF STATUTES

Page references printed in **bold** type indicate where the Act is set out in part or in full.

TABLE OF STATUTORY INSTRUMENTS

Page references printed in **bold** type indicate where the Statutory Instrument is set out in part or in full.

TABLE OF CASES

Page references printed in **bold** type indicate where the case is set out in part or in full.

PART I
BASIC CONCEPTS

1

INTRODUCTORY TOPICS

I. THE SCOPE OF LAND LAW

Land law is concerned with the creation, transfer and protection of rights in and over land. It is often referred to as the law of *real property* which signifies, first, that it is part of the law of property (as opposed to the law governing personal rights, such as the law of contract); and, secondly, that it governs land rather than chattels ('real' property rather than personal property[1]).

---

[1] The language is a legacy of history: 'real property' is so called because, during the formative period of the principles of land law, land was the only form of property which was the subject of actions to obtain specific recovery—the 'real actions'. But the scope of 'real property' is not identical with rights in land, since the lease was not characterised as real property but as a form of personal property (a 'chattel real') for the very reason that the real actions were not available to protect the tenant: C & B, pp. 28, 36–8; below, p. 324.

A. PROPERTY RIGHTS AND PERSONAL RIGHTS[2]

In broad terms,[3] one can say that property rights relating to land are rights in or over the land itself, such as the right to the freehold, or a right of way over a neighbour's land (an *easement*[4]). In their purest form, property rights are rights *in rem*, rights which attach to the property so that they are enforceable against everyone who comes later to that land—the person who acquires an interest in the land or who is seeking to deny the claimant's exercise of the property right. We shall see later in this chapter[5] that English law distinguishes between legal and equitable rights in and over land, and that certain rights—particularly equitable rights—are not automatically enforceable against everyone who comes to the land but their enforceability depends, for example, on whether the right was registered, or whether the defendant had notice of the right. In this respect, the rules governing the circumstances in which rights are binding on the successor to the land vary according to whether the title to the land is registered or unregistered.[6] But for our purposes we can still categorise such rights as property rights, since they are inherently capable of binding those who come to the land. This contrasts with purely personal rights, which are rights against a person, generated by the act of that person and giving rise to obligations owed by the particular person to the claimant. Obligations arising from contract, or from tort, are personal: the defendant is bound to the claimant because he has undertaken the contractual obligation, or committed a tortious wrong against the claimant.

The significance of the distinction between property rights and personal rights is whether they benefit or bind third parties, and the nature of the remedies to which the different rights give rise. Many rights in or over land will have their origin in a contract between the parties who owned the relevant parcels of land at the time when the right was created. A landowner may give his neighbour a right of way (an *easement*); or undertake in favour of his neighbour not to use his premises for business purposes (a *restrictive covenant*). Or he may grant another person exclusive possession of his house for a particular period (a *lease*), or grant the bank a *mortgage* over the house in return for a loan. If a dispute arises as to the enforceability of these rights as between the original parties themselves, the law of contract may offer a solution—it may not be necessary to consider the rights in their quality as

---

[2] C & B, pp. 152–4.

[3] For further discussion of the nature of property rights, see Lawson and Rudden, *The Law of Property*; Bright and Dewar, *Land Law Themes and Perspectives*, chaps 1 (K. Gray and S. F. Gray), 18 (P. Birks); Tee, *Land Law Issues, Debates, Policy*, chap. 1 (M. Dixon); Harris, *Property and Justice*; Honoré, *Oxford Essays in Jurisprudence*, (ed. Guest), p. 107 ff.; Rudden, *Oxford Essays in Jurisprudence* (3rd series, ed. Eekelaar and Bell), pp. 239 ff.

[4] Below, chap. 9.

[5] Below, p. 13. For the argument that equitable estates are rights *in personam* rather than rights *in rem* because of the rule that they do not bind those who come to the property without notice of the right (or, in the modern law, if the right is not registered) see C & B, pp. 56–8.

[6] For the difference between registered and unregistered land, see below, pp. 56 ff.

property rights at all, the personal nature of the rights being adequate to give a remedy to the aggrieved claimant. Sometimes, even as between the parties themselves, land law will enhance the remedies—for example, the (property) rights granted by way of security under a mortgage carry particular remedial consequences for the parties, beyond the purely contractual arrangements for the repayment of the loan.[7] But the point at which one is generally forced to move to the law of property in order to analyse the claimant's rights and remedies is when the original party who undertook the burden of the right has transferred the land over which the right was created and the claimant seeks to enforce his right against the successor. Contractual rights can benefit third parties—either by way of assignment of the benefit of the right[8] or, since the enactment of the Contracts (Rights of Third Parties) Act 1999,[9] if the contract itself gives enforceable rights to third parties. But a third party cannot generally by bound by a contractual obligation undertaken by another person without himself agreeing to undertake a (new) obligation. Land law offers the claimant the opportunity to bind the successor simply because he now has the land over which the right was originally created, or at least because he has acquired the land subject to rights which were registered or of which he had notice when he acquired it.

For rights to bind a successor by virtue of his coming to the land it must be shown that the right was a recognised property right. This was made clear by Lord WILBERFORCE in **National Provincial Bank Ltd v Ainsworth** [1965] AC 1175 at 1247–8:

Before a right or an interest can be admitted into the category of property, or of a right affecting property, it must be definable, identifiable by third parties, capable in its nature of assumption by third parties, and have some degree of permanence or stability.

His Lordship went on to hold that a wife's right to occupy the matrimonial home was not a property right, and therefore could not constitute an overriding interest under s. 70 of the Land Registration Act 1925,[10] which might bind a successor to her husband's registered title to the property (at 1261):

This Act is a registration Act concerned (in this instance) to provide that certain rights are to be binding without registration and without the necessity for actual notice. To ascertain what 'rights' come within this provision, one must look outside the Land Registration Act and see what rights affect purchasers under the general law. To suppose that the subsection makes any right, of howsoever a personal character, which a person in occupation may have, an overriding interest by which a purchaser is bound, would involve two consequences: first that this Act is, in this respect, bringing about a substantive change in real property law by making personal rights bind purchasers; second, that there is a difference *as to the nature of the rights by which a purchaser may be bound* between registered and unregistered land; for purely personal rights including the wife's right to stay in the house (if my analysis of this is correct) cannot affect purchasers of unregistered land even with notice. One may have to accept that there is a

---

[7] Below, chap. 10.   [8] LPA 1925, s. 136; below, p. 777.
[9] Below, p. 771.   [10] See now LRA 2002, Sch. 3, para. 2; below, p. 196.

difference between unregistered land and registered land as regards what kind of notice binds a purchaser, or what kind of inquiries a purchaser has to make. But there is no warrant in the terms of this paragraph or elsewhere in the Act for supposing that the nature of the rights which are to bind a purchaser is to be different, excluding personal rights in one case, including them in another. The whole frame of section 70, with the list that it gives of interests, or rights, which are overriding, shows that it is made against a background of interests or rights whose nature an a whose transmissible character is known, or ascertainable, aliunde, i.e., under other statutes or under the common law. So, if the right of a deserted wife is a purely personal claim against her husband, not specifically related to the house in question, but merely, at its highest, to be provided with a home, there is no difficulty in seeing that this type of right cannot, any more than any purely contractual right, be an overriding interest.

B. THE MEANING OF 'LAND'

(i) Fixtures[11]

Since land and chattels are treated differently by the law and since a chattel may, by being affixed to land, become part of the land, it is necessary to have a test to determine whether or not such a change has taken place. For example, a brick in a builder's yard is a chattel; once used to build a wall, it becomes part of the land; and if the wall is knocked down the bricks become chattels again. When land is sold, the conveyance includes the land but not the chattels,[12] but includes those things which were once chattels but which have become land.[13]

The question whether a chattel remains a chattel or has become part of the land can arise in many contexts, such as whether it passes to a purchaser[14] or sub-purchaser[15]

[11] C & B, pp. 156–161; Gray, paras 1.2.47–1.2.68; M & W, chap. 23; MM, pp. 19–24; Smith, pp. 82–88; LPA 1925, s. 205(1)(ix) as amended by TLATA 1996, s. 25(2), Sch. 4; SLA 1925, s. 117(1)(ix) as amended by TLATA 1996, s. 25(1), Sch. 3, para. 2(13)(a); TA 1925, s. 68(6) as amended by TLATA 1996, s. 25(2), Sch. 4; LCA 1972 s. 17(1); Interpretation Act 1978, s. 5, Sch. 1.

[12] By LPA 1925, s. 62, p. 664, below, a conveyance of land includes buildings, erections and fixtures, in the absence of a contrary intention: *HE Dibble Ltd v Moore* [1970] 2 QB 181 (greenhouses resting on own weight on concrete dollies held to be removable chattels).

[13] See *Melluish v BMI (No 3) Ltd* [1996] AC 454 (contractual term that object shall remain a chattel not decisive: 'the concept of a fixture which remains personal or removable property is a contradiction in terms and an impossibility in law; [1995] Ch 90 at 115, per Dillon LJ in CA).

[14] *Colegrave v Dias Santos* (1823) 2 B & C 76, 107 ER 311 (fixtures, including those which a tenant could have removed, passed on sale of freehold); *Phillips v Lamdin* [1949] 2 KB 33 (purchaser entitled to reinstatement of Adam door removed by vendor); *Hynes v Vaughan* (1985) 50 P & CR 444 (purchaser not entitled to chrysanthemum growing frame and sprinkler system); *Deen v Andrews* (1986) 52 P & CR 17 (purchaser not entitled to large prefabricated greenhouse bolted to concrete plinth resting by its own weight). For the effect of hire-purchase agreements, see (1963) 27 Conv (NS) 30 (A. G. Guest and J. Lever); [1990] Conv 275 (G. McCormack).

[15] *Berkley v Poulett* (1976) 241 EG 911, 242 EG 39. Cf. *Hamp v Bygrave* (1982) 266 EG 720 (stone and lead garden ornaments resting on own weight held to be fixtures because the vendors regarded them as 'features of, and part and parcel of, the garden'; alternatively, if the ornaments were chattels, the vendors were estopped from denying that they formed part of the sale); [1983] LSG 1773 (H. W. Wilkinson). *Berkley v*

on a sale of the land; whether it is included as part of the security on a mortgage of the land,[16] whether it is owned by the estate of a tenant for life of settled land or passes to the remainderman,[17] whether it is owned by a tenant for years or by the freeholder,[18] whether it passes on a death as realty or personalty,[19] and whether a drainpipe, placed underground in the exercise of an easement of drainage, remains the property of the party entitled to the easement.[20]

A related but separate question follows.[21] There are some occasions in which the owner of a one-time chattel may remove it even though it has now become part of the land.

Elitestone Ltd v Morris
[1997] 1 WLR 687 (HL, **Lords Browne-Wilkinson, Lloyd of Berwick, Nolan, Nicholls of Birkenhead** and **Clyde**)[22]

Lord Lloyd of Berwick: My Lords, the plaintiffs, Elitestone Ltd., are the freehold owners of land known as Holt's Field, Murton, near Swansea. The land is divided into 27 lots. The defendant, Mr Morris, is the occupier of a chalet or bungalow on Lot No. 6. It is not known for certain when the chalet was built. But it seems likely that it was before 1945. Mr Morris has lived there since 1971.

Poulett was not cited. See generally [1983] NZLJ 256 (H. W. Wilkinson); *Kennedy v Secretary of State for Wales* [1996] EGCS 17 (three massive ormulu bronze chandeliers and carillon turret clock at Neo-Gothic Grade II listed Leighton Hall, Welshpool, held to be fixtures).

[16] *Holland v Hodgson* (1872) LR 7 CP 328; *Hobson v Gorringe* [1897] 1 Ch 182 (machinery affixed. The judgment of A. L. Smith LJ contains a resumé of the cases up to that time); *Lyon & Co v London City and Midland Bank* [1903] 2 KB 135 (tip-up seats screwed to bolts fastened to floor and hired to mortgagors held to be chattels); *Vaudeville Electric Cinema Ltd v Muriset* [1923] 2 Ch 74 (similar seats owned by mortgagor held to be land); *Reynolds v Ashby & Sons* [1904] AC 466 (machines bolted to the floor held to be land); *Hulme v Brigham* [1943] KB 152 (heavy printing machinery resting by its own weight held by Birkett J to be chattels); *Botham v TSB Bank plc* (1996) 73 P & CR D1 (CA held bathroom fittings, fitted kitchen units and sink to be fixtures, but not fitted carpets, curtains, blinds, gas fires, oven, hob, dishwasher, freezer and washing machine).

[17] *D'Eyncourt v Gregory* (1866) LR 3 Eq 382 (ornamental statues in park, resting by their weight on plinth, held to be part of realty); *Leigh v Taylor* [1902] AC 157 (tapestries stretched over canvas and tacked thereto held to remain chattels); *Re Lord Chesterfield's Settled Estates* [1911] 1 Ch 237 (proceeds of sale of ornamental wood carvings by Grinling Gibbons treated as capital money under SLA 1882).

[18] *Culling v Tufnal* (1694) Bull NP 34; *Elwes v Maw* (1802) 3 East 38, 102 ER 510 (Dutch barn resting by own weight in hollow of brick foundations remained a chattel); *Webb v Frank Bevis Ltd* [1940] 1 All ER 247 (similarly a corrugated iron building held to floor by iron strips); cf. *Elitestone Ltd v Morris*, below (27 chalets resting on timber and block footing held to be part of land).

[19] *Bain v Brand* (1876) 1 App Cas 762 (machinery in colliery passed to heir and not to executor); *Re Whaley* [1908] 1 Ch 615 (pictures and tapestries in dining-room designed as a 'complete specimen of Elizabethan dwelling-house' passed under devise of house and not under bequest of chattels).

[20] *Simmons v Midford* [1969] 2 Ch 415 (plaintiffs drainpipe under road held to be chattel with which neighbour claiming an easement of drainage could not interfere); cf. *Montague v Long* (1972) 24 P & CR 240 (bridge over river).

[21] The two questions are not always kept separate: *Leigh v Taylor* [1902] AC 157; cf. Lords Halsbury and Macnaghten with Lord Shand.

[22] (1997) 147 NLJ 1031 (H. W. Wilkinson); [1997] CLJ 498 (S. Bridge).

The plaintiffs acquired the freehold in 1989 with a view to redevelopment. On 30 April 1991 they issued proceedings in the Swansea County Court claiming possession against all 27 occupiers. Five lead actions were selected, including that in which Mr Morris was defendant. They came on for trial before Mr Bidder, sitting as an assistant recorder, in November 1994. The assistant recorder had a number of issues to decide. He dealt with them in a most impressive manner. So far as Mr Morris is concerned, his defence was that he is a tenant from year-to-year, that he occupies the premises as his residence, and is therefore entitled to the protection of the Rent Act 1966. He claims a declaration to that effect.

The assistant recorder held, correctly, at the end of what was necessarily a very lengthy judgment that the question in Mr Morris's case turned on whether or not the bungalow formed part of the realty. If it did then Mr Morris was entitled to his declaration...

[The assistant recorder held that the bungalow formed part of the realty, but the Court of Appeal disagreed.] The photographs show very clearly what the bungalow is, and especially what it is not. It is *not* like a Portakabin, or mobile home. The nature of the structure is such that it could not be taken down and re-erected elsewhere. It could only be removed by a process of demolition. This, as will appear later, is a factor of great importance in the present case. If a structure can only be enjoyed in situ, and is such that it cannot be removed in whole or in sections to another site, there is at least a strong inference that the purpose of placing the structure on the original site was that it should form part of the realty at that site, and therefore cease to be a chattel....

The sole remaining issue for your Lordships is whether Mr Morris's bungalow did indeed become part of the land, or whether it has remained a chattel ever since it was first constructed before 1945.

It will be noticed that in framing the issue for decision I have avoided the use of the word 'fixture.' There are two reasons for this. The first is that 'fixture,' though a hallowed term in this branch of the law, does not always bear the same meaning in law as it does in everyday life. In ordinary language one thinks of a fixture as being something fixed to a building. One would not ordinarily think of the building itself as a fixture. Thus in *Boswell v Crucible Steel Co* [1925] 1 KB 119 the question was whether plate glass windows which formed part of the wall of a warehouse were landlord's fixtures within the meaning of a repairing covenant. Atkin LJ said, at p. 123:

> '...I am quite satisfied that they are not landlord's fixtures, and for the simple reason that they are not fixtures at all in the sense in which that term is generally understood. A fixture, as that term is used in connection with the house, means something which has been affixed to the freehold as accessory to the house. It does not include things which were made part of the house itself in the course of its construction.'

Yet in *Billing v Pill* [1954] 1 QB 70, 75 Lord Goddard CJ said:

> 'What is a fixture? The commonest fixture is a house which is built into the land, so that in law it is regarded as part of the land. The house and the land are one thing.'

There is another reason. The term fixture is apt to be a source of misunderstanding owing to the existence of the category of so called 'tenants' fixtures' (a term used to cover both trade fixtures and ornamental fixtures), which are fixtures in the full sense of the word (and therefore part of the realty) but which may nevertheless be removed by the tenant in the course of or at the end of his tenancy. Such fixtures are sometimes confused with chattels which have never become fixtures at all....

For my part I find it better in the present case to avoid the traditional twofold distinction between chattels and fixtures, and to adopt the threefold classification set out in *Woodfall, Landlord and Tenant* (looseleaf edn), vol. 1, para. 13.131:

'An object which is brought into land may be classified under one of three broad heads. It may be (a) a chattel; (b) a fixture; or (c) part and parcel of the land itself. Objects in categories (b) and (c) are treated as being part of the land.'

So the question in the present appeal is whether, when the bungalow was built, it became part and parcel of the land itself. The materials out of which the bungalow was constructed, that is to say, the timber frame walls, the feather boarding, the suspended timber floors, the chipboard ceilings, and so on, were all, of course, chattels when they were brought onto the site. Did they cease to be chattels when they were built into the composite structure? The answer to the question, as Blackburn J pointed out in *Holland v Hodgson* (1872) LR 7 CP 328, depends on the circumstances of each case, but mainly on two factors, the degree of annexation to the land, and the object of the annexation.

Degree of annexation

The importance of the degree of annexation will vary from object to object. In the case of a large object, such as a house, the question does not often arise. Annexation goes without saying. So there is little recent authority on the point, and I do not get much help from the early cases in which wooden structures have been held not to form part of the realty, such as the wooden mill in *R v Otley* (1830) 1 B & Ad 161, the wooden barn in *Wansbrough v Maton* (1836) 4 Ad & El 884 and the granary in *Wiltshear v Cottrell* (1853) 1 E & B 674. But there is a more recent decision of the High Court of Australia which is of greater assistance. In *Reid v Smith* (1905) 3 CLR 656, 659 Griffith CJ stated the question as follows:

'The short point raised in this case is whether an ordinary dwelling-house, erected upon an ordinary town allotment in a large town, but not fastened to the soil, remains a chattel or becomes part of the freehold.'

The Supreme Court of Queensland had held that the house remained a chattel. But the High Court reversed this decision, treating the answer as being almost a matter of common sense. The house in that case was made of wood, and rested by its own weight on brick piers. The house was not attached to the brick piers in any way. It was separated by iron plates placed on top of the piers, in order to prevent an invasion of white ants. There was an extensive citation of English and American authorities. It was held that the absence of any attachment did not prevent the house forming part of the realty. Two quotations, at p. 667, from the American authorities may suffice. In *Snedeker v Warring* 12 NY 170,175 (1854) Parker J said: 'A thing may be as firmly affixed to the land by gravitation as by clamps or cement. Its character may depend upon the object of its erection.' In *Goff v O'Connor* 16 Ill 421, 423 (1855), the court said:

'Houses, in common intendment of the law, are not fixtures to, but part of, the land. . . . This does not depend, in the case of houses, so much upon the particular mode of attaching, or fixing and connecting them with the land upon which they stand or rest, as it does upon the uses and purposes for which they were erected and designed.'

Purpose of annexation

Many different tests have been suggested, such as whether the object which has been fixed to the property has been so fixed for the better enjoyment of the object as a chattel, or whether it has been fixed with a view to effecting a permanent improvement of the freehold. This and similar tests are useful when one is considering an object such as a tapestry, which may or may not be fixed to a house so as to become part of the freehold: see *Leigh v Taylor* [1902] AC 157. These tests are less useful when one is considering the house itself. In the case of the house the answer is as much a matter of common sense as precise analysis. A house which is constructed in such away so as to be removable, whether as a unit, or in sections, may well remain a chattel, even though it is connected temporarily to mains services such as water and electricity. But a house which is constructed in such a way that it cannot be removed at all, save by destruction, cannot have been intended to remain as a chattel. It must have been intended to form part of the realty. I know of no better analogy than the example given by Blackburn J in *Holland v Hodgson* (1872) LR 7 CP 328, 335:

> 'Thus blocks of stone placed one on the top of another without any mortar or cement for the purpose of forming a dry stone wall would become part of the land, though the same stones, if deposited in a builder's yard and for convenience sake stacked on the top of each other in the form of a wall, would remain chattels.'

Applying that analogy to the present case, I do not doubt that when Mr Morris's bungalow was built, and as each of the timber frame walls were placed in position, they all became part of the structure, which was itself part and parcel of the land. The object of bringing the individual bits of wood onto the site seems to be so clear that the absence of any attachment to the soil (save by gravity) becomes an irrelevance.

Finally I return to the judgment of the Court of Appeal. I need say no more about the absence of attachment, which was the first of the reasons given by the Court of Appeal for reversing the assistant recorder. The second reason was the intention which the court inferred from the previous course of dealing between the parties, and in particular the uncertainty of Mr Morris's tenure. The third reason was the analogy with the shed in *Webb v Frank Bevis Ltd* [1940] 1 All ER 247, and the greenhouse in *Deen v Andrews* [1986] 1 EGLR 262.

As to the second reason the Court of Appeal may have been misled by Blackburn J's use of the word 'intention' in *Holland v Hodgson*. But as the subsequent decision of the Court of Appeal in *Hobson v Gorringe* [1897] 1 Ch 182 made clear, and as the decision of the House in *Melluish v BMI (No 3) Ltd* [1996] AC 454 put beyond question, the intention of the parties is only relevant to the extent that it can be derived from the degree and object of the annexation. The subjective intention of the parties cannot affect the question whether the chattel has, in law, become part of the freehold, any more than the subjective intention of the parties can prevent what they have called a licence from taking effect as a tenancy, if that is what in law it is: see *Street v Mountford* [1985] AC 809 [p. 383, below].

As for the third of the reasons, I have already pointed out that *Webb v Frank Bevis Ltd* does not support the Court of Appeal's conclusion, because the shed in that case was held to be a fixture, albeit a fixture which the tenant was entitled to remove.

In *Deen v Andrews* the question was whether a greenhouse was a building so as to pass to the purchaser under a contract for the sale of land 'together with the farmhouses and other buildings.' Hirst J held that it was not. He followed an earlier decision in *H E Dibble Ltd v Moore* [1970] 2 QB 181, in which the Court of Appeal, reversing the trial judge, held that a greenhouse was not an 'erection' within section 62(1) of the Law of Property Act 1925. I note that in the latter case Megaw LJ, at p. 187G, drew attention to some evidence 'that it was customary to move such greenhouses every few years to a fresh site.' It is obvious that a greenhouse which can be moved from site to site is a long way removed from a two bedroom bungalow which cannot be moved at all without being demolished.

For the above reasons I would allow this appeal and restore the order of the assistant recorder.[23]

(ii) What fixtures may be removed?

Even if a chattel is affixed to the land so as to become part of the land, the person who affixed it or his successors in title may have a right to remove it.[24] At common law, a tenant for years and a tenant for life were entitled to remove trade,[25] ornamental or domestic fixtures.[26] By Agricultural Holdings Act 1986, section 10, replacing earlier legislation, a tenant for years may also remove agricultural fixtures. As between devisee and personal representative, vendor and purchaser and mortgagor and mortgagee there is no right of removal, and the question of entitlement is dependent upon the question of annexation to the land.[27]

II. ESTATES AND INTERESTS IN LAND

A. FREEHOLD AND LEASEHOLD ESTATES

The theory of the common law is that all land is held of the Crown who is the supreme feudal lord. Subjects may hold directly of the Crown or of other subjects

---

[23] *Chelsea Yacht and Boat Co Ltd v Pope* [2000] 1 WLR 1941 (converted wooden D-Day landing craft fitted inside a steel Thames barge, moored to a pontoon and the bed and bank of a river in which it took the ground at about half tide, held not to be part of the land. 'It is common sense that a boat on a river is not part of the land. A boat, albeit one used as a home, is not of the same genus as real property' per Tuckey LJ at 1946. HL refused leave to appeal: [2000] 1 WLR 2469).

[24] *Herbert v British Railways Board* (2000) 4 L&T Rev D13 (rails and sleepers held to be landlord's fixtures).

[25] *Poole's Case* (1703) 1 Salk 368, 91 ER 320; *Climie v Wood* (1861) LR 4 Exch 328; *Penton v Robart* (1801) 2 East 88, 102 ER 302; *Wardell v Usher* (1841) 3 Scott NR 508; *Elliott v Bishop* (1854) 10 Exch 496; *Smith v City Petroleum Co Ltd* [1940] 1 All ER 260; *New Zealand Government Property Corpn v H M and S Ltd* [1982] QB 1145; *Young v Dalgety plc* [1987] 1 EGLR 116; [1987] Conv 253 (G. Kodilinye). See *Mancetter Development Ltd v Garmaston Ltd* [1986] QB 1212.

[26] *Grymes v Boweren* (1830) 6 Bing 437, 130 ER 1349; *Buckland v Butterfield* (1820) 2 Brod & Bing 54, 129 ER 878; *Beck v Rebow* (1706) 1 P Wms 94, 24 ER 309; *Leach v Thomas* (1836) 7 C & P 327, 173 ER 145; *Spyer v Phillipson* [1931] 2 Ch 183; *Colegrave v Dias Santos* (1823) 2 B & C 76, 107 ER 311; *Darby v Harris* (1841) 1 QB 895, 113 ER 1374; *Lyde v Russell* (1830) 1 B & Ad 394, 109 ER 834.

[27] See p. 6, above.

superior to themselves. Those who hold directly of the Crown are tenants in chief. Intermediate holders between the Crown and the tenants in actual possession are mesne lords.[28]

A holder of land is entitled to a number of legal rights in respect of his land-holding, and these legal rights are 'crystallised into one thing'.[29] This is the tenant's 'estate'. To ascertain his rights, it is necessary to decide what estate he owns and to know what rights and duties the law attaches to that type of estate.

Freehold estates, i.e. the estates held by freehold tenure, are those which were in use in the feudal system. In medieval times that system was the basis of the social, military and economic structure of the state; and the holding of freehold land was itself the basis of social position, wealth and power.[30] It was essential for the security of the state and of the social structure that the ownership of freehold estates should be protected; and it is not surprising that the land law was the first of the fields of private law to be undertaken by the King's Court.[31]

The freehold estates are the fee simple, fee tail, life estate and estate pur autre vie. They are freehold because they were recognised by the feudal order, because persons holding such estates in possession were recognised as standing upon a rung in the feudal ladder, and because the remedies available in the King's Court were available to the owner of such an estate and gave a claimant specific recovery. Such estates are 'real property' or 'realty', and are contrasted with the terms of years, a leasehold estate, whose owners were never on the feudal ladder; they could not protect themselves by the same actions as the freeholder; their estate as personal property, or 'personalty', passed on intestacy with chattels. A convenient way of distinguishing between freeholds and leaseholds is to note that freeholds are always of indefinite duration, leaseholds for a fixed period or such as can be made certain. But this is just a label; it does not help to understand the basic gulf between the two, which was so obvious to the medieval lawyer.

A further sub-division must also be introduced here because of the treatment of estates by the 1925 legislation. This is the distinction between legal estates and equitable interests. Pursuant to the Legislature's insistence upon the legal estate being the

---

[28] Under LRA 2002, s. 79 Her Majesty may grant an estate in fee simple absolute in possession out of demesne land to Herself, thus enabling such land to be registered: p. 134, below. For the abolition of feudal tenure in Scotland, see Abolition of Feudal Tenures etc. (Scotland) Act 2000, which came into force on 28 November 2004. The Law Commission has proposed that it should examine the case for reform of the remaining feudal elements of English land law: Ninth Programme of Law Reform 2005 (Law Com No. 293), paras 1.9, 3.10–3.13. However, this is now under reconsideration and will be put forward again for consideration as a possible project for the Eleventh Programme of Law Reform: Law Commission Forty-Second Annual Report 2007–08 (Law Com No. 310), para. 6.26. See also (2008) 124 LQR 586 (E. Nugee).

[29] Hargreaves, *Introduction to Land Law* (4th edn, 1963), p. 46.

[30] In Victorian times, see the conversation between Major Grantly and his father, Archdeacon Grantly, in the *Last Chronicle of Barset*, by Anthony Trollope (1867), chap. 58: ' "I wonder people are so fond of land", said the Major. "It is a comfortable feeling to know that you stand on your own ground. Land is about the only thing that can't fly away. And then, you see, land gives so much more than the rent. It gives position and influence and political power." '

[31] Maitland, *Forms of Action at Common Law*, pp. 20 ff.

basis of conveyancing with beneficial interests kept off the title, the 1925 legislation permits two estates only to exist as legal estates, one freehold and one leasehold, all other interests being capable of existing in equity only.

B. LEGAL AND EQUITABLE ESTATES AND INTERESTS

In the modern law,[32] the definition of *legal estates and interests* and *equitable interests* is found in the Law of Property Act 1925. Section 1(1) sets out the only two legal estates which can be created; section 1(2) sets out the only legal interests which can be created; and section 1(3) provides that all other estates, interests and charges take effect as equitable interests. In addition, in registered land, the Land Registration Act 2002 requires certain transactions to be completed by registration before the interest takes effect as a legal estate or interest. As we shall see later in this chapter, the significance of the distinction between legal and equitable estates and interests in unregistered land was that a legal estate or interest bound anyone who came to the land; an equitable interest bound anyone except a bona fide purchaser of the legal estate without notice of the equitable interest.[33] In the modern law, registration of equitable interests has been largely substituted for the doctrine of notice, even in unregistered land.[34] In registered land registration of legal estates is required, as well as in many cases the protection of equitable interests by entry on the register.[35] But the distinction between legal and equitable estates and interests, set out in the Law of Property Act 1925, is still applicable to registered land.

LAW OF PROPERTY ACT 1925

1. Legal estates and equitable interests.—(1) The only estates in land which are capable of subsisting or of being conveyed or created at law are—

    (a) An estate in fee simple absolute in possession;[36]

---

[32] For the complex history of the distinction between legal and equitable estates and interests, which formed the context for the reforms of 1925 and other later reforms, see C & B, chaps 1–5. See also Radcliffe, *Real Property Law* (2nd edn, 1938), pp. xxxi-xxxii, setting out the 'five stages in the development of the Law of Real Property': (i) the old common law worked out by the judges of the common law courts, subject to a good deal of intervention by Acts of Parliament, during the later Middle Ages; (ii) the intervention of equity and the development of uses (the forerunner of the trust) during the 14th and 15th centuries; (iii) the Tudor period, during which the intervention of equity was much circumscribed by the Statute of Uses 1535 but the common law was profoundly modified by the introduction of equitable rules; (iv) the period from the Restoration to the death of George III: intervention of equity in the enforcement of trusts, and the development of the Strict Settlement; (v) the period of reform from the Royal Commission on the Law of Real Property in 1828 until the 1925 Acts; 'many of [the] most important rules [of the law of real property], still in force and untouched by recent legislation, were evolved under the old law, and are enshrined in judicial decisions which simply cannot be understood by a reader who does not know the outlines of the old system' (at p. xxxii).

[33] See p. 58, below.   [34] See p. 64, below.
[35] See p. 84, below.   [36] See pp. 302 ff, below.

(*b*) A term of years absolute.[37]

(2) The only interests or charges in or over land which are capable of subsisting or of being conveyed or created at law are—

(*a*) An easement,[38] right, or privilege in or over land for an interest equivalent to an estate in fee simple absolute in possession or a term of years absolute;

(*b*) A rentcharge[39] in possession issuing out of or charged on land being either perpetual or for a term of years absolute;

(*c*) A charge by way of legal mortgage;[40]

(*d*) [41] ... and any other similar charge on land which is not created by an instrument;[42]

(*e*) Rights of entry exercisable over or in respect of a legal term of years absolute, or annexed, for any purpose, to a legal rentcharge.

(3) All other estates, interests, and charges in or over land take effect as equitable interests.

(4) The estates, interests, and charges which under this section are authorised to subsist or to be conveyed or created at law are (when subsisting or conveyed or created at law) in this Act referred to as 'legal estates', and have the same incidents as legal estates subsisting at the commencement of this Act; and the owner of a legal estate is referred to as 'an estate owner' and his legal estate is referred to as his estate.

(5) A legal estate may subsist concurrently with or subject to any other legal estate in the same land in like manner as it could have done before the commencement of this Act.

(6) A legal estate is not capable of subsisting or of being created in an undivided share in land[43] or of being held by an infant.

4. Creation and disposition of equitable interests.—(1) Interests in land validly created or arising after the commencement of this Act, which are not capable of subsisting as legal estates, shall take effect as equitable interests, and, save as otherwise expressly provided by statute, interests in land which under the Statute of Uses or otherwise could before the commencement of this Act have been created as legal interests, shall be capable of being created as equitable interests:

Provided that, after the commencement of this Act (and save as hereinafter expressly enacted), an equitable interest in land shall only be capable of being validly created in any case in which an equivalent equitable interest in property real or personal could have been validly created before such commencement.[44]

---

[37] See pp. 327 ff, below.

[38] See pp. 617 ff, below.

[39] See LP (Entailed Interests) A 1932; s. 2. The Rentcharges Act 1977 is phasing out certain kinds of rentcharge; on rentcharges generally, see C & B, chap. 20; Gray, paras 6.6.2–6.6.7; M & W, paras 31.014–31.039; MM, pp. 407–13.

[40] See pp. 856 ff, below.

[41] As amended by Finance Act 1963, s. 73, Sch. 14, Part VI, and Tithe Act 1936, s. 48, Sch. 9.

[42] E.g. tithe redemption annuity (which replaced tithe rentcharge in 1936. See M & W, para. 18.009). This was itself extinguished as from 2 October 1977: FA 1977, s. 56.

[43] See pp. 564 ff, below.

[44] See the discussion in *National Provincial Bank Ltd v Ainsworth* [1965] AC 1175, on the question of interests capable of existing as proprietary rights; p. 5, above.

LAND REGISTRATION ACT 2002

27 Dispositions required to be registered

(1) If a disposition of a registered estate or registered charge is required to be completed by registration, it does not operate at law until the relevant registration requirements are met.

(2) In the case of a registered estate, the following are the dispositions which are required to be completed by registration—

   (a) a transfer,

   (b) where the registered estate is an estate in land, the grant of a term of years absolute—

      (i) for a term of more than seven years from the date of the grant,

      (ii) to take effect in possession after the end of the period of three months beginning with the date of the grant,

      (iii) under which the right to possession is discontinuous,

      (iv) in pursuance of Part 5 of the Housing Act 1985 (the right to buy), or

      (v) in circumstances where section 171A of that Act applies (disposal by landlord which leads to a person no longer being a secure tenant),

   (c) where the registered estate is a franchise or manor, the grant of a lease,

   (d) the express grant or reservation of an interest of a kind falling within section 1(2)(a) of the Law of Property Act 1925, other than one which is capable of being registered under Part 1 of the Commons Act 2006,[45]

   (e) the express grant or reservation of an interest of a kind falling within section 1(2)(b) or (e) of the Law of Property Act 1925, and

   (f) the grant of a legal charge.

(3) In the case of a registered charge, the following are the dispositions which are required to be completed by registration—

   (a) a transfer, and

   (b) the grant of a sub-charge.

(4) Schedule 2 to this Act (which deals with the relevant registration requirements) has effect.

(5) This section applies to dispositions by operation of law as it applies to other dispositions, but with the exception of the following—

   (a) a transfer on the death or bankruptcy of an individual proprietor,

   (b) a transfer on the dissolution of a corporate proprietor, and

   (c) the creation of a legal charge which is a local land charge.

(6) Rules may make provision about applications to the registrar for the purpose of meeting registration requirements under this section.

(7) In subsection (2)(d), the reference to express grant does not include grant as a result of the operation of section 62 of the Law of Property Act 1925.

---

[45] Substituted by Commons Act 2006, s. 52, Sch. 5, para. 8(1), (2).

III. CREATION AND TRANSFER OF
ESTATES AND INTERESTS

A. THE CONTRACT[46]

A contract usually precedes the conveyance which in unregistered land effects the transfer of the legal estate to a purchaser; and a contract also usually precedes a transfer in registered land. A contract also sometimes precedes the grant of an interest in land other than the freehold, such as a lease, an easement or a charge.

In practice such contracts are generally in standard form. The Standard Conditions of Sale (4th edn, 2003) and the Standard Commercial Property Conditions of Sale (2nd edn, 2004)[47] are standard forms of contract containing a set of general conditions of sale. They are usually employed with such alterations as the parties may make for the purpose of the particular transaction.[48]

A contract for the sale or other disposition of land must comply with the general rules of the law of contract.[49] Thus, it must be a final and complete agreement between the parties on its essential terms,[50] i.e. the parties, the property (and the interest to be granted in it) and the consideration. It is common to make a preliminary agreement

---

[46] C & B, chap. 24; Gray, paras 8.1.4–8.1.83; M & W, chap. 15; MM, pp. 147–157; Barnsley, Part 3; F. Silverman, *Law Society's Conveyancing Handbook* (15th edn, 2008); Kenny, *Conveyancing Practice*.

[47] These are reproduced with Explanatory Notes in Silverman, *Conveyancing Handbook*, Appendix III; Kenny, *Conveyancing Practice*, B001-B033. For a discussion of the original Conditions, see [1980] Conv 179 (J.E. Adams). See also National Conveyancing Protocol of the Law Society (5th edn, 2004), which sets out the steps to be taken by solicitors acting for the vendor and purchaser in domestic conveyancing. The vendor of land has no general duty of disclosure: C&B, pp. 854–7; although under the controversial HA 2004, Part 5, the seller of residential property with vacant possession must provide a 'home information pack', a collection of documents relating to the property or the terms on which it is for sale. Earlier plans to make a 'home condition report' compulsory within the pack were abandoned: Home Information Pack Regulations 2007 (SI 2007 No. 992), reg. 10(a), replacing Home Information Pack Regulations 2006 (SI 2006 No. 1503). The 2007 Regulations were then revoked and replaced by Home Information Pack (No. 2) Regulations 2007 (SI 2007 No. 1997) to allow the introduction of home information packs to be deferred and phased in from 1 August 2007: SI 2007 No. 1525. The Regulations have been further amended: SI 2008 Nos 572, 1266 and 3107 (introducing the requirement of a 'property information questionnaire' with effect from 6 April 2009: regs 9, 10); SI 2009 No. 34.

[48] See also LPA 1925 s. 46 and Statutory Form of Conditions of Sale (SR & O 1925 No. 779) which apply to contracts by correspondence; *Stearn v Twitchell* [1985] 1 All ER 631. This section was not repealed by the LP(MP)A 1989, p. 18, below. It may have been overlooked or left on the statute book out of an abundance of caution: *Commission for the New Towns v Cooper (Great Britain) Ltd* [1995] Ch 259 at 287, per Stuart-Smith LJ, although it may well have a reduced application now, given that an exchange of correspondence will often not fulfil the formality requirements of s. 2 LP(MP)A 1989.

[49] For remedies relating to defects in formation of the contract and for breach of contract, see C & B, pp. 883–893. For third-party rights, see Contracts (Rights of Third Parties) Act 1999; below, p. 772.

[50] See, e.g., *Fletcher v Davies* (1980) 257 EG 1149 (flat in Inner Temple).

'subject to contract', the effect of which is that, until a formal contract has been concluded, there is no contract and either party can withdraw from the negotiations with impunity unless there are some very exceptional circumstances necessitating a different conclusion.[51]

Further, a contract for the sale or other disposition of an interest in land must comply with the formalities required by statute.

(i) Formalities for contracts for the sale or other disposition of an interest in land

Before 27 September 1989 a valid contract for the sale or other disposition of land was only enforceable by action if there was a sufficient memorandum in writing that complied with section 40 of the Law of Property Act 1925 or, failing that, if there was a sufficient act of part performance by the party seeking to enforce the contract.

This was superseded by section 2 of the Law of Property (Miscellaneous Provisions) Act 1989, under which there can be *no* contract unless it is in writing signed by or on behalf of both parties. The doctrine of part performance ceases to exist because there can be no oral contract to be partly performed. If, however, the formalities are not complied with, the facts may nevertheless give rise to proprietary estoppel or a constructive trust.

(a) Formalities before 27 September 1989

LAW OF PROPERTY ACT 1925

40. Contracts for sale, &c., of land to be in writing.—(1) No action may be brought upon any contract for the sale or other disposition of land or any interest in land, unless the agreement upon which such action is brought, or some memorandum or note thereof, is in writing, and signed by the party to be charged or by some other person thereunto by him lawfully authorised.

(2) This section applies to contracts whether made before or after the commencement of this Act and does not affect the law relating to part performance, or sales by the court.

---

[51] *Chillingworth v Esche* [1924] 1 Ch 97; *Alpenstow Ltd v Regalian Properties plc* [1985] 1 WLR 721 (words 'subject to contract' meaningless); *Westway Homes Ltd v Moores* [1991] 2 EGLR 193 (notice served by grantee of option to purchase headed 'subject to contract' held to be surplusage and of no effect); *Prudential Assurance Co Ltd v Mount Eden Ltd* [1997] 1 EGLR 37 (subject to licence). For the continued use of 'subject to contract' after 26 September 1989, see below, p. 27.

(b) Formalities after 26 September 1989

LAW OF PROPERTY (MISCELLANEOUS PROVISIONS) ACT 1989[52]

2. Contracts of sale etc. of land to be made by signed writing.—(1) A contract[53] for the sale or other disposition of an interest[54] in land can only be made in writing and only by incorporating all the terms which the parties have expressly agreed in one document or, where contracts are exchanged, in each.

(2) The terms may be incorporated in a document either by being set out in it or by reference to some other document.

---

[52] Based on Law Commission Report on Formalities for Contracts of Sale etc. of Land 1987 (Law Com No. 164); [1987] Conv 313. For the changes, see Emmet, para. 2.030; and generally, (1989) 105 LQR 555 (R. E. Annand); [1989] Conv 431 (P. H. Pettit); (1990) 10 LS 325 (L. Bently and P. Coughlan). See also Requirements of Writing (Scotland) Act 1995, which has not followed the English approach to formalities. The 1989 Act does not change the scope of contracts which are required to satisfy formality requirements: *Nweze v Nwoko* [2004] 2 P & CR 33 at [34], per Carnwath LJ; but as regards the formalities 'section 2 brought about a markedly different regime': *Firstpost Homes Ltd v Johnson* [1995] 1 WLR 1567 at 1571, per Peter Gibson LJ; see also *McCausland v Duncan Lawrie Ltd* [1997] 1 WLR 38, below, p. 20. See also [2007] Conv 544 (T. Watkin) on the application of s. 2 to compromises of property disputes.

[53] *Tootal Clothing Ltd v Guinea Properties Ltd* (1992) 64 P & CR 452 (agreement supplemental to a contract, which had been duly carried out and therefore no longer executory, held outside s. 2); [1993] Conv 89 (P. Luther); (1993) 109 LQR 191 (D. Wilde); *Record v Bell* [1991] 1 WLR 853 (collateral contract of warranty of title held outside s. 2); (1992) 108 LQR 217 (R. J. Smith); [1991] CLJ 399 (C. Harpum); [1991] Conv 471 (M. Harwood); [1991] All ER Rev 201 (P. J. Clarke); *Pitt v PHH Asset Management Ltd* [1994] 1 WLR 327 (lock-out agreement held outside s. 2); *Lotteryking Ltd v AMEC Properties Ltd* [1995] 2 EGLR 13 (collateral agreement to remedy defects held outside s. 2); *United Bank of Kuwait v Sahib* [1997] Ch 107 (equitable mortgage by deposit of title deeds within s. 2), p. 866, below; *Grossman v Hooper* [2001] 2 EGLR 82 (dicta criticising collateral contract test); *Kilcarne Holdings Ltd v Targetfollow (Birmingham) Ltd* [2005] 2 P & CR 8 at [189] (Lewison J: the courts will not artificially divide what is in truth a composite transaction); *Business Environment Bow Lane Ltd v Deanwater Estates Ltd* [2007] 2 EGLR 51 at [42] (Morritt C: 'the law relating to collateral contracts is well-established but in connection with sales or leases of land needs to be applied with caution if not ... suspicion'). See also *Nweze v Nwoko* [2004] 2 P & CR 33; [2004] Conv 323 (M. P. Thompson) (contract to put property on market and to sell to third party if purchaser found held not within s. 2); distinguishing *Jelson Ltd v Derby City Council* [1999] 3 EGLR 91 (contract between A and B under which A has the right without more to call for the property to be transferred to a buyer whom he nominates on terms set out in the contract was a contract to which s. 2 applied, because it was in effect an option contract relating to the land. Further decision of the judge, to the effect that the contract failed because s. 2 required the signature of the third party, rather than just of the two contracting parties, not approved); *Joyce v Rigolli* [2004] 1 P & CR DG 22 (oral boundary agreement involving trivial exchange of land not a disposition within s. 2); [2004] Conv 226 (M. P. Thompson); *Spiro v Glencrown Properties Ltd* [1991] Ch 537, p. 34, below (grant of option, not exercise, is contract within s. 2). There are practical difficulties, with the application of s. 2 to a right of pre-emption. Since the grant of the right of pre-emption does not itself create an interest in land, p. 38, below, the contract to purchase can arise only at a later date when the right is exercised, and commonly that is not done by a document signed by both parties: *Bircham & Co Nominees (No. 2) Ltd v Worrell Holdings Ltd* (2001) 82 P & CR 34.

[54] *Singh v Briggs* (1995) 71 P & CR 120 (s. 2 applied to executory contract for sale when vendor did not at the time have an interest in land but proposed to acquire it in order to complete sale).

(3) The document incorporating[55] the terms or, where contracts are exchanged,[56] one of the documents incorporating them (but not necessarily the same one) must be signed[57] by or on behalf of each party to the contract.[58]

(4) Where a contract for the sale or other disposition of an interest in land satisfies the conditions of this section by reason only of the rectification of one or more documents in pursuance of an order of a court,[59] the contract shall come into being, or be deemed to have come into being, at such time as may be specified in the order.

(5) This section does not apply in relation to—

> (a) a contract to grant such a lease as is mentioned in section 54(2) of the Law of Property Act 1925 (short leases);[60]
>
> (b) a contract made in the course of a public auction; or
>
> (c) a contract regulated under the Financial Services and Markets Act 2000, other than a regulated mortgage contract, a regulated home reversion plan or a regulated home purchase plan,[61]

and nothing in this section affects the creation or operation of resulting, implied or constructive trusts.

(6) In this section —

'disposition' has the same meaning as in the Law of Property Act 1925;

'interest in land' means any estate, interest or charge in or over land;[62]

'regulated mortgage contract', 'regulated home reversion plan' and 'regulated home purchase plan' must be read with—

> (a) section 22 of the Financial Services and Markets Act 2000,

---

[55] *Firstpost Homes Ltd v Johnson* [1995] 1 WLR 1567 (letter which incorporated plan was signed only by vendor, although plan was signed by both vendor and purchaser: s. 2 not satisfied); [1996] CLJ 192 (A. J. Oakley); cf. *Courtney v Corp Ltd* [2006] All ER (D) 16 (Mar) (s. 2 satisfied).

[56] *Commission for the New Towns v Cooper (Great Britain) Ltd* [1995] Ch 259 (exchange of correspondence concerning oral agreement for sale of land held not to satisfy s. 2; see at 285 for the features of the 'well-recognized concept' of exchange of contracts, 'understood by both lawyers and laymen': per Stuart-Smith LJ); CA refusing to follow its own previous decision in *Hooper v Sherman* [1994] NPC 153; [1995] Conv 319 (M. P. Thompson). See also *Orton v Collins* [2007] 1 WLR 2953 (court has power to order parties to sign single document containing terms of settlement which would otherwise not be compliant with s. 2 because concluded only by correspondence).

[57] *Firstpost Homes Ltd v Johnson*, above, n. 55 (typing in letter of plaintiff's own name held not to constitute a signature; decisions on signatures for the purposes of LPA 1925, s. 40 not followed).

[58] *RG Kensington Management Co Ltd v Hutchinson IDH Ltd* [2003] 2 P & CR 13 at [57] (contract to be signed by 'each party to the contract'; not by 'each party to the prospective conveyance or transfer', per Neuberger J). If the contract is signed by an agent, the agent's authority need not itself be conferred in writing: *McLaughlin v Duffill* [2008] All ER (D) 266 (Nov).

[59] *Wright v Robert Leonard (Development)* [1994] EGCS 69 (contract which referred only to land rectified to include furniture as agreed before exchange of contracts took place); *Commission for New Towns v Cooper (Great Britain) Ltd*, above, n. 56; *Oun v Ahmad* [2008] EWHC 545 (Ch), [2008] 2 P & CR DG3 (no rectification: term omitted by express agreement).

[60] See p. 416, below. Since a short lease may be granted informally, a contract for such a lease need not be formal.

[61] As amended by SI 2001 No. 3649, art. 317(1), (2); SI 2006 No. 2383, art. 27(a). Otherwise, some forms of investment which include interests in land, such as unit trusts, would be within s. 2.

[62] As amended by TLATA 1996, s. 25(2), Sch. 4.

(b) any relevant order under that section, and

(c) Schedule 22 to that Act.[63]

(7) Nothing in this section shall apply in relation to contracts made before this section comes into force.

(8) Section 40 of the Law of Property Act 1925 (which is superseded by this section) shall cease to have effect.[64]

In **McCausland v Duncan Lawrie Ltd** [1997] 1 WLR 38,[65] the plaintiff purchasers made a written contract on 26 January 1995 to purchase 1 Beechmore Road, London, from the defendants (the Bank) for £210,000. The contract satisfied the requirements of section 2 of the Law of Property (Miscellaneous) Provisions Act 1989, and set 26 March as the date for completion. However 26 March was a Sunday, and the vendors' solicitors wrote to the plaintiffs' solicitors suggesting the earlier date of 24 March. This was agreed to in writing. On 24 March the purchasers failed to complete and the vendors served a notice to complete which expired on 7 April. The purchasers were not ready to complete but offered to do so on 10 April. The vendors then purported to rescind the contract. The purchasers sought specific performance and damages for repudiation. They argued that there had been no valid variation of the completion date, and therefore no valid rescission of the contract.

In holding that it was necessary to satisfy the requirements of section 2 when varying a material term of an existing contract, NEILL LJ said at 44:

The principle of construction that Parliament is not to be intended to have amended the law 'by a sidewind' is of importance when one is construing a consolidation Act. But, as Peter Gibson LJ explained in *Firstpost Homes Ltd v Johnson* [1995] 1 WLR 1567, 1571, section 2 of the Act of 1989 was intended to effect a major change in the law. Peter Gibson LJ said:

'Section 2 brought about a markedly different regime from that which obtained hitherto. Whereas under section 40 contracts which did not comply with its requirements were not void but were merely unenforceable by action, contracts which do not comply with section 2 are ineffective: a contract for the sale of an interest in land can only be made in writing and in conformity with the other provisions of section 2. Whereas an oral contract was allowed and enforceable provided that it was evidenced in writing and the memorandum or the note thereof was signed by or on behalf of the party against whom it was sought to be enforced, oral contracts are now of no effect and all contracts must be signed by or on behalf of all the parties. Whereas the contract or the memorandum or note evidencing the contract previously could be contained in more than one document, only one document is now allowed, save where contracts are exchanged, although reference to another document may be permitted in the circumstances laid down in subsections (2) and (3). Whereas the memorandum or note needed for section 40 did not have to contain every term of the contract,

---

[63] As amended by SI 2001 No. 3649, art. 317(1), (3); SI 2006 No. 2383, art. 27(b).

[64] For a suggestion that part performance has not been abolished but may survive as an equitable doctrine, see *Singh v Beggs*, above, n. 54, at 122, per Neill LJ; [1997] Conv 293 (S. I. A. Swann); cf. however *Yaxley v Gotts* [2000] Ch 162 at 172, per Robert Walker LJ, p. 22, below ('It is clear that it has not survived'). See also New Zealand doubts on the English formalities: New Zealand Proposed Property Act; [1994] Conv 428 at 430 (H. W. Wilkinson).

[65] [1996] Conv 366 (M. P. Thompson); (1992) 147 NLJ 219 (H. W. Wilkinson); [2008] Conv 7 (E. Slessenger), giving drafting advice to achieve a variation of a land contract.

all the terms must now be contained in the document in question. Whereas the doctrine of part performance allowed certain contracts otherwise unenforceable to be enforced, that doctrine now has no application.'

It seems to me to be clear that Parliament intended to introduce new and strict requirements as to the formalities to be observed for the creation of a valid disposition of an interest in land. As Stuart-Smith LJ noted in *Commission for the New Towns v Cooper (Great Britain) Ltd* [1995] Ch 259, 287c, the section enacted by Parliament was materially different from that drafted by the Law Commission. Under section 2 all the terms of the contract have to be incorporated in the signed document.

What then is the contract on which the bank seeks to rely? It was said by counsel for the bank that the bank relied on the contract dated 26 January which was created in a form which complied with section 2 and that this contract was later varied in a manner which would have been recognised by the common law and by the courts of equity. In my judgment, however, counsel for the plaintiffs was correct when he submitted that the formalities prescribed by section 2 have to be applied to the contract as varied. This was not a case where the agreement between the parties was concluded by an exchange of contracts. The only document signed by both parties was the contract dated 26 January 1995.

The law in this regard is made plain in the speech of Lord Parmoor in *Morris v Baron & Co* [1918] AC 1, 39 where he referred with approval to the following passage in the judgment of Shearman J in *Williams v Moss' Empires Ltd* [1915] 3 KB 242, 246–247:

'The principle . . . is where there is alleged to have been a variation of a written contract by a new parol contract, which incorporates some of the terms in the old contract, the new contract must be looked at in its entirety, and if the terms of the new contract when thus considered are such that by reason of the Statute of Frauds it cannot be given in evidence unless in writing, then being an unenforceable contract it cannot operate to effect a variation of the original contract. . . . whenever parties vary a material term[66] of an existing contract they are in effect entering into a new contract, the terms of which must be looked at in their entirety, and if the new contract is one which is required to be in writing but is not in writing, then it must be wholly disregarded and the parties are relegated to their rights under the original contract.'

In *Morris v Baron & Co* the House of Lords was concerned with a contract for the sale of goods which was required by section 4 of the Sale of Goods Act 1893 to be evidenced in writing. It seems to me, however, that the principle approved by Lord Parmoor is directly applicable in this case. Furthermore, there are other passages in the speeches in *Morris v Baron & Co* which show that if a contract is required to be in writing variations which are not in writing cannot be relied upon: see Lord Finlay LC, at p. 12, and Viscount Haldane, at p. 16. Lord Atkinson explained the matter, at p. 31:

'The foundation, I think, on which that rule rests is that after the agreed variation the contract of the parties is not the original contract which had been reduced into writing, but that contract as varied, that of this latter in its entirety there is no written evidence, and it therefore cannot in its entirety be enforced' . . .

---

[66] 'There is no doubt that in this case the term was material in that respect as it advanced the contractual date for completion and therefore the time when either party might make time of the essence by the service of a notice to complete. But it does not follow that section 2 must be observed in order to secure the variation of a term which is immaterial.' (per Morritt LJ at 49).

In these circumstances I would allow the appeal and reinstate the statement of claim. The matter should proceed to trial if the parties cannot reach some agreement. If the action does proceed the bank will be able to raise the defence of estoppel if so advised.[67]

(ii) Failure to comply with the required formalities: constructive trust and estoppel

Where a contract does not comply with section 2 of the 1989 Act, the facts may nevertheless give rise to a constructive trust or to proprietary estoppel. The parties' agreement may therefore not be entirely devoid of legal effect.

Yaxley v Gotts
[2000] Ch 162 (CA, **Beldam, Robert Walker** and **Clarke LJJ**)[68]

The plaintiff and second defendant (Brownie Gotts) informally agreed that the latter would purchase a house which the plaintiff would convert into flats. The plaintiff would own the ground floor and would act as the second defendant's managing agent for the four flats in the rest of the house. The house was in fact purchased by the first defendant, the second defendant's son (Alan Gotts), but the plaintiff assumed that the father had bought it. The plaintiff converted the property and acted as managing agent for two and a half years. The plaintiff and father fell out. The son refused to allow the plaintiff to manage the flats and denied that the plaintiff had any interest in the ground floor. The plaintiff commenced proceedings against the defendants. The trial judge held that the plaintiff was entitled to a leasehold interest in the ground floor by virtue of proprietary estoppel. On appeal, the defendants argued that the oral agreement between the plaintiff and the father was void by virtue of section 2 of the Law of Property (Miscellaneous Provisions) Act 1989, which requires contracts of sale of land to be in writing, and that it could not be made effective by the doctrine of proprietary estoppel.

Held. If there was an oral agreement between the parties, the plaintiff was entitled to a leasehold interest under a constructive trust which was expressly saved by section 2 (5) of the 1989 Act.

---

[67] Cf. *Target Holdings Ltd v Priestley* (1999) 79 P & CR 305 (agreement to vary mortgage held to be outside s. 2 because a mortgage is a disposition, not a *contract for* the disposition of land); [1999] Conv 414 (M. P. Thompson).

[68] [2000] CLJ 23 (L. Tee); (2000) 116 LQR 11 (R. J. Smith); (2000) 63 MLR 912 (I. Moore); [2000] Conv 245 (M. Thompson); [2000] All ER Rev 242 (P. J. Clarke); *Shah v Shah* [2002] QB 35 (estoppel applied in relation to s. 1 of the 1989 Act where deed not signed in presence of witnesses); [2001] Conv 441 (P. H. K.). Cf. *Actionstrength Ltd v International Glass Engineering IN.GL.EN.SpA* [2003] 2 AC 541 (no estoppel where creditor acted to its detriment on faith of guarantor's oral promise; held unenforceable as failing to comply with Statute of Frauds 1677, s. 4: 'It would wholly frustrate the continued operation of section 4 in relation to contracts of guarantee if an oral promise were to be treated, without more, as somehow carrying in itself a representation that the promise would be treated as enforceable', per Lord Walker of Gestingthorpe at [52]); [2003] CLJ 551 (E. Cooke).

Robert Walker LJ:

The public policy principle

Mr Allston has not contended that the doctrine of part performance, as such, has survived the repeal of section 40 of the Law of Property Act 1925 and its replacement by section 2 of the Act of 1989. It is clear that it has not survived. But he has contended that a comparable equitable doctrine can and in this case should operate despite section 2, that is the species of equitable estoppel, generally referred as proprietary estoppel, on which the judge relied. Mr Allston has also (although only after some prompting by the court) asserted the existence of a constructive trust and has relied on the exception at the end of section 2(5).

Mr Laurence, appearing with Miss Davies for the defendants (neither appeared below), did not go so far as to contend that no form of estoppel could operate in relation to an oral or documentary consensus not amounting to a contract because of non-compliance with section 2. Nor did he submit that a plaintiff was in such a situation unable to obtain any restitutionary remedy: on the contrary, the defendants' notice of appeal concedes that Mr Yaxley is entitled to claim on a quantum meruit basis. But the defendants rely on the general principle, stated in *Halsbury's Laws of England,* 4th edn reissue, vol. 16 (1992), pp. 849–850, para. 962:

> 'The doctrine of estoppel may not be invoked to render valid a transaction which the legislature has, on grounds of general public policy, enacted . . . is to be invalid.'

The defendants also contend that the saving at the end of section 2(5) has a narrower effect than may at first appear.

Recent cases on section 2 and estoppel

The diligence of counsel has produced five cases, decided in the course of the last three years, in which this court has made some reference to estoppel in connection with section 2 of the Act of 1989. However none of them has decided or even discussed at length the points which the defendants take in relation to proprietary estoppel and section 2(5). I can therefore refer to them fairly briefly and I do so in chronological order.

United Bank of Kuwait Plc v Sahib [1997] Ch 107 [p. 866, below], is an important decision on the effect of a deposit of a land certificate unaccompanied by any document satisfying section 2. Peter Gibson LJ noted, at pp. 139–140, that the old law as to the creation of an equitable mortgage by deposit of deeds had been akin to part performance, and was therefore equally inconsistent with the philosophy of the Act of 1989. He noted, at p. 141, that the Law Commission's Report on Transfer of Land: Formalities for Contracts of Sale etc. of Land (1987) (Law Com. No. 164) had contemplated that equitable remedies such as promissory estoppel and proprietary estoppel might be available to do justice in cases where section 2 had not been complied with. But Peter Gibson LJ did not find it necessary to consider the point further because the claimant bank could not on any view have been bound by any estoppel. Phillips LJ agreed, and at p. 144, and saw no reason to extend the list of exceptions in section 2(5).

His Lordship referred to *McCausland v Duncan Lawrie Ltd* [1997] 1 WLR 38, p. 20, above, and continued:

Godden v Merthyr Tydfil Housing Association [1997] NPC 1; Court of Appeal (Civil Division) Transcript No. 370 of 1997, was another appeal (this time unsuccessful) against a striking-out order. This court rejected an argument based on estoppel by convention which Simon Brown LJ regarded as impossible (a view with which I respectfully agree). The case is of interest mainly for the citation of the passage in *Halsbury's Laws of England,* 4th edn reissue, vol. 16, pp. 849–850, para. 962, stating the public policy principle. That passage was, it seems, pointed out by Sir John Balcombe in the course of argument; Simon Brown LJ saw it as a 'central objection to this whole line of argument'—but not, it is to be noted, in a context in which proprietary estoppel was being relied on.

Barely a month later *Godden* was cited, in what Peter Gibson LJ called a 'somewhat garbled version,' in *Bankers Trust Co v Namdar* (unreported), 14 February 1997; Court of Appeal (Civil Division) Transcript No. 349 of 1997, pp. 19–20. Peter Gibson LJ referred to the view of Morritt LJ in *McCausland v Duncan Lawrie Ltd* [1997] 1 WLR 38, 50 that estoppel may be available. He also referred to the Law Commission's report (Law Com. No. 164), para. 5.4–5.5, and to *Cheshire and Burn's Modern Law of Real Property,* 15th edn (1994), p. 124. Peter Gibson LJ did not accept that estoppel could have no relevance. But as the consequence was that this court decided not to allow the appellant to take a new point, the matter was not further investigated.

Finally, in *King v Jackson* [1998] 1 EGLR 30 this court took account of an oral agreement to surrender an assured shorthold tenancy, relied on by the landlord, in assessing damages for unlawful eviction under sections 27 and 28 of the Housing Act 1988. Morritt LJ gave the leading judgment but did not find it necessary to refer to any of the authorities just mentioned.

I have no hesitation in agreeing with what I take to be the views of Peter Gibson LJ, Neill LJ, and Morritt LJ, that the doctrine of estoppel may operate to modify (and sometimes perhaps even counteract) the effect of section 2 of the Act of 1989. The circumstances in which section 2 has to be complied with are so various, and the scope of the doctrine of estoppel is so flexible, that any general assertion of section 2 as a 'no-go area' for estoppel would be unsustainable. Nevertheless the impact of the public policy principle to which Sir John Balcombe drew attention in *Godden v Merthyr Tydfil Housing Association* does call for serious consideration. It is not concerned with illegality (some confusion may have arisen from the inadequate report or note shown to this court in *Bankers Trust Co v Namdar*) but with what Viscount Radcliffe in *Kok Hoong v Leong Cheong Kweng Mines Ltd* [1964] AC 993, 1016, called a principle of general social policy,

> 'to ask whether the law that confronts the estoppel can be seen to represent a social policy to which the court must give effect in the interests of the public generally or some section of the public, despite any rules of evidence as between themselves that the parties may have created by their conduct or otherwise.'

In this case that principle must of course be applied consistently with the terms in which section 2 of the Act of 1989 has been enacted, including the saving at the end of section 2(5).

Parliament's requirement that any contract for the disposition of an interest in land must be made in a particular documentary form, and will otherwise be void, does not have such an obviously social aim as statutory provisions relating to contracts by or with moneylenders, infants, or protected tenants. Nevertheless it can be seen as embodying Parliament's conclusion, in the general public interest, that the need for certainty as to the formation of contracts of this type must in general outweigh the disappointment of those who make informal bargains in ignorance of the statutory requirement. If an estoppel would have the effect of enforcing a void contract and subverting Parliament's purpose it may have to yield to the statutory law which confronts it, except so far as the statute's saving for a constructive trust provides a means of reconciliation of the apparent conflict....

Proprietary estoppel and constructive trusts

At a high level of generality, there is much common ground between the doctrines of proprietary estoppel and the constructive trust, just as there is between proprietary estoppel and part performance. All are concerned with equity's intervention to provide relief against unconscionable conduct, whether as between neighbouring landowners, or vendor and purchaser, or relatives who make informal arrangements for sharing a home, or a fiduciary and the beneficiary or client to whom he owes a fiduciary obligation. The overlap between estoppel and part performance has been thoroughly examined in the defendants' written submissions, with a survey of authorities from *Gregory v Mighell* (1811) 18 Ves. 328 to *Take Harvest Ltd v Liu* [1993] AC 552.

The overlap between estoppel and the constructive trust was less fully covered in counsel's submissions but seems to me to be of central importance to the determination of this appeal. Plainly there are large areas where the two concepts do not overlap: when a landowner stands by while his neighbour mistakenly builds on the former's land the situation is far removed (except for the element of unconscionable conduct) from that of a fiduciary who derives an improper advantage from his client. But in the area of joint enterprise for the acquisition of land (which may be, but is not necessarily, the matrimonial home) the two concepts coincide.

His Lordship referred to *Gissing v Gissing* [1971] AC 886, 905; *Lloyds Bank Plc v Rosset* [1991] 1 AC 107, 132, and *Grant v Edwards* [1986] Ch 638, 656, and continued:

In this case the judge did not make any finding as to the existence of a constructive trust. He was not asked to do so, because it was not then seen as an issue in the case. But on the findings of fact which the judge did make it was not disputed that a proprietary estoppel arose, and that the appropriate remedy was the grant to Mr Yaxley, in satisfaction of his equitable entitlement, of a long leasehold interest, rent free, of the ground floor of the property. Those findings do in my judgment equally provide the basis for the conclusion that Mr Yaxley was entitled to such an interest under a constructive trust. The oral bargain which the judge found to have been made between Mr Yaxley and Mr Brownie Gotts, and to have been adopted by Mr Alan Gotts, was definite enough to meet the test stated by Lord Bridge in *Lloyds Bank Plc v Rosset* [above]...

To recapitulate briefly: the species of constructive trust based on 'common intention' is established by what Lord Bridge in *Lloyds Bank Plc v Rosset,* called an 'agreement, arrangement or understanding' actually reached between the parties, and relied on and acted on by the claimant. A constructive trust of that sort is closely akin to, if not indistinguishable from, proprietary estoppel. See *Birmingham Midshires Mortgage Services Ltd v Sabherwal* (1999) 80 P & CR 256, [p. 555, below]. Equity enforces it because it would be unconscionable for the other party to disregard the claimant's rights. Section 2(5) expressly saves the creation and operation of a constructive trust.

Clarke LJ:

3. Proprietary Estoppel and the Law Commission

The Act of 1989 expressly refers to resulting, implied or constructive trusts but it does not expressly refer to proprietary estoppel, in so far as its principles are different from those relating to constructive trusts. The Act neither expressly saves the operation of the doctrine of proprietary estoppel nor expressly provides that it should have no application. Whether the principles of proprietary (or indeed other classes of estoppel) can be invoked will no doubt depend upon the principle which Robert Walker LJ has quoted from *Halsbury's Laws of England,* 4th edn reissue, vol. 16, pp. 849–850, para. 962, namely that the doctrine of estoppel may not be invoked to render valid a transaction which the legislature, on grounds of general public policy, has enacted is to be invalid or void.

It seems to me that in considering whether a particular estoppel relied upon would offend the public policy behind a statute it is necessary to consider the mischief at which the statute is directed. Where a statute has been enacted as a result of the recommendations of the Law Commission, it is, as I see it, both appropriate and permissible for the court to consider those recommendations in order to help to identify both the mischief which the Act is designed to cure and the public policy underlying it. Indeed, although I agree with Robert Walker LJ that they cannot be conclusive as to how a particular provision should be construed, I entirely agree with Beldam LJ that the policy behind section 2 of the Act of 1989 can clearly be seen from the Law Commission Report to which he refers. In my opinion the contents of that report will be of the greatest assistance in deciding whether or not the principles of particular types of estoppel should be held to be contrary to the public policy underlying the Act. In this regard it seems to me that the answer is likely to depend upon the facts of the particular case. So, for example, an attempt to apply the principles of estoppel by convention is likely to fail, as in *Godden v Merthyr Tydfil Housing Association* [1997] NPC 1; Court of Appeal (Civil Division) Transcript No. 370 of 1997, whereas an attempt to apply the principles of proprietary estoppel might well succeed, depending upon the facts of the particular case.

Beldam LJ:

For my part I cannot see that there is any reason to qualify the plain words of section 2(5). They were included to preserve the equitable remedies to which the Commission had referred. I do not think it inherent in a social policy of simplifying conveyancing by requiring the certainty of a written document that unconscionable conduct or equitable fraud should be allowed to prevail.

In my view the provision that nothing in section 2 of the Act of 1989 is to affect the creation or operation of resulting, implied or constructive trusts effectively excludes from the operation of the section cases in which an interest in land might equally well be claimed by relying on constructive trust or proprietary estoppel.

The approach taken in *Yaxley v Gotts* has been followed in series of cases in the Court of Appeal.[69] However, in **Cobbe v Yeoman's Row Management Ltd** [2008] 1 WLR 1752[70] at 1769 LORD SCOTT OF FOSCOTE, without reference to *Yaxley* or the

---

[69] See *James v Evans* [2000] 3 EGLR 1 (no estoppel); [2001] Conv 86 (L. McMurtry); *Joyce v Rigolli* [2004] 1 P & CR DG22 at [35]-[36], per Arden LJ; *Kinane v Mackie-Conteh* [2005] 2 P & CR D63; [2005] Conv 247 (M. Dixon), 501 (B. McFarlane); *Oates v Stimson* [2006] All ER (D) 219 (May); *McGuane v Welch* [2008] 2 P & CR 24 at [37], per Mummery LJ; *Cobbe v Yeoman's Row Management Ltd* [2006] 1 WLR 2964 ('section 2 has no application to this proprietary estoppel claim. No concluded agreement was made. There can be no question of an action to enforce the second agreement. The section is irrelevant to an action to enforce a cause of action for proprietary estoppel which does not depend on the existence of a concluded agreement for sale or on the enforcement of it', per Mummery LJ at [68]), rvsd by HL [2008] 1 WLR 1752, below. See also *Representative Body of the Church in Wales v Newton* [2005] EWHC 631 (QB), [2005] 16 EG 145 (CS) (no constructive trust where condition of contract (landlord's giving consent to assignment) had not been satisfied).

[70] For the facts, and for extracts from the opinions of Lord Scott of Foscote and Lord Walker of Gestingthorpe in relation to the claim based on proprietary estoppel, see pp. 1021–1027, below. Followed by Peter Smith J in *Hutchison v B & DF Ltd* [2008] EWHC 2286 (Ch), [2008] All ER(D) 41 (Oct) at [68]. See, however, *Herbert v Doyle* [2008] EWHC 1950 (Ch), [2008] All ER(D) 40 (Aug) at [15], per Herbert QC: 'Lord

arguments discussed in that case, doubted (obiter) whether the doctrine of proprietary estoppel could be relied upon where a contract failed to comply with section 2
of the 1989 Act:[71]

29 Section 2 of the 1989 Act declares to be void any agreement for the acquisition of an interest
in land that does not comply with the requisite formalities prescribed by the section. Subsection
(5) expressly makes an exception for resulting, implied or constructive trusts. These may validly
come into existence without compliance with the prescribed formalities. Proprietary estoppel
does not have the benefit of this exception. The question arises, therefore, whether a complete
agreement for the acquisition of an interest in land that does not comply with the section 2
prescribed formalities, but would be specifically enforceable if it did can become enforceable
via the route of proprietary estoppel. It is not necessary in the present case to answer this question, for the second agreement was not a complete agreement and, for that reason, would not
have been specifically enforceable so long as it remained incomplete. My present view, however,
is that proprietary estoppel cannot be prayed in aid in order to render enforceable an agreement
that statute has declared to be void. The proposition that an owner of land can be estopped from
asserting that an agreement is void for want of compliance with the requirements of section 2
is, in my opinion, unacceptable. The assertion is no more than the statute provides. Equity can
surely not contradict the statute.

(iii) 'Subject to contract'

It would seem at first sight that the practice making the negotiations for a contract
'subject to contract'[72] is no longer necessary, since no contract can come into existence
until a document is signed by both parties. However, it is still used in order to draw
a clear distinction between the communications preparatory to the contract and the
contract itself; and it also thereby makes clear that the parties do not yet intend their
communications to have any binding force, not only as a contract but also outside the
contract, such as through a constructive trust or estoppel. It is unlikely that an estoppel or constructive trust will arise where the negotiations are expressed to be subject
to contract.

In **A-G of Hong Kong v Humphreys Estate (Queen's Gardens) Ltd** [1987] AC 114 A,
as representatives of the Government of Hong Kong, reached an agreement in principle, subject to contract, with B, that, in exchange for 83 flats from B, A would grant a
Crown lease of Government property for development by B. A spent some money on

---

Scott's statement of his present view was avowedly obiter, and in my view it remains the case that, if all the
requirements are otherwise satisfied for a claim based on proprietary estoppel to succeed, the claim will not
fail solely because it also consists of an agreement which falls foul of section 2. The analysis of such a case may
be that the court gives effect to the proprietary estoppel by recognising or imposing a constructive trust, and
it is this which enables section 2(5) to apply'. See also, however, *Thorner v Major* [2009] 1 WLR 776 at [99],
per Lord Neuberger of Abbotsbury, p. 1036, below ('I do not consider that section 2 has any impact on a claim
such as the present, which is a straightforward estoppel claim without any contractual connection').

[71] Cf, however, Lord Walker of Gestingthorpe at [93] ('I do not think it is necessary or appropriate to
consider the issue on section 2 of the Law of Property (Miscellaneous Provisions) Act 1989'). Lord Hoffmann
and Lord Mance agreed with Lord Scott. Lord Browne agreed with both Lord Scott and Lord Walker.

[72] Above, p. 16–17.

the flats and moved civil servants into them; and B did some work on the property. B then withdrew from the agreement. The Privy Council held that there was no estoppel to prevent B withdrawing from the agreement. B had shown that, to A's knowledge, it had retained the right to resile from the agreement, and A had failed to prove that B had created or encouraged A to expect that there would be no withdrawal. Lord TEMPLEMAN said at 127:

In the present case the government acted in the hope that a voluntary agreement in principle expressly made 'subject to contract' and therefore not binding would eventually be followed by the achievement of legal relationships in the form of grants and transfers of property. It is possible but unlikely that in circumstances at present unforeseeable a party to negotiations set out in a document expressed to be 'subject to contract' would be able to satisfy the court that the parties had subsequently agreed to convert the document into a contract or that some form of estoppel had arisen to prevent both parties from refusing to proceed with the transactions envisaged by the document. But in the present case the government chose to begin and elected to continue on terms that either party might suffer a change of mind and withdraw.

In **Cobbe v Yeoman's Row Management Ltd** [2008] 1 WLR 1752, p. 26, above, Lord Scott of Foscote said at 1767, para. 25:

The reason why, in a 'subject to contract' case, a proprietary estoppel cannot ordinarily arise is that the would-be purchaser's expectation of acquiring an interest in the property in question is subject to a contingency that is entirely under the control of the other party to the negotiations: see also *British Steel Corpn v Cleveland Bridge and Engineering Co Ltd* [1984] 1 All ER 504, 511, per Robert Goff J; *Waltons Stores (Interstate) Ltd v Maher* (1988) 164 CLR 387; *London & Regional Investments Ltd v TBI plc* [2002] EWCA Civ 355 at [42], per Mummery LJ and *Pridean v Forest Taverns* (1996) 75 P & CR 447. The expectation is therefore speculative.

(iv) Electronic contracts

Electronic conveyancing is gradually being introduced under the Land Registration Act 2002.[73] In 2001 the Lord Chancellor's Department published draft proposals[74] for the introduction of electronic contracts. A new section 2A would be inserted into the Law of Property (Miscellaneous Provisions) Act 1989 to enable an 'electronic contract' to be as effective for the purposes of section 2 (and any other enactment) as an equivalent paper contract if it meets certain conditions. In 2007 the Land Registry published a revised version of the proposed section 2A, which would apply only to contracts relating to registered land.[75] However, it has now been decided that the facility to use electronic contracts will not be introduced until later in the incremental programme by which electronic conveyancing is to be introduced. This is unlikely before 2010.[76]

[73] P. 226, below.
[74] LCD Consultation Paper, Electronic Conveyancing – A draft order under s. 8 Electronic Communications Act 2000, CP 05/2001, March 2001.
[75] Land Registry Consultation paper, E-conveyancing Secondary Legislation Part 1 (February 2007), pp. 95–102.
[76] Land Registry Report on Responses to E-conveyancing Secondary Legislation Part 1, p. 26.

QUESTIONS

1. What is the position if the formalities of section 2 of the Law of Property (Miscellaneous Provisions) Act 1989 are not observed? How far will equitable doctrines, such as estoppel and constructive trust, be used to render an oral agreement enforceable? How far should they be allowed to do so?

2. How can a purchaser prevent gazumping by a vendor? Consider

   (a) A lock-out agreement: *Walford v Miles* [1992] 2 AC 128 at 139; cf. *Pitt v PHH Asset Management Ltd* [1994] 1 WLR 327; [1993] CLJ 392 (C. MacMillan); [1994] Conv 58 (M. P. Thompson); C & B, pp. 860–1. On the remedy (injunction or damages), see *Tye v House* [1997] 2 EGLR 171; *Dandara Holdings Ltd v Co-operative Retail Services Ltd* [2004] 2 EGLR 163 at [13]-[14]; [2004] EG 151 (J. Murdoch). For precedents, see Conv Prec, pp. 10137–41. On compensation for pre-contractual expenditure in the absence of a lock-out agreement, see *Regalian plc v London Docklands Development Corpn* [1995] 1 WLR 212; [1995] Conv 135 (M. P. Thompson); [1995] CLJ 243 (G. Virgo).

   (b) An option to purchase; p. 34, below.

(v) *Effect of a valid and enforceable contract: the doctrine of* Walsh v Lonsdale

(a) An estate contract is a grant in equity

An enforceable contract to convey or create a legal estate in land is one of the categories of contract which equity will specifically enforce.[77] If that remedy is available in respect of a particular contract, equity looks on that as done which ought to be done, and treats the situation as if the land were already conveyed, or the legal estate were already created. Such a contract is thus effective as a conveyance in equity.[78] This is generally known as the doctrine of *Walsh v Lonsdale*, after the case in which it was

[77] On specific performance, see H & M, chap. 24; Snell, chap. 15; Jones and Goodhart, *Specific Performance* (2nd edn, 1996); Burrows, *Remedies for Torts and Breach of Contract* (3rd edn, 2004), chap. 20.

[78] C & B, pp. 877–80; Gray, paras 4.2.86–4.2.102, 8.1.54–8.1.67; M & W, paras 17.041–17.044; Smith, pp. 378–380; *Lysaght v Edwards* (1876) 2 ChD 499, below. See also *Earl of Egmont v Smith* (1877) 6 ChD 469; *Abdulla v Shah* [1959] AC 124 (vendor must not remove parts of the realty after the date of the contract); *Clarke v Ramuz* [1891] 2 QB 456 (removal of soil by trespasser); *Phillips v Lamdin* [1949] 2 KB 33 (removal of door). The risk passes to the purchaser who should therefore insure: *Paine v Meller* (1801) 6 Ves 349; *Rayner v Preston* (1881) 18 ChD 1; LPA 1925, s. 47 (reversing the decision in *Rayner v Preston*); *Berkeley v Poulett* (1976) 241 EG 911, 242 EG 39 (discussing the rights of a sub-purchaser); *Ware v Verderber* (1978) 247 EG 1081 (duty of vendor to take reasonable care of property); *Englewood Properties Ltd v Patel* [2005] 1 WLR 1961 (duty does not extend to dealing with vendor's adjoining or neighbouring premises). Condition 5.1.4 Standard Conditions of Sale excludes LPA 1925, s. 47; [1989] Conv 1 (H. W. Wilkinson). See Law Commission Report on Risk of Damage After Contract of Sale 1990 (Law Com No. 191). As to the effect of LP(MP)A 1989, s. 2 on this informal conveyance, see [1990] Conv 44 (J. Howell).

applied in the context of leases.[79] The conveyance in equity differs in various ways from a conveyance at law; just as interests in equity differ from estates and interests at law. The doctrine is applicable to contracts for the sale of land, contracts to grant a lease, a mortgage, an easement or profit, indeed a contract to convey or create a legal estate or interest in any hereditament, corporeal or incorporeal.[80] Such a contract is termed an estate contract, and is defined in, and (in unregistered land) made registrable by, the Land Charges Act 1972, section 2(4), Class C (iv).[81]

In **Lysaght v Edwards** (1876) 2 ChD 499 Sir George JESSEL MR said at 506:

The effect of a contract for sale has been settled for more than two centuries; certainly it was completely settled before the time of Lord Hardwicke, who speaks of the settled doctrine of the court as to it. What is that doctrine? It is that the moment you have a valid contract for sale the vendor becomes in equity a trustee for the purchaser of the estate sold, and the beneficial ownership passes to the purchaser, the vendor having a right to the purchase-money, a charge or lien on the estate for the security of that purchase-money, and a right to retain possession of the estate until the purchase-money is paid, in the absence of express contract as to the time of delivering possession.[82]

Walsh v Lonsdale[83]
(1882) 21 ChD 9 (CA, Sir George Jessel MR, Cotton and Lindley LJJ)

On 29 May 1879, the defendant agreed to grant to the plaintiff a lease of a mill for seven years at a rent which varied with the number of looms operated by the plaintiff, and at a rate per loom which depended on whether the lessor or lessee provided the steam power. The minimum rent payable was calculated on the smallest number of looms which the plaintiff was contractually bound to operate, and at the lowest rate was £810. The rent was payable in advance if demanded. The plaintiff entered and paid rent quarterly, not in advance. He was in arrears with rent due in January, 1882, and in March the defendant demanded a year's rent in advance. It was not paid, and the defendant distrained. The plaintiff brought this action for damages for illegal distress and also for specific performance of the agreement and for an interim injunction to restrain the distress.

Held. The landlord (defendant) had a right to distrain. An injunction to restrain the distress would be granted only on payment by the plaintiff of £810, the lowest sum that could be due for rent under the lease.

---

[79] Below, p. 419.

[80] As to the distinction between grants of interests in real property and sales of chattels, see M & W, para. 15.026.

[81] See p. 66–67, below. For registration in registered land, see below, p. 163.

[82] On the unpaid seller's lien, see *Barclays Bank plc v Estates and Commercial Ltd* [1997] 1 WLR 415 at 419 per Millett LJ; Emmet, para. 15.014; [1994] CLJ 263 (S. Worthington).

[83] *Tottenham Hotspur Football and Athletic Co Ltd v Princegrove Publishers Ltd* [1974] 1 WLR 113; (1974) 90 LQR 149 (M. Albery); *Warmington v Miller* [1973] QB 877; *Industrial Properties (Barton Hill) Ltd v Associated Electrical Industries Ltd* [1977] QB 580, below; (1988) 8 OJLS 350 (P. Sparkes); *Re A Company (No. 00792 of 1992), ex p Tredegar Enterprises Ltd* [1992] 2 EGLR 39.

Sir George Jessel MR: The question is one of some nicety. There is an agreement for a lease under which possession has been given. Now since the *Judicature Act*[84] the possession is held under the agreement. There are not two estates as there were formerly, one estate at common law by reason of the payment of the rent from year to year, and an estate in equity under the agreement. There is only one court, and the equity rules prevail in it. The tenant holds under an agreement for a lease. He holds, therefore, under the same terms in equity as if a lease had been granted, it being a case in which both parties admit that relief is capable of being given by specific performance. That being so, he cannot complain of the exercise by the landlord of the same rights as the landlord would have had if a lease had been granted. On the other hand, he is protected in the same way as if a lease had been granted; he cannot be turned out by six months' notice as a tenant from year to year. He has a right to say, 'I have a lease in equity, and you can only re-enter if I have committed such a breach of covenant as would if a lease had been granted have entitled you to re-enter according to the terms of a proper proviso for re-entry.' That being so, it appears to me that being a lessee in equity he cannot complain of the exercise of the right of distress merely because the actual parchment has not been signed and sealed.

In **Industrial Properties (Barton Hill) Ltd v Associated Electrical Industries Ltd** [1977] QB 580, the Parker trustees agreed in 1959 to sell part of an industrial estate to the plaintiff company. The purchase money was paid and the contract registered as a land charge, but, in order to save stamp duty, the legal estate was never conveyed to the company. In 1966 the company, which was a mere equitable owner, entered into negotiations with the defendants for the grant of a lease, and their solicitors inadvertently stated that the plaintiffs were the freeholders. The lease contained a covenant to keep the premises in good and tenantable repair and condition and so to yield them up at the determination of the term. When the lease expired, the defendants gave up possession, leaving the premises badly out of repair. The plaintiff company brought an action for damages for breach of the covenant. The defendants argued that the plaintiff company had no legal title to the premises.

The Court of Appeal (Lord Denning MR, Roskill and Lawton LJJ) held that the defendants were liable. There was a tenancy by estoppel under which the defendants were estopped from denying the plaintiff company's title.[85] The Court of Appeal also held that the defendants were liable under the doctrine of *Walsh v Lonsdale*. Lord DENNING said at 598:

Thus far I have considered the position at common law. But in equity there is a much shorter way to a decision. It is quite plain that, if the lease to A.E.I. was defective in point of law, nevertheless it was good in equity, and for this simple reason. There were two agreements of which specific performance would be granted. One was the agreement by the Parker trustees

---

[84] Supreme Court of Judicature Act 1873 provided for the creation of the Supreme Court of Judicature and for the application in all branches thereof of the rules both of law and of equity. In s. 25(1)-(10) rules applicable to particular points are laid down, and sub-s. (11) (now Supreme Court Act 1981, s. 49(1)) provides:

'Generally in all matters not herein-before particularly mentioned in which there is any conflict or variance between the Rules of Equity and the Rules of the Common Law with reference to the same matter, the Rules of Equity shall prevail.'

[85] P. 337, below.

to convey to the plaintiff company. The other was the agreement by the plaintiff company to grant a lease to A.E.I. In respect of each of these agreements, equity looks upon that as done which ought to be done. It follows that, by combining the two agreements, the tenants, A.E.I., hold upon the same terms as if a lease had actually been granted by the Parker trustees to A.E.I. This is, of course, an extension of the doctrine of *Walsh v Lonsdale* where there was only one agreement. But I see no reason why the doctrine should not be extended to a case like the present, where there were two agreements, each of which was such that specific performance would be granted.[86]

(b) Specific performance is discretionary

The equitable interest created under the doctrine of *Walsh v Londsale* is precarious in that, since it depends on the contract being specifically enforceable, the equitable interest can be created by the contract, and will continue to subsist once created, only as long as there is no obstacle to the remedy of specific performance being available on the facts of the case.

In **Warmington v Miller** [1973] QB 877, STAMP J said at 887:

The equitable interests which the intended lessee has under an agreement for a lease do not exist in vacuo, but arise because the intended lessee has an equitable right to specific performance of the agreement. In such a situation that which is agreed to be and ought to be done is treated as having been done and carrying with it in equity the attendant rights.

Coatsworth v Johnson[87]
(1886) 54 LT 520 (CA, **Lord Esher MR, Lindley** and **Lopes LJJ**)

The plaintiff entered into possession of the defendant's farm under an agreement to execute a lease in accordance with a draft lease which had already been signed but not sealed. This draft contained, among other covenants, a covenant by the tenant to use the land in a good and husbandlike manner, and there was a power of re-entry on breach of any of the covenants.

The plaintiff failed to cultivate the farm properly, and the defendant, before any rent was due or paid, gave notice to quit and, acting under the power of re-entry, turned the plaintiff out of possession. The plaintiff brought this action for damages for trespass, claiming protection under section 14 of the Conveyancing Act 1881.[88]

Held. The plaintiff was not entitled to the protection of the statute.

---

[86] See also *McManus v Cooke* (1887) 35 Ch D 681 (easement of light); *Mason v Clarke* [1955] AC 778 (profit à prendre); *Ex p Wright* (1812) 19 Ves 255 (mortgage by deposit of title deeds, where the contract was enforceable under the doctrine of part performance, p. 17, above; now, however, a written contract is required under LP(MP)A 1989, s. 2: *United Bank of Kuwait Sahib* [1997] Ch 107, p. 866, below).

[87] *Williams v Greatrex* [1957] 1 WLR 31; *Cornish v Brook Green Laundry Ltd* [1959] 1 QB 394; (1959) 75 LQR 168 (R.E.M.); *Kingswood Estate Co Ltd v Anderson* [1963] 2 QB 169; (1963) 79 LQR 19 (R.E.M.); *Bell Street Investments v Wood* (1970) 216 EG 585; *Henry Smith's Charity Trustees v Hemmings* (1982) 45 P & CR 377; *Shelley v United Artists Corpn Ltd* [1990] 1 EGLR 103. For a criticism of the requirement of specific performance, see (1987) 7 OJLS 60 (S. Gardner).

[88] See now LPA 1925, s. 146, p. 429, below.

Lopes LJ: In this case the tenant, the plaintiff, who brings this action for trespass, is in possession of the land in question under an agreement for a lease. No rent has been paid, and that agreement contains a covenant to cultivate the land according to the approved course of husbandry—the usual covenant—and it has been found by the jury that that covenant has been broken. But, as I have said, no rent has been paid. If rent had been paid the position of things would have been very different. Then the plaintiff would have been a tenant from year to year on the terms of that agreement, so far as those terms are not inconsistent with a yearly tenancy. But no rent having been paid, I am clearly of opinion that the plaintiff is a tenant at will only.

But it is said in this case that he is more than a tenant at will, because the court of equity would have decreed specific performance of this agreement for a lease, and that he must be regarded as lessee for the term of years mentioned in that agreement on the ground that we must regard that as done which a court of equity would have done. No doubt that is perfectly correct. But then the point arises, would the court of equity have decreed specific performance under the particular circumstances of this case? The plaintiff, the tenant, when he went to the court of equity and asked for specific performance, would have had to admit that which has been proved here, namely, that he himself had failed to perform a material portion of the contract—in point of fact, that he had broken a portion of the agreement. I take it that, under those circumstances, it is perfectly clear that the court of equity would have refused specific performance. If that is so, he is only a tenant at will. The notice had been given; the tenancy was determined; and the landlord, the defendant, makes out the justification which he sets up in this action. It might have been that a very different and important question might have arisen under section 14 of the Conveyancing Act 1881. I do not think, however, that that arises under the circumstances of this case. It is not necessary for us to consider what the position of the tenant under the lease would have been, and I therefore do not give any opinion with regard to that section.

(c) Registration

Since the enforceable contract for the sale or other disposition of an interest in land creates an equitable interest in favour of the purchaser, the purchaser must protect his interest if it is not to be overridden by a subsequent dealing with the legal title before he acquires the legal title himself. Originally this meant that the equitable interest would be defeated by a bona fide purchaser of the legal estate without notice.[89] Now, however, its protection depends upon registration as a land charge in unregistered land, or upon registration or protection as an overriding interest in registered land.

Maitland, *Equity* (2nd edn), p. 158:

An agreement for a lease is not equal to a lease. An equitable right is not equivalent to a legal right; between the contracting parties an agreement for a lease may be as good as a lease; just so between the contracting parties an agreement for the sale of land may serve as well as a completed sale and conveyance. But introduce the third party and then you will see the difference. I take a lease; my lessor then sells the land to X; notice or no notice my lease is good against X. I take a mere agreement for a lease, and the person who has agreed to grant the lease then sells and conveys to Y, who has no notice of my merely equitable right. Y is not bound to grant me a lease.

---

[89] P. 58, below.

In unregistered land I may protect my equitable interest against a third party by registering it as a land charge Class C(iv) under the Land Charges Act 1972.[90] In registered land I may protect it by the entry of a notice under the Land Registration Act 2002; failing that, by having an overriding interest as a person in discoverable actual occupation of the land.[91]

(vi) Option to purchase and right of pre-emption[92]

(a) Option to purchase

An option to purchase has been analysed in two different ways. (1) As an offer to sell which 'the grantor is contractually precluded from withdrawing so long as the option remains exercisable'.[93] A contract to purchase is formed when the notice exercising the option is given to the grantor. (2) As 'a conditional contract which the grantee is entitled to convert into a concluded contract of purchase'.[94] In *Spiro v Glencrown Properties Ltd*,[95] however, Hoffmann J held that neither analysis was convincing but rather an option creates a relationship *sui generis*.

The option creates an immediate equitable interest in favour of the grantee as soon as it is granted. The grantee's right to call for a conveyance of the land is an equitable interest; as far as the grantor is concerned, 'his estate or interest is taken away from him without his consent, and the right to take it away being vested in another, the covenant giving the option must give that other an interest in the land'.[96]

Spiro v Glencrown Properties Ltd[97]
[1991] Ch 537 (ChD, **Hoffmann J**)

Hoffmann J: This is an action for damages for breach of a contract to buy land. On 14 November 1989 the plaintiff granted an option to the first defendant ('the purchaser') to buy a property

---

[90] LCA 1972, s. 2(4), p. 66, below.

[91] LRA 2002, ss. 28, 29, 32, Sch. 3. para. 2, pp. 170, 172, 196, below.

[92] C & B, pp. 880–3; Gray, paras 8.1.73–8.1.82; M & W, paras 15.012–15.013; MM, p. 150; Smith, p. 94. See generally *Barnsley's Land Options* (4th edn, 2004); (1974) 38 Conv (NS) 8 (A. Pritchard); [1984] CLJ 55 (S. Tromans); (1991) Can BR (P. M. Perell); Blundell Memorial Lecture 1996 (T. Etherton and D. Beales).

[93] *Beesly v Hallwood Estates Ltd* [1960] 1 WLR 549 at 556, per Buckley J. See also *Brown v Gould* [1972] Ch 53 at 58, p. 371, below. The option must be sufficiently certain in its terms: *Sudbrook Trading Estate Ltd v Eggleton* [1983] 1 AC 444, p. 375, below.

[94] *Griffith v Pelton* [1958] Ch 205 at 225, per Jenkins LJ.   [95] Below.

[96] *London and South Western Rly Co v Gomm* (1882) 20 ChD 562 at 581, per Jessel MR; *Griffith v Pelton* [1958] Ch 205 at 225; *Webb v Pollmount Ltd* [1966] Ch 584 at 597; *Mountford v Scott* [1975] Ch 258; *George Wimpey & Co Ltd v IRC* [1974] 1 WLR 975 at 980; affd [1975] 1 WLR 995; *Pritchard v Briggs* [1980] Ch 338 at 418, below, p. 38. See also *Di Luca v Juraise (Springs) Ltd* [1998] 2 EGLR 125 ('The rule that time is of the essence, a settled and invariable rule in relation to options to purchase', per Nourse LJ). If an option is registered, there is no need to register the ensuing contract when the option is exercised: *Armstrong & Holmes Ltd v Holmes* [1993] 1 WLR 1482; [1994] Conv 483 (N. P. Gravells).

[97] [1990] Conv 9 (J. E. Adams); [1990] 47 EG 48 (C. Sydenham and M. Rodrigues); [1991] Conv 140 (P. F. Smith); [1991] CLJ 236 (A. J. Oakley); Emmet, para. 2.080. See also *Bircham & Co Nominees (No 2) Ltd v Worrell Holdings Ltd* [2001] 3 EGLR 83 at [39]-[43], per Chadwick LJ analysing and applying *Spiro v*

in Finchley for £745,000. The option was exercisable by notice in writing delivered to the vendor or his solicitors by 5 p.m. on the same day. The purchaser gave a notice exercising the option within the stipulated time. He failed to complete and the vendor, after serving a notice to complete and issuing a writ for specific performance, rescinded the contract. The second defendant, Mr. Berry, is guarantor of the purchaser's obligations. On 1 May 1990 the vendor obtained judgment in default of defence against the purchaser for damages to be assessed. There are now before me a summons by the vendor for judgment under R.S.C., Ord. 14 against Mr. Berry as guarantor and a summons by the purchaser to set aside the judgment against it. Since both summonses raise the same short point of law and there are no other issues in the case, the parties have agreed to treat this hearing as the trial of the action.

The only question for decision is whether the contract on which the vendor relies complied with the provisions of section 2 of the Law of Property (Miscellaneous Provisions) Act 1989, which came into force on 27 September 1989, some seven weeks before the grant and exercise of the option. It is a question which has produced a lively debate in conveyancing journals. The relevant provisions are as follows:

'(1) A contract for the sale or other disposition of an interest in land can only be made in writing and only by incorporating all the terms which the parties have expressly agreed in one document or, where contracts are exchanged, in each. (2) The terms may be incorporated in a document either by being set out in it or by reference to some other document. (3) The document incorporating the terms or, where contracts are exchanged, one of the documents incorporating them (but not necessarily the same one) must be signed by or on behalf of each party to the contract.'

If the 'contract for the sale ... of an interest in land' was for the purposes of section 2(1) the agreement by which the option was *granted,* there is no difficulty. The agreement was executed in two exchanged parts, each of which incorporated all the terms which had been agreed and had been signed by or on behalf of the vendor and purchaser respectively. But the letter which *exercised* the option was of course signed only on behalf of the purchaser. If the contract was made by this document, it did not comply with section 2.

Apart from authority, it seems to me plain enough that section 2 was intended to apply to the agreement which created the option and not to the notice by which it was exercised. Section 2, which replaced section 40 of the Law of Property Act 1925, was intended to prevent disputes over whether the parties had entered into a binding agreement or over what terms they had agreed. It prescribes the formalities for recording their mutual consent. But only the grant of the option depends upon consent. The exercise of the option is a unilateral act. It would destroy the very purpose of the option if the purchaser had to obtain the vendor's countersignature to the notice by which it was exercised. The only way in which the concept of an option to buy land could survive section 2 would be if the purchaser ensured that the vendor not only signed the agreement by which the option was granted but also at the same time provided him with a countersigned form to use if he decided to exercise it. There seems no conceivable reason why the legislature should have required this additional formality.

The language of section 2 places no obstacle in the way of construing the grant of the option as the relevant contract. An option to buy land can properly be described as a contract for the sale of that land conditional on the exercise of the option. A number of eminent judges have so

Glencrown Properties Ltd; Active Estates Ltd v Parness [2002] 3 EGLR at 18–19 per Neuberger J (put option). A put option is when it is the potential grantee or lessor who is to execute it: a call option (as in *Spiro v Glencrown*) is where it is the potential grantee or purchaser who can execute it.

described it. In *Helby v Matthews* [1895] AC 471 at 482, which concerned the sale of a piano on hire-purchase, Lord Macnaghten said:

> 'The contract, as it seems to me, on the part of the dealer was a contract of hiring coupled with a conditional contract or undertaking to sell. On the part of the customer it was a contract of hiring only until the time came for making the last payment.'

In *Griffith v Pelton* [1958] Ch 205, which raised the question of whether the benefit of an option was assignable, Jenkins LJ said, at 225:

> 'An option in gross for the purchase of land is a conditional contract for such purchase by the grantee of the option from the grantor, which the grantee is entitled to convert into a concluded contract of purchase, and to have carried to completion by the grantor, upon giving the prescribed notice and otherwise complying with the conditions upon which the option is made exercisable in any particular case.'

In the context of section 2, it makes obvious sense to characterise it in this way. So far, therefore, the case seems to me to be clear.

The purchaser, however, submits that I am constrained by authority to characterise an option as an irrevocable offer which does not become a contract for the sale of land until it has been accepted by the notice which exercises the option. It follows that the 'contract for the sale . . . of an interest in land' within the meaning of section 2 can only have been made by the letter.

His Lordship referred to *Helby v Matthews* [1895] AC 471 and continued:

But the concept of an offer is of course normally used as part of the technique for ascertaining whether the parties have reached that mutual consent which is a necessary element in the formation of a contract. In this primary sense, it is of the essence of an offer that by itself it gives rise to no legal obligations. It was for this reason that Diplock LJ said in *Varty v British South Africa Co* [1965] Ch 508, 523:

> 'To speak of an enforceable option as an "irrevocable offer" is juristically a contradiction in terms, for the adjective "irrevocable" connotes the existence of an obligation on the part of the offeror, while the noun "offer" connotes the absence of an obligation until the offer has been accepted.'

Here the underlying principles are clear enough. The granting of the option imposes no obligation on the purchaser and an obligation on the vendor which is contingent on the exercise of the option. When the option is exercised, vendor and purchaser come under obligations to perform as if they had concluded an ordinary contract of sale. And the analogy of an irrevocable offer is, as I have said, a useful way of describing the position of the purchaser between the grant and exercise of the option. Thus in *J Sainsbury plc v O'Connor* [1990] STC 516, Millett J used it to explain why the grantee of an option to buy shares did not become the beneficial owner until he had exercised the option.

But the irrevocable offer metaphor has much less explanatory power in relation to the position of the vendor. The effect of the 'offer' which the vendor has made is, from his point of view, so different from that of an offer in its primary sense that the metaphor is of little assistance. Thus in the famous passage in *London and South Western Rly Co v Gomm* (1882) 20 Ch D 562, 581, Sir George Jessel MR had no use for it in explaining why the grant of an option to buy land confers an interest in the land upon the grantee:

> 'The right to call for a conveyance of the land is an equitable interest or an equitable estate. In the ordinary case of a contract for purchase there is no doubt about this, and an option for repurchase is

not different in its nature. A person exercising the option has to do two things, he has to give notice of his intention to purchase, and to pay the purchase money; but as far as the man who is liable to convey is concerned, his estate or interest is taken away from him without his consent, and the right to take it away being vested in another, the covenant giving the option must give that other an interest in the land.'

The fact that the option binds the vendor contingently to convey was the reason why an option agreement was held to fall within section 40 of the Law of Property Act 1925: see *Richards v Creighton Griffiths (Investments) Ltd* (1972) 225 EG 2104, where Plowman J rejected a submission that it was merely a contract not to withdraw an offer. Similarly in *Weeding v Weeding* (1861) 1 John & H 424, Page-Wood V-C held that the grant of an option to buy land was sufficient to deem that land converted into personalty for the purposes of the grantor's will, even though the option had not yet been exercised when he died. The Vice-Chancellor said, at 430–431:

'I cannot agree with the argument that there is no contract. It is as much a conditional contract as if it depended on any other contingency than the exercise of an option by a third person, such as, for example, the failure of issue of a particular person.'

Thus in explaining the vendor's position, the analogy to which the courts usually appeal is that of a conditional contract. This analogy might also be said to be imperfect, because one generally thinks of a conditional contract as one in which the contingency does not lie within the sole power of one of the parties to the contract. But this difference from the standard case of a conditional contract does not destroy the value of the analogy in explaining the *vendor's* position. So far as he is concerned, it makes no difference whether or not the contingency is within the sole power of the purchaser. The important point is that 'his estate or interest is taken away from him without his consent.'

His Lordship referred to *Griffith v Pelton* [1958] Ch 205; *Laybutt v Amoco Australia Pty Ltd* (1974) 48 ALJR 492, and continued:

The purchaser's argument requires me to say that 'irrevocable offer' and 'conditional contract' are mutually inconsistent concepts and that I must range myself under one or other banner and declare the other to be heretical. I hope that I have demonstrated this to be a misconception about the nature of legal reasoning. An option is not strictly speaking either an offer or a conditional contract. It does not have *all* the incidents of the standard form of either of these concepts. To that extent it is a relationship sui generis. But there are ways in which it resembles each of them. Each analogy is in the proper context a valid way of characterising the situation created by an option. The question in this case is not whether one analogy is true and the other false, but which is appropriate to be used in the construction of section 2 of the Law of Property (Miscellaneous Provisions) Act 1989.

His Lordship referred to *Beesly v Hallwood Estates Ltd* [1960] 1 WLR 549, 556; *London and South Western Rly Co v Gomm* (1882) 20 Ch D 562, 581, and *United Scientific Holdings Ltd v Burnley Borough Council* [1978] AC 904, and continued:

Perhaps the most helpful case for present purposes is *Re Mulholland's Will Trusts* [1949] 1 All ER 460. A testator had let premises to the Westminster Bank on a lease which included an option to purchase. He appointed the bank his executor and trustee and after his death the bank exercised the option. It was argued for his widow and children that the bank was precluded from exercising the option by the rule that a trustee cannot contract with himself. Wynn-Parry J was pressed with the irrevocable offer metaphor, which, it was said, led inexorably to the conclusion that when the bank exercised the option, it was indeed entering into a contract with itself. But Wynn-Parry J held that if one considered the purpose of the self-dealing rule, which was to prevent a trustee from being subjected to a conflict of interest and duty, the only relevant contract was the grant of the option. The rule could only sensibly be applied to a consensual transaction. While for some purposes it might be true to say that the exercise of the option brought the contract into existence, there could be no rational ground for applying the self-dealing rule to the unilateral exercise of a right granted before the trusteeship came into existence. Wynn-Parry J quoted, at p. 464, from Sir George Jessel MR in *Gomm's* case, 20 Ch D 562, 582, and said:

> 'As I understand that passage, it amounts to this, that, as regards this option, there was between the parties only one contract, namely, the contract constituted by the provisions in the lease which I have read creating the option. The notice exercising the option did not lead, in my opinion, to the creation of any fresh contractual relationship between the parties, making them for the first time vendors and purchasers, nor did it bring into existence any right in addition to the right conferred by the option....'

In my judgment there is nothing in the authorities which prevents me from giving section 2 of the Act of 1989 the meaning which I consider to have been the clear intention of the legislature. On the contrary, the purposive approach taken in cases like *Mulholland* [1949] 1 All ER 460 encourages me to adopt a similar approach to section 2. And the plain purpose of section 2 was, as I have said, to prescribe the formalities for recording the consent of the parties. It follows that in my view the grant of the option was the only 'contract for the sale or other disposition of an interest in land' within the meaning of the section and the contract duly complied with the statutory requirements. There must be judgment for the plaintiff against both defendants with costs.

(b) Right of pre-emption

A right of pre-emption does not give the grantee the immediate right to call for the transfer of the property, but will generally give the grantee such a right *if* the grantor decides to sell and thereby converts the pre-emption into an option.[98] The proprietary effect of a right of pre-emption has been disputed, but the majority of the Court of Appeal in *Pritchard v Briggs*[99] held that it creates an equitable interest in the grantee from the moment when the grantor fulfils the conditions for its conversion into an option. In registered land, the Land Registration Act 2002[100] settled the question by providing that a right of pre-emption has proprietary effect from the moment of its creation.

In **Kling v Keston Properties Ltd** (1983) 49 P & CR 212, the question was whether a right of pre-emption over a garage in Chelsea was enforceable by the grantee against a

---

[98] There are various different forms of pre-emption: *Bircham & Co Nominees (No 2) Ltd v Worrell Holdings Ltd* (2001) 82 P & CR 34 at [31], per Chadwick LJ (distinguishing a 'right of first refusal' from a right of pre-emption); *Speciality Shops v Yorkshire and Metropolitan Estates Ltd* [2003] 2 P & CR 31 at [25]–[29], per Park J, identifying three forms of right of pre-emption; 'more may exist'.

[99] [1980] Ch 338; discussed in *Kling v Keston Properties Ltd* (1983) 49 P & CR 212, below.

[100] S. 115; below, p. 40.

purchaser of the garage from the grantor. In holding that it was, VINELOTT J followed the views of the majority of the Court of Appeal in *Pritchard v Briggs* [1980] Ch 338[101] that the right of pre-emption, although not initially an interest in land, became an equitable interest when the grantor agreed to sell the garage to the purchaser. He said at 215:

The question whether a right of pre-emption or first refusal over land creates an equitable interest in the land capable of binding a purchaser was for many years a controversial one. It was settled so far as this court is concerned by the decision of the Court of Appeal in *Pritchard v Briggs*. In that case, the owners of a piece of land granted the defendants' predecessor in title a right of first refusal. It was granted in the form of a negative stipulation 'that so long as the [grantee] shall live and the [owners] or the survivors of them shall also be alive the [owners] will not nor will either of them sell or concur in selling all or any part of the [land] without giving to the [grantee] the option of purchasing [the land]'—at a stated price. Later the owners granted a lease to the plaintiff and the lease contained an option giving the plaintiff the right to purchase the land on three months' notice after the death of the survivor of the owners, again at a fixed price.

A further lease was subsequently granted and the option was repeated in it. Both the right of pre-emption and the option were registered as estate contracts under the Land Charges Act 1925. Under that Act, and under the Land Charges Act 1972 (which is a consolidating Act) the contracts registrable as estate contracts expressly include a contract conferring 'a valid option or right of pre-emption or any other like right.' The survivor of the owners, a Major Lockwood, in fact sold the land to the defendants, purportedly in pursuance of the right of pre-emption. After the death of Major Lockwood, the plaintiff gave notice exercising the option. Goff LJ was of the opinion that the right of pre-emption created a merely personal right and did not create an interest in land even after the conditions for its exercise had been satisfied. Accordingly the defendants could not claim priority over the plaintiff's option. In his opinion the Land Charges Act 1972, in so far as it provided for registration of a right of pre-emption as an estate contract, proceeded on a wrong view of the law.[102] However, Templeman and Stephenson LJJ took a different view of the nature and effect of a right of pre-emption. Templeman LJ explained the effect of a right of pre-emption in a passage which I should, I think, cite in full. He said at 418:

'Rights of option and rights of pre-emption share one feature in common; each prescribes circumstances in which the relationship between the owner of the property which is the subject of the right and the holder of the right will become the relationship of vendor and purchaser. In the case of an option, the evolution of the relationship of vendor and purchaser may depend on the fulfilment of certain specified conditions and will depend on the volition of the option holder. If the option applies to land, the grant of the option creates a contingent equitable interest which, if registered as an estate contract, is binding on successors in title of the grantor and takes priority from the date of its registration. In the case of a right of pre-emption, the evolution of the relationship of vendor and

---

[101] (1980) 96 LQR 488 (H.W.R.W.); [1980] Conv 433 (J. Martin). See also *Manchester Ship Canal Co v Manchester Racecourse Co* [1901] 2 Ch 37; *Murray v Two Strokes Ltd* [1973] 1 WLR 823; (1973) 89 LQR 462 (M. J. Albery); *First National Securities Ltd v Chiltern District Council* [1975] 1 WLR 1075; cf. *Birmingham Canal Co v Cartwright* (1879) 11 ChD 421.

[102] For similar provisions, see LPA 1925, ss. 2(3)(iv), 186; SLA 1925, ss. 58(2), 61(2); PAA 1964, s. 9(2). See also HA 1925, s. 33.

purchaser depends on the grantor, of his own volition, choosing to fulfil certain specified conditions and thus converting the pre-emption into an option. The grant of the right of pre-emption creates a mere spes which the grantor of the right may either frustrate by choosing not to fulfil the necessary conditions or may convert into an option and thus into equitable interest by fulfilling the conditions. An equitable interest thus created is protected by prior registration of the right of pre-emption as an estate contract but takes its priority from the date when the right of pre-emption becomes exercisable and the right is converted into an option and the equitable interest is then created. The holder of a right of pre-emption is in much the same position as a beneficiary under a will of a testator who is still alive, save that the holder of the right of pre-emption must hope for some future positive action by the grantor which will elevate his hope into an interest. It does not seem to me that the property legislation of 1925 was intended to create, or operated to create an equitable interest in land where none existed.'

Accordingly the plaintiff's claim succeeded, for:

'After the grant of Mr Pritchard's option, Major Lockwood was not in a position to make an offer to Mr and Mrs Briggs or to grant an option to them pursuant to their right of pre-emption or at all save subject to Mr Pritchard's option. After the registration of Mr Pritchard's option, Mr and Mrs Briggs could not accept an offer or exercise an option granted by Major Lockwood pursuant to the right of pre-emption or at all save subject to Mr Pritchard's option. In short Major Lockwood could only sell and the Briggs could only purchase subject to Mr Pritchard's option; ...'

Stephenson LJ said at 423:

'The 1944 conveyance—(which created the right of pre-emption)—refers to giving the option of purchasing but as a future act, not as a present right; and Mr Scott has satisfied me that what is granted as a right of pre-emption, on the true construction of the grant, is only properly called an option when the will of the grantor turns it into an option by deciding to sell and thereby binding the grantor to offer it for sale to the grantee. That it thereby becomes an interest in land is a change in the nature of the right to which, unlike Goff LJ, I see no insuperable objection in logic or in principle. And, as I understand his opinion on this point, its consequence would be that a right of pre-emption could never be enforceable against a successor in title whether it is registered or not.

I accordingly prefer the option of Templeman LJ on this point'.[103]

LAND REGISTRATION ACT 2002

115 Rights of pre-emption[104]

(1) A right of pre-emption in relation to registered land has effect from the time of creation as an interest capable of binding successors in title (subject to the rules about the effect of dispositions on priority).

(2) This section has effect in relation to rights of pre-emption created on or after the day on which this section comes into force.[105]

---

[103] For a detailed analysis of the right, see Chadwick LJ in *Bircham & Co Nominees (No 2) Ltd v Worrell Holdings Ltd* [2001] 3 EGLR 83 at [26]-[44]; *Tiffany Investments Ltd v Bircham & Co Nominees (No 2) Ltd* [2004] 2 EGLR 31; *Dear v Reeves* [2002] Ch 1 (right of pre-emption held to be an interest in land for the purposes of Insolvency Act 1986, s. 436 ('*Pritchard v Briggs* was a decision on the construction of LCA 1925', per Mummery LJ at [43]); [2001] Conv 295 (P. H. Kenny).

[104] H & B para. 9.15; R & R, paras 15.026–15.027.   [105] 13 October 2003.

QUESTIONS

1. It has often been said that the Judicature Act effects a fusion of procedure but not of substantive law. 'But the two streams of jurisdiction, though they run in the same channel run side by side, and do not mingle their waters': Ashburner, *Principles of Equity* (2nd edn, 1933), p. 18. What light is thrown on this question by the cases considered in this section? See also (1870) 14 SJ 548; (1954) 70 LQR 326 (Lord Evershed); (1961) 24 MLR 116 (V. T. H. Delany); (1977) 93 LQR 529 (P. V. Baker); (1977) 6 Anglo-Am 119 (T. G. Watkin); H & M, pp. 20–26; Meagher, Gummow and Lehane, *Equity: Doctrines and Remedies* (4th edn, 2002), chap. 2; Pettit, *Equity and the Law of Trusts* (10th edn, 2006), pp. 9–11; *United Scientific Holdings Ltd v Burnley Borough Council* [1978] AC 904; *Tinsley v Milligan* [1994] 1 AC 340 at 370, 375.

2. Work out, step by step, the way in which the *Walsh v Lonsdale* litigation would have proceeded before 1875. H & M para. 1–016.

3. Is a contract for a lease as good as a lease? p. 419, below. What is the effect on this of (a) Land Charges Act 1972; (b) Law of Property (Miscellaneous Provisions) Act 1989, s. 2; [1990] Conv 44 (J. Howell); (c) Land Registration Act 2002?

B. FORMALITIES FOR THE CREATION AND TRANSFER OF ESTATES AND INTERESTS

(i) Legal estates and interests

With some exceptions,[106] the creation or transfer of a legal estate or interest must be made by deed. In addition, in registered land, certain dispositions are required to be completed by registration and do not operate at law until the relevant registration requirements are met.[107]

(a) Requirement of deed[108]

LAW OF PROPERTY ACT 1925

51. Lands lie in grant only.—(1) All lands and all interests therein lie in grant and are incapable of being conveyed by livery or livery and seisin, or by feoffment, or by bargain and sale,[109] and a conveyance of an interest in land may operate to pass the possession or right to possession thereof, without actual entry, but subject to all prior rights thereto.

---

[106] LPA 1925, s. 52(2), below.   [107] LRA 2002, s. 27; below, p. 163.

[108] C & B, pp. 896–902; Gray, paras 8.1.87–8.1.95; MM, pp. 158–86. S. 54(1) follows Statute of Frauds, s. 1; and s. 52(1) follows Real Property Act 1845, s. 3.

[109] For these old methods of conveyancing, see Holdsworth, vol. 3, pp. 217–46; vol. 7, pp. 356–62.

52. Conveyances to be by deed.—(1) All conveyances of land or of any interest therein are void for the purpose of conveying or creating a legal estate unless made by deed.

(2) This section does not apply to—

(a) assents by a personal representative,[110]

(b) disclaimers made in accordance with sections 178 to 180 or sections 315 to 319 of the Insolvency Act 1986,[111] or not required to be evidenced in writing;

(c) surrenders by operation of law, including surrenders which may, by law, be effected without writing;

(d) leases or tenancies or other assurances not required by law to be made in writing;

(e) receipts other than those falling within section 115 below;[112]

(f) vesting orders of the court or other competent authority;

(g) conveyances taking effect by operation of law.[113]

54. Creation of interests in land by parol.—(1) All interests in land created by parol and not put in writing and signed by the persons so creating the same, or by their agents thereunto lawfully authorised in writing, have, notwithstanding any consideration having been given for the same, the force and effect of interests at will only.

(2) Nothing in the foregoing provisions of this Part of this Act shall affect the creation by parol of leases taking effect in possession[114] for a term not exceeding three years (whether or not the lessee is given power to extend the term) at the best rent which can be reasonably obtained without taking a fine.[115]

55. Savings in regard to last two sections.—Nothing in the last two foregoing sections[116] shall—

(a) invalidate dispositions by will; or

(b) affect any interest validly created before the commencement of this Act; or

(c) affect the right to acquire an interest in land by virtue of taking possession; or

(d) affect the operation of the law relating to part performance.

---

[110] But assents to the vesting of a legal estate in land must be in writing, signed by the personal representative: AEA 1925, s. 36(1) (4); *Re Edwards' Will Trusts* [1982] Ch 30; *Re King's Will Trusts* [1964] Ch 542; (1964) 28 Conv (NS) 298 (J. F. Garner); (1976) CLP 60 (E. C. Ryder); Farrand, *Contract and Conveyance* (4th edn), p. 106; Barnsley, p. 321. See Law Commission Report on Title on Death 1989 (Law Com No. 184), paras 1.5–1.6. *Re King's Will Trusts* was not followed in *Mohay v Roche* [1991] 1 IR 560; [1992] Conv 383 (J. A. Dowling).

[111] As amended by Insolvency Act 1986, s. 439, Sch. 14.

[112] Reconveyances of mortgages by endorsed receipts, p. 981, below. As amended by LP(MP)A 1989, s. 1, Sch. 1, para. 2.

[113] E.g. probates and letters of administration.

[114] A reversionary lease conferring no immediate right to take possession is excluded from the ambit of s. 54(2) and can take effect only if made by deed: *Long v Tower Hamlets Borough Council* [1998] Ch 197 at 210–219; [2001] Conv 213 (J.E.A.).

[115] I.e. a premium paid on the granting of the lease and operating in reduction of the rent; LP(MP)A 1989, s. 2, does not apply to a contract to grant such a lease: s. 2(5)(a), p. 19, above.

[116] For s. 53, see p. 47, below.

(b) Form of deed

1. General requirements and execution by individuals

LAW OF PROPERTY (MISCELLANEOUS PROVISIONS) ACT 1989

1. Deeds and their execution.[117]—(1) Any rule of law which—

(a) restricts the substances on which a deed may be written;

(b) requires a seal for the valid execution of an instrument as a deed by an individual; or

(c) requires authority by one person to another to deliver an instrument as a deed on his behalf to be given by deed,

is abolished.

(2) An instrument shall not be a deed unless—

(a) it makes it clear on its face that it is intended to be a deed by the person making it or, as the case may be, by the parties to it (whether by describing itself as a deed or expressing itself to be executed or signed as a deed or otherwise);[118] and

(b) it is validly executed as a deed—

(i) by that person or a person authorised to execute it in the name or on behalf of that person, or

(ii) by one or more of those parties or a person authorised to execute it in the name or on behalf of one or more of those parties.

(2A) For the purposes of subsection (2)(a) above, an instrument shall not be taken to make it clear on its face that it is intended to be a deed merely because it is executed under seal.

(3) An instrument is validly executed as a deed by an individual if, and only if—

(a) it is signed—

(i) by him in the presence of a witness who attests the signature; or

(ii) at his direction and in his presence and the presence of two witnesses who each attest the signature; and

(b) it is delivered as a deed.

(4) In subsections (2) and (3) above 'sign', in relation to an instrument, includes—

(a) an individual signing the name of the person or party on whose behalf he executes the instrument; and

(b) making one's mark on the instrument,

---

[117] As amended by Courts and Legal Services Act 1990, s. 125(2), Sch. 17, para. 20; Regulatory Reform (Execution of Deeds and Documents) Order 2005 (SI 2005 No. 1906). This section is based on Law Commission Report on Deeds and Escrows 1987 (Law Com No. 163). See [1991] LMCLQ 209 (G. Virgo and C. Harpum) for a trenchant criticism of 'the recent reforms which have left the law of deeds both more complex and less rational than it was hitherto'.

[118] *HSBC Trust Co (UK) Ltd v Quinn* [2007] EWHC 1543 (Ch), [2007] All ER(D) 125 (Jul) (use of formal language in the document and witnesses to signatures not sufficient: 'All that they show is that the parties intended it to be legally binding, and in my judgment this is plainly not enough; what is needed is something showing that the parties intended the document to have the extra status of being a deed': at [51], per Nugee QC).

and 'signature' is to be construed accordingly.

(4A) Subsection (3) above applies in the case of an instrument executed by an individual in the name or on behalf of another person whether or not that person is also an individual.

(5) Where a solicitor, duly certificated notary public or licensed conveyancer, or an agent or employee of a solicitor, duly certificated notary public or licensed conveyancer, in the course of or in connection with a transaction, purports to deliver an instrument as a deed on behalf of a party to the instrument, it shall be conclusively presumed in favour of a purchaser that he is authorised so to deliver the instrument.

2. Execution by companies

COMPANIES ACT 2006[119]

44 Execution of documents

(1) Under the law of England and Wales or Northern Ireland a document is executed by a company—

    (a) by the affixing of its common seal, or

    (b) by signature in accordance with the following provisions.

(2) A document is validly executed by a company if it is signed on behalf of the company—

    (a) by two authorised signatories, or

    (b) by a director of the company in the presence of a witness who attests the signature.

(3) The following are 'authorised signatories' for the purposes of subsection (2)—

    (a) every director of the company, and

    (b) in the case of a private company with a secretary or a public company, the secretary (or any joint secretary) of the company.

(4) A document signed in accordance with subsection (2) and expressed, in whatever words, to be executed by the company has the same effect as if executed under the common seal of the company.

45 Common seal

(1) A company may have a common seal, but need not have one.

(2) A company which has a common seal shall have its name engraved in legible characters on the seal.

46 Execution of deeds

(1) A document is validly executed by a company as a deed for the purposes of section 1(2)(b) of the Law of Property (Miscellaneous Provisions) Act 1989...if, and only if—

    (a) it is duly executed by the company, and

    (b) it is delivered as a deed.

(2) For the purposes of subsection (1)(b) a document is presumed to be delivered upon its being executed, unless a contrary intention is proved.

[119] Replacing CA 1985, s. 36A.

For corporations sole, and corporations aggregate[120] which are not companies within the Companies Act 1985, sealing remains a requirement.

3. Electronic documents

For the purposes of electronic conveyancing in registered land, the Land Registration Act 2002 provides that certain electronic documents are to be treated as taking effect as deeds.

LAND REGISTRATION ACT 2002

91 Electronic dispositions: formalities

(1) This section applies to a document in electronic form where—

    (a) the document purports to effect a disposition which falls within subsection (2), and

    (b) the conditions in subsection (3) are met.

(2) A disposition falls within this subsection if it is—

    (a) a disposition of a registered estate or charge,

    (b) a disposition of an interest which is the subject of a notice in the register, or

    (c) a disposition which triggers the requirement of registration,

which is of a kind specified by rules.

(3) The conditions referred to above are that—

    (a) the document makes provision for the time and date when it takes effect,

    (b) the document has the electronic signature of each person by whom it purports to be authenticated,

    (c) each electronic signature is certified, and

    (d) such other conditions as rules may provide are met.

(4) A document to which this section applies is to be regarded as—

    (a) in writing, and

    (b) signed by each individual, and sealed by each corporation, whose electronic signature it has.

(5) A document to which this section applies is to be regarded for the purposes of any enactment as a deed.

(9) In relation to the execution of a document by a company in accordance with section 44(2) of the Companies Act 2006 (signature on behalf of the company)—

    (a) subsection (4) above has effect in relation to paragraph (a) of that provision (signature by two authorised signatories) but not paragraph (b) (signature by director in presence of witness);

---

[120] 'In favour of a purchaser an instrument shall be deemed to have been duly executed by a corporation aggregate if a seal purporting to be the corporation's seal purports to be affixed to the instrument in the presence of and attested by (a) two members of the board of directors, council or the governing body of the corporation, or (b) one such member and the clerk, secretary or other permanent officer of the corporation or his deputy': LPA 1925, s. 74 (1) as substituted by SI 2005 No. 1906, art. 3.

(b) the other provisions of section 44 apply accordingly (the references to a document purporting to be signed in accordance with subsection (2) of that section being read as references to its purporting to be authenticated in accordance with this section);

(c) where subsection (4) above has effect in relation to a person signing on behalf of more than one company, the requirement of subsection (6) of that section is treated as met if the document specifies the different capacities in which the person signs.[121]

(10) In this section, references to an electronic signature and to the certification of such a signature are to be read in accordance with section 7(2) and (3) of the Electronic Communications Act 2000.

(c) Registered land: registration requirements

LAND REGISTRATION ACT 2002

27 Dispositions required to be registered

(1) If a disposition of a registered estate or registered charge is required to be completed by registration, it does not operate at law until the relevant registration requirements are met.

(2) In the case of a registered estate, the following are the dispositions which are required to be completed by registration—

(a) a transfer,

(b) where the registered estate is an estate in land, the grant of a term of years absolute—

(i)   for a term of more than seven years from the date of the grant,

(ii)   to take effect in possession after the end of the period of three months beginning with the date of the grant,

(iii) under which the right to possession is discontinuous,

(iv) in pursuance of Part 5 of the Housing Act 1985 (the right to buy), or

(v)   in circumstances where section 171A of that Act applies (disposal by landlord which leads to a person no longer being a secure tenant),

(c) where the registered estate is a franchise or manor, the grant of a lease,

(d) the express grant or reservation of an interest of a kind falling within section 1(2)(a) of the Law of Property Act 1925, other than one which is capable of being registered under Part 1 of the Commons Act 2006,[122]

(e) the express grant or reservation of an interest of a kind falling within section 1(2)(b) or (e) of the Law of Property Act 1925, and

(f) the grant of a legal charge.

(3) In the case of a registered charge, the following are the dispositions which are required to be completed by registration—

(a) a transfer, and

---

[121] As substituted by SI 2008 No. 948, Sch. 1, para. 224.
[122] As amended by Commons Act 2006, s. 52, Sch. 5, para. 8(1), (2).

(b) the grant of a sub-charge.

(4) Schedule 2 to this Act (which deals with the relevant registration requirements) has effect.[123]

(7) In subsection (2)(d), the reference to express grant does not include grant as a result of the operation of section 62 of the Law of Property Act 1925.

(ii) Equitable interests[124]

LAW OF PROPERTY ACT 1925

53. Instruments required to be in writing.[125]—(1) Subject to the provisions hereinafter contained with respect to the creation of interests in land by parol—

(a) no interest in land can be created or disposed of except by writing signed by the person creating or conveying the same, or by his agent thereunto lawfully authorised in writing, or by will, or by operation of law;

(b) a declaration of trust respecting any land or any interest therein must be manifested and proved by some writing signed by some person who is able to declare such trust or by his will;

(c) a disposition of an equitable interest or trust subsisting at the time of the disposition, must be in writing[126] signed by the person disposing of the same, or by his agent thereunto lawfully authorised in writing or by will.[127]

(2) This section does not affect the creation or operation of resulting, implied or constructive trusts.[128]

55. Savings in regard to last two sections.—p. 42, above.

(iii) Failure to comply with the required formalities: constructive trust and estoppel

In certain circumstances the law will allow a party who has failed to comply with the formalities required for the creation or transfer of an estate or interest in land still to have some form of enforceable right relating to the land. The informal creation

---

[123] Below, p. 164.   [124] C & B, pp. 903–4; M & W, paras 11.036–11.049.

[125] See generally H & M, pp. 79–94; M & B, *Trusts and Trustees* (7th edn, 2008), pp. 111–125.

[126] This may be satisfied by joinder of documents: *Re Danish Bacon Co Ltd Staff Pension Fund Trusts* [1971] 1 WLR 248; cf. LPA 1925, s. 40(1), p. 17, above; LP(MP)A 1989, s. 2(3), p. 19, above; *Timmins v Moreland Street Property Co Ltd* [1958] Ch 110; *Elias v George Sahely & Co (Barbados) Ltd* [1983] 1 AC 646.

[127] *Grey v IRC* [1960] AC 1; (1960) 76 LQR 197 (R. E. Megarry); *Oughtred v IRC* [1960] AC 206; *Bishop Square Ltd v IRC* (1997) 78 P & CR 169; *Neville v Wilson* [1997] Ch 144; *Re Tyler* [1967] 1 WLR 1269; *Vandervell v IRC* [1967] 2 AC 291 at 310–312; [1966] CLJ 19 (G. H. Jones); *Re Vandervell's Trusts (No 2)* [1974] Ch 269; (1975) 38 MLR 557 (J. W. Harris); see generally [1979] Conv 17; (1975) 7 Ottawa LR 483 (G. Battersby); (1984) 47 MLR 385 (B. Green).

[128] *Bannister v Bannister* [1948] 2 All ER 133, p. 1101, below; *Hodgson v Marks* [1971] Ch 892; *Binions v Evans* [1972] Ch 359, p. 1102, below; *Ottaway v Norman* [1972] Ch 698.

of interests in land is within the traditional domain of equity. We have already seen that the failure to comply with the requirements for the creation or transfer of a legal estate or interest in land can, under the doctrine of *Walsh v Lonsdale*,[129] be remedied by the court recognising that the intended beneficiary of the legal right, as long as he has the benefit of a specifically enforceable contract, has the equivalent *equitable* right. In certain other contexts the courts use the doctrines of constructive trust or proprietary estoppel to protect a party against the failure of formality. These will be discussed later.[130]

IV. ALIENABILITY

A. CONDITIONS AGAINST ALIENATION[131]

Cheshire and Burn's Modern Law of Real Property (17th edn, 2006), pp. 574–575

(1) TOTAL RESTRAINTS

In accordance with the cardinal principle that the power of alienation is necessarily and insep-arably incidental to ownership, it has been held in a long line of decisions that if an *absolute* interest is given to a donee—whether it be a fee simple, a fee tail, a life interest or any other interest, and whether it be in possession or *in futuro*—any restriction which *substantially* takes that power away is void as being repugnant to the very conception of ownership.[132] Therefore, a condition[133] that the donee:

> shall not alienate at all;[134] or
> shall not alienate during a particular time, such as the life of a certain person,[135] or during his own life;[136] or
> shall alienate only to one particular person,[137] or to a small and diminishing class of persons, such as to one of his three brothers;[138]

---

[129] (1882) 21 ChD 9; p. 29, above.

[130] Pp. 574–601, below (co-ownership in equity: constructive trust); pp. 1101–1107, below (licence protected by constructive trust); pp. 1007–1079, 1107–1109 (proprietary estoppel). See also C & B, pp. 905–909.

[131] C & B, p. 574; M & W, paras 3.063–3.064; MM, p. 43; (1917) 33 LQR 11 (E. Jenks); (1917) 33 LQR 236, 342 (C. Sweet); (1954) 70 LQR 15 (R.E.M.). See further p. 306, below.

[132] Cf. the position of a tenant for life under SLA 1925 the exercise of whose powers cannot be prohibited or limited, s. 106. But restraints even of a general nature may be valid in the case of a determinable interest: *Re Dugdale* (1888) 38 ChD 176; *Re Leach* [1912] 2 Ch 422; and this is the basis of the protected life interest under TA 1925, s. 33. [For determinable interests, see C & B, pp. 566–569.]

[133] But a *covenant* against alienation is not repugnant: *Caldy Manor Estate Ltd v Farrell* [1974] 1 WLR 1303.

[134] Litt s. 360; Co Litt 206b, 223a; *Re Dugdale*, above.   [135] *Re Rosher* (1884) 26 ChD 801.

[136] *Corbett v Corbett* (1888) 14 PD 7.

[137] *Muschamp v Bluet* (1617) J Bridg 132; *Re Cockerill* [1929] 2 Ch 131.

[138] *Re Brown* [1954] Ch 39 [p. 306, below].

or shall not adopt some particular mode of assurance such as a mortgage,[139] or shall not bar an entail,[140]

is void.

(2) PARTIAL RESTRAINTS

A restraint that is partial, however, and which therefore does not substantially deprive the owner in fee of his power of alienation, is valid. Thus it has been held that a condition is valid which restrains the owner from alienating to a specified person[141] or to anyone except a particular class of persons, provided, however, that the class is not too restricted.[142] But when does a restraint cease to be total? In the case of *Re Macleay*,[143] where there was a devise:

> to my brother J on the condition that he never sells out of the family,

the condition was held by Jessel MR to be valid, though some doubt has been thrown on the correctness of this decision by a later case.[144]

The difficulty, indeed, is to ascertain the principle upon which such restraints have been permitted, for they would seem to be just as repugnant to ownership as a total restraint. Perhaps the truth is that the courts, losing sight of the fundamental doctrine of repugnancy, have, unintentionally and unwittingly, allowed the necessities of public policy to engraft certain exceptions on the main rule.[145]

B. RULES AGAINST PERPETUITIES AND EXCESSIVE ACCUMULATIONS[146]

The policy of the law has always been to prevent property from being tied up in perpetuity.[147] This issue most commonly arises where a property owner attempts to provide for successive interests to come into existence in the property long into the future. Under the Law of Property Act 1925 the only freehold legal estates in land are the fee simple absolute in possession and the term of years absolute.[148] These are

---

[139] *Ware v Cann* (1830) 10 B & C 433.

[140] *Mildmay's Case* (1605) 6 Co Rep 40*a*; *Mary Portington's Case* (1613) 10 Co Rep 35*b*; *Dawkins v Lord Penrhyn* (1878) 4 App Cas 51.

[141] Co Litt 223a.

[142] *Doe d Gill v Pearson* (1805) 6 East 173 ('except to four sisters or their children'). But racial discrimination in the disposal of property is made unlawful by the Race Relations Act 1976, s. 21. See also Sex Discrimination Act 1975, s. 30; Disability Discrimination Act 1995, s. 22.

[143] (1875) LR 20 Eq 186.

[144] *Re Rosher*, above. But the restriction was placed only on a sale, and it was to endure only for the life of J. See too *Re Brown*, above; (1954) 70 LQR 15 (R.E.M.).

[145] *Re Rosher* (1884) 26 Ch D 801 at 813.

[146] C & B, chap. 16; M & W, chap. 9; MM, pp. 210–246; Gray, *Rule Against Perpetuities* (4th edn, 1942); Maudsley, *Modern Law of Perpetuities* (1979); Morris and Leach, *Rule Against Perpetuities* (2nd edn, 1962 and supplement, 1964); Lynn, *The Modern Rule Against Perpetuities* (1965); *Theobald on Wills* (16th edn, 2001), chap. 44.

[147] For the history, see Holdsworth, *History of English Law*, vol. vii, pp. 81–144, 193–238; Simpson, *History of the Land Law* (2nd edn 1986) pp. 208–241.

[148] LPA 1925, s. 1; p. 13, above.

present (not future) estates; interests in land can be created so as to come into existence in the future, but these must take effect as equitable interests. Until 1996, as we shall see,[149] successive interests could be created either under a strict settlement or under a trust for sale, but since 1 January 1997, when the Trusts of Land and Appointment of Trustees Act 1996 came into force, future interests can only be created under a trust of land. A landowner who wishes to create a future interest in his land may do so, within the provisions of the 1996 Act. However, his freedom to create future interests is also restricted by the rule against perpetuities.

The rule against perpetuities was devised by the courts to limit the extent to which estates could be made to vest in the future. The period finally established was that of a life or lives in being plus 21 years plus a period of gestation in respect of a life in being or of a beneficiary if a posthumous child were born.[150] The perpetuity rule was changed—and relaxed—by the Perpetuities and Accumulations Act 1964. A further reform was proposed by the Law Commission in 1998 which will reduce its scope still further. However, the Law Commission stopped short of recommending the outright abolition of the rule.[151] A consequence of the proposed reform is that there will co-exist three different rules against perpetuities: for instruments made (a) prior to the coming into force of the 1964 Act; (b) after the coming into force of that Act but before the recommended reforms are implemented; and (c) after the coming into force of those reforms.

The rule against accumulations was introduced by the Accumulations Act 1800, as a result of the decision in *Thellusson v Woodford*[152] in which a direction in a will to trustees to accumulate income arising from the testator's land was held valid where it was calculated that the accumulation would endure for about 80 years, and produce an amount of approximately £100 million.[153] These statutory provisions were re-enacted and amended by sections 164–166 of the Law of Property Act 1925. The general effect is to limit those accumulations to which the Act applies[154] to any one of four periods: first, the life of the grantor or settlor; second, 21 years from the death of the grantor, settlor or testator, and third and fourth, two alternative periods of certain specified minorities. Two further periods of accumulation were added by the Perpetuities and

---

[149] Chap. 6, below.

[150] *Duke of Norfolk's Case* (1683) 3 Cas in Ch 1; *Lloyd v Carew* (1697) Show Parl Cas 137, 1 Moo PCC 133n; *Stephens v Stephens* (1736) Cas temp Talb 228; *Thellusson v Woodford* (1805) 11 Ves 112; *Cadell v Palmer* (1833) 1 Cl & Fin 372; *Re Wilmer's Trusts* [1903] 2 Ch 411; *Re Stern* [1962] Ch 732.

[151] For arguments in favour of abolition or retention and reform of the rules against perpetuities, see (1984) 4 OJLS 454 (R. Deech).

[152] (1799) 4 Ves 227; affd (1805) 11 Ves 112.

[153] Challis, *Law of Real Property* (3rd edn), p. 201; Holdsworth, *History of English Law*, vol. vii, pp. 228 et seq.; Morris and Leach, p. 267 n. 5; (1970) NILQ 131 (G. W. Keeton); (1997) 147 NLJ 1046 (S. Hooper). 'On the death of the last surviving grandson in 1856, the estate was divided (not without more litigation) between the two male representatives of two of Peter Thellusson's sons who had left issue. But owing to mismanagement and costs of litigation, the estate realised a comparatively small amount': Holdsworth, at p. 230.

[154] For exemptions, see LPA 1925, s. 164 (2).

Accumulations Act 1964, section 13(1)[155] for the benefit of a living settlor, namely 21 years from the date of the disposition, and the minority or respective minorities of any person or persons in being at that date. The effect of a direction which breaks the rule against accumulations depends on whether it also breaks the rule against perpetuities. If it breaks both rules, then the direction is totally void i.e. there is no accumulation at all. If, however, it satisfies the rule against perpetuities but only breaks the rule against accumulations, then it is good pro tanto and only void as to the excess beyond the appropriate statutory period. There is, then, a gap from the end of the statutory period until the end of the period chosen during which the income is in effect undisposed of; during this gap the income so released either reverts to the settlor or his representatives or falls into residue or goes to the next of kin. There is no acceleration of the interests of those entitled after the accumulation is over.[156]

The following extracts from the Law Commission's Report give an outline of the rule against perpetuities under the present law, and the position which will hold if, as is expected, the Report is implemented. Lack of space forbids further detailed treatment of this topic.[157]

Law Commission Report on The Rules Against Perpetuities and Excessive Accumulations 1998 (Law Com No. 251), paras 1.1–1.4, 1.6–1.8, 3.2, 4.2–4.6, 4.33, 1.15

1.1 A property owner is thinking of making a will or creating a trust. How far into the future should the law allow him or her to reach when tying up that property? Can he or she control the devolution of that property indefinitely? For a lifetime? For a fixed period of years? How far should one generation be given freedom to dispose of property in ways that will restrict the freedom of the next? These fundamental questions, which are the substance of this Report, are ancient ones, and different answers have been given to them at different times.[158] Those answers—whatever they may have been—have always involved striking a balance between complete freedom to tie up property in perpetuity on the one hand and the right to prescribe only the immediate devolution of the property on the other. Where that balance has been struck has varied from time to time, as have the factors that have been relevant in striking it. The rules grew up in relation to the devolution of estates and interests under family settlements. They have since been extended piecemeal to a wide range of rights over property unconnected with family arrangements, including options, rights of pre-emption and easements. This extension has not always occurred with a proper consideration of its appropriateness.

---

[155] Following the recommendations of the Law Reform Committee Fourth Report, paras 56, 57; (1964) 80 LQR 529–530; Morris and Leach Supp., 19.

[156] *Green v Gascoyne* (1865) 4 De GJ & Sm 565.

[157] For extracts from the case law on the common law rule, and the Perpetuities and Accumulations Act 1964, see the 8th edn of this book, chap. 7.

[158] During the Second Reading of the Perpetuities and Accumulations Bill (which became the Perpetuities and Accumulations Act 1964), the then Lord Chancellor Lord (later Viscount) Dilhorne commented that the problem addressed by the rule against perpetuities was 'a straightforward one. It arises from the fact that the law has for centuries set its face against the possibility of a person's tying up his property in perpetuity': Hansard (HL) 5 March 1964, vol. 256, col. 236.

1.2 Since the end of the seventeenth century, there has been a 'rule against perpetuities'[159] which has two effects. First, it restricts future dispositions of property by prescribing a time limit—the perpetuity period—in which those dispositions must take effect. Secondly, it now makes void those dispositions that actually fall outside it, and prior to the Perpetuities and Accumulations Act 1964,[160] it invalidated those that might possibly have done so.[161] The rule has been significantly modified by statute, principally the 1964 Act. In addition to the rule against perpetuities, which had a common law origin, there are statutory restrictions, dating back to 1800, which limit the time for which a direction to accumulate income can be validly made.

1.3 This Report, which follows our earlier Consultation Paper,[162] reconsiders the rules against perpetuities and excessive accumulations and attempts to reformulate them in a way that reflects contemporary needs. As we explain, our aims have been to restrict the two rules to those cases where they still perform an essential role and to simplify the law to make it easier to understand and apply. It has been made abundantly clear to us from the responses to the Consultation Paper that the rule against perpetuities causes particular difficulty in the context of commercial transactions, and it is this consideration above all that has prompted us to reconsider it. The rule against perpetuities places restrictions on the creation of future options and easements, for example, that are a significant obstacle to properly planned developments. Its application is especially hard to justify (and for practitioners to explain to clients) when there are no similar limitations on options in leases (whether for renewal or for the purchase of the freehold reversion). Furthermore, cases inevitably occur where the non-application of the rule to options in leases and its application to other property rights leads to a mismatch. These problems are intractable: the rule against perpetuities is an absolute one. Its effects cannot be circumvented by skilful drafting. We were told on consultation that the rule against excessive accumulations works a similar mischief in relation to trusts. It long predates the emergence of the modern discretionary trust, in which powers to accumulate are an important element. The reasonable wishes of settlors will often be incapable of fulfilment or will run the risk of being defeated by an absolute rule that cannot be side-stepped.

1.4 We anticipate that the reforms which we propose should have the following beneficial effects (amongst others)—

(1) they should greatly facilitate dealings with land by enabling parties to enter into reasonable contracts and other arrangements which at present they cannot, and as a result, should allow for the more effective use of land;

(2) they should allow for much greater flexibility in dealings with property and in drafting trusts;

(3) they should make the law much easier to understand for those who have to apply it, and should thereby significantly reduce the scope for making errors, something which can easily be done given the complexities of the present law;

[159] The content of which has varied.

[160] Referred to throughout this Report as 'the 1964 Act'.

[161] Dispositions made prior to 16 July 1964, when the 1964 Act was brought into force, are still subject to this rule: see below, para. 1.7.

[162] The Rules Against Perpetuities and Excessive Accumulations, Consultation Paper No. 133 (1993), referred to through this Report as 'the Consultation Paper'. The delay in publishing this Report has been caused by a combination of staff shortages and the pressure to complete other more urgent projects.

(4) they should simplify and shorten the drafting of legal documents; and

(5) they should reduce legal and perhaps other professional costs.

1.6 As we have indicated above,[163] the rule against perpetuities restricts the time within which future interests in property created by a disposition must either vest or take effect. Despite its name, the rule against perpetuities is therefore concerned with the commencement of interests rather than with their duration, though by restricting the time within which future interests may be created, the rule may (and commonly will) have the effect of limiting the life of a trust.[164] Furthermore, to describe the rule as being against perpetuities is also somewhat misleading—

> The rule against perpetuities, to be comprehended, must be understood as permitting them within limits, and most modern discussion of the rule in England is distorted by a failure to appreciate that the contemporary oddity of the rule lies not in what it prevents, but in how much it allows.[165]

1.7 The rule against perpetuities has to be stated in two parts. For dispositions made before the 1964 Act came into force on 16 July 1964, the rule is as follows[166]—

(1) A future interest in any type of property will be void from the date that the instrument which attempts to create it takes effect,[167] if there is any possibility that the interest may vest or commence outside the perpetuity period.[168]

(2) For these purposes, the perpetuity period consists of one or more lives in being plus a period of 21 years and, where relevant, a period of gestation.[169]

1.8 Where an instrument creates a future interest after 15 July 1964—

(1) that interest will only be void where it must vest or take effect (if at all) outside the perpetuity period;

(2) it is therefore necessary to 'wait and see', if need be for the whole perpetuity period, to determine whether the interest is valid;[170] and

---

[163] See para. 1.2.

[164] A leading authority on the rule observed that 'The Rule against Perpetuities should have been called the Rule against Remoteness. It is aimed at the control of future interests; it has nothing to do, save incidentally, with present interests. But its name is a constant temptation to treat it as aimed against restraints on the alienation of present interests': J. C. Gray, *Gray on Perpetuities* (4th edn, 1942) p. x, quoting the preface to the first edition (1886).

[165] A. W. B. Simpson, 'Entails and Perpetuities' (1979) 24 Jur Rev 1, 17.

[166] See Sir Robert Megarry and Sir William Wade, *The Law of Real Property* (5th edn, 1984) pp. 241, 242, upon which our formulation is based. The rule is explained in more detail in Part IV.

[167] A deed takes effect on delivery. A will, however, takes effect only on the death of the testator.

[168] The rule is almost invariably couched in terms of an interest 'vesting' outside the perpetuity period. That is appropriate where the future estate or interest arises under a trust or settlement. But, as we explain below, the rule has come to apply to the creation of most future rights in property, such as future easements or restrictive covenants and options. For these, the language of 'vesting' does not seem apposite.

[169] A child *en ventre sa mère* is treated as a life in being for the purposes of the rule against perpetuities: this is explained more fully below, para. 4.11.

[170] The doctrine of 'wait and see', which was introduced by the 1964 Act, s. 3(1), is explained below, paras 4.37 and following.

(3) an alternative perpetuity period of up to 80 years may be employed instead of a life in being plus 21 years.[171]

In addition to these general principles, the 1964 Act lays down a 21-year perpetuity period for options.[172]

APPLICATION OF THE RULE AGAINST PERPETUITIES TO SUCCESSIVE ESTATES AND INTERESTS

3.2 The usual situation in which the rule applies is in relation to successive estates and interests in property. The example may be given of a testator who leaves property by will to A for life, thereafter to A's eldest daughter for life, thereafter to A's eldest granddaughter absolutely. The rule against perpetuities applies to each of these gifts. To be valid at common law, it would have to be certain that the gift would vest within the perpetuity period. If, however, the will took effect on or after 16 July 1964, so that the 1964 Act applied, the gift would be valid if it did in fact vest within the perpetuity period.[173]

THE NATURE OF THE RULE

The rule is concerned with the *vesting* of future interests

4.2 An interest in property may be either vested or contingent. An interest is vested only if—

(1) the person or persons entitled to the property is or are in existence and ascertained;

(2) all contingencies attached to the disposition are satisfied, so that the interest takes effect in possession or is ready to take effect in possession subject only to some prior interest; and

(3) in relation to classes, the exact size of each beneficiary's interest is ascertained.[174]

Should any of these conditions remain unsatisfied, the interest is merely contingent.

4.3 Even if these conditions are satisfied and the interest is vested, it is still necessary to determine whether the interest is vested *in possession* (a present right to the present enjoyment of the property) or *in interest* (a present right to the future enjoyment of the property, where the owner must await the determination of some prior interest before he or she is entitled in possession). For example, if there is a gift to A for life, remainder to the first of A's children to attain 21, where A is alive and has minor children at the date of the gift, A has an interest vested in possession but the children have merely contingent interests. When one child attains 21, he or she will acquire an interest vested in interest. However, only when A later dies will that child acquire an interest vested in possession.

4.4 The rule against perpetuities is concerned only with interests that have not yet satisfied the conditions for vesting, that is, with interests which are contingent in the sense explained in paragraph 4.2 above.[175] Thus, in the above example, the rule would apply only so as to ensure that the remainder is certain to vest in the first child of A to attain 21 within the perpetuity

---

[171] See below, paras 4.34 and following.   [172] See below, para. 3.42.

[173] This is because of the principle of 'wait and see' introduced by s. 3(1) of that Act: see above, para. 1.8; and more fully below, paras 4.37 and following.

[174] For similar definitions, see R. H. Maudsley, *The Modern Law of Perpetuities* (1979) pp. 10–11; E. H. Burn, *Cheshire and Burn's Modern Law of Real Property* (15th edn, 1994) p. 279; and A. J. Oakley, *Parker and Mellows: The Modern Law of Trusts* (6th edn, 1994) pp. 164–165.

[175] See too above, para. 1.6.

period. It is not concerned to regulate when that interest subsequently vests in possession on the death of A.

The rule is concerned with the commencement and not the duration of future interests

4.5 The rule sets limits on the length of the period within which future interests created by a disposition must vest: interests that vest too remotely are void. The rule applies, therefore, to the commencement of interests. It is not concerned with their duration. The point may be illustrated by the example of a gift in a will to a corporation of a fee simple in land that is contingent on the fulfilment of some condition precedent. In order to satisfy the rule against perpetuities the fee simple must be certain to vest in interest within the prescribed period. However, if that is the case, it is wholly irrelevant that the corporation may hold that fee simple for much longer than the perpetuity period.

THE COMMON LAW RULE AGAINST PERPETUITIES

4.6 The common law rule against perpetuities may be expressed in the following terms[176]—

a future interest in property is void from the outset if, at the time of its creation, it is not certain to vest (if at all) within the perpetuity period.

THE RULE AGAINST PERPETUITIES AS MODIFIED BY THE 1964 ACT

4.33 This Act modified the rule against perpetuities in relation to instruments taking effect on or after 16 July 1964[177] in three main ways—

(1) It became possible to stipulate expressly a fixed perpetuity period not exceeding 80 years as an alternative to the common law measure of 'lives in being plus 21 years'.[178]

(2) 'Wait and see' was introduced. A future interest which is not certain from the outset to vest within the perpetuity period is not automatically void; instead it is treated as exempt from the rule against perpetuities until such time, if any, as it becomes established that the vesting must occur (if at all) after the end of the 'wait and see' period.[179]

THE PRINCIPAL REFORMS THAT WE PROPOSE

Summary

1.15 In this Report we make three principal recommendations[180]—

(1) The rule against perpetuities should be restricted in its application to successive estates and interests in property and to powers of appointment, thereby restoring it to its original function. It would cease to apply to rights over property such as options, rights of pre-emption and future easements. The existing exclusion from the rule of some pension schemes would be widened to include virtually all such schemes.

---

[176] See also the famous formulation in J. C. Gray, *Gray on Perpetuities* (4th edn, 1942) § 201: '[n]o interest is good unless it must vest, if at all, not later than 21 years after some life in being at the creation of the interest'.

[177] The Act was not retrospective in effect, save for one provision relating to the exclusion of the administrative powers of trustees from the scope of the rule against perpetuities: s. 15(5). Therefore, in respect of instruments taking effect before 16 July 1964, the unamended common law rule continues to apply.

[178] See s. 1.   [179] See s. 3.

[180] [For a complete list of the Law Commission's recommendations, see Part XI of the Report.]

(2) There should be a single perpetuity period of 125 years and the principle of 'wait and see' should apply for this period.

(3) The rule against excessive accumulations should be abolished except in relation to charitable trusts (to which, as we shall explain, special considerations apply).[181]

Subject to certain minor exceptions, these recommendations would be prospective and not retrospective in effect. They would apply only to estates, rights and interests created after any legislation was brought into force.

On 6 March 2001 the Government accepted the recommendations in the Law Commission Report, and at last on 1 April 2009 a Perpetuities and Accumulations Bill was introduced in the House of Lords to give effect, subject to minor modifications, to the Law Commission's Report.[182]

V. PROTECTION OF PROPERTY RIGHTS BY REGISTRATION

A. INTRODUCTION: UNREGISTERED LAND AND REGISTERED LAND

A knowledge of the estates and interests recognised at law and in equity is necessary to an understanding of conveyancing; that is, the practice of creating and transferring estates and interests in land. The owner of an estate may transfer it to another, as on the sale of a house, or create a series of smaller interests out of it, as on the creation of a lease; or create other rights which are recognised at law or in equity, but which are not estates in land, such as an easement or a restrictive covenant. Details of the practice of

---

[181] In the case of charitable trusts, the accumulation should be restricted to a period of 21 years, after which the charity could still build up *reserves of income* if it could satisfy the Charity Commission that the reasons for retaining income were reasonable.

[182] The Lord Chancellor's Department issued a consultation paper in September 2002 on the partial implementation of the Report (on accumulations) by way of a Regulatory Reform Order, but no progress was made at that stage. In January 2006, a Legislative and Regulatory Reform Bill was introduced into Parliament which would have replaced the existing procedures for Regulatory Reform Orders under the Regulatory Reform Act 2001, and would allow a Minister to implement by Statutory Instrument recommendations of the Law Commission, with or without changes, as long as certain preconditions were met. The Law Commission Report on Rules against Perpetuities and Excessive Accumulations 1998 (Law Com No. 251) was identified as containing recommendations which would be suitable for implementation under this procedure: see Notes on the Bill, produced by the Cabinet Office. However, the Bill (which in due course became the Legislative and Regulatory Reform Act 2006) was amended and these wide powers of implementation were removed. On 3 April 2008 the House of Lords approved a new procedure for uncontroversial Law Commission Bills, under which a significant part of the legislative process in the Lords would be taken in Committee off the floor of the House, and the draft Bill which accompanied the Law Commission's report on Perpetuities and Accumulations was a suitable candidate for this new special Parliamentary procedure: Law Commission Forty-Second Annual Report 2007–2008 (Law Com No. 310), pp. 1, 18.

conveyancing are beyond our present scope; but it is material to say here that there are two quite separate and distinctive methods of conveyancing in operation in England and Wales at the present day; that relating to unregistered land and that relating to registered land.

The former is the development of techniques which reach back to medieval times. The system in essence is one whereby the estate owner proves his title to land by showing from deeds and documents in his possession that he derives his title lawfully from some person or persons who have been in peaceful possession for a long period of time. In the nature of things, the title to his estate can never be proved absolutely, for there may have been an interference with the rights of the true owner many years back. However, with the assistance of the Limitation Acts[183] and other statutory provisions proof of title during the last fifteen years is, for practical purposes, sufficient; and a purchaser is required to trace the title back to a good root of title at least fifteen years old.[184] On completion of the purchase, the deeds are handed over to the purchaser. Before the introduction of compulsory registration of title, the purchaser would then make title in a similar manner when he decided to sell. However, nowadays the sale of land to which the title is not yet registered—and which still follows the method of proof of title set out above—is always followed by the registration of the title.

Registration of the title in a central registry is a much more satisfactory system of proof of title. The change involves the recording of all interests in land which need to be placed on the register. In England and Wales, a system of registration of title, introduced in 1862,[185] was superseded by more comprehensive legislation in 1925,[186] which was substantially revised by the Land Registration Act 2002. The compulsory registration of title is triggered by a number of specified events; for example, where unregistered land is sold. Subsequent conveyancing of the land is then based on the title so registered. There is also provision for voluntary registration of title. The system of registration of title is explained in detail in chapter 2.

At the present time the transition from unregistered to registered conveyancing continues. Compulsory registration of title was finally extended to the whole of England and Wales as from 1 November 1990 and so every sale (and certain other transactions) of unregistered land since that date has resulted in the land being transferred from the unregistered system to the registered system. However, since it will be some years until all land appears on the register,[187] it is still necessary to understand the unregistered system, and to distinguish between the doctrines applicable to the two.

We have seen above the formalities required for the creation and transfer of estates and interests in land. A question which then follows is whether the person who takes

---

[183] See p. 246, below.   [184] LPA 1969, s. 23. For earlier (longer) periods, see p. 79, below.

[185] Land Registry Act 1862, repealed by LRA 2002, s. 135, Sch. 13.

[186] LRA 1925, p. 116, below.

[187] The Land Registry has a strategic objective to create a comprehensive land register for England and Wales. Until the 2005–06 Annual Report (p. 112) the target was stated as 2012, but now the Land Registry sets annual targets for increasing the total area of freehold land which is on the register: Land Registry Annual Reports 2006–07, pp. 8, 95; 2007–08, pp. 23–24, 96. See further pp. 116–118, below.

an estate or interest in the land is bound by rights of another—generally referred to as a 'third party'—who already held an estate or interest in the land. This is a fundamental question in land law: the circumstances in which a person (the third party) who has rights in or over land, can assert those rights against successors in title to the land. Where the successor can be bound by the third party's earlier right, it marks it out as being a property right, rather than a purely personal right.[188]

In the modern law, the approach to the question of whether the third party's right is binding on a successor to the land depends on whether the land is registered or unregistered. We shall see the detail of registered land in chapter 2. But the rules of registered land in this respect cannot be properly understood without first understanding the approach which was developed by the old courts of equity in relation to the binding force of third-party rights: the doctrine of the 'bona fide purchaser of a legal estate for value without notice'. Although in its original form, based on the principle of notice, the doctrine of the bona fide purchaser is now applied only in very limited circumstances in unregistered land, and not in registered land, we shall see that the general approach to the protection of third-party rights throughout the modern law is still based on the original doctrine. Registration of third-party rights has largely superseded the principle of notice. But the underlying rationale of the system of registration of third-party rights can be said to be a modern solution to the same concerns which the courts sought to address by developing the doctrine of notice.

B. THE OLD DOCTRINE OF THE BONA FIDE PURCHASER OF A LEGAL ESTATE FOR VALUE WITHOUT NOTICE[189]

The recognition of the trust has given to English law a unique form of duality of ownership. The trustees own a legal estate which, like other forms of legal ownership, is valid against all the world. They obtain, however, no personal benefit from their legal ownership, for they must hold the land and all the income from it for the benefit of the beneficiaries.

The interest of the beneficiaries has its origin in the willingness of the Chancellor to give relief in a situation in which the owner of the legal estate had undertaken to hold his legal estate *to the use of* another. The 'use' was the predecessor of the modern trust.[190] The conscience of the legal owner (then referred to as the 'feoffee to uses'—later the 'trustee') was affected and the Chancellor compelled him to observe his obligation. So long as the original parties to the arrangement remained, the position is comparatively simple; but complications arise where the legal or equitable ownership changes.

---

[188] See p. 4–6, above.

[189] C & B, pp. 58–65; Gray, paras 1.4.25–1.4.40, 8.3.18–8.3.32; M & W, paras 8.005–8.025; MM, pp. 58–63; Smith, pp. 207–211; H & M, pp. 34–40; Snell, paras 4.08–4.32; Maitland, *Equity* (2nd edn), pp. 106–116.

[190] C & B, pp. 42–54. See generally Holdsworth, vol. 4, pp. 407–480 and Simpson, *A History of the Land Law* (2nd edn, 1986), pp. 173–207.

A change of legal ownership raises the question whether the use is enforceable against a person other than the original feoffee.

The use was based upon conscience. If a feoffee to uses transferred to a purchaser with notice, the purchaser was bound as being a party to the fraud; if he had no notice, the use was 'transferred' to him. A donee was bound, notice or no notice; for, without consideration being given, the original use was not changed. A use was however only binding on persons claiming through the original feoffee; and a disseisor therefore took free.[191] With the rise of the trust, however, this technicality disappeared; and an interest under a trust is now valid against all the world with the exception of a bona fide purchaser[192] of the legal estate for value[193] without notice, actual, constructive[194] or imputed.[195]

It may be helpful to add three comments upon the application of this doctrine in the modern law. First, in respect of rights and interests which are registrable as land charges under the Land Charges Act 1972,[196] registration is deemed to constitute actual notice. Thus, a purchaser takes subject to registered land charges whether he knows about them or not; and, conversely, he takes free from unregistered (but registrable) land charges even if he knows about them.[197]

Secondly, where there are concurrent or successive beneficial interests in land, a trust of land exists; the trustees have power to sell the fee simple, and as long as the sale is by at least two trustees (or a trust corporation) the equitable interests are 'overreached', that is, transferred from the land to the purchase money.[198] Thus, the purchaser takes the land free of the equitable interests, even if he knows that some exist; and, after the sale, the equitable interests exist in a fund of money derived from the sale of the land. A similar result is reached where land is held under a strict settlement. The pattern of the 1925 legislation was that all interests in land, other than the fee simple absolute

---

[191] Simpson, above, n. 190, pp. 179–181.

[192] As to the meaning of 'purchaser', see C & B, pp. 59, 171, n. 20; M & W, para. 8.008; MM, p. 59.

[193] M & W, para. 8.008: 'It means any consideration in money, money's worth...or marriage. "Money's worth" extends to all forms of non-monetary consideration in the sense used in the law of contract, but it also includes the satisfaction of an existing debt. "Marriage", however, extends only to a future marriage. An ante-nuptial agreement...is deemed to have been made for value as regards both the spouses and the issue of the marriage. However, a promise made in respect of a past marriage...is not.'

[194] See *Macmillan Inc v Bishopsgate Investment Trust plc (No 3)* [1995] 1 WLR 978, where Millett J said at 1000: 'In English law notice...includes not only actual notice (including "wilful blindness" or "contrived ignorance", where the purchaser deliberately abstains from an inquiry in order to avoid learning the truth) but also constructive notice, that is to say notice of such facts as he would have discovered if he had taken proper measures to investigate them'.

[195] For the meaning of imputed notice, see LPA 1925, s. 199 (1) (ii) and p. 80, n. 278, below.

The doctrine of constructive notice applies differently with personalty. A transferee cannot disregard equitable interests of which he is aware or which present themselves to his notice: *Nelson v Larholt* [1948] 1 KB 339: but, as there are no title deeds to chattels, there is no duty to examine the title: *Joseph v Lyons* (1884) 15 QBD 280 (pledgee under no obligation to search register of bills of sale, and not bound by a bill of sale assigning after-acquired property); H & M, p. 37.

Similarly with negotiable instruments; a holder may be 'in due course' without having taken steps to examine the title of the transferor: *London Joint Stock Bank v Simmons* [1892] AC 201.

[196] See pp. 64–71, below. LCA 1972 consolidates LCA 1925 (apart from local land charges) and other enactments relating to the registration of land charges. It does not make any substantive alterations.

[197] Pp. 71–84, below.   [198] For overreaching, see pp. 548–558, below.

in possession and the term of years absolute[199] should be either registrable or over-reachable.[200] Situations have arisen to destroy the tidiness of this pattern, and in these cases the old doctrine of the bona fide purchaser will apply.[201] An understanding of the doctrine is essential to an appreciation of the relationship between law and equity.

Thirdly, the doctrine of the purchaser for value of the legal estate without notice is relevant only to *un*registered land i.e. where the title to land is derived from title deeds relating to a previous transaction. The concept of the duality of ownership, legal and equitable, developed in that context. Where a totally new system of registration of *title* to and of certain *interests* in land is introduced, wholly different concepts apply. It will be seen from chapter 2 that such a system was made available in 1925 by the Land Registration Act, and since 1990 has been made compulsory for all dealings with land in England and Wales. The 1925 Act was reformed and replaced by the Land Registration Act 2002. The essence of a system of registration of title is that the Register controls and that any person dealing with the land will be safe in relying on the Register. The basic division is thus between estates and interests which appear on the Register and those which do not, rather than between legal estates and equitable interests.[202] But it will be seen that some cases do seem to allow this old distinction to penetrate the registered land system, and cause confusion in its administration[203] and that the Land Registration Act 2002 itself follows the thinking of the old doctrine of the bona fide purchaser.[204]

(i) *The doctrine*

Pilcher v Rawlins

(1872) 7 Ch App 259 (Lord Hatherley LC, James and Mellish LJJ)

In 1851 the trustees of Jeremiah Pilcher's settlement advanced the funds to Rawlins on the security of land including the 'Whitchurch' property, which was conveyed by Rawlins to the trustees in a deed which noticed the trusts.

---

[199] P. 13, above.

[200] See Russell LJ in *Shiloh Spinners Ltd v Harding* [1972] Ch 326 at 340–341.

[201] P. 84, below.

[202] *Williams & Glyn's Bank Ltd v Boland* [1981] AC 487 at 503, where Lord Wilberforce said: 'The registered system is designed to free the purchaser from the hazards of notice—real or constructive... The only kind of notice recognised is by entry on the register'; *Parkash v Irani Finance Ltd* [1970] Ch 101 at 109, where Plowman J found a plaintiff's reliance on the doctrine 'a little surprising, since one of the essential features of registration of title is to substitute a system of registration of rights for the doctrine of notice.' See also Cross J in *National Provincial Bank Ltd v Hastings Car Mart Ltd* [1964] Ch 9 at 16; *Miles v Bull (No 2)* [1969] 3 All ER 1585; *Lloyds Bank plc v Carrick* [1996] 4 All ER 630.

[203] *Barclays Bank Ltd v Taylor* [1974] Ch 137; *Peffer v Rigg* [1977] 1 WLR 285, p. 222, below; *Lyus v Prowsa Developments Ltd* [1982] 1 WLR 1044, p. 223, below *Lloyds Bank plc v Rosset* [1989] Ch 350 at 404, per Purchas LJ; *Abbey National Building Society v Cann* [1989] 2 FLR 265, at 278, per Ralph Gibson and Woolf LJJ. See also *Hodgson v Marks* [1971] Ch 892; *Williams & Glyn's Bank Ltd v Boland*, above, n. 202; p. 203, below; [1996] Conv 34 (J. Howell).

[204] P. 85, n. 296, below.

In 1856 W. H. Pilcher, the surviving trustee of the settlement, reconveyed the Whitchurch property to Rawlins, who repaid only part of the loan. Rawlins, with W. H. Pilcher's connivance, mortgaged that property to Stockwell and Lamb, showing only the title deeds prior to the 1851 mortgage and thus appearing as unincumbered owner in fee simple.

Stockwell and Lamb thus received the legal estate, not under the title deeds which showed that Rawlins had a good title prior to 1851, but through the 1851 mortgage and later reconveyance also. The complete deeds thus disclosed the trusts. There was no way in which Stockwell and Lamb could have discovered the missing deeds, or learned of their contents. The question was whether the fact that the title deeds disclosed the trusts constituted constructive notice.

Held. Stockwell and Lamb took free from the trusts as bona fide purchasers of the legal estate for value without notice.

James LJ: I propose simply to apply myself to the case of a purchaser for valuable consideration, without notice, obtaining, upon the occasion of his purchase, and by means of his purchase deed, some legal estate, some legal right, some legal advantage; and, according to my view of the established law of this Court, such a purchaser's plea of a purchase for valuable consideration without notice is an absolute, unqualified, unanswerable defence, and an unanswerable plea to the jurisdiction of this Court. Such a purchaser, when he has once put in that plea, may be interrogated and tested to any extent as to the valuable consideration which he has given in order to shew the *bona fides* or *mala fides* of his purchase, and also the presence or the absence of notice; but when once he has gone through that ordeal, and has satisfied the terms of the plea of purchase for valuable consideration without notice, then, according to my judgment, this Court has no jurisdiction whatever to do anything more than to let him depart in possession of that legal estate, that legal right, that legal advantage, which he has obtained, whatever it may be. In such a case a purchaser is entitled to hold that which, without breach of duty, he has had conveyed to him.

In the case of *Carter v Carter* (1857) 3 K & J 617, which was decided by the present Lord Chancellor, and which was followed by the Master of the Rolls in this case, and with which I am bound to say I am unable to agree, an exception from that rule was, under the circumstances, supposed to exist.

It is very clearly expressed in a few lines of the judgment in that case: 'But here the purchaser taking the conveyance under one will, supposed by all parties to be really the last will of the testator, finds himself driven to rely upon another and a second will containing on the face of it all the trusts which the testator has created;'—and that circumstance is supposed to create the exception. To my mind there are to that supposition two short and conclusive answers—the one a matter of principle, and the other a matter of fact. My view of the principle is, that when once you have arrived at the conclusion that the purchaser is a purchaser for valuable consideration without notice, the Court has no right to ask him, and has no right to put him to contest the question, how he is going to defend himself, or what he is going to rely on. He may say, honestly and justly, 'I am not going to tell you. I have got the deeds; I defend them, and you will never be able to make me produce them, and you will never be able to produce secondary evidence of them. I am not obliged to produce them at all; probably before you get halfway through your action of ejectment you will find a *jus tertii* which you will not dispose of the estate is in the hands of a legal tenant to whom I have let it, and no one can determine that tenancy without notice, and no one can give that notice but myself; I will not give that notice, and no Court has any power to compel me to give it. I have a right to rely, as every person defending his position has, on the weakness of the title of the person who is seeking to displace me.' That seems to be exactly the position of such a purchaser as this....

I am therefore of opinion that whatever may be the accident by which a purchaser has obtained a good legal title, and in respect of which he has paid his money and is in possession of the property, he is entitled to the benefit of that accident, just as a purchaser would be entitled to avail himself of the possession so acquired, without any reference to the rights of the persons who may be otherwise interested....

The decision in the case of *Carter v Carter* (1857) 3 K & J 617, which has been so much referred to, is a decision which I have considered for some years, and I have more than once thought it right to express my views of that case. I differ in some respects in my views from those of the Lord Chancellor with regard to that case, but I say that the right of a person without notice is absolute and unqualified, when once he has made it out.

In **Wilkes v Spooner** [1911] 2 KB 473, Spooner, the lessee of two premises, No. 137 and No. 170, in High St., East Ham, assigned the lease of No. 170 to the plaintiff and covenanted, in effect, not to compete with the plaintiff's business of general butcher. Spooner then surrendered the lease of No. 137 to the landlord with a view to terminating the restrictive covenant. The landlord knew nothing of the covenant; he accepted the surrender and granted a new lease to Spooner's son, who did. The son opened a business in competition with the plaintiff, who sued to restrain this breach of the covenant. The Court of Appeal (Vaughan Williams, Fletcher Moulton and Farwell LJJ, reversing Scrutton J) held that the restrictive covenant was not binding. The landlord was a bona fide purchaser for value without notice; and the covenant, once destroyed, did not revive on the passing of the land to the son. VAUGHAN WILLIAMS LJ said at 483:

I think that this appeal must be allowed. This case has been very well argued, but really, when certain conclusions of fact are arrived at, there is very little left to argue. It cannot seriously be disputed that the proposition which I quoted from Ashburner's Principles of Equity, p. 75, is good law. It is as follows: 'A purchaser for valuable consideration without notice can give a good title to a purchaser from him with notice. The only exception is that a trustee who has sold property in breach of trust, or a person who has acquired property by fraud, cannot protect himself by purchasing it from a bona fide purchaser for value without notice.' The learned author cites as authorities for that proposition the cases *Sweet v Southcote* (1786) 2 Bro CC 66, and *Re Stapleford Colliery Co, Barrow's Case* (1880) 14 ChD 432.

(ii) Constructive notice

In **Midland Bank Ltd v Farmpride Hatcheries Ltd** (1980) 260 EG 493, the bank lent money in 1971 to the company to enable it to expand its chicken hatchery business. The loan was secured by a mortgage on a 'well-preserved 16th century mansion at Mundford, in Norfolk, together with two cottages and hatcheries and other outbuildings. Under a service agreement with the company in 1968, Mr Willey had been given a licence for himself and his family to live rent free on the premises for

20 years. Mr Willey and his wife were the sole shareholders and the only directors of the company. The licence was never disclosed to nor discovered by the bank when it was negotiating the mortgage with Mr Willey, who was acting as the company's agent. The bank's negotiator, Mr Timbers, was aware that the family was living in the house.

The company defaulted on the mortgage repayment, and the bank brought an action for possession. Mr Willey claimed that his licence was binding on the bank because it had taken the mortgage with constructive notice.[205] The Court of Appeal held that the bank was entitled to possession. SHAW LJ said at 497:

In my judgment Mr Willey set up a smoke-screen designed to hide even the possible existence of some interest in himself which could derogate from the interest of the company ostensibly conferred by the mortgage. To change the metaphor, he deliberately put Mr Timbers off the scent and the bank accepted the mortgage as a consequence. They would not have done so but for Mr Willey's subtle but positive indication that he had communicated all that had to be told which could be relevant to the bank's consideration of the company's application.

This being so, I am of the opinion that Mr Willey is estopped from setting up any facts which would go to show that he held an interest which overrides or stands in priority to their interest as mortgagees from the company.[206]

And OLIVER LJ said at 498:

Now of course, an agent who negotiates a sale or mortgage on his principal's behalf does not thereby make any representation that his principal has an indefeasible title to the property offered for sale or as security. As to that the purchaser or mortgagee must satisfy himself by making the usual enquiries before he completes. But in negotiating on his principal's behalf he does, in my judgment, at least represent that he has his principal's authority to offer the property free from any undisclosed adverse interest of his own. I would therefore be prepared to hold that the purchaser or mortgagee dealing with such an agent can reasonably assume that if the agent with whom he is dealing has himself an interest adverse to the title which he offers on his principal's behalf, he will disclose it. It was in my judgment reasonable for Mr Timbers not to make enquiry about an adverse interest of the negotiating agent which that agent's own reticence entitled him to assume did not exist and he did not, therefore, have constructive notice of it.[207]

---

[205] The issues of the binding effect of a licence on a third party (p. 1095, below), and of the lifting of the veil of corporate personality, were not raised. See (1982) 132 NLJ 68 (H. W. Wilkinson); [1982] Conv 67 (R. E. Annand); (1982) 79 LSG 464 (H. Lowless and J. Alder). On constructive notice generally, see *Northern Bank Ltd v Henry* [1981] IR 1.

[206] Cf. in registered land, LRA 2002, Sch. 3, para. 2 (b), pp. 85, 196, below.

[207] *Hervey v Smith* (1856) 22 Beav 299 (purchaser of house held to have constructive notice of equitable easement to use two chimneys for the passage of smoke from the mere fact of there being fourteen chimney pots on top of the chimney stack and only twelve flues in the house); *Kingsnorth Finance Co Ltd v Tizard* [1986] 1 WLR 783, p. 216, below (mortgagee held to have constructive notice of mortgagor's wife's equitable interest in matrimonial home due to (a) his agent's inspection at a time prearranged with the mortgagor (b) his failure to make further inquiries after his agent (i) found evidence of occupation by twin 15 year old children of the mortgagor and (ii) was informed by the mortgagor, who had described himself as single on the mortgage application form, that he was separated from his wife who was residing nearby). The decision is criticised in [1986] Conv 283 (M. P. Thompson); (1986) 136 NLJ 771 (P. Luxton); [1986] All ER Rev 181

C. UNREGISTERED LAND: REGISTRATION UNDER LAND CHARGES ACT 1972[208]

The Land Charges Act 1972[209] provides for a number of registers to be maintained in which third-party rights over land can be registered. The most important register is the register of land charges. The general principle is that registration in one of the registers constitutes actual notice of the right for the purposes of determining whether a purchaser of the land is affected by it. And that the failure to register constitutes in law an absence of notice, whether or not the purchaser in fact knows about it. For interests covered by the Act, therefore, registration is intended to replace the old doctrine of notice. The Act makes provision for the effect of non-registration of registrable interests.

The Land Charges Act 1972 applies only to unregistered land.[210] The protection of such rights in registered land is covered by the Land Registration Act 2002.[211]

(i) Registration constitutes actual notice

LAW OF PROPERTY ACT 1925

198. Registration under the Land Charges Act, 1925, to be notice.—(1) The registration of any instrument or matter in any register, kept under the Land Charges Act 1972 or any local land charges register[212] shall be deemed to constitute actual notice of such instrument or matter, and of the fact of such registration, to all persons and for all purposes connected with the land affected, as from the date of registration or other prescribed date and so long as the registration continues in force.

(2) This section operates without prejudice to the provisions of this Act respecting the making of further advances by a mortgagee,[213] and applies only to instruments and matters required or authorised to be registered in any such register.[214]

Under the normal practice of conveyancing in unregistered land the parties will enter into the contract of sale before the purchaser has the opportunity of investigating the vendor's title—and so before he has the opportunity of searching the land charges register.[215] It is therefore provided that at the stage at which the contract is entered into the purchaser is only affected by registrable charges of which he has actual knowledge,

---

(P. J. Clarke); *Abbey National plc v Tufts* [1999] 2 FLR 399 (bank had no constructive notice of wife's credit status where bankrupt husband applied for loan on her behalf).

[208] C & B, pp. 97–8, 111–12, 937–47; Gray, paras 8.3.4–8.3.17; M & W, paras 8.061–8.106; MM, pp. 93–108; Barnsley, pp. 383–407; Report of the Committee on Land Charges 1956 (Cmd 9825); [1956] CLJ 216 (H. W. R. Wade); Law Commission Report on Land Charges Affecting Unregistered Land 1969 (Law Com. No. 18).

[209] Replacing LCA 1925.

[210] LCA 1972, s. 14(1), as amended by LRA 2002, s. 133, Sch. 11, para. 10(1), (2).

[211] See p. 84, below.   [212] As amended by LLCA 1975, s. 17(2), Sch. 1.

[213] See p. 989, below.   [214] As amended by LLCA 1975, s. 17(2), Sch. 1.

[215] The search under LCA 1972 is against the names of previous estate owners: p. 79, below; and until he is given access to the documents of title the purchaser has no information about the names against which he should search.

and not unknown charges which are in fact registered. It is therefore still open to him to challenge the vendor's title when he later discovers registered charges.

LAW OF PROPERTY ACT 1969

24. Contracts for purchase of land affected by land charge, etc.—(1) Where under a contract for the sale or other disposition of any estate or interest in land the title to which is not registered under the Land Registration Act 2002[216]...any question arises whether the purchaser had knowledge, at the time of entering into the contract, of a registered land charge, that question shall be determined by reference to his actual knowledge and without regard to the provisions of section 198 of the Law of Property Act 1925...

(ii) What interests are registrable as land charges

LAND CHARGES ACT 1972[217]

1. The registers and the index.—(1) The registrar shall continue to keep at the registry[218] in the prescribed manner the following registers, namely—

    (a) a register of land charges;

    (b) a register of pending actions;

    (c) a register of writs and orders affecting land;

    (d) a register of deeds of arrangement affecting land;

    (e) a register of annuities,[219]

and shall also continue to keep there an index whereby all entries made in any of those registers can readily be traced.

(6) Subject to the provisions of this Act, registration may be vacated pursuant to an order of the court.[220]

(7) In this section 'index' includes any device or combination of devices serving the purpose of an index.

2. The register of land charges.—(1) If a charge on or obligation affecting land falls into one of the classes described in this section, it may be registered in the register of land charges as a land charge of that class.[221]

---

[216] As amended by LRA 2002, s. 133, Sch. 11, para. 9.

[217] See also LC Rules 1974 (SI 1974 No. 1286); 1994 (SI 1994 No. 287); 1995 (SI 1995 No. 287); LC Fees Rules 1990; Fees (Amendment) Rules 1994 (SI 1994 No. 286); LC (Amendment) Rules 1990 (SI 1990 No. 485), 1995 (SI 1995 No. 1355), 2005 (SI 2005 No. 1981).

[218] In Plymouth.

[219] Sch. 1. No entries have been possible in this register since 1925.

[220] This is wider than the corresponding LCA 1925, s. 10(8): *Calgary and Edmonton Land Co Ltd v Dobinson* [1974] Ch 102 at 109, per Megarry J. See also (1968) 118 New LJ 1167 (S. M. Cretney pointing out that a charge can be registered without any proof of its validity, the function of the Registry being purely ministerial; but the registration of such a charge might in practice make the land unsaleable); *Hooker v Wyle* [1974] 1 WLR 235; *Jones v Morgan* (1973) 231 EG 1167; *Mens v Wilson* (1973) 231 EG 843; *Haslemere Estates Ltd v Baker* [1982] 1 WLR 1109; [1983] Conv 69 (J.E.M.).

Cf. the position in registered land: LRA 2002, ss. 35, 36, replacing LRA 1925, ss. 56(3), 82; p. 174, below.

[221] For the date of effective registration and priority notices, see LCA 1972, s. 11; (1977) 74 LSG 136 (P. Freedman).

(2) A Class A land charge is—

    (a) a rent or annuity or principal money payable by instalments or otherwise, with or without interest, which is not a charge created by deed but is a charge upon land (other than a rate) created pursuant to the application of some person under the provisions of any Act of Parliament, for securing to any person either the money spent by him or the costs, charges and expenses incurred by him under such Act, or the money advanced by him for repaying the money spent or the costs, charges and expenses incurred by another person under the authority of an Act of Parliament,[222] or

    (b) a rent or annuity or principal money payable as mentioned in paragraph (a) above which is not a charge created by deed but is a charge upon land (other than a rate) created pursuant to the application of some person under any of the enactments mentioned in Schedule 2 to this Act.[223]

(3) A Class B land charge is a charge on land (not being a local land charge)[224] of any of the kinds described in paragraph (a) of subsection (2) above, created otherwise than pursuant to the application of any person.[225]

(4) A Class C land charge is any of the following (not being a local land charge),[226] namely—

    (i) a puisne mortgage,[227]

    (ii) a limited owner's charge,[228]

    (iii) a general equitable charge,[229]

    (iv) an estate contract,[230]

and for this purpose—

    (i) a puisne[231] mortgage is a legal mortgage which is not protected by a deposit of documents relating to the legal estate affected;

    (ii) a limited owner's charge is an equitable charge acquired by a tenant for life or statutory owner under the Inheritance Tax Act 1984 or under any other statute by reason of the discharge by him of any inheritance tax[232] or other liabilities and to which special priority is given by the statute;

    (iii) a general equitable charge is any equitable charge which—

        (a) is not secured by a deposit of documents relating to the legal estate affected; and

---

[222] E.g. a statutory charge under the Improvement of Land Act 1864.

[223] E.g. LTA 1927, s. 12, Sch. 1, para. 7 (charge in respect of improvements to business premises).

[224] As amended by LLCA 1975, s. 19, Sch. 2.

[225] E.g. a charge on property recovered or preserved for an assisted person arising under Access to Justice Act 1999, s. 17(3)(g).

[226] As amended by LLCA 1975, s. 17(1)(b).   [227] P. 986, below.

[228] Below.

[229] This does not include mortgages of equitable interests which are treated separately; p. 987, below.

[230] P. 29, above.

[231] Puisne is derived from the old French *puis* (after) *né* (born); hence a later or subsequent mortgage.

[232] As amended by FA 1975, s. 52, Sch. 12, para. 18; IHTA 1984, s. 276, Sch. 8, para. 3(1)(a). See IHTA 1984, ss. 237, 238.

(b) does not arise or affect an interest arising under a trust of land[233] or a settlement; and

(c) is not a charge given by way of indemnity against rents equitably apportioned or charged exclusively on land in exoneration of other land and against the breach or non-observance of covenants or conditions; and

(d) is not included in any other class of land charge;

(iv) an estate contract is a contract by an estate owner or by a person entitled at the date of the contract to have a legal estate conveyed to him to convey or create a legal estate, including a contract conferring either expressly or by statutory implication a valid option to purchase,[234] a right of pre-emption[235] or any other like right.

(5) A Class D land charge is any of the following (not being a local land charge)[236] namely—

(i) an Inland Revenue charge;

(ii) a restrictive covenant;[237]

(iii) an equitable easement;[238]

and for this purpose—

(i) an Inland Revenue charge is a charge on land, being a charge acquired by the Board under the Inheritance Tax Act 1984;[239]

(ii) a restrictive covenant is a covenant or agreement (other than a covenant or agreement between a lessor and a lessee) restrictive of the user of land and entered into on or after 1st January 1926;

(iii) an equitable easement is an easement, right or privilege over or affecting land created or arising on or after 1st January 1926, and being merely an equitable interest.

(6) A Class E land charge is an annuity created before 1st January 1926 and not registered in the register of annuities.

(7) A Class F land charge is a charge affecting any land by virtue of Part IV of the Family Law Act 1996.[240]

(8) A charge or obligation created before 1st January 1926 can only be registered as a Class B land charge or a Class C land charge if it is acquired under a conveyance made on or after that date.

---

[233] As amended by TLATA 1996, s. 25(1), Sch. 3, para. 12(2).

[234] *Beesly v Hallwood Estates Ltd* [1960] 1 WLR 549; *Taylors Fashions Ltd v Liverpool Victoria Trustees Co Ltd* [1982] QB 133n, p. 1012, below (option to renew, contained in lease, held registrable as option to purchase); approved in *Phillips v Mobil Oil Co Ltd* [1989] 1 WLR 888; [1990] Conv 168, 250 (J. Howell); [1989] All ER Rev 193 (P. H. Pettit).

[235] *Pritchard v Briggs* [1980] Ch 338, p. 38, above; (1980) 39 CLJ 35 (C. Harpum); A. Rosenthal, M. Dray and C. Groves, *Barnsley's Land Options* (4th edn, 2004), chap. 7.

[236] As amended by LLCA 1975, s. 17(1)(b).

[237] P. 750, below.   [238] P. 648, below.

[239] As amended by FA 1975, s. 52, Sch. 12, para. 18; IHTA 1984, s. 276, Sch. 8, para. 3(1)(b).

[240] As amended by Family Law Act 1996, s. 27, Sch. 8, para. 47 (replacing Matrimonial Homes Act 1983), pp. 602–606, below.

3. Registration of land charges.—(1) A land charge shall be registered in the name of the estate owner[241] whose estate is intended to be affected.[242]

(1A) Where a person has died and a land charge created before his death would apart from his death have been registered in his name, it shall be so registered notwithstanding his death.[243]

(2) A land charge registered before 1st January 1926 under any enactment replaced by the Land Charges Act 1925 in the name of a person other than the estate owner may remain so registered until it is registered in the name of the estate owner in the prescribed manner.

(3) A puisne mortgage created before 1st January 1926 may be registered as a land charge before any transfer of the mortgage is made.

The types of application to the Land Charges Department in 2007–08 were as follows:[244]

Land Registry Annual Report and Accounts 2007–08, p. 23

Type of application	Number of applications or names in 2007/8	% variation compared with 2006/7
New registrations, rectifications and renewals	171,518	-2.4
Cancellations	24,769	-17.8
Official Searches:		
- Full Searches	642,559	-9.0
- Searches limited to insolvency	3,920,020	-7.0
Official copies	75,833	-14.5
Total	4,834,699	-7.3

In **Shiloh Spinners Ltd v Harding** [1973] AC 691[245] the respondents were assignees of part of leasehold premises which was subject to covenants. The appellants had the right to re-enter and retake the premises in the event of breach. The respondents were aware of this all the time, and, in breach of covenant, they demolished the premises, and argued that the right of entry was void against them because it was not registered.

[241] P. 79, below. The name of the estate owner means the name as disclosed by the conveyance: *Standard Property Investment plc v British Plastics Federation* (1985) 53 P & CR 25; [1987] Conv 135 (J.E.A.). A person entitled to have the legal estate conveyed to him is not an estate owner: *Barrett v Hilton Developments Ltd* [1975] Ch 237; *Property Discount Corpn Ltd v Lyon Group Ltd* [1981] 1 WLR 300.

[242] On the mechanics of the register see *Oak Co-operative Building Society v Blackburn* [1968] Ch 730 at 741, per Russell LJ.

[243] Inserted by LP(MP)A 1994, s. 15(2). See Law Commission Report: Title on Death 1989 (Law Com No. 184, Cm 777), paras 2–2 to 2–9; [1995] Conv 476 (L. Clements).

[244] The Report for 1995–1996 was the last to give a breakdown of new registrations. The most numerous classes were C(i) (puisne mortgages); C(iv) (estate contracts); and D(ii) (restrictive covenants).

[245] (1973) 32 CLJ 218 (P. B. Fairest).

The House of Lords held that the right of entry was not registrable, and was enforceable against purchasers with notice. LORD WILBERFORCE said at 718:

The right of entry, it is said, is unenforceable against the respondent, although he took with actual notice of it, because it was not registered as a charge under the Land Charges Act 1925. There is no doubt that if it was capable of registration under that Act, it is unenforceable if not registered: the appellants deny that it was so capable either (i) because it was a legal right, not an equitable right, or (ii) because, if equitable, it does not fall within any of the classes or descriptions of charges registration of which is required.

His Lordship held that the right of entry was equitable and continued:

So I pass, as did the Court of Appeal, to the Land Charges Act 1925. The original contention of the respondents was that the equitable right of entry was capable of registration under Class D(iii) of the Act. In the Court of Appeal an alternative contention was raised, apparently at the court's suggestion, that it might come within Class C(iv). In my opinion this is unmaintainable. Class C(iv) embraces:

'Any contract by an estate owner or by a person entitled at the date of the contract to have a legal estate conveyed to him to convey or create a legal estate, including a contract conferring either expressly or by statutory implication a valid option of purchase, a right of pre-emption or any other like right (in this Act referred to as "an estate contract").'

The only words capable of including a right of entry are 'any other like right', but, in my opinion, no relevant likeness can be found. An option or right of pre-emption eventuates in a contract for sale at a price; this is inherent in 'purchase' and 'pre-emption'; the right of entry is penal in character and involves the revesting of the lease, in the event of default, in a previous owner. There is no similarity in law or fact between these situations.[246]

Class D(iii) reads:

'A charge or obligation affecting land of any of the following kinds, namely:— ... (iii) Any easement right or privilege over or affecting land created or arising after the commencement of this Act, and being merely an equitable interest (in this Act referred to as an "equitable easement").'

The argument for inclusion in this class falls into two parts. First it is said that a right of entry falls fairly within the description, or at least that, if the words do not appear to include it, they are sufficiently open in meaning to admit it. Secondly it is said that the provisions of the Law of Property Act as to 'overreaching'[247] compel the conclusion that a right of entry must fall under some class or sub-class of the Land Charges Act, and since this is the only one whose words can admit it, they should be so interpreted as to do so. Thus the argument depends for its success upon a combination of ambiguity, or openness of Class D(iii) with compelling consideration brought about in the overreaching provisions. In my opinion it fails

---

[246] But a proviso in a lease requiring a lessee, who wishes to assign, first to offer a surrender of the lease to the lessor is registrable as an estate contract: *Bocardo SA v S and M Hotels Ltd* [1980] 1 WLR 17; *Adler v Upper Grosvenor Street Investment Ltd* [1957] 1 WLR 227; (1957) 73 LQR 157 (R. E. M.); *Creer v P and O Lines of Australia Pty Ltd* (1971) 45 ALJR 697; (1972) 88 LQR 317. This surrender proviso was doubted by CA in *Greene v Church Comrs for England* [1974] Ch 467. On registrability, see LCA 1972, s. 2(4); *Greene v Church Comrs for England*, above. For the position of business tenancies under LTA 1954, Part II, see *Allnatt London Properties Ltd v Newton* [1981] 2 All ER 290; [1980] Conv 418 (C. G. Blake); (1983) 127 SJ 855 (C. Coombe).

[247] P. 548, below.

under both limbs: Class D(iii) cannot be interpreted so as to admit equitable rights of entry, and no conclusive, compelling, or even clear conclusions can be drawn from the overreaching provisions which can influence the interpretation of Class D(iii).

Dealing with Class D(iii), I reject at once the suggestion that any help (by way of enlarging the content of this class) can be derived either from the introductory words, for they limit themselves to the 'following kinds,' or from the words 'and being merely an equitable interest,' for these are limiting, not enlarging, words. I leave out of account the label at the end—though I should think it surprising if so expert a draftsman had attached that particular label if the class included a right of entry. To include a right of entry in the description of 'equitable easement' offends a sense both of elegance and accuracy. That leaves 'easement right or privilege over or affecting land.' If this were the only place where the expression occurred in the legislation, I should find it difficult to attribute to 'right' a meaning so different in quality from easement and privilege as to include a right of entry. The difference between a right to use or draw profit from another man's land, and a right to take his land altogether away, is one of quality, not of degree. . . . I do not further elaborate this point because a reading of their judgments leaves little doubt that the Lords Justices would themselves have read Class D(iii) as I can only read it but for the influence of the overreaching argument.

So I turn to the latter. This, in my opinion, only becomes compelling if one first accepts the conclusion that all equitable claims relating to land are either registrable under the Land Charges Act, or capable of being overreached under section 2 of the Law of Property Act; i.e., are capable by use of the appropriate mechanism of being transferred to the proceeds of sale of the land they affect. If this dilemma could be made good, then there could be an argument for forcing, within the limits of the possible, an equitable right of entry into one of the registrable classes, since it is obviously not suitable for overreaching. But the dilemma cannot be made good. What may be overreached is any 'equitable interest or power affecting that estate': yet 'equitable interest' (for powers do not enter into the debate) is a word of most uncertain content. The searcher after a definition has to be satisfied with section 1(8) 'Estates, interests, and charges in or over land which are not legal estates are in this Act referred to as "equitable interests"'—a tautology rather than a definition. There is certainly nothing exhaustive about the expression 'equitable interests'—just as certainly it has no clear boundaries. The debate whether such rights as equity, over the centuries, has conferred against the holder of the legal estate are truly proprietary in character, or merely rights in personam, or a hybrid between the two, may have lost some of its vitality in the statutory context but the question inevitably rises to mind whether the 'curtain' or 'overreaching' provisions of the 1925 legislation extend to what are still conveniently called 'equities' or 'mere equities,' such as rights to rectification, or to set aside a conveyance. There is good authority, which I do not presume to doubt, for a sharp distinction between the two—I instance Lord Upjohn in *National Provincial Bank Ltd v Ainsworth* [1965] AC 1175 at 1238, and *Snell's Principles of Equity,* 25th edn (1960) p. 38. I am impressed by the decision in *E R Ives Investment Ltd v High* [1967] 2 QB 379 [p. 1074, below], in which the Court of Appeal held that a right by estoppel—producing an effect similar to an easement—was not registrable under Class D(iii). Lord Denning MR referred to the right as subsisting only in equity. Danckwerts LJ thought it was an equity created by estoppel or a proprietary estoppel: plainly this was not an equitable interest capable of being overreached, yet no member of the court considered that the right—so like an easement—could be brought within Class D(iii). The conclusion followed, and the court accepted it, that whether it was binding on a purchaser depended on notice. All this seems to show that there may well be rights, of an equitable character, outside the provisions as to registration and which are incapable of being overreached.

That equitable rights of entry should be among them is not in principle unacceptable. First, rights of entry, before 1925, were not considered to confer an interest in the land. They were described as bare possibilities *(Challis's Real Property,* 3rd edn (1911), p. 76) so that it is not anomalous that equitable rights of entry should not be treated as equitable interests. Secondly, it is important that section 10 of the Land Charges Act 1925[248] should be given a plain and ordinary interpretation. It is a section which involves day to day operation by solicitors doing conveyancing work: they should be able to take decisions and advise their clients upon a straight-forward interpretation of the registration classes, not upon one depending upon a sophisticated, not to say disputable, analysis of other statutes. Thirdly, the consequence of equitable rights of entry not being registrable is that they are subject to the doctrine of notice, preserved by section 199 of the Law of Property Act. This may not give complete protection, but neither is it demonstrable that it is likely to be less effective than the present system of registration against names. I am therefore of opinion that Class D(iii) should be given its plain prima facie meaning and that so read it does not comprise equitable rights of entry. It follows that non-registration does not make the appellants' right unenforceable in this case.

The consequence is that the appellants' claim to re-enter must succeed unless the respondent can and should be relieved in equity against the appellants' legal right.'

Relief against forfeiture was refused.[249]

(iii) *Effect of non-registration*

LAND CHARGES ACT 1972

4. Effect of land charges and protection of purchasers.[250] — (5) A land charge of Class B and a land charge of Class C (other than an estate contract) created or arising on or after 1st January 1926 shall be void as against a purchaser of the land charged with it, or of any interest in such land, unless the land charge is registered in the appropriate register before the completion of the purchase.

(6) An estate contract and a land charge of Class D created or entered into on or after 1st January 1926 shall be void as against a purchaser for money or money's worth[251] (or, in the case of an Inland Revenue charge, a purchaser within the meaning of the Inheritance Tax Act 1984)[252] of a legal estate in the land charged with it, unless the land charge is registered in the appropriate register before the completion of the purchase.

(7) After the expiration of one year from the first conveyance occurring on or after 1st January 1926 of a land charge of Class B or Class C created before that date the person entitled to the land charge shall not be able to enforce or recover the land charge or any part of it as against a purchaser of the land charged with it, or of any interest in the land, unless the land charge is registered in the appropriate register before the completion of the purchase.

---

[248] Now LCA 1972, s. 2.   [249] P. 458, n. 252, below.

[250] Sub-ss. (l)–(4) contain provisions relating to land charges Class A.

[251] *Midland Bank Trust Co Ltd v Green* [1981] AC 513, below. *Lloyds Bank plc v Carrick* [1996] 4 All ER 630 p. 86, n. 299, below.

[252] As amended by FA 1975 s. 52, Sch. 12; IHTA 1984, s. 276, Sch. 8, para. 3(2).

(8) A land charge of Class F shall be void as against a purchaser of the land charged with it, or of any interest in such land, unless the land charge is registered in the appropriate register before the completion of the purchase.

17. Interpretation.—(1) In this Act, unless the context otherwise requires,—

'purchaser' means any person (including a mortgagee or lessee) who, for valuable consideration, takes any interest in land or in a charge on land, and 'purchase' has a corresponding meaning.

Midland Bank Trust Co Ltd v Green
[1981] AC 513 (HL, **Lords Wilberforce, Edmund-Davies, Fraser of Tullybelton, Russell of Killowen** and **Bridge of Harwich**)[253]

In 1961 a father (Walter) granted to his son (Geoffrey) a 10 year option to purchase Gravel Hill Farm, Thornton-le-Moor, Lincolnshire, of which the son was his tenant. The option was not registered under LCA 1925. In 1967 the father, wishing to deprive the son of his option, conveyed the farm, then worth about £40,000, to the mother (Evelyne) for £500. When the son discovered this, he registered the option and purported to exercise it.

The son's executors claimed that the option was binding on the mother's estate.

Held (reversing CA, and restoring the decision of Oliver J). Option void. The mother was a 'purchaser of a legal estate for money or money's worth' under LCA 1925, ss. 13(2) and 20(8).[254]

Lord Wilberforce: This option was, in legal terms, an estate contract and so a legal charge, class C, within the meaning of the Land Charges Act 1925. The correct and statutory method for protection of such an option is by means of entering it in the Register of Land Charges maintained under the Act. If so registered, the option would have been enforceable, not only (contractually) against Walter, but against any purchaser of the farm.

The option was not registered, a failure which inevitably called in question the responsibility of Geoffrey's solicitor. To anticipate, Geoffrey in fact brought proceedings against his solicitor which have been settled for a considerable sum, payable if the present appeal succeeds....

His Lordship stated the history of the case, read LCA 1925, ss. 13(2), 20(8), and continued:

Thus the case appears to be a plain one. The 'estate contract,' which by definition includes an option of purchase, was entered into after January 1, 1926; Evelyne took an interest (in fee simple) in the land 'for valuable consideration'— so was a 'purchaser': she was a purchaser for

---

[253] The 'Green Saga', which 'bids fair to rival in time and money the story of *Jarndyce v Jarndyce*' (see [1980] Ch 590 at 622, per Lord Denning MR), continued. For the liability of the solicitor for failing to advise the son to register the option and for failing to register it, see *Midland Bank Trust Co Ltd v Hett, Stubbs and Kemp* [1979] Ch 384; and for conspiracy between husband and wife, see *Midland Bank Trust Co Ltd v Green (No 3)* [1982] Ch 529. For a full review of all three cases by Sir Peter Oliver, who tried them at first instance, see *The Green Saga* (1983) Child & Co Oxford Lecture. See also [1981] CLJ 213 (C. Harpum); (1981) 97 LQR 518 (B. Green).

[254] Now LCA 1972, ss. 4(6) and 17(1), above, p. 71.

money—namely £500: the option was not registered before the completion of the purchase. It is therefore void as against her.

In my opinion this appearance is also the reality. The case is plain: the Act is clear and definite. Intended as it was to provide a simple and understandable system for the protection of title to land, it should not be read down or glossed: to do so would destroy the usefulness of the Act. Any temptation to remould the Act to meet the facts of the present case, on the supposition that it is a hard one and that justice requires it, is, for me at least, removed by the consideration that the Act itself provides a simple and effective protection for persons in Geoffrey's position—viz.—by registration.

The respondents submitted two arguments as to the interpretation of section 13(2): the one sought to introduce into it a requirement that the purchaser should be 'in good faith'; the other related to the words 'in money or money's worth.'

The argument as to good faith fell into three parts: first, that 'good faith' was something required of a 'purchaser' before 1926; secondly, that this requirement was preserved by the 1925 legislation and in particular by section 13(2) of the Land Charges Act 1925. If these points could be made good, it would then have to be decided whether the purchaser (Evelyne) was in 'good faith' on the facts of the case.

My Lords, the character in the law known as the bona fide (good faith) purchaser for value without notice was the creation of equity. In order to affect a purchaser for value of a legal estate with some equity or equitable interest, equity fastened upon his conscience and the composite expression was used to epitomise the circumstances in which equity would or rather would not do so. I think that it would generally be true to say that the words 'in good faith' related to the existence of notice. Equity, in other words, required not only absence of notice, but genuine and honest absence of notice. As the law developed, this requirement became crystallised in the doctrine of constructive notice which assumed a statutory form in the Conveyancing Act 1882, section 3. But, and so far I would be willing to accompany the respondents, it would be a mistake to suppose that the requirement of good faith extended only to the matter of notice, or that when notice came to be regulated by statute, the requirement of good faith became obsolete. Equity still retained its interest in and power over the purchaser's conscience. The classic judgment of James LJ in *Pilcher v Rawlins* (1872) 7 Ch App 259 at 269, p. 60, above, is clear authority that it did: good faith there is stated as a separate test which may have to be passed even though absence of notice is proved. And there are references in cases subsequent to 1882 which confirm the proposition that honesty or bona fides remained something which might be inquired into (see *Berwick & Co v Price* [1905] 1 Ch 632 at 639; *Taylor v London and County Banking Co* [1901] 2 Ch 231 at 256; *Oliver v Hinton* [1899] 2 Ch 264 at 273).

But did this requirement, or test, pass into the property legislation of 1925?

My Lords, I do not think it safe to seek the answer to this question by means of a general assertion that the property legislation of 1922–25 was not intended to alter the law, or not intended to alter it in a particular field, such as that relating to purchases of legal estates. All the Acts of 1925, and their precursors, were drafted with the utmost care, and their wording, certainly where this is apparently clear, has to be accorded firm respect. As was pointed out in *Grey v IRC* [1960] AC 1, the Acts of 1922–24 effected massive changes in the law affecting property and the House, in consequence, was persuaded to give to a plain word ('disposition') its plain meaning, and not to narrow it by reference to its antecedents. Certainly that case should firmly discourage us from muddying clear waters. I accept that there is merit in looking at the corpus as a whole in order to produce if possible a consistent scheme. But there are limits to the possibilities of this process: for example it cannot eliminate the difference between registered and unregistered land, or the respective charges on them.

As to the requirement of 'good faith' we are faced with a situation of some perplexity. The expression 'good faith,' appears in the Law of Property Act 1925 definition of 'purchaser' ('a purchaser in good faith for valuable consideration'), section 205(1)(xxi); in the Settled Land Act 1925, section 117(1)(xxi) (ditto); in the Administration of Estates Act 1925, section 55(1) (xviii) ('"Purchaser" means a lessee, mortgagee or other person who in good faith acquires an interest in property for valuable consideration') and in the Land Registration Act 1925, section 3(xxi) which does not however, as the other Acts do, include a reference to nominal consideration. So there is certainly some indication of an intention to carry the concept of 'good faith' into much of the 1925 code. What then do we find in the Land Charges Act 1925? We were taken along a scholarly peregrination through the numerous Acts antecedent to the final codification and consolidation in 1925—the Land Charges Registration and Searches Act 1888, the Law of Property Act 1922, particularly Schedule 7, the Law of Property (Amendment) Act 1924 as well as the Yorkshire and Middlesex Deeds Registration Acts. But I think, with genuine respect for an interesting argument, that such solution as there is of the problem under consideration must be sought in the terms of the various Acts of 1925 themselves. So far as concerns the Land Charges Act 1925, the definition of 'purchaser' quoted above does not mention 'good faith' at all. 'Good faith' did not appear in the original Act of 1888, nor in the extension made to that Act by the Act of 1922, Schedule 7, nor in the Act of 1924, Schedule 6. It should be a secure assumption that the definition of 'purchaser for value' which is found in section 4 of the Act of 1888 (...'person who for valuable consideration takes any interest in land') together with the limitation which is now the proviso to section 13(2) of the Act of 1925, introduced in 1922, was intended to be carried forward into the Act of 1925. The expression 'good faith' appears nowhere in the antecedents. To write the word in, from the examples of contemporaneous Acts, would be bold. It becomes impossible when it is seen that the words appear in section 3(1) and in section 7(1), in each case in a proviso very similar, in structure, to the relevant proviso in section 13(2). If canons of constructions have any validity at all, they must lead to the conclusion that the omission in section 13(2) was deliberate.

My Lords, I recognise that the inquiring mind may put the question: why should there be an omission of the requirement of good faith in this particular context? I do not think there should be much doubt about the answer. Addition of a requirement that the purchaser should be in good faith would bring with it the necessity of inquiring into the purchaser's motives and state of mind. The present case is a good example of the difficulties which would exist. If the position was simply that the purchaser had notice of the option, and decided nevertheless to buy the land, relying on the absence of notification, nobody could contend that she would be lacking in good faith. She would merely be taking advantage of a situation, which the law has provided, and the addition of a profit motive could not create an absence of good faith. But suppose, and this is the respondents' argument, the purchaser's motive is to defeat the option, does this make any difference? Any advantage to oneself seems necessarily to involve a disadvantage for another: to make the validity of the purchase depend upon which aspect of the transaction was prevalent in the purchaser's mind seems to create distinctions equally difficult to analyse in law as to establish in fact: avarice and malice may be distinct sins, but in human conduct they are liable to be intertwined. The problem becomes even more acute if one supposes a mixture of motives. Suppose—and this may not be far from the truth—that the purchaser's motives were in part to take the farm from Geoffrey, and in part to distribute it between Geoffrey and his brothers and sisters, but not at all to obtain any benefit for herself, is this acting in 'good faith': or not? Should family feeling be denied a protection afforded to simple greed? To eliminate the necessity for inquiries of this kind may well have been part of the legislative intention. Certainly there is here no argument for departing—violently—from the wording of the Act.

Before leaving this part of the case, I must comment on *Re Monolithic Building Co* [1915] 1 Ch 643, which was discussed in the Court of Appeal. That was a case arising under section 93 of the Companies (Consolidation) Act 1908 which made an unregistered mortgage void against any creditor of the company. The defendant Jenkins was a managing director of the company, and clearly had notice of the first unregistered mortgage: he himself subsequently took and registered a mortgage debenture and claimed priority over the registered mortgage. It was held by the Court of Appeal, first that this was not a case of fraud: 'It is not fraud to take advantage of legal rights, the existence of which may be taken to be known to both parties' (per Lord Cozens-Hardy MR, at 663), secondly that section 93 of the Act was clear in its terms, should be applied according to its plain meaning, and should not be weakened by infusion of equitable doctrines applied by the courts during the 19th century. The judgment of Lord Cozens-Hardy MR contains a valuable critique of the well known cases of *Le Neve v Le Neve* (1747) 3 Atk 646 and *Greaves v Tofield* (1880) 14 ChD 563 which, arising under the Middlesex Registry Act 1708 and other enactments, had led the judges to import equitable doctrines into cases of priority arising under those Acts, and establishes that the principles of those cases should not be applied to modern Acts of Parliament.

My Lords, I fail to see how this authority can be invoked in support of the respondents' argument, or of the judgments of the majority of the Court of Appeal. So far from supporting them, it is strongly the other way. It disposes, for the future, of the old arguments based, ultimately, upon *Le Neve v Le Neve* for reading equitable doctrines (as to notice, etc.) into modern Acts of Parliament: it makes it clear that it is not 'fraud' to rely on legal rights conferred by Act of Parliament: it confirms the validity of interpreting clear enactments as to registration and priority according to their tenor.

The judgment of Philimore LJ in *Re Monolithic Building Co* [1915] 1 Ch 643 at 669, 670 does indeed contain a passage which appears to favour application of the principle of *Le Neve v Le Neve* and to make a distinction between a transaction designed to obtain an advantage, and one designed to defeat a prior (unregistered) interest. But, as I have explained, this distinction is unreal and unworkable: this whole passage is impossible to reconcile with the views of the other members of the Court of Appeal in the case, and I respectfully consider that it is not good law.

My Lords, I can deal more shortly with the respondents' second argument. It relates to the consideration for the purchase. The argument is that the protection of section 13(2) of the Land Charges Act 1925 does not extend to a purchaser who has provided only a nominal consideration and that £500 is nominal. A variation of this was the argument accepted by the Court of Appeal that the consideration must be 'adequate'—an expression of transparent difficulty. The answer to both contentions lies in the language of the subsection. The word 'purchaser,' by definition (section 20(8)), means one who provides valuable consideration—a term of art which precludes any inquiry as to adequacy. This definition is, of course, subject to the context. Section 13(2), proviso, requires money or money's worth to be provided: the purpose of this being to exclude the consideration of marriage. There is nothing here which suggests, or admits of, the introduction of a further requirement that the money must not be nominal.

The argument for this requirement is based upon the Law of Property Act 1925 which, in section 205(1)(xxi) defining 'purchaser' provides that 'valuable consideration' includes marriage but does not include a 'nominal consideration in money.' The Land Charges Act 1925 contains no definition of 'valuable consideration,' so it is said to be necessary to have resort to the Law of Property Act definition: thus 'nominal consideration in money' is excluded. An indication that this is intended is said to be provided by section 199(1)(i). I cannot accept this. The fallacy lies in supposing that the Acts—either of them—set out to define 'valuable consideration'; they do not: they define 'purchaser,' and they define the word differently (see the first part of the argument). 'Valuable consideration' requires no definition: it is an expression denoting an advantage conferred or detriment suffered. What each Act does is, for its own purposes, to exclude some things from this general expression: the Law of Property Act includes marriage but not a nominal sum in money; the Land Charges Act excludes marriage but allows 'money or money's worth.' There is no coincidence between these two; no link by reference or necessary logic between them. Section 199(1)(i) by referring to the Land Charges Act 1925, necessarily incorporates—for the purposes for this provision—the definition of 'purchaser' in the latter Act, for it is only against such a 'purchaser' that an instrument is void under that Act. It cannot be read as incorporating the Law of Property Act definition into the Land Charges Act. As I have pointed out the land charges legislation has contained its own definition since 1888, carried through, with the addition of the reference to 'money or money's worth' into 1925. To exclude a nominal sum of money from section 13(2) of the Land Charges Act would be to rewrite the section.

This conclusion makes it unnecessary to determine whether £500 is a nominal sum of money or not. But I must say that for my part I should have great difficulty in so holding. 'Nominal consideration' and a 'nominal sum' in the law appear to me, as terms of art, to refer to a sum or consideration which can be mentioned as consideration but is not necessarily paid. To equate 'nominal' with 'inadequate' or even 'grossly inadequate' would embark the law upon inquiries which I cannot think were contemplated by Parliament.

I would allow the appeal.

In **McCarthy & Stone Ltd v Julian S Hodge & Co Ltd** [1971] 1 WLR 1547 the plaintiffs, who were engaged in building work on the premises of Cityfield Properties Ltd, obtained on 17 February 1964 an option to purchase. On 14 March 1964, Cityfield Properties Ltd created an equitable mortgage by deposit of title deeds[255] with the defendant bank. On 13 April 1964, the bank registered the equitable mortgage under the Companies Act 1948, s. 95.[256]

On 27 September 1965 the plaintiffs registered their option as an estate contract. On 21 June 1967, Cityfield Properties Ltd were in liquidation.

One question was whether the plaintiffs' estate contract had priority over the bank's equitable mortgage. Foster J held that it had. The Land Charges Act 1925, s. 13(2) (now Land Charges Act 1972, s. 4(6)) did not apply, because the bank was not a purchaser for value of a legal estate. The bank was only an *equitable* mortgagee, and the priority as between the plaintiffs and the bank depended on the time of creation, in accordance with the equitable principle *Qui potior est tempore, potior est jure* (the first in time has

---

[255] P. 864, below.   [256] Now CA 2006, s. 860, p. 93, below.

the stronger right). The option was created before the mortgage and therefore the bank took subject to it.[257]

(iv) Other registers under the Land Charges Act 1972

LAND CHARGES ACT 1972

5. The register of pending actions.—(1) There may be registered in the register of pending actions—

(a) a pending land action;[258]

(b) a petition in bankruptcy filed on or after 1st January 1926.

(4) The registrar shall forthwith enter the particulars in the register, in the name of the estate owner or other person whose estate or interest is intended to be affected.

(4A) Where a person has died and a pending land action would apart from his death have been registered in his name, it shall be so registered notwithstanding his death.[259]

(7) A pending land action shall not bind a purchaser without express notice of it unless it is for the time being registered under this section.

(8) A petition in bankruptcy shall not bind a purchaser of a legal estate in good faith, for money or money's worth, unless it is for the time being registered under this section.[260]

(10) The court, if it thinks fit, may, upon the determination of the proceedings, or during the pendency of the proceedings if satisfied that they are not prosecuted in good faith, make an order vacating a registration under this section, and direct the party on whose behalf it was made to pay all or any of the costs and expenses occasioned by the registration and by its vacation.[261]

6. The register of writs and orders affecting land.—(1) There may be registered in the register of writs and orders affecting land—

(a) any writ or order affecting land[262] issued or made by any court for the purpose of enforcing a judgment or recognisance;[263]

---

[257] At 1555; [1972A] CLJ 34 (P. B. Fairest), where the point is made that if the plaintiffs' interest had been a land charge in a different category within Class C (e.g. a puisne mortgage), the bank would not have been bound. An unregistered puisne mortgage is void against a purchaser for value of any interest in the land. See also (1976) CLP 25 (D. J. Hayton).

[258] Defined in LCA 1972, s. 17 (1) as 'any action or proceeding in court relating to land or any interest in or charge on land.' See *Calgary and Edmonton Land Co Ltd v Dobinson* [1974] Ch 102; *Whittingham v Whittingham* [1979] Fam 9; *Greenhi Builders Ltd v Allen* [1979] 1 WLR 156; *Selim Ltd v Bickenhall Engineering Ltd* [1981] 1 WLR 1318; *Regan & Blackburn Ltd v Rogers* [1985] 1 WLR 870; *Sowerby v Sowerby* (1982) 44 P & CR 192; *Haslemere Estates Ltd v Baker* [1982] 1 WLR 1109; [1983] Conv 69 (J. E. M.); *Perez-Adamson v Perez Rivas* [1987] Fam 89; [1987] Conv 58 (J. E. Martin); *Kemmis v Kemmis* [1988] 1 WLR 1307; and generally (1986) 136 NLJ 157 (H. W. Wilkinson); *Willies-Williams v National Trust* (1993) 65 P & CR 359.

[259] As inserted by LP(MP)A 1994, s. 15(3).

[260] As amended by Insolvency Act 1985, s. 235, Sch. 8, para. 21(2), and Sch. 10.

[261] *Calgary and Edmonton Land Co Ltd v Discount Bank (Overseas) Ltd* [1971] 1 WLR 81; *Norman v Hardy* [1974] 1 WLR 1048; *Northern Development (Holdings) Ltd v UDT Securities Ltd* [1976] 1 WLR 1230. Cf. LCA 1972, s. 1(6), p. 67, above.

[262] *Perry v Phoenix Assurance plc* [1988] 1 WLR 940.

[263] E.g. an order charging the land of a judgment debtor with the payment of the money due: Charging Orders Act 1979, p. 866, below. See *Stockler v Fourways Estates Ltd* [1984] 1 WLR 25 (Mareva injunction (now, freezing order) prohibiting a party from disposing of his assets held not registrable).

(b) any order appointing a receiver[264] or sequestrator of land;

(c) any bankruptcy order, whether or not the bankrupt's estate is known to include land;[265]

(d) any access order under the Access to Neighbouring Land Act 1992.[266]

(1A) No writ or order affecting an interest under a trust of land may be registered under subsection (1) above.[267]

(2A) Where a person has died and any such writ or order as is mentioned in subsection (1) (a) or (b) above would apart from his death have been registered in his name, it shall be so registered notwithstanding his death.[268]

(4) Except as provided by subsection (5) below and by section 37(5) of the Supreme Court Act 1981[269] and section 107(3) of the County Courts Act 1984 (which make special provision as to receiving orders in respect of land of judgment debtors) every such writ and order as is mentioned in subsection (1) above, and every delivery in execution or other proceeding taken pursuant to any such writ or order, or in obedience to any such writ or order, shall be void as against a purchaser of the land unless the writ or order is for the time being registered under this section.

(5) Subject to subsection (6) below, the title of a trustee in bankruptcy shall be void as against a purchaser of a legal estate in good faith for money or money's worth, unless the bankruptcy order is for the time being registered under this section.[270]

(6) Where a petition in bankruptcy has been registered under section 5 above, the title of the trustee in bankruptcy shall be void as against a purchaser of a legal estate in good faith for money or money's worth claiming under a conveyance made after the date of registration, unless at the date of the conveyance either the registration of the petition is in force or a receiving order on the petition is registered under this section.

7. The register of deeds of arrangement affecting land.—(1) A deed of arrangement affecting land may be registered in the register of deeds of arrangement affecting land, in the name of the debtor, on the application of a trustee of the deed or a creditor assenting to or taking the benefit of the deed.

(2) Every deed of arrangement shall be void as against a purchaser of any land comprised in it or affected by it unless it is for the time being registered under this section.

8. Expiry and renewal of registrations.—A registration under section 5, section 6 or section 7 of this Act shall cease to have effect at the end of the period of five years from the date on which it is made, but may be renewed from time to time and, if so renewed, shall have effect for five years from the date of renewal.

---

[264] *Clayhope Properties Ltd v Evans* [1986] 1 WLR 1223 (receivership order made against landlord for specific performance of repairing covenants held registrable). In registered land, this is registrable as a restriction under LRA 2002, s. 87(2).

[265] As amended by Insolvency Act 1985, s. 235, Sch. 8, para. 21(3), and Sch. 10.

[266] As inserted by Access to Neighbouring Land Act 1992, s. 5(1), p. 650, below.

[267] As inserted by TLATA 1996, s. 25(1), Sch. 3, para. 12(3).

[268] As inserted by LP(MP)A 1994, s. 15(4).

[269] As amended by Supreme Court Act 1981, s. 152(1), Sch. 5.

[270] As amended by County Courts Act 1984, s. 148(1), Sch. 2, para. 18.

(v) Registration against estate owners prior to root of title

Since the system of registration of land charges provides for the registration of charges against the name of the estate owner, a purchaser can only search against those persons whom he knows to have been estate owners. He will find their names from the deeds. But if the number of years between 1926, when the Register of Land Charges began, and the date of the purchase is greater than 15 years, which is the statutory period of search,[271] then it is possible that persons may have been estate owners since 1925 without the purchaser knowing about them. He would then be bound by land charges registered against their names without having any way of searching against them. This hazard began in 1956, 30 years (then the statutory period of search[272]) after registration began.

When the statutory period of search was reduced in 1969 to 15 years,[273] the purchaser's risk greatly increased, and some protection was needed.

LAW OF PROPERTY ACT 1969

25. Compensation in certain cases for loss due to undisclosed land charges.—(1) Where a purchaser of any estate or interest in land under a disposition to which this section applies has suffered loss by reason that the estate or interest is affected by a registered land charge, then if—

    (a) the date of completion was after the commencement of this Act; and

    (b) on that date the purchaser had no actual knowledge of the charge; and

    (c) the charge was registered against the name of an owner of an estate in the land who was not as owner of any such estate a party to any transaction, or concerned in any event, comprised in the relevant title; the purchaser shall be entitled to compensation for the loss.[274]

(2) For the purposes of subsection (1)(b) above, the question whether any person had actual knowledge of a charge shall be determined without regard to the provisions of section 198 of the Law of Property Act 1925 (under which registration under the Land Charges Act 1925 or any enactment replaced by it is deemed to constitute actual notice).[275]

(9) This section applies to the following dispositions, that is to say—

    (a) any sale or exchange and, subject to the following provisions of this subsection, any mortgage of an estate or interest in land;

    (b) any grant of a lease for a term of years derived out of a leasehold interest;

    (c) any compulsory purchase, by whatever procedure, of land; and

    (d) any conveyance of a fee simple in land under Part I of the Leasehold Reform Act 1967;

---

[271] P. 57, above.   [272] LPA 1925, s. 44(1).
[273] LPA 1969, s. 23.
[274] Payable by the Chief Land Registrar out of public funds: LPA 1969, s. 25(4).
[275] P. 64, above.

but does not apply to the grant of a term of years derived out of the freehold or the mortgage of such a term by the lessee; and references in this section to a purchaser shall be construed accordingly.

(10) In this section—

'relevant title' means—

   (a) in relation to a disposition made under a contract, the title which the purchaser was, apart from any acceptance by him (by agreement or otherwise) of a shorter or an imperfect title, entitled to require; or

   (b) in relation to any other disposition,[276] the title which he would have been entitled to require if the disposition had been made under a contract to which section 44(1) of the Law of Property Act 1925[277] applied and that contract had been made on the date of completion.

(11) For the purposes of this section any knowledge acquired in the course of a transaction by a person who is acting therein as counsel, or as solicitor or other agent, for another shall be treated as the knowledge of that other.

(vi) Actual and constructive notice are irrelevant under the Land Charges Act

LAW OF PROPERTY ACT 1925

199. Restrictions on constructive notice.—(1) A purchaser shall not be prejudicially affected by notice of—

   (i) any instrument or matter capable of registration under the provisions of the Land Charges Act, 1925, or any enactment which it replaces, which is void or not enforceable as against him under that Act or enactment, by reason of the non-registration thereof;

   (ii) any other instrument or matter or any fact or thing unless—

      (a) it is within his own knowledge, or would have come to his knowledge if such inquiries and inspections had been made as ought reasonably to have been made by him; or

      (b) in the same transaction with respect to which a question of notice to the purchaser arises, it has come to the knowledge of his counsel, as such, or of his solicitor or other agent, as such, or would have come to the knowledge of his solicitor or other agent, as such, if such inquiries and inspections had been made as ought reasonably to have been made by the solicitor or other agent.[278]

---

[276] E.g. compulsory purchase or acquisition under Leasehold Reform Act 1967.

[277] N. 272, above.

[278] This re-enacts Conveyancing Act 1882, s. 3. See also *Sharpe v Foy* (1868) 4 Ch App 35; *Re Cousins* (1886) 31 ChD 671; *Kingsnorth Finance Co Ltd v Tizard* [1986] 1 WLR 783; *Halifax Mortgage Services Ltd v Stepsky* [1996] Ch 207 (notice not imputed to client where solicitor was under duty to another client not to communicate the information); *Woolwich plc v Gomm* (2000) 79 P & CR 61 (imputed notice under LPA 1925, s. 199(i),(ii)(b); standard is objective and does not depend on particular instructions given by building society to its solicitor).

In **Hollington Bros Ltd v Rhodes** [1951] 2 TLR 691 the plaintiffs purported to take an unsealed 7 year underlease from the defendants at a rent of £612 a year. They went into possession and paid rent, but did not register the informal lease as a land charge. The defendants then sold the legal reversion to Daymar Estates Ltd 'subject to and with the benefit of such tenancies as may affect the premises'. On the same day Daymar Estates Ltd served half a year's notice to quit on the plaintiffs, contending that Daymar Estates Ltd were not bound by the equitable lease but only by the legal tenancy from year to year. The plaintiffs agreed to take a new lease from Daymar Estates Ltd at a premium and an increased rent and sued the defendants for the difference between their old rent and the new payments.

Harman J held that there was no concluded agreement between the plaintiffs and the defendants, and so the plaintiffs failed. He then considered what the position would have been had there been a contract. He referred to the pre-1926 law and quoted Farwell J in *Hunt v Luck* [1901] 1 Ch 45 at 51:[279]

'(1) A tenant's occupation is notice of all that tenant's rights, but not of his lessor's title or rights; (2) actual knowledge that the rents are paid by the tenants to some person whose receipt is inconsistent with the title of the vendor is notice of that person's rights.'

HARMAN J continued at 695:

After 1925, however, by virtue of section 10 of the Land Charges Act 1925,[280] this contract came within Class C(iv) as a charge on or obligation affecting land, and therefore might be registered as a land charge in the Registry of Land Charges. Accordingly, by virtue of section 13(2),[281] this being a land charge of Class C is void 'against a purchaser of the land charged therewith, or of any interest in such land, unless the land charge is registered in the appropriate register before the completion of the purchase.' Moreover, by section 199 of the Law of Property Act 1925, a purchaser is not to be prejudicially affected by notice of any instrument or matter capable of registration under the Land Charges Act 1925, which is void against him by reason of non-registration. This land charge was not registered, and accordingly it is said that it was void against Daymar Estates, Limited, notwithstanding their notice or knowledge, and, moreover, that there was no duty lying on the plaintiffs to register the contract in order to prevent this result. This has been held to be so by Wynn-Parry J in *Wright v Dean* [1948] Ch 686 where he said that it could not be urged that there was any such duty on the plaintiff. I propose to follow that decision, although I may observe in passing that there is in section 200(4) of the Law of Property Act 1925, a reference to 'the obligation to register a land charge in respect of . . . any estate contract.'

The defendants' answer to this point was that in fact Daymar Estates, Limited, did not contract to obtain, and did not by the assignment get, any estate in the land expressed to override the plaintiffs' rights, and that consequently they took subject to those rights which are expressly mentioned, and that the land which they purchased was in fact only an interest in the

---

[279] Approved by CA [1902] 1 Ch 428 at 432. The principle is preserved by LPA 1925, s. 14: *City of London Building Society v Flegg* [1988] AC 54 at 80, per Lord Oliver of Aylmerton; p. 551, below.

[280] Now LCA 1972, s. 2, p. 65, above.

[281] Now LCA 1972, s. 4(6), p. 71, above. An estate contract is void only against a purchaser for money or money's worth of the legal estate.

land subject to the rights of the plaintiffs in it. This argument seemed to me attractive because it appears at first glance wrong that a purchaser, who knows perfectly well of rights subject to which he is expressed to take, should be able to ignore them. It was, moreover, pointed out that *Wright v Dean* was distinguishable in this respect because there the option which was overridden by the conveyance was not mentioned in it, nor did the purchaser take expressly subject to it. It seems to me, however, that this argument cannot prevail having regard to the words in section 13(2) of the Land Charges Act 1925 which I have quoted, coupled with the definition of 'land' in the Act. The fact is that it was the policy of the framers of the 1925 legislation to get rid of equitable rights of this sort unless registered....

Finally, as under section 13 of the Land Charges Act 1925 ... an unregistered estate contract is void, and under section 199 of the Law of Property Act 1925, the purchaser is not to be prejudicially affected by it, I do not see how that which is void and which is not to prejudice the purchaser can be validated by some equitable doctrine.[282]

In **Smith v Jones** [1954] 1 WLR 1089 the defendant Jones purchased, at an auction, a farm which the plaintiff, to Jones' knowledge, occupied as a tenant.

Disputes arose between the plaintiff and defendant as to the liability for certain repairs, and eventually the plaintiff brought this action claiming that his tenancy agreement should be rectified so as to make the defendant liable for structural repairs.

The defendant contended that, even if a case for rectification could be established against the original lessor, he, as a bona fide purchaser for value, was not bound by the equity to rectify. UPJOHN J held that there was no equity for rectification; and even if there had been, the defendant would have taken free of it. On the second point, he said at 1091:

Lastly, Mr Arnold for the plaintiff argued that as the plaintiff was in actual occupation as tenant, the defendant was affected with notice of all his rights and all his equities, including an equity to rectify. On the view I have formed of the facts and law as to rectification, this point does not strictly arise, but as it has been fully argued, I think that I ought to express my views thereon.

In *Barnhart v Greenshields* (1853) 9 Moo PCC 18, where the law is clearly and compendiously stated, the judgment of the Privy Council was delivered by Mr Pemberton Leigh, afterwards Lord Kingsdown, who said at 32: 'With respect to the effect of possession merely, we take the law to be, that if there be a tenant in possession of land, a purchaser is bound by all the equities which the tenant could enforce against the vendor, and that the equity of the tenant extends not only to interests connected with his tenancy, as in *Taylor v Stibbert* (1794) 2 Ves 437, but also to interests under collateral agreements, as in *Daniels v Davison* (1809) 16 Ves 249, *Allen v Anthony* (1816) 1 Mer 282, the principle being the same in both classes of cases; namely, that the possession of the tenant is notice that he has some interest in the land, and that a purchaser having notice of that fact, is bound, according to the ordinary rule, either to inquire what that interest is, or to give effect to it, whatever it may be.'

---

[282] *Markfaith Investment Ltd v Chiap Hua Flashlights Ltd* [1991] 2 AC 43 ('indistinguishable from the decision of Harman J in *Hollington Bros Ltd v Rhodes*': per Lord Templeman). See also *Lyus v Prowsa Developments Ltd* [1982] 1 WLR 1044, p. 223, below, where a sale of *registered* land expressly subject to an estate contract gave rise to a constructive trust; *Ashburn Anstalt v Arnold* [1989] Ch 1, p. 1097, below, per Fox LJ, at 25.

Then a little later on he cited the language of Lord Eldon in *Allen v Anthony* at 284: 'It is so far settled as not to be disputed, that a person purchasing, where there is a tenant in possession, if he neglects to inquire into the title, must take, subject to such rights as the tenant may have.'

On the other hand, Mr. Arnold has not produced any case which goes so far as to say that an equity of rectification is an equity which is enforceable against a purchaser. In my judgment it would be extending the doctrine of notice and the obligation to make inquiry far too much if the doctrine was intended to cover an equity of rectification. Of course the purchaser is bound by the rights of the tenant in occupation—that is quite clear. He is not entitled to assume—as was argued in the earlier cases, notably, I think, *Taylor v Stibbert*—that the tenant is in possession from year to year. He must look at the agreement and he is bound by the agreement, and if, as in *Daniels v Davidson,* the tenant not only has a tenancy agreement but an option to purchase, he is also bound by that.

But, in my judgment, a purchaser is not only entitled but bound to assume, when he is looking at the agreement under which the tenant holds, that that agreement correctly states the relationship between the tenant and the landlord; and he is not bound to assume or to ask or make inquiry whether the tenant has any rights to rectify that contract.

Barnhart v Greenshields (1853) 9 Moo PCC 18 was followed in the Court of Appeal by the well-known case of *Hunt v Luck* [1902] 1 Ch 428, where the principle was again stated, but as Cozens-Hardy LJ pointed out in argument, and Vaughan Williams LJ pointed out at the beginning of his judgment, the real question for determination was the true construction of the Conveyancing Act 1882; Farwell J, who heard the case at first instance [1901] 1 Ch 45, having dealt with the matter without reference to the statutory enactment. I have no doubt that that was because he treated the Act as merely declaratory of the existing law; but it is after all a matter of construction of the Act, although I have already expressed an opinion as though the matter rested solely upon decided cases.

The relevant section which re-enacts exactly, so far as relevant, the provisions of the Conveyancing Act 1882, is to be found in s. 199(1) of the Law of Property Act 1925 [His Lordship read sub-ss. (i) and (ii)(a) and continued]:

The question which I have to answer is this: What inspection and inquiries ought reasonably to have been made by the defendant of the tenant before the sale, so far as relevant to this question? I think the only relevant inquiry that he would have made would have been this: 'May I see your tenancy agreement? I want to see whether it corresponds with the copy agreement I have seen in the auction rooms.' That is the document which governed the rights of the parties.

He ought to have asked whether he had seen a correct copy, but he was under no obligation, in my view, to proceed further and say: 'Does that correctly represent your rights?' In fact, if he had asked that question, the answer honestly but erroneously given would have been 'Yes'. Still less was he bound to take the tenant step by step through the document and ask how the tenant interpreted its provisions. He could not be so bound, and it would be most unwise for any intending purchaser to do so.

In my judgment the defendant is entitled and bound to rely on the terms of the document, and the document speaks for itself. Accordingly, had I come to a contrary conclusion upon the claim for rectification, I should have found that this action was barred by the plea of bona fide purchaser of value without notice. In the circumstances, I must dismiss the action.[283]

---

[283] For registered land, see *Nurdin & Peacock plc v Ramsden & Co Ltd* [1999] 1 EGLR 119, p. 199, n. 268, below.

(vii) The residual role of the doctrine of the bona fide purchaser in unregistered land

We have seen that a purchaser's actual or constructive notice of a third party's interest which is registrable under the Land Charges Act 1972 is irrelevant. If the interest is properly registered it is binding; otherwise he takes free of it.[284]

However, in the case of an equitable interest which is not registrable,[285] and as long as the interest is not overreached by the conveyance to the purchaser,[286] the doctrine of the bona fide purchaser still applies: the purchaser takes free of it only if he is the purchaser of a legal estate, and has no notice (actual, constructive or imputed) of it.[287]

An *equitable interest* must be distinguished from a *mere equity*, such as the right to claim rescission for misrepresentation or undue influence, or rectification for mistake, and the rights to consolidation or to reopen a foreclosure.[288] In unregistered land[289] a mere equity is less potent than an equitable interest, and not even binding on a bona fide purchaser of an *equitable interest* for value without notice.

D. REGISTERED LAND: PROTECTION BY ENTRY ON THE REGISTER OR AS AN OVERRIDING INTEREST

The Land Charges Act 1972 is not applicable where the title to land is registered.[290] Interests or charges which are registrable against the name of the estate owner under the Land Charges Act 1972 in the case of unregistered land must be protected in the case of registered land by the entry of a notice on the register of title to the land itself. However, within the scheme for registered land there is also provision for rights to be protected by taking effect as *overriding interests*—that is, certain interests which will bind a disponee for valuable consideration of registered land even though the interests are not protected by entry of a notice on the register.[291] Registered land is considered

---

[284] Pp. 71 ff, above.

[285] E.g. beneficial interest under trust of land: *Kingsnorth Finance Co Ltd v Tizard* [1986] 1 WLR 783, p. 216, below; restrictive covenant entered into before 1926: LCA 1972, s. 2(5), Class D (ii); equitable right of re-entry on breach of covenant: *Shiloh Spinners Ltd v Harding* [1973] AC 691, p. 68, above; equity by estoppel: *ER Ives Investment Ltd v High* [1967] 2 QB 379, p. 1074, below; right of entry to remove fixtures at end of lease: *Poster v Slough Estates Ltd* [1969] 1 Ch 495.

[286] *Caunce v Caunce* [1969] 1 WLR 286; (1974) 38 Conv (NS) 226; *Kingsnorth Finance Co Ltd v Tizard*, above, n. 285 (capital money paid to only one trustee). For overreaching, see pp. 548–558, below.

[287] 'Notice' is now defined in LPA 1925, s. 199(1)(ii); above, p. 80.

[288] For further discussion of mere equities, see chap. 11.

[289] In registered land, LRA 2002, s. 116(b) provides that a mere equity has effect from the time it arises as an interest capable of binding successors in title, and comes within the priority rules of the Act; no distinction is therefore now made between an equitable interest and a mere equity for the purposes of registered land: below, p. 1006.

[290] LCA 1972, s. 14(1) as amended by LRA 2002, s. 133, Sch. 11, para. 10.

[291] LRA 2002 s. 29(1), (2) and Sch. 3; pp. 194 ff, below.

in detail in chapter 2.[292] But for present purposes we should note one particularly significant category of overriding interest: the interest of a person in actual occupation of the Land Registration Act, Schedule 3, paragraph 2.[293]

LAND REGISTRATION ACT 2002

SCHEDULE 3

UNREGISTERED INTERESTS WHICH OVERRIDE REGISTERED DISPOSITIONS

Interests of persons in actual occupation

2 An interest belonging at the time of the disposition to a person in actual occupation, so far as relating to land of which he is in actual occupation, except for—

(a) an interest under a settlement under the Settled Land Act 1925;

(b) an interest of a person of whom inquiry was made before the disposition and who failed to disclose the right when he could reasonably have been expected to do so;

(c) an interest—

    (i) which belongs to a person whose occupation would not have been obvious on a reasonably careful inspection of the land at the time of the disposition, and

    (ii) of which the person to whom the disposition is made does not have actual knowledge at that time;

(d) a leasehold estate in land granted to take effect in possession after the end of the period of three months beginning with the date of the grant and which has not taken effect in possession at the time of the disposition.

The principles of notice work differently in the two systems. An interest or charge which is not registrable under the Land Charges Act 1972 may be enforceable under the old doctrine of notice in the case of unregistered land;[294] but in the case of registered land, it must either be protected by an entry on the register or take effect as an overriding interest.[295] There is theoretically no room in the registered system for a residual category of third party rights whose enforceability depends on the old doctrine of notice.[296]

On the other hand there is no place in the unregistered system for the safety net provision of an overriding interest under Schedule 3 of the Land Registration Act 2002 under which the rights of persons in actual occupation are protected even if the occupant has not registered them.[297] In the case of unregistered land, however, the

---

[292] For the entry of notices and restrictions on the register, see pp. 171 ff, below; and for overriding interests, see p. 179, below.

[293] Replacing (with amendments) LRA 1925, s. 70(1)(*g*).   [294] P. 84, above.

[295] Rights such as those in p. 84, n. 285, above, may be protected under LRA 2002 by a notice or a restriction: p. 171, below.

[296] However, the operation of the overriding interests, and in particular of LRA 2002, Sch. 3, para. 2, above, is closely related to the doctrine of notice, since the purchaser will not be bound by the rights of persons of whose occupation he does not know and which would not have been obvious on a reasonably careful inspection of the land: Sch. 3, para. 2(c). See further p. 194, below.

[297] P. 195, below; *Williams & Glyn's Bank Ltd v Boland* [1981] AC 487, p. 203, below.

Draconian solution was adopted whereby the failure to register a registrable interest under the Land Charges Act 1925 renders it void against a purchaser, even though he is in bad faith or actually knows,[298] and even though the holder of the right is in possession.[299] This vital difference between the two systems may well have been due to an error on the part of the draftsmen of the 1925 legislation.

[1982] Conv 213 (M. Friend and J. Newton), pp. 215–217

It is as well ... to quote section 14 [of the Law of Property Act 1925] in full: '14. This part of this Act shall not prejudicially affect the interest of any person in possession or in actual occupation of land to which he may be entitled in right of such possession or occupation.'

The crucial words are, *This part of this Act,* for this makes it clear that it is only Part I of the Act (i.e. the first 39 sections) which are relevant....

The root of the problem may be traced back to the Law of Property Act 1922,[300] most of whose provisions were repealed before they ever came into force, where this particular provision originally appeared as section 33, and where it made a good deal more sense than it makes as it stands in the 1925 Act which replaced it. Part I of the Law of Property Act 1922 dealt with the 'Assimilation and amendment of the law of real and personal estate.' In particular, section 10 dealt with undivided shares (by reference to Schedule 3 to the Act); section 11 dealt with dispositions on trust for sale (by reference to Schedule 4); and section 14 dealt with land charges (by reference to Schedule 7). The various schedules to the 1922 Act contained provisions broadly similar to those contained in the main body of the 1925 Act. Moreover, paragraph 1(1)(f) of Schedule 7 introduced a new category of land charge, namely: '(f) Any contract, by an estate owner or by a person entitled to have a legal estate conveyed to him, to convey a legal estate (including a contract conferring a valid option of purchase, a right of pre-emption and any other like right) entered into after the commencement of this Act...'

In other words, the idea behind this provision seems to have been that estate contracts (e.g. contracts to convey a legal estate, agreements for a lease, etc.) should have been registrable as land charges, but that a person who did not so protect his interest and who was in possession or actual occupation, and who was entitled to such land in right of his possession or occupation should not thereby be prejudiced. This idea seems to be an extension of the rule

---

[298] *Midland Bank Trust Co Ltd v Green* [1981] AC 513, p. 72, above; *Hollington Bros Ltd v Rhodes* [1951] 2 TLR 691, p. 81, above; *Markfaith Investment Ltd v Chiap Hua Flashlights Ltd* [1991] 2 AC 43. These cases would have been decided differently in registered land. As to whether such a purchaser might be bound by a constructive trust, see (1981) 97 LQR at pp. 521–522 (B. Green); p. 222, below.

[299] The purchaser may nevertheless be bound by an unregistered registrable land charge (a) by estoppel: *Taylors Fashions Ltd v Liverpool Victoria Trustees Co Ltd* [1982] QB 133n, p. 1013, below, (b) by failure to plead the non-registration when sued: *Balchin v Buckle* (1982) Times, 1 June ('One would have thought that the purchaser could waive its effect and agree to be bound by the covenant (Class D (ii)). If he chose, whether from incompetence of his own or his legal advisers or from gentlemanly consideration for the rights or convenience of others, to be bound by the covenant or not to raise the point that it was void, there was no reason why the court should raise the point for him' per Stephenson LJ). But he is not bound by a bare trust 'which is merely an equitable consequence of a specifically enforceable contract of sale': *Lloyds Bank plc v Carrick* [1996] 4 All ER 630; (1996) 112 LQR 549 (P. Ferguson); [1996] Conv 295 (M. P. Thompson); [1997] CLJ 32 (M. Oldham); [1996] All ER Rev 257 (P. J. Clarke).

[300] This idea is not new. The writers wish to acknowledge the views expressed by Mr Charles Harpum of Downing College, Cambridge, and by Mr David Ibbetson in (1977) 41 Conv (NS) 415, 419, n. 31.

in *Hunt v Luck*.[301] Had section 33 of the 1922 Act found an appropriate context in the 1925 legislation many of the present problems could have been avoided. If the section had been re-enacted in the Land Charges Act 1925, the enforceability of unregistered estate contracts in registered and unregistered conveyancing would have been identical: this would also have accorded with the general scheme of the 1925 legislation, which must surely have been to ensure that there should be no differences of substantive law between registered and unregistered conveyancing. The absence of section 33 of the 1922 Act from the Land Charges Act 1925 may be regarded as merely an error in the final stages of drafting; the consequences for property law, however, were serious. One such consequence was the decision in *Hollington Bros Ltd v Rhodes*[302] to the effect that a purchaser (as defined[303]) takes free from an unregistered estate contract where the title to the land is unregistered, even though the holder of the estate contract is in possession of the land.

This is clearly anomalous. There can be no doubt that the Law of Property Act 1922, s. 33 (as replaced by the Law of Property Act 1925, s. 14) was designed to have the same effect in unregistered conveyancing as the Land Registration Act 1925, s. 70(1)(g) has for registered land.[304] The Land Registration Act 1925, s. 70(1)(g) refers to 'the rights of every person in actual occupation of the land or in receipt of the rents and profits thereof....' The Law of Property Act 1925, s. 14 refers to '...the interest of any person in possession or in actual occupation of land....' The definition of 'possession' in the Law of Property Act 1925, s. 205(1) (xix) includes 'the receipt of rents and profits'; in other words, both the Law of Property Act 1925, s. 14 and the Land Registration Act 1925, s. 70(1)(g) were designed to protect the rights of those in actual or constructive possession of land. Yet as the law now stands, the protection afforded to such persons is radically different, depending on whether the title to the land is registered or not. There is no good reason, legal or historical for an arbitrary distinction of this sort; the fact that the law now requires it to be made suggests a need for legislative reform.[305]

E. OTHER REGISTERS

(i) *Local land charges*[306]

Registers are maintained under the Local Land Charges Act 1975 by all district councils in England and Wales, and also by Welsh county councils, county borough

---

[301] [1901] 1 Ch 45.   [302] [1951] 2 All ER 578n [p. 81, above].

[303] LCA 1925, ss. 13(2), 20(8); and cf. LCA 1972, ss. 4(6), 17(1).

[304] [Now LRA 2002, Sch. 1, para. 2 and Sch. 3, para. 2].

[305] [See M & W, para. 8.096; MM, p. 88, which adds the point that the Lords and Commons Joint Committee had erroneously certified that the consolidation of LPA 1922 and LP(A)A 1924 into the various 1925 Acts made no change in the law. See Lord Oliver of Aylmerton in *City of London Building Society v Flegg* [1988] AC 54 at 80: 'The ambit of section 14 is a matter which has puzzled conveyancers ever since the Law of Property Act was enacted.... What section 14 does not do, on any analysis, is to enlarge or add to whatever interest it is that the occupant has in right of his occupation.' He then agreed with Wolstenholme and Cherry (13th edn), vol. i. p. 69, that s. 14 was designed to preserve the principle of *Hunt v Luck* [1902] 1 Ch 428; p. 81, above; *Lloyds Bank plc v Carrick* [1996] 4 All ER 630 at 642.]

[306] LLC Rules 1977 (SI 1977 No. 985); LLC (Amendment) Rules 1978 (SI 1978 No. 1638); 1995 (SI 1995 No. 260); 2003 LLC (Amendment) Rules (SI 2003 No. 2502). On searches for and information on contaminated land, see Tromans and Clarke, *Contaminated Land* (2000); (2001) 145 SJ 827. The Act came into force on

councils, London boroughs and the Common Council of the City of London.[307] Only those land charges which would not normally be disclosed by an inspection of the property or the title deeds have been made registrable. The register relates to both unregistered and registered land. In registered land, a local land charge takes effect as an overriding interest.[308]

The register, and the index by which all entries made in the register can readily be traced, need not be kept in documentary form.[309]

LAW OF PROPERTY ACT 1925

198. Registration under the Land Charges Act, 1925, to be notice.—p. 64, above.

LOCAL LAND CHARGES ACT 1975

1. Local land charges.[310]—(1) A charge or other matter affecting land is a local land charge if it falls within any of the following descriptions and is not one of the matters set out in section 2 below:—

    (a) any charge acquired either before or after the commencement of this Act by a local authority or National Park authority, water authority, sewerage undertaker or new town development corporation under the Public Health Acts 1936 and 1937, the Public Health Act 1961 or the Highways Act 1980 (or any Act repealed by that Act) or the Building Act 1984 or any similar charge acquired by a local authority or National Park authority under any other Act, whether passed before or after this Act, being a charge that is binding on successive owners of the land affected;

    (b) any prohibition of or restriction on the use of land—

        (i) imposed by a local authority or National Park authority on or after 1st January 1926 (including any prohibition or restriction embodied in any condition attached to a consent, approval or licence granted by a local authority on or after that date), or

        (ii) enforceable by a local authority or National Park authority under any covenant or agreement made with them on or after that date,

    being a prohibition or restriction binding on successive owners of the land affected;

---

1 August 1977 and replaces LCA 1925, s. 15 and other sections set out in LCA 1972, s. 18, Sch. 4. See Law Commission Report on Local Land Charges 1974 (Law Com No. 62); *Garner's Local Land Charges* (13th edn, 2005) which has a useful table of all local land charges arranged alphabetically (pp. 209–28). For other registers maintained by local authorities, see *Garner's Local Land Charges*, chap. 10. See generally Silverman, *Conveyancing Handbook* (15th edn, 2008), chap. B10. For local authority search forms, see CON 29 Parts 1 and 2; (2002) 152 NLJ 1022; Silverman, *Conveyancing Handbook*, Appendix III; and for searches in commercial conveyancing (2001) 151 NLJ 1346 (A. Boulton).

[307] LLCA 1975, s. 3(1) as amended by Local Government (Wales) Act 1994, s. 66(6), Sch. 16, para. 49. This includes the Inner Temple and the Middle Temple, s. 3(4).

[308] See LRA 2002, Sch. 1, para. 6; Sch. 3, para. 6, pp. 193, 196, below.

[309] LLCA 1975, s. 3(3) as substituted by the Local Government (Miscellaneous Provisions) Act 1982, s. 34(a).

[310] As amended by Highways Act 1980, s. 343(2), Sch. 24, para. 26; Building Act 1984, s. 133, Sch. 6, para. 16; Water Act 1989, s. 190, Sch. 25, para. 52; Environment Act 1995, s. 78, Sch. 10, para. 14; Norfolk and Suffolk Broads Act 1988, s. 21, Sch. 6, para. 14.

(c) any prohibition of or restriction on the use of land—

    (i) imposed by a Minister of the Crown or government department on or after the date of the commencement of this Act (including any prohibition or restriction embodied in any condition attached to a consent, approval or licence granted by such a Minister or department on or after that date), or

    (ii) enforceable by such a Minister or department under any covenant or agreement made with him or them on or after that date, being a prohibition or restriction binding on successive owners of the land affected;

(d) any positive obligation affecting land enforceable by a Minister of the Crown, government department or local authority or National Park authority under any covenant or agreement made with him or them on or after the date of the commencement of this Act and binding on successive owners of the land affected;

(e) any charge or other matter which is expressly made a local land charge by any statutory provision not contained in this section.

(2) For the purposes of subsection (1)(a) above, any sum which is recoverable from successive owners or occupiers of the land in respect of which the sum is recoverable shall be treated as a charge, whether the sum is expressed to be a charge on the land or not.

(3) For the purposes of this section and section 2 of this Act, the Broads Authority shall be treated as a local authority or National Park authority.

2. Matters which are not local land charges.[311]—The following matters are not local land charges:—

(a) a prohibition or restriction enforceable under a covenant or agreement made between a lessor and a lessee;

(b) a positive obligation enforceable under a covenant or agreement made between a lessor and a lessee;

(c) a prohibition or restriction enforceable by a Minister of the Crown, government department or local authority or National Park authority under any covenant or agreement, being a prohibition or restriction binding on successive owners of the land affected by reason of the fact that the covenant or agreement is made for the benefit of land of the Minister, government department or local authority or National Park authority;

(d) a prohibition or restriction embodied in any bye-laws;

(e) a condition or limitation subject to which planning permission was granted at any time before the commencement of this Act or was or is (at any time) deemed to be granted under any statutory provision relating to town and country planning, whether by a Minister of the Crown, government department or local authority or National Park authority;

(f) a prohibition or restriction embodied in a scheme under the Town and Country Planning Act 1932 or any enactment repealed by that Act;

(g) a prohibition or restriction enforceable under a forestry dedication covenant entered into pursuant to section 5 of the Forestry Act 1967;

[311] As amended by Environment Act 1995, s. 78, Sch. 10, para. 14.

(h) a prohibition or restriction affecting the whole of any of the following areas:—

   (i) England, Wales or England and Wales;

   (ii) England, or England and Wales, with the exception of, or of any part of, Greater London;

   (iii) Greater London.

5. Registration.—(1) Subject to subsection (6) below, where the originating authority as respects a local land charge are the registering authority, it shall be their duty to register it in the appropriate local land charges register.

(2) Subject to subsection (6) below, where the originating authority as respects a local land charge are not the registering authority, it shall be the duty of the originating authority to apply to the registering authority for its registration in the appropriate local land charges register and upon any such application being made it shall be the duty of the registering authority to register the charge accordingly.

(3) The registration in a local land charges register of a local land charge, or any matter which when registered becomes a local land charge, shall be carried out by reference to the land affected or such part of it as is situated in the area for which the register is kept.

(4) In this Act, 'the originating authority', as respects a local land charge, means the Minister of the Crown, government department, local authority or other person by whom the charge is brought into existence or by whom, on its coming into existence, the charge is enforceable;[312] ...

(5) The registration of a local land charge may be cancelled pursuant to an order of the court.

(6) Where a charge or other matter is registrable in a local land charges register and before the commencement of this Act was also registrable in a register kept under the Land Charges Act 1972, then, if before the commencement of this Act it was registered in a register kept under that Act, there shall be no duty to register it, or to apply for its registration, under this Act and section 10 below shall not apply in relation to it.

10. Compensation for non-registration or defective official search certificate.—(1) Failure to register a local land charge in the appropriate local land charges register shall not affect the enforceability of the charge but where a person has purchased any land affected by a local land charge, then—

   (a) in a case where a material personal search[313] of the appropriate local land charges register was made in respect of the land in question before the relevant time, if at the time of the search the charge was in existence but not registered in that register; or

   (aa) in a case where the appropriate local land charges register is kept otherwise than in documentary form and a material personal search of that register was made in respect of the land in question before the relevant time, if the entitlement to search in that register conferred by section 8 above was not satisfied as mentioned in sub-section (1A) of that section; or[314]

---

[312] In the case of charges under the Highways Act 1980, s. 224, the originating authority is the street works authority for the street concerned.

[313] S. 8.

[314] As added by Local Government (Miscellaneous Provisions) Act 1982, s. 34.

(*b*) in a case where a material official search[315] of the appropriate local land charges register was made in respect of the land in question before the relevant time, if the charge was in existence at the time of the search but (whether registered or not) was not shown by the official search certificate as registered in that register, the purchaser shall (subject to section 11(1) below[316]) be entitled to compensation for any loss suffered by him in consequence.[317]

(3) For the purposes of this section—

(*a*) a person purchases land where, for valuable consideration, he acquires any interest in land or the proceeds of sale of land, and this includes cases where he acquires as lessee or mortgagee and shall be treated as including cases where an interest is conveyed or assigned at his direction to another person;

(*b*) the relevant time—

(i) where the acquisition of the interest in question was preceded by a contract for its acquisition, other than a qualified liability contract, is the time when that contract was made;

(ii) in any other case, is the time when the purchaser acquired the interest in question or, if he acquired it under a disposition which took effect only when registered in the register of title kept under the Land Registration Act 2002,[318] the time when that disposition was made;

and for the purposes of sub-paragraph (i) above, a qualified liability contract is a contract containing a term the effect of which is to make the liability of the purchaser dependent upon, or avoidable by reference to, the outcome of a search for local land charges affecting the land to be purchased.

(*c*) a personal search is material if, but only if—

(i) it is made after the commencement of this Act, and

(ii) it is made by or on behalf of the purchaser or, before the relevant time, the purchaser or his agent has knowledge of the result of it;

(*d*) an official search is material if, but only if—

(i) it is made after the commencement of this Act, and

(ii) it is requisitioned by or on behalf of the purchaser or, before the relevant time, the purchaser or his agent has knowledge of the contents of the official search certificate.

(4) Any compensation for loss under this section shall be paid by the registering authority in whose area the land affected is situated; and where the purchaser has incurred expenditure for the purpose of obtaining compensation under this section, the amount of the compensation shall include the amount of the expenditure reasonably incurred by him for that purpose (so far as that expenditure would not otherwise fall to be treated as loss for which he is entitled to compensation under this section).

---

[315] S. 9.   [316] S. 11 (1) deals with the position of mortgagees in respect of a claim.

[317] The valuation date for the correct assessment of compensation is the date of the compensation assessment hearing: *Alcoa Minerals of Jamaica Inc v Broderick* [2002] 1 AC 371; *Pound v Ashford Borough Council* [2004] 1 P & CR 2 (criteria for awarding compensation).

[318] As amended by LRA 2002, s. 133, Sch. 11, para. 13.

(7) In the case of an action to recover compensation under this section the cause of action shall be deemed for the purposes of the Limitation Act 1939[319] to accrue at the time when the local land charge comes to the notice of the purchaser; and for the purposes of this subsection the question when the charge came to his notice shall be determined without regard to the provisions of section 198 of the Law of Property Act 1925[320] (under which registration under certain enactments is deemed to constitute actual notice).

LOCAL LAND CHARGES RULES 1977

3. Parts of the Register.—The register shall continue to be divided into parts, for the registration of different types of charge, as follows:

Part 1, for general financial charges;[321]

Part 2, for specific financial charges;

Part 3, for planning charges;

Part 4, for charges not registrable in another part of the register ('miscellaneous charges');[322]

Part 5, for charges falling within section 8(4) of the Agriculture (Miscellaneous Provisions) Act 1941 ('fenland ways maintenance charges');

Part 6, for charges falling within section 8(4) or 52(8) of the Land Compensation Act 1973 ('land compensation charges');

Part 7, for charges falling within section 1(4) or 9 of the New Towns Act 1965 ('new towns charges');[323]

Part 8, for charges falling within section 33 of the Civil Aviation Act 1949, section 21 of the Civil Aviation Act 1968 or section 16(2) of the Civil Aviation Act 1971 ('civil aviation charges');[324]

Part 9, for charges falling within section 11(1) or 16(6) of the Opencast Coal Act 1958 ('opencast coal charges');

Part 10, for charges falling within section 54(6) of the Town and Country Planning Act 1971 ('listed buildings charges');

Part 11, for charges falling within section 2(4) of the Rights of Light Act 1959 ('light obstruction notices');[325]

Part 12, for charges falling within section 31(4) of the Land Drainage Act 1976 ('drainage scheme charges').

(ii) Companies and limited liability partnerships

A register is maintained by the Registrar of Companies under the Companies Act 2006[326] of land charges created by a company for securing money.[327] The provisions of

---

[319] P. 252, below.   [320] P. 64, above.   [321] LLCA 1975, s. 6.

[322] This includes a variety of prohibitions of and restrictions on the user or mode of user of land or buildings, other than planning charges.

[323] Now New Towns Act 1981, ss. 1(5), 12.

[324] Now Civil Aviation Act 1982, s. 55(1).   [325] P. 733, below.

[326] Formerly CA 1985. The 2006 Act received royal assent on 8 November 2006. It is gradually being brought into force, and other statutory provisions which refer to the provisions of CA 1985 will be amended accordingly, but many remain in place for the time being. Provisions for registration of company charges were first introduced by CA 1900, s. 14, and were later contained in CA 1948, s. 95.

[327] Records can be inspected at Crown Way, Cardiff and Companies House, Bloomsbury Street, London, although between 1999 and 2005 there was a very significant shift to electronic searches of the register

the Companies Act in relation to registration of charges also apply (with appropriate modifications) to limited liability partnerships.[328]

A charge created by a company or a limited liability partnership[329] over registered land must be registered under the Land Registration Act 2002,[330] as well as under the Companies Act.

LAND CHARGES ACT 1972

3. Registration of land charges.—(7) In the case of a land charge for securing money created by a company before 1st January 1970 or so created at any time as a floating charge, registration under Part XII, or Chapter III of Part XXIII, of the Companies Act 1985 (or corresponding earlier enactments)[331] shall be sufficient in place of registration under this Act, and shall have effect as if the land charge had been registered under this Act.[332]

(8) The corresponding earlier enactments referred to in subsection (7) above are section 93 of the Companies (Consolidation) Act 1908, section 79 of the Companies Act 1929, section 95 of the Companies Act 1948 and sections 395 to 398 of the Companies Act 1985 as originally enacted.

COMPANIES ACT 2006

860 Charges created by a company

(1) A company that creates a charge to which this section applies must deliver the prescribed particulars of the charge, together with the instrument (if any) by which the charge is created or evidenced, to the registrar for registration before the end of the period allowed for registration.[333]

(2) Registration of a charge to which this section applies may instead be effected on the application of a person interested in it.

(e.g. by e-mail or online viewing): Companies House Annual Report and Accounts 2004/05, p. 34. Almost 100% of company searches are now made electronically: Companies House Annual Report and Accounts 2007/08, p. 48. A company must also keep a register of charges at its registered office: CA 2006, s. 876. See generally McCormack, *Registration of Company Charges* (2nd edn, 2005); Gough, *Company Charges* (2nd edn, 1995); *Gore-Brown on Companies* (45th edn, 2004), chap. 31.

[328] Limited Liability Partnerships Regulations 2001 (SI 2001 No. 1090), reg. 4, Sch. 2, referring to CA 1985; above, n. 326.

[329] A new form of legal entity created by Limited Liability Partnerships Act 2000. Under s. 1 it is a body corporate with unlimited capacity but with legal personality separate from that of its members, who have a limited liability to contribute to its assets in the event of it being wound up.

[330] LRA 2002, s. 27(2)(f), p. 163, below. It is envisaged that a single application for registration can be made to the Land Registrar, which will then be forwarded to the Registrar of Companies: LRA 2002, s. 121, but rules to provide for this have not yet been made. At present, the company or limited liability partnership must provide to the Land Registrar a certificate that the charge has already been registered under the Companies Act: LRR 2003, r. 111.

[331] As substituted by Companies Act 1989, s. 107, Sch. 16, para. 1; now Companies Act 2006; above, n. 326.

[332] *Property Discount Corpn Ltd v Lyon Group Ltd* [1981] 1 WLR 300 (registration in companies register held sufficient, even though it was not in name of estate owner as required by LCA 1972, s. 3 (1), p. 68, above); [1982] Conv 43 (D. M. Hare and T. Flanagan).

[333] For liability in negligence of company's solicitors to director and secretary (personal guarantors of company's debt) for failing to register a charge, see *Re Foster* [1986] BCLC 307 (CA 1948, s. 95).

(3) Where registration is effected on the application of some person other than the company, that person is entitled to recover from the company the amount of any fees properly paid by him to the registrar on registration.

(4) If a company fails to comply with subsection (1), an offence is committed by—

(a) the company, and

(b) every officer of it who is in default.

(5) A person guilty of an offence under this section is liable—

(a) on conviction on indictment, to a fine;

(b) on summary conviction, to a fine not exceeding the statutory maximum.

(6) Subsection (4) does not apply if registration of the charge has been effected on the application of some other person.

(7) This section applies to the following charges—

(a) a charge on land or any interest in land, other than a charge for any rent or other periodical sum issuing out of land...[334]

861 Charges which have to be registered: supplementary

(1) The holding of debentures entitling the holder to a charge on land is not, for the purposes of section 860(7)(a), an interest in the land.

(2) It is immaterial for the purposes of this Chapter where land subject to a charge is situated.

(5) In this Chapter—

(a) 'charge' includes mortgage, and

(b) 'company' means a company registered in England and Wales or in Northern Ireland.

869 Register of charges to be kept by registrar[335]

(1) The registrar shall keep, with respect to each company, a register of all the charges requiring registration under this Chapter.

(4) In the case of any other charge,[336] the registrar shall enter in the register the following particulars—

(a) if it is a charge created by a company, the date of its creation and, if it is a charge which was existing on property acquired by the company, the date of the acquisition,

---

[334] *Re Molton Finance Ltd* [1968] Ch 325 (equitable sub-mortgage); *Re Wallis & Simmonds (Builders) Ltd* [1974] 1 WLR 391 (equitable charge by deposit of title deeds). A vendor's lien arises by operation of law, not by contract, and is not a charge against property which requires registration: *London and Cheshire Insurance Co Ltd v Laplagrene Property Co Ltd* [1971] Ch 499, p. 217, below. All these cases were decided under CA 1948, s. 95.

[335] See also ss. 871 (registration of enforcement of security, where receiver or manager of company's property is appointed), 872 (entry in register of satisfaction in whole or in part of debt for which charge was given, or release in whole or in part of company's property or undertaking from charge), 873 (rectification of register of charges), 875 (company to keep copies of instruments creating charges), 876 (company to keep register of charges), 877 (instruments creating charges and company's register of charges to be available for inspection).

[336] I.e., other than charges to the benefit of which the holders of a series of debentures are entitled (s. 869(2)) and charges imposed under the Judgments Enforcement (Northern Ireland) Order 1981 (s. 869(3)).

(b) the amount secured by the charge,

(c) short particulars of the property charged, and

(d) the persons entitled to the charge.

(5) The registrar shall give a certificate of the registration of any charge registered in pursuance of this Chapter, stating the amount secured by the charge.

(6) The certificate—

(a) shall be signed by the registrar or authenticated by the registrar's official seal, and

(b) is conclusive evidence that the requirements of this Chapter as to registration have been satisfied.

(7) The register kept in pursuance of this section shall be open to inspection by any person.

870 The period allowed for registration

(1) The period allowed for registration of a charge created by a company is—

(a) 21 days beginning with the day after the day on which the charge is created, or

(b) if the charge is created outside the United Kingdom, 21 days beginning with the day after the day on which the instrument by which the charge is created or evidenced (or a copy of it) could, in due course of post (and if despatched with due diligence) have been received in the United Kingdom.

874 Consequence of failure to register charges created by a company

(1) If a company creates a charge to which section 860 applies, the charge is void (so far as any security on the company's property or undertaking is conferred by it) against—

(a) a liquidator of the company,

(b) an administrator of the company, and

(c) a creditor of the company,

unless that section is complied with.

(2) Subsection (1) is subject to the provisions of this Chapter.

(3) Subsection (1) is without prejudice to any contract or obligation for repayment of the money secured by the charge; and when a charge becomes void under this section, the money secured by it immediately becomes payable.

(iii) Agricultural charges

AGRICULTURAL CREDITS ACT 1928[337]

5. Agricultural charges on farming stock and assets.—(1) It shall be lawful for a farmer as defined by this Act by instrument in writing to create in favour of a bank as so defined a charge (hereinafter referred to as an agricultural charge) on all or any of the farming stock and other agricultural assets belonging to him as security for sums advanced or to be advanced to him or

---

[337] Agricultural Credits Regulations 1928 (SR & O 1928 No. 667); Agricultural Credits Fees Order 1985 (SI 1985 No. 372). In 2007–08 there were 1,267 new registrations, 808 cancellations and rectifications and 4,269 searches: Land Registry Annual Report and Accounts 2007–08, p. 23. The register is kept at the Land Registry at Plymouth.

paid or to be paid on his behalf under any guarantee by the bank and interest, commission and charges thereon.

9. Registration of agricultural charges.—(1) Every agricultural charge shall be registered under this Act within seven clear days after the execution thereof, and, if not so registered, shall be void as against any person other than the farmer:

Provided that the High Court on proof that omission to register within such time as aforesaid was accidental or due to inadvertence may extend the time for registration on such terms as the Court thinks fit.

(2) The Land Registrar shall keep at the Land Registry a register of agricultural charges in such form and containing such particulars as may be prescribed.

(8) Registration of an agricultural charge under this section shall be deemed to constitute actual notice of the charge, and of the fact of such registration, to all persons and for all purposes connected with the property comprised in the charge, as from the date of registration or other prescribed date, and so long as the registration continues in force:

Provided that, where an agricultural charge created in favour of a bank is expressly made for securing a current account or other further advances, the bank, in relation to the making of further advances under the charge, shall not be deemed to have notice of another agricultural charge by reason only that it is so registered if it was not so registered at the time when the first-mentioned charge was created or when the last search (if any) by or on behalf of the bank was made, whichever last happened.

(iv) Commons and town and village greens[338]

The registration provisions of the Commons Act 2006 replace the Commons Registration Act 1965.[339]

---

[338] C & B, pp. 645–8; Gray, paras 10.7.40–10.7.45; M & W, paras 27.039–27.042, 27.046–27.053; MM, p. 442. See generally N. Ubhi and B. Denyer-Green, *Law of Commons and of Town and Village Greens* (2nd edn, 2006); P. Clayden, *Our Common Land* (6th edn, 2007); Jessel, *Law of the Manor* (1998) and *Law of the Manor: the Twenty-First Century* (2004). For a recent account of the history of the common law and legislation on towns and village greens, see *Oxfordshire County Council v Oxford City Council* [2006] 2 AC 674 at [1]-[28], per Lord Hoffmann; [2006] All ER Rev 246 (P. J. Clarke). There are 373,570 hectares of registered common land in England (about 3% of the total land area), and 175,000 hectares in Wales (about 8.4% of the total land area). Nearly 57% of common land is designated as a Site of Special Scientific Interest, and over half of England's common land is in Cumbria and North Yorkshire (31% and 21% respectively) (figures as at January 2009 from Defra website, where further statistics can be found). For the liability of a solicitor who failed to search the register, see *G & K Ladenbau (UK) Ltd v Crawley and de Reya* [1978] 1 WLR 266.

For the rights of the public over commons and waste lands, see LPA 1925, ss. 193; *Mienes v Stone* (1985) CO/1217/84 noted [1985] Conv 415 (J. R. Montgomery); *R v Secretary of State for the Environment, ex p Billson* [1999] QB 374. See also National Parks and Access to the Countryside Act 1949, ss. 59–60, 64–82; Countryside Act 1968, ss. 6, 9; *R v Doncaster MBC, ex p Braim* (1986) 57 P & CR 1 (Doncaster Common 'best known as the site of the St. Leger' held to be an open space within LGA 1972, s. 123 (2A)); [1988] Conv 369 (J. Hill); Countryside and Right of Way Act 2000, Part I, which gives to the general public a right of access on foot to open countryside for the purpose of open-air recreation (the 'right to roam'). As to whether this is compatible with the Human Rights Act 1998, see Rook, *Property Law and Human Rights*, pp. 211–19. An even more extensive provision has been adopted by the Scottish Parliament: Land Reform (Scotland) Act 2003.

[339] The 2006 Act is being brought progressively into force: see commencement orders SI 2006 No. 2504; SI 2007 Nos 456 and 2584; SI 2008 No. 1960. S. 15 was brought into force on 6 April 2007: see below, n. 357. The principal sections were brought into force with effect from 1 October 2008 in relation to seven pilot

Explanatory Notes to Commons Act 2006
(The Stationery Office Ltd, 2006)

16 The [Commons Registration Act 1965] was intended to establish definitive registers of common land and town and village greens in England and Wales and to record details of rights of common. Commons registration authorities (generally county councils) were appointed to draw up the registers. Applications were invited between 2 January 1967 and 2 January 1970[340] for the provisional registration of common land, greens, and rights of common, and registration authorities were also able to register land on their own initiative. The registers remained open for objection until 31 July 1972.[341] Disputed provisional registrations were referred to a Commons Commissioner[342] (appointed under the 1965 Act) for determination, but unopposed provisional registrations became final automatically. The 1965 Act provided that, where land was eligible for registration under the Act (whether as common land or a town or village green), a failure to register it resulted in the land being deemed not to be common land or a green (as the case may be) after 31 July 1970.[343] Similarly, a failure to register rights of common which were eligible for registration caused the rights to cease to be exercisable[344] after the same date.

17 In practice the task of establishing registers was complex and the 1965 Act proved to have deficiencies. For example, some land provisionally registered under the Act was wrongly struck out, and other common land was overlooked and never registered. Many greens became registered as common land. Some grazing rights were registered far in excess of the carrying capacity of the common. The scope for correcting errors was limited.[344a] Furthermore, regulations made under the Act did not provide for sufficient notification of applications made for provisional registration of common land and rights of common, so that many provisional registrations became final without any objections and thus without independent appraisal of the claim made in the application. The Court of Appeal held that even where land had clearly been wrongly registered as common land, the Act provided no mechanism to enable such land to be removed from the register once the registration had become final.[345]

18 Moreover, although the 1965 Act made provision for amendments to be made to the registers consequent on events which occurred after 1970, there was no obligation on persons

registration authority areas in England. A review of the pilot will take place during 2009 and national roll-out is expected to commence in stages from October 2010 (information as at January 2009 from Defra website).

[340] Commons Registration (Time Limits) Order 1966 (SI 1966 No. 470) (a later date of 31 July 1970 applied in relation to land registered on the initiative of the registration authority).

[341] Article 4(2) of the Commons Registration (Objections and Maps) Regulations 1968 (SI 1968 No. 989), as amended by the Commons Registration (Objections and Maps) (Amendment) Regulations 1970 (SI 1970 No. 384).

[342] [The Commissioners' decisions covering the period from 1965 to 1990 are recorded in 78 bound volumes, in one volume or sometimes two volumes for each county in England and Wales. Most matters were determined by 1990, though any later decisions are all recorded: [1997] Conv 248 (A. Samuels). Decisions were reported in Campbell, *Decisions of the Commons Commissioners* (1972), in Current Law, and in the Annual Reports of the Commons, Open Spaces and Footpaths Preservation Society. See (1973) 117 SJ 537; (1974) 118 SJ 424 (I. Campbell).]

[343] Section 1(2) of the 1965 Act, as prescribed by the Commons Registration (Time Limits) Order 1966 (SI 1966 No. 1470), as amended.

[344] Section 1(2)(b) of the 1965 Act states that such rights are rendered not 'exercisable'. In *Central Electricity Generating Board v Clwyd County Council* [1976] 1 WLR 151, Goff J concluded that the fact that rights of common were no longer exercisable meant that they were extinguished, and this finding is now generally accepted.

[344a] *Betterment Properties (Weymouth) Ltd v Dorset CC* [2009] 1 WLR 334 (procedure to be followed for rectification)

[345] *Corpus Christi College, Oxford v Gloucestershire County Council* [1982] 3 All ER 995.

interested in any entry in the register to seek such an amendment. Many events which in principle affected entries in the registers have not been registered, and the registers have become significantly out-of-date since 1970.

19 The 1965 Act also explicitly postponed action on the Royal Commission's recommendations to improve management of common land and introduce public access in the wake of registration.

20 Several initiatives were promoted over the intervening period in support of further legislation. An inter-Departmental working party reported in 1977 with recommendations for reform to commons legislation.[346] The (then) Countryside Commission set up the Common Land Forum which reported in 1986,[347] reflecting a broad consensus between landowning, farming, nature conservation and recreational interests as the basis for legislation. Comprehensive legislation was later ruled out by the 1995 White Paper 'Rural England', and instead research was proposed to develop guidance for the management of common land (the conclusions of the research were subsequently published in 1998[348]). However, the Rural White Paper in 2000[349] included a commitment to legislate on common land as soon as parliamentary time allowed. Part I of the Countryside and Rights of Way Act 2000 provided for a public right of access (on foot) to all registered common land, which was fully implemented across England and Wales by October 2005.

21 The Government published a consultation paper in February 2000,[350] to coincide with the introduction of the Countryside and Rights of Way Bill, on proposed reforms to legislation relating to common land and town and village greens. Two years later, building on responses to the consultation, the Common Land Policy Statement 2002[351] set out in broad terms the Government's intentions for future legislation relating to common land and town and village greens. A Stakeholder Working Group was set up in 2002 to seek a consensus on more detailed proposals on agricultural use and management of common land,[352] on which there was further public consultation in 2003.[353]

22 The Commons Act gives effect to the recommendations set out in the Common Land Policy Statement with respect to the registration of common land and town or village greens, works and fencing on common land, and the agricultural use and management of common land (sections 2, 3 and 5 of the Policy Statement). It also makes more limited changes to the law with regard to town or village greens (section 4), principally in relation to the registration of greens, and the criteria for registering new greens.

---

[346] Common Land: preparations for comprehensive legislation—report of an inter-departmental working party, Department of the Environment (September 1978), unpublished.

[347] *Report of the Common Land Forum*, Countryside Commission (now the Countryside Agency), 1986, CCP215. Available on the internet at: www.countryside.gov.uk/Publications/articles/Publication_tcm2–29827.asp.

[348] Good Practice Guide on Managing the Use of Common Land, DETR, June 1998. Available from Defra: see www.defra.gov.uk/wildlife-countryside/issues/common/manage/guides.htm for how to obtain a copy.

[349] *Rural White Paper*, Defra, November 2000. Available on the internet at: www.defra.gov.uk/rural/ruralwp/.

[350] Greater Protection and Better Management of Common Land in England and Wales. DETR, February 2000. Available on the internet at: www.defra.gov.uk/wildlife-countryside/consult/common/index.htm.

[351] Defra, July 2002. Available on the internet at: www.defra.gov.uk/wildlife-countryside/issues/common/policy.htm.

[352] The report and proceedings of the Stakeholder Working Group are available on the internet at: www.defra.gov.uk/wildlife-countryside/issues/common/manage/workgroup.htm.

[353] Consultation on agricultural use and management of common land. Defra, August 2003. Available on the internet at: www.defra.gov.uk/corporate/consult/common-land/.

27 Part 1 of the Act provides for commons registration authorities to continue to keep registers of common land and town or village greens ('the commons registers'), and to permit amendments to be made to the registers in accordance with the provisions in that Part. This replaces and improves the registration system under the 1965 Act, but using the same registers prepared under that Act.

28 In particular, Part 1 includes provisions for:

the amendment of the registers upon the occurrence of registrable events, such as the disposition of rights of common, statutory dispositions of common land (*e.g.* under compulsory purchase legislation) and the creation of new town or village greens;

the prohibition of the severance of a registered right of common from any land to which it is attached, subject to certain exceptions;

the deregistration of common land and registration of other land as common land in exchange, subject to the consent of the appropriate national authority;

the correction of errors in the registers by commons registration authorities;

the establishment of electronic registers;

transitional powers to rectify mistakes made in registers under the 1965 Act, and to register events which occurred while the 1965 Act was in force; and

ensuring that only registered rights of common may be exercised over land to which Part 1 applies.

COMMONS ACT 2006[354]

1 Registers of common land and greens

Each commons registration authority shall continue to keep—

(a) a register known as a register of common land; and

(b) a register known as a register of town or village greens.

2 Purpose of registers[355]

(1) The purpose of a register of common land is—

(a) to register land as common land; and

(b) to register rights of common exercisable over land registered as common land.

(2) The purpose of a register of town or village greens is—

(a) to register land as a town or village green; and

(b) to register rights of common exercisable over land registered as a town or village green.

3 Content of registers

(1) The land registered as common land in a register of common land is, subject to this Part, to be—

(a) the land so registered in it at the commencement of this section;[356] and

---

[354] Replacing Commons Registration Act 1965. See also Commons Registration (England) Regulations 2008 (SI 2008 No. 1961).

[355] Regulations may require or permit the whole or any part of a register kept under this Part to be kept in electronic form: s. 25. For inspection of the registers, see s. 20.

[356] Throughout this section such references are to existing registrations under Commons Registration Act 1965.

    (b) such other land as may be so registered in it under this Part.

  (2) The land registered as a town or village green in a register of town or village greens is, subject to this Part, to be—

    (a) the land so registered in it at the commencement of this section; and

    (b) such other land as may be so registered in it under this Part.

  (3) The rights of common registered in a register of common land or town or village greens are, subject to this Part, to be—

    (a) the rights registered in it at the commencement of this section; and

    (b) such other rights as may be so registered in it under this Part.

  (4) The following information is to be registered in a register of common land or town or village greens in respect of a right of common registered in it—

    (a) the nature of the right;

    (b) if the right is attached to any land, the land to which it is attached;

    (c) if the right is not so attached, the owner of the right.

  (5) Regulations may—

    (a) require or permit other information to be included in a register of common land or town or village greens;

    (b) make provision as to the form in which any information is to be presented in such a register.

  (6) Except as provided under this Part or any other enactment—

    (a) no land registered as common land or as a town or village green is to be removed from the register in which it is so registered;

    (b) no right of common registered in a register of common land or town or village greens is to be removed from that register.

  (7) No right of common over land to which this Part applies is to be registered in the register of title.

4 Commons registration authorities

  (1) The following are commons registration authorities—

    (a) a county council in England;

    (b) a district council in England for an area without a county council;

    (c) a London borough council; and

    (d) a county or county borough council in Wales.

  (2) For the purposes of this Part, the commons registration authority in relation to any land is the authority in whose area the land is situated.

  (3) Where any land falls within the area of two or more commons registration authorities, the authorities may by agreement provide for one of them to be the commons registration authority in relation to the whole of the land.

5 Land to which Part 1 applies

  (1) This Part applies to all land in England and Wales, subject as follows.

(2) This Part does not apply to—

(a) the New Forest; or

(b) Epping Forest.

(3) This Part shall not be taken to apply to the Forest of Dean.

(4) If any question arises under this Part whether any land is part of the forests mentioned in this section it is to be referred to and decided by the appropriate national authority.

6 Creation

(1) A right of common cannot at any time after the commencement of this section be created over land to which this Part applies by virtue of prescription.

(2) A right of common cannot at any time after the commencement of this section be created in any other way over land to which this Part applies except—

(a) as specified in subsection (3); or

(b) pursuant to any other enactment.

(3) A right of common may be created over land to which this Part applies by way of express grant if—

(a) the land is not registered as a town or village green; and

(b) the right is attached to land.

(4) The creation of a right of common in accordance with subsection (3) only has effect if it complies with such requirements as to form and content as regulations may provide.

(5) The creation of a right of common in accordance with subsection (3) does not operate at law until on an application under this section—

(a) the right is registered in a register of common land; and

(b) if the right is created over land not registered as common land, the land is registered in a register of common land.

(6) An application under this section to register the creation of a right of common consisting of a right to graze any animal is to be refused if in the opinion of the commons registration authority the land over which it is created would be unable to sustain the exercise of—

(a) that right; and

(b) if the land is already registered as common land, any other rights of common registered as exercisable over the land.

15 Registration of greens[357]

(1) Any person may apply to the commons registration authority to register land to which this Part applies as a town or village green in a case where subsection (2), (3) or (4) applies.

---

[357] S. 15 was brought into force on 6 April 2007: Commons Act 2006 (Commencement No. 2, Transitional Provisions and Savings) (England) Order 2007 (SI 2007 No. 456). See also Commons (Registration of Town or Village Greens) (Interim Arrangements) (England) Regulations 2007 (SI 2007 No. 457) which provide for registration of new greens within the new scheme provided by the Commons Act 2006, but in the registers under the Commons Registration Act 1965 Act until ss. 1–3 of the 2006 Act are in force. The 2007 Regulations were revoked by Commons Registration (England) Regulations 2008 (SI 2008 No. 1961), reg. 55, in relation to the registration areas covered by the current pilot implementation of the 2006 Act; p. 96, n. 339, above.

(2) This subsection applies where—

    (a) a significant number of the inhabitants of any locality,[358] or of any neighbourhood within a locality, have indulged as of right[359] in lawful sports and pastimes[360] on[361] the land for a period of at least 20 years; and

    (b) they continue to do so at the time of the application.

(3) This subsection applies where—

    (a) a significant number of the inhabitants of any locality, or of any neighbourhood within a locality, indulged as of right in lawful sports and pastimes on the land for a period of at least 20 years;

    (b) they ceased to do so before the time of the application but after the commencement of this section; and

---

[358] *R (Cheltenham Builders Ltd) v South Gloucestershire DC* [2004] 1 EGLR 85 ('locality' must be a distinct and identifiable community; drawing a line on a map is not sufficient).

[359] *R v Oxfordshire County Council, ex p Sunningwell Parish Council* [2000] 1 AC 355, 355–356 ('as of right' reflects common law concept of *nec vi nec clam nec precario* and does not require subjective belief in the existence of the right); [1998] Conv 526 (T. Sutton); *R (Beresford) v Sunderland City Council* [2004] 1 AC 889 (mowing the grass and providing benches not sufficient to render use *precario* so as negative claim to user as of right: for this, landowner's permission, whether express or implied, must be shown to be temporary or revocable); *R (Lewis) v Redcar & Cleveland Borough Council* [2009] 15 EG 100 (extensive and frequent user for more than 20 years but inhabitants had deferred to alternative use as a golf course. No *principle* of deference, but on facts deference may be relevant to whether user has been sufficient to bring home to reasonable owner that local inhabitants have been asserting a right to use the land).

[360] Unaccompanied local children, picnicking, fishing in a pond, collecting bullrushes and picking mushrooms; local children, accompanied by adults, playing, picking blackberries, and studying fish and plant life; local adults picnicking, taking dogs for walks, and fishing in the pond held to amount to pastimes indulged in as of right: *Re White Lane Pond, Four Dales and Clay Pits, Thorne and Stainforth, South Yorkshire* [1984] CLY 287; cf. *Re River Don and its Banks* [1984] CLY 284, where it was held that walking with or without dogs along the banks of the River was not indulging; *Re Foreshore, East Bank of River Ouse, Naburn, Selby District, North Yorkshire* [1989] CLY 276 (pastime of idling by a river held to be customary right, which may be proved by walking, fishing and picnicking on the foreshore as of right by usage); [1992] Conv 434 (A. Samuels); *R v Buckinghamshire County Council* [2004] 1 EGLR 69 (agricultural use incompatible with use as of right for recreation as a village green). See also *R v Oxfordshire County Council, ex p Sunningwell Parish Council*, above, n. 359, at 356–357, per Lord Hoffmann ('sports and pastimes' is a not two classes of activities but a single composite class which uses two words in order to avoid arguments about whether an activity is a sport or a pastime); [1999] All ER Rev 223 (P. J. Clarke). Once registered, 'land registered as a town or village green can be used generally for sports and pastimes. It seems to me that Parliament must have thought that if the land had to be kept available for one form of recreation, it would not matter a great deal to the owner whether it was used for others as well. This would be in accordance with the common law, under which proof of a custom to play one kind of game gave rise to a right to use the land for other games': *Oxfordshire County Council v Oxford City Council* [2006] 2 AC 674 at [50], per Lord Hoffmann.

[361] 'The present question concerns what counts as indulging in such sports and pastimes "on" the land: must the "significant number" of inhabitants have set their feet everywhere on the land and must such activity be exclusively referable to indulging in sports and pastimes rather than exercising or creating rights of way?... If the area is in fact intersected with paths and clearings, the fact that these occupy only 25% of the land area would not in my view be inconsistent with a finding that there was recreational use of the scrubland as a whole. For example, the whole of a public garden may be used for recreational activities even though 75% of the surface consists of flower beds, borders and shrubberies on which the public may not walk': *Oxfordshire County Council v Oxford City Council*, above, n. 360, at [63], [67], per Lord Hoffmann.

(c) the application is made within the period of two years beginning with the cessation referred to in paragraph (b).[362]

(4) This subsection applies (subject to subsection (5)) where—

(a) a significant number of the inhabitants of any locality, or of any neighbourhood within a locality, indulged as of right in lawful sports and pastimes on the land for a period of at least 20 years;

(b) they ceased to do so before the commencement of this section; and

(c) the application is made within the period of five years beginning with the cessation referred to in paragraph (b).

(5) Subsection (4) does not apply in relation to any land where—

(a) planning permission was granted before 23 June 2006 in respect of the land;

(b) construction works were commenced before that date in accordance with that planning permission on the land or any other land in respect of which the permission was granted; and

(c) the land—

(i) has by reason of any works carried out in accordance with that planning permission become permanently unusable by members of the public for the purposes of lawful sports and pastimes; or

(ii) will by reason of any works proposed to be carried out in accordance with that planning permission become permanently unusable by members of the public for those purposes.

(6) In determining the period of 20 years referred to in subsections (2)(a), (3)(a) and (4)(a), there is to be disregarded any period during which access to the land was prohibited to members of the public by reason of any enactment.

(7) For the purposes of subsection (2)(b) in a case where the condition in subsection (2)(a) is satisfied—

(a) where persons indulge as of right in lawful sports and pastimes immediately before access to the land is prohibited as specified in subsection (6), those persons are to be regarded as continuing so to indulge; and

(b) where permission is granted in respect of use of the land for the purposes of lawful sports and pastimes, the permission is to be disregarded in determining whether persons continue to indulge in lawful sports and pastimes on the land 'as of right'.

(8) The owner of any land may apply to the commons registration authority to register the land as a town or village green.

(9) An application under subsection (8) may only be made with the consent of any relevant leaseholder of, and the proprietor of any relevant charge over, the land.

---

[362] Sub-ss. (3) and (4) reverse the effect of the decision of HL in *Oxfordshire County Council v Oxford City Council*, above, n. 360, on the interpretation of Commons Registration Act 1965, s. 22(1A), which required the use necessary for registration as a town or village green to continue to the date of application. S. 15 also changes the law relating to greens in other respects, such as requiring any period of statutory closure to be disregarded (s. 15(6)) and allowing the landowner to register voluntarily (s. 15(8)).

(10) In subsection (9)—

'relevant charge' means-

(a) in relation to land which is registered in the register of title, a registered charge within the meaning of the Land Registration Act 2002;

(b) in relation to land which is not so registered—

(i) a charge registered under the Land Charges Act 1972; or

(ii) a legal mortgage, within the meaning of the Law of Property Act 1925, which is not registered under the Land Charges Act 1972;

"relevant leaseholder" means a leaseholder under a lease for a term of more than seven years from the date on which the lease was granted.

18 Conclusiveness[363]

(1) This section applies to land registered as common land, or as a town or village green, which is registered as being subject to a right of common.

(2) If the land would not otherwise have been subject to that right, it shall be deemed to have become subject to that right, as specified in the register, upon its registration.

(3) If the right is registered as attached to any land, the right shall, if it would not otherwise have attached to that land, be deemed to have become so attached upon registration of its attachment.

(4) If the right is not registered as attached to any land, the person registered as the owner of the right shall, if he would not otherwise have been its owner, be deemed to have become its owner upon his registration.

(5) Nothing in subsection (2) affects any constraint on the exercise of a right of common where the constraint does not appear in the register.

(6) It is immaterial whether the registration referred to in subsection (2), (3) or (4) occurred before or after the commencement of this section.

61 Interpretation

(1) In this Act—

'appropriate national authority' means—

(a) the Secretary of State, in relation to England; and

(b) the National Assembly for Wales, in relation to Wales;

'land' includes land covered by water;

'regulations' means regulations made by the appropriate national authority;

'register of title' means the register kept under section 1 of the Land Registration Act 2002;

'right of common' includes a cattlegate or beastgate[364] (by whatever name known) and a right of sole or several vesture[365] or herbage or of sole or several

---

[363] For correction of the register, see s. 19.

[364] Cattlegate or beastgate, sometimes called *stinted pasture*, is a right to pasture a fixed number of beasts on the land of another, generally for a part of the year only. See e.g. *Rigg v Earl of Lonsdale* (1857) 1 H & N 923; *Brackenbank Lodge Ltd v Peart* (1993) 67 P & CR 249.

[365] The right of sole vesture, *vestura terrae*, is not merely to graze cattle, but to take away the product of the land, such as grass, corn, underwood, turf, peat, and so forth.

pasture, but does not include a right held for a term of years or from year to year.[366]

QUESTIONS

1. Why is no provision made in unregistered land for the registration of equitable beneficial interests?

2. Francis David Blackburn entered into a contract to sell a house, title to which is not registered, to a purchaser who registered the contract in the land charges register as an estate contract against the name of Frank David Blackburn, which was the name in which Francis David Blackburn carried on business as an estate agent. Is the registration valid:

   (a) against a mortgagee who does not search?

   (b) against a mortgagee who searches against the name of Francis David Blackburn and receives a nil certificate?

   (c) against a mortgagee who searches against the name of Francis Davis Blackburn and receives a nil certificate?

   See *Oak Co-Operative Building Society v Blackburn* [1967] Ch 1169; revsd [1968] Ch 730; LCA 1972, s. 10(4); *Du Sautoy v Symes* [1967] Ch 1146; (1968) 84 LQR 303 (P.V.B.); *Diligent Finance Co Ltd v Alleyne* (1972) 23 P & CR 346; Ruoff, *Searching Without Tears* (1974), chaps 9, 10, 11. As to errors in searches in respect of registered titles under LRA 2002, see s. 103, Sch. 8, para. 1(1)(c), p. 158, below.

   Of what significance would be the fact that the erroneous entry or certificate was due to the negligence of a clerk in the Land Registry? See *Ministry of Housing and Local Government v Sharp* [1970] 2 QB 223; *Coats Patons (Retail) Ltd v Birmingham Corpn* (1971) 69 LGR 356; LCA 1972, s. 10.

3. In unregistered land, is a decision that an equitable right or interest is registrable likely to improve or reduce its prospects of being enforceable against third parties? See *ER Ives Investment Ltd v High* [1967] 2 QB 379, p. 1074, below; *Shiloh Spinners Ltd v Harding* [1973] AC 691, p. 68, above.

4. Consider how the registration of a non-existent land charge can prejudicially affect a land owner. Should the Land Registrar be required to find a prima facie case for registration before adding a charge to the register? See Megarry J in *Thomas v Rose* [1968] 1 WLR 1797 at 1805, and *Rawlplug Co Ltd v Kamvale Properties Ltd* (1969) 20 P & CR 32 at 39; (1968) 118 NLJ 1167; and Brightman J in *Jones v Morgan* (1973) 231 EG 1167.

   Consider this in the context of the Family Law Act 1996 (formerly Matrimonial Homes Act 1983); see Megarry J in *Miles v Bull* [1969] 1 QB 258 at 261; *Wroth v Tyler* [1974] Ch 30, p. 602, below.

---

[366] Under Commons Registration Act 1965 'common land' also included waste land of a manor not subject to rights of common: s. 22(1). See Commons Act 2006, s. 22, Sch. 2, para. 4, for registration of waste land of a manor which was not registered under the 1965 Act.

5. Could/should the Land Charges Act 1925 have established a better system of registration than that of registration against the name of the estate owner? Report of the Committee on Land Charges (the Roxburgh Committee) 1956 (Cmd 9825); Report on Land Charges Affecting Unregistered Land 1969 (Law Com No. 18); LPA 1969, s. 25, p. 79, above.

6. Consider

   (i)   the moral and other difficulties which are raised by allowing a purchaser with notice to ignore an equitable interest of which he is aware;

   (ii) the legal difficulties of allowing the Register to be overridden by the doctrine of constructive notice;

   (iii) the absurdity of putting a purchaser with his eyes shut in a better position than one with his eyes open.

7. Read *Lloyds Bank plc v Carrick* [1996] 4 All ER 630, and the articles on p. 86, n. 299, above and

   (a) Analyse the interrelationship between estate contracts, constructive trusts, the Land Charges Act 1972, and proprietary estoppel.

   (b) Consider whether, and if so, why, Mrs Carrick might have won if

       (i) the case had been one of registered land (LRA 2002, Sch. 3, para. 2, p. 85, above; p. 196);

       (ii) Mrs Carrick's agreement had been a contractual nullity under the Law of Property (Miscellaneous Provisions) Act 1989, s. 2, p. 18, above.

   (c) Do you sympathise with Mrs Carrick or with Lloyds Bank plc?

VI. LAND LAW AND HUMAN RIGHTS[367]

In recent years the Human Rights Act 1998 has been invoked in a significant number of cases involving real property rights. The United Kingdom has been bound by the European Convention on Human Rights since 1953, but before the enactment of the Human Rights Act the only recourse was against the State, in an action brought before the European Court of Human Rights at Strasbourg.[368] Under the Act, however,

---

[367] M & W, paras 1.021–1.032; Gray, paras 1.6.1–1.6.30; Rook, *Property Law & Human Rights*; Allen, *Property and The Human Rights Act 1998*.

[368] Such recourse is still possible, and a litigant who cannot obtain an appropriate remedy in the domestic courts may seek to obtain an order from the European Court of Human Rights for compensation from the UK Government for its failure to protect his human rights in accordance with the Convention. See, e.g., the litigation in *J A Pye (Oxford) Ltd v United Kingdom* [2005] 3 EGLR 1 (combined operation of Limitation Act 1980 and LRA 1925 incompatible with Article 1 of the First Protocol), reversed by the Grand Chamber, (2008) 46 EHRR 45; p. 290, below. See *Ofulue v Bossert* [2009] Ch 1 at [32] on the duty of English courts to follow Strasbourg jurisprudence.

the domestic courts now have a limited jurisdiction[369] in relation to alleged breaches of the Convention. In the context of land law, the courts have interpreted the succession provisions of the Rent Act 1977 so as to apply to same-sex partners, in order to eliminate their discriminatory effect and so to comply with the Convention;[370] and have interpreted the provisions of the Land Registration Act 1925[371] on adverse possession in order to comply with Article 1 of the First Protocol to the Convention on deprivation of possessions.[372] They have also considered a number of cases in which public authorities have been alleged to have infringed Convention rights—for example in the exercise by public authority landlords of their right to possession of premises against residential occupiers.[373]

HUMAN RIGHTS ACT 1998

1 The Convention Rights

(1) In this Act 'the Convention rights' means the rights and fundamental freedoms set out in—

(a) Articles 2 to 12 and 14 of the Convention,

(b) Articles 1 to 3 of the First Protocol, and

(c) Articles 1 and 2 of the Sixth Protocol,

as read with Articles 16 to 18 of the Convention.

3 Interpretation of legislation

(1) So far as it is possible to do so, primary legislation and subordinate legislation must be read and given effect in a way which is compatible with the Convention rights.

6 Acts of public authorities

(1) It is unlawful for a public authority to act in a way which is incompatible with a Convention right.

(2) Subsection (1) does not apply to an act if—

(a) as the result of one or more provisions of primary legislation, the authority could not have acted differently; or

---

[369] E.g. they can only declare legislation incompatible with the Convention (Human Rights Act 1998, s. 4) and cannot disapply the legislation, nor require the legislature to enact amending legislation to comply with the Convention. But they must interpret legislation in a way which is compliant with the Convention 'so far as it is possible to do so': s. 3, below.

[370] *Ghaidan v Godin-Mendoza* [2004] 2 AC 557, p. 109, below (HRA 1998, s. 3; art. 14 of the Convention, read with art. 8).

[371] S. 75; below, p. 289. LRA 2002 has a different regime for adverse possession which complies with the Convention: below, p. 297.

[372] *Beaulane Properties Ltd v Palmer* [2006] Ch 79, p. 289, below; [2005] Conv 345 (M. Dixon); but see *J A Pye (Oxford) Ltd v United Kingdom* (2008) 46 EHRR 45, p. 290, below.

[373] *Harrow LBC v Qazi* [2004] 1 AC 983; [2004] Conv 406 (J. Howell); (2004) 120 LQR 398 (S. Bright); [2004] PL 594 (I. Loveland); *Kay v Lambeth LBC* [2006] 2 AC 465, p. 113, below (HRA 1998, s. 6 and art. 1 of the First Protocol); *Smith v Evans* [2008] 1 WLR 661 (Caravan Sites Act 1968, s. 4, as amended, and art. 8). See also *McCann v United Kingdom* [2008] 2 EGLR 45, p. 334, n. 32, below (European Court of Human Rights; art. 8).

    (b) in the case of one or more provisions of, or made under, primary legislation which cannot be read or given effect in a way which is compatible with the Convention rights, the authority was acting so as to give effect to or enforce those provisions.

(3) In this section 'public authority' includes—

    (a) a court or tribunal, and

    (b) any person certain of whose functions are functions of a public nature,

but does not include either House of Parliament or a person exercising functions in connection with proceedings in Parliament.

(5) In relation to a particular act, a person is not a public authority by virtue only of subsection (3)(b) if the nature of the act is private.

(6) 'An act' includes a failure to act but does not include a failure to—

    (a) introduce in, or lay before, Parliament a proposal for legislation; or

    (b) make any primary legislation or remedial order.

21 Interpretation, etc.

(1) In this Act—

'the Convention' means the Convention for the Protection of Human Rights and Fundamental Freedoms, agreed by the Council of Europe at Rome on 4th November 1950 as it has effect for the time being in relation to the United Kingdom;

'the First Protocol' means the protocol to the Convention agreed at Paris on 20th March 1952.

SCHEDULE 1

THE ARTICLES

PART I THE CONVENTION

ARTICLE 8 RIGHT TO RESPECT FOR PRIVATE AND FAMILY LIFE

1. Everyone has the right to respect for his private and family life, his home and his correspondence.

2. There shall be no interference by a public authority with the exercise of this right except such as is in accordance with the law and is necessary in a democratic society in the interests of national security, public safety or the economic well-being of the country, for the prevention of disorder or crime, for the protection of health or morals, or for the protection of the rights and freedoms of others.

ARTICLE 14 PROHIBITION OF DISCRIMINATION

The enjoyment of the rights and freedoms set forth in this Convention shall be secured without discrimination on any ground such as sex, race, colour, language, religion, political or other opinion, national or social origin, association with a national minority, property, birth or other status.

PART II THE FIRST PROTOCOL

ARTICLE 1 PROTECTION OF PROPERTY

Every natural or legal person is entitled to the peaceful enjoyment of his possessions. No one shall be deprived of his possessions except in the public interest and subject to the conditions provided for by law and by the general principles of international law. The preceding provisions shall not, however, in any way impair the right of a State to enforce such laws as it deems necessary to control the use of property in accordance with the general interest or to secure the payment of taxes or other contributions or penalties.

In **Ghaidan v Godin-Mendoza** [2004] 2 AC 557[374] LORD NICHOLLS OF BIRKENHEAD said at 564:

1 My Lords, on the death of a protected tenant of a dwelling-house his or her surviving spouse, if then living in the house, becomes a statutory tenant by succession. But marriage is not essential for this purpose. A person who was living with the original tenant 'as his or her wife or husband' is treated as the spouse of the original tenant: see paragraph 2(2) of Schedule 1 to the Rent Act 1977. In *Fitzpatrick v Sterling Housing Association Ltd* [2001] 1 AC 27 your Lordships' House decided this provision did not include persons in a same-sex relationship. The question raised by this appeal is whether this reading of paragraph 2 can survive the coming into force of the Human Rights Act 1998. In *Fitzpatrick's* case the original tenant had died in 1994.

2 In the present case the original tenant died after the Human Rights Act 1998 came into force on 2 October 2000. In April 1983 Mr Hugh Wallwyn-James was granted an oral residential tenancy of the basement flat at 17 Cresswell Gardens, London SW5. Until his death on 5 January 2001 he lived there in a stable and monogamous homosexual relationship with the defendant Mr Juan Godin-Mendoza. Mr Godin-Mendoza is still living there. After the death of Mr Wallwyn-James the landlord, Mr Ahmad Ghaidan, brought proceedings in the West London County Court claiming possession of the flat. Judge Cowell held that on the death of Hugh Wallwyn-James Mr Godin-Mendoza did not succeed to the tenancy of the flat as the surviving spouse of Hugh Wallwyn-James within the meaning of paragraph 2 of Schedule 1 to the Rent Act 1977, but that he did become entitled to an assured tenancy of the flat by succession as a member of the original tenant's 'family' under paragraph 3(1) of that Schedule.

3 Mr Godin-Mendoza appealed, and the Court of Appeal, comprising Kennedy, Buxton and Keene LJJ, allowed the appeal: [2003] Ch 380. The court held he was entitled to succeed to a tenancy of the flat as a statutory tenant under paragraph 2. From that decision Mr Ghaidan, the landlord, appealed to your Lordships' House.

4 I must first set out the relevant statutory provisions and then explain how the Human Rights Act 1998 comes to be relevant in this case. Paragraphs 2 and 3 of Schedule 1 to the 1977 Act provide:[375]

'2(1) The surviving spouse (if any) of the original tenant, if residing in the dwelling-house immediately before the death of the original tenant, shall after the death be the statutory tenant if and so long as he or she occupies the dwelling-house as his or her residence.

(2) For the purposes of this paragraph, a person who was living with the original tenant as his or her wife or husband shall be treated as the spouse of the original tenant...

---

[374] [2005] PL 23 (A. Young). See also C & B, pp. 356–357, 361–362.

[375] Para. 2 was later amended by Civil Partnership Act 2004, Sch. 8, para. 13, to include surviving civil partners and persons living as if they were civil partners, therefore removing for the future the need to interpret the original provisions as in *Ghaidan v Godin-Mendoza*. However, the general approach of HL in this case remains instructive. Lord Millett dissented on the question of whether it was proper to construe the Rent Act provision by 'adopting an interpretation of the existing legislation which it not only does not bear but which is manifestly inconsistent with it': at [101]. He drew attention (at [96]]) to the fact that Parliament was already considering corrective legislation in the Civil Partnership Bill.

3(1) Where paragraph 2 above does not apply, but a person who was a member of the original tenant's family was residing with him in the dwelling-house at the time of and for the period of two years immediately before his death then, after his death, that person or if there is more than one such person such one of them as may be decided by agreement, or in default of agreement by the county court, shall be entitled to an assured tenancy of the dwelling-house by succession.'

5 On an ordinary reading of this language paragraph 2(2) draws a distinction between the position of a heterosexual couple living together in a house as husband and wife and a homosexual couple living together in a house. The survivor of a heterosexual couple may become a statutory tenant by succession, the survivor of a homosexual couple cannot. That was decided in *Fitzpatrick's* case. The survivor of a homosexual couple may, in competition with other members of the original tenant's 'family', become entitled to an assured tenancy under paragraph 3. But even if he does, as in the present case, this is less advantageous. Notably, so far as the present case is concerned, the rent payable under an assured tenancy is the contractual or market rent, which may be more than the fair rent payable under a statutory tenancy, and an assured tenant may be evicted for non-payment of rent without the court needing to be satisfied, as is essential in the case of a statutory tenancy, that it is reasonable to make a possession order. In these and some other respects the succession rights granted by the statute to the survivor of a homosexual couple in respect of the house where he or she is living are less favourable than the succession rights granted to the survivor of a heterosexual couple.

6 Mr Godin-Mendoza's claim is that this difference in treatment infringes article 14 of the European Convention on Human Rights read in conjunction with article 8. Article 8 does not require the state to provide security of tenure for members of a deceased tenant's family. Article 8 does not in terms give a right to be provided with a home: *Chapman v United Kingdom* (2001) 33 EHRR 399, 427, para 99. It does not 'guarantee the right to have one's housing problem solved by the authorities': *Marzari v Italy* (1999) 28 EHRR CD 175, 179. But if the state makes legislative provision it must not be discriminatory. The provision must not draw a distinction on grounds such as sex or sexual orientation without good reason. Unless justified, a distinction founded on such grounds infringes the Convention right embodied in article 14, as read with article 8. Mr Godin-Mendoza submits that the distinction drawn by paragraph 2 of Schedule 1 to the Rent Act 1977 is drawn on the grounds of sexual orientation and that this difference in treatment lacks justification.

7 That is the first step in Mr Godin-Mendoza's claim. That step would not, of itself, improve Mr Godin-Mendoza's status in his flat. The second step in his claim is to pray in aid the court's duty under section 3 of the Human Rights Act 1998 to read and give effect to legislation in a way which is compliant with the Convention rights. Here, it is said, section 3 requires the court to read paragraph 2 so that it embraces couples living together in a close and stable homosexual relationship as much as couples living together in a close and stable heterosexual relationship. So read, paragraph 2 covers Mr Godin-Mendoza's position. Hence he is entitled to a declaration that on the death of Mr Wallwyn-James he succeeded to a statutory tenancy.

20 In the present case the only suggested ground for according different treatment to the survivor of same sex couples and opposite sex couples cannot withstand scrutiny. Rather, the present state of the law as set out in paragraph 2 of Schedule 1 of the Rent Act 1977 may properly be described as continuing adherence to the traditional regard for the position of surviving spouses, adapted in 1988 to take account of the widespread contemporary trend for men and women to cohabit outside marriage but not adapted to recognise the comparable position of cohabiting same sex couples. I appreciate that the primary object of introducing the regime

of assured tenancies and assured shorthold tenancies in 1988 was to increase the number of properties available for renting in the private sector. But this policy objective of the Housing Act 1988 can afford no justification for amending paragraph 2 so as to include cohabiting heterosexual partners but not cohabiting homosexual partners. This policy objective of the Act provides no reason for, on the one hand, extending to unmarried cohabiting heterosexual partners the right to succeed to a statutory tenancy but, on the other hand, withholding that right from cohabiting homosexual partners. Paragraph 2 fails to attach sufficient importance to the Convention rights of cohabiting homosexual couples.

24 In my view, therefore, Mr Godin-Mendoza makes good the first step in his argument: paragraph 2 of Schedule 1 to the Rent Act 1977, construed without reference to section 3 of the Human Rights Act, violates his Convention right under article 14 taken together with article 8.

25 I turn next to the question whether section 3 of the Human Rights Act 1998 requires the court to depart from the interpretation of paragraph 2 enunciated in *Fitzpatrick's* case.

26 Section 3 is a key section in the Human Rights Act 1998. It is one of the primary means by which Convention rights are brought into the law of this country. Parliament has decreed that all legislation, existing and future, shall be interpreted in a particular way. All legislation must be read and given effect to in a way which is compatible with the Convention rights 'so far as it is possible to do so'. This is the intention of Parliament, expressed in section 3, and the courts must give effect to this intention.

27 Unfortunately, in making this provision for the interpretation of legislation, section 3 itself is not free from ambiguity. Section 3 is open to more than one interpretation. The difficulty lies in the word 'possible'. Section 3(1), read in conjunction with section 3(2) and section 4, makes one matter clear: Parliament expressly envisaged that not all legislation would be capable of being made Convention-compliant by application of section 3. Sometimes it would be possible, sometimes not. What is not clear is the test to be applied in separating the sheep from the goats. What is the standard, or the criterion, by which 'possibility' is to be judged? A comprehensive answer to this question is proving elusive. The courts, including your Lordships' House, are still cautiously feeling their way forward as experience in the application of section 3 gradually accumulates.

28 One tenable interpretation of the word 'possible' would be that section 3 is confined to requiring courts to resolve ambiguities. Where the words under consideration fairly admit of more than one meaning the Convention-compliant meaning is to prevail. Words should be given the meaning which best accords with the Convention rights.

29 This interpretation of section 3 would give the section a comparatively narrow scope. This is not the view which has prevailed. It is now generally accepted that the application of section 3 does not depend upon the presence of ambiguity in the legislation being interpreted. Even if, construed according to the ordinary principles of interpretation, the meaning of the legislation admits of no doubt, section 3 may none the less require the legislation to be given a different meaning. The decision of your Lordships' House in *R v A (No 2)* [2002] 1 AC 45 is an instance of this. The House read words into section 41 of the Youth Justice and Criminal Evidence Act 1999 so as to make that section compliant with an accused's right to a fair trial under article 6. The House did so even though the statutory language was not ambiguous.

30 From this it follows that the interpretative obligation decreed by section 3 is of an unusual and far-reaching character. Section 3 may require a court to depart from the unambiguous meaning the legislation would otherwise bear. In the ordinary course the interpretation of legislation involves seeking the intention reasonably to be attributed to Parliament in using the

language in question. Section 3 may require the court to depart from this legislative intention, that is, depart from the intention of the Parliament which enacted the legislation. The question of difficulty is how far, and in what circumstances, section 3 requires a court to depart from the intention of the enacting Parliament. The answer to this question depends upon the intention reasonably to be attributed to Parliament in enacting section 3.

31 On this the first point to be considered is how far, when enacting section 3, Parliament intended that the actual language of a statute, as distinct from the concept expressed in that language, should be determinative. Since section 3 relates to the 'interpretation' of legislation, it is natural to focus attention initially on the language used in the legislative provision being considered. But once it is accepted that section 3 may require legislation to bear a meaning which departs from the unambiguous meaning the legislation would otherwise bear, it becomes impossible to suppose Parliament intended that the operation of section 3 should depend critically upon the particular form of words adopted by the parliamentary draftsman in the statutory provision under consideration. That would make the application of section 3 something of a semantic lottery. If the draftsman chose to express the concept being enacted in one form of words, section 3 would be available to achieve Convention-compliance. If he chose a different form of words, section 3 would be impotent.

32 From this the conclusion which seems inescapable is that the mere fact the language under consideration is inconsistent with a Convention-compliant meaning does not of itself make a Convention-compliant interpretation under section 3 impossible. Section 3 enables language to be interpreted restrictively or expansively. But section 3 goes further than this. It is also apt to require a court to read in words which change the meaning of the enacted legislation, so as to make it Convention-compliant. In other words, the intention of Parliament in enacting section 3 was that, to an extent bounded only by what is 'possible', a court can modify the meaning, and hence the effect, of primary and secondary legislation.

33 Parliament, however, cannot have intended that in the discharge of this extended interpretative function the courts should adopt a meaning inconsistent with a fundamental feature of legislation. That would be to cross the constitutional boundary section 3 seeks to demarcate and preserve. Parliament has retained the right to enact legislation in terms which are not Convention-compliant. The meaning imported by application of section 3 must be compatible with the underlying thrust of the legislation being construed. Words implied must, in the phrase of my noble and learned friend, Lord Rodger of Earlsferry, 'go with the grain of the legislation'. Nor can Parliament have intended that section 3 should require courts to make decisions for which they are not equipped. There may be several ways of making a provision Convention-compliant, and the choice may involve issues calling for legislative deliberation.

35 In some cases difficult problems may arise. No difficulty arises in the present case. Paragraph 2 of Schedule 1 to the Rent Act 1977 is unambiguous. But the social policy underlying the 1988 extension of security of tenure under paragraph 2 to the survivor of couples living together as husband and wife is equally applicable to the survivor of homosexual couples living together in a close and stable relationship. In this circumstance I see no reason to doubt that application of section 3 to paragraph 2 has the effect that paragraph 2 should be read and given effect to as though the survivor of such a homosexual couple were the surviving spouse of the original tenant. Reading paragraph 2 in this way would have the result that cohabiting heterosexual couples and cohabiting homosexual couples would be treated alike for the purposes of succession as a statutory tenant. This would eliminate the discriminatory effect of paragraph 2 and would do so consistently with the social policy underlying paragraph 2. The

precise form of words read in for this purpose is of no significance. It is their substantive effect which matters.

In **Kay v Lambeth LBC** [2006] 2 AC 465[376] the House of Lords held that a possession order made by a court in respect of the defendant's home will be an interference with the right to respect for his home, and therefore article 8 of the Convention will normally be engaged where a local authority landlord seeks possession. However, their Lordships disagreed over the circumstances in which a defendant can challenge the claim to possession on the basis of the Convention. The majority held that the challenge is not based on the defendant's individual personal circumstances, or the particular facts of the case, but only as to the compatibility with the Convention of the domestic rules under with possession is sought. LORD HOPE OF CRAIGHEAD said at 516:

109 The contrary conclusion, for which the appellants contend, is that procedures must exist in the domestic system for a consideration of the interests safeguarded by article 8 in every case where a person is evicted from his home by the making of a possession order. A requirement that the article 8 issue must be considered by the court in every case by taking into account the defendant's personal circumstances would...drive a deep wedge into the domestic system for the handling of possession cases and would be a colossal waste of time and money.... [J]udges in the county courts, when faced with such a defence, should proceed on the assumption that domestic law strikes a fair balance and is compatible with the occupier's Convention rights.

J. Howell, 'The Human Rights Act: Land, Private Citizens and the Common Law' (2007) LQR 618 at pp. 632–635

On one view, the HRA is to be welcomed: land law has never operated in a vacuum. Legislation and judgments are already driven by social, economic and to an extent, moral, considerations, whose weight and content change over time. Land law is already going through a period of unprecedented but largely unremarked change.[377] The HRA is simply one more factor to be absorbed and given its own value....

But the seductive effects of the HRA should be resisted. Land law must, it is suggested, keep to the narrow and stony path. Land law is essentially pragmatic and practical and, most importantly, has consequences for third parties: certainty is almost always justice. Already the uncertainty over the circumstances in which the courts will find that a beneficial interest has arisen under a constructive trust or through estoppel is making life difficult for practitioners.[378] The introduction of human rights values is a wild card which is wholly unpredictable in effect. Parties will not enter into agreements over land if they cannot be sure of their effect, and practitioners will not be able to advise them. The Convention is a 'living instrument', but

---

[376] [2006] Conv 294 (S. Bright), 526 (D. Hughes and M. Davis). See also C & B, pp. 333–335.

[377] The proposals for electronic conveyancing will arguably undermine traditional principles; Howell 'Land Law in an E-Conveyancing World' (2006) 70 Conv 553.

[378] There is still considerable uncertainty for example over the effect of *Midland Bank Plc v Cooke* [1995] 4 All ER 563 and *Oxley v Hiscock* [2004] EWCA Civ 546, [2005] Fam 211, still left unresolved after *Stack v Dowden* [2007] UKHL 17, [2007] 2 WLR 831 [p. 580, below].

it will be unfortunate indeed if this principle were to be applied to agreements relating to land.[379]

So far, little damage has been done.[380] In *Ghaidan v Godin-Mendoza*[381] and *Beaulane Properties Ltd v Palmer*[382] no third parties were involved. It may be that the courts when faced directly with, for example, a claim that the overreaching provisions of the Law of Property Act 1925 or the provisions for registration under the Land Registration Act 2002 may lead to a breach of Arts 1 and 8—all the necessary elements are there—will take the view that the provisions are 'in the public interest' or 'necessary in a democratic society', that in fact they strike the necessary balance.[383] But it may be that every settled principle of land law is at least to be open to scrutiny under the HRA. There are here issues which go beyond land law but are not being addressed by the higher courts. It is hoped that the House of Lords will take the first opportunity to give a strong guide one way or the other.[384] The present uncertainty is the worst possible position for anyone who has any dealings with land.

---

[379] Kay, 'The European Convention on Human Rights and the Control of Private Law', EHRLR 2005, 5, 466–479, p. 471, discussing *Pla and Puncernau v Andora* [2004] FCR 630 (ECHR) (where the exclusion of an adopted son from rights under a will was held to breach both Art. 8 and Art. 14) says, surely correctly, that the application of Convention rights to the private law would 'wreak havoc in commercial transactions if contracts were to be treated as "living instruments"'.

[380] Hughes and Davis in 'Human Rights and the Triumph of Property: the Marginalisation of the European Convention on Human Rights in Housing Law' (2006) 70 Conv. 527 suggest that the HRA is having little impact in housing matters.

[381] [2004] 2 AC 557 [p. 109, above].   [382] [2006] Ch 79 [p. 289, below].

[383] The courts will need to explain how overreaching and the overriding provisions of the Land Registration Act 2002 can be reconciled.

[384] It is unfortunate that the House of Lords did not take the opportunity in *YL v Birmingham CC* [2007] 3 WLR 112 to clarify these points. It is true that this was not necessary for the decision, and in *Oxfordshire County Council v Oxford City Council* [2006] AC 674, the House of Lords objected to being set an 'examination paper' in the law of village greens—but did answer it.

2

REGISTERED LAND[1]

---

[1] C & B, pp. 100–113, 952–987; Gray, paras 2.2.16–2.2.72, part 8.2; M & W, chap. 7; MM, pp. 111–145; Smith, chap. 13. For the current regime in relation to registered land under LRA 2002, see Ruoff and Roper, *Registered Conveyancing* (2003 looseleaf edn); Harpum and Bignell, *Registered Land: The New Law* (2002) and *Registered Land: Law and Practice under the Land Registration Act 2002* (2004); Wolstenholme and Cherry's *Annotated Land Registration Act 2002* (ed. I. Clarke and J. Farrand, 2004) which contains LRA 1925 and 2002, and LRR 1925 and 2003; Wontner's *Guide to Land Registry Practice*; Abbey and Richards, *Blackstone's Guide to the Land Registration Act 2002*; Cooke, *The New Law of Land Registration*; Current Law Statutes 2002 (ch. 9) annotated by P.H. Kenny; [2002] Conv 11 (E. Cooke); [2003] Conv 136 (M. Dixon); Law Commission Consultative Document on Land Registration for the Twenty-First Century 1998 (Law Com No. 254); Law Commission Report on Land Registration for the Twenty-First Century—a Conveyancing Revolution 2001 (Law Com No. 271).

For the law as it used to be under LRA 1925 and before LRA 2002, see Ruoff and Roper, *Law and Practice of Registered Conveyancing* (1991 looseleaf edn, updated to 2002 before its replacement by the new 2003 looseleaf edn); Ruoff and Pryer, *Concise Land Registration Handbook*; Wolstenholme and Cherry, *Conveyancing Statutes* (13th edn), vol. 6; Barnsley, chaps 2, 3, 4, 11, 15; Potter, *Principles and Practice of Conveyancing under the Land Registration 1925* (1934; 2nd edn, 1948); Brickdale and Stewart-Wallace, *The Land Registration Act 1925*.

For registration of a freehold estate in land as commonhold under CLRA 2002, see pp. 309–322, below.

I. INTRODUCTION

We have seen[2] that the basic doctrines of land law developed at common law under a system in which title to land was proved by the production of deeds recording the history of transactions affecting the land; this system is rapidly being overtaken by one which is based upon the registration of title to land. Under the latter system, all transfers of the legal title are required to be by registration in an individual register of the transferee's property, name and any charges on that property. The old cumbrous method of conveyancing by title deeds is dispensed with; and a registered title is thenceforth guaranteed by the State.

A system of registration of title was introduced into England as far back as 1862, but only on an optional basis. A revised system of registration of title was set out in the Land Registration Act 1925[3] and the Land Registration Rules 1925—which must be kept wholly distinct from systems of registration of charges (such as that under the Land Charges Acts 1925 and 1972 which is applicable to *unregistered land*[4]). Since 1990 registration of title has been compulsory over the whole of England and Wales;[5] compulsory in the sense that dealings in land must now be carried out under the new and not the old system of conveyancing.[6] Therefore, as unregistered land changes hands, or is subject to other dealings which trigger compulsory registration, the whole of England and Wales will be brought onto the register. By 2007 the register comprised

---

[2] Above, pp. 56–58.
[3] For a history of land registration before 1926, see (1972) 36 Conv (NS) 390 (H. W. Wilkinson); Rowton Simpson, *Land Law and Registration*, pp. 39–47. For land registration systems in European countries, see Cooke, *The New Law of Land Registration*, chap. 9.
[4] Above, pp. 64–84.
[5] Land registration is being extended to Scotland by area: Land Registration (Scotland) Act 1979. The Scottish system of land law is, however, fundamentally different from that in England and Wales.
[6] Registration of Title Order 1989.

59 per cent of area of England and Wales, and the Land Registry[7] now sets annual targets for increasing the total area of freehold land which is on the register.[8]

The Land Registration Act 1925 and the Land Registration Rules 1925 were repealed and replaced by the Land Registration Act 2002 and the Land Registration Rules 2003, implementing the Law Commission Report on Land Registration for the Twenty-First Century.[9] The new Act and Rules came into force on 13 October 2003. There are substantial transitional provisions which make the former Act and Rules relevant.[10]

In many respects the principles of the 1925 scheme are maintained, although the object of the new Act and Rules is to provide a legislative framework which will enable conveyancing to be carried out electronically. Conveyancing will thus take advantage of information technology and develop alongside similar transactions such as

[7] The Land Registry is charged with the business of registration of title to land: LRA 2002, s. 99(1). Its headquarters is in Lincoln's Inn Fields, London, and it has 21 offices around England and Wales which deal with land registry applications relating to land situated in their respective administrative areas: Land Registration (Proper Office) Order 2008 (SI 2008 No. 3201). The Office of the Land Registry was first created by the Land Transfer Act 1875, s. 106. The Land Registry produces Practice Guides on many aspects of its practice and procedure, and the Chief Land Registrar publishes an Annual Report. Current and recent versions can be seen on the Land Registry website: www.landregistry.gov.uk.

[8] Land Registry Annual Report 2006–07, pp. 8, 95. The target for 2006–07 (which was exceeded) was 700 hectares and the target for 2007–08 was 550 hectares. The 59% of the area of England and Wales comprises just over 21 million titles; the Land Registry estimates the complete register will comprise around 23 million titles: 2006–07 Report, pp. 16, 99. Land can also be registered voluntarily, even when there is no trigger for compulsory registration, and a lower fee is now charged for voluntary registration to encourage this. Until the 2005–06 Annual Report the Land Registry stated a strategic objective of completing the register by 2012.

[9] Law Com No. 271, 2001. See also the earlier Law Commission Consultative Document: Land Registration for the Twenty-First Century (Law Com No. 254, 1998). For earlier proposals of the Law Commission on registered conveyancing, see the first report 1983 (Law Com No. 125) on Identity and Boundaries, Conversion of Title, the Treatment of Leases and the Minor Interests Index; second report 1985 on Inspection of the Register (Law Com No. 148); third report 1987 on Overriding Interests, Rectification and Indemnity and Minor Interests (Law Com No. 158); [1987] Conv 334 (R. J. Smith). The recommendations on the last three topics of the 1983 Report were implemented in LRA 1986, and the 1985 Report was implemented in LRA 1988. Its fourth report was in 1988 which presented a Land Registration Bill incorporating the recommendations of the third report and 'is a modern, and we hope, simpler version of the 1925 Act'. In advance of this, the Law Commission published in 1995 a First Report on the Implementation of its Third and Fourth Reports (Law Com No. 235); and this was implemented in LRA 1997.

[10] For transitional provisions, see LRA 2002, s. 134, Sch. 12, paras 1–3 (existing entries in the register); 4 (existing cautions against first registration); 5–6 (pending applications); 7–13 (former overriding interests); 14–16 (cautions against first registration); 17 (applications under ss. 34 or 43 by cautioners); 18 (adverse possession), p. 279, n. 129, below; 19 (indemnities); 20 (implied indemnity covenants on transfers of pre-1996 leases); LRR 2003 rr. 218–223 (cautions against dealings); 224 (rentcharges and adverse possession); LRA 2002 (Transitional Provisions) Order, arts 2–5 (general and administrative); 6–9 (disputes, objections, appeals and proceedings); 6–13 (souvenir land), 14–18 (cautions); 19 (outline applications); 20 (matrimonial home rights cautions); 21 (index of relating franchises and manors); 22–23 (compulsory first registration); 24 (land and charge certificates); 25 (obligation to make further advances); 26–27 (Forms); 28–29 (official searches and official copies); LRA 2002 (Transitional Provisions) (No. 2) Order 2003 (No. 2) (right to repair of church chancel), p. 197, n. 262, below.

For amendments to LRR, see LR (Amendment) Rules 2005 (SI 2005 No. 1766); 2005 (No. 2) (SI 2005 No. 1982); 2008 (SI 2008 No. 1919).

banking and business. To this end the register of a parcel of land must be as complete a mirror of title as possible.

The Law Commission said in its Report on Land Registration for the Twenty-First Century[11] that:

The fundamental objective of the [Act] is that, under the system of electronic dealing with land that it seeks to create, the register should be a complete and accurate reflection of the state of the title of the land at any given time, so that it is possible to investigate title to land on line, with the absolute minimum of additional enquiries and inspections.

A. CONTEMPORARY RELEVANCE OF THE LAND REGISTRATION ACT 1925

Until there is a new body of case law under the new Act and Rules, it will be necessary to look back at some of the cases decided in relation to the former provisions on points which are unchanged in substance. The scheme of registered land which is presented in this chapter is the scheme of the 2002 Act.[12] But there will be some reference to the provisions of the 1925 Act, and to cases decided under the former Act, in order to explain and illuminate the current law. Cases decided under the former Act must always be read with caution, checking the extent to which the legislative provisions in question have been changed by the new Act.

B. SIMILARITY OF 1925 AND 2002 ACTS

There are similarities of policy and structure between the two Acts. The 2002 Act is presented in a more coherent and logical form.[13] The main similarities between the two Acts are:

1. A disposition of registered land will not take effect at law unless the registration requirements are met.

2. There is a tripartite register for each title to a parcel of registered land.

3. There is voluntary and compulsory registration of title, with the latter being triggered by specified events.

4. The register of title is conclusive, but the effect of this is qualified by the court's powers of alteration and indemnity.

5. Indemnity is an integral part of the State guarantee of title.

---

[11] 2001 (Law Com No. 271), para. 1.5.

[12] For detail on LRA 1925 and LRR 1925, see the 7th edn of this book, chap. 2, and C & B 16th edn (2000), pp. 100–8, 855–76.

[13] LRA 1925 was the only part of the 1925 Legislation which was not drafted by Sir Benjamin Cherry.

6. The registrar is not to be affected with notice of a trust, and overreaching continues to apply to interests in registered land.

7. There is a distinction between interests which can be registered under their own separate title numbers, and those interests which should be protected against a registered estate.

8. There are overriding interests which bind even though they do not appear on the register.

C. MAIN CHANGES IN THE LAND REGISTRATION ACT 2002

Important changes have been made by the Land Registration Act 2002 and the Land Registration Rules 2003. These are:

1. An increase in the number of triggers for compulsory first registration, with the promise of more to come until the register is complete.

2. The length of leases subject to compulsory registration is reduced from 21 to 7 years—with the result that most business leases now become registrable.

3. Voluntary registration has a reduced fee in order to encourage owners of unregistered land to register.[14]

4. A decrease in the number and extent of overriding interests.

5. The Limitation Act 1980 is disapplied in relation to registered land, and is replaced by a new law of adverse possession. This is advantageous to a landowner, but disadvantageous to a squatter, so much so that a landowner may decide to register voluntarily.

6. Land held by Her Majesty the Queen as demesne land becomes registrable for the first time. This includes extensive parts of the foreshore in England and Wales.

7. The redrafting of classes of title, the methods of protection of minor interests (and the terminology, but not the concept, of 'minor interests' is abandoned), and the restructuring of rectification and indemnity.

8. A simplification of the principles of priority.

9. Mortgages can no longer be created by demise and sub-demise (they were already obsolescent).

10. The creation of a new system of independent adjudication arising out of disputed applications to the registrar.[15]

[14] LR Fee Order 2006, arts 2(6), 6(3), replacing LR Fee Order 2004. The normal fee is reduced by 25%, and adjusted to the nearest £10.

[15] LRA 2002, ss. 107–114; The Adjudicator to Her Majesty's Land Registry (Practice and Procedure) Rules 2003 (SI 2003 No. 2171); LR (Referral to Adjudicator to HM Land Registry) Rules 2003 (SI 2003 No. 2114);

11. No further land or charge certificates will be issued, and, if a certificate is lodged with the Land Registry, it will be destroyed.[16] In its place a Title Information Document will be issued which comprises a copy of the register and a copy of the title plan.

These changes are designed to pave the way for the introduction of a system of paper-less transfer of land by electronic conveyancing. This is a fundamental change and will not be fully implemented overnight.[17]

The new Act and Rules create a coherent framework in which the land law of England and Wales can continue to develop.

D. REQUIREMENT OF REGISTRATION
FOR EFFECT AT LAW

A fundamental principle is that certain dispositions of registered land shall not have effect at law unless registered in accordance with the Act.[18]

LAND REGISTRATION ACT 2002

27 Disposition required to be registered

(1) If a disposition of a registered estate or registered charge is required to be completed by registration, it does not operate at law until the relevant registration requirements are met.

E. CONCLUSIVENESS OF REGISTER

Registration is conclusive of title to the legal estate and is said to confer a new root of title on the proprietor. There are limited powers of rectification of the register, subject to payment of an indemnity from public funds to any person suffering loss thereby.[19]

Land Registration (Acting Adjudicator) Regs. 2003 (SI 2003 No. 2342); The Adjudicator to Her Majesty's Land Registry (Practice and Procedure) (Amendment) Rules 2008 (SI 2008 No. 1731); Land Registry Practice Guide No. 37 Objections and disputes—A guide to Land Registry practice and procedures (2007, replacing 2003 edn).

[16] LRA 2002 (Transitional Provisions) Order 2003, art. 24. For copies of the original land certificate and its successor, see the 7th edn of this book at pp. 105–108. The borders were decorated with the arms of six Lord Chancellors, Lords Birkenhead, Haldane, Halsbury, Cairns, Selborne and Westbury. See the tribute paid to these Lord Chancellors by Sir Leslie Scott when moving the second reading of the Law of Property Bill 1922; Scott, *The New Law of Property Acts Explained* (1925) 'It is not revolution, but evolution.'

[17] Below, pp. 226–233.

[18] For the list of dispositions which are required to be registered, and the registration requirements, see below, pp. 163–166. Pending registration, dispositions may be given effect in equity: below, p. 163.

[19] On alteration of the register (including rectification) and indemnity, see pp. 141–160, below.

LAND REGISTRATION ACT 2002

58 Conclusiveness

(1) If on the entry of a person in the register as the proprietor of a legal estate, the legal estate would not otherwise be vested in him, it shall be deemed to be vested in him as a result of the registration.

(2) Subsection (1) does not apply where the entry is made in pursuance of a registrable disposition in relation to which some other registration requirement remains to be met.

Law Commission Report on Land Registration for the Twenty-First Century 2001 (Law Com No. 271), paras 9.4, 9.6

9.4 One of the most fundamental principles of registered conveyancing is that it is registration that vests the legal estate in the registered proprietor. [Section 58 of the Act] provides accordingly that if, on the entry of a person in the register as the proprietor of a legal estate, the legal estate would not otherwise be vested in him or her, it shall be deemed to be vested in him or her as a result of registration. Thus, for example, if a person is registered as proprietor on the strength of a forged transfer, the legal estate will vest in that transferee even though the transfer was a nullity.

9.6 The following events will exemplify how the provision in [section 58(2)] will operate. X applies to be registered as the grantee of a 99-year lease. The lease is registered with its own title. However, the registrar fails to enter a notice of the lease on the superior freehold title. The legal estate is not vested in X by virtue of [section 58(1)].[20]

F. TRUSTS

LAND REGISTRATION ACT 2002

78 Notice of trust not to affect registrar

The registrar shall not be affected with notice of a trust.[21]

G. CRITIQUE OF LAND REGISTRATION ACT 2002

Law Commission Consultative Document on Land Registration for the Twenty-First Century 1998 (Law Com No. 254), para. 11.9.

As any system is likely to be introduced in stages, we regard it as essential that the eventual goal that we wish to achieve should be clear from the outset. Only in this way can developments be

---

[20] The grant will, however, be effective in equity.

[21] Cf. LRA 1925, s. 74. For the operation of constructive trusts *outside* the register, see pp. 222–226, below.

properly directed. That eventual goal is to eliminate so far as possible the present three-stage process by which a document is executed, lodged with the Registry and then registered. The only way to achieve this is to provide that the transaction should be executed electronically by registration. Thus any transfer would be completed by registering it, and any right that it was intended to create over registered land would not be created until it was registered. This is only possible with an electronic system.

Law Commission Report on Land Registration for the Twenty-First Century 2001 (Law Com No. 271), para. 1.10.

These changes will necessarily alter the perception of title to land. It will be the fact of registration and registration alone that confers title. This is entirely in accordance with the fundamental principle of a conclusive register which underpins the Bill.

C. Harpum in *Rationalizing Property, Equity and Trusts: Essays in Honour of Edward Burn* (ed. Getzler), p. 203

[LRA 2002] is a very different Act from its predecessor. First, it has the coherent objective of securing a conclusive register. Secondly, it creates a system under which, when electronic conveyancing is introduced, there will be title by registration rather than registration of title.[22] Thirdly, it sets out to create a system of substantive law that reflects the principles of registered conveyancing. The two Law Commission reports, that respectively preceded and accompanied the Land Registration Bill,[23] provide a substantial corpus of material to guide the courts in interpreting the new legislation and the mischief it is intended to remedy.[24] Furthermore, the draftsman of LRA 2002 went to considerable trouble to define the relationship between land registration and the general principles of real property law. It is much clearer under the new Act than it is under LRA 1925. However, no draftsman, however good, can foresee all possibilities, nor address all those situations that he can. The modern approach to statutory interpretation is purposive and, it is suggested, principles that might be applicable in unregistered conveyancing should not be applied to dealings with registered land if to do so would be inconsistent with the scheme found in the new Act. In the final report that accompanied the draft Land Registration Bill, the Law Commission commented that 'unregistered land has had its day'.[25] If LRA 2002 is to achieve its objective the registered system has to be recognised in its own right and can no longer be regarded as mere gloss on the unregistered system.

---

[22] LRA 2002, s. 93 [p. 228, below].

[23] Land Registration for the Twenty-First Century: A Consultative Document (Law Com No. 254) and Land Registration for the Twenty-First Century: A Conveyancing Revolution (Law Com No. 271).

[24] Although Lord Nicholls has warned that the use of external aids to the construction of legislation (including Law Commission Reports, which he expressly mentioned) need to be used with circumspection (*R v Secretary of State for the Environment, ex p. Spath Holme Ltd* [2001] 2 AC 349 at 398), the courts can and do frequently refer to them. As Clarke LJ explained in *Yaxley v Gotts* [2000] Ch 162 at 182, 'Where a statute has been enacted as a result of the recommendations of the Law Commission, it is, as I see it, both appropriate and permissible for the court to consider those recommendations in order to help to identify both the mischief which the Act is designed to cure and the public policy underlying it.'

[25] Land Registration for the Twenty-First Century: A Conveyancing Revolution (Law Com No. 271) para. 1.6.

II. SCOPE OF TITLE REGISTRATION

LAND REGISTRATION ACT 2002

2 Scope of title registration

This Act makes provision about the registration of title to—

(a) unregistered legal estates which are interests of any of the following kinds—

    (i)   an estate in land,

    (ii) a rentcharge,[26]

    (iii) a franchise,[27]

    (iv) a profit a prendre in gross,[28] and

    (v)   any other interest or charge which subsists for the benefit of, or is a charge on, an interest the title to which is registered, and

(b) interests capable of subsisting at law which are created by a disposition of an interest the title to which is registered.

III. THE REGISTER OF TITLE

LAND REGISTRATION ACT 2002

1 Register of title

(1) There is to continue to be a register of title kept by the registrar.[29]

(2) Rules may make provision about how the register is to be kept and may, in particular, make provision about—

(a) the information to be included in the register,

(b) the form in which information included in the register is to be kept, and

(c) the arrangement of that information.

LAND REGISTRATION RULES 2003

Form and arrangement of the register of title

2.—(1) The register of title may be kept in electronic or paper form, or partly in one form and partly in the other.

(2) Subject to rule 3, the register of title must include an individual register for each registered estate which is—

    (a) an estate in land, or

---

[26] On rentcharges in registered land, see R & R, chap. 29.

[27] A franchise is 'a royal privilege or branch of the royal prerogative subsisting in the hands of a subject, by grant from the King': *Spook Erection Ltd v Secretary of State for the Environment* [1989] QB 300 at 305, per Nourse LJ. The most important franchise is that of the market.

[28] Under this provision profits à prendre in gross (i.e. without a dominant tenement, p. 615, below) became registrable with their own titles. Manors are no longer registrable.

[29] R & R, chap. 4.

(b) a rentcharge, franchise, manor or profit a prendre in gross,

vested in a proprietor.

Arrangement of individual registers

4.—(1) Each individual register must have a distinguishing number, or series of letters and numbers, known as the title number.

(2) Each individual register must consist of a property register, a proprietorship register and, where necessary, a charges register.

(3) An entry in an individual register may be made by reference to a plan or other document; in which case the registrar must keep the original or a copy of the document.

(4) Whenever the registrar considers it desirable, he may make a new edition of any individual register so that it contains only the subsisting entries, rearrange the entries in the register or alter its title number.

Contents of the property register

5.[30] Except where otherwise permitted, the property register of a registered estate must contain—

(a) a description of the registered estate which in the case of a registered estate in land, rentcharge or registered franchise which is an affecting franchise must refer to a plan based on the Ordnance Survey map and known as the title plan;[31]

(b) where appropriate, details of—

(i)   the inclusion or exclusion of mines and minerals in or from the registration under rule 32,

(ii) easements, rights and privileges benefiting the registered estate and other similar matters,

(iii) all exceptions or reservations arising on enfranchisement of formerly copyhold land, and

(iv) any matter otherwise required to be entered in any other part of the register which the registrar considers may more conveniently be entered in the property register, and

(c) such other matters as are required to be entered in the property register by these rules.

Property register of a registered leasehold estate

6.—(1) The property register of a registered leasehold estate must also contain sufficient particulars of the registered lease to enable that lease to be identified.

---

[30] Amended by LR (Amendment) Rules 2008 (SI 2008 No. 1919), Sch. 1, para. 1.

[31] LRA 2002, s. 60; the boundary as shown for the purposes of the register is a general boundary and does not determine the exact line of the boundary. That line, however, may be fixed in accordance with s. 60(3), (4); LRR 2003, rr. 117–123; R & R, chap. 5; Law Com No. 271 (2001), paras 9.9–9.15; *Chadwick v Abbotswood Properties Ltd* [2005] 1 P & CR 10 (reviewing the authorities). For accretion and diluvian, see s. 61 and *Southern Centre of Theosophy Inc v State of South Australia* [1982] AC 706, 716, per Lord Wilberforce.

In *Alan Wibberley Building Ltd v Insley* [1999] 1 WLR 894 at 895 Lord Hoffmann said: 'Boundary disputes are a particularly painful form of litigation. Feelings run high as disproportionate amounts of money are spent. Claims to small and valueless pieces of land are pressed with the zeal of Fortinbras's army. It is therefore important that the law on boundaries should be as clear as possible.' On boundaries generally, see Aldridge, *Boundaries, Walls and Fences* (9th edn, 2004).

(2) Subject to rule 72A,[32] if the lease contains a provision that prohibits or restricts dispositions of the leasehold estate, the registrar must make an entry in the property register stating the lease prohibits or restricts dispositions of the estate.[33]

Property register of a registered estate in a rentcharge, a franchise or a profit a prendre in gross

7. Where practicable,[34] the property register of a registered estate in a rentcharge, franchise or a profit a prendre in gross must, if the estate was created by an instrument, also contain sufficient particulars of the instrument to enable it to be identified.

Contents of the proprietorship register

8.[35]—(1) The proprietorship register of a registered estate must contain, where appropriate—

(a) the class of title,

(b) the name of the proprietor of the registered estate including, where the proprietor is a company registered under the Companies Acts, or a limited liability partnership incorporated under the Limited Liability Partnerships Act 2000, its registered number,

(c) an address for service of the proprietor of the registered estate in accordance with rule 198,

(d) restrictions under section 40 of the Act,[36] including one entered under section 86(4) of the Act, in relation to the registered estate,

(e) notices under section 86(2) of the Act in relation to the registered estate,[37]

(f) positive covenants by a transferor or transferee and indemnity covenants by a transferee entered under rules 64 or 65,

(g) details of any modification of the covenants implied by paragraphs 20(2) and (3) of Schedule 12 to the Act entered under rule 66,[38]

(h) details of any modification of the covenants implied under the Law of Property (Miscellaneous Provisions) Act 1994[39] entered under rule 67(6), and

(i) such other matters as are required to be entered in the proprietorship register by these rules.

(2) Where practicable, the registrar must enter in the proprietorship register—

(a) on first registration of a registered estate,

(b) following completion by registration of a lease which is a registrable disposition, and

(c) on a subsequent change of proprietor of a registered estate,

the price paid or value declared for the registered estate.

(3) An entry made under paragraph (2) must remain until there is a change of proprietor, or some other change in the register of title which the registrar considers would result in the entry being misleading.

---

[32] Amended by LR (Amendment) (No. 2) Rules 2005 (SI 2005 No. 1982), Pt. 2, r. 4.
[33] Amended by LR (Amendment) Rules 2008 (SI 2008 No. 1919), Sch. 1, para. 2.
[34] Amended by LR (Amendment) Rules 2008 (SI 2008 No. 1919), Sch. 1, para. 3.
[35] Amended by LR (Amendment) Rules 2008 (SI 2008 No. 1919), Sch. 1, para. 4.
[36] P. 175, below.
[37] Notice in respect of a pending action after registration of petition in bankruptcy.
[38] Implied indemnity covenants on transfer of pre-1996 leases, p. 472, below.
[39] P. 188, below.

Contents of the charges register

9.[40] Except where otherwise permitted, the charges register of a registered estate must contain, where appropriate—

(a) details of leases, charges, and any other interests which adversely affect the registered estate subsisting at the time of first registration of the estate or created thereafter,

(b) any dealings with the interests referred to in paragraph (a), or affecting their priority, which are capable of being noted on the register,

(c) sufficient details to enable any registered charged to be identified,

(d) the name of the proprietor of any registered charge including, where the proprietor is a company registered under the Companies Acts, or a limited liability partnership incorporated under the Limited Liability Partnerships Act 2000, its registered number,

(e) an address for service of the proprietor of any registered charge in accordance with rule 198,

(f) restrictions under section 40 of the Act,[41] including one entered under section 86(4) of the Act, in relation to a registered charge,

(g) notices under section 86(2) of the Act in relation to a registered charge,[42]

(h) such other matters affecting the registered estate or any registered charge as are required to be entered in the charges register by these rules, and

(i) any matter otherwise required to be entered in any other part of the register which the registrar considers may more conveniently be entered in the charges register.

There is also:

(1) an index which records all registered estates and land affected by any caution against first registration: LRA 2002, s. 68; LRR 2003, r. 10;

(2) an index of proprietors' names: LRR 2003, r. 11;

(3) a record (the 'day list') showing the date and time at which every pending application was made and of every application for an official search with priority under LRR 2003 r. 147: LRR 2003, r. 12;

(4) a register of cautions against first registration (p. 140, below): LRA 2002, s. 19; LRR 2003, rr. 40, 41.

The registers of title and cautions against first registration are open to the public; any person may inspect and make copies: LRA 2002, ss. 66, 67;[43] but not if the document contains prejudicial information: LRR 2003, rr. 133, 136.[44]

A purchaser may make an official search with priority protection under LRA 2002 ss. 70, 72 and LRR 2003, rr. 147–154.

---

[40] Amended by LR (Amendment) Rules 2008 (SI 2008 No. 1919), Sch. 1, para. 5.
[41] P. 175, below.   [42] Pending action in respect of a bankruptcy petition.
[43] For the problems of potential fraud arising from the right for the public to inspect the register, see (2008) 124 LQR 351 (P. Matthews); Land Registry Practice Guide 67 (2008).
[44] As amended by LR (Amendment) Rules 2008 (SI 2008 No. 1919), Sch.1, para. 46; R & R, para. 31.005.

Specimen extract from the Register[45]

Title number: CS72510

This title is dealt with by Land Registry, Plymouth Office.

The following extract contains information taken from the register of the above title number. A full copy of the register accompanies this document and you should read that in order to be sure that these brief details are complete.

Neither this extract nor the full copy is an 'official copy' of the register. An official copy of the register is admissible in evidence in a court to the same extent as the original. A person is entitled to be indemnified by the registrar if he suffers loss by reason of a mistake in an official copy.

This extract shows information current on [date and time] and so does not take account of any application made after that time even if pending in the Land Registry when this extract was issued.

REGISTER EXTRACT

Title Number	: CS72510
Address of Property	: 23 Cottage Lane, Kerwick, PL14 3JP.
Price Paid/Value Stated	: £128,000
Registered Owners	: Peter Andrew Bartram and Susan Helen Bartram of : 23 Cottage Lane, Kerwick, (PL14 3JP).
Lender	: ILKINGHAM BUILDING SOCIETY

The title number is Land Registry's unique reference number for this registered land.

The price paid/value stated information has been entered in the register since 1 April 2000. It is based on information contained in the transfer or application form lodged with us. It has not been verified by us and may not represent the full market value of the property. For further information please click here.

---

[45] The extract is taken from www.landregisteronline.gov.uk/lro/resources/example_register.pdf. There is also a title plan.

Specimen register

This is a copy of the register of the title number set out immediately below, showing the entries in the register on [date and time]. This copy does not take account of any application made after that time even if still pending in the Land Registry when this copy was issued.

This copy is not an 'official copy' of the register. An official copy of the register is admissible in evidence in a court to the same extent as the original. A person is entitled to be indemnified by the registrar if he suffers loss by reason of a mistake in an official copy. If you want to obtain an official copy, you will need to complete form OC1.

TITLE NUMBER : CS72510   PROPERTY REGISTER

CORNSHIRE : MARADON

1. (29 August 1974) The Freehold land shown edged with red on the plan of the above Title filed at the Registry and being 23 Cottage Lane, Kerwick, (PL14 3JP).

2. (29 August 1974) The land tinted yellow on the title plan has the benefit of the following rights granted by the Conveyance dated 27 July 1968 referred to in the charges register:-

   "TOGETHER WITH the benefit of a right of way on foot only over that part of the shared accessway belonging to 25 Cottage Lane."

3. (29 August 1974) The land has the benefit of the rights granted by the Transfer dated 21 August 1974 referred to in the Charges Register.

END OF PROPERTY REGISTER

The title number is Land Registry's unique reference number for this registered land.

This is the date that the entry was made in the register.

The **property register** identifies the geographical location and extent of the registered property by means of a short verbal description (usually the address) and by reference to an official plan which is prepared for each title. It may also give particulars of any rights that benefit the land. In the case of a leasehold title, it gives brief details of the lease.

TITLE NUMBER : CS72510   PROPRIETORSHIP REGISTER - ABSOLUTE FREEHOLD

---

1. (18 December 2001): PROPRIETOR: PETER ANDREW BARTRAM and SUSAN HELEN
    BARTRAM of 23 Cottage Lane, Kerwick, (PL14 3JP).

2. (18 December 2001) The price stated to have been paid on 3 December 2001 was £128,000.

3. (18 December 2001) Except under an order of the registrar no disposition by the proprietor
    of the land is to be registered without the consent of the proprietor of the charge dated 3
    December 2001 in favour of the Ilkingham Building Society referred to in the Charges
    Register.

END OF PROPRIETORSHIP REGISTER

This type of entry has been entered in the register
since 1 April 2000. It is based on information
contained in the transfer or application form
lodged with us. It has not been verified by us and
may not represent the full market value of the
property.

The **proprietorship register** specifies the quality of title. It also gives the name and address of
the legal owner(s) and shows whether there are any restrictions on their power to sell, mortgage
or otherwise deal with the land. It **may** give details of price paid or value information relating to
the title.

TITLE NUMBER : CS72510   CHARGES REGISTER- ABSOLUTE FREEHOLD

---

1. (29 August 1974) A Conveyance of the land tinted pink on the title plan dated 14 February 1965 made between (1) Archibald Henry Dawson (Vendor) and (2) Thomas Yorke (Purchaser) contains the following covenants:-

   "THE Purchaser hereby covenants with the Vendor so as to bind the land hereby conveyed into whosoever hands the same may come that the Purchaser and his successors in title will not use the premises hereby conveyed for the retail sale of grocery or as a butchers shop."

2. (29 August 1974) The land in this title is subject to the following rights reserved by a Conveyance dated 27 July 1968 made between (1) Maradon Borough Council (Vendor) and (2) John Robertson (Purchaser):-

   "subject to

   (i) An exception and reservation in favour of the Vendor of the right to enter upon the land hereby conveyed for the purpose of constructing a public sewer the approximate line of which is shown coloured red on the plan annexed hereto and at all times hereafter for the purpose of inspecting cleaning repairing or renewing the said sewer."

   NOTE:- The red line referred to is shown by a blue broken line on the title plan.

3. (29 August 1974) A Transfer of the land in this title dated 21 August 1974 made between (1) Henry Smith and (2) David Stanley Charles and Susan Charles contains restrictive covenants.

   NOTE: Copy in Certificate.

4. REGISTERED CHARGE dated 3 December 2001 to secure the moneys including the further advances therein mentioned.

   PROPRIETOR Ilkingham Building Society of 101 Cambridge Street, Ilkingham IL1 3FC.

Where the matters contained in a deed are lengthy, we normally do not set out the full details in the register. This is because it allows us to process applications quicker so providing a more efficient service to our customers and also because the matters are sometimes best understood when read with the rest of the deed. Where this method has been used, the deed will be referred to in the register as "copy in certificate" or "copy filed". To obtain an official copy of a deed referred to on the register in this way you will need to complete form OC2.

A registered mortgage, called a charge, affecting the title. It gives the date of the charge and the name and address of the lender.

The **charges register** contains identifying particulars of registered mortgages and notice of other financial burdens secured on the property (but does not disclose details of the amounts of money involved). It also gives notice of other rights and interests to which the property is subject such as leases, rights of way or covenants restricting the use of the property.

IV. FIRST REGISTRATION OF TITLE[46]

First registration of title may be either voluntary or compulsory. Since 1990 it has been compulsory throughout England and Wales when there are certain dealings with unregistered land. The events which trigger compulsory registration of unregistered land were extended by the Land Registration Act 1997 and further extended by the Land Registration Act 2002. The Lord Chancellor has power under section 5 of the 2002 Act to add further triggers. The eventual aim is to have a complete register of title of all land.[47] We shall then have a second Domesday Book over nine hundred years after its more picturesque ancestor of 1086.

A. VOLUNTARY FIRST REGISTRATION

LAND REGISTRATION ACT 2002

3 When title may be registered

(1) This section applies to any unregistered legal estate which is an interest of any of the following kinds—

(a) an estate in land,

(b) a rentcharge,

(c) a franchise, and

(d) a profit a prendre in gross.

(2) Subject to the following provisions, a person may apply to the registrar to be registered as the proprietor of an unregistered legal estate to which this section applies if—

(a) the estate is vested in him, or

(b) he is entitled to require the estate to be vested in him.

(3) Subject to subsection (4), an application under subsection (2) in respect of a leasehold estate may only be made if the estate was granted for a term of which more than seven years are unexpired.

(4) In the case of an estate in land, subsection (3) does not apply if the right to possession under the lease is discontinuous.[48]

(5) A person may not make an application under subsection (2)(a) in respect of a leasehold estate vested in him as a mortgagee where there is a subsisting right of redemption.

(6) A person may not make an application under subsection (2)(b) if his entitlement is as a person who has contracted to buy under a contract.

---

[46] LRR 2003, rr. 21–38; R & R, chaps 5–11; H & B, Part 1; Law Com No. 271 (2001), Part III.

[47] No firm date is now given for the completion of the register, but annual targets are set for increasing the total area of freehold land on the register: above, n 8.

[48] Pp. 328, 357–358, 418, below.

(7) If a person holds in the same right both—

    (a) a lease in possession, and

    (b) a lease to take effect in possession on, or within a month of, the end of the lease in possession,

then, to the extent that they relate to the same land, they are to be treated for the purposes of this section as creating one continuous term.

B. COMPULSORY FIRST REGISTRATION[49]

(i) Triggers for registration

LAND REGISTRATION ACT 2002

4 When title must be registered

(1) The requirement of registration applies on the occurrence of any of the following events—

    (a) the transfer of a qualifying estate—

        (i) for valuable or other consideration,[50] by way of gift or in pursuance of an order of any court,

        (ii) by means of an assent (including a vesting assent) or

        (iii) giving effect to a partition of land subject to a trust of land;[51]

    (aa) the transfer of a qualifying estate—

        (i) by a deed that appoints, or by virtue of section 83 of the Charities Act 1993 has effect as if it appointed, a new trustee or is made in consequence of the appointment of a new trustee, or

        (ii) by a vesting order under section 44 of the Trustee Act 1925 that is consequential on the appointment of a new trustee;[52]

    (b) the transfer of an unregistered legal estate in land in circumstances where section 171A of the Housing Act 1985 applies (disposal by landlord which leads to a person no longer being a secure tenant);

    (c) the grant out of a qualifying estate of an estate in land—

        (i) for a term of years absolute of more than seven years from the date of the grant, and

---

[49] R & R, chaps. 8, 9; H & B, paras 2.8–2.24; Law Com No. 271 (2001), paras 3.22–3.41. Cf. LRA 1925, ss. 123, 123A, as amended by LRA 1997, s. 1.

[50] 'Valuable consideration' does not include marriage consideration or a nominal consideration in money: LRA 2002, s. 132(1): cf. LRA 1925, s. 3(xxxi), which included marriage but not nominal consideration in money.

[51] Sub-para. (ii) inserted by LRA 2002 (Amendment) Order 2008 (SI 2008 No. 2872), art. 2.

[52] Para. (aa) inserted by LRA 2002 (Amendment) Order 2008 (SI 2008 No. 2872), art. 2.

(ii) for valuable or other consideration, by way of gift or in pursuance of an order of any court;[53]

(d) the grant out of a qualifying estate of an estate in land for a term of years absolute to take effect in possession after the end of the period of three months beginning with the date of the grant;

(e) the grant of a lease in pursuance of Part 5 of the Housing Act 1985 (the right to buy) out of an unregistered legal estate in land;

(f) the grant of a lease out of an unregistered legal estate in land in such circumstances as are mentioned in paragraph (b);

(g) the creation of a protected first legal mortgage of a qualifying estate.

(2) For the purposes of subsection (1), a qualifying estate is an unregistered legal estate which is—

(a) a freehold estate in land, or

(b) a leasehold estate in land for a term which, at the time of the transfer, grant or creation, has more than seven years to run.

(3) In subsection (1)(a), the reference to transfer does not include transfer by operation of law.

(4) Subsection (1)(a) does not apply to—

(a) the assignment of a mortgage term, or

(b) the assignment or surrender of a lease to the owner of the immediate reversion where the term is to merge in that reversion.

(5) Subsection (1)(c) does not apply to the grant of an estate to a person as a mortgagee.

(6) For the purposes of subsection (1)(a) and (c), if the estate transferred or granted has a negative value, it is to be regarded as transferred or granted for valuable or other consideration.

(7) In subsection (1)(a) and (c), references to transfer or grant by way of gift include transfer or grant for the purpose of—

(a) constituting a trust under which the settlor does not retain the whole of the beneficial interest, or

(b) uniting the bare legal title and the beneficial interest in property held under a trust under which the settlor did not, on constitution, retain the whole of the beneficial interest.[54]

(8) For the purposes of subsection (1)(g)—

(a) a legal mortgage is protected if it takes effect on its creation as a mortgage to be protected by the deposit of documents relating to the mortgaged estate,[55] and

---

[53] Under LRA 1925 leases granted for more than 21 years were subject to compulsory registration. Leases granted for more than seven years became subject to compulsory registration under LRA 2002. So did leases granted to take effect in possession more than three months in advance (reversionary leases) and discontinuous leases (p. 418, below).

[54] Thus a settlement by S to trustees on trust for S and B would amount to a gift triggering registration. Transfers to trustees on a bare trust (e.g. by S to trustees on trust for S alone absolutely: p. 520, below) would not.

[55] P. 856, below.

(b) a first legal mortgage is one which, on its creation, ranks in priority ahead of any other mortgages then affecting the mortgaged estate.

(9) In this section—

'land' does not include mines and minerals held apart from the surface;

'vesting assent' has the same meaning as in the Settled Land Act 1925.

(ii) Special case: the Crown[56]

Before the 2002 Act the Crown was unable to register its demesne land (land which it holds in its capacity as ultimate feudal overlord) because it had no *estate* in such land: 'a major, but unremarked, lacuna in the system of land registration in England and Wales', per Burnton QC in *Scmlla Properties Ltd v Gesso Properties (BVI) Ltd* [1995] BCC 793 at 798. Under LRA 2002, s. 79 the Crown can grant to itself a freehold estate which it can then register, and s. 80 provides for compulsory registration of demesne land.

LAND REGISTRATION ACT 2002

79 Voluntary registration of demesne land

(1) Her Majesty may grant an estate in fee simple absolute in possession out of demesne land to Herself.

80 Compulsory registration of grants out of demesne land

(1) Section 4(1) shall apply as if the following were included among the events listed—

(a) the grant by Her Majesty out of demesne land of an estate in fee simple absolute in possession, otherwise than under section 79;

(b) the grant by Her Majesty out of demesne land of an estate in land—

(i) for a term of years absolute of more than seven years from the date of the grant, and

(ii) for valuable or other consideration, by way of gift or in pursuance of an order of any court.

(iii) Duty to apply for registration

LAND REGISTRATION ACT 2002

6 Duty to apply for registration of title

(1) If the requirement of registration applies, the responsible estate owner, or his successor in title, must, before the end of the period for registration, apply to the registrar to be registered as the proprietor of the registrable estate.

---

[56] R & R, chap. 40; H & B, chap. 6; Law Com No. 271 (2001), paras 11.2–11.19. See also ss. 81 (demesne land: cautions against first registration); 82 (escheat etc.); 83 (Crown and Duchy land: representation); 84 (disapplication of requirements relating to Duchy land); 85 (bona vacantia).

(2) If the requirement of registration applies because of section 4(1)(g)—

    (a) the registrable estate is the estate charged by the mortgage, and

    (b) the responsible estate owner is the owner of that estate.

(3) If the requirement of registration applies otherwise than because of section 4(1)(g)—

    (a) the registrable estate is the estate which is transferred or granted, and

    (b) the responsible estate owner is the transferee or grantee of that estate.

(4) The period for registration is 2 months beginning with the date on which the relevant event occurs, or such longer period as the registrar may provide under subsection (5).

(5) If on the application of any interested person the registrar is satisfied that there is good reason for doing so, he may by order provide that the period for registration ends on such later date as he may specify in the order.

(6) Rules may make provision enabling the mortgagee under any mortgage falling within section 4(1)(g) to require the estate charged by the mortgage to be registered whether or not the mortgagor consents.

(iv) Effect of failure to register[57]

LAND REGISTRATION ACT 2002

7 Effect of non-compliance with section 6

(1) If the requirement of registration is not complied with, the transfer, grant or creation becomes void as regards the transfer, grant or creation of a legal estate.[58]

(2) On the application of subsection (1)—

    (a) in a case falling within section 4(1)(a) or (b),[59] the title to the legal estate reverts to the transferor who holds it on a bare trust for the transferee,

    (aa) in a case falling within section 4(1)(aa), the title to the legal estate reverts to the person in whom it was vested immediately before the transfer,[60] and

    (b) in a case falling within section 4(1)(c) to (g),[61] the grant or creation has effect as a contract made for valuable consideration to grant or create the legal estate concerned.

(3) If an order under section 6(5) is made in a case where subsection (1) has already applied, that application of the subsection is to be treated as not having occurred.

(4) The possibility of reverter under subsection (1) is to be disregarded for the purposes of determining whether a fee simple is a fee simple absolute.[62]

---

[57] R & R, paras 8.013–8.016.

[58] See also LRA 2002, s. 8 (transferee, grantee or mortgagor who fails to comply with registration require-ments is liable for other party's consequential costs and liabilities).

[59] P. 132, above.

[60] Para. (aa) inserted by LRA 2002 (Amendment) Order 2008, SI 2008 No. 2872, art. 3 (with effect from date to be appointed).

[61] Pp. 132–133, above.

[62] On possibility of reverter, see LPA 1925, s. 7, p. 302, below.

C. CLASSES OF TITLE[63]

Once registered, the title is guaranteed by the State. There are different classes of registered title, reflecting the level of assurance which the Registrar is able to give on behalf of the State as to the quality of the proprietor's title on the basis of the information available at the time of registration. Provision is also made for titles which are less than the highest class, 'absolute title', to be upgraded in specified circumstances.

(i) Freehold estates

LAND REGISTRATION ACT 2002

9 Titles to freehold estates

(1) In the case of an application for registration under this Chapter of a freehold estate, the classes of title with which the applicant may be registered as proprietor are—

    (a) absolute title,

    (b) qualified title, and

    (c) possessory title;

and the following provisions deal with when each of the classes of title is available.

(2) A person may be registered with absolute title if the registrar is of the opinion that the person's title to the estate is such as a willing buyer could properly be advised by a competent professional adviser to accept.

(3) In applying subsection (2), the registrar may disregard the fact that a person's title appears to him to be open to objection if he is of the opinion that the defect will not cause the holding under the title to be disturbed.

(4) A person may be registered with qualified title if the registrar is of the opinion that the person's title to the estate has been established only for a limited period or subject to certain reservations which cannot be disregarded under subsection (3).

(5) A person may be registered with possessory title if the registrar is of the opinion—

    (a) that the person is in actual possession of the land, or in receipt of the rents and profits of the land, by virtue of the estate, and

    (b) that there is no other class of title with which he may be registered.

(ii) Leasehold estates

LAND REGISTRATION ACT 2002

10 Titles to leasehold estates

(1) In the case of an application for registration under this Chapter of a leasehold estate, the classes of title with which the applicant may be registered as proprietor are—

    (a) absolute title,

---

[63] R & R, chap. 6; H & B, chap. 3. Law Com No. 271 (2001), paras 3.42–3.44, cf. LRA 1925, s. 4.

    (b) good leasehold title,

    (c) qualified title, and

    (d) possessory title;

and the following provisions deal with when each of the classes of title is available.

(2) A person may be registered with absolute title if—

    (a) the registrar is of the opinion that the person's title to the estate is such as a willing buyer could properly be advised by a competent professional adviser to accept, and

    (b) the registrar approves the lessor's title to grant the lease.

(3) A person may be registered with good leasehold title if the registrar is of the opinion that the person's title to the estate is such as a willing buyer could properly be advised by a competent professional adviser to accept.

(4) In applying subsection (2) or (3), the registrar may disregard the fact that a person's title appears to him to be open to objection if he is of the opinion that the defect will not cause the holding under the title to be disturbed.

(5) A person may be registered with qualified title if the registrar is of the opinion that the person's title to the estate, or the lessor's title to the reversion, has been established only for a limited period or subject to certain reservations which cannot be disregarded under subsection (4).

(6) A person may be registered with possessory title if the registrar is of the opinion—

    (a) that the person is in actual possession of the land, or in receipt of the rents and profits of the land, by virtue of the estate, and

    (b) that there is no other class of title with which he may be registered.

(iii) Upgrading of titles[64]

LAND REGISTRATION ACT 2002

62 Power to upgrade title

(1) Where the title to a freehold estate is entered in the register as possessory or qualified, the registrar may enter it as absolute if he is satisfied as to the title to the estate.

(2) Where the title to a leasehold estate is entered in the register as good leasehold, the registrar may enter it as absolute if he is satisfied as to the superior title.

(3) Where the title to a leasehold estate is entered in the register as possessory or qualified the registrar may—

    (a) enter it as good leasehold if he is satisfied as to the title to the estate, and

    (b) enter it as absolute if he is satisfied both as to the title to the estate and as to the superior title.

(4) Where the title to a freehold estate in land has been entered in the register as possessory for at least twelve years, the registrar may enter it as absolute if he is satisfied that the proprietor is in possession of the land.

---

[64] R & R, chap. 12; Law Com No. 271 (2001), paras 9.16–9.27. Cf. LRA 1925, s. 77 (as amended).

(5) Where the title to a leasehold estate in land has been entered in the register as possessory for at least twelve years, the registrar may enter it as good leasehold if he is satisfied that the proprietor is in possession of the land.

(6) None of the powers under subsections (1) to (5) is exercisable if there is outstanding any claim adverse to the title of the registered proprietor which is made by virtue of an estate, right or interest whose enforceability is preserved by virtue of the existing entry about the class of title.

(7) The only persons who may apply to the registrar for the exercise of any of the powers under subsections (1) to (5) are—

(a) the proprietor of the estate to which the application relates,

(b) a person entitled to be registered as the proprietor of that estate,

(c) the proprietor of a registered charge affecting that estate, and

(d) a person interested in a registered estate which derives from that estate.

(8) In determining for the purposes of this section whether he is satisfied as to any title, the registrar is to apply the same standards as those which apply under section 9 or 10 to first registration of title.

(9) The Lord Chancellor may by order amend subsection (4) or (5) by substituting for the number of years for the time being specified in that subsection such number of years as the order may provide.[65]

63 Effect of upgrading title

(1) On the title to a registered freehold or leasehold estate being entered under section 62 as absolute, the proprietor ceases to hold the estate subject to any estate, right or interest whose enforceability was preserved by virtue of the previous entry about the class of title.

(2) Subsection (1) also applies on the title to a registered leasehold estate being entered under section 62 as good leasehold, except that the entry does not affect or prejudice the enforcement of any estate, right or interest affecting, or in derogation of, the title of the lessor to grant the lease.

D. EFFECT OF FIRST REGISTRATION[66]

(i) *Freehold estates*

LAND REGISTRATION ACT 2002

11 Freehold estates[67]

(1) This section is concerned with the registration of a person under this Chapter as the proprietor of a freehold estate.

---

[65] See Law Commission Report on Limitation of Actions 2001 (Law Com No. 270), which recommends that the limitation period for recovery of unregistered land be reduced from 12 years to 10 years; p. 274, below; if enacted, this might suggest that the Lord Chancellor should substitute 10 years for 12 years in sub-ss (4) and (5): Law Com No. 271 (2001), para. 9.17(2).

[66] R & R, para. 3.007; H & B, chap. 4; Law Com No. 271 (2001), paras 3.45–3.51.

[67] Cf. LRA 1925, ss. 5, 6, 7(2).

(2) Registration with absolute title has the effect described in subsections (3) to (5).

(3) The estate is vested in the proprietor together with all interests subsisting for the benefit of the estate.

(4) The estate is vested in the proprietor subject only to the following interests affecting the estate at the time of registration—

(a) interests which are the subject of an entry in the register in relation to the estate,[68]

(b) unregistered interests which fall within any of the paragraphs of Schedule 1,[69] and

(c) interests acquired under the Limitation Act 1980 of which the proprietor has notice.[70]

(5) If the proprietor is not entitled to the estate for his own benefit, or not entitled solely for his own benefit, then, as between himself and the persons beneficially entitled to the estate, the estate is vested in him subject to such of their interests as he has notice of.[71]

(6) Registration with qualified title has the same effect as registration with absolute title, except that it does not affect the enforcement of any estate, right or interest which appears from the register to be excepted from the effect of registration.

(7) Registration with possessory title has the same effect as registration with absolute title, except that it does not affect the enforcement of any estate, right or interest adverse to, or in derogation of, the proprietor's title subsisting at the time of registration or then capable of arising.

(ii) Leasehold estates

LAND REGISTRATION ACT 2002

12 Leasehold estates[72]

(1) This section is concerned with the registration of a person under this Chapter as the proprietor of a leasehold estate.

(2) Registration with absolute title has the effect described in subsections (3) to (5).

(3) The estate is vested in the proprietor together with all interests subsisting for the benefit of the estate.

(4) The estate is vested subject only to the following interests affecting the estate at the time of registration—

(a) implied and express covenants, obligations and liabilities incident to the estate,

(b) interests which are the subject of an entry in the register in relation to the estate,

(c) unregistered interests which fall within any of the paragraphs of Schedule 1, and

(d) interests acquired under the Limitation Act 1980 of which the proprietor has notice.

---

[68] For example, a notice entered by the registrar on the charges register of the servient land in respect of an easement.

[69] Unregistered interests which override first registration; p. 193, below.

[70] P. 246, below. See H & B, paras 4.5–4.6; Explanatory Notes on the Land Registration Bill, cited Wolstenholme and Cherry, *Annotated Land Registration Act 2002*, para. 3.011.

[71] This includes not only the rights of a beneficiary under a trust: chaps 6 and 7, below, but also the rights of a person who has an equity arising by proprietary estoppel: chap. 11, below.

[72] Cf. LRA 1925, ss. 9, 10, 11, 12(2).

(5) If the proprietor is not entitled to the estate for his own benefit, or not entitled solely for his own benefit, then, as between himself and the persons beneficially entitled to the estate, the estate is vested in him subject to such of their interests as he has notice of.

(6) Registration with good leasehold title has the same effect as registration with absolute title, except that it does not affect the enforcement of any estate, right or interest affecting, or in derogation of, the title of the lessor to grant the lease.

(7) Registration with qualified title has the same effect as registration with absolute title except that it does not affect the enforcement of any estate, right or interest which appears from the register to be excepted from the effect of registration.

(8) Registration with possessory title has the same effect as registration with absolute title, except that it does not affect the enforcement of any estate, right or interest adverse to, or in derogation of, the proprietor's title subsisting at the time of registration or then capable of arising.

E. CAUTIONS AGAINST FIRST REGISTRATION

Any person who has an interest in unregistered land may apply for a caution against first registration of that land. The object is to ensure that on first registration his interest will be protected on the register. The caution gives the cautioner the right to be notified of the application to register and to object to it. It is a procedural device and gives no substantive right.[73]

LAND REGISTRATION ACT 2002

15 Right to lodge

(1) Subject to subsection (3), a person may lodge a caution against the registration of title to an unregistered legal estate if he claims to be—

    (a) the owner of a qualifying estate, or

    (b) entitled to an interest affecting a qualifying estate.

(2) For the purposes of subsection (1), a qualifying estate is a legal estate which—

    (a) relates to land to which the caution relates, and

    (b) is an interest of any of the following kinds—

        (i)   an estate in land,

        (ii)   a rentcharge,

        (iii) a franchise, and

        (iv)   a profit a prendre in gross.

(3) No caution may be lodged under subsection (1)—

    (a) in the case of paragraph (a), by virtue of ownership of—

        (i)   a freehold estate in land, or

---

[73] LRA 2002 replaces the caution against dealings under LRA 1925, s. 53 and creates a new special register of cautions: LRR 2003, rr. 39–53; R & R, chap. 11; H & B, chap. 5; Law Com No. 271 (2001), paras 3.54–3.65. See also LRA 2002, ss. 17 (cautioner may withdraw caution); 19 (cautions register); 20, 21 (alteration of register by court and by registrar). For transitional provisions, see Sch. 12, paras 4, 14–17.

    (ii) a leasehold estate in land granted for a term of which more than seven years are unexpired;

  (b) in the case of paragraph (b), by virtue of entitlement to such a leasehold estate as is mentioned in paragraph (a) (ii) of this subsection.

(4) The right under subsection (1) is exercisable by application to the registrar.

16 Effect

(1) Where an application for registration under this Part relates to a legal estate which is the subject of a caution against first registration, the registrar must give the cautioner notice of the application and of his right to object to it.

(2) The registrar may not determine an application to which subsection (1) applies before the end of such period as rules may provide, unless the cautioner has exercised his right to object to the application or given the registrar notice that he does not intend to do so.

(3) Except as provided by this section, a caution against first registration has no effect and, in particular, has no effect on the validity or priority of any interest of the cautioner in the legal estate to which the caution relates.

(4) For the purposes of subsection (1), notice given by a person acting on behalf of an applicant for registration under this Part is to be treated as given by the registrar if—

  (a) the person is of a description provided by rules, and

  (b) notice is given in such circumstances as rules may provide.

18 Cancellation

(1) A person may apply to the registrar for cancellation of a caution against first registration if he is—

  (a) the owner of the legal estate to which the caution relates, or

  (b) a person of such other description as rules may provide.

V. ALTERATION AND RECTIFICATION OF THE REGISTER AND INDEMNITIES[74]

A. RECTIFICATION OF THE REGISTER AND INDEMNITY UNDER THE LAND REGISTRATION ACT 1925

Law Commission Report on Land Registration for the Twenty-First Century 2001 (Law Com No. 271), paras 10.1–10.3

10.1 ... The Land Registration Act 1925 makes detailed provision for one particular type of alteration to the register, namely rectification. There are presently ten grounds on which

---

[74] C & B, pp. 106, 959–62; Gray, paras 2.2.59–2.2.72; M & W, paras 7.131–7.145; MM, pp. 138–143; Smith, pp. 259–266; R & R, chaps 46, 47; H & B, chaps 22, 23; Law Com No. 271 (2001), Part X; Land Registry

rectification may be ordered under the Land Registration Act 1925 or the Land Registration Rules 1925.[75] These can be broadly summarised as follows—

(1) Where a court either makes an order which gives effect to an established property right or interest, or orders the removal from the register of an entry in respect of a right which has not been established.[76]

(2) Where the court or the registrar decides that the register is incorrect in some way.[77]

(3) Where the registrar decides that a clerical error needs to be corrected.[78]

Under that Act, rectification is always discretionary.[79] However, in practice, it is only where rectification is concerned with the correction of some mistake in the register—the cases summarised in (2) and (3) above—that the discretion is normally exercised. In cases where a court has concluded that a person is entitled to a right or interest in the land, rectification will usually, though not invariably, be ordered.[80] Indeed, it would be strange if it were otherwise. Where a person establishes his or her entitlement to some such right or interest, there will not often be any reason why a court should refuse to give effect to it, as this would leave the successful claimant with a mere right to indemnity.

10.2 Where the register is changed for some reason other than one of the statutory grounds for rectification, as where the registrar removes an entry on the register that is spent because the interest to which it relates has terminated, that alteration is not 'rectification' for the purposes of the Act. Indeed, the Act has no specific name for it. It is simply part of the process of ensuring that the register is kept up to date. Although this distinction between rectification of the register and its alteration is implicit in the Land Registration Act 1925, it is not spelt out explicitly.[81]

10.3 Indemnity is, in some senses, the correlative of rectification. It is payable where a person suffers loss as a result of an error or omission in the register, whether or not the register is rectified, and in certain other circumstances.[82] The availability of indemnity is of great importance to the system of land registration. It is the basis of the so-called 'State guarantee of title' which registration confers.[83]

Practice Guide 39. On rectification and indemnity under LRA 1925, see Barnsley, chap. 4; Hayton, *Registered Land*, chap. 9; Farrand, *Contract and Conveyance* (2nd edn), pp. 209–222.

[75] See Law Com No. 254, paras 2.37–2.39; summary, paras 8.6–8.22 (where the provisions are analysed in detail).

[76] Land Registration Act 1925, s. 82(1)(a), (b).

[77] Ibid., s. 82(1)(d)–(h). There is also a power to rectify where all interested persons consent: ibid., s. 82(1)(c).

[78] Land Registration Rules 1925, rr. 13, 14.   [79] See Law Com No. 254, para. 8.5.

[80] See *Norwich & Peterborough Building Society v Steed* [1993] Ch 116, 139; Law Com No. 254, paras 8.12–8.13. However, see now *Kingsalton Ltd v Thames Water Developments Ltd* [2001] EWCA Civ 20; [2001] EGCS 12 where rectification was refused in a case that was held to fall within Land Registration Act 1925, s. 82(1)(a) (though in reality, on the facts, it appears to have been a case involving a mistake that fell within s. 82(1)(g), that is 'where the legal estate has been registered in the name of a person who if the land had not been registered would not have been the estate owner'). On the power of the court to refuse rectification when s. 82(1)(a) applied, see in particular the comments of Arden LJ at [2001] EWCA Civ 20, [39].

[81] Compare, for example, Land Registration Act 1925, ss. 35 (discharge of charges), 46 (determination of leases and other registered estates), 50(3) (discharge of restrictive covenants), 75 (registration of adverse possessor) on the one hand with s. 82 (rectification) on the other.

[82] See Land Registration Act 1925, s. 83 (as substituted by Land Registration Act 1997, s. 2).

[83] On this, see Ruoff & Roper, *Registered Conveyancing*, 2–10; 2–13; 40–02.

B. ALTERATION OF THE REGISTER AND INDEMNITY UNDER THE LAND REGISTRATION ACT 2002

(i) Alteration of the register

The provisions for alteration of the register have been recast so as to reflect the present practice in relation to rectification and amendment of the register. The basic concept is *alteration* of the register, with rectification as one form of alteration. Rectification is defined in paragraph 1 of Schedule 4 to the 2002 Act as an alteration which (a) involves the correction of a mistake; and (b) prejudicially affects the title of a registered proprietor. In respect of this kind of alteration, the proprietor of land may have a claim to an indemnity under Schedule 8.

LAND REGISTRATION ACT 2002

65 Alteration of register[84]

Schedule 4 (which makes provision about alteration of the register) has effect.

SCHEDULE 4
ALTERATION OF THE REGISTER

Introductory

1 In this Schedule, references to rectification, in relation to alteration of the register, are to alteration which—

   (a) involves the correction of a mistake,[85] and

   (b) prejudicially affects the title of a registered proprietor.[86]

Alteration pursuant to a court order

2 (1) The court may make an order for alteration of the register for the purpose of—

   (a) correcting a mistake,

   (b) bringing the register up to date, or

   (c) giving effect to any estate, right or interest excepted from the effect of registration.

   (2) An order under this paragraph has effect when served on the registrar to impose a duty on him to give effect to it.

---

[84] LRR, Part 12.

[85] No mistake for rectification where charge properly executed and registered, but proprietor of charged land was itself not entitled to be registered as proprietor, unless mortgagee had actual or 'Nelsonian' notice of the defect in mortgagor's title: *Barclays Bank plc v Guy* [2008] 2 EGLR 74 at [23], per Lloyd LJ.

[86] *Derbyshire CC v Fallon* [2007] 3 EGLR 44 (no prejudice where boundary on land registry plan showed wrong title; correcting the plan would only give effect to actual property rights); criticised [2007] Conv 238.

3 (1) This paragraph applies to the power under paragraph 2, so far as relating to rectification.

(2) If alteration affects the title of the proprietor of a registered estate in land, no order may be made under paragraph 2 without the proprietor's consent in relation to land in his possession unless—

(a) he has by fraud or lack of proper care caused or substantially contributed to the mistake, or

(b) it would for any other reason be unjust for the alteration not to be made.[87]

(3) If in any proceedings the court has power to make an order under paragraph 2, it must do so, unless there are exceptional circumstances which justify its not doing so.

(4) In sub-paragraph (2), the reference to the title of the proprietor of a registered estate in land includes his title to any registered estate which subsists for the benefit of the estate in land.

4 Rules[88] may—

(a) make provision about the circumstances in which there is a duty to exercise the power under paragraph 2, so far as not relating to rectification;

(b) make provision about the form of an order under paragraph 2;

(c) make provision about service of such an order.

Alteration otherwise than pursuant to a court order

5 The registrar may alter the register for the purpose of—

(a) correcting a mistake,

(b) bringing the register up to date,

(c) giving effect to any estate, right or interest excepted from the effect of registration, or

(d) removing a superfluous entry.

6 (1) This paragraph applies to the power under paragraph 5, so far as relating to rectification.

(2) No alteration affecting the title of the proprietor of a registered estate in land may be made under paragraph 5 without the proprietor's consent in relation to land in his possession unless—

(a) he has by fraud or lack of proper care caused or substantially contributed to the mistake, or

(b) it would for any other reason be unjust for the alteration not to be made.

---

[87] *James Hay Pension Trustees Ltd v Cooper Estates Ltd* [2005] All ER (D) 144 (Jan) (proprietor in possession was accidental owner of small piece of land it never intended to acquire, useful only to extract ransom payment: transfer and register rectified); *Sainsbury's Supermarkets Ltd v Olympia Homes Ltd* [2006] 1 P & CR 17, p. 157, below, at para. 88 (registered proprietor in possession, registered with legal title by mistake, had believed that its title would be subject to prior rights belonging to party seeking rectification, and so refusal of rectification would confer a very substantial and unfair windfall on it).

[88] LRR 2003, rr. 126–127.

(3) If on an application for alteration under paragraph 5 the registrar has power to make the alteration, the application must be approved, unless there are exceptional circumstances which justify not making the alteration.

(4) In sub-paragraph (2), the reference to the title of the proprietor of a registered estate in land includes his title to any registered estate which subsists for the benefit of the estate in land.

7 Rules[89] may—

   (a) make provision about the circumstances in which there is a duty to exercise the power under paragraph 5, so far as not relating to rectification;

   (b) make provision about how the register is to be altered in exercise of that power;

   (c) make provision about applications for alteration under that paragraph, including provision requiring the making of such applications;

   (d) make provision about procedure in relation to the exercise of that power, whether on application or otherwise.

Rectification and derivative interests

8 The powers under this Schedule to alter the register, so far as relating to rectification, extend to changing for the future the priority of any interest affecting the registered estate or charge concerned.

Cases under the 1925 Act will be relevant in interpreting the new provisions under Schedule 4.

(a) Fraud. Forgery

Norwich and Peterborough Building Society v Steed (No 2)
[1993] Ch 116 (CA, Purchas, Butler-Sloss and Scott LJJ)[90]

In 1964 Mr Steed became the registered freehold proprietor of 2 Arlow Road, Winchmore Hill, London. In 1976 he went to the United States, leaving in the house his mother, and his sister and her husband, Mr and Mrs Hammond. He alleged that in 1979 his sister induced him to sign a power of attorney to enable his mother to sell the house on his behalf; and that a transfer of the house took place by way of a forged deed in favour of the sister and her husband who were then registered as joint proprietors. They borrowed £15,000 by way of registered legal charge from the Argyle Building Society. On default the Building Society obtained an order for possession. Mr Steed applied to have the registered charge rectified against the Building Society. The Court of Appeal in *Argyle Building Society v Hammond* (1984) 49 P & CR 148 held that it had jurisdiction under section 82 of the Land Registration Act 1925 to order rectification and stayed the order for possession.

In subsequent proceedings for possession by the Norwich Building Society (successor of the Argyle Building Society) Mr Steed no longer alleged forgery but relied

---

[89] LRR 2003, rr. 128–129.

[90] On forgeries and registered land generally, see (1985) 101 LQR 79 (R. J. Smith); (1993) 109 LQR 187 (R. J. Smith); [1993] All ER Rev 245, (P. J. Clarke); [1992] Conv 293 (C. Davis).

on new pleas of non est factum and fraud. Knox J held that non est factum did not apply on the facts but that the transfer was voidable for fraud. He ordered rectification against the Hammonds but refused it against the Building Society. On appeal against this refusal.

Held. No rectification against the Building Society.

Scott LJ: The transfer of 4 September 1979 was induced by the fraud of Mr and Mrs Hammond. It was voidable but not void. The building society advanced £15,000 to the Hammonds on the security of the charge which they executed and which was subsequently registered. The question is whether the court has power under section 82 of the Land Registration Act 1925 to order the register to be rectified by deletion of the entry of the building society's registered charge in the charges register. The question is primarily one of construction of the statutory language used in section 82. Section 82, as amended by sections 24 and 32 of, and Schedule 5 to, the Administration of Justice Act 1977, provides:

'(1) The register may be rectified pursuant to an order of the court or by the registrar, subject to an appeal to the court, in any of the following cases, but subject to the provisions of this section:—(a) Subject to any express provisions of this Act to the contrary, where a court of competent jurisdiction has decided that any person is entitled to any estate right or interest in or to any registered land or charge, and as a consequence of such decision such court is of opinion that a rectification of the register is required, and makes an order to that effect; (b) Subject to any express provision of this Act to the contrary, where the court, on the application in the prescribed manner of any person who is aggrieved by any entry made in, or by the omission of any entry from, the register, or by any default being made, or unnecessary delay taking place, in the making of any entry in the register, makes an order for the rectification of the register; (c) In any case and at any time with the consent of all persons interested; (d) Where the court or the registrar is satisfied that any entry in the register has been obtained by fraud; (e) Where two or more persons are, by mistake, registered as proprietors of the same registered estate or of the same charge; (f) Where a mortgagee has been registered as proprietor of the land instead of as proprietor of a charge and a right of redemption is subsisting; (g) Where a legal estate has been registered in the name of a person who if the land had not been registered would not have been the estate owner; and (h) In any other case where, by reason of any error or omission in the register, or by reason of any entry made under a mistake, it may be deemed just to rectify the register. (2) The register may be rectified under this section, notwithstanding that the rectification may affect any estates, rights, charges, or interests acquired or protected by registration, or by any entry on the register, or otherwise. (3) The register shall not be rectified, except for the purpose of giving effect to an overriding interest or an order of the court, so as to affect the title of the proprietor who is in possession—(a) unless the proprietor has caused or substantially contributed to the error or omission by fraud or lack of proper care; or (c) unless for any other reason, in any particular case, it is considered that it would be unjust not to rectify the register against him.... (5) The registrar shall obey the order of any competent court in relation to any registered land on being served with the order or an official copy thereof.'

It is convenient to refer at this point to section 83 of the Act, which makes provision for an indemnity to be given to those suffering loss by reason of the rectification of the register and, in certain circumstances, to those suffering loss where rectification is refused.

Section 83, as amended by section 3 of the Land Registration and Land Charges Act 1971, provides so far as relevant:

'(1) Subject to the provisions of this Act to the contrary, any person suffering loss by reason of any rectification of the register under this Act shall be entitled to be indemnified. (2) Where an error or omission has occurred in the register, but the register is not rectified, any person suffering loss by reason of such error or omission, shall, subject to the provisions of this Act, be entitled to be indemnified.... (4) Subject as hereafter provided, a proprietor of any registered land or charge claiming in good faith under a forged disposition shall, where the register is rectified, be deemed to have suffered loss by reason of such rectification and shall be entitled to be indemnified under this Act. (5) No indemnity shall be payable under this Act in any of the following cases:—(a) where the applicant or a person from whom he derives title (otherwise than under a disposition for valuable consideration which is registered or protected on the register) has caused or substantially contributed to the loss by fraud or lack of proper care; ... (6) Where an indemnity is paid in respect of the loss of an estate or interest in or charge on land the amount so paid shall not exceed—(a) Where the register is not rectified, the value of the estate, interest or charge at the time when the error or omission which caused the loss was made; (b) Where the register is rectified, the value (if there had been no rectification) of the estate, interest or charge, immediately before the time of rectification.'

If an order of rectification is to be made the case must be brought within at least one of paragraphs (a) to (h) of section 82(1). The dispute in the present case is as to the breadth of the power conferred by paragraphs (a) and (b) and, to a lesser extent, (d) and (h). There is no doubt but that, if Mrs Steed's signature had been forged or if the non est factum plea had been made good, the case would have fallen squarely within paragraph (g). In neither case, if the land had been unregistered, would the Hammonds or the building society have obtained a legal estate. I cannot see any reasonable basis on which an order of rectification could have been withheld. If, however, as is the case, the transfer is only voidable, paragraph (g) does not apply. It is plain that, if title to the property had been unregistered, Mr Steed would have had no remedy against the building society. He would have recovered the property from the Hammonds but the property would have remained subject to the charge. It is submitted, however, that paragraphs (a), (b), (d) or (h) can, since title is registered, be prayed in aid. This submission is made on the footing that, under one or more of these paragraphs, the court is given a general discretion to order rectification in any case in which it may be thought just to do so. If the submission is right, then section 82, or its statutory predecessors, achieved a remarkable and unnoticed change in the substantive law. If the discretion can be exercised where there has been a fraudulent misrepresentation, as in the present case, it must be exercisable also where a merely innocent misrepresentation has been made. It would, as Mr Lloyd conceded, be exercisable also in a case where no misrepresentation inducing the transaction could be pointed to but where a registered proprietor had entered into a transaction under a misapprehension for which the other party to the transaction was not responsible, a misapprehension as to the value of the property, for example. Mr Lloyd said that in such a case the discretion to order rectification against a bona fide purchaser, such as the building society in the present case, would be very unlikely ever to be exercised. But the proposition that the discretionary power contended for can be spelled out of the statutory language is, to me, so startling as to require the premise of the proposition to be very carefully examined.

There is a sense in which the power to rectify under section 82 is undoubtedly discretionary. The words, in subsection (1) are 'may be rectified'. Section 83(2) shows that rectification is not automatic. The power to rectify may, in a particular case, be present but, nonetheless, there is a general discretion to refuse rectification. It does not follow, however, that there is, in every case, a general discretion to grant rectification. The power to grant rectification is limited in subsection (1) to 'any of the following cases.' The power to order rectification must, therefore, be found within one or other of the subsection (1) paragraphs and cannot be spelled out of the words 'may be rectified.'

Paragraphs (a) and (b) provide a power to rectify that can only be exercised by the court. The power conferred by the other paragraphs can be exercised either by the registrar or by the court. Paragraph (a) enables an order of rectification to be made where the court 'has decided that any person is entitled to any estate right or interest in or to any registered land or charge....' This, in my judgment, is a clear reference to an entitlement under the substantive law. An example would be a case, such as Mr Steed's case against the Hammonds, for the setting aside of a transaction on the ground of misrepresentation or some other sufficient cause. Another example would be the successful assertion of a possessory title. A third example might be the assertion of a right by a beneficiary under a trust who had become absolutely entitled to the land. In each of these cases, once the entitlement had been established the court would have power under paragraph (a) to order the register to be rectified so as to reflect the entitlement. But paragraph (a) does not, in my judgment, give any substantive cause of action where none before existed. It does not enable a voidable transaction to be set aside as against a bona fide purchaser who has acquired by registration a legal estate. And if no entitlement as against such a purchaser can be established, paragraph (a) does not, in my judgment, enable the register to be rectified as against such a purchaser. Paragraph (a) does not assist Mr Steed in his rectification claim against the building society.

Paragraph (b) is the paragraph on which Mr Lloyd pinned his main hopes. It applies, he submitted, whenever any person is 'aggrieved' by an entry on the register. Paragraph (b) is something of a puzzle, not least because the form of the 'application' is not 'prescribed' by any rules made under the Act. The same language was used in section 96 of the [Land Transfer] Act of 1875, but there, too, no form of application was 'prescribed'. The legislative intention underlying paragraph (b) and its statutory predecessor is difficult to identify with clarity. The reference to 'the application in the prescribed manner' makes me believe that it was contemplated that some form of summary process would be prescribed in order to enable speedy relief to be given in clear cases. Be that as it may, the real question at issue is whether the provision was intended simply to provide a remedy in respect of proprietary rights that either entitled the proprietor to have some entry made on the register or entitled the proprietor to have some entry removed from the register or whether the provision should be construed as creating a new cause of action entitling the court to make rectification orders as it might in its discretion think fit in favour of persons who would not under substantive law, apart from paragraph (b), have any proprietary rights which they could assert against the registered proprietor or chargee. In my judgment, the question has only to be put for the answer to be apparent. Parliament could not have intended paragraph (b) to produce new substantive rights in respect of registered land, enabling registered dispositions to be set aside and removed from the register in circumstances where, if the land had not been registered, no cause of action would have existed. In my judgment, paragraph (b), like paragraph (a), provides a remedy but does not create any new substantive rights or causes of action.

The scope of paragraph (c) is self-evident but not relevant in the present case.

Paragraph (d) too was relied on by Mr Lloyd. He contended that since the transfer had been induced by the Hammonds' fraud, both the registration of the Hammonds as proprietors and the registration of the building society's legal charge could be described as having been 'obtained by fraud.' In my judgment, that is a misreading of the paragraph. The paragraph is directed, in my opinion, to fraud practised upon the Land Registry in order to obtain the entry in question. No fraud was used to obtain the entry on the charges register of the building society's legal charge.

This construction of paragraph *(d)* derives support from the language used in section 174(1) *(c)* of the Law of Property Act 1922, the statutory predecessor of paragraph *(d)*. Section 174(1)*(c)* enabled the register to be rectified:

'Where the court or the registrar is satisfied that the registration of . . . a charge, mortgage, or other entry in the register . . . has been obtained by fraud, by annulling the registration, notice or other entry . . .'

This provision was reduced to its present succinct form in the Law of Property (Amendment) Act 1924: see section 8 and Schedule 8, paragraph 16. It is the *registration* that must be obtained by fraud.

The registration of a forged transfer could, in my opinion, at least if the application for registration had been made by the forger, be annulled under paragraph *(d)*. The entry would have been obtained by fraud in the presenting of a forged transfer for registration. But if a voidable disposition were registered before being avoided, I would doubt whether the register could be rectified under paragraph *(d)*, even if the disposition were voidable on account of fraud. In such a case the entry on the register would not, it seems to me, have been obtained by fraud. Rectification could, of course, in such a case be obtained under paragraph *(a)* or paragraph *(b)*. Whether or not that is right, and it need not be decided in this case, a registered disposition made by the fraudster to a bona fide purchaser cannot in my judgment be removed from the register under paragraph *(d)*. The registration would not have been obtained by fraud. So paragraph *(d)* cannot in my judgment assist Mr Steed as against the building society.

Paragraphs *(e)* and *(f)* are self-explanatory and are of no relevance to this case.

Paragraph *(g)* does not, in the event that the transfer is voidable, assist Mr Steed as against the building society. It is, however, an important paragraph so far as an understanding of the scheme of section 82(1) is concerned.

In my opinion the scheme is reasonably clear. Paragraphs *(a)* and *(b)* give power to the court to make orders of rectification in order to give effect to property rights which have been established in an action or which are clear. Paragraph *(c)* enables orders to be made by consent. The remaining paragraphs, *(d)* to *(h)*, are intended to enable errors to be corrected. Paragraph *(d)*, paragraph *(e)*, Paragraph *(f)* and paragraph *(g)* each deals with an error of a particular character. But, since these paragraphs might not cover comprehensively all errors, paragraph *(h)* was added as a catch-all provision to cover any other errors. The breadth of the catch-all provision was, I imagine, the reason why it was thought appropriate to make the power exercisable 'where . . . it may be deemed just to rectify the register.' There are no comparable words in any of the other paragraphs.

Paragraph *(h)* is relied on by Mr Lloyd. But in order for the paragraph to be applicable some 'error or omission in the register' or some 'entry made under a mistake' must be shown. The entry in the charges register of the building society's legal charge was not an error and was not made under a mistake. The legal charge was executed by the Hammonds, who were at the time transferees under a transfer executed by Mrs Steed as attorney for the registered proprietor. The voidable transfer had not been set aside. The registration of the Hammonds as proprietors took place at the same time as the registration of the legal charge. Neither registration was an error. Neither entry was made under a mistake. So the case for rectification cannot be brought under paragraph *(h)*.

As a matter of principle, if, as I think, the defendant's case for rectification as against the building society cannot be brought under any of the paragraphs of section 82(1), I would conclude that that must be an end to the rectification claim. Mr Lloyd, however, has relied strongly on passages in the judgment of Slade LJ in *Argyle Building Society v Hammond* (1984) 49 P & CR 148. Before I come to those passages, it is convenient to refer to such earlier authority as there is.

His Lordship referred to *Chowood v Lyall (No 2)* [1930] 2 Ch 156 and *Calgary & Edmonton Co Ltd v Discount Bank (Overseas) Ltd* [1971] 1 WLR 81, and continued:

In *Re Leighton's Conveyance* [1936] 1 All ER 667 a non est factum case was raised. The plaintiff sought rectification first, against her daughter, who had fraudulently induced the plaintiff to sign a transfer leading to the daughter's registration as proprietor and, secondly, against chargees who, without any notice of the daughter's fraud, had advanced money to the daughter on the security of registered charges. The case was, therefore, very similar to the present case. Luxmoore J ordered rectification as against the daughter but, having concluded that the non est factum plea failed, he dismissed the rectification claim against the chargees. He said, at p. 673:

'I am satisfied that there are no grounds on which I can say that these charges are bad, but with regard to the equity of redemption I am satisfied on the evidence that what Mrs Wardman did was at the request of and in reliance on her daughter, and under her influence.... It follows that the conveyance to Mrs Bergin can have no effect as against Mrs Wardman, and she is still entitled to the equity of redemption in the property.... With regard to the charges register, there is no ground for interfering with it and directing any rectification. They are good charges and remain enforceable against the property.'

It was not stated in the judgment which paragraph or paragraphs of section 82(1) Luxmoore J regarded as applicable, but the report of the argument of counsel and an editorial note at p. 667 suggest that the judge was invited to act under paragraph (d). It appears also from the report of argument that rectification as against the daughter was conceded and that the only issue in the case against the chargees was the non est factum issue. In my opinion, paragraph (a), rather than paragraph (d), provided the power to rectify as against the daughter. If the non est factum case had succeeded, paragraph (g) also would have been in point, both against the daughter and against the chargees. It was not suggested by counsel for the mother that, if the non est factum plea failed, she might nonetheless be entitled to rectification against the chargees. And there is nothing in the judgment of Luxmoore J to indicate that, having rejected the non est factum plea, he thought that he had any discretionary power to order rectification of the charges register.

I now come to the judgment of Slade LJ in *Argyle Building Society v Hammond* (1984) 49 P & CR 148. For the purposes of his judgment Slade LJ assumed that the allegation of forgery would succeed. He assumed nothing else. References to the 'assumed facts' are references to the facts regarding the forgery. At p. 157, having set out the text of section 82(1), he said:

'First, registers of title made pursuant to the Act of 1925 consist of three parts, namely the property register, the proprietorship register and the charges register. The jurisdiction to rectify under the subsection plainly extends to all or any of these parts. Secondly, on the assumed facts in the present case, the court would, in our judgment, have clear jurisdiction to rectify the proprietorship register of the house by substituting the name of the appellant for that of Mr and Mrs Hammond, since the case would fall within all or any of sub-paragraphs (a), (b), (d), (g) and (h) of section 82(1). The present argument relates to the possibility or otherwise of rectification of the charges register.'

At p. 158 he made clear the opinion of the court that, on the assumed facts, the court would have power to rectify the charges register against the mortgagees as well as the proprietorship register against the Hammonds. I would respectfully agree, save that, for the reasons I have given, I do not think the case would come within paragraph *(d)*. It would come, in my opinion, within paragraphs *(a)*, *(b)*, *(g)* and, perhaps, *(h)*.

Slade LJ then referred to *Re Leighton's Conveyance* [1936] 1 All ER 667, cited the passage from the judgment of Luxmoore J that I have cited and continued, at p. 160:

'Reverting to the decision at first instance in the *Leighton* case, the report of the argument shows that the provisions of section 82(1) and (2) of the Act of 1925 were drawn to the attention of Luxmoore J. We feel no doubt that he would have appreciated that, even in the absence of a successful plea of forgery or non est factum, the section would in terms have conferred a discretion on the court to rectify the charges register, even as against the innocent chargees. Nevertheless, it is readily intelligible that Luxmoore J should have considered that, when the discretion fell to be exercised, the equities were all on one side—that is to say in favour of the chargees, who had acted on the faith of a document of transfer which the mother had herself executed after having failed to make inquiries which would have revealed that the document related to the property. If the title to the land had not been registered, the title of the daughter would, at worst, have been voidable, not void; and under general principles of equity, mortgagees from the daughter in good faith and for value, without notice of the facts giving rise to the voidability, would have acquired a good title to their mortgages. We can see no reason why the court in the *Leighton* case should have regarded the equities as being any different, as between the mother and the chargees, merely because the land happened to be registered land.'

In my respectful opinion, this analysis of *Re Leighton's Conveyance* is not justified by Luxmoore J's judgment. There is nothing in the judgment or in the report of counsel's argument to suggest that the possibility of rectification against the chargees, in the absence of a successful plea of forgery or non est factum, was ever considered. At p. 162 of his judgment Slade LJ commented:

'in a case where one or more of the conditions of section 82(1) are fulfilled, the court always has at least theoretical discretion to rectify any part of the register, even as against innocent third parties...'

I would respectfully agree with this comment, based as it is on the premise that the case can be brought within one or other of the paragraphs of section 82(1). But Slade LJ then went on to distinguish the case of a party 'deprived of his title as a result of a forged document which he did not execute' from the case where the party 'has been deprived as a result of a document which he himself executed, albeit under a mistake induced by fraud' and commented that 'when the court comes to exercise its discretion, different considerations may well apply.' The paragraph of section 82(1) under which the latter case could be brought was not identified. On the true construction of section 82(1) there is not, in my opinion, any paragraph under which the latter case could be brought.

Mr Lloyd's argument that the court has a general discretionary power to order rectification of the register was based on the passages from Slade LJ's judgment to which I have referred. The passages were not part of the ratio of the decision by which we are bound and with which I respectfully agree. A voidable transfer was not part of the 'assumed facts' on which the ratio was based. In my judgment, the obiter passages, regarding voidable transfers and innocent third parties claiming thereunder, were based on an incorrect construction of section 82(1) and should not be followed.

In my opinion, if the defendant's non est factum case is rejected, the court has no power under section 82(1) to order rectification as against the building society.

It is strictly unnecessary for me to deal with the issue of discretion which only arises if the court has power to rectify. Knox J refused rectification as a matter of discretion. He held that as between the defendant and the building society 'all the equities are on the building society's side'. This would certainly be so if the land were unregistered. But under section 83(1) the building society, if rectification were ordered, would have what seems to me to be an unimpeachable statutory right to an indemnity against the loss it would thereby suffer. On the other hand, if rectification were refused, the defendant would not be able to claim an indemnity under section 83(2). Mr Lloyd accepted, rightly, that, since the registration of the building society's charge was not an 'error or omission,' the case would not come within section 83(2). The financial consequences to the parties of ordering or refusing rectification make it difficult to weigh the 'equities.' If rectification were ordered, the loss would fall not upon the building society but upon the public purse. If rectification were refused, the public purse would be saved the burden of paying an indemnity. I mention these matters not in order to indicate any disagreement with Knox J's conclusions on discretion but because the indemnity provisions in section 83 seem to me to underline that the legislature did not contemplate the power of rectification being exercisable under section 82 except in cases either where an error or omission had occurred in the register, i.e. paragraphs (d) to (h), or where a substantive cause of action against the registered proprietor required the register to be rectified, i.e. paragraphs (a) and (b).

In 'error or omission' cases, i.e. in cases coming within paragraphs (d) to (h), an indemnity would, if rectification were refused, be available under section 83(2), subject always to section 83(5) (a). In cases within paragraphs (a) and (b) but not within any of paragraphs (d) to (h), e.g. cases in which voidable transactions are set aside and, as a consequence, rectification of the register is required, it is difficult to construct any scenario in which rectification could be withheld. The construction of section 82(1) that I have suggested seems to me to mesh with and to explain the scheme of indemnity contained in section 83. The 'general discretion' approach to section 82(1) does not.

For the reasons I have given I would dismiss this appeal.

(b) Double conveyance. Overriding interest

Epps v Esso Petroleum Co Ltd
[1973] 1 WLR 1071[91] (ChD, **Templeman J**)

In 1935 Alfred Clifford owned 4 Darland Avenue, Gillingham, Kent, and, on the north side of it, the adjoining Darland Garage. In that year he leased both to Mr Jones. In 1955 his personal representatives conveyed the house to Mrs Jones in fee simple, together with an extra 11 foot strip of frontage on the north side of the wall dividing the home from the garage. The object was to provide space for a garage at the home. Mrs Jones covenanted to erect a new wall on the new boundary, but never did. In 1956 Clifford's personal representatives granted a new lease of Darland Garage to Mr Jones, and in error the plan included the 11 foot strip. In 1959 they conveyed the garage, subject to the lease, to Julian Ball, and included the strip. The Land Registration Act 1925 had become applicable, and Ball became first registered proprietor of the garage

---

[91] (1973) 37 Conv (NS) 284 (F. R. Crane).

and strip, with the consequence that LRA 1925, section 5 deprived Mrs Jones of the strip and vested it in Ball, subject to any overriding interests affecting the strip. In 1964 Ball conveyed the garage and strip to the defendants who became the second registered proprietors with absolute title. In 1968 the personal representatives of Mrs Jones conveyed 4 Darland Avenue and the strip to Mr and Mrs Epps, who obtained first registration of the house without the strip.

On a summons by Mr and Mrs Epps for rectification of the register, so as to exclude the strip from the defendant's title on the register, the plaintiffs argued that Mrs Jones was in possession of the strip at the time of the conveyance to the defendant in 1964; and, therefore, Mrs Jones and her estate had an overriding interest under LRA 1925, section 70(1)(*g*)[92] by virtue of that possession.

Held. Rectification refused.

Templeman J: Section 82(1) of the Land Registration Act provides that the register may be rectified where, inter alia, as in the present case, a legal estate has been registered in the name of a person who, if the land had not been registered, would not have been the estate owner. That describes the defendants. Section 82(3) limits the exercise of the power of rectification conferred by section 82(1). The limitation is in these terms:

> 'The register shall not be rectified, except for the purpose of giving effect to an overriding interest, so as to affect the title of the proprietor who is in possession—unless...'

and then it specifies three conditions,[93] one of which must be satisfied, if rectification is to be granted....

Condition *(c)* provides for rectification and I quote:

> 'unless for any other reason, in any particular case, it is considered that it would be unjust not to rectify the register against...' [the registered proprietor][94]

Mr Cullen, for the plaintiffs, submitted that when Mrs Jones was deprived of her legal estate in fee simple by the mistaken registration of Mr Ball as proprietor, Mrs Jones retained or acquired, and her successors in title, down to and including the plaintiffs, acquired an equitable interest in fee simple. The registered proprietor, first Mr Ball and now the defendants, acquired the legal estate, subject to the equitable interest of Mrs Jones and her successors. Effect should be given to that equitable interest by rectification. The limitation on the exercise of the power of rectification, which is to be found in section 82(3), does not apply where rectification is required to give effect to an overriding interest. The equitable interest of Mrs Jones and her successors in title is an overriding interest.

By section 70(1)(*g*)[95] overriding interests include the rights of every person in actual occupation of the land or in receipt of the rents and profits thereof, save where inquiry is made of such person and the rights are not disclosed. Mrs Jones and her successors in title were in actual occupation, because Mrs Jones, and later the plaintiffs, parked a car on the disputed

---

[92] See now LRA 2002, Sch. 3, para. 2; p. 196, below.
[93] Reduced to two by AJA 1977, s. 24.
[94] See now LRA 2002, Sch. 4, para. 3(2)(b) and para. 6(2)(b); p. 144, above.
[95] See now LRA 2002, Sch. 3, para. 2; p. 196, below. The words 'or in receipt of the rents and profits thereof' no longer appear in the 2002 Act.

strip. Mr Ball and the defendants acquired the disputed strip subject to the overriding interests of Mrs Jones and her successors constituted by an equitable interest protected by actual occupation. The defendants never were in possession or, at any rate, ceased to be in possession when the plaintiffs erected their fence in 1968. Thus far Mr Cullen. . . .

The claim put forward by Mr Cullen on behalf of the plaintiffs to an overriding interest depends on whether Mr Jones was in actual occupation of the disputed strip when the defendants became the registered proprietor of the disputed strip in 1964. The contention put forward by Mr Cullen that the defendants were not in possession depends on whether they went into possession of the disputed strip when they became the registered proprietor and remained in possession until after the plaintiffs completed their purchase in 1968. Mr Brodie for the defendants took up a position at the opposite pole. He submitted that even if Mr Jones was in actual occupation he occupied in his capacity as tenant of Mr Ball. Alternatively, the occupation of Mr Jones could not protect any equitable interest vested in the probate judge at the date when the defendants became the registered proprietors of the disputed strip in 1964.

I reject these submissions of Mr Brodie. If Mr Jones was in actual occupation when the defendants completed their purchase of the disputed strip then his occupation in the present circumstances sufficed to assert and protect any equitable interest of Mrs Jones and her estate so as to constitute an overriding interest, and sufficed also to defeat the claim by the defendants to be in possession. . . .

In my judgment, the fact that the defendants were not the original proprietors, but subsequent transferees, is only one element to be considered in the exercise of the discretion conferred by section 82(1) and section 82(3)(c) of the Land Registration Act 1925. In the confrontation envisaged by section 82(1) and in particular by section 82(1)(g), between, on the one hand, the registered proprietor, who is a victim of double conveyancing, and the first purchaser or his successors, deprived of the legal estate by registration, the court must first determine whether the registered proprietor is in possession. If the registered proprietor is not in possession then section 82(3) does not apply, and the court will normally grant rectification: see *Chowood Ltd v Lyall (No 2)* [1930] 2 Ch 156. A fortiori if the registered proprietor is not in possession but the applicant has an overriding interest constituted by an equitable interest protected by actual occupation, the court will grant rectification; see *Bridges v Mees* [1957] Ch 475 at 486. However, the power of rectification given by section 82(1) never ceases to be discretionary, so that where section 82(3) does not apply there may still be circumstances which defeat the claim for rectification.

If the registered proprietor is in possession, the applicant for rectification will not normally be in actual occupation, and one of the conditions specified in section 82(3) must be satisfied if rectification is to be granted. . . .

It follows that the crucial questions in the present case are, first, whether Mr Jones was in actual occupation of the disputed strip when the defendants completed purchase in 1964; secondly, whether the defendants were in possession at the date when the plaintiffs completed their purchase of 4 Darland Avenue in 1968; and if those questions are decided in favour of the defendants, thirdly, whether it would be unjust not to rectify against them.

In *Hodgson v Marks* [1971] Ch 892 at 931, Russell LJ said, on actual occupation as an ingredient of an overriding interest, that he was prepared for the purpose of that case to assume, without necessarily accepting, that section 70(1)(g) of the Land Registration Act 1925 is designed only to apply to a case in which the occupation is such in point of fact as would in the case of unregistered land affect a purchaser with constructive notice of the rights of the occupier. Then Russell LJ said, at 932:

> 'I do not think it desirable to attempt to lay down a code or catalogue of situations in which a person other than the vendor should be held to be in occupation of unregistered land for the purpose of constructive notice of his rights, or in actual occupation of registered land for the purposes of section 70(1)(g). It must depend on the circumstances, and a wise purchaser or vendor will take no risks. Indeed, however wise he may be he may have no ready opportunity of finding out; but, nevertheless, the law will protect the occupier.'

In my judgment Mr Jones was not in actual occupation of the disputed strip when the defendants completed their purchase of Darland Garage and was not thereafter in actual occupation.

Mr Jones gave evidence that every night he parked his car on the disputed strip, and sometimes the car was there during the day. Mr Jones's recollection, not unnaturally, was not very reliable, and I find that he sometimes parked his car on the disputed strip, but how often and when no one can now determine with any certainty. But even if Mr Jones regularly parked his car on the disputed strip I do not consider that this constituted actual occupation of the disputed strip in the circumstances of the present case. I reach this conclusion for the following reasons: first, the parking of a car on a strip 11 feet wide by 80 feet long does not actually occupy the whole, or a substantial, or any defined part of that disputed strip for the whole or any defined time. Secondly, the parking of a car on an unidentified piece of land, apparently comprised in garage premises, is not an assertion of actual occupation of anything.

In addition to these two reasons there are circumstances which show that, not only was Mr Jones not in actual occupation, but on the contrary that the defendants were.

His Lordship reviewed the evidence and continued:

In my judgment, therefore, section 82(3) does apply because the Jones's and the plaintiffs had no overriding interest protected by actual occupation and because the defendants were in possession. There remains the question, under condition (c) of section 82(3) whether it would be unjust not to rectify against the defendants.

In my judgment, justice in the present case lies wholly with the defendants and not with the plaintiffs....

In my judgment, whereas the defendants bought the disputed strip, the plaintiffs bought a law suit, thanks to the default of their vendor in not taking steps to assert ownership and possession of the disputed strip, and thanks to the failure of the plaintiffs to make before completion the inquiries which they made immediately after completion.

Mr Cullen put forward one additional circumstance which he argued, with some force, tilted the balance of justice in favour of rectification. That circumstance, he submitted, was that if the register is rectified the defendants can recover compensation based on the 1973 value of the disputed strip, but if the register is not rectified the plaintiffs cannot recover compensation. This argument is founded on section 83 of the Land Registration Act 1925 which deals with compensation. Section 83(1) provides that, subject to the provisions of the Act to the contrary, any person suffering loss by reason of any rectification of the register under the Act shall be entitled to be indemnified. That will be the position of the defendants if I rectify. Section 83(2) provides that where an error or omission has occurred in the register but the register is not rectified, any person suffering loss by reason of such error or omission shall, subject to the provisions of the Act, be entitled to be indemnified. That is the position of the plaintiffs, if I do not rectify.

By section 83[8][96] where indemnity is paid in respect of the loss of an estate or interest in or charge on land the amount so paid shall not exceed (a), where the register is not rectified the value of the estate interest or charge at the time when the error or omission which caused the loss was made. In other words, if I do not rectify then the plaintiffs' indemnity is reduced to the value of the disputed strip as at 1959 when the error was made. Subsection [8](*b*), on the other hand, says that where the register is rectified the indemnity is not to exceed the value if there had been no rectification of the estate, interest or charge immediately before the time of rectification. This would apply to the defendants. So that the legislature provides 1959 values for the plaintiffs and 1973 values for the defendants. The matter does not end there, however, because by subsection [12] there is a further limitation on indemnity. Subsection [12] provides that a liability to pay indemnity under the Act shall be deemed a simple contract debt and for the purposes of the Limitation Act the cause of action shall be deemed to arise at the time when the claimant knows or, but for his own default, might have known of the existence of his claim. Whether or not that applies to the plaintiffs, it clearly does not affect the defendants; first, because they are not claimants; and, secondly, because they must have been in complete innocence of anything wrong until the plaintiffs came on the scene and raised the question of where the true boundary lay . . .

This is a case, in my judgment, in which if an order for rectification is made the defendants will be entitled to indemnity on 1973 values, and if the claim for rectification is refused then they will keep the land, but the plaintiffs will not get compensation.

The question I have to determine is whether that is sufficient to upset the justice of the defendants' claim that there should not be rectification in the present instance. Is it sufficient—and this is the test—to make it unjust not to rectify the register against the defendants? Mr Cullen pointed out that as far as the defendants are concerned the disputed strip formed, he calculated, 4 per cent of the garage premises. He said it could not make a lot of difference to the defendant's garage; on the other hand, it was of importance to 4 Darland Avenue because it provided a private garage, an asset which is important in commuter territory.

In my judgment, however, this cannot be solved merely on the question of money. The defendants bought the land; they bought it to exploit for their commercial purposes; they did not buy it in order to sell a strip for a 1973 value, which in real terms will not, in my judgment, adequately indemnify them. Although the strip is at the back of the garage, in the same way as it could be used as a private garage for 4 Darland Avenue, so it could be used by the defendants for commercial purposes, and in fact they say now they intend to use it in connection with a car wash; if they are deprived of it they will be in considerable difficulty, and will not have all the facilities which a modern garage requires. I think that may be putting it a bit high, but the fact of the matter is that this strip is worth more to the defendants than the pounds, shillings and pence which they will receive by indemnity, even on a 1973 basis.

Accordingly, in my judgment, that argument is not sufficient to overturn all the other arguments in favour of the defendants, and I decline to order rectification of the register.[97]

[96] These sections are renumbered as a result of the substituted s. 83 by LRA 1997, s. 2.

[97] See also *Malory Enterprises Ltd v Cheshire Homes (UK) Ltd* [2002] Ch 216; H & B, para. 15.7, and criticism by C. Harpum in *Rationalizing Property, Equity and Trusts: Essays in Honour of Edward Burn* (ed. Getzler), chap. 9; [2009] Conv 127 (A. Hill-Smith).

(c) Effect of rectification

In **Sainsbury's Supermarkets Ltd v Olympia Homes Ltd** [2006] 1 P & CR 17 Olympia was registered as first proprietor of a parcel of land by mistake: the conveyance was by a person who had only an equitable charge over the property and could therefore not convey the legal title to Olympia. Sainsbury's had a prior equitable interest in the land. MANN J said at 328, para. 96:

I therefore grant the rectification sought by Sainsbury's so as to reflect its interest in the gas board site. [Counsel for Olympia]'s skeleton argument sought to argue that since rectification of the register operates only from the date of the rectification, Olympia took free from such rights as the rectification would seek to protect because Olympia had become the registered owner of the gas board site at a time when the interest was not registered. Registration was not retrospective. In this respect he relied on *Freer v Unwins* [1976] Ch. 288 as setting out the law under the 1925 Act, and Sch. 4 para.8 of the 2002 Act as codifying it. He also relied on a passage in Ruoff & Roper at paras 47.017 and 47.018. This point was not much pressed in oral argument, and in my view rightly so. It is not a good point. What *Freer v Unwins* decides is that where A gets registered as proprietor, then makes a registered disposition to B, and A's title is then rectified to reflect some third party interest, the rectification does not bind B because B took from a registered proprietor at a time when the third party interest was not protected. It does not purport to deal (or deal fully) with how the interest affects A and A's estate. It presupposes that for the future A's estate will be affected by the third party interest, and that therefore A is affected by it for the future. If Mr Gaunt's argument were right it is hard to see how there could ever be a useful rectification. The proprietor could always say that he took his title free from the interest because it was not protected by registration when he was registered with his title; the rectification is not retrospective; therefore it cannot bind him. That cannot be right. In cases such as the present the question is whether the proprietor should have been registered free from the interest in the first place. Rectification is allowed to bring the situation into line with what it should have been had the mistake not been made at the time of registration. To allow the registration itself to bar the effect of that would be to let the tail wag the dog. The non-retrospective aspect of rectification means that pending rectification the land is treated as not being subject to the relevant interest, so that those relying on the state of the register at that time would not be bound by it; but it is not saying any more than that. Once registration takes place the land, and the proprietor against whom it is ordered, is bound. Accordingly, rectification prevents Olympia from saying that it now holds the land free from the relevant rights. It is now that matters.

(ii) *Indemnities*

Schedule 8 sets out the eight grounds which govern the payment of indemnities. They reflect the similar grounds under section 83 of the 1925 Act, which were amended by section 2 of the Land Registration Act 1997. Although redrafted in the 2002 Act, their substance is unimpaired.

LAND REGISTRATION ACT 2002

103 Indemnities

Schedule 8 (which makes provision for the payment of indemnities by the registrar) has effect.

SCHEDULE 8
INDEMNITIES

Entitlement

1 (1) A person is entitled to be indemnified by the registrar if he suffers loss by reason of—

    (a) rectification of the register,

    (b) a mistake whose correction would involve rectification of the register,

    (c) a mistake in an official search,

    (d) a mistake in an official copy,

    (e) a mistake in a document kept by the registrar which is not an original and is referred to in the register,

    (f) the loss or destruction of a document lodged at the registry for inspection or safe custody,

    (g) a mistake in the cautions register, or

    (h) failure by the registrar to perform his duty under section 50.

  (2) For the purposes of sub-paragraph (1)(a)—

    (a) any person who suffers loss by reason of the change of title under section 62 is to be regarded as having suffered loss by reason of rectification of the register, and

    (b) the proprietor of a registered estate or charge claiming in good faith under a forged disposition is, where the register is rectified, to be regarded as having suffered loss by reason of such rectification as if the disposition had not been forged.

  (3) No indemnity under sub-paragraph (1)(b) is payable until a decision has been made about whether to alter the register for the purpose of correcting the mistake; and the loss suffered by reason of the mistake is to be determined in the light of that decision.

Mines and minerals

2 No indemnity is payable under this Schedule on account of—

    (a) any mines or minerals, or

    (b) the existence of any right to work or get mines or minerals, unless it is noted in the register that the title to the registered estate concerned includes the mines or minerals.

Claimant's fraud or lack of care

5 (1) No indemnity is payable under this Schedule on account of any loss suffered by a claimant—

    (a) wholly or partly as a result of his own fraud, or

    (b) wholly as a result of his own lack of proper care.

(2) Where any loss is suffered by a claimant partly as a result of his own lack of proper care, any indemnity payable to him is to be reduced to such extent as is fair having regard to his share in the responsibility for the loss.

(3) For the purposes of this paragraph any fraud or lack of care on the part of a person from whom the claimant derives title (otherwise than under a disposition for valuable consideration which is registered or protected by an entry in the register) is to be treated as if it were fraud or lack of care on the part of the claimant.

Valuation of estates etc.

6 Where an indemnity is payable in respect of the loss of an estate, interest or charge, the value of the estate, interest or charge for the purposes of the indemnity is to be regarded as not exceeding—

(a) in the case of an indemnity under paragraph 1(1)(a), its value immediately before rectification of the register (but as if there were to be no rectification), and

(b) in the case of an indemnity under paragraph 1(1)(b), its value at the time when the mistake which caused the loss was made.

Determination of indemnity by court

7 (1) A person may apply to the court for the determination of any question as to—

(a) whether he is entitled to an indemnity under this Schedule, or

(b) the amount of such an indemnity.

(2) Paragraph 3(1) does not apply to the costs of an application to the court under this paragraph or of any legal proceedings arising out of such an application.

Time limits

8 For the purposes of the Limitation Act 1980—

(a) a liability to pay an indemnity under this Schedule is a simple contract debt, and

(b) the cause of action arises at the time when the claimant knows, or but for his own default might have known, of the existence of his claim.

Interest

9 Rules may make provision about the payment of interest on an indemnity under this Schedule, including[98]—

(a) the circumstances in which interest is payable, and

(b) the periods for and rates at which it is payable.

Recovery of indemnity by registrar

10 (1) Where an indemnity under this Schedule is paid to a claimant in respect of any loss, the registrar is entitled (without prejudice to any other rights he may have)—

(a) to recover the amount paid from any person who caused or substantially contributed to the loss by his fraud, or

---

[98] LRR 2003, r. 195.

(b) for the purpose of recovering the amount paid, to enforce the rights of action referred to in sub-paragraph (2).

(2) Those rights of action are—

(a) any right of action (of whatever nature and however arising) which the claimant would have been entitled to enforce had the indemnity not been paid, and

(b) where the register has been rectified, any right of action (of whatever nature and however arising) which the person in whose favour the register has been rectified would have been entitled to enforce had it not been rectified.

(3) References in this paragraph to an indemnity include interest paid on an indemnity under rules under paragraph 9.

Interpretation

11 (1) For the purposes of this Schedule, references to a mistake in something include anything mistakenly omitted from it as well as anything mistakenly included in it.

(2) In this Schedule, references to rectification of the register are to alteration of the register which—

(a) involves the correction of a mistake, and

(b) prejudicially affects the title of a registered proprietor.

Re Chowood's Registered Land
[1933] Ch 574 (ChD, **Clauson J**)

Lyall had, before the registration of Chowood Ltd (the purchaser of certain freeholds from Ralli) as proprietor of those freeholds with an absolute title, acquired a right under the Limitation Acts[99] to a part thereof. The register was rectified and Chowood Ltd claimed an indemnity under section 83.

Held. Chowood Ltd was not entitled to be indemnified.

Clauson J: Chowood's title was all along subject to the rights which Lyall has succeeded in establishing; and the loss, if it may properly be so called, which Chowood has suffered is that they have not got, and since the Act of 1925 came into force (whatever may have been the position before) have never had title to the strip, except subject to an overriding right in Lyall. That loss was occasioned by Chowood failing to ascertain that, when they bought, Lyall was in possession, and in possession under such circumstances that Ralli could not make a title to the strip. The loss was occasioned by paying Ralli for a strip to which Ralli could not make title. The rectification of the register merely recognised the existing position, and put Chowood in no worse a position than they were in before.

In these circumstances I must hold that Chowood have suffered no loss by reason of the rectification of the register.

---

[99] The Limitation Act 1980 is now however disapplied in relation to registered land: LRA 2002, s. 96; p. 282, below.

QUESTION

What is the effect of registration of a transfer which was

(i) void by virtue of being a forgery, or executed under the doctrine of *non est factum*?

(ii) voidable by virtue of being executed under a misrepresentation (whether fraudulent or not)?

Can the court rectify the register in such cases to remedy the situation?

See LRA 2002, s. 58(1), p. 121, above; Sch. 4, p. 143, above; Law Commission Report on Land Registration for the Twenty-First Century 2001 (Law Com No. 271), para. 9.4; *Norwich and Peterborough Building Society v Steed (No 2)* [1993] Ch 116, p. 145, above; *Malory Enterprises Ltd v Cheshire Homes (UK) Ltd* [2002] Ch 216; H & B, para. 15.7; C. Harpum in *Rationalizing Property, Equity and Trusts: Essays in Honour of Edward Burn* (ed. Getzler), chap. 9; [2009] Conv 127 (A. Hill-Smith). Note carefully the way in which the relevant provisions of LRA 2002 are similar to, or differ from, the provisions of LRA 1925 which were considered in those cases.

VI. DISPOSITIONS OF REGISTERED LAND[100]

A. POWERS OF DISPOSITION[101]

Part III of the Act is concerned with dispositions of registered land by an owner—that is, dealings of various kinds with land which is already registered. Sections 23–26 set out the powers of disposition. Section 26 provides that an owner's right to exercise them is to be taken to be free from any limitation affecting the validity of the disposition, unless the limitation is reflected by an entry in the register (by a notice or a restriction). This follows from the fundamental basis of the registration system that those who rely on the register can assume that its contents are true.[102]

LAND REGISTRATION ACT 2002

23 Owner's powers

(1) Owner's powers in relation to a registered estate consist of—

(a) power to make a disposition of any kind permitted by the general law in relation to an interest of that description, other than a mortgage by demise or sub-demise,[103] and

---

[100] H & B, part 2; Law Com No. 271 (2001), Part IV.

[101] R & R, chap. 13; H & B, chap. 7; Law Com No. 271 (2001), paras 4.2–4.11.

[102] See LRA 2002, s. 58, p. 121, above.

[103] Thereby abolishing the creation of a mortgage by demise or sub-demise; p. 859, below.

(b) power to charge the estate at law with the payment of money.[104]

24 Right to exercise owner's powers

A person is entitled to exercise owner's powers in relation to a registered estate or charge[105] if he is—

(a) the registered proprietor, or

(b) entitled to be registered as the proprietor.[106]

26 Protection of disponees

(1) Subject to subsection (2), a person's right to exercise owner's powers in relation to a registered estate or charge is to be taken to be free from any limitation affecting the validity of a disposition.

(2) Subsection (1) does not apply to a limitation—

(a) reflected by an entry in the register, or

(b) imposed by, or under, this Act.

(3) This section has effect only for the purpose of preventing the title of a disponee being questioned (and so does not affect the lawfulness of a disposition).

Harpum and Bignall, *Registered Land: Law and Practice under the Land Registration Act 2002*, paras 7.7–7.8

7.7 ... This example demonstrates that the protection given by the LRA 2002 does not apply to the transferor who has acted in breach of his obligations. It also shows that although the transferee's title is inviolable, he may be under other forms of liability if he was knowingly implicated in the breach of duty by the transferor.[107]

7.8 A and B hold registered land on trust for C for life, thereafter for D absolutely. Under the terms of the trust, A and B may not sell the land without the prior written consent of D. There is no restriction in the register to ensure that no sale can take place without D's consent. A and B sell the land to E without obtaining D's consent. E's title cannot be challenged by D. A and B are in breach of trust and D can take proceedings against them accordingly. If D could show that E knew that A and B were acting in breach of trust by transferring the land:

– she could not challenge E's title; but

– she could take proceedings against him on the basis that he was liable in equity for the knowing receipt of property transferred in breach of trust.[108]

Liability for knowing receipt is merely a personal liability to account for the loss suffered by D. It does not give rise to a proprietary claim by D against the land which E acquired.

---

[104] Similarly for owner's powers in relation to a registered charge: LRA 2002, s. 23(2), (3), p. 860, below.

[105] Ibid.

[106] On the mode of exercise of owner's powers, see LRA 2002, s. 25.

[107] Cf. (2001) Law Com No. 271, paras 4.10, 4.11.

[108] [See H & M, paras 12.010–12.025; Maudsley & Burn, *Trusts and Trustees: Cases and Materials* (7th edn, 2008), pp. 968–982.]

B. REGISTRABLE DISPOSITIONS[109]

Section 27 of the Land Registration Act 2002 provides that a disposition of a registered estate or charge is required to be completed by registration. Until it is registered, it does not take effect at law. However it may take effect in equity and be valid as an estate contract[110] which needs to be protected by entry of a notice in the register, or as an overriding interest by actual occupation.[111]

LAND REGISTRATION ACT 2002

27 Dispositions required to be registered

(1) If a disposition of a registered estate or registered charge is required to be completed by registration, it does not operate at law until the relevant registration requirements are met.

(2) In the case of a registered estate, the following are the dispositions which are required to be completed by registration—

(a) a transfer,

(b) where the registered estate is an estate in land, the grant of a term of years absolute—

(i) for a term of more than seven years from the date of the grant,

(ii) to take effect in possession after the end of the period of three months beginning with the date of the grant,

(iii) under which the right to possession is discontinuous,[112]

(iv) in pursuance of Part 5 of the Housing Act 1985 (the right to buy), or

(v) in circumstances where section 171A of that Act applies (disposal by landlord which leads to a person no longer being a secure tenant),

(c) where the registered estate is a franchise or manor, the grant of a lease,

(d) the express grant or reservation of an interest of a kind falling within section 1(2) (a) of the Law of Property Act 1925,[113] other than one which is capable of being registered under Part 1 of the Commons Act 2006.[113a]

(e) the express grant or reservation of an interest of a kind falling within section 1(2)(b) or (e) of the Law of Property Act 1925,[114] and

(f) the grant of a legal charge.

[109] R & R, chap. 16; H & B, chap. 8; Law Com No. 271 (2001), paras 4.12–4.31.

[110] Above, p. 29.

[111] For protection of an estate contract in registered land, see above, pp. 84–7; below, pp. 171–220. The importance of s. 27 will be diminished when electronic conveyancing is introduced. Dispositions will then occur and be registered simultaneously. Hence s. 27(1) is disapplied by s. 93(4), p. 228, below. Section 27 replaces similar but not identical provisions of LRA 1925, ss. 18, 21, 123, 123A.

[112] Pp. 328, 357–358, 418, below.

[113] P. 14, above (easement, right or privilege in or over land for an interest equivalent to an estate in fee simple absolute in possession or term of years absolute).

[113a] Amended by Commons Act 2006, Sch. 5, para. 8.

[114] P. 14, above (rentcharge in possession, or right of entry over term of years absolute or annexed to legal rentcharge).

(3) In the case of a registered charge, the following are the dispositions which are required to be completed by registration—

(a) a transfer, and

(b) the grant of a sub-charge.

(4) Schedule 2 to this Act (which deals with the relevant registration requirements) has effect.[115]

(5) This section applies to dispositions by operation of law as it applies to other dispositions, but with the exception of the following—

(a) a transfer on the death or bankruptcy of an individual proprietor,

(b) a transfer on the dissolution of a corporate proprietor, and

(c) the creation of a legal charge which is a local land charge.

(6) Rules may make provision about applications to the registrar for the purpose of meeting registration requirements under this section.

(7) In subsection (2)(d), the reference to express grant does not include grant as a result of the operation of section 62 of the Law of Property Act 1925.[116]

C. REGISTRATION REQUIREMENTS

LAND REGISTRATION ACT 2002

SCHEDULE 2
REGISTRABLE DISPOSITIONS: REGISTRATION REQUIREMENTS

PART 1

REGISTERED ESTATES

Introductory

1 This Part deals with the registration requirements relating to those dispositions of registered estates which are required to be completed by registration.

Transfer

2 (1) In the case of a transfer of whole or part, the transferee, or his successor in title, must be entered in the register as the proprietor.

(2) In the case of a transfer of part, such details of the transfer as rules may provide must be entered in the register in relation to the registered estate out of which the transfer is made.

Lease of estate in land

3 (1) This paragraph applies to a disposition consisting of the grant out of an estate in land of a term of years absolute.

(2) In the case of a disposition to which this paragraph applies—

---

[115] Below.   [116] P. 664, below (easements created by 'implied' grant).

(a) the grantee, or his successor in title, must be entered in the register as the proprietor of the lease, and

(b) a notice in respect of the lease must be entered in the register.

Lease of franchise or manor

4 (1) This paragraph applies to a disposition consisting of the grant out of a franchise or manor of a lease for a term of more than seven years from the date of the grant.

(2) In the case of a disposition to which this paragraph applies—

(a) the grantee, or his successor in title, must be entered in the register as the proprietor of the lease, and

(b) a notice in respect of the lease must be entered in the register.

5 (1) This paragraph applies to a disposition consisting of the grant out of a franchise or manor of a lease for a term not exceeding seven years from the date of the grant.

(2) In the case of a disposition to which this paragraph applies, a notice in respect of the lease must be entered in the register.

Creation of independently registrable legal interest

6 (1) This paragraph applies to a disposition consisting of the creation of a legal rentcharge or profit a prendre in gross, other than one created for, or for an interest equivalent to, a term of years absolute not exceeding seven years from the date of creation.

(2) In the case of a disposition to which this paragraph applies—

(a) the grantee, or his successor in title, must be entered in the register as the proprietor of the interest created, and

(b) a notice in respect of the interest created must be entered in the register.

(3) In sub-paragraph (1), the reference to a legal rentcharge or profit a prendre in gross is to one falling within section 1(2) of the Law of Property Act 1925.[117]

Creation of other legal interest

7 (1) This paragraph applies to a disposition which—

(a) consists of the creation of an interest of a kind falling within section 1(2) (a), (b) or (e) of the Law of Property Act 1925, and

(b) is not a disposition to which paragraph 4, 5 or 6 applies.

(2) In the case of a disposition to which this paragraph applies—

(a) a notice in respect of the interest created must be entered in the register, and

(b) if the interest is created for the benefit of a registered estate, the proprietor of the registered estate must be entered in the register as its proprietor.

(3) Rules may provide for sub-paragraph (2) to have effect with modifications in relation to a right of entry over or in respect of a term of years absolute.

Creation of legal charge

8 In the case of the creation of a charge, the chargee, or his successor in title, must be entered in the register as the proprietor of the charge.

---

[117] P. 14, above.

Introductory

9 This Part deals with the registration requirements relating to those dispositions of registered charges which are required to be completed by registration.[118]

Transfer

10 In the case of a transfer, the transferee, or his successors in title, must be entered in the
register as the proprietor.

Creation of sub-charge

11 In the case of the creation of a sub-charge, the sub-chargee, or his successor in title, must
be entered in the register as the proprietor of the sub-charge.

D. LAND REGISTRY FORM FOR TRANSFER OF
WHOLE OF REGISTERED TITLE

The Land Registration Rules 2003[119] prescribe many forms for particular purposes, including several forms for the transfer of registered land. Form TR1 is to be
used for the transfer of the whole of a registered title or titles: it is reproduced on
pages 167–169.[120]

E. EFFECT OF DISPOSITIONS ON PRIORITIES[121]

Sections 28–31 the Land Registration Act 2002 establish a new statutory scheme of
priorities for registered land.[122] In section 28 the basic rule is that the priority of any
interest, whether the interest is entered on the register or not, is not affected by a disposition of the estate or charge which it affects. In substance, this means that under the
basic rule the relative priority of interests is determined by the date of their creation,
and those who come to the land are bound by all property interests which already
affect the land. To this there are two important exceptions.

---

[118] P. 859, below.

[119] R. 206, Sch. 1. The forms were revised and Sch. 1 was substituted by LR (Amendment) Rules 2008
(SI 2008 No. 1919), r. 11, Sch. 2, with effect from 10 November 2008. The forms are also available for down-
loading from the Land Registry website.

[120] Source acknowledgement: TR1 produced by Land Registry. © Crown copyright material is reproduced with the permission of Land Registry. For an explanation of the provisions of form TR1, see C & B,
pp. 966–969.

[121] R & R, chap. 15; H & B, chap. 9; Law Commission Consultative Document on Land Registration
for the Twenty-First Century 1998 (Law Com No. 254), paras 7.15–7.19; Law Commission Report on Land
Registration for the Twenty-First Century 2001 (Law Com No. 271), Part V. For a useful example on the
operation of the principal rules, see R & R, paras 15.032–15.039.

[122] For the approach of LRA 1925, see C & B, pp. 106–108.

Land Registry
Transfer of whole of registered title(s)

If you need more room than is provided for in a panel, and your software allows, you can expand any panel in the form. Alternatively use continuation sheet CS and attach it to this form.

Leave blank if not yet registered.	**1** Title number(s) of the property:
Insert address including postcode (if any) or other description of the property, for example 'land adjoining 2 Acacia Avenue'.	**2** Property:
	3 Date:
Give full name(s).	**4** Transferor:
Complete as appropriate where the transferor is a company.	**For UK incorporated companies/LLPs** Registered number of company or limited liability partnership including any prefix: **For overseas companies** (a) Territory of incorporation: (b) Registered number in England and Wales including any prefix:
Give full name(s).	**5** Transferee for entry in the register:
Complete as appropriate where the transferee is a company. Also, for an overseas company, unless an arrangement with Land Registry exists, lodge either a certificate in Form 7 in Schedule 3 to the Land Registration Rules 2003 or a certified copy of the constitution in English or Welsh, or other evidence permitted by rule 183 of the Land Registration Rules 2003.	**For UK incorporated companies/LLPs** Registered number of company or limited liability partnership including any prefix: **For overseas companies** (a) Territory of incorporation: (b) Registered number in England and Wales including any prefix:
Each transferee may give up to three addresses for service, one of which must be a postal address whether or not in the UK (including the postcode, if any). The others can be any combination of a postal address, a UK DX box number or an electronic address.	**6** Transferee's intended address(es) for service for entry in the register:
	7 The transferor transfers the property to the transferee

Place 'X' in the appropriate box. State the currency unit if other than sterling. If none of the boxes apply, insert an appropriate memorandum in panel 11.	**8 Consideration** ☐ The transferor has received from the transferee for the property the following sum (in words and figures): ☐ The transfer is not for money or anything that has a monetary value ☐ Insert other receipt as appropriate:
Place 'X' in any box that applies. Add any modifications.	**9 The transferor transfers with** ☐ full title guarantee ☐ limited title guarantee
Where the transferee is more than one person, place 'X' in the appropriate box. Complete as necessary.	**10 Declaration of trust. The transferee is more than one person and** ☐ they are to hold the property on trust for themselves as joint tenants ☐ they are to hold the property on trust for themselves as tenants in common in equal shares ☐ they are to hold the property on trust:
Insert here any required or permitted statement, certificate or application and any agreed covenants, declarations and so on.	**11 Additional provisions**

| The transferor must execute this transfer as a deed using the space opposite. If there is more than one transferor, all must execute. Forms of execution are given in Schedule 9 to the Land Registration Rules 2003. If the transfer contains transferee's covenants or declarations or contains an application by the transferee (such as for a restriction), it must also be executed by the transferee. | 12   Execution |

WARNING
If you dishonestly enter information or make a statement that you know is, or might be, untrue or misleading, and intend by doing so to make a gain for yourself or another person, or to cause loss or the risk of loss to another person, you may commit the offence of fraud under section 1 of the Fraud Act 2006, the maximum penalty for which is 10 years' imprisonment or an unlimited fine, or both.

Failure to complete this form with proper care may result in a loss of protection under the Land Registration Act 2002 if, as a result, a mistake is made in the register.

Under section 66 of the Land Registration Act 2002 most documents (including this form) kept by the registrar relating to an application to the registrar or referred to in the register are open to public inspection and copying. If you believe a document contains prejudicial information, you may apply for that part of the document to be made exempt using Form EX1, under rule 136 of the Land Registration Rules 2003.

© Crown copyright (ref: LR/HO) 07/08

First, under section 29, where there is a *registered* disposition of a registered estate or charge which is made for *valuable consideration*,[123] the basic rule of the order of creation does not apply, and the disponee of the estate or charge is bound only by interests which were already 'protected' at the time of registration of the disposition in his favour—that is:

(a) a registered charge;

(b) an interest which is the subject of a notice in the register;[124]

(c) an unregistered interest which overrides a registered disposition under Schedule 3;[125]

(d) an interest which appears from the register to be excepted from the effect of registration where title is other than absolute, for example, possessory title;

(e) an interest which is incident to a leasehold estate, for example, restrictive covenants in a lease which do not have to be protected by a notice on the register.

The second exception to the basic rule in section 28 is the Inland Revenue charge for unpaid tax (section 31).

LAND REGISTRATION ACT 2002

28 Basic rule

(1) Except as provided by sections 29 and 30, the priority of an interest affecting a registered estate or charge is not affected by a disposition of the estate or charge.

(2) It makes no difference for the purposes of this section whether the interest or disposition is registered.

29 Effect of registered dispositions: estates

(1) If a registrable disposition of a registered estate is made for valuable consideration,[126] completion of the disposition by registration has the effect of postponing to the interest under the disposition any interest affecting the estate immediately before the disposition whose priority is not protected at the time of registration.

(2) For the purposes of subsection (1), the priority of an interest is protected—

(a) in any case, if the interest—

(i) is a registered charge or the subject of a notice in the register,

(ii) falls within any of the paragraphs of Schedule 3, or

(iii) appears from the register to be excepted from the effect of registration, and

---

[123] 'Valuable consideration' does not include marriage consideration or a nominal consideration in money: LRA 2002, s. 132(1) of the 2002 Act. This is narrower than under LRA 1925: above, p. 132, n. 50. This is the modern statutory application of the old equitable doctrine of the bona fide purchaser: above, p. 58.

[124] For the different method of protection of interests under a trust by way of restriction, see p. 175, below.

[125] Pp. 179–220, below.

[126] *Halifax plc v Curry Popeck* [2009] 1 P & CR D7 (fraudulent transaction not for valuable consideration so did not defeat bank's prior charge).

    (b) in the case of a disposition of a leasehold estate, if the burden of the interest is incident to the estate.

  (3) Subsection (2)(a)(ii) does not apply to an interest which has been the subject of a notice in the register at any time since the coming into force of this section.

  (4) Where the grant of a leasehold estate in land out of a registered estate does not involve a registrable disposition, this section has effect as if—

    (a) the grant involved such a disposition, and

    (b) the disposition were registered at the time of the grant.

30 Effect of registered dispositions: charges

  (1) If a registrable disposition of a registered charge is made for valuable consideration, completion of the disposition by registration has the effect of postponing to the interest under the disposition any interest affecting the charge immediately before the disposition whose priority is not protected at the time of registration.

  (2) For the purposes of subsection (1), the priority of an interest is protected—

    (a) in any case, if the interest—

      (i)   is a registered charge or the subject of a notice in the register,

      (ii) falls within any of the paragraphs of Schedule 3, or

      (iii) appears from the register to be excepted from the effect of registration, and

    (b) in the case of a disposition of a charge which relates to a leasehold estate, if the burden of the interest is incident to the estate.

  (3) Subsection (2)(a)(ii) does not apply to an interest which has been the subject of a notice in the register at any time since the coming into force of this section.

31 Inland Revenue charges

The effect of a disposition of a registered estate or charge on a charge under section 237 of the Inheritance Tax Act 1984 (charge for unpaid tax) is to be determined, not in accordance with sections 28 to 30 above, but in accordance with sections 237(6) and 238 of that Act (under which a purchaser in good faith for money or money's worth takes free from the charge in the absence of registration).

VII. PROTECTION OF INTERESTS BY ENTRY ON THE REGISTER[127]

As we have seen, the priority of an interest is protected as against a purchaser of the registered estate for valuable consideration if it is the subject of a notice in the register.[128] The Land Registration Act 1925 designated as 'minor interests'[129]

---

[127] C & B, pp. 973–975; Gray, paras 2.2.49–2.2.52 (restrictions), 8.2.12–8.2.23 (notices); M & W, paras 7.069–7.084; Smith, pp. 232–234; R & R, chaps 42–45; H & B, chap. 10.

[128] LRA 2002, s. 29(2)(a)(i). Similarly, for protection as against a registered chargee for value, s. 30(2)(a)(i); above.

[129] LRA 1925, s. 3(xv).

those interests which needed to be protected on the register, and provided for four categories of entry on the register: notices, cautions, inhibitions and restrictions.[130] The Land Registration Act 2002 provides a simpler scheme: the language of 'minor interests' is not used, and there are only two forms of entry on the register: notices and restrictions, which together cover the whole range of interests which may affect a registered estate.

A. NOTICES[131]

Under the 2002 Act notices are of two kinds: agreed notices and unilateral notices. An agreed notice will be entered on the application of or with the agreement of the registered proprietor of the land affected. A unilateral notice, on the other hand, may be entered without the consent of the proprietor, but the registrar must inform him of the entry so that he may exercise his right to apply for its cancellation. The mere fact of registration of a notice does not mean that the interest is valid; only that, if valid, its priority is protected against a later disposition of the estate for valuable consideration.[132]

Section 33 sets out interests which cannot be protected by a notice. The most important are:

(a) beneficial interests under a trust of land or strict settlement;[133]

(b) leases for a term of three years or less, the title to which is not required to be registered;[134]

(c) restrictive covenants between lessor and lessee so far as relating to the demised premises.[135]

LAND REGISTRATION ACT 2002

32 Nature and effect

(1) A notice is an entry in the register in respect of the burden of an interest affecting a registered estate or charge.

---

[130] LRA 1925, Part IV. Actual notice of the interest which should have been protected, but was not so protected, was irrelevant: LRA 1925, s. 59(6); see, however, *Peffer v Rigg* [1977] 1 WLR 285, p. 222, below. For the detail of the scheme of LRA 1925, see the 8th edn of this book, pp. 165–169. Existing entries made under LRA 1925 continue to have effect: LRA 2002, Sch. 12, paras 1–6.

[131] LRR 2003, Part 7, as amended.   [132] LRA 2002, s. 32(3), below.

[133] The purchaser has no concern with such interests if they are overreached: below, p. 548; and the appropriate method of protection to ensure that overreaching is applied is the entry of a *restriction* on the register: below, p. 175.

[134] Leases granted for more than seven years must be registered; the effect is therefore to allow notices to be entered on the register only of leases granted for a term of more that three years but not more than seven years. Most leases not exceeding seven years will in any event be protected by virtue of being overriding interests: LRA 2002, Sch. 3, para. 1; below, p. 195.

[135] The purchaser will be able to inspect the lease, and therefore discover the covenants. The burden of covenants incident to the leasehold estate have priority in any event on the disposition of the estate: LRA 2002, s. 29(2)(b); above, p. 171.

(2) The entry of a notice is to be made in relation to the registered estate or charge affected by the interest concerned.

(3) The fact that an interest is the subject of a notice does not necessarily mean that the interest is valid, but does mean that the priority of the interest, if valid, is protected for the purposes of sections 29 and 30.

33 Excluded interests

No notice may be entered in the register in respect of any of the following—

  (a) an interest under—

    (i) a trust of land, or

    (ii) a settlement under the Settled Land Act 1925[136]

  (b) a leasehold estate in land which—

    (i) is granted for a term of years of three years or less from the date of the grant, and

    (ii) is not required to be registered,[137]

  (c) a restrictive covenant made between a lessor and lessee, so far as relating to the demised premises,[138]

  (d) an interest which is capable of being registered under Part 1 of the Commons Act 2006,[139] and

  (e) an interest in any coal or coal mine, the rights attached to any such interest and the rights of any person under section 38, 49 or 51 of the Coal Industry Act 1994.

34 Entry on application

(1) A person who claims to be entitled to the benefit of an interest affecting a registered estate or charge may, if the interest is not excluded by section 33, apply to the registrar for the entry in the register of a notice in respect of the interest.

(2) Subject to rules, an application under this section may be for—

  (a) an agreed notice,[140] or

  (b) an unilateral notice.

(3) The registrar may only approve an application for an agreed notice if—

  (a) the applicant is the relevant registered proprietor, or a person entitled to be registered as such proprietor,

  (b) the relevant registered proprietor, or a person entitled to be registered as such proprietor, consents to the entry of the notice, or

  (c) the registrar is satisfied as to the validity of the applicant's claim.

(4) In subsection (3), references to the relevant registered proprietor are to the proprietor of the registered estate or charge affected by the interest to which the application relates.

---

[136] P. 508, below.   [137] P. 418, below.   [138] P. 753, n. 73, below.
[139] Amended by Commons Act 2006, Sch. 5, para. 8; p. 96, above.
[140] LRR 2003, r. 81.

35 Unilateral notices

(1) If the registrar enters a notice in the register in pursuance of an application under section 34(2)(b) ('a unilateral notice'[141]), he must give notice of the entry to—

(a) the proprietor of the registered estate or charge to which it relates, and

(b) such other persons as rules may provide.

(2) A unilateral notice must—

(a) indicate that it is such a notice, and

(b) identify who is the beneficiary of the notice.

(3) The person shown in the register as the beneficiary of a unilateral notice, or such other person as rules may provide, may apply to the registrar for the removal of the notice from the register.

36 Cancellation of unilateral notices[142]

(1) A person may apply to the registrar for the cancellation of a unilateral notice if he is—

(a) the registered proprietor of the estate or charge to which the notice relates, or

(b) a person entitled to be registered as the proprietor of that estate or charge.

(2) Where an application is made under subsection (1), the registrar must give the beneficiary of the notice of the application and of the effect of subsection (3).

(3) If the beneficiary of the notice does not exercise his right to object to the application before the end of such period as rules may provide, the registrar must cancel the notice.

(4) In this section—

'beneficiary', in relation to a unilateral notice, means the person shown in the register as the beneficiary of the notice, or such other person as rules may provide;

'unilateral notice' means a notice entered in the register in pursuance of an application under section 34(2)(b).

37 Unregistered interests

(1) If it appears to the registrar that a registered estate is subject to an unregistered interest which—

(a) falls within any of the paragraphs of Schedule 1,[143] and

(b) is not excluded by section 33,

he may enter a notice in the register in respect of the interest.

(2) The registrar must give notice of an entry under this section to such persons as rules may provide.

38 Registrable dispositions

Where a person is entered in the register as the proprietor of an interest under a disposition falling within section 27(2)(b) to (e),[144] the registrar must also enter a notice in the register in respect of that interest.

---

[141] LRR 2003, r. 83.   [142] Ibid., r. 86.

[143] An unregistered interest which overrides first registration; p. 193, below.

[144] Above, p. 163: the grant of certain leases, easements, rentcharges and rights of entry. The object is to provide for a cross-entry.

39 Supplementary

Rules may make provision about the form and content of notices in the register.

LAND REGISTRATION RULES 2003

Certain interests to be protected by agreed notices

80. A person who applies for the entry of a notice in the register must apply for the entry of an agreed notice where the application is for—

   (a) a home rights notice,[145]

   (b) an inheritance tax notice,

   (c) a notice in respect of an order under the Access to Neighbouring Land Act 1992,[146]

   (d) a notice of any variation of a lease effected by or under an order under section 38 of the Landlord and Tenant Act 1987 (including any variation as modified by an order under section 39(4) of that Act),

   (e) a notice in respect of a—

      (i)   public right, or

      (ii) customary right.

Entry of a notice in the register

84.—(1) A notice under section 32 of the Act must be entered in the charges register of the registered title affected.

B. RESTRICTIONS[147]

These are similar to restrictions under the 1925 Act. They cannot be used to protect interests which are capable of being protected by a notice.

LAND REGISTRATION ACT 2002

40 Nature

   (1) A restriction is an entry in the register regulating the circumstances in which a disposition of a registered estate or charge may be the subject of an entry in the register.

   (2) A restriction may, in particular—

      (a) prohibit the making of an entry in respect of any disposition, or a disposition of a kind specified in the restriction;

      (b) prohibit the making of an entry—

         (i)   indefinitely,

         (ii) for a period specified in the restriction, or

         (iii) until the occurrence of an event so specified.

---

[145] P. 602, below. It used to be called a 'matrimonial home rights notice' but r. 80 was amended by LR (Amendment) (No 2) Rules 2005 (SI 2005 No. 1982), Pt. 4, r. 10 to delete 'matrimonial'.

[146] P. 650, below.   [147] LRR 2003, Part 8, as amended.

(3) Without prejudice to the generality of subsection (2)(b)(iii), the events which may be specified include—

    (a) the giving of notice,

    (b) the obtaining of consent, and

    (c) the making of an order by the court or registrar.

(4) The entry of a restriction is to be made in relation to the registered estate or charge to which it relates.

41 Effect

(1) Where a restriction is entered in the register, no entry in respect of a disposition to which the restriction applies may be made in the register otherwise than in accordance with the terms of the restriction, subject to any order under subsection (2).

(2) The registrar may by order—

    (a) disapply a restriction in relation to a disposition specified in the order or dispositions of a kind so specified, or

    (b) provide that a restriction has effect, in relation to a disposition specified in the order or dispositions of a kind so specified, with modifications so specified.[148]

(3) The power under subsection (2) is exercisable only on the application of a person who appears to the registrar to have a sufficient interest in the restriction.

42 Power of registrar to enter

(1) The registrar may enter a restriction in the register if it appears to him that it is necessary or desirable to do so for the purpose of—

    (a) preventing invalidity or unlawfulness in relation to dispositions of a registered estate or charge,

    (b) securing that interests which are capable of being overreached[149] on a disposition of a registered estate or charge are overreached, or

    (c) protecting a right or claim in relation to a registered estate or charge.

(2) No restriction may be entered under subsection (1)(c) for the purpose of protecting the priority of an interest which is, or could be, the subject of a notice.

(3) The registrar must give notice of any entry made under this section to the proprietor of the registered estate or charge concerned, except where the entry is made in pursuance of an application under section 43.

(4) For the purposes of subsection (1)(c), a person entitled to the benefit of a charging order relating to an interest under a trust shall be treated as having a right or claim in relation to the trust property.

43 Applications

(1) A person may apply to the registrar for the entry of a restriction under section 42(1) if—

    (a) he is the relevant registered proprietor, or a person entitled to be registered as such proprietor,

    (b) the relevant registered proprietor, or a person entitled to be registered as such proprietor, consents to the application, or

---

[148] LRR 2003, r. 96.   [149] P. 548, below.

(c) he otherwise has a sufficient interest in the making of the entry.[150]

(2) Rules may—

(a) require the making of an application under subsection (1) in such circumstances, and by such person, as the rules may provide;

(b) make provision about the form of consent for the purposes of subsection (1)(b);

(c) provide for classes of person to be regarded as included in subsection (1)(c);

(d) specify standard forms of restriction.[151]

(3) If an application under subsection (1) is made for the entry of a restriction which is not in a form specified under subsection (2)(d), the registrar may only approve the application if it appears to him—

(a) that the terms of the proposed restriction are reasonable, and

(b) that applying the proposed restriction would—

(i) be straightforward, and

(ii) not place an unreasonable burden on him.

(4) In subsection (1), references to the relevant registered proprietor are to the proprietor of the registered estate or charge to which the application relates.

44 Obligatory restrictions

(1) If the registrar enters two or more persons in the register as the proprietor of a registered estate in land, he must also enter in the register such restrictions as rules may provide for the purpose of securing that interests which are capable of being overreached on a disposition of the estate are overreached.

(2) Where under any enactment the registrar is required to enter a restriction without application, the form of the restriction shall be such as rules may provide.[152]

45 Notifiable applications

(1) Where an application under section 43(1) is notifiable, the registrar must give notice of the application, and of the right to object to it, to—

(a) the proprietor of the registered estate or charge to which it relates, and

(b) such other persons as rules may provide.

(2) The registrar may not determine an application to which subsection (1) applies before the end of such period as rules may provide,[153] unless the person, or each of the persons, notified under that subsection has exercised his right to object to the application or given the registrar notice that he does not intend to do so.

(3) For the purposes of this section, an application under section 43(1) is notifiable unless it is—

(a) made by or with the consent of the proprietor of the registered estate or charge to which the application relates, or a person entitled to be registered as such proprietor,

[150] LRR 2003, r. 93, p. 178, below.

[151] LRR 2003, Part 8, and Sch. 4 (Standard Forms of Restriction) as substituted by LR (Amendment) Rules 2008 (SI 2008 No. 1919), Sch. 4, para. 1.

[152] Ibid., r. 95.   [153] Ibid., r. 92.

(b) made in pursuance of rules under section 43(2)(a), or

(c) an application for the entry of a restriction reflecting a limitation under an order of the court or registrar, or an undertaking given in place of such an order.

46 Power of court to order entry

(1) If it appears to the court that it is necessary or desirable to do so for the purpose of protecting a right or claim in relation to a registered estate or charge, it may make an order requiring the registrar to enter a restriction in the register.

(2) No order under this section may be made for the purpose of protecting the priority of an interest which is, or could be, the subject of a notice.

(3) The court may include in an order under this section a direction that an entry made in pursuance of the order is to have overriding priority.

(4) If an order under this section includes a direction under subsection (3), the registrar must make such entry in the register as rules may provide.[154]

(5) The court may make the exercise of its power under subsection (3) subject to such terms and conditions as it thinks fit.

47 Withdrawal

A person may apply to the registrar for the withdrawal of a restriction if—

(a) the restriction was entered in such circumstances as rules may provide, and

(2) he is of such a description as rules may provide.[155]

LAND REGISTRATION RULES 2003

Persons regarded as having a sufficient interest to apply for a restriction

93. The following persons are to be regarded as included in section 43(1)(c) of the Act—

(a) any person who has an interest in a registered estate held under a trust of land where a sole proprietor or a survivor of joint proprietors (unless a trust corporation) will not be able to give a valid receipt for capital money, and who is applying for a restriction in Form A to be entered in the register of that registered estate,

(b) any person who has a sufficient interest in preventing a contravention of section 6(6) or section 6(8) of the Trusts of Land and Appointment of Trustees Act 1996[156] and who is applying for a restriction in order to prevent such a contravention,

(c) any person who has an interest in a registered estate held under a trust of land where the powers of the trustees are limited by section 8 of the Trusts of Land and Appointment of Trustees Act 1996, and who is applying for a restriction in Form B to be entered in the register of that registered estate,

(d) any person who has an interest in the due administration of the estate of a deceased person, where—

(i) the personal representatives of the deceased hold a registered estate on a trust of land created by the deceased's will and the personal representatives' powers

---

[154] LRR 2003, r. 100.   [155] Ibid., r. 98.   [156] P. 521, below.

are limited by section 8 of the Trusts of Land and Appointment of Trustees Act 1996, and

(ii) he is applying for a restriction in Form C to be entered in the register of that registered estate,

(e) the donee of a special power of appointment in relation to registered land affected by that power,

(f) the Charity Commissioners in relation to registered land held upon charitable trusts...

C. ANTI-ABUSE PROVISION

A person who fails to exercise reasonable care when applying for the entry of a notice or a restriction may be liable in damages to anyone who suffers damage in consequence. Section 77(2) creates a statutory tort. The object is to dissuade anyone from using the procedure as tactics in neighbour or business disputes.

LAND REGISTRATION ACT 2002

77 Duty to act reasonably

(1) A person must not exercise any of the following rights without reasonable cause—

   (a) the right to lodge a caution under section 15,[157]

   (b) the right to apply for the entry of a notice or restriction,[158] and

   (c) the right to object to an application to the registrar.

(2) The duty under this section is owed to any person who suffers damage in consequence of its breach.[159]

VIII. OVERRIDING INTERESTS[160]

A. INTRODUCTION

Overriding interests are enforceable without being protected on the register, and bind a registered proprietor and his transferee even if he does not know of their existence.

---

[157] P. 140, above.   [158] Pp. 173, 176, above.

[159] *Anderson Antiques (UK) Ltd v Anderson Wharf (Hull) Ltd* [2007] All ER (D) 409 (May) (company which could not establish interest in registered land by virtue of oral agreement to purchase made application for notices to be entered against title. Held, declaration under s. 77 that notices had been applied for without reasonable cause; liability for damages (if loss established) would attach primarily to company but also to sole director and shareholder of the company who had procured the application for notices against claimant's title).

[160] C & B, pp. 107–108, 975–987; Gray, paras 8.2.41–8.2.119; M & W, paras 7.086–7.101; MM, pp. 121–129; Smith, pp. 241–259; R & R, chaps. 10, 17; H & B, chap. 11; Land Registry Practice Guide 15.

They thus detract from the principle that the register should be a mirror of the title. They consist of third party rights which on policy grounds should bind the registered proprietor, and a purchaser from him, even though they have not been entered on the register. If, however, a right which could be protected as an overriding interest does appear on the register, then its protection under this category is superfluous; it ceases to bind as an overriding interest and its protection is then the protection of an interest entered on the register.

The Land Registration Act 1925 listed overriding interests in section 70(1), and further additions were made by later enactments.[161] There was criticism of the wide scope of overriding interests under the 1925 Act,[162] especially of the wide-ranging safety-net of paragraph (g), which accorded protection to 'the rights of every person in actual occupation of the land or in receipt of the rents and profits thereof, save where enquiry is made of such person and the rights are not disclosed'. This paragraph protected an occupier who had failed either to register a title or to protect an interest by an entry on the register. This is diametrically opposed to the Draconian provisions of the Land Charges Act 1972 in the case of unregistered land under which a purchaser takes free of an unregistered land charge even if the person entitled to it is in possession.[163] On principle, however, the Land Registration Act rule is sounder than the Land Charges Act rule. In most cases, of course, vacant possession will be given to the purchaser on completion, and the problem does not arise. Where the purchaser completes when some other person is in occupation, he will almost always, if he is careful, discover the occupation.

The Land Registration Act 2002 reduced the number and extent of overriding interests in pursuance of its policy of creating as complete a register of land as possible. Some of the old categories of overriding interests were abolished; others will be phased out after 10 years; others are reduced in extent or otherwise modified.[164] The basic principle is now said to be that[165] 'the *only* overriding interests should be those where

'Overriding interests' was a defined term under LRA 1925, s. 3 (xvi). It is no longer so used under LRA 2002, although the concept is the same, and the Land Registry still uses the old terminology: Practice Guide 15. On overriding interests under the LRA 1925, see R & R (1991 edn), chap. 6; W & C, vol. 6, pp. 63–67; Farrand (2nd edn), pp. 184–209; Barnsley, pp. 50–69; Hayton, *Registered Land*, chap. 6.

[161] LRR 1925, r. 258; Tithe Act 1936, s. 13(11); Coal Act 1938, s. 41; Leasehold Property (Temporary Provisions) Act 1951, s. 2(4); Coal Industry Act 1987, s. 1; Coal Industry Act 1994, Sch. 9, para. 1(2); Greater London Authority Act 1999, s. 219(7).

[162] Part II of the Law Commission's Third Report on Land Registration (Law Com No. 158), contains a valuable and critical account of the existing law. See also Consultative Document on Land Registration for the Twenty-First Century 1998 (Law Com No. 254), Part IV; *Overseas Investment Services Ltd v Simcobuild Construction Ltd* [1996] 1 EGLR 49 at 51, per Peter Gibson LJ 'As they constitute an exception [to the mirror of title principle] the court should, in my opinion, not be astute to give a wide meaning to any item constituting an overriding interest'.

[163] LCA 1972, s. 4, p. 71, above.

[164] There are transitional provisions which preserve any overriding interests acquired under the 1925 Act: LRA 2002, Sch. 12, paras 7–13.

[165] Law Commission Consultative Document on Land Registration for the Twenty-First Century 1998 (Law Com No. 254), para. 4.17, adopting Third Report on Land Registration 1987 (Law Com No. 158), para. 2.6. See also Report on Land Registration for the Twenty-First Century 2001 (Law Com No. 271),

protection against purchasers is needed, yet it is either not reasonable to expect nor sensible to require any entry on the register'.

However, although the scope of overriding interests under the 2002 Act is changed, the language of the provisions of the 2002 Act is in many respects similar to the equivalent provisions of the 1925 Act. Cases on Land Registration Act 1925, section 70(1), may therefore still be relevant to the interpretation of the equivalent provisions of LRA 2002. In the following pages of this section we therefore include a brief account of the provisions of the 1925 Act, and we include many cases which were decided under the provisions of the 1925 Act, although it should be noted from the outset that the cases on the former Act must be approached with some caution, and not applied to the 2002 Act without a careful consideration of the similarities and differences between the provisions in question.

Law Commission Report on Land Registration for the Twenty-First Century 2001 (Law Com No. 271), paras 8.1, 8.6

8.1 We have explained that one of the principal objectives of the Bill is to create a faster and simpler conveyancing system, electronically based, under which it is possible to investigate title to the land almost entirely on-line with the bare minimum of additional enquiries.[166] A major obstacle to achieving that goal is the existence of a category of interests in registered land that are not on the register but which will, nonetheless, bind any person who acquires an interest in the land.[167] These unregistered interests have been known as overriding interests since the enactment of the Land Registration Act 1925.[168] To achieve the objective mentioned at the beginning of this paragraph, the Bill seeks to minimise the circumstances in which new overriding interests can arise and also to provide mechanisms to ensure that existing overriding interests are brought on to the register wherever possible.

8.6 It is the fact that overriding interests do not appear on the register, yet bind any person who acquires any interest in registered land, that makes them such an unsatisfactory feature of the system of registered conveyancing.[169] The existence of such rights means that inquiries

---

para. 8.6. An earlier rationale for overriding interests was that the system of registration of title was designed to replace the title deeds; and so it was still to be expected that a purchaser should make enquiries outside the register for those 'various minor liabilities which are not usually, or at any rate not invariably, shown in title-deeds or mentioned in abstracts of title, and as to which, therefore, it is impracticable to form a trustworthy record on the register': Brickdale & Stewart Wallace, *Land Registration Act 1925*, p. 190, quoted and criticised in Law Com No. 254, at para. 4.4.

[166] See above, para. 1.5.

[167] Cf. *Secretary of State for the Environment, Transport and the Regions v Baylis (Gloucester) Ltd* (2000) 80 P & CR 324, 338, where Kim Lewison QC (sitting as a Deputy High Court Judge) said, '[i]t is not in doubt that the purpose of a system of land registration is to promote certainty of title. To achieve that objective it is necessary to keep to a minimum the number of matters which may defeat the title of a registered proprietor'.

[168] See particularly Land Registration Act 1925, ss. 3(xvi) and 70. The term was not found in the Land Transfer Act 1875.

[169] As we explained in the Consultative Document, '[b]ecause such rights subsist and operate outside the register, they are an inevitable source of tension within the land registration system': Law Com No. 254, para. 4.1.

as to title cannot be confined to a search of the register. We devoted a substantial part of the Consultative Document to a discussion of overriding interests and how their impact might be reduced without causing any disadvantage to those who have the benefit of them.[170] Our conclusion was that interests should only have overriding status where protection against buyers was needed, but where it was neither reasonable to expect nor sensible to require any entry on the register.[171] We suggested a number of strategies to ensure that the only overriding interests were those which met these criteria.[172] As we have explained above,[173] the introduction of electronic conveyancing will, of itself, substantially reduce the circumstances in which those criteria are met...

B. THE OLD LAW: LAND REGISTRATION ACT 1925

LAND REGISTRATION ACT 1925

3. Interpretation.—(xvi) 'Overriding interests' mean all the incumbrances, interests, rights, and powers not entered on the register but subject to which registered dispositions are by this Act to take effect, and in regard to land registered at the commencement of this Act include the matters which are by any enactment repealed by this Act declared not to be incumbrances;

70. Liability of registered land to overriding interests.[174]—(1) All registered land shall, unless under the provisions of this Act the contrary is expressed on the register, be deemed to be subject to such of the following overriding interests as may be for the time being subsisting in reference thereto, and such interests shall not be treated as incumbrances within the meaning of this Act, (that is to say):—

(a) Rights of common, drainage rights, customary rights (until extinguished), public rights, profits à prendre, rights of sheep-walk, rights of way, watercourses, rights of water, and other easements not being equitable easements required to be protected by notice on the register;[175]

(b) Liability to repair highways by reason of tenure, quit-rents, crown rents, heriots, and other rents and charges (until extinguished) having their origin in tenure;

(c) Liability to repair the chancel of any church;

(d) Liability in respect of embankments, and sea and river walls;

(e) ...,[176] payments in lieu of tithe, and charges or annuities payable for the redemption of tithe rentcharges;

---

[170] See Law Com No. 254, Parts IV, V.   [171] Law Com No. 254, para. 4.17.
[172] See Law Com No. 254, paras 4.23–4.39.   [173] See para. 8.2.

[174] For further detailed references on LRA 1925, s. 70, see the footnotes in the 8th edn of this book, pp. 129–32. For references which continue to be relevant to the interpretation of LRA 2002, Schs 1 and 3, see pp. 198–219, below.

[175] Read together with LRR 1925, r. 258, this was interpreted as including 'equitable easements other than such as by reason of some other statutory provision or applicable principle of law, could obtain protection otherwise than by notice on the register': *Celsteel Ltd v Alton House Holdings Ltd* [1985] 1 WLR 204, 220 (Scott J).

[176] Amended by Tithe Act 1936, s. 48, Sch. 8, and Finance Act 1963, ss. 68, 73(8)(b), Sch. 14, Pt. VI. Tithe redemption annuities were extinguished as from 2 October 1977; FA 1977, s. 56.

(f) Subject to the provisions of this Act, rights acquired or in course of being acquired under the Limitation Acts;[177]

(g) The rights[178] of every person in actual occupation of the land or in receipt of the rents and profits thereof, save where enquiry is made of such person and the rights are not disclosed;

(h) In the case of a possessory, qualified, or good leasehold title[179] all estates, rights, interests and powers excepted from the effect of registration;

(i) Rights under local land charges unless and until registered or protected on the register in the prescribed manner,[180]

(j) Rights of fishing and sporting, seignorial and manorial rights of all descriptions (until extinguished), and franchises;

(k) Leases granted[181] for a term not exceeding twenty-one years;[182]

(kk) PPP leases[183]

(l) In respect of land registered before the commencement of this Act, rights to mines and minerals, and rights of entry, search, and user, and other rights and reservations incidental to or required for the purpose of giving full effect to the enjoyment of rights to mines and minerals or of property in mines or minerals, being rights which, where the title was first registered before the first day of January, eighteen hundred and ninety-eight, were created before that date, and where the title was first registered after the thirty-first day of December, eighteen hundred and ninety-seven, were created before the date of first registration;

(m) Any interest or right which is an overriding interest by virtue of paragraph 1(1) of Schedule 9 to the Coal Industry Act 1994;[184]

---

[177] LRA 1925, s. 75. LRA 2002 effected a fundamental change in the position of a squatter in relation to registered land, in consequence of which a squatter no longer has an overriding interest under LRA 2002: p. 279, below.

[178] There were statutory exclusions from para. (g) under Family Law Act 1996, s. 31(10)(b) (spouse or civil partner's right of occupation); Leasehold Reform Act 1967, s. 5(5) (tenant's right to acquire freehold or apply for extended lease); HA 1985 Sch. 9A, para. 6(1), inserted by Housing and Planning Act 1986, s. 8(2), Sch. 2 (tenant's right to buy); Access to Neighbouring Land Act 1992, s. 5 (rights conferred by, or access order under, the Act); Landlord and Tenant (Covenants) Act 1995, s. 20(6) (right to overriding lease), all of which have been now amended by LRA 2002, Sch. 11, to confer similar exclusions on the provisions which replaced para. (g), LRA 2002, Sch. 1, para. 2, and Sch. 3, para. 2. And also excluded by implication was an interest under a strict settlement: LRA 1925, s. 86(2).

[179] LRA 1925, ss. 6, 7, 10, 11, 12.   [180] Ibid., s. 49(1)(c), s. 59(2).

[181] This did not include an agreement for a lease; City Permanent Building Society v Miller [1952] Ch 840, p. 198, below; nor a statutory tenancy under the Rent Act 1977: Barclays Bank plc v Zaroovabli [1997] Ch 321 at 328; (1997) 113 LQR 390 (M. Robinson). But these could be overriding interests under para. (g). No application could be made under LRA 1925 for the entry of a notice of a lease for 21 years or less: LRA 1925, s. 48(1).

[182] As amended by LRA 1986, s. 4(1), following Law Commission Report on Land Registration Part IV Treatment of Leases 1983 (Law Com No. 121), para. 4.37, which recommended that the exclusion of gratuitous leases and of leases granted at a premium should be removed.

[183] Added by Greater London Authority Act 1999, s. 219(7).

[184] Added by Coal Industry Act 1994, Sch. 9, para. 1(2).

Provided that, where it is proved to the satisfaction of the registrar that any land registered or about to be registered is exempt from land tax, or tithe rentcharge or payments in lieu of tithe, or from charges or annuities payable for the redemption of tithe rentcharge, the registrar may notify the fact on the register in the prescribed manner.

(2) Where at the time of first registration any easement, right, privilege, or benefit created by an instrument and appearing on the title adversely affects the land, the registrar shall enter a note thereof on the register.

(3) Where the existence of any overriding interest mentioned in this section is proved to the satisfaction of the registrar or admitted, he may (subject to any prescribed exceptions) enter notice of the same or of a claim thereto on the register, but no claim to an easement, right, or privilege not created by an instrument shall be noted against the title to the servient land if the proprietor of such land (after the prescribed notice is given to him) shows sufficient cause to the contrary.

(3A) Neither subsection (2) nor subsection (3) of this section shall apply in the case of a PPP lease.[185]

(4) Neither subsection (2) nor subsection (3) of this section shall apply in the case of any such interest or right as is mentioned in subsection (1)(*m*) of this section.[186]

Law Commission: Land Registration For The Twenty-First Century: A Consultative Document 1998 (Law Com No. 254), paras 4.4–4.15

THE RATIONALE OF OVERRIDING INTERESTS

Why do we have overriding interests?

4.4 The orthodox explanation for the existence of overriding interests is that they are—

> various minor liabilities which are not usually, or at any rate not invariably, shown in title-deeds or mentioned in abstracts of title, and as to which, therefore, it is impracticable to form a trustworthy record on the register . . . As to these, persons dealing with registered land must obtain information aliunde in the same manner and from the same sources as persons dealing with unregistered land obtain it.[187]

The way in which the law on overriding interests has developed over the last seventy-two years has demonstrated that overriding interests are by no means only 'minor liabilities'. Furthermore, as will become apparent from the analysis of individual overriding interests in Part V of this Report, this explanation of the rationale of such interests is no longer correct in all respects, whatever the position may have been perceived to be when the legislation was first enacted. Most overriding interests do appear to have one shared characteristic, however, that is related to the orthodox explanation of them, namely that *it is unreasonable to expect the person who has the benefit of the right to register it as a means of securing its protection.* As we shall explain, not every overriding interest can be justified on that basis, and this in itself is a reason for examining such interests in detail. An examination of the list of overriding interests—at

---

[185] Added by Greater London Authority Act 1999, s. 219(7).

[186] As added by Coal Industry Act 1994, Sch. 9, para. 1(2).

[187] Brickdale & Stewart Wallace's *Land Registration Act, 1925* (4th edn, 1939), p. 190. The substance of the passage is retained in Ruoff & Roper, *Registered Conveyancing*, 6–04.

least as they have come to be understood in practice—suggests that most of them fall into five tolerably clear categories.

Categories of overriding interests

Those which provide a means of accommodating rights which may be created informally or where the origins of the rights may be obscure

4.5 First, overriding interests provide a means of accommodating rights which can be created (or may arise) informally, and where registration at the time of creation may therefore be unrealistic. These include—

(1) easements that arise by prescription or by implied grant or reservation;[188]

(2) the rights of adverse possessors;[189] and

(3) in the case of persons in actual occupation, rights arising by estoppel or constructive trust.[190]

4.6 The inclusion of customary and public rights as overriding interests,[191] is justifiable on a similar basis, namely the obscurity that may surround their origins. Customary rights can only be established by long user—in theory (but not in practice) this must be shown from the beginning of legal memory in 1189.[192] Although public rights can of course arise in other ways, it is not uncommon for their origins to be uncertain and undocumented and, in effect, to depend upon proof of long exercise.[193]

Rights that had overriding status prior to 1926

4.7 Secondly, rights which were the equivalent of overriding interests under the previous land registration legislation[194] became overriding interests under the Land Registration Act 1925.[195] Most of these rights were of a kind that could no longer be created. The overriding interests that fall within this category are—

(1) liability to repair highways by reason of tenure, quit-rents, crown rents, heriots, and other rents and charges having their origin in tenure;[196]

(2) chancel repair liability;[197]

(3) liability in respect of embankments, and sea and river walls;[198]

---

[188] See LRA 1925, s. 70(1)(*a*); but note the doubts about whether such rights arising by implied grant and reservation really are accommodated by the system of registered title: below, para. 5.11.

[189] LRA 1925, s. 70(1)(*f*).   [190] Ibid., s. 70(1)(*g*).

[191] Ibid., s. 70(1)(*a*).

[192] See Sir Robert Megarry & Sir William Wade, *The Law of Real Property* (5th edn, 1984), p. 849. There is in fact some uncertainty as to the sense in which the expression 'customary rights' is employed in the Land Registration Act 1925.

[193] Sir Robert Megarry & Sir William Wade, *The Law of Real Property* (5th edn, 1984), p. 844.

[194] See Land Transfer Act 1875, s. 18, as amended by the Land Transfer Act 1897. The rights were rather clumsily described as interests which were not deemed to be encumbrances within the meaning of the Land Transfer Act 1875.

[195] The five categories of overriding interest that were introduced for the first time in the Land Registration Act 1925 were (i) customary and public rights (s. 70(1)(*a*)); (ii) the rights of adverse possessors (s. 70(1)(*f*)); (iii) the rights of persons in actual occupation (s. 70(1)(*g*)); (iv) the rights excepted from the effect of registration in cases where title was registered with some title other than absolute (s. 70(1)(*h*)); and (v) rights under local land charges (s. 70(1)(*i*)).

[196] See Land Registration Act 1925, s. 70(1)(*b*).

[197] Ibid., s. 70(1)(*c*).   [198] Ibid., s. 70(1)(*d*).

(4) liability to make various payments in lieu of tithe or tithe rentcharge;[199]

(5) seignorial and manorial rights and franchises;[200]

(6) in relation to land registered—

    (a) prior to 1898, mineral rights created before that date; and

    (b) after 1897 and before 1926, mineral rights created prior to first registration.[201]

It would obviously have been unreasonable in those circumstances to impose an obligation to register such rights.[202]

Incorporeal rights in existence at the time of first registration but not registered

4.8 Thirdly, incorporeal rights such as easements and profits, which were in existence but were not noted on the register at the time of the first registration of the land burdened by them, take effect as overriding interests.[203] The status of overriding interest here acts as a 'fail-safe' mechanism to protect such rights in case they do not come to light on first registration.[204]

Rights which it would be inconvenient or pointless to register

4.9 Fourthly, some rights are overriding interests because it would be either inconvenient or even pointless to register them. Leases granted for a term not exceeding 21 years,[205] and rights in coal[206] both fall into this category.

Rights which are otherwise protected

4.10 Finally, there are rights which are otherwise protected and where it may therefore be regarded as otiose to expect them to be registered. An obvious example of this is the category of local land charges which are protected by registration on a register kept by the relevant local authority.[207] More controversially, the rights of those in actual occupation[208] are also explicable on this basis. At common law, the rights over land of a person in occupation—and perhaps in possession as well—were protected by that occupation or possession.[209] The exact scope of this principle was never precisely defined.[210] Sometimes it was explained on the basis that occupation gave notice of the rights of the occupier.[211] On other occasions, it was formulated more widely. The mere *fact* of occupation, whether or not it was apparent, was notice of the rights of the occupier.[212] Whatever the extent of the principle, the idea that an occupier was not required to take any further steps to protect his or her rights in the property was an ancient and deeply engrained one.

---

[199] LRA 1925, s. 70(1)(*e*).   [200] Ibid., s. 70(1)(*j*).   [201] Ibid., s. 70(1)(*l*).

[202] There are other situations in the 1925 property legislation where a registration requirement was imposed prospectively, so as not to affect the existing method of protecting rights that had already been created. Thus restrictive covenants and equitable easements created before 1926 are not registrable as land charges in unregistered land, but continue to be protected by the doctrine of notice: see Land Charges Act 1972, s. 2(5)(ii), (iii).

[203] This can be inferred from Land Registration Act 1925, ss. 70(1)(*a*); 70(2); and 70(3).

[204] Cf. ibid., s. 70(2).   [205] Ibid., s. 70(1)(*k*).   [206] Ibid., s. 70(1)(*m*).

[207] Ibid., s. 70(1)(*i*).   [208] Ibid., s. 70(1)(*g*).

[209] For a discussion, see Charles Harpum, 'Overreaching, Trustees' Powers and the Reform of the 1925 Legislation' [1990] CLJ 277, 315–320.

[210] Nor, given the effect upon it of the provisions of the Law of Property Act 1925 and what is now the Land Charges Act 1972, is it ever likely to be.

[211] See, e.g. *Barnhart v Greenshields* (1853) 9 Moo PCC 18, 32; 14 ER 204, 209.

[212] *Holmes v Powell* (1856) 8 De GM & G 572, 580–581; 44 ER 510, 514.

CRITICISMS OF OVERRIDING INTERESTS

Introduction

4.11 Although, as we have explained, it is possible to explain the rationale of most of the categories of overriding interests,[213] such interests have nonetheless been much criticised. In the following paragraphs we set out the most important grounds of criticism.

Title not absolute

4.12 First, the existence of overriding interests means that absolute title cannot be absolute in the true sense, because the register may not be a true mirror of the state of the title. However, the register could only be a wholly accurate reflection of the title at a price, namely the suppression of many third party rights. This is because in practice the nature of overriding interests is such that if they were now required to be registered, some at least might not be.[214] They would therefore be defeated by any subsequent disposition for value of the land burdened by them.[215] There are in fact only two other ways in which such rights can be accommodated with the land registration system. First, they could simply be extinguished wholesale by statute. To do this in accordance with the European Convention of Human Rights, it would almost certainly be necessary to pay compensation to those deprived of their rights.[216] To adopt this option would involve an unquantifiable commitment to pay compensation on a potentially large scale. The second option is to accept (as the Land Registration Act 1925 does accept) that such rights can exist independently of the register.

Undiscoverability

4.13 Secondly, overriding interests are not necessarily discoverable from a reasonable inspection of land.[217] For example, to ascertain whether a property is subject to a liability to pay for chancel repairs,[218] it may be necessary to search the tithe records which are kept in several different branches of the Public Record Office. As those records are incomplete, there is in fact no certainty that a property is free from liability even when such a search has been made. As regards the rights of occupiers, it has been said that 'there can be cases where a purchaser may make the most searching enquiries without discovering that the land in question is in the actual occupation of a third party'.[219] A purchaser of registered land may find that he or she is bound by a right that has not been protected by an entry on the register, notwithstanding that there is no person other than the vendor in apparent occupation of the property and that careful inspection and inquiry has failed to reveal anything which might give the purchaser

---

[213] See above, paras 4.4 and following.

[214] See the discussion below, paras 4.25, 4.26.

[215] Where it can be demonstrated that a category of overriding interests is almost certainly obsolete, these considerations do not apply. In such cases we consider that the category should be removed from the list of overriding interests: see below, para. 4.31.

[216] See Article 1 of the First Protocol of the Convention, considered below, para. 4.27.

[217] This appears to have been recognised as a defect since the Act was passed: see Brickdale & Stewart Wallace's *Land Registration Act, 1925* (4th edn, 1939), p. 193; below, para. 5.57.

[218] Which is an overriding interest under Land Registration Act 1925, s. 70(1)(c).

[219] *Kling v Keston Properties Ltd* (1983) 49 P & CR 212, 222, per Vinelott J. Factually similar situations can produce different results: compare *Epps v Esso Petroleum Co Ltd* [1973] 1 WLR 1071 (parking a car on a strip 11' x 80' was *not* actual occupation) with *Kling v Keston Properties Ltd*, above (parking a car within a garage *was* actual occupation).

any reason to suspect that someone other than the vendor had any interest in or rights over the property.[220]

Rectification but no indemnity

4.14 The third criticism that is often made of overriding interests is one that is, in our view, unjustified. Where an overriding interest exists, the register may be rectified even as against a proprietor in possession in order to give effect to an overriding interest.[221] Furthermore, because a purchaser of registered land takes it subject to overriding interests,[222] when the register is so rectified, no indemnity is payable. This is because the proprietor is not a 'person suffering loss by reason of any rectification of the register' within the meaning of the Land Registration Act 1925.[223] In such a case, all that the rectification of the register does is to ensure that it reflects the true state of affairs.[224] It is for this reason that we are unconvinced by this particular criticism of overriding interests. It should be noted that in this regard the position of registered land is exactly the same as unregistered land. A purchaser of unregistered land would not expect to receive state compensation because it transpired that part of the land that he or she had purchased belonged in fact to a squatter who had acquired title to it by adverse possession. Any remedy which the purchaser might have would be against the vendor on the implied covenants for title. It is not obvious to us that this outcome is wrong, particularly as the covenants for title now provide a more effective remedy in many such instances than was formerly the case.[225]

Unsatisfactory drafting

4.15 Fourthly, the drafting of section 70(1) of the Land Registration Act 1925 is unsatisfactory for the following reasons—

(1) the range of rights which may exist as overriding interests is not clearly or precisely defined;

(2) a number of rights that are listed as overriding interests in the section are now obsolete;

(3) certain rights which must in practice be treated as overriding interests are omitted from the section;

(4) it fails to exclude—as in principle it should—expressly created easements,[226] which have in consequence been held to be overriding interests;[227]

(5) the wording of the section is verbose and several of the rights listed are no more than examples of broader categories contained within it.

4.16 Given that overriding interests operate in effect outside the register, it is clearly important that the range of such rights should be defined with as much precision and clarity as possible and that the list should be no wider than is necessary. We note that in a recent decision,

---

[220] *Kling v Keston Properties Ltd*, above, at p. 222.
[221] Land Registration Act 1925, s. 82(3). It is only in the four exceptional cases listed in that subsection, of which this is one, that the register may be rectified against a proprietor who is in possession. We consider this matter further below, at paras 8.23 and following.
[222] Land Registration Act 1925, ss. 20(1), 23(1).
[223] Section 83(1) (as substituted).   [224] *Re Chowood's Registered Land* [1933] Ch 574.
[225] See the Law of Property (Miscellaneous Provisions) Act 1994.
[226] Which ought of course to be completed by registration as registered dispositions.
[227] See below, paras 5.8, 5.9.

Staughton LJ expressed a similar sentiment when he said that '[i]t is desirable that overriding interests should be in a narrow rather than a wide class and should be clearly defined'.[228]

C. THE NEW LAW: LAND REGISTRATION ACT 2002

The Land Registration Act 2002 implemented the recommendations of the Law Commission's Report on Land Registration for the Twenty-First Century, which had criticised the scope of overriding interests under the Land Registration Act 1925 and sought to restrict such interests.

Law Commission Report on Land Registration for the Twenty-First Century 2001 (Law Com No. 271), paras 2.24–2.27

2.24 Overriding interests are interests that are not protected in the register but are, none-theless, binding on any person who acquires an interest in registered land, whether on first registration or where there has been a registrable disposition of a registered estate that has been completed by registration. The range of interests that are presently overriding is sig-nificant. They include many easements (whether or not these have been expressly granted or reserved),[229] the rights of persons in actual occupation,[230] leases granted for 21 years or less,[231] as well as some obscure interests that may have very serious effects on the registered proprietor (such as manorial rights). Overriding interests therefore present a very significant impediment to one of the main objectives of the Bill, namely that the register should be as complete a record of the title as it can be, with the result that it should be possible for title to land to be investigated almost entirely on-line.

2.25 The Bill seeks to restrict such interests so far as possible.[232] The guiding principle on which it proceeds is that interests should be overriding only where it is unreasonable to expect them to be protected in the register.[233] The Bill incorporates a number of strategies to achieve this objective. These include, in particular, the following—

(1) defining the categories of overriding interests more narrowly;

(2) excluding some expressly created interests from overriding status;

(3) phasing out the overriding status of the more obscure interests after 10 years and allowing for them to be entered on the appropriate register without charge in the interim;[234] and

(4) strengthening mechanisms for ensuring that overriding interests are protected in the register if they are capable of being so protected.

---

[228] *Overseas Investment Services Ltd v Simcobuild Construction Ltd* (1995) 70 P & CR 322, 330. See too Peter Gibson LJ at p. 327: 'the court should ... not be astute to give a wide meaning to any item constituting an overriding interest'.

[229] Land Registration Act 1925, s. 70(1)(*a*).   [230] Ibid., s. 70(1)(*g*).

[231] Ibid., s. 70(1)(*k*).   [232] See below, Part VIII.

[233] See below, para. 8.6 [above, p. 181].

[234] At the end of that period, the interests in question would not be extinguished. But if they were not appropriately protected, they would be vulnerable.

2.26 The move to electronic conveyancing, described below,[235] will itself facilitate the process of eliminating overriding interests. This is because it is envisaged that many interests in land will only be capable of being created when simultaneously registered.[236] Such interests will never be overriding, therefore.

2.27 It may be helpful to summarise the likely extent of overriding interests that will be binding on registered disponee of registered land ten years after the Bill is brought into force and the provisions mentioned in paragraph 2.25(3) have taken effect. They are likely to comprise—

(1) most leases granted for three years or less;

(2) the interests of persons in actual occupation where—

    (a) that actual occupation is apparent; and

    (b) the interest—

        (i) is a beneficial interest under a trust; or

        (ii) arose informally (such as an equity arising by estoppel);

(3) legal easements and *profits à prendre* that have arisen by implied grant or reservation or by prescription;

(4) customary and public rights;

(5) local land charges; and

(6) certain mineral rights.

Each of these can be justified under the guiding principle mentioned above in paragraph 2.25.

The 2002 Act substantially changed the law on overriding interests in pursuance of its policy of creating as complete a register of land as possible. It reduced the number and extent of the interests, by abolishing some of them, by phasing out others after 10 years, and by reducing the extent of some of those that remain. There are transitional provisions which preserve any overriding interests acquired under the 1925 Act.[237]

In three of the categories of overriding interests (short leases, legal easements and profits à prendre, and the interests of persons in actual occupation), the requirements for the overriding interest depend on whether it is a case of first registration (Schedule 1) or a case of subsequent registered disposition (Schedule 3). This division is new.

Law Commission Report on Land Registration for the Twenty-First Century 2001 (Law Com No. 271), para. 8.3

8.3 Overriding interests are not different in their nature from any other unregistered interests that subsist in relation to registered land. However, for various reasons of policy, they are given a special status in two circumstances, namely—

---

[235] See paras 2.41 and following. [See below, p. 229.]

[236] See above, para. 2.1(2) and below, paras 2.59 and following.

[237] For transitional provisions to preserve former overriding interests, see LRA 2002, Sch. 12, paras 7–13.

(1) on first registration, when the estate is vested in the first registered proprietor subject to overriding interests but free from most other interests not entered on the register;[238] and

(2) where a registrable disposition for valuable consideration is completed by registration, when the disponee takes subject to overriding interests but free from most other unregistered interests.[239]

These two situations are intrinsically different. In general, first registration has no dispositionary effect because the first registered proprietor will already have the legal title vested in him or her.[240] Whether or not the first registered proprietor is bound by an interest that can be an overriding interest on first registration will have been determined prior to that date.[241] By contrast, where there is a registrable disposition for valuable consideration, the registration of that disposition is dispositionary and vests the legal title in the disponee. An issue of priority therefore arises at the time of the disposition and whether or not the disponee is bound by an interest has to be determined then. This distinction has an effect in some cases on the substantive requirements for what amounts to an overriding interest. For example, the rights of persons in actual occupation constitute an overriding interest both under the present law[242] and under the Bill.[243] However, whether a disponee has made enquiries of a person in actual occupation is irrelevant on first registration because the issue of whether or not the first registered proprietor is bound by the rights of such an occupier will already have been decided.[244] By contrast it *is* material in relation to a registered disposition to decide whether registration vests the legal title in the disponee free of the rights of the occupier or not.[245] If the disponee has made appropriate enquiries prior to the disposition, the occupier is, in effect, estopped from asserting his or her interest.

(i) Unregistered interests which override first registration

When a person becomes the proprietor of registered land on first registration, he takes the estate subject to those overriding interests which are set out in Schedule 1 to the 2002 Act. Important changes from the 1925 Act arise in three cases:

(a) Short leases for a term not exceeding seven years from the date of the grant (paragraph 1)

This is a reduction from 21 years under the 1925 Act (section 70(1)(*k*)). A notice of such a lease should be entered on the register of the title out of which it has been granted. There are exceptions which are not overriding interests even if they are for seven years

---

238 See [LRA 2002, ss. 11(4)(b); 12(4)(c)].

239 See [LRA 2002, ss. 29(2)(a)(ii), 30(2)(a)(ii)].

240 For a case where it does, see [LRA 2002, ss. 11(4)(c); 12(4)(d)].

241 Where first registration is voluntary, the overriding interest may have arisen or been created after the first registered proprietor acquired the land, but before he or she applied for the registration of his or her title. Even where a disposition triggered compulsory first registration (under [LRA 2002, s. 4]) the interests to which the disponee took subject will have been determined according to the rules of unregistered conveyancing applicable to that disposition.

242 See Land Registration Act 1925, s. 70(1)(*g*).   243 See Schedules 1, para. 2; 3, para. 2.

244 See [Law Com No. 271], para. 8.21.   245 See [Law Com No. 271], para. 8.60.

or less (LRA 2002, section 4(1)(d)-(f), p. 133 above). These must be registered with their own individual titles.

(b) Interests of persons in actual occupation (paragraph 2)

There are four major changes from the equivalent interests in section 70(1)(g) of the 1925 Act. First, persons who are in receipt of the rent and profits of the land no longer have overriding interests. Secondly, if a person is in actual occupation of part of the land, he no longer has an overriding interest over the whole of that land.[246] Thirdly, the exclusion of the rights of a beneficiary under the Settled Land Act 1925 is confirmed.[247] And, fourthly, the qualification in section 70(1)(g) 'save where enquiry is made of such person and the rights are not disclosed' is left out.[248]

(c) Legal easements and profits à prendre (paragraph 3)

Section 70(1)(a) of the Land Registration Act 1925 is replaced. Equitable easements and profits à prendre can no longer be overriding interests.[249] There may be fewer legal easements and profits à prendre under paragraph 3, because of the duty of disclosure under section 71, p. 197, below.

There are no changes of substance in paragraphs 4 to 9. The miscellaneous interests in paragraphs 10 to 14 are to be phased out over ten years from the date when the Act came into force (13 October 2003). Section 117 permits those with the benefit of those rights to protect them on the register during the ten years without payment of fees; by a caution against first registration in the case of unregistered land, or by a notice in the case of registered land. Paragraph 16 (church chancel repair liability) was added in 2003,[250] to reinstate the protection to such rights given by section 70(1)(c) of the Land Registration Act 1925, but this will also be phased out on 13 October 2013. Section 90 of the 2002 Act also adds as a further overriding interest a PPP lease relating to transport in London.

---

[246] Reversing the decision in *Ferrishurst Ltd v Wallcite Ltd* [1999] Ch 355 on the interpretation of LRA 1925, s. 70(1)(g).

[247] In spite of the recommendations of the Law Commission Consultative Document on Land Registration for the Twenty-First Century (Law Com No. 254), para. 5.63, which was not supported on consultation: Law Com No. 271, para. 8.17.

[248] However, this follows from the fact that the effect of first registration is to confirm the existing rights, and not (as in the case of disposition of registered land) to determine competing priorities: (Law Com No. 271), para. 8.3, above, p. 190.

[249] Reversing *Celsteel Ltd v Alton House Holdings Ltd* [1987] 1 WLR 291, p. 182, n. 175, above.

[250] After the decision of HL in *Aston Cantlow Parochial Church Council v Wallbank* [2004] 1 AC 546 that the recovery of costs of chancel repair is not contrary to HRA 1998; LRA 2002, Sch. 1, para. 16, below, n. 253; Sch. 3, para. 16; below, n. 262. Law Commission Report on Liability for Chancel Repairs 1985 (Law Com No. 152) recommended that liability should be abolished after 10 years; but, if not abolished promptly, it should be registered in Local Land Charges registers, and failure to register would exonerate a purchaser of the land; (1984) 100 LQR 185 (J. H. Baker). For the liability in unregistered land, see *Hauxton Parochial Church Council v Stevens* [1929] P 240; *Chivers & Sons Ltd v Air Ministry and Queen's College, Cambridge* [1955] Ch 585.

LAND REGISTRATION ACT 2002

SCHEDULE 1

UNREGISTERED INTERESTS WHICH OVERRIDE FIRST REGISTRATION

Leasehold estates in land

1 A leasehold estate in land granted for a term not exceeding seven years from the date of the grant, except for a lease the grant of which falls within section 4(1)(d), (e) or (f).

Interests of persons in actual occupation

2 An interest belonging to a person in actual occupation, so far as relating to land of which he is in actual occupation, except for an interest under a settlement under the Settled Land Act 1925.

Easements and profits a prendre

3 A legal easement or profit a prendre.

Customary and public rights

4 A customary right.
5 A public right.[251]

Local land charges

6 A local land charge.

Mines and minerals

7 An interest in any coal or coal mine, the rights attached to any such interest and the rights of any person under section 38, 49 or 51 of the Coal Industry Act 1994.
8 In the case of land to which title was registered before 1898, rights to mines and minerals (and incidental rights) created before 1898.
9 In the case of land to which title was registered between 1898 and 1925 inclusive, rights to mines and minerals (and incidental rights) created before the date of registration of the title.

Miscellaneous[252]

10 A franchise.
11 A manorial right.
12 A right to rent which was reserved to the Crown on the granting of any freehold estate (whether or not the right is still vested in the Crown).
13 A non-statutory right in respect of an embankment or sea or river wall.
14 A right to payment in lieu of tithe.
16 A right in respect of the repair of a church chancel.[253]

---

[251] *Overseas Investment Services Ltd v Simcobuild Construction Ltd* (1995) 70 P & CR 322 ('public rights' under LRA 1925, s. 70(1)(a) limited to present rights, exercisable by anyone merely by virtue of being a member of the public and under the general law, and did not include agreement for a future highway made between the previous owners of their land and local authority).

[252] Paras 10 to 14 cease to have effect at the end of the period of ten years beginning with the day on which the Schedules came into force (i.e., 13 October 2003): LRA 2002, s. 117(1).

[253] Added by LRA 2002 (Transitional Provisions) (No 2) Order 2003 (SI 2003 No. 2431), art. 2(1), for a period of 10 years beginning on 13 October 2003. It was added as para. 16, because para. 15 originally

(ii) Unregistered interests which override registered dispositions

There are 16 interests which override registered dispositions. Fifteen are set out in Schedule 3; and a further interest is added by section 90 (PPP leases relating to transport in London). Of these 16 interests 13 are identical with those in Schedule 1. There are, however, important changes in the other three:

(a) Short leases (paragraph 1)

The three categories in Schedule 1 in which leases granted for a term not exceeding seven years are not overriding interests on first registration also apply in Schedule 3. To these are added five further exceptions in respect of dispositions which are granted out of a registered estate; they cannot be overriding interests because they are registrable in their own right. They are specified in section 27(2)(b) (p. 163, above).

(b) Interests of person in actual occupation (paragraph 2)

In this paragraph there is a new and very important replacement of section 70(1)(*g*) of the 1925 Act, which attempts to provide a fairer balance between the interests of a person in actual occupation and that of a purchaser for valuable consideration. The interest is not overriding if it (i) belongs to a person whose occupation would not have been obvious on a reasonably careful inspection of the land at the time of the disposition, and (ii) of which the person to whom the disposition is made does not have actual knowledge at that time. The Law Commission in its Report,[254] makes three important points:

(1) For the purposes of the Bill, it is not the *interest* that has to be apparent (as is the case in relation to contracts for the sale of land), but the *occupation* of the person having the interest.

(2) The test is not one of constructive notice of the occupation. It is the less demanding one (derived from the test applicable to intending buyers of land) that it should be obvious on a reasonably careful inspection of the land.[255]

(3) Even if a person's occupation is not apparent, the exception does not apply where a buyer has actual knowledge of that occupation.

The object of this exception is, therefore, to protect buyers and other registered disponees for valuable consideration in cases where the fact of occupation is neither subjectively known to them nor readily ascertainable. Once an intending buyer becomes aware of the occupation, he or she should make inquiry of the occupier because of the second exception mentioned above.

(c) Legal easements and profits à prendre (paragraph 3)

Far-reaching changes are made under Schedule 3 to the scope of overriding interests in relation to easements and profits à prendre. No such rights which are expressly

---

contained a temporary provision under which a right already acquired under the Limitation Act 1980 constituted an overriding interest until 13 October 2006.

[254] Report on Land Registration for the Twenty-First Century 2001 (Law Com No. 271), para. 8.62.

[255] See M & W, para. 12.068; Law Com No. 25, para. 5.72. [Cf. the view of Wolstenholme and Cherry, *Annotated Land Registration Act 2002*, para. 3.173B: 'Not only does the asserted distinction from constructive notice seem elusive, but the asserted derivation of the test is suspect'.]

created or reserved out of registered land[256] can take effect as overriding interests; and no equitable easements or profits, however created, are capable of overriding a registered disposition.[257] The only legal easements and profits which will be capable of being overriding interests are:

(i) those already in existence at the time the 2002 Act came into force which have not been registered;

(ii) those arising by implied grant or reservation; and

(iii) those arising by prescription.

There is a further curtailment of the category. Legal easements and profits à prendre which are not easily discoverable cannot be overriding interests. The effect of paragraph 3 is that a purchaser of an interest for valuable consideration under a registered disposition is only bound by an easement or profit à prendre which is an overriding interest if:

(i) he actually knows of it; or

(ii) if it would have been obvious on a reasonably careful inspection of the land over which the easement or profit à prendre is exercisable; or

(iii) it has been exercised within one year before the disposition. This is intended to cover the numerous invisible easements such as rights of drainage or the right to run a water supply over a neighbour's land.

There were significant transitional provisions. An easement or profit à prendre which was an overriding interest in relation to a registered estate immediately before the coming into force of Schedule 3 (i.e. 13 October 2003), but which would not fall within paragraph 3 of that Schedule if created after that date, retains its overriding status.[258] Moreover, for a period of three years after the Act came into force (i.e. until 13 October 2006) all legal easements and profits à prendre which had not been registered constituted overriding status.[259]

LAND REGISTRATION ACT 2002

SCHEDULE 3

UNREGISTERED INTERESTS WHICH OVERRIDE REGISTERED DISPOSITIONS

Leasehold estates in land

1 A leasehold estate in land granted for a term not exceeding seven years from the date of the grant, except for—

(a) a lease the grant of which falls within section 4(1)(d), (e) or (f);

(b) a lease the grant of which constitutes a registrable disposition.

---

[256] See p. 655, below, for the express or implied creation of easements and profits à prendre.
[257] See R & R, para. 17.027.   [258] LRA 2002, s. 134, Sch. 12, para. 9.
[259] Ibid., para. 10 ('For the period of three years beginning with the day on which Schedule 3 comes into force, paragraph 3 of the Schedule has effect with the omission of the exception').

Interests of persons in actual occupation

2 An interest belonging at the time of the disposition to a person in actual occupation, so far as relating to land of which he is in actual occupation, except for—

  (a) an interest under a settlement under the Settled Land Act 1925;

  (b) an interest of a person of whom inquiry was made before the disposition and who failed to disclose the right when he could reasonably have been expected to do so;

  (c) an interest —

    (i) which belongs to a person whose occupation would not have been obvious on a reasonably careful inspection of the land at the time of the disposition, and

    (ii) of which the person to whom the disposition is made does not have actual knowledge at that time;

  (d) a leasehold estate in land granted to take effect in possession after the end of the period of three months beginning with the date of the grant and which has not taken effect in possession at the time of the disposition.

Easements and profits a prendre

3 (1) A legal easement or profit a prendre, except for an easement, or a profit a prendre which is not registered under Part 1 of the Commons Act 2006,[259a] which at the time of the disposition —

    (a) is not within the actual knowledge of the person to whom the disposition is made, and

    (b) would not have been obvious on a reasonably careful inspection of the land over which the easement or profit is exercisable.

  (2) The exception in sub-paragraph (1) does not apply if the person entitled to the easement or profit proves that it has been exercised in the period of one year ending with the day of the disposition.

Customary and public rights

4 A customary right.

5 A public right.[260]

Local land charges

6 A local land charge.

Mines and minerals

7 An interest in any coal or coal mine, the rights attached to any such interest and the rights of any person under section 38, 49 or 51 of the Coal Industry Act 1994.

8 In the case of land to which title was registered before 1898, rights to mines and minerals (and incidental rights) created before 1898.

9 In the case of land to which title was registered between 1898 and 1925 inclusive, rights to mines and minerals (and incidental rights) created before the date of registration of the title.

Miscellaneous[261]

10 A franchise.

[259a] Amended by Commons Act 2006, Sch. 5, para. 8.

[260] *Overseas Investment Services Ltd v Simcobuild Construction Ltd* (1995) 70 P & CR 322, above, p. 193, n. 251.

[261] Paras 10 to 14 cease to have effect at the end of the period of ten years beginning with the day on which the Schedules came into force (i.e., 13 October 2003): LRA 2002, s. 117(1). Land Registry Practice Guide 66.

11 A manorial right.

12 A right to rent which was reserved to the Crown on the granting of any freehold estate (whether or not the right is still vested in the Crown).

13 A non-statutory right in respect of an embankment or sea or river wall.

14 A right to payment in lieu of tithe.

16 A right in respect of the repair of a church chancel.[262]

(iii) Abolition of certain overriding interests

Three categories of overriding interests were abolished by the Land Registration Act 2002. First, rights acquired or in course of being acquired under the Limitation Acts (LRA 1925, section 70(1)(*f*));[263] a new scheme of adverse possession is introduced by the 2002 Act (p. 279, below). Secondly, 'in the case of a possessory qualified or good leasehold title, all rights interests and powers excepted from the effect of registration' (section 70(1)(*h*)). The third category abolished, 'liability to repair the chancel of any church' (section 70(1)(*c*)), was reinstated in the light of the reversal of *Aston Cantlow Parochial Church Council v Wallbank* by the House of Lords.[264]

(iv) Duty to disclose unregistered interests

There is a new duty of disclosure in an application for registration to provide information about overriding interests under both Schedules 1 and 3. Although there is no specific penalty for failure to do so, the object of section 71 of the Act is to ensure that as many rights as possible are brought onto the register.

LAND REGISTRATION ACT 2002

71 Duty to disclose unregistered interests

Where rules so provide[265]—

(a) a person applying for registration under Chapter 1 of Part 2 must provide to the registrar such information as the rules may provide about any interest affecting the estate to which the application relates which—

(i) falls within any of the paragraphs of Schedule 1, and

(ii) is of a description specified by the rules;

---

[262] Added by LRA 2002 (Transitional Provisions) (No 2) Order 2003 (SI 2003 No. 2431), art. 2(2), for a period of 10 years beginning on 13 October 2003. It was added as para. 16, because para. 15 originally contained a temporary provision under which a right already acquired by a squatter under the Limitation Act 1980 to be registered as proprietor of the estate constituted an overriding interest until 13 October 2006: LRA 2002, s. 134, Sch. 12, para. 11.

[263] Subject to transitional provisions until 13 October 2006: above, n. 262.

[264] [2004] 1 AC 546, above, p. 192, n. 250.

[265] LRR 2003, rr. 28, 57. Land Registry Practice Guide 15. There is no requirement to disclose interests that cannot be protected by notice on the register, public rights, local land charges and leases which have one year or less still to run and, in the case of first registration, interests that are apparent from the deeds and documents of title accompanying the application. Under LRA 1925 the applicant had no duty of disclosure, but the registrar had a mandatory duty to enter a notice on first registration of 'any easement, right, privilege, or benefit created by an instrument' which appeared on the title and adversely affected the land: LRA 1925, s. 70 (2).

(b) a person applying to register a registrable disposition of a registered estate must provide to the registrar such information as the rules may provide about any unregistered interest affecting the estate which—

(i) falls within any of the paragraphs of Schedule 3, and

(ii) is of description specified by the rules.

D. PARAGRAPH 1: LEGAL LEASES

Under the Land Registration Act 2002 the interest of the tenant under a lease will have priority against a purchaser for value from the landlord if the lease fulfils the requirements of paragraph 1 of Schedule 3:

1 A leasehold estate in land granted for a term not exceeding seven years from the date of the grant, except for —

(a) a lease the grant of which falls within section 4(1)(d), (e) or (f);

(b) a lease the grant of which constitutes a registrable disposition.

The opening words (leasehold *estate* in land *granted* for a term...) show that this is limited to legal leases.[266] The language of 'grant' also appeared in the equivalent provision in the Land Registration Act 1925, section 70(1)(k); its significance was explained by JENKINS LJ in **City Permanent Building Society v Miller** [1952] Ch 840 at 853:

In my judgment, the use [in Land Registration Act 1925, s. 70(1)(k)] of the word 'granted' clearly imports the actual creation of a term of years, whether it is done by deed or by an agreement under hand only, in that class of cases in which a legal term can be created by a document not under seal, or indeed by parol in any case in which an actual tenancy taking effect at law may be created without writing. But in my judgment the word 'granted' necessarily imports the actual creation of a term, and that excludes, by force of the context, the case of a mere agreement for a lease, having no more than a contractual effect. To include such a case, in my judgment, section 70(1)(k) should have read 'granted or agreed to be granted.'

E. PARAGRAPH 2: INTERESTS OF PERSONS IN ACTUAL OCCUPATION

(i) The 'interest'

Paragraph 2 protects as an overriding interest an '*interest* belonging at the time of the disposition to a person in actual occupation'. The occupation is not itself an overriding interest; the occupier must have a right which is separately identifiable as a property right before it can be given priority as against a purchaser for value by virtue of the

---

[266] For the distinction between legal and equitable leases, and the requirements for the creation of a legal lease, see pp. 416–421, below.

occupier's actual occupation. This was made clear by LORD WILBERFORCE in relation to section 70 of the Land Registration Act 1925 in **National Provincial Bank Ltd v Ainsworth** [1965] AC 1175 at 1261:

[The Land Registration] Act is a registration Act concerned (in this instance) to provide that certain rights are to be binding without registration and without the necessity for actual notice. To ascertain what 'rights' come within this provision, one must look outside the Land Registration Act and see what rights affect purchasers under the general law. To suppose that the subsection makes any right, of howsoever a personal character, which a person in occupation may have, an overriding interest by which a purchaser is bound, would involve two consequences: first that this Act is, in this respect, bringing about a substantive change in real property law by making personal rights bind purchasers; second, that there is a difference *as to the nature of the rights by which a purchaser may be bound* between registered and unregistered land; for purely personal rights including the wife's right to stay in the house (if my analysis of this is correct) cannot affect purchasers of unregistered land even with notice. One may have to accept that there is a difference between unregistered land and registered land as regards what kind of notice binds a purchaser, or what kind of inquiries a purchaser has to make. But there is no warrant in the terms of this paragraph or elsewhere in the Act for supposing that the nature of the rights which are to bind a purchaser is to be different, excluding personal rights in one case, including them in another. The whole frame of section 70, with the list that it gives of interests, or rights, which are overriding, shows that it is made against a background of interests or rights whose nature and whose transmissible character is known, or ascertainable, aliunde, i.e., under other statutes or under the common law. So, if the right of a deserted wife is a purely personal claim against her husband, not specifically related to the house in question, but merely, at its highest, to be provided with a home, there is no difficulty in seeing that this type of right cannot, any more than any purely contractual right,[267] be an overriding interest.

But the interest which can be overriding under paragraph 2 need not be the interest by virtue of which the occupier occupies the land. And so, for example, a tenant's option to purchase the freehold can be an overriding interest.[268]

---

[267] *Nationwide Anglia Building Society v Ahmed and Balakrishnan* (1995) 70 P & CR 381 (vendor of premises who remained in possession of part under contractual licence after completion held not to have overriding interest).

[268] Other examples of rights which were held to be sufficient within LRA 1925, s. 70(1)(*g*), and which would now constitute 'interests' within para. 2 of Scheds 1 and 3 of the 2002 Act, are (1) an equitable interest under a trust of land: *Williams & Glyn's Bank Ltd v Boland* [1981] AC 487, p. 203, below; cf. *City of London Building Society v Flegg* [1988] AC 54, p. 551, below (equitable interests of parents as tenants in common arising from contribution to purchase price of house, registered in names of their daughter and son-in-law, were an interest under s. 70(1)(ii)); (2) a right of pre-emption: *Kling v Keston Properties Ltd* (1983) 49 P & CR 212 (see also LRA 2002, s. 115, above, p. 40: right of pre-emption 'has effect from the time of creation as an interest capable of binding successors in title'); (3) an unpaid vendor's lien where the vendor remains in occupation under a lease-back by the purchaser: *London and Cheshire Insurance Co Ltd v Laplagrene Property Co Ltd* [1971] Ch 499; (4) an equity by estoppel: *Habermann v Koehler* (1996) 73 P & CR 515 (see also LRA 2002, s. 116, an equity by estoppel 'has effect from the time the equity arises as an interest capable of binding successors'); (5) a right to rectify an instrument: *Blacklocks v JB Developments (Godalming) Ltd* [1982] Ch 183 (cf. *Smith v Jones* [1954] 1 WLR 1089, where Upjohn J held that a right to rectify a tenancy agreement would not be enforceable by a tenant against a purchaser of the reversion who had inspected the agreement; [1983] Conv 169, 257 (J.T.F.), 361 (D. G. Barnsley); distinguished in *Nurdin & Peacock plc v Ramsden & Co Ltd* [1999] 1 EGLR 119 as being a

Webb v Pollmount Ltd
[1966] Ch 584 (ChD, **Ungoed-Thomas J**)

The plaintiff held under a lease granted by the defendant's predecessor in title. The lease gave to the plaintiff the option to purchase the freehold but, as the register contained no mention of the option, the defendant claimed that it could not be exercised as against him. The issue was whether the option constituted an overriding interest within section 70(1)(g).

Held. The option was an overriding interest.

Ungoed-Thomas J: The defendant submits that overriding interests or rights in section 70(1)(g) are limited to rights of a person in an estate in the land, and he makes this submission with a view to establishing that the plaintiff's overriding interest is here limited to his leasehold estate exclusive of the option to purchase. It was first sought to establish this by limiting 'land' in sub-paragraph (g) to an estate in the land....

As a matter of first impression, 'land' in section 70(1)(g) does not appear to me to refer to an estate in land, but to the physical land. The references which are contained in the sub-paragraph to 'actual occupation' and 'receipt of the rents and profits thereof' indicate this conclusion: and (g) is not limited to the rights of every tenant or estate owner, but extends to the rights of every person in actual occupation. 'Registered land' and 'land' are by definition not limited to estates in land, but include physical land....

As the definition of 'overriding interests' expressly excludes matters entered on the register, it indicates that matters registrable but not registered, are not excluded. Overriding interests may include registrable matters, provided they have not been entered on the register....

The opening words of section 70(1) provide a further limit on overriding interests within the section, namely, that they be 'for the time being subsisting in reference' to the registered land.[269] The result is that, so far as material to this case, rights within section 70(1)(g) must fall within such rights as (1) are 'not entered on the register', (2) are 'affecting the estate transferred' to the defendant, (3) 'may be for the time being subsisting in reference' to the registered land. The option was not entered on the register, and there is no difficulty about the first of these limitations. So, the question in this case is whether the option to purchase contained in the lease affects the reversion transferred to the defendant and subsists in reference to the registered

case on unregistered land; [1999] [Conv] 421 (S. Pascoe). See also LRA 2002, s. 116: a mere equity 'has effect from the time the equity arises as an interest capable of binding successors in title'); (6) the right to seek rectification of the register: *Malory Enterprises Ltd v Cheshire Homes (UK) Ltd* [2002] Ch 216; (7) the right of a beneficiary under a bare trust to the fee simple in equity: *Hodgson v Marks* [1971] Ch 892; *Collings v Lee* [2001] 2 All ER 332 (rights of beneficiary under bare trust arising as a result of transfer induced by fraudulent misrepresentation); [2001] CLJ 477 (R. Nolan); [2001] All ER Rev 253 (P. J. Clarke)).

For statutory exclusions from para. 2 (carried over from LRA 1925, s. 70(1)(*g*)), see Family Law Act 1996, s. 31(10)(*b*) (spouse's right of occupation); Leasehold Reform Act 1967, s. 5(5) (tenant's right to acquire freehold or apply for extended lease); HA 1985 Sch. 9A, para. 6(1), inserted by Housing and Planning Act 1986, s. 8(2), Sch. 2 (secure tenant's right to buy); Access to Neighbouring Land Act 1992, s. 5 (rights conferred by, or access order under, the Act); L & T(C)A 1995, s. 20(6) (right to overriding lease), all amended by LRA 2002, Sch. 11.

[269] LRA 2002, Schs 1 and 3 do not contain this language. However, s. 29(1) limits interests which can have priority (including overriding interests under s. 29(2)(a)(ii)) to interests 'affecting the estate'.

land. The statute itself does not answer this question: it raises it. The answer is only to be found by reference to the general law in whose context the statute was enacted.

In *National Provincial Bank Ltd v Hastings Car Mart Ltd*,[270] the House of Lords, in considering the rights of a deserted wife in respect of the matrimonial home, dealt with section 70. Russell LJ's observations in the Court of Appeal in that case were quoted with approval in the House of Lords. He said:

> 'It seems to me that section 70 in all its parts is dealing with rights in reference to land which have the quality of being capable of enduring through different ownerships of the land, according to normal conceptions of title to real property.'

Lord Upjohn said:

> '...notice itself does not create the right. To create a right over the land of another that right must (apart from statute) create a burden on the land, i.e., an equitable estate or interest in the land.'

Thus, for a right to be within section 70(1)(*g*), it must be an 'interest in the land' 'capable of enduring through different ownerships of the land according to normal conceptions of title to real property.'

An option to purchase is an interest in the land in respect of which it is exercisable, whether contained in a lease or not....

It was suggested for the defendant that 'the right of every person in actual occupation of the land' should be construed as the right by virtue of which a person is in actual occupation of the land. The short answer to this, it seems to me, is that it does not say so; and the wording is in marked contrast with the wording in section 14 of the Law of Property Act 1925, where reference is made to the interest of a person in possession or occupation of land 'to which he may be entitled in right of such possession or occupation'. It is neither, in my view, consistent with the wording of section 70(1)(*g*) of the Land Registration Act 1925, nor with the authorities from which I have quoted.

Although an option to purchase does not, like an option to renew, 'touch', 'concern' or 'affect' the land demised and regarded as the subject-matter of the lease' (so as, e.g., to bind the reversion under the Grantees of Reversions Act 1540[271]), what we are concerned with here is not whether it so 'affects' 'the land demised' and is within the relationship of landlord and tenant as considered in the judgment of the Court of Appeal in *Woodall v Clifton* [1905] 2 Ch 257, but whether within section 20(1)(*b*) it is an interest 'affecting the estate transferred' to the defendant. That it is capable of affecting the estate transferred to the defendant is not disputed; e.g., if the defendant had notice of it before transfer to him. So, it seems to me to fall within Russell LJ's test in *National Provincial Bank Ltd v Hastings Car Mart Ltd* of 'being capable of enduring through different ownerships of the land according to normal conceptions of title to real property.' And if it, thus, in the circumstances of this case, is a right 'affecting the estate transferred', within the requirement of section 20(1)(*b*), it seems to me that it is 'for the time being subsisting in reference to' registered land within the requirement of section 70(1). My conclusion, therefore, is that subject to deciding the question as to the effect of section 59, the option to purchase appears to be an overriding interest.

---

[270] *National Provincial Bank Ltd v Ainsworth* [1965] AC 1175, on appeal from *National Provincial Bank Ltd v Hastings Car Mart Ltd* [1964] Ch 665.
[271] Below, p. 463.

(ii) 'belonging at the time of the disposition'

Law Commission: Land Registration For The Twenty-First Century: A Consultative Document 1998 (Law Com No. 254), paras 5.112–5.113

THE 'REGISTRATION GAP'

5.112 One problem that was a source of uncertainty until comparatively recently was the so-called 'registration gap' in relation to overriding interests. The question arises because there is at present an inevitable gap between the completion of a sale, lease of, or charge over registered land and the registration of the transfer or charge. Which is the appropriate date for ascertaining the existence of an overriding interest, the date of the transfer or the date of registration? The latter is the more logical in a system of title registration. A purchaser of registered land takes it *when registered* subject to entries on the register and overriding interests but free from all other estates and interests.[272] As one commentator has observed—

> The essence of any registration system lies in registration. If a purchaser fails to register then he cannot expect to assert priority over unprotected interests. Similarly, he should not be protected if he delays in registering. We should set out to encourage prompt registration. After all, registration might in some cases be delayed for years…[273]

However, the advantage of the transfer date is that it provides protection against overriding interests which are deliberately created between transfer and registration and which may therefore prejudice a chargee who has provided funding for the purchase. In its Third Report, the Law Commission recommended that the transfer date should be accepted as the relevant date for ascertaining the existence of an overriding interest.[274] To adopt this recommendation without more however, could lead to some very odd consequences. It would mean (for example) that if a local land charge were to arise between transfer and registration, the purchaser would take free of it for the reasons set out above.[275]

5.113 The Law Commission's proposals have, however, been overtaken by events. In *Abbey National Building Society v Cann*,[276] the House of Lords held that—

(1) the relevant date for ascertaining the existence of an overriding interest was *the date of registration*;[277] but

(2) in relation to overriding interests under section 70(1)(g)—the rights of persons in actual occupation—the actual occupation had to be one 'which preceded and existed

---

272 Land Registration Act 1925, ss. 20(1), 23(1).

273 Roger J. Smith, 'Land Registration and Conveyancing Absurdity' (1988) 104 LQR 507, 509–510.

274 Law Com No. 158, para. 2.77.

275 See *Abbey National Building Society v Cann* [1991] 1 AC 56, 85. It should be noted that, in the Third Report, the Law Commission had recommended that local land charges should take effect as general burdens and bound all transferees: Law Com No. 158, para. 2.94. This particular oddity would not therefore have arisen under their proposals.

276 [1991] 1 AC 56 [below, p. 214; (1990) 106 LQR 32, 545 (R. J. Smith); [1990] CLJ 397 (A. J. Oakley); (1990) 87 LSG 19–24, 34–19 (M. Beaumont, junior counsel for Mrs Cann); [1991] Conv 116 (S. Baughen), 155 (P. T. Evans)]. See too *Barclays Bank Plc v Zaroovabli* [1997] Ch 321, 327, 328.

277 Registration is deemed to take place when the application to register is delivered to the proper office: Land Registration Rules 1925, r. 83. [See now LRR 2003, r. 15.]

at completion of a transfer or disposition',[278] because it was only at that date that the inquiry contemplated by the paragraph[279] could be made.

We consider that this rule achieves a fair balance between the principles of registration and the interests of encumbrancers on the one hand and the need to ensure security for the interests of purchasers and chargees on the other....

We note that, in time, the 'registration gap' should become a thing of the past. If electronic transfer of land is introduced, transfers (and other dispositions of registered land) will be simultaneous with their registration.[280]

The 2002 Act follows this consultation proposal, and therefore for the purposes of para. 2 of Sch. 3[281] the date for deciding whether there is actual occupation is the date for completion of the purchase (the disposition), when the transfer is executed and exchanged for the purchase money, rather than the (later) date of registration of the transferee as proprietor.[282]

(iii) 'in actual occupation'

Paragraph 2 of Schedules 1 and 3 of the Land Registration Act 1925 provide that the person must be 'in actual occupation' of the land. This phrase also appeared in section 70(1)(g) of the Land Registration Act 1925, on which there was extensive case law.

(a) 'Actual occupation' as ordinary words of plain English

Williams & Glyn's Bank Ltd v Boland
[1981] AC 487 (HL, **Lord Wilberforce, Viscount Dilhorne, Lords Salmon, Scarman** and **Roskill**)

In each of two cases the husband was registered as sole proprietor of the matrimonial home where he and his wife lived. The wife had made a substantial contribution to the purchase, which entitled her to a share in the house. She had not protected her interest by entering a notice, caution or restriction on the register. The husband, without the wife's consent, charged the house to the plaintiff bank to secure his business indebtedness. The bank made no enquiry as to whether the wife had any interest in the house. It now claimed repayment of the loan and possession of the house. In both cases the wife claimed an overriding interest under Land Registration Act 1925, section 70(1)(g).

---

[278] [1991] 1 AC 56 at 88, *per* Lord Oliver.

[279] '...save where enquiry is made of such person and the rights are not disclosed'.

[280] [See below, p. 226.]

[281] The date for other overriding interests is the date of registration, except for para. 3 of Sch. 3 (legal easements and profits à prendre) where the discoverability test is applied at the time of the disposition: p. 220, below. Under Sch. 1 (first registration,), all overriding interests (including actual occupation under para. 2, and easements and profits under para. 3), are tested at the date of registration because first registration does not presuppose any disposition: p. 191, above.

[282] For a different view, based on the assumption that the 'time of the disposition' is registration because under LRA 2002, s. 27 (1), the disposition does not operate at law until registration, see Wolstenholme and Cherry, *Annotated Land Registration Act 2002*, para. 3–173A.

Held. The wife had an overriding interest.

Lord Wilberforce: My Lords, these appeals, . . . raise for decision the same question: whether a husband or a wife, (in each actual case a wife) who has a beneficial interest in the matrimonial home, by virtue of having contributed to its purchase price, but whose spouse is the legal and registered owner, has an 'overriding interest' binding on a mortgagee who claims possession of the matrimonial home under a mortgage granted by that spouse alone. Although this statement of the issue uses the words 'spouse,' 'husband and wife,' 'matrimonial home,' the appeals do not, in my understanding, involve any question of matrimonial law, or of the rights of married women or of women as such. Exactly the same issue could arise if the roles of husband and wife were reversed, or if the persons interested in the house were not married to each other. The solution must be derived from a consideration in the light of current social conditions of the Land Registration Act 1925 and other property statutes. . . .

The legal framework within which the appeals are to be decided can be summarised as follows:

Under the Land Registration Act 1925, legal estates in land are the only interests in respect of which a proprietor can be registered. Other interests take effect in equity as 'minor interests,' which are overriden by a registered transfer. But the Act recognises also an intermediate, or hybrid, class of what are called 'overriding interests': though these are not registered, legal dispositions take effect subject to them. The list of overriding interests is contained in section 70 [above, p. 182] and it includes such matters as easements, liabilities having their origin in tenure, land tax and tithe rentcharge, seignorial and manorial rights, leases for terms not exceeding 21 years, and finally, the relevant paragraph being section 70(1)(g):

> 'The rights of every person in actual occupation of the land or in receipt of the rents and profits thereof, save where enquiry is made of such person and the rights are not disclosed; . . .'

The first question is whether the wife is a 'person in actual occupation' and if so, whether her right as a tenant in common in equity is a right protected by this provision.

The other main element arises out of the Law of Property Act 1925. Since that Act, undivided shares in land can only take effect in equity, behind a trust for sale upon which the legal owner is to hold the land.[283] Dispositions of the land, including mortgages, may be made under this trust and, provided that there are at least two trustees, or a trust corporation, 'overreach' the trusts.[284] This means that the 'purchaser' takes free from them, whether or not he has notice of them, and that the trusts are enforceable against the proceeds of sale: see Law of Property Act 1925, section 2(2) and (3) which lists certain exceptions.

The second question is whether the wife's equitable interest under the trust for sale, if she is in occupation of the land, is capable of being an overriding interest, or whether, as is generally the rule as regards equitable interests it can only take effect as a 'minor interest.' In the latter event a registered transferee, including a legal mortgagee, would take free from it.

The system of land registration, as it exists in England, which long antedates the Land Registration Act 1925, is designed to simplify and to cheapen conveyancing. It is intended to replace the often complicated and voluminous title deeds of property by a single land certificate, on the strength of which land can be dealt with. In place of the lengthy and often technical investigation of title to which a purchaser was committed, all he has to do is to consult

---

[283]　Since 1997, trusts of land under TLATA 1996; see chap. 6, below.

[284]　For overreaching, see pp. 548–558, below.

the register; from any burden not entered on the register, with one exception, he takes free. Above all, the system is designed to free the purchaser from the hazards of notice—real or constructive—which, in the case of unregistered land, involved him in enquiries, often quite elaborate, failing which he might be bound by equities. The Law of Property Act 1925 contains provisions limiting the effect of the doctrine of notice, but it still remains a potential source of danger to purchasers. By contrast, the only provisions in the Land Registration Act 1925 with regard to notice are provisions which enable a purchaser to take the estate free from equitable interests or equities whether he has notice or not. (See, for example, section 3(xv) s.v. 'minor interests'). The only kind of notice recognised is by entry on the register.

The exception just mentioned consists of 'overriding interests' listed in section 70. As to these, all registered land is stated to be deemed to be subject to such of them as may be subsisting in reference to the land, unless the contrary is expressed on the register. The land is so subject regardless of notice actual or constructive. In my opinion therefore, the law as to notice as it may affect purchasers of unregistered land, whether contained in decided cases, or in a statute (the Conveyancing Act 1882, section 3, Law of Property Act, section 199) has no application even by analogy to registered land. Whether a particular right is an overriding interest, and whether it affects a purchaser, is to be decided upon the terms of section 70, and other relevant provisions of the Land Registration Act 1925, and upon nothing else.

In relation to rights connected with occupation, it has been said that the purpose and effect of section 70(1)(g) of the Land Registration Act 1925 was to make applicable to registered land the same rule as previously had been held to apply to unregistered land: see per Lord Denning MR in *National Provincial Bank Ltd v Hastings Car Mart Ltd* [1964] Ch 665 at 689, and in this House [1965] AC 1175 at 1259.

I adhere to this, but I do not accept the argument which learned counsel for the appellant sought to draw from it. His submission was that, in applying section 70(1) (g), we should have regard to and limit the application of the paragraph in the light of the doctrine of notice. But this would run counter to the whole purpose of the Act. The purpose, in each system, is the same, namely, to safeguard the rights of persons in occupation, but the method used differs. In the case of unregistered land, the purchaser's obligation depends upon what he has notice of—notice actual or constructive. In the case of registered land, it is the fact of occupation that matters. If there is actual occupation, and the occupier has rights, the purchaser takes subject to them. If not, he does not. No further element is material.

I now deal with the first question. Were the wives here in 'actual occupation'? These words are ordinary words of plain English, and should, in my opinion, be interpreted as such. Historically they appear to have emerged in the judgment of Lord Loughborough LC in *Taylor v Stibbert* (1794) 2 Ves 437 at 439–440, in a passage which repays quotation:

'...whoever purchases an estate from the owner, knowing it to be in possession of tenants, is bound to inquire into the estates those tenants have. It has been determined, that a purchaser being told, particular parts of the estate were in possession of a tenant, without any information as to his interest, and taking it for granted it was only from year to year, was bound by a lease, that tenant had, which was a surprise upon him. That was rightly determined; for it was sufficient to put the purchaser upon inquiry, that he was informed, the estate was not in the *actual possession* of the person, with whom he contracted; that he could not transfer the ownership and possession at the same time; that there were interests, as to the extent and terms of which it was his duty to inquire.'

They were taken up in the judgment of the Privy Council in *Barnhart v Greenshields* (1853) 9 Moo PCC 18. The purpose for which they were used, in that case, was evidently to distinguish the case of a person who was in some kind of legal possession, as by receipt of the rents and profits, from that of a person actually in occupation as tenant. Given occupation, i.e. presence on the land, I do not think that the word 'actual' was intended to introduce any additional quali-fication, certainly not to suggest that possession must be 'adverse': it merely emphasises that what is required is physical presence, not some entitlement in law. So even if it were necessary to look behind these plain words into history, I would find no reason for denying them their plain meaning.

Then, were the wives in actual occupation? I ask: why not? There was physical presence, with all the rights that occupiers have, including the right to exclude all others except those having similar rights. The house was a matrimonial home, intended to be occupied, and in fact occupied by both spouses, both of whom have an interest in it: it would require some special doctrine of law to avoid the result that each is in occupation. Three arguments were used for a contrary conclusion. First, it was said that if the vendor (I use this word to include a mortgagor) is in occupation, that is enough to prevent the application of the paragraph. This seems to be a proposition of general application, not limited to the case of husbands, and no doubt, if correct, would be very convenient for purchasers and intending mortgagees. But the presence of the vendor, with occupation, does not exclude the possibility of occupation of others.[285] There are observations which suggest the contrary in the unregistered land case of *Caunce v Caunce* [1969] 1 WLR 286, but I agree with the disapproval of these, and with the assertion of the proposition I have just stated by Russell LJ in *Hodgson v Marks* [1971] Ch 892 at 934. Then it was suggested that the wife's occupation was nothing but the shadow of the husband's—a version I suppose of the doctrine of unity of husband and wife. This expression and the argument flowing from it was used by Templeman J in *Bird v Syme-Thomson* [1979] 1 WLR 440 at 444, a decision preceding and which he followed in the present case. The argu-ment was also inherent in the judgment in *Caunce v Caunce* which influenced the decisions of Templeman J. It somewhat faded from the arguments in the present case and appears to me to be heavily obsolete. The appellant's main and final position became in the end this: that, to come within the paragraph, the occupation in question must be apparently inconsistent with the title of the vendor. This, it was suggested, would exclude the wife of a husband-vendor because her apparent occupation would be satisfactorily accounted for by his. But, apart from the rewriting of the paragraph which this would involve, the suggestion is unacceptable. Consistency, or inconsistency, involves the absence, or presence, of an independent right to occupy, though I must observe that 'inconsistency' in this context is an inappropriate word. But how can either quality be predicated of a wife, simply qua wife? A wife may, and everyone knows this, have rights of her own; particularly, many wives have a share in a matrimonial home. How can it be said that the presence of a wife in the house, as occupier, is consistent or inconsistent with the husband's rights until one knows what rights she has? And if she has rights, why, just because she is a wife (or in the converse case, just because an occupier is the husband), should these rights be denied protection under the paragraph? If one looks beyond the case of husband and wife, the difficulty of all these arguments stands out if one considers the case of a man living with a mistress, or of a man and a woman—or for that matter two persons of the same sex—living in a house in separate or partially shared rooms. Are these cases of apparently consistent occupation, so that the rights of the other person (other than

---

[285] 'Occupation need not be in one single person. Two persons can be in actual occupation, by themselves jointly, or each of them severally': *Williams & Glyn's Bank Ltd v Boland* [1979] Ch 312 at 331, per Lord Denning MR.

the vendor) can be disregarded? The only solution which is consistent with the Act (section 70(1)(g)) and with common sense is to read the paragraph for what it says. Occupation, existing as a fact, may protect rights if the person in occupation has rights. On this part of the case I have no difficulty in concluding that a spouse, living in a house, has an actual occupation capable of conferring protection, as an overriding interest, upon rights of that spouse.[286]

This brings me to the second question, which is whether such rights as a spouse has under a trust for sale are capable of recognition as overriding interests—a question to my mind of some difficulty.[287] The argument against this is based upon the structure of the Land Registration Act 1925 and upon specific provisions in it.

As to structure, it is said that the Act recognises three things: (a) legal estates, (b) minor interests, which take effect in equity, (c) overriding interests. These are mutually exclusive: an equitable interest, which is a minor interest, is incapable of being at the same time an overriding interest. The wife's interest, is incapable of being at the same time an overriding interest. The wife's interest, existing under or behind a trust for sale, is an equitable interest and nothing more. To give it the protection of an overriding interest would, moreover, contradict the principle according to which such an equitable interest can be overreached by an exercise of the trust for sale. As to the provisions of the Act, particular emphasis is placed on section 3(xv) which, in defining 'minor interests' specifically includes in the case of land held on trust for sale 'all interests and powers which are under the Law of Property Act 1925 capable of being overridden by the trustees for sale' and excludes, expressly, overriding interests. Reliance is also placed on section 86, which, dealing analogously, so it is said, with settled land, prescribes that successive or other interests created by or arising under a settlement take effect as minor interests and not otherwise, and on section 101 which, it is argued, recognises the exclusive character of minor interests, which in all cases can be overridden.

My Lords, I find this argument formidable. To reach a conclusion upon it involves some further consideration of the nature of trusts for sale, in relation to undivided shares. The trusts upon which, in this case, the land is to be held are defined—as 'statutory trusts'—in section 35 of the Law of Property Act 1925, i.e.:

'...upon trust to sell the same and to stand possessed of the net proceeds of sale, after payment of costs, and of the net rents and profits until sale after payment of rates, taxes, costs of insurance, repairs, and other outgoings, upon such trusts, and subject to such powers and provisions, as may be requisite for giving effect to the rights of the persons...interested in the land'.

In addition to this specific disposition, the general provisions as to trusts for sale in sections 23 to 31, where not inconsistent, appear to apply. The right of occupation of the land pending sale is not explicitly dealt with in these sections and the position as to it is obscure. Before the Act the position was that owners of undivided shares (which could exist at law) had

---

[286] This argument may not, however, hold in the case of children: *Hypo-Mortgage Services Ltd v Robinson* [1997] 2 FLR 71 (minors aged 1 and 3 with equitable beneficial interests under a trust for sale held not to be capable of being in actual occupation: 'They were there because their parent is there. They have no right of occupation of their own...they are only there as shadows of occupation of their parents': per Nourse LJ, citing *Bird v Syme-Thompson* [1979] 1 WLR 440).

[287] Since 1997 the interest of the spouse takes effect under a trust of land; and the doctrine of conversion has been 'abolished' with retrospective effect so that the interest under a trust for sale of land, even if created before 1997, is no longer to be regarded as personal property: TLATA 1996, ss. 1, 3; p. 519, below. This removes one argument which had to be addressed in *Boland* about whether the beneficiary's interest is an interest 'subsisting in reference to' the land within LRA 1925, s. 70(1).

concurrent rights of occupation. In *Bull v Bull* [1955] 1 QB 234 it was held by the Court of Appeal, applying *Re Warren* [1932] 1 Ch 42, that the conversion of these legal estates into equitable interests by the Law of Property Act 1925 should not affect the mutual rights of the owners. Denning LJ, in a judgment which I find most illuminating, there held, at 238, in a factual situation similar to that of the instant cases, that 'when there are two equitable tenants in common, then, until the place is sold, each of them is entitled concurrently with the other to the possession of the land and to the use and enjoyment of it in a proper manner'. And he referred to section 14 of the Law of Property Act 1925 which provides that the Act 'shall not prejudicially affect the interest of any person in possession or in actual occupation of land to which he may be entitled in right of such possession or occupation'.

How then are these various rights to be fitted into the scheme of the Land Registration Act 1925? It is clear, at least, that the interests of the co-owners under the 'statutory trusts' are minor interests—this fits with the definition in section 3(xv). But I can see no reason why, if these interests, or that of any one of them, are or is protected by 'actual occupation' they should remain merely as 'minor interests'. On the contrary, I see every reason why, in that event, they should acquire the status of overriding interests. And, moreover, I find it easy to accept that they satisfy the opening, and governing, words of section 70, namely, interests subsisting in reference to the land. As Lord Denning MR points out, to describe the interests of spouses in a house jointly bought to be lived in as a matrimonial home as merely an interest in proceeds of sale, or rents and profits until sale, is just a little unreal: see also *Elias v Mitchell* [1972] Ch 652, per Pennycuick V-C with whose analysis I agree, and contrast, *Cedar Holdings Ltd v Green* [1981] Ch 129 (which I consider to have been wrongly decided).

There are decisions, in relation to other equitable interests than those of tenants in common, which confirm this line of argument. In *Bridges v Mees* [1957] Ch 475, Harman J decided that a purchaser of land under a contract for sale, who had paid the price and so was entitled to the land in equity, could acquire an overriding interest by virtue of actual occupation, and a similar position was held by the Court of Appeal to arise in relation to a resulting trust: *Hodgson v Marks* [1971] Ch 892. These decisions (following the law as it undoubtedly existed before 1925—see *Barnhart v Greenshields* (1853) 9 Moo PCC 18 at 32, *Daniels v Davison* (1809) 16 Ves 249, *Allen v Anthony* (1816) 1 Mer 282, 284 per Lord Eldon LC) provide an answer to the argument that there is a firm dividing line, or an unbridgeable gulf, between minor interests and overriding interests, and, on the contrary, confirm that the fact of occupation enables protection of the latter to extend to what without it would be the former. In my opinion, the wives' equitable interests, subsisting in reference to the land, were by the fact of occupation, made into overriding interests, and so protected by section 70(1)(*g*). I should add that it makes no difference to this that these same interests might also have been capable of protection by the registration of a caution: see *Bridges v Mees* [1957] Ch 475 at 487, and Land Registration Act 1925, section 59(6).

There was finally an argument based upon section 74 of the Land Registration Act 1925.[288] The section provides:

'Subject to the provisions of this Act as to settled land, neither the registrar nor any person dealing with a registered estate or charge shall be affected with notice of a trust express implied or constructive, and references to trusts shall, so far as possible, be excluded from the register.'

[288] See now LRA 2002, s. 78.

The argument was that if the overriding interest sought to be protected is, under the general law, only binding on a purchaser by virtue of notice, the section has the effect of denying the protection. It is obvious—and indeed conceded—that if this is right, *Hodgson v Marks* and *Bridges v Mees* must have been wrongly decided.

I am of opinion that this section has no such effect. Its purpose is to make clear, as I have already explained, that the doctrine of notice has no application to registered conveyancing, and accordingly to establish, as an administration measure, that entries may not be made in the register which would only be appropriate if that doctrine were applicable. It cannot have the effect of cutting down the general application of section 70(1).

I would only add, in conclusion, on the appeal as it concerns the wives a brief observation on the conveyancing consequences of dismissing the appeal. These were alarming to Templeman J, and I can agree with him to the extent that whereas the object of a land registration system is to reduce the risks to purchasers from anything not on the register, to extend (if it be an extension) the area of risk so as to include possible interests of spouses, and indeed, in theory, of other members of the family or even outside it, may add to the burdens of purchasers, and involve them in enquiries which in some cases may be troublesome.

But conceded, as it must be, that the Act, following established practice, gives protection to occupation, the extension of the risk area follows necessarily from the extension, beyond the paterfamilias, of rights of ownership, itself following from the diffusion of property and earning capacity. What is involved is a departure from an easy-going practice of dispensing with enquiries as to occupation beyond that of the vendor and accepting the risks of doing so. To substitute for this a practice of more careful enquiry as to the fact of occupation, and if necessary, as to the rights of occupiers can not, in my view of the matter, be considered as unacceptable except at the price of overlooking the widespread development of shared interests of ownership. In the light of section 70 of the Act, I cannot believe that Parliament intended this, though it may be true that in 1925 it did not foresee the full extent of this development.[289]

(b) Nature and state of the property

Lloyds Bank plc v Rosset
[1989] Ch 350 (CA, **Purchas, Mustill** and **Nicholls LJJ**)[290]

In 1982 Mr and Mrs Rosset decided to purchase a semi-derelict farmhouse in Thanet, Kent, which was registered land. The purchase was to be funded by Mr Rosset's family trust in Switzerland, and the legal estate was to be in his sole name. It was their common intention that the renovation should be a joint venture and that Mrs Rosset should have a beneficial interest in the farmhouse.

On 7 November the vendors allowed Mr and Mrs Rosset's builders to enter and start work. Mrs Rosset spent nearly every day on the site and generally urged on the builders. On 23 November contracts were exchanged. On 14 December, Mr Rosset, without his

---

[289] Cf. *City of London Building Society v Flegg* [1988] AC 54, p. 551, below, where HL distinguished *Boland* (mortgage money paid to *two* trustees; equitable beneficial interests overreached under LPA 1925, s. 2(1)(ii) even though their holders were in actual occupation).

[290] [1988] Conv 453 (M. P. Thompson); [1989] CLJ 180 (P. G. McHugh); [1988] All ER Rev 163 (P. J. Clarke); (1988) 104 LQR 507 (R. J. Smith); [1989] Conv 342 (P. Sparkes).

wife's knowledge, sought a short term loan from the Bank. On 17 December completion took place, and Mr Rosset executed a charge in favour of the Bank. On 3 February
the transfer and the charge were registered. Mr and Mrs Rosset and their two children
moved into the farmhouse, where Mrs Rosset had been spending occasional evenings
since completion.

Following matrimonial difficulties, Mr Rosset, who was a courier accompanying
coach parties abroad, left the farm and his wife and children in May 1984. The loan to
Mr Rosset was not repaid, and the Bank sought an order for possession. Mrs Rosset
claimed an equitable beneficial interest under a trust, and an overriding interest under
Land Registration Act 1925, section 70(1)(*g*).

Held. (1) The relevant date for determining the overriding interest was the date of
completion (17 December) and not registration (3 February).

(2) (Mustill LJ dissenting) Mrs Rosset was in actual occupation on 17 December.

The House of Lords affirmed (1) in [1991] 1 AC 107, following *Abbey National
Building Society v Cann* [1991] 1 AC 56, p. 214, below, but reversed the Court of
Appeal on the ground that Mrs Rosset had no equitable beneficial interest under a
trust. Accordingly, no views were expressed on the question of actual occupation.

Nicholls LJ: Lord Wilberforce observed in *Williams & Glyn's Bank Ltd v Boland* [1981] AC
487, 504, that the words 'actual occupation' are ordinary words of plain English and that they
should be interpreted as such. The bank submitted that in ordinary, every day speech the wife
would not have been regarded as being in occupation of Vincent Farmhouse on 17 December.
Residential premises are occupied only by those who live in them.

I agree with this submission to the extent that I accept that in ordinary speech one normally
does equate occupation in relation to a house with living there. If a person is intending to move
into a house but has not yet done so, he would not normally be regarded as having gone into
occupation. That is the normal position, with a house which is fit for living in. But that does not
provide the answer in the present case, where the house was semi-derelict. In the first place, I do
not think that in every day speech actual occupation of a house can never exist short of residence.
Take Vincent Farmhouse. I do not think that it is as clear as the bank suggests that in every day
speech the wife would not have been regarded as being in occupation on 17 December 1982 when
the purchase was completed. Had the defendants been asked on the day 'are you in occupation?'
I am not sure that their answer would have been a simple 'no'. Their answer might well have been
to the effect 'We are not living there yet. The farmhouse was semi-derelict when we found it.
No one could have lived there with the house as it was then. But we have the builders in. They
have been there for over five weeks now. Diana spends almost every day there. Progress has been
slower than we had hoped. We had intended to move in by Christmas but that will not be possible
now.' Secondly, if the words 'actual occupation' are given the rigid, restricted meaning submitted by the bank in relation to residential premises, and that meaning is applied to a house in
course of being built or renovated, the result in some cases will be to defeat the purpose intended
to be achieved by paragraph (*g*) of section 70(1). If, day after day, workmen are actively building
a house on a plot of land, or actively and substantially renovating a semi-derelict house, it would
be contrary to the principle underlying paragraph (*g*) if a would be purchaser or mortgagee were
entitled to treat that site as currently devoid of an occupant for the purpose of the paragraph. If,
for example, the owner had granted a tenancy in return for a premium, so that the tenancy did not

qualify as an overriding interest under section 70(1)(k),[291] but the tenant himself and workmen employed by him were on site, building or renovating as I have described, why should he not be as much entitled to the protection afforded to occupants by section 70(1)(g) as he would be once the work had been finished and he was living in the house?

In my view, the test of residence propounded by the bank is too narrow. As the judge observed, what constitutes occupation will depend upon the nature and state of the property in question. I can see no reason, in principle or in practice, why a semi-derelict house such as Vincent Farmhouse should not be capable of actual occupation whilst the works proceed and before anyone has started to live in the building.

The bank further submitted that the presence of the builder and his men in the property could not constitute actual occupation by the defendants. I am unable to agree. I can detect nothing in the context in which the expression 'actual occupation' is used in paragraph (g) to suggest that the physical presence of an employee or agent cannot be regarded as the presence of the employer or principal when determining whether the employer or principal is in actual occupation. Whether the presence of an employee or agent is to be so regarded will depend on the function which the employee or agent is discharging in the premises in the particular case.

His Lordship referred to *Williams & Glyn's Bank Ltd v Boland* [1979] Ch 312, 338, per Ormrod LJ: and *Strand Securities Ltd v Caswell* [1965] Ch 958, 981, 984, p. 212, below, per Lord Denning MR and Russell LJ and continued:

I turn to the facts of the present case, which I have already summarised. The vendors had ceased to be in actual occupation long before 17 December. The house was empty and semi-derelict. They permitted the husband to go on to the property before completion. From 7 November until after Christmas the builder and his men were there every working day. One of them slept in the property on most nights. The wife spent almost every weekday at the property, from 10 a.m. to 4 p.m. Thus, there was physical presence on the property throughout the period leading up to completion on 17 December and that physical presence was to the extent that one would expect of an occupier, having regard to the then state of the property.

Thus far I am in agreement with the judge. Where I feel obliged to part company from him is his conclusion that, although (as I read his judgment) the husband, through the presence of the building and his men, was in actual occupation of the property on 17 December, the wife was not. As appears from the second extract from his judgment that I have quoted above, in reaching that conclusion the judge attached importance to the answer which Mr Griffin, the builder, would have given to the question, 'who occupies the building?' With all respect to the judge, I do not think that was the right question to pose. What mattered was not the builder's views on who occupied the building, but on whose behalf the builder was in the building. The judge himself had observed earlier that that was the vital question. As to that, the facts seem reasonably clear. Mr Griffin regarded himself as being employed by both the husband and the wife. There was no clear evidence that in this he was mistaken. Mr Griffin addressed his invoices to both Mr and Mrs Rosset. He looked to both of them for payment. In those circumstances, even though the husband alone was the contracting purchaser of the property, it seems to me that the presence of the builder and his men on the property was as much on behalf of the wife as it was on behalf of

---

[291] The exclusion of leases granted for a premium from the category of overriding interests under LRA 1925, s. 70(1)(k) was removed by LRA 1986, s. 4(1); p. 183, n. 182, above; and no such exclusion was made in the new provisions of LRA 2002, Sch. 1, para. 1 and Sch. 3, para. 1.

the husband. Mr Griffin was working there under a contract made with both of them, renovating the property for both of them. He was there on behalf of both of them. There was no sound basis for distinguishing between the two of them. If the builder's presence was sufficient to constitute occupation by the husband, it was equally sufficient to constitute occupation by the wife. This was so even after the incident mentioned by the judge. A stage was reached when the workmen complained that both the husband and wife were giving them instructions. The husband then 'laid it down' that the workmen should take their instructions from him alone.

So the position was that the builder and his men were in the building, carrying out a contract made with the husband and the wife. Additionally, the wife herself was there almost every weekday. In my view, those facts amounted to actual occupation of the property by the wife on 17 December 1982. There was, I repeat, physical presence on the property by the wife and her agent of the nature, and to the extent, that one would expect of an occupier having regard to the then state of the property: namely, the presence involved in actively carrying out the renovation necessary to make the house fit for residential use.

In my view, therefore, the judge erred in the inference he drew from the primary facts which he found. The reality was that before completion the husband and the wife had already taken over this semi-derelict house, under a revocable licence granted to the husband by the vendors. By 17 December renovation was well under way. Completion took place on 17 December, but no physical change then took place in their use of the property, save that the wife slept there more frequently. Eventually in February 1983 the family began to live there.

This conclusion has the attraction that it gives effect to the purpose of paragraph (g). Had a representative of the bank inspected the property before 17 December to check if anyone was in actual occupation, he would have seen that, indeed, someone was there. Builders were working there, day after day, plainly on behalf of someone. Had he gone up to the door, he would probably have found the wife in the house. In such circumstances the bank really has only itself to blame if it lends money without looking into the position further. In particular, I find it surprising that the bank, knowing that this was to be the matrimonial home, did not seek the wife's written consent to the grant of the charge. This was in December 1982. The *Boland* case [1981] AC 487 was decided by the House of Lords over two years earlier, in June 1980.[292]

(c) Actual occupation through others

Strand Securities Ltd v Caswell[293]
[1965] Ch 958 (CA, **Lord Denning MR** and **Harman** and **Russell LJJ**)

The first defendant was the sub-lessee of a flat, the 42-year head lease of which had been registered with good leasehold title. The sub-lease of 39¼ years, less three days, was not, at the material date, entered in any way on the register. The question arose

---

[292] See also *Epps v Esso Petroleum Co Ltd* [1973] 1 WLR 1071, p. 152, above (intermittent parking of car on undefined space not actual occupation); *Stockholm Finance Ltd v Garden Holdings Inc* [1995] NPC 162 (intermittent presence held to be 'pattern of alternating presence and absence rather than continuous occupation marked by absences', and therefore not an overriding interest); *Goodger v Willis* [1999] EGCS 302 (demolition of buildings and laying of concrete held to be actual occupation); *Malory Enterprises Ltd v Cheshire Homes (UK) Ltd* [2002] Ch 216 (derelict block of flats only used for temporary storage; gates in fence kept locked and ground floor windows blocked up held to be actual occupation): 'The requisite physical presence must, as it seems to me, in fairness be such as to put a person inspecting the land on notice that there was some person in occupation', per Arden LJ at para. 81).

[293] LRA 1925, s. 70(1)(k) did not apply; the first defendant's sub-lease exceeded 21 years; the second defendant was a gratuitous licensee. Under LRA 2002 the person 'in receipt of the rents and profits' of

whether the first defendant had an overriding interest within section 70(1)(g) which prevailed against a purchaser from the freeholders. He lived in the country but used the flat as a London base. He allowed his stepdaughter, the second defendant (who had been deserted by her husband) to live in the flat rent free.

Held. The first defendant had no overriding interest.

Russell LJ: It is to be remarked that if [the first defendant]...had moved up to London and occupied the bedroom or received from or demanded of his step-daughter...a penny a week for the privilege of remaining there, he would have had an unanswerable claim to his sublease being an overriding interest under section 70(1)(g) as he would be in the one case a person in actual occupation and in the other in receipt of the rents and profits. Of course he did neither of these things. Their possibility, however, serves to show how rare it must be that an actual sublessee entitled to possession is not a person either in actual occupation or in receipt of the rents and profits....

On the facts, was the first defendant...a person in actual occupation, though he was not in any ordinary sense residing there or treating it as his home, and the second defendant and her family were allowed by him to reside there? As a matter of the ordinary use of language I would not consider the first defendant to be such. For him it was argued that the phrase 'in actual occupation' derives from cases in which 'actual occupation' and 'actual possession' are used indifferently to describe a condition of enjoyment of the land itself, and that the phrase 'actual occupation' here involves that form of the legal concept of possession as distinct from the other or notional forms of that concept consisting of the receipt of money payments derived from land, or of the right to possession though the land be vacant. And it was argued that 'actual possession' was avoided by the draftsman as a phrase because of the difficulty which would flow from the definition of 'possession', in section 3(xviii) of the Land Registration Act, 1925. Reference was made to the number of authorities, including cases in the fields of rating, poor law, and landlord and tenant, with a view to showing that possession, and therefore occupation, may be had through the medium of another. Suppose, it was said, that the first defendant employed a resident caretaker to look after the flat in question, would the first defendant not be a person in actual occupation? I think that is correct. Then, it was argued, that is because the caretaker would be his licensee, bound to go at his will, and that was the position of the second defendant. But I think that here is the distinction between occupation by the caretaker as a matter of duty on behalf of the first defendant and the occupation of the second defendant on her own behalf; both were licensees, but the former, by her occupation for which she was employed, was the representative of the first defendant and her occupation may therefore be regarded as his. The proposition that in each case the first defendant was in actual occupation because neither the caretaker nor the second defendant had a right to occupy independently of him seems to me too broadly stated and to ignore that distinction. I do not say that a contract of employment or agency with the person residing there is essential to actual occupation by

the land is no longer protected: only the person in actual occupation is covered by para. 2 of Sch. 1 and Sch. 3.

The decision was applied in *Lloyd v Dugdale* [2002] 2 P & CR 13: where D Ltd, rather than D, major shareholder and managing director of D Ltd, was in occupation as licensee of D, it was held that D was not in actual occupation. '*Strand Securities v Caswell* is clear authority for the proposition that where A permits B to occupy land on B's own behalf by way of gratuitous licence, A's capacity as licensor will not by itself entitle him to claim to be in actual occupation of the land': per Sir Christopher Slade at para. 45. Nor did D's regular presence help, since he was there as managing director and not on his own account.

the other person. I think that it might well be that if a house was used as a residence by a wife, separated from the tenant, her husband (whether or not in desertion), he could also be regarded as in actual occupation through her; the question whether the husband was also a person in actual occupation did not, of course, arise in *National Provincial Bank Ltd v Hastings Car Mart Ltd (No 3)* [1964] Ch 665. But this conception, even if valid, could not extend to the relationship in the present case.

Nor, it seems to me, can the presence on the premises of some of the first defendant's furniture,[294] nor the previously mentioned use by him and others of the family of the flat, nor the fact, which I am prepared to assume though it was not proved, that he had a key, nor a combination of those matters, constitute actual occupation by him.[295]

(d) Acts of preparatory character

In **Abbey National Building Society v Cann** [1991] 1 AC 56,[296] George Cann applied in May 1984 to the Building Society for a loan of £25,000 to be secured on a mortgage of a registered leasehold house, 7 Hillview, Mitcham, which he proposed to purchase. He stated that the house was being purchased for his sole occupation. He intended, however, that the house should be occupied by his elderly mother and her 81-year-old husband-to-be, Abraham. Of the £25,000 loan, only £4,000 was required for the purchase of the house, and George used the balance to pay his creditors. Completion was to be on 13 August.

On 6 August the Building Society gave a cheque for £25,000 to George's solicitors, and prior to 13 August, George executed a legal charge in their favour. On 13 August completion of the purchase and of the charge took place simultaneously at 12.30 p.m.

At that time Mrs Cann was on holiday in the Netherlands, but at 10.00 a.m. George and Abraham arrived at the house; and at 11.45 a.m., with the vendor's consent, carpet-layers, acting on behalf of Mrs Cann, laid the carpets, and her furniture was taken into the house. The house was thereafter occupied by Mrs Cann and Abraham. On 13 September George was registered as sole proprietor, and the Building Society as proprietors of the charge.

George defaulted in his payments and the Building Society brought an action for possession. Mrs Cann claimed that, by reason of a contribution which she had made to the purchase of a property previously purchased by George, and of an assurance given by him that she would always have a roof over her head, she had an equitable interest in the house; and that this interest took priority over the charge as an overriding interest under Land Registration Act 1925, section 70(1)(*g*) by virtue of her actual occupation at the date of registration.

---

[294] See *Chhokar v Chhokar* [1984] FLR 313, p. 217, below, where furniture was relevant.

[295] The first defendant succeeded on another ground; when he had made application for first registration of his sub-lease, he was unable to produce the head-lessor's land certificate. CA held that there was no need to produce it, and that the register should be rectified. This gave the sub-lease priority over the transfer of the head-lease to the purchaser, which had not been registered until after the date of the first defendant's application.

[296] (1990) 106 LQR 32, 545 (R. J. Smith); [1990] CLJ 397 (A. J. Oakley); (1990) 87 LSG 19–24, 34–39 (M. Beaumont, junior counsel for Mrs Cann); [1991] Conv 116 (S. Baughen), 155 (P. T. Evans).

The House of Lords held

(1) (upholding the Court of Appeal (1989) 57 P & CR 381) Mrs Cann had impliedly authorised George to obtain the charge so as to preclude her from relying on any interest as prevailing over that of the Building Society.[297]

(2) The relevant date for determining the existence of overriding interests was the date of registration, but the date of actual occupation under paragraph (g) was that of completion.[298]

(3) There was no scintilla temporis between completion and charge, during which Mrs Cann's equitable interest could crystallise and then take priority over that of the Building Society (p. 340, below).

(4) In any event, Mrs Cann was not in actual occupation.

LORD OLIVER OF AYLMERTON said at 93:

I have, up to this point, been content to assume that the facts of the instant case justify the proposition which found favour with Dillon LJ, that [Mrs Cann] was in actual occupation of the property at the material time. This is, of course, essentially a question of fact, but there is the serious question of what, in law, can amount to 'actual occupation' for the purposes of section 70(1)(g). In Williams & Glyn's Bank Ltd v Boland [1981] AC 487, 504, Lord Wilberforce observed that these words should be interpreted for what they are, that is to say, ordinary words of plain English. But even plain English may contain a variety of shades of meaning. At the date of completion Mrs Cann was not personally even in England, leave alone in personal occupation of the property, and the trial judge held that the acts done by Mr Abraham Cann and Mr George Cann amounted to

'no more than the taking of preparatory steps leading to the assumption of actual residential occupation on or after completion, whatever the moment of the day when completion took place...'

For my part, I am content to accept this as a finding of fact which was amply justified by the evidence before him, and I share the reservations expressed by Ralph Gibson and Woolf LJJ in the Court of Appeal. It is, perhaps dangerous to suggest any test for what is essentially a question of fact, for 'occupation' is a concept which may have different connotations according to

---

[297] Mrs Cann was well aware that there was a shortfall which would have to be met from somewhere...Dillon LJ inferred that 'she left it to George Cann to raise the balance', from which he further inferred that George Cann had authority to raise that sum from the society': per Lord Oliver of Aylmerton at 94. See also Bristol and West Building Society v Henning [1985] 1 WLR 778; Paddington Building Society v Mendelsohn (1985) 50 P & CR 244; Equity and Law Home Loans Ltd v Prestridge [1992] 1 WLR 137; (1992) 108 LQR 371 (R. J. Smith) (X, sole legal owner of house in Penzance, mortgaged it to Britannia Building Society for £30,000, with the knowledge of Y, who had an equitable interest in the house arising from her contribution of £10,000 to its purchase price. X then remortgaged the house to the plaintiff for £43,000, without Y having any knowledge of the mortgagee's identity or of the mortgage details. CA held, extending Henning, that Y's interest was subject to that of the plaintiff to the extent of £30,000: 'the substituted encumbrance should rank ahead of the beneficial interest as far as, but no further than, the consent which was to be imputed to Y' per Mustill LJ); [1992] CLJ 223 (M. Dixon); [1992] Conv 206 (M. P. Thompson); (1992) 108 LQR 371 (R. J. Smith); Locabail (UK) Ltd v Waldorf Investment Corpn (1999) Times, 31 March; Woolwich Building Society v Dickman [1996] 3 All ER 204; [1996] All ER Rev 254 (P. J. Clarke); [1998] CLJ 1328 (L. Tee). And the mortgage itself may be invalid if the registered proprietor has no power to create it.

[298] On this point, see p. 202, above.

the nature and purpose of the property which is claimed to be occupied. It does not necessarily, I think, involve the personal presence of the person claiming to occupy. A caretaker or the representative of a company can occupy, I should have thought, on behalf of his employer. On the other hand, it does, in my judgment, involve some degree of permanence and continuity which would rule out mere fleeting presence. A prospective tenant or purchaser who is allowed, as a matter of indulgence, to go into property in order to plan decorations or measure for furnishings would not, in ordinary parlance, be said to be occupying it, even though he might be there for hours at a time. Of course, in the instant case, there was, no doubt, on the part of the persons involved in moving Mrs Cann's belongings, an intention that they would remain there and would render the premises suitable for her ultimate use as a residential occupier. Like the trial judge, however, I am unable to accept that acts of this preparatory character carried out by courtesy of the vendor prior to completion can constitute 'actual occupation' for the purposes of section 70(1)(g). Accordingly, all other considerations apart, Mrs Cann fails, in my judgment, to establish the necessary condition for the assertion of an overriding interest.

(e) Effect of absence on acquisition of overriding interest

In **Kingsnorth Finance Co Ltd v Tizard** [1986] 1 WLR 783,[299] Mr and Mrs Tizard lived at Willowdown, Lechlade, Gloucestershire. The unregistered title was in the sole name of the husband, who held it on trust for sale for himself and his wife. In 1982 the marriage broke down, and the wife moved into the spare bedroom. She began to spend some nights at her sister's house, but returned to sleep at Willowdown, especially during the frequent absences of the husband on business. She still kept her clothes in cupboards in their bedroom, and frequently returned to the house in the mornings to look after their twin children and to prepare herself for work.

In March 1983, the husband negotiated a loan with the plaintiffs, describing himself on the application form as single. A surveyor, acting as agent for the plaintiffs, visited the house and saw only the husband, who told him that he was married, but that his wife had left him some months ago to live with someone nearby. No further enquiries were made, and on the basis of the surveyor's report, the plaintiffs granted a mortgage. The husband emigrated and they claimed possession of the house.

In rejecting the claim, JUDGE JOHN FINLAY QC held that the surveyor had constructive notice of the wife's equitable interest, and that this notice was imputed to the plaintiffs. He considered the position if it were a case of registered land, and said at 788:

Mrs Tizard was, in my judgment, in occupation of Willowdown notwithstanding that Mr Tizard was living there also; and notwithstanding the fact that on numerous occasions she slept elsewhere. 'The physical presence' to which Lord Wilberforce refers[300] does not connote continuous and uninterrupted presence; such a notion would be absurd. Nor, indeed, do I consider that the requisite 'presence' is negatived by regular and repeated absence. I find that Mrs Tizard was in Willowdown virtually every day for some part of the day; that her life and activities were based on her presence, interrupted though it was, in Willowdown; there she prepared herself for work; there she cared for her children; she went in the morning and returned in the evening

---

[299] [1987] CLJ 28 (P. G. McHugh); [1986] Conv 283 (M. P. Thompson); p. 63, n. 207, above.
[300] *Williams & Glyn's Bank Ltd v Boland* [1981] AC 487 at 505–506.

to discharge her duties as housewife and mother. It is clear that prior to the time, November 1982, when she ceased always to sleep in the house when her husband was there, she had been in occupation; and, in my judgment she did not cease to be in occupation simply because she made that change in her habits, significant though the change was.

Willowdown, however, is not registered land. If it were, my findings that Mrs Tizard had equitable rights in the house and was at the material time in occupation would protect those rights against the mortgagee by reason of section 70 (1)(g) of the Land Registration Act 1925.

In **Chhokar v Chhokar** [1984] FLR 313, a husband and wife purchased the registered freehold of 5 Lady Margaret Road, Southall, as a matrimonial home in 1977. Both contributed to the purchase price and upkeep of the house which was registered in the name of the husband only. In 1978 the husband and wife went to India, where the husband deserted his wife and returned home. She followed him a few weeks later, being seven months' pregnant. In December the husband, without the knowledge of his wife, arranged to sell the house to a Mr Parmar at a price well below market value. As Cumming-Bruce LJ said in the Court of Appeal 'there was an obvious similarity between this discussion and a discussion that might take place in similar circumstances in relation to property which was asserted to have fallen off the back of a lorry'. EWBANK J said at 317:

On 19 February 1979, the date of completion, the husband made special arrangements to have the net proceeds of sale in cash in his hands. He paid his debts and then set off for India. That was the last the wife saw of him for some 2 years. The wife and the baby were discharged from hospital on 22 February. They went home. They found the locks had been changed and so they went to spend the night with an aunt with whom the elder child had been staying while the wife was in hospital. On the following day, 23 February, the wife went home. Mr Parmar, who had bought the house, ejected her. On 1 March 1979 Mr Parmar registered the conveyance to him at the Land Registry. The wife on that date[301] was not in the house because he had put her out, but some of her furniture was there. I have to consider whether she was in actual occupation on the day of the registration of the conveyance. I have no difficulty in deciding that she was in actual occupation. Her interest, accordingly, in the house is an overriding interest and Mr Parmar, in my judgment, took the conveyance of the house into his name subject to her overriding interest. He accordingly has held the house since then, subject to a half share belonging to the wife.[302]

(f) Effect of absence on loss of overriding interest

In **London and Cheshire Insurance Co Ltd v Laplagrene Property Co Ltd** [1971] Ch 499 the unpaid vendors of registered land,[303] who remained in occupation under

---

[301] The relevant date was later held to be that of completion: *Abbey National Building Society v Cann* [1991] 1 AC 56, reproduced in LRA 2002, Sch. 3, para. 2; p. 202, above.

[302] This part of the judgment was not challenged in the Court of Appeal, where Mr Parmar's application for sale under LPA 1925, s. 30 [see now TLATA 1996, s. 14; below, p. 532] and for rent failed. 'Is there any room for crocodile tears because his unlawful enterprise did not succeed? I can see no room for giving him anything more than the court in an unreported case gave to the moneylender who had rights over a debtor. The proceedings are recorded in a play of Shakespeare.' The story had a happy ending: Mr and Mrs Chhokar were reconciled, and Mr Parmar was left owning a house which he could neither occupy nor sell and from which he could get no rent.

[303] (1971) 35 Conv (NS) 188 (F.R. Crane). On conveyancing liens generally, see [1997] Conv 336 (D. G. Barnsley), especially pp. 344–345.

a leaseback by the purchasers, were held to have an overriding interest under section
70(1)(*g*). This entitled the vendors to enforce their lien against chargees of the purchaser, even though they had gone out of occupation subsequent to the purchase.
BRIGHTMAN J said at 505:

I can see nothing in section 20,[304] read with section 70, which causes a paragraph (*g*) overriding interest, subject to which a disposition was made, to be extinguished merely because the
owner of the right ceases occupation after that disposition but before there has been any other
material dealing with the land. The extinction of the overriding interest in such a case, for the
fortuitous benefit of the proprietor of the land, seems to me both unsupported by the wording
of the Act and an unreasonable result. A right exists as an overriding interest for the very good
reason that the owner of the right is in occupation of the land, ought to have been asked to define
his rights by the intending transferee or grantee, but is ignored and has no inquiry made of him.
In such circumstances, it is reasonable to provide that the transferee or grantee takes subject
to the right as an overriding interest. The transferee or grantee has no one but himself to blame
for that result. If the overriding interest were extinguished when the owner of the right went out
of occupation, that would be a windfall for the transferee or grantee. He would be freed from a
burden for no good reason that I can discern.

(iv) 'so far as relating to land of which he is in actual occupation'

These words are new in paragraph 1 of Schedule 1 and Schedule 3 of the Land
Registration Act 2002. Under the 1925 Act it was held in *Ferrishurst Ltd v Wallcite
Ltd*[305] that a person who had the benefit of an option to purchase the leasehold interest
in the whole of a building comprising offices and a garage, but occupied only part of
it, had an overriding interest in respect of the whole. Now, however, the overriding
interest, and therefore the priority afforded by it, can exist only in relation to the part
actually occupied.

(v) Exceptions from paragraph 2

Paragraph 2 contains exceptions to the rule that the rights of a person in actual occupation will be overriding interests. Two are particularly significant.[306] A purchaser is
not bound by[307]

an interest of a person of whom inquiry was made before the disposition and who failed to
disclose the right when he could reasonably have been expected to do so.

This reproduces an exception contained in section 70(1)(*g*) of the Land Registration
Act 1925, although it is an improvement in providing that the occupier loses his right

---

[304] [Effect of registration of disposition of freeholds. See now LRA 2002, s. 29.]
[305] [1999] Ch 355; [1999] Conv 144 (S. Pascoe); [1999] CLJ 483 (L. Tee); (2000) 63 MLR 113 (J. Hill).
[306] The other two relate to particular types of interests in land: an interest under a settlement under SLA
1925 (LRA 2002, Sch. 3, para. 2(a): but no new settlements can be created after TLATA 1996: p. 516, below);
and leases granted to take effect in possession more than three months after the grant (reversionary leases:
Sch. 3, para. 2(d); such leases must be registered: LRA 2002, s. 4(1)(d), p. 133, above).
[307] LRA 2002, Sch. 3, para. 2(b).

to assert his interest as overriding after failing to disclose it only if he could *reasonably* have been expected to do so.

But there is also a new exception, in Schedule 3, paragraph 2(c), of the 2002 Act. A purchaser is not bound by an interest—

(i) which belongs to a person whose occupation would not have been obvious on a reasonably careful inspection of the land at the time of the disposition, and

(ii) of which the person to whom the disposition is made does not have actual knowledge at that time.

Law Commission Report on Land Registration for the Twenty-First Century 2001 (Law Com No. 271), para. 8.62

8.62   There are a number points to note about the exception in [Schedule 3, paragraph 2(c)]. It has obvious similarities with the rule of conveyancing law that a seller of land must disclose to an intending buyer prior to contract all latent defects in title (those that are not apparent on a reasonable inspection of the land) and which are not known to the buyer.[308] Three points should be noted about this exception—

(1) For the purposes of the [Act], it is not the *interest* that has to be apparent (as is the case in relation to contracts for the sale of land), but the *occupation* of the person having the interest.[309]

(2) The test is not one of constructive notice of the occupation. It is the less demanding one (derived from the test applicable to intending buyers of land) that it should be obvious on a reasonably careful inspection of the land.[310]

(3) Even if a person's occupation is not apparent, the exception does not apply where a buyer has actual knowledge of that occupation.

The object of this exception is, therefore, to protect buyers and other registered disponees for valuable consideration in cases where the fact of occupation is neither subjectively known to them nor readily ascertainable. Once an intending buyer becomes aware of the occupation, he or she should make inquiry of the occupier because of the second exception mentioned above.[311]

F. PARAGRAPH 3: LEGAL EASEMENTS AND PROFITS À PRENDRE

Under the Land Registration Act 2002 the interest of the owner of the dominant tenement by way of an easement or a profit à prendre will have priority against a purchaser

---

[308] See Megarry & Wade's *Law of Real Property* (6th edn, 2000), 12–068.

[309] We stress this point because although it was made in the Consultative Document (see Law Com No. 254, para. 5.73), one correspondent took the view that we had confused the two issues. We had not. We had earlier explained that the authorities were in some disarray as to whether the occupation had to be apparent or not: see Law Com No. 254, para. 5.58.

[310] See Megarry & Wade's *Law of Real Property* (6th edn, 2000), 12–068; Law Com No. 254, para. 5.72.

[311] [LRA 2002. Sch. 3, para. 2(b).]

for value of the servient tenement if the lease fulfils the requirements of paragraph 3 of Schedule 3:

> 3 (1) A legal easement or profit a prendre, except for an easement, or a profit a prendre which is not registered under Part 1 of the Commons Act 2006, which at the time of the disposition—
>
> > (a) is not within the actual knowledge of the person to whom the disposition is made, and
> >
> > (b) would not have been obvious on a reasonably careful inspection of the land over which the easement or profit is exercisable.
>
> (2) The exception in sub-paragraph (1) does not apply if the person entitled to the easement or profit proves that it has been exercised in the period of one year ending with the day of the disposition.

The opening words make clear that this is limited to legal easements.[312] The equivalent provision in the Land Registration Act 1925, section 70(1)(a), read together with the Land Registration Rules 1925, rule 258, was interpreted as including 'equitable easements other than such as by reason of some other statutory provision or applicable principle of law, could obtain protection otherwise than by notice on the register'.[313] However, equitable easements can no longer take effect as overriding interests under the 2002 Act.

QUESTIONS

1. How far is notice or actual knowledge relevant in the Land Registration Act 2002? See Law Commission Report on Land Registration for the Twenty-First Century 2001 (Law Com No. 271), paras 5.16–5.27; H & B para. 9.13; Emmet, para. 5.124. In particular, consider the relevance of notice to determine the existence of an overriding interest: *Malory Enterprises Ltd v Cheshire Homes (UK) Ltd* [2002] Ch 216 at para. 81 (Arden LJ), p. 212, n. 292, above; LRA 2002 Sch. 3, para. 2(b), (c) and para. 3(1)(a), (b), p. 196, above; LRA 2002, ss. 11(4)(c), (5), p. 139, above, s. 12(4)(d), (5), p. 139–140, above; and the effect of *Lyus v Prowsa Developments Ltd* [1982] 1 WLR 1044, p. 223, below, and *Peffer v Rigg* [1977] 1 WLR 285, p. 222, below.

2. You are advising the mortgagee bank in a Boland situation.

   (a) How would you set about discovering whether there is a 'person in actual occupation'? And when would you inspect the property? See Hayton, *Registered Land*, pp. 88–91, and the criticisms of Vinelott J in *Kling v Keston Properties Ltd* (1983) 49 P & CR 212 at 221–222.

---

[312] For the distinction between legal and equitable easements, and the requirements for the creation of a legal easement, see pp. 646–649, below.

[313] *Celsteel Ltd v Alton House Holdings Ltd* [1985] 1 WLR 204 at 220 (Scott J).

(b) You discover an actual occupant who discloses to you a beneficial interest under a trust. The mortgagee nevertheless still wishes to lend money to the registered proprietor. How would you seek to neutralise the occupant's rights? Consider in particular

(i) The appointment of an additional trustee. Should this entitle the bank to overreach the occupant's interest? *City of London Building Society v Flegg* [1988] AC 54, p. 551, below; Law Commission Report on Overreaching: Beneficiaries in Occupation 1989 (Law Com No. 188).

(ii) The express release of rights by the occupant. See *Gracegrove Estates v Boateng* [1997] NPC 98. Are there any difficulties—

(a) If the occupant is a minor?

(b) In the construction of the release given by the occupant: *Woolwich Building Society v Dickman* [1996] 3 All ER 204; (1996) 140 SJ 1108 (M. Draper); [1997] CLJ 37 (L. Tee).

(iii) The implied release of rights by the occupant

(a) By estoppel: *Spiro v Lintern* [1973] 1 WLR 1002; Emmet, para. 11.031.

(a) By an imputed intention that his interest is subject to the rights of the purchaser: *Abbey National Building Society v Cann* [1991] 1 AC 56 at 94, p. 214, above; *Bristol and West Building Society v Henning* [1985] 1 WLR 778; *Paddington Building Society v Mendelsohn* (1985) 50 P & CR 244; *Equity and Law Homes Loans Ltd v Prestidge* [1992] 1 WLR 137, p. 215, n. 297, above.

3. In 1982 Lord Hailsham of St. Marylebone LC, speaking in the House of Lords (Hansard volume 437 col. 663, 15 December) made the point that, if the bank in *Boland* had made Mr Boland bankrupt, it could then have forced a sale of the property in spite of the wife's overriding interest.

(a) Advise the bank on the possible success of this course of action. See TLATA 1996, ss. 14, 15; *Re Lowrie* [1981] 3 All ER 353; *Re Citro* [1991] Ch 142; Insolvency Act 1986, s. 335A, as added by TLATA 1996, s. 25(1), Sch. 3, para. 23; pp. 536–543, below.

(b) What further advice would you give to the bank in the light of s. 267(2)(b) of the Insolvency Act 1986, which provides that the debt must be unsecured at the time of the presentation of the petition. If the bank wishes to make Mr Boland bankrupt, it must forego the priority afforded to him by the mortgage under s. 269.

4. You are advising the purchaser of a dwelling house. On inspection you discover on the premises the vendor and a baby in a pram. There are no other occupants. To what legal problems does the baby give rise? See *Hypo-Mortgage Services Ltd v Robinson* [1997] 2 FLR 71, p. 207, n. 286, above.

5. How would you decide the actual occupation point in the following cases, if the events took place after the Land Registration Act 2002 came into force

  (a) *Chhokar v Chhokar* [1984] FLR 13, p. 217, above;

  (b) *Kling v Keston Properties* (1983) 49 P & CR 212, p. 38, above;

  (c) *Malory Enterprises Ltd v Cheshire Homes (UK) Ltd* [2002] Ch 216, p. 212, n. 292, above?

IX. REGISTERED LAND AND CONSTRUCTIVE TRUSTS

In **Williams & Glyn's Bank Ltd v Boland** [1981] AC 487 at 504, the House of Lords confirmed that the doctrine of notice has no relevance to registered land. As Lord Wilberforce said: 'The only kind of notice recognised is by entry on the register.'[314]

However, the constructive trust has been used in two cases at first instance to avoid the consequences of the failure to register a right as a minor interest under the Land Registration Act 1925.[315]

A. PURCHASER WITH NOTICE

In **Peffer v Rigg** [1977] 1 WLR 285[316] a purchaser with notice of an interest under a trust for sale was held to take subject to it, applying general equitable principles. By section 20(1) of the Land Registration Act 1925,[317] a transferee for valuable consideration takes free from unprotected minor interests. GRAHAM J held that the requirement of good faith could be read into this provision, so that a transferee with notice of the minor interest could not rely on it; but that the same result could be achieved by the device of a constructive trust. He said at 294:

On the evidence in this case I have found that the second defendant knew quite well that the first defendant held the property on trust for himself and the plaintiff in equal shares. The second defendant knew this was so and that the property was trust property when the transfer was made to her, and therefore she took the property on a constructive trust in accordance with general equitable principles: see *Snell's Principles of Equity* 27th edn (1973), pp. 98–99. This

---

314 P. 205, above. *Peffer v Rigg*, below, was not cited.

315 On resulting trusts and registered land, see [1995] Conv 383 (D. Wilde). On constructive trusts, see M & B, *Trusts & Trustees* (7th edn, 2008), Chaps. 5, 7, 8.

316 (1977) 41 Conv (NS) 207 (F. R. Crane); 93 LQR 341 (R. J. Smith); [1977] CLJ 227 (D. Hayton); (1977) 40 MLR 602 (S. Anderson); [1978] Conv 52 (J. Martin). See also *Orakpo v Manson Investments Ltd* [1977] 1 WLR 347 at 360; (1978) 94 LQR 239 (D. C. Jackson).

317 See now LRA 2002, s. 29.

is a new trust imposed by equity and is distinct from the trust which bound the first defendant. Even if, therefore, I am wrong as to the proper construction of sections 20 and 59, when read together, and even if section 20 strikes off the shackles of the express trust which bound the first defendant, this cannot invalidate the new trust imposed on the second defendant.

B. A STATUTE CANNOT BE USED AS AN INSTRUMENT OF FRAUD

In **Lyus v Prowsa Developments Ltd** [1982] 1 WLR 1044 a development company was the registered proprietor of St Martin's Green Estate, Trimley, Suffolk. In 1978 it mortgaged the estate to the bank, and in 1979 contracted to build a house on Plot 29 and sell it to the plaintiffs. It then went insolvent, leaving the house unfinished. The bank, although not subject to the plaintiffs' contract, sold Plot 29 as mortgagees to Prowsa Developments Ltd (the first defendants) 'subject to and with the benefit of' the plaintiffs' contract. Prowsa Developments Ltd then contracted to re-sell Plot 29 to the second defendants, subject to the plaintiffs' contract of 1978 'so far, if at all, as it may be enforceable against' Prowsa Developments Ltd. The second defendants were registered as proprietors after a transfer which did not mention the contract of 1978.

The plaintiffs sought a declaration that the 1978 contract was binding on Prowsa Developments Ltd and on the second defendants, and for an order for specific performance.

DILLON J held that the defendants were bound by a constructive trust on the ground that the Land Registration Act was not to be used as an instrument of fraud. Having applied *Bannister v Bannister* [1948] 2 All ER 133 and a dictum of Lord Denning MR in *Binions v Evans* [1972] Ch 359 at 368, p. 1101, below, his Lordship said at 1054:

This does not, however, conclude the matter since I also have to consider the effect of the provisions of the Land Registration Act 1925, plot 29 having at all material times, as I have mentioned, been registered land. In the course of the argument, emphasis was laid on the effect of section 34(4) of the Land Registration Act 1925, which is concerned with the effect on subsequent interests of a transfer of registered land by a mortgagee. Section 34 has, however, to be read with section 20[318], which is concerned with the effect of the registration of a transfer of registered land by the registered proprietor. The protection conferred by section 34 on a transfer by a mortgagee is thus additional to the protection which is conferred by section 20 on registration of a transfer by a registered proprietor.

It has been pointed out by Lord Wilberforce in *Midland Bank Trust Co Ltd v Green* [1981] AC 513 at 531 [p. 78, above] that it is not fraud to rely on legal rights conferred by Act of Parliament. Under section 20, the effect of the registration of the transferee of a freehold title is to confer an absolute title subject to entries on the register and overriding interests, but, 'free from all other estates and interests whatsoever, including estates and interests of His Majesty...' In *Miles v Bull (No 2)* [1969] 3 All ER 1585, Bridge J expressed the view that the words which I have quoted embraced, prima facie, not only all kinds of legal interests, but

---

[318] See now LRA 2002, s. 29.

all kinds of equitable interests: see 1589.[319] He therefore held, at 1590, as I read his judgment, that actual or constructive notice on the part of a purchaser of an unregistered interest would not have the effect of imposing a constructive trust on him. The interest in *Miles v Bull (No 2)* was the interest in the matrimonial home of a deserted wife who had failed to protect her interest by registration under the Matrimonial Homes Act 1967.[320] The contract for sale between the husband, who was the registered proprietor, and the purchaser provided that the house concerned was sold subject to such rights of occupation as might subsist in favour of the wife, with a proviso that this was not to imply that the wife had, or would after completion have any such rights as against the purchaser. Plainly, therefore, the cause was only included in the contract for the protection of the husband who was the vendor. The wife was to get no fresh rights, and it was not in *Miles v Bull (No 2)* a stipulation of the bargain between the vendor and the purchaser that the purchaser should give effect to the rights as against the vendor of the deserted wife. *Miles v Bull (No 2)* is thus distinguishable from the facts of the present case as I interpret those facts.

It seems to me that the fraud on the part of the defendants in the present case lies not just in relying on the legal rights conferred by an Act of Parliament, but in the first defendant reneging on a positive stipulation in favour of the plaintiffs in the bargain under which the first defendant acquired the land. That makes, as it seems to me, all the difference. It has long since been held, for instance, in *Rochefoucauld v Boustead* [1897] 1 Ch 196, that the provisions of the Statute of Frauds 1677 now incorporated in certain sections of the Law of Property Act 1925, cannot be used as an instrument of fraud, and that it is fraud for a person to whom land is agreed to be conveyed as trustee for another to deny the trust and relying on the terms of the statute to claim the land for himself. *Rochefoucauld v Boustead* was one of the authorities on which the judgment in *Bannister v Bannister* [1948] 2 All ER 133[321] was founded.

It seems to me that the same considerations are applicable in relation to the Land Registration Act 1925. If, for instance, the agreement of October 18, 1979, between the bank and the first defendant had expressly stated that the first defendant would hold Plot 29 upon trust to give effect for the benefit of the plaintiffs to the plaintiffs' agreement with the vendor company, it would be difficult to say that that express trust was overreached and rendered nugatory by the Land Registration Act 1925. The Land Registration Act 1925 does not, therefore, affect the conclusion which I would otherwise have reached in reliance on *Bannister v Bannister* and the judgment of Lord Denning MR in *Binions v Evans* [1972] Ch 359, had Plot 29 been unregistered land.

The plaintiffs are, therefore, entitled to succeed in this action. The appropriate relief in that event is that specific performance should be ordered as against the second defendants of the sale to the plaintiffs of Plot 29, with the completed house thereon, on the terms of the agreement of January 30, 1978, made between the plaintiffs and the vendor company.

(1983) 46 MLR 96 (P. H. Kenny) at p. 98:

The case is as important for what was omitted as for what was decided. Key sections of the Land Registration Act were not referred to: section 74 which states that no 'person dealing

---

[319] See also *Ashburn Anstalt v Arnold (No. 2)* [1989] Ch 1, which upheld the decision in *Lyus v Prowsa*, at the same time holding that more than notice is required for the creation of the constructive trust: p. 1102, below; cf. *Chattey v Farndale Holdings Inc* (1996) 75 P & CR 298 (where a purchaser from the constructive trustee was not bound by mere knowledge of the trustee's obligation).

[320] Now Family Law Act 1996, p. 602, below.   [321] See generally [1984] CLJ 306 (T.G. Youdan).

with a registered estate or charge shall be affected with notice of a trust express implied or constructive' was ignored. Similarly, section 59(1) providing that matters registrable in the case of unregistered land under the Land Charges Act 1972 are to be 'protected only by lodging a creditor's notice, a bankruptcy inhibition or a caution against dealings with the land or charge' was ignored.[322] Presumably, the same sweeping principles of equity would have sidestepped these provisions.

The court here showed the usual judicial reluctance to grapple firmly with the mechanics of land registration. This arm's-length approach to the registration system led it not to give effect to the prescriptive system of registration in the Land Registration Act 1925. In the same way that the effect of non-registration of an estate contract is prescribed by section 4 of the Land Charges Act 1972 and had to be given effect to in *Midland Bank Trust Co Ltd v Green,* so the need to register an equivalent interest in registered land is prescribed by section 59(1) of the Land Registration Act 1925 which, with section 20 and section 34(4), should have been given effect to by the court. The legislation for both registered and unregistered land makes mandatory provision for registration and is specific on the effect of non-registration. The estate contract could, under the Land Registration Act, have been protected against the charge only by registration giving priority over the charge with the bank's consent. If there is a principle of equity which allows such transparently clear provisions to be sidestepped it should at least be described with greater precision and result from a less cavalier treatment of the relevant legislation.[323]

It is important, however, to recognise that the constructive trust which was imposed in *Lyus v Prowsa Developments Ltd* constituted a *new* right: the purchaser was not bound by a pre-existing (unregistered) property right simply by having notice of it; but notice of a prior property right (the estate contract[324]) was held in the particular circumstances of the case, to give rise to a new right under the constructive trust. The second defendant's conscience was affected in a similar way to the first defendant's conscience—so as to impose a constructive trust also on the second defendant personally. This was explained in **Chattey v Farndale Holdings Inc** (1998) 75 P & CR 298 where MORRITT LJ said at 316–317:

In dealing with the effect of the Land Registration Act 1925, Dillon J. said

His Lordship quoted the two paragraphs at p. 224, above, beginning 'It seems to me that the fraud on the part of the defendants in the present case lies not just on relying on the legal rights conferred by an Act of Parliament...'

---

[322] *De Lusignan v Johnson* (1973) 230 EG 499 was also ignored although it could have been distinguished in the same way as *Miles v Bull (No 2)*.

[323] See Oakley, *Constructive Trusts* (1978), at p. 28: 'the imposition of a constructive trust on the joint and equitable grounds may well seriously undermine established principles of property law'. [See also Oakley, *Constructive Trusts* (3rd edn, 1997), chap. 2; [1982] All ER Rev (P. J. Clarke); [1983] CLJ 54 (C.J. Harpum); [1983] Conv 64 (P. Jackson); (1983) 133 NLJ 798 (C. T. Emery and B. Smythe); cf. (1984) 47 MLR 476 (P. Bennett); [1985] CLJ 280 (M. P. Thompson); *Du Boulay v Raggett* (1988) 58 P & CR 138. On constructive trusts generally, see H & M, chap. 12; Maudsley & Burn, *Trusts and Trustees: Cases and Materials* (7th edn, 2008), chap. 7.]

[324] Pp. 29–34, above.

Though Dillon J does not in that passage refer expressly to the necessity for a constructive trust to have been imposed on the second defendant he must have intended to apply the same principles to him for otherwise that defendant would not have been 'a person to whom land is agreed to be conveyed as trustee for another' and it could not have been a fraud for the second defendant 'to rely on the terms of the statute to claim the land for himself.'

X. ELECTRONIC CONVEYANCING[325]

The changes made by the Land Registration Act 2002 prepare the way for the move from a paper-based system of conveyancing to one which is entirely electronic. The enabling provisions for its introduction are set out in Part 8 of the Act (sections 91 to 95). Schedule 5 sets out the details for the Land Registry network agreement under which electronic conveyancing takes place.

The full system will take time to introduce.[326] It is already possible to notify the Registry of the discharge of a registered charge by electronic means, and applications to register dealings with registered land can be lodged electronically.

LAND REGISTRATION ACT 2002

91 Electronic dispositions: formalities

(1) This section applies to a document in electronic form where—

    (a) the document purports to effect a disposition which falls within subsection (2), and

    (b) the conditions in subsection (3) are met.

(2) A disposition falls within this subsection if it is—

    (a) a disposition of a registered estate or charge,[327]

    (b) a disposition of an interest which is the subject of a notice in the register, or

    (c) a disposition which triggers the requirement of registration, which is of a kind specified by rules.

(3) The conditions referred to above are that—

    (a) the document makes provision for the time and date when it takes effect,

---

[325] C & B, pp. 110–111, 987; Gray, paras 2.2.31–2.2.32; M & W, paras 7.157–7.163; Smith, pp. 103–106; R & R, chap. 19; H & B, Part 5; Law Com No. 271 (2001), Part XIII; Land Registry Consultations on E-conveyancing 2002 (on general principles of e-conveyancing) 2006 (on electronic funds transfer), 2007 (with draft Land Registration (Network Access) Rules and draft Land Registration (Electronic Communications) Order). The responses to the Consultations are available in the e-conveyancing section of the Land Registry website: www.landregistry.gov.uk. Land Registration (Network Access) Rules 2008 (SI 2008 No. 1748); Land Registration (Electronic Conveyancing) Rules 2008 (SI 2008 No. 1750). See also p. 28, above (electronic contracts); p. 45 above (electronic documents as deeds); p. 983, below (electronic discharge of mortgages).

[326] The current state of progress can be discovered by consulting the e-conveyancing section of the Land Registry website.

[327] Land Registration (Electronic Conveyancing) Rules 2008 (SI 2008 No. 1750) (creation of legal charges in electronic form, and information which such legal charges must contain).

(b) the document has the electronic signature of each person by whom it purports to be authenticated,

(c) each electronic signature is certified, and

(d) such other conditions as rules may provide are met.

(4) A document to which this section applies is to be regarded as—

(a) in writing, and

(b) signed by each individual, and sealed by each corporation, whose electronic signature it has.

(5) A document to which this section applies is to be regarded for the purposes of any enactment as a deed.

(6) If a document to which this section applies is authenticated by a person as agent, it is to be regarded for the purposes of any enactment as authenticated by him under the written authority of his principal.

(7) If notice of an assignment made by means of a document to which this section applies is given in electronic form in accordance with rules, it is to be regarded for the purposes of any enactment as given in writing.

(8) The right conferred by section 75 of the Law of Property Act 1925 (purchaser's right to have the execution of a conveyance attested) does not apply to a document to which this section applies.

(9) In relation to the execution of a document by a company in accordance with section 44(2) of the Companies Act 2006 (signature on behalf of the company)—

(a) subsection (4) above has effect in relation to paragraph (a) of that provision (signature by two authorised signatories) but not paragraph (b) (signature by director in presence of witness);

(b) the other provisions of section 44 apply accordingly (the references to a document purporting to be signed in accordance with subsection (2) of that section being read as references to its purporting to be authenticated in accordance with this section);

(c) where subsection (4) above has effect in relation to a person signing on behalf of more than one company, the requirement of subsection (6) of that section is treated as met if the document specifies the different capacities in which the person signs.[328]

(9A) If subsection (3) of section 29C of the Industrial and Provident Societies Act 1965 (execution of documents) applies to a document because of subsection (4) above, subsection (5) of that section (presumption of due execution) shall have effect in relation to the document with the substitution of 'authenticated' for 'signed'.[329]

(10) In this section, references to an electronic signature and to the certification of such a signature are to be read in accordance with section 7(2) and (3) of the Electronic Communications Act 2000.

---

[328] Substituted by CA 2006 (Consequential Amendments etc.) Order 2008 (SI 2008 No. 948), Sch. 1(2), para. 224.

[329] Inserted by Co-operatives and Community Benefit Societies Act 2003, s. 5(8).

92 Land registry network[330]

(1) The registrar may provide, or arrange for the provision of, an electronic communications network for use for such purposes as he thinks fit relating to registration or the carrying on of transactions which—

    (a) involve registration, and

    (b) are capable of being effected electronically.

(2) Schedule 5 (which makes provision in connection with a network provided under subsection (1) and transactions carried on by means of such a network) has effect.

93 Power to require simultaneous registration

(1) This section applies to a disposition of—

    (a) a registered estate or charge, or

    (b) an interest which is the subject of a notice in the register, where the disposition is of a description specified by rules.

(2) A disposition to which this section applies, or a contract to make such a disposition, only has effect if it is made by means of a document in electronic form and if, when the document purports to take effect—

    (a) it is electronically communicated to the registrar, and

    (b) the relevant registration requirements are met.

(3) For the purposes of subsection (2)(b), the relevant registration requirements are—

    (a) in the case of a registrable disposition, the requirements under Schedule 2,[331] and

    (b) in the case of any other disposition, or a contract, such requirements as rules may provide.

(4) Section 27(1) does not apply to a disposition to which this section applies.[332]

(5) Before making rules under this section the Lord Chancellor must consult such persons as he considers appropriate.

(6) In this section, 'disposition', in relation to a registered charge, includes postponement.

94 Electronic settlement

The registrar may take such steps as he thinks fit for the purpose of securing the provision of a system of electronic settlement in relation to transactions involving registration.

95 Supplementary

Rules may—

    (a) make provision about the communication of documents in electronic form to the registrar;

    (b) make provision about the electronic storage of documents communicated to the registrar in electronic form.

---

[330] Land Registration (Network Access) Rules 2008 (SI 2008 No. 1748).
[331] P. 164, above.   [332] P. 163, above.

Law Commission Report on Land Registration for the Twenty-First Century 2001 (Law Com No. 271), paras 2.48 to 2.61

Electronic conveyancing: the anticipated model

Introduction

2.48 ... Before examining how a typical dematerialised conveyancing transaction involving registered land[333] might work, two points should be emphasised.

2.49 The first is that the Land Registry's involvement in the conveyancing process will begin earlier than at present. This will be either—

(1) before the parties to a disposition of either—

    (a) registered land; or

    (b) unregistered land that will trigger compulsory registration;

    conclude a contract that is to precede that disposition;[334] or if there is no such contract,[335]

(2) before the relevant disposition is made.

2.50 In many cases the disposition and, where title is already registered, its simultaneous registration will be the *last* stage of the conveyancing process. That means that all the conveyancing work must be completed by that date.[336] One of the intended objectives of the new system is to identify errors and discrepancies at the earliest possible stage, and to resolve any difficulties so far as possible before registration.[337]

2.51 The second point is that changes to the register will be made as a result of the actions of the solicitors or licensed conveyancers acting for the parties to the transactions. This is explained more fully below.[338] We also explain that do-it-yourself conveyancers will not be excluded from electronic conveyancing.[339]

How a typical conveyancing transaction might operate

2.52 The manner in which electronic conveyancing might operate may be illustrated by the example of a typical contract to sell a parcel of registered land and its subsequent completion.

---

[333] For electronic conveyancing and applications for first registration, see below, para. 2.65.

[334] In other words, an estate contract such as a contract to sell land.

[335] As where a registered proprietor intends to charge his land, or where (as is commonly the case) there is to be a lease without any prior agreement for a lease.

[336] Ironically, this will bring the registered system into line with what formerly happened with unregistered conveyancing, where the deed of conveyance was the final stage of the conveyancing process. Many dispositions of unregistered land now trigger compulsory registration, so that the deed of conveyance is no longer the final stage. There has to be an application for first registration and the registrar will need to be satisfied as to the title before he can register the disposition. See Ruoff & Roper, *Registered Conveyancing*, 12–45.

[337] We have been told by many practitioners that it is not always possible for them to finalise the details of ancillary rights (typically cross-easements) in a complex conveyancing transaction, and that such matters are presently resolved *after* the application for registration is made. However, in future, such matters could be resolved by contract between the parties. That contract will be protected in the register, so that its priority is preserved. When the details are finalised between the parties, the easements or other rights can then be entered in the register.

[338] See below, para. 2.57.   [339] See below, para. 2.68.

It should be stressed that this is necessarily tentative and that what eventually appears is likely to differ in some details at least from what is set out here.[340] The system is likely to be based on a secure electronic communications network that will only be accessible by contractually authorised professionals, whether those are solicitors, licensed conveyances, estate agents or mortgage lenders.[341] The network will not just be used for the specifically legal stages of the transaction, but also for the provision of information about the property. It is also likely to be employed to co-ordinate and manage chains of transactions,[342] provided that those transactions are dispositions of registered land or are of a kind that will trigger the requirement of compulsory registration. It is anticipated that some body—which might or might not be the Land Registry—will be made responsible for managing chain sales in order to facilitate them. When a party instructs a solicitor or licensed conveyancer to act on his or her behalf in a purchase or sale of a property in circumstances in which there is likely to be a chain, that agent will be required[343] to notify the 'chain manager' of the fact of that instruction. There will be further requirements for that agent to provide information to the chain manager as to the completion of the various pre-contractual stages of the transaction, such as investigating title, carrying out local searches, obtaining mortgage offers, etc. The chain manager will then be able to build up a picture of the chain and so that he can identify any persons in the chain who are delaying the process. This information will be made available via the secure Intranet to all parties in the chain. Although it is not anticipated that the chain manager will have any compulsive powers,[344] he will be able to encourage the offending parties to complete the steps that are still to be performed. There will inevitably be pressure from others in the chain who are ready to contract. The power to manage chains in this way is an important feature of our proposals on electronic conveyancing. Chains are a major cause of disquiet in the conveyancing process, particularly in relation to domestic conveyancing. By providing a means of controlling and expediting chains, the Bill should do much to alleviate the frustrations that are suffered by so many buyers and sellers of land. It is anticipated that it should prevent chains from collapsing.

2.53 When the parties have agreed the terms of the contract,[345] they will send a copy in electronic form to HM Land Registry, where it will be checked electronically. This will enable any discrepancies in the contract on matters such as property address, title number and seller's name to be identified at that stage and rectified before the contract is concluded.

2.54 The contract will be made in electronic form and signed electronically by the parties or their agents. It is anticipated that, under the Bill, estate contracts will be required to be protected in the register by the entry of a notice as pre-requisite to their validity. This noting in the register will occur simultaneously with the making of the contract and one effect of it will be to confer priority protection on the buyer.[346] The form of notice will have been agreed with the Registry in advance. The Registry will store the contract in electronic form and this is likely

---

[340] Formal consultation on the Land Registry's model for electronic conveyancing is planned for the autumn of this year [i.e. 2001. See Land Registry Consultation on E-conveyancing 2002.]

[341] The extent to which professionals may be permitted to access the secure Intranet will obviously depend on their role.

[342] In particular a chain of house sales. There may be no need for 'chain management' in relation to a chain of commercial transactions.

[343] The basis of this requirement will be contractual.

[344] Indeed, it is not easy to see what effective forms of compulsion there could be.

[345] The draft contract will be an electronic document.

[346] See cl. 72(6)(a)(ii) of the Bill, below, para. 9.68. [See LRA 2002, s. 72(6)(a)(ii).]

to be for a period that will be set in accordance with rules and is likely to reflect the nature of the contract.[347]

2.55 In relation to the disposition itself, a similar process will be undertaken. The draft transfer and any charge will be prepared in electronic form and agreed between the parties. Once again, the draft will be submitted to the Registry. The details in the transfer will be checked electronically against the contract to ensure that there are no discrepancies. A 'notional' register will then be prepared by the Registry in consultation with the parties to indicate the form that the register will take when the transaction is completed. Completion, when it occurs, will entail the simultaneous occurrence of the following events—

(1) the execution of the transfer and any charges in electronic form and their transmission to the Registry, where they will be stored;

(2) the registration of the dispositions so that the register conforms with the notional register previously agreed with the Registry; and

(3) the appropriate (and automatic) movement of funds[348] and the payment of stamp duty[349] and Land Registry fees.

2.56 The proposed system will eliminate the 'registration gap'. There will no longer be any period of time between the disposition and its registration. In time it will also mean that the register becomes conclusive as to the priority of all expressly created interests. This is because, if it is only possible to create interests validly if they are registered simultaneously, the date on which they are created will be the date of their registration. The register will therefore become a record of the priority of such rights.

2.57 As we have indicated above—

(1) Changes to the register will be made automatically as a consequence of electronic documents and applications created by solicitors or licensed conveyancers, who are acting for the parties to the transactions.[350]

(2) Only those solicitors or licensed conveyancers who have been authorised do so will be permitted to conduct electronic conveyancing.[351] The relationship with the Registry will be contractual, under a 'network access agreement',[352] and the Registry will be obliged to contract with any solicitor or licensed conveyancer who meets the specified criteria.[353] Those specified criteria will be the subject of wide consultation and discussion with the relevant professional and other interested bodies. One of the important aims of those criteria is, as we explain in Part XIII of this Report, to raise the standards of conveyancing.[354]

---

[347] In the case of a normal estate contract, the period of storage is likely to be comparatively short. This is because most contractual obligations are merged on completion. Where the contract is likely to have a longer life, such as an option or a right of pre-emption, the period of storage will be longer. It will be possible to obtain official copies of such contracts.

[348] See below, para. 2.62.   [349] See below, para. 2.64. [See FA 2003, s. 48(1), (2).]

[350] See below, para. 2.51.   [351] See below, para. 2.52.

[352] For such agreements, see Sch. 5, para. 1; below, para. 13.36.

[353] The criteria are necessary to ensure the integrity of the register. For the criteria, see Sch. 5, para. 10; below, paras 13.40 and following.

[354] See below, para. 13.42.

2.58 However, it will also be noted from the examples given above,[355] that the Registry will still exercise a substantial measure of control over the registration process. This is because it will not be possible to change the register except in the form agreed in advance with the Registry.

Compulsory use of electronic conveyancing

2.59 There is power in the Bill to make the use of electronic conveyancing compulsory. The way that the power will operate, if exercised, is that a disposition (or a contract to make such a disposition) will only have effect if it is—

(1) made by means of an electronic document;

(2) communicated in electronic form to the Registry; and

(3) simultaneously registered.[356]

2.60 This is a power that will not be exercised lightly. When solicitors and licensed conveyancers enter into network access agreements with the Registry, they will be required to conduct electronic conveyancing in accordance with network transaction rules.[357] Those transaction rules are likely to provide that the dispositions and contracts to make dispositions are made in the manner explained in the previous paragraph. In other words, those rules will ensure that electronic dispositions are simultaneously registered, which is the single most important technical objective of the Bill. However, as we explain in Part XIII of this Report,[358] it may be necessary to exercise the statutory power to secure that technical objective notwithstanding what can be done under the network transaction rules.[359]

2.61 There are, in any event, other reasons why the Bill has to contain a power to make electronic conveyancing compulsory. It is inevitable that the move from a paper-based to an all-electronic system of conveyancing will take some years and that the two systems will necessarily co-exist during this period of transition. However, that period of transition needs to be kept to a minimum for two principal reasons. The first is that it will be very difficult both for practitioners and for the Land Registry to have to operate two distinct systems side by side. Secondly, if electronic conveyancing is to achieve its true potential and deliver the savings and benefits that it promises, it must be the only system. This can be illustrated by the example of a typical chain of domestic sales. As we have indicated above, it will be possible to manage chains in an all-electronic system.[360] However, if just one link in that chain is conducted in the conventional paper-based manner, the advantages of electronic chain management are likely to be lost. A chain moves at the speed of the slowest link. A paper-based link is in its nature likely to be slower than an electronic one[361] and will not be subject to the scrutiny and controls of those links in the chain that are electronic and therefore managed. There must, therefore, be a residual power to require transactions to be conducted in electronic form. It is hoped that the eventual exercise of the power will be merely a formality because solicitors and licensed conveyancers will have chosen to conduct conveyancing electronically in view of the advantages that it offers to them and to their clients. Not only will it make the conduct of conveyancing

---

[355] See below, paras 2.54, 2.55.   [356] S. 93; below, para. 13.75.

[357] See Sch. 5, paras 2, 5; below, paras 13.47, 13.52.

[358] See below, paras 13.74 and following.

[359] This could be quite important in relation to priorities: see above, para. (2).

[360] See para. 2.52.

[361] Because it will not be able to take advantage of the time-saving features that electronic conveyancing will be able to offer.

easier and faster for them, but they will also have to compete with other practitioners who have elected to adopt the electronic system.

Land Registry E-conveyancing Consultation 2007, p. 47

We propose to gradually phase in e-conveyancing services over the next few years to make the transition to electronic working as straightforward as possible for both users and Land Registry.

We have already introduced some building blocks that are taking us towards e-conveyancing. For example, some lenders are using e-discharges, which is a machine-to-machine operation, resulting in the removal of charges from the register without human intervention. Also, many of our customers will be familiar with our e-lodgement service, which allows you to lodge certain applications, such as restrictions and notices, electronically. E-lodgement services will be developed further to complement e-conveyancing.

The introduction of e-conveyancing services is starting in a small way with a trial of a Chain Matrix[362] prototype by volunteer users in Bristol, Portsmouth and Fareham.

Once the secondary legislation is in place, e-conveyancing can properly begin. Users will be able to sign up to network access agreements, giving them the capability to submit for registration electronic documents with electronic signatures. At first, e-conveyancing will be limited to simpler transactions such as transfers of whole, discharges and charges. As with Chain Matrix, we envisage piloting e-conveyancing in a limited way before rolling it out nationally.

As the system develops, more services will be introduced, such as the lodging of electronic contracts, the notional register, an enhanced Chain Matrix and Electronic Funds Transfer. In time, it will be possible to carry out a wider range of transactions electronically, with leases and transfers of part, for example, being included.

The ultimate goal is, of course, that e-conveyancing becomes the norm. A provision exists in the Act (s. 93) to make e-conveyancing compulsory. Further consultation will take place, however, before this final step is taken.

QUESTIONS

1. Legal and equitable estates in land have existed for centuries. Since 1925, we speak of legal estates and equitable interests. To what extent is this nomenclature meaningful in the context of

   (a) unregistered land;

   (b) registered land?

See Maitland, *Equity*, pp. 210–215.

---

[362] ['Chain Matrix is an internet-based information and coordination tool. It allows buyers, sellers, their legal representatives, estate agents and lenders to view the progress of every transaction in their property chain. It allows them to see at a glance where their transactions sit within the chain and shows the progress of each transaction against the key stages in the conveyancing process. It facilitates decision-making about when to complete, for example, or whether to remarket a property if one transaction is holding up the chain': Land Registry E-conveyancing Consultation 2007, p. 48. 'The Land Registry Board made the decision in December 2007 to focus resources on electronic discharges, charges and transfers—thus automating our core business of registering land as the priority in the e-conveyancing programme'; further work on Chain Matrix has been deferred for the time being: Land Registry Annual Report 2007/8, p. 49. The Chain Matrix prototype evaluation is available on the Land Registry website.]

2. Is the Land Registration Act 2002 evolutionary or revolutionary?

3. How far is a purchaser bound, and how far should he be bound, by an unregistered registrable interest of which he actually knows?

   (a) Unregistered land: see LPA 1925, s. 199; LCA 1972, s. 4; *Hollington Bros
       Ltd v Rhodes* [1951] 2 TLR 691, p. 81, above; *Industrial Properties (Barton
       Hill Ltd) v Associated Electrical Industries Ltd* [1977] QB 580 at 608–609,
       per Roskill LJ; *Midland Bank Trust Co Ltd v Green* [1981] AC 513, p. 72,
       above.

   (b) Registered land: see *Hodges v Jones* [1935] Ch 657 at 671, per Luxmoore
       J; *De Lusignan v Johnson* (1973) 230 EG 499, p. 225, n. 322, above; *Peffer
       v Rigg* [1977] 1 WLR 285, p. 222, above; *Lyus v Prowsa Developments Ltd*
       [1982] 1 WLR 1044, p. 223, above.

See also Question 1 on p. 220, above.

3

ADVERSE POSSESSION AND LIMITATION OF ACTIONS[1]

I. INTRODUCTION

All legal systems have to decide whether there is a time limit within which a person who has been unlawfully dispossessed of his land, or has been deprived of some right over his land, must bring a claim. The most common situation in which such a question arises is where a squatter takes possession of someone else's land: what rights, if any, does the squatter acquire to the land by virtue of his uninterrupted possession? The answer to this question in English law has varied over time.[2] In the modern law

---

[1] C & B, chap. 26; Gray, part 9.1; M & W, chap. 35; MM, chap. 14; Smith, pp. 62–82. See the annotation of the Limitation Act 1980 in Current Law Statutes (D. Morgan), and generally McGee, *Limitation Periods* (5th edn, 2006); Preston and Newsom, *Limitation of Actions* (3rd edn, 1953; 4th edn, 1989); Franks, *Limitation of Actions* (1959); Josling, *Periods of Limitation* (7th edn, 1989); Prime and Scanlan, *Modern Law of Limitation* (1993); Redmond-Cooper, *Limitation of Actions* (1992); Oughton, Lowry and Merkin, *Limitation of Actions* (1998); Jourdan, *Adverse Possession* (2003). For the history of the old law: Holdsworth, vol. iv, pp. 484–486, vol. vii, p. 29 et seq.; Simpson, *History of the Land Law* (2nd edn, 1986), pp. 151–155; Hayes, *Introduction to Conveyancing* (5th edn), pp. 222 et seq. In 2001 the Law Commission published a Report on Limitation of Actions (Law Com No. 270), pp. 274–278, below, which included proposals relating to land, although substantial reforms were made in relation to registered land by LRA 2002; below, pp. 279–287.

[2] C & B, pp. 114–117.

the answer depends on whether the title to the land is registered or unregistered. In very broad terms, in unregistered land under the Limitation Act 1980 the squatter can acquire an indefeasible title to the land by virtue of his adverse possession of the land for 12 years. The Land Registration Act 1925 adopted this principle, and so a squatter could also acquire title to registered land by 12 years' adverse possession. However, the Land Registration Act 2002 displaced the law in the Land Registration Act 1925 and substituted a radical new scheme which reflects the principles underlying registered conveyancing, and which seriously restricts the squatter's ability to obtain title to registered land.[3]

In order to understand the current law in relation to registered land it is necessary to understand the position in unregistered land under the Limitation Act 1980 (which still governs land the title to which has not yet been registered), and the Land Registration Act 1925. First, however, it is important to grasp the concept of 'adverse possession', which is an essential element of the squatter's claim to title to the land, whether in unregistered land or registered land.

II. ADVERSE POSSESSION

In order to establish a title by adverse possession, a squatter must be shown to have both factual possession and the requisite intention to possess ('animus possidendi'). In *JA Pye (Oxford) Ltd v Graham* [2003] 1 AC 419, at para. 43, Lord Browne-Wilkinson approved the test, set out by Slade LJ in *Buckinghamshire County Council v Moran* [1990] Ch 623 at 640, that the requisite intention was 'an intention to exclude the world at large, including the owner with the paper title, so far as reasonably practicable and so far as the processes of the law will allow.[4]

J A Pye (Oxford) Ltd v Graham
[2003] 1 AC 419 (HL, **Lords Bingham of Cornhill, Mackay of Clashfern, Browne-Wilkinson, Hope of Craighead** and **Hutton**)[5]

Pye was the registered proprietor of land which it intended to develop. In February 1983 Pye entered into a contract with Graham to allow Graham to use a portion of the land, which was adjacent to Graham's farm, and was accessible only through Graham's own land, for the purposes of grazing. This grazing contract ended on 31 December 1983, and Pye required Graham to vacate the land but Graham continued to use it for grazing and Pye took no steps to evict him. Graham knew of Pye's intention to develop the land, and continued to use it knowing that he might be requested to vacate it or to

---

[3] The details of the new scheme are set out in LRA 2002, Sched. 6 and LRR 2003, rr. 187–194; below, pp. 279–287.

[4] See also *Powell v McFarlane* (1977) 38 P & CR 452 at 470, per Slade J.

[5] [2003] CLJ 36 (L. Tee).

pay for its continued use for grazing, but no such request was made by Pye. In August 1984 Pye allowed Graham to cut and remove hay, in return for payment. In December 1984 Graham asked Pye whether he might have a further formal grazing contract, but Pye did not reply. Graham made no further attempts to contact Pye, but would have been prepared to pay for occupation if asked. In 1997 Graham registered cautions at the Land Registry claiming that he had obtained title by adverse possession. On 30 April 1998 Pye brought an action seeking the cancellation of the cautions, and on 20 January 1999 Pye brought a further action for possession of the land.

Held (reversing the Court of Appeal [2001] Ch 804 and restoring Neuberger J [2002] Ch 676). Graham had established a possessory title under the Limitation Act 1980, section 15(1), Schedule 1, paragraphs 1, 8(1).[6]

Lord Browne-Wilkinson:

The issues

27 The action was brought by Pye at the earliest on 30 April 1998. The question therefore is whether, prior to that date, there was a period of 12 years during which the Grahams were in possession of the disputed land to the exclusion of Pye. More accurately, there are two questions viz: (1) did Pye discontinue possession or was it 'dispossessed' of the disputed land (within the meaning of paragraph 1 of Schedule 1 to the 1980 Act) before 30 April 1986; and if so (2) did the Grahams thereafter remain in possession of the land for a period of 12 years?

28 It is common ground that Pye did not 'discontinue' possession within the meaning of the Act. Further I did not understand there to be any claim by Pye that, if the Grahams had at any time prior to 30 April 1986 dispossessed Pye, the Grahams thereafter ceased to be in possession for the purposes of the Act.

29 It was further common ground that so long as the Grahams were occupying the disputed land with Pye's consent, they could not be treated as having dispossessed Pye. Accordingly no relevant right of action can have accrued to Pye under Schedule 1, paragraph 1 until after the expiry on or about 31 August 1984 of the grass-cutting permission.

30 The relevant question therefore is whether at some time between 1 September 1984 and 30 April 1986 Pye were 'dispossessed' of the disputed land so that, at that date, Pye's right of action accrued for the purposes of Schedule 1, paragraph 1 to the 1980 Act.

The law

31 The apparently straightforward statutory provisions have given rise to considerable difficulties, most of which flow from the remarks of the Court of Appeal in *Leigh v Jack* (1879) 5 Ex D 264 and *Littledale v Liverpool College* [1900] 1 Ch 19. In a remarkable judgment at first instance, *Powell v McFarlane* (1977) 38 P & CR 452,[7] Slade J traced his way successfully through a number of Court of Appeal judgments which were binding on him so as to restore a degree of order to the subject and to state clearly the relevant principles. Although there are one or two minor points on which (unlike Slade J) your Lordships are not bound by authority and can therefore make necessary adjustments, for the most part the principles set out by Slade J as subsequently approved by the Court of Appeal in *Buckinghamshire County Council v Moran*

---

6 Below, pp. 249–250.

7 [Infant who at age of 14 began to graze the cow Kashla, otherwise known as Ted's cow, held not to have requisite intent.]

[1990] Ch 623 cannot be improved upon. Hereafter I adopt them without specific recognition beyond marking with inverted commas those passages which I have quoted verbatim.

Possession, dispossession, ouster and adverse possession

32 In *Powell's* case Slade J was considering the Limitation Act 1939. However, apart from paragraph 8(4) of Schedule 1 to the 1980 Act the statutory provisions applicable in the present case are identical in the 1939 Act and the 1980 Act. Slade J first addressed himself to the question what was the meaning of possession and dispossession in the statutory provisions. After noticing that possession and dispossession were not defined in the 1939 Act he continued, at p. 469:

'Possession of land, however, is a concept which has long been familiar and of importance to English lawyers, because (inter alia) it entitles the person in possession, whether rightfully or wrongfully, to maintain an action of trespass against any other person who enters the land without his consent, unless such other person has himself a better right to possession. In the absence of authority, therefore, I would for my own part have regarded the word "possession" in the 1939 Act as bearing the traditional sense of that degree of occupation or physical control, coupled with the requisite intention commonly referred to as animus possidendi, that would entitle a person to maintain an action of trespass in relation to the relevant land; likewise I would have regarded the word "dispossession" in the Act as denoting simply the taking of possession in such sense from another without the other's licence or consent; likewise I would have regarded a person who has "dispossessed" another in the sense just stated as being in "adverse possession" for the purposes of the Act.'

Save as to the last sentence I have quoted (as to which I will make certain further comments below), I entirely agree with that statement of the law. Slade J felt doubts whether, in the light of certain Court of Appeal judgments then binding on him, he could properly adhere to the view that he expressed. Decisions (for example *Wallis's Cayton Bay Holiday Camp Ltd v Shell-Mex and BP Ltd* [1975] QB 94) appeared to hold that use of the land by a squatter which would have been sufficient to constitute possession in the ordinary sense of the word was not enough: it was said that such use by the squatter did not constitute 'adverse possession' which was required for the purposes of limitation unless the squatter's use conflicted with the intentions of the paper title owner as to his present or future use of the disputed land. In those cases it was held that the use by the squatter was, as a matter of law, to be treated as enjoyed with the implied consent of the paper owner. Not surprisingly, Slade J found this line of reasoning difficult to follow. It is hard to see how the intentions of the paper title owner (unless known to the squatter) can affect the intention of the squatter to possess the land. In my judgment, Slade J was right and the decision of the Court of Appeal in those cases wrong. In any event Parliament (on the advice of the Law Reform Committee) has intervened to reverse the principle of implied licence: see the 1980 Act, Schedule 1, paragraph 8(4). However there remains a long standing confusion as to what constitutes 'dispossession' and the place, if any, of 'adverse possession' in the modern law.

33 The root of the problem is caused by the concept of 'non-adverse possession'. This was a concept engrafted by the common law and equity onto the limitation statute of James I (21 Jac 1, c 16). Before the passing of the Real Property Limitation Acts 1833 (3 & 4 Will 4, c 27) and 1874 (37 & 38 Vict c 57), the rights of the paper owner were not taken away save by a 'disseisin' or an ouster and use of the land by the squatter of a kind which was clearly inconsistent with the paper title. Such inconsistent use was called adverse possession: see Professor Dockray, 'Adverse Possession and Intention' [1982] Conveyancer 256, 260. Under the 1833 Act (sections 2 and 3 of which were substantially to the same effect as the 1980 Act, section 15(1)

and Schedule 1, paragraph 1) the right of action was barred 20 years after 'the right... to bring such action shall have first accrued' and 'such right shall be deemed to have first accrued at the time of such dispossession or discontinuance of possession'. Soon after the passing of the 1833 Act it was held that 'the second and third sections of that Act ... have done away with the doctrine of non-adverse possession, and...the question is whether 20 years have elapsed *since the right accrued,* whatever the nature of the possession': Denman CJ in *Nepean v Doe d Knight* (1837) 2 M & W 894, 911. The same statement of the new law was made in *Culley v Doe d Taylerson* (1840) 11 Ad & E 1008, 1015 where Denman CJ said:

'The effect of [section 2] is to put an end to all questions and discussions, whether the possession of lands, etc., be adverse or not; and, if one party has been in the actual possession for 20 years, whether adversely or not, the claimant, whose original right of entry accrued above 20 years before bringing the ejectment, is barred by this section.'

34 The same was held to be the law by the Privy Council in a carefully reasoned advice delivered by Lord Upjohn in *Paradise Beach and Transportation Co Ltd v Price-Robinson* [1968] AC 1072; see also Professor Dockray [1982] Conveyancer 256.

35 From 1833 onwards, therefore, old notions of adverse possession, disseisin or ouster from possession should not have formed part of judicial decisions. From 1833 onwards the only question was whether the squatter had been in possession in the ordinary sense of the word. That is still the law, as Slade J rightly said. After 1833 the phrase 'adverse possession' did not appear in the statutes until, to my mind unfortunately, it was reintroduced by the Limitation Act 1939, section 10 of which is in virtually the same words as para 8(1) of Schedule 1 to the 1980 Act. In my judgment the references to 'adverse possession' in the 1939 and 1980 Acts did not reintroduce by a side wind after over 100 years the old notions of adverse possession in force before 1833. Paragraph 8(1) of Schedule 1 to the 1980 Act defines what is meant by adverse possession in that paragraph as being the case where land is in the possession of a person in whose favour time 'can run'. It is directed not to the nature of the possession but to the capacity of the squatter. Thus a trustee who is unable to acquire a title by lapse of time against the trust estate (see section 21) is not in adverse possession for the purposes of paragraph 8. Although it is convenient to refer to possession by a squatter without the consent of the true owner as being 'adverse possession' the convenience of this must not be allowed to reintroduce by the back door that which for so long has not formed part of the law.[8]

36 Many of the difficulties with these sections which I will have to consider are due to a conscious or subconscious feeling that in order for a squatter to gain title by lapse of time he has to act adversely to the paper title owner. It is said that he has to 'oust' the true owner in order to dispossess him; that he has to intend to exclude the whole world including the true owner; that the squatter's use of the land has to be inconsistent with any present or future use by the true owner. In my judgment much confusion and complication would be avoided if reference to adverse possession were to be avoided so far as possible and effect given to the clear words

---

8 See, however, *Beaulane Properties Ltd v Palmer* [2006] Ch 79 at [213]-[214], below, p. 290, where Nicholas Strauss QC interpreted LRA 1925 s. 75, in relation to the acquisition of title by a trespasser between October 2000 and October 2003, as requiring 'adverse' possession to be inconsistent with the registered proprietor's use or intended use of the land, in order to avoid an incompatibility with the European Convention on Human Rights. The Grand Chamber of the European Court of Human Rights later held that s. 75 was not in fact incompatible with the Convention: *JA Pye (Oxford) Ltd v United Kingdom* (2008) 46 EHRR 45, below, p. 290; but the Land Registry maintains that *Beaulane* represents English law on the question: Land Registry Additional Practice Guide affecting Practice Guide 5 (2007).

of the Acts. The question is simply whether the defendant squatter has dispossessed the paper owner by going into ordinary possession of the land for the requisite period without the consent of the owner.

37 It is clearly established that the taking or continuation of possession by a squatter with the actual consent of the paper title owner does not constitute dispossession or possession by the squatter for the purposes of the Act. Beyond that, as Slade J said, the words possess and dispossess are to be given their ordinary meaning.

38 It is sometimes said that ouster by the squatter is necessary to constitute dispossession: see for example *Rains v Buxton* (1880) 14 ChD 537, 539 per Fry J. The word 'ouster' is derived from the old law of adverse possession and has overtones of confrontational, knowing removal of the true owner from possession. Such an approach is quite incorrect. There will be a 'dispossession' of the paper owner in any case where (there being no discontinuance of possession by the paper owner) a squatter assumes possession in the ordinary sense of the word. Except in the case of joint possessors, possession is single and exclusive. Therefore if the squatter is in possession the paper owner cannot be. If the paper owner was at one stage in possession of the land but the squatter's subsequent occupation of it in law constitutes possession the squatter must have 'dispossessed' the true owner for the purposes of Schedule 1, paragraph 1: see *Treloar v Nute* [1976] 1 WLR 1295, 1300; Professor Dockray [1982] Conveyancer 256. Therefore in the present case the relevant question can be narrowed down to asking whether the Grahams were in possession of the disputed land, without the consent of Pye, before 30 April 1986. If they were, they will have 'dispossessed' Pye within the meaning of paragraph 1 of Schedule 1 to the 1980 Act.

39 What then constitutes 'possession' in the ordinary sense of the word?

Possession

40 In *Powell's* case 38 P & CR 470 Slade J said, at p. 470:

'(1) In the absence of evidence to the contrary, the owner of land with the paper title is deemed to be in possession of the land, as being the person with the prime facie right to possession. The law will thus, without reluctance, ascribe possession either to the paper owner or to persons who can establish a title as claiming through the paper owner. (2) If the law is to attribute possession of land to a person who can establish no paper title to possession, he must be shown to have both factual possession and the requisite intention to possess ("animus possidendi").'

Counsel for both parties criticised this definition as being unhelpful since it used the word being defined—possession—in the definition itself. This is true: but Slade J was only adopting a definition used by Roman law and by all judges and writers in the past. To be pedantic the problem could be avoided by saying there are two elements necessary for legal possession: (1) a sufficient degree of physical custody and control ('factual possession'); (2) an intention to exercise such custody and control on one's own behalf and for one's own benefit ('intention to possess'). What is crucial is to understand that, without the requisite intention, in law there can be no possession. Remarks made by Clarke LJ in *Lambeth London Borough Council v Blackburn* (2001) 82 P & CR 494, 499 ('It is not perhaps immediately obvious why the authorities have required a trespasser to establish an intention to possess as well as actual possession in order to prove the relevant adverse possession') provided the starting point for a submission by Mr Lewison for the Grahams that there was no need, in order to show possession in law, to show separately an intention to possess. I do not think that Clarke LJ was under any misapprehension, but in any event there has always, both in Roman law and in common law, been a requirement to show an intention to possess in addition to objective acts of physical possession. Such intention may be, and frequently is, deduced from the physical acts themselves, but there is no doubt in my judgment that there are two separate elements in legal possession. So far as English law is concerned intention as a separate element is obviously necessary. Suppose a case where A is found to be in occupation of a locked house. He may be there as a squatter, as an overnight trespasser, or as a friend looking after the house of the paper owner during his absence on holiday. The acts done by A in any given period do not tell you whether there is legal possession. If A is there as a squatter he intends to stay as long as he can for his own benefit: his intention is an intention to possess. But if he only intends to trespass for the night or has expressly agreed to look after the house for his friend he does not have possession. It is not the nature of the acts which A does but the intention with which he does them which determines whether or not he is in possession.

Factual possession

41 In *Powell's* case Slade J said at pp. 470–471:

'(3) Factual possession signifies an appropriate degree of physical control. It must be a single and [exclusive] possession, though there can be a single possession exercised by or on behalf of several persons jointly. Thus an owner of land and a person intruding on that land without his consent cannot both be in possession of the land at the same time. The question what acts constitute a sufficient degree of exclusive physical control must depend on the circumstances, in particular the nature of the land and the manner in which land of that nature is commonly used or enjoyed... Everything must depend on the particular circumstances, but broadly, I think what must be shown as constituting factual possession is that the alleged possessor has been dealing with the land in question as an occupying owner might have been expected to deal with it and that no one else has done so.'

I agree with this statement of the law which is all that is necessary in the present case. The Grahams were in occupation of the land which was within their exclusive physical control. The paper owner, Pye, was physically excluded from the land by the hedges and the lack of any key to the roadgate. The Grahams farmed it in conjunction with Manor Farm and in exactly the same way. They were plainly in factual possession before 30 April 1986.

Intention to possess

(a) To own or to possess?

42 There are cases in which judges have apparently treated it as being necessary that the squatter should have an intention to own the land in order to be in possession. In *Littledale v Liverpool College* [1900] 1 Ch 19, 24 Sir Nathaniel Lindley MR referred to the plaintiff relying on 'acts of ownership': see also *George Wimpey & Co Ltd v Sohn* [1967] Ch 487, 510. Even Slade J in *Powell,* at pp. 476 and 478, referred to the necessary intention as being an 'intention to own'. In the *Moran* case (1988) 86 LGR 472, 479 the trial judge (Hoffmann J) had pointed out that what is required is 'not an intention to own or even an intention to acquire ownership but an intention to possess'. The Court of Appeal in that case [1990] Ch 623, 643 adopted this proposition which in my judgment is manifestly correct. Once it is accepted that in the Limitation Acts, the word 'possession' has its ordinary meaning (being the same as in the law of trespass or conversion) it is clear that, at any given moment, the only relevant question is whether the person in factual possession also has an intention to possess: if a stranger enters on to land occupied by a squatter, the entry is a trespass against the possession of the squatter whether or not the squatter has any long term intention to acquire a title.

43 A similar manifestation of the same heresy is the statement by Sir Nathaniel Lindley MR in *Littledale v Liverpool College* [1900] 1 Ch 19, 23 that the paper owners 'could not be dispossessed unless the plaintiffs obtained possession themselves; and possession by the plaintiffs involves an animus possidendi—i.e., occupation with the intention of excluding the owner as well as other people'. This requirement of an intention to exclude the owner as well as everybody else has been repeated in subsequent cases. In *Powell's* case 38 P & CR 452, 471–472 Slade J found difficulty in understanding what was meant by this dictum since a squatter will normally know that until the full time has run the paper owner can recover the land from him. Slade J reformulated the requirement (to my mind correctly) as requiring an 'intention, in one's own name and on one's own behalf, to exclude the world at large, including the owner with the paper title if he be not himself the possessor, so far as is reasonably practicable and so far as the processes of the law will allow'.

(b) Must the acts of the squatter be inconsistent with the intentions of the paper owner?

44 The decision of the Court of Appeal in *Leigh v Jack* 5 Ex D 264 has given rise to repeated trouble in later cases. In that case the plaintiff's predecessor in title (Mr Leigh) had laid out part of his estate as proposed streets to be known as Grundy Street and Napier Place. He conveyed to the defendant certain land described as being 'bounded by' Grundy Street and Napier Place: therefore the intention to use the adjoining land for streets was known to all parties. Within the 20-year limitation period, both Mr Leigh and the defendant had carried out work on a fence separating Grundy Street from other land of Mr Leigh, Regent Road. From 1854 onwards the defendant had placed on Grundy Street and Napier Place old graving dock materials, screw propellers, boilers and refuse from his foundry. In 1872 (four years before action brought) the defendant completely enclosed Grundy Street and Napier Place. The Court of Appeal held that the defendant had not acquired title to the enclosed land under the Limitation Act 1833.

45 The decision on the facts is not a surprising one. Quite apart from anything else, during the 20-year limitation period relied on, the paper owner (Mr Leigh) carried out works on the fence separating Grundy Street from Regent Road. This was inconsistent with a claim that he had either discontinued possession or been dispossessed. Unfortunately, other reasons were given. Cockburn CJ said that the defendant's storage of goods on the disputed land was not 'done with the view of defeating the purpose of the parties to the conveyances'. It will be noted that the defendant was well aware of Mr Leigh's intention to use the land as a public road since he was party to the conveyance so stating. Cotton LJ relied solely on the repair of the fence by Mr Leigh which I have mentioned as showing that there had been possession by him during the limitation period. The real difficulty has arisen from the judgment of Bramwell LJ. He said, at p. 273:

> 'I do not think that there was any dispossession of the plaintiff by the acts of the defendant: acts of user are not enough to take the soil out of the plaintiff and her predecessors in title and to vest it in the defendant; in order to defeat a title by dispossessing the former owner, acts must be done which are inconsistent with his enjoyment of the soil for the purposes for which he intended to use it…'

The suggestion that the sufficiency of the possession can depend on the intention not of the squatter but of the true owner is heretical and wrong. It reflects an attempt to revive the pre-1833 concept of adverse possession requiring inconsistent user. Bramwell LJ's heresy led directly to the heresy in the *Wallis's Cayton Bay* line of cases to which I have referred, which heresy was abolished by statute. It has been suggested that the heresy of Bramwell LJ survived this statutory reversal but in the *Moran* case the Court of Appeal rightly held that however one formulated the proposition of Bramwell LJ as a proposition of law it was wrong.[9] The highest it can be put is that, if the squatter is aware of a special purpose for which the paper owner uses or intends to use the land and the use made by the squatter does not conflict with that use, that may provide some support for a finding as a question of fact that the squatter had no intention to possess the land in the ordinary sense but only an intention to occupy it until needed by the paper owner. For myself I think there will be few occasions in which such inference could be properly drawn in cases where the true owner has been physically excluded from the land. But it remains a possible, if improbable, inference in some cases.

(c) Squatters' willingness to pay if asked

46 In a number of cases (such as the present case) squatters have given evidence that if they had been asked by the paper owner to pay for their occupation of the disputed land or to take a lease they would have been prepared to do so. In *Ocean Estates Ltd v Pinder* [1969] 2 AC 19, 24 Lord Diplock giving the advice of the Privy Council said that an admission by the squatter to that effect 'which any candid squatter hoping in due course to acquire a possessory title would be almost bound to make' did not indicate an absence of an intention to possess. In my judgment in the present case the Court of Appeal did not give full weight to that decision. In my judgment the decision of the Court of Appeal in *R v Secretary of State for the Environment, Ex p Davies* (1990) 61 P & CR 487 (the decision in *Pinder* not having been cited) was wrong. The decision in *Pinder* is to be preferred because it is consistent with principle. Once it is accepted that the necessary intent is an intent to possess not to own and an intention to exclude the paper owner only so far as is reasonably possible, there is no inconsistency between a squatter being willing to pay the paper owner if asked and his being in the meantime in possession. An admission of title by the squatter is not inconsistent with the squatter being in possession in the meantime. . . .

His Lordship reviewed the judgments of Neuberger J and the Court of Appeal and continued:

64 . . . Despite Pye's notification to quit the land in December 1983, its peremptory refusal of a further grazing licence in 1984 and the totally ignored later requests for a grazing licence, after 31 December 1983 the Grahams stayed in occupation of the disputed land using it for what purposes they thought fit. Some of those purposes (i.e. the grazing) would have fallen within a hypothetical grazing agreement. But the rest are only consistent with an intention, verified by Mr Michael Graham, to use the land as they thought best. That approach was adopted from the outset. In my judgment, when the Grahams remained in factual possession of the fully enclosed land after the expiry of the mowing licence they manifestly intended to assert their possession against Pye.

65 Finally I should mention one further point. In the Court of Appeal Pye unsuccessfully contended that the Human Rights Act 1998 affected the appeal which came on for hearing on 4 December 2000, i.e. after the Act had come into effect on 2 October 2000. Before your Lordships' House, it was conceded that the Human Rights Act 1998 did not have a retrospective effect. But Pye submitted that, even under the common law principles of construction applicable before the Human Rights Act 1998 came into effect, the court should seek to apply the law so as to make it consistent with the European Convention for the Protection of Human Rights and Fundamental Freedoms. Any such old principle of construction only applied where

---

[9] Similarly disapproved in *London Borough of Hounslow v Minchinton* (1997) 74 P & CR 221.

there was an ambiguity in the language of a statute. No such ambiguity in the 1980 Act was demonstrated to your Lordships.[10]

66 For these reasons I would allow the appeal and restore the judgment of Neuberger J.[11]

[10] For the impact of the European Convention on Human Rights, and the Human Rights Act 1998, on claims to land based on adverse possession, see below, pp. 288–97.

[11] On factual possession, see *Seddon v Smith* (1877) 36 LT 168; *Littledale v Liverpool College* [1900] 1 Ch 19; *George Wimpey & Co Ltd v Sohn* [1967] Ch 487 (where the plaintiff had an easement over the land in question); *Bligh v Martin* [1968] 1 WLR 804; *Tecbild Ltd v Chamberlain* (1969) 20 P & CR 633 (playing by children and tethering of ponies held to be acts too trivial for adverse possession): *Basildon District Council v Manning* (1975) 237 EG 879 (erecting fence and dumping poultry manure held not to be adverse possession); *Red House Farms (Thorndon) Ltd v Catchpole* (1976) 244 EG 295 (shooting over marshy ground held to be adverse possession); *Treloar v Nute* [1976] 1 WLR 1295 (grazing of two cows and a yearling, storing timber and stone and filling in a gully held to be adverse possession); *Hyde v Pearce* [1982] 1 WLR 560 (continued occupation by purchaser, after termination of licence to occupy pending completion, held not to be adverse possession since 'he had at no time made it clear that he was no longer bound by the contract of sale') cf. *Bridges v Mees* [1957] Ch 475 (contracting purchaser having equitable ownership held adverse possessor); [1982] Conv 383 (J.E.M.); 46 MLR 89 (M. Dockray); *Bills v Fernandez-Gonzalez* (1981) 132 NLJ 60 (compost pens, bonfires, free-ranging chickens and planting trees and shrubs, together with adjoining owner's walking along line of fence for purposes of his garden, held not to be adverse possession); *Williams v Usherwood* (1983) 45 P & CR 235 (enclosure of land by fence, parking of three cars in enclosed curtilage of private dwelling-house and paving of driveway with decorative crazy-paving stones held to be adverse possession); [1983] Conv 398 (M. Dockray); (1984) 134 NLJ 144 (H. Wilkinson); *Dear v Woods* [1984] CA Transcript 318 (playing of children, single perambulation by male plaintiff and laying of tar macadam on strip half the width of a brick held not to be adverse possession: this note was cited by Sir David Cairns as containing examples of trivial acts that will not suffice); *Boosey v Davis* (1987) 55 P & CR 83 (grazing of goats, cutting down of scrub and erection of secondary wire mesh fence held not to be adverse possession); *Buckinghamshire County Council v Moran* [1990] Ch 623 (placing of new lock and chain on access gate held to be adverse possession); [1990] CLJ 23 (C. Harpum); [1989] Conv 211 (G. McCormack); [1989] All ER 176 (P. J. Clarke); *Marsden v Miller* (1992) 64 P & CR 239 (erection of fence for 24 hours held not to be adverse possession by person having no documentary title against another such person); *Wilson v Martin's Executors* [1993] 1 EGLR 178 (walking boundary, cutting chestnuts for repair of fence, clearing fallen timber for firewood, repairing wire fence and cutting trees for sale held not to be adverse possession); *London Borough of Hounslow v Minchinton* (1997) 74 P & CR 221 (keeping of compost heap, trimming of hawthorn and elderberry hedges and erection of fencing to prevent dogs from escaping held to be adverse possession); (1997) 147 NLJ 1662 (H. W. Wilkinson); *Prudential Assurance Co Ltd v Waterloo Real Estate Inc* [1999] 2 EGLR 85 (adverse possession of one face of a divided wall); *Burns v Anthony* (1997) 74 P & CR D41 (concreting over an enclosed area and parking cars regularly and apparently as of right, close to someone else's conservatory, held to be adverse possession); *Central Midlands Estates Ltd v Leicester Dyers Ltd* [2003] 2 P & CR DG1 (no possession where car parking was on an unenclosed strip of land with no erection of car parking signs); *Inglewood Investment Co Ltd v Baker* [2003] 2 P & CR 319 (erection of portakabins for use as lavatories for those attending car boot sales; shooting of rabbits and foxes; children playing and deposit of rubbish held not to be adverse possession; nor was the erection of a fence, the object of which was to keep sheep in and not to keep the paper owner out); *Purbrick v Hackney London Borough* [2004] 1 P & CR 34 (placing makeshift door with two locks on entrance to dilapidated 'burnt-out shell' held to be adverse possession, even though squatter was aware that he was liable to be dispossessed); *Topplan Estates Ltd v Townley* [2005] 1 EGLR 89 (no obligation in law on squatter to alert owner that time is running against him); *Ashe v National Westminster Bank plc* [2008] 1 WLR 710 (adverse possession by mortgagor against mortgagee).

On animus possidendi, see *Pavledes v Ryesbridge Properties Ltd* (1989) 58 P & CR 459 (intention to possess absent where claimant of land for car-parking asked the true owner 'to do its duty as the person entitled to possession to keep out trespassers'); *Battersea Freehold and Leasehold Property Co Ltd v Battersea London Borough Council* (2001) 82 P & CR 137 (distribution of access keys to other persons entitled to use land indicates lack of animus); *Ellis v Lambeth London Borough Council* (1999) 32 HLR 596 (squatter not estopped by failure to return community charge forms sent to the property); *Wills v Wills* [2004] 1 P & CR 612 (dispossession or discontinuance, where co-owner husband acquired title by possession from co-owner wife: only

In **Topplan Estates Ltd v Townley** [2005] 1 EGLR 89 at 96 JONATHAN PARKER LJ summarised the law in the light of *Powell v McFarlane* (1977) 38 P & CR 452 and *J A Pye (Oxford) Ltd v Graham* [2003] 1 AC 419, p. 236, above:

71 First, the epithet 'adverse' in the expression 'adverse possession', in para. 8 of Part I of Schedule 1 to the 1980 Act refers not to the quality of the possession but to the capacity of the party claiming possessory title (the squatter) as being a person 'in whose favour the period of limitation can run': per Lord Browne-Wilkinson in [35].... In particular, it does not connote any element of aggression, hostility or subterfuge (per Lord Hope of Craighead in [69]...), nor does it throw any light on the question as to whether the squatter is in possession of the land (ibid).

72 Second, the word 'possession' in the expression 'adverse possession' means no more than 'ordinary possession of the land': per Lord Browne-Wilkinson in [36].... However, in order to establish possession in this context, the squatter must prove: (a) sufficient objective acts to constitute physical possession (factual possession); coupled with (b) an intention to possess (animus possidendi). 'Occupation of the land alone is not enough, nor is an intention to occupy that is not put into effect by action': per Lord Hope of Craighead in [70]....

73 Third, an intention to possess must be distinguished from an intention to own: it is only the former that is relevant in the context of adverse possession: per Lord Browne-Wilkinson in [42].... An intention to possess might be, and frequently is, deduced from the objective acts of physical possession: per Lord Browne-Wilkinson in [40]...; per Lord Hope of Craighead in [70]...; and per Lord Hutton in [76].... However, where the acts relied upon as objective acts of physical possession are equivocal, further evidence of intention might be required: see, for example, per Lord Hutton ibid. An intention to possess means, in this context, 'an intention to occupy and use the land as one's own': per Lord Hope of Craighead in [71].... It is not necessary for the squatter to establish that he had a deliberate intention to exclude the true owner (ibid): it is enough that he intends to exclude the owner 'as best he can' (per Slade J in *Powell* at p. 472...); or, to put it another way (as Slade J did in *Powell* at pp. 471–472...), 'to exclude the world at large, including the owner with the paper title if he be not the possessor, so far as is reasonably practicable and so far as the processes of the law will allow'. The intention to possess must be manifested to the true owner, but where the objective acts of physical possession are clear and unequivocal, those acts themselves will generally constitute a sufficient manifestation of the intention to possess: per Lord Hope of Craighead in [71]... and per Lord Hutton in [76]....

74 Fourth, as to factual possession, as Slade J said in *Powell* (at pp. 470–471) in the passage cited with approval by Lord Browne-Wilkinson in [41]... :

'The question what acts constitute a sufficient degree of exclusive physical control must depend on the circumstances, in particular the nature of the land and the manner in which land of that nature is

possession of wife on premises was her discarded wedding ring); *Clowes Developments (UK) Ltd v Walters* [2006] 1 P & CR 1 (daughter and son-in-law of former licensee had no intention to possess; intention to remain in factual possession only for so long as the true owner continues so to permit not sufficient animus); *Tennant v Adamczyk* [2006] 1 P & CR 28 (mere intention to use own land and to make additional use of other land only so far as necessary for parking and unloading not sufficient); *Ofulue v Bossert* [2009] Ch 1 at [63] (person who wrongly believes he is a tenant can occupy property in such a way that he has possession, just as much as a squatter). See also [2001] Conv 155 (O. Radley-Gardner and C. Harpum).

Once a person has taken possession a mere temporary absence does not prevent his continuing in possession unless he does an act which is sufficient to exclude himself from possession: *Generay Ltd v Containerised Storage Co Ltd* [2005] 2 EGLR 7 (three months' exclusion from part of land by erection of line of rods and orange tape).

commonly used or enjoyed ... Everything must depend on the particular circumstances, but broadly, I think what must be shown as constituting factual possession is that the alleged possessor has been dealing with the land in question as an occupying owner might have been expected to deal with it and that no one else has done so.'

75 In general, therefore, a squatter will establish factual possession if he can show that he used the land in the way one would expect him to use it if he were the true owner, and in such a way that the owner is excluded: per Lord Hope of Craighead in [71]...and per Lord Hutton in [76]...

76 To the above propositions, I would venture to add one further proposition. Just as the issue as to factual possession depends crucially upon the facts of the particular case, so also, in my judgment, must the issue as to the existence of the requisite intention to possess. In particular, whether the existence of factual possession is sufficient in itself to establish the existence of the requisite intention to possess, or whether some further evidence of intention is required, must depend upon the particular facts of the case.

QUESTIONS

1. What weight do you think should be given, in determining whether adverse possession has been taken, to the fact that

   (a) the owner did not currently need the land but had plans for future development;

   (b) the trespasser did or did not intend to acquire the land as his own;

   (c) the owner knew or did not know or should have known of the trespass?

2. Consider the very difficult questions which arise in determining whether the owner (claimant) impliedly permitted the defendant to occupy; and whether an earlier express permission is still operative. A similar question arises in connection with the acquisition of easements by prescription. See *Healey v Hawkins* [1968] 1 WLR 1967, p. 692, below; Limitation Act 1980, Sch. 1, para. 8(4), p. 250, below; Law Reform Committee 21st Report (1977), paras 3.47–3.52.

III. UNREGISTERED LAND: LIMITATION ACT 1980

The Limitation Act 1980[12] consolidates the law of limitation of civil actions.[13] It still applies to land to which title has not yet been registered, and its general principle is that no action may be brought for the recovery of land after the expiration of a prescribed

---

[12] As amended by the Latent Damage Act 1986; p. 260, n. 66, below.

[13] Previous statutes on actions to recover land were: Limitation Act 1623; Real Property Limitation Acts 1833, 1874; Limitation Act 1939 (based upon Law Revision Committee Fifth Interim Report (Statutes of

period from the time when the right of action first accrues. This period is now in general 12 years,[14] and the Act deals specifically 'with the accrual of the right of action in the case of present interests, future interests, settled land and land held under a trust of land, forfeiture or breach of condition, and tenancies. For an action to accrue, and consequently for time to start running, there must be an 'adverse possessor' against whom an action can be brought.[15]

The policy of limitation was stated by STREATFIELD J in **R B Policies at Lloyd's v Butler** [1950] 1 KB 76 at 81[16]:

It is a policy of the Limitation Acts that those who go to sleep upon their claims should not be assisted by the courts in recovering their property, but another, and, I think, equal policy behind these Acts, is that there shall be an end of litigation.

What is the effect of such a policy? What is the effect of the expiration of the limitation period on D (the person who has been dispossessed or has discontinued his possession) and on A (the person in adverse possession)?[17]

(a) On D

The effect of the Limitation Act is purely negative. Not only is D's right of action to recover the land from A extinguished, but also his title to the land.[18] D cannot revive his title by a later acknowledgement or payment made to him,[19] nor by a judgment obtained by default.[20] He cannot restore his position by re-entry on the land (in this case, he can only regain it by lapse of time as an adverse possessor), and if he brings an action for recovery of the land, A need not plead the Limitation Act.[21]

(b) On A

Here the Act is silent. It is now clear that D's title is not transferred to A: there is no 'Parliamentary Conveyance'.[22] But by a combination of the negative effect of the Act

Limitation) 1936 (Cmd. 5334)); Limitation Amendment Act 1980 (based upon Law Reform Committee 21st Report (Final Report on Limitations of Actions) 1977 (Cmnd 6923), which contains a valuable discussion of all aspects of limitation).

[14] Limitation Act 1980, s. 15(1); the general period of 20 years, fixed by the Real Property Limitation Act 1833, was reduced to 12 years by the Real Property Limitation Act 1874.

[15] Ibid., s. 15(6), Sch. 1, para. 8. On the meaning of 'adverse possession', see pp. 236–246, above.

[16] *A'Court v Cross* (1825) 3 Bing 329 at 332, per Best CJ 'It is...an Act of peace. Long dormant claims have often more of cruelty than of justice in them.' See also See [1985] Conv 272 (M. Dockray).

[17] C & B, pp. 135–138; Gray, paras 2.2.3, 9.1.5; M & W, paras 4.003–4.004, 35.055–35.057; MM, pp. 559–564; Smith, pp. 78–79, 81–82; Pollock and Wright, *Possession* (1888), pp. 93–100; Franks, pp. 131–133, 141–143; (1925) 41 LQR 139 (S.A. Wiren); (1940) 56 LQR 376 (A.D. Hargreaves), 479 (W.S. Holdsworth); (1962) 78 LQR 541 (H.W.R. Wade); (1964) 80 LQR 63 (B. Rudden); (1973) 32 Conv (NS) 85 (J.A. Omotola); Section E, below.

[18] Limitation Act 1980, s. 17, p. 265, below; s. 25(3) (advowsons).

[19] *Sanders v Sanders* (1881) 19 ChD 373, p. 264, below; *Nicholson v England* [1926] 2 KB 93.

[20] *Irish Land Commission v Ryan* [1900] 2 IR 565.

[21] *Dawkins v Lord Penrhyn* (1878) 4 App Cas 51; Franks, pp. 131, 265.

[22] *Tichborne v Weir* (1892) 67 LT 735, p. 272, below.

on D's title, and the positive effect of his adverse possession, A has a new estate of his own, a fee simple subject to the unextinguished rights of other persons.[23] If D is a fee simple owner, then, as Megarry and Wade say:[24]

A's possession at once gives him all the rights and powers of ownership...[25] A has, in fact, a legal estate, a fee simple absolute in possession. But so also has D, until such time as his title is extinguished by limitation....There is thus no absurdity in speaking of two or more[26] adverse estates in the land, for their validity is relative. If D allows his title to become barred by lapse of time, A's title becomes the better, and A then becomes absolute owner. But if D brings his action within the time allowed, he can successfully assert his better title based on his prior possession; as against D, A's legal estate is nothing.

If D is a lessee of L, and A has been in adverse possession for twelve years, A's possession extinguishes D's title. This has no effect on L's title, because L's right of action does not accrue until the end of the lease.[27] A 'has a legal fee simple, subject to [L's] right of entry at the end of the period of the original term.'[28] But A may be evicted before then (a) by L, if he has taken a surrender of the lease from D,[29] or if he has forfeited the lease,[30] (b) by D, if he has taken a conveyance of the fee simple from L.[31] If, however, A acknowledges L as the freeholder, he may become a tenant for a term of years, or a yearly tenant or a tenant at will.

Whatever interest A gets, it is subject to the legal and equitable rights of third parties which run with the land and have not themselves been independently extinguished e.g. easements and restrictive covenants.[32] If the land is leasehold and A has extinguished the title of the lessee but not that of the lessor, he is not an assignee of the lease, and so is not bound by any covenants in the lease, unless they are enforceable as restrictive covenants.[33] If A pays rent to the lessor and becomes a yearly tenant, he is

---

[23] Co Litt 271a (also 2a, 297a) 'For a disseisor, abator, intruder, usurper, etc., have a fee simple, but it is not a lawful fee'; *Leach v Jay* (1878) 9 ChD 44 at 45; *Rankin v M'Murtry* (1889) 24 LR Ir 290; (1962) 78 LQR at 543–545.

[24] At paras 4.008–4.009. The symbols have been changed, and footnotes omitted.

[25] [If A dies, the land passes under his will or intestacy; *Asher v Whitlock* (1865) LR 1 QB 1, p. 251, below; *Allen v Roughley* (1955) 94 CLR 98; [1956] CLJ 177 (H.W.R. Wade).]

[26] [In the case of successive adverse possessors, the last in possession may be evicted by an earlier adverse possessor, until that possessor's title has itself been extinguished by lapse of time. See *Mount Carmel Investments Ltd v Peter Thurlow Ltd* [1988] 1 WLR 1078 where D was dispossessed by A, who in turn transferred his possession to X, another squatter; CA held that X could add both periods and acquire title by limitation.]

[27] Limitation Act 1980, s. 15(2), p. 253, below.   [28] M & W, para. 35.063.

[29] *Fairweather v St Marylebone Property Co Ltd* [1963] AC 510, p. 269, below. For a different solution in registered land under LRA 1925, see *Spectrum Investment Co v Holmes* [1981] 1 WLR 221, p. 278, n. 125, below.

[30] *Tickner v Buzzacott* [1965] Ch 426 (adverse possessor not entitled to apply to court for relief against forfeiture of lease for non-payment of rent).

[31] *Taylor v Twinberrow* [1930] 2 KB 16; *Chung Ping Kwan v Lam Island Development Co Ltd* [1997] AC 38, p. 266, below.

[32] *Re Nisbet and Potts' Contract* [1906] 1 Ch 386, p. 273, below; *Scott v Scott* (1854) 4 HL Cas 1065.

[33] For the enforceability of restrictive covenants, see chap. 9.

not, by the mere payment of rent, estopped from denying that he is bound by the terms of the original lease.[34]

The Limitation Act 1980, then, operates negatively; not positively as did the Prescription Act 1832.[35] It does not create a title in A, it merely prevents D from enforcing his. The effect of this as between vendor and purchaser is that a title based on adverse possession alone for the limitation period or longer is not necessarily a good title. The claims of the reversioner or a remainderman may have yet to be extinguished:[36] the reversion may be on a 99 year lease, the remainderman's interest may not vest in possession for over 100 years.[37] But if a vendor can establish that the flaw in an otherwise good title is one that can be cured by the running of time in his favour under the Act, he can force a purchaser to take the title.[38] Proof that rival claims have been extinguished by the lapse of time may be very difficult, and in practice a purchaser of unregistered land often agrees to accept an imperfect title.

LIMITATION ACT 1980

15. Time limit for actions to recover land.—(1) No action shall be brought by any person to recover any land after the expiration of twelve years from the date on which the right of action accrued to him or, if it first accrued to some person through whom he claims, to that person.[39]

(6) Part I of Schedule 1 to this Act contains provisions for determining the date of accrual of rights of action to recover land in the cases there mentioned.

38. Interpretation.—(1) In this Act, unless the context otherwise requires—'land' includes corporeal hereditaments, tithes and rent-charges and any legal or equitable estate or interest therein, but except as provided above in this definition does not include any incorporeal hereditament.[40]

(5) Subject to subsection (6) below, a person shall be treated as claiming through another person if he became entitled by, through, under, or by the act of that other person to the right claimed, and any person whose estate or interest might have been barred by a person entitled to an entailed interest in possession shall be treated as claiming through the person so entitled.

(6) A person becoming entitled to any estate or interest by virtue of a special power of appointment shall not be treated as claiming through the appointor.

---

[34] *Tichborne v Weir* (1892) 67 LT 735, p. 272, below.

[35] See *Buckinghamshire County Council v Moran* [1990] Ch 623 at 644, per Nourse LJ.

[36] Limitation Act 1980, s. 15(2). Time runs against the landlord even if the lease is immediately renewed; p. 259, below.

[37] *Cadell v Palmer* (1833) 1 Cl & Fin 372: vesting postponed for over 100 years (note to *Re Villar* [1928] Ch 471 at 478).

[38] *Re Atkinson's and Horsell's Contract* [1912] 2 Ch 1; *Re Spencer and Hauser's Contract* [1928] Ch 598, distinguished in *George Wimpey & Co Ltd v Sohn* [1967] Ch 487; Farrand (4th edn), pp. 108–109.

[39] For special rules relating to future interests, settlements and trusts of land, forfeiture and tenancies, and for redemption actions, actions to recover rent and actions to recover money secured by a mortgage or charge, see below, pp. 253–260.

[40] As amended by TLATA 1996, s. 25(2), Sch. 4.

A. ADVERSE POSSESSION

LIMITATION ACT 1980

SCHEDULE 1
RIGHT OF ACTION NOT TO ACCRUE OR CONTINUE UNLESS
THERE IS ADVERSE POSSESSION

8.—(1) No right of action to recover land shall be treated as accruing unless the land is in the possession of some person[41] in whose favour the period of limitation can run (referred to below in this paragraph as 'adverse possession'); and where under the preceding provisions of this Schedule any such right of action is treated as accruing on a certain date and no person is in adverse possession on that date, the right of action shall not be treated as accruing unless and until adverse possession is taken of the land.

(2) Where a right of action to recover land has accrued and after its accrual, before the right is barred, the land ceases to be in adverse possession, the right of action shall no longer be treated as having accrued and no fresh right of action shall be treated as accruing unless and until the land is again taken into adverse possession.[42]

(3) For the purposes of this paragraph—

(a) possession of any land subject to a rentcharge by a person (other than the person entitled to the rentcharge) who does not pay the rent shall be treated as adverse possession of the rentcharge; and

(b) receipt of rent under a lease by a person wrongfully claiming to be entitled to the land in reversion immediately expectant on the determination of the lease[43] shall be treated as adverse possession of the land.[44]

(4) For the purpose of determining whether a person occupying land is in adverse possession of the land it shall not be assumed by implication of law that his occupation is by permission of the person entitled to the land merely by virtue of the fact that his occupation is not inconsistent with the latter's present or future enjoyment of the land.[45]

This provision shall not be taken as prejudicing a finding to the effect that a person's occupation of any land is by implied permission of the person entitled to the land in any case where such a finding is justified on the actual facts of the case.[46]

---

[41] The Crown can acquire by adverse possession: Limitation Act 1980, s. 37(1); *Roberts v Swangrove Estates Ltd* [2008] Ch 439.

[42] Enacting the rule in *Trustees, Executors and Agency Co Ltd v Short* (1888) 13 App Cas 793. The mere sending and receipt of a letter demanding possession of land does not amount to termination of adverse possession: *Mount Carmel Investments Ltd v Peter Thurlow Ltd* [1988] 1 WLR 1078. Cf. *BP Properties Ltd v Buckler* (1987) 55 P & CR 337 where possession ceased to be adverse when claimant occupied by unilateral licence from true owner; [1994] Conv 196 (H. Wallace); *Sze To Chun Keung v Kung Kwok Wai David* [1997] 1 WLR 1232 (the last appeal to PC from Hong Kong); *Smith v Lawson* (1997) 75 P & CR 466 (time held not to run against freeholder in favour of occupier of land protected by promissory estoppel from claim by owner to possession of the land).

[43] See p. 253, below.   [44] *Bligh v Martin* [1968] 1 WLR 804.

[45] This reverses the doctrine of implied or hypothetical licence suggested by Lord Denning MR in *Wallis's Cayton Bay Holiday Camp Ltd v Shell-Mex and BP Ltd* [1975] QB 94; *Gray v Wykeham-Martin and Goode* [1977] Bar Library Transcript No 10A (CA, affirming the decision of Goulding J, who had followed *Wallis* by implying a licence without any factual basis). In *Powell v McFarlane* (1979) 38 P & CR 452 at 484 Slade J explained 'the substantial conceptual difficulties of the doctrine.'

[46] Implied licences were found on the facts in *Colin Dawson Windows Ltd v King's Lynn and West Norfolk BC* [2005] 2 P & CR 19; *Batsford Estates (1983) Co Ltd v Taylor* [2005] 2 EGLR 12.

The meaning of 'adverse possession' has already been discussed: see above, pp. 236–246.

B. SUCCESSIVE ADVERSE POSSESSORS[47]

The right to possession, or seisin, was developed by the common law as the basis of title to unregistered land.[48] This creates a system of relativity of title, based on the relative strengths of the right to possession. From the first day of his possession, the disseisor has a title to the land which is good against all except those with a better right to possession of the land. The right to recover the land, and the corresponding loss of the right to recover the land by virtue of the passage of time under the Limitation Act, therefore concerns the right to bring an action against the particular adverse possessor, based on the claimant's better claim to possession—even if that claim to possession is itself based on the claimant himself having earlier taken adverse possession of the land.

Asher v Whitlock
(1865) LR 1 QB 1 (Ct Exch Ch, **Cockburn CJ** and **Mellor** and **Lush JJ**)

In 1842 Williamson enclosed some manorial land, which he occupied until his death in 1860. At that time (the period of limitation being 20 years) the title of the Lord of the Manor was not yet extinguished. He devised the land by will to his widow so long as she remained unmarried, with remainder to his daughter in fee simple. After his death the widow remained in possession, and in 1861 married the defendant, who came to live with the widow and daughter. The daughter died in February and the widow in May 1863. The defendant remained in possession of the property, and in 1865 the daughter's heir-at-law brought ejectment against him.

Held. The heir-at-law was entitled to recover the property.

Cockburn CJ: Assuming the defendant's possession to have been adverse, we have then to consider how far it operated to destroy the right of the devisee and her heir-at-law....I take it as clearly established, that possession is good against all the world except the person who can shew a good title; and it would be mischievous to change this established doctrine. In *Doe d Hughes v Dyeball* (1829) Mood & M 346 one year's possession by the plaintiff was held good against a person who came and turned him out; and there are other authorities to the same effect. Suppose the person who originally inclosed the land had been expelled by the defendant, or the defendant had obtained possession without force, by simply walking in at the open door in the absence of the then possessor, and were to say to him, 'You have no more title than I have, my possession is as good as yours,' surely ejectment could have been maintained by the original possessor against the defendant. All the old law on the doctrine of disseisin was founded on the principle that the disseisor's title was good against all but the disseisee. It is too clear to admit of doubt, that if the devisor had been turned out of possession he could have maintained ejectment. What is the position of the devisee? There can be no doubt that a man has a right to devise that

---

[47] C & B, pp. 120–121; Gray, para. 2.1.33; M & W, para. 4.008; MM, pp. 563–564.
[48] C & B, pp. 27–31, 114–115; M & W, paras 4.008–4.011.

estate, which the law gives him against all the world but the true owner. Here the widow was a prior devisee, but *durante viduitate* only, and as soon as the testator died, the estate became vested in the widow; and immediately on the widow's marriage the daughter had a right to possession; the defendant however anticipates her, and with the widow takes possession. But just as he had no right to interfere with the testator, so he had no right against the daughter, and had she lived she could have brought ejectment; although she died without asserting her right, the same right belongs to her heir. Therefore I think the action can be maintained, inasmuch as the defendant had not acquired any title by length of possession. The devisor might have brought ejectment, his right of possession being passed by will to his daughter, she could have maintained ejectment, and so therefore can her heir, the female plaintiff. We know to what extent encroachments on waste lands have taken place; and if the lord has acquiesced and does not interfere, can it be at the mere will of any stranger to disturb the person in possession? I do not know what equity may say to the rights of different claimants who have come in at different times without title; but at law, I think the right of the original possessor is clear. On the simple ground that possession is good title against all but the true owner, I think the plaintiffs entitled to succeed.[49]

C. ACCRUAL OF RIGHT OF ACTION[50]

The Limitation Act 1980 makes separate provision for the accrual of the right of action for various different types of interests and different claims.

(i) Present interests

LIMITATION ACT 1980

SCHEDULE 1

ACCRUAL OF RIGHT OF ACTION IN CASE OF PRESENT INTERESTS IN LAND

1. Where the person bringing an action to recover land, or some person through whom he claims, has been in possession of the land, and has while entitled to the land been dispossessed or discontinued his possession, the right of action shall be treated as having accrued on the date of the dispossession or discontinuance.

2. Where any person brings an action to recover any land of a deceased person (whether under a will or on intestacy) and the deceased person—

(a) was on the date of his death in possession of the land or, in the case of a rentcharge created by will or taking effect upon his death, in possession of the land charged; and

(b) was the last person entitled to the land to be in possession of it;

the right of action shall be treated as having accrued on the date of his death.

---

[49] *Perry v Clissold* [1907] AC 73; *Ezekiel v Fraser* [2002] EWHC 2066 (Ch), [2002] NPC 132, where Judge Rich followed *Oxford Meat Pty Co Ltd v McDonald* (1963) 63 SR (NSW) 423.

[50] C & B, pp. 122–133; Gray, paras 9.1.3; M & W, paras 35.014–35.043; MM, pp. 550–557.

3.   Where any person brings an action to recover land, being an estate or interest in possession assured otherwise than by will to him, or to some person through whom he claims, and—

(a) the person making the assurance was on the date when the assurance took effect in possession of the land or, in the case of a rentcharge created by the assurance, in possession of the land charged; and

(b) no person has been in possession of the land by virtue of the assurance;

the right of action shall be treated as having accrued on the date when the assurance took effect.

(ii) Future interests

LIMITATION ACT 1980

SCHEDULE 1

ACCRUAL OF RIGHT OF ACTION IN CASE OF FUTURE INTERESTS

4.   The right of action to recover any land shall, in a case where—

(a) the estate or interest claimed was an estate or interest in reversion or remainder or any other future estate or interest; and

(b) no person has taken possession of the land by virtue of the estate or interest claimed;

be treated as having accrued on the date on which the estate or interest fell into possession by the determination of the preceding estate or interest.

15. Time limit for actions to recover land.—(2) Subject to the following provisions of this section, where —

(a) the estate or interest claimed was an estate or interest in reversion or remainder or any other future estate or interest and the right of action to recover the land accrued on the date on which the estate or interest fell into possession by the determination of the preceding estate or interest; and

(b) the person entitled to the preceding estate or interest (not being a term of years absolute) was not in possession of the land on that date;

no action shall be brought by the person entitled to the succeeding estate or interest after the expiration of twelve years from the date on which the right of action accrued to the person entitled to the preceding estate or interest or six years from the date on which the right of action accrued to the person entitled to the succeeding estate or interest, whichever period last expires.[51]

(3) Subsection (2) above shall not apply to any estate or interest which falls into possession on the determination of an entailed interest and which might have been barred by the person entitled to the entailed interest.[52]

---

[51] Where the Crown or a spiritual or eleemosynary corporation sole is entitled to the succeeding estate or interest, the periods are 30 years and 12 years (instead of 12 years and six years respectively): Limitation Act 1980, Sch. 1, para. 13. This longer period applies even if the Crown has succeeded to the estate or interest since the adverse possessor first took possession (but before the limitation period had expired); and the extended period also benefits a successor to the Crown: *Hill v Transport for London* [2005] Ch 379.

[52] See also ss. 15(1) and 38(5); M & W, para. 35.025. The combined effect of these three sections is that a 'reversioner or remainderman expectant upon an entail in possession is not entitled to the alternative six-year period, if his interest could have been barred by the tenant in tail.'

(iii) Settlements and trusts of land

LIMITATION ACT 1980

18. Settled land and land held on trust.[53]—(1) Subject to section 21(1) and (2) of this Act, the provisions of this Act shall apply to equitable interests in land as they apply to legal estates.

Accordingly a right of action to recover the land shall, for the purposes of this Act but not otherwise, be treated as accruing to a person entitled in possession to such an equitable interest in the like manner and circumstances, and on the same date, as it would accrue if his interest were a legal estate in the land (and any relevant provision of Part I of Schedule 1 to this Act shall apply in any such case accordingly).

(2) Where the period prescribed by this Act has expired for the bringing of an action to recover land by a tenant for life or a statutory owner of settled land —

(a) his legal estate shall not be extinguished if and so long as the right of action to recover the land of any person entitled to a beneficial interest in the land either has not accrued or has not been barred by this Act: and

(b) the legal estate shall accordingly remain vested in the tenant for life or statutory owner and shall devolve in accordance with the Settled Land Act 1925;

but if and when every such right of action has been barred by this Act, his legal estate shall be extinguished.

(3) Where any land is held upon trust and the period prescribed by this Act has expired for the bringing of an action to recover the land by the trustees, the estate of the trustees shall not be extinguished if and so long as the right of action to recover the land of any person entitled to a beneficial interest in the land either has not accrued or has not been barred by this Act; but if and when every such right of action has been so barred the estate of the trustees shall be extinguished.

(4) Where —

(a) any settled land is vested in a statutory owner; or

(b) any land is held upon trust;

an action to recover the land may be brought by the statutory owner or trustees on behalf of any person entitled to a beneficial interest in possession in the land whose right of action has not been barred by this Act, notwithstanding that the right of action of the statutory owner or trustees would apart from this provision have been barred by this Act.

SCHEDULE 1

POSSESSION OF BENEFICIARY NOT ADVERSE TO OTHERS INTERESTED IN SETTLED LAND OR LAND HELD ON TRUST

9. Where any settled land or any land subject to a trust of land is in the possession of a person entitled to a beneficial interest in the land (not being a person solely or absolutely entitled to the land), no right of action to recover the land shall be treated for the purposes of this Act as accruing during that possession to any person in whom the land is vested as tenant for life, statutory owner or trustee, or to any other person entitled to a beneficial interest in the land.[54]

---

[53] As amended by TLATA 1996, s. 25(2), Sch. 4.

[54] As amended by TLATA 1996, s. 25(1), Sch. 3, para. 18; s. 25(2), Sch. 4. *Bridges v Mees* [1957] Ch 475; *Re Cussons Ltd* (1904) 73 LJ Ch 296; M & W, para. 35.040; *Earnshaw v Hartley* [2000] Ch 155 (beneficial interest in unadministered estate held to be sufficient for purposes of para. 9); (2000) 150 NLJ 940 (G. Miller).

21. Time limit for actions in respect of trust property.—(1) No period of limitation prescribed by this Act shall apply to an action by a beneficiary under a trust, being an action—

   (*a*) in respect of any fraud or fraudulent breach of trust to which the trustee was a party or privy;[55] or

   (*b*) to recover from the trustee trust property or the proceeds of trust property in the possession of the trustee, or previously received by the trustee and converted to his use.[56]

(2) Where a trustee who is also a beneficiary under the trust receives or retains trust property or its proceeds as his share on a distribution of trust property under the trust, his liability in any action brought by virtue of sub-section (1) (*b*) above to recover that property or its proceeds after the expiration of the period of limitation prescribed by this Act for bringing an action to recover trust property shall be limited to the excess over his proper share.

This subsection only applies if the trustee acted honestly and reasonably in making the distribution.

(3) Subject to the preceding provisions of this section, an action by a beneficiary to recover trust property or in respect of any breach of trust, not being an action for which a period of limitation is prescribed by any other provision of this Act, shall not be brought after the expiration of six years from the date on which the right of action accrued.

For the purposes of this subsection, the right of action shall not be treated as having accrued to any beneficiary entitled to a future interest in the trust property until the interest fell into possession.[57]

(iv) Forfeiture

LIMITATION ACT 1980

SCHEDULE 1

ACCRUAL OF RIGHT OF ACTION IN CASE OF FORFEITURE OR BREACH OF CONDITION

7.—(1) Subject to sub-paragraph (2) below, a right of action to recover land by virtue of a forfeiture or breach of condition shall be treated as having accrued on the date on which the forfeiture was incurred or the condition broken.

(2) If any such right has accrued to a person entitled to an estate or interest in reversion or remainder and the land was not recovered by virtue of that right, the right of action to recover the land shall not be treated as having accrued to that person until his estate or interest fell into possession, as if no such forfeiture or breach of condition had occurred.

---

[55] *Armitage v Nurse* [1998] Ch 241 (deliberate but honest breach by trustee not fraud); *Paragon Finance plc v DB Thakerar & Co* [1999] 1 All ER 400. On constructive trustees and breach of fiduciary duty, see *Paragon Finance v DB Thakerar & Co; Coulthard v Disco Mix Club Ltd* [2000] 1 WLR 707; *Cia de Seguros Imperio v Heath (REBX) Ltd* [2001] 1 WLR 112; Maudsley & Burn, *Trusts & Trustees: Cases & Materials* (7th edn, 2008), pp. 878–884.

[56] *Armitage v Nurse*, above, n. 55 (beneficiaries under discretionary trust did not have an interest in possession).

[57] The section does not apply to an action by the Attorney-General to enforce a charitable trust, because there is no relevant beneficiary: *A-G v Cocke* [1988] Ch 414.

(v) Tenancies

(a) Periodic tenancies

LIMITATION ACT 1980

15. Time limit for actions to recover land.—(2) p. 253, above.

SCHEDULE 1

ACCRUAL OF RIGHT OF ACTION IN CASE OF FUTURE INTERESTS

4. P. 253, above.

5.—(1) Subject to sub-paragraph (2) below, a tenancy from year to year or other period, without a lease in writing,[58] shall for the purposes of this Act be treated as being determined at the expiration of the first year or other period; and accordingly the right of action of the person entitled to the land subject to the tenancy shall be treated as having accrued at the date on which in accordance with this sub-paragraph the tenancy is determined.[59]

(2) Where any rent has subsequently been received in respect of the tenancy, the right of action shall be treated as having accrued on the date of the last receipt of rent.

6.—(1) Where —

    (a) any person is in possession of land by virtue of a lease in writing by which a rent of not less than ten pounds a year is reserved; and

    (b) the rent is received by some person wrongfully claiming to be entitled to the land in reversion immediately expectant on the determination of the lease; and

    (c) no rent is subsequently received by the person rightfully so entitled;

the right of action to recover the land of the person rightfully so entitled shall be treated as having accrued on the date when the rent was first received by the person wrongfully claiming to be so entitled and not on the date of the determination of the lease.

(2) Sub-paragraph (1) above shall not apply to any lease granted by the Crown.

In **Hayward v Chaloner** [1968] 1 QB 107 the Saville Estate leased in 1938 to the rector of the parish of Bilsthorpe part of Redcote Farm for use as a garden on an oral tenancy at the rent of 10s. a year. The rent was paid by successive rectors until 1942, but not subsequently. In 1955 the plaintiffs purchased Redcote Farm including the part let to the rector.

In 1966 the incumbent rector, the defendant, claimed title under the Limitation Act 1939. The plaintiffs' application for possession failed before the Court of Appeal (Lord Denning MR dissenting). RUSSELL LJ said at 122:

In the present case there was a periodic tenancy, not in writing: the last payment of rent was in May, 1942, by the then rector, Mr McCormick, so that the right of action must by

---

[58] A document is not a lease in writing unless it is dispositive, that is a document which at law creates, of and by itself, a leasehold estate in land. A document which is merely an agreement for a lease, or merely evidential of the terms of a lease is not a lease in writing. *Long v Tower Hamlets London Borough Council* [1998] Ch 197 at 208–9.

[59] *Moses v Lovegrove* [1952] 2 QB 533 (rent-book is not a lease in writing: and the Rent Acts do not prevent time from running); *Jessamine Investment Co v Schwartz* [1978] QB 264; *Smith v Lawson* (1998) 75 P & CR 466.

section 9(2)[60] for the purposes of the Limitation Act be deemed to have then accrued, and the plaintiffs' action in 1966 to recover possession was clearly forbidden by section 4(3).[61]

It was argued for the plaintiffs, and the argument found favour with the county court judge, that section 10(1)[62] operated to prevent the right of action being deemed to accrue at any time because no person was in adverse possession at any time, adverse possession being the label applied by section 10 to 'the possession of some person in whose favour the period of limitation can run.' I do not think it necessary to discuss here the history of the conception of 'adverse possession' beyond a reference to Preston and Newsom's Limitation of Actions, 3rd edn (1953), p. 86. I have no doubt that for this purpose the possession of a tenant is to be considered adverse once the period covered by the last payment of rent has expired so that section 10(1) does not bear further upon section 9(2). Nor do I doubt the applicability of section 9(2) to the present case just because the freeholders were content that the rector should not pay his rent and did not bother to ask for it for all those years. In *Moses v Lovegrove* [1952] 2 QB 533, in this court it was assumed on all hands that when section 9 apparently operates, adverse possession starts: see especially Lord Evershed, and Romer LJ, at 538–540, 543. The principle clearly accepted was that once the period covered by the last payment of rent expired, the tenant ceased to be regarded by the Limitation Acts as the tenant. This case was not cited to the county court judge. A similar assumption was made in *Nicholson v England* [1926] 2 KB 93 under the then existing principles which section 10(1) was designed to embody. Textbooks to the same effect include Cheshire's Modern Law of Real Property, 9th edn (1962), pp. 797, 798; Megarry and Wade's Textbook of the Law of Real Property, 3rd edn (1966), p. 1010; and Preston & Newsom on Limitation of Actions, 3rd edn (1953), p. 89. I am not aware that the contrary view has been anywhere expressed, and in my judgment the cases relied upon by the county court judge of *Leigh v Jack* (1879) 5 Ex D 264, and *Williams Bros Direct Supply Ltd v Raftery* [1958] 1 QB 159, have no bearing on a question arising under section 9(2) of the Act. In my judgment, therefore, a possessory title has been acquired to this property....

The generous indulgence of the plaintiffs and their predecessors in title, loyal churchmen all, having resulted in a free accretion at their expense to the lands of their church, their reward may be in the next world. But in this jurisdiction we can only qualify them for that reward by allowing the appeal and dismissing their action.[63]

(b) Occupation for benefit of landlord

Smirk v Lyndale Developments Ltd
[1975] Ch 317 (ChD, **Pennycuick V-C,** and CA, **Cairns and Lawton LJJ** and **Walton J**)

A tenant of a house, first of British Railways, and, from 1967, of the defendants, occupied other land belonging to British Railways which adjoined the house (the blue land) and enclosed it. The defendants in 1973 began to develop the blue land, and the

---

[60] Now Limitation Act 1980, s. 15(6), Sch. 1, para. 5, above.

[61] Ibid. s. 15(1), p. 260, below.   [62] Ibid., s. 15(6), Sch. 1, para. 8(1), p. 250, above.

[63] *Lodge v Wakefield Metropolitan City Council* [1995] 2 EGLR 124 (occupier who wrongly believed that he was a rent paying tenant held to have necessary animus possidendi); *Price v Hartley* [1995] EGCS 74; *Williams v Jones* [2002] 3 EGLR 69 (former tenant holding over without payment of rent in continuous possession did not have to satisfy requirements of animus possidendi).

plaintiff brought this action claiming (i) that he had a good possessory title to the land, or alternatively (ii) that he held it as an extension of the tenanted land.

Held. (i) (expressly agreeing with Pennycuick V-C) the plaintiff held the land as an addition to the demised land; and (ii) (reversing Pennycuick V-C) the purchase of the blue land by the defendants in 1967 did not, on the facts, operate as a surrender and regrant of the lease.

Pennycuick V-C:[64] I turn now to the law applicable where a tenant takes possession of adjoining land—a tenant, during the currency of his tenancy, who takes possession of adjoining land belonging to his landlord. The law on this point, if I may respectfully say so, has got into something of a tangle.

His Lordship referred to *Kingsmill v Millard* (1855) 11 Exch 313 and quoted from the judgments of Alderson and Parke BB and continued:

It will be observed that in his judgment Parke B in terms states that the presumption that the tenant has inclosed for the benefit of the landlord applies, irrespective of whether the inclosed land is part of the waste or belongs to the landlord; and indeed he uses the word 'encroachment' as appropriate in either case. He then goes on to state in terms, following and agreeing what Alderson B said in the course of the argument, that in order to displace the presumption there must be communication to the landlord. That decision of high authority seems to me to be in accordance with justice and common sense, and unless I were compelled to do otherwise by subsequent authority, I would certainly adopt it. I should add, as is perhaps obvious, as appears in some of the later cases, that the presumption may be rebutted by any form of express or implied agreement or, in some cases, as Parke B says, by estoppel.

The next case is *Whitmore v Humphries* (1871) LR 7 CP 1, where Willes J says, at pp. 4–5:

> 'This case raises a question upon a branch of the law which involves considerations of some nicety. By the rule of law applicable to this subject the landlord is entitled at the determination of the tenancy to recover from the tenant, not only the land originally demised, but also any land which the tenant may have added to it by encroachment from the waste, such encroachment being deemed to be made by him as tenant as an addition to his holding, and consequently for the benefit of his landlord, unless it is made under circumstances which show an intention to hold it for his own benefit alone, and not as part of his holding under the landlord. This rule undoubtedly applies when the encroachment is made over land belonging to the landlord, and no inquiry appears ever to have been made in such cases, whether it was made with the consent of the landlord or not. In such cases the reasonableness of the rule is very obvious; it only gives back to the landlord that which is rightly his, and prevents the tenant, who has taken advantage of his tenancy to encroach, from keeping that which it would be a breach of the duty arising from the relation of the landlord and tenant not to give up. The rule, however, goes further than this. It is not confined to cases where the encroachment is upon land to which the landlord is entitled, it applies to cases where the land encroached upon does not belong to the landlord'

and he then goes on to deal with the position where the encroachment is upon land to which the landlord is not entitled. Willes J continues, at p. 5:

> 'The rule is based upon the obligation of the tenant to protect his landlord's rights, and to deliver up the subject of his tenancy in the same condition, fair wear and tear excepted, as that in which he enjoyed it. There is often great temptation and opportunity afforded to the tenant to take in adjoining land which

---

[64] The present extract covers the judgment of Pennycuick V-C on the first point.

may or may not be his landlord's and it is considered more convenient and more in accordance with the rights of property that the tenant who has availed himself of the opportunity afforded him by his tenancy to make encroachments, should be presumed to have intended to make them for the benefit of the reversioner, except under circumstances pointing to an intention to take the land for his own benefit exclusively. The result is to avoid questions which would otherwise frequently arise as to the property in land, and to exclude persons who have come in as tenants, and who are likely to encroach, from raising such questions. The reason of the rule appears on the one hand to be entirely independent of any notion of encroachment being a wrong done, and so also on the other hand it appears to be quite independent of the question, whether the encroachment was made with the assent of the landlord.'

His Lordship said that this principle was applied also in *Tabor v Godfrey* (1895) 64 LJQB 245. But statements in other cases (*Lord Hastings v Saddler* (1898) 79 LT 355 and *JF Perrott & Co Ltd v Cohen* [1951] 1 KB 705) apply the presumption only to cases where the land occupied by the tenant is waste and adjacent to the demised land.

Having been through the authorities I propose, as I have said earlier, to adopt and apply the principle laid down in *Kingsmill v Millard* (1855) 11 Exch 313.

To return to the present case, there is nothing on the facts which could in any way rebut the presumption, which it seems to me is applicable here, namely, that the tenant, the plaintiff, was occupying the plots by way of an addition to land comprised with his tenancy, and not otherwise adversely to the landlord. I need only add on this point that if, contrary to my view, the unilateral intention of the plaintiff was relevant, the plaintiff's very candid evidence of intention would be fatal to his own case.

In **Tower Hamlets LBC v Barrett** [2006] 1 P & CR 9 Neuberger LJ said at 140:

28 It is difficult to discern the precise basis upon which the courts have decided that a tenant, who squats on a third party's land and thereby acquires title to that land, does so for the benefit of his landlord....

30 ... In my view, it is right to proceed on the basis that the doctrine is too well-established by the cases considered at first instance in *Smirk*'s case to be overruled, at any rate in this court, not least because of the approval by Lawton LJ in that case of the analysis and conclusions of Pennycuick V-C.

31 However, I would be sceptical about the application of the doctrine...unless the land to which possessory title is acquired is very close to the demised land and occupied by the tenant together with that demised land. That appears to accord with principle, in that Willes J in [*Whitmore v Humphries* (1871–2) LR 7 CP 1] at 5 referred to the 'opportunity afforded to the tenant to *take in adjoining land*'. He went on to explain, on the same page, that the doctrine was not only 'in accordance with the rights of property', but was also based on the fact that it was 'convenient'. It is hard to see how convenience could be invoked in a case where the two pieces of land are not very close and are used and occupied together.

(c) Time runs even if the lease is immediately renewed

In **Gray v Wykeham-Martin and Goode** [1977] Bar Library Transcript No. 10A Geoffrey Lane LJ said:

A person coming to this type of situation freshly may well wonder by what possible rule of law a life tenant[65] could be affected [where there have been continual renewals]. It would seem to

---

[65] The landlord.

the uninitiated that the land has been in the possession of tenants throughout and that even if the freeholder had wanted to remove the chicken houses or the rabbit hutches from the land and to ensure thereby that the plaintiff had no claim to the land, he could not have done so. Such it seems is not the case; because it is not disputed by the defendants that the decision of the House of Lords in *Ecclesiastical Comrs of England and Wales v Rowe* (1880) 5 App Cas 736 governs the situation and that, where a tenancy comes to an end, even if it is followed immediately by a fresh tenancy, there is a moment of time, however short, in which the freeholder notionally regains possession of the land and a moment when time can start to run against the freeholder or life tenant; ... Consequently if during that moment of time, or one of those moments of time, the squatter is in the necessary adverse possession of the disputed land, time under the Limitation Act starts to run against the life tenant.

D. LIMITATION PERIOD[66]

LIMITATION ACT 1980

15. Time limit for actions to recover land.—(1) No action shall be brought by any person to recover any land after the expiration of twelve years from the date on which the right of action accrued to him or, if it first accrued to some person through whom he claims, to that person.[67]

16. Time limit for redemption actions.—When a mortgagee of land has been in possession of any of the mortgaged land for a period of twelve years, no action to redeem the land of which the mortgagee has been so in possession shall be brought after the end of that period by the mortgagor or any person claiming through him.[68]

19. Time limit for actions to recover rent.—No action shall be brought, or distress made, to recover arrears of rent, or damages in respect of arrears of rent, after the expiration of six years from the date on which the arrears became due.[69]

---

[66] The Limitation Act 1980 also contains provisions in relation to other actions, such as those founded on tort (s. 2: six years from accrual of cause of action), simple contract (s. 5: six years from accrual of cause of action) and actions on a specialty (s. 8: 12 years from accrual of cause of action); claims in negligence for latent damage to property (s. 14A: the longer of six years from accrual of cause of action and three years from sufficient knowledge of claim) with 15-year long-stop from negligent act or omission (s. 14B); ss. 14A and 14B were introduced by Latent Damage Act 1986. A 'specialty' includes a covenant under seal: Re *Compania de Electricidad de la Provincia de Buenos Aires Ltd* [1980] Ch 146 (the obligation must be created or secured by the specialty); *Collin v Duke of Westminster* [1985] QB 581 (tenant's claim to enfranchisement under Leasehold Reform Act 1967 held to be a claim upon a specialty). See *Global Financial Recoveries Ltd v Jones* (2000) Times, 23 February (claim to recover shortfall on personal covenant after realisation of mortgage held to be on a specialty, where loan founded on express agreement under seal, and therefore subject to a limitation period of 12 years under Limitation Act 1980, s. 8(1)).

[67] After a judgment for possession has been obtained in an action begun in due time, the successful plaintiff has twelve years from the date of judgment: *BP Properties Ltd v Buckler* (1987) 55 P & CR 337. Sch. 1, Pt II, contains provisions modifying s. 15 in their application to actions brought by the Crown or any spiritual or eleemosynary corporation sole: the period for s. 15(1) is 30 years (in place of 12 years), and for an action to recover foreshore the period is 60 years. For an action brought by a successor of the Crown, see Sch. 1, para. 12. On advowsons, see Limitation Act 1980, s. 25.

[68] *Young v Clarey* [1948] Ch 191.

[69] *Romain v Scuba TV Ltd* [1997] QB 887 (time limit applies to guarantor in respect of his undertaking to pay rent reserved by lease); *Tabarrok v EDC Lord & Co* (1997) Times, 14 February (where negligent advice causes plaintiff to guarantee another's debts, time runs as soon as plaintiff suffers loss).

20. Time limit for actions to recover money secured by a mortgage or charge or to recover proceeds of the sale of land.—(1) No action shall be brought to recover—

(a) any principal sum of money secured by a mortgage or other charge on property (whether real or personal); or

(b) proceeds of the sale of land;

after the expiration of twelve years from the date on which the right to receive the money accrued.[70]

(3) The right to receive any principal sum of money secured by a mortgage or other charge and the right to foreclose on the property subject to the mortgage or charge shall not be treated as accruing so long as that property comprises any future interest or any life insurance policy which has not matured or been determined.

(4) Nothing in this section shall apply to a foreclosure action in respect of mortgaged land, but the provisions of this Act relating to actions to recover land shall apply to such an action.

(5) Subject to subsections (6) and (7) below, no action to recover arrears of interest payable in respect of any sum of money secured by a mortgage or other charge or payable in respect of proceeds of the sale of land, or to recover damages in respect of such arrears shall be brought after the expiration of six years from the date on which the interest became due.[71]

(6) Where—

(a) a prior mortgagee or other incumbrancer has been in possession of the property charged; and

(b) an action is brought within one year of the discontinuance of that possession by the subsequent incumbrancer;

the subsequent incumbrancer may recover by that action all the arrears of interest which fell due during the period of possession by the prior incumbrancer or damages in respect of those arrears, notwithstanding that the period exceeded six years.

(7) Where—

(a) the property subject to the mortgage or charge comprises any future interest or life insurance policy; and

(b) it is a term of the mortgage or charge that arrears of interest shall be treated as part of the principal sum of money secured by the mortgage or charge;

interest shall not be treated as becoming due before the right to recover the principal sum of money has accrued or is treated as having accrued.

---

[70] *British & West plc v Bartlett* [2003] 1 WLR 284 (even if mortgagee has exercised power of sale before issuing proceedings for recovery of principal and interest); *Scottish Equitable plc v Thompson* [2003] HLR 48; *Gotham v Doodes* [2007] 1 WLR 86 (charge under s. 313 Insolvency Act 1986 did not create a present right to receive money, so time did not start to run until order for sale); *Yorkshire Bank Finance Ltd v Mulhall* [2008] 50 EG 74 (s. 20(1) does not apply to defeat creditor's claim to enforce charging order, following *Ezekiel v Orakpo* [1997] 1 WLR 340, n. 71, below).

[71] *Barclays Bank plc v Walters* (1988) Times, 20 October. Section 20(5) does not apply to defeat creditor's claim to enforce charging order: *Ezekiel v Orakpo* [1997] 1 WLR 340.

E. EXTENSION, POSTPONEMENT OR RE-STARTING OF LIMITATION PERIOD

In certain circumstances the start of the limitation period may be delayed, or a period which is already running may be extended, or a fresh limitation period may begin.

(i) Disability[72]

LIMITATION ACT 1980

28. Extension of limitation period in case of disability.—(1) Subject to the following provisions of this section, if on the date when any right of action accrued for which a period of limitation is prescribed by this Act, the person to whom it accrued was under a disability, the action may be brought at any time before the expiration of six years from the date when he ceased to be under a disability or died (whichever first occurred) notwithstanding that the period of limitation has expired.

(2) This section shall not affect any case where the right of action first accrued on some person (not under a disability) through whom the person under a disability claims.

(3) When a right of action which has accrued to a person under a disability accrues, on the death of that person while still under a disability, to another person under a disability, no further extension of time shall be allowed by reason of the disability of the second person.

(4) No action to recover land or money charged on land shall be brought by virtue of this section by any person after the expiration of thirty years from the date on which the right of action accrued to that person or some person through whom he claims.

38. Interpretation.—(2) For the purposes of this Act a person shall be treated as under a disability while he is an infant, or of unsound mind.

(ii) Fraud, concealment and mistake[73]

LIMITATION ACT 1980

32. Postponement of limitation period in case of fraud, concealment or mistake.—(1) Subject to subsection (3)...below, where in the case of any action for which a period of limitation is prescribed by this Act, either—

(a) the action is based upon the fraud of the defendant;[74] or

(b) any fact relevant to the plaintiff's right of action has been deliberately concealed from him by the defendant;[75] or

---

[72] C & B, p. 139, M & W, paras 35.045–35.047; MM, pp. 557–558.

[73] C & B, pp. 140–141; M & W, paras 35.048–35.050; MM, p. 558.

[74] *Beaman v ARTS Ltd* [1949] 1 KB 550 at 558, per Lord Greene MR.

[75] *Rains v Buxton* (1880) 14 Ch D 537; *Vane v Vane* (1873) 8 Ch App 383; *Clark v Woor* [1965] 1 WLR 650; *Applegate v Moss* [1971] 1 QB 406; *King v Victor Parsons & Co* [1973] 1 WLR 29; *Tito v Waddell* (No 2) [1977] Ch 106 at 224–225; *Lewisham London Borough v Leslie & Co Ltd* (1978) 250 EG 1289; *Bartlett v Barclays Bank Trust Co Ltd* [1980] Ch 515 at 537; *Westlake v Bracknell District Council* [1987] 1 EGLR 161; *Johnson v Chief Constable of Surrey* (1992) Times 23 November.

(c) the action is for relief from the consequences of a mistake;[76]

the period of limitation shall not begin to run[77] until the plaintiff has discovered the fraud, concealment or mistake (as the case may be) or could with reasonable diligence have discovered it.[78]

References in this subsection to the defendant include references to the defendant's agent and to any person through whom the defendant claims[79] and his agent.

(2) For the purposes of subsection (1) above, deliberate commission of a breach of duty in circumstances in which it is unlikely to be discovered for some time amounts to deliberate concealment of the facts involved in that breach of duty.[80]

(3) Nothing in this section shall enable any action—

(a) to recover, or recover the value of, any property; or

(b) to enforce any charge against, or set aside any transaction affecting, any property;

to be brought against the purchaser of the property or any person claiming through him in any case where the property has been purchased for valuable consideration by an innocent third party since the fraud or concealment or (as the case may be) the transaction in which the mistake was made took place.

(4) A purchaser is an innocent third party for the purposes of this section—

(a) in the case of fraud or concealment of any fact relevant to the plaintiff's right of action, if he was not a party to the fraud or (as the case may be) to the concealment of that fact and did not at the time of the purchase know or have reason to believe that the fraud or concealment had taken place; and

(b) in the case of mistake, if he did not at the time of the purchase know or have reason to believe that the mistake had been made.

(iii) Acknowledgment and part payment[81]

LIMITATION ACT 1980

29. Fresh accrual of action on acknowledgment or part payment.—(1) Subsections (2) and (3) below apply where any right of action (including a foreclosure action) to recover land or an advowson[82] . . . has accrued.

---

[76] See *Phillips-Higgins v Harper* [1954] 1 QB 411, per Pearson J. Mistake must be an essential ingredient of the cause of action, for example, an action to recover money paid under a mistake: see *Kleinwort Benson Ltd v Lincoln City Council* [1999] 2 AC 349; [1999] CLJ 478 (G. Virgo) (s. 32(1)(c) held to apply to claim for recovery of money paid under a mistake of law, including cases where mistake based on a settled understanding of the law which is shown by a later judicial decision to have been mistaken). See also *Nurdin & Peacock plc v DB Ramsden & Co Ltd* [1999] 1 WLR 1249.

[77] *Sheldon v RHM Outhwaite (Underwriting Agencies) Ltd* [1996] AC 102 (even though time started to run after cause of action arose, subsequent concealment starts time running again).

[78] See *Peco Arts Inc v Hazlitt Gallery Ltd* [1983] 1 WLR 1315 at 1322–1323 (drawing Études Pour le Bain Turc by Ingres), per Warner J.

[79] *Eddis v Chichester Constable* [1969] 2 Ch 345 (painting attributed to Caravaggio).

[80] *Cave v Robinson Jarvis & Rolf* [2003] 1 AC 384 (deliberate concealment does not include failure to disclose a negligent breach of duty which the actor was unaware of committing). See Emmet, para. 1.026.

[81] C & B, pp. 141–143; M & W, paras 35.051–35.054; MM, p. 559; *Colchester Borough Council v Smith* [1992] Ch 421 (claimant estopped from asserting that he had title under Limitation Act 1980).

[82] Limitation Act 1980, s. 25.

(2) If the person in possession of the land...acknowledges the title of the person to whom the right of action has accrued—

(a) the right shall be treated as having accrued on and not before the date of the acknowledgment...

(3) In the case of a foreclosure or other action by a mortgagee, if the person in possession of the land, ... or the person liable for the mortgage debt makes any payment in respect of the debt (whether of principal or interest) the right shall be treated as having accrued on and not before the date of the payment.

(4) Where a mortgagee is by virtue of the mortgage in possession of any mortgaged land and either—

(a) receives any sum in respect of the principal or interest of the mortgage debt; or

(b) acknowledges the title of the mortgagor, or his equity of redemption;

an action to redeem the land in his possession may be brought at any time before the expiration of twelve years from the date of the payment or acknowledgment.

(5) Subject to subsection (6) below, where any right of action has accrued to recover—

(a) any debt or other liquidated pecuniary claim,[83] or

(b) any claim to the personal estate of a deceased person or to any share or interest in any such estate;

and the person liable or accountable for the claim acknowledges the claim[84] or makes any payment in respect of it the right shall be treated as having accrued on and not before the date of the acknowledgment or payment.

(6) A payment of a part of the rent or interest due at any time shall not extend the period for claiming the remainder then due, but any payment of interest shall be treated as a payment in respect of the principal debt.

(7) Subject to subsection (6) above, a current period of limitation may be repeatedly extended under this section by further acknowledgments or payments, but a right of action, once barred by this Act, shall not be revived by any subsequent acknowledgment or payment.[85]

30. Formal provisions as to acknowledgments and part payments.—(1) To be effective for the purposes of section 29 of this Act, an acknowledgment must be in writing and signed by the person making it.[86]

(2) For the purposes of section 29, any acknowledgment or payment—

(a) may be made by the agent of the person by whom it is required to be made under that section; and

---

[83] As, for example, rent due under a lease.

[84] Acknowledgement of a claim includes admission of the existence of a debt even though its quantum is disputed: *Bradford & Bingley plc v Rashid* [2006] 1 WLR 2066; *Good v Parry* [1963] 2 QB 418; *Dungate v Dungate* [1965] 1 WLR 1477; *Surrendra Overseas Ltd v Government of Sri Lanka* [1977] 1 WLR 565; *Kamouh v Associated Electrical Industrial International Ltd* [1980] QB 199; *Re Overmark Smith Warden Ltd* [1982] 1 WLR 1195.

[85] *Sanders v Sanders* (1881) 19 ChD 373; *Nicholson v England* [1926] 2 KB 93.

[86] *See Browne v Perry* [1991] 1 WLR 1297 at 1301, per Lord Templeman; *Bigden v Lambeth London Borough Council* (2001) 33 HLR 43; *Archangel v Lambeth London Borough Council* (2001) 33 HLR 44; *Rehman v Benfield* [2007] 2 P & CR 16 (document which purported to be a lease of the property, signed by possessors as 'tenants' but without paper owner's knowledge, constituted acknowledgement when signed by possessors or when sent to paper owner's solicitor).

(b) shall be made to the person, or to an agent of the person, whose title or claim is being acknowledged or, as the case may be, in respect of whose claim the payment is being made.[87]

31. Effect of acknowledgment or part payment on persons other than the maker or recipient.—(1) An acknowledgment of the title to any land…by any person in possession of it shall bind all other persons in possession during the ensuing period of limitation.

(2) A payment in respect of a mortgage debt by the mortgagor or any other person liable for the debt, or by any person in possession of the mortgaged property, shall, so far as any right of the mortgagee to foreclose or otherwise to recover the property is concerned, bind all other persons in possession of the mortgaged property during the ensuing period of limitation.

F. EFFECT OF EXPIRATION OF LIMITATION PERIOD[88]

LIMITATION ACT 1980

17. Extinction of title to land after expiration of time limit.—Subject to—

(a) section 18 of this Act;[89]

at the expiration of the period prescribed by this Act for any person to bring an action to recover land (including a redemption action)[90] the title of that person to the land shall be extinguished.[91]

It is important to understand the limits of this provision. The expiration of the limitation period extinguishes the former person's title only *as against the squatter*. It does not transfer the title to the squatter, but only gives to the squatter an indefeasible title *as against the person against whom he adversely possessed*. The effect of the expiration of the limitation period is therefore only *relative to the two parties concerned*. This becomes particularly significant in examining the rights of a landlord in the case of adverse possession of a squatter against his tenant; and the extent to which the squatter is bound by covenants, either leasehold or freehold.

---

[87] *Edginton v Clark* [1964] 1 QB 367 (letter to owner's agent offering to purchase land held to be effective acknowledgment); *Re Compania de Electricidad de la Provincia de Buenos Aires Ltd* [1980] Ch 146 (balance sheet effective acknowledgment if received by creditor). But the acknowledgment is not effective if not made by the person in possession: *Tower Hamlets LBC v Barrett* [2006] 1 P & CR 9 at [95] (offer to purchase made by landlord of person in possession, even though the tenant was by his possession acquiring title for the landlord); *Allen v Matthews* [2007] 2 P & CR 21 (acknowledgement by solicitors acting not for person in possession but for his company).

[88] C & B, pp. 135–138; M & W, paras 35.055–35.069; MM, pp. 559–564.

[89] See p. 254, above: in the case of settled land and land held on trust, the title of the trustee to the legal estate is not extinguished until all the beneficiaries have been barred.

[90] Limitation Act 1980, s. 16, p. 260, above.

[91] The extinguishment of title also extinguishes the rights to claim rent and mesne profits during the period of adverse possession: *Mount Carmel Investments Ltd v Peter Thurlow Ltd* [1988] 1 WLR 1078; and adverse possession by the mortgagor extinguishes the mortgagee's right to take possession of the land, as well as his right to payment of the mortgage debt: *Ashe v National Westminster Bank plc* [2008] 1 WLR 710.

(i) Landlord, tenant and squatter

Chung Ping Kwan v Lam Island Development Co Ltd
[1997] AC 38 (PC, Lords Keith of Kinkel, Jauncey of Tullichettle, Nicholls of Birkenhead and **Steyn** and **Sir Christopher Slade)**

The Crown granted a lease of land on an island in the New Territories of Hong Kong for a term of 75 years from 1 July 1898 to Lam Island Development Co Ltd. The lease expired in 1973 but was renewable for a further term of 24 years less three days. Chung Ping Kwan had been in continuous possession adverse to Lam Island Development Co Ltd since 1959.

The question was whether the tenant, having exercised its option to renew the lease could recover possession from the squatter, who had, by virtue of his adverse possession, barred its rights against him under the original lease.

Held. For Chung Ping Kwan, the squatter.

Lord Nicholls of Birkenhead: Their Lordships will consider first the basic principles applicable in this area of the law, before turning to the provisions of the Renewable Leases Ordinance. The Limitation Ordinance is closely modelled on the English Limitation Acts: the Limitation Act 1939, since replaced by the Limitation Act 1980.[92]

His Lordship read the relevant provisions and continued:

From these provisions several conclusions emerge. Time begins to run against a lessee when he is dispossessed by a trespasser. In the present case time ran against the plaintiff's predecessor Mak Yung from the date when the defendants took possession and thereby dispossessed him: [Limitation Act 1980, Sch. 1, para. 1]. If continued for the prescribed period of 20 years, this adverse possession would have barred the right of Mak Yung to recover possession. It would similarly have barred those claiming under him.

However, dispossession of a lessee by a squatter does not set time running against the lessee's landlord. The landlord's right to recover possession from the squatter on the determination of the lease is not barred by a squatter's adverse possession against the lessee, however long this continues. In the ordinary course the landlord's right of action accrues when, but only when, the lease ends and the landlord's reversionary interest falls into possession: [Limitation Act 1980, Sch. 1, para. 4, p. 253, above]. Only then does time start running against the landlord.

The rationale of this provision is that so long as the legal estate created by the lease remains in existence, the landlord has no right to obtain possession of the land from a squatter. The squatter dispossessed the lessee, not his landlord. If the lessee seeks to recover possession it will be sufficient for him to prove he was in possession and that the squatter dispossessed him. But if the landlord, not having been dispossessed by the squatter, comes along and seeks to eject the squatter he must set up and rely upon his title. He has to show a better title to possession than the squatter. Herein will be his difficulty. So long as the lease is extant, his title to present possession of the land is deficient. This is so even if the title of the lessee, as between himself and the squatter, has been extinguished by [Limitation Act 1980, s. 17, p. 265, above].

---

92 The sections of the Limitation Act 1980 have been substituted for those of the Ordinance.

These established principles are conveniently displayed in Megarry & Wade, *The Law of Real Property,* 5th edn (1984), pp. 103–109, 1037.

On the determination of the lease, therefore, the landlord is entitled to oust the squatter however long he may have been on the land. Those claiming through the landlord are similarly entitled: their right to possession is no better, and no worse, than the right of the landlord from whom they derive their title. So if the landlord grants a new lease, the lessee of the new lease may eject the squatter.

In principle the position cannot be different if the lessee under the new lease is the same person as the lessee under the original lease. There seems to be no sensible reason why the landlord's ability to confer on a new lessee a title as good as his own should be subject to an exception when the new lessee is the original lessee. Lord Bledisloe argued otherwise. He submitted that the combined effect of [Limitation Act 1980, s. 15(1), p. 260, above and Sch. 1, para. 1, p. 252, above] is that once the prescribed period of 20 years has run against a lessee, the lessee is barred from bringing an action to recover the land from the squatter and that he remains barred even if he acquires another source of title he did not have when the 20-year period expired. It would be extraordinary, so the argument runs, if a lessee whose right to bring possession proceedings against a squatter has become time-barred could set time running anew against the same squatter by obtaining another lease.

Their Lordships are unable to accept this submission. A lessee's ability to regain possession in reliance on a new lease is no more than a striking illustration of the principle that dispossession of a lessee sets time running against the lessee and those claiming through him as lessee, but not against the landlord and those claiming through him as reversioner. A trespasser on leased property is more vulnerable than a trespasser on property occupied by the freeholder. In the latter case the title which the squatter bars is the freehold title. In the former case the title which is barred is leasehold only, because that is the extent of the title of the person who has been dispossessed. Adverse possession defeats the rights, whatever they may be, of the person against whom the possession is adverse. It does not defeat the rights of others.

Their Lordships consider that *Taylor v Twinberrow* [1930] 2 KB 16 was correctly decided. It is unnecessary for their Lordships to express a view on the controversial decision in *Fairweather v St Marylebone Property Co Ltd* [1963] AC 510:[93] see the powerful critique by Professor H.W.R. Wade in 'Landlord, Tenant and Squatter', (1962) 78 LQR 541. The actual decision in that case turned on the effect of the surrender of a lease by a lessee whose title has been barred by a trespasser's adverse possession. The answer to that conundrum throws no light on the problem arising in the present appeal.

A right to renew

Thus far consideration has been given to the straightforward position of a simple lease for a term of years. The next step is to consider the case of a lease containing an option for the lessee to renew the lease. Mr Nugee submitted this makes no difference. In such a case, just as much as in the case where there is no option to renew, the estate to which the squatter's possession was adverse was the term of years created by the lease. Only that estate was extinguished. As between the landlord and the lessee the lease still subsists, and the lessee can still enforce the option. If he does so, he acquires from the landlord a new legal estate, and in respect of that estate time runs from the determination of the original lease, in accordance with [Sch. 1,

---

[93] P. 269, below.

para. 4]. The lessee's claim for possession is then based on the new lease, not the original lease. The pre-existing contractual right of renewal is not itself an estate.

Clearly, until the new lease is granted the lessee does not have a legal estate in the property for the term of years which is the subject of the option. Equally clearly, in the ordinary course the option will be specifically enforceable. The lessee has a right in respect of the property which he can enforce against the landlord. Thus the question to be addressed is whether adverse possession bars the lessee from asserting against the squatter this specifically enforceable right, *and the legal estate which flows from this right,* as much as it bars the lessee from asserting against the squatter the other rights granted to him by the lease.

Their Lordships consider that an affirmative answer to this question will accord better with the legislative intention inherent in the scheme of the Limitation Act 1980 and the Limitation Ordinance. The principle underlying [Sch. 1, para.4] is that time should not run against a reversioner so long as there is a prior estate or interest standing between him and the right to retake the property. Until the preceding estate or interest determines, and the reversionary estate or interest falls into possession, the reversioner is not sleeping on his rights.

This principle applies to a prior legal estate such as a lease. This principle seems apt to be applied also to a specifically enforceable prior right to call for a legal estate, such as a lessee's renewal option, when the person having the right is already lawfully in possession. In the latter case, as much as the former, the reversioner has no right to enter and eject the trespasser. If the lessee validly exercises the option the landlord is bound to renew the lease. He can be compelled to do so. He is not entitled to eject the lessee at the expiration of the lease. This is the crucial feature. The landlord is not entitled to possession. This pre-existing interest of the lessee, precluding the landlord from ejecting the lessee, would be a fatal flaw in a claim by the landlord to oust a trespasser. The trespasser is as much entitled to set up and rely upon this interest as a deficiency in the landlord's right to possession as he is entitled to set up and rely upon a lease for this purpose.

Conversely, and unlike the reversioner, the lessee has slept on his rights. There seems to be no compelling reason why, as between him and the trespasser, his rights under the renewal option in the lease should not be defeated just as much as his other rights under the lease. It is true that when he exercises the option the lessee obtains a new legal estate, but this is no more than implementation of a preexisting contract. He acquires a new legal estate by virtue only of a right included in the lease whose title has been extinguished as against the trespasser. To ignore the legal source of the lessee's entitlement to his new legal estate would be to exalt form (a new legal estate) over substance (a pre-existing right to the estate).

There seems to be no authority on this point. The point was not raised clearly in the recent Hong Kong cases until the present one. Some assistance can be derived from considering the closely analogous situation which arose in the Australian case of *Bree v Scott* (1904) 29 VLR 692....

In their Lordships' view, where a new lease is granted pursuant to a lessee's option in the original lease the right to bring an action to recover the land from a trespasser within the meaning of section [15] accrues to the lessee on the date of the dispossession. [Sch. 1, para. 1] is applicable in such a case, and as against the trespasser section 17 operates to extinguish his title to the new lease as much as the original lease. Conversely, in such a case [Sch. 1, para. 4] is inapplicable and does not operate to set a new limitation period running in favour of the lessee. The lessee's claim in right of the new lease is not a claim to an estate or interest in reversion within the meaning of [Sch. 1, para. 4], because the lessee's right to the new lease, subject to satisfying any prescribed conditions, was a right he already had as lessee.

(ii) Surrender of lease by squatter

Fairweather v St Marylebone Property Co Ltd
[1963] AC 510 (HL, **Lords Radcliffe, Denning, Morris of Borth-y-Gest**[94] and **Guest**)

Lord Denning: My Lords, at the back of a leasehold house in Hampstead there is a shed. In the year 1920 the next-door neighbour, Mr Millwood, saw it was unused and out of repair. He went in and repaired it and has treated it as his own ever since. Mr Millwood has actually sub-let it as part of his own house. Now a property company has bought the freehold of the property on which the shed stands and wants to recover possession of the shed. Can it do so? or is it barred by the Statutes of Limitation? There are three important persons to consider:

(1) The *freeholder* who, in 1893, let the premises on which the shed stands on a lease for 99 years at a ground rent with a repairing covenant and a proviso for re-entry. The 99 years will not expire till 1992.

(2) The *leaseholder* who has taken no steps for more than 12 years to recover possession of the shed which stands on part of his leasehold premises. His right of action first accrued in 1920. So the 12 years for him to sue expired in 1932.

(3) The *squatter,* who has been in possession of the shed since 1920, by himself or his sub-tenants.

And there is one important event to consider. The *surrender* in 1959 by the *leaseholder* to the *freeholder* of the rest of the term of 99 years. Whereupon the freeholder claims that he is entitled to possession of the shed. But the *squatter* says he is entitled to stay in it until 1992.

It is quite clear from the Statutes of Limitation that in the year 1932 the 'title' of the lease-holder to the land was 'extinguished'. What does this mean? There are four suggestions to consider.

The first suggestion is that the title of the leaseholder to the shed is extinguished completely, not only against the squatter, but also against the freeholder. So that the leasehold interest disappears altogether, and the freeholder becomes entitled to the land. I reject this suggestion completely. It would mean in this case that the freeholder would have become entitled to possession of the shed in the year 1932 and time would have begun to run against him from 1932. So that 12 years later the title of the freeholder to the shed would have been extinguished, that is, in 1944. That cannot be right, and it was not seriously suggested. In 99 cases out of 100, the freeholder has no knowledge that the squatter is on the premises at all. It would be utterly wrong if the title of the freeholder could be eroded away during the lease without his knowledge. The correct view is that the freehold is an estate in reversion within section 6(1) of the Act of 1939,[95] and time does not run against the freeholder until the determination of the lease: see *Doe d Davy v Oxenham* (1840) 7 M & W 131.

The second suggestion is that the title of the leaseholder to the shed is extinguished so far as the leaseholder is concerned—so that he is no longer entitled to the shed—but that the lease-hold interest itself persists and is vested in the squatter. In other words, the squatter acquired a title which is 'commensurate' with the leasehold interest which has been extinguished. This suggestion was made in 1867 in the first edition of Darby and Bosanquet's book [Statutes of

---

[94] Lord Morris dissented. For criticism of the majority view, see (1962) 78 LQR 541 (H. W. R. Wade).

[95] Now Limitation Act 1980, Sch. 1, para. 4, p. 253, above.

Limitation] at p. 390, and it was accepted in 1889 as correct by the court in Ireland in *Rankin v M'Murtry* (1889) 24 LR Ir 290. But it has since been disapproved. If it were correct, it would mean that the squatter would be in the position of a statutory assignee of the shed, and he would by reason of privity of estate, be liable on the covenants and subject to the conditions of the lease. I reject this suggestion also: for the simple reason that the operation of the Statutes of Limitation is merely negative. It destroys the leaseholder's title to the land but does not vest it in the squatter. The squatter is not liable on the repairing covenants: see *Tichborne v Weir* (1892) 67 LT 735 [p. 272, below]. Nor, when the leasehold is a tenancy from year to year, does he step into the shoes of the tenant so as to be himself entitled to six months' notice to quit: see *Taylor v Twinberrow* [1930] 2 KB 16.

The third suggestion is that the *title* of the leaseholder is extinguished but that his *estate* in the land is not. This is too fine a distinction for me. And so it was for Parliament. For Parliament itself uses the two words as if they meant the same: see section 16 of the Limitation Act 1939, and section 75 of the Land Registration Act 1925.

The fourth suggestion is that the title of the leaseholder to the shed is extinguished as *against the squatter,* but remains good as *against the freeholder.* This seems to me the only acceptable suggestion. If it is adopted, it means that time does not run against the freeholder until the lease is determined—which is only just. It also means that until that time the freeholder has his remedy against the leaseholder on the covenants, as he should have; and can also re-enter for forfeiture, as he should be able to do: see *Humphry v Damion* (1612) Cro Jac 300, and can give notice to determine on a 'break' clause or notice to quit, as the case may be. Further, it means that if the leaseholder should be able to induce the squatter to leave the shed—or if the squatter quits and the leaseholder resumes possession—the leaseholder is at once in the same position as he was originally, being entitled to the benefits and subject to the burdens of the lease in regard to the shed. All this seems to me eminently reasonable but it can only be achieved if, despite the presence of the squatter, the title of the leaseholder remains good as against the freeholder.

On this footing it is quite apparent that at the date of the surrender, the leaseholder had something to surrender. He still had his title to the shed as against the freeholder and was in a position to surrender it to him. The maxim nemo dat quod non habet has no application to the case at all.

But there still remains the question: What was the effect of the surrender?[96] There are here two alternatives open:

(1) On the one hand, it may be said that the surrender operated to *determine* the term, just as a forfeiture does. If this is correct, it would mean that the freeholder would be entitled to possession at once as soon as the leaseholder surrendered the house. He could evict the squatter by virtue of his freehold estate against which the squatter could say nothing. And time would begin to run against the freeholder as soon as the surrender took place. This view is based on *Ecclesiastical Commissioners of England and Wales v Rowe* (1880) 5 App Cas 736, and section 6(1) of the Limitation Act 1939.

(2) On the other hand, it may be said that the surrender operated as an *assignment* by the leaseholder to the freeholder of the rest of the 99 years. If this is correct, it would mean that the freeholder could not evict the squatter because the freeholder would be 'claiming through' the leaseholder and would be barred for the rest of the 99 years, just as the leaseholder would

---

[96] On surrender generally, see C & B, pp. 325–327, 897; Gray, paras 4.2.128–4.2.137; M & W, paras 18.066–18.070; MM, pp. 364–365.

be: see section 4(3) of the Limitation Act.[97] Time would not begin to run against the freeholder until the 99 years expired. This view is based on *Walter v Yalden* [1902] 2 KB 304.

My Lords, I have come to the clear conclusion that a surrender operates as a determination of the term. It is not an assignment of it. I am aware that no less an authority than Lindley LJ once said that 'the surrender of the term only operated as an assignment of the surrenderor's interest in it': see *David v Sabin* [1893] 1 Ch 523, 533. But if that be true, it is not by any rule of the common law, only by force of statute: and then only in the case of underleases, not in the case of trespasser or squatter.

At common law, if a leaseholder made an underlease and afterwards surrendered his term to the freeholder, then the freeholder could not evict the underlessee during the term of the under-lease: see *Pleasant (Lessee of Hayton) v Benson* (1811) 14 East 234. But this was not because there was any assignment from surrenderor to surrenderee. It is clear that, upon the surrender, the head term was determined altogether. It was extinguished completely, so much so that the freeholder could not sue the underlessee on the covenants or enforce the proviso for re-entry: see *Webb v Russell* (1789) 3 Term Rep 393. The underlessee could enjoy the property without payment of rent and without performance of the covenants and conditions until the end of the term of the underlease: see *Ecclesiastical Comrs for England v Treemer* [1893] 1 Ch 166, 174. This was remedied by the statutes of 1740 and 1845, which have been re-enacted in sections 139 and 150 of the Law of Property Act 1925. Under those statutes, on a surrender of the head lease, an underlessee becomes a direct tenant of the freeholder on the terms of his underlease. So that the surrender does operate as if it were an assignment of the surrenderor's interest. But those statutes have no application to trespassers or squatters.

The question may be asked: why did the common law on a surrender protect the underlessee from eviction? The answer is to be found in Coke upon Littleton II, p. 338b, where it is said that 'having regard to the parties to the surrender, the estate is absolutely drowned... But having regard to strangers, who were not parties or privies thereunto, lest by a voluntary surrender they may receive prejudice touching any right or interest they had before the surrender, the estate surrendered hath in consideration of law a continuance.' This passage applies in favour of an underlessee so as to protect him from eviction during the term of his underlease: but it does not apply in favour of a trespasser. The reason for the difference is because the underlessee comes in under a grant from the lessee; and the lessee cannot, by a surrender, derogate from his own grant: see *Davenport's case* (1610) 8 Co Rep 144b and *Mellor v Watkins* (1874) LR 9 QB 400, 405, by Blackburn J. But a trespasser comes in by wrong and not by grant of the lessee. If the lessee surrenders his term, the freeholder is at once entitled to evict the trespasser for the simple reason that, on the surrender, the lease is determined, and there is no bar whatever to the freeholder recovering possession: see *Ecclesiastical Commissioners of England and Wales v Rowe* (1880) 5 App Cas 736. And I see no reason why the same reasoning should not apply even though, at the date of the surrender, the trespasser is a squatter who has been there more than 12 years. For, as against the freeholder, he is still a trespasser. The freeholder's right to possession does not arise until the lease is determined by the surrender. It then comes into being and time begins to run against him under section 6(1) of the Limitation Act, 1939.

The only reason, it seems to me, which can be urged against this conclusion is that it means that a squatter's title can be destroyed by the leaseholder and freeholder putting their heads together. It is said that they can by a surrender—or by a surrender and regrant—destroy the

---

[97] Now Limitation Act 1980, s. 15(1), p. 260, above.

squatter's title completely and get rid of him. So be it. There is no way of preventing it. But I would point out that, if we were to deny the two of them this right, they could achieve the same result in another way. They could easily do it by the leaseholder submitting to a forfeiture. If the leaseholder chooses not to pay the rent, the freeholder can determine the lease under the proviso for re-entry. The squatter cannot stop him. He cannot pay the rent without the authority of the leaseholder. He cannot apply for relief against forfeiture. The squatter's title can thus be defeated by a forfeiture—or by a forfeiture and regrant—just as it can by a surrender—or by a surrender and regrant. So there is nothing in the point.

My Lords, so far as these questions under the Limitation Acts are concerned, I must say that I see no difference between a surrender or merger or a forfeiture. On each of those events the lease is determined and the freeholder is entitled to evict the squatter, even though the squatter has been on the land during the lease for more than 12 years: and on the determination of the lease, time then begins to run against the freeholder. It follows that, in my opinion, *Walter v Yalden* [1902] 2 KB 304 was wrongly decided and *Taylor v Twinberrow* [1930] 2 KB 16 was rightly decided....I would dismiss this appeal.[98]

(iii) Covenants

In **Tichborne v Weir** (1892) 67 LT 735[99] KAY LJ said at 737:

On the occasion of the conveyance [between Giraud and Weir] Giraud made a statement that he had no assignment of the lease, but only a title by a possession of forty years. The question is, what is the effect of that title. There is no doubt that covenants running with the land would bind anyone coming into possession of the estate which Baxter had, and if the lease is any-how vested in the defendant, he would be bound by such covenants. Therefore the question is, whether Baxter's estate is vested in the defendant. It was argued that the effect of the statute was to transfer the term from Baxter to Giraud, and so it would be vested in the defendant. Under section 34 of 3 & 4 Will 4, c27,[100] 'the right and title' of Baxter to 'the land' (which by the interpretation clause includes chattel interest) was 'extinguished'. That is the operation of the section, and we are now asked to construe the Act of Parliament so as to make it say that Baxter's right and title was transferred to Giraud....The defendant got an estate in the land which he has admitted, by paying rent, is not the fee simple, and by operation of the statute Baxter's right to claim the term was extinguished. It follows that Giraud during the test of the term was free from liability to Baxter or anyone claiming under him, but it does not follow that he acquired Baxter's estate. There is another point as to whether the defendant is estopped from denying that he was in possession of Baxter's lease. He admits he is in possession of the land, he and Giraud have paid rent agreed on in the lease of 1802, and they have claimed posses-sion for the rest of the term. The landlord's title to the land has been completely admitted, but there is no other evidence of the defendant's being bound by all the terms of the lease, or of his holding all Baxter's estate. There being no such admission, either express or implied, we must

---

98 *Jessamine Investment Co v Schwartz* [1978] QB 264 (sub-tenant, protected as statutory tenant under Rent Acts, acquired possessory title against his immediate landlord, whose title continued to exist as against the freeholder until head lease expired. Sub-tenant held still protected under Rent Acts thereafter against freeholder); (1977) 41 Conv (NS) 213 (F.R. Crane).

99 See p. 759, below, where the facts are given.

100 Reproduced with amendments as Limitation Act 1980, s. 17, p. 265, above.

hold that there is no evidence of such an extensive estoppel as that which has been contended for.[101] I think that the defendant, for the reasons I have stated, is not liable on the covenants of the lease, and that this appeal should be dismissed.

In **Re Nisbet and Potts' Contract** [1906] 1 Ch 386,[102] COZENS-HARDY LJ said at 409:

The suggestion which is at the root of the appellant's argument is this, that a squatter can wholly disregard restrictive covenants affecting a building estate. That is so startling a proposition, and so wide-reaching, that it must be wrong. The value of estates in the neighbourhood of London and all large towns, and the amenity of those estates, depend almost entirely upon the continuance of the mutual restrictive covenants affecting the user and the enjoyment of the property; and when we are told that the squatter, notwithstanding that he is a mere trespasser, is to be in a better position than that occupied by a person deriving a title strictly through the original covenantor, one feels that there must be an answer to the argument; and I think the authorities, when carefully examined, make the answer quite plain. The benefit of a restrictive covenant of this kind is a paramount right in the nature of a negative easement not in any way capable of being affected by the provisions of the Statute of Limitations on which the squatter relies. The only rights extinguished for the benefit of the squatter under section 34[103] are those of persons who might, during the statutory period, have brought, but did not in fact bring, an action to recover possession of the land. But the person entitled to the benefit of a restrictive covenant like this never had any cause of action which he could have brought, because unless and until there is a breach, or a threatened breach, of such a covenant, it is impossible for the person entitled to the benefit of it to bring any action. It appears, therefore, so far as the squatter is himself concerned, that both during the currency of the twelve years and after the expiration of the twelve years, there could be no possible answer to the claim of anyone seeking to enforce the covenant. In fact, there would, so far as he is concerned, be no difference between this covenant, which is in the nature of an equitable easement, and a legal easement strictly and properly so called. But although the squatter took the property subject to this equitable burden, it maybe that the present vendor, who purchased from or through the squatter, is able to say that the burden does not affect the property in his hands. But what must he prove in order to claim this exemption? He must prove that he is a purchaser for value of the legal estate without notice.... Now can the present vendor allege and prove that he was a purchaser for value without notice? I think not.

G. LAW REFORM

In 2001 the Law Commission recommended that the provisions on actions to recover land should be reformed.[104] The main recommendation was that such actions should

---

[101] *Tickner v Buzzacott* [1965] Ch 426 (payment of rent due under lease not estoppel); *Ashe v Hogan* [1920] 1 IR 159; *O'Connor v Foley* [1906] 1 IR 20.

[102] See p. 759, below, where the facts are given.

[103] Reproduced with amendments as Limitation Act 1980, s. 17.

[104] The Report also proposed a general reform of the law on limitation of actions to introduce a 'core regime' which would apply to most claims for a remedy for a wrong, claims for the enforcement of a right and claims to restitution: a 'primary limitation period' of three years starting from the date on which the

be subject to a long-stop period of 10 years from the date on which the action accrued; a reduction from the 12 years of the Limitation Act 1980.

In July 2002 the Government accepted in principle the recommendations in the Report, although time was not found for its implementation, and in 2007 the Government announced a further consultation on the implementation of the Law Commission's recommendations.[105] The law on limitation of actions in relation to registered land was reformed in the Land Registration Act 2002.[106]

Law Commission Report on Limitation of Actions 2001 (Law Com No. 270), paras 4.126–4.135 and 4.149–4.150

4.126 Generally, claims to recover land are subject to a limitation period of twelve years, which runs from the date on which the claimant's right of action accrued, or, if the right first accrued to some other person through whom the claimant claims, then the date on which the right accrued to that person. This date will usually be when the land first came to be in adverse possession, but special provision is made in certain cases, in particular when the claimant has only a future interest in the land.[107]

4.127 In the Consultation Paper we provisionally recommended that the primary limitation period of three years running from the date of knowledge should not apply to claims to recover land.[108] We explained that in many cases the defendant's trespass will be discoverable immediately, or very soon after. Applying the core regime would therefore mean that the limitation period would have been reduced from twelve years to three, and we believed this to be unacceptably short. On the other hand, in cases where there was an issue as to whether the claimant had knowledge of the adverse possession, there could be enormous uncertainty. It would be necessary to ascertain not only when the adverse possession commenced, but also when the claimant knew (or ought to have known) that the defendant was in possession of the piece of land in question and had the necessary *animus possidendi*. Although we are generally content that the degree of uncertainty inherent in any test for the 'date of knowledge' is a price worth paying for the fairness of the result, we explained that in the case of ownership of land we believed that the need for certainty was of particular importance. Moreover, we explained that the date of knowledge test did not sit easily with the existing rule that time runs against an owner regardless of his or her knowledge of the adverse possession, and we were reluctant to put forward any reform that would alter the nature of adverse possession.

4.128 Instead, therefore, we provisionally recommended that a long-stop limitation period commencing on the date of adverse possession should be the sole limitation period applying to such claims. We asked consultees whether that limitation period should be ten years (as under the core regime) or twelve years (the period applying under the current law).[109]

4.129 The suggestion that a single limitation period running from the date of adverse possession (as defined under the current law) should apply to claims to recover land received

---

claimant knows, or ought reasonably to know, certain facts relevant to his claim, subject in most cases to a 'long-stop period' of 10 years.

[105] Law Commission Annual Report 2007–2008 (Law Com No. 310), paras 3.26–3.27.

[106] Below, pp. 279 ff.

[107] Limitation Act 1980, s. 15 and Sch. 1. See further paras 2.52–2.59 above and paras 4.133–4.134 below.

[108] Limitation of Actions, Consultation Paper No 151 (1998), para. 13.121.

[109] Limitation of Actions, Consultation Paper No 151 (1998), para. 13.121.

substantial support from consultees: over seventy-five per cent agreed. There was less agreement as to the length of that period. The largest proportion of consultees (around twenty-five per cent) would accept a limitation period of ten years. A smaller proportion argued in favour of a period of twelve years. Periods of fifteen years or twenty years were also suggested.[110]

4.130 It has been suggested that, as land-related claims need to be given special treatment, the attempt to bring them partially within the core regime by applying the long-stop limitation period to them is misguided. We accept that the regime applying to claims to recover land is substantially different to other claims within the core regime, not least because the effect of the expiry of the limitation period is to extinguish the claimant's title to the land rather than to provide the defendant with a defence to any claim made by the claimant. We propose therefore, instead of legislating for a defence to a claim to recover land, to retain the existing statutory formula that no claim to recover land may be brought after the expiry of the limitation period. This is however a change in emphasis rather than in substance. The limitation period applying to claims to recover land will be ten years—the length of the long-stop limitation period. It will start on the day on which the claimant's cause of action accrues (as would be the case with the long-stop limitation period), and we propose to re-enact the current provisions in relation to the accrual of the cause of action for a claim to recover land. In addition, the provisions of the core regime in relation to the extension of limitation period (namely in relation to agreements, concealment, acknowledgments and part payments and disability) will apply.

4.131 It was suggested that the doctrine of adverse possession should be abolished. One of the original justifications for the doctrine of adverse possession (to prevent claims when all evidence is lost and to ensure certainty of title) no longer applies because of the existence of the Land Register. We noted in our Consultation Paper that any radical reform of the concept of adverse possession was beyond the remit of a project reviewing the law on limitation periods.[111] In fact the existence of the system of land registration seems to strengthen the case for a ten year period. Proposals for the reform of adverse possession of registered land have now been put forward by the Law Commission in Land Registration for the Twenty-First Century: A Consultative Document.[112] Under these proposals, a person in adverse possession of land which has a registered title would be able to apply for registration as proprietor of that land following ten years of adverse possession. Notice of the application would be given to anyone who appeared from the Land Register to have title to the land, who would thereupon have the opportunity to object to the application. Any such objection would lead to the dismissal of the application for registration, unless the adverse possessor could show: (i) that it would be unconscionable for registered proprietor to seek to dispossess the applicant, and that the adverse possessor ought to be registered as proprietor; (ii) that he had some independent right to the land that entitled him to be registered as proprietor; or (iii) that the land in adverse possession is adjacent to his own land and the exact line of the boundary between the two has never been determined, that he has been in adverse possession of the land in question in the reasonable belief that the land in question belonged to him, and that the estate he seeks was registered more than one year ago. The registered proprietor would then have two years within which to bring a claim to recover

---

[110] Three per cent favoured each of the following options: 15 years, 20 years, and a period between 10 and 15 years (unspecified).

[111] Limitation of Actions, Consultation Paper No 151 (1998), para. 13.113.

[112] Law Com No. 254 (1998). [Followed by Report on Land Registration for the Twenty-First Century 2001, Law Com No. 271: see below, p. 280.]

the land from the adverse possessor.[113] If these proposals are accepted,[114] it is likely that the recommendations made in this report will only apply to unregistered land, and claims in respect of interests in registered land which are not themselves capable of registration.[115]

4.132   The proposals contained in the Consultative Document on Land Registration give the landowner significantly greater protection against the squatter where title to the land is registered. If the owner of unregistered land wishes to benefit from the same protection, he or she can apply for registration of his or her land. This removes much (if not all) of the cause for concern expressed over our provisional proposal that the general limitation period for claims to recover land should be reduced to ten years.

4.133   The general rule we recommend in this Report, of ten years running from the date of adverse possession, would, however, require modification where the claimant has only a future interest in the land. Such an interest might include not only the reversionary interest expectant on the determination of a life interest, but also the reversion of a lease. Under the present law, time does not generally run in such cases until the interest falls into possession.[116] That is, the right of action is treated as arising when the interest falls into possession through the determin- ation of the preceding interest, provided that the person entitled to the preceding interest was in possession of the land at that time, and that no one had already taken possession by virtue of the future interest claimed.[117] Where the person entitled to the preceding interest in the land was not in possession at the date when that interest determined, the limitation period is the longer of (i) twelve years from the date the right of action accrued to the person entitled to the preceding interest or (ii) six years from the date on which the right of action accrued to the person entitled to the succeeding interest.[118]

4.134   As we explained in the Consultation Paper, we do not think it appropriate, in the course of this review, to change the law so as to accelerate the running of time against future interests. We therefore recommend that the general rule is subject to an exception so that where the claimant's interest is a future interest, the limitation period should not begin to run until that interest falls into possession, where this is later than the date of adverse possession. This exception would itself be subject to the exceptions which currently allow time to run against a claimant with a future interest,[119] though where the person entitled to the preceding interest was not in possession when that interest determined, we do not propose to impose a separate limitation period as in section 15(2) of the 1980 Act. Instead, the normal limitation period will apply.

---

[113]   If the registered proprietor failed to do so within this time, the adverse possessor could apply to be registered as proprietor as of right.

[114]   [The proposals in relation to registered land were implemented by LRA 2002; below, p. 279.]

[115]   Such as a short lease, or a tenancy or licence at will of registered land.

[116]   See further, Limitation of Actions, Consultation Paper No 151 (1998), para. 13.118.

[117]   Limitation Act 1980, Sch. 1, para. 4. The same general rule also applies to leases.

[118]   Limitation Act 1980, s. 15(2). But this provision does not apply in the case of any estate or interest which falls into possession on the determination of an entailed interest and which might have been barred by the person entitled to the entailed interest. Here, time will run against a person entailed in remainder, even though he or she may have no entitlement to possession of the land during the limitation period: Limitation Act 1980, s. 15(3). In addition, where the claimant has both a present and a future interest in land, and his or her right to bring an action to recover the present interest has become time-barred, he or she may not bring an action to recover the future interest unless in the meantime someone has recovered possession of the land under an intermediate interest: Limitation Act 1980, s. 5(5).

[119]   Limitation Act 1980, s. 15(3) and (5). See para. 4.133 n. 137 above.

4.135 We therefore recommend that:[120]

(1) a long-stop limitation period of ten years commencing on the date that the claimant's right to recover the land accrued[121] (or, if later, the date on which the claimant's interest becomes an interest in possession) should apply to, and (subject to the recommendation in paragraph 4.147 below) be the sole limitation period for claims to recover land[122] (Draft Bill, Cl 16(1), (2));

(2) that a claimant entitled to a future interest to land which was in adverse possession before that interest fell into possession should be subject to a limitation period of ten years from the date on which his or her interest fell into possession rather than a reduced period;

(3) the expiry of the limitation period will extinguish the claimant's rights to the land in question, and after that period, no claim may be made. (Draft Bill, Cl 18(1)). But we would emphasise that, if the Law Commission's proposals on adverse possession in registered land are accepted, the recommendation will only be applicable to interest in unregistered land and unregistrable interests in registered land.

4.149 Subject to one point, we do not propose to change the present law as to the date on which the cause of action accrues in relation to a claim to recover land. As under the current law, this will depend on the date on which the defendant, or some person from whom he derived title, has taken adverse possession of the land in question, and the rules laid down in Schedule 1 to the Limitation Act 1980 will be re-enacted. The one change we wish to make relates to the position where there has been a series of adverse possessors of the land in question. Under the current law, a change in the identity of those in adverse possession of the land will not affect the running of the limitation period against the claimant. Even if a second squatter has dispossessed an earlier squatter, he or she is able to claim the benefit of the adverse possession by that squatter to allege that the limitation period has expired against the claimant.[123] This seems unreasonable. We therefore propose that a new cause of action should accrue to the claimant when there is a change in the identity of the people in adverse possession of the land. Where more than one person is in possession of the land, this will not apply unless all the existing squatters leave. There will be two other exceptions to this principle. If the second squatter claims through the first squatter because, for example, he 'bought' the land in dispute from the first squatter, no new cause of action will accrue to the claimant. The same will apply where a squatter who was himself dispossessed of the land in question returns to resume his adverse possession. In each case the squatter will continue to be able to claim the benefit of the earlier adverse possession by the squatter who has been replaced.

---

[120] [For further recommendations relating to claims by the Crown, claims to the foreshore, claims to recover the proceeds of sale of land, claims to recover rent, and claims relating to mortgages and other charges, see paras 4.137–4.196.]

[121] We do not intend to change the date of accrual of the cause of action from that provided for under the present law. This will generally be the date of the commencement of adverse possession as provided under Part I of Sch. I to the Limitation Act 1980 (Draft Bill, Sch. 1). We also recommend that provision should be made to retain the special rules in respect of the relation back of actions to recover land by an administrator of an estate (Limitation Act 1980, s. 26) and the cure of defective disentailing assurances (Limitation Act 1980, s. 27) (Draft Bill, cll. 17(4) and 21).

[122] Subject to the exceptions presently set out in Limitation Act 1980, s. 15(3) and (5).

[123] See *Mount Carmel Investments Ltd v Peter Thurlow Ltd* [1988] 1 WLR 1078, CA.

4.150 We therefore recommend that

(1) Where the identity of the person in adverse possession of the land changes, a new cause of action shall accrue to the claimant, unless anyone in adverse possession of the land before the change continues to be in adverse possession after that date. (Draft Bill, Sch 1, para. 1(4), (5)(a))

(2) However, no new cause of action will accrue to the claimant

(a) where the second person in adverse possession claims possession through his or her predecessor (Draft Bill, Sch 1, para. 1(5)(b)) and

(b) where the squatter coming into possession is recovering possession of the land from a squatter who had previously dispossessed him or her (Draft Bill, Sch 1, para. 1(6)).

IV. REGISTERED LAND

A. LAND REGISTRATION ACT 1925[124]

The limitation provisions in the Land Registration Act 1925 were based on the principles applicable to unregistered land under the Limitation Act 1980. However, there was a fundamental difference.[125] In unregistered land there is no Parliamentary conveyance of the title of the dispossessed person to the squatter.[126] However, the language of section 75(1) of the Land Registration Act had the effect that the squatter acquired (on registration) his predecessor's title.

LAND REGISTRATION ACT 1925

75. Acquisition of title by possession.—(1) The Limitation Acts shall apply to registered land in the same manner and to the same extent as those Acts apply to land not registered, except that where, if the land were not registered, the estate of the person registered as proprietor would be extinguished, such estate shall not be extinguished but shall be deemed to be held by the proprietor for the time being in trust for the person who, by virtue of the said Acts, has acquired title against any proprietor,[127] but without prejudice to the estates and interests of any other person interested in the land whose estate or interest is not extinguished by those Acts.

---

[124] C & B, pp. 143–145; R & R (1991), chap. 29.

[125] For a further difference, see *Spectrum Investment Co v Holmes* [1981] 1 WLR 221, in which Browne-Wilkinson J held that the principle of *Fairweather v St Marylebone Property Co Ltd* [1963] AC 510, p. 269, above, did not apply to land registered under LRA 1925 once the squatter had acquired title as against the tenant and had been registered as proprietor in place of the tenant. The tenant could no longer defeat the squatter's title by surrendering his lease because, once the squatter had been registered, the tenant no longer had an estate to surrender.

[126] Above, p. 247.

[127] The rights of the squatter, acquired or in the course of being acquired under the Limitation Acts, constituted an overriding interest under LRA 1925 s. 70(1)(*f*).

(2) Any person claiming to have acquired a title under the Limitation Acts to a registered estate in the land may apply to be registered as proprietor thereof.

(3) The registrar shall, on being satisfied as to the applicant's title, enter the applicant as proprietor either with absolute, good leasehold, qualified, or possessory title, as the case may require, but without prejudice to any estate or interest protected by any entry on the register which may not have been extinguished under the Limitation Acts, and such registration shall, subject as aforesaid, have the same effect as the registration of a first proprietor; but the proprietor or the applicant or any other person interested may apply to the court for the determination of any question arising under this section.

In **Central London Commercial Estates Ltd v Kato Kagaku Ltd** [1998] 4 All ER 948 SEDLEY J said at 959:

The squatter, unlike an underlessee, has no legal relationship at all with the leaseholder during the 12 initial years of trespass (except in the negative sense that the leaseholder may at any time evict him and claim damages); and at the end of the 12 years by operation of law the leaseholder's right and title to do even this are extinguished wherever the Limitation Acts apply. At law the squatter is then in a position to make a good title, independent of the lease although always subject to the freeholder's eventual reversion. In relation to a registered leasehold, however, s. 75 lifts the extinguishing effect of the Limitation Act and substitutes a trust of the leasehold interest, benefits and burdens alike, from the moment of extinction of the leasehold title. The squatter becomes entitled, without regard to merits, to be placed in the same relationship with the freeholder as had previously been enjoyed by the leaseholder. The trust preserves not the squatter's common law title but a new statutory right to be substituted by registration for the leaseholder—carrying with it, as Mr Nugee accepts, an obligation to indemnify the leaseholder against outgoings. This is to all appearances a statutory conveyance of the entire leasehold interest....

B. LAND REGISTRATION ACT 2002[128]

The Land Registration Act 2002 disapplies the Limitation Act 1980 in relation to registered land with effect from the date when the 2002 Act came into force (13 October 2003).[129] It substitutes a new scheme which reflects the principle underlying registered conveyancing that the basis of title to registered land is registration, not possession. The details of the scheme are set out in Schedule 6 to the Act, as supplemented by the Land Registration Rules 2003.

[128] C & B, pp. 145–148; Gray, paras 9.1.20–9.1.34; M & W, paras 35.070–35.095; MM, pp. 549–550, 562–563; R & R (2003) chap. 33; H & B, chap. 8; Law Commission Report on Land Registration for the Twenty-First Century 2001 (Law Com No. 271), Part XIV; (2007) 27 Legal Studies 236 (N. Cobb and L. Fox); Land Registry Practice Guide 4.

[129] For transitional provisions, see LRA 2002, s. 134, Sch. 12, para. 18 (where at that date a registered estate in land was already held in trust for an adverse possessor by virtue of the operation of LRA 1925, s. 75, the adverse possessor remained entitled to be registered as proprietor, and the right constituted an overriding interest for a period of three years after 13 October 2003). But if the period of limitation had not yet been completed by 13 October 2003, the provisions of the 2002 Act apply.

Certain features of the law on limitation of actions which had been developed for both registered and unregistered land are preserved in the 2002 Act. The basis for a squatter's claim is still his adverse possession of the land—the meaning of which will be determined in accordance with the old cases.[130] And, where the squatter is registered as proprietor, he becomes the successor in title to the previous proprietor, as was the case under the Land Registration Act 1925.[131]

However, the mere fact that the squatter has been in possession of the land for a period of time does not give him a right to the land; merely a right to apply to be registered—a right which the registered proprietor can resist. The registered proprietor remains the estate owner as against an adverse possessor, both at law and in equity, unless and until the adverse possessor is registered. It is therefore now much more difficult for a squatter to acquire title to registered land than to unregistered land.[132]

Law Commission Report on Land Registration for the Twenty-First Century 2001 (Law Com No. 271), paras 1.13, 14.5–14.7

1.13 The Bill abandons the notion that a squatter acquires title once he or she has been in adverse possession for 12 years. It creates new rules in relation to registered land that will confer greater protection against the acquisition of title by persons in adverse possession. This is consistent with one of the objectives of the Bill—that it is registration alone that should confer title. The essence of the new scheme is that a squatter will be able to apply to be registered as proprietor after 10 years' adverse possession. However, the registered proprietor will be notified of that application and will, in most cases, be able to object to it.[133] If he or she does, the application will be rejected. However, the proprietor will then have to take steps to evict the squatter or otherwise regularise his or her position within two years. If the squatter is still in adverse possession after two years, he or she will be entitled to be registered as proprietor. We consider that this new scheme strikes a fairer balance between landowner and squatter than does the present law. It also reflects the fact that the basis of title to registered land is the fact of registration, not (as is the case with unregistered land) possession.

14.5 The essence of the scheme is that—

(1) adverse possession of itself, for however long, will not bar the owner's title to a registered estate;

(2) a squatter will be entitled to apply to be registered as proprietor after 20 years' adverse possession, and the registered proprietor, any registered chargee, and certain other persons interested in the land will be notified of the application;

(3) if the application is not opposed by any of those notified the squatter will be registered as proprietor of the land;

---

[130] See especially *JA Pye (Oxford) Ltd v Graham* [2003] 1 AC 416; above, p. 236.
[131] LRA 1925, s. 75; above, p. 278.
[132] This provides an incentive for the owner of unregistered land to apply for voluntary first registration.
[133] If there is no objection to the application, the squatter will be registered.

(4) if any of those notified oppose the application it will be refused, unless the adverse possessor can bring him or herself within one of three limited exceptions;[134]

(5) if the application for registration is refused but the squatter remains in adverse possession for a further two years,[135] he or she will be entitled to apply once again to be registered and will this time be registered as proprietor whether or not the registered proprietor objects;

(6) where the registered proprietor brings proceedings to recover possession from a squatter, the action will succeed unless the squatter can establish certain limited exceptions which are consistent with those in (4) above.

There are certain particular rules for special cases and there are transitional provisions to protect the rights of squatters who had barred the rights of the registered proprietor prior to the coming into force of the legislation.[136]

14.6 The aims of the scheme are as follows.

(1) Registration should of itself provide a means of protection against adverse possession, though it should not be unlimited protection. Title to registered land is not possession-based as is title to unregistered land. It is registration that vests the legal estate in the owner and the person's ownership is apparent from the register. The registered proprietor and other interested persons, such as the proprietor of a registered charge, are therefore given the opportunity to oppose an application by a squatter to be registered as proprietor.

(2) If the application is not opposed, however, whether because the registered proprietor has disappeared or is unwilling to take steps to evict the squatter, the squatter will be registered as proprietor instead. This ensures that land which has (say) been abandoned by the proprietor, or which he or she does not consider to be worth the price of possession proceedings, will remain in commerce.

(3) If the registered proprietor (or other interested person) opposes the registration, then it is incumbent on him or her to ensure that the squatter is either evicted or his or her position regularised[137] within two years. If the squatter remains in adverse possession for two years after such objection has been made, he or she will be entitled to apply once again to be registered, and this time the registered proprietor will not be able to object. In other words, the scheme provides a registered proprietor with one chance, but only one chance, to prevent a squatter from acquiring title to his or her land. The proprietor who fails to take appropriate action following his or her objection will lose the land to the squatter.

(4) Consistently with the approach set out above, a registered proprietor who takes possession proceedings against a squatter will succeed, unless the squatter can bring him or herself within some very limited exceptions.

[134] Explained below, paras 14.36–14.52. [See also para. 14.7, below.]

[135] Which might happen if no steps were taken to evict the squatter, or to regularise his or her possession so that it would no longer be adverse, as where the squatter agreed to be the tenant or licensee of the registered proprietor.

[136] [LRR 2003, s. 134, Sch. 12, para. 18; the squatter can protect this right by being in actual occupation: para. 18(2).]

[137] In other words, where the squatter agrees to become the tenant or licensee of the registered proprietor.

It will be apparent from this summary that one of the essential features of the scheme is that it must produce a decisive result. Either the squatter is evicted or otherwise ceases to be in *adverse* possession, or he or she is registered as proprietor of the land.

14.7 As we have mentioned above, there are certain very limited cases in which either—

(1) a squatter's application to be registered will be successful notwithstanding the registered proprietor's objections; or

(2) he or she may successfully resist possession proceedings brought by the proprietor.

This will be so where the squatter—

(a) was otherwise entitled to the land, as for example—

(i) where he or she was a purchaser in possession who had paid the whole of the contract price; or

(ii) by application of the principles of proprietary estoppel; or

(b) had been in adverse possession of land adjacent to his or her own under the mistaken but reasonable belief that he or she was the owner of it.

The situation in (a) is self-evident, but that in (b) needs explanation. As mentioned above, the register is not normally conclusive as to boundaries.[138] Furthermore, cases often occur where the physical boundaries of the land and the legal boundaries as they appear from the register do not coincide. A common case is where a developer lays out an estate and constructs the fences between properties otherwise than in accordance with the boundaries as they are set out on the plan on the register. In these cases, we think that the squatter, whose conduct has been perfectly reasonable, should prevail over the registered proprietor.

LAND REGISTRATION ACT 2002

96 Disapplication of periods of limitation

(1) No period of limitation under section 15 of the Limitation Act 1980[139] (time limits in relation to recovery of land) shall run against any person, other than a chargee, in relation to an estate in land or rentcharge the title to which is registered.

(2) No period of limitation under section 16 of that Act[140] (time limits in relation to redemption of land) shall run against any person in relation to such an estate in land or rentcharge.

(3) Accordingly, section 17[141] of that Act (extinction of title on expiry of time limit) does not operate to extinguish the title of any person where, by virtue of this section, a period of limitation does not run against him.

97 Registration of adverse possessor

Schedule 6 (which makes provision about the registration of an adverse possessor of an estate in land or rentcharge) has effect.[142]

---

[138] See above, para. 14.1; and see paras 9.9 and following.   [139] P. 249, above.
[140] P. 265, above.   [141] P. 260, above.
[142] Below. See LRR 2003, rr. 187–194.

98 Defences

(1) A person has a defence to an action for possession of land if—

(a) on the day immediately preceding that on which the action was brought he was entitled to make an application under paragraph 1 of Schedule 6 to be registered as the proprietor of an estate in the land, and

(b) had he made such an application on that day, the condition in paragraph 5(4) of that Schedule would have been satisfied.

(2) A judgment for possession of land ceases to be enforceable at the end of the period of two years beginning with the date of the judgment if the proceedings in which the judgment is given were commenced against a person who was at that time entitled to make an application under paragraph 1 of Schedule 6.

(3) A person has a defence to an action for possession of land if on the day immediately preceding that on which the action was brought he was entitled to make an application under paragraph 6 of Schedule 6 to be registered as the proprietor of an estate in the land.

(4) A judgment for possession of land ceases to be enforceable at the end of the period of two years beginning with the date of the judgment if, at the end of that period, the person against whom the judgment was given is entitled to make an application under paragraph 6 of Schedule 6 to be registered as the proprietor of an estate in the land.

(5) Where in any proceedings a court determines that—

(a) a person is entitled to a defence under this section, or

(b) a judgment for possession has ceased to be enforceable against a person by virtue of subsection (4),

the court must order the registrar to register him as the proprietor of the estate in relation to which he is entitled to make an application under Schedule 6.

(6) The defences under this section are additional to any other defences a person may have.

(7) Rules may make provision to prohibit the recovery of rent due under a rentcharge from a person who has been in adverse possession of the rentcharge.[143]

SCHEDULE 6

REGISTRATION OF ADVERSE POSSESSOR

Right to apply for registration

1 (1) A person may apply to the registrar to be registered as the proprietor of a registered estate in land if he has been in adverse possession of the estate for the period of ten years ending on the date of the application.

(2) A person may also apply to the registrar to be registered as the proprietor of a registered estate in land if—

(a) he has in the period of six months ending on the date of the application ceased to be in adverse possession of the estate because of eviction by the registered proprietor, or a person claiming under the registered proprietor,

---

[143] LRR 2003, rr. 191–193.

(b) on the day before his eviction he was entitled to make an application under sub-paragraph (1), and

(c) the eviction was not pursuant to a judgment for possession.

(3) However, a person may not make an application under this paragraph if—

(a) he is a defendant in proceedings which involve asserting a right to possession of the land, or

(b) judgment for possession of the land has been given against him in the last two years.

(4) For the purposes of sub-paragraph (1), the estate need not have been registered throughout the period of adverse possession.

Notification of application

2 (1) The registrar must give notice of an application under paragraph 1 to—

(a) the proprietor of the estate to which the application relates,[144]

(b) the proprietor of any registered charge on the estate,

(c) where the estate is leasehold, the proprietor of any superior registered estate,

(d) any person who is registered in accordance with rules as a person to be notified under this paragraph, and

(e) such other persons as rules may provide.

(2) Notice under this paragraph shall include notice of the effect of paragraph 4.

Treatment of application

3 (1) A person given notice under paragraph 2 may require that the application to which the notice relates be dealt with under paragraph 5.

(2) The right under this paragraph is exercisable by notice to the registrar given before the end of such period as rules may provide.

4 If an application under paragraph 1 is not required to be dealt with under paragraph 5, the applicant is entitled to be entered in the register as the new proprietor of the estate.

5 (1) If an application under paragraph 1 is required to be dealt with under this paragraph, the applicant is only entitled to be registered as the new proprietor of the estate if any of the following conditions is met.

(2) The first condition is that—

(a) it would be unconscionable because of an equity by estoppel for the registered proprietor to seek to dispossess the applicant,[145] and

(b) the circumstances are such that the applicant ought to be registered as the proprietor.

(3) The second condition is that the applicant is for some other reason entitled to be registered as the proprietor of the estate.

---

[144] In practice, however, the registered proprietor is given an earlier, informal notice because the Land Registry, before accepting that the applicant has an arguable case for registration, will normally require one of its own surveyors to inspect the land; both the registered proprietor and the applicant are notified of the inspection: Land Registry Practice Guide 4, para. 5.1.

[145] [2004] Conv 123 (S. Nield).

(4) The third condition is that—

    (a) the land to which the application relates is adjacent to land belonging to the applicant,

    (b) the exact line of the boundary between the two has not been determined under rules under section 60,[146]

    (c) for at least ten years of the period of adverse possession ending on the date of the application, the applicant (or any predecessor in title) reasonably believed that the land to which the application relates belonged to him, and

    (d) the estate to which the application relates was registered more than one year prior to the date of the application.

(5) In relation to an application under paragraph 1(2), this paragraph has effect as if the reference in sub-paragraph (4)(c) to the date of the application were to the day before the date of the applicant's eviction.

Right to make further application for registration

6 (1) Where a person's application under paragraph 1 is rejected, he may make a further application to be registered as the proprietor of the estate if he is in adverse possession of the estate from the date of the application until the last day of the period of two years beginning with the date of its rejection.

  (2) However, a person may not make an application under this paragraph if—

    (a) he is a defendant in proceedings which involve asserting a right to possession of the land,

    (b) judgment for possession of the land has been given against him in the last two years, or

    (c) he has been evicted from the land pursuant to a judgment for possession.

7 If a person makes an application under paragraph 6, he is entitled to be entered in the register as the new proprietor of the estate.

Restriction on applications

8 (1) No one may apply under this Schedule to be registered as the proprietor of an estate in land during, or before the end of twelve months after the end of, any period in which the existing registered proprietor is for the purposes of the Limitation (Enemies and War Prisoners) Act 1945—

    (a) an enemy, or

    (b) detained in enemy territory.

  (2) No one may apply under this Schedule to be registered as the proprietor of an estate in land during any period in which the existing registered proprietor is—

    (a) unable because of mental disability to make decisions about issues of the kind to which such an application would give rise, or

    (b) unable to communicate such decisions because of mental disability or physical impairment.

---

[146] P. 124, n. 31, above; LRR 2003 rr. 117–123.

(3) For the purposes of sub-paragraph (2), 'mental disability' means a disability of disorder of the mind or brain, whether permanent or temporary, which results in an impairment or disturbance of mental functioning.

(4) Where it appears to the registrar that sub-paragraph (1) or (2) applies in relation to an estate in land, he may include a note to that effect in the register.

Effect of registration

9 (1) Where a person is registered as the proprietor of an estate in land in pursuance of an application under this Schedule, the title by virtue of adverse possession which he had at the time of the application is extinguished.

(2) Subject to sub-paragraph (3), the registration of a person under this Schedule as the proprietor of an estate in land does not affect the priority of any interest affecting the estate.

(3) Subject to sub-paragraph (4), where a person is registered under this Schedule as the proprietor of an estate, the estate is vested in him free of any registered charge affecting the estate immediately before his registration.

(4) Sub-paragraph (3) does not apply where registration as proprietor is in pursuance of an application determined by reference to whether any of the conditions in paragraph 5 applies.

Appointment and discharge of charges

10 (1) Where—

    (a) a registered estate continues to be subject to a charge notwithstanding the registration of a person under this Schedule as the proprietor, and

    (b) the charge affects property other than the estate,

the proprietor of the estate may require the chargee to apportion the amount secured by the charge at that time between the estate and the other property on the basis of their respective values.

(2) The person requiring the apportionment is entitled to a discharge of his estate from the charge on payment of—

    (a) the amount apportioned to the estate, and

    (b) the costs incurred by the chargee as a result of the apportionment.

(3) On a discharge under this paragraph, the liability of the chargor to the chargee is reduced by the amount apportioned to the estate.

(4) Rules may make provision about apportionment under this paragraph, in particular, provision about—

    (a) procedure,

    (b) valuation,

    (c) calculation of costs payable under sub-paragraph (2) (b), and

    (d) payment of the costs of the chargor.

Meaning of 'adverse possession'

11 (1) A person is in adverse possession of an estate in land for the purposes of this Schedule if, but for section 96, a period of limitation under section 15 of the Limitation Act 1980 would run in his favour in relation to the estate.

(2) A person is also to be regarded for those purposes as having been in adverse possession of an estate in land—

(a) where he is the successor in title to an estate in the land, during any period of adverse possession by a predecessor in title to that estate, or

(b) during any period of adverse possession by another person which comes between, and is continuous with, periods of adverse possession of his own.

(3) In determining whether for the purposes of this paragraph a period of limitation would run under section 15 of the Limitation Act 1980, there are to be disregarded—

(a) the commencement of any legal proceedings, and

(b) paragraph 6 of Schedule 1 to that Act.

Trusts

12 A person is not to be regarded as being in adverse possession of an estate for the purposes of this Schedule at any time when the estate is subject to a trust, unless the interest of each of the beneficiaries in the estate is an interest in possession.

Crown foreshore

13 (1) Where—

(a) a person is in adverse possession of an estate in land,

(b) the estate belongs to Her Majesty in right of the Crown or the Duchy of Lancaster or to the Duchy of Cornwall,[147] and

(c) the land consists of foreshore,

paragraph 1(1) is to have effect as if the reference to ten years were to sixty years.

(2) For the purposes of sub-paragraph (1), land is to be treated as foreshore if it has been foreshore at any time in the previous ten years.

(3) In this paragraph, 'foreshore' means the shore and bed of the sea and of any tidal water, below the line of the medium high tide between the spring and neap tides.

Rentcharges

14 Rules must make provision to apply the preceding provisions of this Schedule to registered rentcharges, subject to such modifications and exceptions as the rules may provide.

Procedure

15 Rules may make provision about the procedure to be followed pursuant to an application under this Schedule.

---

[147] P. 134, above.

QUESTIONS

1. What is meant by saying that the new scheme of adverse possession under the Land Registration Act 2002 reflects the fact that the basis of title to registered land is the fact of registration, not (as is the case with unregistered land) possession? See Law Commission Report on Land Registration for the Twenty-First Century 2001 (Law Com No. 271), para. 1.13.

2. Does the new scheme under the 2002 Act reflect the correct balance between the rights of the landowner and the rights of the squatter? See Law Commission Report on Land Registration for the Twenty-First Century 2001 (Law Com No. 271), Part XIV; (2007) 27 Legal Studies 236 (N. Cobb and L. Fox).

3. A takes adverse possession of B's land and remains there for 12 years before B seeks to recover possession. Compare A's rights where

   (a) the land is unregistered;

   (b) the land is registered and the expiry of the 12-year period fell on 12 October 2003;

   (c) the land is registered and the expiry of the 12-year period fell on 14 October 2003.

V. ADVERSE POSSESSION AND HUMAN RIGHTS

In recent years questions have been about the compatibility of the rules on adverse possession of land with the European Convention on Human Rights. The issue arises differently in relation to unregistered land and the old provisions under the Land Registration Act 1925, on the one hand, and the new regime under the Land Registration Act 2002, on the other hand. The effect of the expiration of the limitation period in unregistered land is automatically to extinguish the title of the former owner, without any requirement for the adverse possessor to give him formal notice of his possession, or that he is approaching the completion of the limitation period, and without any compensation for the former owner. At first, both the domestic courts[148] and the European Court of Human Rights[149] took the view that such a regime contravenes Article 1 of the First Protocol to the Convention.[150] However, the Grand Chamber of the European Court of Human Rights[151] has overturned this and by a majority of ten votes to seven has held that the regime in the Land Registration

---

[148] *Beaulane Properties Ltd v Palmer* [2006] Ch 79; below, p. 289.

[149] *JA Pye (Oxford) Ltd v United Kingdom* [2005] 3 EGLR 1 (majority of four to three).

[150] Set out above, p. 108.

[151] *JA Pye (Oxford) Ltd v United Kingdom* (2008) 46 EHRR 45; below, p. 290.

Act 1925 does not violate Article 1 of the First Protocol. In consequence, it appears to be beyond doubt that the regime under the 2002 Act complies with the European Convention.

A. UNREGISTERED LAND AND LAND REGISTRATION ACT 1925

In **Beaulane Properties Ltd v Palmer** [2006] Ch 79[152] Nicholas Strauss QC held that the registered proprietor's loss of the disputed land in accordance with section 75 of the Land Registration Act 1925 was incompatible with Article 1 of the First Protocol. However, rather than declaring section 75 incompatible with the Convention, he re-interpreted it[153] so as to make it compatible. He said at 139:

210 Mr Knox submits first that the legislation should be construed as being inapplicable to registered land. This invites me to commit judicial vandalism. Section 75 of the Land Registration Act 1925 deliberately applied the law relating to adverse possession to registered land by imposing a statutory trust. That is its plain meaning. As to the submission that section 3(xii) of the 1925 Act is to be treated as applicable only to the Limitation Acts then in force, the definition includes 'any Acts amending those Acts' and the Limitation Act 1939 and now the Limitation Act 1980 are clearly within that definition. The preamble to the 1980 Act states that it is an 'Act to consolidate the Limitation Acts 1939 to 1980' and the 1939 Act repeals and replaces the previous Real Property Limitation Acts: see section 34 of the 1939 Act and the schedule thereto.

211 Mr Knox's alternative submission is that (a) section 75 of the Land Registration Act 1925 should be read as being applicable only when the same was consistent with a good conscience, and/or (b) that a person is not 'a person in whose favour the period of limitation can run' within the meaning of paragraph 8(1) of Schedule 1 to the Limitation Act 1980, unless he reasonably believes that when in possession the land belongs to him, and/or (c) the registered owner of land has not been dispossessed and has not discontinued his possession within the meaning of paragraph 1 of the Schedule, when the person occupying his land does not interfere with such use (if any) as he then makes of it.

212 I do not think that it is open to me to read a requirement of consistency with equity and good conscience into the legislation. This would create a 'wholly different scheme' (cf per Lord Rodger [Ghaidan v Godin-Mendoza] [2004] 2 AC 557, para. 110), which is consistent neither with the old provisions, which were never based on considerations of fault or equitable considerations (that is part of the objection to them), or with the new scheme which has replaced them, which is far more precise than that. Nor do I think that it is open to me to re-interpret paragraph 8(1) to exclude, from the definition of persons in whose favour the period of limitation can run, all except the trespasser who reasonably believes that the land belongs to him. This again would create a fault-based system, which is inconsistent with the old provisions and with

---

[152] [2005] Conv 345 (M. Dixon); [2005] All ER Rev 262 (P. J. Clarke). An 'impressive judgment': *Tower Hamlets LBC v Barrett* [2006] 1 P & CR 9 at [120], per Neuberger LJ.

[153] Human Rights Act 1998, s. 3. On the relationship between the Convention and English law, see also pp. 106–114, above.

the new scheme which can, in some circumstances, operate in favour of the person who has no reasonable belief, e.g. if registration of title is unopposed.

213 However, I do in substance accept the last part of Mr Knox's submissions. In my view, there is a simpler solution, namely to interpret section 75 of the Land Registration Act 1925 as being applicable to those cases in which the trespasser establishes 'possession' in accordance with the case law in existence at the time of its enactment. Thus 'adverse possession' in the Schedule to the Limitation Act 1980 is given the meaning it had under the post-1879 case law. Since Mr Palmer's action is not inconsistent with any use or intended use of the land by Beaulane, his possession of it was not 'adverse'. This may be a novel application of section 3 of the Human Rights Act 1998, but I think it is justifiable in circumstances in which it is the duty of the court to avoid a declaration of incompatibility 'unless it is plainly impossible to do so' such as where there is a clear limitation on Convention rights stated in terms: per Lord Steyn in R v A (No 2) [2002] 1 AC 45, para. 44. Indeed, such an interpretation has the possibly unique and certainly unusual merit that it accords as nearly as possible with what is likely to have been the actual intention of the statutory draftsman and of Parliament at the time.

214 It is true that Lord Browne-Wilkinson said in the Pye case [2003] 1 AC 419, para. 35[154] that the phrase 'adverse possession' in section 10 of the Limitation Act 1939 and paragraph 8(1) of Schedule 1 to the 1980 Act did not reintroduce the old pre-1833 notions of adverse possession, and that the use of the term 'must not be allowed to reintroduce by the back door that which for so long has not formed part of the law', but I do not think that he had the possible need to reinterpret in accordance with section 3 in mind when he said this. In any event, in view of the Land Registration Act 2002, the need to apply section 3 in this area is only likely to arise in relation to the acquisition of title by a trespasser between October 2000 and October 2003,[155] so this may well be positively the last reappearance of the ghost of the old law of adverse possession. Certainly, it is unlikely that there will be many more.[156]

JA Pye (Oxford) Ltd v United Kingdom[157]
(2008) 46 EHRR 45 (ECHR, Grand Chamber)

The decision of the House of Lords in *JA Pye (Oxford) Ltd v Graham* [2003] 1 AC 419 was set out above, p. 236. Having lost title to the land to an adverse possessor under section 75 of the Land Registration Act 1925 in accordance with that decision, Pye sought compensation from the UK Government on the basis that it had failed to ensure that section 75 complied with Pye's rights under the European Convention on

---

154 [Above, p. 239.]

155 I.e., from the date when the Human Rights Act 1998 came into force until the date when LRA 2002 superseded LRA 1925. For a contrary view, see [2005] Conv 345 at 350–351 (M. Dixon).

156 In spite of the decision of the Grand Chamber of the European Court of Human Rights in *JA Pye (Oxford) Ltd v United Kingdom*, below, the Land Registry still regards the decision in *Beaulane Properties Ltd v Palmer* [2006] Ch 79 as reflecting English Law in the interpretation of s. 75 LRA 1925 in relation to applications made under LRA 2002, Sch. 12, para. 18 (transitional provisions): Land Registry Additional Practice Guide affecting Practice Guide 5 (2007), criticised in [2007] Conv 552 at 557–8 and [2008] Conv 160 at 165 (M. Dixon).

157 [2007] Conv 552; [2007] 0737 EG 228 (O. Radley-Garder and J. Small); (2008) 71 MLR 878 (L. Fox O'Mahony and N Cobb); *Ofulue v Bossert* [2009] Ch 1 at [52] (the determination of the Grand Chamber in *Pye* applies to all decisions on adverse possession and it is not open to the English court not to follow it because the case is distinguishable on its facts); [2008] Conv 160 (M. Dixon).

Human Rights. The Grand Chamber of the European Court of Human Rights rejected the claim by a majority of ten votes to seven. The following extract is from the majority judgment.

2. Applicability of Article 1 of Protocol No.1

58 The Court will first turn to the question of whether the case should be dealt with under Art. 1 of Protocol No. 1, or whether, as the Government contended, it should be considered only under Art. 6 of the Convention.

59 In *Stubbings v United Kingdom*, the Court dealt with limitation periods under Arts 6, 8 and 14 of the Convention. Under Art. 6, the Court found that a non-extendable time-limit of six years from the applicants' 18th birthdays did not impair the very essence of the applicants' right of access to court.[158] The Court also considered the case under Art. 8 in the context of the positive obligations inherent in an effective respect for private or family life, finding that overall such protection was afforded.[159]

60 The Court finds nothing in its case law to suggest that the present case should be dealt with only under Art. 6 of the Convention, and indeed, given the different content of the two rights, it would be unusual if the Court were to decline to deal with a complaint under one head solely because it were capable of raising different issues under a separate Article. The Court agrees with the Chamber that there is nothing in principle to preclude the examination of a claim under Art. 1 of Protocol No.1 where the complaint is directed against legislation concerning property rights.

61 Article 1 of Protocol No.1 protects 'possessions', which can be either 'existing possessions' or assets, including claims, in respect of which the applicant can argue that he or she has at least a 'legitimate expectation' of obtaining effective enjoyment of a property right. It does not, however, guarantee the right to acquire property.[160] Where there is a dispute as to whether an applicant has a property interest which is eligible for protection under Art. 1 of Protocol No. 1, the Court is required to determine the legal position of the applicant.[161]

62 In the present case, the applicant companies were the beneficial owners of the land in Berkshire, as they were successive registered proprietors. The land was not subject to a right of pre-emption, as in the case of *Beyeler*, but it was subject to the ordinary law of the land, including, by way of example, town and country planning legislation, compulsory purchase legislation, and the various rules on adverse possession. The applicant companies' possessions were necessarily limited by the various rules of statute and common law applicable to real estate.

63 It remains the case, however, that the applicant companies lost the beneficial ownership of 23ha of agricultural land as a result of the operation of the 1925 and 1980 Acts. The Court finds inescapable the Chamber's conclusion that Art. 1 of Protocol No. 1 is applicable.

3. The nature of the interference

64 The Court has, on a number of occasions, considered cases in which a loss of ownership of possessions was not categorised as a 'deprivation' within the meaning of the second sentence of the first paragraph of Art. 1 of Protocol No. 1. In the cases of *AGOSI* and *Air Canada*, the forfeiture of the applicant companies' possessions was considered to amount to a control of

---

[158] App. No. 22083/93, *Stubbings v United Kingdom*, October 22, 1996 at [52].

[159] App. No. 22083/93, *Stubbings*, October 22, 1996 at [60]-[67].

[160] See *Kopecky v Slovakia* (2005) 41 EHRR 43 at [35].

[161] See *Beyeler v Italy* (2001) 33 EHRR 52.

use of gold coins and a control of the use of aircraft which had been employed for the import of prohibited drugs, respectively.[162] The applicant company in the case of *Gasus* had sold a concrete-mixer to a third party subject to a retention of title clause. The tax authorities' seizure of the concrete-mixer was considered as an exercise of the State's right to 'secure the payment of taxes', although the tax debts were not those of the applicant company.[163] The Court declined, in the case of *Beyeler*, to determine whether the interference with the applicant's property rights constituted a 'deprivation of possessions', as it sufficed to examine the situation complained of in the light of the general rule in the first sentence of the first paragraph of Art.1.[164]

65 The applicant companies did not lose their land because of a legislative provision which permitted the State to transfer ownership in particular circumstances,[165] or because of a social policy of transfer of ownership,[166] but rather as the result of the operation of the generally applicable rules on limitation periods for actions for recovery of land. Those rules provided that at the end of the limitation period, the paper owner's title to unregistered land was extinguished.[167] In the case of registered land, the position was amended to take into account the fact that until the register was rectified, the former owner continued to appear as registered proprietor. Thus in the present case, s. 75(1) of the 1925 Act provided that on expiry of the limitation period the title was not extinguished, but the registered proprietor was deemed to hold the land in trust for the adverse possessor.

66 The statutory provisions which resulted in the applicant companies' loss of beneficial ownership were thus not intended to deprive paper owners of their ownership, but rather to regulate questions of title in a system in which, historically, 12 years' adverse possession was sufficient to extinguish the former owner's right to re-enter or to recover possession, and the new title depended on the principle that unchallenged lengthy possession gave a title. The provisions of the 1925 and 1980 Acts which were applied to the applicant companies were part of the general land law, and were concerned to regulate, amongst other things, limitation periods in the context of the use and ownership of land as between individuals. The applicant companies were therefore affected, not by a 'deprivation of possessions' within the meaning of the second sentence of the first paragraph of Art. 1, but rather by a 'control of use' of land within the meaning of the second paragraph of the provision.

4. The aim of the interference

67 The applicable provisions of the 1925 and 1980 Acts were concerned to apply the limitation period for actions for recovery of land which had been fixed at 20 years since the Limitation Act 1623 and at 12 years since the Real Property Limitation Act 1874, and they were concerned then to regulate the subsequent position that the paper owner was no longer able to recover possession, and the adverse possessor had been in possession for sufficiently long to establish title.

---

[162] *AGOSI* [1986] EHRR 1 at [51]; *Air Canada v United Kingdom* (1995) 20 EHRR 150 at [34]; see also App. No. 28078/95, *CM v France*, June 26, 2001.

[163] *Gasus Dosier und Fördertechnik GmbH v Netherlands* (1995) 20 EHRR 403 at [59].

[164] *Beyeler v Italy* (2001) 33 EHRR 52 at [106].

[165] As in the cases of *AGOSI* [1986] EHRR 1, *Air Canada* (1995) 20 EHRR 150 and *Gasus* (1995) 20 EHRR 403.

[166] As in the case of *James* (1995) 20 EHRR 403.

[167] Section 17 of the 1980 Act.

68 The Court has considered limitation periods as such in the context of Art. 6 of the Convention in the case of *Stubbings v United Kingdom.* It held as follows:

'It is noteworthy that limitation periods in personal injury cases are a common feature of the domestic legal systems of the Contracting States. They serve several Important purposes, namely to ensure legal certainty and finality, protect potential defendants from stale claims which might be difficult to counter and prevent the injustice which might arise if courts were required to decide upon events which took place in the distant past on the basis of evidence which might have become unreliable and incomplete because of the passage of time.'[168]

69 Although that statement referred to limitation periods in personal injury cases in the context of Art. 6, the Court considers that it can also be applied to the situation where limitation periods in actions for recovery of land are being assessed in the light of Art.1 of Protocol No.1. Indeed, the parties do not suggest that limitation periods for actions for recovery of land do not pursue a legitimate aim in the general interest.

70 The Court finds that the existence of a 12-year limitation period for actions for recovery of land as such pursues a legitimate aim in the general interest.

71 As to the existence, over and above the general interest in the limitation period, of a specific general interest in the extinguishment of title and the attribution of new title at the end of the limitation period, the Court recalls that in discussing the public interest present in the case of Jahn, in the context of a deprivation of property, it stated that:

'[F]inding it natural that the margin of appreciation available to the legislature in implementing social and economic policies should be a wide one [the Court] will respect the legislature's judgment as to what is 'in the public interest' unless that judgment is manifestly without reasonable foundation.'[169]

This is particularly true in cases such as the present one where what is at stake is a longstanding and complex area of law which regulates private law matters between individuals.

72 It is plain from the comparative material submitted by the parties that a large number of Member States possesses some form of mechanism for transferring title in accordance with principles similar to adverse possession in the common law systems, and that such transfer is effected without the payment of compensation to the original owner.

73 The Court further notes, as did the Chamber, that the amendments to the system of adverse possession contained in the Land Registration Act 2002 did not abolish the relevant provisions of the 1925 and the 1980 Acts. Parliament thus confirmed the domestic view that the traditional general interest remained valid.

74 It is a characteristic of property that different countries regulate its use and transfer in a variety of ways. The relevant rules reflect social policies against the background of the local conception of the importance and role of property. Even where title to real property is registered, it must be open to the legislature to attach more weight to lengthy, unchallenged possession than to the formal fact of registration. The Court accepts that to extinguish title where the former owner is prevented, as a consequence of the application of the law, from recovering possession of land cannot be said to be manifestly without reasonable foundation.

---

[168] App. No. 22083/93, *Stubbings v United Kingdom*, October 22, 1996 at [51].

[169] *Jahn v Germany* (2006) 42 EHRR 49 at [91], with reference back to the cases of *James* (1986) 8 EHRR 123 and *The Former King of Greece v Greece* (2001) 33 EHRR 21, and to App. No. 46129/99, *Zvolsky and Zvolská v Czech Republic*, November 12, 2002 at [67].

There existed therefore a general interest in both the limitation period itself and the extinguishment of title at the end of the period.

5. Whether there was a fair balance

75 The second paragraph of Art. 1 is to be construed in the light of the general principle enunciated in the opening sentence. There must, in respect of a 'control of use', also exist a reasonable relationship of proportionality between the means employed and the aim sought to be realised. In other words, the Court must determine whether a fair balance has been struck between the demands of the general interest and the interest of the individuals concerned. In determining whether a fair balance exists, the Court recognises that the State enjoys a wide margin of appreciation, with regard both to choosing the means of enforcement and to ascertaining whether the consequences of enforcement are justified in the general interest for the purpose of achieving the object of the law in question.[170] In spheres such as housing, the Court will respect the legislature's judgment as to what is in the general interest unless that judgment is manifestly without reasonable foundation.[171] In other contexts, the Court has underlined that it is not in theory required to settle disputes of a private nature. It can nevertheless not remain passive, in exercising the European supervision incumbent on it, where a domestic court's interpretation of a legal act appeared 'unreasonable, arbitrary or . . . inconsistent . . . with the principles underlying the Convention'.[172] When discussing the proportionality of a refusal of a private television company to broadcast a television commercial, the Court considered that a margin of appreciation was particularly essential in commercial matters.[173] In a case concerning a dispute over the interpretation of patent law, and at the same time as noting that even in cases involving litigation between individuals and companies the State has obligations under Art.1 of Protocol No.1 to take measures necessary to protect the right of property, the Court reiterated that its duty is to ensure the observance of the engagements undertaken by the contracting parties to the Convention, and not to deal with errors of fact or law allegedly committed by a national court unless Convention rights and freedoms may have been infringed.[174]

76 The Chamber[175] found that the relevant provisions—s. 75 of the 1925 Act in particular—went further than merely precluding the applicant companies from invoking the assistance of the courts to recover possession of their property. The Court recalls that the Court of Appeal in the present case was of the view that the Grahams had not established the requisite intention to possess the land, so that time had not started to run against the applicant companies.[176] It nevertheless considered that the extinguishment of title at the end of the limitation period of an action for recovery of land was a logical and pragmatic consequence of the barring of the right to bring an action after the expiration of the limitation period. The House of Lords disavowed the Court of Appeal's interpretation of the law on intention to possess, but did not comment on the suggestion that to terminate title at the end of the limitation period was 'logical and pragmatic'. Even though the general position in English law is that the expiry of a limitation period bars the remedy but not the right, the Court accepts that where an action for recovery

---

[170] See *AGOSI* [1986] EHRR 1 at [52] and, for a more recent authority concerning a deprivation of possessions, the case of *Jahn* (2006) 42 EHRR 49 at [93].

[171] *Immobiliare Saffi v Italy* (2000) 30 EHRR 756 at [49].

[172] App. No. 69498/01, *Pla and Puncernau v Andorra*, October 10, 2006 at [59].

[173] *Vgt Verein gegen Tierfabriken v Switzerland* (2002) 34 EHRR 4 at [69].

[174] App. No. 73049/01, *Anheuser-Busch Inc v Portugal*, January 11, 2007 at [83].

[175] App. No. 73049/01, *Anheuser-Busch Inc v Portugal*, January 11, 2007 at [55].

[176] See [17] above.

of land is statute-barred, termination of the title of the paper owner does little more than regularise the respective positions, namely to confirm that the person who has acquired title by 12 years' adverse possession is the owner. Moreover, the law reflected the aim of the land registration legislation, which was to replicate the pre-registration law so far as practicable. As already noted above,[177] such a regime cannot be considered as 'manifestly without reasonable foundation'.

77 The Court has rejected the Government's contention that the pre-existing nature of the regime of adverse possession excluded the facts of the case from consideration under Art. 1 of Protocol No. 1.[178] The fact that the rules contained in both the 1925 and the 1980 Acts had been in force for many years before the first applicant even acquired the land is nevertheless relevant to an assessment of the overall proportionality of the legislation. In particular, it is not open to the applicant companies to say that they were not aware of the legislation, or that its application to the facts of the present case came as a surprise to them. Indeed, although the case proceeded domestically as far as the House of Lords, the applicant companies do not suggest that the conclusions of the domestic courts were unreasonable or unforeseeable, in the light of the legislation.

78 In connection with the limitation period in the present case, the Court notes that the Chamber took the view that the period was relatively long.[179] It has been unable, however, to derive any assistance from the comparative material submitted by the parties in this connection, beyond noting that there is no clear pattern as regards the length of limitation periods. It is in any event the case that very little action on the part of the applicant companies would have stopped time running. The evidence was that if the applicant companies had asked for rent, or some other form of payment, in respect of the Grahams' occupation of the land, it would have been forthcoming, and the possession would no longer have been 'adverse'. Even in the unlikely event that the Grahams had refused to leave and refused to agree to conditions for their occupation, the applicant companies need only have commenced an action for recovery, and time would have stopped running against them.

79 The Chamber and the applicant companies emphasised the absence of compensation for what they both perceived as a deprivation of the applicant companies' possessions. The Court has found that the interference with the applicant companies' possessions was a control of use, rather than a deprivation of possessions, such that the case law on compensation for deprivations is not directly applicable. Further, in the cases in which a situation was analysed as a control of use, even though the applicant had lost possessions,[180] no mention was made of a right to compensation. The Court would note, in agreement with the Government, that a requirement of compensation for the situation brought about by a party failing to observe a limitation period would sit uneasily alongside the very concept of limitation periods, whose aim is to further legal certainty by preventing a party from pursuing an action after a certain date. The Court would also add that, even under the provisions of the Land Registration Act 2002, which the applicant companies use as confirmation that the provisions of the earlier legislation were not compatible with the Convention, no compensation is payable by a person who is ultimately registered as a new owner of registered land on expiry of the limitation period.

80 The Chamber and the applicant companies were also exercised by the absence of procedural protection for a paper owner whose property rights are about to be extinguished by

---

177 See [74] above.   178 See [62] and [63] above.
179 See [73] above.   180 *AGOSI* [1986] EHRR 1 and *Air Canada* (1995) 20 EHRR 150.

the running of the limitation period under s. 15 of the 1980 Act, at least in so far as it applied to registered land. The Court would recall here that the applicant companies were not without procedural protection. While the limitation period was running, and if they failed to agree terms with the Grahams which put an end to the 'adverse possession', it was open to them to remedy the position by bringing a court action for repossession of the land. Such an action would have stopped time running. After expiry of the period, it remained open to the applicant companies to argue before the domestic courts, as they did, that the occupiers of their land had not been in 'adverse possession' as defined by domestic law.

81 It is true that since the entry into force of the Land Registration Act 2002, the paper owner of registered land against whom time has been running is in a better position than were the applicant companies at the relevant time. The 2002 Act requires, in effect, the giving of notice to a paper owner before the expiry of the limitation period, to give him time, if he wishes, to take action to deal with the adverse possessor. It improves the position of the paper owner and, correspondingly, makes it more difficult for an adverse possessor to acquire a full 12 years' adverse possession. The provisions of the 2002 Act do not, however, apply to the present case, and the Court must consider the facts of the case as they are. In any event, legislative changes in complex areas such as land law take time to bring about, and judicial criticism of legislation cannot of itself affect the conformity of the earlier provisions with the Convention.

82 The Government contended that it could not be the role of Art. 1 of Protocol No. 1 to protect commercial operators against their own failings. The Court regards this suggestion as related to those aspects of the Court's case law which underline that the Court is not in theory required to settle disputes of a private nature, in respect of which states enjoy a wide margin of appreciation.[181] In a case such as the present, where the Court is considering, principally, the statutory regime by which title is extinguished at the end of the limitation period, rather than the specific facts of the case, the relevance of the individual applicant's conduct is correspondingly restricted.

83 The applicant companies contended that their loss was so great, and the windfall to the Grahams so significant, that the fair balance required by Art. 1 of Protocol No. 1 was upset. The Court would first note that, in the case of James, the Court found that the view taken by Parliament as to the tenant's 'moral entitlement' to ownership of the houses at issue fell within the State's margin of appreciation. In the present case, too, whilst it would be strained to talk of the 'acquired rights' of an adverse possessor during the currency of the limitation period, it must be recalled that the registered land regime in the United Kingdom is a reflection of a long-established system in which a term of years' possession gave sufficient title to sell. Such arrangements fall within the State's margin of appreciation, unless they give rise to results which are so anomalous as to render the legislation unacceptable. The acquisition of unassailable rights by the adverse possessor must go hand in hand with a corresponding loss of property rights for the former owner. In James, the possibility of 'undeserving' tenants being able to make 'windfall profits' did not affect the overall assessment of the proportionality of the legislation,[182] and any windfall for the Grahams must be regarded in the same light in the present case.

84 As to the loss for the applicant companies, it is not disputed that the land lost by them, especially those parts with development potential, will have been worth a substantial sum of

181 See [75] above.   182 James (1986) 8 EHRR 123 at [69].

money. However, limitation periods, if they are to fulfil their purpose,[183] must apply regardless of the size of the claim. The value of the land cannot therefore be of any consequence to the outcome of the present case.

85 In sum, the Court concludes that the fair balance required by Art. 1 of Protocol No. 1 to the Convention was not upset in the present case.

B. LAND REGISTRATION ACT 2002

In **Beaulane Properties Ltd v Palmer** [2006] Ch 79[184] at 137 NICHOLAS STRAUSS QC considered (obiter) the compatibility of the provisions of the Land Registration Act 2002 on adverse possession with the European Convention on Human Rights:

198 ... What the 2002 Act does is to place the burden where it lies, on the party seeking to override a registered title. This reflects the Law Commission's view that there is no need for an owner who has established his claim by registering it to make a further claim. It is for the trespasser to establish his claim, if he has good grounds to do so.

199 What happens under the new provisions is that notice is given to the registered owner of the application, so that—as the Law Commission says, at paras 10.45 and 10.47 of the consultative document (Cm 4027[185]), the registered owner would have 'ample opportunity...to evict the squatter'. The squatter would not normally be awarded a title to the land, unless the registered owner did not oppose the application. If he did, the application would succeed only in the limited classes of cases envisaged by the Law Commission and provided for in Schedule 6.

200 Thus, the objectionable feature of the pre-2003 law, which as Lord Hope said in the *Pye* case [2003] 1 AC 419, para. 73, is the inadvertent loss of land, sometimes without any fault, and sometimes in favour of the deliberate land-grabber, is avoided. Save in the exceptional cases, the title to the land can only be lost by ten years' adverse possession, followed by a failure to respond to notification of the application, in which case it is legitimate for the law to infer abandonment.

---

[183] See [67]–[74] above.
[184] For the decision in this case in relation to s. 75 LRA 1925, see above, p. 289.
[185] Law Com No. 254 (1998).

PART II

FREEHOLD AND LEASEHOLD ESTATES IN LAND

4

FREEHOLD ESTATES

I. INTRODUCTION

We saw in chapter 1 the distinction between freehold estates and leasehold estates in land; and between estates which can exist at common law and estates which exist only in equity.[1] The freehold estates are those which have no fixed duration; leasehold estates are those which exist for a fixed period or a period which can be made certain. We shall consider leasehold estates in detail in chapter 5. In this chapter we consider freehold estates.

The freehold estates which were recognised by the common law are the fee simple, the fee tail (or 'entail'), the life estate and the estate pur autre vie. These are freeholds because they may endure for as long as the estate owner has heirs to whom to pass his estate (the fee simple); or as long as he has heirs of a particular class (the fee tail: for example, an estate which can pass only to his male heirs); or as long as he may live (the life estate) or as long as some other identified individual may live (the estate pur autre vie—'for another life').

However, the Law of Property Act 1925[2] provided that the only freehold estate which can exist at common law is the fee simple absolute in possession.[3] There can

---

[1] Above, pp. 11–15.   [2] S. 1; below, p. 302.

[3] A fee simple may be absolute, determinable, subject to a condition (below, p. 303; C & B, Chap. 17) or base (C & B, p. 484) A fee simple may also be (a) a 'flying freehold', where 'a man may have an inheritance in an upper chamber though the lower buildings and soil be in another': Co Litt 48b; Lincoln's Inn Act 1860 which regulates flying freeholds in New Square, Lincoln's Inn; (1977) 41 Conv 11 (M. Vitoria). See the claim to a 'subterranean flying freehold' of a cellar in *Grigsby v Melville* [1974] 1 WLR 80 at 83; (b) a 'movable fee', where the 'fee itself is a continuing estate, but it is an estate in land which from time to time changes its position': *Baxendale v Instow Parish Council* [1982] Ch 14 at 20, per Megarry V-C (foreshore capable of being granted as it might be from time to time); *Welden v Bridgewater* (1595) Cro Eliz 421, 78 ER 662 (lot meadows, where two or more have a fee simple in a measured part of a meadow, but the precise part owned is determined by lots at specified times); [1982] Conv 208 (R. E. Annand).

no longer be a legal fee tail, life estate or estate pur autre vie: such interests take effect only in equity, and such interests can now be created only under a trust of land.[4] Commonhold, a new form in which the legal freehold in registered land can be held, was introduced by the Commonhold and Leasehold Reform Act 2002. In this chapter we therefore consider the fee simple absolute in possession, and commonhold.

II. FEE SIMPLE ABSOLUTE IN POSSESSION[5]

Challis, *Law of Real Property* (3rd edn, 1911), p. 218

A *fee simple* is the most extensive in *quantum,* and the most absolute in respect to the rights which it confers, of all estates known to the law. It confers, and since the beginning of legal history it always has conferred, the lawful right to exercise over, upon, and in respect to, the land, every act of ownership which can enter into the imagination, including the right to commit unlimited waste; and, for all practical purposes of ownership, it differs from the absolute dominion of a chattel, in nothing except the physical indestructibility of its subject.

The rights of a fee simple owner are, however, limited by the rights of his neighbour— for example, where the neighbour has the benefit of an easement[6] or a restrictive covenant[7] which burdens the fee simple owner's land—and by statute, such as the Town and Country Planning Acts[8] and the Rent Acts.[9]

A. DEFINITION

LAW OF PROPERTY ACT 1925

1. Legal estates and equitable interests.—(1) The only estates in land which are capable of subsisting or of being conveyed or created at law are—

(a) An estate in fee simple absolute in possession...

7. Saving of certain legal estates and statutory powers.—(1) A fee simple which, by virtue of the Lands Clauses Acts... or any similar statute,[10] is liable to be divested,[11] is for the purposes of this Act a fee simple absolute,[12] and remains liable to be divested as if this Act had not been

---

[4] TLATA 1996; below, chap. 6.

[5] C & B, chap. 8; Gray, part 3.1; M & W, paras 3.005, 3.035–3.069; MM, pp. 40–45; Smith, pp. 34–39.

[6] Chap. 8, below.   [7] Chap. 9, below.   [8] P. 834, below.

[9] P. 379, below.

[10] *Tithe Redemption Commission v Runcorn UDC* [1954] Ch 383 (highway vested in the local highway authority; Local Government Act 1929 held to be 'a similar statute' within LPA 1925, s. 7(1)).

[11] These Acts provide that land granted for certain public purposes shall revert to the grantor, his successors or some other person, if the purpose fails or is not carried out.

[12] As amended by Reverter of Sites Act 1987, which excludes from s. 7(1) the School Sites Acts, the Literary and Scientific Institutions Act 1854 and the Places of Worship Sites Act 1873. The right of reverter in those

passed, [and a fee simple subject to a legal or equitable right of entry or re-entry is for the purposes of this Act a fee simple absolute].[13]

(2) A fee simple vested in a corporation which is liable to determine by reason of the dissolution of the corporation is, for the purposes of this Act, a fee simple absolute.[14]

205. General definitions.—(1) (xix) 'Possession' includes receipt of rents and profits or the right to receive the same, if any.

Preston, *An Elementary Treatise on Estates* (2nd edn, 1820–7), vol. i, pp. 125-6

The epithet *absolute* is used to distinguish an estate extended to any given time, without any condition to defeat, or collateral limitation to determine the estate in the mean time, from an estate subject to a condition or collateral limitation. The term absolute is of the same signification with the word pure, or *simple*, a word which expresses that the estate is not determinable by any event besides the event marked by the clause of limitation.

In **District Bank Ltd v Webb** [1958] 1 WLR 148[15] the question was whether an estoppel was raised against vendors by reason of a recital that they were 'seised in unencumbered fee simple in possession upon trust for sale,' when the property was subject to a

---

cases is replaced by a trust of land. Where, for example, a school site ceases to be used for purposes mentioned in the School Sites Act 1841, the charitable trustees continue to hold the legal estate on a trust of land for the revertee: Reverter of Sites Act 1987, s. 1 (as amended by TLATA 1996, s. 5; Sch. 2, para. 6); *Fraser v Canterbury Diocesan Board of Finance (No 2)* [2006] 1 AC 377. They may apply to the Charity Commissioners to have the interests of the revertee extinguished: s. 2. A revertee in some circumstances may be entitled to compensation: s. 2(4). For the difficulties caused by the original s. 7(1), see Law Commission Report on Rights of Reverter 1981 (Law Com No. 111, Cmnd 8410). The Act departs in a significant number of respects from the Report's recommendations. See Current Law Statutes Annotated (J. Hill); [1987] Conv 408 (D. Evans).

[13] The words in square brackets were added by LP (A) A 1926 Sch., and the intention of the Legislature appears to have been to include as legal estates certain holdings, common in the North of England, where a fee simple is purchased in return for a perpetual rentcharge upon the land. But the enactment is, in its terms, wider than this, and appears to include a grant to A in fee simple subject to a right of entry in the grantor on the happening of some event, such as, for example, A's marrying outside a certain religious persuasion. One would have expected a fee simple subject to such a condition to have been an equitable interest, and for such a grant to have created a settlement. Indeed SLA 1925, s. 1(1)(ii)(*b*) provides that a grant of a fee simple subject to an executory limitation over on the happening of some event created a settlement; it would be strange if the distinction were to depend upon the difference between an executory gift over and the right of the grantor to re-enter and terminate for breach of condition. It is tempting to suggest that the words of the amendment are wider than the Legislature intended; how they will be construed is not known. C & B, p. 170; M & W, para. 6.013–6.014; [1985] Conv 311. Since 1996 no new strict settlements can be created, and base and determinable fees take effect behind a trust of land: TLATA 1996, s. 25(1), Sch. 3, para. 2.

[14] As to whether the lands of a corporation upon its dissolution reverted to the donor or escheated to the lord, see Co Litt 13b; Gray, *Rule against Perpetuities* (4th edn), ss. 44–52; Challis, *Law of Real Property* (3rd edn), pp. 35–36, 467–468; *Hastings Corpn v Letton* [1908] 1 KB 378; *Re Woking UDC (Basingstoke Canal) Act 1911* [1914] 1 Ch 300; *Re Sir Thomas Spencer Wells* [1933] Ch 29; (1933) 49 LQR 240; (1934) 50 LQR 33 (F. E. Farrer); (1935) 51 LQR 347 (M. W. Hughes), 361 (F. E. Farrer).

[15] See also *Re Morgan* (1883) 24 ChD 114 at 116.

lease. DANCKWERTS J held that the representation was not sufficiently unambiguous to create an estoppel, and added at 150:

Secondly, the words 'in possession' are relied upon, but I do not think that 'in possession' means vacant possession. It seems to me that the meaning is 'fee simple in possession' as opposed to 'fee simple in reversion' and there again it seems to me impossible for the bank to rely upon such representation in the recital to cause the vendors to be bound by any estoppel.

B. CREATION AND TRANSFER[16]

As a legal estate, the fee simple can be created or transferred only by deed, and in registered land the transfer must be completed by registration if the transferee is to acquire the legal title to the estate.[17] At common law particular words were required for the conveyance of a fee simple, but this was simplified by the Conveyancing Act 1881 and the Law of Property Act 1925.

LAW OF PROPERTY ACT 1925

52. Conveyances to be by deed.—(1) All conveyances of land or of any interest therein are void for the purpose of conveying or creating a legal estate unless made by deed.[18]

60. Abolition of technicalities in regard to conveyances and deeds.—(1) A conveyance of freehold land to any person without words of limitation,[19] or any equivalent expression, shall pass to the grantee the fee simple or other the whole interest which the grantor had power to convey in such land, unless a contrary intention appears in the conveyance.

(2) A conveyance of freehold land to a corporation sole by his corporate designation without the word 'successors' shall pass to the corporation the fee simple or other the whole interest which the grantor had power to convey in such land, unless a contrary intention appears in the conveyance.

(4) The foregoing provisions of this section apply only to conveyances and deeds executed after the commencement of this Act:

Provided that in a deed executed after the thirty-first day of December, eighteen hundred and eighty-one,[20] it is sufficient—

    (a) In the limitation of an estate in fee simple, to use the words 'in fee simple,' without the word 'heirs'.

205. General definitions.—(1) In this Act unless the context otherwise requires, the following expressions have the meanings hereby assigned to them respectively, that is to say:—

---

[16] C & B, pp. 170–173; Gray, para. 1.3.16; M & W, paras 3.026–3.032; MM, pp. 37–39; Smith, p. 40.

[17] For further details see above, pp. 41–48 (formalities for creation and transfer of estates and interests in land) and chap. 2 (registered land).

[18] For exceptions, see s. 52(2); above, p. 42.

[19] [2008] Conv 129 (J. Mee), criticising the drafting of s. 60(1) and discussing the proposal to adopt it in a reform of Irish land law.

[20] The Conveyancing Act 1881 came into force on 1 January 1882.

(ii) 'Conveyance' includes a mortgage, charge, lease, assent, vesting declaration, vesting instrument, disclaimer, release and every other assurance of property or of an interest therein by any instrument, except a will....

LAND REGISTRATION ACT 2002

3 When title may be registered

(1) This section applies to any unregistered legal estate which is an interest of any of the following kinds—

(a) an estate in land...

4 When title must be registered

(1) The requirement of registration applies on the occurrence of any of the following events—

(a) the transfer of a qualifying estate—

(i) for valuable or other consideration, by way of gift or in pursuance of an order of any court, or

(ii) by means of an assent (including a vesting assent)...

(2) For the purposes of subsection (1), a qualifying estate is an unregistered legal estate which is—

(a) a freehold estate in land...

11 Freehold estates

(1) This section is concerned with the registration of a person under this Chapter as the proprietor of a freehold estate.

(2) Registration with absolute title has the effect described in subsections (3) to (5).

(3) The estate is vested in the proprietor together with all interests subsisting for the benefit of the estate.

(4) The estate is vested in the proprietor subject only to the following interests affecting the estate at the time of registration—

(a) interests which are the subject of an entry in the register in relation to the estate,

(b) unregistered interests which fall within any of the paragraphs of Schedule 1,[21] and

(c) interests acquired under the Limitation Act 1980 of which the proprietor has notice.

27 Dispositions required to be registered

(1) If a disposition of a registered estate or registered charge is required to be completed by registration, it does not operate at law until the relevant registration requirements are met.

(2) In the case of a registered estate, the following are the dispositions which are required to be completed by registration—

(a) a transfer...

---

[21] Overriding interests; p. 193, above.

132 General interpretation

(1) In this Act—

'legal estate' has the same meaning as in the Law of Property Act 1925.

C. ALIENABILITY

A condition attached to the grant of an interest which is inconsistent with the nature of the interest itself is void.[22] Since a fee simple is an inherently alienable interest, a question can arise as to the extent to which a restriction on alienation is permissible in law.

Re Brown
[1954] Ch 39 (ChD, **Harman J**)

The testator devised freehold properties in trust for his wife for life, and after her death, on his youngest son attaining 21, for all the sons then living in equal shares as tenants in common. Clause 6 of the will provided that if any son should allow his share to be vested in any person other than one of the brothers, that share should be held on discretionary trusts for the son and his wife and children. The question, on one son wishing to sell outside the family, was whether the restriction upon alienation was good.

Held. No.

Harman J: This is a point on which it appears that the authorities give no certain guide, and the various editors of Jarman on Wills give it up, as textbook writers, therein more fortunate than judges, are entitled to do with the bland statement that the law is uncertain.

The point is a very narrow one, and it is whether a restriction on alienation appended to an absolute devise of real estate is good or no. The instinct of any equity lawyer is, to start with, to say that all restraints on absolute interests which tend to negative the rights attached to those interests are abhorred by the law and disallowed. That is a general rule cited by Jarman (8th edn, vol. 2, p. 1477): 'A power of alienation is necessarily and inseparably incidental to an estate in fee.'

The view at the outset is that anything which seeks to deprive the feoffee (so to call him) of his rights is void, but there is no doubt that some degree of restriction may be put upon him . . .

As I have said, the instinct of any Chancery lawyer is to say that this is a restriction quite inconsistent with an absolute interest in real estate (or in proceeds of sale, for that matter) and that the restriction is not good. Mr Thompson,[23] however, has been able to persuade me that there is a great deal to be said for the view that a restriction of this sort may be good, if it do not amount to a total restriction. He starts with Coke upon Littleton (11th edn., Part 1,

---

[22] P. 48, above. A life interest may be made determinable upon the happening of various events, including alienation. This is the basis of protective trusts: *Brandon v Robinson* (1811) 18 Ves 429; *Rochford v Hackman* (1852) 9 Hare 475; H & M, para. 7.002.

[23] Counsel for infants interested under the discretionary trusts.

book 3, section 360), where the translation is as follows: 'Also if a feoffment be made upon this condition, that the feoffee shall not alien the land to any, this condition is void because when a man is enfeoffed of lands or tenements, he hath power to alien them to any person by the law: For if such a condition should be good, then the condition should oust him of all the power which the law gives him, which should be against reason; and therefore such a condition is void.' That is to say, it is repugnant to the gift. The passage following (section 361) is in these terms: 'But if the condition be such that the feoffee shall not alien to such a one, naming his name, or to any of his heirs, or of the issues of such a one, etc. or the like, which conditions do not take away all power of alienation from the feoffee, etc., then such condition is good.' That merely says that you may point out a certain person (or, I suppose, persons) and prohibit alienation to him or them: quaere as to how many persons may you extend that prohibition? According to two cases to which I shall refer in a moment, you may extend it to all the world except a certain class of people; but that seems to me to be a very curious way to read the doctrine of Coke, which, after all, merely says that you may exclude A or B from the world of people to whom it is permissible to alienate.

The earliest case to which I was referred is a decision of the Court of King's Bench, where the judgment was given by Lord Ellenborough CJ, *Doe d Gill v Pearson* (1805) 6 East 173, 174, 180. The gift in that case was of a piece of land to 'my daughters...Ann and Hannah, their heirs and assigns for ever, as tenants in common, and not as joint tenants; *upon this special proviso and condition,* that in case my said daughters Ann and Hannah Collett, or either of them, shall have no lawful issue, that then and in such case they or she having no lawful issue as aforesaid shall have no power to dispose of her share in the said estates so above given to them except to her sister or sisters, or to their children.' The exception was confined to sisters and the children of sisters, which is a narrow enough class, although one does not know exactly how many there were in the class. There were five daughters...[T]he whole court, the Court of King's Bench, decided apparently that the condition not to alienate except to a class consisting of four sisters and their children was good.

That case was considered in *Attwater v Attwater* (1853) 18 Beav 330, where Sir John Romilly MR refused to follow the Court of King's Bench, and merely said that, notwithstanding *Doe d Gill v Pearson,* he held the opposite. The limitation in *Attwater v Attwater* was: 'I bequeath to *Gay Thomas Attwater,* jun., eldest son of my niece, the family estate at *Charlton, Wilts.,* to become his property on attaining the age of 25 years, with an injunction never to sell it out of the family; but, if sold at all, it must be to one of his brothers hereafter named.' He had three brothers. Sir John Romilly declined to hold that condition good; in his judgment he said: 'It is obvious, that if the introduction of one person's name, as the only person to whom the property may be sold, renders such a proviso valid, a restraint on alienation may be created, as complete and perfect as if no person whatever was named; inasmuch as the name of the person who alone is permitted to purchase, might be so selected, as to render it reasonably certain that he would not buy the property, and that the property could not be aliened at all. It appears to me also, that this is the true construction of the words used by the testator; it is, in truth, an injunction never to sell the hereditaments devised at all....It is not, in my opinion, desirable to impose fresh fetters on the enjoyment of property, and it appears to me, that this proviso is distinctly at variance with the rules laid down by Lord Coke, and which have always been considered and treated as good law. I am of opinion, therefore, that this clause is merely inoperative.'

That is a decision on a limitation exactly in pari materia to the one before me. I should feel no difficulty about following it, rather than *Doe d Gill v Pearson* (1805) 6 East 173, but for the fact that in *Re Macleay* (1875) LR 20 Eq 186 the great authority of Sir George Jessel appears to be on the other side. In that case the devise was 'to my brother J. on the condition that he never sells out of the family'. The limitation was not, therefore, to named persons, it was 'out of the family'. Sir George Jessel said at 187: '... It has been suggested, however, that it is void as being repugnant to the quality of the estate, that is to say, that you cannot restrict the right of an owner in fee of alienating in anyway in which he may think fit. If that were the law, the condition would be plainly void. But, with the exception of one authority, a case decided by my immediate predecessor, I am not aware that the law has ever been laid down in that way.' Sir George Jessel then discussed the point in Coke on Littleton, *Muschamp v Bluet* (1617) J Bridge 132, *Attwater v Attwater* (1853) 18 Beav 330, and *Jacobs v Brett* (1875) LR 20 Eq 1. He decided at 189: 'So that, according to the old books, Sheppard's Touchstone being to the same effect, the test is whether the condition takes away the whole power of alienation substantially: it is a question of substance, and not of mere form.' ...[H]e came to the conclusion that the words were not sufficiently restrictive to be in substance an absolute bar. His reason was that 'the family' was a larger term than 'sister or sisters, or their children' and that the only restriction was to sell and not to dispose, which might include leases or mortgages. He came to the conclusion that the limitation in that case was a good one.

That decision, therefore, inclines to the view for which Mr. Thompson has argued. In *Re Rosher* (1884) 26 ChD 801, however, Pearson J felt it necessary to make an elaborate attack upon Sir George Jessel's decision in *Re Macleay* (1875) LR 20 Eq 186. Although the decision in *Re Rosher* was, as a matter of construction that the restriction was in effect an absolute one, Pearson J delivered a long judgment explaining why he could not agree that *Re Macleay* was well decided. The restriction in *Re Rosher* was that if the testator's 'son, his heirs or devisees' wished to sell over a certain period, property worth £15,000 had to be offered to the testator's wife during her lifetime at a price of £3,000; and the judge held that that meant in effect that it could not be sold at all, because nobody would give away property worth £15,000 for £3,000. Although *Re Rosher,* qua its decision, is not of much help, it shows that in the view of Pearson J, *Re Macleay* was wrongly decided.

I need take the law no further. I have to choose one way or the other ...

It is most pertinent to remember, as Mr. Armstrong[24] has also pointed out to me, that the class to whom it is permissible to alienate begins with three for any one share and that the prohibition goes on not only during the joint lives of all the brothers, but during the lives of the survivors and survivor of them, and therefore a period will be reached when there are two, and then only one, and at last no person to whom any alienation is allowed. If none it is plainly bad. If it is only one, that in substance, as in *Muschamp v Bluet,* is equivalent to none. If one be bad, are two good? It seems to me that a class of this sort, which is bound to be a diminishing class, brings it about, in substance, that this is a general prohibition on alienation. It would be an extraordinary thing if no one could postulate of any one of these brothers that he would or would not during his lifetime be able to dispose of his own share; and that it must depend on whether he outlives two of his brothers. In my view, this is the kind of restriction which the law views, or should view, with dislike. It is exactly the same kind of condition as in *Attwater v Attwater,* and I think that I should be at liberty to follow that decision were it necessary for me to do so, but I do not think that I need follow any case in this region, because the cases are inconsistent with one another, and I am entitled to take my own view. It is pertinent that a number of persons, as in this clause, is in

---

[24] Counsel for the sons.

essence different from a class consisting, for instance, as Sir George Jessel's did in *Re Macleay*, of members of the family, which he said was a large indeterminate class of people and might, of course, increase as time went on; whereas, if alienation be restricted to three or four or five persons such as brothers, the class is bound to diminish as death takes its toll of the members. I hold therefore, that the restriction in clause 6 of the will is an attempt to fetter the natural qualities of the interest given, and is accordingly void and can be disregarded.[25]

III. COMMONHOLD[26]

In 1987 the Aldridge Working Group on Freehold Flats and Freehold Ownership of Other Independent Buildings[27] recommended the introduction of a new scheme for the freehold ownership of properties which lie in close proximity to each other and are interdependent—such as the separate flats within a single building. This new scheme was designed to facilitate the regulation of the relationship between the several owners of the separate units, and so, for example, to allow the enforcement of covenants between the owners for the time being of the units. As we shall see, the burden of positive covenants does not normally run between freeholders.[28] And although positive covenants can be enforced between landlord and tenant,[29] the use of leasehold estates for the ownership of flats can present problems, since the lease is a wasting asset which towards the end of its term becomes increasingly difficult to sell or to use as security. In theory, therefore, the use of a commonhold scheme should place the owners of the units in a stronger position, with a better-regulated scheme binding all associated unit holders, and holding a freehold asset, rather than simply a leasehold.

[25] Cf. *Caldy Manor Estate Ltd v Farrell* [1974] 1 WLR 1303. A fee simple determinable (whether on alienation or for any other reason) became settled land under SLA 1925, s. 1(1)(ii)(c) (as amended by TLATA 1996, s. 25(1), Sch. 3, para. 2(2)), and the land thus became alienable by the tenant for life (p. 508, below). Any term which would operate to restrict the tenant for life's freedom of alienation is void: SLA 1925, s. 106. No new settlements can be created after 1996: p. 516, below; and where a person is granted a determinable fee after 1996 the land is held on trust under TLATA 1996 with the grantor as trustee. See also on sterilisation of land, *Overseas & Commercial Developments Ltd v Cox* [2002] All ER (D) 253 (Apr).

[26] C & B, chap. 9; Gray, part 3.2; M & W, chap. 33; Smith, chap. 21. Fetherstonhaugh, Sefton and Peters, *Commonhold* (2004); Cowen, Driscoll and Target, *Commonhold Law and Practice* (2005); Hill and Redman, *The Commonhold and Leasehold Reform Act 2002*, chap. 2; Clarke, *Commonhold: The New Law* (2002); *Clark on Commonhold: Law, Practice and Precedents* (2004); Aldridge, *Commonhold Law*; R & R, chap. 22.

[27] Cm 79. The Working Group was established in 1986 by the Chairman of the Law Commission as a result of the initiative of the Lord Chancellor: p.v. See also Commonhold—A Consultation Paper 1990 (Cm 1345), which contained a draft bill; [1991] Conv 170 (H. W. Wilkinson). In 1996 the Lord Chancellor's Department issued a further Consultation paper, [1997] Conv 6; (1996) IL & T Rev 3 (J. C. Williams). A third draft Bill published in 2000 (Cm 4843) fell when the general election of 2001 was called. See also Blundell Memorial Lecture 1991: *Commonhold—Can we make it work* (J. Wylie and E. Nugee QC); [1997] Conv 169 (L. Charlebois); [1998] Conv 283 (L. Crabb); [2002] Conv 349 (D. N. Clarke); [2006] Conv 14 (S.M.J. Wong); [2009] 0917 EG 98 (M. Dowden).

[28] Below, pp. 745–750.   [29] Below, pp. 462–499.

Commonhold was introduced by Part I of the Commonhold and Leasehold Reform Act 2002, which came into force on 27 September 2004.[30] It provides a new means by which the freehold estate in registered land can be held.[31] A commonhold association is the registered proprietor of the common parts, but the holder of each unit is registered as the proprietor of the freehold estate in that unit. The commonhold association is a company limited by guarantee; and only members of the association are the owners of the individual units. Their rights and duties, as between themselves and as between themselves and the commonhold association, are specified in a Commonhold Community Statement.

It remains to be seen how widely commonhold will be used.[32]

Aldridge Working Group on Freehold Flats and Freehold Ownership of Other Independent Buildings (1987) Cm 79, paras 1.1, 1.3–1.4, 1.10–1.24

1.1 This Report proposes a new land ownership scheme, for England and Wales, called commonhold. The purpose of the scheme is to regulate relations between owners of separate properties which lie in close proximity to each other and are interdependent. The scheme is suitable for, but not limited to, residential property. It gives people the chance to own flats freehold, without the present drawbacks, but the scheme can also apply to offices, commercial and industrial premises and other properties.

BACKGROUND

The Problem

1.3 When the owner of a freehold property enters into a positive obligation connected with his ownership, English law provides no direct way to enforce that obligation against successive owners of the property. For example, the purchaser of a new house built in what was the garden of the neighbouring house may undertake to maintain the fence dividing the two gardens. The owner of the older house, who sold the new one, can oblige the purchaser to do all necessary repairs to the fence. However, when the new house is subsequently sold, he cannot insist that the new owner does that work. In the case of a block of flats, this problem is accentuated. The very

---

[30] CLRA 2002 (Commencement No. 4) Order 2004 (SI 2004 No. 1832). The Act is supplemented by Commonhold Regulations 2004 (SI 2004 No 1829); Commonhold (LR) R 2004 (SI 2004 No 1830); Commonhold (LR) (Amendment) R 2008 (SI 2008 No. 1920). See also LCD Consultation Paper on Proposals for Commonhold Regulations 2002 and Analysis of the Responses to the Consultation Paper 2003; DCA Non-Statutory Guidance on the Commonhold Regulations 2004; Guidance on the Drafting of a Commonhold Community Statement including Specimen Local Rules 2005.

[31] Commonhold is similar to Condominium legislation in Canada, the United States of America and, under the name of strata titles, in Australia and New Zealand. Similar legislation has been in force in Europe since the 1930s, and it has been introduced in many other parts of the world. On strata titles in Australia, see (1991) 9107 EG 92 (N. Carter); and for other comparisons, see [2005] Conv 53 (C. G. van der Merwe and P. F. Smith). The suggestion that 'strata title' be introduced in England was first made in the Report of the Committee on Positive Covenants Affecting Land 1965, Cmnd 2719. For proposals to introduce 'Multi-unit development' in Irish law, see [2009] Conv 21 (P. F. Smith).

[32] At first it appeared that developers were slow to adopt commonhold: (2006) 156 NLJ 226 (F. Larcombe); [2005] 35 EG 104 (G. Fetherstonhaugh), but they are now beginning to do so: [2006] 09 EG 173; (2005) 154 PLJ 5 (J. Hopkins). For common misconceptions amongst property developers about commonhold which appear to have discouraged its use, see (2008) 158 NLJ 1137 (J. Driscoll).

stability of a building divided into separate units depends on the proper maintenance and repair both of the individual flats and of the common parts. If either falls into disrepair, that affects the value of all parts of the property and the enjoyment of all the flats. One unit often depends on another for support and shelter. The owner of each therefore needs to be able to enforce the positive obligations undertaken by the others.

1.4 Until now, most satisfactory subdivisions of buildings have had to be organised by the owner of the whole block granting leases of each separate unit within it. This provides a satisfactory solution to the problem of enforcing positive obligations, because each successive owner of the lease is liable to comply with all the obligations which relate to the property and are set out in the lease. However, this leads to further problems. A lease necessarily lasts only for the period for which it is granted. Although this period can be, and often is, as long as 99 years or more, there is a period towards the end of the lease when it is not considered satisfactory security for a mortgage loan. As the period of unmortgageability is generally 40–45 years, this is particularly unsatisfactory in relation to flats, most of which are bought with the aid of a mortgage. Besides this drawback, there is no standard form of lease, with the result that buying and selling leases can add to the cost and delays of conveyancing and some of the leases themselves are not in a satisfactory form.

COMMONHOLDS

The Scheme

1.10 Commonhold is a new term for a system of land ownership where the emphasis is on co-operation between owners living within a defined area. So long as the commonhold continues, the owner of each unit is the freeholder with exclusive ownership of a specified piece of property (e.g., a flat). In certain circumstances, the commonhold can be ended . . . The ownership of the unit will then automatically be converted into a share, fixed in advance, of the ownership of the entire property within the commonhold.

1.11 To keep conveyancing as simple as possible, with the additional benefits of speed and cheapness which that brings, the commonhold system will only be available where the land is registered at HM Land Registry with absolute title. To introduce separate rules to allow commonholds on unregistered land would be unnecessarily complicated, bearing in mind that it is settled Government policy to extend compulsory registration of title to the whole country within the next few years.[33] The way ahead for any new property law must lie with registered title. We do not, however, wish to exclude any property from the commonhold scheme merely because its title is not currently registered and therefore suggest that if an owner intends to create a commonhold, that should be an acceptable ground for applying for voluntary registration of title.

1.12 As soon as a commonhold is registered at the Land Registry, a management association will automatically be created. The members of the association will be the unit owners. The association will own the common parts of the property, including the structural walls of the buildings (except in a case where the document creating the commonhold expressly varies this rule), and will be responsible for their repair and maintenance. The association will also be liable to provide services (e.g., heating, light, lifts, etc.) which will be financed by a service charge payable by the unit owners.

1.13 Statutory constitution rules will govern the conduct of the management association, and statutory regulations the rights and obligations of the unit owners in relation to each other.

---

[33] [Compulsory registration of title was extended to the whole country in 1990: above, p. 116.]

These regulations will include all the rights which unit owners need for the support of their properties and access to them.

1.14 In making our recommendations, we have constantly borne in mind the need to devise a scheme which is easy to understand and easy to operate. This policy has affected the conclusions we have reached on details. For instance, we have thought it better to devise a single scheme which can apply universally, rather than several schemes to cater for individual circumstances. We have also opted, where possible, for standardisation of regulations and documents.

1.15 There is no need for commonholds to be the compulsory way in which to organise a block of flats, or a similar commercial development. Many properties will clearly be suitable for the commonhold scheme, and others not. It is impossible to tell in advance whether the simplification explained in the last paragraph will be a disincentive to developers to use the scheme in borderline cases, or whether the advantages of commonholds will outweigh the restrictions. Ultimately, the market will determine whether commonhold is adopted as the most advantageous way of owning the development in each particular case.

1.16 Nevertheless, if other circumstances dictate that compulsion would be appropriate in the adoption of the commonhold scheme in particular situations, or for particular types of property, this could be done. For example, it could be available if the owners of the leases of all flats in a block were given the right to purchase the freehold from their common landlord. Or, it could be made the model for all future developments of flats.

THE ADVANTAGES

Automatic Rights and Obligations

1.17 A small number of developments of freehold flats already exist. Generally, they have proved less than satisfactory, mainly because as explained above, it has been impossible to provide adequate means of ensuring that the whole property is properly maintained and repaired and such flats are difficult to sell as financial institutions are reluctant to lend on them. The commonhold system will solve these problems by statutory regulations. The rights which will be enjoyed by the unit owner will be automatic and standard. His position will not depend on the skill and negotiating power of his particular lawyer, or—even more uncertainly—of the lawyer who represented a former owner.

Ownership of a share in the site

1.18 One disadvantage of freehold flats is that if a building is totally destroyed then all that the unit owner has (unless he is the owner of a ground floor unit) is the ownership of a block of air. Under the commonhold scheme all unit owners will have a proportionate share in the site itself.

Freehold rather than Leasehold

1.19 Although for the reasons explained above, we now have many multi-ownership leasehold developments, people often find it difficult to understand why they should not be able to obtain a freehold when they buy a flat. They resent continuing to pay a ground rent, even though it may not be a high one 'for nothing'. The foreign purchaser or investor in commercial units also finds difficulty in our leasehold system. Freehold units will give more consumer satisfaction, as they do in other countries.

Mortgageability

1.20 The security of a building society, or any other lender, rests on its ability, in the final analysis, to sell the mortgaged property and recoup the amount of its loan as well as outstanding interest and expenses. Building societies are lending, and therefore putting at risk, other people's money, that of their investors. They therefore rightly act with caution, and are legally obliged to do so. The result, as we pointed out earlier, is that leases which are coming towards expiry cease to be mortgageable. Someone may happily buy a 55 year lease, thinking it will outlast his lifetime, but if he wants to move 30 years later and seeks to sell his flat he may have difficulty. If on the other hand, the flat is a freehold unit in a commonhold, the legal interest will not expire and it will, subject always to the physical state of the property, permanently provide a good security for a loan.

Democratic Management

1.21 One major problem with leases is that decisions on, and the provision of, repairs, services and other matters are often in the hands of the landlord whose interests may be opposed to those of the tenants. Indeed, the landlord may have ceased to have any real interest in the property at all. In a commonhold, the management of the property will be in the hands of a democratically run commonhold association, composed of the unit owners themselves. The interests of the unit owners and the commonhold association are identical.

Protection for Minorities and Majorities

1.22 Fundamental decisions affecting a commonhold require a resolution supported by a unanimous vote. This protects the interests of minorities. However it is also important that a few recalcitrant unit owners should not be able to hinder the effective management of the commonhold. There are therefore provisions for the majority to make an application to the court where the vote in favour of a resolution is at least 80%. As it is only where there is a substantial majority that an application can be made to the court this will reduce the amount of court work necessary. We therefore do not expect commonholds to create too heavy a demand on court resources.

Simplified Conveyancing

1.23 Commonholds, with their standard forms and regulations, will make conveyancing simpler and cheaper. By way of illustration, we have included an example of a typical set of commonhold documents in Appendix B. At present, the purchaser of leasehold property has no automatic right to see evidence of the freeholder's title, nor in some cases, superior leases. (There will be, however, a limited right under The Landlord and Tenant Act 1987 for a residential tenant to inspect the register at the Land Registry to ascertain the name and address of his landlord.)[34] There are cases in which it transpires that a landlord has no right to grant the lease, or that the property is subject to some right in favour of a third party which the tenant had no means to discover. The commonhold scheme, by giving satisfactory freehold ownership of units, eliminates these drawbacks.

1.24 We are aware of two inescapable limitations of the commonhold scheme: the human factor, and the physical wasting nature of buildings. Neither commonholds, nor any other system, can solve all the problems inherent in people living close together. Commonholds will only work if people co-operate in abiding by regulations and participating in management. Again, no

---

[34] [At the time when this report was written there was no general right of inspection of the register of title to registered land, and so specific provision was made by LTA 1987, s. 51, to allow a residential tenant to search for his landlord's name and address. The register was however opened to public inspection by LRA 1988. See now LRA 2002, s. 66; above, p. 126.]

legal arrangements can prolong the life of a building. However, we hope that the commonhold scheme will give a framework within which co-operation is likely to be achieved, and that this will maximise the care taken in repairing and maintaining buildings.

COMMONHOLD AND LEASEHOLD REFORM ACT 2002

Nature of commonhold

1 Commonhold land

(1) Land is commonhold land if—

(a) the freehold estate in the land is registered as a freehold estate in commonhold land,

(b) the land is specified in the memorandum of association of a commonhold association as the land in relation to which the association is to exercise functions, and

(c) a commonhold community statement makes provision for rights and duties of the commonhold association and unit-holders (whether or not the statement has come into force).

Registration[35]

2 Application[36]

(1) The Registrar shall register a freehold estate in land as a freehold estate in commonhold land if—

(a) the registered freeholder of the land makes an application under this section, and

(b) no part of the land is already commonhold land.

(3) A person is the registered freeholder of land for the purposes of this Part if—

(a) he is registered as the proprietor of a freehold estate in the land with absolute title, or

(b) he has applied, and the Registrar is satisfied that he is entitled, to be registered as mentioned in paragraph (a).[37]

4 Land which may not be commonhold

Schedule 2 (which provides that an application under section 2 may not relate wholly or partly to land of certain kinds[38]) shall have effect.

---

[35] Commonhold Regulations 2004, Part II; Commonhold (LR) R 2004; Commonhold (LR) (Amendment) R 2008; Land Registry Practice Guide 60.

[36] An application requires the consent of anyone who is the registered proprietor of the freehold of the whole or part of the land, or of a lease granted for more than 21 years, or of a charge over the whole or part of the land; or of other persons prescribed by regulations: s. 3. For the consequences of registration in error, see s. 6.

[37] This includes a transferee of a registered estate who has not yet been registered, and a transferee of unregistered land where the estate is now to be registered for the first time. The application for first registration is completed first, before the title is then re-registered as commonhold: Land Registry Practice Guide 60, para. 4.1.

[38] Flying freeholds (p. 301, n. 3, above), certain agricultural land, and contingent estates (liable to revert or vest in another person on particular events).

5 Registered details

(1) The Registrar shall ensure that in respect of any commonhold land the following are kept in his custody and referred to in the register—

    (a) the prescribed details of the commonhold association;[39]

    (b) the prescribed details of the registered freeholder of each commonhold unit;

    (c) a copy of the commonhold community statement;[40]

    (d) a copy of the memorandum and articles of association of the commonhold association.

Effect of registration

9 Registration with unit-holders[41]

(1) This section applies in relation to a freehold estate in commonhold land if—

    (a) it is registered as a freehold estate in commonhold land in pursuance of an application under section 2, and

    (b) the application is accompanied by a statement by the applicant requesting that this section should apply.

(2) A statement under subsection (1)(b) must include a list of the commonhold units giving in relation to each one the prescribed details of the proposed initial unit-holder or joint unit-holders.

(3) On registration—

    (a) the commonhold association shall be entitled to be registered as the proprietor of the freehold estate in the common parts,

    (b) a person specified by virtue of subsection (2) as the initial unit-holder of a commonhold unit shall be entitled to be registered as the proprietor of the freehold estate in the unit,

    (c) a person specified by virtue of subsection (2) as an initial joint unit-holder of a commonhold unit shall be entitled to be registered as one of the proprietors of the freehold estate in the unit,

    (d) the Registrar shall make entries in the register to reflect paragraphs (a) to (c) (without applications being made),

    (e) the rights and duties conferred and imposed by the commonhold community statement shall come into force, and

    (f) any lease of the whole or part of the commonhold land shall be extinguished by virtue of this section.[42]

(4) For the purpose of subsection (3)(f) 'lease' means a lease which—

    (a) is granted for any term, and

    (b) is granted before the commonhold association becomes entitled to be registered as the proprietor of the freehold estate in the common parts.

---

[39] S. 34; p. 321, below.   [40] S. 31; p. 320, below.

[41] For registration without unit-holders, see s. 7.

[42] If a tenant or sub-tenant was not required to give consent, he has an action for his loss against his superior landlord or the freeholder who did give consent: s. 10.

Commonhold unit[43]

11 Definition

(1) In this Part 'commonhold unit' means a commonhold unit specified in a commonhold community statement in accordance with this section.

(2) A commonhold community statement must—

    (a) specify at least two parcels of land as commonhold units, and

    (b) define the extent of each commonhold unit.

(3) In defining the extent of a commonhold unit a commonhold community statement—

    (a) must refer to a plan which is included in the statement and which complies with prescribed requirements,

    (b) may refer to an area subject to the exclusion of specified structures, fittings, apparatus or appurtenances within the area,

    (c) may exclude the structures which delineate an area referred to, and

    (d) may refer to two or more areas (whether or not contiguous).

(4) A commonhold unit need not contain all or any part of a building.

12 Unit-holder

A person is the unit-holder of a commonhold unit if he is entitled to be registered as the proprietor of the freehold estate in the unit (whether or not he is registered).

13 Joint unit-holders

(1) Two or more persons are joint unit-holders of a commonhold unit if they are entitled to be registered as proprietors of the freehold estate in the unit (whether or not they are registered).

14 Use and maintenance

(1) A commonhold community statement must make provision regulating the use of commonhold units.

(2) A commonhold community statement must make provision imposing duties in respect of the insurance, repair and maintenance of each commonhold unit.

(3) A duty under subsection (2) may be imposed on the commonhold association or the unit-holder.

15 Transfer

(1) In this Part a reference to the transfer of a commonhold unit is a reference to the transfer of a unit-holder's freehold estate in a unit to another person—

    (a) whether or not for consideration,

    (b) whether or not subject to any reservation or other terms, and

    (c) whether or not by operation of law.

(2) A commonhold community statement may not prevent or restrict the transfer of a commonhold unit.

---

[43] Commonhold Regulations 2004, Part III.

(3) On the transfer of a commonhold unit the new unit-holder shall notify the commonhold association of the transfer.

16 Transfer: effect

(1) A right or duty conferred or imposed—

   (a) by a commonhold community statement, or

   (b) in accordance with section 20,

   shall affect a new unit-holder in the same way as it affected the former unit-holder.

(2) A former unit-holder shall not incur a liability or acquire a right—

   (a) under or by virtue of the commonhold community statement, or

   (b) by virtue of anything done in accordance with section 20.

(3) Subsection (2)—

   (a) shall not be capable of being disapplied or varied by agreement, and

   (b) is without prejudice to any liability or right incurred or acquired before a transfer takes effect.

(4) In this section—

   'former unit-holder' means a person from whom a commonhold unit has been transferred (whether or not he has ceased to be the registered proprietor), and

   'new unit-holder' means a person to whom a commonhold unit is transferred (whether or not he has yet become the registered proprietor).

17 Leasing: residential

(1) It shall not be possible to create a term of years absolute in a residential commonhold unit unless the term satisfies prescribed conditions.[44]

(2) The conditions may relate to—

   (a) length;

   (b) the circumstances in which the term is granted;

   (c) any other matter.

(3) Subject to subsection (4), an instrument or agreement shall be of no effect to the extent that it purports to create a term of years in contravention of subsection (1).

(4) Where an instrument or agreement purports to create a term of years in contravention of subsection (1) a party to the instrument or agreement may apply to the court for an order—

   (a) providing for the instrument or agreement to have effect as if it provided for the creation of a term of years of a specified kind;

   (b) providing for the return or payment of money;

   (c) making such other provision as the court thinks appropriate.

---

[44] The principal restrictions are that the lease must not be granted for a premium, nor for longer than 7 years: Commonhold Regulations 2004, reg. 11.

(5) A commonhold unit is residential if provision made in the commonhold community statement by virtue of section 14(1) requires it to be used only—

    (a) for residential purposes, or

    (b) for residential and other incidental purposes.

18 Leasing: non-residential

An instrument or agreement which creates a term of years absolute in a commonhold unit which is not residential (within the meaning of section 17) shall have effect subject to any provision of the commonhold community statement.

20 Other transactions

(1) A commonhold community statement may not prevent or restrict the creation, grant or transfer by a unit-holder of—

    (a) an interest in the whole or part of his unit, or

    (b) a charge over his unit.

(2) Subsection (1) is subject to sections 17 to 19 (which impose restrictions about leases).

(3) It shall not be possible to create an interest of a prescribed kind in a commonhold unit unless the commonhold association—

    (a) is a party to the creation of the interest, or

    (b) consents in writing to the creation of the interest.

(4) A commonhold association may act as described in subsection (3)(a) or (b) only if—

    (a) the association passes a resolution to take the action, and

    (b) at least 75 per cent of those who vote on the resolution vote in favour.

(5) An instrument or agreement shall be of no effect to the extent that it purports to create an interest in contravention of subsection (3).

(6) In this section 'interest' does not include—

    (a) a charge, or

    (b) an interest which arises by virtue of a charge.

21 Part-unit: interests

(1) It shall not be possible to create an interest in part only of a commonhold unit.

(2) But subsection (1) shall not prevent—

    (a) the creation of a term of years absolute in part only of a residential commonhold unit where the term satisfies prescribed conditions,

    (b) the creation of a term of years absolute in part only of a non-residential commonhold unit, or

    (c) the transfer of the freehold estate in part only of a commonhold unit where the commonhold association consents in writing to the transfer.

(3) An instrument or agreement shall be of no effect to the extent that it purports to create an interest in contravention of subsection (1).

22 Part–unit: charging

(1) It shall not be possible to create a charge over part only of an interest in a commonhold unit.

(2) An instrument or agreement shall be of no effect to the extent that it purports to create a charge in contravention of subsection (1).

23 Changing size

(1) An amendment of a commonhold community statement which redefines the extent of a commonhold unit may not be made unless the unit-holder consents—

    (a) in writing, and

    (b) before the amendment is made.

(2) But regulations may enable a court to dispense with the requirement for consent on the application of a commonhold association in prescribed circumstances.

Common parts

25 Definition

(1) In this Part 'common parts' in relation to a commonhold means every part of the commonhold which is not for the time being a commonhold unit in accordance with the commonhold community statement.

(2) A commonhold community statement may make provision in respect of a specified part of the common parts (a 'limited use area') restricting—

    (a) the classes of person who may use it;

    (b) the kind of use to which it may be put.

(3) A commonhold community statement—

    (a) may make provision which has effect only in relation to a limited use area, and

    (b) may make different provision for different limited use areas.

26 Use and maintenance

A commonhold community statement must make provision—

    (a) regulating the use of the common parts;

    (b) requiring the commonhold association to insure the common parts;

    (c) requiring the commonhold association to repair and maintain the common parts.

27 Transactions

(1) Nothing in a commonhold community statement shall prevent or restrict—

    (a) the transfer by the commonhold association of its freehold estate in any part of the common parts, or

    (b) the creation by the commonhold association of an interest in any part of the common parts.

(2) In this section 'interest' does not include—

(a) a charge,[45] or

(b) an interest which arises by virtue of a charge.

Commonhold community statement

31 Form and content: general[46]

(1) A commonhold community statement is a document which makes provision in relation to specified land for—

(a) the rights and duties of the commonhold association, and

(b) the rights and duties of the unit-holders.

(2) A commonhold community statement must be in the prescribed form.[47]

(3) A commonhold community statement may—

(a) impose a duty on the commonhold association;

(b) impose a duty on a unit-holder;

(c) make provision about the taking of decisions in connection with the management of the commonhold or any other matter concerning it.

(4) Subsection (3) is subject to—

(a) any provision made by or by virtue of this Part, and

(b) any provision of the memorandum or articles of the commonhold association.

(5) In subsection (3)(a) and (b) 'duty' includes, in particular, a duty—

(a) to pay money;

(b) to undertake works;

(c) to grant access;

(d) to give notice;

(e) to refrain from entering into transactions of a specified kind in relation to a commonhold unit;

(f) to refrain from using the whole or part of a commonhold unit for a specified purpose or for anything other than a specified purpose;

(g) to refrain from undertaking works (including alterations) of a specified kind;

(h) to refrain from causing nuisance or annoyance;

(i) to refrain from specified behaviour;

(j) to indemnify the commonhold association or a unit-holder in respect of costs arising from the breach of a statutory requirement.

(6) Provision in a commonhold community statement imposing a duty to pay money (whether in pursuance of subsection (5)(a) or any other provision made by or by virtue

---

[45] For the restrictions on the commonhold association charging the common parts, see ss. 28, 29.

[46] For amendment of the commonhold community statement, see s. 33. For the operation of commonhold, see ss. 37–42; and for termination (both voluntary and by the court), see ss. 43–56.

[47] Commonhold Regulations 2004, reg. 15, Sch. 3. For an example, see Cowan, Driscoll and Target, *Commonhold Law and Practice*, Appendix B.

of this Part) may include provision for the payment of interest in the case of late payment.

(7) A duty conferred by a commonhold community statement on a commonhold association or a unit-holder shall not require any other formality.

(8) A commonhold community statement may not provide for the transfer or loss of an interest in land on the occurrence or non-occurrence of a specified event.

(9) Provision made by a commonhold community statement shall be of no effect to the extent that—

(a) it is prohibited by virtue of section 32,[48]

(b) it is inconsistent with any provision made by or by virtue of this Part,

(c) it is inconsistent with anything which is treated as included in the statement by virtue of section 32, or

(d) it is inconsistent with the memorandum or articles of association of the commonhold association.

Commonhold association[49]

34 Constitution

(1) A commonhold association is a private company limited by guarantee the memorandum of which—

(a) states that an object of the company is to exercise the functions of a commonhold association in relation to specified commonhold land, and

(b) specifies £1 as the amount required to be specified in pursuance of section 2(4) of the Companies Act 1985 (members' guarantee).

(2) Schedule 3 (which makes provision about the constitution of a commonhold association) shall have effect.

35 Duty to manage

(1) The directors of a commonhold association shall exercise their powers so as to permit or facilitate so far as possible—

(a) the exercise by each unit-holder of his rights, and

(b) the enjoyment by each unit-holder of the freehold estate in his unit.

(2) The directors of a commonhold association shall, in particular, use any right, power or procedure conferred or created by virtue of section 37[50] for the purpose of preventing, remedying or curtailing a failure on the part of a unit-holder to comply with a requirement or duty imposed on him by virtue of the commonhold community statement or a provision of this Part.

---

[48] S. 32 provides that Regulations shall make provisions about the content of a commonhold community statement': see Commonhold Regulations 2004, reg. 15, Sch. 3.

[49] Commonhold Regulations 2004, Part IV; Sch. 1 and 2.

[50] Enforcement of rights or duties imposed by (inter alia) the commonhold community statement, under powers to be provided by regulations; see Commonhold Regulations 2004, reg. 15, Sch. 3, section 4.11.

(3) But in respect of a particular failure on the part of a unit-holder (the 'defaulter') the directors of a commonhold association—

    (a) need not take action if they reasonably think that inaction is in the best interests of establishing or maintaining harmonious relationships between all the unit-holders, and that it will not cause any unit-holder (other than the defaulter) significant loss or significant disadvantage, and

    (b) shall have regard to the desirability of using arbitration, mediation or conciliation procedures (including referral under a scheme approved under section 42[51]) instead of legal proceedings wherever possible.

(4) A reference in this section to a unit-holder includes a reference to a tenant of a unit.

Miscellaneous

57 Multiple site commonholds

(1) A commonhold may include two or more parcels of land, whether or not contiguous.

(2) But section 1(1) of this Act is not satisfied in relation to land specified in the memorandum of association of a commonhold association unless a single commonhold community statement makes provision for all the land.

---

[51] An ombudsman scheme, to be approved by the Lord Chancellor. No scheme has yet been approved.

5

LEASES[1]

---

[1] C & B, pp. 36–37, chap. 10; Gray, part 4; M & W, paras 3.009–3.016, chaps 17–20; MM, chap. 9; Smith, chaps 18–20; Aldridge, *Leasehold Law*; Bright, *Landlord and Tenant Law Past Present and Future* (2006); Bright, *Landlord and Tenant Law in Context* (2007); Evans and Smith, *Law of Landlord and Tenant* (6th edn, 2002); *Hill and Redman's Law of Landlord and Tenant*; Hill and Redman: *Guide to Landlord and Tenant Law* (1999); Sparkes, *A New Landlord and Tenant* (2001); Woodfall, *Landlord and Tenant*.

The Law Commission has published numerous reports on the law of landlord and tenant: (a) The Obligations of Landlords and Tenants 1975 (Law Com No. 67); (b) Covenants Restricting Dispositions, Alterations and Change of User 1985 (Law Com No. 141); (1985) 135 NLJ 991, 1015 (P. F. Smith); (c) Forfeiture of Tenancies 1985 (Law Com No. 142); (d) Leasehold Conveyancing 1987 (Law Com No. 161); (e) Landlord and Tenant: Reform of the Law 1987 (Law Com No. 162, Cm 145) which reviews the law and identifies areas which require reform; (f) Privity of Contract and Estate 1988 (Law Com No. 174); (g) Compensation for Tenants' Improvements 1989 (Law Com No. 178); (h) Distress for Rent 1991 (Law Com No. 194); (i) Business Tenancies: A Periodic Review of the Landlord and Tenant Act 1954 Part II 1992 (Law Com No. 208); [1993] Conv 334 (M. Haley); (j) Implied Covenants for Title 1991 (Law Com No. 199); (k) Termination of Tenancies Bill 1994 (Law Com No. 221); (l) Responsibility for State and Condition of Property 1996 (Law Com No. 238); (m) Land, Valuation and Housing Tribunals 2003 (Law Com No. 281); (n) Renting Homes 2003 (Law Com No. 284; a 'narrative report'); (o) Renting Homes 2006 (Law Com No. 297); (p) Termination of Tenacies for Tenant Default 2006 (Law Com No. 303); (q) Housing: Proportionate Dispute Resolution 2008 (Law Com No. 309); (r) Housing: Encouraging Responsible Letting 2008 (Law Com No. 312).

Consultation papers have been published by
(a) the Lord Chancellor's Department on Distress for Rent 2001 (Cm 5096);
(b) the DTLR on Landlord and Tenant: Responsibility for State and Condition of Property (2001); and on Business Tenancies Legislation in England and Wales: The Government's Proposals for Reform (2001); [2002] Conv 261 (R. Hewitson). On the voluntary Code of Practice for Commercial Leases, see (2002) 152 NLJ 1033 (J. Keating);
(c) the Office of the Deputy Prime Minister on Commercial Property Leases (2004);
(d) the Department of the Environment on the Reform of the Caravan Sites Act 1968 (1992); [1993] Conv 39, 111 (G. Holgate); LTA 1954 Part II (1996); Residential Leasehold Reform (1999);
(e) the Department for Communities and Local Government on Tolerated Trespassers (2007).

Many cases on leases are reported only in the Property, Planning and Compensation Reports (until 1967, Planning and Compensation Reports; from 1968 until 1985, Property and Compensation Reports); the Estates Gazette (issued weekly); the Estates Gazette Digest (published annually until 1984) and (since 1985) the Estates Gazette Law Reports; Landlord and Tenant Reports (since 1998). Specialist periodicals are Landlord and Tenant Law Review (which began in 1997) and Rent Review and Lease Journal (1981).

I. GENERAL BACKGROUND

Other than the estate in fee simple absolute in possession, the only *legal* estate which can subsist after 1925 is the term of years absolute.[2] These two legal estates are different in nature, in that the former is a freehold, the latter a leasehold estate; the former, in other words, is held, theoretically, of a feudal superior by freehold tenure, the latter is held of the freeholder by leasehold tenure.[3] The two estates can therefore exist contemporaneously in one piece of land,[4] the fee simple being held by the freeholder.

It was essential for the feudal system of landholding that one person or a group of persons should be responsible for each piece of land; as freeholders they were protected, in the days before the action of trespass, by the Real Actions, the Writs of Right, Writs of Entry and the Possessory Assizes, all of which were available to, and only to, persons seised.[5] The leaseholder's position was not important to the feudal system, and he never received the protection of the Real Actions; his interest never became 'Real' property, and is, to the present day, personalty; he was never seised; he was originally left to his action on the covenant against his landlord, the freeholder, if he were evicted.[6]

Better remedies became available to the leaseholder as soon as remedies dependent on *possession,* as opposed to *seisin,* were developed in the King's Court. Trespass was such an action, and a leaseholder, being *possessed* of the land, could bring the writ of trespass, without being *seised.*[7] By the thirteenth century,[8] the action of trespass

---

[2] LPA 1925, s. 1(1); p. 327, below.

[3] See p. 12, above. The expressions 'term of years', 'lease' and 'tenancy' are for most practical purposes synonymous in the modern law: all refer to the relationship between a landlord (or 'lessor') and a tenant (or 'lessee').

[4] LPA 1925, s. 1(5).

[5] Maitland, *Forms of Action at Common Law,* pp. 20 et seq; Simpson, *A History of the Land Law* (2nd edn, 1986), pp. 25–46; M & W, paras 4.015–4.017.

[6] Pollock and Maitland, *History of English Law* (2nd edn, reissued 1968), vol. ii, pp. 106–117; Plucknett, *Concise History of the Common Law* (5th edn, 1956), pp. 570–574; Jouon des Longrais, *La Conception Anglaise de la Saisine,* pp. 141–148; Simpson, pp. 71–78.

[7] In the ordinary case of land being owned by A, the freeholder, and leased to B, the leaseholder, A is seised and B possessed of the land.

[8] Maitland, *Forms of Action,* p. 48; C & B, pp. 26–29.

quare clausum fregit was available to persons in possession of land and lay for damages against anyone who was guilty of unlawful physical interference with land. This was an improvement, but the leaseholder needed something more than damages; he needed an action by which he could recover his lease. This came with Ejectment at the end of the fifteenth century.[9] From that time a leaseholder has had a 'real' remedy; but leasehold property was already established as 'personalty' and it was too late then for it to become 'realty' for the purposes of the general law.

The tables were now turned on the freeholder. He had a 'real' remedy, but it was cumbrous and old-fashioned. The leaseholder now had a modern action for specific recovery, the action of Ejectment. Freeholders began to use this action by alleging a fictitious lease. This practice began in the sixteenth century, and continued until the abolition of the old Real Actions in the first half of the nineteenth century. A possession claim now lies in respect of any wrongful deprivation of possession of land.[10]

This chapter deals with some of the principles of the law relating to leases. Superimposed upon the general law is a large body of statutory material dealing with specialised topics. The general policy of these statutes is to limit the rent which a landlord can obtain, and restrict his right to recover possession of the premises at the end of the lease. The Leasehold Reform Act 1967 and the Leasehold Reform, Housing and Urban Development Act 1993 go further, and grant to certain long leaseholders of residential premises at low rents the right to acquire the freehold or an extended lease.[11] These statutes and books dealing with them must be consulted before a working knowledge of the law of leaseholds can be obtained; but lack of space forbids their treatment here.[12]

[9] *Trespass de ejectione firmae*: Pollock and Maitland, p. 109; Simpson, pp. 144–147; M & W, paras 4.018–4.022.

[10] Maitland, *Forms of Action*, pp. 57–60; C & B, p. 87; M & W, paras 4.026–4.028; Simpson, pp. 147–151. On the modern law, see pp. 422–424, below.

[11] C & B, pp. 363–375; see also p. 749, below.

[12] C & B, pp. 336–395; Gray, parts 4.6, 4.7; M & W, chap. 22; MM, pp. 580–619; Aldridge, *Leasehold Law*; Hill and Redman, *Law of Landlord and Tenant*; Woodfall, *Landlord and Tenant*. The main statutes are:

(a) *Agricultural Lettings*
 (i) Agricultural holdings before September 1995: Agricultural Holdings Act 1986.
 (ii) Farm business tenancies after August 1995: Agricultural Tenancies Act 1995.
 (iii) Agricultural tied accommodation. Rent (Agriculture) Act 1976.
Lennon, *Agricultural Law, Tax and Tenancies*; Muir Watt and Moss, *Agricultural Holdings* (14th edn, 1998); Rodgers, *Agricultural Law* (3rd edn, 2008); Scammell and Densham's *Law of Agricultural Holdings* (9th edn, 2007).

(b) *Business Tenancies.* Landlord and Tenant Act 1954, Part II as amended by Regulatory Reform (Business Tenancies) (England and Wales) Order 2003 (SI 2003 No 3096); (2004) 148 SJ 520, 565, 593, 617, 651, 679 (G. Webber); LPA 1969, Part I. Aldridge, *Letting Business Premises* (8th edn, 2004); *Lewison's Drafting Business Leases* (7th edn, 2006); *Ross on Commercial Leases* looseleaf edn; Tromans, *Commercial Leases* (2nd edn, 1996); Reynolds and Clark, *Renewal of Business Tenancies* (3rd edn, 2007); Williams and Brand, *Handbook of Business Tenancies*; Haley, *Statutory Regulation of Business Tenancies*.

(c) *Private Residential Lettings before 15 January 1989.* Rent Act 1977; Housing Act 1980; Rent (Amendment) Act 1985. Megarry, *Rent Acts* vols 1 and 2.

Office for National Statistics Social Trends 34 (2004 edn), pp. 152–154[13]

The increase in owner-occupation has been a notable feature of the past century. At the start of the 20th century, almost all dwellings in England, 89 per cent, were privately rented and only a small proportion, 10 per cent, were owner-occupied. The 1950s saw a period of growth in prosperity alongside initiatives to improve housebuilding; this was accompanied by deregulation in both planning and the building industry. Thus, owner-occupation increased from 29 per cent in 1951 to 45 per cent in 1964. Between 1981 and 2002 the number of owner-occupied dwellings in Great Britain increased by almost 43 per cent to reach 17.4 million, more than double the number of rented dwellings. During the same period the number of private rented dwellings increased by 5 per cent to 2.5 million and the number of dwellings rented in the social sector decreased by 23 per cent to 5.1 million.[14]

The growth in owner occupation since the early 1980s has in part been due to a number of schemes that aim to increase low-cost home ownership, such as the right to buy scheme. Owner occupation is lower in Scotland (64 per cent) than in either England or Wales (70 and 73 per cent, respectively). The only sector where there has been a decline in stock since 1981 is in dwellings rented from local authorities. This reflects large scale stock transfers to registered social landlords whose stock rose by 256 per cent during this period.

The Census provided a comprehensive picture of the type of tenure and accommodation. In April 2001, 81 per cent of households in England and Wales lived in a house or bungalow, with semi-detached and terraced being the most common type of dwelling. The type of accommodation varies by tenure. Owner occupiers are far more likely to live in houses than renters in either the social or private sectors. The proportion of those in shared ownership properties (part-rent part-buy) who lived in a house of bungalow was lower than for those who owned outright or with a mortgage. In contrast social sector renters were far more likely than owners to live in purpose-built flats. Those living in shared ownership properties were also more likely than other owner occupiers to live in a flat, although less likely to do so than social renters.

Tenure varies markedly according to the type of household. In 2001 lone parents with dependent children were far more likely than any other type of household to rent their property. While

(d) *Private Residential Lettings on and after 15 January 1989.* Housing Act 1988; *on and after 28 Feb. 1997* Housing Act 1996 Part III (assured tenancies and assured shorthold tenancies). Megarry, *Rent Acts,* vol. 3; Martin, *Residential Security* (2nd edn, 1996); Rodgers, *Housing Law;* Bridge, *Assured Tenancies* (1999).

(e) *Public Sector Housing (Secure Tenancies).* Housing Act 1985, Parts IV and V, Leasehold Reform, Housing and Urban Development Act 1993, Part II; Housing Act 1996, Part V; Housing Act 2004, Part 6. Hughes, *Public Sector Housing Law* (3rd edn, 2001).

(f) *Long Tenancies.* Landlord and Tenant Act 1954, Part I; Leasehold Reform Act 1967, Part I; Leasehold Reform Act 1979; Leasehold Reform, Housing and Urban Development Act 1993; Housing Act 1996, Part III; Commonhold and Leasehold Reform Act 2002. Barnes, *Leasehold Reform Act 1967; Hague on Leasehold Enfranchisement* (5th edn, 2008); Megarry, *Rent Acts,* chap. 13.

(g) *Mobile Homes.* Caravan Sites Act 1968, Part 1; Mobile Homes Act 1983. Brand, *Mobile Homes and the Law* (1986); Clayden, *The Law of Mobile Homes and Caravans* (2nd edn, 2003).

[13] The full report contains tables of statistical data, and is available on the National Statistics website: www.statistics.gov.uk.

[14] [This trend has continued: by 2006 the number of owner-occupied dwellings had reached 18.5 million; the number of private rented dwellings had reached 3 million, and in the social rented sector the number of homes rented from local authorities had fallen to 2.7 million, although 2.2 million were rented from registered social landlords: Social Trends 38 (2008 edn), pp. 137–138).]

only 34 per cent of lone parents with dependent children households lived in owner-occupier property, 46 per cent lived in accommodation rented from the social sector and 19 per cent rented privately. In contrast, 80 per cent of households comprising a couple with dependent children owned their own property and only 13 per cent rented from the social sector. Similarly, 81 per cent of pensioner households were owner occupiers, compared with only 58 per cent of lone pensioner households.

Owner occupation in the United Kingdom, at 71 per cent, is just above the average for all EU countries. In 2000 the highest rates of owner occupation in the EU were in Spain, Greece and Ireland, at over 80 per cent. Germany had the lowest level of owner occupation at just over 40 per cent. In all EU countries owner occupiers were more likely to live in a house than a flat. On average, 80 per cent of those living in a house in the EU were owner occupiers compared with only 38 per cent of those living in a flat. Tenure is also linked to economic activity status. At the time of the 2001 Census, over thee quarters of employed, self-employed and retired heads of household were owner occupiers. In contrast, less than a third of unemployed heads of household and just over a fifth of full-time students who were also in paid employment owned their own home, either outright or with a mortgage. Renting from a council was the most common form of tenure among those who were looking after a home or family, or those who were permanently sick or disabled. In contrast, less than a tenth of employed or self-employed heads of household rented from a council.

II. GENERAL CHARACTERISTICS

A. A LEASE MAY BE A LEGAL ESTATE

A lease may be a legal estate if it is a 'term of years absolute' within the meaning of section 1 of the Law of Property Act 1925, and as long as its creation fulfils the formality requirements prescribed by statute for the creation of a legal estate.[15] A lease which does not satisfy the definition of a term of years absolute, or which has not been created in the required form, may take effect as an equitable lease.[16]

LAW OF PROPERTY ACT 1925

1. Legal estates and equitable interests.—(1) The only estates in land which are capable of subsisting or of being conveyed or created at law are—

   (a) An estate in fee simple absolute in possession;[17]

   (b) A term of years absolute.

   (3) All other estates, interests, and charges in or over land take effect as equitable interests.

---

[15] Below, pp. 416–419. In the case of registered land, this can include the requirement that the lease be registered: LRA 1925, s. 27(1), (2)(b); above, p. 163; below, p. 418.

[16] Below, pp. 418–421.   [17] Chap. 4, above.

205. General definitions.—(1)...(xxvii) 'Term of years absolute' means a term of years (taking effect in possession or in reversion whether or not at a rent) with or without impeachment for waste,[18] subject or not to another legal estate, and either certain or liable to determination by notice, re-entry,[19] operation of law, or by a provision for cesser on redemption,[20] or in any other event (other than the dropping of a life, or the determination of a determinable life interest); but does not include any term of years determinable with life or lives or with the cesser of a determinable life interest,[21] nor, if created after the commencement of this Act, a term of years which is not expressed to take effect in possession within twenty-one years after the creation thereof where required by this Act to take effect within that period,[22] and in this definition the expression 'term of years' includes a term for less than a year,[23] or for a year or years and a fraction of a year or from year to year.

B. FIXED TERM LEASES, PERIODIC AND OTHER TENANCIES

A lease may take any one of a number of different forms. It may be for a single fixed period, usually a fixed number of years, although the period might equally well be (for example) a week or a month or a discontinuous succession of days or months.[24] On the other hand, it may be a tenancy at will or at sufferance; or a periodic tenancy (a tenancy which will continue from one period to another in succession until either party determines it); or even a tenancy 'by estoppel'. This section outlines the nature of such tenancies and particular rules relating to their creation and termination.

(i) Tenancies at will and at sufferance

Entry into possession as a tenant, or holding over with the landlord's consent after the expiration of the tenancy, creates a tenancy at will.[25] A tenant who holds over without the landlord's consent becomes a tenant at sufferance. There is a presumption that such tenancies expand to become periodic (weekly, monthly or yearly) tenancies where rent is paid and accepted, the length of the tenancy being related to the period in respect of which the rent is paid.[26]

---

[18] See C & B, p. 239, below.   [19] See p. 422, below.

[20] I.e., where a lease is used as the mechanism for a mortgage: see pp. 856–857, below. Mortgages by demise of *registered* land are no longer possible: p. 859, below.

[21] LPA 1925, s. 149(6); p. 366, below.   [22] Ibid., s. 149(3); p. 364, below.

[23] See *Re Land and Premises at Liss, Hants* [1971] Ch 986 at 991, per Goulding J; *Trustees of Henry Smith's Charity Trustees v Willson* [1983] QB 316 at 326–328, per Slade J.

[24] A 'discontinuous' lease, such as a timeshare lease: below, p. 358, n. 74. A 'term of years' within LPA 1925, s. 205(1)(xxvii), above, need not be defined by a period of *years*.

[25] It is occasionally created by express agreement: *Morgan v William Harrison Ltd* [1907] 2 Ch 137; *Manfield & Sons Ltd v Botchin* [1970] 2 QB 612; *Hagee (London) Ltd v A B Erikson and Larson* [1976] QB 209; *Cardiothoracic Institute v Shrewdcrest Ltd* [1986] 1 WLR 368; *Javad v Mohammed Aqil* [1991] 1 WLR 1007, p. 332, below; *Dean and Chapter of the Cathedral and Metropolitan Church of Canterbury v Whitbread plc* (1995) 72 P & CR 9.

[26] *Clayton v Blakey* (1798) 8 Term Rep 3; *Dougal v McCarthy* [1893] 1 QB 736; *Marcroft Wagons Ltd v Smith* [1951] 2 KB 496; *Longrigg, Burrough and Trounson v Smith* (1979) 251 EG 847; *Javad v Mohammed*

In **Wheeler v Mercer** [1957] AC 416 VISCOUNT SIMONDS said at 426:

It may, I think, be truly said that, since a tenant at will is regarded at law as being in possession by his own will and at the will, express or implied, of his landlord, he is a tenant by their mutual agreement.... He is distinguished from a tenant at sufferance in that such a tenant is said to be in possession without either the agreement or disagreement of the landlord.... A tenancy at will, though called a tenancy, is unlike any other tenancy except a tenancy at sufferance, to which it is next-of-kin. It has been properly described as a personal relation between the landlord and his tenant: it is determined by the death of either of them or by any one of a variety of acts, even by an involuntary alienation, which would not affect the subsistence of any other tenancy.[27]

In **Heslop v Burns** [1974] 1 WLR 1241 SCARMAN LJ said at 1253:

It may be that the tenancy at will can now serve only one legal purpose, and that is to protect the interests of an occupier during a period of transition. If one looks to the classic cases in which tenancies at will continue to be inferred, namely, the case of someone who goes into possession prior to a contract of purchase, or of someone who, with the consent of the landlord, holds over after the expiry of his lease,[28] one sees that in each there is a transitional period during which negotiations are being conducted touching the estate or interest in the land that has to be protected, and the tenancy at will is an apt legal mechanism to protect the occupier during such a period of transition: he is there and can keep out trespassers: he is there with the consent of the landlord and can keep out the landlord as long as that consent is maintained.

In **Ramnarace v Lutchman** [2001] 1 WLR 1651, LORD MILLETT, in delivering the judgment of the Privy Council on appeal from the Court of Appeal of Trinidad and Tobago, said:

16 A tenancy at will is of indefinite duration, but in all other respects it shares the characteristics of a tenancy. As Lord Templeman observed in *Street v Mountford* [1985] AC 809, 818

Aquil, below; *Dreamgate Properties Ltd v Arnot* (1998) 76 P & CR 25 (new tenancy not implied after expiry of lease; demand for rent computer generated and not result of conscious decision); *London Baggage Co (Charing Cross Ltd) v Railtrack plc* [2000] L & TR 439 (test of intention objective); *Walji v Mount Cook Land Ltd* [2002] 1 P & CR 13.

[27] Cf. the tolerated trespasser, who is a public sector tenant who remains in possession after the tenancy has been ended by a possession order, and pays for occupation, without the local authority taking any active steps to evict: *Burrows v Brent London Borough Council* [1996] 1 WLR 1448; *Newham LBC v Hawkins* [2005] 2 EGLR 51; (2003) 119 LQR 495 (S. Bright). He was described by Clarke LJ in *Pemberton v Southwark London Borough Council* [2000] 1 WLR 1672 at 1683 as 'a recent, somewhat bizarre, addition to the dramatis personae of the law', and the Housing and Regeneration Act 2008, s. 299, Sch. 11, Part 1, makes provisions designed to prevent the creation in future of tolerated trespassers, and to give a new tenancy to existing tolerated trespassers; [2009] Conv 1 (ed.).

[28] Under LTA 1730, s. 1, a tenant who wilfully holds over after demand made and written notice given for delivery up of possession, is liable to pay double the yearly value of the lands for the time the premises are detained: *French v Elliott* [1960] 1 WLR 40; *Dun & Bradstreet Software Services (England) Ltd v Provident Mutual Life Assurance Association* [1998] 2 EGLR 175. See also Distress for Rent Act 1737, s. 18; *Ballard (Kent) Ltd v Oliver Ashworth (Holdings) Ltd* [2000] Ch 12. LTA 1954 Part II (security of tenure, etc., for business tenancies) does not apply to a tenancy at will: *London Baggage Co (Charing Cross) Ltd v Railtrack (No 2)* [2003] 1 EGLR 141. For doubts whether HA 1985 Part IV (public sector secure tenancies), applies, see *Banjo v Brent LBC* [2005] 1 WLR 2520 at [25]–[26], [31]–[35], per Chadwick LJ, and [40]–[43], per Buxton LJ. However, the Rent Acts did apply to a tenancy at will, and some of the modern statutory codes which replaced them similarly apply: e.g. assured tenancies under HA 1988; Megarry, *Rent Acts*, vol. 1, p. 66; vol. 3, p. 72.

[p. 383 below], there can be no tenancy unless the occupier enjoys exclusive possession; but the converse is not necessarily true. An occupier who enjoys exclusive possession is not necessarily a tenant. He may be the freehold owner, a trespasser, a mortgagee in possession, an object of charity or a service occupier. Exclusive possession of land may be referable to a legal relationship other than a tenancy or to the absence of any legal relationship at all. A purchaser who is allowed into possession before completion and an occupier who remains in possession pending the exercise of an option each has in equity an immediate interest in the land to which his possession is ancillary. They are not tenants at will: see *Essex Plan Ltd v Broadminster* (1988) 56 P & CR 353, 356 per Hoffmann J.

17 A person cannot be a tenant at will where it appears from the surrounding circumstances that there was no intention to create legal relations. A tenancy is a legal relationship; it cannot be created by a transaction which is not intended to create legal relations. This provides a principled rationalisation of the statement of Denning LJ in *Facchini v Bryson* [1952] 1 TLR 1386, 1389 [p. 389, below,] on which the Court of Appeal relied in the present case. Before an occupier who is in exclusive occupation of land can be treated as holding under a licence and not a tenancy there must be something in the circumstances such as a family arrangement, an act of friendship or generosity or suchlike, to negative any intention to create legal relations.

18 In the present case the plaintiff was allowed into occupation of the land as part of a family arrangement and at least in part as an act of generosity. But not wholly so, for the plaintiff testified that the intention of the parties was that she would buy the land when she could afford to do so, and the judge accepted her evidence. Her uncle was generous in that he allowed her to remain indefinitely and rent-free pending her purchase, and in that he did not press her to negotiate. But a tenancy at will commonly arises where a person is allowed into possession while the parties negotiate the terms of a lease or purchase. He has no interest in the land to which his possession can be referred, and if in exclusive and rent-free possession is a tenant at will. In *Hagee (London) Ltd v AB Erikson and Larson* [1976] QB 209, 217, Scarman LJ described this as one of the 'classic circumstances' in which a tenancy at will arose.

19 Whether the parties intended to create legal relations, and whether there was any genuine intention on their part to negotiate a sale of the land when the plaintiff could afford to buy it, were questions of fact for the judge. Although he made no express findings in this regard, there was evidence which he accepted from which he could properly conclude that the plaintiff entered into possession as tenant at will.

(ii) Periodic tenancies

(a) Creation

Adler v Blackman
[1952] 2 All ER 41 (QBD, Ormerod J)[29]

Blackman had held shop premises under a weekly tenancy until December 1947, from which date the tenancy was changed to a yearly tenancy on the following terms: 'To

---

[29] Affirmed by CA (Somervell, Jenkins and Hodson LJJ) [1953] 1 QB 146, where the decision of Macnaghten J in *Covered Markets Ltd v Green* [1947] 2 All ER 140 was overruled.

hold for the term of one year… at the exclusive weekly rent of £3 payable weekly…'. After the expiration of the year, Blackman held over and Adler served on him a notice to quit, which was valid if he held a weekly, void if he held a yearly, tenancy. The notice to quit was first accepted by Blackman, whose first reaction was to claim compensation or a new lease under the Landlord and Tenant Act 1927. He subsequently claimed that the notice was invalid.

Held. Notice valid, as Blackman was a weekly tenant.

Ormerod J: The questions to be decided are: Was the tenant holding these premises as a tenant from year to year, in which case, of course, this notice was invalid, or was he holding them on a weekly tenancy, in which case admittedly the notice is good? Secondly, even if the notice was invalid, as the tenant elected to treat it as valid by taking proceedings under the Landlord and Tenant Act, 1927, can he now say that the notice was invalid and that he is entitled to remain in possession of the premises? So far as the first point is concerned, it is clearly established that, if a tenant holds over with the consent of the landlord at the expiration of a period reserved by a lease or tenancy agreement, an implied tenancy is set up, and the presumption is that that tenancy is a yearly tenancy on the terms of the instrument creating the original tenancy so far as they are consistent with a yearly tenancy, but that presumption may be rebutted by various circumstances including, of course, the terms of the agreement itself. I am asked by the landlord to say that the fact that the original tenancy was admittedly a weekly tenancy is a circumstance which should be taken into account in rebutting this presumption. The agreement for a tenancy for twelve months, in which the rent was expressed to be payable by the week and was calculated by the week and not by the year, says the landlord, is also a very strong circumstance to take into account. Further, he says that the conduct of the parties after the expiration of the period of tenancy, and, particularly, when the notice to quit was served by the landlord on the tenant, establishes beyond doubt the inference that the tenancy was not a tenancy from year to year….

In *Covered Markets Ltd v Green* [1947] 2 All ER 140 a tenant held over at the expiration of a tenancy for seven years at a rent of £3, payable weekly. Macnaghten J decided that the presumption was that the tenancy was a yearly one, and he saw no reason to rebut that presumption. He distinguished that case from Maugham J's decision on the ground that the premises were a fishmonger's shop, whereas the premises in [*Ladies' Hosiery & Underwear Ltd v Parker* [1930] 1 Ch 304] were merely a piece of ground. I find it difficult to appreciate the distinction, but Macnaghten J very clearly held that the proper inference from the circumstances was that there was a yearly tenancy on the termination of the seven years.

I have to consider whether in the present case there is a yearly tenancy or whether the circumstances are such that the presumption of a yearly tenancy has been rebutted and the tenant holds the premises on a weekly tenancy only. I have come to the conclusion that I ought to hold that the presumption has been rebutted and that the tenancy is a weekly one. I am not influenced by the situation before the agreement for a yearly tenancy was entered into. I do not think I ought to regard that as relevant to the consideration of the circumstances because it may well be that the parties decided that they would have the tenancy on an entirely new basis. There is no evidence about that one way or the other. The terms of the tenancy under the agreement were very different from the terms of the tenancy before it, including the rent, the terms relating to repairs, and so on, but I do take into consideration strongly the fact that the rent was expressed to be the rent of £3 per week and was never calculated by reference to a yearly sum. It was always paid weekly, and, after the term of the agreement had expired, it continued to be paid weekly right up to the time when the notice to quit was given.... The notice to quit was served on the basis that the tenancy was a weekly one, and was accepted without question by the tenant. Clearly the tenant's view was that he was holding on a weekly tenancy and not on a yearly tenancy, and I see no reason why that should not be taken into account in deciding whether the presumption of a yearly tenancy has been rebutted. Even if that were not the case, however, I think that, where as here, the original tenancy is not for a period of years, but is for only one year, and where the rent payable is expressed as a weekly sum and not by reference to a yearly rent, the presumption is rebutted that there is a yearly tenancy and the tenant must be taken to be holding over on the basis of a weekly tenancy on the terms of the agreement so far as they are consistent therewith. It follows that the notice was valid and the landlord is entitled to succeed in this action.

Ormerod J found it unnecessary to decide the second question. If it had been necessary to decide it, he would have held that the tenant, by claiming a new lease under the Landlord and Tenant Act 1927, had elected to accept the notice and could not now say that it was invalid.

In **Javad v Mohammed Aqil** [1991] 1 WLR 1007[30] the defendant was let into occupation of business premises owned by the plaintiff while negotiations proceeded for the grant to him of a 10-year lease. On three occasions he paid rent on a quarterly basis before negotiations broke down, and the plaintiff told him to leave. The question was whether the defendant was a tenant at will, in which case the notice to quit was valid, or whether he was a quarterly tenant, in which case he was protected under the Landlord and Tenant Act 1954 Part II. In holding that the defendant was a tenant at will, NICHOLLS LJ said at 1012:

A tenancy, or lease, is an interest in land. With exceptions immaterial for present purposes, a tenancy springs from a consensual arrangement between two parties: one person grants to another the right to possession of land for a lesser term than he, the grantor, has in the land. The extent of the right thus granted and accepted depends primarily upon the intention of the parties.

As with other consensually-based arrangements, parties frequently proceed with an arrangement whereby one person takes possession of another's land for payment without having agreed or directed their minds to one or more fundamental aspects of their transaction. In such cases the law, where appropriate, has to step in and fill the gaps in a way which is sensible and reasonable. The law will imply, from what was agreed and all the surrounding circumstances, the terms the parties are to be taken to have intended to apply. Thus if one party permits another to go into possession of his land on payment of a rent of so much per week or month, failing more the inference sensibly and reasonably to be drawn is that the parties intended that there should be a weekly or monthly tenancy. Likewise, if one party permits another to remain in possession after the expiration of his tenancy. But I emphasise the qualification: 'failing more.'

---

[30] (1990) 140 NLJ 1538 (H. W. Wilkinson); [1991] CLJ 232 (S. Bridge); *Brent London Borough Council v O'Bryan* [1993] 1 EGLR 59; *Walji v Mount Cook Land Ltd* [2002] 1 P & CR 13.

Frequently there will be more. Indeed, nowadays there normally will be other material surrounding circumstances. The simple situation is unlikely to arise often, not least because of the extent to which statute has intervened in landlord-tenant relationships. Where there is more than the simple situation, the inference sensibly and reasonably to be drawn will depend upon a fair consideration of all the circumstances, of which the payment of rent on a periodical basis is only one, albeit a very important one. This is so, however large or small may be the amount of the payment.

To this I add one observation, having in mind the facts of the present case. Where parties are negotiating the terms of a proposed lease, and the prospective tenant is let into possession or permitted to remain in possession in advance of, and in anticipation of, terms being agreed, the fact that the parties have not yet agreed terms will be a factor to be taken into account in ascertaining their intention. It will often be a weighty factor. Frequently in such cases a sum called 'rent' is paid at once in accordance with the terms of the proposed lease: for example, quarterly in advance. But, depending on all the circumstances, parties are not to be supposed thereby to have agreed that the prospective tenant shall be a quarterly tenant. They cannot sensibly be taken to have agreed that he shall have a periodic tenancy, with all the consequences flowing from that, at a time when they are still not agreed about the terms on which the prospective tenant shall have possession under the proposed lease, and when he has been permitted to go into possession or remain in possession merely as an interim measure in the expectation that all will be regulated and regularised in due course when terms are agreed and a formal lease granted.

Of course, when one party permits another to enter or remain upon his land on payment of a sum of money, and that other has no statutory entitlement to be there, almost inevitably there will be some consensual relationship between them. It may be no more than a licence determinable at any time, or a tenancy at will. But when and so long as such parties are in the throes of negotiating larger terms, caution must be exercised before inferring or imputing to the parties an intention to give to the occupant more than a very limited interest, be it licence or tenancy. Otherwise the court would be in danger of inferring or imputing from conduct, such as payment of rent and the carrying out of repairs, whose explanation lies in the parties' expectation that they will be able to reach agreement on the large terms, an intention to grant a lesser interest, such as a periodic tenancy, which the parties never had in contemplation at all.

(b) Terms

Where a tenant obtains a yearly (or other periodic) tenancy by entry followed by payment of rent in pursuance of an agreement to grant a lease or of a purported grant which is void for lack of formality, the terms of the tenancy include such of those of the void grant as are consistent with a tenancy for the period in question.[31]

---

[31] *Doe d Rigge v Bell* (1793) 5 Term Rep 471; *Doe d Thomson v Amey* (1840) 12 Ad & El 476; C & B, p. 217; M & W, para. 17.066; MM, pp. 347–348.

(c) Termination of periodic joint tenancy

Hammersmith and Fulham London Borough Council v Monk[32]
[1992] 1 AC 478 (HL, **Lords Bridge of Harwich, Brandon of Oakbrook, Ackner, Jauncey of Tullichettle** and **Browne-Wilkinson**)[33]

Lord Bridge of Harwich. My Lords, the issue in this appeal is whether a periodic tenancy held by two or more tenants jointly can be brought to an end by a notice to quit by one of the joint tenants without the consent of the others....

...[B]efore examining the relevant authorities I think it helpful to consider whether the application of first principles suggests the answer to the question at issue. For a large part of this century there have been many categories of tenancy of property occupied for agricultural, residential and commercial purposes where the legislature has intervened to confer upon tenants extra-contractual rights entitling them to continue in occupation without the consent of the landlord, either after the expiry of a contractual lease for a fixed term or after notice to quit given by the landlord to determine a contractual periodic tenancy. It is primarily in relation to joint tenancies in these categories that the question whether or not notice to quit given by one of the joint tenants can determine the tenancy is of practical importance, particularly where, as in the instant case, the effect of the determination will be to deprive the other joint tenant of statutory protection. This may appear an untoward result and may consequently provoke a certain reluctance to hold that the law can permit one of two joint tenants unilaterally to deprive his co-tenant of 'rights' which both are equally entitled to enjoy. But the statutory consequences are in truth of no relevance to the question which your Lordships have to decide. That question is whether, at common law, a contractual periodic tenancy granted to two or more joint tenants is incapable of termination by a tenant's notice to quit unless it is served with the concurrence of all the joint tenants. That is the proposition which the appellant must establish in order to succeed.

As a matter of principle I see no reason why this question should receive any different answer in the context of the contractual relationship of landlord and tenant than that which it would receive in any other contractual context. If A and B contract with C on terms which are to continue in operation for one year in the first place and thereafter from year to year unless determined by notice at the end of the first or any subsequent year, neither A nor B has bound himself contractually for longer than one year. To hold that A could not determine the contract at the end of any year without the concurrence of B and vice versa would presuppose that each had assumed a potentially irrevocable contractual obligation for the duration of their joint lives, which, whatever the nature of the contractual obligations undertaken, would be such an improbable intention to impute to the parties that nothing less than the clearest express

---

[32] For discussion of possible challenges to the rule in *Hammersmith v Monk* based on the European Convention on Human Rights, see [2005] Conv 123 (I. Loveland); *Bradney v Birmingham City Council* [2004] HLR 27; *Harrow LBC v Qazi* [2004] 1 AC 983; (2004) 120 LQR 398 (S. Bright); *McCann v United Kingdom* [2008] 2 EGLR 45 (held by European Court of Human Rights that art. 8 (right to respect for a person's home) was violated by notice to quit and possession proceedings by public authority landlord against one joint tenant where the other joint tenant (his wife) signed notice terminating tenancy without realizing that it would extinguish the husband's right to live in the house). For the Law Commission's proposals in this respect in relation to residential leases and licenses ('occupation contracts'), see Renting Homes 2006 (Law Com No. 297), paras 4.84–4.103; (2008) 11 JHL 81 (M. Partington).

[33] [1992] Conv 279 (S. Goulding); CLJ 218 (L. Tee); 108 LQR 375 (J. Dewar).

contractual language would suffice to manifest it. Hence, in any ordinary agreement for an initial term which is to continue for successive terms unless determined by notice, the obvious inference is that the agreement is intended to continue beyond the initial term only if and so long as all parties to the agreement are willing that it should do so. In a common law situation, where parties are free to contract as they wish and are bound only so far as they have agreed to be bound, this leads to the only sensible result.

Thus the application of ordinary contractual principles leads me to expect that a periodic tenancy granted to two or more joint tenants must be terminable at common law by an appropriate notice to quit given by any one of them whether or not the others are prepared to concur. But I turn now to the authorities to see whether there is any principle of the English law of real property and peculiar to the contractual relationship of landlord and tenant which refutes that expectation or whether the authorities confirm it. A useful starting point is the following passage from *Blackstone's Commentaries,* Book II (1766), ch. 9, pp. 145–147:

His Lordship read the passage and continued:

Hence, from the earliest times a yearly tenancy has been an estate which continued only so long as it was the will of both parties that it should continue, albeit that either party could only signify his unwillingness that the tenancy should continue beyond the end of any year by giving the appropriate advance notice to that effect. Applying this principle to the case of a yearly tenancy where either the lessor's or the lessee's interest is held jointly by two or more parties, logic seems to me to dictate the conclusion that the will of the joint parties is necessary to the continuance of the interest.

In *Doe d Aslin v Summersett* (1830) 1 B & Ad 135, the freehold interest in land let on a yearly tenancy was vested jointly in four executors of a will to whom the land had been jointly devised. Three only of the executors gave notice to the tenant to quit. It was held by the Court of King's Bench that the notice was effective to determine the tenancy. Delivering the judgment, Lord Tenterden CJ said, at pp. 140–141:

> 'Upon a joint demise by joint tenants upon a tenancy from year to year, the true character of the tenancy is this, not that the tenant holds of each the share of each so long as he and each shall please, but that he holds the *whole* of *all* so long as he *and all* shall please; and as soon as any one of the joint tenants gives a notice to quit, he effectually puts an end to *that* tenancy; the tenant has a right upon such a notice to give up *the whole,* and unless he comes to a new arrangement with the other joint tenants as to their shares, he is compellable so to do. The hardship upon the tenant, if he were not entitled to treat a notice from one as putting an end to the tenancy as to the whole, is obvious; for however willing a man might be to be sole tenant of an estate, it is not very likely he should be willing to hold undivided shares of it; and if upon such a notice the tenant is entitled to treat it as putting an end to the tenancy as to the whole, the other joint tenants must have the same right. It cannot be optional on one side, and on one side only.' ...

There are three principal strands in the argument advanced for the appellant. First, reliance is placed on the judgment in *Gandy v Jubber* (1865) 9 B & S 15, for the proposition that a tenancy from year to year, however long it continues, is a single term, not a series of separate lettings. ...

The passage relied on reads, at p. 18:

> 'There frequently is an actual demise from year to year so long as both parties please. The nature of this tenancy is discussed in 4 Bac. Abr. tit. Leases and Terms for Years, pp. 838, 839, 7th edn; and

this article has always been deemed of the highest authority being said to be the work of Gilbert CB. It seems clear that the learned author considered that the true nature of such a tenancy is that it is a lease for two years certain, and that every year after it is a springing interest arising upon the first contract and parcel of it, so that if the lessee occupies for a number of years, these years by computation from time past, make an entire lease for so many years, and that after the commencement of each new year it becomes an entire lease certain for the years past and also for the year so entered on, and that it is not a reletting at the commencement of the third and subsequent years. We think this is the true nature of a tenancy from year to year created by express words, and that there is not in contemplation of law a recommencing or reletting at the beginning of each year.'

It must follow from this principle, Mr Reid submits, that the determination of a periodic tenancy by notice is in all respects analogous to the determination of a lease for a fixed term in the exercise of a break clause, which in the case of joint lessees clearly requires the concurrence of all. But reference to the passage from *Bacon's Abridgment,* 7th edn, vol. IV, p. 839, on which the reasoning is founded shows that this analogy is not valid....

Thus the fact that the law regards a tenancy from year to year which has continued for a number of years, considered retrospectively, as a single term in no way affects the principle that continuation beyond the end of each year depends on the will of the parties that it should continue or that, considered prospectively, the tenancy continues no further than the parties have already impliedly agreed upon by their omission to serve notice to quit.

The second submission for the appellant is that, whatever the law may have been before the enactment of the Law of Property Act 1925, the effect of that statute, whereby a legal estate in land vested in joint tenants is held on trust for sale for the parties beneficially entitled, coupled with the principle that trustees must act unanimously in dealing with trust property, is to reverse the decision in *Summersett's* case and to prevent one of two joint tenants determining a periodic tenancy without the concurrence of the other. It is unnecessary to consider the position where the parties beneficially entitled are different from those who hold the legal interest. But where, as here, two joint tenants of a periodic tenancy hold both the legal and the beneficial interest, the existence of a trust for sale can make no difference to the principles applicable to the termination of the tenancy. At any given moment the extent of the interest to which the trust relates extends no further than the end of the period of the tenancy which will next expire on a date for which it is still possible to give notice to quit. If before 1925 the implied consent of both joint tenants, signified by the omission to give notice to quit, was necessary to extend the tenancy from one period to the next, precisely the same applies since 1925 to the extension by the joint trustee beneficiaries of the periodic tenancy which is the subject of the trust.[34]

Finally, it is said that all positive dealings with a joint tenancy require the concurrence of all joint tenants if they are to be effective. Thus, a single joint tenant cannot exercise a break clause in a lease,[35] surrender the term, make a disclaimer, exercise an option to renew the term or apply for relief from forfeiture.[36] All these positive acts which joint tenants must concur in performing are said to afford analogies with the service of notice to determine a periodic tenancy which is likewise a positive act. But this is to confuse the form with the substance. The action of giving

---

[34] The position is not changed by TLATA 1996, s. 11, p. 526, below. The giving of a notice is not an exercise of any *function* relating to land subject to the trust: *Notting Hill Housing Trust v Brackley* [2001] 3 EGLR 11; [2004] Conv 370 (S. Pascoe). Nor is the failure to consult a breach of trust: *Crawley Borough Council v Ure* [1996] QB 13.

[35] *Hounslow London Borough Council v Pilling* [1993] 1 WLR 1242.

[36] On the unilateral grant of a tenancy, see [2000] Conv 208 (L. Fox).

notice to determine a periodic tenancy is in form positive; but both on authority and on the principle so aptly summed up in the pithy Scottish phrase 'tacit relocation' the substance of the matter is that it is by his omission to give notice of termination that each party signifies the necessary positive assent to the extension of the term for a further period.

For all these reasons I agree with the Court of Appeal that, unless the terms of the tenancy agreement otherwise provide, notice to quit given by one joint tenant without the concurrence of any other joint tenant is effective to determine a periodic tenancy.

(iii) Tenancy by estoppel[37]

If a person purports to grant a lease of land of which he has no estate, both parties may be estopped from denying that a tenancy exists.

(a) Nature, effects and termination of tenancy by estoppel

In **Webb v Austin** (1844) 7 Man & G 701, 135 ER 282, Tindal CJ said at 724, at 291:

The doctrine on this subject, as it has been generally understood by the profession, may be collected from Mr Preston's Treatise on Abstracts vol. ii, p. 210, and the authorities there cited. That general understanding appears to be, that 'An indenture of lease, or a fine sur concessit, for years, will be an estoppel only during the term. It first operates by way of estoppel, and finally, when the grantor obtains an ownership, it attaches on the seisin and creates an interest, or produces the relation of landlord and tenant; and there is a term commencing by estoppel, but for all purposes it becomes an estate or interest. It binds the estate of the lessor, &c., and therefore continues in force against the lessor, his heirs, &c. It also binds the assigns of the lessor and of the lessee'.

In **Bruton v London & Quadrant Housing Trust** [2000] 1 AC 406, Lord Hoffmann said at 416:

[T]he estoppel arises when one or other of the parties wants to deny one of the ordinary incidents or obligations of the tenancy on the ground that the landlord had no legal estate. The basis of the estoppel is that having entered into an agreement which constitutes a lease or tenancy, he cannot repudiate that incident or obligation.

Industrial Properties (Barton Hill) Ltd v Associated Electrical Industries Ltd
[1977] QB 580 (CA, **Lord Denning MR, Roskill** and **Lawton LJJ**)[38]

Lord Denning MR: In the course of the discussion we were referred to many authorities, old and new. I have considered them all[39]—and others, too—but the result can be stated thus: If a

---

[37] Spencer Bower and Turner, *Estoppel by Representation* (4th edn, 2004), paras IX.3.1-IX.3.32; C & B, pp. 217–219; M & W, paras 17.095–17.102; MM, pp. 352–353; (1964) 80 LQR 370 (A. M. Prichard). A tenant by estoppel of business premises is entitled to the protection of L & TA 1954: *Bell v General Accident Fire & Life Assurance Corpn Ltd* [1998] 1 EGLR 69.

[38] The facts are stated at p. 31, above. (1977) 40 MLR 718 (P. Jackson); [1978] Conv 137 (J. Martin).

[39] His Lordship approved *Cuthbertson v Irving* (1859) 4 H & N 742; affd (1860) 6 H & N 135, and overruled *Harrison v Wells* [1967] 1 QB 263, on the ground that it was decided per incuriam.

landlord lets a tenant into possession under a lease, then, so long as the tenant remains in possession *undisturbed by any adverse claim*—then the tenant cannot dispute the landlord's title. Suppose the tenant (not having been disturbed) goes out of possession and the landlord sues the tenant on the covenant for rent or for breach of covenant to repair or to yield up in repair. The tenant cannot say to the landlord: 'You are not the true owner of the property.' Likewise, if the landlord, on the tenant's holding over, sues him for possession or for use and occupation or mesne profits, the tenant cannot defend himself by saying: 'The property does not belong to you, but to another.'

But if the tenant is disturbed *by being evicted by title paramount or the equivalent* of it, then he can dispute the landlord's title. Suppose the tenant is actually turned out by the third person—or if the tenant, without going out, acknowledges the title of the third person by attorning to him—or the tenant contests the landlord's claim on an indemnity from the third person—or there is anything else done which is equivalent to an eviction by title paramount then the tenant is no longer estopped from denying the landlord's title: see *Wilson v Anderton* (1830) 1 B & Ad 450 at 457, per Littledale J. The tenant, being thus disturbed in his possession, can say to the landlord: 'You were not truly the owner at the time when you demanded and received the rent from me. I am liable to pay mesne profits to this other man. So you must repay me the rent which I overpaid you. Nor am I liable to you on the covenants during the time you were not the owner.' See *Newsome v Graham* (1829) 10 B & C 234, *Mountnoy v Collier* (1853) 1 E & B 630 and *Watson v Lane* (1856) 11 Exch 769. The tenant can also claim damages for the eviction if there is, as here, an express covenant for quiet enjoyment covering interruption by title paramount.

Short of eviction by title paramount, or its equivalent, however, the tenant is estopped from denying the title of the landlord. It is no good his saying: 'The property does not belong to you but to a third person' unless that third person actually comes forward and successfully makes an adverse claim—by process in the courts or by the tenant's attornment; or acknowledgment of it as by the tenant defending on an indemnity. If the third person, for some reason or other, makes no adverse claim or is debarred from making it, the tenant remains estopped from denying the landlord's title. This is manifestly correct: for, without an adverse claim, it would mean that the tenant would be enabled to keep the property without paying any rent to anybody or performing any covenants. That cannot be right. That was the reasoning adopted by the Court of Queen's Bench in *Biddle v Bond* (1865) 6 B & S 225, a case of a bailor and bailee, but the court treated it as the same as landlord *v* tenant....

In the present case the tenants, A.E.I., are not subject to any adverse claim whatever. The lessor to A.E.I. was the plaintiff company which was the equitable owner. The legal owners were the Parker trustees. They were also the directors and shareholders of the plaintiff company. They acquiesced in the lease being made by the plaintiff company to A.E.I. They could not by any possibility make any adverse claim against A.E.I. on their own account. Not only that. They have actually come in as plaintiffs in these proceedings jointly with the plaintiff company—so as to make sure that the benefit of these proceedings goes to the plaintiff company only.

Seeing that A.E.I. are absolved from any adverse claim by the legal owners, it is a very proper case for the doctrine of tenancy by estoppel. A.E.I. have had the full benefit of the lease for the stipulated term of years. They should perform the covenants—or pay damages in lieu—to the only persons entitled to sue them, namely, the plaintiff company. Even though A.E.I. have gone out of possession, they cannot avoid their responsibilities by reliance on a technical rule of law—which on investigation is found to be groundless.

National Westminster Bank Ltd v Hart
[1983] QB 773 (CA, **Waller LJ** and **Sir David Cairns**)[40]

42 Haggard Road, Twickenham, was let under a 99 year lease expiring in 1967. In 1921 Cowles acquired the residue of the lease, and in 1947 sub-let the house to Mr and Mrs Hart. The sub-lease expired in 1965. Thereafter the Harts continued to pay rent to Cowles until 1978, when, on the death of Cowles, they claimed that Cowles's title had expired in 1967. They refused to pay rent to Cowles's executor, the plaintiff bank, until it proved title. In the county court the plaintiff recovered arrears of rent on the ground that the Harts were estopped from denying its title, since there was no third party claim to a better title.

Held (reversing the county court judge). The Harts were not estopped from denying the bank's title.

Waller LJ: The defendants submit that they became tenants of this house before 1965, at which time they became tenants of the Cowles, and that the Cowles made no communication to them in 1967 when the headlease expired. The defendants cannot be estopped by the fact that they paid rent from March 1967 until August 1978, because they did not know the facts, and the Cowles did not tell them. They submit that neither the Cowles nor their personal representatives have title to 42, Haggard Road. They rely on *Fenner v Duplock* (1824) 2 Bing 10 and *Serjeant v Nash, Field & Co* [1903] 2 KB 304, and submit that the judge was in error in his conclusions.

The bank submit that the defendants are not entitled to succeed because they are unable to prove an adverse claim by a third party. They rely on *Carlton v Bowcock* (1884) 51 LT 659 and *Hindle v Hick Bros Manufacturing Co Ltd* [1947] 2 All ER 825.

The judge, being of opinion that the reasoning in *Carlton's* case and *Hindle's* case was inconsistent with *Fenner's* case and *Serjeant's* case, preferred *Carlton* and *Hindle,* and since there was no adverse claim by a third party on the facts of this case, gave judgment for the bank....

Can the reasoning of these two lines of cases be reconciled? The bank submit that they are not inconsistent because in *Fenner v Duplock,* and in *Serjeant v Nash, Field & Co* although in neither case did the judges mention it, there was in each case a third party claimant. There was in each case a possible third party claimant, but in my judgment the existence of such a person was not regarded by the judge as important. In *Fenner's* case, Best CJ, having said that a tenant may show that his title has expired, said, at 11, that the rule was founded on good sense, 'because if it were otherwise, the tenant might be called on to pay his rent twice over.' And in *Serjeant v Nash, Field & Co* the observations of each member of the court were quite specific, and I cannot believe that the necessity would have gone unmentioned by each member of the court if it was regarded as a requirement.

Mr Parker, on behalf of the defendants, submits that the decisions are quite consistent because when considering estoppel there is a great difference between the case of the landlord's title determining without informing a tenant so that the tenant in ignorance continues to pay rent, and the case of the landlord assigning his interest and the tenant, aware that there has been an assignment, paying rent to the assignee. In the latter case he is on notice that there has been a change of landlord and it is for him to decide whether to pay his rent to the assignee or not. If he does, he cannot be heard to complain about the assignee's title unless there is somebody else

[40] [1984] Conv 64 (J. W. Price).

claiming title. It is clear from the care with which Cave J set out the receipts in his judgment
that he regarded them as important because they gave notice of the change. In the former case
of the landlord's title determining, the tenant does not know because nothing has happened to
give him notice of the change. There can be no estoppel unless the tenant knows the facts or he
has had notice which should have warned him.

As Mr Parker pointed out, there is a logical difference between the assignee and the landlord
whose title has determined. When the tenant has freely entered into a tenancy agreement with
the landlord and has as a consequence entered into possession, so long as he is in possession he
is estopped from denying his landlord's title. However, the tenant whose landlord has assigned
the tenancy and he, with notice, has accepted the assignee, cannot challenge the assignee's title
unless there is a third party claiming to be the landlord.

Finally, in the case of the landlord whose title has determined and who has not informed the
tenant:

> 'It is clear law that though a tenant cannot deny the title of his landlord to deal with the premises, he
> may prove that the title has determined.' (See per Sir Richard Henn Collins MR in *Serjeant's* case
> [1903] 2 KB 304, 312.)

In the present case in my opinion if the Cowles had told the defendants in 1967 that title had
determined, the tenants would have been under no obligation to pay rent to them. The Cowles
not having disclosed the fact that their title had determined, the defendants cannot now be
estopped from relying on the determination. I have come to the conclusion that the defendants
are not liable to pay rent to the bank, and I would allow this appeal.

Sir David Cairns: I would add that it seems to me that the bank in this case might have contended
that they and their predecessors had been in possession of the rents and profits for more than
12 years, paying no rent and in no way recognising the rights of whoever may have been the
freeholder, and that in that way they might have acquired a possessory title. But no such case
was open to them on the pleadings, nor discussed in the court below.

(b) Feeding the estoppel

If, after creating a tenancy by estoppel, the owner/lessor acquires the legal estate, for
example, where he purchases the fee simple, the effect is to 'feed' the estoppel; the
lessee then at once acquires a legal lease and ceases to rely on the estoppel.

Suppose that P agrees to purchase a house from V and is let into possession by
V before completion of the purchase. He grants a lease of the house to T, and, later
on completion, mortgages the house to M in order to raise the purchase price. The
question arises whether the lease (which, until it is fed by completion of the purchase,
is only a lease by estoppel) is binding on M. It is common practice for the conveyance
of the house by V to P and the mortgage by P to M to be executed simultaneously.
It is now settled that there is no *scintilla temporis* between the conveyance and the
mortgage, which would enable a legal lease to be acquired by T and so take priority
over M's mortgage.

This was decided by the House of Lords in **Abbey National Building Society v
Cann** [1991] 1 AC 56, p. 214, above,[41] where it was held that there was no possibility of

---

[41]   (1992) 108 LQR 380 (G. Goldberg).

a prior equitable interest gaining priority over such a mortgage through the doctrine of feeding the estoppel. Lord OLIVER OF AYLMERTON said at 89:

It is argued, however, that because the creation of a charge on property in favour of the society necessarily posits that the chargor has acquired an interest out of which the charge can be created, there must notionally be a point of time at which the estate vested in him free from the charge and in which the estoppel affecting him could be 'fed' by the acquisition of the legal estate so as to become binding on and take priority over the interest of the chargee. This is a puzzling problem upon which it is not easy to reconcile the authorities.

The appellants rely upon the decision of the Court of Appeal in *Church of England Building Society v Piskor* [1954] Ch 553, a case concerned with unregistered conveyancing.... On the other side of the line are *Re Connolly Bros Ltd (No 2)* [1912] 2 Ch 25 and *Security Trust Co v Royal Bank of Canada* [1976] AC 503 ...

One is therefore presented with a stark choice between them. Of course, as a matter of legal theory, a person cannot charge a legal estate that he does not have, so that there is an attractive legal logic in the ratio in *Piskor's* case. Nevertheless, I cannot help feeling that it flies in the face of reality. The reality is that, in the vast majority of cases, the acquisition of the legal estate and the charge are not only precisely simultaneous but indissolubly bound together. The acquisition of the legal estate is entirely dependent upon the provision of funds which will have been provided before the conveyance can take effect and which are provided only against an agreement that the estate will be charged to secure them. Indeed, in many, if not most, cases of building society mortgages, there will have been, as there was in this case, a formal offer of acceptance of an advance which will ripen into a specifically enforceable agreement immediately the funds are advanced which will normally be a day or more before completion. In many, if not most, cases, the charge itself will have been executed before the execution, let alone the exchange, of the conveyance or transfer of the property. This is given particular point in the case of registered land where the vesting of the estate is made to depend upon registration, for it may well be that the transfer and the charge will be lodged for registration on different days so that the charge, when registered, may actually take effect from a date prior in time to the date from which the registration of the transfer takes effect: see section 27(3) of the Act of 1925 and the Land Registration Rules 1925, rule 83(2). Indeed, under rule 81 of the Rules of 1925, the registrar is entitled to register the charge even before registration of the transfer to the chargor if he is satisfied that both are entitled to be registered. The reality is that the purchaser of land who relies upon a building society or bank loan for the completion of his purchase never in fact acquires anything but an equity of redemption, for the land is, from the very inception, charged with the amount of the loan without which it could never have been transferred at all and it was never intended that it should be otherwise. The 'scintilla temporis' is no more than a legal artifice and, for my part, I would adopt the reasoning of the Court of Appeal in *Re Connolly Bros Ltd* and of Harman J in *Coventry Permanent Economic Building Society v Jones* [1951] 1 All ER 901 and hold that *Piskor's* case was wrongly decided. It follows, in my judgment, that Mrs Cann can derive no assistance from this line of argument.[42]

---

[42] *Walthamstow Building Society v Davies* (1989) 60 P & CR 99 (where mortgagee took a second charge to replace a first charge, held no scintilla temporis between discharge of first and creation of second charge during which unauthorised tenancy granted by mortgagor became binding on mortgagee).

The doctrine also applies in registered land: *First National Bank plc v Thompson* [1996] Ch 231 (creation of charge of registered land); (1995) 139 SJ 1040 (P. Cowell); [1996] All ER Rev 253 (P. J. Clarke).

C. MULTIPLE AND CONCURRENT LEASES

There may be several leasehold estates in the same parcel of land. The freeholder may grant a lease to T1, who may in turn grant a lease (often referred to as a 'sub-lease', and which must be for a term which is no longer than T1's own estate) to T2, and T2 may in turn grant a lease to T3, and so on.

When a landlord grants a lease, and then later grants another lease of the same land (for more or less than the period of the first lease), there are concurrent leases, and he is said to have granted a lease of the reversion.[43] This creates the relationship of landlord and tenant between the first and second lessees; the second lessee does not need to go into possession,[44] but, by virtue of his legal estate, he can as reversioner claim rent, distrain, and enforce covenants. This is so, even if the second lease is for a term shorter than the first one.[45] If his lease continues after the end of the first lease, he is entitled to possession when the first lease terminates.

LAW OF PROPERTY ACT 1925

149. Abolition of interesse termini, and as to reversionary leases and leases for lives.—(5) Nothing in this Act affects the rule of law that a legal term, whether or not being a mortgage term, may be created to take effect in reversion expectant on a longer term, which rule is hereby confirmed.

In **Re Moore and Hulm's Contract** [1912] 2 Ch 105, leaseholds were mortgaged by sub-demise for the residue of the original term less one day. Afterwards by another mortgage they were sub-demised to a second mortgagee (Worrell) for the same period, subject to the first mortgage. The second mortgage was paid off during the continuance of the first mortgage and the deed effecting the second mortgage was handed back to the mortgagor. A purchaser of the leaseholds from the mortgagor declined to complete without a formal surrender being obtained of the term created by the second mortgage. JOYCE J held that a surrender was necessary and said at 109:

[Counsel for the vendor] says, first, that there was no necessity or reason for Worrell, the second mortgagee, to surrender the term granted to him by the second mortgage because no legal term or interest passed to him. Bearing in mind, however, the cases cited to me by [counsel for the purchaser], I think that a legal estate or interest did pass to the second mortgagee. I think that Worrell acquired a legal reversion upon the term created by the first mortgage. I think that he got a legal term under his mortgage. If the money secured by the earlier mortgage had been paid to the first mortgagee on the date fixed for payment I think that the second mortgagee would have had a right to the actual possession of the leasehold premises,[46] and if the lease granted by the first mortgage had been terminated in any manner during the continuance of the second mortgage, the second mortgagee would have been entitled to possession for the rest of

---

[43] Distinguish a reversionary lease: p. 364, n. 77, below.

[44] LPA 1925, s. 149(2); p. 364, below.

[45] *Neale v Mackenzie* (1836) 1 M & W 747; *Re Moore and Hulm's Contract* [1912] 2 Ch 105, below.

[46] For a mortgagee's right to possession, see p. 928, below.

the term created by his mortgage. Therefore I think that the argument for the vendor on the first point fails.

D. CONTRACTUAL NATURE OF A LEASE

A lease is not only an estate; it is also a contract between landlord and tenant. In recent years the courts have emphasised the contractual nature of a lease and in some cases have applied contractual rules, for example, the doctrines of frustration and repudiation.[47]

'A lease is a hybrid, part contract, part property'.[48] In the controversial case of *Bruton v London & Quadrant Housing Trust* [2000] 1 AC 406, p. 348 below, the House of Lords has created a hybrid within a hybrid. An agreement with an occupant by an owner which had the capacity but not the power to grant a lease was held to create a lease as between the parties without creating any property relationship so as to bind third parties.[49]

In **Hussein v Mehlman** [1992] 2 EGLR 87,[50] Mehlman granted to the plaintiff tenants a three-year assured shorthold tenancy of 27 Kenneth Crescent, Brent, London. The

[47] *Hussein v Mehlman* [1992] 2 EGLR 87, below (repudiation); *National Carriers Ltd v Panalpina (Northern) Ltd* [1981] AC 675 (frustration); cf. *Graves v Graves* [2008] HLR 10 (CA held implied condition, so not necessary to consider whether judge correct to hold assured shorthold tenancy void for mistake or discharged by frustration); [2008] Conv 70 (J. Brown). See also *Killick v Roberts* [1991] 1 WLR 1146 (rescission for fraud), [1992] Conv 269 (J. Martin); [1992] CLJ 21 (L. Tee); cf. *Islington London Borough Council v Uckac* [2006] 1 WLR 1303 (remedy of rescission of secure tenancy excluded by HA 1985, ss. 82, 84); [2008] Conv 81 (J. Morgan); *Liverpool City Council v Irwin* [1977] AC 239 (implied terms). The Unfair Contract Terms Act 1977 does not apply to a covenant in a lease 'in so far as it relates to the creation or transfer of an interest in land': Sch. 1, para. 1(b); *Electricity Supply Nominees Ltd v IAF Group Ltd* [1993] 1 WLR 1059 (anti-set-off clause excluded); *Star Rider Ltd v Inntrepreneur Pub Co* [1998] 1 EGLR 53 (agreement for lease). But the Unfair Terms in Consumer Contract Regulations 1999 do apply to contracts relating to land, and therefore to a lease: *R (Khatun) v Newham LBC* [2005] QB 37; Office of Fair Trading, Guidance on Unfair Terms in Tenancy Agreements 2005 (OFT 356). The Law Commission proposes to replace the Unfair Contract Terms Act 1977 and the Unfair Terms in Consumer Contracts Regulations 1999 with a single statute which, in relation to land contracts, would apply only to *consumer* contracts (thereby broadly maintaining the position under the 1977 Act and the 1999 Regulations): Unfair Terms in Contracts 2005 (Law Com No. 293, Cm 6464), paras 3.80, 4.84, 5.77. The Law Commission has also emphasized the contractual nature of residential leases in Renting Homes 2006 (Law Com No. 297) (see esp. Part 3: residential leases and licences to be 'occupation contracts').

[48] *Linden Gardens Trust Ltd v Lenester Sludge Disposals Ltd* [1994] 1 AC 85 at 108, per Lord Browne-Wilkinson. See S. Bridge in L. Tee (ed), *Land Law Issues, Debates, Policy*, chap. 4.

[49] See M & W, para. 17.003; Smith, pp. 384–387. However, in *Prudential Assurance Co Ltd v London Residuary Body* [1992] 2 AC 386, p. 358, below, HL rejected a contractual approach; *PW & Co v Milton Gate Investments Ltd* [2004] Ch 142, where Neuberger J held that as a matter of law it was not possible to contract out of the general rule in *Pennell v Payne* [1995] QB 192 and *Barrett v Morgan* [2000] 2 AC 264, that a sub-tenancy comes to an end on determination of the head tenancy, p. 354, n. 68. See also *Street v Mountford* [1985] AC 809, p. 383, below, at 819, per Templeman J: 'Both parties enjoyed freedom to contract or not to contract and both parties exercised that freedom by contracting on the terms set forth in the written agreement and on no other terms. But the consequences in law of the agreement, once concluded, can only be determined by consideration of the effect of the agreement'.

[50] [1995] Conv 379 (M. Pawlowski); [1993] Conv 71 (S. Bright); [1993] CLJ 212 (C. Harpum). See also *WG Clark (Properties) Ltd v Dupre Properties Ltd* [1992] Ch 297 (tenant's disclaimer of lease a repudiation);

tenancy was subject to a covenant to repair on the part of the landlord implied by section 11 of the Landlord and Tenant Act 1985. By March 1991 one of the bedrooms had been made uninhabitable by the collapse of its ceiling; the sitting-room was letting in rainwater and part of its ceiling was bulging dangerously; the outside toilet was unusable and the hall wall was affected by damp. This situation was not improved by ill-fitting doors and windows and the effects of burst pipes. The landlord refused to carry out repairs in spite of several complaints by the tenants, who in the end returned the keys to the landlord's agents and vacated the property.

SEDLEY QC, in holding that there had been a repudiatory breach by the landlord of the implied covenant to repair, and that the tenants had accepted that repudiation as putting an end to the tenancy, said at 88:

The single most important point in the case is this: is it possible in law for a contract of letting to be terminated by one party's acceptance of the other's repudiatory conduct? . . .

Although a contract of letting, whether for a term of years certain or for a periodic 'springing' term, differs from other contracts in creating an estate in land, it is nevertheless a contract: see *United Scientific Holdings Ltd v Burnley Borough Council* [1978] AC 904, at pp. 929E, 935B, 944B, 947B-C, 956F-H, 962A and 963H-964B, approving *CH Bailey Ltd v Memorial Enterprises Ltd* [1974] 1 WLR 728; and, most recently, *Hammersmith and Fulham London Borough Council v Monk* [1991] 3 WLR 1144 at pp. 1147C, G and 1156 C, G-H.[51] Since, in the ordinary way, any contract may be brought to an end by one party's repudiatory conduct, the question to be answered is whether a contract of letting is an exception to the rule.

In *CH Bailey Ltd v Memorial Enterprises Ltd* at 732C, Lord Denning MR said:

'It is time to get away from the medieval concept of rent. That appears from a passage in *Holdsworth, A History of English Law,* vol. VII (1900), p. 262 . . . : . . . in modern law, rent is not conceived of as a thing, but rather as a payment which a tenant is bound by his contract to make to his landlord for the use of the land.

The time and manner of the payment is to be ascertained according to the true construction of the contract, and not by reference to out-dated relics of medieval law.'

Sir Eric Sachs at p. 735E said:

'Whatever the position last century, the word "rent" today can often simply refer to any contractual sum to which a landlord becomes entitled for the use of his land.'

He endorsed the following passage in *Foa, General Law of Landlord and Tenant* (8th edn, 1957) at p. 101:

'There has been a considerable development from the medieval conception of rent as a 'thing' or proprietary interest to the modern conception of rent as a contractual obligation to pay for the use of property let, and the notion that 'rent' must have the quality that it can be distrained for is more appropriate to the medieval than the modern conception. Accordingly, the question in each case is to determine what in substance is the subject-matter of the tenancy granted to the tenant by the

---

GS Fashions Ltd v B & Q plc [1995] 1 WLR 1088; *Progressive Mailing House Pty Ltd v Tabili Pty Ltd* (1985) 157 CLR 17; [1986] Conv 262 (J. W. Carter and J. Hill); (1988) 14 Monash LR 83 (J. Effron).

[51] P. 334, above.

contract: *prima facie* rent is the monetary compensation payable by the tenant in consideration for the grant, however it be described or allocated...'

It seems clear, then, that, although the modern law of landlord and tenant has not made obsolete the availability of distress for rent[52] or the concept of an estate in land arising out of the relationship, these are no longer the foundation of the relationship but are its incidents: its foundation is the contract to pay money or give other consideration in return for the exclusive right to occupy land. (It may or may not be that the rent-free tenancy is an anomaly in this context, but that rare species cannot swim very far against the tide of the general law.)

The anchor by which Mr Russen, in his able argument, seeks to secure his client's boat against this tide is the decision of the Court of Appeal in *Total Oil Great Britain Ltd v Thompson Garages (Biggin Hill) Ltd* [1972] 1 QB 318...

Lord Denning MR [said] at p. 324A:

'...A lease is a demise. It conveys an interest in land. It does not come to an end like an ordinary contract on repudiation and acceptance. There is no authority on the point, but there is one case which points that way. It is [*Cricklewood Property & Investment Trust Ltd v Leighton's Investment Trust Ltd*] [1945] AC 221. Lord Russell of Killowen and Lord Goddard at pp. 234 and 244 were both of opinion that frustration does not bring a lease to an end.[53] Nor I think does repudiation and acceptance.'...

The *Total Oil* decision, at its fullest, is therefore to be found in the judgment of Lord Denning. If it stood by itself it would, at this level, be binding authority for the proposition that because of the special character of a demise of land a lease is not terminable by frustration nor, therefore, by repudiation and acceptance.

However, since the *Total Oil* case was decided in 1971, both the major and the minor premises upon which Lord Denning's second holding was based appear to have been destroyed by decisions of the House of Lords. As I have already indicated, the major premise that a lease of land is in its essence different from other contracts has been overset, in particular by the decision of the House of Lords in *United Scientific Holdings Ltd v Burnley Borough Council*. The minor premise that a lease cannot be determined by frustration has been overset by the decision of the House of Lords in *National Carriers Ltd v Panalpina (Northern) Ltd* [1981] AC 675, in which a demised warehouse became unusable because of a street closure, and the tenants withheld rent, claiming that the lease had been frustrated. The House of Lords (Lord Russell of Killowen dissenting) held that the doctrine of frustration was in principle applicable to leases but that it did not operate on the facts of the instant case. Their lordships declined to follow the *dicta* in

---

[52] The common law remedy of distress has now been abolished, although a new equivalent statutory procedure has been introduced for the benefit of commercial landlords: p. 421, n. 174, below.

[53] The third Lord Russell of Killowen, with filial piety, dissented, and followed the views of the second Lord Russell and Lord Goddard in the *Cricklewood* case. For him also 'the second answer of the *Pinafore's* captain on the subject of mal de mer is to be preferred to his first.' See C & B, pp. 328–329. Lord Russell of Killowen at 223 recognised obiter that there may be excuses for the non-performance of a building covenant short of full frustration: 'It may well be that circumstances may arise during the currency of the term which render it difficult, or even impossible, for one party or the other to carry out some of its obligations as landlord or tenant, circumstances which might afford a defence to a claim for damages for their breach, but the lease would remain.' This dictum was applied in *John Lewis Properties plc v Viscount Chelsea* [1993] 2 EGLR 77 where a tenant was unable to perform a covenant to demolish and rebuild property owing to his inability to obtain planning permission, which had become necessary on its subsequent listing as a Grade II building (25 Cadogan Gardens, once described as the most beautiful building in the world).

the *Cricklewood* case. The *Total Oil* case was cited but was not referred to in the speeches. Lord Hailsham, at p. 690D, said:

'I conclude that the matter is not decided by authority and that the question is open to your Lordships to decide on principle. In my view your Lordships ought now so to decide it. Is there anything in principle which ought to prevent a lease from ever being frustrated? I think there is not. In favour of the opposite opinion, the difference in principle between real and chattel property was strongly urged. But I find it difficult to accept this, once it has been decided, as has long been the case, that time and demise charters even of the largest ships and of considerable duration can in principle be frustrated.'

Lord Wilberforce at p. 694E, said:

'It was pointed out, however, by Atkin LJ in Matthey v Curling [1922] 2 AC 180, 200, in a passage later approved by Viscount Simon [1945] AC 221, 230, that as a lease can be determined, according to its terms, upon the happening of certain specified events, there is nothing illogical in implying a term that it should be determined on the happening of other events—namely, those which in an ordinary contract work a frustration...

A man may desire possession and use of land or buildings for, and only for, some purpose in view and mutually contemplated. Why is it an answer, when he claims that this purpose is 'frustrated', to say that he has an estate if that estate is unusable and unsaleable? In such a case the lease, or the conferring of an estate, is a subsidiary means to an end, not an aim or end of itself.'

He concluded at p. 696G:

'It was not until the *Cricklewood* case that the argument was put on principle and fully explored. The governing decision (of the Court of Appeal) was summary, unargued, and based upon previous cases which will not bear the weight of a generalisation. I think that the movement of the law of contract is away from a rigid theory of autonomy towards the discovery—or I do not hesitate to say imposition—by the Courts of just solutions, which can be ascribed to reasonable men in the position of the parties.'

This reasoning, it seems to me, not only takes away the minor premise of the *Total Oil* judgment but has fundamental implications for its major premise: it continues the process, to which I have referred, of assimilating leases to other contracts. It follows, in my judgment, that unless some special exception can be established for acts of repudiation, not only has *Total Oil* ceased to be authority for the proposition that a lease cannot be repudiated: the decisions which have rendered it obsolete point powerfully in the direction of repudiation being a legitimate ground for termination of a lease. I bear in mind, however, that the House of Lords was extremely cautious about the range of situations in which it would allow the doctrine of frustration to operate on a lease and that Lord Hailsham posed the choice, in the language of *HMS Pinafore,* as lying only between 'never' and 'hardly ever', coming down in favour of the latter.

Very recently the Court of Appeal has held, apparently without argument to the contrary and without any citation of authority, that a tenancy agreement which one party is induced to enter into by the fraud of the other can be rescinded at the innocent party's election: *Killick v Roberts* [1991] 4 All ER 289 at p. 292d. This seems another step down the same road.

It is perhaps a relief that the *Total Oil* case is no longer good law, because it appears to have silently overruled an important line of cases (not cited in argument) in which, throughout the 19th century, the courts took it as axiomatic that a contract of letting could be terminated by the innocent party without notice if the other party failed to fulfil a fundamental term of the contract. I will refer to them because they are of assistance in deciding the next question, namely what breaches of a lessor's covenant are of a sufficiently fundamental character to amount to repudiation.

His Lordship referred to *Edwards v Etherington* (1825) Ry & M 268; *Collins v Barrow* (1831) 1 Mood & R 112; *Izon v Gorton* (1839) 5 Bing NC 501; and *Arden v Pullen* (1842) 10 M & W 321; and continued:

It was this well-established line of authority that the Court of Exchequer followed in the celebrated case of *Smith v Marrable* (1843) 11 M & W 5. The defendant had taken a furnished house for his family, who found it infested with bugs and left. On an action for the rent for the remainder of the term of five weeks, Lord Abinger CB directed the jury that:

> 'in point of law every house must be taken to be let upon the implied condition that there was nothing about it so noxious as to render it uninhabitable.'

Parke B, giving the leading judgment on a motion for a new trial, cited a number of the authorities to which I have referred and concluded:

> 'These authorities appear to me fully to warrant the position, that if the demised premises are incumbered with a nuisance of so serious a nature that no person can reasonably be expected to live in them, the tenant is at liberty to throw them up.'

Lord Abinger CB, sitting as was the custom on the appeal against his own direction to the jury, expressed relief that authorities supported what he had taken to be a proposition of common sense and concluded:

> 'I entertain no doubt whatever on the subject, and think the defendant was fully justified in leaving these premises as he did: indeed, I only wonder that he remained so long, and gave the landlord so much opportunity of remedying the evil.'

It will be seen that this case is authority not only for the proposition for which it is known, that there is an implied covenant of fitness for habitation in a letting of a furnished house, but also for the proposition that a contract of tenancy may be repudiated by a breach of such a condition, and—incidentally—that it is not to be held against the tenant that he has endured the breach for longer than he needed to.

Although the vocabulary of repudiation is not consistently used in these cases—the earliest, for example, speaks of 'exempting' the defendant from the demand for rent and others speak of the tenant being allowed to 'throw up' the letting or 'to withdraw', by 1842 Lord Abinger is using the phrase 'the contract of letting' and Alderson B is speaking about the tenant 'avoiding' the lease for the landlord's default. When in 1877 the Exchequer division decided *Wilson v Finch Hatton* (1877) 2 Ex D 336 and followed *Smith v Marrable,* all three barons used the language of repudiation and Pollock B sought to cut away furnished lettings from the doctrine that rent issues out of the realty and to hold instead that this was simply 'a sum paid for the accommodation afforded by the use of the house'. (The divergent patch which Parke B charted in relation to demises of real property in *Hart v Windsor* (1843) 12 M & W 68, shortly after he decided *Smith v Marrable,* has now, it appears, all but converged again with the path of contract, at least since the decision in *C H Bailey Ltd v Memorial Enterprises Ltd.*)...

I recognise that the proposition that a contract of tenancy can be repudiated like any other contract has a number of important implications, which it is not appropriate to explore on the facts of this case. For example, if the obligation to pay rent is as fundamental as the obligation to keep the house habitable, it will follow that a default in rent payments is a repudiatory act on the tenant's part. That this may follow is not, however, a reason for going back on what appears to me to be the inexorable effect of binding authority. It will, however, have effect subject not only to all the statutory provisions which now hedge the right to recover possession but also, I would think, to the provisions contained in the contract of letting itself in relation to forfeiture (where there is a term certain): in other words, the right to terminate by acceptance of repudiatory conduct may itself be modified by further contractual provisions which lay down conditions, supported by statute, for the exercise of the right.

Bruton v London & Quadrant Housing Trust
[2000] 1 AC 406[54] (HL, Lords Slynn of Hadley, Jauncey of Tullichettle, Hoffmann, Hope of Craighead and Hobhouse of Woodborough)

The London Borough of Lambeth owned a block of flats in Brixton of which it had no statutory authority to grant a tenancy. It therefore entered into a licence agreement with the Housing Trust, which prohibited it from granting a tenancy. The Trust then entered into a 'weekly licence agreement' with Mr Bruton, who had exclusive possession of the flat. He brought an action against the Trust for breach of repairing obligations implied by section 11 of the Landlord and Tenant Act 1985. This section applied only to 'a lease of dwelling-house granted . . . for a term of less than seven years' (section 13(1)).

Held (reversing the Court of Appeal [1988] QB 834) for Mr Bruton. The fact that the Trust had no estate in the land to support a lease binding on third parties was irrelevant.

Lord Hoffmann: Did this agreement create a 'lease' or 'tenancy' within the meaning of the Landlord and Tenant Act 1985 or any other legislation which refers to a lease or tenancy? The decision of this House in *Street v Mountford* [1985] AC 809 [p. 383, below] is authority for the proposition that a 'lease' or 'tenancy' is a contractually binding agreement, not referable to any other relationship between the parties, by which one person gives another the right to exclusive occupation of land for a fixed or renewable period or periods of time, usually in return for a periodic payment in money. An agreement having these characteristics creates a relationship of landlord and tenant to which the common law or statute may then attach various incidents. The fact that the parties use language more appropriate to a different kind of agreement, such as a licence, is irrelevant if upon its true construction it has the identifying characteristics of a lease. The meaning of the agreement, for example, as to the extent of the possession which it grants, depends upon the intention of the parties, objectively ascertained by reference to the language and relevant background. The decision of your Lordships' House in *Westminster City Council v Clarke* [1992] 2 AC 288 [p. 381, n. 111, below] is a good example of the importance of background in deciding whether the agreement grants exclusive possession or not. But the classification of the agreement as a lease does not depend upon any intention additional to that

---

[54] [1999] All ER Rev 229 (P. J. Clarke); (1999) 3 L & TR 124 (M. Pawlowski); (2000) 116 LQR 7 (S. Bright); [2002] CLJ 25 (M. Dixon); (2000) 4 L&TR 119 (M. Pawlowski and J. Brown); S. Bridge in L. Tee (ed.), *Land Law Issues, Debates, Policy*, chap. 4, p. 351, below.

expressed in the choice of terms. It is simply a question of characterising the terms which the parties have agreed. This is a question of law.

In this case, it seems to me that the agreement, construed against the relevant background, plainly gave Mr Bruton a right to exclusive possession. There is nothing to suggest that he was to share possession with the trust, the council or anyone else. The trust did not retain such control over the premises as was inconsistent with Mr Bruton having exclusive possession, as was the case in *Westminster City Council v Clarke*. The only rights which it reserved were for itself and the council to enter at certain times and for limited purposes. As Lord Templeman said in *Street v Mountford* at 818, such an express reservation 'only serves to emphasise the fact that the grantee is entitled to exclusive possession and is a tenant.' Nor was there any other relationship between the parties to which Mr Bruton's exclusive possession could be referable.

Mr Henderson, who appeared for the trust, submitted that there were 'special circumstances' in this case which enabled one to construe the agreement as a licence despite the presence of all the characteristics identified in *Street v Mountford*. These circumstances were that the trust was a responsible landlord performing socially valuable functions, it had agreed with the council not to grant tenancies. Mr Bruton had agreed that he was not to have a tenancy and the trust had no estate out of which it could grant one.

In my opinion none of these circumstances can make an agreement to grant exclusive possession something other than a tenancy. The character of the landlord is irrelevant because although the Rent Acts and other Landlord and Tenant Acts do make distinctions between different kinds of landlords, it is not by saying that what would be a tenancy if granted by one landlord will be something else if granted by another. The alleged breach of the Trust's licence is irrelevant because there is no suggestion that the grant of a tenancy would have been ultra vires either the trust or the council: see section 32(3) of the Housing Act 1985. If it was a breach of a term of the licence from the council, that would have been because it was a tenancy. The licence could not have turned it into something else. Mr Bruton's agreement is irrelevant because one cannot contract out of the statute. The trust's lack of title is also irrelevant, but I shall consider this point at a later stage. In *Family Housing Association v Jones* [1990] 1 WLR 779, where the facts were very similar to those in the present case, the Court of Appeal construed the 'licence' as a tenancy. Slade LJ gave careful consideration to whether any exceptional ground existed for making an exception to the principle in *Street v Mountford* and came to the conclusion that there was not. I respectfully agree. For these reasons I consider that the agreement between the trust and Mr Bruton was a lease within the meaning of section 11 of the Landlord and Tenant Act 1985.

My Lords, in my opinion, that is the end of the matter. But the Court of Appeal did not stop at that point. In the leading majority judgment, Millett LJ said [1998] QB 834, 845 that an agreement could not be a lease unless it had a further characteristic, namely that it created a legal estate in the land which 'binds the whole world.' If, as in this case, the grantor had no legal estate, the agreement could not create one and therefore did not qualify as a lease. The only exception was the case in which the grantor was estopped from denying that he could not create a legal estate. In that case, a 'tenancy by estoppel' came into existence. But an estoppel depended upon the grantor having purported to grant a lease and in this case the trust had not done so. It had made it clear that it was only purporting to grant a licence.

My Lords, I hope that this summary does justice to the closely reasoned judgment of Millett LJ. But I fear that I must respectfully differ at three critical steps in the argument.

First, the term 'lease' or 'tenancy' describes a relationship between two parties who are designated landlord and tenant. It is not concerned with the question of whether the agreement creates an estate or other proprietary interest which may be binding upon third parties. A lease may, and usually does, create a proprietary interest called a leasehold estate or, technically, a 'term of years absolute.' This will depend upon whether the landlord had an interest out of which he could grant it. Nemo dat quod non habet. But it is the fact that the agreement is a lease which creates the proprietary interest. It is putting the cart before the horse to say that whether the agreement is a lease depends upon whether it creates a proprietary interest.

His Lordship referred to *Lewisham Borough Council v Roberts* [1949] 2 KB 608, and continued:

Millett LJ, at p. 846, distinguished *Family Housing Association v Jones,* where, as I have said, the facts were very similar to those in the present case, on the ground that 'the fact that the grantor had no title was not referred to in argument or the judgments.' In my opinion this is easily explained by the fact that the grantor's title or lack of title was irrelevant to the issue in the case.

Secondly, I think that Millett LJ may have been misled by the ancient phrase 'tenancy by estoppel' into thinking that it described an agreement which would not otherwise be a lease or tenancy but which was treated as being one by virtue of an estoppel. In fact, as the authorities show, it is not the estoppel which creates the tenancy, but the tenancy which creates the estoppel. The estoppel arises when one or other of the parties wants to deny one of the ordinary incidents or obligations of the tenancy on the ground that the landlord had no legal estate. The basis of the estoppel is that having entered into an agreement which constitutes a lease or tenancy, he cannot repudiate that incident or obligation. So in *Morton v Woods* (1869) LR 4 QB 293, a factory owner granted a second mortgage to a bank to secure advances. But the mortgagor had no legal estate, having conveyed it to the first mortgagee, and therefore could not confer one upon the second mortgagee. As additional security, the borrower 'attorned tenant' to the second mortgagee, that is to say, acknowledged a relationship of landlord and tenant between them. This was a device commonly used in old mortgages to give the mortgagee the rights of a landlord—a speedier procedure for recovery of possession which was then available and the right to levy distress upon goods and chattels on the mortgaged premises: see Megarry & Wade, *The Law of Real Property,* 5th edn (1984), p. 946. When the borrower failed to pay, the bank levied a distress. The owner of the goods sued for damages, claiming that the bank had no right to levy distress because that ancient common law remedy was available only to the holder of a legal estate. A recital to the mortgage made it plain that the bank was a second mortgagee and therefore had no legal estate. The Court of Queen's Bench held that the mortgagor was estopped from denying the bank's legal title. Kelly CB said, at p. 304:

'it is the creation of the tenancy, or the estoppel, which arises from the creation of the relation of landlord and tenant by agreement between the parties, that makes the actual legal estate unnecessary to support the distress...'

Thus it is the fact that the agreement between the parties constitutes a tenancy that gives rise to an estoppel and not the other way round. It therefore seems to me that the question of tenancy by estoppel does not arise in this case. The issue is simply whether the agreement is a tenancy. It is not whether either party is entitled to deny some obligation or incident of the tenancy on the ground that the trust had no title.

Thirdly, I cannot agree that there is no inconsistency between what the trust purported to do and its denial of the existence of a tenancy. This seems to me to fly in the face of *Street v Mountford.* In my opinion, the trust plainly did purport to grant a tenancy. It entered into an agreement on terms which constituted a tenancy. It may have agreed with Mr Bruton to say that it was not a tenancy. But the parties cannot contract out of the Rent Acts or other landlord and tenant statutes by such devices. Nor in my view can they be used by a landlord to avoid being estopped from denying that he entered into the agreement he actually made.

For these reasons I would allow the appeal and declare that Mr Bruton was a tenant. I should add that I express no view on whether he was a secure tenant or on the rights of the council to recover possession of the flat.

Lord Hobhouse of Woodborough: My Lords, I agree that this appeal should be allowed as proposed by my noble and learned friend, Lord Hoffmann, and for the reasons which he has given. I would add only this.

The claim made in the action seeks to enforce a contractual cause of action....

Counsel for the housing trust accepted before your Lordships that a contractual relationship of landlord and tenant suffices to make the provisions of the Act applicable. The question therefore is whether the agreement creates such a relationship. The answer to this question is, in my judgment, determined by the decision in *Street v Mountford*. The agreement was an agreement to give Mr Bruton the exclusive possession of the flat for a period or periods of time in return for the periodic payment of money; the grant of exclusive possession was not referable to any other relationship between the parties. It follows that the relationship created was that of landlord and tenant and the provisions of the Act apply to the agreement. Mr Bruton is entitled to succeed.

The relevant question is simply one of ascertaining the effect in law of the agreement which the parties made. It is true that before the court construes an agreement it must inform itself of the surrounding circumstances existing at the time that the contract was made: *Reardon Smith Line Ltd v Yngvar Hansen-Tangen* [1976] 1 WLR 989. This rule applies as much to contracts relating to property as to any other contract. In the present case, it is correct that both parties knew that the housing trust was a mere licensee of the council and, in so far as they may have thought about it, should have realised that for the housing trust to grant Mr Bruton the exclusive possession of the flat probably amounted to a breach of the housing trust's obligations to the council. But this cannot contradict what was actually agreed between the housing trust and Mr Bruton or its legal effect as between them (*Family Housing Association v Jones*). It would be different if it could be shown that the housing trust had no capacity to make the agreement (*Minister of Agriculture and Fisheries v Matthews* [1950] 1 KB 148). Lack of capacity renders an apparent agreement without legal effect; this is an application of the ordinary principles of the law of contract. But the present case is not such a case. The housing trust had the requisite capacity to make the agreement with Mr Bruton (as for that matter had the council: section 44(1) of the Housing Act 1985).

S. Bridge in L. Tee (ed.), *Land Law Issues, Debates, Policy*, pp. 116–120

The process of contractualisation of leases was now growing apace. Frustration, rescission for fraud, termination for breach, implication of terms for business efficacy (contractual doctrines all) have been applied in recent years to leases, unobjectionably in my view, on the ground that a lease is as much a contract as an estate.[55] But the *coup de grace*, or some might say the *reductio ad absurdum*, of the contractualists, was to come in the decision of the House

---

[55] See also the central role assumed by contract in the future version of the landlord occupier relationship in Law Commission Consultation Paper No. 162, *Renting Homes*, 1.32 et seq, Part VI.

of Lords in *Bruton v London & Quadrant Housing Trust.* A lease is a contract, and it may be nothing more than a contract. It need not be an estate at all....

Lord Hoffmann, giving the leading speech, held that the agreement conferred exclusive possession on the occupier. Under normal *Street v Mountford* principles, therefore, this would be a tenancy unless 'special circumstances' could be shown. Lord Hoffmann rightly rejected the defendant's argument that the identity of the landlord, or its agreement with the council not to grant tenancies, or the plaintiff's agreement that he was not to be a tenant, comprised 'special circumstances'. But he went on to hold, much more controversially, that the defendant's lack of any property interest in the land was immaterial. Although the defendant trust could not grant a legal estate in the land, the plaintiff had nevertheless obtained a lease in the flat.

Lord Hoffmann advanced two arguments in support of this result. First, the term 'lease' (or 'tenancy') refers to a bilateral relationship between the landlord and the tenant, and nothing more:

> 'It is not concerned with the question of whether the agreement creates an estate or other proprietary interest which may be binding upon third parties. A lease may, and usually does, create a proprietary interest called a leasehold estate or, technically, a "term of years absolute". This will depend upon whether the landlord had an interest out of which he could grant it. Nemo dat quod non habet. But it is the fact that the agreement is a lease which creates the proprietary interest. It is putting the cart before the horse to say that whether the agreement is a lease depends upon whether it creates a proprietary interest.'[56]

This has been aptly described as advancing a 'relative' or 'relational' concept of exclusive possession, pursuant to which the court asks simply whether the occupier has exclusive possession as against their immediate landlord.[57] By adopting this focused approach, it is possible to concentrate on the two parties to the contract and to disregard wider issues such as capacity to grant a proprietary interest. But its undoubted effect is to recognise that an agreement which does not confer an estate in the property can nevertheless be a lease. This kind of lease, being non-proprietary, is unique.

Lord Hoffmann held that a tenancy also arose by virtue of estoppel. Here, the articulation of principle ('it is not the estoppel which creates the tenancy, but the tenancy which creates the estoppel') is unexceptionable.[58] But its application to the facts of the case is. While it may be necessary for there to be a tenancy to create the estoppel, there was no tenancy in *Bruton,* for the reasons given above. There are two accepted circumstances in which a tenancy by estoppel may arise. The estoppel may be by deed (the grantor being precluded from disputing the validity of his or her grant[59]), or by representation (the grantor being estopped by an unambiguous and material representation as to his or her title on the strength of which the tenant takes a lease[60]). The facts of *Bruton* cannot be forced into either analysis. The trust took great care to communicate the limited nature of their interest in the flat to the plaintiff, and throughout the agreement referred to him only as a licensee. The trust had never purported to grant the plaintiff a tenancy—on the contrary.[61]...

---

[56] [2001] 1 AC 406 at 415.   [57] See Bright (2000) 116 LQR 7.

[58] For subsequent citation by way of approval, see *Wroe (t/a Telepower) v Exmos Cover Ltd* [2000] EGLR 66.

[59] *First National Bank plc v Thompson* [1996] Ch 231 at 237.

[60] See Harpum, Megarry & Wade: *The Law of Real Property,* 6th edn, 2000, para. 14.095.

[61] Millett LJ set out the position lucidly in the Court of Appeal: 'In the present case both parties knew that the trust had no title and could not grant a tenancy. That is not sufficient to prevent the creation of a tenancy

The one speech that takes a slightly different tack is that of Lord Hobhouse. As befits a commercial judge, he adopts what might be described as a 'contractual' approach. The claim was to enforce a contractual course of action. The existence of a contractual relationship of landlord and tenant sufficed to trigger the statutory implication of the repairing covenant. The housing trust had capacity to enter into the contractual agreement. No problem arose from the fact that the trust had no legal estate, as no interest was being asserted by the plaintiff against any third party to the agreement. Lord Hobhouse's speech does not satisfactorily answer the objections already outlined, but it may indicate a possible way for future courts to deal with the precedent set by *Bruton*. Indeed, on policy grounds—that a landlord should not be able to escape statutorily repairing obligations by denying that they had capacity to grant a tenancy—the decision is perfectly acceptable. As a precedent it is much more difficult, as it creates a hybrid interest of a seemingly non-proprietary nature, the full implications of which we will only come to understand and appreciate with its further judicial exposition.[62] ...

Prior to *Bruton*, one would have thought that the conferment of a proprietary interest was absolutely essential to the characterisation of an agreement as a lease. The bare minima of a lease would have seemed to be the grant of exclusive possession for a term, and the capacity to make a grant of exclusive possession in the absolute sense (so that the tenant can defend his or her possession against all-comers) of the very essence. In an earlier House of Lords decision, *Prudential Assurance Co Ltd v London Residuary Body*,[63] an attack was made on the necessity for the 'term' of a lease to fulfil the requirement of certainty. Previous cases had held that it must be possible to say, at the beginning of a lease, when it would terminate by effluxion of time.[64] However, despite argument that the contractual autonomy of the parties should be respected and their freely negotiated agreement duly enforced, the House of Lords held that the principle must prevail. This assertion of the power of property law to limit the extent to which parties can modify property interests was welcomed in some quarters.[65] Most conveyancers would agree that freedom of contract must occasionally be sacrificed on the altar of property, and Lord Templeman did not seem unduly concerned by the consequences of applying strict property principles to the facts before him. However, Lord Browne-Wilkinson, while accepting that under the current law it was necessary for an effective lease to satisfy tests of certainty, considered that the result in *Prudential Assurance* was unsatisfactory, and proposed that the issue should be referred to the Law Commission so that it could contemplate future reform.[66] The decision in *Bruton* presents a further challenge for those who believe that the division between contract and property should be clear and easily drawn.

In **Kay v Lambeth London Borough Council** [2006] 2 AC 465[67] the House of Lords held that the tenancy which was held by Mr Bruton and other similar occupiers of the block of flats in the *Bruton* case did not bind Lambeth, the freeholder. In 1995

by estoppel. But the trust did not purport to grant a tenancy. The document was carefully drawn by the trust and accepted by Mr Bruton as a licence. There is no inconsistency between the terms of the document and the trust's assertion that it has not granted a tenancy. There is no ground for holding that the parties must be taken to have adopted an assumed basis for the transaction. They did not agree that the trust should grant a tenancy even though it had no title; they agreed that it should grant a licence because it could not grant a tenancy.'

[62] See Bright (2000) 116 LQR 7 at 9.   [63] [1992] 2 AC 386.
[64] *Lace v Chantler* [1944] KB 368.   [65] Sparkes (1993) 109 LQR 93.
[66] [1992] 2 AC 386 at 396, below.   [67] [2006] All ER Rev 260 (P. H. Pettit).

Lambeth had granted the Housing Trust a lease of the block of flats, to replace the licence. But this did not mean that the occupiers acquired estates in the land which became binding on the freeholder. LORD SCOTT OF FOSCOTE said at 524:

143 ... LQHT [the Housing Trust] was, when it granted the *Bruton* tenancies, merely a licensee of Lambeth. The tenancies were not granted by Lambeth and were not carved by LQHT out of any estate that Lambeth had granted to LQHT. They were not derivative estates. LQHT, prior to the grant of the 1995 lease, had no estate in the land. It merely had a contractual licence. In these circumstances the *Mellor v Watkins*[68] point that the intermediate landlord cannot by a consensual surrender give away an interest that belongs to a subtenant has no substance. True it is that LQHT could not by a surrender of its licence give away or prejudice the rights of the *Bruton* tenants against itself, LQHT. But these rights never were enforceable against Lambeth. Once the LQHT licence had been terminated the appellants were trespassers as against Lambeth.

144 An analogous situation would arise if a person not the owner of land but in adverse possession of it were to grant a tenancy of the land to another. As between the grantor and grantee there would be a valid 'non-estate' tenancy. But unless and until the adverse possession had continued for the requisite 12 years the tenancy would not bind the true owner of the land. An agreement by the adverse possessor to deliver up the land to the true owner would not affect the rights of his tenant against him, the landlord, but equally could not turn the tenant into the true owner's tenant or give the tenant any rights against the true owner.

145 So, too, the consensual termination of LQHT's contractual licence from Lambeth could not, in my opinion, turn the *Bruton* 'non-estate' tenants into estate tenants of Lambeth. I agree with Mr Luba, counsel for the appellants, that the *Bruton* tenants were not bound by a transaction between Lambeth and LQHT to which they were not parties. But the contended for conclusion that they therefore became tenants of Lambeth is a non sequitur. They never were *sub* tenants holding, via a grant from LQHT, an interest created by Lambeth. They were tenants of LQHT holding an interest created by LQHT. The *Mellor v Watkins* principle has, in my opinion, no application to such a case.

146 As to the effect on the *Bruton* tenancies of the grant of the 1995 lease to LQHT and the termination of that lease in 2000, there are two points to be made. First, I agree with the appellants that when in 1995 LQHT were granted a term of years by Lambeth the *Bruton* tenancies became, vis-à-vis Lambeth, no longer 'non-estate' tenancies but estate tenancies. The *Bruton* tenancies were, so to speak, fed by the estate that their landlord, LQHT, had acquired.

147 But that estate was from the outset subject to the terms of the 1995 lease. The termination of that lease in 2000 in accordance with the termination provisions contained in it terminated the entitlement of the *Bruton* tenants to claim an estate derived from and binding on Lambeth: see *Barrett v Morgan* [2000] 2 AC 264, 272 where Lord Millett referred to a subtenant's derivative title as precarious 'for it cannot survive the natural termination of the head tenancy in accordance with its terms agreed before his subtenancy was created'. The 'estate'

---

68 '[T]he appellants rely on the principle established by *Mellor v Watkin* (1874) LR 9 QB 400, namely, that where A has granted a tenancy to B and B has granted a subtenancy to C, a surrender by B to A of B's tenancy does not determine C's subtenancy but has the effect that A becomes C's landlord i.e. C holds his tenancy directly from A': *Kay v Lambeth*, above, at [140], per Lord Scott of Foscote. If, however, the termination takes effect not by surrender, but under the terms of the head lease itself, the subtenancy comes to an end on the termination of the head lease: *Pennell v Payne* [1995] QB 192; *Barrett v Morgan* [2000] 2 AC 264.

tenancies held by the appellants were derived from and could not survive the termination of the 1995 lease. The 'non-estate' *Bruton* tenancies could survive as against the grantor of them, LQHT, but they were not binding as against Lambeth.

E. THE PARTIES TO A LEASE

The landlord and tenant under a lease must be different legal persons. One cannot simply grant a lease to oneself.

LAW OF PROPERTY ACT 1925

72. Conveyances by a person to himself, &c.—(3) After the commencement of this Act a person may convey land to or vest land in himself.

(4) Two or more persons (whether or not being trustees or personal representatives) may convey, and shall be deemed always to have been capable of conveying, any property vested in them to any one or more of themselves in like manner as they could have conveyed such property to a third party; provided that if the persons in whose favour the conveyance is made are, by reason of any fiduciary relationship or otherwise, precluded from validly carrying out the transaction, the conveyance shall be liable to be set aside.

Rye v Rye
[1962] AC 496 (HL, **Viscount Simonds, Lords MacDermott, Reid, Radcliffe** and **Denning**)

In 1942 Arthur Rye, the appellant, and his brother Frank, who were in partnership as solicitors, became owners of freehold premises in London as tenants in common in equal shares. They decided to transfer the practice there and orally agreed that the firm should be granted a yearly tenancy of the premises at a rent of £500 a year to be paid out of the partnership assets. In 1948 Frank died, and the freehold was vested in Arthur and the two trustees of Frank's will, one of whom was Frank's son, Ralph, the respondent. In 1950 Arthur took Ralph into a partnership, which was dissolved in 1957. Ralph refused to leave the premises, where he continued to occupy a room. Arthur claimed possession of the room, on the ground that the firm was the tenant under the oral yearly tenancy of 1942, and that he was the surviving partner.

Held (affirming CA). No tenancy was created in 1942, and, therefore, the claim for possession failed.

Viscount Simonds: The first [question] is whether it is competent for two persons orally to grant to themselves an annual tenancy of premises of which they are the owners....

It is common ground, my Lords, that before the Law of Property Act, 1925, came into force it could not. But the appellant claims that the law has been altered by the combined effect of sections 72 and 205 of that Act. In the courts below the meaning and effect of section 205(1) (ii) has been the main topic of discussion, and it appears to have been readily assumed that, if 'conveyance' includes the oral grant (or agreement to make a grant) of an annual tenancy, then either subsection (3) or subsection (4) of section 72 validates the transaction. I do not differ from those of your Lordships who think that section 205(1)(ii) has not this effect, nor do I think that any assistance is given by section 52 or section 54. But I would briefly examine the position if the contrary view prevails and an oral grant of a tenancy is a 'conveyance' within the meaning of the Act and 'convey' has a corresponding meaning.

I turn, then, to section 72 ... Let me take subsection (4) first. In this subsection I do not find it provided that two persons may convey property to themselves or three persons to themselves. On the contrary, I read the subsection literally as meaning that where property is vested in two persons they may convey it to one of themselves and where it is vested in three persons they may convey it to one or two of themselves. I see no reason for giving a more extended meaning to this subsection, and I would point out that, if it did have the meaning claimed for it, it would add nothing to subsection (3) except to provide a plain inconsistency in respect of the date of commencement. I come back to subsection (3). I accept that in this subsection the singular 'person' must include the plural so that two persons may now convey land to, or vest land in, themselves. What, then, is the scope of this subsection? It is said on behalf of the appellant that it enables A., the owner of property, to grant a lease of it to himself and similarly enables A. and B., the joint owners of property, to grant a lease of it to themselves. It was not, I think, suggested that A. and B. could do what A. could not do. The question, then, can conveniently be examined by asking whether the subsection enables A. to grant a lease to himself of land of which he is the owner, or, in other words, to carve out of his larger estate a lesser estate which creates (I know not how to put it otherwise) the relationship of landlord and tenant between himself and himself. I find this a strange conception. In *Grey v Ellison* (1856) 1 Giff 438, 444, Stuart V-C describes as fanciful and a whimsical transaction the proposal that a man should grant a lease to himself. He had, no doubt, in mind that a lease is in one aspect contractual. Of things necessary to a lease, says Sheppard's Touchstone of Assurances (see 7th edn., vol. II. p. 268), one is that: 'There must be an acceptance, [actual or presumed], of the thing demised.' Yet it is meaningless to say that a man accepts from himself something which is already his own. I recognise that a lease not only has a contractual basis between lessor and lessee, but operates also to vest an estate in the lessee. But what sort of estate is in these circumstances vested in the lessee? I will assume that it will not at once merge in the higher estate from which it springs, though I see no reason why it should not. Yet it must be an estate hitherto unknown to the law. Even a bare demise implies certain covenants at law: but to such an estate as this no covenants can be effectively attached. Nor can the common law remedy of distress operate to enable the lessor to distrain on his own goods. Again, at law in the absence of some special provision the lessee is entitled to exclusive possession of the demised premises. What meaning is to be attributed to this where the lessee is also the lessor? My Lords, my mind recoils against an interpretation of the Act which leads to so fanciful and whimsical a result, and it appears to me to be quite unnecessary.[69]

[69] A person who holds land as a nominee for his principal may grant a valid lease to that principal: *Ingram v IRC* [2000] 1 AC 293 (as part of an inheritance tax avoidance scheme HL held that Lady Ingram's solicitor, as nominee for her, granted a valid lease to her. The tax advantage has been negatived by FA 1999, s. 104); (1999) 115 LQR 351 (R. Kerridge). The convincing dissenting judgment of Millett LJ in CA was approved: [1997] STC 1234 at 1255. See also Lord Radcliffe in *Rye v Rye* at 511: 'In effect, putting aside conveyancing forms, a man was able to convey to himself before the 1925 Act. He could, of course, put land in trust for himself by conveying it to a nominee, and, I suppose, if there was any conceivable point in the operation, he could similarly demise land to a nominee.' Cf. *Kildrummy (Jersey) Ltd v IRC* [1990] STC 657, where it was held by the Court of Session that land could not be demised to a nominee. *Rye v Rye* was not cited; See also

If, then, it is asked what meaning can be given to the subsection, I think that the answer is that it is intended partly to supersede the old conveyancing device of a conveyance to uses or of a grant and regrant and partly to provide an essential step in the new machinery set up by the series of Acts passed in 1925. To the latter the word 'vest' itself supplies a clue. It appears to refer to the statutory provisions for vesting the legal estate in a tenant for life or statutory owner, which are to be found, for example, In Schedule II, paragraph 1, to the Settled Land Act 1925.

Thirty-five years have now passed since the Law of Property Act came into operation. I have not found in any of the textbooks that I have been able to consult dealing with real property or the relation of landlord and tenant any suggestion that section 72 of the Act has given birth to such a monstrous child ... I am not prepared in this case to give it currency, and for this reason I would dismiss this appeal.

F. THE ESSENTIALS OF A LEASE

In **Street v Mountford** [1985] AC 809, p. 383, below, the House of Lords considered the essential elements of a lease in the context of the occupation of residential accommodation. LORD TEMPLEMAN said at 827:

where as in the present case the only circumstances are that residential accommodation is offered and accepted with exclusive possession for a term at a rent, the result is a tenancy.

Lord Templeman here indicated that if these three hallmarks—*exclusive possession*, for a *term*, at a *rent*—are present, then there will be a tenancy unless there are exceptional circumstances to negative it.[70] In fact, rent is not essential, although if payable it must be certain. And the term—the period of time for which the estate exists—must also be certain. We shall first consider the certainty of time, and of rent, and then the grant of exclusive possession, which distinguishes the lease from a licence.

(i) Time certain[71]

A lease must commence at,[72] and exist for,[73] a 'time certain', or at or for a time which can be rendered certain. It may even be for a single discontinuous term, for example,

---

Clydesdale Bank plc v Davidson [1998] SLT 522 (under Scots law pro diviso heritable proprietors cannot create a lease over a property in favour of one of their number).

[70] For possible exceptional circumstances, see below, pp. 381–382.

[71] C & B, pp. 207–211; Gray, paras 4.1.41–4.1.58; M & W, paras 17.055–17.060, 17.064; MM, pp. 342, 346, 350–352, 411–413; Smith, pp. 348–351.

[72] *Harvey v Pratt* [1965] 1 WLR 1025 (a contract for a lease failed to specify the date of its commencement); *James v Lock* (1977) 246 EG 395; cf. *Secretary of State for Social Services v Beavington* (1981) 262 EG 551. See generally *Liverpool City Council v Walton Group plc* [2001] 1 EGLR 149.

[73] *Birrell v Carey* (1989) 58 P & CR 184 (grant for a term 'so long as the company is trading' held uncertain); [1990] Conv 288 (J. E. Martin).

a single letting for three successive bank holidays,[74] or where possession is limited to certain hours of the day.[75]

The rule of certainty applies both to fixed and to periodic tenancies.

Prudential Assurance Co Ltd v London Residuary Body
[1992] 2 AC 386 (HL, **Lords Templeman, Griffiths, Goff of Chieveley, Browne-Wilkinson** and **Mustill**)

In 1930 the London County Council, predecessor in title of the London Residuary Body, entered into a sale and lease back agreement with Mr Nathan concerning a strip of land with a frontage of 36 feet to Walworth Road, Southwark, at a rent of £30 a year. Mr Nathan retained the freehold of his adjacent shop premises (Nos. 263–265). The tenancy was to continue 'until the said land is required by the council for the purposes of the widening of Walworth Road,' in which case the landlord could recover possession on giving two months' notice.

In 1988 the landlord issued a notice, and the tenant sought a declaration that the tenancy could only be determined on the land being required for road widening.

Held (reversing the Court of Appeal). Declaration refused.

(i)   The term was of uncertain duration

(ii) A periodic tenancy arising from payment and acceptance of rent failed since its terms were inconsistent with those of a yearly tenancy.

Lord Templeman: The agreement was clearly intended to be of short duration and could have been secured by a lease for a fixed term, say five or ten years with power for the landlord to determine before the expiry of that period for the purposes of the road widening. Unfortunately the agreement was not so drafted. Over 60 years later Walworth Road has not been widened, and it does not appear that the road will ever be widened. The agreement purported to grant a term of uncertain duration which, if valid, now entitles the tenant to stay there for ever and a day at the 1930 rent of £30; valuers acting for both parties have agreed that the annual current commercial rent exceeds £10,000.

A demise for years is a contract for the exclusive possession and profit of land for some determinate period. Such an estate is called a 'term.' Thus *Co.Litt.*, 19th edn (1832), vol. 1, para. 45b said that:

'["Terminus"] in the understanding of the law does not only signify the limits and limitation of time, but also the estate and interest that passes for that time.'

---

[74] *Smallwood v Sheppards* [1895] 2 QB 627; *Cottage Holiday Associates Ltd v Customs and Excise Comrs* [1983] QB 735 (lease of holiday cottage on time sharing basis of one week in each year for 80 consecutive years held to be lease for a discontinuous term of 80 weeks); [1983] All ER Rev 229 (P. J. Clark).

See Timeshare Act 1992; Timeshare Regulations 1997 (SI 1997 No. 1081); The Act and the Regs were both amended by Timeshare Act 1992 (Amendment) Regulations 2003 (SI 2003 No. 1922); Timeshare (Cancellation Information) 2003 (SI 2003 No. 2579); [1992] Conv 30; [1993] Conv 248 (H. W. Wilkinson).

[75] *Graysim Holdings Ltd v P&O Property Holdings Ltd* [1996] AC 329.

Blackstone's Commentaries on the Laws of England, 2nd edn (1766), vol. II, said, at p. 143:

> 'Every estate which must expire at a period certain and prefixed, by whatever words created, is an estate for years. And therefore this estate is frequently called a term, *terminus*, because its duration or continuance is bounded, limited and determined: for every such estate must have a certain beginning, and certain end.'

In *Say v Smith* (1563) 1 Plowd 269 a lease for a certain term purported to add a term which was uncertain; the lease was held valid only as to the certain term. Anthony Brown J is reported to have said, at p. 272:

> 'every contract sufficient to make a lease for years ought to have certainty in three limitations, viz. in the commencement of the term, in the continuance of it, and in the end of it; so that all these ought to be known at the commencement of the lease, and words in a lease, which don't make this appear, are but babble...And these three are in effect but one matter, showing the certainty of the time for which the lessee shall have the land, and if any of these fail, it is not a good lease, for then there wants certainty.'

The Law of Property Act 1925, taking up the same theme provided, by section 1(1), that:

> 'The only estates in land which are capable of subsisting or of being conveyed or created at law are—(a) An estate in fee simple absolute in possession; (b) A term of years absolute.'

Section 205 (1) (xxvii) was in these terms:

> '"Term of years absolute" means a term of years...either certain or liable to determination by notice, re-entry, operation of law, or by a provision for cesser on redemption, or in any other event (other than the dropping of a life, or the determination of a determinable life interest); ... and in this definition the expression 'term of years' includes a term for less than a year, or for a year or years and a fraction of a year or from year to year;'...

The term expressed to be granted by the agreement in the present case does not fall within this definition.

Ancient authority, recognised by the Act of 1925, was applied in *Lace v Chantler* [1944] KB 368. A dwelling house was let at the rent of 16s. 5d. per week. Lord Greene MR (no less) said, at pp. 370–371:

> 'Normally there could be no question that this was an ordinary weekly tenancy, duly determinable by a week's notice, but the parties in the rent-book agreed to a term which appears there expressed by the words "furnished for duration," which must mean the duration of the war. The question immediately arises whether a tenancy for the duration of the war creates a good leasehold interest. In my opinion, it does not. A term created by a leasehold tenancy agreement must be expressed either with certainty and specifically or by reference to something which can, at the time when the lease takes effect, be looked to as a certain ascertainment of what the term is meant to be. In the present case, when this tenancy agreement took effect, the term was completely uncertain. It was impossible to say how long the tenancy would last. Mr Sturge in his argument has maintained that such a lease would be valid, and that, even if the term is uncertain at its beginning when the lease takes effect, the fact that at some future time it will be rendered certain is sufficient to make it a good lease. In my opinion, that argument is not to be sustained. I do not propose to go into the authorities on the matter, but in *Foa's Landlord and Tenant*, 6th edn (1924), p. 115, the law is stated in this way, and, in

my view, correctly: "The habendum in a lease must point out the period during which the enjoyment of the premises is to be had; so that the duration, as well as the commencement of the term, must be stated. The certainty of a lease as to its continuance must be ascertainable either by the express limitation of the parties at the time the lease is made, or by reference to some collateral act which may, with equal certainty, measure the continuance of it, otherwise it is void."'

The legislature concluded that it was inconvenient for leases for the duration of the war to be void and therefore by the Validation of Wartime Leases Act 1944 Parliament provided, by section 1(1), that any agreement entered into before or after the passing of the Act which purported to grant a tenancy for the duration of the war:

> 'shall have effect as if it granted or provided for the grant of a tenancy for a term of 10 years, subject to a right exercisable either by the landlord or the tenant to determine the tenancy, if the war ends before the expiration of that term, by at least one month's notice in writing given after the end of the war;'...

Parliament granted the fixed and certain term which the agreements between the parties lacked in the case of tenancies for the duration of the war and which the present agreement lacks.

When the agreement in the present case was made, it failed to grant an estate in the land. The tenant however entered into possession and paid the yearly rent of £30 reserved by the agreement. The tenant entering under a void lease became by virtue of possession and the payment of a yearly rent, a yearly tenant holding on the terms of the agreement so far as those terms were consistent with the yearly tenancy. A yearly tenancy is determinable by the landlord or the tenant at the end of the first or any subsequent year of the tenancy by six months' notice unless the agreement between the parties provides otherwise. Thus in *Doe d Rigge v Bell* (1793) 3 Durn & E 471 a parol agreement for a seven-year lease did not comply with the Statute of Frauds 1677 but the tenant entered and paid a yearly rent and it was held that he was tenant from year to year on the terms of the agreement. Lord Kenyon CJ said, at p. 472:

> 'Though the agreement be void by the Statute of Frauds as to the duration of the lease, it must regulate the terms on which the tenancy subsists in other respects, as to the rent, the time of year when the tenant is to quit, etc.... Now, in this case, it was agreed, that the defendant should quit at Candlemas; and though the agreement is void as to the number of years for which the defendant was to hold, if the lessor chooses to determine the tenancy before the expiration of the seven years, he can only put an end to it at Candlemas.'

Now it is said that when in the present case the tenant entered pursuant to the agreement and paid a yearly rent he became a tenant from year to year on the terms of the agreement including clause 6 which prevents the landlord from giving notice to quit until the land is required for road widening. This submission would make a nonsense of the rule that a grant for an uncertain term does not create a lease and would make nonsense of the concept of a tenancy from year to year because it is of the essence of a tenancy from year to year that both the landlord and the tenant shall be entitled to give notice determining the tenancy.

In *Doe d Warner v Browne* (1807) 8 East 165 there was an agreement to lease at a rent of £40 per annum and it was agreed that the landlord, W. Warner, should not raise the rent nor turn out the tenant 'so long as the rent is duly paid quarterly, and he does not expose to sale or sell any article that may be injurious to W. Warner in his business.' The tenant duly paid his rent and did not commit any breach of covenant. The landlord gave six months' notice and it was held that the notice was good. These were the days when it was possible to have a lease for life. Lord Ellenborough CJ asked, at p. 166:

'What estate the defendant was contended to have? And whether he was not in this dilemma; that either his estate might enure for life, at his option; and then according to Lord Coke such an estate would, in legal contemplation, be an estate for life; which could not be created by parol: or if not for life, being for no assignable period, it must operate as a tenancy from year to year; in which case it would be inconsistent with, and repugnant to the nature of such an estate, that it should not be determinable at the pleasure of either party giving the regular notice.'

Lawrence J said, at p. 167:

'If this interest be not determinable so long as the tenant complies with the terms of the agreement, it would operate as an estate for life; which can only be created by deed... The notion of a tenancy from year to year, the lessor binding himself not to give notice to quit, which was once thrown out by Lord Mansfield, has been long exploded.'

In *Cheshire Lines Committee v Lewis & Co* (1880) 50 LJQB 121 an agreement for a weekly tenancy contained an undertaking by the landlord not to give notice to quit until the landlord required to pull down the demised buildings. Lush J, after citing *Doe d Warner v Browne* 8 East 165 said of that case, 50 LJQB 121, 124:

'This reasoning applies with at least equal force to the present case. This is not a mere constructive tenancy as that was. It is as explicit as words can make it that the defendants are to hold 'upon a weekly tenancy at a weekly rental, and that the tenancy is to be determined by either of the parties on giving a week's notice to the other.' There is this difference between the two cases, that in *Doe d Warner v Browne* the lessor engaged not to turn out the tenant so long as he observed the conditions, and in this case [the company's agent] engages that the tenant shall hold until the company require to pull down the buildings. But, as that is an event which may never happen, the distinction is merely between the contingency of the tenant breaking the conditions and the contingency of the company wanting the premises in order to pull them down. The restriction is as repugnant to the nature of the tenancy in the one case as in the other. It is therefore no legal answer to the ejectment to say that the contingency provided for has not happened.'

These authorities indicate plainly enough that the agreement in the present case did not create a lease and that the tenancy from year to year enjoyed by the tenant as a result of entering into possession and paying a yearly rent can be determined by six months' notice by either landlord or tenant. The landlord has admittedly served such a notice. The Court of Appeal have however concluded that the notice was ineffective and that the landlord cannot give a valid notice until the land is required 'for the purposes of the widening of Walworth Road' in conformity with clause 6 of the agreement.

The notion of a tenancy from year to year, the landlord binding himself not to give notice to quit, which was exploded long before 1807 according to Lawrence J in *Doe d Warner v Browne* 8 East 165, 167, was however revived and applied by the Court of Appeal in *Re Midland Rly Co's Agreement* [1971] Ch 725. In that case a lease for a period of six months from 10 June 1920 was expressed to continue from half year to half year until determined. The agreement provided for the determination of the agreement by three months' written notice given by either party to the other subject to a proviso that the landlords should not exercise that right unless they required the premises for their undertaking. The successors to the landlords served a six months' written notice to quit under section 25 of the Landlord and Tenant Act 1954 although they did not require the premises for their undertaking. The Court of Appeal, upholding Foster J, declared that the notice to quit was invalid and of no effect because the landlords did not require the premises for their undertaking. The Court of Appeal held that the decision in *Lace v Chantler* [1944] KB 368 did not apply to a periodic tenancy and declined to follow *Doe d Warner v Browne* 8 East 165 or *Cheshire Lines Committee v Lewis & Co* 50 LJQB 121. Russell LJ delivering the judgment of the court held that the decision in *Lace v Chantler* [1944] KB 368 did not apply to a tenancy from year to year and said [1971] Ch 725, 733:

> 'we are persuaded that, there being no authority to prevent us, it is preferable as a matter of justice to hold parties to their clearly expressed bargain rather than to introduce for the first time in 1971 an extension of a doctrine of land law so as to deny the efficacy of that bargain'.

My Lords, I consider that the principle in *Lace v Chantler* [1944] KB 368 reaffirming 500 years of judicial acceptance of the requirement that a term must be certain applies to all leases and tenancy agreements. A tenancy from year to year is saved from being uncertain because each party has power by notice to determine at the end of any year. The term continues until determined as if both parties made a new agreement at the end of each year for a new term for the ensuing year. A power for nobody to determine or for one party only to be able to determine is inconsistent with the concept of a term from year to year: see *Doe d Warner v Browne* 8 East 165 and *Cheshire Lines Committee v Lewis & Co* 50 LJQB 121. In *Re Midland Rly Co's Agreement* there was no 'clearly expressed bargain' that the term should continue until the crack of doom if the demised land was not required for the landlord's undertaking or if the undertaking ceased to exist. In the present case there was no 'clearly expressed bargain' that the tenant shall be entitled to enjoy his 'temporary structures' in perpetuity if Walworth Road is never widened. In any event principle and precedent dictate that it is beyond the power of the landlord and the tenant to create a term which is uncertain.

A lease can be made for five years subject to the tenant's right to determine if the war ends before the expiry of five years. A lease can be made from year to year subject to a fetter on the right of the landlord to determine the lease before the expiry of five years unless the war ends. Both leases are valid because they create a determinable certain term of five years. A lease might purport to be made for the duration of the war subject to the tenant's right to determine before the end of the war. A lease might be made from year to year subject to a fetter on the right of the landlord to determine the lease before the war ends. Both leases would be invalid because each purported to create an uncertain term. A term must either be certain or uncertain. It cannot be partly certain because the tenant can determine it at any time and partly uncertain because the landlord cannot determine it for an uncertain period. If the landlord does not grant and the tenant does not take a certain term the grant does not create a lease.

The decision of the Court of Appeal in *Re Midland Rly Co's Agreement* [1971] Ch 725 was taken a little further in *Ashburn Anstalt v Arnold* [1989] Ch 1. That case, if it was correct, would make it unnecessary for a lease to be of a certain duration. In an agreement for the sale of land the vendor reserved the right to remain at the property after completion as licensee and to trade therefrom without payment of rent

> 'save that it can be required by Matlodge [the purchaser] to give possession on not less than one quarter's notice in writing upon Matlodge certifying that it is ready at the expiration of such notice forthwith to proceed with the development of the property and the neighbouring property involving, inter alia, the demolition of the property'.

The Court of Appeal held that this reservation created a tenancy. The tenancy was not from year to year but for a term which would continue until Matlodge certified that it was ready to proceed with the development of the property. The Court of Appeal held that the term was not uncertain because the vendor could either give a quarter's notice or vacate the property without giving notice. But of course the same could be said of the situation in *Lace v Chantler* [1944] KB 368. The cumulative result of the two Court of Appeal authorities *Re Midland Rly Co's Agreement* and *Ashburn's* case would therefore destroy the need for any term to be certain.

In the present case the Court of Appeal were bound by the decisions in *Re Midland Rly Co's Agreement* and *Ashburn's* case. In my opinion both these cases were wrongly decided. A grant for an uncertain term does not create a lease. A grant for an uncertain term which takes the form of a yearly tenancy which cannot be determined by the landlord does not create a lease. I would allow the appeal.

Lord Browne-Wilkinson: My Lords, I agree with the speech of my noble and learned friend, Lord Templeman, that this appeal must be allowed for the reasons he gives. However, I reach that conclusion with no satisfaction.

Before 1930, Mr Nathan owned shop premises, 263–265 Walworth Road, with a frontage to the street. The agreement made in 1930 between the London County Council and Mr Nathan was part of a sale and leaseback arrangement whereby a part of Mr Nathan's land ('the strip') was sold to the L.C.C. for road widening. Mr Nathan retained the freehold of the remainder of No. 263–265. By the agreement, the strip was leased back to Mr Nathan for continued use, with the rest of 263–265, Walworth Road until required for road widening as commercial premises. Up until today, the remainder of No. 263–265 together with the strip has been let and occupied as one single set of retail shop premises with a frontage to the Walworth Road. As a result of our decision Mr Nathan's successor in title will be left with the freehold of the remainder of No. 263–265 which, though retail premises, will have no frontage to a shopping street: the L.C.C.'s successors in title will have the freehold to a strip of land with a road frontage but probably incapable of being used save in conjunction with the land from which it was severed in 1930, i.e. the remainder of No. 263–265.

It is difficult to think of a more unsatisfactory outcome or one further away from what the parties to the 1930 agreement can ever have contemplated. Certainly it was not a result their contract, if given effect to, could ever have produced. If the 1930 agreement had taken effect fully, there could never have come a time when the freehold to the remainder of No. 263–265 would be left without a road frontage.

This bizarre outcome results from the application of an ancient and technical rule of law which requires the maximum duration of a term of years to be ascertainable from the outset. No one has produced any satisfactory rationale for the genesis of this rule. No one has been able to point to any useful purpose that it serves at the present day. If, by overruling the existing authorities, this House were able to change the law for the future only I would have urged your Lordships to do so. But for this House to depart from a rule relating to land law which has been established for many centuries might upset long established titles. I must therefore confine myself to expressing the hope that the Law Commission might look at the subject to see whether there is in fact any good reason now for maintaining a rule which operates to defeat contractually agreed arrangements between the parties (of which all successors in title are aware) and which is capable of producing such an extraordinary result as that in the present case.[76]

---

[76] Lords Griffiths and Mustill concurred with this view.

(a) Interesse termini

At common law the rule was that, until he entered into possession of the land, the tenant in certain circumstances had only a right to the term (an *interesse termini*) rather than the actual estate. This doctrine was abolished by the Law of Property Act 1925.

LAW OF PROPERTY ACT 1925

149. Abolition of interesse termini, and as to reversionary leases and leases for lives.—(1) The doctrine of interesse termini is hereby abolished.

(2) As from the commencement of this Act all terms of years absolute shall, whether the interest is created before or after such commencement, be capable of taking effect at law or in equity, according to the estate interest or powers of the grantor, from the date fixed for commencement of the term, without actual entry.

(b) Reversionary leases

A 'reversionary lease' is one in which the term is to commence only at a future date.[77]

LAW OF PROPERTY ACT 1925

149. Abolition of interesse termini, and as to reversionary leases and leases for lives.—(3) A term, at a rent or granted in consideration of a fine,[78] limited after the commencement of this Act to take effect more than twenty-one years from the date of the instrument purporting to create it, shall be void, and any contract made after such commencement to create such a term shall likewise be void; but this subsection does not apply to any term taking effect in equity under a settlement, or created out of an equitable interest under a settlement, or under an equitable power for mortgage, indemnity or other like purposes.

Re Strand and Savoy Properties Ltd[79]
[1960] Ch 582 (ChD, **Buckley J**)

A 35 year lease contained a provision that the lessors would 'at the written request of the lessee made 12 months before the expiration of the term hereby created' grant a further term of 35 years at the same rent.

The tenants took out a summons to determine whether the Law of Property Act 1925, section 149(3) invalidated their option to renew the lease on the ground that it was a contract to take effect more than 21 years from the date of the lease granting the option.

Held. The option for renewal was valid.

Buckley J: Sir Milner Holland, who appears for the tenants, ... says that subsection (3) makes it impossible for any man to create a reversionary term—that is to say, a term to take effect more

---

[77] A reversionary lease can take effect only if created by deed: *Long v Tower Hamlets London Borough Council* [1998] Ch 197 at 210–219; above, p. 42, n. 114. A reversionary lease is not to be confused with the *reversion*, the interest retained by the landlord under every lease, and which is a *present estate* conferring the right to the possession of the land when all inferior leases have determined. The landlord can grant a (present) lease of his reversion: LPA 1925, s. 149(5); p. 342, above.

[78] P. 366, n. 81, below.   [79] (1960) 76 LQR 352 (R.E.M.).

than 21 years from the date of the instrument creating the term—and that it also invalidates any contract by which a man undertakes to create a reversionary term, that is to say, a term which will not commence until 21 years after the date of the instrument creating such a term. He says that the subsection does not invalidate a contract to create a lease, at however remote a date in the future, which, when it is granted, will create a term which will take effect within 21 years of the date of that lease....

Mr Albery, on the other hand, points out that the contention advanced by Sir Milner really gives no operative effect to that part of subsection (3) which deals with contracts at all, because if a lease granting a term to commence at a date later than 21 years from the date of the lease is void, a contract to grant such a lease must also necessarily be void without any express provision to that effect in the statute....

[T]he subsection is confined, so far as contracts are concerned, to contracts to create terms which, when created, will only take effect more than 21 years from the dates of the instruments creating them; that is to say, it invalidates contracts for the granting of leases which will, when granted, be reversionary leases, the postponement of the commencement of the term being for more than 21 years from the date of the lease.

Weg Motors Ltd v Hales
[1962] Ch 49 (CA, **Lord Evershed MR, Harman** and **Donovan LJJ**)

In July 1938 the plaintiffs were granted a lease of premises for a term of 21 years from December 1938, with an option of 'taking a further lease' of the premises for a period of 21 years from the date of the exercise of the option; and the option was expressed to be exercisable at any time before 25 December 1959. The defendants claimed that the option agreement was void under section 149 (3).

Held. The option agreement was valid.

Lord Evershed MR: [T]he question is, in our judgment, an extremely short one—namely, does the option agreement of July, 1938, fall within the scope of the language in subsection (3) of section 149 of the Act of 1925 as being a contract 'to create such a term' as therein mentioned? The view of the learned author of the note to the section in volume 1 of Wolstenholme and Cherry's *Conveyancing Statutes,* 12th edn (1952), p. 497, appears clearly to have been that a contract to create a term of years, which might begin to take effect more than 21 years from the date of the contract, fell within the vice of the subsection. It was this view that Buckley J rejected in the case already cited;[80] and he did so upon the basis that the phrase 'such a term' could in its context refer, and refer only, to a term commencing more than 21 years from the instrument purporting to create the term, that is to say, the lease executed in pursuance of the contract and not the contract itself. We must not be taken to be expressing any doubt of the correctness of Buckley J's decision. But in the present case we are concerned not with a contract, that is a binding agreement, to grant and take a lease but with an option which might never be exercised and cannot, until exercised, be in any event said, in our judgment, to create a term of years at all. It follows, therefore, in our view, that the option agreement with which we are concerned cannot be said to be such a contract as is comprehended in section 149(3) of the Act of 1925. The challenge to the plaintiffs based upon that section must, therefore, fail.

[80] *Re Strand and Savoy Properties Ltd* [1960] Ch 582 [p. 364, above].

(c) Leases for lives

LAW OF PROPERTY ACT 1925

149. Abolition of interesse termini, and as to reversionary leases and leases for lives.—(6)[81] Any lease or underlease, at a rent, or in consideration of a fine,[82] for life or lives or for any term of years determinable with life or lives, or on the marriage of the lessee, or on the formation of a civil partnership between the lessee and another person, or any contract therefor, made before or after the commencement of this Act, or created by virtue of Part V of the Law of Property Act, 1922, shall take effect as a lease, underlease or contract therefor, for a term of ninety years determinable after (as the case may be) the death or marriage of, or the formation of a civil partnership by, the original lessee or the survivor of the original lessees, by at least one month's notice in writing given to determine the same on one of the quarter days applicable to the tenancy, either by the lessor or the persons deriving title under him, to the person entitled to the leasehold interest, or if no such person is in existence by affixing the same to the premises, or by the lessee or other persons in whom the leasehold interest is vested to the lessor or the persons deriving title under him:

Provided that—

(a) this subsection shall not apply to any term taking effect in equity under a settlement or created out of an equitable interest under a settlement for mortgage, indemnity, or other like purposes; ...

(d) if there are no quarter days specially applicable to the tenancy, notice may be given to determine the tenancy on one of the usual quarter days.[83]

In **Bass Holdings Ltd v Lewis** [1986] 2 EGLR 40, Bass Holdings Ltd, the respondent, entered into a tenancy agreement with Lewis, by which it sub-let to him the Railway Tavern, Deptford for three years, terminable by Bass on giving six months' notice, or, if Lewis died, not less than fourteen days' notice to his personal representatives. In November 1984, Bass served a notice to quit on Lewis who denied Bass's right to possession, on the ground that under section 149(6) the term granted to him had been converted into one for 90 years, determinable only by notice after his death. Hoffmann J rejected this claim. Affirming that decision, NOURSE LJ said at 40:

The essence of Hoffmann J's decision is to be found at p. 3 B–C of the transcript where, having described the appellant's claim and its consequences in tones of some irony, he said this:

'In my judgment the short answer to this remarkable claim is that Mr Lewis's tenancy was not granted for life or lives or any term of years determinable with life or lives within the meaning of section 149(6) of the Law of Property Act 1925. The statute is dealing with leases which are granted

[81] Amended by Civil Partnership Act 2004, s. 81, Sch. 8, para. 1(2), (3).

[82] A fine is usually the single payment of a lump sum made by the tenant, and is additional to the rent. By statute the word includes 'a premium or foregift and any payment, consideration or benefit in the nature of a fine, premium or foregift': LPA 1925, s. 205(1)(xxiii); *Skipton Building Society v Clayton* (1993) 66 P & CR 223. The rent or fine excludes beneficial tenancies for life under a settlement; these are equitable interests and subject to SLA 1925 or, after 1996, to a trust of land: *Binions v Evans* [1972] Ch 359 at 366, p. 1102, below; *Ivory v Palmer* [1975] ICR 340.

[83] Lady Day (March 25), Midsummer Day (June 24); Michaelmas Day (September 29) or Christmas Day (December 25).

either for a term limited by reference to a life or lives, or for a term of years limited conditionally upon the survival of a life or lives'.

I entirely agree. I add by way of illustration that the simplest example of a term of years limited conditionally upon the survival of a life or lives is a lease 'to A for a term of 20 years if he shall so long live.'

The learned judge[84] then went on to consider the aim of the 1925 property legislation, implemented in part by section 149(6), to reduce the legal estates which are capable of existing in land to estates in fee simple absolute in possession and to terms of years absolute. He pointed out, correctly, that a lease for a fixed period with a proviso which allows for its determination by notice, even if the dropping of a life is a condition precedent to the service of a valid notice, is none the less a term of years absolute.

The appellant's construction of section 149(6) as advanced by Mr Wood on his behalf, necessitates reading the words 'for any term of years determinable with life or lives' as including a term of years determinable by notice after the dropping of a life or lives. It seems to me that there are a number of conclusive objections to that construction.

First, the word 'determinable' is capable of meaning 'liable to determine' and no more. It does not necessarily also mean 'determinable by notice' or by some other positive act.

Second, it seems to me to be very important to pay attention to the prepositions which are used in the two parts of the subsection. In describing the leases to which it is to apply, the subsection refers to leases determinable *with* life or lives, or *on* the marriage of the lessee. That suggests that it is referring to leases which will determine automatically, in the one case on death and in the other on marriage. By contrast, when you get to the provision dealing with the new lease, you find that it is to be determinable by notice *after* the death or marriage as the case may be of the lessee. That is a distinction which I do not think can be ignored and it is further emphasised by the terms of proviso *(c)*.

Third, the contrast between the use of the word 'determinable' *simpliciter* in the first part of the subsection and the reference to determinability after the death or marriage *by notice* in the second conclusively confirms that in the first part 'determinable' does not mean determinable by notice.

For these reasons, as well as for those given by the learned judge, it seems to me that this is a very clear case. In my view the learned judge arrived at an entirely correct decision. I would therefore dismiss this appeal.

(d) Perpetually renewable leases

A lease must be determinable by both landlord and tenant at some definite or definable time: it cannot be perpetual. A very long lease—for, say, 999 years—is acceptable, and so is a lease which will be renewed from time to time until one party gives notice to quit—such as a periodic tenancy.[85] But a lease under which the tenant for the time being has the *right* of *perpetual renewal* is not tolerated. Perpetually renewable leases are converted into terms of 2,000 years; those already existing on 1 January 1926 date

---

[84] See Hoffmann J (unreported) who said: 'Why should a term of 3 years "if X shall so long live" automatically become a term of 90 years determinable by notice after X's death? It is possible (although one hardly dare whisper such a suggestion about the great conveyancers who drafted the statute) that it was simply a mistake.'

[85] Above, p. 334.

from the commencement of the existing tenancy, and those created after 1925 from the date fixed for the commencement of the tenancy. Perpetually renewable subleases are converted into terms of 2,000 years less one day.[86]

In **Caerphilly Concrete Products Ltd v Owen** [1972] 1 WLR 372[87] a grant in 1963 of a five year term of 4,800 square feet in an industrial area of Caerphilly at £10 a year contained a provision that 'the landlord will on the written request of the tenant...grant to him a lease of the said demised land for the further term of five years from the expiration of the said term hereby granted at the same rent and containing the like covenants and provisos as are herein contained (including an option to renew such lease for the further term of five years at the expiration thereof)'. The Court of Appeal (Russell, Sachs and Stamp LJJ) held that the grant took effect as a lease for 2,000 years.

RUSSELL LJ said at 374:

The approach to the question whether a lease is perpetually renewable is not in doubt. The language used must plainly lead to that result: though the fact that an argument is capable of being sustained at some length against that result does not of course suffice. As a matter of history, when a covenant by a lessor conferred a right to renewal of the lease, the new grant to contain the same or the like covenants and provisos as were contained in the lease, the courts refused to give literal effect to that language, which if taken literally would mean that the second lease would contain the same covenant (or option) to renew, totidem verbis, and so on perpetually. The reference to the same covenants was construed as not including the option covenant itself. This limited the tenant's right to one renewal. In order therefore to make it plain that the covenants to be contained in the second lease (to be granted under the exercise of the option to renew) were to include also the covenant to renew, draftsmen were accustomed to insert phrases such as 'including this covenant', so as to achieve a perpetually renewable lease. As I have indicated, if they did not do this, the second lease would not contain any option clause.

The operation of the words of inclusion was not limited to requiring the second lease to contain a covenant to renew once more only, which would have been the outcome if the words of inclusion had been omitted in the second lease. This was because the words of inclusion could not properly be construed as requiring the second lease to contain the same covenants other than the covenant to renew but additionally to include an option to renew once more only—a total of three terms. The words of inclusion defined or explained what was meant by 'the same covenants,' that is to say, as including the covenant to renew. Consequently in the second lease, in order to comply with the words of definition or explanation, the covenants referred to therein to be contained in the second lease must contain the same wording including the inclusion.

In the present case the brackets make it abundantly plain that the parties are explaining that 'containing the like covenants and provisos' is a phrase intended to embrace an option. That is to say that the covenants and provisos contained in the first lease, which the first lease requires the second lease to contain, are not to be construed as a reference to those covenants and provisos other than an option to renew, but as a reference to all those covenants including an option to renew.... If the words...are repeated in the second lease without the words in parenthesis

---

86 LPA 1922, s. 145 and Sch. 15.   87 (1972) 88 LQR 173.

the second lease will not be carrying out the requirement of the first lease: it will not be granting an option for a further lease containing 'the like covenants' as defined.

SACHS LJ said at 375:

I, too, have underlined the words in brackets. It is trite to say that when construing a document such as a lease it is the prime purpose of the courts to seek to adopt a meaning that conforms to the intentions of the parties. Not even the most impeccable conveyancing logic, however neatly expressed, can convince me that in the instant case it was the mutual intention of the parties that the lease should be perpetually renewable. So far as the landlord is concerned it seems to me highly unlikely that he really intended that this particular lease could or should be 'for ever'. My doubts on that question of intention extend also to the tenant—for I would acquit him of any intent to lay a trap through the operation of the words enclosed in the brackets, which we know to have been added to the draft at the very last moment by his solicitors. It is difficult indeed, at any rate so far as I am concerned, to think that two business men would be talking in terms of five years if both—or indeed either—of them truly meant that a lease should be granted which went on ad infinitum.

Were I in a position to give effect to the views just expressed that would result in the landlord succeeding in this appeal: but it is necessary to consider whether the authorities which were so fully and so helpfully cited to us permit such a result. An examination of the relevant decisions discloses an area of law in which the courts have manoeuvred themselves into an unhappy position... [T]hey appear to have bound themselves to hold that the use of a certain set of words (to which I will refer as 'the formula') causes the lease to be perpetually renewable, even when no layman—at least if he has some elementary knowledge of business—would dream of granting such a lease and, if aware of the technical meaning of the particular phraseology would almost certainly be aghast at its devastating effect and refuse to sign. One reason for the courts so binding themselves is said to be that the formula is one the effect of which is well known to trained conveyancers, and that this is advantageous, however much of a trap it may constitute for others.

As already mentioned, the prime purpose of the courts when construing a lease is to interpret it according to the true intentions of the parties. Already 20 years ago judicial unease at having to determine those intentions in cases of the instant type by a blinkered approach is reflected in the judgments in *Parkus v Greenwood,* both at first instance [1950] Ch 33 and on appeal [1950] Ch 644.

His Lordship referred to *Green v Palmer* [1944] Ch 328 and continued:

The judicial unease of 1950 is, so far as I am concerned, by now increased by two factors. First, more and more leases over the two succeeding decades have tended to come from pens not fully trained in the art of conveyancing. Secondly, over the same period the value of the pound sterling has been decreasing rapidly, thus making it even more unlikely that a man of business in the course of a normal transaction would knowingly part 'for ever' with his rights over land in return for a static rent. Moreover, when residential property is concerned a landlord could indeed now find himself in the position of having to relinquish a freehold when the document which he signed appeared on the face of it to be a lease for relatively short periods of years.

In those circumstances I, too, have great sympathy with the line of approach adopted by Uthwatt J [in *Green v Palmer*] and Harman J in [*Parkus v Greenwood*]. I could wish that the courts had followed the apparent preference of Lord FitzGerald in *Swinburne v Milburn* (1884) 9 App Cas 844, 855 for confining interpretations of perpetual renewability to leases where words such as 'for ever' or 'from time to time for ever hereafter' or some equivalent were used in the relevant document. This approach would have avoided that sort of path by which good logic can on occasion make bad law, and would have been in accord with the aphorism that at times 'logic is only the art of going wrong with confidence'.

Having, however, examined the authorities, I feel bound in this court to say that the matter is concluded by them in that the words in brackets, as inserted at the last moment, have in law the same effect as those considered in *Parkus v Greenwood*.

In **Marjorie Burnett Ltd v Barclay** [1981] 1 EGLR 41,[88] there was a grant in 1971 of a seven year lease of a shop with residential accommodation above in Boscombe at a yearly rent of £650. Clause 6 contained a covenant to renew. The plaintiff sought a declaration that this was not perpetually renewable. In holding that it was not, NOURSE J said at 41:

[Clause 6] reads as follows:

'If the tenant shall be desirous of taking a new lease of the demised premises after the expiration of the term hereby granted...'

There are then provisions which are in a not very elegant form, but the effect of them is clear enough. It is that the tenant can give the landlord notice of the desire to take a new lease. Then clause 6 goes on as follows:

'Then the landlord will at or before the expiration of the term hereby granted, if there shall then be no subsisting breach of any of the tenant's obligations under this present lease—and now I come to some important words—grant to the tenant a new lease of the premises hereby demised for a further term of seven years, to commence from and after the expiration of the term hereby granted at a rent to be agreed between the parties'.

There are then provisions for the rent to be fixed in default of agreement. Then come the final words of the clause, which are also important. They read as follows:

'And such lease shall also contain a like covenant for renewal for a further term of seven years on the expiration of the term thereby granted....'

His Lordship referred to *Parkus v Greenwood* [1950] Ch 33 and *Caerphilly Concrete Products Ltd v Owen* [1972] 1 WLR 372, above, p. 368, and continued:

In construing clause 6 of the lease in the present case I must therefore approach the matter in this way. I must bear in mind that the leaning of the courts has been against perpetual renewals. I have to find expressly in the lease a covenant or obligation for perpetual renewal. And I have to look ahead to see what the second lease will contain when the requirements of the covenant for renewal in the first have been duly observed.

I now return to clause 6 of the lease. What the landlord has to do, if the tenant gives it notice of his desire to take a new lease, is to grant to the tenant a new lease of the demised premises for a further term of seven years at a rent to be agreed, and if not agreed to be fixed in the manner specified. Then it is provided that such lease shall also contain a like covenant for renewal for a further term of seven years on the expiration of the term thereby granted.

Mr Henty really puts his case on this primary question in two ways. First, he takes the simple course of asking me to see what provisions the second lease would contain if it were to be granted pursuant to clause 6. He says that it would inevitably be at a different rent from the

---

[88] (1981) 131 NLJ 683 (H. W. Wilkinson).

£650 reserved by the first lease. Then he says that the second lease would contain a like covenant for renewal for a further term of seven years as that contained in clause 6 of the first lease.
But that covenant ends with the part of clause 6 which deals with the provisions for fixing the
rent in default of agreement. It does not seem to me that the second lease could possibly contain
the words 'and such lease shall also contain a like covenant for renewal for a further term of
seven years on the expiration of the term thereby granted,' because those words are not part
of the covenant for renewal and to include them would be to go further than clause 6 requires.
And so I agree with Mr Henty that the second lease would be at a new rent and that it would
contain the whole of clause 6, except for the last three lines or so which I have just quoted. On
that footing it is clear that there is no express covenant or obligation for perpetual renewal.
Indeed the contrary is the case. There is an express provision in the lease to the effect that it
can be renewed twice only.

That would in itself be enough to dispose of the primary question in these proceedings. But
Mr Henty goes on to take a second point, which appears to me to be one of equal force, and that
is this. He says that even supposing his first argument were wrong I must bear in mind that what
will happen if this is a perpetually renewable lease is that it will be converted by the 1922 Act into
a lease for a term of 2,000 years. He says, and I can see no answer to this, that the notion of a
2,000-year term is completely inimical to a lease which contains provisions for rent review every
seven years. And so again he says that as a matter of construction clause 6 could not possibly
have the effect for which the defendant has contended. I agree with that contention also.

(ii) Certainty of rent

Rent is not essential for a lease.[89] However, where rent is payable it must be certain.[90]
That does not mean that it must be certain at the date of the lease. Rent is sufficiently
certain if it can be calculated with certainty at the time when payment comes to be
made.[91] This problem has been considered in connexion with options to renew a lease
and rent revision at the time of renewal.

(a) Option to renew lease

Brown v Gould[92]
[1972] Ch 53 (ChD, **Megarry J**)

In 1949 Margaret Gould leased part of Albion Granaries, 250 High Road, Loughton,
Essex to Frank Brown[93] for 21 years from 29 September 1949, at a rent of £500 a year.
Clause 3(c) of the lease granted to the tenant an option to renew the tenancy for a

---

[89] LPA 1925, s. 205 (1) (xxvii); *Ashburn Anstalt v Arnold,* [1989] Ch 1, p. 380, n. 108 below.

[90] On the meaning of rent, see [1991] Conv 270 (R. G. Lee); C & B, pp. 241, 265–266.

[91] *Greater London Council v Connolly* [1970] 2 QB 100 ('rent liable to be increased or decreased on notice
being given' held to be valid); *CH Bailey Ltd v Memorial Enterprises Ltd* [1974] 1 WLR 728 (increased rent
ascertained retrospectively); *Bradshaw v Pawley* [1980] 1 WLR 10 (rent payable from a date prior to execution of lease). For the validity of an index-linked rent, see *Blumenthal v Gallery Five Ltd* (1971) 220 EG 31
(index of retail prices); *Cumshaw Ltd v Bowen* [1987] 1 EGLR 30; (1987) 132 NLJ 288 (H. W. Wilkinson);
(1994) 138 SJ 552 (R. Castle and A. MacFarquhar).

[92] (1972) 36 Conv (NS) 317 (P. Robertshaw).

[93] 'He had the good fortune to live at Arabin House, High Beech, Essex', at 55. See Megarry, *Arabinesque-
at-law* (1969), p. xi.

further term of 21 years at a rent 'to be fixed having regard to the market value of the premises at the time of exercising the option taking into account to the advantage of the tenant any increased value of such premises attributable to structural improvements made by the tenant during the currency of this present lease'. Frank Brown spent nearly £30,000 rebuilding the premises, and in 1969 served notice in accordance with the terms of the lease purporting to exercise the option. The trustees of Margaret Gould, in whom the reversion had vested on her death, contended that the option was void for uncertainty.

Held. The option was valid.

Megarry J: The landlords... contend that the option for renewal contained in the lease is void for uncertainty. That is the sole question that I have to determine. Stated briefly, the proper approach, I think, is that the court is reluctant to hold void for uncertainty any provision that was intended to have legal effect. In this case it is very properly accepted that the option was intended to have business efficacy.

In an unreported case, *Re Lloyd's Trust Instruments* 24th June, 1970, to which I referred counsel, I endeavoured to state the basic principles applicable in cases of uncertainty. What I said there was:

'I think the starting point on any question of uncertainty must be that of the court's reluctance to hold an instrument void for uncertainty. Lord Hardwicke LC once said "A court never construes a devise void, unless it is so absolutely dark, that they cannot find out the testator's meaning": *Minshull v Minshull* (1737) 1 Atk 411, 412. Lord Brougham said: "The difficulty must be so great that it amounts to an impossibility, the doubt so grave that there is not even an inclination of the scales one way": *Doe d Winter v Perratt* (1843) 9 Cl & F 606, 689. In a well-known statement, Sir George Jessel MR said that the court would not hold a will void for uncertainty "unless it is utterly impossible to put a meaning upon it. The duty of the court is to put a fair meaning on the terms used, and not, as was said in one case, to repose on the easy pillow of saying that the whole is void for uncertainty": *Re Roberts* (1881) 19 ChD 520, 529. That this is not a doctrine confined to wills but is one which applies to other instruments, such as planning permissions, is shown by cases such as *Fawcett Properties Ltd v Buckingham County Council* [1961] AC 636, where, by a majority, the delphic language of a condition in a planning permission escaped from being held void for uncertainty largely because of its resemblance to a section to be found in a modern Act of Parliament. The second question is that of the types of uncertainty. The basic type (and on one view the only true type) is uncertainty of concept, as contrasted with mere difficulty of application: see, for example, *Re Gape* [1952] Ch 418, affirmed at 743, where the question was one of a condition subsequent, in which special considerations apply. In *Fawcett's* case [1961] AC 636, 670, Lord Keith of Avonholm said: "The point is one of uncertainty of concept. If it is impossible, on construction of the condition, to reach a conclusion as to what was in the draftsman's mind, the condition is meaningless and must be read as pro non scripto." Putting it another way, the question is one of linguistic or semantic uncertainty, and not of difficulty of ascertainment: see *Re Baden's Deed Trusts* [1971] AC 424, 457, per Lord Wilberforce. If there is a trust for "my old friends," all concerned are faced with uncertainty as to the concept or idea enshrined in these words. It may not be difficult to resolve that "old" means not "aged" but "of long standing"; but then there is the question how long is "long". Friendship, too, is a concept with almost infinite shades of meaning. Where the concept is uncertain, the gift is void. Where the concept is certain, then mere difficulty in tracing and discovering those who are entitled normally does not invalidate the gift.'

To the authorities mentioned in that passage must now be added *Greater London Council v Connolly* [1970] 2 QB 100, a landlord and tenant case concerning a condition on the rent card of a council tenant. This condition provided that the rent and other sums shown on the rent card 'are liable to be increased or decreased on notice being given'; and the Court of Appeal unanimously held that the condition was not void for uncertainty. Lord Denning MR said, at 108:

> 'The courts are always loath to hold a condition bad for uncertainty. They will give it a reasonable interpretation whenever possible. It is possible here.' . . .

No doubt there may be cases in which the draftsman's ineptitude will succeed in defeating the court's efforts to find a meaning for the provision in question; but only if the court is driven to it will it be held that a provision is void for uncertainty.

With that in mind, I approach the attack made on the present clause. Mr Scamell [counsel for the defendants] concentrated on three phrases in the clause, the words 'a rent to be fixed', the words 'having regard to' the market value of the premises at the time of exercising the option, and the words 'taking into account' to the advantage of the tenant any increased value of the premises attributable to his structural improvements. In addition, he pointed to the absence of any machinery for working out this formula, by contrast with the other provisions in the lease that I have mentioned. Taken together, he said, these considerations showed that the clause provided neither a clear basis for determining the rent nor any means of quantifying that basis, and accordingly the option was void for uncertainty.

At least three types of option may be distinguished. First, the option may be for renewal simply 'at a rent to be agreed'. In that case, no formula for quantifying the rent is laid down, and prima facie the option will, as in *King's Motors (Oxford) Ltd v Lax* [1970] 1 WLR 426, be void as being a mere contract to make a contract, or, perhaps more properly, as being an agreement to make a contract, or a contract dependent upon the making of an agreement.[94] In *Smith v Morgan* [1971] 1 WLR 803, my brother Brightman held that a right of pre-emption in a conveyance 'at a figure to be agreed upon' was not void for uncertainty, but imposed upon the person granting it an obligation to offer the land to the grantee at the price at which she was willing to sell it. On this, I would make two comments. First, it illustrates the attitude of the court in striving to avoid holding a provision void for uncertainty. Second, it illustrates one of the differences between an option and a right of pre-emption. Under an option, only one step is normally needed to constitute a contract, namely, the exercise of the option. Under a right of pre-emption, two steps will usually be necessary, the making of the offer in accordance with the right of pre-emption, and the acceptance of that offer. The failure to provide either a price or a formula for ascertaining the price is accordingly far more serious in the case of an option than under a pre-emption: he who exercises such an option may well be virtually signing a blank cheque, whereas he who is entitled to a right of pre-emption can at least refrain from accepting the grantor's offer if the price be too high.[95]

The second type of option is one that is expressed to be exercisable at a price to be determined according to some stated formula, without any effective machinery being in terms

---

[94] See also *Courtney and Fairbairn Ltd v Tolaini Bros (Hotels) Ltd* [1975] 1 WLR 297 (building agreement 'to negotiate fair and reasonable contract sums' held to be void for uncertainty); *Walford v Miles* [1992] 2 AC 128 (agreement 'to continue to negotiate in good faith' held to be void for uncertainty).

[95] See pp. 34–40, above. *Smith v Morgan* was doubted in *Miller v Lakefield Estates Ltd* (1988) 57 P & CR 104, where May LJ thought it arguable that 'the judge there might have implied too much into the option clause.'

provided for the working out of that formula. That is the present case. Thirdly, the option may be one which provides both a formula and the machinery, as, for example, arbitration. In this last case, it may be that the machinery can do something to cure defects in the formula: I do not have to decide that. What is before me is a formula that is assailed for its uncertainty, and the absence of any specified machinery that can do anything to cure that uncertainty. I shall consider the question of machinery first.

His Lordship rejected the landlords' argument that there was no adequate machinery for determining the rent, and continued:

I readily accept that the words of clause 3(c) might have been more precise. But that is not the point: the point is whether it is void for uncertainty. If one approaches the formula stated in the clause with reasonable goodwill, as I think I am entitled and, indeed, required to do, does it appear to embody such uncertainty of concept as to make it void? Without saying that there is no room for argument on the details, I would answer No to that question, or, indeed, to any other reasonable way of formulating the question that I can conceive. The question is not, I think, whether the clause is proof against wilful misinterpretation, but whether someone genuinely seeking to discover its meaning is able to do so. To that question I would answer Yes.

In **Corson v Rhuddlan Borough Council** (1989) 59 P & CR 185,[96] the lease of Prestatyn Golf course included an option to renew for a further lease 'and at a rent to be agreed', such rent not to exceed the previous rent of £1,150. The Court of Appeal rejected the landlord's claim that the option was void for uncertainty, and implied a term for a fair rent with an upper limit of £1,150. RALPH GIBSON LJ said at 194:

It seems plain to me, therefore, that, in the absence of authority requiring us to take a different course, it is proper to apply to this clause the principle applied by Lord Tomlin to the document in *Hillas & Co v Arcos* (1932) 147 LT 503 namely that the court should, if it can: 'so balance matters that without violation of essential principle the dealings of men may as far as possible be treated as effective.'

In *Brown v Gould,* Megarry J referred to the reluctance of the court to hold an instrument void for uncertainty as a basic principle. If we are free to do so, I would hold that in this case the contractual intention of the parties is clear that, upon proper notice being given, the council should be under an obligation to grant a new lease at a fair rent to be agreed between the parties, that fair rent not to be in excess of £1,150. It is just and necessary to imply the provision for the rent to be a fair rent.

There is said to be authority in the way of taking that course. In *King's Motors (Oxford) Ltd v Lax* the option clause was contained in a seven-year lease of a petrol station and provided for a further term of seven years. As in this case, there was a requirement as to the giving of notice six months before the end of the term and of due performance of the covenants in the lease, but the rent was to be 'as may be agreed between the parties.' There was no statement as to the maximum rent. Mr Orr submitted that that case had been approved in *Beer v Bowden* [1981]

---

[96] [1990] Conv 290 (J. E. Martin). See also *Miller v Lakefield Estates Ltd,* above (option to purchase 'at a price to be agreed', but if no sale took place within six months of notice given to exercise option, then property should be sold at public auction, held valid). Cf. *ARC Ltd v Schofield* [1990] 2 EGLR 52 (option to renew lease at a rent 'to be agreed between the landlord and tenant, being a fair and reasonable market rent at that time' held valid).

1 WLR 522n, p. 377, below, by this court and that the reference in the option clause in this case to a maximum rent did not serve to distinguish this case from the grounds of decision in *Lax's* case. As was pointed out in the course of argument by Balcombe LJ, the correctness of the decision in *Lax's* case was not treated as a matter of decision for this court in *Beer v Bowden.* The *Lax* case was concerned with an option clause, as contrasted with the rent revision clause before the court in *Beer v Bowden,* and was thus regarded as distinguishable. It is, again, I think, not necessary for this court to decide whether the decision in the *Lax* case was correct because the provision for a maximum rent is, in my judgment, a material distinction. For my part, however, I incline to the view that it was, as Mr George submitted, wrongly decided, and I would respectfully differ from the view of Goff LJ that the option clause was in that case precluded from being a valid contract because the rent was not ascertainable. I see no reason why different principles should be applicable to the construction, so far as concerns voidness for uncertainty, of a rent revision clause in an existing lease as contrasted with an option for a 'new' lease or further lease in an existing lease. *Foley v Classique Coaches Ltd* [1934] 2 KB 1, established that the presence of the words 'to be agreed by the parties' is not fatal to the existence of an enforceable contract if it is otherwise plain, upon the construction of the whole of the document in its context, including of course those words, that there was a clear contractual intention of the parties to be bound by the clause. A provision that the rent should be a fair rent could, I think, have been implied in the *Lax* case. I can see no risk of difficulty arising from such a conclusion. If parties intend an option clause to be no more than an indication that the landlord will be willing to consider a request for a new lease without obligation and on terms to be agreed, there is no difficulty in making that intention clear if there is thought to be any utility in including such a statement in the document.

Sudbrook Trading Estate Ltd v Eggleton
[1983] 1 AC 444[97] (HL, **Lords Diplock, Fraser of Tullybelton, Russell of Killowen, Scarman** and **Bridge of Harrow**)

In a series of leases of industrial properties in Gloucester, the lessees were granted an option 'to purchase the reversion in fee simple in the premises hereby demised...at such price not being less than £12,000 as may be agreed upon by two valuers one to be nominated by the lessor and the other by the lessee and in default of such agreement by an umpire appointed by the valuers.' The lessees purported to exercise the option, but the lessors refused to appoint a valuer, claiming that machinery for the ascertainment of the option price was defectively uncertain. The lessees sought specific performance of the options.

Held (Lord Russell of Killowen dissenting). Specific performance granted.

Lord Fraser of Tullybelton: I recognise the logic of the reasoning which has led to the courts' refusing to substitute their own machinery for the machinery which has been agreed upon by the parties. But the result to which it leads is so remote from that which parties normally intend and expect, and is so inconvenient in practice, that there must in my opinion be some defect in the reasoning. I think the defect lies in construing the provisions for the mode of ascertaining the value as an essential part of the agreement. That may have been perfectly true early in the 19th

---

[97] [1983] Conv 76 (K. Hodkinson); (1982) 98 LQR 539 (J. Murdoch).

century, when the valuer's profession and the rules of valuation were less well established than they are now. But at the present day these provisions are only subsidiary to the main purpose of the agreement which is for sale and purchase of the property at a fair or reasonable value. In the ordinary case parties do not make any substantial distinction between an agreement to sell at a fair value, without specifying the mode of ascertaining the value, and an agreement to sell at a value to be ascertained by valuers appointed in the way provided in these leases. The true distinction is between those cases where the mode of ascertaining the price is an essential term of the contract, and those cases where the mode of ascertainment, though indicated in the contract, is subsidiary and non-essential: see *Fry on Specific Performance,* 6th edn (1921), pp. 167, 169, paragraphs 360, 364. The present case falls, in my opinion, into the latter category. Accordingly when the option was exercised there was constituted a complete contract for sale, and the clause should be construed as meaning that the price was to be a fair price. On the other hand where an agreement is made to sell at a price to be fixed by a valuer who is named, or who, by reason of holding some office such as auditor of a company whose shares are to be valued, will have special knowledge relevant to the question of value, the prescribed mode may well be regarded as essential. Where, as here, the machinery consists of valuers and an umpire, none of whom is named or identified, it is in my opinion unrealistic to regard it as an essential term. If it breaks down there is no reason why the court should not substitute other machinery to carry out the main purpose of ascertaining the price in order that the agreement may be carried out.

In the present case the machinery provided for in the clause has broken down because the respondents have declined to appoint their valuer. In that sense the breakdown has been caused by their fault, in failing to implement an implied obligation to co-operate in making the machinery work. The case might be distinguishable in that respect from cases where the breakdown has occurred for some cause outside the control of either party, such as the death of an umpire, or his failure to complete the valuation by a stipulated date. But I do not rely on any such distinction. I prefer to rest my decision on the general principle that, where the machinery is not essential, if it breaks down for any reason the court will substitute its own machinery...

The appropriate means for the court to enforce the present agreements is in my opinion by ordering an inquiry into the fair value of the reversions. That was the method used in *Talbot v Talbot* [1968] Ch 1 [option to purchase 'at a reasonable valuation' held valid by CA]. The alternative of ordering the respondents to appoint a valuer would not be suitable because in the event of the order not being obeyed, the only sanction would be imprisonment for contempt of court which would clearly be inappropriate.

Lord Russell of Killowen (dissenting): I felt considerable sympathy for counsel for the respondents when he was told that he had all the law on his side, but was (in effect) facing the prophets. (This is a paraphrase of my own remark in argument, when he was told that he had all equity behind him and I intervened to suggest that he had less in front of him.)

In the result I would dismiss this appeal. I can only exclaim with Macduff—'What! All my pretty chickens and their dam, at one fell swoop?' (Macbeth, Act IV, Sc. 3).[98]

---

[98] *Re Malpass* [1985] Ch 42 (testamentary option to purchase farm 'at the agricultural value thereof determined for agricultural purposes...as agreed with the District Valuer'; the valuer declined to act). See also *Campbell v Edwards* [1976] 1 WLR 403 (valuation fixed by an agreed valuer held binding);*Trustees of National Deposit Friendly Society v Beatties of London Ltd* [1985] 2 EGLR 59, where Goulding J held valid an option agreement for a new lease in favour of tenants who had carried on a business of selling model railways for 75 years 'the rent payable...to be the greater of £33,000 per annum exclusive or such rent as may be agreed as from the architect's certificate of completion'. In rejecting claims that it was void for uncertainty in

(b) Rent review[99]

In **Beer v Bowden** [1981] 1 WLR 522n a lease was granted in 1968 for 14 years. The rent was £1,250 for the first five years and was to be reviewed every five years thereafter, being 'such rent as shall thereupon be agreed between the landlords and the tenant...and in any case not less than the yearly rental payable hereunder'. The lease contained no machinery for fixing the rent in default of agreement. On failure to agree at the end of the first five years, the question arose as to what rent was payable. The Court of Appeal held that the rent should be a fair rent.

GOFF LJ said at 525:

King's Motors (Oxford) Ltd v Lax [1970] 1 WLR 426 ..., in my judgment, is wholly distinguishable and does not really assist at all. That was a case of an option to renew, and the exercise of the option could operate, if at all, only to create a contract. Valid contract it could not be, because an essential term—namely, the rent—was neither agreed nor ascertainable. That, in my judgment, poses an entirely different problem from that which arises where one starts with the premise that there is a subsisting lease which creates an estate in the land and with the premise that the court must imply some term, because it is conceded that rent is payable.

BUCKLEY LJ said at 528:

It appears to me that the introduction by implication of a single word in the clause in the lease relating to the rent to be payable solves the problem of this case; that is, the insertion of the word 'fair' between the words 'such' and 'rent.' If some such implication is not made, it seems to me that this would be a completely inoperative rent review provision, because it is not to be expected that the tenant would agree to an increase in the rent if the rent to be agreed was absolutely at large. Clearly the parties contemplated that at the end of five years some adjustment might be necessary to make the position with regard to the rent a fair one, and the rent review provision with which we are concerned was inserted in the lease to enable such an adjustment to be made. The suggestion that upon the true construction of the clause it provides that the rent shall continue to be at the rate of £1,250 a year unless the parties otherwise agree

---

regard to the date of the commencement of the term, the amount of rent and the covenants and conditions, he said at 61: 'There has been such performance on the tenant's side as to justify the court in a much more liberal approach to the validity of the document than in the case of a purely executory option where nothing but perhaps a nominal consideration has been given on either side'; *R & A Millett (Shops) Ltd v Leon Allan International Fashions Ltd* [1989] 1 EGLR 138 (sub-lease rent to be 78/85ths of fair market rent as fixed in manner provided by head lease); *Harben Style Ltd v Rhodes Trust* [1995] 1 EGLR 118 (only landlord had power to apply to President of RCIS for appointment of third party to determine rent; on his refusal to apply, tenant not entitled to have rent determined by court); cf. *Royal Bank of Scotland v Jennings* [1997] 1 EGLR 101 (where both landlord and tenant had such power); *Addin v Secretary of State for the Environment* [1997] 1 EGLR 99; *Black Country Housing Association v Shand and Shand* [1998] NPC 92 (land to be transferred at a price which reflected its use being restricted as a garden held valid).

[99] On rent review clauses, see *United Scientific Holdings Ltd v Burnley Borough Council* [1978] AC 904 where HL held that there was a presumption that time was not of the essence in construing clauses which specify time limits for the operation of the rent review procedure. See generally C & B, pp. 243–245; Aldridge, *Leasehold Law,* paras 4.045–4.060; Reynolds and Fetherstonhaugh, *Handbook of Rent Review;* Bernstein and Reynolds, *Essentials of Rent Review* (1995); Reynolds and Clark, *Renewal of Business Tenancies* (3rd edn, 2007); Emmet, paras 26.080–26.152; Barnsley, *Land Options* (4th edn, 2005), chap. 9; Rent Review Journal (which began in 1981), superseded in 1992 by Rent Review and Lease Renewal Journal.

would, in my opinion, render the provision entirely inoperative, because, as I say, one could not expect the tenant voluntarily to agree to pay a higher rent.[100]

In **Thomas Bates & Son Ltd v Wyndham's (Lingerie) Ltd** [1981] 1 WLR 505 a seven year lease was granted in 1956 with an option for a further lease 'of the demised premises ... at a rent to be agreed between the lessor and the lessees but in default of such agreement at a rent to be fixed by a single arbitrator appointed by the President for the time being of the Royal Institution of Chartered Surveyors.' In 1963 the option was exercised and a further seven-year lease was granted with an option in terms identical to the original lease. In 1970, when the lessees exercised the option, the lessor sought to introduce a review clause. A new lease was executed for 14 years with a review at the fifth and tenth years. By a mistake, the lease contained no provision for arbitration in default of agreement on the rent review, and merely provided that the rent during the second five years and the final four years should be 'such rents as shall have been agreed between the lessor and the lessee.' The lessees, though aware of the omission, did not bring it to the lessor's notice.

In proceedings for rectification, the Court of Appeal held:

(i)   the rent review clause should be rectified by inserting a reference to arbitration;

(ii) the arbitrator should assess not the market rent but the rent which it would have been reasonable for the parties themselves to have agreed under the lease.

BUCKLEY LJ said at 519:

In my judgment, in default of agreement between the parties, the arbitrator would have to assess what rent it would have been reasonable for these landlords and these tenants to have agreed under this lease having regard to all the circumstances relevant to any negotiations between them of a new rent from the review date.

If I were wrong on a point of rectification, then, on construction and by a process of implication, the rent to be ascertained in default of agreement must, I think, be a fair rent as between the landlords and the tenants. It would be most unjust that the landlords should receive no rent because of failure of the parties to agree. The landlords have granted a 14-year term and the court must endeavour to fill any gap in the terms of the lease by means of a fair and reasonable implication as to what the parties must have intended their bargain to be. See in this connection the decision of this court in F & G Sykes (Wessex) Ltd v Fine Fare Ltd [1967] 1 Lloyd's Rep 53, which was a case very different on its facts from the present, but in which the court explained the function of any court of construction where parties have embarked upon any commercial relationship but under terms that are not altogether adequate to cover the eventualities. The court would ascertain by inquiry what rent the landlords and the tenants, as willing negotiators anxious to reach agreement, would arrive at for each of the two rent review periods. In short, the standard would be the same, as I see it, as would have to be adopted by an arbitrator under the clause if it is rectified in the way in which I consider that it should be rectified.[101]

---

[100] See *Corson v Rhuddlan Borough Council* (1989) 59 P & CR 185, p. 374, above; *Coventry Motor Mart Ltd v Corner Coventry Ltd* [1997] NPC 48.

[101] *Lear v Blizzard* [1983] 3 All ER 662 where there was an option to renew a lease for a further term of 21 years 'at a rent to be agreed between the parties or in default of agreement at a rent to be determined by

(iii) The grant of exclusive possession: the distinction between a lease and a licence[102]

(a) The distinction

In the 19th century the critical issue was whether the party in question had exclusive possession of the land.[103] If a person were in exclusive possession (other than a freeholder or copyholder) he was a tenant, if not he was a licensee.[104] In the mid 20th century the emphasis shifted from the simple test of exclusive possession to that of the intention of the parties to be inferred from all the circumstances. Contrary to views expressed in many of the older cases, exclusive possession did not necessarily mean that the person in enjoyment must be a tenant and not a licensee. As Sachs LJ said in *Barnes v Barratt* [1970] 2 QB 657 at 669: 'In this case, as always, it is necessary to give weight to the fact that exclusive possession has been given to the occupiers. That, however, is a factor which is no longer conclusive and, indeed, appears nowadays to have diminishing weight... The law has adapted itself so as to deal with the complexities of the Rent Acts without causing patently unintended injustice to landlords, whilst guarding against improper avoidance by the latter of the provisions of those Acts.' This statement draws attention to the fact that the context in which the courts have most commonly had to consider whether the occupier is a tenant or merely a licensee is that of residential occupation, where the 'Rent Acts' conferred on a tenant, but not on a licensee, substantial benefits: principally security of tenure and control over the level of rent chargeable.[105]

a single arbitrator.' Tudor Evans J held that the rent to be determined by the arbitrator was to be a fair rent for the particular tenant and the particular landlord, account being taken of all considerations which would affect the mind of either party to negotiations between them. Cf. *Ponsford v HMS Aerosols Ltd* [1979] AC 63, where HL, by a majority of 3 to 2, applied an objective test; 'a reasonable rent for the demised premises' was construed as that which was reasonable for the premises and not what would be reasonable for the tenant to pay. See [1983] All ER Rev 239 (P. H. Pettit).

[102] C & B, pp. 197–207; Gray, paras 4.1.59–4.1.120; M & W, paras 17.010–17.027; MM, pp. 339–342; Smith, pp. 351–372; Megarry, *Rent Acts* (11th edn, 1988), vol 1, chap. 3; Martin, *Residential Security* (2nd edn, 1995), pp. 7–31; Evans and Smith, *Law of Landlord and Tenant* (6th edn, 2002), chap. 3.

[103] The giving of a right of exclusive possession should be distinguished from the giving of an exclusive or sole right to use the premises for a particular purpose which has never been held to create a tenancy: *Hill v Tupper* (1863) 2 H & C 121, p. 620, below; *Wilson v Tavener* [1901] 1 Ch 578; *Clore v Theatrical Properties Ltd and Westby & Co Ltd* [1936] 3 All ER 483; *Moncrieff v Jamieson* [2007] 1 WLR 2620, p. 631, below (grant of sole use for limited purpose not inconsistent with owner's retention of possession and can therefore constitute an easement).

[104] In *Lynes v Snaith* [1899] 1 QB 486, Lawrence J said: 'As to the first question, I think it is clear [the defendant] was a tenant at will and not a licensee; for the admissions state that she was in exclusive possession, a fact which is wholly inconsistent with her having been a mere licensee'; *Allan v Liverpool Overseers* (1874) LR 9 QB 180, p. 386, below; *Glenwood Lumber Co Ltd v Phillips* [1904] AC 405, p. 385, below. Cf. *Taylor v Caldwell* (1863) 3 B & S 826, p. 386, below.

[105] The distinction is also relevant in the application of the LTA 1954 (business tenancies), p. 395, below; the duty of care owed to an occupier in respect of his chattels by a licensor but not by a landlord: *Appah v Parncliffe Investments Ltd* [1964] 1 WLR 1064; the warranty of suitability of premises for their intended purpose implied into a licence: *Wettern Electric Ltd v Welsh Development Agency* [1983] QB 796; (1983) 80 LSG 2195 (H. W. Wilkinson): there is no such warranty in respect of a lease, apart from express guarantee by the landlord; the length of notice required for the termination of a licence: *Smith v Northside Developments Ltd* [1987] 2 EGLR 151; and, under FA 2003, s. 48(1) and (2) a lease is a stamp duty chargeable interest, but a licence to use or occupy land, (or a tenancy at will) is not. And, more importantly, a lease (but not a 'Bruton tenancy': above, p. 348) is enforceable against third parties as a legal estate or an equitable interest, whereas a

The high-water mark of this approach was seen in the line of Court of Appeal decisions which began with *Somma v Hazelhurst* [1978] 1 WLR 1014, in which agreements were drafted as licences and exclusive possession was denied to the occupier by the device of reserving to the licensor the right to enter upon the premises himself or to introduce other licensees. The general principle was stated by Cumming-Bruce LJ at 1024: 'We can see no reason why an ordinary landlord should not be able to grant a licence to occupy an ordinary house. If that is what both he and the licensee intend and if they can frame any written agreement in such a way as to demonstrate that it is not really an agreement for a lease masquerading as a licence, we can see no reason in law or justice why they should be prevented from achieving that object.' The House of Lords Appellate Committee refused leave to appeal from the decision in *Somma v Hazelhurst*,[106] and subsequent decisions in the Court of Appeal continued to restate the principle, even when the agreement was held to be a sham.[107]

In *Street v Mountford* [1985] AC 809, p. 383, below, the House of Lords (in the first case to be heard there on the distinction) decisively rejected this approach. In this case there was a licence agreement, under which the occupant was given exclusive possession but had signed a statement at the end of the agreement that she accepted that it 'does not and is not intended to give me a tenancy protected under the Rent Acts'. As Slade LJ said in the Court of Appeal (1984) 271 EG 1261 at 1262: 'It was a plain expression of the intentions of both parties that what she was being given was a licence rather than a tenancy. There is no plea by her of misrepresentation, undue influence or *non est factum* and no claim for rectification.' The House of Lords reversed the Court of Appeal and held that the agreement was a tenancy. It also disapproved at 825 of the 'sham device and artificial transaction' of *Somma v Hazlehurst*.

Street v Mountford thus decides that 'where the only circumstances are that residential accommodation is offered and accepted with exclusive possession for a term at a rent,[108]

contractual licence is not, unless the circumstances give rise to a constructive trust or proprietary estoppel: *Ashburn Anstalt v Arnold* [1989] Ch 1, p. 1096, below. Certain other differences between leases and licences have been removed in recent years, e.g. the doctrines of frustration and termination for repudiatory breach now apply to leases as well as to licences: pp. 343–355, above. It can also sometimes also be necessary for the purposes of value added tax to know whether a transaction is a lease or a licence to occupy land: VAT Act 1994, s. 31 and Sch. 9 Part II Group 1. This provision, which implements Council Directive 77/388, must however be construed in accordance with Community law: *Sinclair Collis Ltd v Customs and Excise Commissioners* [2001] STC 989 (HL); [2003] STC 898 (ECJ); *Belgium v Temco Europe SA* [2005] STC 1451; *Abbey National plc v Customs and Excise Commissioners* [2006] 3 EGLR 153.

106 [1978] 2 All ER 1011 at 1025 (Lords Wilberforce, Salmon and Fraser of Tullybelton).

107 Followed in *Aldrington Garages Ltd v Fielder* (1978) 247 EG 557; *Sturolson & Co v Weniz* (1984) 272 EG 326. Cf. *O'Malley v Seymour* (1978) 250 EG 1083; *Walsh v Griffiths-Jones* [1978] 2 All ER 1002, where the agreements were held to be sham. For a detailed review, see (1980) 130 NLJ 939, 959 (A. Waite).

108 Rent is not essential for a lease; LPA 1925, s. 205 (1) (xxvii); *Ashburn Anstalt v Arnold*, [1989] Ch 1, p. 1096, below (occupier let into possession for business purposes under rent-free arrangement pending re-development; only outgoings payable during occupation; held to be a tenant: 'We are unable to read Lord Templeman's speech in *Street v Mountford* as laying down a principle of "no rent, no lease"', per Fox LJ at 9); *Skipton Building Society v Clayton* (1993) 66 P & CR 223; [1983] Conv 478 (L. Crabb).

For a residential tenancy to be protected under the Rent Act 1977, the rent had to be not less than two-thirds of the rateable value or, if not in money, quantifiable: *Barnes v Barratt* [1970] 2 QB 657; *Bostock v Bryant* (1990) 61 P & CR 23 (Uncle Joe who owned a house and lived in one room paid general and water rates

the result is a tenancy[109] ... The courts will, save in exceptional circumstances, only be concerned to inquire whether as a result of an agreement relating to residential accommodation the occupier is a lodger or a tenant'.[110] Lord Templeman (who delivered the only speech) identified as exceptional cases those where:

> (a) the occupancy is within one of a number of special categories, for example,[111] 'under a contract for the sale of land,[112] or pursuant to a contract of employment or referable to the holding of an office';[113]

in respect of the whole house, and the respondents, who lived in the rest of the house, the gas and electricity likewise for the whole; CA held that, assuming the respondents were tenants, the rent was not quantifiable).

Where no rent is payable, a licence may be the more likely construction: *Barnes v Barratt,* above; *Onyx (UK) Ltd v Beard* [1996] EGCS 55. See also *Vesely v Levy* [2008] L & TR 9 (rent-free arrangement for exclusive use and occupation of premises does not create tenancy if no intention to create landlord and tenant relationship; sharing of the expenses of a joint household by two friends not rent).

[109] A simple example of the rule is *Caplan v Mardon* [1986] CLY 1873 (held in the county court that three students were joint tenants in spite of a signed agreement that nothing in it should create a tenancy). Cf. *Mehta v Royal Bank of Scotland* [1999] 3 EGLR 153 (licence even though the three hallmarks of *Street v Mountford* were present; ten other equally significant factors based on the parties' intentions and surrounding circumstances to be taken into account; no deliberate intention to exclude the Rent Acts); (1999) 3 L & TR 64.

[110] [1985] AC 809 at 827. 'He will be a lodger if the landlord provides attendance or services which require the landlord or his servants to have unrestricted access to the premises': *Royal Philanthropic Society v County* [1985] 2 EGLR 109 at 110, per Fox LJ; *Brillouet v Landless* (1996) 28 HLR 836. But the fact that the occupier chooses not to avail himself of the attendance or services cannot convert a licence into a tenancy: *Uratemp Ventures Ltd v Collins* [2002] 1 EGLR 156 at 157, per Peter Gibson LJ. The presence or absence of cooking facilities is not relevant: *Uratemp Ventures Ltd v Collins* [2002] 1 AC 301.

[111] The categories are 'illustrative and not exhaustive': *Dellneed Ltd v Chin* (1986) 53 P & CR 172 at 187, per Millett J. See *Royal Philanthropic Society v County* [1985] 2 EGLR 109, where CA rejected a number of submitted exceptional circumstances; [1986] Conv 215 (P. F. Smith); *Whitbread West Pennines Ltd v Reedy* [1988] ICR 807.

Another possible exception is homeless persons: *Westminster City Council v Clarke* [1992] 2 AC 288; [1992] Conv 112 (J. E. Martin), 285 (D. S. Cowan); [1992] All ER Rev 225 (P. J. Clarke) (grant of 'licence to occupy' to occupant of single room in men's hostel run by appellant council, in pursuance of its duty to house the homeless under HA 1985, s. 65(2), held to be a licence and not a secure tenancy; 'a very special case which depends on the peculiar nature of the hostel maintained by the council, the use of the hostel by the council, the totality, immediacy, and objectives of the powers exercisable by the council and the immediate restrictions imposed on Mr Clarke. The decision in this case will not allow a landlord, private or public, to free himself from the Rent Acts or from the restrictions of a secure tenancy merely by adopting or adapting the language of the licence to occupy': per Lord Templeman at 302); *Parkins v Westminster City Council* [1998] 1 EGLR 22; *Bruton v London and Quadrant Housing Trust* [2000] 1 AC 456, p. 348, above (not a special circumstance that the Trust was a responsible landlord performing socially valuable functions). See also HA 1985, s. 79(3), Sch. 1, para. 4, which excludes most tenancies granted in such circumstances from statutory protection.

[112] See *Bretherton v Paton* [1986] 1 EGLR 172, where CA interpreted this exception narrowly, in holding that a *potential* purchaser of a dwelling house who had entered into exclusive possession for a term at a rent under an arrangement with the ultimate intention of negotiating for its sale was held to be a tenant. See also *Essex Plan Ltd v Broadminster Ltd* (1988) 56 P & CR 353 (licence where occupier continued in possession after expiry of option; no exclusive possession); [1989] Conv 55 (J. E. Martin); cf. *Heslop v Burns* [1974] 1 WLR 1241, p. 329, below, where Scarman LJ held that occupation prior to a contract of sale was a paradigm case of a tenancy at will; *Vandersteen v Agius* (1992) 65 P & CR 266 (occupation pursuant to sale of goodwill of osteopathy practice not an exception); *Cameron v Rolls-Royce plc* [2007] All ER (D) 397 (business tenant remaining in exclusive possession at end of lease was granted, pending negotiation for renewal, a 'licence' in substance on same terms as proposed leases: held, only licence).

[113] *Street v Mountford* [1985] AC 809 at 827. *Mayhew v Suttle* (1854) 4 E & B 347; *Smith v Seghill Overseers* (1875) LR 10 QB 422, p. 387, below. Distinguish a service occupant who is a licensee from a service tenant who is not. The latter is a person to whom a dwelling-house is let in consequence of his employment, but who

(*b*) the owner has no power to grant a tenancy;[114]

(*c*) the circumstances show that there is no intention to create legal relationships as, for example, 'where there has been something in the circumstances such as a family arrangement, an act of friendship or such like, to negative any intention to create a tenancy'.[115]

It would appear that the test of intention is relevant in deciding whether there is an intention to create a legal relationship, but irrelevant in deciding which legal relationship is created.

Five years later the House of Lords considered the matter further in joint appeals: *AG Securities v Vaughan* and *Antoniades v Villiers* [1990] 1 AC 417, p. 399, below. The House followed and elaborated *Street v Mountford* in the complex area of multiple occupation.

The effect of *Street v Mountford* and the subsequent cases is to prevent a landlord from driving a coach and horses through the Rent Acts.[116] Its rejection of the relevance of the *intention* of the parties is of paramount importance; and the consequent rigidity

is not required to live there for the better performance of his duties: *Torbett v Faulkner* [1952] 2 TLR 659. See *Royal Philanthropic Society v County*, above; *Norris v Checksfield* [1991] 1 WLR 1241 (semi-skilled mechanic held to be service licensee, even though he was never in a position to perform the duties required of him); *Burgoyne v Griffiths* [1991] 13 EG 164 (farm cottage); [1991] All ER Rev 214 (P. J. Clarke); *South Glamorgan County Council v Griffiths* [1992] 2 EGLR 232; *Hughes v Greenwich London Borough Council* [1994] 1 AC 170; *Surrey County Council v Lamond* [1999] 1 EGLR 32 (employer providing facility but not imposing obligation). The occupant may also be an object of charity; *Gray v Taylor* [1998] 1 WLR 1093 (occupant of Peterborough Almshouse held to be a licensee); [1998] 2 L & TR 40.

[114] *Street v Mountford* [1985] AC 809 at 821; *Camden London Borough Council v Shortlife Community Housing Ltd* (1992) 90 LGR 358 (which contains a critique on the exceptions by Millett J); [1993] Conv 157 (D. S. Cowan); *Bruton v London and Quadrant Housing Trust*, p. 348, above (whittling down this exception).

[115] *Facchini v Bryson* [1952] 1 TLR 1386 at 1389–1390, per Denning LJ, cited in *Street v Mountford* at 821, p. 389, below; *Ramnarace v Lutchman* [2001] 1 WLR 1651, p. 329, See *Booker v Palmer* [1942] 2 All ER 674, p. 387, below; *Marcroft Wagons Ltd v Smith* [1951] 2 KB 496; p. 388, below; *Heslop v Burns* [1974] 1 WLR 1241, p. 329, below; *Sharp v McArthur* (1986) 19 HLR 364 (where owner of flat, with 'For Sale' notice board prominently displayed, let defendant into possession as a favour pending sale. Held by CA to be a licence, even though defendant had exclusive possession and was given a rent book for the purpose of enabling him to obtain payment from the DHSS for outgoings for accommodation); *Carr Gomm Society v Hawkins* [1990] CLY 2811 (self-employed gardener held to be licensee of registered charity which had 60 homes in London and a continuing need to move people if necessary); *Westminster City Council v Basson* [1991] 1 EGLR 277 (girl friend who remained in exclusive possession of flat after her boy friend's tenancy had been terminated held to be licensee, even though she had received rent rebates from the council, which had made it clear that no tenancy was intended); [1992] Conv 113 (J. E. Martin); *Colchester Borough Council v Smith* [1992] Ch 421 (no intention to create legal relations where occupant's implied offer to pay reasonable rent was rejected, and where there was insistence on his occupation at his own risk and on his giving up possession at short notice if land required for other purposes). Cf. *Nunn v Dalrymple* (1989) 59 P & CR 231; *Ward v Warnke* (1990) 22 HLR 496 (in both cases a *family* arrangement in which exclusive possession of a cottage in return for regular payments was held to be a tenancy). See also *Abbeyfield (Harpenden) Society v Woods* [1968] 1 WLR 374, p. 391, below; *Barnes v Barratt* [1970] 2 QB 657 (house-sharing arrangement without rent or fixed term held to be licence).

[116] *Street v Mountford* [1985] AC 809 at 819. In *Brooker Settled Estates Ltd v Ayers* [1987] 1 EGLR 50, O'Connor LJ said at 51: 'Lord Templeman reviewed the authorities dealing with this tortured question, and sought to introduce some order into the law for the better administration of the law and guidance of the learned judges, particularly in the county courts, who have to deal with this problem.'

of the test for distinguishing between a lease and a licence may have led to the over-protection of the tenant at the expense of the landlord.

The crux of the matter is that an owner of residential property is reluctant to grant a lease to a tenant which will have the consequences of rent control and of security of tenure after the end of the contractual term. A status of irremovability is particularly unattractive to an owner. However, the Housing Act of 1988 phased out the Rent Act 1977 by introducing the assured tenancy and the assured shorthold tenancy. The object was to provide an incentive to landlords to let premises and to ease the housing shortage in the private rented sector. The new regime preserved the basic principle of security of tenure, but the grounds of possession were strengthened and only minimal rights of succession and rent control were provided. But tenancies created before 15 January 1989 were not affected. The Housing Act 1996 reduced the rights of tenants still further, by providing that, subject to limited exceptions, future tenancies (save those outside the Act) were to take effect as assured shortholds, which offer less security than assured tenancies.[117]

There is now less incentive for the landlord of residential property to create a licence instead of a lease. There will, however, still be cases of licences created before *Street v Mountford* which will have to be interpreted in the light of that decision; and the distinction between a lease and a licence has significance beyond the context of the occupation of residential property and the application of the Rent Acts.[118]

(b) Residential tenant or lodger

Street v Mountford
[1985] AC 809 (HL, **Lords Scarman, Keith of Kinkel, Bridge of Harwich, Brightman** and **Templeman**)

Lord Templeman: My Lords, by an agreement dated 7 March 1983, the respondent Mr Street granted the appellant Mrs Mountford the right to occupy the furnished rooms numbers 5 and 6 at 5, St. Clements Gardens, Boscombe, from 7 March 1983 for £37 per week, subject to termination by 14 days' written notice and subject to the conditions set forth in the agreement. The question raised by this appeal is whether the agreement created a tenancy or a licence.

A tenancy is a term of years absolute. This expression, by section 205(1)(xxvii) of the Law of Property Act 1925, reproducing the common law, includes a term from week to week in possession at a rent and liable to determination by notice or re-entry. Originally a term of years was not an estate in land, the lessee having merely a personal action against his lessor. But a legal estate in leaseholds was created by the Statute of Gloucester 1278 and the Act of 1529 21 Hen VIII, c 15. Now by section 1 of the Law of Property Act 1925 a term of years absolute is an estate in land capable of subsisting as a legal estate. In the present case if the agreement dated 7 March 1983 created a tenancy, Mrs Mountford having entered into possession and made weekly payments acquired a legal estate in land. If the agreement is a tenancy, the occupation of Mrs Mountford is protected by the Rent Acts.

[117] For assured tenancies and assured shorthold tenancies, see C & B, pp. 337–358.
[118] Above, p. 379, n. 105.

A licence in connection with land while entitling the licensee to use the land for the purposes authorised by the licence does not create an estate in the land. If the agreement dated 7 March 1983 created a licence for Mrs Mountford to occupy the premises, she did not acquire any estate in the land. If the agreement is a licence then Mrs Mountford's right of occupation is not protected by the Rent Acts. Hence the practical importance of distinguishing between a tenancy and a licence.

In the course of argument, nearly every clause of the agreement dated 7 March 1983 was relied upon by the appellant as indicating a lease and by the respondent as indicating a licence. The agreement, in full, was in these terms:

'I Mrs Wendy Mountford agree to take from the owner Roger Street the single furnished room number 5 and 6 at 5 St. Clements Gardens, Boscombe, Bournemouth, commencing 7 March 1983 at a licence fee of £37 per week.

I understand that the right to occupy the above room is conditional on the strict observance of the following rules:

1. No paraffin stoves, or other than the supplied form of heating, is allowed in the room.

2. No one but the above-named person may occupy or sleep in the room without prior permission, and this personal licence is not assignable.

3. The owner (or his agent) has the right at all times to enter the room to inspect its condition, read and collect money from meters, carry out maintenance works, install or replace furniture or for any other reasonable purpose.

4. All rooms must be kept in a clean and tidy condition.

5. All damage and breakages must be paid for or replaced at once. An initial deposit equivalent to 2 weeks' licence fee will be refunded on termination of the licence subject to deduction for all damage or other breakages or arrears of licence fee, or retention towards the cost of any necessary possession proceedings.

6. No nuisance or annoyance to be caused to the other occupiers. In particular, all music played after midnight to be kept low so as not to disturb occupiers of other rooms.

7. No children or pets allowed under any circumstances whatsoever.

8. Prompt payment of the licence fee must be made every Monday in advance without fail.

9. If the licence fee or any part of it shall be seven days in arrear or if the occupier shall be in breach of any of the other terms of this agreement or if (except by arrangement) the room is left vacant or unoccupied, the owner may re-enter the room and this licence shall then immediately be terminated (without prejudice to all other rights and remedies of the owner).

10. This licence may be terminated by 14 days' written notice given to the occupier at any time by the owner or his agent, or by the same notice by the occupier to the owner or his agent.

Occupier's signature

Owner/agent's signature

Date 7 March 1983

I understand and accept that a licence in the above form does not and is not intended to give me a tenancy protected under the Rent Acts.

Occupier's signature.'

On 12 August 1983 on Mrs Mountford's application a fair rent was registered. Mr Street then made application under section 51(a) of the County Courts Act for a declaration that Mrs Mountford's occupancy was a licence and not a tenancy. The recorder in the county court held that Mrs Mountford was a tenant entitled to the protection of the Rent Acts and made a declaration accordingly. The Court of Appeal held that Mrs Mountford was a licensee not entitled to the protection of the Rent Acts. Mrs Mountford appeals.

On behalf of Mrs Mountford her counsel, Mr Hicks QC seeks to reaffirm and re-establish the traditional view that an occupier of land for a term at a rent is a tenant providing the occupier is granted exclusive possession. It is conceded on behalf of Mr Street that the agreement dated 7 March 1983 granted exclusive possession to Mrs Mountford. The traditional view that the grant of exclusive possession for a term at a rent creates a tenancy is consistent with the elevation of a tenancy into an estate in land. The tenant possessing exclusive possession is able to exercise the rights of an owner of land, which is in the real sense his land albeit temporarily and subject to certain restrictions. A tenant armed with exclusive possession can keep out strangers and keep out the landlord unless the landlord is exercising limited rights reserved to him by the tenancy agreement to enter and view and repair. A licensee lacking exclusive possession can in no sense call the land his own and cannot be said to own any estate in the land. The licence does not create an estate in the land to which it relates but only makes an act lawful which would otherwise be unlawful.

On behalf of Mr Street his counsel, Mr Goodhart QC, relies on recent authorities which, he submits, demonstrate that an occupier granted exclusive possession for a term at a rent may nevertheless be a licensee if, in the words of Slade LJ in the present case [1985] 49 P & CR 324, 332:

'there is manifested the clear intention of both parties that the rights granted are to be merely those of a personal right of occupation and not those of a tenant.'

In the present case, it is submitted, the provisions of the agreement dated 7 March 1983 and in particular clauses 2, 4, 7 and 9 and the express declaration at the foot of the agreement manifest the clear intention of both parties that the rights granted are to be those of a personal nature and not those of a tenant.

My Lords, there is no doubt that the traditional distinction between a tenancy and a licence of land lay in the grant of land for a term at a rent with exclusive possession. In some cases it was not clear at first sight whether exclusive possession was in fact granted. For example, an owner of land could grant a licence to cut and remove standing timber. Alternatively the owner could grant a tenancy of the land with the right to cut and remove standing timber during the term of the tenancy. The grant of rights relating to standing timber therefore required careful consideration in order to decide whether the grant conferred exclusive possession of the land for a term at a rent and was therefore a tenancy or whether it merely conferred a bare licence to remove the timber.

In *Glenwood Lumber Co Ltd v Phillips* [1904] AC 405, the Crown in exercise of statutory powers 'licensed' the respondents to hold an area of land for the purpose of cutting and removing timber for the term of 21 years at an annual rent. Delivering the advice of the Judicial Committee of the Privy Council, Lord Davey said, at 408–409:

'The appellants contended that this instrument conferred only a licence to cut timber and carry it away, and did not give the respondent any right of occupation or interest in the land itself. Having regard to the provisions of the Act under the powers of which it was executed and to the language of the document itself, their Lordships cannot adopt this view of the construction or effect of it. In the so-called licence itself it is called indifferently a licence and a demise, but in the Act it is spoken of as a lease, and the holder of it is described as the lessee. It is not, however, a question of words but of substance. If the effect of the instrument is to give the holder an exclusive right of occupation of the land, though subject to certain reservations or to a restriction of the purposes for which it may be used, it is in law a demise of the land itself. By [the Act] it is enacted that the lease shall vest in the lessee the right to take and keep exclusive possession of the lands described therein subject to the conditions in the Act provided or referred to, and the lessee is empowered (amongst other things) to bring any actions or suits against any party unlawfully in possession of any land so leased, and to prosecute all trespassers thereon. The operative part and habendum in the licence is framed in apt language to carry out the intention so expressed in the Act. And their Lordships have no doubt that the effect of the so-called licence was to confer a title to the land itself on the respondent.'

This was a case in which the court after careful consideration of the purposes of the grant, the terms of the grant and the surrounding circumstances, came to the conclusion that the grant conferred exclusive possession and was therefore a tenancy.

A contrary conclusion was reached in *Taylor v Caldwell* (1863) 3 B & S 826 in which the defendant agreed to let the plaintiff have the use of the Surrey Gardens and Music Hall on four specified days giving a series of four concerts and day and night fetes at the gardens and hall on those days, and the plaintiff agreed to take the gardens, and the hall and to pay £100 for each day. Blackburn J said, at 832:

'The parties inaccurately call this a 'letting,' and the money to be paid a 'rent,' but the whole agreement is such as to show that the defendants were to retain the possession of the hall and gardens so that there was to be no demise of them, and that the contract was merely to give the plaintiffs the use of them on those days.'

That was a case where the court after considering the purpose of the grant, the terms of the grant and the surrounding circumstances came to the conclusion that the grantee was not entitled to exclusive possession but only to use the land for limited purposes and was therefore a licensee.

In the case of residential accommodation there is no difficulty in deciding whether the grant confers exclusive possession. An occupier of residential accommodation at a rent for a term is either a lodger or a tenant.[119] The occupier is a lodger if the landlord provides attendance or services which require the landlord or his servants to exercise unrestricted access to and use of the premises.[120] A lodger is entitled to live in the premises but cannot call the place his own. In *Allan v Liverpool Overseers* (1874) LR 9 QB 180 at 191–192 Blackburn J said:

'A lodger in a house, although he has the exclusive use of rooms in the house, in the sense that nobody else is to be there, and though his goods are stowed there, yet he is not in exclusive occupation in that sense, because the landlord is there for the purpose of being able, as landlords commonly do in the case of lodgings, to have his own servants to look after the house and the furniture, and has retained to himself the occupation, though he has agreed to give the exclusive enjoyment of the occupation to the lodger.'

If on the other hand residential accommodation is granted for a term at a rent with exclusive possession, the landlord providing neither attendance nor services, the grant is a tenancy; any express reservation to the landlord of limited rights to enter and view the state of the

[119] 'I think it wiser and safer to say that the question whether a man is a lodger, or whether he is occupying as a tenant, must depend on the circumstances of each case': *Bradley v Baylis* (1881) 8 QBD 195 at 218, per Jessel MR.

[120] 'This does not mean that an occupier is a lodger, if and only if such attendance or services are provided: *Crancour Ltd v De Silvaesa* [1986] 1 EGLR 80 at 85, per Ralph Gibson LJ; *Brooker Settled Estates Ltd v Ayers* (1987) 54 P & CR 165; *Huwyler v Ruddy* (1996) 72 P & CR D3 (provision of cleaning and linen once a week which entailed only twenty minutes labour held to be unrestricted access).

premises and to repair and maintain the premises only serves to emphasise the fact that the grantee is entitled to exclusive possession and is a tenant. In the present case it is conceded that Mrs Mountford is entitled to exclusive possession and is not a lodger. Mr Street provided neither attendance nor services and only reserved the limited rights of inspection and maintenance and the like set forth in clause 3 of the agreement. On the traditional view of the matter, Mrs Mountford not being a lodger must be a tenant.

There can be no tenancy unless the occupier enjoys exclusive possession; but an occupier who enjoys exclusive possession is not necessarily a tenant. He may be owner in fee simple, a trespasser, a mortgagee in possession, an object of charity or a service occupier. To constitute a tenancy the occupier must be granted exclusive possession for a fixed or periodic term certain in consideration of a premium or periodical payments. The grant may be express, or may be inferred where the owner accepts weekly or other periodical payments from the occupier.

Occupation by service occupier may be eliminated. A service occupier is a servant who occupies his master's premises in order to perform his duties as a servant. In those circumstances the possession and occupation of the servant is treated as the possession and occupation of the master and the relationship of landlord and tenant is not created; see *Mayhew v Suttle* (1854) 4 E & B 347. The test is whether the servant requires the premises he occupies in order the better to perform his duties as a servant:

> 'Where the occupation is necessary for the performance of services, and the occupier is required to reside in the house in order to perform those services, the occupation being strictly ancillary to the performance of the duties which the occupier has to perform, the occupation is that of a servant;' per Mellor J in *Smith v Seghill Overseers* (1875) LR 10 QB 422, 428.

The cases on which Mr Goodhart relies begin with *Booker v Palmer* [1942] 2 All ER 674. The owner of a cottage agreed to allow a friend to install an evacuee in the cottage rent free for the duration of the war. The Court of Appeal held that there was no intention on the part of the owner to enter into legal relationships with the evacuee. Lord Greene MR said at 677:

> 'To suggest there is an intention there to create a relationship of landlord and tenant appears to me to be quite impossible. There is one golden rule which is of very general application, namely, that the law does not impute intention to enter into legal relationships where the circumstances and the conduct of the parties negatives any intention of the kind. It seems to me that this is a clear example of the application of that rule.'

The observations of Lord Greene MR were not directed to the distinction between a contractual tenancy and a contractual licence. The conduct of the parties (not their professed intentions) indicated that they did not intend to contract at all.

In the present case, the agreement dated 7 March 1983 professed an intention by both parties to create a licence and their belief that they had in fact created a licence. It was submitted on behalf of Mr Street that the court cannot in these circumstances decide that the agreement created a tenancy without interfering with the freedom of contract enjoyed by both parties. My Lords, Mr Street enjoyed freedom to offer Mrs Mountford the right to occupy the rooms comprised in the agreement on such lawful terms as Mr Street pleased. Mrs Mountford enjoyed freedom to negotiate with Mr Street to obtain different terms. Both parties enjoyed freedom to contract or not to contract and both parties exercised that freedom by contracting on the terms set forth in the written agreement and on no other terms. But the consequences in law of the agreement, once concluded, can only be determined by consideration of the effect of the agreement. If the agreement satisfied all the requirements of a tenancy, then the agreement produced a tenancy and the parties cannot alter the effect of the agreement by insisting that they only created a licence. The manufacture of a five-pronged implement for manual digging results in a fork even if the manufacturer, unfamiliar with the English language, insists that he intended to make and has made a spade.[121]

It was also submitted that in deciding whether the agreement created a tenancy or a licence, the court should ignore the Rent Acts. If Mr Street has succeeded, where owners have failed these past 70 years, in driving a coach and horses through the Rent Acts, he must be left to enjoy the benefit of his ingenuity unless and until Parliament intervenes. I accept that the Rent Acts are irrelevant to the problem of determining the legal effect of the rights granted by the agreement. Like the professed intention of the parties, the Rent Acts cannot alter the effect of the agreement.

In *Marcroft Wagons Ltd v Smith* [1951] 2 KB 496 the daughter of a deceased tenant who lived with her mother claimed to be a statutory tenant by succession and the landlords asserted that the daughter had no rights under the Rent Acts and was a trespasser. The landlords expressly refused to accept the daughter's claims but accepted rent from her while they were considering the position. If the landlords had decided not to apply to the court for possession but to accept the daughter as a tenant, the moneys paid by the daughter would have been treated as rent. If the landlords decided, as they did decide, to apply for possession and to prove, as they did prove, that the daughter was not a statutory tenant, the moneys paid by the daughter were treated as mesne profits. The Court of Appeal held with some hesitation that the landlords never accepted the daughter as tenant and never intended to contract with her although the landlords delayed for some six months before applying to the court for possession. Roxburgh J said, at 507:

> 'Generally speaking, when a person, having a sufficient estate in land, lets another into exclusive possession, a tenancy results, and there is no question of a licence. But the inference of a tenancy is not necessarily to be drawn where a person succeeds on a death to occupation of rent-controlled premises and a landlord accepts some rent while he or the occupant, or both of them, is or are considering his or their position. If this is all that happened in this case, then no tenancy would result.'

In that case, as in *Booker v Palmer* the court deduced from the conduct of the parties that they did not intend to contract at all.

Errington v Errington and Woods [1952] 1 KB 290 concerned a contract by a father to allow his son to buy the father's house on payment of the instalments of the father's building society loan. Denning LJ referred, at 297, to the judgment of Lord Greene MR in *Booker v Palmer* [1942] 2 All ER 674, 677 where, however, the circumstances and the conduct of the parties negatived any intention to enter into legal relationships. Denning LJ continued, at 297–298:

> 'We have had many instances lately of occupiers in exclusive possession who have been held to be not tenants, but only licensees. When a requisitioning authority allowed people into possession at a weekly rent: . . . when a landlord told a tenant on his retirement that he could live in a cottage rent free for the rest of his days: . . . when a landlord, on the death of the widow of a statutory tenant, allowed her daughter to remain in possession, paying rent for six months: *Marcroft Wagons Ltd v Smith*

---

[121] See *Antoniades v Villiers* [1990] 1 AC 417 at 444, where Bingham LJ said: 'The House of Lords [in *Street v Mountford*] has not, I think, held that assertions in a document that it is a licence should be ignored. It has held that the true legal nature of a transaction is not to be altered by the description the parties choose to give it. A cat does not become a dog because the parties have agreed to call it a dog. But in deciding whether an animal is a cat or a dog the parties' agreement that it is a dog may not be entirely irrelevant.'

[1951] 2 KB 496; when the owner of a shop allowed the manager to live in a flat above the shop, but did not require him to do so, and the value of the flat was taken into account at £1 a week in fixing his wages: ... in each of those cases the occupier was held to be a licensee and not a tenant.... The result of all these cases is that, although a person who is let into exclusive possession is prima facie to be considered a tenant, nevertheless he will not be held to be so if the circumstances negative any intention to create a tenancy. Words alone may not suffice. Parties cannot turn a tenancy into a licence merely by calling it one. But if the circumstances and the conduct of the parties show that all that was intended was that the occupier should be granted a personal privilege, with no interest in the land, he will be held to be a licensee only.'

In *Errington v Errington and Woods* and in the cases cited by Denning LJ at 297 there were exceptional circumstances which negatived the prima facie intention to create a tenancy, notwithstanding that the occupier enjoyed exclusive occupation. The intention to create a tenancy was negatived if the parties did not intend to enter into legal relationships at all, or where the relationship between the parties was that of vendor and purchaser, master and service occupier, or where the owner, a requisitioning authority, had no power to grant a tenancy. These exceptional circumstances are not to be found in the present case where there has been the lawful, independent and voluntary grant of exclusive possession for a term at a rent.

If the observations of Denning LJ are applied to the facts of the present case it may fairly be said that the circumstances negative any intention to create a mere licence. Words alone do not suffice. Parties cannot turn a tenancy into a licence merely by calling it one. The circumstances and the conduct of the parties show that what was intended was that the occupier should be granted exclusive possession at a rent for a term with a corresponding interest in the land which created a tenancy.

In *Cobb v Lane* [1952] 1 TLR 1037, an owner allowed her brother to occupy a house rent free. The county court judge, who was upheld by the Court of Appeal, held that there was no intention to create any legal relationship and that a tenancy at will was not to be implied. This is another example of conduct which negatives any intention of entering into a contract, and does not assist in distinguishing a contractual tenancy from a contractual licence.

In *Facchini v Bryson* [1952] 1 TLR 1386, an employer and his assistant entered into an agreement which, inter alia, allowed the assistant to occupy a house for a weekly payment on terms which conferred exclusive possession. The assistant did not occupy the house for the better performance of his duty and was not therefore a service occupier. The agreement stipulated that 'nothing in this agreement shall be construed to create a tenancy between the employer and the assistant.' Somervell LJ said, at 1389:

'If, looking at the operative clauses in the agreement, one comes to the conclusion that the rights of the occupier, to use a neutral word, are those of a lessee, the parties cannot turn it into a licence by saying at the end 'this is deemed to be a licence;' nor can they, if the operative paragraphs show that it is merely a licence, say that it should be deemed to be a lease.'

Denning LJ referred to several cases including *Errington v Errington and Woods* and *Cobb v Lane* and said, at 1389–1390:

'In all the cases where an occupier has been held to be a licensee there has been something in the circumstances, such as a family arrangement, an act of friendship or generosity, or such like, to negative any intention to create a tenancy.... In the present case, however, there are no special circumstances. It is a simple case where the employer let a man into occupation of a house in consequence of his employment at a weekly sum payable by him. The occupation has all the features of a service tenancy, and the parties cannot by the mere words of their contract turn it into something else. Their relationship is determined by the law and not by the label which they choose to put on it:...'

The decision, which was thereafter binding on the Court of Appeal and on all lower courts, referred to the special circumstances which are capable of negativing an intention to create a tenancy and reaffirmed the principle that the professed intentions of the parties are irrelevant. The decision also indicated that in a simple case a grant of exclusive possession of residential accommodation for a weekly sum creates a tenancy.

In *Murray, Bull & Co Ltd v Murray* [1953] 1 QB 211 a contractual tenant held over, paying rent quarterly. McNair J found at 217:

'both parties intended that the relationship should be that of licence and no more... The primary consideration on both sides was that the defendant, as occupant of the flat, should not be a controlled tenant.'

In my opinion this case was wrongly decided. McNair J citing the observations of Denning LJ in *Errington v Errington and Woods* [1952] 1 KB 290 at 297 and *Marcroft Wagons Ltd v Smith* [1951] 2 KB 496 failed to distinguish between first, conduct which negatives an intention to create legal relationships, secondly, special circumstances which prevent exclusive occupation from creating a tenancy and thirdly, the professed intention of the parties. In *Murray, Bull & Co Ltd v Murray* the conduct of the parties showed an intention to contract and there were no relevant special circumstances. The tenant holding over continued by agreement to enjoy exclusive possession and to pay a rent for a term certain. In those circumstances he continued to be a tenant notwithstanding the professed intention of the parties to create a licence and their desire to avoid a controlled tenancy.

In *Addiscombe Garden Estates Ltd v Crabbe* [1958] 1 QB 513, the Court of Appeal considered an agreement relating to a tennis club carried on in the grounds of a hotel. The agreement was:

'described by the parties as a licence... the draftsman has studiously and successfully avoided the use either of the word landlord' or the word 'tenant' throughout the document:' per Jenkins LJ at 522.

On analysis of the whole of the agreement the Court of Appeal came to the conclusion that the agreement conferred exclusive possession and thus created a tenancy. Jenkins LJ said, at 522:

'The whole of the document must be looked at; and if, after it has been examined, the right conclusion appears to be that, whatever label may have been attached to it, it in fact conferred and imposed on the grantee in substance the rights and obligations of a tenant, and on the grantor in substance the rights and obligations of a landlord, then it must be given the appropriate effect, that is to say, it must be treated as a tenancy agreement as distinct from a mere licence.'

In the agreement in the *Addiscombe* case it was by no means clear until the whole of the document had been narrowly examined that exclusive possession was granted by the agreement. In the present case it is clear that exclusive possession was granted and so much is conceded. In these circumstances it is unnecessary to analyse minutely the detailed rights and obligations contained in the agreement.

In the *Addiscombe* case Jenkins LJ referred, at 528, to the observations of Denning LJ in *Errington and Errington and Woods* to the effect that 'The test of exclusive possession is by no means decisive.' Jenkins LJ continued:

'I think that wide statement must be treated as qualified by his observations in *Facchini v Bryson* [1952] 1 TLR 1386, 1389; and it seems to me that, save in exceptional cases of the kind mentioned by Denning LJ in that case, the law remains that the fact of exclusive possession, if not decisive against the view that there is a mere licence, as distinct from a tenancy, is at all events a consideration of the first importance.'

Exclusive possession is of first importance in considering whether an occupier is a tenant; exclusive possession is not decisive because an occupier who enjoys exclusive possession is not necessarily a tenant. The occupier may be a lodger or service occupier or fall within the other exceptional categories mentioned by Denning LJ in *Errington v Errington and Woods.*

In *Isaac v Hotel de Paris Ltd* [1960] 1 WLR 239, an employee who managed a night bar in a hotel for his employer company which held a lease of the hotel negotiated 'subject to contract' to complete the purchase of shares in the company and to be allowed to run the nightclub for his own benefit if he paid the head rent payable by the company for the hotel. In the expectation that the negotiations 'subject to contract' would ripen into a binding agreement, the employee was allowed to run the nightclub and he paid the company's rent. When negotiations broke down the employee claimed unsuccessfully to be a tenant of the hotel company. The circumstances in which the employee was allowed to occupy the premises showed that the hotel company never intended to accept him as a tenant and that he was fully aware of that fact. This was a case, consistent with the authorities cited by Lord Denning in giving the advice of the Judicial Committee of the Privy Council, in which the parties did not intend to enter into contractual relationships unless and until the negotiations 'subject to contract' were replaced by a binding contract.

In *Abbeyfield (Harpenden) Society Ltd v Woods* [1968] 1 WLR 374 the occupier of a room in an old people's home was held to be a licensee and not a tenant. Lord Denning MR said, at 376:

'The modern cases show that a man may be a licensee even though he has exclusive possession, even though the word 'rent' is used, and even though the word 'tenancy' is used. The court must look at the agreement as a whole and see whether a tenancy really was intended. In this case there is, besides the one room, the provision of services, meals, a resident housekeeper, and such like. The whole arrangement was so personal in nature that the proper inference is that he was a licensee.'

As I understand the decision in the *Abbeyfield* case the court came to the conclusion that the occupier was a lodger and was therefore a licensee not a tenant.

In *Shell-Mex and BP Ltd v Manchester Garages Ltd* [1971] 1 WLR 612, the Court of Appeal after carefully examining an agreement whereby the defendant was allowed to use a petrol company's filling station for the purposes of selling petrol, came to the conclusion that the agreement did not grant exclusive possession to the defendant who was therefore a licensee.[122] At 615 Lord Denning MR in considering whether the transaction was a licence or a tenancy said:

'Broadly speaking, we have to see whether it is a personal privilege given to a person (in which case it is a licence), or whether it grants an interest in land (in which case it is a tenancy). At one time it used to be thought that exclusive possession was a decisive factor. But that is not so. It depends on broader considerations altogether. Primarily on whether it is personal in its nature or not: see *Errington v Errington and Woods.*'

---

[122] *Esso Petroleum Co Ltd v Fumegrange Ltd* [1994] 2 EGLR 90 (three year 'partnership licence' agreement, which reserved control to licensor over physical layout of premises and way in which the business was run held to be licence).

In my opinion the agreement was only 'personal in its nature' and created 'a personal priv-ilege' if the agreement did not confer the right to exclusive possession of the filling station. No other test for distinguishing between a contractual tenancy and a contractual licence appears to be understandable or workable.

Heslop v Burns [1974] 1 WLR 1241 was another case in which the owner of a cottage allowed a family to live in the cottage rent free and it was held that no tenancy at will had been created on the ground that the parties did not intend any legal relationship. Scarman LJ cited with approval, at 1252, the statement by Denning LJ in *Facchini v Bryson* [1952] 1 TLR 1386, 1389:

'In all the cases where an occupier has been held to be a licensee there has been something in the circumstances, such as a family arrangement, an act of friendship or generosity, or such like, to negative any intention to create a tenancy.'

In *Marchant v Charters* [1977] 1 WLR 1181, a bedsitting room was occupied on terms that the landlord cleaned the rooms daily and provided clean linen each week. It was held by the Court of Appeal that the occupier was a licensee and not a tenant. The decision in the case is sustainable on the grounds that the occupier was a lodger and did not enjoy exclusive posses-sion. But Lord Denning MR said, at 1185:

'What is the test to see whether the occupier of one room in a house is a tenant or a licensee? It does not depend on whether he or she has exclusive possession or not. It does not depend on whether the room is furnished or not. It does not depend on whether the occupation is permanent or temporary. It does not depend on the label which the parties put upon it. All these are factors which may influence the decision but none of them is conclusive. All the circumstances have to be worked out. Eventually the answer depends on the nature and quality of the occupancy. Was it intended that the occupier should have a stake in the room or did he have only permission for himself personally to occupy the room, whether under a contract or not? In which case he is a licensee'.

But in my opinion in order to ascertain the nature and quality of the occupancy and to see whether the occupier has or has not a stake in the room or only permission for himself personally to occupy, the court must decide whether upon its true construction the agreement confers on the occupier exclusive possession. If exclusive possession at a rent for a term does not constitute a tenancy then the distinction between a contractual tenancy and a contractual licence of land becomes wholly unidentifiable.

In *Somma v Hazlehurst* [1978] 1 WLR 1014, a young unmarried couple H. and S. occupied a double bedsitting room for which they paid a weekly rent. The landlord did not provide services or attendance and the couple were not lodgers but tenants enjoying exclusive possession. But the Court of Appeal did not ask themselves whether H. and S. were lodgers or tenants and did not draw the correct conclusion from the fact that H. and S. enjoyed exclusive possession. The Court of Appeal were diverted from the correct inquiries by the fact that the landlord obliged H. and S. to enter into separate agreements and reserved power to determine each agreement separately. The landlord also insisted that the room should not in form be let to either H. or S. or to both H. and S. but that each should sign an agreement to share the room in common with such other persons as the landlord might from time to time nominate. The sham nature of this obligation would have been only slightly more obvious if H. and S. had been married or if the room had been furnished with a double bed instead of two single beds. If the landlord had served notice on H. to leave and had required S. to share the room with a strange man, the notice would only have been a disguised notice to quit on both H. and S. The room was let and taken as residential accommodation with exclusive possession in order that H. and S. might live together in undisturbed quasi-connubial bliss making weekly payments. The agreements signed by H. and S. constituted the grant to H. and S. jointly of exclusive possession at a rent for a term for the purposes for which the room was taken and the agreement therefore created a tenancy. Although the Rent Acts must not be allowed to alter or influence the construction of an agreement, the court should, in my opinion, be astute to detect and frustrate sham devices and artificial transactions[123] whose only object is to disguise the grant of a tenancy and to evade the Rent Acts. I would disapprove of the decision in this case that H. and S. were only licensees and for the same reason would disapprove of the decision in *Aldrington Garages Ltd v Fielder* (1978) 37 P & CR 461 and *Sturolson & Co v Weniz* (1984) 272 EG 326.

In the present case the Court of Appeal, 49 P & CR 324 held that the agreement dated 7 March 1983 only created a licence. Slade LJ at 329 accepted that the agreement and in particular clause 3 of the agreement 'shows that the right to occupy the premises conferred on the defendant was intended as an exclusive right of occupation, in that it was thought necessary to give a special and express power to the plaintiff to enter....' Before your Lordships it was conceded that the agreement conferred the right of exclusive possession on Mrs Mountford. Even without clause 3 the result would have been the same. By the agreement Mrs Mountford was granted the right to occupy residential accommodation. The landlord did not provide any services or attendance. It was plain that Mrs Mountford was not a lodger. Slade LJ proceeded to analyse all the provisions of the agreement, not for the purpose of deciding whether his finding of exclusive possession was correct, but for the purpose of assigning some of the provisions of the agreement to the category of terms which he thought are usually to be found in a tenancy agreement and of assigning other provisions to the category of terms which he thought are usually to be found in a licence. Slade LJ may or may not have been right that in a letting of a furnished room it was 'most unusual to find a provision in a tenancy agreement obliging the tenant to keep his rooms in a "tidy condition"': (p. 329). If Slade LJ was right about this and other provisions there is still no logical method of evaluating the results of his survey. Slade LJ reached the conclusion that 'the agreement bears all the hallmarks of a licence, rather than a tenancy, save for the one important feature of exclusive occupation': p. 329. But in addition to the hallmark of exclusive occupation of residential accommodation there were the hallmarks of weekly payments for a periodical term. Unless these three hallmarks are decisive, it really becomes impossible to distinguish a contractual tenancy from a contractual licence save by reference to the professed intention of the parties or by the judge awarding marks for drafting. Slade LJ was finally impressed by the statement at the foot of the agreement by Mrs Mountford 'I understand and accept that a licence in the above form does not and is not intended to give me a tenancy protected under the Rent Acts.' Slade LJ said, at 330:

> 'it seems to me that if the defendant is to displace the express statement of intention embodied in the declaration, she must show that the declaration was either a deliberate sham or at least an inaccurate statement of what was the true substance of the real transaction agreed between the parties;'...

---

[123] 'It would have been more accurate and less liable to give rise to misunderstandings if I had substituted the word "pretence" for the references to "sham devices" and "artificial transactions"'; *AG Securities v Vaughan* [1990] 1 AC 417 at 462, per Lord Templeman, p. 399, below. See also *Stribling v Wickham* [1989] 2 EGLR 35 at 38, per Sir Denys Buckley, p. 405, below.

My Lords, the only intention which is relevant is the intention demonstrated by the agreement to grant exclusive possession for a term at a rent. Sometimes it may be difficult to discover whether, on the true construction of an agreement, exclusive possession is conferred.[124] Sometimes it may appear from the surrounding circumstances that there was no intention to create legal relationships. Sometimes it may appear from the surrounding circumstances that the right to exclusive possession is referable to a legal relationship other than a tenancy. Legal relationships to which the grant of exclusive possession might be referable and which would or might negative the grant of an estate or interest in the land include occupancy under a contract for the sale of the land, occupancy pursuant to a contract of employment or occupancy referable to the holding of an office. But where as in the present case the only circumstances are that residential accommodation is offered and accepted with exclusive possession for a term at a rent, the result is a tenancy.

The position was well summarised by Windeyer J sitting in the High Court of Australia in *Radaich v Smith* (1959) 101 CLR 209, 222, where he said:

'What then is the fundamental right which a tenant has that distinguishes his position from that of a licensee? It is an interest in land as distinct from a personal permission to enter the land and use it for some stipulated purpose or purposes. And how is it to be ascertained whether such an interest in land has been given? By seeing whether the grantee was given a legal right of exclusive possession of the land for a term or from year to year or for a life or lives. If he was, he is a tenant. And he cannot be other than a tenant, because a legal right of exclusive possession is a tenancy and the creation of such a right is a demise. To say that a man who has, by agreement with a landlord, a right of exclusive possession of land for a term is not a tenant is simply to contradict the first proposition by the second. A right of exclusive possession is secured by the right of a lessee to maintain ejectment and, after his entry, trespass. A reservation to the landlord, either by contract or statute, of a limited right of entry, as for example to view or repair, is, of course, not inconsistent with the grant of exclusive possession. Subject to such reservations, a tenant for a term or from year to year or for a life or lives can exclude his landlord as well as strangers from the demised premises. All this is long established law: see *Cole on Ejectment* (1857) pp. 72, 73, 287, 458.'

My Lords, I gratefully adopt the logic and the language of Windeyer J. Henceforth the courts which deal with these problems will, save in exceptional circumstances, only be concerned to inquire whether as a result of an agreement relating to residential accommodation the occupier is a lodger or a tenant. In the present case I am satisfied that Mrs Mountford is a tenant, that the appeal should be allowed, that the order of the Court of Appeal should be set aside and that the respondent should be ordered to pay the costs of the appellant here and below.[125]

---

[124] See *Appah v Parncliffe Investments Ltd* [1964] 1 WLR 1064; *University of Reading v Johnson-Houghton* (1985) 276 EG 1353; *Wigan Borough Council v Green & Son (Wigan) Ltd* [1985] 2 EGLR 242.

[125] 'The original rent of £37 per week was a compromise between Mr Street's suggestion for £39 and Mrs Mountford's suggestion for £35. The rent officer then fixed a "fair" rent of £14. Costs as claimed (but not yet taxed) at the county court, Court of Appeal and House of Lords amount to some £40,000. Meanwhile, Mrs Mountford has vacated in return for a cash sum of £1,800. This can, in effect, be deducted from the £2,410 rent she paid whilst occupying the flat for 2½ years.' (1985) 129 SJ 852 in a letter from G. Cutting, Chairman, Small Landlords Association.

For a checklist of the points raised by Lord Templeman, see *Crancour Ltd v De Silvaesa* [1986] 1 EGLR 80 at 88; (1987) 50 MLR 226 (A. J. Waite).

(c) Business tenant or licensee

The decision in *Street v Mountford*, which related to residential accommodation, has been applied to business tenancies.[126] In the context of premises occupied for business purposes, however, Lord Templeman's test, 'tenant or lodger?', has to be adapted, since 'lodger' is the language of residential occupation. Moreover, the policies underlying the statutory regulation of business tenancies differ from those underlying the regulation of residential tenancies,[127] and so the courts' reluctance to allow the parties to agree to create a licence, rather than a lease, may not be so strict in the case of business premises.

In **Dresden Estates Ltd v Collinson** [1987] 1 EGLR 45,[128] where 'an unusual provision' in a licence agreement reserved to the licensor of an industrial unit the right to relocate the licensee to an adjoining unit, the Court of Appeal held that this effectively deprived the licensee of the right to exclusive possession. GLIDEWELL LJ said at 46–47:

Street v Mountford...was concerned with residential premises. Mr. Coveney conceded that there was no material difference, at least for present purposes, between the law applicable to residential premises and the law applicable to business premises. As a broad, general proposition that may be right, but I am not sure that his concession may not have gone too far in this respect, that the attributes of residential premises and business premises are often quite different.

---

[126] *London and Associated Investment Trust plc v Calow* [1986] 2 EGLR 80; [1987] Conv 137 (S. Bridge); *Dellneed Ltd v Chin* (1986) 53 P & CR 172 (Mai Toi agreement); [1987] Conv 298 (S. Bridge); cf. *Smith v Northside Developments Ltd* [1987] 2 EGLR 151 (*oral* agreement where occupier said that he 'would take unit 17 on my own' held not to be grant of exclusive possession); *University of Reading v Johnson-Houghton* [1985] 2 EGLR 113 (grant of right to 'gallops for racehorses at Blewbury in Berkshire' held to be a lease 'on the balance of probabilities... despite its title ['licence'] and much of its language), per Leonard J at 116; [1986] Conv 275 (C. P. Rodgers); *Wigan Borough Council v Green & Son (Wigan) Ltd* [1985] 2 EGLR 242 ('permission to use exclusively' stalls in covered market for 'a very substantial butcher's shop' held to be tenancy); *McCarthy v Bence* [1990] 1 EGLR 1 (joint venture in form of sharing milk arrangement held to be licence for purposes of s. 2(2)(b) of the Agricultural Holdings Act 1986; agreement would not involve 'exclusive occupation', and area of land and fields available for licensee's cows might be altered from time to time by the licensor, who also enjoyed access for several purposes such as the exercise of sporting rights, felling dead elm trees, hedging and ditching and 'walking with his dog, taking his thistle spud in the thistle season to pull out thistles or doing any other minor tidying up that caught his eye' [1991] Conv 58 (C. Rodgers), 207 (M. Slater)); *Graysim Holdings Ltd v P & O Property Holdings Ltd* [1996] AC 329 (stallholder in covered market at Wallasey held to be tenant); *Hunts Refuse Disposals v Norfolk Environmental Waste Services Ltd* [1997] 1 EGLR 16 (agreement giving waste disposal firm access to part of active quarry for 21 years for disposal of waste on payment held to be licence); *Venus Investment Ltd v Stocktop Ltd* [1996] EGCS 173 (vendor of garage permitted to remain after completion under written agreement intended to create licence and not lease held to be licensee); *National Car Parks Ltd v Trinity Development Co (Banbury) Ltd* [2002] 2 P & CR 18 (agreement to operate shoppers' car park held to be licence because grantee had no right to exclude grantor), following *Esso Petroleum Co Ltd v Fumegrange Ltd* [1994] 2 EGLR 90 p. 391, n. 122, above [2001] Conv 348 (M. Haley); *Clear Channel UK Ltd v Manchester City Council* [2006] 1 EGLR 27, below, p. 396. See also *Bracey v Read* [1962] 3 All ER 472 at 475, per Cross J.

[127] In particular, although business tenants are given protection by way of security of tenure and rent control under LTA 1954, Part II, the parties are permitted to contract out of those protective provisions: C & B, p. 385.

[128] [1987] Conv 220 (P. F. Smith); (1987) 50 MLR 655 (S. Bridge).

The passage that I have already quoted from the speech of Lord Templeman, where he says in effect that all you have to decide in relation to residential premises is whether the occupier is a tenant or a lodger is, of course, of itself not applicable to business premises because there is no such person as a lodger in relation to business premises. For myself, I think that the indicia, which may make it more apparent in the case of a residential tenant or a residential occupier that he is indeed a tenant, may be less applicable or be less likely to have that effect in the case of some business tenancies.

And LLOYD LJ said at 48:

I would only add, like my Lord, that our decision today should not be regarded as providing a way round the decision of the House of Lords in *Street v Mountford*. It will be in only a limited class of case that a provision, such as is found in clause 4(b), would be appropriate. If it is included in an agreement where it is not appropriate, then it will not carry the day.

In **London and Associated Investment Trust plc v Calow** (1986) 53 P & CR 340, JUDGE PAUL BAKER QC said at 352:

Certainly it seems to me that self-contained business offices stand in the same case as do residential properties. Lord Templeman mentioned residence because that was the actual case that he was dealing with there. It was not meant to lay down a separate doctrine for residential properties as opposed to business properties. There might be special cases of some sort of trading properties, areas in shops and so forth, or stalls in markets, and there might be difficulties with agricultural properties, where licences are frequent, but I cannot see differentiation for this purpose between a residence on the one hand and a solicitor's office on the other.

In **Clear Channel UK Ltd v Manchester City Council** [2006] 1 EGLR 27 the Court of Appeal held that the agreement pursuant to which Clear Channel erected and maintained 13 large advertising displays at various prominent sites in Manchester owned by the council constituted a licence, not a tenancy. Although the hoardings were set in concrete bases embedded in the ground, the agreement gave Clear Channel only the right to erect them at undefined locations within a wider area of land (the 'Sites') and so did not grant exclusive possession of any parcel of land. The agreement referred to a 'term' and provided for a 'rent'; but clause 14.1 provided:

'This Agreement shall constitute a licence in respect of each Site and confers no tenancy on [Clear Channel] and possession of each Site is retained by [the council] subject however to the rights and obligations created by this Agreement.'

JONATHAN PARKER LJ said at 29, para. 28:

I find it surprising and (if I may say so) unedifying that a substantial and reputable commercial organisation like Clear Channel, having (no doubt with full legal assistance) negotiated a contract with the intention expressed in the contract (see clause 14.1, quoted above) that the contract should not create a tenancy, should then invite the court to conclude that it did.

In making that comment I intend no criticism whatever of Mr McGhee, who sought valiantly to make bricks without straw. Nor, of course, do I intend to cast any doubt whatever upon the principles established in *Street v Mountford*. On the other hand, the fact remains that this was a contract negotiated between two substantial parties of equal bargaining power and with the benefit of full legal advice. Where the contract so negotiated contains not merely a label but a clause that sets out in unequivocal terms the parties' intention as to its legal effect, I would in any event have taken some persuading that its true effect was directly contrary to that expressed intention. In the event, however, as the judge so clearly demonstrated, the case admits of only one result.

(d) Multiple occupation. Sham devices or pretence[129, 130]

Before 1985 some landlords had drafted residential occupation agreements in terms designed to ensure that the premises were occupied under a licence and not under a lease. Their object was to avoid the application of the Rent Acts. A simple device was to deny the occupant the right to exclusive possession of the premises by incorporating a term that their use was 'to be in common with the licensor and such other licensees as the licensor may permit from time to time to use the said rooms'. This term was upheld by the Court of Appeal in *Somma v Hazlehurst* [1978] 1 WLR 1014, p. 380, above. A further green light was given when the Appellate Committee of the House of Lords refused leave to appeal: [1978] 2 All ER 1011 at 1025.

As we have seen, the House of Lords in *Street v Mountford* [1985] AC 809, p. 383, above, strongly disapproved of *Somma v Hazlehurst*, and in two cases in 1990 disapproved it as being a mere pretence and inconsistent with the Rent Acts,[131]

[129, 130] P. 393, n. 123, above. See *Snook v London and West Riding Investments Ltd* [1967] 2 QB 786 at 802, where Diplock LJ defined 'this popular and pejorative word': 'If it has any meaning in law, it means acts done or documents executed by the parties to the "sham" which are intended by them to give to third parties or to the court the appearance of creating between the parties legal rights and obligations different from the actual legal rights and obligations (if any) which the parties intend to create.'

Cf. the similar approach in the House of Lords to tax avoidance schemes which involve 'a pre-ordained series of transactions (whether or not they include the achievement of a legitimate commercial end) into which there are inserted steps which have no commercial purpose apart from the avoidance of a liability to tax which in the absence of those particular steps would have been payable': *IRC v Burmah Oil Co Ltd* [1982] STC 30 at 32, per Lord Diplock. See also *WT Ramsay Ltd v IRC* [1982] AC 300; *Furniss v Dawson* [1984] AC 474; *Craven v White* [1989] AC 398; *Hatton v IRC* [1992] STC 140; *IRC v Fitzwilliam* [1993] 1 WLR 1189; *IRC v McGuckian* [1997] 1 WLR 991; *MacNiven v Westmoreland Investments Ltd* [2003] 1 AC 311. See M & B, *Trusts and Trustees* (7th edn, 2008), pp. 32–38. See also *Gisborne v Burton* [1989] QB 390, where CA invoked the tax doctrine to strike down a scheme to deny a sub-tenant the protection of the Agricultural Holdings Act 1948, s. 24(1); cf. *Hilton v Plustitle Ltd* [1989] 1 WLR 149 (company let scheme held not to be a sham because the company tenant, rather than the occupier, performed all the obligations under the tenancy), distinguished in *Bankway Properties Ltd v Pensfold-Dunsford* [2001] 1 WLR 1369; [2001] CLJ 146 (S. Bright); *Kaye v Massbetter Ltd* (1990) 62 P & CR 558 (letting to limited company tenant with a view to excluding the Rent Acts held to be genuine); [1992] Conv 58 (P. Luther); *Estavest Investments Ltd v Commercial Express Travel Ltd* [1988] 2 EGLR 91: (1991) 11 OJLS 136 (S. Bright); *Belvedere Court Management v Frogmore Developments Ltd* [1997] QB 858. See also the 1986 Blundell Memorial Lecture, summarised at (1986) 83 LSG 3736 (K. Lewison); (1987) 84 LSG 403 (P. Freedman) (2001) 117 LQR 575 (Lord Templeman); *Rationalizing Property, Equity and Trusts: Essays in Honour of Edward Burn* (ed. Getzler), chap. 7 (Lord Templeman), chap. 8 (B. McFarlane and E. Simpson); [2008] LMCLQ 488 (J. Vella).

[131] *Aldrington Garages Ltd v Fielder* (1978) 37 P & CR 461, *Sturolson v Weniz* (1984) 272 EG 326, and *Hadjiloucas v Crean* [1988] 1 WLR 1006 were also reversed.

AG Securities v Vaughan and *Antoniades v Villiers* [1990] 1 AC 417, below, which were heard simultaneously.[132] Both concerned separate flat-sharing agreements, both were described as 'licences', and both denied exclusive possession (in terms drafted before *Street v Mountford*). In both cases the House of Lords reversed the Court of Appeal, holding that in the first there was a licence, and in the second a joint tenancy.

In **AG Securities v Vaughan** four young men signed separate agreements on different dates with different amounts of payment. The documents were described as licences, denied exclusive possession of any part and required the occupier to share with not more than three other persons. When there was a change, there was a pecking order for the best rooms. The House of Lords held that the four occupiers were individual licensees, and not joint tenants. The differences of date and payment made it impossible for the four unities (of possession, interest, time and title) of a joint tenancy to exist.[133] As Lord BRIDGE OF HARWICH said at 454:

The arrangement seems to have been a sensible and realistic one to provide accommodation for a shifting population of individuals who were genuinely prepared to share the flat with others introduced from time to time who would, at least initially, be strangers to them. There was no artificiality in the contracts concluded to give effect to this arrangement.

In **Antoniades v Villiers** there were two separate agreements based on the *Somma v Hazelhurst* precedent. They were entered into by a man and a woman who wished to live together in a small flat in undisturbed quasi-connubial bliss.[134] They chose a double bed rather than single beds. They were to use the flat in common with the owner or other licensees permitted by him. Unlike *AG Securities v Vaughan*, 'the two agreements were interdependent, not independent of one another. Both would have been signed or neither. The two agreements must therefore be read together' (per Lord Templeman at 460). The sharing term was 'contrary to the provisions of the Rent Acts and, in addition was, in the circumstances, a pretence intended only to get round the Rent Acts' (at 464).

AG Securities v Vaughan
Antoniades v Villiers
[1990] 1 AC 417 (Lords Bridge of Harwich, Templeman, Ackner, Oliver of Aylmerton and Jauncey of Tullichettle)

Lord Templeman: My Lords, ever since 1915 the Rent Acts have protected some tenants of residential accommodation with security of tenure and maximum rents. The scope and effect

---

132 [1989] CLJ 19 (C. Harpum); (1989) 105 LQR 165 (P. V. Baker); (1989) Conv 128 (P. F. Smith); (1989) 52 MLR 408 (J. Hill); [1988] All ER Rev 171 (P. J. Clarke).
133 On the four unities, see C & B, pp. 454–455; Gray, paras 7.4.21–7.4.27; M & W, paras 13.004–13.008; MM, pp. 304–306; Smith, pp. 284–286.
134 *Street v Mountford* [1985] AC 809 at 825, per Lord Templeman.

of the Rent Acts have been altered from time to time and the current legislative protection is contained in the Rent Act 1977. Section 1 of the Act of 1977, reproducing earlier enactments, provides:

> 'Subject to this Part of this Act, a tenancy under which a dwelling-house (which may be a house or part of a house) is let as a separate dwelling is a protected tenancy for the purposes of this Act.'

Parties to an agreement cannot contract out of the Rent Acts; if they were able to do so the Acts would be a dead letter because in a state of housing shortage a person seeking residential accommodation may agree to anything to obtain shelter. The Rent Acts protect a tenant but they do not protect a licensee. Since parties to an agreement cannot contract out of the Rent Acts, a document which expresses the intention genuine or bogus of both parties or of one party to create a licence will nevertheless create a tenancy if the rights and obligations enjoyed and imposed satisfy the legal requirements of a tenancy. A person seeking residential accommodation may concur in any expression of intention in order to obtain shelter. Since parties to an agreement cannot contract out of the Rent Acts, a document expressed in the language of a licence must nevertheless be examined and construed by the court in order to decide whether the rights and obligations enjoyed and imposed create a licence or a tenancy. A person seeking residential accommodation may sign a document couched in any language in order to obtain shelter. Since parties to an agreement cannot contract out of the Rent Acts, the grant of a tenancy to two persons jointly cannot be concealed, accidentally or by design, by the creation of two documents in the form of licences. Two persons seeking residential accommodation may sign any number of documents in order to obtain joint shelter. In considering one or more documents for the purpose of deciding whether a tenancy has been created, the court must consider the surrounding circumstances including any relationship between the prospective occupiers, the course of negotiations and the nature and extent of the accommodation and the intended and actual mode of occupation of the accommodation. If the owner of a one-bedroomed flat granted a licence to a husband to occupy the flat provided he shared the flat with his wife and nobody else and granted a similar licence to the wife provided she shared the flat with the husband and nobody else, the court would be bound to consider the effect of both documents together. If the licence to the husband required him to pay a licence fee of £50 per month and the licence to the wife required her to pay a further licence fee of £50 per month, the two documents read together in the light of the property to be occupied and the obvious intended mode of occupation would confer exclusive occupation on the husband and wife jointly and a tenancy at the rent of £100.

Landlords dislike the Rent Acts and wish to enjoy the benefits of letting property without the burden of the restrictions imposed by the Acts. Landlords believe that the Rent Acts unfairly interfere with freedom of contract and exacerbate the housing shortage. Tenants on the other hand believe that the Acts are a necessary protection against the exploitation of people who do not own the freehold or long leases of their homes. The court lacks the knowledge and the power to form any judgment on these arguments which fall to be considered and determined by Parliament. The duty of the court is to enforce the Acts and in so doing to observe one principle which is inherent in the Acts and has been long recognised, the principle that parties cannot contract out of the Acts.

Lord Oliver of Aylmerton:

ANTONIADES V VILLIERS

The appellants in this appeal are a young couple who at all material times were living together as man and wife. In about November 1984 they learned from a letting agency that a flat was available in a house at 6 Whiteley Road, London S. E. 19, owned by the respondent, Mr Antoniades. They inspected the flat together and were told that the rent would be £174 per month. They were given the choice of having the bedroom furnished with a double bed or two single beds and they chose a double bed. So, right from the inception, there was never any question but that the appellants were seeking to establish a joint home and they have, at all material times, been the sole occupants of the flat.

There is equally no question but that the premises are not suitable for occupation by more than one couple, save on a very temporary basis. The small living-room contains a sofa capable of being converted into a double bed and also a bed-table capable of being opened out to form a narrow single bed. The appellants did in fact have a friend to stay with them for a time in what the trial judge found to be cramped conditions, but the size of the accommodation and the facilities available clearly do not make the flat suitable for multiple occupation. When it came to drawing up the contractual arrangements under which the appellants were to be let into possession, each was asked to and did sign a separate licence agreement in the terms set out in the speech of my noble and learned friend, Lord Templeman, under which each assumed an individual, but not a joint, responsibility for payment of one half of the sum of £174 previously quoted as the rent.

There is an air of total unreality about these documents read as separate and individual licences in the light of the circumstance that the appellants were together seeking a flat as a quasi-matrimonial home. A separate licensee does not realistically assume responsibility for all repairs and all outgoings. Nor in the circumstances can any realistic significance be given to clauses 16 and 17[135] of the document. It cannot realistically have been contemplated that the respondent would either himself use or occupy any part of the flat or put some other person in to share accommodation specifically adapted for the occupation by a couple living together. These clauses cannot be considered as seriously intended to have any practical operation or to serve any purpose apart from the purely technical one of seeking to avoid the ordinary legal consequences attendant upon letting the appellants into possession at a monthly rent. The unreality is enhanced by the reservation of the right of eviction without court order, which cannot seriously have been thought to be effective, and by the accompanying agreement not to get married, which can only have been designed to prevent a situation arising in which it would be quite impossible to argue that the 'licensees' were enjoying separate rights of occupation.

The conclusion seems to me irresistible that these two so-called licences, executed contemporaneously and entered into in the circumstances already outlined, have to be read together as constituting in reality one single transaction under which the appellants became

---

[135] '(16) The licensor shall be entitled at any time to use the rooms together with the licensee and permit other persons to use all of the rooms together with the licensee...(17) This licence is personal to the licensee and shall not permit the use of the rooms by any person whatsoever and only the licensor will have the right to use or permit the use of the room as described in clause 16. The licensee under no circumstances will have the right to allow any other people of his choice to use the rooms in any way...'

joint ccupiers. That of course does not conclude the case because the question still remains, what is the effect?

The document is clearly based upon the form of document which was upheld by the Court of Appeal as an effective licence in *Somma v Hazlehurst* [1978] 1 WLR 1014 [p. 380, above]. That case, which rested on what was said to be the impossibility of the two licensees having between them exclusive possession, was overruled in *Street v Mountford* [1985] AC 809. It was, however, a case which related to a single room and it is suggested that a similar agreement relating to premises containing space which could, albeit uncomfortably, accommodate another person is not necessarily governed by the same principle. On the other hand, the trial judge found that apart from the few visits by the respondent (who, on all but one occasion, sought admission by knocking on the door) no one shared with the appellants and that they had exclusive possession. He held that the licences were 'artificial transactions designed to evade the Rent Acts,' that a tenancy was created and that the appellants occupied as joint tenants.

His decision was reversed by the Court of Appeal, [1990] 1 AC 438E, on, broadly, the grounds that he had erred in treating the subsequent conduct of the parties as admissible as an aid to construction of the agreements and that in so far as the holding above referred to constituted a finding that the licences were a sham, that was unsupported by the evidence inasmuch as the appellants' intention that they should enjoy exclusive possession was not shared by the respondent. The licences could not, therefore, be said to mask the real intention of the parties and fell to be construed by reference to what they said in terms.

If the documents fall to be taken seriously at their face value and to be construed according to their terms, I see, for my part, no escape from the conclusion at which the Court of Appeal arrived. If it is once accepted that the respondent enjoyed the right—whether he exercised it or not—to share the accommodation with the appellants, either himself or by introducing one or more other persons to use the flat with them, it is, as it seems to me, incontestable that the appellants cannot claim to have had exclusive possession. The appellants' case therefore rests, as Mr Colyer frankly admits, upon upholding the judge's approach that the true transaction contemplated was that the appellants should jointly enjoy exclusive possession and that the licences were mere sham or window-dressing to indicate legal incidents which were never seriously intended in fact, but which would be inconsistent with the application to that transaction of the Rent Acts. Now to begin with, I do not, for my part, read the notes of the judge's judgment as showing that he construed the agreement in the light of what the parties subsequently did. I agree entirely with the Court of Appeal that if he did that he was in error. But though subsequent conduct is irrelevant as an aid to construction, it is certainly admissible as evidence on the question of whether the documents were or were not genuine documents giving effect to the parties' true intentions. Broadly what is said by Mr Colyer is that nobody acquainted with the circumstances in which the parties had come together and with the physical lay-out and size of the premises could seriously have imagined that the clauses in the licence which, on the face of them, contemplate the respondent and an apparently limitless number of other persons moving in to share the whole of the available accommodation, including the bedroom with what, to all intents and purposes, was a married couple committed to paying £174 a month in advance, were anything other than a smoke-screen; and the fact that the respondent, who might be assumed to want to make the maximum profit out of the premises, never sought to introduce anyone else is at least some indication that that is exactly what it was. Adopting the definition of a sham formulated by

Purchas LJ in *Hadjiloucas v Crean* [1988] 1 WLR 1006, 1013, Mr Colyer submits that the licences clearly incorporate clauses by which neither party intended to be bound and which were obviously a smoke-screen to cover the real intentions of both contracting parties. In the Court of Appeal, [1990] 1 AC 417, 446H–447A, Bingham LJ tested the matter by asking two questions, viz (1) on what grounds, if one party had left the premises, could the remaining party have been made liable for anything more than the £87 which he or she had agreed to pay, and (2) on what ground could they have resisted a demand by the respondent to introduce a further person into the premises? For my part, however, I do not see how this helps. The assumed negative answers prove nothing, for they rest upon the assumption that the licences are not sham documents, which is the very question in issue.

If the real transaction was, as the judge found one under which the appellants became joint tenants with exclusive possession, on the footing that the two agreements are to be construed together, then it would follow that they were together jointly and severally responsible for the whole rent. It would equally follow that they could effectively exclude the respondent and his nominees.

Although the facts are not precisely on all fours with *Somma v Hazlehurst* [1978] 1 WLR 1014, they are strikingly similar and the judge was, in my judgment, entitled to conclude that the appellants had exclusive possession of the premises. I read his finding that, 'the licences are artificial transactions designed to evade the Rent Acts' as a finding that they were sham documents designed to conceal the true nature of the transaction. There was, in my judgment, material on which he could properly reach this conclusion and I, too, would allow the appeal.

AG SECURITIES V VAUGHAN

The facts in this appeal are startlingly different from those in the case of *Antoniades*. To begin with the appeal concerns a substantial flat in a mansion block consisting of four bedrooms, a lounge, a sitting-room and usual offices. The trial judge found, as a fact, that the premises could without difficulty provide residential accommodation for four persons. There is no question but that the agreements with which the appeal is concerned reflect the true bargain between the parties. It is the purpose and intention of both parties to each agreement that it should confer an individual right on the licensee named, that he should be liable only for the payment which he had undertaken, and that his agreement should be capable of termination without reference to the agreements with other persons occupying the flat. The judge found that the agreements were not shams and that each of the four occupants had arrived independently of one another and not as a group. His finding was that there was never a group of persons coming to the flat all together. That has been challenged because, it is said, the evidence established that initially in 1977 and 1978 there was one occupant who was joined by three others who, although they came independently and not as a trio, moved in at about the same time. Central heating was then installed, so that the weekly payments fell to be increased and new agreements were signed by the four occupants contemporaneously. Speaking for myself, I cannot see how this can make any difference to the terms upon which the individuals were in occupation. If they were in as licensees in the first instance, the mere replacement of their agreements by new agreements in similar form cannot convert them into tenants, and the case has, in my judgment, to be approached on the footing that agreements with the occupiers were entered into separately and individually. The only questions are those of the effect of each agreement vis-a-vis the individual licensee and whether the agreements collectively had the effect of creating a joint tenancy among the occupants of the premises for the time being by virtue of their having between them exclusive possession of the premises.

Taking first, by way of example, the position of the first occupier to be let into the premises on the terms of one of these agreements, it is, in my judgment, quite unarguable, once any question of sham is out of the way, that he has an estate in the premises which entitles him to exclusive possession. His right, which is, by definition, a right to share use and occupation with such other persons not exceeding three in number as the licensor shall introduce from time to time, is clearly inconsistent with any exclusive possession in him alone even though he may be the only person in physical occupation at a particular time. He has no legal title which will permit him to exclude other persons to whom the licensor may choose to grant the privilege of entry. That must equally apply to the additional licensees who join him. None of them has individually nor have they collectively the right or power lawfully to exclude a further nominee of the licensor within the prescribed maximum.

I pause to note that it has never been contended that any individual occupier has a tenancy of a particular room in the flat with a right to use the remainder of the flat in common with the tenants of other rooms. I can envisage that as a possibility in cases of arrangements of this kind if the facts support the marking out with the landlord's concurrence of a particular room as the exclusive domain of a particular individual. But to support that there would, I think, have to be proved the grant of an identifiable part of the flat and that simply does not fit with the system described in the evidence of the instant case.

The real question—and it is this upon which the respondents rely—is what is the position when the flat is occupied concurrently by all four licensees? What is said then is that since the licensor has now exhausted, for the time being, his right of nomination, the four occupants collectively have exclusive possession of the premises because they can collectively exclude the licensor himself. Because, it is argued, (1) they have thus exclusive possession and, (2) there is an ascertainable term during which all have the right to use and occupy, and (3) they are occupying in consideration of the payment of periodic sums of money, *Street v Mountford* [1985] AC 809 shows that they are collectively tenants of the premises. They are not lodgers. Therefore they must be tenants. And because each is not individually a tenant, they must together be joint tenants.

My Lords, there appear to me to be a number of fallacies here. In the first place, the assertion of an exclusive possession rests, as it seems to me, upon assuming what it is sought to prove. If, of course, each licence agreement creates a tenancy, each tenant will be sharing with other persons whose rights to be there rest upon their own estates which, once they have been granted, they enjoy in their own right independently of the landlord. Collectively they have the right to exclude everyone other than those who have concurrent estates. But if the licence agreement is what it purports to be, that is to say, merely an agreement for permissive enjoyment as the invitee of the landlord, then each shares the use of the premises with other invitees of the same landlord. The landlord is not excluded for he continues to enjoy the premises through his invitees, even though he may for the time being have precluded himself by contract with each from withdrawing the invitation. Secondly, the fact that under each agreement an individual has the privilege of user and occupation for a term which overlaps the term of user and occupation of other persons in the premises, does not create a single indivisible term of occupation for all four consisting of an amalgam of the individual overlapping periods. Thirdly, there is no single sum of money payable in respect of use and occupation. Each person is individually liable for the amount which he has agreed, which may differ in practice from the amounts paid by all or some of the others.

The respondents are compelled to support their claims by a strange and unnatural theory that, as each occupant terminates his agreement, there is an implied surrender by the other three and an implied grant of a new joint tenancy to them together with the new incumbent when he enters under his individual agreement. With great respect to the majority in the Court of Appeal, this appears to me to be entirely unreal. For my part, I agree with the dissenting judgment of Sir George Waller in finding no unity of interest, no unity of title, certainly no unity of time and, as I think, no unity of possession. I find it impossible to say that the agreements entered into with the respondents created either individually or collectively a single tenancy either of the entire flat or of any part of it. I agree that the appeal should be allowed.

(e) Shifting population of individuals

AG Securities v Vaughan was applied in **Stribling v Wickham** [1989] 2 EGLR 35,[136] where PARKER LJ, in holding that the agreement was a licence, said at 35:

The appellant, Mr Nigel Stribling, is the freehold owner of a large flat known as Garden Flat, 10a St Quintin Avenue, London W10. On May 23 1987, by three separate agreements each of which was in identical terms, he granted (or purported to grant) to each of the two respondents and a Mr Wickham a licence to use the premises on a shared basis from May 24 1987 to April 23 1988 in consideration of the payment by each of £1,254 by 11 instalments of £114, payable on May 24 1987 and thereafter on the 24th of each month until March 24 1988.

The respondents and Mr Wickham occupied the premises on a shared basis and duly paid the amounts provided for by the agreements. On the expiry of the agreements, despite the appellant's demand, the respondents and Mr Wickham refused to leave the premises and on May 16 1988 the appellant commenced proceedings for possession against them in the Bloomsbury County Court.

The action was tried in September 1988 by Mr Assistant Recorder Harris. By that time Mr Wickham had left the premises and did not defend. The respondents resisted the claim, contending that the three agreements, notwithstanding their terms, had created a joint tenancy of the flat in the respondents and Mr Wickham, and that they were accordingly entitled to protection under the Rent Act 1977.

It was, and is, common ground that if the respondents' contention is correct, the claim for possession fails but that if the contention fails the claim for possession succeeds.

The assistant recorder upheld the contention and accordingly dismissed the claim. The appellant now appeals to this court....

His Lordship referred to *AG Securities v Vaughan* and *Antoniades v Villiers* and continued:

In the two above-mentioned appeals, their lordships were dealing with two very different factual situations described by Lord Oliver as being at different ends of the scale. The present situation falls midway between the two....

---

[136] [1989] Conv 192 (J. E. Martin).

It is not, and could not be, suggested that each agreement constituted a tenancy of a particular room together with a right to share living-room, kitchen and bathroom. The contest is between three individual licences and a joint tenancy.

As a matter of pure construction, it could not, in my view, possibly be suggested that, taken together, the agreements created a joint tenancy. One has therefore to see if any, and if so which, parts of the agreement should be regarded as a pretence or a sham or window dressing, the purpose of which was to disguise the grant of a tenancy.

The flat was suitable for use by a multiple but shifting population and was so used. Each occupant was given a specific right to terminate on 28 days' notice, and James Mavor specifically did so. His letter makes it plain that he considered that he was intending to terminate his own rights and obligations only, and that the positions of the other two would be unaffected. The owner was given a specific right against each to terminate on notice, and each agreement was expressed to terminate automatically if the 'licensee' were in breach. Each licensee had a specific obligation to pay the amount reserved by his agreement only.

In my judgment, there is no process of 'legal alchemy' by which the agreements can be placed into the mould of a tenancy. They represent the realities of the transaction and a genuine and sensible arrangement for the benefit of both sides.

The three licences were in substance and reality just what they purported to be. The right, specifically given under each of termination on 28 days' notice by either side, and the provision whereby each was responsible only for a specific sum which was in fact one-third of the total required by the landlord, are wholly inconsistent with a joint tenancy. That they were intended to operate is clear from events. They cannot be ignored nor can they, in my judgment, be converted by any legitimate process into a joint obligation to pay the whole rent or a form of authority to each occupant by the others to terminate a joint tenancy on notice by him, but by some magical process to re-create on the instant a joint tenancy in the remaining two until expiry of the current agreements.

I would allow this appeal, set aside the judgment and order that judgment for possession should be entered against the respondents.

Sir Denys Buckley said at 38:

I only want to add very few words in relation to the passage in the speech of Lord Templeman in *Street v Mountford* [1985] AC 809 at 825, where he refers to the court being astute to detect and frustrate sham devices. Of course a court should always be astute to give effect to the intention of Parliament, although the word 'astute' may be a rather emotive one to use in such a context. This does not mean that the court should lean in favour of any particular approach to construction, or any particular inference from the facts of the case.

The question whether there is a sham device, an artificial transaction or a pretence involved in the transaction under consideration must be approached evenhandedly. Only if an evenhanded approach to all the relevant considerations leads to the conclusion that some feature of the transaction in question is in fact a pretence can the court proceed to consider whether that constitutes a ground for holding that that feature amounts to an attempt to evade the Rent Acts. I am satisfied that Lord Templeman did not intend to imply anything other than this in the passage to which I have referred.

(f) Sharing part of demised premises

Street v Mountford principles also apply as between a tenant and the occupant of part of his demised premises.

In **Monmouth Borough Council v Marlog** [1994] 2 EGLR 68, Mr Roberts became the tenant of 5 Charles Close, Abergavenny. He moved in, accompanied by Mrs Marlog and her two children. Mr Roberts occupied one bedroom; Mrs Marlog and her children occupied the other two bedrooms. The kitchen, bathroom and living accommodation were shared. Mrs Marlog paid Mr Roberts £20 a week.

The Court of Appeal held that, although Mrs Marlog and her children had exclusive occupation of their two bedrooms, she was not the sub-tenant of Mr Roberts, but his licensee. She was therefore not entitled to remain as a secure tenant when Mr Roberts's tenancy from the local authority ended. NOURSE LJ said at 70:

Where two persons move into residential premises together under a tenancy granted to one but not the other of them, each occupying a bedroom or bedrooms and the remainder of the premises being shared between them, the court will be slow to infer a common intention that the one who is not the tenant shall be the subtenant of the one who is. The natural inference is that what is intended is a contractual house-sharing arrangement under the tenancy of one of them. The inference is greatly strengthened where, as here, there is a written agreement between the landlord and the tenant and none between the tenant and the other occupant.

(g) Joint and several liability for payment

In **Mikeover Ltd v Brady** [1989] 3 All ER 618, Mr Brady and Miss Guile occupied the plaintiff's second floor flat (which had been advertised in the Evening Standard as a flat for two people to share on the basis of two separate but identical agreements). Each agreement provided that the 'Owner grants to the Licensee the right to use in common with others who had been granted the like right the rooms on the second floor', and also that the Licensee shall 'pay the sum of £86.66 per month for the right to share in the use of the said rooms.' Two years later Miss Guile moved out, but Mr Brady remained and with the consent of the plaintiffs, paid £86.66 a month. When he fell into arrears, the plaintiffs sought possession of the flat. The defendant argued that the agreements together created a joint tenancy and that he was entitled to Rent Act protection.

In rejecting the claim, SLADE LJ said at 623:

The agreements have to be construed against the plaintiffs who proffered them. If they wished to reserve the right to impose on the defendant or Miss Guile a substitute co-occupant during the currency of the agreements, it was, in our judgment, incumbent on the plaintiffs to do so in much clearer terms.

It follows that, in our judgment, the defendant's agreement on its true construction conferred on him the *right* (by cl 1) to exclusive occupation of the flat in common only with Miss Guile during its currency. Clause 2(4) is to be read simply as imposing on him a corresponding *obligation* not to impede the use of the rooms etc. by Miss Guile during the currency of the term. Thus it is not necessary or relevant to consider the alternative argument of the defendant's counsel to the effect that, in so far as the agreement purported to reserve to the plaintiffs the right to impose on the defendant a substitute co-occupier in place of Miss Guile, it was a 'sham'....

We have already given reasons for concluding that the agreements in the present case did not on their proper reading purport to reserve to the plaintiffs the right to impose a co-occupant on the defendant or Miss Guile during the term of either agreement. Nevertheless, their effect was to confer on the defendant and Miss Guile together, so long as Miss Guile remained, a right of joint exclusive occupation of the property. The decision in *Street v Mountford* [1985] AC 809, establishes that the enjoyment by one person of exclusive occupation of premises for a term in consideration of periodical payments creates a tenancy save in exceptional circumstances not relevant to this appeal: see *Antoniades v Villiers* [1990] AC 417 at 459, per Lord Templeman. Similarly, as the last-mentioned decision illustrates, the enjoyment by more than one person of joint exclusive occupation of premises for the same term in consideration of periodical payments is capable of creating a joint tenancy.

It is, however, well settled that four unities must be present for the creation of a joint tenancy, namely the unities of possession, interest, title and time: see Megarry and Wade *The Law of Real Property* (5th edn, 1984) pp. 419–422. In the present case there is no dispute that the two agreements of 6 June 1984 operated to confer on the defendant and Miss Guile unity of possession and title. Likewise, there was unity of time in that each of their interests arose simultaneously and was expressed to endure for six months. The dispute concerns unity of interest. The general principle, as stated in Megarry and Wade p. 240, is:

> 'The interest of each joint tenant is the same in extent, nature and duration, for in theory of law they hold but one estate'.

'Interest' in this context must, in our judgment, include the bundle of rights and obligations representing that interest. The difficulty, from the defendant's point of view, is that the two agreements, instead of imposing a joint liability on him and Miss Guile to pay a deposit of £80 and monthly payments of £173.32, on their face imposed on each of them individual and separate obligations to pay only a deposit of £40 and monthly payments of only £86.66. On the face of it, the absence of joint obligations of payment is inconsistent with the existence of a joint tenancy.

Counsel for the defendant sought to meet this difficulty in three ways. First, he contended that the two agreements were, as he put it, 'interdependent' and must be read together. When so read, he submitted, they should be construed as placing on the two parties joint obligations. However, it seems to us quite impossible to rewrite the two agreements in this manner as a matter of construction: cf *Aldrington Garages Ltd v Fielder* (1978) 37 P & CR 461 at 471 per Geoffrey Lane LJ. One cannot add up two several obligations to pay £X so as to construct a joint obligation to pay £2X....

In agreement with the judge we thus conclude that as a matter of substance and reality each of the two parties to the agreements placed himself or herself under merely individual obligations to pay monthly sums of £86.66 and a deposit of £40, but no joint monetary obligations. What then is the effect?

Counsel for the defendant, as his last line of defence, submitted that even on this footing the defendant and Miss Guile were in law capable of being (and were in fact) joint tenants. In this context he invoked the authority of a dictum of Lord Templeman in *Antoniades v Villiers* [1990] 1 AC 417 at 461, where he said:

> 'Mr Antoniades required each of them, Mr Villiers and Miss Bridger, to agree to pay one-half of each aggregate periodical payment, but this circumstance cannot convert a tenancy into a licence. A tenancy remains a tenancy even though the landlord may choose to require each of two joint tenants to agree expressly to pay one-half of the rent.'

Lord Templeman was saying this in the context of two agreements which he regarded as shams. With great respect, however, if he was intending to say that a joint tenancy can exist even though the supposed joint tenants are not jointly liable for the whole rent, the weight of authority appears to go the other way. In *Antoniades v Villiers* at 469, Lord Oliver said:

> 'If the real transaction was, as the judge found, one under which the appellants became joint tenants with exclusive possession, on the footing that the two agreements are to be construed together, then it would follow that they were together jointly and severally responsible for the whole rent. It would equally follow that they could effectively exclude the respondent and his nominees.'

In the same case Lord Jauncey said at 473:

> 'Normal attributes of a lease to joint tenants include a demise for a specific period with exclusive possession at a single rent for payment of which each joint tenant is liable to the lessor in full subject to relief from his co-tenants.'

Finally, very recently in *Stribling v Wickham* [1989] 2 EGLR 35 [p. 493, above], Parker LJ, with whose judgment Fox LJ and Sir Denys Buckley agreed, said:

> 'The three licences were in substance and reality just what they purported to be. The right, specifically given under each of termination on 28 days' notice by either side, and the provision whereby each was responsible only for a specific sum which was in fact one-third of the total required by the landlord, are wholly inconsistent with a joint tenancy.'

The entire inconsistency with a joint tenancy of a provision rendering each licensee responsible only for one-third of the total required by the landlord was, as we read *Stribling v Wickham*, part of the essential reasoning which led this court to its final decision.

On these authorities, it appears to us that unity of interest imports the existence of joint rights and joint obligations. We therefore conclude that the provisions for payment contained in these two agreements (which were genuinely intended to impose and did impose on each party an obligation to pay no more than the sums reserved to the plaintiffs by his or her separate agreement) were incapable in law of creating a joint tenancy, because the monetary obligations of the two parties were not joint obligations and there was accordingly no complete unity of interest. It follows that there was no joint tenancy. Since inter se Miss Guile and the defendant had no power to exclude each other from occupation of any part of the premises, it also follows that their respective several rights can never have been greater than those of licensees during the period of their joint occupation. It has not been submitted (and we think in all the circumstances it could not be submitted) that the defendant's status became that of tenant after Miss Guile's departure, if it was not that before....

[E]very case where the question of lease or licence arises must depend on its own facts. All we need say is that in our view and on the judge's findings, on the particular facts of the present case, no sham device or artificial transaction is involved. At first sight it appeared to us that the employment of two forms of agreement, rather than one, had an air of artificiality about it. However, once it is accepted that the monetary obligations of each licensee were genuinely intended to be entirely independent from those of the other, it seems to us that this course was understandable, even though not essential, and is not fairly open to criticism. We have already accepted that each agreement has to be construed in the light of the other. However, we do not accept the submission of counsel for the defendant that they were 'interdependent'. While each had to be read with the other, each was perfectly capable of being operated on its own.

For the reasons stated, and despite counsel's admirable argument for the defendant, we dismiss this appeal.

(h) Construction of terms of occupation. Introduction of others. Retention of keys

Antoniades v Villiers was applied in *Aslan v Murphy* and *Duke v Wynne* [1990] 1 WLR 766 (a joint appeal to the Court of Appeal).

In **Asian v Murphy**[137] the plaintiff was the owner of a small basement room in Redcliffe Gardens, London. It was occupied by the defendant under a written agreement which provided that 'the licensor is not willing to grant the licensee exclusive possession of any part of the room'; that the licensor might permit others to use the room; and that the licensee had no occupation rights at all between 10.30 a.m. and 12 noon each day; and that the licensor would retain the keys to the room and have absolute right of entry at all times. Virtually no services were provided by the plaintiff during the defendant's occupation. The plaintiff obtained an order for possession of the room.

In **Duke v Wynne,** the plaintiff was the owner of a three bedroom house in Dunkeld Road, South Norwood, London. It was occupied by the defendants and their two sons. The written agreement recited that the owner wished to be able to obtain vacant possession at very short notice, that the occupiers accepted as a fundamental term of the agreement that they had no right of exclusive occupation in any part of the house, but would have to share it with other persons as directed by the plaintiff who retained a key and reserved the right to enter the house at any time. The plaintiff wished to emigrate to Canada and to sell the house with vacant possession. Negotiations took place with a view to the defendants buying the house, but agreement could not be reached on the price. Eventually the plaintiff obtained an order for possession.

In holding that in both cases the occupiers were tenants and therefore protected under the Rent Acts, LORD DONALDSON OF LYMINGTON said at 770:

General principles

The status of a tenant is essentially different from that of a lodger and owners of property are free to make accommodation available on either basis. Which basis applies in any particular case depends upon what was the true bargain between the parties. It is the ascertainment of that true bargain which lies at the heart of the problem.

Labelling

The labels which parties agree to attach to themselves or to their agreements are never conclusive and in this particular field, in which there is enormous pressure on the homeless to agree to any label which will facilitate the obtaining of accommodation, they give no guidance at all. As Lord Templeman said in *Street v Mountford* [1985] AC 809, 819.

---

[137] [1989] All ER Rev 172 (P. J. Clarke). There were two cases: *Aslan v Murphy (Nos 1 and 2)*; case No. 2 related to separate possession proceedings between the same parties as case No. 1. *Antoniades v Villiers* was also applied in *Nicolaou v Pitt* [1989] 1 EGLR 84 ('after a certain amount of humming and hawing the owner said he did contemplate introducing a stranger into the flat. I do not believe him'. CA held that there was a tenancy, even though the flat had a spare bedroom and had been previously occupied by three persons).

'The manufacture of a five-pronged implement for manual digging results in a fork even if the manufacturer, unfamiliar with the English language, insists that he intended to make and has made a
spade.'

Exclusive or non-exclusive occupation

This is the touchstone by which the 'spade' of tenancy falls to be distinguished from the 'fork'
of lodging. In this context it is necessary to consider the rights and duties of the person making
the accommodation available ('the owner') and the rights of other occupiers. The occupier has
in the end to be a tenant or a lodger. He cannot be both. But there is a spectrum of exclusivity
ranging from the occupier of a detached property under a full repairing lease, who is without
doubt a tenant, to the overnight occupier of a hotel bedroom who, however upmarket the hotel,
is without doubt a lodger. The dividing line—the sorting of the forks from the spades—will not
necessarily or even usually depend upon a single factor, but upon a combination of factors.

Pretences

Quite apart from labelling, parties may succumb to the temptation to agree to pretend to have
particular rights and duties which are not in fact any part of the true bargain. Prima facie,
the parties must be taken to mean what they say, but given the pressures on both parties to
pretend, albeit for different reasons, the courts would be acting unrealistically if they did not
keep a weather eye open for pretences, taking due account of how the parties have acted in
performance of their apparent bargain. This identification and exposure of such pretences does
not necessarily lead to the conclusion that their agreement is a sham, but only to the conclusion
that the terms of the true bargain are not wholly the same as those of the bargain appearing on
the face of the agreement. It is the true rather than the apparent bargain which determines the
question 'tenant or lodger?'

The effect of the Rent Acts

If an occupier would otherwise be protected by the Rent Acts, he does not lose that protection
by agreeing that he will surrender it either immediately or in the future and whether directly and
in terms or indirectly, e.g. by agreeing to substitute a shared for an exclusive right of occupation
should the owner so require: *Antoniades v Villiers* [1990] AC 417, 461.

Aslan v Murphy (No.1)

His Lordship stated the facts and the decision of the trial judge to the effect that the
defendant was a licensee, and continued:

In fairness to the judge, it should be said that he gave judgment before the House of Lords
reversed the decision of this court in *Antoniades v Villiers,* and therefore without the benefit
of the guidance contained in the speeches. In the light of that guidance, the judge's decision is
unsupportable on this ground and no attempt was made to support it.

The judge was, of course, quite right to approach the matter on this basis that it is not a crime,
nor is it contrary to public policy, for a property owner to license occupiers to occupy a property
on terms which do not give rise to a tenancy. Where he went wrong was in considering whether
the whole agreement was a sham and, having concluded that it was not, giving effect to its terms
i.e. taking it throughout at face value. What he should have done, and I am sure would have done
if he had known of the House of Lords approach to the problem, was to consider whether the
whole agreement was a sham and, if it was not, whether in the light of the factual situation the

provisions for sharing the room and those depriving the defendant of the right to occupy it for 90 minutes out of each 24 hours[138] were part of the true bargain between the parties or were pretences. Both provisions were wholly unrealistic and were clearly pretences.

In this court an attempt to uphold the judge's decision was made upon a different basis, namely, the landlord's right to retain the keys....

Provisions as to keys are often relied upon in support of the contention that an occupier is a lodger rather than a tenant. Thus in *Duke v Wynne,* to which we turn next, the agreement required the occupier 'not to interfere with or change the locks on any part of the premises, [or] give the key to any other than an authorised occupier of the premises.' Provisions as to keys, if not a pretence which they often are, do not have any magic in themselves. It is not a requirement of a tenancy that the occupier shall have exclusive possession of the keys to the property. What matters is what underlies the provisions as to keys. Why does the owner want a key, want to prevent keys being issued to the friends of the occupier or want to prevent the lock being changed?

A landlord may well need a key in order that he may be able to enter quickly in the event of emergency: fire, burst pipes or whatever. He may need a key to enable him or those authorised by him to read meters or to do repairs which are his responsibility. None of these underlying reasons would of themselves indicate that the true bargain between the parties was such that the occupier was in law a lodger. On the other hand, if the true bargain is that the owner will provide genuine services which can only be provided by having keys, such as frequent cleaning, daily bed-making, the provision of clean linen at regular intervals and the like, there are materials from which it is possible to infer that the occupier is a lodger rather than a tenant. But the inference arises not from the provisions as to keys, but from the reason why those provisions formed part of the bargain. On the facts of this case, the argument based upon the provisions as to keys must and does fail for the judge found that 'during the currency of the present agreement virtually "no services" had been provided.' These provisions may or may not have been pretences, but they are without significance in the context of the question which we had to decide.[139]

Duke v Wynne

Here the facts were very different from those in *Asian v Murphy*...

Tenants or lodgers?

Were the defendants tenants or lodgers? Unlike the facts in *Asian v Murphy* it would have been possible for them to have shared the house with another occupant. There were three bedrooms. One could have been used by the defendants, one by the children and the third, which was a very small room, by a lodger. However, the evidence did not disclose any immediate intention on the part of the plaintiff to make such an arrangement and she never in fact did so. Meanwhile, the defendants in fact occupied the whole house. In cases such as this the court has to determine whether the true bargain is that the occupiers are entitled to exclusive possession of the premises, unless and until the owner requires them to share, or whether the true bargain is that their entitlement is only to their share in the right to occupy, although, as there is currently no other occupant, it will be impracticable and unreasonable to seek to prevent their de facto occupation

---

[138] A similar provision in *Crancour Ltd v Da Silvaesa* [1986] 1 EGLR 80 was described by Nicholls LJ at 86 as being 'so extraordinary in a grant of a right to use residential accommodation for a period of six months that it calls for an explanation'.

[139] *Family Housing Association v Jones* [1990] 1 WLR 779 at 789.

of the whole premises. If the former is the case and, for the time being, they have an entitlement to exclusive occupation, they are tenants and their status cannot at some future date be unilaterally converted into that of lodgers by the owner requiring them to share their occupation: *Antoniades v Villiers*. If the latter is the case, they never achieve the status of tenants.

In the instant appeal it is quite clear that the true bargain was that the defendants should be entitled to exclusive occupation unless and until the plaintiff wanted to exercise her right to authorise someone else to move in as a lodger and she never suggested that this was a serious possibility. The provision about the key was no pretence in the sense that the plaintiff retained a key and no doubt did not wish the defendants to change the locks without at least giving her new keys. But her wish to have a key was not dictated by any obligation to provide services or anything else from which it could be inferred that she was herself occupying the house as well as the defendants.

But the situation could have been different. If the plaintiff had determined to have two couples as lodgers, she might not have been able to find them simultaneously. The first couple might have de facto occupation of the whole house meanwhile, but could not have claimed to be tenants since the plaintiff would de jure herself have been a co-occupier until the second pair of lodgers arrived. Applying the test of what was the true bargain between the parties, the court would have wanted to know what steps (if any) were being taken by the owner to fill the vacancy. If the owner was not actively seeking another occupant, it would be inherently more likely that the first couple were *entitled* to exclude possession of the whole in the meanwhile and so were tenants.

On the facts of this case and the law as now declared by the House of Lords, the defendants are clearly to be regarded as tenants, their appeal must be allowed and the order for possession set aside.

G. LAW REFORM

In 2006 the Law Commission published its Report on Renting Homes 2006 (Law Com No. 297).[140] Its recommendations for the reform of housing law represent radical legislative change to the regulation of the rented sector of the housing market:

1.4 First, we recommend the creation of a single social tenure. At present, local authorities can only let on secure tenancies; registered social landlords only on assured tenancies. Our recommendations are 'landlord-neutral'. They enable social housing providers, referred to in the Bill as 'community landlords', and those private sector landlords who so wish to rent on identical terms. This has long been sought by local authorities and registered social landlords. This offers the prize of vastly increased flexibility both to policy makers and landlords in the provision and management of social housing.

1.5 Secondly, we recommend a new 'consumer protection' approach which focuses on the contract between the landlord and the occupier (the contract-holder), incorporating consumer

---

[140] The Report followed two Consultation Papers: (a) Renting Homes (1) Status and Security 2002 (Law Com No. 162); and (b) Renting Homes (2) Co-occupation, Transfer and Succession 2002 (Law Com No. 168), and a 'Narrative Report' 2003 (Law Com No. 284). See also [2006] 18 EG 146, [2007] 35 EG 131 (M. Partington).

protection principles of fairness and transparency. Thus our recommended scheme does not depend on technical legal issues of whether or not there is a tenancy as opposed to a licence (as has usually been the case in the past). This ensures that both landlords and occupiers have a much clearer understanding of their rights and obligations.

1.6 The terms of the contract, underpinned by our statutory scheme, will be set out in model contracts that we anticipate will be free and easily downloadable.[141] They will benefit landlords by explaining their rights and obligations, thus reducing the ignorance many landlords have about their responsibilities. They will benefit occupiers who will also have a clear statement of their rights and obligations, which sets out the basis on which they occupy accommodation, and the circumstances in which their rights to occupy may come to an end.

It is recommended that there should be two basic types of occupation contract:

(1) the *secure contract,* with a high degree of security of tenure protected by the Act; these would be periodic contracts only.

(3) the standard contract with a low degree of security of tenure provided by statute. Landlords would be able to enter either fixed-term or periodic contracts.

Secure contracts are modelled on the present (local authority) secure tenancy; standard contracts are modelled on the present assured shorthold tenancy agreement, and most relevant existing tenancies and licences will be converted into occupation contracts. (paras 2.3, 2.4; 3.19–3.21.)

The broad policy objective is that, unless there are compelling reasons for exclusion, all contracts to occupy premises as a home should come within the scheme. A number of types of agreement currently outside the existing statutory scheme would be brought within it; for example, service occupancies and student accommodation provided by universities and local authorities. There would, however, be two classes of exemption from the scheme:

(1) contracts covered by other statutory schemes; these include business tenancies, tenancies protected by the Rent Act 1977 or the Rent (Agriculture) Act 1976, long tenancies and agricultural tenancies;

(2) certain types of contract excluded on social policy grounds, such as tenancies or licences relating to direct access accommodation, tenancies or licences where no rent or other consideration is payable, holiday lets, provision of accommodation in a care institution, provision of accommodation in barracks, provision of accommodation as a temporary expedient to persons who entered premises as trespassers, and accommodation shared with the landlord. (paras 2.56–2.59.)

Under the scheme there must be a contractual agreement between the landlord and the occupier; if it is made orally, a written statement of it must be provided by the landlord to the occupier, there would be model agreements. (paras 3.34–3.54.)

---

[141] Two sample model contracts appear at the end of this Report (Appendix B).

The agreements would contain a clear statement of the rights and obligations of both landlords and occupiers and the grounds for possession, which would be terms of the contract rather than the present situations where the grounds for possession are prescribed in detail in statutory texts which operate outside the agreement. (Part 4).

On the core provision—the occupation contract—the Report says:

3.7 At the heart of the scheme is the occupation contract.[142] So long as a contract conferring the right to occupy premises satisfies normal common law rules relating to the creation of contracts—that there should be an offer, acceptance of the offer, and consideration[143]—it is potentially an occupation contract within the scope of the scheme. A landlord and a contract-holder can reach a binding occupation contract orally without the need for any written formality.[144]...

3.9 A number of points about the definition of 'occupation contract' should be noted at the outset.

(1) It is specifically provided that an occupation contract can be either a tenancy or a licence.[145] This avoids historic complications whereby statutory schemes only applied where premises were 'let'.[146] This definition recognises that the distinction between a lease/tenancy and a licence exists. This will often be important. For example, where a landlord sells their legal estate in a property to another, it is highly relevant whether that estate is subject to a lease or a licence. These issues continue to be determined by application of the current law. We also make explicit that, where an occupation contract is a tenancy, any land registration requirements must be satisfied.[147]

(2) The contract must be made between a landlord and an individual[148] (the 'contract-holder'[149]). The contract must confer the right to occupy premises as a home.[150] Where the contract is made with two or more persons, at least one must be an individual.[151] Contracts relating to the occupation of premises for purposes other than occupation as a home fall outside the scope of our scheme. In many situations, such agreements fall within the scope of other statutory schemes, for example business tenancies. These exceptions are set out in schedule 1 to the Bill and are discussed below at paragraphs 3.13 to 3.17.

---

[142] Cl. 1(1) [of the Draft Bill]. In Renting Homes (2003) Law Com No. 284 this was called the occupation agreement.

[143] It will be possible for a landlord to bring a tenancy or licence in relation to which there is no consideration within the scheme by giving the occupier notice: see Sch. 1, para. 1(2).

[144] The Bill specifically provides that any requirements in the Land Registration Act 2002 for tenancies must be satisfied: cl. 217. Nothing in the Bill prevents the creation of leases, though long leases are outside the scope of the scheme: see below at para. 3.14.

[145] Cl. 1(1).

[146] A phrase interpreted by the courts to mean that there must be an agreement which satisfied the criteria for the creation of a tenancy. The most important restatement of these rules was made by the House of Lords in *Street v Mountford* [1985] AC 809 [above, p. 383]. Land law purists argued that their interpretation was not in strict accord with the law as previously understood. The new concept is designed to avoid these problems.

[147] Cl. 217.   [148] The individual must be at least 16 years old: cl. 1(5).

[149] Cl. 1(4). In Renting Homes (2003) Law Com No. 284 we referred to the contract-holder as the occupier.

[150] Cl. 1(2).

[151] Cl. 1(3). A contract made exclusively with a company could still be an occupation contract if it is confers the right to occupy premises as a home on an individual and the landlord gives notice that the contract is to be an occupation contract. See Sch. 1, para. 1(1) and para. 2.

(3) Despite the breadth of the definition, not all contracts which confer the right to occupy premises as a home fall within the scope of the Bill.[152] These exceptions are set out in schedule 1 and discussed in more detail below.

(4) Most of the ancillary tests currently used to define the scope of statutory protection are removed. Thus, there is no requirement that the rent should be above or below a defined rent limit. Nor is there any requirement that the premises must be occupied as the 'only or principal home'.[153]

(5) Most importantly in the context of the social rented sector, there is no 'landlord condition'. Our emphasis on the principle of landlord neutrality means that the scheme will, for the first time, enable the creation of a single type of contract that can apply throughout the social rented sector, irrespective of the identity of the landlord.

(6) Once created, an occupation contract continues in existence either until it is terminated in accordance with the provisions of the scheme, or unless the premises or the contract come within the scope of the exceptions listed in paragraph 3 of schedule 1.[154] In the latter case, the underlying tenancy or licence would continue to exist.[155]

QUESTIONS

1. Is there any good reason why freedom of contract should not prevail in

    (a) a *Street v Mountford* situation;

    (b) a *Somma v Hazlehurst* situation?

    Is the unlikely but possible intrusion into quasi-connubial bliss (*Street v Mountford* [1985] AC 809 at 825) a sufficient reason for preventing the parties from being held to a genuine bargain?

2. Draft an occupation agreement so as to avoid granting exclusive possession to the occupant.

3. How far should professional drafting be relevant when construing an agreement for the occupation of premises? See *IDC Group Ltd v Clark* [1992] 1 EGLR 187; affd [1992] 2 EGLR 184, p. 1106, below; *Clear Channel UK Ltd v Manchester City Council* [2006] 1 EGLR 27 at 29, p. 396, above.

4. Could the agreements in *AG Securities v Vaughan* [1990] 1 AC 417 and *Stribling v Wickham* [1989] 2 EGLR 35 be tenancies in common? See (1992) 142 NLJ 575 (S. Bright). Note, however, that as against the landlord, the (legal) lease must be held as a joint tenancy: LPA 1925, s. 1(6); above, p. 14.

---

[152] Cl. 1(6).

[153] A landlord who wishes to impose this requirement will be able to do so in the agreement. A contract holder who has more than one occupation contract is then in breach of the agreement and liable to face proceedings for possession. But as the purpose of the scheme is to ensure that *all* contract holders are informed about their contractual rights and obligations, there is no statutory rule preventing more than one contract from falling within the scope of the scheme.

[154] See below, at paras 3.13–3.17.

[155] Sch. 1, para. 3(1).

III. CREATION[156]

A. STATUTORY REQUIREMENTS FOR THE CREATION OF A LEGAL LEASE

The Law of Property Act 1925 and the Land Registration Act 2002 set out requirements of formality for the creation of legal leases, although exceptions allow certain short leases to be legal even though they are created informally, without writing or registration.

(i) Law of Property Act 1925

LAW OF PROPERTY ACT 1925

52. Conveyances to be by deed.—(1) All conveyances of land or of any interest therein are void for the purpose of conveying or creating a legal estate unless made by deed.

   (2) This section does not apply to—

      (d) leases or tenancies or other assurances not required by law to be made in writing...

54. Creation of interest in land by parol.—(1) All interests in land created by parol and not put in writing and signed by the persons so creating the same, or by their agents thereunto lawfully authorised in writing, have, notwithstanding any consideration having been given for the same, the force and effect of interests at will only.

   (2) Nothing in the foregoing provisions of this Part of this Act shall affect the creation by parol of leases taking effect in possession for a term not exceeding three years (whether or not the lessee is given power to extend the term) at the best rent which can be reasonably obtained without taking a fine.[157]

Section 54(2) applies only to the *creation* of a lease. In **Crago v Julian** [1992] 1 WLR 372[158] SIR DONALD NICHOLLS V-C, in holding that a legal *assignment* of an oral lease created within the ambit of section 54(2) of the Law of Property Act 1925 must be by deed, said at 375:

I turn first to the question of law: could this tenancy be assigned effectively only by deed? I can start with the summary of the law set out in Megarry & Wade, *The Law of Real Property*, 5th edn (1984), p. 665:

---

[156] C & B, pp. 219–229; Gray, paras 4.2.20–4.2.39; M & W, paras 17.029–17.053; MM, pp. 342–353; Smith, pp. 101–102.

[157] This does not exclude from the formality requirement of s. 52 a lease for a period exceeding three years even though it may be determinable within the period: *Kushner v Law Society* [1952] 1 KB 264. See also *Fitzkriston LLP v Panayi* [2008] L & TR 26 (one-year tenancy at rent of £4,000 per annum, by document which was not properly executed as a deed, took effect at will only because not at the best rent reasonably obtainable); [2008] 47 EG 110 (G. Fetherstonhaugh);(2008) 12 L & T Rev 215 (B. Baruch); [2009] Conv 54 (J. Brown).

[158] [1992] Conv 375 (P. Sparkes); *London Borough of Camden v Alexandrou* (1997) 74 P & CR D33.

'A legal lease, once created, can be transferred inter vivos only by deed, in accordance with the general rule. This applies to all legal leases, even those created orally, e.g. a yearly tenancy. However, on principles similar to those applicable to the creation of leases, an oral or written assignment will be effective in equity as between the assignor and the assignee as a contract to assign, if sufficiently evidenced by writing or part performance.'

In the present case nothing less than an assignment at law will assist Mrs Julian. The view stated in Megarry & Wade is also expressed in all the other leading textbooks on this subject. Undaunted, Mr Phillips contended that these views are erroneous. The general rule mentioned by Megarry & Wade is a reference to certain provisions in the Law of Property Act 1925. Mr Phillips submitted that, properly interpreted, these provisions do not preclude a valid assignment otherwise than by deed of a lease which has been created orally.

The statutory provisions are to be found in Part II of the Law of Property Act 1925. The material parts of the relevant sections, sections 52 to 54, provide:

His Lordship read ss. 52 (p. 416, above), 53(1) (p. 47, above) and 54 (p. 416, above) and continued:

This is a hotchpotch of sections reproducing, with some amendments, provisions which before 1925 were to be found in the Statute of Frauds 1677 and the Real Property Act 1845. I consider section 53 first. The grant of a tenancy is the creation of an interest in land. An assignment of a tenancy of land is the disposal of an interest in land. Thus, both the grant of a tenancy, and the assignment of a tenancy, fall four-square within section 53(1)(a). A tenancy of land cannot be created or assigned save by writing, or by will, or by operation of law. Paragraph (a), however, is expressed to be 'subject to the provisions hereinafter contained with respect to the *creation* of interests in land by parol.' (Emphasis added.) Section 54(2) is such a provision. Section 54(2) provides that the statutory requirements of Part II of the Act do not affect 'the creation' by parol of leases taking effect in possession for a term not exceeding three years at a full market rent.

I pause to observe that, thus far, there can be no doubt as to the meaning of the statutory provisions: interests in land cannot be created or disposed of except in writing, but a lease in possession at a market rent for up to three years can be validly created orally. Hence, and this is to be noted, the effect of these statutory provisions is indubitably to draw a distinction between the manner in which a short lease may be created and the manner in which it may be assigned.

The point is not wholly free from authority. Section 53(1)(a) derives from section 3 of the Statute of Frauds, and section 54 derives from sections 1 and 2. In *Botting v Martin* (1808) 1 Camp 317 Serjeant Best argued that by the leases mentioned in section 3, as requiring to be assigned in writing, must be intended such leases as are required by sections 1 and 2 to be created in writing, viz., leases conveying a larger interest to the party than a term for three years. He submitted:

'As a lease from year to year could be originally made by parol, there was no reason why it might not be assigned by parol, and the words of the statute would bear this interpretation, which was clearly consistent with its general import.'

McDonald CB rejected the submission.

In my view section 53 provides an insuperable obstacle for Mrs Julian in the present case. Like McDonald CB, I consider the statutory language really leaves no room for reaching a different conclusion, even though the result is the curious distinction I have mentioned. Even if there were room for doubt I would be slow to upset an interpretation of statutory provisions which has been accepted by conveyancers for a very long time.

This conclusion is sufficient to dispose of this appeal, because here there was no assignment in writing.

(ii) Land Registration Act 2002

The Land Registration Act 2002 lays down an additional requirement of registration for certain leases. Failure to register has the consequence that the lease, even if it complies with the formalities required by the Law of Property Act 1925, will not take effect at law.[159]

LAND REGISTRATION ACT 2002

27 Dispositions required to be registered

  (1) If a disposition of a registered estate or registered charge is required to be completed by registration, it does not operate at law until the relevant registration requirements are met.

  (2) In the case of a registered estate, the following are the dispositions which are required to be completed by registration—

    (a) a transfer,

    (b) where the registered estate is an estate in land, the grant of a term of years absolute—

      (i)   for a term of more than seven years[160] from the date of the grant,

      (ii) to take effect in possession after the end of the period of three months beginning with the date of the grant,

      (iii) under which the right to possession is discontinuous,[161]

      (iv) in pursuance of Part 5 of the Housing Act 1985 (the right to buy), or

      (v)   in circumstances where section 171A of that Act applies (disposal by landlord which leads to a person no longer being a secure tenant).

B. EQUITABLE LEASES

A lease may fail to satisfy the formalities required for its creation as a legal lease, but may still take effect as an equitable lease. This is so where there is:

---

[159] In addition, most leases which are required to be completed by registration must also, if granted on or after 19 June 2006, comply with requirements as to their form and content. Failure to comply with these requirements will result in the Land Registry rejecting the application for registration as defective. See LRR 2003, r. 58A, Sch. 1A, inserted by LR (Amendment) (No. 2) Rules 2005 (SI 2005 No. 1982), r. 5; Land Registry Practice Guide 64.

[160] This is a reduction from the period of 21 years under LRA 1925. The effect of the shorter period is that most business leases, which are usually granted for 10 or 15 years, are now registrable. The Lord Chancellor has power to shorten the seven-year period still further: LRA 2002, s. 5.

[161] Pp. 357–358, above.

(i) a contract to grant a legal lease, of which equity is prepared, in the circumstances, to grant specific performance. The contract must itself satisfy the formality requirements for a contract for the sale or other disposition of an interest in land.[162] Equity (following the maxim that 'equity looks on that as done which ought to be done') will treat the intended tenant as having already, in equity, a lease which satisfies the requirement of formalities for its creation. This is an application of the doctrine of *Walsh v Lonsdale*[163] or

(ii) a 'void' lease, i.e. a lease in writing for more than three years which is void at law owing to the lack of a deed, but is construed in equity as an agreement for a lease and the doctrine of *Walsh v Lonsdale* accordingly applies;[164] or

(iii) a lease in registered land which has not satisfied the requirements for registration.

C. DIFFERENCES BETWEEN A LEGAL LEASE AND AN EQUITABLE LEASE[165]

In certain significant respects an equitable lease is not as good as a legal lease.

(i) Third parties

An equitable lease gives the tenant less protection against third parties, such as a purchaser from the landlord. In unregistered land, a legal lease is binding on the purchaser, but the purchaser takes free of an equitable lease unless the lease is registered as a land charge under the Land Charges Act 1972.[166] In registered land the purchaser will be bound by a legal lease, either because it is registered with its own title,[167] or because it takes effect as an overriding interest.[168] But the equitable lease will be binding only if it is protected either by a notice in the register, or as an overriding interest by virtue of the tenant being in discoverable actual occupation.[169]

(ii) Law of Property Act 1925, section 62

An agreement for a lease is not a 'conveyance' within the meaning of the Law of Property Act 1925, section 62,[170] and therefore the equitable tenant cannot claim the benefit of rights which would be conferred by that section on a legal tenant—such as the creation of

---

[162] LP (MP) A 1989, s. 2; p. 18, above.   [163] (1882) 21 ChD 9, p. 30, above.

[164] *Parker v Taswell* (1858) 2 De G & J 559; *Bond v Rosling* (1861) 1 B & S 371; *Tidey v Mollett* (1864) 16 CBNS 298.

[165] C & B, pp. 225–227; Gray, paras 4.2.96–4.2.102; M & W, paras 17.041–17.053; MM, pp. 343–346; Smith, pp. 378–380.

[166] An equitable lease arising under the doctrine of *Walsh v Lonsdale* is an estate contract, and so registrable as a Class C(iv) land charge: pp. 33–34, 66, above.

[167] Above, pp. 123, 131, 132–133.   [168] LRA 2002, Sch. 3, para. 1; above, p. 195.

[169] LRA 2002, Sch. 3, para. 2. Only *legal* leases are protected under para. 1.

[170] 'Conveyance' is defined in LPA 1925, s. 205(1) (ii), p. 305, above.

an easement by implication in the conveyance. However, the rule in *Wheeldon v Burrows*, another doctrine by which easements can be implied, does apply to equitable leases.[171]

Borman v Griffith
[1930] 1 Ch 493 (ChD, **Maugham J**)

In 1923 James agreed to grant a lease to Borman of a house which was situated in a large park containing a mansion. The house was approached only by the drive leading to the mansion and not by a public road. The agreement contained no express grant of a right of way over the drive. In 1926 James leased the mansion to Griffith for 14 years.

Subsequent to the agreement of 1923, James constructed an unmetalled road to the rear of Borman's house. The road was not adequate for heavy traffic, and was unsuitable for Borman's trade as a poultry dealer, and Borman continued to use the drive. In 1928 Griffith obstructed Borman's use of the drive, and Borman sued to establish his right of way.

Held. (i) Section 62 of the Law of Property Act 1925 did not apply to an agreement for a lease, and the plaintiff could not claim an easement on that ground.

(ii) The plaintiff was entitled to claim the right of way under the rule in *Wheeldon v Burrows*.

Maugham J: . . . The date of the contract is a date before the coming into force of the Law of Property Act 1925, and is a date at which the Conveyancing Act, 1881, was still in force. The plaintiff relies on section 62, subsections 1 and 2 of the Law of Property Act 1925, under which certain general words are deemed to be included in a conveyance, and, in particular, the words 'ways . . . reputed to appertain to the land, houses, etc.' and 'reputed or known as part or parcel of or appurtenant to the land, houses, etc.,': he asserts that the way along the drive in the front of his house, and the branch drive leading directly to the back of his house, were ways enjoyed with the premises demised by the contract; and he points out that under subsection 6, the section applies to conveyances executed after 31 December 1881, and that 'conveyance' is defined in section 205, subsection 1 (ii), to include 'a lease . . . and every other assurance of property or of an interest therein by any instrument, except a will'. . . .

On the whole, I think that it is not a 'conveyance', because it is not an 'assurance of property or of an interest therein'. It is true that, under the decision in *Walsh v Lonsdale* (1882) 21 ChD 9 at 14 [p. 30, above] it has been held that, where there is an agreement for a lease under which possession has been given, the tenant holds, for many purposes, as if a lease had actually been granted. [His Lordship then quoted from the judgment of Jessel MR and continued:] That is the well known judgment of Sir George Jessel MR, with which Cotton and Lindley LJJ agreed. But no court has yet declared that an agreement for a lease for a term of more than three years is an 'assurance'. It has to be borne in mind that a lease for any term of more than three years must be by deed, and it is well known that, under section 3 of the Real Property Act, 1845,' . . . a lease required by law to be in writing, of any tenements or hereditaments . . . shall . . . be void at law unless made by deed.' (See now section 52 of the Law of Property Act, 1925, and the repeal section.)

In my opinion, a contract for a lease exceeding a term of three years does not come within the meaning of the phrase 'assurance of property or of an interest therein' as that phrase is used in

---

[171] For the application of LPA 1925, s. 62, in the context of easements, and the rule in *Wheeldon v Burrows* (1879) 12 ChD 31, see pp. 655–686, below.

section 205, subsection 1(ii), of the Law of Property Act, 1925: and accordingly I am unable to construe the agreement of 10 October 1923, as if the general words of section 62 of that Act were included in it...

In my view, the principles laid down in such cases as *Wheeldon v Burrows* (1879) 12 ChD 31; *Brown v Alabaster* (1887) 37 ChD 490; and *Nicholls v Nicholls* (1899) 81 LT 811 are applicable. Without going through all those cases in detail, I may state the principle as follows— namely, that where, as in the present case, two properties belonging to a single owner and about to be granted are separated by a common road, or where a plainly visible road exists over the one for the apparent use of the other, and that road is necessary for the reasonable enjoyment of the property, a right to use the road will pass with the quasi-dominant tenement, unless by the terms of the contract that right is excluded: and in my opinion, if the present position were that the plaintiff was claiming against the lessor specific performance of the agreement of 10 October 1923, he would be entitled to be given a right of way for all reasonable purposes along the drive, including the part that passes the farm on the way to the orchard.

(iii) Availability of specific performance

The doctrine of *Walsh v Lonsdale* is dependent upon the availability of specific performance, which is discretionary; and the willingess of a court to exercise its discretion in favour of the tenant can be affected by the tenant's conduct.[172] The position of an equitable tenant, whose status against the landlord depends upon the application of the doctrine, is therefore more precarious than that of a legal tenant.

(iv) The effect of an assignment on covenants

Under the Landlord and Tenant (Covenants) Act 1995 the benefit and burden of covenants in both legal and equitable leases entered into after 1995 run with the land and with the reversion on assignment. However, in the case of equitable leases entered into before 1996 it is not clear on the authorities that the burden of covenants runs with the land.[173]

IV. REMEDIES OF THE LANDLORD

It is not possible, in the available space, to deal with all the landlord's remedies.[174] This section will be confined to a consideration of some of the restrictions upon the landlord's right to recover possession of the demised premises, and his right to forfeit the lease for the tenant's breach of covenant.

---

[172] *Coatsworth v Johnson* (1885) 55 LJQB 220, p. 32, above.

[173] See pp. 476–482, below. A further difference was removed by *National Carriers Ltd v Panalpina (Northern) Ltd* [1981] AC 675, where HL held that the doctrine of frustration is applicable to a lease; for an agreement for a lease, see *Rom Securities Ltd v Rogers (Holdings) Ltd* (1967) 205 EG 427.

[174] See C & B, pp. 249–251 (specific performance and damages for breach of tenant's covenant to repair), 265–273 (distress and action to recover unpaid rent); Gray, part 4.4. The common law right of distress for arrears of rent was abolished by Tribunals, Courts and Enforcement Act 2007, s. 71, but a new procedure was

A. STATUTORY RESTRICTIONS ON
RECOVERY OF POSSESSION[175]

When a lease comes to an end, whether by the expiry of the term or by notice to quit, the landlord's common law right to recover possession is subject to certain statutory restrictions.[176]

(a) The landlord may be liable criminally, under Criminal Law Act 1977, section 6, for using of threatening violence to secure entry; under Protection from Eviction Act 1977, section 1,[177] for unlawful eviction and harassment, and under Protection from Harassment Act 1997.

(b) The landlord may be liable under Housing Act 1988, sections 27 and 28 to pay damages when he has committed acts which amount to unlawful eviction and harassment.[178]

(c) The tenant may be protected under the statutory codes set out on p. 325, n. 12, above, for example by having the right to a new lease or to an extension of the existing lease.

(d) Or, more generally, under the following provisions:

PROTECTION FROM EVICTION ACT 1977[179]

2. Restriction on re-entry without due process of law.—Where any premises are let as a dwelling on a lease which is subject to a right of re-entry or forfeiture it shall not be lawful to enforce

---

put in place by s. 72 and Sch. 12 for a commercial landlord to take control of the tenant's goods and sell them to recover unpaid rent later. The Law Commission had proposed the abolition of distress for both commercial and residential premises: Report on Distress for Rent 1991 (Law Com No. 194). For the *tenant's* remedies, see C & B, pp. 232–238 (repudiation and damages for breach of landlord's implied obligations in respect of state of premises), 251–253 (specific performance, damages and appointment of receiver or manager for breach of landlord's covenant to repair).

[175] C & B, pp. 330–335; Gray, paras 4.4.11–4.4.26; M & W, paras 19.034–19.037; MM, pp. 616–617; Report of the Committee on the Rent Acts (1971) (Cmnd 4609), pp. 105–106.

[176] On the landlord's right to terminate by physical re-entry, see Law Commission Report on Termination of Tenancies for Tenant Default 2006 (Law Com No. 303, p. 459, post). In the case of a public authority landlord, art. 8 of the European Convention on Human Rights (right to respect for a person's home) is engaged by the claim for possession, although the courts hearing summary claims for possession are entitled to assume that domestic law strikes a fair balance and is compatible with the occupier's Convention rights and should therefore apply the domestic statutory regimes in favour of landlords seeking possession: *Kay v Lambeth London Borough Council* [2006] 2 AC 465; C & B, pp. 333–335.

[177] As amended by HA 1988, s. 29. See *R v Burke* [1991] 1 AC 135.

[178] For the measure of damages, see *Tagro v Cafane* [1991] 1 WLR 378 (£31,000); [1991] Conv 297 (C. Rogers); *Jones v Miah* [1992] 2 EGLR 50 (£8,000); [1993] Conv 84 (S. Bridge); *Haniff v Robinson* [1993] QB 419 (£26,000); *Regalgrand Ltd v Dickerson* (1996) 74 P & CR 312 (reduction by mitigating conduct); *King v Jackson* [1998] 1 EGLR 30. Such decisions are reported regularly in the monthly issues of Legal Action. For a review, see (1995) 145 NLJ 937, 1061 (N. Madge). See also *Sampson v Wilson* [1996] Ch 39 (landlord's agent not liable).

[179] See generally Martin, *Residential Security* (2nd edn, 1995), chap. 3; [2001] Conv 249 (D. Cowan).

that right otherwise than by proceedings in the court while any person is lawfully residing in the premises or part of them.[180]

3. Prohibition of eviction without due process of law.—(1) Where any premises have been let as a dwelling[181] under a tenancy which is neither a statutorily protected tenancy nor an excluded tenancy[182] and—

    (a) the tenancy (in this section referred to as the former tenancy) has come to an end, but

    (b) the occupier continues to reside in the premises or part of them,

it shall not be lawful for the owner to enforce against the occupier, otherwise than by proceedings in the court, his right to recover possession of the premises.

(2) In this section 'the occupier', in relation to any premises, means any person lawfully residing in the premises or part of them at the termination of the former tenancy.

(2B) Subsections (1) and (2) above apply in relation to any premises occupied as a dwelling under a licence, other than an excluded licence, as they apply in relation to premises let as a dwelling under a tenancy, and in those subsections the expressions 'let' and 'tenancy' shall be construed accordingly.[183]

5. Validity of notices to quit.—Subject to subsection (1B) below no notice by a landlord or a tenant to quit any premises let (whether before or after the commencement of this Act) as a dwelling shall be valid unless—

    (a) it is writing and contains such information as may be prescribed, and

    (b) it is given not less than 4 weeks before the date on which it is to take effect.[184]

(1A)[185] Subject to subsection (1B) below, no notice by a licensor or a licensee to determine a periodic licence[186] to occupy premises as a dwelling (whether the licence was granted before or after the passing of this Act) shall be valid unless—

    (a) it is in writing and contains such information as may be prescribed, and

    (b) it is given not less than 4 weeks before the date on which it is to take effect.

(1B) Nothing in subsection (1) or subsection (1A) above applies to—

    (a) premises let on an excluded tenancy which is entered into on or after the date on which the Housing Act 1988 came into force unless it is entered into pursuant to a contract made before that date; or

    (b) premises occupied under an excluded licence.

---

[180] *Iperion Investments Corpn v Broadwalk House Residents Ltd* [1992] 2 EGLR 235 (tenants' housekeeper resident in premises); *Patel v Pirabakaran* [2006] 1 WLR 3112 ('let as a dwelling' means 'let wholly or partly as a dwelling' and so applies to premises let for mixed residential and business purposes, an interpretation which is compliant with the European Convention on Human Rights).

[181] See also *National Trust v Knipe* [1998] 1 WLR 230.

[182] As amended by HA 1988, s. 30(1). For a definition of excluded tenancies and licences, see s. 3A, added by HA 1988, s. 31. The most important exclusion is where accommodation is shared with either the landlord or with a member of the landlord's family (in the latter case the landlord must also reside in the same building, which must not be a purpose-built block of flats).

[183] As added by HA 1988, s. 30(2).   [184] As amended by HA 1988, s. 32(1).

[185] As amended by HA 1988, s. 32(2).

[186] *Norris v Checksfield* [1991] 1 WLR 1241.

8. **Interpretation.**—(1) In this Act 'statutorily protected tenancy' means—

(a) a protected tenancy within the meaning of the Rent Act 1977 or a tenancy to which Part I of the Landlord and Tenant Act 1954 applies;

(b) a protected occupancy or statutory tenancy as defined in the Rent (Agriculture) Act 1976;

(c) a tenancy to which Part II of the Landlord and Tenant Act 1954 applies;

(d) a tenancy of an agricultural holding within the meaning of the Agricultural Holdings Act 1986, which is a tenancy in relation to which that Act applies;[187]

(e) an assured tenancy or assured agricultural occupancy under Part I of the Housing Act 1988;[188]

(f) a tenancy to which Schedule 10 to the Local Government and Housing Act 1989 applies;[189]

(g) a farm business tenancy within the meaning of the Agricultural Tenancies Act 1995.[190]

(2) For the purposes of Part I of this Act a person who, under the terms of his employment, had exclusive possession of any premises other than as a tenant shall be deemed to have been a tenant and the expressions 'let' and 'tenancy' shall be construed accordingly.

(3) In Part I of this Act 'the owner', in relation to any premises, means the person who, as against the occupier, is entitled to possession thereof.

9. **The court for purposes of Part I.**—(3) Nothing in this Act shall affect the jurisdiction of the High Court in proceedings to enforce a lessor's right of re-entry or forfeiture or to enforce a mortgagee's right of possession in a case where the former tenancy was not binding on the mortgagee.[191]

B. FORFEITURE AND RELIEF AGAINST FORFEITURE[192]

A written lease usually includes a forfeiture clause which provides for the landlord's right to forfeit the remainder of the lease if there is a breach by the tenant of any

---

[187] As amended by the Agricultural Holdings Act 1986, Sch. 14, para. 61; Agricultural Tenancies Act 1995, s. 40, Sch. 8, para. 29(a).

[188] As amended by HA 1988, s. 33(2).

[189] As amended by Local Government and Housing Act 1989, Sch. 11, para. 54.

[190] As inserted by Agricultural Tenancies Act 1995, s. 40, Sch. 8, para. 29(b).

[191] See p. 925, below.

[192] C & B, pp. 273–293; Gray, paras 4.4.27–4.4.92; M & W, paras 18.004–18.065; MM, pp. 354–384; Smith, pp. 400–417; Pawlowski, *The Forfeiture of Leases* (1993). See Anti-social Behaviour Act 2003, under which a public sector landlord may apply to the county court for a demotion order, which temporarily removes security of tenure from an anti-social tenant: (2004) 148 SJ 771 (D. Underwood); Collins and Cattermole, *Anti-Social Behaviour: Powers and Remedies* (2004). For 'forfeiture by estoppel', where landlord purported to forfeit before it became legal proprietor by registration, and so registration 'fed' the estoppel, see *Rother District Investments Ltd v Corke* [2004] 1 EGLR 47 at [15], [16]. For proposals to abolish the remedy of forfeiture as part of a reform of the landlord's rights to terminate the tenancy for tenant default, see Law Commission Report on Termination of Tenacies for Tenant Default 2006 (Law Com No. 303); p. 459, below.

covenants in the lease.[193] The burden of proof lies on the landlord to establish an act of forfeiture on the part of the tenant.[194]

Unlimited application of such a clause could inflict hardship on the tenant out of all proportion to the damage suffered by the landlord. For example, a tenant who is in arrears with his rent may subsequently pay everything that is due, with interest; a breach of a covenant to insure may cause no loss to the landlord, but it used to be treated as sufficient to produce forfeiture under a forfeiture clause.

It has long been settled that equity will relieve a tenant against forfeiture in respect of non-payment of rent, but as a general rule not in other cases. The position is now regulated by statute.

Under the Civil Procedure Rules 1998 all claims for the recovery of possession of land, including those by a landlord, must be started in the County Court; they may only be started in the High Court where there are complicated disputes of fact or points of law of general importance.[195] It is the issue of the claim form by the Court which is equivalent to re-entry by the landlord.

(i) Non-payment of rent[196]

COMMON LAW PROCEDURE ACT 1852

210. Proceedings in ejectment by landlord for non-payment of rent.[197]—In all cases between landlord and tenant, as often as it shall happen that one half year's rent shall be in arrear, and the landlord or lessor, to whom the same is due, hath right by law to re-enter for the non-payment thereof, such landlord or lessor shall and may without any formal demand or re-entry, serve a writ in ejectment for the recovery of the demised premises, which service shall stand in the place and stead of a demand and re-entry;[198] and in case of judgment against the defendant for

---

[193] See *Richard Clarke & Co Ltd v Widnall* [1976] 1 WLR 845, where a clause in a lease under which the landlord was entitled to serve a notice to terminate in the event of a breach of a covenant to pay rent was construed as a forfeiture clause. Cf. *Clays Lane Housing Co-operative Ltd v Patrick* (1984) 49 P & CR 72 (for a clause to be a forfeiture clause it must bring the lease to an end earlier than the actual termination date). A forfeiture may also be incurred where the tenant denies his landlord's title: *WG Clark Properties Ltd v Dupre Properties Ltd* [1992] Ch 297 (disclaimer of title as to part of demised premises held not sufficient); [1993] Conv 299 (J. E. Martin); *British Telecommunications plc v Department of the Environment* [1996] NPC 148 (denial must be unequivocal); *Abidogun v Frolan Health Cares Ltd* [2002] L & TR 16 (no denial of title by submitting question of title to court for determination); [2001] Conv 399 (M. Pawlowski).

[194] *Doe d Bridger v Whitehead* (1838) 8 Ad & El 571; *Hagee (London) Ltd v Co-operative Insurance Society Ltd* [1992] 1 EGLR 57; [1992] Conv 345 (J. E. Martin).

[195] CPR 55; PD 1.3.

[196] For a useful summary of the law, see *Billson v Residential Apartments Ltd* [1992] 1 AC 494 at 510, per Sir Nicolas Browne-Wilkinson V-C.

[197] As amended by Statute Law Revision Act 1892.

[198] *Canas Property Co Ltd v KL Television Services Ltd* [1970] 2 QB 433; *Richards v De Freitas* (1975) 29 P & CR 1; *Ashton v Sobelman* [1987] 1 WLR 177; *Hammersmith and Fulham London Borough Council v Top Shop Centres Ltd* [1990] Ch 237; *Capital and City Holdings Ltd v Dean Warburg Ltd* (1988) 58 P & CR 346; *GS Fashions Ltd v B & Q Ltd* [1995] 1 WLR 1088.

The forfeiture does not become final until the landlord has obtained unconditional judgment for possession. Until then the covenants in the lease remain potentially good in favour of the tenant: *Driscoll v Church*

non-appearance, if it shall be made appear to the court where the said action is depending, by affidavit, or be proved upon the trial in case the defendant appears, that half a year's rent was due before the said writ was served, and that no sufficient distress was to be found on the demised premises, countervailing the arrears then due, and that the lessor had power to re-enter, then and in every such case the lessor shall recover judgment and execution, in the same manner as if the rent in arrear had been legally demanded, and a re-entry made; and in case the lessee or his assignee, or other person claiming or deriving under the said lease, shall permit and suffer judgment to be had and recovered on such trial in ejectment, and execution to be executed thereon, without paying the rent and arrears, together with full costs, and without proceeding for relief in equity within six months after such execution executed, then and in such case the said lessee, his assignee, and all other persons claiming and deriving under the said lease, shall be barred and foreclosed from all relief or remedy in law or equity, other than by bringing error for reversal of such judgment, in case the same shall be erroneous, and the said landlord or lessor shall from thenceforth hold the said demised premises discharged from such lease...

211. Lessee proceeding in equity not to have injunction or relief without payment of rent and costs.—In case the said lessee, his assignee, or other person claiming any right, title, or interest, in law or equity, of, in, or to the said lease, shall, within the time aforesaid, proceed for relief in any court of equity, such person shall not have or continue any injunction against the proceedings at law on such ejectment, unless he does or shall, within forty days next after a full and perfect answer shall be made by the claimant in such ejectment, bring into court, and lodge with the proper officer such sum and sums of money as the lessor or landlord shall in his answer swear to be due and in arrear over and above all just allowances, and also the costs taxed in the said suit, there to remain till the hearing of the cause, or to be paid out to the lessor or landlord on good security, subject to the decree of the court; and in case such proceedings for relief in equity shall be taken within the time aforesaid, and after execution is executed, the lessor or landlord shall be accountable only for so much and no more as he shall really and bona fide, without fraud, deceit, or wilful neglect, make of the demised premises from the times of his entering into the actual possession thereof; and if what shall be so made by the lessor or landlord happen to be less than the rent reserved on the said lease, then the said lessee or his assignee, before he shall be restored to his possession, shall pay such lessor or landlord what the money so by him made fell short of the reserved rent for the time such lessor or landlord held the said lands.

212. Tenant paying all rent, with costs, proceedings to cease.—If the tenant or his assignee do or shall, at any time before the trial in such ejectment, pay or tender to the lessor or landlord, his executors or administrators, or his or their attorney in that cause, or pay into the court where the same cause is depending, all the rent and arrears,[199] together with the costs, then

---

Comrs for England [1957] 1 QB 330; *Peninsular Maritime Ltd v Padseal Ltd* (1981) 259 EG 860 (landlord's covenant to repair lift held enforceable by tenant while seeking relief against forfeiture). See also *Meadows v Clerical Medical and General Life Assurance Society* [1981] Ch 70 ('The tenancy has a trance-like existence pendente lite; none can assert with assurance whether it is alive or dead', per Sir Robert Megarry at 75); *Associated Deliveries Ltd v Harrison* (1984) 50 P & CR 91; [1985] Conv 285 (J. E. Martin); *Official Custodian for Charities v Mackey (No 2)* [1985] 1 WLR 1308; *Hillgate House Ltd v Expert Clothing Service and Sales Ltd* [1987] 1 EGLR 65; *Ivory Gate Ltd v Spetale* (1998) 77 P & CR 141; *Mount Cook Land Ltd v Media Business Centre Ltd* [2004] 2 P & CR 25.

[199] *Standard Pattern Co Ltd v Ivey* [1962] Ch 432 (limiting the tenant's right to cases where at least half a year's rent is in arrear); (1962) 78 LQR 168 (R. E. Megarry).

and in such case all further proceedings on the said ejectment shall cease and be discontinued; and if such lessee, his executors, administrators, or assigns, shall, upon such proceedings as aforesaid, be relieved in equity, he and they shall have, hold, and enjoy the demised lands, according to the lease thereof made, without any new lease.

LAW OF PROPERTY ACT 1925

146. Restrictions on and relief against forfeiture of leases and underleases.—(4) p. 430, below.

SUPREME COURT ACT 1981

38. Relief against forfeiture for non-payment of rent.[200]—(1) In any action in the High Court for the forfeiture of a lease for non-payment of rent, the court shall have power to grant relief against forfeiture in a summary manner, and may do so subject to the same terms and conditions as to the payment of rent, costs or otherwise as could have been imposed by it in such an action immediately before the commencement of this Act.

(2) Where the lessee or a person deriving title under him is granted relief under this section, he shall hold the demised premises in accordance with the terms of the lease without the necessity for a new lease.

(ii) Breach of covenants other than non-payment of rent

(a) Law of Property Act 1925, section 146

Before a landlord can enforce a right of forfeiture for breach of covenant other than one for the payment of rent, he must serve a notice on the tenant under section 146(1) of the Law of Property Act 1925. Whether a breach is capable of remedy under para. *(b)*

---

[200] See *Belgravia Insurance Co Ltd v Meah* [1964] 1 QB 436; *Stanhope v Haworth* (1886) 3 TLR 34; *Re Brompton Securities Ltd (No 2)* [1988] 3 All ER 677, where Vinelott J said at 680: 'Save in very exceptional circumstances, the court will grant relief against forfeiture to a tenant, and will do so notwithstanding that actions have been brought on previous occasions to recover the rent'. The court will refuse relief if 'the landlord has, not unreasonably or precipitously, granted rights in the premises to third parties; *Silverman v AFCO (UK) Ltd* [1988] 1 EGLR 51 at 53, per Slade LJ. See also *Khar v Delbounty Ltd* (1998) 75 P & CR 232 (unless lease contains an agreement that a maintenance or service charge is to be treated as or deemed to be rent or additional rent, it is not 'rent' within the statutory provisions conferring jurisdiction to grant relief from forfeiture).

Under the ancient jurisdiction of the Court of Chancery, the court has power, independent of statute, to grant relief from forfeiture where there has been a peaceable entry; *Howard v Fanshawe* [1895] 2 Ch 581; *Lovelock v Margo* [1963] 2 QB 786; *Thatcher v CH Pearce & Sons (Contractors) Ltd* [1968] 1 WLR 748 (tenant granted relief, in spite of bringing action six months and four days after landlord regained possession); *Ladup Ltd v Williams & Glyn's Bank plc* [1985] 1 WLR 851. See [1969] JPL pp. 251–252. See also *Billson v Residential Apartments Ltd* [1992] 1 AC 494 at 516, where CA held that there was no similar inherent jurisdiction in the case of relief for breach of covenant other than the covenant to pay rent; p. 453, below.

For the statutory jurisdiction of the county court to grant relief, see the County Courts Act 1984, s. 138, as amended by AJA 1985, s. 55; High Court and County Courts Jurisdiction Order 1991, art. 2 (SI 1991 No. 724); *United Dominions Trust Ltd v Shellpoint Trustees Ltd* [1993] 4 All ER 310 (containing a detailed examination of the sections); (1994) 110 LQR 15 (N. P. Gravells); *Maryland Estates Ltd v Bar-Joseph* [1999] 1 WLR 83; *Croydon (Unique) Ltd v Wright* [2001] Ch 318 (charging order).

has given rise to difficulty. If the covenant is positive, e.g. to repair, the breach is clearly capable of remedy.[201] In the case of a negative covenant, 'the attractive and easy ratio'[202] of MacKinnon J in *Rugby School (Governors) v Tannahill* [1934] 1 KB 695, 700–701 was to hold that all negative covenants are incapable of remedy, and that recovery of possession by the landlord depends solely on whether the tenant can persuade the court to grant relief from forfeiture under section 146(2). In *Scala House & District Property Co Ltd v Forbes* [1974] QB 575, p. 434, below, the Court of Appeal held that the breach of a covenant not to assign, underlet or part with possession without the consent of the landlord is incapable of remedy. 'It is a complete breach once for all.'[203] The Court also considered that the breach of a user covenant, e.g. not to use the premises for illegal or immoral purposes, where the user has ceased before the service of a section 146 notice, is also incapable of remedy; the stigma attaching to the premises cannot be removed by mere cesser of the immoral or illegal user.'[204]

In *Savva v Houssein* [1996] 2 EGLR 65, p. 437, below, however, the Court of Appeal, in holding that the breach of a covenant not to make alterations without the consent of the landlord was capable of remedy, changed tack and considered whether the harm caused by the breach was remediable, rather than whether the breach itself could be remedied. And in *Akici v LR Butlin Ltd* [2006] 1 WLR 201, p. 439, below, the Court of Appeal went further. Holding that the breach of a covenant against parting with possession of the premises is capable of remedy, Neuberger LJ accepted that *Scala House* might be binding authority on whether the breach of a covenant against assignment can be remedied, but said that it should not be given any wider authority. However, in the light of this latest decision, there must be some doubt whether *Scala House* will survive, even in the context of covenants against assignment.

The effect of the grant of relief to a tenant by the court is to reinstate the old lease, which is deemed to have been continuously in force. The court may impose conditions on granting relief. Where a lease is forfeited, any under-leases created out of it automatically come to an end.[205] But an underlessee or mortgagee has the same right of applying to the court for relief against forfeiture of the head lease as the tenant has under the head lease. In this case, however, the effect of granting relief to an underlessee is to grant and vest a new term in him; the lease forfeited by the landlord is not revived and continued.[206]

---

[201] *Expert Clothing Service and Sales Ltd v Hillgate House Ltd* [1986] Ch 340, p. 444, below.

[202] *Hoffmann v Fineberg* [1949] Ch 245 at 254, per Harman J.

[203] At 588, per Russell LJ, p. 436, below; *Billson v Residential Apartments Ltd* [1992] 1 AC 494 (where Sir Nicolas Browne-Wilkinson V-C doubted whether breach of covenant not to make alterations without prior consent of landlord was irremediable).

[204] *Rugby School (Governors) v Tannahill* [1935] 1 KB 87, p. 432, below; *Egerton v Esplanade Hotels, London Ltd* [1947] 2 All ER 88; *Hoffmann v Fineberg*, n. 202, above; p. 435, below; *Borthwick-Norton v Romney Warwick Estates Ltd* [1950] 1 All ER 798; *Glass v Kencakes Ltd* [1966] 1 QB 611, p. 435, below; *Dunraven Securities Ltd v Holloway* (1982) 264 EG 709; (1983) 133 NLJ 485 (H. W. Wilkinson); *British Petroleum Pension Trust Ltd v Behrendt* (1985) 52 P & CR 117, p. 432, n. 226, below; *Van Haarlam v Kasner* [1992] 2 EGLR 59.

[205] *Pennell v Payne* [1995] QB 192 at 197; *Barrett v Morgan* [2000] 2 AC 264; *PW & Co v Milton Gate Investments Ltd* [2004] Ch 142, p. 343, n. 49, above.

[206] The new term cannot be any longer than the one forfeited, and the words 'any longer term ... sub-lease' in LPA 1925 s. 146(4) refer to the position immediately before forfeiture: *Cadogan v Dimovic* [1984] 1 WLR

LAW OF PROPERTY ACT 1925

146. Restrictions on and relief against forfeiture of leases and underleases.—(1) A right of re-entry or forfeiture under any proviso or stipulation in a lease for a breach of any covenant or condition in the lease[207] shall not be enforceable, by action or otherwise, unless and until the lessor serves on the lessee[208] a notice[209]

> (a) specifying the particular breach complained of;[210] and

> (b) if the breach is capable of remedy, requiring the lessee to remedy the breach; and

> (c) in any case requiring the lessee to make compensation in money for the breach;[211]

and the lessee fails, within a reasonable time thereafter,[212] to remedy the breach, if it is capable of remedy, and to make reasonable compensation in money, to the satisfaction of the lessor, for the breach.

609 (sub-lease terminated by forfeiture of head lease, which was a business tenancy subject to extension under L & T Act 1954; sub-lessee granted a new term of appropriate duration but within the limits of the extension imposed by the 1954 Act); *Official Custodian for Charities v Mackey* [1985] Ch 168 (rent for under-leases payable to lessor during period between forfeiture of the old lease and the creation of the new one); [1985] Conv 50 (J. Martin).

[207] A s. 146 notice cannot be validly served under a long lease of a dwelling, unless the fact that there has been a breach has been determined by a court or admitted by the tenant: Commonhold and Leasehold Reform Act 2002, ss. 168, 169; for further restrictions, see s. 167 (failure to pay small amount for short period); s. 170 (forfeiture for failure to pay service charge etc.), amending HA 1996, ss. 81, 82.

[208] Where a lessee assigns his lease in breach of covenant, the assignment is effective, and the notice must be served on the assignee and not on the original lessee: *Old Grovebury Manor Farm Ltd v W Seymour Plant Sales and Hire Ltd (No 2)* [1979] 1 WLR 1397; *Governors of the Peabody Donation Fund v Higgins* [1983] 1 WLR 1091; *Fuller v Judy Properties Ltd* [1992] 1 EGLR 75; [1992] Conv 343 (J. E. Martin) (second notice served on assignee after taking possession held invalid); *Greenwich London Borough Council v Discreet Selling Estates Ltd* [1990] 2 EGLR 65; [1991] Conv 222 (J. E. Martin) (landlord who had served notice for breach of covenant to repair and then waived breach by acceptance of rent need not serve a fresh notice). The notice should be served on the tenant, and not on a mortgagee of the term: *Church Commissioners for England v Ve-Ri-Best Manufacturing Co Ltd* [1957] 1 QB 238; *Smith v Spaul* [2003] QB 983.

[209] The notice may be served under LPA 1925 s. 196: it may be left at the tenant's address even though he is in prison and unlikely to receive it: *Van Haarlam v Kasner* [1992] 2 EGLR 59; and even though he is suffering from mental disorder: *Tadema Holdings Ltd v Ferguson* [1999] NPC 144. It may be sent there by registered letter or recorded delivery (Recorded Delivery Service Act 1962, s. 1); *WX Investments Ltd v Begg* [2002] 1 WLR 2849 (deemed delivery in the ordinary course of post); [2003] Conv 90 (M. Haley); *Blunden v Frogmore Investments Ltd* [2002] 2 EGLR 29 (notice affixed to premises); [2002] Conv 312 (J. E. Adams). See also p. 565, n. 12, below.

[210] The landlord is not required to give particulars of each defect: *Fox v Jolly* [1916] 1 AC 1; *Adagio Properties Ltd v Ansari* [1998] 2 EGLR 69; but the lessee should not have any reasonable doubt as to the particular breach or breaches of covenant complained of: *Akici v Butlin Ltd* [2006] 1 WLR 201.

[211] This does not make it necessary for the lessor to claim compensation if he does not want it: *Lock v Pearce* [1893] 2 Ch 271; *Rugby School (Governors) v Tannahill*, p. 432, below.

[212] *Civil Service Co-operative Society Ltd v McGrigor's Trustee* [1923] 2 Ch 347; *Scala House and District Property Co Ltd v Forbes* [1974] QB 575 (fourteen days held to be sufficient where breach of covenant against assigning or sub-letting held to be incapable of remedy); *Cardigan Properties Ltd v Consolidated Property Investments Ltd* [1991] 1 EGLR 64 (ten days to comply with insurance covenant held to be insufficient); [1991] Conv 223 (J. E. Martin); *Bhojwani v Kingsley Investment Trust Ltd* [1992] 2 EGLR 70; [1993] Conv 296 (J. E. Martin); *Fuller v Judy Properties Ltd* [1992] 1 EGLR 75 (seven days reasonable for breach of covenant against assignment); *Van Haarlam v Kasner* [1992] 2 EGLR 59 (twenty days reasonable for breach of covenant not to use premises for illegal or immoral purposes); *Courtney Lodge Management Ltd v Blake* [2005] 1 P & CR 17 (four working days inadequate for tenant to remedy nuisance caused by sub-tenants to neighbours).

(2) Where a lessor is proceeding,[213] by action[214] or otherwise,[215] to enforce such a right of re-entry or forfeiture, the lessee[216] may, in the lessor's action, if any, or in any action brought by himself, apply to the court for relief; and the court may grant or refuse relief, as the court, having regard to the proceedings and conduct of the parties under the foregoing provisions of this section, and to all the other circumstances, thinks fit; and in case of relief may grant it on such terms, if any, as to costs, expenses, damages, compensation, penalty, or otherwise, including the granting of an injunction to restrain any like breach in the future, as the court, in the circumstances of each case, thinks fit.[217]

(4) Where a lessor is proceeding by action or otherwise to enforce a right of re-entry or forfeiture under any covenant, proviso, or stipulation in a lease, or for non-payment of rent, the court may, on application by any person claiming as under-lessee[218] any estate or interest in the property comprised in the lease or any part thereof, either in the lessor's action (if any) or in any action brought by such person for that purpose, make an order vesting, for the whole term of the lease or any less term, the property comprised in the lease or any part thereof in any person entitled as under-lessee to any estate or interest in such property upon such conditions as to execution of any deed or other document, payment of rent, costs, expenses, damages, compensation, giving security, or otherwise, as the court in the circumstances of each case may think fit, but in no case shall any such under-lessee be entitled to require a lease to he granted to him for any longer term than he had under his original sub-lease.[219]

---

[213] The right to relief does not terminate upon peaceable re-entry by the lessor: *Billson v Residential Apartments Ltd* [1992] 1 AC 494, p. 453, below.

[214] Such an action is a pending land action under LCA 1972, s. 17(1) and is registrable under s. 5; and, in the case of registered land, is required to be protected by a notice under LRA 2002, s. 87; H & B, paras 10.102–10.105; *Selim Ltd v Bickenhall Engineering Ltd* [1981] 1 WLR 1318.

[215] I.e., by the service of a notice under s. 146: *Pakwood Transport Ltd v 15 Beauchamp Place Ltd* (1977) 36 P & CR 112.

[216] Where there are joint lessees, relief cannot be granted on the application of only one of them: *TM Fairclough & Sons Ltd v Berliner* [1931] 1 Ch 60.

[217] In some circumstances the court may be able to grant relief as to part of the demised premises by restricting the order for possession to a part only: *GMS Syndicate Ltd v Gary Elliot Ltd* [1982] Ch 1. Nourse J said at 12: 'I emphasise that I do not intend to go beyond the circumstances of the present case, where the two parts of the demised property are physically separated one from the other and are capable of being distinctly enjoyed, and where the breaches complained of were committed on one part of the property and on that part alone'.

[218] See *Grand Junction Co Ltd v Bates* [1954] 2 QB 160, p. 859, n. 29, below, where it was held that a mortgagee by way of legal charge can claim as underlessee. So can an equitable chargee: *Re Good's Lease* [1954] 1 WLR 309.

On relief for underlessees generally, see [1986] Conv 187 (S. Tromans). If relief is granted to a head-tenant's mortgagee, any sub-lease is forfeited, but the sub-tenant in turn has a right to relief: *Hammersmith and Fulham London Borough Council v Top Shop Centres Ltd* [1990] Ch 237; [1989] All ER Rev 194 (P. J. Clarke); *Escalus Properties Ltd v Robinson* [1996] QB 231 (relief granted retrospectively under s. 146(2) to mortgagee by sub-demise); [1995] All ER Rev 334 (P. J. Clarke); cf. *Pellicano v MEPC plc* [1994] 1 EGLR 104 (vesting order under s. 146(4) not retrospective; sub-lessee had no right to possession between date of forfeiture and grant of relief); *Barclays Bank plc v Prudential Assurance Ltd* [1998] 1 EGLR 44 (disclaimer of lease held not to prevent granting of relief to mortgagee as under-lessee).

On relief for the holder of an equitable charge over a lease, see *Bland v Ingrams Estates Ltd* [2001] Ch 767; [2002] All ER Rev 737 (P. H. Pettit); leave to appeal to HL refused: [2003] 1 WLR 1810.

[219] For the inherent jurisdiction of the court to grant relief outside sub-s. (4) where the lessor has re-entered peaceably for breach of covenant to pay a sum of money other than for payment of rent, see *Billson v Residential Apartments Ltd* [1992] 3 WLR 264 (reversed on other grounds by HL, [1992] 1 AC 494, p. 453,

(5) For the purposes of this section—

(a) 'Lease' includes an original or derivative under-lease; also an agreement for a lease where the lessee has become entitled to have his lease granted; also a grant at a fee farm rent, or securing a rent by condition;

(b) 'Lessee' includes an original or derivative under-lessee, and the persons deriving title under a lessee,[220] also a grantee under any such grant as aforesaid and the persons deriving title under him;

(c) 'Lessor' includes an original or derivative under-lessor, and the persons deriving title under a lessor; also a person making such grant as aforesaid and the persons deriving title under him;

(d) 'Under-lease' includes an agreement for an under-lease where the under-lessee has become entitled to have his under-lease granted;

(e) 'Under-lessee' includes any person deriving title under an under-lessee.

(8) This section does not extend—

(i) To a covenant or condition against assigning, underletting, parting with the possession, or disposing of the land leased where the breach occurred before the commencement of this Act; or

(ii) In the case of a mining lease, to a covenant or condition for allowing the lessor to have access to or inspect books, accounts, records, weighing machines or other things, or to enter or inspect the mine or the workings thereof.

(9) This section does not apply to a condition for forfeiture on the bankruptcy of the lessee[221] or on taking in execution of the lessee's interest if contained in a lease of—

(a) Agricultural or pastoral land;

(b) Mines or minerals;

(c) A house used or intended to be used as a public-house or beershop;

(d) A house let as a dwelling-house, with the use of any furniture, books, works of art, or other chattels not being in the nature of fixtures;

(e) Any property with respect to which the personal qualifications of the tenant are of importance for the preservation of the value or character of the property,[222] or on the ground of neighbourhood to the lessor,[223] or to any person holding under him.

---

below, inherent jurisdiction not being raised), where CA preferred *Smith v Metropolitan City Properties Ltd* [1986] 1 EGLR 52, where Walton J held that the inherent jurisdiction has been replaced by s. 146(2) (otherwise 'it would make complete nonsense of subsection (2)') and *Official Custodian for Charities v Parway Estates Developments Ltd* [1985] Ch 151, where CA held that it had no inherent jurisdiction where the lessee was outside the time limits for relief under sub-s. 10, below; [1984] All ER Rev 195 (P. H. Pettit) and rejected *Abbey National Building Society v Maybeech Ltd* [1985] Ch 190. But the mortgagee can apply outside the time limits under sub-s. (4): *Official Custodian for Charities v Mackey (No 2)* [1985] 1 WLR 1308.

[220] *High Street Investments Ltd v Bellshore Property Investments Ltd* [1996] 2 EGLR 40 (equitable assignee); *Escalus Properties Ltd v Robinson*, above, n. 218 (mortgagee by sub-demise).

[221] But it does apply on the bankruptcy of a lessee's surety: *Halliard Property Co Ltd v Jack Segal Ltd* [1978] 1 WLR 377.

[222] *Earl of Bathurst v Fine* [1974] 1 WLR 905; (1974) 90 LQR 441.

[223] *Hockley Engineering Co Ltd v V & P Midlands Ltd* [1993] 1 EGLR 76.

(10) Where a condition of forfeiture on the bankruptcy of the lessee or on taking in execution of the lessee's interest is contained in any lease, other than a lease of any of the classes
mentioned in the last subsection, then—

>   (a) if the lessee's interest is sold within one year from the bankruptcy or taking in execu-
>   tion, this section applies to the forfeiture condition aforesaid;

>   (b) if the lessee's interest is not sold before the expiration of that year, this section only
>   applies to the forfeiture condition aforesaid during the first year from the date of the
>   bankruptcy or taking in execution.[224]

(11) This section does not, save as otherwise mentioned, affect the law relating to re-entry
or forfeiture or relief in case of non-payment of rent.

(12) This section has effect notwithstanding any stipulation to the contrary.

LAW OF PROPERTY (AMENDMENT) ACT 1929

1. Relief of under-lessees against breach of covenant.—Nothing in subsection (8), subsection (9) or subsection (10) of section one hundred and forty-six of the Law of Property Act,
1925...shall affect the provisions of subsection (4) of the said section.

In **Plymouth Corpn v Harvey** [1971] 1 WLR 549[225] the tenant executed an undated
deed of surrender in escrow. When he was in breach, the landlord dated the deed
and demanded possession. The deed was held void as being a device to circumvent section 146. The statutory notices were required. 'A forfeiture in the guise of a
surrender...remains a forfeiture for the purposes of section 146,' said Plowman J.

1. Breach of negative covenant

(a) Not to use premises for immoral or illegal user. Stigma

Rugby School (Governors) v Tannahill
[1935] 1 KB 87 (CA, **Greer, Maugham** and **Roche LJJ**)[226]

The Governors of Rugby School let premises in London to tenants who assigned them
with their consent to the defendant, a woman who was convicted of using the premises
for the purpose of habitual prostitution. The lease contained a covenant that the premises should not be used for illegal or immoral purposes, and contained a proviso for
re-entry for breach of covenant. The Governors served a notice under Law of Property
Act 1925, s. 146, requiring the defendant to surrender possession. The defence was that

---

[224] See *Official Custodian for Charities v Parway Estates Developments Ltd* [1985] Ch 151, p. 431, n. 219,
above.

[225] See also *Hussein v Mehlman* [1992] 2 EGLR 87, above, p. 343, per Sedley QC at 90 (termination of lease
by landlord's acceptance of tenant's repudiatory breach would still be subject to 'all the statutory provisions
which now hedge the right to recover possession' as well as 'the provisions contained in the contract of
letting itself in relation to forfeiture').

[226] *British Petroleum Pension Trust Ltd v Behrendt* (1985) 52 P & CR 117, where Purchas LJ said at 124:
'I have found nothing in the recent authorities which enables me to accede to Mr Brook's submissions that
the concept that breaches of the negative covenant in "stigma" cases are irremediable has in any way been
relaxed.'

the notice to quit was bad in that it did not require the defendant to remedy the breach under s. 146(1)(b), nor to make compensation in money under s. 146(1)(c).

Held. (i) The breach was not capable of remedy and omission to require it to be remedied did not invalidate the notice;

(ii) As the landlords did not require compensation, omission to demand it did not invalidate the notice.

Greer LJ: The first point is, whether this particular breach is capable of remedy. In my judgment MacKinnon J was right in coming to the conclusion that it was not. I think perhaps he went further than was really necessary for the decision of this case in holding that a breach of any negative covenant—the doing of that which is forbidden—can never be capable of remedy.[227] It is unnecessary to decide the point on this appeal; but in some cases where the immediate ceasing of that which is complained of, together with an undertaking against any further breach, it might be said that the breach was capable of remedy. This particular breach, however—conducting the premises, or permitting them to be conducted, as a house of ill-fame—is one which in my judgment was not remedied by merely stopping this user. I cannot conceive how a breach of this kind can be remedied. The result of committing the breach would be known all over the neighbourhood and seriously affect the value of the premises. Even a money payment together with the cessation of the improper use of the house could not be a remedy. Taking the view as I do that this breach was incapable of remedy, it was unnecessary to require in the notice that the defendant should remedy the breach.

The further question is whether the absence of any statement in the notice requiring compensation in money in respect of the breach is fatal to the validity of the notice. As to that, the decision of the Court of Appeal in *Lock v Pearce* [1893] 2 Ch 271 binds us to hold that the plaintiffs were under no obligation to require compensation in money. I can well understand that a body like the plaintiffs would be averse to touch money coming from a tenant in such circumstances. In any event, whatever might have been our view in the absence of authority, it is plain from the judgments in *Lock v Pearce* that the point is not open in this court. Lindley LJ there used these words at 279: 'Then, as regards the notices required by s. 14, sub-s. 1 [of the Conveyancing Act 1881], the statute requires notice to be given specifying the breach complained of, as the first thing, and, if the breach is capable of remedy, requiring the lessee to remedy it, and "in any case requiring the lessee to make compensation in money for the breach." Supposing the lessor does not want compensation, is the notice to be held bad because he does not ask for it? There is no sense in that. The meaning is to be found by looking a little further on. The sub-section begins by saying that the right of re-entry or forfeiture shall not be enforceable unless proper notice is given and the lessee fails within a reasonable time afterwards to remedy the breach and to make reasonable compensation in money to the satisfaction of the lessor. The sense of that is that the lessor must tell the lessee what he wants done. The lessee is entitled to know what his landlord complains of, and, if his landlord is entitled to compensation, whether he wants compensation.' The Lord Justice there concluded his judgment in a paragraph of two sentences which are specially applicable to the present case; he said: 'On these grounds I am of opinion that this appeal fails. Upon the merits as well as upon the technicalities, all the points are against the appellants.' In the later case of *Civil Service Co-operative Society Ltd v McGrigor's Trustee*

---

[227] [1934] 1 KB 695 at 701: 'A promise to do a thing, if broken, can be remedied by the thing being done. But breach of a promise not to do a thing cannot in any sense be remedied; that which was done cannot be undone. There cannot truly be a remedy; there can only be abstention, perhaps accompanied with apology.'

[1923] 2 Ch 347, Russell J followed *Lock v Pearce* as applicable to a case where the breach was incapable of remedy. The appeal must be dismissed.

(b) Not to assign or sublet without consent of landlord.
Once for all breach

Scala House & District Property Co Ltd v Forbes[228]
[1974] QB 575 (CA, **Russell** and **James LJJ** and **Plowman J**)

By a lease dated 8 February 1968, the lessees covenanted not to assign underlet or part with the possession of a shop in Dean Street, London, without the permission of the landlords. The lease contained a proviso for re-entry on breach of covenant. In March the lease was assigned to the first defendant with the landlords' consent. He used the premises as a restaurant, and then in November entered into an agreement with Pierto and Elisa Delpoio, the second and third defendants, to manage the restaurant for him. This agreement, which was intended to be a management agreement, in fact created a sub-lease in breach of the covenant. The plaintiff, who had acquired the reversion of the lease, served on the defendants a notice under Law of Property Act 1925, section 146(1), requiring them to remedy the breach, and 14 days later then issued a writ for possession. Nield J held that the breach was capable of remedy, and since 14 days was insufficient time for the defendants to remedy the breach, dismissed the action. On appeal by the plaintiff:

Held. (i) The breach was not capable of remedy, and therefore 14 days was a sufficient time.

(ii) Relief from forfeiture was granted to the first defendant.

Russell LJ: It is a remarkable fact that this case raises questions under section 146 of the Law of Property Act 1925, which, except in a case at first instance reported only in the Estates Gazette Digest,[229] have never been considered for decision....

So the first question is whether a breach of covenant such as is involved in the present case is capable of remedy. If it is capable of remedy, and is remedied in reasonable time, the lessor is unable to prove that a condition precedent to his ability to seek to forfeit by action or otherwise has been fulfilled. Here at once is a problem. An unlawful subletting is a breach once and for all. The subterm has been created.

I turn to the authorities. In *Jackson v Simons* [1923] 1 Ch 373 there was a breach of a covenant against sharing the premises let: such a breach was not excluded from section 14 of the Act of 1881: no notice at all was served before the writ for possession issued and this was fatal to the action. The sharing apparently ended shortly after the writ: but there was no discussion whether a subsequent notice based on a 'past' breach, followed by a writ, would have resulted in either forfeiture or relief. *Rugby School (Governors) v Tannahill* [1935] 1 KB 87 was a case of user by the lessee for immoral purposes contrary to covenant in the lease sought to be forfeited. Apparently before the section 146 notice the prostitutes had left and the premises had ceased to be used for immoral purposes. The notice did not call upon the lessee to remedy the breach. At first instance the judge decided in favour of the lessor on the short ground that breach of a

228 (1973) 89 LQR 460 (P.V.B.); (1973) 57 Conv (NS) 445 (D. Macintyre).
229 *Capital and Counties Property Co Ltd v Mills* [1966] EGD 96.

negative covenant could never be remedied. This court did not call upon counsel for the lessor, who thus had no opportunity to support the judge's short ground: this court expressed the view that breach of negative covenants might be capable of remedy, but not this one, on the ground that the stigma attaching to the premises would not be removed by mere cesser of the immoral user. I observe that it does not appear to have been considered whether the breach in that case was incapable of remedy on another ground, viz.: that the wrongful user had ceased before the section 146 notice. It might perhaps be argued that reliance by this court on the 'stigma' point suggests that it was considered that a wrongful user in breach wholly in the past, without continuing adverse effect, would not entitle the lessor to seek to forfeit at all. But the question does not seem to have been canvassed.

His Lordship referred to *Borthwick-Norton v Romney Warwick Estates Ltd* [1950] 1 All ER 798, and continued:

In *Hoffmann v Fineberg* [1949] Ch 245 (Harman J), the lessee, in breach of user covenants, allowed the premises to be used for illegal gambling, for which there were convictions. The section 146 notice did not call for the breach to be remedied. It is not clear whether the illegal user continued at the date of the notice. Again the decision was based on the 'stigma' aspect as making the breach incapable of remedy within a reasonable time. Harman J said, at 257: '. . . on the facts of this case this is a breach where mere cesser is no remedy.' The judgment referred to another immoral user case of *Egerton v Esplanade Hotels London Ltd* [1947] 2 All ER 88 (Morris J), in which the notice did not call for the breach to be remedied: it was decided on the stigma point, on the facts of that case, that the breach was not capable of remedy within a reasonable time. Morris J said, at 91:

> 'Merely desisting from the wrongful user or not continuing to commit further breaches is not, . . . on the facts of this case, a way of remedying the breach.'

Neither case was considered on the possible shorter ground that a user covenant breach when the user had ceased before the section 146 notice was incapable of remedy for that very reason.

Glass v Kencakes Ltd [1966] 1 QB 611, a decision of Paull J was of this nature. The lease forbade the use of the upper part of the premises otherwise than for residential purposes. The lessee sublet that part to D, who caused and permitted their use for the business of prostitution unknown to the lessee. The sublease contained a similar covenant. The section 146 notice was simply based upon the fact of business use. It asserted that the breach was incapable of remedy. The judge held that the breach of the sublease by D was incapable of remedy by him: apparently he considered that the person who caused or permitted such a use could not, by the cesser of such use, remedy the breach, because the stigma on the premises could not be blotted out within a reasonable time so long as the man responsible remained subtenant. He therefore could not remedy his breach. Paull J pointed out that in the *Rugby School* case, in *Egerton v Esplanade Hotels London Ltd* (both cases of immoral user) and in *Hoffmann v Fineberg* (the illegal gambling case) it was in each case the tenant under the lease sought to be forfeited who was directly responsible for the breach: and that in the *Borthwick-Norton* case the lessee had in breach suffered and permitted the immoral user by a subtenant. Paull J decided, however, that where the breach alleged was merely of a user by a subtenant for which the lessee whose lease was sought to be forfeited could not be said to have permitted or suffered or to be in anyway responsible for, the breach was not incapable of remedy by that lessee, the remedy required

being not only the cesser of the user in breach but also the ending of the subterm with all exped-
ition by forfeiture. Paull J was much impressed by the argument that where there was a lease
for a large block of flats, one of which, without any fault of the lessee, was used for a short time
in breach of the user covenant in the lease by a subtenant, he should not be put in the situation
that he was not capable of remedying the breach and must therefore be put to the expense of
seeking relief from forfeiture. He held in that case that the notice was bad since it asserted that
the breach was not capable of remedy.[230]

Two points are to be noticed in that case. First: Paull J did not address his mind, particularly
in the case of the large block of flats mentioned, to the possible situation of the lessee if the
subletting in question, and therefore the unlawful user, had come to an end before discovery by
the head lessor, when no remedial step would have been available to the lessee, and whether in
such case the lessee could only have sought relief. Second: the decision in terms says nothing
of a case (other than 'stigma' cases) where the lessee is directly responsible for the breach by a
business user contrary to covenant....

In summary upon the cases we have therefore a number of cases of user of premises in breach
of covenant in which the decision that the breach is not capable of remedy has gone upon the
'stigma' point, without considering whether a short answer might be—if the user had ceased
before the section 146 notice—that it was ex hypothesi incapable of remedy, leaving the lessee
only with the ability to seek relief from forfeiture and the writ unchallengeable as such. If a user
in breach has ceased before the section 146 notice (quite apart from the stigma cases) then
either it is incapable of remedy and after notice there is nothing in the way of a writ: or the cesser
of use has somehow deprived the lessor of his ability to seek to forfeit though he has done nothing to waive the breach, a situation in law which I find extremely difficult to spell out of section
146. But whatever may be the position in user breach cases, which are of a continuing nature,
there is no authority, other than that of *Capital and Counties Property Co Ltd v Mills* [1966]
EGD 96 to suggest that the creation of a subterm in breach of covenant is capable of remedy.
I would make two particular comments on that decision, as reported. First: I find it difficult to
see how a breach is said to be capable of remedy because the lessor can waive the breach, which
would be involved in the suggestion that he could below hoc consent to the subletting. Second:
I do not see how a breach by unlawful subletting can be said to be remedied by the lessee when
he does nothing except wait for the subterm to come to an end by effluxion of time.

After this review of the cases I come to the conclusion that breach by an unlawful subletting is
not capable of remedy at all. In my judgment the introduction of such breaches into the relevant
section for the first time by section 146 of the Act of 1925 operates only to confer a statutory
ability to relieve the lessee from forfeiture on that ground. The subterm has been effectively
created subject only to risks of forfeiture: it is a complete breach once for all: it is not in any
sense a continuing breach. If the law were otherwise a lessee, when a subtenancy is current
at the time of the section 146 notice, would have a chance of remedying the situation without
having to apply for relief. But if the unlawful subletting had determined before the notice, the
lessee could only seek relief from forfeiture. The only escape from that wholly unsatisfactory
difference would be to hold that in the second example by some analogy the lessor was disabled
from issuing a writ for possession. But I can find nothing in the section to justify that limitation
on the common law right of re-entry, bearing especially in mind that a lessor might discover

---

[230] Cf. *British Petroleum Pension Trust Ltd v Behrendt* (1985) 52 P & CR 117, where 'the tenant either knew
of or deliberately shut his eyes to the use of the premises for prostitution' by his licensee.

a whole series of past expired unlawful sublettings which might well justify a refusal to grant relief in forfeiture proceedings.

I stress again that where there has been an unlawful subletting which has determined (and which has not been waived) there has been a breach which at common law entitles the lessor to re-enter: nothing can be done to remedy that breach: the expiry of the subterm has not annulled or remedied the breach: in such case the lessor plainly need not, in his section 146 notice, call upon the lessee to remedy the breach which is not capable of remedy, and is free to issue his writ for possession, the possibility of relief remaining. Can it possibly be that, while that is the situation in such case, it is otherwise if the lessee has failed to get rid of the subterm until after a notice served? Is the lessee then in a stronger position and the lessor in a weaker position? In my judgment not so. These problems and questions arise only if such a breach is capable of remedy, which in my judgment it is not.[231] I consider that *Capital and Counties Property Co Ltd v Mills*, if correctly reported, was wrongly decided. I should add that I find some support for my opinion in the comments of Fraser J in *Abrahams v MacFisheries Ltd* [1925] 2 KB 18, 35, who expressed the view that the exceptions in section 14(6) of the Act of 1881 (as to, inter alia, subletting) were made to cover cases where the breach cannot be remedied specifically.

In those circumstances in judging whether the 14 days that here elapsed between the section 146 notice and the writ, the time which it might reasonably take the lessee to come to terms with the subtenants, the second and third defendants, so as to end the subterm, which in fact was done in June 1972, is irrelevant. In those circumstances it is in my view plain that the writ was not prematurely issued, even assuming, as with all familial piety I must having regard to *Civil Service Co-operative Society Ltd v McGrigor's Trustee* [1923] 2 Ch 347, citing *Horsey Estate v Steiger* [1899] 2 QB 79, that reasonable time in the case of an irremediable breach is related to something other than making compensation in money, notwithstanding the language of the section.

(c) Other breaches of negative covenants

Savva v Houssein
[1996] 2 EGLR 65 (CA, **Staughton** and **Aldous LJJ** and **Sir John May**)[232]

In 1991 Mr and Mrs Savva granted a lease of premises to Mr Houssein for their use as a cafe, a snack bar and a place for operating mini-cabs. Mr Hussein covenanted not to display on the outside of the premises any sign or advertisement and not to make any alterations or additions to them without the prior consent of the landlords. The tenant broke both covenants. The landlords served a section 146 notice asserting the breach of the covenants and claiming that they were incapable of remedy.

Held. The breaches were capable of remedy; the notice was invalid because it did not require the tenant to remedy the breach.

---

[231] See the general criticism of this reasoning in *Expert Clothing Service and Sales Ltd v Hillgate House Ltd* [1986] Ch 340 at 364, per O'Connor LJ: 'It seems to me that it cannot be right to describe a breach which has been remedied as a breach which *is* incapable of remedy, and thereafter to say that it was incapable of remedy before it was remedied. To my mind a breach which has been remedied has been demonstrated to have been a breach which was ab initio capable of remedy.'

[232] [1997] 1 L & TLR 70 (J. Brown and R. Duddridge).

Staughton LJ: In this case the question is whether the breaches, if there were breaches, were capable of remedy. They amount to doing things without the consent of the landlord. That is what the covenant did not allow. In the case of *Billson v Residential Apartments Ltd* (1990) 60 P & CR 392, Mummery J touched on the question whether such a breach could ever be capable of remedy. He said at p. 406:

'I reject the defendants' arguments on the ground that the breach of covenant committed by making the alterations in the property without the plaintiffs' consent "first had and obtained" was not capable of remedy by the defendants. It was a breach of the covenant for the defendants to embark on alterations to the property without first applying for and seeking to obtain the plaintiffs' consent. Now that the alterations have been made without consent it is impossible for the defendants to comply with the covenant which required them first to apply for consent so that they could either obtain it or, if they did not obtain it, be in a position to contend that they were entitled to make improvements because the plaintiffs had unreasonably withheld consent. In those circumstances I hold that the breach was not capable of remedy...'

When that case reached the Court of Appeal, the Vice Chancellor said:

'The judge held, first, that since the alterations had been started without prior consent of the plaintiffs the breach was irremediable. Second, he held that even if he were wrong on the first point, remedying the breach would consist, not in doing the works of reinstatement but in stopping the works, submitting the necessary plans and specifications and then awaiting the giving or unreasonable withholding of consent.

I prefer to express no view on the judge's first ground of decision, beyond expressing some doubt as to whether he was right in holding that the breach was irremediable.'

It is established law in this court that the breach of a covenant not to assign without consent cannot be remedied. That was decided in *Scala House & District Property Co Ltd v Forbes* [1974] QB 575 [p. 434, above]. Even then relief from forfeiture was granted, so that may not be of any great consequence.

In my judgment, except in a case of breach of a covenant not to assign without consent, the question is: whether the remedy referred to is the process of restoring the situation to what it would have been if the covenant had never been broken, or whether it is sufficient that the mischief resulting from a breach of the covenant can be removed. When something has been done without consent, it is not possible to restore the matter wholly to the situation which it was in before the breach. The moving finger writes and cannot be recalled. That is not to my mind what is meant by a remedy, it is a remedy if the mischief caused by the breach can be removed. In the case of a covenant not to make alterations without consent or not to display signs without consent, if there is a breach of that, the mischief can be removed by removing the signs or restoring the property to the state it was in before the alterations.

I would hold that all the breaches complained of in this case were capable of remedy. It follows that the notice under section 146 should have required them to be remedied.

Auld LJ: In one sense a breach can never be remedied because there must have been non-compliance with the covenant for there to be a breach. That cannot be the solution. Thus, the fact there has been a breach does not determine whether it can be remedied in the way contemplated by the Law of Property Act 1925 section 146. That was decided in *Expert Clothing Service & Sales Ltd v Hillgate House Ltd* [1986] Ch 340, below, Slade LJ p. 357F:

'...breach of a positive covenant to do something...can ordinarily, for practical purposes, be remedied by the thing being actually done...'

I can see no reason why similar reasoning should not apply to some negative covenants. An important purpose of section 146 is to give tenants, who have not complied with their obligations, one last chance to do so before the landlord reenters. Slade LJ in *Expert Clothing* proposed this test at p. 358D:

> '... if the section 146 notice had required the lessee to remedy the breach and the lessors had then allowed a reasonable time to elapse to enable the lessee fully to comply with the relevant covenant, would such compliance, coupled with the payment of any appropriate monetary compensation, have effectively remedied the harm which the lessors had suffered or were likely to suffer from the breach?'

It is only if the answer to that question is 'no' can it be said that the breach is not capable of being remedied.

What was proposed as the question to ask by Slade LJ, albeit in relation to a case of dispute about a positive covenant, is relevant to consideration as to whether a negative covenant can be remedied. There is, in my view, nothing in the statute, nor in logic, which require different considerations between a positive and negative covenant, although it may be right to differentiate between particular covenants. The test is one of effect. If a breach has been remedied then it must have been capable of being remedied.

For the reasons given by Staughton LJ I agree with the order proposed.

Akici v LR Butlin Ltd
[2006] 1 WLR 201 (CA, **Mummery and Neuberger LJJ**)[233]

On 5 August 2002 Mr Akici became tenant under a lease which contained a covenant not to charge, assign, underlet or part with possession of part of the premises, nor to hold the whole or any part of the premises on trust for another, 'nor to share possession of the whole or any part of the ... premises nor to part with possession of the whole of the ... premises'. Shortly thereafter a company, in which Mr Akici had no direct interest, began trading from the premises in the business of preparing and selling takeaway pizzas. In June 2004 the landlord served a section 146 notice on Mr Akici asserting that he had assigned, sublet or parted with possession of the premises to the company. On 10 August 2004 Mr Akici acquired all the shares in the company which was trading from the premises, and became its sole director. The trial judge held that there had been no assignment, subletting or parting with possession of the premises by Mr Akici to the company, but that he was in breach of the covenant by sharing possession; and that that breach was incapable of remedy but, if it had been capable of remedy, the breach would have been remedied by Mr Akici's acquisition of ownership and control of the company. On appeal by Mr Akici:

Held. Mr Akici had shared possession of the premises with the company, and so was in breach of covenant, but the landlord's section 146 notice was ineffective because it failed clearly to specify sharing of possession as a breach of covenant. But breach of a covenant against sharing possession is capable of remedy within section 146, and the judge was entitled to conclude that Mr Akici had remedied the breach by acquiring all

---

[233] [2006] Conv 382 (P. F.Smith); [2006] All ER Rev 270 (P. H. Pettit).

the shares in the company and becoming its sole director, so that it became possible to treat the tenant as in possession through the medium of the company.

Neuberger LJ:

Was the section 146 notice valid?

48 [T]he judge found, rightly in my view, that Mr Akici had not parted with possession of the premises to the company, but that he had shared possession of the premises with the company. However, the section 146 notice upon which Butlins relied alleged that the particular breach complained of was assigning, underletting or parting with possession of the premises. There was no express allegation of sharing possession.

52 If one confines oneself to the contents of the notice, it is very difficult to see how it can fairly be construed as specifying the sharing of possession as a breach of covenant complained of. The notice quotes clause 4.18, which includes covenants not to assign, not to sublet, not to part with possession, and not to share possession, and then goes on to allege the breach complained of, which is assigning, subletting or parting with possession. On any rational approach, it seems to me that a reasonable recipient of the notice would have understood that sharing of possession was not being complained of....

53 I was at one time attracted by Mr Lloyd's point that this objection to the notice is unduly technical, because it would have been clear to the reasonable recipient that what was being complained of was the presence of the company on the premises. In those circumstances, it was argued, the notice made clear the nature of the lessors' complaint and, in so far as the breach was capable of remedy, it also made it clear what the lessee had to do to put matters right. In that connection Mr Lloyd relied on the approach to the construction of contractual notices under leases adopted by the majority of the House of Lords in *Mannai Investment Co Ltd v Eagle Star Life Assurance Co Ltd* [1997] AC 749.

54 I accept the submission that the approach of the majority of the House of Lords in *Mannai* to contractual notices[234] would apply to section 146 notices... However... even applying the *Mannai* case the notice has to comply with the requirements of section 146(1) of the 1925 Act, and if, as appears pretty plainly to be the case, it does not specify the right breach, then nothing in the *Mannai* case can save it.

55 Quite apart from this, if, on its true construction, the section 146 notice did not specify sharing possession as a breach complained of, it can be said with considerable force that it neither informed the recipient of the breach complained of, nor indicated to him whether, and if so how, he must remedy any breach. On the basis that there was a sharing of possession, a reasonable recipient of the section 146 notice would have been entitled to take the view that he need do nothing, because the lessors were only complaining about the presence of the company if there was a parting with possession (or assigning or underletting) by Mr Akici to it.

56 Accordingly, a reasonable recipient in this case (and it is the understanding of such a hypothetical person by reference to which the validity of the notice is to be assessed according to the *Mannai* case) could, to put it at its lowest, reasonably have taken the view that the lessors were not objecting to any sharing of possession, and consequently that no steps need to be taken, either with a view to remedying the breach or with a view to improving the prospects of obtaining relief from forfeiture.

---

[234] Treitel, para. 6.008.

57 We were referred to authorities relating to the validity of notices served under section 146 and its statutory predecessor. I do not consider that they provide much assistance on the point that we have to determine in the present case. It is, however, appropriate to mention the decision of the House of Lords in *Fox v Jolly* [1916] 1 AC 1, 23 where the last sentence of the speech of Lord Parmoor appears to me to encapsulate the proper approach to section 146 notices and, it may be said, to notices generally:

'I think that the notice should be construed as a whole in a common-sense way, and that no lessee could have any reasonable doubt as to the particular breaches which are specified.'

58 In this case I think it is impossible to say that no lessee would have been in any doubt but that the lessors were not contending that he was sharing possession of the premises.

Was the breach capable of remedy?

62 The judge was of the view that a breach of covenant against sharing possession was not capable of remedy within the meaning of section 146 in the light of the reasoning of the Court of Appeal in *Scala House and District Property Co Ltd v Forbes* [p. 434, above], although he made it clear that he would have decided otherwise in the absence of that authority....

63 Considering the matter free of authority I would, like the judge, be firmly of the view that a covenant against sharing possession, indeed a covenant against parting with possession, should be capable of remedy. It seems to me that there are two principal purposes of section 146 in relation to forfeiture clauses in leases. The first is to enable a lessee in breach of covenant to have the opportunity to remedy the breach, where that is possible, and thereby to avoid the forfeiture altogether, provided the lessors are fully reimbursed with regard to damages and costs. The second principal purpose of the section, which only arises where the lessee fails to remedy the breach or where the breach is incapable of remedy, is to enable the court to accord the lessee relief from forfeiture, where the lessors enforce the forfeiture.

64 In those circumstances it seems to me that the proper approach to the question of whether or not a breach is capable of remedy should be practical rather than technical. In a sense it could be said that any breach of covenant is, strictly speaking, incapable of remedy. Thus, where a lessee has covenanted to paint the exterior of demised premises every five years, his failure to paint during the fifth year is incapable of remedy, because painting in the sixth year is not the same as painting in the fifth year, an argument rejected in *Hoffmann v Fineberg* [1949] Ch 245, 253, cited with approval by this court in *Expert Clothing Service and Sales Ltd v Hillgate House Ltd* [1986] Ch 340, 351c-d [below, p. 444]. Equally it might be said that where a covenant to use premises only for residential purpose is breached by use as a doctor's consulting room, there is an irremediable breach because even stopping the use will not, as it were, result in the premises having been unused as a doctor's consulting room during the period of breach. Such arguments, as I see it, are unrealistically technical.

65 In principle I would have thought that the great majority of breaches of covenant should be capable of remedy, in the same way as repairing or most user covenant breaches. Even where stopping, or putting right, the breach may leave the lessors out of pocket for some reason, it does not seem to me that there is any problem in concluding that the breach is remediable. That is because section 146(1) entitles the lessors to 'compensation in money ... for the breach' and, indeed, appears to distinguish between remedying the breach and paying such compensation.

66 On this basis I consider that it would follow, as a matter of both principle and practicality, that breaches of covenants involving parting with or sharing possession should be capable of remedy. One can see an argument, albeit that it strikes me as somewhat technical, for saying

that the breach of covenant against assigning or subletting is incapable of remedy, because such a breach involves the creation or transfer of an interest in land, and a surrender or assignment back does not alter the fact that an interest in land has been created or transferred. Were the point free of authority, I would see much force in the contention that such an analysis is over-technical, and I would be attracted to the view that a surrender or assignment back could be a sufficient remedy, at least in most cases, for the purposes of section 146.

67   So far as the authorities are concerned it appears to me that, at least short of the House of Lords, there are two types of breach of covenant which are as a matter of principle incapable of remedy. The first is a covenant against subletting: that is the effect of the reasoning of this court in the *Scala House* case [1974] QB 575 [above, p. 434]. At least part of the reasoning in the leading judgment of Russell LJ, at p. 588, justifying that conclusion is defective, as was explained by O'Connor LJ in the *Expert Clothing* case [1986] Ch 340, 364e-f in a judgment with which Bristow J agreed (at p. 365c). However, as O'Connor LJ also said, the *Scala House* case is a decision which is binding on this court. In terms of principle (which may not be a wholly safe touchstone in this field) this is, I think, based on the proposition that one cannot, as it were, uncreate an underlease. It therefore appears to me that it should very probably follow that the general assumption that an unlawful assignment also constitutes an irremediable breach is correct. (This would suggest that breach of a covenant against charging a lease is irremediable, which strikes me as arguably unsatisfactory; failure to comply with a covenant to give notice of a charge, a somewhat different breach, is remediable: see the *Expert Clothing* case at p. 355d.)

68   The other type of breach of covenant which is incapable of remedy is a breach involving illegal or immoral use: see *Rugby School (Governors) v Tannahill* [1935] 1 KB 87 [above, p. 432] and *British Petroleum Pension Trust Ltd v Behrendt* [1985] 2 EGLR 97. This has been justified on the basis of illegal or immoral user fixing the premises with some sort of irremovable 'stigma', which results in the breach being incapable of remedy. Especially in the light of the provision for damages in section 146, it is not entirely easy to justify this, particularly as it does not appear to apply where the lessee himself does not know of the illegal or immoral user: see *Glass v Kencakes Ltd* [1966] 1 QB 611. However, in terms of policy there is force in the view that a lessee, who has used premises for an illegal or immoral purpose, should not be able to avoid the risk of forfeiture simply by ceasing that use on being given notice of it, particularly as relief from forfeiture would still be available. Another example, mentioned in the *Expert Clothing* case [1986] Ch 340, 355a, might be a breach of covenant to insure against damage by fire, where the property burns down before insurance can be effected.

69   In the *Expert Clothing* case itself the Court of Appeal held that a covenant to carry out substantial building works was capable of remedy at the time of the service of the section 146 notice, even though the work should have been completed by the date of service and had not even been started. Slade LJ said, at p. 357, that breach of a positive covenant could 'ordinarily, for practical purposes, be remedied by the thing being actually done'. However, the notion that any breach of a negative covenant will be irremediable plainly cannot be right, as is demonstrable by considering an innocuous and innocent breach of a user covenant.

70   There are three types of classification of covenants. They are (a) positive and negative (relevant to the transmission of the burden of freehold covenants, equitable in origin), (b) continuing and 'once and for all' (relevant to waiver of forfeiture, with a common law origin), and (c) remediable and irremediable (relevant for section 146, and thus statutory in origin). These three types of classification are thus for different purposes and have different

origins. Attempting to equate one class of one type with one class of a different type is therefore likely to be worse than unhelpful.

71 Any idea that negative covenants are by their nature irremediable has been put to rest by the decision of this court in *Savva v Hussein* (1996) 73 P & CR 150 [above, p. 437]. In that case the breach of covenant consisted of carrying out alterations in breach of a covenant not to do so. After quoting the passage I have just cited from the *Expert Clothing* case, Aldous LJ said, at p.157, that he could 'see no reason why similar reasoning should not apply to some negative covenants'. He went on to quote with approval of a subsequent passage in Slade LJ's judgment [1986] Ch 340, 358:

> 'if the section 146 notice had required the lessee to remedy the breach and the lessors had then allowed a reasonable time to elapse to enable the lessee fully to comply with the relevant coven- ant, would such compliance, coupled with the payment of any appropriate monetary compensation, have effectively remedied the harm which the lessors had suffered or were likely to suffer from the breach?'

72 As Aldous LJ, with whom Sir John May agreed, then went on to say 73 P & CR 150, 157: 'It is only if the answer to that question is "no" it can be said that the breach is not capable of being remedied.'

73 In these circumstances it appears to me that, unless there is some binding authority, which either calls into question the conclusion or renders it impermissible, both the plain pur- pose of section 146(1) and the general principles laid down in two relatively recent decisions in this court, namely the *Expert Clothing* and *Savva* cases, point strongly to the conclusion that, at least in the absence of special circumstances, a breach of covenant against parting with possession or sharing possession, falling short of creating or transferring of legal interest, are breaches of covenant which are capable of remedy within the meaning of section 146.

74 The only authority which could be cited to call that conclusion into question is the *Scala House* case itself, but that does not deter me from my conclusion. First, it was only concerned with underletting; secondly, the reasoning of the leading judgment in the case is, at least in part, demonstrably fallacious and inconsistent with common sense and many other authorities; thirdly, it has been overtaken and marginalised by the *Expert Clothing* and *Savva* cases; fourthly, there is no reason of logic or principle why the reasoning or conclusion in the *Scala House* case should be extended to apply to a breach which falls short of creating a legal interest.

75 It is true that Slade LJ said in the *Expert Clothing* case [1986] Ch 340, 354G that the principle in the *Scala House* case extends to parting with possession, as well as assigning and underletting. That was an obiter observation, which I do not regard as binding. Bristow J, at p. 365C, agreed with Slade LJ's judgment but he also agreed with the judgment of O'Connor LJ who, at p. 365A-B, said that the *Scala House* case, while authority for the proposition that breach of a covenant against underletting was irremediable, was not 'authority for any wider proposition'. As I have indicated, my present view is an intermediate one. I think that principle and precedent probably require one to go along with Slade LJ and conclude that the *Scala House* case applies to assigning but, in agreement with O'Connor LJ, I certainly do not see why it extends to parting with (let alone sharing) possession.

Was the breach in this case remedied?

76 The judge appears to have formed the provisional view that if, contrary to his conclusion, the breach consisting of sharing possession in this case was capable of remedy, it had been remedied by 10 August 2004....

77 As I see it the judge's conclusion that the breach was remedied was based on the fact that, by ensuring that he had acquired all the shares and had become the sole director of the company, Mr Akici procured a situation whereby he was no longer sharing possession of the premises with the company. In my judgment, that was a conclusion to which the judge was entitled to come, at least on the facts of this case.

79 As I see it the judge considered that, by acquiring all the shares in the company and becoming the sole director of the company, Mr Akici regained the exclusive possession he was granted at the start of the lease, but which he then relinquished by sharing possession with the company while it was effectively, or mainly, owned and controlled by [a third party]. In my view, at least as present advised, that was a conclusion to which he was entitled to have come. Where a lessee owns all the shares in, and exclusively controls, a company which is operating the only activity conducted in the demised premises, it appears to me that, unless it is inconsistent with other facts, it is permissible to treat the company as the agent of the lessee for the purposes of identifying who is in possession of those premises.

81 It is true that the very fact that a person chooses to conduct his business through a company is because the company is treated as a different entity in law from him, and that there is therefore nothing unfairly artificial in treating him as sharing possession with (or, depending on the facts, as parting with possession to) the company. However, where the lessee owns all the shares in, and is in sole control of a company, it seems to me that it is justifiable in principle, as well as commercially sensible, to treat the lessee as in possession through the medium of the company (possibly as well as through his own presence). In such a case it is no more artificial to treat the lessee as being in possession through the company than it is to treat an employer who requires an employee to reside in premises as enjoying possession through his employee: see *Street v Mountford* [1985] AC 809, 818F-G.

2. Breach of positive covenant

Expert Clothing Service & Sales Ltd v Hillgate House Ltd
[1986] Ch 340 (CA, **O'Connor** and **Slade LJJ** and **Bristow J**)

In 1972 the plaintiff landlords granted a 25-year lease of Hillgate House, London W8 to the defendants, who covenanted to reconstruct the premises into a gymnasium and health club and to make them ready for occupation by or before 28 September 1982. The defendants failed to carry out the work. The plaintiffs served a s. 146 notice, alleging the breach of covenant and stating that the breach was incapable of remedy. They then brought proceedings claiming possession of the premises.

Held (reversing Judge Paul Baker QC). Claim for possession refused. The breach was capable of remedy, and, therefore the notice was invalid.[235]

Slade LJ: In a case where the breach is 'capable of remedy' within the meaning of the section, the principal object of the notice procedure provided for by section 146(1), as I read it, is to afford the lessee two opportunities before the lessor actually proceeds to enforce his right of re-entry, namely (1) the opportunity to remedy the breach within a reasonable time after service of the notice, and (2) the opportunity to apply to the court for relief from forfeiture. In a case where the breach is not 'capable of remedy,' there is clearly no point in affording the first

---

[235] The court further held that the plaintiffs had not waived their right to forfeit the lease.

of these two opportunities; the object of the notice procedure is thus simply to give the lessee the opportunity to apply for relief.

Unfortunately the authorities give only limited guidance as to what breaches are capable of remedy within the meaning of the section. As Harman J pointed out in *Hoffmann v Fineberg* [1949] Ch 245 at 253:

'In one sense, no breach can ever be remedied, because there must always, ex concessis, be a time in which there has not been compliance with the covenant, but the section clearly involves the view that some breaches are remediable, and therefore it cannot mean that.'

His Lordship referred to MacKinnon J in *Rugby School (Governors) v Tannahill* [1934] 1 KB 695 at 701, p. 433, n. 227, above, and to Greer LJ in [1935] 1 KB 87 at 90–91, p. 433, above, and Maugham LJ at 93, and continued:

In supporting the judge's conclusion that the breach relating to reconstruction of the premises was irremediable, Mr Collins, on behalf of the plaintiffs, has submitted to us three principal arguments. First, he pointed out that (as is common ground) the first defendant's failure to build by 28 September 1982 was a 'once and for all' breach of the relevant covenant, and not a continuing breach: see, for example, *Stephens v Junior Army and Navy Stores Ltd* [1914] 2 Ch 516, 523, *per* Lord Cozens-Hardy MR. He submitted that the breach of a covenant such as this, which can only be broken once, is ex hypothesi in no case capable of remedy.

Some superficial support for this conclusion is perhaps to be found in the judgments in *Scala House and District Property Co Ltd v Forbes* [1974] QB 575 [p. 434, above], in which the Court of Appeal held that the breach of a covenant not to assign, underlet or part with possession was not a breach capable of remedy within the meaning of section 146(1)....

His Lordship referred to Russell LJ at 588, p. 436, above, and continued:

It might well be regarded as anomalous if the once and for all breach of a negative covenant not to sublet were to be regarded as 'capable of remedy' within section 146, provided that the unlawful subtenancy was still current at the date of the section 146 notice, but (as Russell LJ considered) were not to be regarded as 'capable of remedy' if the unlawful subtenancy had been determined at that date. Russell LJ and James LJ who agreed with his reasoning (see particularly at 591C-D), were clearly much influenced by this anomaly in reaching the conclusion that the breach of a covenant against underletting is never capable of remedy.

However, in the *Scala House* case this court was addressing its mind solely to the once and for all breach of a negative covenant. No corresponding anomaly arises if the once and for all breach of a positive covenant is treated as capable of remedy. While the *Scala House* decision is, of course, authority binding on this court for the proposition that the breach of a negative covenant not to assign, underlet or part with possession is never 'capable of remedy,' it is not, in my judgment, authority for the proposition that the once and for all breach of a positive covenant is never capable of remedy.

Mr Neuberger, on behalf of the defendants, did not feel able to go so far as to support the view of MacKinnon J that the breach of a positive covenant is *always* capable of remedy. He accepted, for example, that the breach of a covenant to insure might be incapable of remedy at a time when the premises had already been burnt down. Another example might be the breach of a positive covenant which in the event would be only capable of being fully performed, if at all, after the expiration of the relevant term.

Nevertheless, I would, for my part, accept Mr Neuberger's submission that the breach of a positive covenant (whether it be a continuing breach or a once and for all breach) will ordinarily be capable of remedy. As Bristow J pointed out in the course of argument, the concept of capability of remedy for the purpose of section 146 must surely be directed to the question whether the harm that has been done to the landlord by the relevant breach is for practicable purposes capable of being retrieved. In the ordinary case, the breach of a promise to do something by a certain time can for practical purposes be remedied by the thing being done, even out of time. For these reasons I reject the plaintiffs' argument that the breach of the covenant to reconstruct by 28 September 1982 was not capable of remedy *merely* because it was not a continuing breach....

His Lordship rejected the second main argument that the breach of covenant was incapable of remedy because of the operation of a rent review clause and continued:

I therefore turn to the third, and far the most important point, relied on by Mr Collins in support of the decision of the court below. His submissions in this context were to the following effect. The judgment of Maugham LJ in the *Rugby School* case [1935] 1 KB 87, 93 and other judicial dicta indicate that if a breach is to be 'capable of remedy' at all within the meaning of section 146, it must be capable of remedy *within a 'reasonable time.'* As was observed by Lord Herschell LC in *Hick v Raymond and Reid* [1893] AC 22, 29: 'there is of course no such thing as a reasonable time in the abstract. It must always depend upon circumstances.' In the present case, it was submitted, what was a reasonable time was a question of fact. In deciding that the breach of the covenant to reconstruct was not capable of remedy within a reasonable time, the judge expressed himself as 'having regard to the facts as I have found them.'...

...[I]n my opinion, in considering whether or not remedy within a reasonable time is possible, a crucial distinction (which I infer from the judgment did not feature prominently in argument before the judge) falls to be drawn between breaches of negative user covenants, such as those under consideration in the *Rugby School* and the *Esplanade Hotels* [1947] 2 All ER 88 cases, and breaches of positive covenants. In the two last-mentioned cases, where the relevant breaches consisted of allowing premises to be used as a brothel, even full compliance with the covenant within a reasonable time and for a reasonable time would not have remedied the breach. As Maugham LJ pointed out in the *Rugby School* case, at p. 94:

'merely ceasing for a reasonable time, perhaps a few weeks or a month, to use the premises for an immoral purpose would be no remedy for the breach of covenant which had been committed over a long period.'

On the facts of cases such as those, mere cesser by the tenant of the offending use within a reasonable period and for a reasonable period of time could not have remedied the breaches because it could not have removed the stigma which they had caused to attach to the premises. The harm had been irretrievably done. In such cases, as Harman J pointed out in *Hoffmann v Fineberg* [1949] Ch 245, 257, mere cesser will not enable the tenant to 'make his record clean, as he could by complying, though out of time, with a failure to lay on the prescribed number of coats of paint.'

In contrast with breaches of negative user covenants, the breach of a positive covenant to do something (such as to decorate or build) can ordinarily, for practical purposes, be remedied by the thing being actually done if a reasonable time for its performance (running from the service of the section 146 notice) is duly allowed by the landlord following such service and the tenant duly does it within such time.

In the present case there is no question of the breach of the covenant to reconstruct having given rise to any 'stigma' against the lessors or the premises. Significantly, the lease in 1982 still had 20 years to run. Mr Collins has, I think, been able to suggest no convincing reasons why the plaintiffs would still have suffered irremediable damage if (i) the section 146 notice had required the lessee to remedy the breach and (ii) the lessors had then allowed a reasonable time to elapse sufficient to enable the lessee to comply with the relevant covenant, and (iii) the lessee had complied with the covenant in such reasonable time and had paid any appropriate monetary compensation. Though he has submitted that a requirement directed to the defendants to remedy the breach would have been purposeless, on the grounds that they had neither the financial means nor the will to do the necessary work, these are matters which, in my opinion, a landlord is not entitled to prejudge in drafting his notice. An important purpose of the section 146 procedure is to give even tenants who have hitherto lacked the will or the means to comply with their obligations one last chance to summon up that will or find the necessary means before the landlord re-enters. In considering what 'reasonable time' to allow the defendants, the plaintiffs, in serving their section 146 notice, would, in my opinion, have been entitled to take into account the fact that the defendants already had enjoyed 15 months in which to fulfil their contractual obligations to reconstruct and to subject the defendants to a correspondingly tight time-table running from the date of service of the notice, though, at the same time, always bearing in mind that the contractual obligation to reconstruct did not even arise until 29 June 1981, and that as at 8 October 1982 the defendants had been in actual breach of it for only some 10 days. However, I think they were not entitled to say, in effect: 'We are not going to allow you any time at all to remedy the breach, because you have had so long to do the work already.'

In my judgment, on the remediability issue, the ultimate question for the court was this: if the section 146 notice had required the lessee to remedy the breach and the lessors had then allowed a reasonable time to elapse to enable the lessee fully to comply with the relevant covenant, would such compliance, coupled with the payment of any appropriate monetary compensation, have effectively remedied the harm which the lessors had suffered or were likely to suffer from the breach? If, but only if, the answer to this question was 'No,' would the failure of the section 146 notice to require remedy of the breach have been justifiable. In *Rugby School (Governors) v Tannahill* [1935] 1 KB 87; *Egerton v Esplanade Hotels, London Ltd* [1947] 2 All ER 88 and *Hoffmann v Fineberg* [1949] Ch 245 the answer to this question plainly would have been 'No.' In the present case, however, for the reasons already stated, I think the answer to it must have been 'Yes.'

My conclusion, therefore, is that the breach of the covenant to reconstruct . . . was 'capable of remedy.' In reaching this conclusion, I find it reassuring that no reported case has been brought to our attention in which the breach of a positive covenant has been held incapable of remedy, though I do not suggest that cases of this nature, albeit perhaps rarely, could not arise.

3. Covenants to repair

Where the landlord sues in respect of a covenant to keep or put the premises in repair, he is subject to further statutory restrictions under the Landlord and Tenant Act 1927, and the Leasehold Property (Repairs) Act 1938.[236]

---

[236] For the special provisions relating to internal decorative repair, see LPA 1925, s. 147.

LANDLORD AND TENANT ACT 1927

18. **Provisions as to covenants to repair.**—(2) A right of re-entry or forfeiture for a breach of any such covenant or agreement as aforesaid shall not be enforceable, by action or otherwise, unless the lessor proves that the fact that such a notice as is required by section one hundred and forty-six of the Law of Property Act, 1925, had been served on the lessee was known either—

    (a) to the lessee; or

    (b) to an under-lessee holding under an under-lease which reserved a nominal reversion only to the lessee; or

    (c) to the person who last paid the rent due under the lease either on his own behalf or as agent for the lessee or under-lessee;

and that a time reasonably sufficient to enable the repairs to be executed had elapsed since the time when the fact of the service of the notice came to the knowledge of any such person.

Where a notice has been sent by registered post[237] addressed to a person at his last known place of abode in the United Kingdom, then, for the purposes of this subsection, that person shall be deemed, unless the contrary is proved, to have had knowledge of the fact that the notice had been served as from the time at which the letter would have been delivered in the ordinary course of post.

This subsection shall be construed as one with section one hundred and forty-six of the Law of Property Act, 1925.

LEASEHOLD PROPERTY (REPAIRS) ACT 1938

1.[238] **Restriction on enforcement of repairing covenants in long leases of small houses.**—(1) Where a lessor serves on a lessee under subsection (1) of section one hundred and forty-six of the Law of Property Act, 1925, a notice that relates to a breach of a covenant or agreement to keep or put in repair[239] during the currency of the lease all or any of the property comprised in the lease, and at the date of the service of the notice three years or more of the term of the lease remain unexpired, the lessee may within twenty-eight days from that date serve on the lessor a counter-notice to the effect that he claims the benefit of this Act.

(2) A right to damages[240] for a breach of such a covenant as aforesaid shall not be enforceable by action commenced at any time at which three years or more of the term of the lease remain unexpired unless the lessor has served on the lessee not less than one month before the commencement of the action such a notice as is specified in subsection (1) of

---

[237] The recorded delivery service may be used as an alternative to registered post; Recorded Delivery Service Act 1962, s. 1(1). [1990] Conv 47 (J. E. Adams); *Beanby Estates Ltd v Egg Stores (Stamford Hill) Ltd* [2003] 1 WLR 2064 (where notice sent by recorded delivery to addressee at place of abode, it was irrebuttably deemed to have been served); see *CA Webber (Transport) Ltd v Railtrack plc* [2004] 1 WLR 320 (*Beanby Estates Ltd* not inconsistent with Human Rights Act 1998).

[238] As amended by Landlord and Tenant Act 1954, s. 51(2). On the Act generally, see [1986] Conv 85 (P. F. Smith).

[239] *Starrokate Ltd v Burry* (1982) 265 EG 871 (an obligation to cleanse is not an obligation to repair).

[240] A landlord's action to recover a sum expended on carrying out repairs for which the tenant was liable was held to be for debt and not for damages and therefore no leave of the court is required under the Act: *Hamilton v Martell Securities Ltd* [1984] Ch 266; *Jervis v Harris* [1996] 1 All ER 303; [1997] Conv 299 (R. Hewitson). See also *SEDAC Investments Ltd v Tanner* [1982] 1 WLR 1342; (1984) 134 NLJ 791 (H. W. Wilkinson).

section one hundred and forty-six of the Law of Property Act, 1925,[241] and where a notice is served under this subsection, the lessee may, within twenty-eight days from the date of the service thereof, serve on the lessor a counter-notice to the effect that he claims the benefit of this Act.

(3) Where a counter-notice is served by a lessee under this section, then, notwithstanding anything in any enactment or rule of law, no proceedings, by action or otherwise, shall be taken by the lessor for the enforcement of any right of re-entry or forfeiture under any proviso or stipulation in the lease for breach of the covenant or agreement in question, or for damages for breach thereof, otherwise than with the leave of the court.

(4) A notice served under subsection (1) of section one hundred and forty-six of the Law of Property Act, 1925, in the circumstances specified in subsection (1) of this section, and a notice served under subsection (2) of this section shall not be valid unless it contains a statement, in characters not less conspicuous than those used in any other part of the notice,[242] to the effect that the lessee is entitled under this Act to serve on the lessor a counter-notice claiming the benefit of this Act, and a statement in the like characters specifying the time within which, and the manner in which, under this Act a counter-notice may be served and specifying the name and address for service of the lessor.[243]

(5) Leave for the purposes of this section shall not be given unless the lessor proves[244] —

    (a) that the immediate remedying of the breach in question is requisite for preventing substantial diminution in the value of his reversion, or that the value thereof has been substantially diminished by the breach;

    (b) that the immediate remedying of the breach is required for giving effect in relation to the premises to the purposes of any enactment, or of any byelaw or other provision having effect under an enactment, or for giving effect to any order of a court or requirement of any authority under any enactment or any such byelaw, or other provision as aforesaid;

    (c) in a case in which the lessee is not in occupation of the whole of the premises as respects which the covenant or agreement is proposed to be enforced, that the immediate remedying of the breach is required in the interests of the occupier of those premises or of part thereof;

    (d) that the breach can be immediately remedied at an expense that is relatively small in comparison with the much greater expense that would probably be occasioned by postponement of the necessary work; or

---

[241] A notice cannot be served after the breach has been remedied, even if it is remedied by the landlord, since the s. 146 notice cannot then require the tenant to remedy the breach; *SEDAC Investments Ltd v Tanner*, above, n. 240 ('a conclusion reached' by Michael Wheeler QC 'with surprise and regret'). In *Hamilton v Martell Securities Ltd*, above, n. 240, Vinelott J was 'not persuaded that the decision was wrong.' [1983] Conv 72 (P. F. Smith).

[242] To be read as 'equally readable': *Middlegate Properties Ltd v Messimeris* [1973] 1 WLR 168 at 172 (Lord Denning MR).

[243] *Middlegate Properties Ltd v Messimeris*, above, n. 242; *BL Holdings Ltd v Marcolt Investments Ltd* (1978) 249 EG 849.

[244] The landlord has to prove one of the statutory grounds on the balance of probabilities: *Associated British Ports v CH Bailey plc* [1990] 2 AC 703; [1990] CLJ 401 (S. Bridge); [1990] Conv 305 (P. F. Smith). The relevant date for proving one or more of the s. 1(5) grounds is the date of the application for leave to bring forfeiture proceedings: *Landmaster Properties Ltd v Thackeray Property Service* [2003] 2 EGLR 30.

(e) special circumstances which in the opinion of the court, render it just and equitable
     that leave should be given.[245]

(6) The court may, in granting or in refusing leave for the purposes of this section, impose
such terms and conditions on the lessor or on the lessee as it may think fit.

(iii) Waiver

(a) The doctrine

In **Matthews v Smallwood** [1910] 1 Ch 777, PARKER J said at 786:

I think that the law on the subject of waiver is reasonably clear. The right to re-enter is a legal
right which, apart from release or abandonment or waiver, will exist and can be exercised, at
any time within the period fixed by the Statutes of Limitation; and if a defendant in an action of
ejectment based upon that right of re-entry alleges a release or abandonment or waiver, logically speaking the onus ought to lie on him to shew the release or the abandonment or the waiver.
Waiver of a right of re-entry can only occur where the lessor, with knowledge of the facts
upon which his right to re-enter arises, does some unequivocal act recognizing the continued
existence of the lease. It is not enough that he should do the act which recognizes, or appears to
recognize, the continued existence of the lease, unless, at the time when the act is done, he has
knowledge of the facts under which, or from which, his right of entry arose. Therefore we get
the principle that, though an act of waiver operates with regard to all known breaches, it does
not operate with regard to breaches which were unknown to the lessor at the time when the act
took place. It is also, I think, reasonably clear upon the cases that whether the act, coupled with
the knowledge, constitutes a waiver is a question which the law decides, and therefore it is not
open to a lessor who has knowledge of the breach to say 'I will treat the tenancy as existing, and
I will receive the rent, or I will take advantage of my power as landlord to distrain; but I tell you
that all I shall do will be without prejudice to my right to re-enter, which I intend to reserve'.
That is a position which he is not entitled to take up. If, knowing of the breach, he does distrain,
or does receive the rent, then by law he waives the breach, and nothing which he can say by way
of protest against the law will avail him anything. Logically, therefore, a person who relies upon
waiver ought to shew, first, an act unequivocally recognizing the subsistence of the lease, and
secondly, knowledge of the circumstances from which the right of re-entry arises at the time
when the act is performed.[246]

---

[245] *Landmaster Properties Ltd v Thackeray Property Services*, above, n. 244.

[246] *Goodright d Charter v Cordwent* (1795) 6 Term Rep 219; *Dendy v Nicholl* (1858) 4 CBNS 376; *Ward v
Day* (1864) 5 B & S 359; *Grimwood v Moss* (1872) LR 7 CP 360; *Segal Securities Ltd v Thoseby* [1963] 1 QB 887
(demand for rent made without prejudice held to be waiver); cf. *Expert Clothing Service & Sales Ltd v Hillgate
House Ltd* [1986] Ch 340, p. 444, above (proffering of negotiating document held not to be waiver where no
acceptance of rent or demand for rent involved); *Re National Jazz Centre Ltd* [1988] 2 EGLR 57 (mere entry
into negotiations held not to be waiver); *Church Comrs for England v Nodjoumi* (1985) 51 P & CR 155 (service
of s. 146 notice held not to be waiver of right to forfeit lease on grounds other than those set out in notice);
Central Estates (Belgravia) Ltd v Woolgar (No 2) [1972] 1 WLR 1048 (clerk of landlord's agents accepted rent
by mistake); *David Blackstone Ltd v Burnetts (West End) Ltd* [1973] 1 WLR 1487, p. 451, below (demand
for future rent); *Welch v Birrane* (1974) 29 P & CR 102; (1976) 40 Conv (NS) 327; (1977) 41 Conv (NS) 220
(E. L. G. Tyler); (1988) 138 NLJ (H. W. Wilkinson); *Metropolitan Properties Co Ltd v Cordery* (1979) 39 P &
CR 10 (landlords' acceptance of rent for flat with knowledge, through their porters, of facts which pointed
to breach of covenant held to be waiver); *Cornillie v Saha* (1996) 72 P & CR 147. Cf. *Trustees of Henry Smith's*

LAW OF PROPERTY ACT 1925

148. Waiver of a covenant in a lease.—(1) Where any actual waiver by a lessor or the persons deriving title under him of the benefit of any covenant or condition in any lease is proved to have taken place in any particular instance, such waiver shall not be deemed to extend to any instance, or to any breach of covenant or condition save that to which such waiver specially relates, nor operate as a general waiver of the benefit of any such covenant or condition.

(2) This section applies unless a contrary intention appears and extends to waivers effected after the twenty-third day of July, eighteen hundred and sixty.

In **David Blackstone Ltd v Burnetts (West End) Ltd** [1973] 1 WLR 1487 SWANWICK J, in holding that there had been waiver by a landlord who was demanding future rent, said at 1498:

My view, both on principle and on such persuasive authority as has been cited to me, is that an unambiguous demand for future rent in advance such as was made here does in law amount to an election and does constitute a waiver if, at the time when it is made, the landlord has sufficient knowledge of the facts to put him to his election. To my perhaps simple mind there is a fundamental inconsistency between contending that a lease has been determined and demanding rent on the basis of its future continuance.

This leads me to the second main issue in this case: what knowledge must the landlord or his agent be proved to have had in order that a demand for rent should amount to a waiver; what is the point in time at which such knowledge is to be assessed; and, therefore, are the second plaintiffs proved to have had the necessary knowledge at the relevant time so as to make their demand a waiver?

I will deal first with the appropriate point in time. . . .

I consider that . . . for there to be a valid election to waive a breach, the landlord or his agent must have sufficient knowledge of the breach before despatching the document making the election, but that such election does not become effective until it is communicated to the tenant. . . .

This leaves the final branch of the final question. At the relevant time, did the second plaintiffs possess sufficient knowledge of the breach to render the demand a waiver in law? . . .

In my judgment, again without the guidance of any direct authority, the knowledge required to put a landlord to his election is knowledge of the basic facts which in law constitute a breach of covenant entitling him to forfeit the lease. Once he or his agent knows those facts an appropriate act by himself or any agent will in law effect a waiver or a forfeiture. His knowledge or

Charity v Willson [1983] QB 316 (uncommunicated rent demand); *Re A Debtor (No 13A)* [1995] 1 WLR 1127 (demand for rent due before right to forfeit not waiver); *Official Custodian for Charities v Parway Estates Development Ltd* [1985] Ch 151 (publication in London Gazette of compulsory liquidation held not to be imputed knowledge so as to constitute waiver); *Chrisdell Ltd v Johnson* [1987] 2 EGLR 123 (landlord's failure to take action because he thinks that he will not be able to prove suspected breach of contract held not to be waiver); *Van Haarlam v Kasner* [1992] 2 EGLR 59; *Iperion Investments Corpn v Broadwalk House Residents Ltd* [1992] 2 EGLR 235; *Seahive Investments Ltd v Osibanjo* [2008] EWCA Civ 1282, [2009] 9 EG 194 (processing of cheque, where part retained in discharge of outstanding bankruptcy debt and part returned which had been tendered as outstanding rent, was not conclusive of whether payment accepted as rent). However, it has not yet been authoritatively settled at the level of CA that unequivocal demand for future rent constitutes waiver: *Greenwood Reversion Ltd v World Environment Foundation Ltd* [2008] HLR 31 at [26]-[27].

ignorance of the law is, in my judgment, irrelevant. If it were not so, a vast gap would be opened in the administration of the law of landlord and tenant and a facile escape route for landlords would be provided. Indeed, if this were the position unscrupulous landlords could hardly have failed in the past to take advantage of it long before now.

(b) Waiver of continuing breach

In **City and Westminster Properties (1934) Ltd v Mudd** [1959] Ch 129[247] a lease contained a covenant by the tenant 'to use the demised premises as and for showrooms, workrooms and offices only'. The tenant admitted that he was sleeping there. In an action for forfeiture for breach of covenant, the tenant alleged, inter alia, a release or waiver by the landlord by reason of his knowledge of the breach prior to and during the currency of the lease. In refusing the claim of waiver, HARMAN J said at 143:

The next issue is that of waiver. Now residence, contrary to the covenants of the lease, is a continuing breach and therefore prima facie it is only waived by the acceptance of rent down to the date of that acceptance and there is a new breach immediately thereafter which is not waived. My attention was called to a number of cases which show that acts of waiver may be so continuous that the court is driven to the conclusion that there has been a new agreement for letting or a licence or a release of the covenant. The cases cited on this subject show acquiescence continuing for a very long period of years. For instance, in *Gibson v Doeg* (1858) 2 H & N 623 the period was 20 years, in *Gibbon v Payne* (1905) 22 TLR 54 it was 40 years, and in *Hepworth v Pickles* [1900] 1 Ch 108, 24 years. In the more recent case of *Lloyds Bank Ltd v Jones* [1955] 2 QB 298, Singleton LJ points out that no particular period such as 20 years is required....

   Again, in *Wolfe v Hogan* [1949] 2 KB 194, I find this in the headnote: 'The mere acceptance of rent by the landlord from the tenant, after he had knowledge of the change of user by the tenant, though it continues for some time, does not, by itself, constitute such acceptance by the landlord of the changed position as to show that the house has been let as a separate dwelling'; and Denning LJ, after dealing with the facts, says this at 205: 'A house or a part of a house originally let for business purposes does not become let for dwelling purposes unless it can be inferred from the acceptance of rent that the landlord has affirmatively consented to the change of user. Let me illustrate that from the common law doctrine as to waiver of forfeiture. A breach of covenant not to use premises in a particular way is a continuing breach. Any acceptance of rent by the landlord, after knowledge, only waives the breaches up to the time of the acceptance of rent. It does not waive the continuance of the breach thereafter and, notwithstanding his previous acceptance of rent, the landlord can still proceed for forfeiture on that account. Indeed, in the case of a continuing breach, the acceptance of rent, after knowledge, is only a bar to a claim for forfeiture if it goes on for so long, or is accepted in such circumstances, that it can be inferred that the landlord has not merely waived the breach but has affirmatively consented to the tenant continuing to use the premises as he has done.' I cannot think that anything proved here amounts to a release by the landlord of his rights. He knew, indeed, that the tenant was using the property to sleep in, but I do not think he knew more than that. At that he was willing to wink, but I am unable to find a release of the covenant or an agreement for a new letting. In my judgment, therefore, the plea of waiver fails.

[247] *Cooper v Henderson* (1982) 263 EG 592.

(iv) Relief against forfeiture

Billson v Residential Apartments Ltd[248]
[1992] 1 AC 494 (HL, Lords Keith of Kinkel, Templeman, Oliver of Aylmerton, Goff of Chieveley and Jauncey of Tullichettle)

The plaintiff landlords owned the freehold reversion of 17 Gledlow Gardens in London, a lease of which was assigned to the defendant tenants in May 1989 for £280,000. The lease contained a covenant by the tenant against alterations or additions without the written consent of the landlords. The defendants started on a major conversion scheme at a cost of between £260,000 and £375,000 without written consent. After correspondence between the parties, the landlords eventually served a notice under section 146 of the Law of Property Act 1925 on 4 July, requiring the breaches of covenant to be remedied 'within a reasonable time...in so far as they are capable of remedy'. The tenants however continued their building works. At 6 a.m. on 18 July the landlords peaceably re-entered the vacant premises and changed the locks. By 10 a.m. on the same day the tenants regained possession. Before the trial judge and the Court of Appeal, the landlords successfully claimed possession on the ground that the court had no jurisdiction to grant relief against forfeiture under section 146(2) of the Law of Property Act 1925.

Held (reversing the Court of Appeal [1991] 3 WLR 264). The court had jurisdiction. Application for relief was remitted to the High Court.[249]

Lord Templeman: By the writ in this action dated 19 July 1989 the landlords claim possession, damages for breach of covenant and damages for trespass. By their defence and counterclaim the tenants counterclaim for relief against forfeiture. By their reply the landlords claim that the court has no jurisdiction to grant the tenants relief from forfeiture. The trial judge, Mummery J (1990) 60 P & CR 392, and the Court of Appeal (Sir Nicolas Browne-Wilkinson V-C, and Parker and Nicholls LJJ), considered that they were constrained by authority to hold that the court had no jurisdiction to grant the tenants relief against forfeiture pursuant to section 146(2) because the tenants had not applied to the court for relief prior to the re-entry into possession by the landlords on 18 July 1989.[250] The tenants now appeal.

By the common law, when a tenant commits a breach of covenant and the lease contains a proviso for forfeiture, the landlord at his option may either waive the breach or determine the lease. In order to exercise his option to determine the lease the landlord must either re-enter the premises in conformity with the proviso or must issue and serve a writ claiming possession. The bringing of an action to recover possession is equivalent to an entry for the forfeiture. Thus in *Jones v Carter* (1846) 15 M & W 718, 726, Parke B said:

> 'the bringing of an ejectment for a forfeiture, and serving it on the lessee in possession, must be considered as the exercise of the lessor's option to determine the lease; and the option must be exercised once for all...for after such an act, by which the lessor treats the lessee as a trespasser,

---

[248] [1992] CLJ 216 (S. Bridge); [1992] Conv 273 (P. F. Smith); (1992) 02 EG 154 (P. Dollar and C. Peet).

[249] This was refused: [1993] EGCS 150.

[250] CA also held that (Nicholls LJ dissenting) that the court had no inherent jurisdiction to grant relief. This was not raised in HL. See p. 427, n. 200, above.

the lessee would know that he was no longer to consider himself as holding under the lease, and bound to perform the covenants contained in it; ...'

This observation was cited and applied by Lord Denning MR in *Canas Property Co Ltd v KL Television Services Ltd* [1970] 2 QB 433, 440.[251]

Before the intervention of Parliament, if a landlord forfeited by entering into possession or by issuing and serving a writ for possession, equity could relieve the tenant against forfeiture but only in cases under the general principles of equity whereby a party may be relieved from the consequences of fraud, accident or mistake or in cases where the breach of covenant entitling the landlord to forfeit was a breach of the covenant for payment of rent.

Mr Reid, who appeared for the landlords, conceded that where equity claimed power to relieve against forfeiture, the tenant could apply for relief irrespective of the method by which the landlord had exercised his option to determine the lease. Relief could be granted whether the landlord had forfeited by entering into possession or had forfeited by issuing and serving a writ claiming possession.

In 1881 Parliament interfered to supplement equity and to enable any tenant to be relieved from forfeiture. The need for such intervention was and is manifest because otherwise a tenant who had paid a large premium for a 999-year lease at a low rent could lose his asset by a breach of covenant which was remediable or which caused the landlord no damage. The forfeiture of any lease, however short, may unjustly enrich the landlord at the expense of the tenant. In creating a power to relieve against forfeiture for breach of covenant Parliament protected the landlord by conferring on the court a wide discretion to grant relief on terms or to refuse relief altogether. In practice this discretion is exercised with the object of ensuring that the landlord is not substantially prejudiced or damaged by the revival of the lease.

Section 14(1) and (2) of the Conveyancing and Law of Property Act 1881 were provisions which conferred on the court power to relieve against forfeiture and those provisions were reproduced in section 146(1) and (2) of the Law of Property Act 1925 in identical terms. In referring to a section 146 notice I shall therefore mean and include a notice served under section 14(1) of the Act of 1881 and in referring to section 146(1) and (2) I shall mean and include section 14(1) and (2) of the Act of 1881 where appropriate.

Section 146(1) prevents the landlord from enforcing a right of re-entry or forfeiture by action or otherwise so that the landlord cannot determine the lease by issuing and serving a writ or by re-entering the premises until the tenant has failed within a reasonable time to remedy the breach and make reasonable compensation. Section 146(2) enables the tenant to apply to the court for relief where the landlord 'is proceeding, by action or otherwise' to enforce his right of re-entry or forfeiture. If the landlord 'is proceeding' to determine the lease by issuing and serving a writ, the tenant may apply for relief after the writ has been served. If the landlord 'is proceeding' to determine the lease by re-entering into possession, the tenant may apply for relief after the landlord has re-entered.

Mr Reid submitted and referred to authority for the proposition that on the true construction of section 146(2) a tenant cannot apply for relief against forfeiture after the landlord has re-entered without obtaining a court order. Thereafter the landlord is no longer 'proceeding' to enforce his rights; he has succeeded in enforcing them. The proposition is in my opinion historically unsound because the effect of issuing and serving a writ is precisely the same as

---

[251] And also in *GS Fashions Ltd v B & Q plc* [1995] 1 WLR 1088; *Kingston upon Thames London Borough Council v Marlow* [1996] 1 EGLR 101 (tenant by relinquishing tenancy in response to forfeiture proceedings no longer entitled to possession, nor liable to pay rates).

the effect of re-entry; in each case the lease is determined. The landlord is entitled to remain in possession if he has re-entered and he is entitled to possession if he has issued and served a writ because the lease no longer exists. In each case the tenant seeks relief because the lease has been forfeited. The proposition is also inconsistent with the language of section 146(2). The tenant may apply for relief where the landlord is 'proceeding, by action or otherwise' to enforce his rights. The tenant may apply for relief where the landlord is 'proceeding' by action and also where the landlord is proceeding 'otherwise' than by action. This can only mean that the tenant may apply for relief where the landlord is proceeding to forfeit by re-entry after the expiry of a section 146 notice. If re-entry bars relief, the right of the tenant to apply for relief where the landlord is proceeding otherwise than by action is substantially inoperative and the words 'or otherwise' in section 146(2) have no application. In my opinion those words must have been·included because Parliament intended that a tenant should be able to obtain relief against a landlord whether the landlord has asserted his rights by a writ or by re-entering. It is said that a tenant served with a section 146 notice could during and after the expiration of the notice apply for relief under section 146(2) but if he fails to do so he is at the mercy of the landlord who decides to re-enter and whose rights are therefore, it is said, quite unaffected by the provisions of section 146(2) designed to relieve tenants from the consequences of breach of covenant. In my opinion the ambiguous words 'is proceeding' can mean 'proceeds' and should not be construed so as to produce the result that a tenant served with a section 146 notice can only ensure that he will be able to apply for relief if he does so before he knows whether or not the landlord intends to proceed at all or whether, if the landlord decides to proceed, he will issue and serve a writ or will attempt to re-enter.

When a tenant receives a section 146 notice he will not know whether the landlord can be persuaded that there is no breach or persuaded to accept in due course that any breach has been remedied and that he has been offered adequate and satisfactory compensation or whether the landlord will seek to determine the lease by issuing and serving a writ or will seek to determine the lease by re-entering the premises. The tenant will not wish to institute proceedings seeking relief from forfeiture if those proceedings will be aggressive and hostile and may be premature and unnecessary. Parliament cannot have intended that if the landlord employs the civilised method of determining the lease by issuing and serving a writ, then the tenant will be entitled to apply for relief, but if the landlord employs the dubious and dangerous method of determining the lease by re-entering the premises, then the tenant will be debarred from applying for relief.

Mr Reid concedes that re-entry can only avail the landlord if the entry is lawful. Re-entry is unlawful where the premises are occupied by the tenant but not unlawful where the premises are occupied by the tenant's goods. If the argument of the landlords is correct, section 146 provides a method by which a landlord can sneak up on a shop at night, break into the shop, and install new locks so that the tenant loses his lease and can only press his nose against the shop window being unable to obtain the assistance of the court because he has become a trespasser entitled to no rights and to no relief. The farce in the present case when the landlords occupied the premises for four hours should not be allowed to defeat the statutory rights of the tenants.

The right conferred by section 146(2) on a tenant to apply for relief against forfeiture may without violence to the language, be construed as a right to apply 'where a lessor *proceeds*, by action or otherwise' to enforce a right of re-entry. So construed, section 146(2) enables the tenant to apply for relief whenever and however the landlord claims that the lease has been determined for breach of covenant. I have no doubt that this was the object and intention and is the effect of section 146.

In *Quilter v Mapleson* (1882) 9 QBD 672 a landlord forfeited a lease before the Act of 1881 came into force by issuing and serving a writ for possession. He recovered judgment, the tenant appealed and the Act of 1881 came into force before the appeal was heard. The Court of Appeal held that the Act was retrospective and granted relief to the tenant. Lindley LJ, at p. 676, decided that section 146(2) was applicable:

> 'The action was brought by the landlord on the ground of breaches committed before the Act, and he obtained judgment before the Act came into operation, but execution was stayed, so that he has never obtained possession. The original action then is not yet at an end.... So long as the tenant has not been turned out of possession he is within the terms of the enactment, for the lessor is proceeding to enforce his right of re-entry. The enactment then being in terms retrospective must be construed according to its terms as being retrospective.'

The judgments of Sir George Jessel MR and Bowen LJ were to the like effect and it is now settled law that where a landlord forfeits a lease by issuing and serving a writ for possession the tenant may apply for relief before but not after the landlord has recovered judgment and re-entered. But although the court limited the time during which a tenant could apply for relief against forfeiture constituted by the issue and service of the writ, the court had no power and in my opinion did not intend to deprive a tenant of any right to apply for relief after a forfeiture constituted by re-entry without judgment. *Quilter v Mapleson* is authority for a case where the landlord forfeits by issue and service of a writ but is not authority for a case where the landlord forfeits by re-entry.

In *Rogers v Rice* [1892] 2 Ch 170 a landlord forfeited by the issue and service of a writ, recovered judgment and re-entered pursuant to the writ of possession then issued and was held to be no longer 'proceeding by action' within section 146(2). The tenant sought and was refused leave to set aside the verdict and the judgment. The tenant later issued an originating summons seeking relief from forfeiture under section 146(2). Lord Coleridge CJ said that a section 146 notice had been given and ignored, and continued, at pp. 171–172:

> 'The action proceeded to judgment, the judgment was executed, so far as possession was concerned, and at the time when the present proceeding was commenced the lessor was in possession. The action then, so far as related to enforcing the right of re-entry, was at an end, and it cannot be said that the landlord was "proceeding" to enforce his right of re-entry. The case is clear on the terms of the Act, but I cannot omit to notice that the same view was taken by the judges of the Court of Appeal in *Quilter v Mapleson,* 9 QBD 672, 677, where all three judges gave their opinion to this effect, though that was not the point on which their decision turned.'

The decision can be supported on the grounds that no court could properly exercise its discretion to relieve against forfeiture after the landlord had issued and served a writ, recovered judgment in the action and entered into possession pursuant to that judgment. The decision can also be supported on the grounds set out in the speech of my noble and learned friend, Lord Oliver of Aylmerton. But the court had no power and in my opinion did not intend to deprive a tenant of any right to apply for relief after a forfeiture constituted by re-entry without judgment.

In *Pakwood Transport Ltd v 15, Beauchamp Place Ltd* (1977) 36 P & CR 112 the Court of Appeal rejected an argument by a landlord who had served a section 146 notice that the tenant could not apply for relief from forfeiture until proceedings for forfeiture has been instituted by the landlord. All three Lords Justices derived from *Quilter v Mapleson* and *Rogers v Rice* the proposition that, in the words of Orr LJ, at 117:

> 'a lessee could not apply for relief against re-entry or forfeiture after the landlord had obtained a judg-
> ment of the court entitling him to re-enter on a forfeiture; and it is claimed, and in my judgment rightly

claimed, that the same principle must apply where the landlord has peaceably recovered possession. In other words, once he has either recovered possession or obtained an order for possession he can no longer be said to be "proceeding by action or otherwise to enforce a right of re-entry or forfeiture." '

My Lords, I accept that it is now settled law that a tenant cannot apply for relief after the landlord has recovered judgment for possession and has reentered in reliance on that judgment. But I do not accept that any court has deprived or is entitled to deprive a tenant of any right to apply for relief if the landlord proceeds to forfeit otherwise than by an action instituted for that purpose. Orr LJ continued, at p. 117:

'On this basis the argument for the lessor appears to me to involve an absurdity, in that if the landlord has done no more than serve a section 146 notice, it is too early for the tenant to apply for relief; but if the landlord's next step is peaceably to recover possession, it is then too late for the tenant to apply. For my part, I am not prepared to accept an argument which leads to this absurdity, and I have no hesitation in holding that a landlord who serves a section 146 notice is at that stage "proceeding to enforce a right of re-entry or forfeiture" in that the service of such a notice is a step which the law requires him to take in order to re-enter or forfeit.'

My Lords, I accept the conclusion that a landlord who serves a notice under section 146(1) can be said, for the purposes of section 146(2) to be proceeding to enforce his rights under the lease. A tenant authorised by section 146(2) to apply to the court for relief against forfeiture if he fails to comply with a section 146 notice may make that application after service of the notice for the purpose of elucidating the issues raised by the notice, ascertaining the intentions of the landlord, and setting in train the machinery by which the dispute between the landlord and the tenant can be determined by negotiation or by the court. But the fact that the tenant may apply to the court for relief after service of the section 146 notice does not mean that if he does not do so he loses the right conferred on him by section 146(2) to apply for relief if and when the landlord proceeds, not by action but 'otherwise' by exercising a right of re-entry. No absurdity follows from a construction which allows the tenant to apply for relief before and after a landlord re-enters without first obtaining a court order.

In the words of Laskin JA in *Re Rexdale Investments Ltd and Gibson* [1967] 1 OR 251, 259 dealing with provisions in the Ontario legislation indistinguishable from section 146(2), the argument that a tenant cannot apply for relief after a landlord has determined the lease by re-entry:

'depends on a detached grammatical reading of the phrase "is proceeding"...which makes nonsense of the phrase "or otherwise" (as covering physical re-entry) by making ineffective, in any practical sense, the provision for relief from forfeiture applicable to such re-entry. We do not construe statutes, especially when they are remedial...to the point of self-contradiction. In my opinion, the phrase "is proceeding" is more properly read in the sense of "has proceeded," and I am fortified in this view by the fact that the exercise of the power of termination is manifested effectively by the mere taking of proceedings as well as by physical re-entry. What [section 146(2)] means, therefore, is that when the landlord has terminated the lease by action or by actual re-entry without action, the tenant may seek relief from forfeiture in the pending action, if any, or, if none, by proceedings initiated by him. In the latter case, one would expect prompt reaction by the tenant.... The English cases relied on...[*Rogers v Rice* [1892] 2 Ch 170; *Lock v Pearce* [1893] 2 Ch 271 and *Quilter v Mapleson*, 9 QBD 672] are distinguishable, if need be...by the fact...that they relate to re-entry in pursuance of a judgment for possession.'

These observations by a distinguished Canadian judge who subsequently became Chief Justice of the Supreme Court of Canada, support the views which I have formed concerning the construction of section 146 and the ambit and effect of the earlier decisions.

Mr Reid argued that your Lordships should not interfere with 19th century decisions and for my part I do not intend to do so on this occasion or to question the result of the decision of the Court of Appeal in *Pakwood Transport Ltd v 15, Beauchamp Place Ltd* (1977) 36 P & CR 112. But the authorities were never directed to the point now in issue and certainly never decided that issue.

It was suggested that Parliament in 1925 accepted the views expressed in the 19th century cases. I agree that Parliament accepted that a tenant cannot apply for relief under section 146(2) after the landlord has forfeited the lease by issuing and serving a writ for possession and in his action has recovered and enforced judgment. The 19th century cases were not directed to the problem which has now emerged.

We were informed that the researches of counsel had not disclosed any reported case in which a landlord has forfeited by re-entry and then successfully denied the right of the tenant to apply for relief.

The landlords or their advisers, perhaps incensed by the activities of the tenants in the present case, conceived and carried out a dawn raid which fortunately did not result in bloodshed. Since the decision of the Court of Appeal in the instant case there has been a proliferation of section 146 notices followed by pressure on tenants to surrender on terms favourable to the landlord. If this appeal were not allowed, the only safe advice for a tenant would be to issue proceedings for relief against forfeiture as soon as a section 146 notice is received at a time when the tenant cannot know whether relief will be necessary. A tenant ignorant of the development in the law pioneered by the landlords in the present case will be at the mercy of an aggressive landlord. The conclusions which I have reached will not entail these consequences and will not again involve Parliament in correcting judicial constructions of statute by further legislation.

The results of section 146 and the authorities are as follows. A tenant may apply for appropriate declarations and for relief from forfeiture under section 146(2) after the issue of a section 146 notice but he is not prejudiced if he does not do so. A tenant cannot apply for relief after a landlord has forfeited a lease by issuing and serving a writ, has recovered judgment and has entered into possession pursuant to that judgment. If the judgment is set aside or successfully appealed the tenant will be able to apply for relief in the landlord's action but the court in deciding whether to grant relief will take into account any consequences of the original order and repossession and the delay of the tenant. A tenant may apply for relief after a landlord has forfeited by re-entry without first obtaining a court order for that purpose but the court in deciding whether to grant relief will take into account all the circumstances, including delay, on the part of the tenant. Any past judicial observations which might suggest that a tenant is debarred from applying for relief after the landlord has re-entered without first obtaining a court order for that purpose are not to be so construed.

I would therefore allow the appeal and set aside the orders of the trial judge and the Court of Appeal.[252]

---

[252] See also *Shiloh Spinners Ltd v Harding* [1973] AC 691, p. 68, above (refusal of relief in 'a case of clear and wilful breaches of more than one covenant'); *Scala House and District Property Co Ltd v Forbes* [1974] QB 575 at 584, p. 434, above; *Southern Depot Co Ltd v British Railways Board* [1990] 2 EGLR 39 (relief granted despite wilful breaches involving 'a thoroughly deceptive course of conduct towards the landlord'). For the grant of relief in wholly exceptional circumstances in favour of a tenant who was in breach of a covenant against immoral user, see *Central Estates (Belgravia) Ltd v Woolgar (No 2)* [1972] 1 WLR 1048; *Ropemaker Properties Ltd v Noonhaven Ltd* [1989] 2 EGLR 50; (1989) 139 NLJ 1747 (H. W. Wilkinson); cf. *British Petroleum Pension Trust Ltd v Behrendt* (1985) 52 P & CR 117.

(v) Law reform

(2007) 157 NLJ 54 (S. Bridge)[253]

In January 2004, the Law Commission's (the commission's) consultation paper, *Termination of Tenancies for Tenant Default* (Law Com No 174) (see 154 NLJ 7113, p. 113), stated that the law of forfeiture was 'complex...lacks coherence and...can lead to injustice'. It provisionally proposed that forfeiture should be replaced with a statutory scheme for the termination of tenancies. The scheme would make the law easier to understand, simpler to use, and would assist landlords and tenants to resolve disputes out of court. Responses to the consultation paper revealed widespread dissatisfaction with the current law and strong support for reform. The commission has now published its final report (Law Com No 303) and the draft Landlord and Tenant (Termination of Tenancies) Bill.[254] This article briefly sets out the main recommendations, which are largely of significance in relation to commercial tenancies and long residential tenancies.

Landlords will no longer be able to terminate a tenancy by using the law of forfeiture or by peaceable re-entry; under the commission's recommendations, a tenancy can only be terminated for breach of covenant by using the statutory scheme. The gateway to the scheme is 'tenant default', broadly defined as any breach by the tenant of a covenant or condition of the tenancy, unless the parties have agreed otherwise. In response to tenant default, the landlord may take termination action, either making a termination claim to the court or using the summary termination procedure.

Default notice for termination claims

A landlord who wishes to make a termination claim must serve a tenant default notice on the tenant detailing the breach, any remedial action that the tenant must take, and a deadline for completion of that action. This notice, to be given within six months of the landlord having knowledge of the tenant default, must also be served on those who hold 'qualifying interests' deriving out of the tenancy, of whom the landlord has knowledge. These include subtenants, chargees, and those with options or rights of pre-emption. The notice has a shelf life. If the tenant does not complete the remedial action specified in the notice by the deadline, the landlord has six months in which to go to court. The doctrine of waiver has no part to play.

Available court orders

The draft Bill lists the orders available under the scheme. The court, guided by a checklist of factors that it must take into account, may make such order as is appropriate and proportionate in the circumstances. A termination order ends the tenancy on a specified date and any interest deriving out of the tenancy ends simultaneously. A remedial order requires the tenant to remedy the default. If the tenant fails to do so, the landlord can apply for a termination order. In deciding whether to make a termination order then, the court will take into account the tenant's failure to comply with the remedial order. An order for sale directs that the tenancy is sold and the proceeds distributed. The proceeds will be applied to discharge any debt owed to the landlord, to satisfy the claims of secured creditors and the residue will be paid to the tenant. It may be appropriate and proportionate to make this order where the tenancy has a high capital value

---

[253] See also (2007) 11 L & T Rev 140 (J. Bignell), 145 (S. Bridge).

[254] [Law Commission Report on Termination of Tenancies for Tenant Default 2006 (Law Com No. 303, Cm 6946). For previous proposals, see Law Commission Reports on Forfeiture of Tenancies 1985 (Law Com No. 142); and on Termination of Tenancies Bill 1994 (Law Com No. 221)].

and termination would confer a large windfall on the landlord. There are two orders which are only available to qualifying interest holders: orders transferring the tenancy, or granting a new tenancy, to the applicant.

Summary termination procedure

A summary termination procedure is available. How and when it can be used is restricted. For example, it cannot be used where there is someone lawfully residing in the premises or where the unexpired term of the tenancy exceeds 25 years. The procedure is commenced by the service of a summary termination notice on the tenant, any qualifying interest holder, and at the premises addressed to 'the occupier'. If there is no response to the notice, the tenancy ends one month later. However, the notice can be opposed by a tenant, or qualifying interest holder, who may apply for a discharge order which prevents the automatic termination of the tenancy. On hearing a discharge application, the onus is on the landlord to show that, if a termination claim were made, there would be no realistic prospect of the applicant persuading the court not to make a termination order. For a period of six months after the tenancy has terminated pursuant to the summary termination procedure, a former tenant or qualifying interest holder can apply to the court for a post-termination order. Such an order could require the payment of compensation to the applicant, or the grant of a new tenancy. The terminated tenancy cannot, however, be revived. The principal function of the summary termination procedure will be to provide landlords with an expeditious means of termination where the premises have been abandoned, or where the tenant has ceased trading.

Merits of the statutory scheme

The draft Bill contains provisions that retain the statutory protections for tenants contained in the Commonhold and Leasehold Reform Act 2002 and the Leasehold Property (Repairs) Act 1938. The scheme operates subject to the provisions of the Insolvency Acts.

The report and draft Bill have now been laid before Parliament. Implementing the recommendations would replace an area of the law which is archaic—and notoriously difficult to understand for those who are unfamiliar with its operation—with a system which is clear, straightforward and an application of common sense. It would both simplify and modernise a vital part of the law of landlord and tenant.

V. THE TITLE TO THE FREEHOLD

A. UNREGISTERED LAND[255]

LAW OF PROPERTY ACT 1925

44. Statutory commencements of title.—(2) Under a contract to grant or assign a term of years, whether derived or to be derived out of freehold or leasehold land, the intended lessee or assign shall not be entitled to call for the title to the freehold.

---

[255] C & B, pp. 935–935; M & W, paras 21.005–21.010.

(3) Under a contract to sell and assign a term of years derived out of a leasehold interest in land, the intended assign shall not have the right to call for the title to the leasehold reversion.

(4) On a contract to grant a lease for a term of years to be derived out of a leasehold interest, with a leasehold reversion, the intended lessee shall not have the right to call for the title to that reversion.

(4A) Subsections (2) and (4) of this section do not apply to a contract to grant a term of years if the grant will be an event within section 4(1) of the Land Registration Act 2002 (events which trigger compulsory first registration of title).[256]

(5) Where by reason of any of subsections (2) to (4) of this section[257] an intending lessee or assign is not entitled to call for the title to the freehold or to a leasehold reversion, as the case may be, he shall not, where the contract is made after the commencement of this Act, be deemed to be affected with notice of any matter or thing of which, if he had contracted that such title should be furnished, he might have had notice.

(12) Nothing in this section applies in relation to registered land or to a term of years to be derived out of registered land.[258]

In **Shears v Wells** [1936] 1 All ER 832 the first defendant was the owner, and the second defendant, Cooper, the tenant of premises under a tenancy commencing in 1929.[259] The plaintiff brought this action for an injunction to restrain the breach of a restrictive covenant contained in the conveyance to the first defendant. The second defendant pleaded that he had no notice of the restrictive covenant. Holding that, by virtue of the Law of Property Act 1925, section 44(5), the second defendant was only bound by matters of which the plaintiff could prove he had notice at the commencement of his tenancy, LUXMOORE J said at 834:

I think that Cooper is not liable under the covenant at all. He took the tenancy of the garage in 1929 after the passing of the Law of Property Act 1925. Section 44 enacts as follows: [His Lordship read section 44(2), (4), (5):] It follows that the onus of proving that the defendant Cooper had notice when he took the tenancy is on the plaintiff. There is no evidence here that he had notice and the onus is not discharged. The defendant Cooper is therefore not subject to the covenants in the deed.

This case illustrates the reversal of the rule in *Patman v Harland* (1881) 17 ChD 353, where Jessel MR held that a tenant had constructive notice of a restrictive covenant affecting the freehold, which covenant was disclosed in the deeds. The tenant was not protected even if the lessor told her that there was no such covenant, nor by the Vendor and Purchaser Act 1874, section 2 which provides 'subject to any stipulation to the contrary' that 'under a contract to grant or assign a term of years, whether derived or to be derived out of a freehold or leasehold estate, the intended lessee or assign shall not be entitled to call for the title to the freehold.'

[256] Added by LRA 2002, s. 133, Sch. 11, para. 2(1), (2).
[257] Substituted by LRA 2002, s. 133, Sch. 11, para. 2(1), (3).
[258] Added by LRA 2002, s. 133, Sch. 11, para. 2(1), (4).
[259] In the statement of facts this date is given as 1931 but this is at variance with the date given in the judgment which is used here.

Shears v Wells does not, however, solve all the problems. The person entitled to the benefit of the covenant needs to ensure that the lessee has notice of the covenant. Presumably he could do this by registration and rely on the provisions of the Law of Property Act 1925, section 198(1) that registration is deemed to constitute 'actual notice...to all persons...connected with the land affected.'[260] The result is not satisfactory; for the procedure for registration under the Land Charges Act 1925 provides for registration under personal names and not under the land concerned.[261] Unless therefore the incumbrance is registered against the present lessor, the tenant (a fortiori, a sub-tenant), not seeing the earlier deeds, will not know under whose name to search. And neither pre-1926 covenants nor covenants originally entered into between landlord and tenant are registrable.[262]

B. REGISTERED LAND

Section 44(12) of the Law of Property Act 1925 disapplies section 44 (p. 460, above) as regards registered land for a term of years to be derived out of registered land. This follows from the register being proof of the title of a registered estate, and the register being open to public inspection.[263] Therefore any prospective lessee can inspect the title of his landlord.[264]

VI. THE EFFECT OF ASSIGNMENT ON COVENANTS [265]

The Landlord and Tenant (Covenants) Act 1995 radically changed the law relating to the enforcement of covenants in leases.[266] It is not retrospective. It provides a new code for covenants in leases granted after 1995. The existing law continues where the lease was created before 1996.[267]

---

[260] In *White v Bijou Mansions* [1937] Ch 610 at 619 Simonds J suggested 'that s. 198...appears, notwithstanding the unqualified language of s. 44, sub-s. 5, to affect a lessee with notice of all those charges which are registered under the Land Charges Act 1925'.

[261] Above, p. 79.

[262] (1940) 56 LQR 361 (D. W. Logan); [1956] CLJ 230–234 (H. W. R. Wade).

[263] Above, p. 126.

[264] Law Com Report No. 217, paras 12.9–12.13; H & B, para. 24.6.

[265] C & B, pp. 294–316; Gray, part 4.5; M & W, paras 17.050–17.052, 17.108–17.114, chap. 20; MM, pp. 381–406; Smith, chap. 20.

[266] (1996) 59 MLR (M. Davey); [1996] CLJ 313 (S. Bridge); [1996] Conv 432 (P. Walter); (1996) 49 CLP Part I 95 (A. Clarke). See generally Fancourt: *Enforceability of Landlord and Tenant Covenants* (2nd edn, 2006).

[267] Sections 17–20 apply to all leases whenever granted; p. 475, below. In *First Penthouse Ltd v Channel Hotels & Properties (UK) Ltd* [2004] 1 EGLR 16, Lightman J said at [43]: 'The 1995 Act is the product of rushed drafting, and its provisions create exceptional difficulties.'

A. COVENANTS IN PRE-1996 LEASES

(i) Covenants which touch and concern the land[268]

The only covenants which can be enforced by or against assignees of the leasehold estate or the reversion, are those which 'touch and concern the land',[269] or (which means the same thing) have 'reference to the subject-matter of the lease.'[270] In Lord Ellenborough's words, the test is satisfied if the covenant 'affected the nature, quality or value of the thing demised, independently of collateral circumstances; or if it affected the mode of enjoying it.'[271] The simplest test is that put forward by Cheshire,[272] that is to consider whether the covenant affects 'the landlord *qua* landlord or the tenant *qua* tenant'.

In **P & A Swift Investments v Combined English Stores Group plc** [1989] AC 632 the House of Lords held that a covenant in a lease by a surety who guaranteed payment of the rent by the tenant was a covenant which touched and concerned the land. LORD TEMPLEMAN said at 637:

The landlord replies that a covenant by a surety, in whatever form or expression the surety covenant may take, is a covenant that the tenant's covenants shall be performed and observed. A covenant by a surety that a tenant's covenant which touches and concerns the land shall be performed and observed must itself be a covenant which touches and concerns the land; the benefit of that surety's covenant will run with the reversion, and the covenant is therefore enforceable without express assignment. I agree. A surety for a tenant is a quasi tenant who volunteers to be a substitute or twelfth man for the tenant's team and is subject to the same rules and regulations as the player he replaces. A covenant which runs with the reversion against the tenant runs with the reversion against the surety.[273]

LORD OLIVER OF AYLMERTON said at 642:

Formulations of definitive tests are always dangerous, but it seems to me that, without claiming to expound an exhaustive guide, the following provides a satisfactory working test for whether, in any given case, a covenant touches and concerns the land: (1) the covenant benefits only the reversioner for time being, and if separated from the reversion ceases to be of benefit to the covenantee; (2) the covenant affects the nature, quality, mode of user or value of the land of the reversioner; (3) the covenant is not expressed to be personal (that is to say neither being given only to a specific reversioner nor in respect of the obligations only of a specific tenant[274]);

---

[268] C & B, pp. 295–297; Gray, paras 4.5.42–4.5.54; M & W, paras 20.022–20.028; MM, pp. 387–388.

[269] *Spencer's Case* (1583) 5 Co Rep 16a, p. 465, below; *Smith's Leading Cases* (13th edn, 1929), vol. 1, p. 51.

[270] LPA 1925, ss. 141, 142; *Davis v Town Properties Investment Corpn Ltd* [1903] 1 Ch 797.

[271] *Mayor of Congleton v Pattison* (1808) 10 East 130 at 135.

[272] Below, p. 464. This was approved in *Breams Property Investment Co Ltd v Stroulger* [1948] 2 KB 1 at 7; *Hua Chiao Commercial Bank Ltd v Chiaphua Industries Ltd* [1987] AC 99 at 107, below, p. 464.

[273] See *Milverton Group Ltd v Warner World Ltd* [1995] 2 EGLR 28 at 31.

[274] *System Floors Ltd v Ruralpride Ltd* [1995] 1 EGLR 48 (benefit of covenant runs against assignee of reversion even though personal to original tenant).

(4) the fact that a covenant is to pay a sum of money will not prevent it from touching and concerning the land so long as the three foregoing conditions are satisfied and the covenant is connected with something to be done on, to or in relation to the land.[275]

In **Hua Chiao Commercial Bank Ltd v Chiaphua Industries Ltd** [1987] AC 99 the Privy Council held that a covenant by a tenant to pay the landlord a substantial security deposit on the terms that it would be repayable at the end of the lease if there was no breach of the tenant's covenants, did not touch and concern the land. LORD OLIVER OF AYLMERTON said at 107:

Their Lordships have been referred to and are content to adopt the following passage from *Cheshire and Burn's Modern Law of Real Property,* 13th edn (1982), pp. 430–431:

> 'If the covenant has direct reference to the land, if it lays down something which is to be done or is not to be done upon the land, or, and perhaps this is the clearest way of describing the test, if it affects the landlord in his normal capacity as landlord or the tenant in his normal capacity as tenant, it may be said to touch and concern the land.
>
> Lord Russell CJ [in *Horsey Estate Ltd v Steiger* [1899] 2 QB 79, 89] said: "The true principle is that no covenant or condition which affects merely the person, and which does not affect the nature, quality, or value of the thing demised or the mode of using or enjoying the thing demised, runs with the land;" and Bailey J at an earlier date asserted the same principle [in *Congleton Corporation v Pattison* (1808) 10 East 130, 138]: "In order to bind the assignee, the covenant must either affect the land itself during the term, such as those which regard the mode of occupation, or it must be such as per se, and not merely from collateral circumstances, affects the value of the land at the end of the term."
>
> If a simple test is desired for ascertaining into which category a covenant falls, it is suggested that the proper inquiry should be whether the covenant affects either the landlord qua landlord or the tenant qua tenant. A covenant may very well have reference to the land, but, unless it is reasonably incidental to the relation of landlord and tenant, it cannot be said to touch and concern the land so as to be capable of running therewith or with the reversion.'

(ii) Covenants running with the leasehold estate

The common law rule was that covenants which touched and concerned the land were enforceable by and against the assignee of the tenant. There was however an exception to the effect that the burden of a covenant relating to something not '*in esse*' (i.e. not already in existence) at the date of the covenant only ran with the leasehold estate if assigns were expressly mentioned; but this exception was abolished in 1925.[276]

---

[275] See also *Kumar v Dunning* [1989] QB 193, approved by Lord Oliver; *Coronation Street Industrial Properties Ltd v Ingall Industries plc* [1989] 1 WLR 304 (covenant to accept a new lease on the disclaimer of the lease by the tenant's liquidator held to touch and concern); *Clegg v Hands* (1890) 44 Ch D 503; *Caerns Motor Services Ltd v Texaco Ltd* [1994] 1 WLR 1249 (solus agreement to purchase products held to touch and concern).

[276] LPA 1925, s. 79, p. 466, below; and, in respect of covenants entered into before 1996, L & T(C)A 1995, s. 3(7), p. 486, below.

Spencer's Case
(1583) 5 Co Rep 16a (KB)

Spencer and his wife leased land to S for 21 years. S covenanted for himself, his executors and administrators that he, his executors, administrators, or assigns would build a brick wall thereon. He assigned his lease to J, who assigned it to the defendant Clark. The question is as to the liability of Clark on the covenant to build.

Held. Since the covenant was in respect of something to be done on the land demised, and was not made expressly on behalf of the assigns, the defendant was not liable.

The report records that after many arguments at the Bar, the case was excellently argued and debated by the justices at the Bench. Three of the resolutions were:

1. When the covenant extends to a thing *in esse,* parcel of the demise, the thing to be done by force of the covenant is *quodammodo* annexed and appurtenant to the thing demised, and shall go with the land, and shall bind the assignee although he be not bound by express words: but when the covenant extends to a thing which is not in being at the time of the demise made, it cannot be appurtenant or annexed to the thing which hath no being: as if the lessee covenants to repair the houses demised to him during the term, that is parcel of the contract, and extends to the support of the thing demised, and therefore is *quodammodo* annexed appurtenant to houses, and shall bind the assignee although he be not bound expressly by the covenant: but in the case at bar, the covenant concerns a thing which was not *in esse* at the time of the demise made, but to be newly built after, and therefore shall bind the covenantor, his executors, or administrators, and not the assignee, for the law will not annex the covenant to a thing which hath no being.

2. It was resolved that in this case, if the lessee had covenanted for him and his assigns, that they would make a new wall upon some part of the thing demised, that for as much as it is to be done upon the land demised, that it should bind the assignee; for although the covenant doth extend to a thing to be newly made, yet it is to be made upon the thing demised, and the assignee is to take the benefit of it, and therefore shall bind the assignee by express words. So on the other side, if a warranty be made to one, his heirs and assigns, by express words, the assignee shall take benefit of it, and shall have a *Warrantia chartae.* ... But although the covenant be for him and his assigns, yet if the thing to be done be merely collateral to the land, and doth not touch or concern the thing demised in any sort, there the assignee shall not be charged. As if the lessee covenants for him and his assigns to build a house upon the land of the lessor which is no parcel of the demise, or to pay any collateral sum to the lessor, or to a stranger, it shall not bind the assignee, because it is merely collateral, and in no manner touches or concerns the thing that was demised, or that is assigned over; and therefore in such case the assignee of the thing demised cannot be charged with it, no more than any other stranger.

4. It was resolved, that if a man makes a feoffment by this word *dedi,* which implies a warranty, the assignee of the feoffee shall not vouch; but if a man makes a lease for years by this word *concessi* or *demisi,* which implies a covenant, if the assignee of the lessee be evicted, he shall have a writ of covenant; for the lessee and his assignee hath the yearly profits of the land which shall grow by his labour and industry for an annual rent, and therefore it is reasonable when he hath applied his labour, and employed his cost upon the land, and be evicted (whereby he loses all), that he shall take such benefit of the demise and grant, as the first lessee might,

and the lessor hath no other prejudice than what his special contract with the first lessee hath bound him to.

LAW OF PROPERTY ACT 1925[277]

78. Benefit of covenants relating to land.—(1) A covenant relating to any land of the covenantee shall be deemed to be made with the covenantee and his successors in title and the persons deriving title under him or them, and shall have effect as if such successors and other persons were expressed.

For the purposes of this subsection in connexion with covenants restrictive of the user of land 'successors in title' shall be deemed to include the owners and occupiers for the time being of the land of the covenantee intended to be benefited.

(2) This section applies to covenants made after the commencement of this Act, but the repeal of section fifty-eight of the Conveyancing Act, 1881, does not affect the operation of covenants to which that section applied.

79. Burden of covenants relating to land.—(1) A covenant relating to any land of a covenantor or capable of being bound by him, shall, unless a contrary intention is expressed, be deemed to be made by the covenantor on behalf of himself his successors in title and the persons deriving title under him or them, and, subject as aforesaid, shall have effect as if such successors and other persons were expressed.

This subsection extends to a covenant to do some act relating to the land, notwithstanding that the subject-matter may not be in existence when the covenant is made.

(2) For the purposes of this section in connexion with covenants restrictive of the user of land 'successors in title' shall be deemed to include the owners and occupiers for the time being of such land.

(3) This section applies only to covenants made after the commencement of this Act.

(iii) Covenants running with the reversion

At common law the benefit and burden of covenants other than 'usual' or 'implied' covenants (e.g. the covenant to pay rent) did not run with the landlord's reversion. Statutory provision was made in 32 Hen 8 c 34 and in the Conveyancing Act 1881. These provisions were superseded by the Law of Property Act 1925.[278]

(a) Benefit

LAW OF PROPERTY ACT 1925

141. Rent and benefit of lessee's covenants to run with the reversion.—(1) Rent reserved by a lease, and the benefit of every covenant or provision therein contained, having reference to the subject-matter thereof, and on the lessee's part to be observed or performed, and every

---

[277] See also pp. 761–762, 773–777, 783–797, below.

[278] See also LPA 1925, s. 63 which provides that, subject to a contrary intention in the conveyance, 'Every conveyance is effectual to pass all the estate, right, title, interest, claim, and demand which the conveying parties respectively have, in, to, or on the property conveyed, or expressed or intended so to be, or which they respectively have power to convey in, to, or on the same'; *Harbour Estates Ltd v HSBC Bank plc* [2005] Ch 194 (benefit of break clause in lease held to touch and concern land, and therefore, to pass to assignee).

condition of re-entry and other condition therein contained, shall be annexed and incident to and shall go with the reversionary estate in the land, or in any part thereof, immediately expectant on the term granted by the lease, notwithstanding severance of that reversionary estate,[279] and without prejudice to any liability affecting a covenantor or his estate.

(2) Any such rent, covenant or provision shall be capable of being recovered, received, enforced, and taken advantage of, by the person from time to time entitled, subject to the term, to the income of the whole or any part, as the case may require, of the land leased.

(3) Where that person becomes entitled by conveyance or otherwise, such rent, covenant or provision may be recovered, received, enforced or taken advantage of by him notwithstanding that he becomes so entitled after the condition of re-entry or forfeiture has become enforceable, but this subsection does not render enforceable any condition of re-entry or other condition waived or released before such person becomes entitled as aforesaid.[280]

(4) This section applies to leases made before or after the commencement of this Act, but does not affect the operation of—

(a) any severance of the reversionary estate; or

(b) any acquisition by conveyance or otherwise of the right to receive or enforce any rent covenant or provision;

effected before the commencement of this Act.

Re King[281]
[1963] Ch 459 (CA, Lord Denning MR, Upjohn and Diplock LJJ)

In 1895 Edward Graves-Tagg granted a lease of land and a factory in Bethnal Green to Mrs Elven, who covenanted for herself, her executors, administrators and assigns (a) to keep the premises in repair, (b) to insure the premises and keep them insured against loss or damage by fire and (c) to lay out all moneys received under any such policy in rebuilding or repairing the premises destroyed or damaged by fire and, if necessary, to reinstate the premises. In 1907 the lease was assigned to King. In 1944 the factory was severely damaged by fire, but could not be repaired or rebuilt owing to wartime restrictions. The insurance moneys were duly paid. In 1946 Edward Graves-Tagg assigned his reversion to Edward Ernest Graves-Tagg ('Tagg') and in 1949 King died. The factory had never been repaired or rebuilt. In 1960 Tagg assigned his reversion to the London County Council as a result of a compulsory purchase order. In 1961, during negotiations between the London County Council and King's executors for the transfer of the lease to the London County Council, King's executors issued a summons to determine, inter alia, whether Tagg could still sue them for the breach

---

[279] When the reversion is severed i.e. different parts come into different ownerships, the benefit of any covenant, condition or right of entry is apportioned and annexed to the severed parts: LPA 1925, s. 140. The severance must be genuine: *Persey v Bazley* (1983) 47 P & CR 37 (landlord conveyed part of reversion to bare trustees for himself); [1985] Conv 292 (J. Martin). The tenancy itself remains a single tenancy: *Jelley v Buckman* [1974] QB 488; *Nevill Lang & Co (Boards) Ltd v Firmenich & Co* (1983) 47 P & CR 59. See also *Lester v Ridd* [1990] 2 QB 430 (severance of tenancy).

[280] *Kataria v Safeland plc* [1998] 1 EGLR 39.

[281] (1966) 30 Conv (NS) 429 (D. Macintyre). On the construction of a covenant to insure, see *Farimani v Gates* (1984) 271 EG 887; *Beacon Carpets Ltd v Kirby* [1985] QB 755.

of the covenant to repair and to reinstate, which had occurred before the assignment of 1960. If he could, then King's executors argued that an indemnity by the London County Council should be included in the transfer of the lease.

Held. King's executors were not liable to Tagg.

Upjohn LJ: The first question may be briefly stated in this way: Can a landlord, who has assigned his reversion to a lease, after the date of such assignment, sue the lessee in respect of breaches of covenant which occurred before the assignment? . . .

This case is concerned with express covenants in a lease, and in such case it cannot possibly be doubted that section 141 of the Law of Property Act 1925 governs the situation.

His Lordship read sections (1) and (2) and continued:

I turn, then, to a consideration of the meaning of section 141 and construe the language used in its ordinary and natural meaning, which seems to me quite plain and clear. To illustrate this, consider the case of a lease containing a covenant to build a house according to certain detailed specifications before a certain day. Let me suppose that after that certain day the then lessor assigns the benefit of the reversion to an assignee, and at the time of the assignment the lessee has failed to perform the covenant to build. Who can sue the lessee for breach of covenant? It seems to me clear that the assignee alone can sue. Upon the assignment the benefit of every covenant on the lessee's part to be observed and performed is annexed and incident to and goes with the reversionary estate. The benefit of that covenant to build, therefore, passed; as it had been broken, the right to sue also passed as part of the benefit of the covenant and, incidentally, also the right to re-enter, if that has not been waived. I protest against the argument that because a right to sue is itself a chose in action it, therefore, has become severed from, and independent of, the parent covenant; on the contrary it remains part of it. The right to sue on breach is merely one of the bundle of rights that are contained in the concept 'benefit of every covenant'. . . . To return to my example. Suppose the right to sue for breach of that covenant did not pass, and that right remained in the assignor, then the assignee would take the lease without the benefit of that covenant and he could never enforce it. So he has not got the benefit of every covenant contained in the lease and the words of the section are not satisfied. That cannot be right. . . .

Then suppose the lease contains a covenant to keep in repair which is broken at the date of the assignment, and that at all material times the premises were out of repair; that is, a continuing breach. It is an a fortiori case to the example I have just dealt with. Indeed, with all respect to the argument to the contrary, you cannot give any sensible meaning to the words of the section unless the entire benefit of a repairing covenant had passed, leaving the assignor without remedy against the lessee. Look at the absurd results if that were not so. The assignor of the reversion remains at liberty to sue the lessee for breaches down to the moment of the assignment. After assignment he sues and obtains judgment for certain damages. But then the premises are still out of repair and the breach continues. The assignee claims to re-enter or to sue because the premises are out of repair. What is the situation of the lessee? Either he has to pay damages twice or pay damages to the assignor and then reinstate the premises because otherwise the assignee will re-enter. This is impossible. Alternatively, the assignee's right to re-enter or to sue in respect of post assignment breaches is in some way adversely affected by reason of the fact that the assignor has recovered a judgment for damages for pre-assignment breaches; therefore, the benefit of the covenant to keep in repair did not pass wholly to him even in respect of post-assignment breaches. That directly contradicts the words of the section. . . .

In my judgment Tagg's claims fail and I would allow this part of the appeal.

In **London and County (A and D) Ltd v Wilfred Sportsman Ltd** [1971] Ch 764 the Court of Appeal held that section 141 should be similarly interpreted in the case of a covenant to pay rent. RUSSELL LJ said at 784:

The language of section 141 (substantially re-enacting the earlier legislation from 1881 onwards) is such as, in my judgment, to indicate plainly that an assignee of the reversion may sue and re-enter for rent in arrear at the date of the assignment when the right of re-entry has arisen before the assignment.[282] The decision in *Rickett v Green* [1910] 1 KB 253 [p. 480, below] was, therefore, correct.

(b) Burden

LAW OF PROPERTY ACT 1925

142. Obligation of lessor's covenants to run with reversion.—(1) The obligation under a condition or of a covenant entered into by a lessor with reference to the subject-matter of the lease[283] shall, if and as far as the lessor has power to bind the reversionary estate immediately expectant on the term granted by the lease, be annexed and incident to and shall go with that reversionary estate, or the several parts thereof, notwithstanding severance of that reversionary estate, and may be taken advantage of and enforced by the person in whom the term is from time to time vested by conveyance, devolution in law, or otherwise; and, if and as far as the lessor has power to bind the person from time to time entitled to that reversionary estate, the obligation aforesaid may be taken advantage of and enforced against any person so entitled.

(2) This section applies to leases made before or after the commencement of this Act, whether the severance of the reversionary estate was effected before or after such commencement:

Provided that, where the lease was made before the first day of January eighteen hundred and eighty-two, nothing in this section shall affect the operation of any severance of the reversionary estate effected before such commencement.

This section takes effect without prejudice to any liability affecting a covenantor or his estate.

Section 142 has been interpreted differently from section 141. It is the tenant and not the assignee who is entitled to sue for breach of a covenant committed by the landlord before the tenant assigned the lease.

In **City and Metropolitan Properties Ltd v Greycroft Ltd**[284] [1987] 1 WLR 1085 the landlord bought a flat in Belsize Court, London NW3 subject to a 99-year lease. In

---

[282] *Arlesford Trading Co Ltd v Servansingh* [1971] 1 WLR 1080 (assignee of reversion recovered rent against lessee who had assigned his lease before the reversion was assigned, so that there was neither privity of contract nor of estate between the parties).

[283] The obligation may be expressed in a side-letter; *System Floors Ltd v Ruralpride Ltd* [1995] 1 EGLR 48; *Lotteryking Ltd v AMEC Properties Ltd* [1995] NPC 55; cf. s. 141, where the covenant must be contained in the lease: *Weg Motors Ltd v Hales* [1962] Ch 49 at 73.

[284] [1987] Conv 374 (P. F. Smith).

1982 the tenant acquired the lease by assignment when the landlord was in serious breach of the covenant to repair. In 1984 the tenant sold the lease again and claimed damages for losses suffered while it was tenant. In holding that the landlord was liable, JOHN MOWBRAY QC said at 1086:

The landlord's first defence is that, when the tenant assigned the lease, all its rights passed to the assignee, including any right to damages such as are claimed under the pre-existing specially indorsed writ, so the tenant has no cause of action left to support its claim. In my view that defence is not well founded. No authority was cited on the precise question whether a tenant who has assigned his lease can afterwards recover damages from the landlord for breaches of the landlord's covenants committed while the tenant held the lease. It is common ground, though, that a tenant (not the original lessee) who has assigned his lease again remains liable to the landlord for breaches of covenant which he committed while tenant: see Megarry and Wade, *The Law of Real Property*, 5th edn (1984), p. 750, para. 5, Woodfall, *Landlord and Tenant*, 28th edn (1978), vol. 1, para. 1–1095 and *Halsbury's Laws of England*, 4th edn, vol. 27 (1981), para. 395. Both this liability and the benefit of the landlord's covenants run with the lease at common law by privity of estate under *Spencer's Case* (1583) 5 Co.Rep. 16a: see *Smith's Leading Cases*, 13th edn (1929), vol. 1, p. 51. There is a close analogy between the two. I take the view that, by this analogy, the landlord's liability to the tenant for existing breaches survives the assignment of the lease, in the same way as the tenant's liability to the landlord.

Mr Moss argued for the landlord here that the tenant's rights against the landlord did not survive the assignment of the lease, because on the assignment section 142(1) of the Law of Property Act 1925 made a statutory transfer of the tenant's rights to the assignee of the lease. Section 142(1) reads: ...

Mr Moss argued that the middle part of section 142(1) carried out the transfer, that is the words 'and may be taken advantage of and enforced by the person in whom the tenant is from time to time vested by conveyance, devolution in law, or otherwise.' He pointed out that the Court of Appeal has held section 141(1) to make a statutory transfer of the whole benefit of a tenant's covenant to an assignee of the reversion: *Re King* [1963] Ch 459 [p. 467, above] and *London and County (A & D) Ltd v Wilfred Sportsman Ltd.* [1971] Ch 764 [p. 469, above]. He asked me to apply that principle by analogy to an assignment of the lease.

It is not possible to apply those decisions. They turned on words corresponding to the first part of section 142(1), 'shall ... be annexed and incident to and shall go with that reversionary estate ...' The middle passage of section 142(1) is quite different. It does not say that the right to take advantage of the landlord's covenants is annexed or incident to the term, or "shall go with" it, the graphic phrase specially relied on by Diplock LJ in *Re King* [1963] Ch 459, 497. It is not possible to apply the Court of Appeal decisions to the middle passage. If the intention had been to effect a statutory transfer of the right to an assignee of the term, I should have expected words to have been used similar to those in section 141(1) and the beginning of section 142(1) itself. What is more, the middle passage of section 142(1) does not on its separate interpretation show any intention to restrict a tenant's proceedings to any particular period. The words 'from time to time' mean as occasion may require. If the intention had been to limit the tenant's right to recover damages to the time when he was tenant, I should have expected the subsections to say 'for the time being.'

Mr Moss said that these conclusions could lead to anomaly and injustice, particularly that both assignor and assignee tenants might attack the landlord for the disrepair and both recover damages for it, which could overlap. He very reasonably referred to *Re King,* on this point, in the judgment of Upjohn LJ, at p. 489, and Diplock LJ, at p. 498. I do not see how there can be any overlap in the present case, because the repairs were done before the assignment. The mere consequential damages of the assignor are personal and could not overlap any consequential damages of an assignee, who, in the present case, could not suffer any damage anyhow. It is true that a possible overlap of rights could occur in a case where disrepair continued over the assignment, but section 142 would not prevent the assignee's damages from being reduced to allow for his having bought cheaply because of the disrepair: contrast section 141(1) and *Re King* at p. 489.

Mr Moss also said that there could be several successive assignors who sold at depressed prices during the disrepair and each sued the landlord for the shortfall. I think this is a rather fanciful apprehension. It could only arise if the landlord delayed so long that a number of successive tenants sold in despair or disgust. Even where the disrepair lasted over the assignment, I do not see how any consequential damage to assignor or assignee could overlap, because each would be personal damages arising from the plaintiff's personal circumstances. I conclude that the first defence which I have been considering, based on section 142(1) of the Law of Property Act 1925, fails.

(iv) Privity of estate and privity of contract

Subject to the situation discussed in (e) below, liability under, and the right to sue upon, covenants running with the land or the reversion exists only between persons between whom there is privity of estate. The original contracting parties are liable to each other contractually and remain so liable: assignees are liable and able to sue only if, and so long as, they hold the estate with which the covenant runs; and such persons must be assignees and not sub-lessees or squatters.[285]

(a) General principles

In **City of London Corporation v Fell** [1994] 1 AC 458 LORD TEMPLEMAN said at 464:

The principle that the benefit and burden of covenants in a lease which touch and concern the land run with the term and with the reversion is necessary for the effective operation of the law of landlord and tenant. Common law, and statute following the common law, recognise two forms of legal estate in land, a fee simple absolute in possession and a term of years absolute: see section 1 of the Act of 1925. Common law, and statute following the common law, were faced with the problem of rendering effective the obligations under a lease which might endure for a period of 999 years or more beyond the control of any covenantor. The solution was to annex to the term and the reversion the benefit and burden of covenants which touch and concern the land. The covenants having been annexed, every legal owner of the term granted by the lease and every legal owner of the reversion from time to time holds his estate with the benefit of and subject to the covenants which touch and concern the land. The system of leasehold tenure requires that the obligations in the lease shall be enforceable throughout the term, whether those obligations are affirmative or negative. The owner of a reversion must be able

---

[285] Below, pp. 475–476.

to enforce the positive covenants to pay rent and keep in repair against an assignee who in turn must be able to enforce any positive covenants entered into by the original landlord. Common law retained the ancient rule that the burden of a covenant does not run with the land of the covenantor except in the case of a lease, but even that rule was radically modified by equity so far as negative covenants were concerned: see *Tulk v Moxhay* (1848) 2 Ph 774 [p. 754, below].

The effect of common law and statute on a lease is to create rights and obligations which are independent of the parallel rights and obligations of the original human covenantor who and whose heirs may fail or the parallel rights and obligations of a corporate covenantor which may be dissolved. Common law and statute achieve that effect by annexing those rights and obligations so far as they touch and concern the land to the term and to the reversion. Nourse LJ neatly summarised the position when he said in an impeccable judgment [1993] QB 589, 604:

> 'The contractual obligations which touch and concern the land having become imprinted on the estate, the tenancy is capable of existence as a species of property independently of the contract.'

The common law did not release the original tenant from liability for breaches of covenant committed after an assignment because of the sacred character of covenant in English law. I understand that Scots law releases the original tenant once he has been replaced by a permitted or accepted assignee. This only means that the fortunate English landlord has two remedies after an assignment, namely his remedy against the assignee and his remedy against the original tenant. It does not follow that if the liability of the original tenant is released or otherwise disappears then the term granted by the lease will disappear or that the assignee will cease to be liable on the covenants.

As between landlord and assignee the landlord cannot enforce a covenant against the assignee because the assignee does not covenant. The landlord enforces against the assignee the provisions of a covenant entered into by the original tenant, being provisions which touch and concern the land, because those provisions are annexed by the lease to the term demised by the lease. The assignee is not liable for a breach of covenant committed after the assignee has himself in turn assigned the lease because once he has assigned over he has ceased to be the owner of the term to which the covenants are annexed.

Covenants are introduced on the creation of a lease but are not necessary to sustain a lease. Upon an assignment of a lease, the provisions of the covenants by the original tenant continue to attach to the term because those provisions touch and concern the land and not because there continues to exist an original tenant who has ceased to own any interest in the demised land but remains liable in contract to fulfil the promises he made under covenant.

(b) Plight of original parties

1. Original tenant

The continuing liability of an original tenant in contract is a serious hazard. He may have long since disposed of his property and then find himself being made liable for breaches of covenant which occurred after the assignment, in particular, where an assignee over whom he has no control breaks the covenant to pay rent or to repair.[286]

---

[286] See *City of London Corpn v Fell* [1994] 1 AC 458 (where lease assigned by original tenant had run its term and been extended under Landlord and Tenant Act 1954, Part II, original tenant's obligations held to cease on completion of term); [1994] CLJ 28 (S. Bridge); cf. *Herbert Duncan Ltd v Gluttons* [1993] QB 589;

M. Davey, 'Privity of Contract and Leases' (1996) 59 MLR 78 at pp. 81–83

The original tenant had very few means of protecting himself save by verifying the credit-worthiness of his immediate assignee as well as insisting on the presence of a clause in the original lease which compelled the landlord to take a direct covenant from that assignee.[287] The most obvious form of protection was for the first assignor to take an express indemnity[288] from his assignee who on a further assignment would have taken an indemnity from his assignee and so on, enabling liability to be ultimately revisited on the assignee in default. In addition the original tenant had a quasi-contractual claim against the defaulting assignee.[289] The weakness of these remedies was obvious. As far as the express (or statutory) indemnity was concerned it was always possible that there would turn out to have been an assignment at some stage where an indemnity had not been taken, thereby breaking the chain. But even more serious, in the case of both the express (or statutory) indemnity and the quasi-contractual claim, was the fact that the assignee in default would prove to be not worth suing. Indeed this would usually be the case if the landlord had felt it necessary to resort to the original tenant. Furthermore, if the defaulting tenant became insolvent and the lease was disclaimed by the trustee in bankruptcy, the assignee and his guarantor would be freed from liability.[290] But this afforded no relief to the former tenant, because his liability (and that of his surety[291]) remained unaffected.[292] Even if the former tenant was in a position to have recourse by way of indemnity to an insolvent tenant he would only have been an ordinary creditor of the insolvent estate. However, a small measure of relief was provided by the rule that if there were a solvent guarantor of a later assignee, an original tenant who was sued was entitled to be indemnified by that guarantor.[293]

[1993] Conv 164 (P. F. Smith). See also *Norwich Union Life Insurance Society v Low Profile Fashions Ltd* [1992] 1 EGLR 86; [1992] CLJ 425 (S. Bridge) (no duty of care on landlord to ensure solvency of assignee when consenting to assignment, and no equitable principle which obliges landlord to sue assignees and his surety before original tenant).

[287] By this means the assignee could be made liable for breaches which occurred even after any further disposal of the lease by assignment when privity of estate between himself and the landlord would have ceased: *Estates Gazette Ltd v Benjamin Restaurants Ltd* [[1994] 1 WLR 1528]. Qualified covenants against disposition have usually made this a condition of granting a licence to assign. By contrast it was not usual practice for an assignee of the reversion to covenant directly with the original tenant.

[288] An express indemnity would extend the liability of the assignee to breaches of any of the lease covenants committed at any time during the remainder of the term. A statutory indemnity to the same effect applied in the case of assignments for valuable consideration of leases to which title was unregistered: LPA 1925, s. 77(1)(c), Sch. 2, Pt IX whilst in the case of registered titles the indemnity applied to all transfers by way of assignment: LRA 1925, s. 24(1). [The implied statutory covenant is one of indemnity and not guarantee: *Scottish & Newcastle plc v Raguz (No. 1)* [2004] L & TR 11.]

[289] *Moule v Garrett* (1872) LR 7 Exch 101, 104.

[290] Insolvency Act 1986, s. 315. A similar rule applies in relation to a disclaimer by the liquidator of an insolvent company; ibid., s. 178.

[291] *Warnford Investments v Duckworth* [1979] Ch 127.

[292] See *Hindcastle Ltd v Barbara Attenborough Associates Ltd* [1995] QB 95 [affd [1997] AC 707; *Doleman v Shaw* [2009] 14 EG 86 (cs)].

[293] *Becton Dickinson UK Ltd v Zwebner* [1989] QB 208, 217. [*Re A Debtor (No 21 of 1995)* [1995] NPC 170. Other defences available are fraught with difficulty:

(a) surrender and regrant: *Jenkin R. Lewis Ltd v Kerman* [1971] Ch 477; [1995] Conv 124 (A. Dowling); *Friends' Provident Life Office v British Railways Board* [1996] 1 All ER 336;

(b) release by accord and satisfaction: *Deanplan Ltd v Mahmoud* [1993] Ch 151, [1993] 143 NLJ 23 (H. W. Wilkinson); *Sun Life Assurance Society plc v Tantofex (Engineers) Ltd* [1999] 2 EGLR 135; *Allied*

The unfortunate plight of former tenants was highlighted by a series of reported cases in the early 1980s when a number of tenants were held liable for very large sums attributable to breaches of covenant by assignees.[294]

2. Original landlord

In **Stuart v Joy** [1904] 1 KB 362 Cozens-Hardy LJ said at 368:

In my opinion, the position of the lessor with respect to covenants running with the reversion is now precisely similar to the position of the lessee with respect to covenants running with the lease. In neither case is liability extinguished by assignment.[295]

M. Davey, 'Privity of Contract and Leases' (1996) 59 MLR 78 at pp. 83, 81

The precarious position of former tenants was in marked contrast to that of the landlord who would invariably have reserved to himself the power to approve the identity of a proposed assignee. In addition the landlord had the powerful remedy of forfeiture in the event of non compliance with a covenant by the present tenant. Even worse from the tenant's point of view, were cases where the landlord preferred to have recourse to the original tenant for unpaid rent because market rental levels had fallen since the lease was granted and therefore he would not benefit by repossessing and reletting the property which might be occupied by the tenant in default or have been abandoned. In those circumstances the original tenant might have preferred to be able to have recourse to the leasehold property, but was unable to do so in the absence of a provision for re-entry in the assignment itself.

Finally, it should be noted that it had long been standard practice for landlords to require a tenant or, in cases where a direct covenant was required, an assignee, to provide a surety for performance of the tenant's covenants in the lease. The contractual liability of such a surety was normally, unless restricted, co-extensive with that of the principal debtor.[296] The benefit of

---

London Investments Ltd v Hambro Life Assurance Ltd [1984] 1 EGLR 16; *Mytre Investments Ltd v Reynolds* [1995] 3 All ER 588; *March Estates plc v Gunmark Ltd* [1996] 2 EGLR 38.

(c) disclaimer by liquidator or trustee in bankruptcy: *Hindcastle Ltd v Barbara Attenborough Associates Ltd*, above; [1997] Conv 24 (T. Taylor); *Scottish Widows plc v Tripipatkul* [2004] 1 P & CR 29; *Groveholt Ltd v Hughes*. See generally [1996] CLJ 313 at 319 (S. Bridge).

[294] See also the examples cited by the Law Commission which included claims against a retired couple whose income was barely above social security level and a former shopkeeper who faced a claim for £10,000 under a lease which he had assigned when the rent was £450 a year. Law Com No. 174, (1988) para. 3.8.

The catalyst for the Landlord and Tenant (Covenants) Act 1995 was *Centrovincial Estates plc v Bulk Storage Ltd* (1983) 46 P & CR 393, where an original tenant was held to be contractually liable for a substantial increase in rent due to the operation by the landlord and his assignee of a rent review clause in the lease. This decision was undermined by CA in *Friends Provident Life Office v British Railways Board* [1996] 1 All ER 336; *Beegas Nominees Ltd v BHP Petroleum Ltd* [1998] 2 EGLR 57. See now Landlord and Tenant (Covenants) Act 1995, s. 18, p. 475, below.

On release of a surety by variation, see *Metropolitan Properties Co Ltd v Bartholomew* [1996] 1 EGLR 82; *Howard de Walden Estates Ltd v Pasta Place Ltd* [1995] 1 EGLR 79.]

[295] See *City and Metropolitan Properties Ltd v Greycroft Ltd* [1987] 1 WLR 1085, p. 469, above; *Celsteel Ltd v Alton House Holdings Ltd (No 2)* [1987] 1 WLR 291 at 296.

[296] *Thames Manufacturing Co Ltd v Perrotts (Nichol & Peyton) Ltd* (1984) 271 EG 284, 287, cf. *Johnsey Estates Ltd v Webb* [[1990] 1 EGLR 80]. But note that under the general law, if the obligation of the principal

such a covenant would pass to any subsequent assignee of the landlord's estate by virtue of the common law rules governing covenants affecting freehold land.[297]

(c) Statutory protection for original tenant

The Landlord and Tenant (Covenants) Act 1995 imposes restrictions on the contractual liability of a former tenant or his guarantor after assignment of the tenancy. Sections 17–20, which apply to all tenancies whether created before or after the Act, are mentioned here in brief outline.

1. Restriction on liability for fixed charge

Under section 17 there can only be liability for a 'fixed charge' (i.e. arrears of rent or service charge, or liquidated damages for breach of a tenant covenant) if the landlord serves a prescribed notice[298] on the former tenant or his guarantor within six months of the date when the fixed charge becomes due.

2. Right to overriding lease

Under sections 19 and 20 a former tenant or his guarantor who has paid a fixed charge under section 17 may have an overriding lease granted to him. He can then pursue remedies directly against the defaulting tenant, if he is still in occupation, or take possession and make use of the property so that he can set off the return against his liability. In estate terms the former tenant is slotted into the hierarchy of interests.

3. Restriction on liability for post assignment variation

Under section 18 a former tenant or his guarantor are not liable to pay any amount which is attributable to the variation of a covenant effected after assignment.

(d) Assignees and sub-tenants

Assignees are liable and able to sue only if, and so long as, they hold the estate with which the covenant runs; and such persons must be assignees and not sublessees[299] or squatters.[300]

---

debtor were changed or if the creditor allowed him any time or indulgence, his guarantor was released unless, as was frequently the case in practice, the guarantee provided otherwise.

[297] *P & A Swift Investments v Combined English Stores Group plc* [[1989] AC 632, p. 463, above].

[298] Landlord and Tenant (Covenants) Act 1995 (Notices) Regulations 1995, Sch., Form 1 (SI 1995 No. 2964); *Cheverell Estates Ltd v Harris* [1998] 1 EGLR 27 (where guarantor is to be sued, notice need not also be served on former tenant as well); *Commercial Union Life Assurance Co Ltd v Moustafa* [1999] 2 EGLR 44 (notice is properly served if sent to intended recipient at his last residential address, whether it was received by that recipient or not); *Scottish & Newcastle plc v Raguz* [2008] 1 WLR 2494 (sum to be specified in notice is the sum of rent currently payable, not unquantified sum that would become quantified and accordingly payable at some unknown date in the future). The amount recoverable may be less than the amount specified in the notice under s. 17(4); *Kellogg v Tobin* [1999] L & TR 513; [1999] EG 25 May p. 152 (D. Stevens) (former tenants must receive notices from landlord in order to obtain indemnity).

[299] *South of England Dairies Ltd v Baker* [1906] 2 Ch 631. A restrictive convenant can be enforced against a sub-tenant: *Hemingway Securities Ltd v Dunraven Ltd* [1995] 1 EGLR 61 (breach of covenant against subletting).

[300] *Tichborne v Weir* (1982) 67 LT 735, p. 759, below.

In **South of England Dairies v Baker** [1906] 2 Ch 631, the freeholder of certain property demised it for 21 years and covenanted to pay all rates and taxes (except one third of the water rate). In the following year, the lessee sub-demised the premises to the plaintiff (a company formed by the lessee) for the remainder of his term less three days. Seven years later the freeholder sold the fee simple subject to the lease to the defendant, who in the following year accepted the surrender of the lease from the original lessee. The plaintiff, the sub-tenant, was compelled by the Local Authority to pay the rates, and sought to recover damages from the defendant under the landlord's covenant to pay all rates and taxes. Joyce J held that the defendant was not liable since the plaintiff was not an assignee of the original lessee and was unable therefore to enforce the covenant originally given to the lessee.

In **Milmo v Carreras** [1946] KB 306, the plaintiff was tenant of a flat under a 7-year lease, expiring on 28 November 1944. In October 1943, he agreed to sublet the flat to the defendant for one year from 1 November 1943, 'and thereafter quarterly until such time as' one of the parties should give three months' notice to terminate. The plaintiff gave such notice on returning from active service in 1945.

The Court of Appeal (Lord Greene MR, Morton and Bucknill LJJ) held that the notice was bad because the plaintiff retained no reversion. LORD GREENE MR said at 310:

> For the purposes of this case, I think it is sufficient to say that, in accordance with a very ancient and established rule, where a lessee, by a document in the form of a sub-lease, divests himself of everything that he has got (which he must necessarily do if he is transferring to his so-called sub-lessee an estate as great as, or purporting to be greater than, his own) he from that moment is a stranger to the land, in the sense that the relationship of landlord and tenant, in respect of tenure, cannot any longer exist between him and the so-called sub-lessee. That relationship must depend on privity of estate. I myself find it impossible to conceive of a relationship of land-lord and tenant which has not got that essential element of tenure in it, and that implies that the tenant holds of his landlord, and he can only do that if the landlord has a reversion. You cannot have a purely contractual tenure. Tenure exists by reason of privity of estate. That seems to me to be the effect of all the decisions, and that position is recognised by all the decisions.[301]

(e) Agreements for leases

The question of the enforcement of covenants after assignment raises different issues where there has been no grant of a lease, but merely an agreement for a lease.[302] First, it used to be said that covenants could run with land at common law only if created under seal,[303] but this rule has since been changed.[304] Secondly, there is no privity of estate between persons who have entered into a contract for a lease or between their

---

[301] *Parc Battersea Ltd v Hutchinson* [1999] 2 EGLR 35 (oral sub-tenancy effective on assignment by operation of law).

[302] See pp. 29–34, 418–421, above.

[303] *Manchester Brewery Co v Coombs* [1901] 2 Ch 608, p. 478, below.

[304] *Boyer v Warbey* [1953] 1 QB 234, p. 481, below.

assigns;[305] nor between the lessor and one who has contracted to take an assignment from a lessee.[306]

Since the benefit of a covenant can be assigned at law, there is no difficulty in holding that the benefit of a covenant runs with the freehold reversion;[307] and it appears that the benefit will run also by virtue of Law of Property Act 1925, section 141,[308] and, if this is so, the burden will run also with the reversion under section 142. It is usually held that the benefit but not the burden of covenants will run on the assignment of an agreement for a lease;[309] an assignee may be liable under an implied agreement if he enters into possession and pays rent,[310] or on grounds of estoppel.[311] His freedom from liability under the covenant may cause great hardship to the lessor, and the question is whether this is a necessary limitation.

The rule seems to have developed from the independence of law and equity before the Judicature Acts. There could be no liability at law after the assignment because there was no privity of estate; in equity, the question was whether or not specific performance of the agreement would be given, and the question of monetary liability under the covenants pending the grant of specific performance did not arise. There appears to be no reason why, since the Judicature Acts, the doctrine of *Walsh v Lonsdale* should not be applied and the monetary liability of the defendant determined *as if* the decree of specific performance had been granted. The dicta in *Boyer v Warbey* [1953] 1 QB 234, p. 481, below, indicate that 'nowadays' the rules relating to the running of covenants should be the same, whether the lease which has been assigned is legal or equitable. Further, as has been seen, the Court of Appeal in *Industrial Properties (Barton Hill) Ltd v Associated Electrical Industries Ltd* [1977] QB 580, p. 31, above held, as an alternative ground for supporting the judgment, that the doctrine of *Walsh v Lonsdale* applied where an equitable owner had purported to grant a lease; the effect was to treat the equitable lease as a legal lease, and thus enable the owner to sue for damages for breach of covenant in the lease.

The older cases are to the contrary. The only case in which the issue appears to have arisen since the Judicature Acts is *Purchase v Lichfield Brewery* [1915] 1 KB 184, which was, however, one of assignment by way of mortgage. It is submitted that the trend of the modern cases should be supported, and that the court should hold that the liability, both of the assignee of an equitable lease and that of the equitable assignee of a legal lease, is the same as it would be if specific performance had been granted.[312]

---

[305] *Purchase v Lichfield Brewery Co* [1915] 1 KB 184, p. 480, below.

[306] *Cox v Bishop* (1857) 8 De GM & G 815, p. 480, below; *Friary, Holroyd, and Healey's Breweries Ltd v Singleton* [1899] 1 Ch 86.

[307] *Manchester Brewery Co v Coombs*, above.

[308] *Rickets v Green* [1910] 1 KB 253; *Rye v Purcell* [1926] 1 KB 446; *London and County (A and D) Ltd v Wilfred Sportsman Ltd* [1971] Ch 764.

[309] *Marquis of Camden v Batterbury* (1860) 7 CBNS 864; *Purchase v Lichfield Brewery Co*, above.

[310] *Buckworth v Simpson* (1835) 1 Cr M & R 834; *Cornish v Stubbs* (1870) LR 5 CP 334 at 338–339.

[311] *Ashe v Hogan* [1920] 1 IR 159; *Rodenhurst Estates Ltd v WH Barnes Ltd* [1936] 2 All ER 3.

[312] [1978] CLJ 98 (R. J. Smith).

These problems disappear where a lease or an agreement for a lease are created after 1995. Under section 28(1) of the Landlord and Tenant (Covenants) Act 1995, p. 484, below, equitable leases and equitable assignments are treated in the same way as their legal counterparts.

1. Benefit

Manchester Brewery Co v Coombs
[1901] 2 Ch 608 (ChD, **Farwell J**)

By an agreement under seal dated 10 December 1892 between the defendant and Broadbents Ltd, who were brewers, the defendant, who alone executed the deed, undertook to take a yearly tenancy of a hotel, and covenanted with 'Broadbents Ltd and their successors in business' to buy all his liquor from them. The covenant did not mention 'assigns'.

In June 1899, Broadbents sold their business to the plaintiffs, who gave notice of the purchase to the defendant. The defendant continued to take his supplies from the plaintiffs until December, when he ceased to buy from them. They brought this action for an injunction to restrain a breach of the covenant contained in the deed of 1892.

Held. The plaintiffs were entitled to the benefit of the covenant.

Farwell J (after holding that the covenant was not, on its construction, a mere personal covenant confined to beer brewed at the original brewery which no longer operated): The last point taken by Mr Younger rests on the fact that the agreement of 10 December 1892 was not executed by the landlords. Having regard to the construction that I have put on the covenant, it could not be contended that it is not of such a nature as to run with the land. But it is said that, in order to arrive at the conclusion that it does run with the land, the Court must first find that an estate has been duly created at law in the land with which the covenant can run, or, in other words, that there must be privity of estate between lessor and lessee, and that such estate can only be created by deed duly executed by the lessor, and that this is borne out by 32 Hen 8, c 34, which applies only to leases by deed. This is undoubtedly sound—e.g., it has been held that a lease by mortgagor and mortgagee, in which the covenants to repair were with the mortgagor and his assigns, did not enable an assign of the mortgagee to maintain an action on the covenant.

His Lordship referred to *Webb v Russel* (1789) 3 Term Rep 393 per Lord Kenyon at 402, and to *Standen v Christmas* (1847) 10 QB 135, and continued:

But it by no means follows that the plaintiffs would have failed in every form of action, even before the Judicature Acts; still less that they must fail now. Before the Judicature Acts the plaintiffs might have succeeded if they had sued on the new contract implied from the conduct of the tenant and the assignee of the landlord, instead of suing on the original contract between the tenant and the landlord....

His Lordship then found that the defendant agreed that the plaintiffs should occupy the position of landlords to him in the same way as Broadbents Ltd had done, and continued:

There is, moreover, another point which is fatal to the defendant. The defendant holds under an agreement for a lease from Broadbents Limited, under which he has been in possession and paid rent for several years. The whole contract has been performed up to the present time, except that the legal estate has not been actually demised. The defendant would have no defence to an action for specific performance, the sole object of which would be to compel him to accept the legal estate. If Broadbents Limited had not parted with the legal estate, I see no reason why they should not now execute the deed in order to complete the transaction. The present plaintiffs are the assigns of the benefit of the agreement both by implication from the conveyance of the land subject to the lease, and by the express words of clause 26 of the agreement of 29 March 1899. The plaintiffs could, therefore, obtain specific performance in this court of the contract so far as it is incomplete... Holding, therefore, as I do, that the plaintiffs could obtain specific performance against the defendant, I find it laid down by the Court of Appeal that since the Judicature Acts there are not in such a case as this two estates as there were formerly, one at common law by reason of the payment of the rent, and another in equity under the agreement, but the tenant holds under the same terms, and has the same rights and liabilities as if a lease had been granted: *Walsh v Lonsdale* (1882) 21 ChD 9, approved by Cotton LJ in *Lowther v Heaven* (1889) 41 ChD 248, 264, and explained by Lord Esher in *Swain v Ayres* (1888) 21 QBD 289, 292 and *Foster v Reeves* [1892] 2 QB 255. Although it has been suggested that the decision in *Walsh v Lonsdale* takes away all differences between the legal and equitable estate, it, of course, does nothing of the sort, and the limits of its applicability are really somewhat narrow. It applies only to cases where there is a contract to transfer a legal title, and an act has to be justified or an action maintained by force of the legal title to which such contract relates. It involves two questions: (1) Is there a contract of which specific performance can be obtained? (2) If Yes, will the title acquired by such specific performance justify at law the act complained of, or support at law the action in question? It is to be treated as though before the Judicature Acts there had been, first, a suit in equity for specific performance, and then an action at law between the same parties; and the doctrine is applicable only in those cases where specific performance can be obtained between the same parties in the same court, and at the same time as the subsequent legal question falls to be determined. Thus, in *Walsh v Lonsdale*, the landlord under an agreement for a lease for a term of seven years distrained. Distress is a legal remedy and depends on the existence at law of the relation of landlord and tenant; but the agreement between the same parties, if specifically enforced, created that relation. It was clear that such an agreement would be enforced in the same court and between the same parties: the act of distress was therefore held to be lawful. So in the present case I have already stated that specific performance can be granted between the parties to this action. I must treat it therefore as granted, and I then find that the result justifies this action. It is not necessary to call in aid this doctrine in matters that are purely equitable; its existence is due entirely to the divergence of legal and equitable rights between the same parties, nor does it affect the rights of third parties. Thus, a contract by a landowner to sell the fee simple of land in possession to A. would not enable A. to maintain an action of ejectment or trespass against a third person because such actions are purely legal actions requiring the legal estate and possession respectively to support them, and the contract relied on is not made with the defendant....

I hold, therefore, on this point, that the plaintiffs, being clearly entitled in this court against the defendant to specific performance of the agreement under which the defendant has been for years and still is in possession of the land, can sue him on the covenants in the same manner as they could have done if Broadbents had actually executed the original agreement....

The result is that I grant the injunction as asked, and order the defendant to pay the costs of the action.

In **Rickett v Green** [1910] 1 KB 253, one of the questions was whether or not the plaintiff, as assignee of the freehold, was entitled to demand rent from the defendant who held the premises under an agreement for a lease. Darling and Phillimore JJ held that he was entitled to sue by virtue of the Conveyancing Act 1881, section 10 (now Law of Property Act 1925, section 141). DARLING J said at 259:

The question occurred to [the county court judge] whether this tenancy agreement was a 'lease' within the meaning of section 10 of the Act of 1881, inasmuch as the agreement was dated 19 December 1907, and the three years were to run from 25 December 1907, so that the lease was one exceeding three years from the making thereof and, not being under seal, was void at law under section 3 of the Real Property Act 1845. Though at law it may be void as a lease, still in equity it is looked upon as a lease, and in my judgment it must be treated, as between the parties, as if it were a lease under seal. A Court of Equity would look upon the matter as if a lease under seal had been granted. Upon the case to which we have been referred the county court judge came to a right conclusion upon this point, and the agreement must be treated as a 'lease' for the purposes of section 10 of the Act of 1881, and for other purposes also.

2. Burden

In **Cox v Bishop** (1857) 8 De GM & G 815, 44 ER 604, the freeholder brought an action for rent due and for breaches of covenant in a lease. The lessees had contracted to assign the lease to persons who assigned to the defendants. Knight Bruce and Turner LJJ held that the defendants were not liable on the covenants, TURNER LJ saying at 823, at 608:

If, on the other hand, these Defendants are not at law liable to the Plaintiffs, what are the grounds alleged by this bill upon which they are in equity to be made liable? Simply that they have contracted to purchase interests in the lease and have been in possession. The contracts to purchase, however, are not contracts with the Plaintiffs, and there is nothing in the bill to shew that the Plaintiffs are in any manner entitled to the benefit of those contracts, and if the Defendants are liable by virtue of their possession, the liability, as I apprehend, is to be enforced at law and not in equity. Courts of equity do not, as I think, in ordinary cases, decree the payment of rent or the performance of covenants upon a mere agreement for a lease. In such cases the Court does not treat the relation of landlord and tenant as completed by the agreement, and decree the rent to be paid and the covenants to be performed accordingly, but it decrees the execution of the lease, and leaves the parties to their remedies at law consequent upon the relation created by the execution of it. To take, however, a case more near to the present, suppose, in the case of an agreement for a lease the intended lessee has assigned the benefit of the contract, can this Court, at the instance of the intended lessor, enforce the payment of the rent or the performance of the covenants by the assignee of the contract. I take it most clearly not; for there is no privity of contract between the lessor and the assignee; but if this cannot be done where there is a mere contract for a lease, upon what principle it is to be done where there is an actual lease and the lessee has agreed to assign.

Purchase v Lichfield Brewery Co
[1915] 1 KB 184 (KBD, **Horridge and Lush JJ**)

The plaintiff, in writing but not under seal, purported to grant to Lunnis a 15-year lease of a house, the agreement containing a proviso that Lunnis would not assign the term without the plaintiff's consent, such consent not to be unreasonably refused. On the following day Lunnis assigned by way of mortgage his interest to the defendant, who never went into possession. The rent being unpaid, the plaintiff claimed from the defendant (mortgagee) the rent due under the agreement.

Held. In the absence of privity of contract or estate the defendant was not liable.

Lush J (agreeing with Horridge J): I am of the same opinion. The only point which the county court judge decided was that the present case was governed by *Williams v Bosanquet* (1819) 1 Brod & Bing 238. In my view that case does not apply. The lease in question there was under seal. It was assigned by deed to mortgagees. That was a valid assignment. The only question was whether the mortgagees, not having taken possession, were bound by the covenants in the lease. It was held that they were bound. In this case there was no lease under seal. No term was created as between lessor and lessee. Therefore the question decided in *Williams v Bosanquet* does not arise in this case. Consequently the judgment of the county court judge cannot stand on the grounds on which he has based it.

Then can the judgment be supported on other grounds? I do not think it is necessary to say how the case might have stood if the defendants had ever taken possession. They are liable, if at all, on the principle of *Walsh v Lonsdale* (1882) 21 ChD 9. In that case the tenant was in possession under the agreement. In the present case the defendants never did take possession. The agreement contained a provision against assigning. The defendants were only mortgagees. It does not follow from *Walsh v Lonsdale* that a Court of Equity would decree specific performance against mere mortgagees who only took an assignment by way of security. In my opinion it would leave the parties to their position at law. Accordingly the matter stands thus: A tenant under an agreement, whose only title to call himself a lessee depends on his right to specific performance of the agreement, assigns his right to assignees. The assignees never had a term vested in them because no term was ever created; therefore there was never privity of estate. They never went into possession or were recognised by the landlord; therefore there was never privity of contract. It is impossible that specific performance of a contract can be decreed against a person with whom there is neither privity of contract nor privity of estate. Therefore these assignees are not liable to perform the terms of the agreement and this appeal must be allowed.

In **Boyer v Warbey** [1953] 1 QB 234 one question was whether a covenant by a tenant in a written lease of a flat within the Rent Restriction Acts to pay £40 towards the cost of redecoration 'immediately after the expiration or determination of the tenancy' was binding on an assignee of the tenant.

The lease was for 3 years; within nine days of the expiration of term, the lessee assigned the lease to the defendant who, on the expiry of the nine days, became a statutory tenant, subject to all the terms of the original tenancy 'so far as the same are consistent with the provisions of this Act.'[313] It was held, inter alia, that the covenant to pay the £40 became a term of the statutory tenancy.

DENNING LJ said at 245:

Seeing that the agreement touched and concerned the thing demised, it ran with the land so as to bind the assignee, the tenant, as soon as he entered into possession. I know that before

---

[313] Increase of Rent and Mortgage Interest (Restrictions) Act 1920, s. 15(1); now Rent Act 1977, s. 3(1).

the Judicature Act 1873, it was said that the doctrine of covenants running with the land only applied to covenants under seal and not to agreements under hand. See *Elliot v Johnson* (1868) LR 2 QB 120. But since the fusion of law and equity, the position is different. The distinction between agreements under hand and covenants under seal has been largely obliterated. There is no valid reason nowadays why the doctrine of covenants running with the land—or with the reversion—should not apply equally to agreements under hand as to covenants under seal; and I think we should so hold, not only in the case of agreements for more than three years which need the intervention of equity to perfect them, but also in the case of agreements for three years or less which do not.

QUESTION

A agreed to grant a lease for 99 years to B of valuable land at a rent of £25,000 a year. B assigned his interest to C, and disappeared. C has not yet taken possession. Is he liable for the rent? See C & B, pp. 226–227; Gray, paras 4.5.84–4.5.88; M & W, paras 17.051–17.052; Smith, pp. 380, 441–443; *Purchase v Lichfield Brewery Co* [1915] 1 KB 184, p. 480, above; [1978] CLJ 98 (R. J. Smith).

B. COVENANTS IN POST-1995 LEASES

(i) General nature of the post-1995 code

Law Commission Report on Privity of Contract: Contracts for the Benefit of Third Parties 1996 (Law Com No. 242) Cm 3329, para. 2.11

The law on covenants relating to leasehold land has recently been reformed by the Landlord and Tenant (Covenants) Act 1995.[314] The effect of the 1995 Act can be briefly explained in the following four points:—

(i) The benefit and burden of covenants in a lease granted prior to 1996 would pass on an assignment of the lease or reversion so as to benefit or bind the assignee of the lease or the reversion, provided that the covenant 'touched and concerned' the land.[315] As a result of the Landlord and Tenant (Covenants) Act 1995, in relation to leases granted after 1995, the benefit and burden of *all* covenants in a lease pass on an assignment of the lease or reversion unless the covenant is expressed to be personal.[316] It is now for the parties to decide whether a covenant is to be regarded as personal. It is no longer for the court to try to decide it objectively according to whether it is thought to 'touch and concern' the land.

---

[314] Based on the recommendations made in Landlord and Tenant Law: Privity of Contract and Estate (1988) Law Com No 174.

[315] *Spencer's Case* (1583) 5 Co Rep 16a; 77 ER 72 (leases); LPA 1925, ss. 141–142 (reversions) [p. 465, above].

[316] Landlord and Tenant (Covenants) Act 1995, s. 3(6) [p. 486, below].

(ii) Where, prior to 1996, L granted a lease to T and T then sublet to S, the burden of the covenants in the headlease did *not* bind S, the sublessee, because there was no privity of estate[317] between L and S. This was subject to an exception. If the covenant was a restrictive covenant, it would bind S as an equitable property right, provided that, where the title was unregistered, he had notice of the covenant (as he would in practice)[318] or, where the title was registered, in any event.[319] In leases granted after 1995, this rule is codified. A restrictive covenant in the headlease binds any sublessee automatically.[320]

(iii) Where, prior to 1996, L granted a lease to T and T then sublet to S, S *could* enforce the benefit of any landlord covenants which touched and concerned the land against L, despite the absence of privity of contract. This is because the benefit of such covenants was annexed under section 78 of the Law of Property Act 1925 and could be enforced by a person with a derivative interest.[321] In a lease granted after 1995, this is no longer possible.[322] S cannot enforce any covenant in the headlease against L.

(iv) For leases granted prior to 1996, the original tenant and landlord remained liable for a breach of covenant in the lease despite assignment. For leases granted after 1995 the original tenant[323] will generally be released from covenants in the lease once the lease has been assigned.[324] This aspect of the reforms is concerned to cut back a normal feature of privity of contract rather than being concerned with the exception to privity of contract constituted by covenants running with land.

LANDLORD AND TENANT (COVENANTS) ACT 1995[325]

1. Tenancies to which the Act applies.—(1) Sections 3 to 16 and 21 apply only to new tenancies.

(2) Sections 17 to 20 apply to both new and other tenancies.[326]

(3) For the purposes of this section a tenancy is a new tenancy if it is granted on or after the date on which this Act comes into force[327] otherwise than in pursuance of—

(a) an agreement entered into before that date, or

(b) an order of a court made before that date.

---

[317] Which simply means the relationship of landlord and tenant.

[318] See LPA 1925, s. 44; *White v Bijou Mansions Ltd* [1937] Ch 610 [p. 462, n. 260, above].

[319] LRA 1925, s. 23(1)(*a*).

[320] Landlord and Tenant (Covenants) Act 1995, s. 3(5) [p. 486, below].

[321] *Smith v River Douglas Catchment Board* [1949] 2 KB 500 (lessee able to enforce annexed freehold covenant on the wording of s. 78). As it is clear that s. 78 applies to leases as well as to freeholds: *Caerns Motor Services Ltd v Texaco Ltd* [1994] 1 WLR 1249, S must be able to enforce the covenant against L. [On the enforcement of freehold restrictive covenants, see below, pp. 773–797.]

[322] LPA 1925, s. 78 does not apply to such leases (Landlord and Tenant (Covenants) Act 1995, s. 30(4)) and this effect of that section is not replicated: cf. Landlord and Tenant (Covenants) Act 1995, s. 15 [p. 486, below].

[323] Somewhat different provisions apply in respect of an assignment of the reversion by the landlord. The landlord must apply to the tenant to be released from the landlord covenants. If the tenant refuses to do so, the court may release the landlord if it considers it reasonable to do so. See Landlord and Tenant (Covenants) Act 1995, ss. 6–8 [pp. 488–490, below].

[324] Landlord and Tenant (Covenants) Act 1995, ss. 3 and 5 [pp. 485, 487, below]; although under s. 16 [p. 495, below] a tenant may enter into an 'authorised guarantee agreement' to guarantee compliance with the covenants by the assignee.

[325] Landlord and Tenant (Covenants) Act 1995 (Notices) Regulations 1995 (SI 1995 No. 2964).

[326] P. 475, above.   [327] 1 January 1996.

(4) Subsection (3) has effect subject to section 20(1) in the case of overriding leases granted under section 19.

(5) Without prejudice to the generality of subsection (3), that subsection applies to the grant of a tenancy where by virtue of any variation of a tenancy there is deemed surrender and regrant as it applies to any other grant of a tenancy.

(6) Where a tenancy granted on or after the date on which this Act comes into force is so granted in pursuance of an option granted before that date, the tenancy shall be regarded for the purposes of subsection (3) as granted in pursuance of an agreement entered into before that date (and accordingly is not a new tenancy), whether or not the option was exercised before that date.

(7) In subsection (6) 'option' includes right of first refusal.

2. Covenants to which the Act applies.—(1) This Act applies to a landlord covenant or a tenant covenant of a tenancy—

(a) whether or not the covenant has reference to the subject matter of tenancy, and

(b) whether the covenant is express, implied or imposed by law,

but does not apply to a covenant falling within subsection (2).

(2) Nothing in this Act affects any covenant imposed in pursuance of—

(a) section 35 or 155 of the Housing Act 1985 (covenants for repayment of discount on early disposals);

(b) paragraph 1 of Schedule 6A to that Act (covenants requiring redemption of landlord's share); or

(c) section 11 or 13 of the Housing Act 1996 or[328] paragraph 1 or 3 of Schedule 2 to the Housing Associations Act 1985 (covenants for repaying of discount on early disposals or for restricting disposals).

28. Interpretation.—(1) In this Act (unless the context otherwise requires)—

'assignment' includes equitable assignment, and in addition (subject to section 11) assignment in breach of a covenant of a tenancy or by operation of law;

'covenant' includes term, condition and obligation, and references to a covenant (or any description of covenant) of a tenancy include a covenant (or a covenant of that description) contained in a collateral agreement;

'landlord' and 'tenant', in relation to a tenancy, mean the person for the time being entitled to the reversion expectant on the term of the tenancy and the person so entitled to that term respectively;

'landlord covenant', in relation to a tenancy, means a covenant falling to be complied with the landlord of premises demised by the tenancy;

'reversion' means the interest expectant on the termination of a tenancy;

'tenancy' means any lease or other tenancy and includes—

(a) a sub-tenancy, and

(b) an agreement for a tenancy,

but does not include a mortgage term;

---

[328] As added by HA 1996 (Consequential Provisions) Order 1996 art 5, Sch. 2, para. 22 (SI 1996 No. 2325).

'tenant covenant', in relation to a tenancy, means a covenant falling to be complied with by the tenant of premises demised by the tenancy.[329]

(ii) Transmission of covenants

Under the Act the benefit and burden of all leasehold covenants automatically pass on an assignment of the lease or of the reversion. If a covenant is not to pass, it must be expressed to be personal. The effect of an equitable assignment (for example, where there is an agreement for a lease) is the same as that of a legal assignment.[330]

The Act also provides for covenants to be enforceable by and against persons other than the reversioner who are for the time being entitled to the rents and profits under the tenancy, and mortgagees in possession of the reversion who are similarly entitled.[331]

LANDLORD AND TENANT (COVENANTS) ACT 1995

3. Transmission of benefit and burden of covenants.—(1) The benefit and burden of all land-lord and tenant covenants of a tenancy—

(a) shall be annexed and incident to the whole, and to each and every part, of the prem-ises demised by the tenancy and of the reversion in them, and

(b) shall in accordance with this section pass on an assignment of the whole or any part of those premises or of the reversion in them.[332]

(2) Where the assignment is by the tenant under the tenancy, then as from the assignment the assignee—

(a) becomes bound by the tenant covenants of the tenancy except to the extent that—

(i)   immediately before the assignment they did not bind the assignor, or

(ii) they fall to be complied with in relation to any demised premises not comprised in the assignment; and

(b) becomes entitled to the benefit of the landlord covenants of the tenancy except to the extent that they fall to be complied with in relation to any such premises.

(3) Where the assignment is by the landlord under the tenancy, then as from the assignment the assignee—

(a) becomes bound by the landlord covenants of the tenancy except to the extent that—

(i)   immediately before the assignment they did not bind the assignor, or

(ii) they fall to be complied with in relation to any demised premises[333] not com-prised in the assignment; and

---

[329] *First Penthouse Ltd v Channel Hotels (UK) Ltd* [2004] 1 EGLR 16 (obligations to grant sub-lease and pay commission held not to be tenant covenants).

[330] S. 28(1), above (meanings of 'assignment' and 'tenancy').

[331] S. 15, p. 486, below.

[332] For the non-applicability of LPA 1925, ss. 78, 79, 141 and 142 in the case of covenants in post-1995 leases, see s. 30(4).

[333] *Oceanic Village Ltd v United Attractions Ltd* [2000] Ch 234 ('any demised premises' refers only to premises demised by the lease in question, and not to all premises demised by the landlord, if only to have

(b) becomes entitled to the benefit of the tenant covenants of the tenancy except to the extent that they fall to be complied with in relation to any such premises.

(4) In determining for the purposes of subsection (2) or (3) whether any covenant bound the assignor immediately before the assignment, any waiver or release of the covenant (in whatever terms) is expressed to be personal to the assignor shall be disregarded.

(5) Any landlord or tenant covenant of a tenancy which is restrictive of the user of land shall, as well as being capable of enforcement against an assignee, be capable of being enforced against any other person who is the owner or occupier of any demised premises to which the covenant relates, even though there is no express provision in the tenancy to that effect.[334]

(6) Nothing in this section shall operate—

(a) in the case of a covenant which (in whatever terms) is expressed to be personal to any person, to make the covenant enforceable by or (as the case may be) against any other person; or

(b) to make a covenant enforceable against any person if, apart from this section, it would not be enforceable against him by reason of its not having been registered under the Land Registration Act 2002[335] or the Land Charges Act 1972.

(7) To the extent that there remains in force any rule of law by virtue of which the burden of a covenant whose subject matter is not in existence at the time when it is made does not run with the land affected unless the covenantor covenants on behalf of himself and his assigns, that rule of law is hereby abolished in relation to tenancies.[336]

4. Transmission of rights of re-entry.—The benefit of a landlord's right of re-entry under a tenancy—

(a) shall be annexed and incident to the whole, and to each and every part of the reversion in the premises demised by the tenancy, and

(b) shall pass on an assignment of the whole or any part of the reversion in those premises.

15. Enforcement of covenants.—(1) Where any tenant covenant of a tenancy, or any right of re-entry contained in a tenancy, is enforceable by the reversioner in respect of any premises demised by the tenancy, it shall also be so enforceable by—

(a) any person (other than the reversioner) who, as the holder of the immediate reversion in those premises, is for the time being entitled to the rents and profits under the tenancy in respect of those premises, or

(b) any mortgagee in possession of the reversion in those premises who is so entitled.

(2) Where any landlord covenant of a tenancy is enforceable against the reversioner in respect of any premises demised by the tenancy, it shall also be enforceable against any person falling within subsection (1)(a) or (b).

---

conformity with s. 3(2) and (3) where 'any demised premises' can only refer to the premises comprised in the relevant lease).

[334] This preserves the right to sue in equity in respect of restrictive covenants, p. 750, below. See *Hemingway Securities Ltd v Dunraven Ltd* [1995] 1 EGLR 61.

[335] As substituted by LRA 2002, s. 133, Sch. 1, para. 33(2).

[336] This abolishes the rule contained in *Spencer's Case* (1583) 3 Co Rep 16a, p. 465, above, governing covenants made before 1926 to do some act relating to the use where the subject-matter is not in existence at the time the covenant was made (for example, to erect a new house).

(3) Where any landlord covenant of a tenancy is enforceable by the tenant in respect of any premises demised by the tenancy, it shall also be so enforceable by any mortgagee in possession of those premises under a mortgage granted by the tenant.

(4) Where any tenant covenant of a tenancy, or any right of re-entry contained in a tenancy, is enforceable against the tenant in respect of any premises demised by the tenancy, it shall also be so enforceable against any such mortgagee.[337]

(5) Nothing in this section shall operate—

(a) in the case of a covenant which (in whatever terms) is expressed to be personal to any person, to make the covenant enforceable by or (as the case may be) against any other person;[338] or

(b) to make a covenant enforceable against any person if, apart from this section, it would not be enforceable against him by reason of its not having been registered under the Land Registration Act 2002 or the Land Charges Act 1972.

(iii) *Release of covenants on assignment*

(a) Release of tenant

Section 5 of the Act, under which a tenant is released from the tenant covenants (and also ceases to be entitled to enforce the landlord covenants) is the raison d'être of the legislation. At the same time, a guarantor of the tenant's liability is released to the same extent.

LANDLORD AND TENANT (COVENANTS) ACT 1995

5. Tenant released from covenants on assignment of tenancy.—(1) This section applies where a tenant assigns premises demised to him under a tenancy.

(2) If the tenant assigns the whole of the premises demised to him, he—

(a) is released from the tenant covenants of the tenancy, and

(b) ceases to be entitled to the benefit of the landlord covenants of the tenancy,

as from the assignment.

(3) If the tenant assigns part only of the premises demised to him, then as from the assignment he—

(a) is released from the tenant covenant of the tenancy, and

(b) ceases to be entitled to the benefit of the landlord covenants of the tenancy,

only to the extent that those covenants fall to be complied with in relation to that part of the demised premises.[339]

---

[337] On covenants with management companies, see s. 12.

[338] A covenant is not personal if it would endure throughout the term and be binding on the landlord's successors in title, even though the liability of one particular landlord's liability under the covenant is limited to the period during which it holds the reversion: *London Diocesan Fund v Phithwa* [2005] 1 WLR 3956 at [27], per Lord Nicholls of Birkenhead. For a personal covenant, see *BHP Petroleum Great Britain Ltd v Chesterfield Properties Ltd* [2002] Ch 194, p. 488, below (landlord's obligations, contained in agreement for lease and expressed to be personal to the landlord, to remedy defects in building within specified period).

[339] For joint and several liability on covenants binding two or more persons, see s. 13; and for apportionment of liability, see ss. 9 and 10.

(4) This section applies as mentioned in subsection (1) whether or not the tenant is tenant of the whole of the premises comprised in the tenancy.

(b) Release of landlord and former landlord

There is no automatic release for the landlord on his assignment of the reversion. He must apply to the tenant by serving a notice and requesting release within four weeks of the assignment. The reason for this difference is that a tenant cannot vet the landlord's assignee and prevent assignment to a nominee.

LANDLORD AND TENANT (COVENANTS) ACT 1995

6. Landlord may be released from covenants on assignment of reversion.—(1) This section applies where a landlord assigns the reversion in premises of which he is the landlord under a tenancy.

(2) If the landlord assigns the reversion in the whole of the premises of which he is the landlord—

(a) he may apply to be released from the landlord covenants of the tenancy in accordance with section 8; and

(b) if he is so released from all of those covenants, he ceases to be entitled to the benefit of the tenant covenants of the tenancy as from the assignment.

(3) If the landlord assigns the reversion in part only of the premises of which he is the landlord—

(a) he may apply to be so released from the landlord covenants of the tenancy to the extent that they fall to be complied with in relation to that part of those premises; and

(b) if he is, to that extent, so released from all of those covenants, then as from the assignment he ceases to be entitled to the benefit of the tenant covenants only to the extent that they fall to be complied with in relation to that part of those premises.

(4) This section applies as mentioned in subsection (1) whether or not the landlord is landlord of the whole of the premises comprised in the tenancy.

In **BHP Petroleum Great Britain Ltd v Chesterfield Properties Ltd** [2002] Ch 194, the question arose as to whether a landlord was entitled to be relieved by the service of a section 8 notice from his liability for covenants which were expressed in the lease to be 'personal obligations of the landlord'. In holding that he was not, JONATHAN PARKER LJ said:

59 The crux, as we see it, is the definition of 'landlord' in section 28(1) [p. 484, post] as meaning 'the person *for the time being* entitled to the reversion expectant on the term of the tenancy'. (My emphasis.) We find it impossible to read that definition as meaning only the original landlord. In agreement with the judge [2002] Ch 12, 21, para 22, we consider that those words clearly connote the person who may *from time to time* be entitled to the reversion on the tenancy. It follows that, transposing that definition into the definition of the expression 'landlord covenant', what one has is an obligation 'falling to be complied with by [the person who may from time to time be entitled to the reversion on the tenancy]'. An obligation that (that

is to say, the burden of which) is personal to the original landlord is, by definition, not such an obligation, since it does not fall to be performed by the person who may from time to time be entitled to the reversion on the tenancy.

60 It follows that in our judgment Chesterfield's obligations in clause 12 of the agreement, being expressed to be personal to Chesterfield, are not 'landlord covenants' within the meaning of the 1995 Act, and that the notice was accordingly ineffective to release Chesterfield from such obligations.

61 With respect to Mr Lewison, Chesterfield's argument on the 1995 Act issue seems to us to be based upon the fallacy that there is a direct antithesis between a personal covenant (that is to say, a covenant that is personal in the sense that the burden of it is expressed to be personal to the covenantor), on the one hand, and a covenant which 'touches and concerns', or which relates to, the land on the other. As Mr Barnes correctly submits, there is no such direct antithesis. A covenant that relates to the land may nevertheless be expressed to be personal to one or other or both of the parties to it. That is a matter for the contracting parties.

62 Nor can we see anything in the 1995 Act to fetter the freedom of contracting parties to place a contractual limit on the transmissibility of the benefit or burden of obligations under a tenancy. On the contrary, that no such fetter was intended by Parliament is clearly demonstrated, in our judgment, by section 3(6)(a) [p. 486, above].

The same would apply to personal covenants by a tenant; they would not automatically be released on a lawful assignment by section 5, p. 487, above.

LANDLORD AND TENANT (COVENANTS) ACT 1995

7. Former landlord may be released from covenants on assignment of reversion.—(1) This section applies where—

   (a) a landlord assigns the reversion in premises of which he is the landlord under a tenancy, and

   (b) immediately before the assignment a former landlord of the premises remains bound by a landlord covenant of the tenancy ('the relevant covenant').

(2) If immediately before the assignment the former landlord does not remain the landlord of any other premises demised by the tenancy, he may apply to be released from the relevant covenant in accordance with section 8.

(3) In any other case the former landlord may apply to be so released from the relevant covenant to the extent that it falls to be complied with in relation to any premises comprised in the assignment.

(4) If the former landlord is so released from every landlord covenant by which he remained bound immediately before the assignment, he ceases to be entitled to the benefit of the tenant covenants of the tenancy.

(5) If the former landlord is so released from every such landlord covenant to the extent that it falls to be complied with in relation to any premises comprised in the assignment, he ceases to be entitled to the benefit of the tenant covenants of the tenancy to the extent that they fall to be so complied with.

(6) This section applies as mentioned in subsection (1)—

   (a) whether or not the landlord making the assignment is landlord of the whole of the premises comprised in the tenancy; and

(b) whether or not the former landlord has previously applied (whether under section 6 or this section) to be released from the relevant covenant.[340]

(c) Effect of release

LANDLORD AND TENANT (COVENANTS) ACT 1995

24. Effects of release from liability under, or loss of benefit of, covenant.—(1) Any release of a person from a covenant by virtue of this Act does not affect any liability of his arising from a breach of the covenant occurring before the release.

(2) Where—

(a) by virtue of this Act a tenant is released from a tenant covenant of a tenancy, and

(b) immediately before the release another person is bound by a covenant of the tenancy imposing any liability or penalty in the event of a failure to comply with that tenant covenant,

then, as from the release of the tenant, that other person is released from the covenant mentioned in paragraph (b) to the same extent as the tenant is released from that tenant covenant.

(3) Where a person bound by a landlord or tenant covenant of a tenancy—

(a) assigns the whole or part of his interest in the premises demised by the tenancy, but

(b) is not released by virtue of this Act from the covenant (with the result that subsection (1) does not apply),

the assignment does not affect any liability of his arising from a breach of the covenant occurring before the assignment.

(4) Where by virtue of this Act a person ceases to be entitled to the benefit of a covenant, this does not affect any rights of his arising from a breach of the covenant occurring before he ceases to be so entitled.[341]

23. Effects of becoming subject to liability under, or entitled to benefit of, covenant etc.—(1) Where as a result of an assignment a person becomes by virtue of this Act, bound by or entitled to the benefit of a covenant, he shall not by virtue of this Act have any liability or rights under the covenant in relation to any time falling before the assignment.

(2) Subsection (1) does not preclude any such rights being expressly assigned to the person in question.[342]

(d) Excluded assignments

LANDLORD AND TENANT (COVENANTS) ACT 1995

11. Assignments in breach of covenant or by operation of law.—(1) This section provides for the operation of sections 5 to 10 in relation to assignments in breach of a covenant of a tenancy or assignments by operation of law ('excluded assignments').[343]

---

[340] For the procedure for seeking release from a covenant under ss. 6 and 7, see s. 8.

[341] This represents a change from the pre-1996 law in *Re King* [1963] Ch 459, p. 467, above.

[342] By LPA 1925, s. 136.

[343] By devolution to a trustee in bankruptcy or on death to personal representatives.

(2) In the case of an excluded assignment subsection (2) or (3) of section 5—

    (a) shall not have the effect mentioned in that subsection in relation to the tenant as from that assignment, but

    (b) shall have that effect as from the next assignment (if any) of the premises assigned by him which is not an excluded assignment.

(3) In the case of an excluded assignment subsection (2) or (3) of section 6 or 7—

    (a) shall not enable the landlord or former landlord to apply for such a release as is mentioned in that subsection as from that assignment, but

    (b) shall apply on the next assignment (if any) of the reversion assigned by the landlord which is not an excluded assignment so as to enable the landlord or former landlord to apply for any such release as from that subsequent assignment.

'Where the property is a lease which was granted after 1995, the registration of the squatter as the new proprietor will operate as an "excluded assignment" under the Landlord and Tenant (Covenants) Act 1995, s. 11. This is one case under that Act where the former tenant will remain liable on the covenants of the lease': Law Commission Report on Land Registration for the Twenty-First Century 2001 (Law Com No. 271), para. 14.71, n. 242.

(iv) Anti-avoidance provisions

The court has wide powers to strike down any schemes to circumvent purposes of the Act.

LANDLORD AND TENANT (COVENANTS) ACT 1995

25. Agreement void if it restricts operation of the Act.—(1) Any agreement relating to a tenancy is void to the extent that—

    (a) it would apart from this section have effect to exclude, modify or otherwise frustrate the operation of any provision of this Act, or

    (b) it provides for—

        (i) the termination or surrender of the tenancy, or

        (ii) the imposition on the tenant of any penalty, disability or liability,

    in the event of the operation of any provision of this Act, or

    (c) it provides for any of the matters referred to in paragraph (b) (i) or (ii) and does so (whether expressly or otherwise) in connection with, or in consequence of, the operation of any provision of this Act.

(2) To the extent that an agreement relating to a tenancy constitutes a covenant (whether absolute or qualified) against the assignment, or parting with the possession, of the premises demised by the tenancy or any part of them—

    (a) the agreement is not void by virtue of subsection (1) by reason only of the fact that as such the covenant prohibits or restricts any such assignment or parting with possession; but

(b) paragraph (a) above does not otherwise affect the operation of that subsection in relation to the agreement (and in particular does not preclude its application to the agreement to the extent that it purports to regulate the giving of, or the making of any application for, consent to any such assignment or parting with possession).

(3) In accordance with section 16(1) nothing in this section applies to any agreement to the extent that it is an authorised guarantee agreement; but (without prejudice to the generality of subsection (1) above) an agreement is void to the extent that it is one falling within section 16(4)(a) or (b).[344]

(4) This section applies to an agreement relating to a tenancy whether or not the agreement is—

(a) contained in the instrument creating the tenancy; or

(b) made before the creation of the tenancy.

London Diocesan Fund v Phithwa
[2005] 1 WLR 3956 (HL, Lords Nicholls of Birkenhead, Hoffmann, Scott of Foscote and Walker of Gestingthorpe, and Baroness Hale of Richmond)[345]

Lord Nicholls of Birkenhead:

1 This appeal raises a question on the effect of the Landlord and Tenant (Covenants) Act 1995. A sublease invariably contains a covenant by the lessor to pay the rent due under the headlease. Before the enactment of the 1995 Act a lessor could, by the use of appropriate wording, limit his liability under such a covenant in whatever way he and the subtenant might agree. In particular, the lessor's liability could be restricted to the period while the reversion to the sublease remained vested in him. This was legally possible, if seldom met in practice. When the lessor's liability was confined in this way, and the lessor assigned the reversion, his successor would be liable under this covenant by virtue of privity of estate but the lessor's own liability by virtue of privity of contract would be at an end. The issue on this appeal is whether the 1995 Act precludes a lessor from now limiting his liability in this way. The Court of Appeal held it does: [2005] 1 WLR 236.

2 The context is as follows. In February 2002 Avonridge Property Co Ltd acquired by assignment a lease of seven small shop units at Wealdstone, Middlesex. The lease was for a term of 99 years expiring in 2067, at an annual rent of £16,700 subject to review. Avonridge granted subleases of six of these shops for substantially the same term as its own lease, or headlease as the lease then became. The rent payable under each sublease was a peppercorn. The sublessees paid Avonridge substantial premiums for their subleases, of the order of £75,000 for each sublease.

3 Each sublease contained, in clause 6, a landlord's covenant for quiet enjoyment and for payment of the rent reserved by the headlease. The words of the covenant read as follows (commas have been added to assist reading): 'The landlord covenants with the tenant as follows

---

[344] P. 496, below.
[345] [2007] Conv 1; [2006] All ER Rev 264 (P. H. Pettit). The case is also known in some reports as *Avonridge Property Co Ltd v Mashru* ([2006] 1 P & CR 25; [2006] L & TR 4). Avonridge was the appellant and Mashru the respondent before the House of Lords.

(but not, in the case of Avonridge Property Co Ltd only, so as to be liable after the landlord has disposed of its interest in the Property)...'

4 On 2 April 2002 Avonridge assigned the headlease to a Mr Dhirajlal Phithwa. Mr Phithwa was, to use the old legal phrase, a man of straw. He disappeared, leaving unpaid the rent due under the headlease. The headlessor, the London Diocesan Fund and the Parochial Church Council of Holy Trinity, Wealdstone, commenced forfeiture proceedings. The subtenants were granted relief, on unexceptional terms: they had to pay the rent arrears under the headlease with interest and costs, and take new leases of their individual units. The new leases were for the same term as their former subleases and at a rent equal to an apportioned part of the rental payable under the forfeited headlease. This meant that for the future, under the new leases, the former subtenants had to pay an annual rent of £2,376 or, in one instance, £2,441. This is to be contrasted with the nominal rent payable under the subleases they had bought from Avonridge.

5 The subtenants brought proceedings against Avonridge, claiming damages for breach of the landlord's covenant in clause 6 of their leases. Judge Copley sitting in Willesden County Court gave judgment for the subtenants, for damages to be assessed. He held that the 1995 Act rendered void the words in clause 6 limiting Avonridge's liability to the time it was the landlord. The Court of Appeal, comprising Pill, Jonathan Parker and Hooper LJJ, dismissed Avonridge's appeal. Avonridge has now appealed to your Lordships' House....

10 The 1995 Act gave effect, with amendments, to the recommendations of the Law Commission in its report 'Landlord and Tenant Law—Privity of Contract and Estate': Law Com No 174 (1988). One of the principal mischiefs the Act was intended to remedy was that, as the law stood, the original tenant of a lease remained liable for performance of the tenant's covenants throughout the entire duration of the lease. A tenant might part with his lease and many years later find himself liable for substantial amounts of unpaid rent, perhaps much increased under rent review provisions, and for the cost of making good extensive dilapidations.

11 This was considered unfair. This potential liability was not widely understood by tenants, and it could lead to hardship. Section 5 of the Act remedied this defect in the law. Section 5 provides that where a tenant assigns the whole of the premises demised to him under a tenancy, he is released from the tenant covenants of the tenancy. A tenant covenant is a covenant falling to be complied with by the tenant of premises demised by the tenancy. Tenancy includes a subtenancy: section 28(1).

12 Section 6 contains a corresponding provision for the benefit of landlords in respect of landlord covenants, but this provision is not so far-reaching in its effect. Unlike the automatic release of tenant covenants brought about by assignment of the whole of the demised premises, assignment of the reversion in the whole of the demised premises does not automatically relieve the landlord from his liability under the landlord covenants. The Law Commission considered the new provision regarding landlord covenants could not mirror precisely the position regarding tenant covenants. Tenants rarely, if ever, have a right to give or withhold consent to dispositions by their landlord. Moreover, there was less need for radical change with landlord covenants because landlords undertake far fewer obligations than tenants, and landlords may not be troubled by the prospect of continuing responsibility: see para. 4.16 of its report.

13 So sections 6 to 8 of the Act provide a landlord with a means which may result in his being released from the landlord covenants but will not necessarily do so. If the landlord assigns the whole of the premises of which he is landlord he may apply to be released from the landlord covenants of the tenancy. A landlord covenant is a covenant falling to be complied with by the

landlord of the premises demised by a tenancy. An application for release is made by the land-lord serving an appropriate notice on the tenant requesting a release of the landlord covenant wholly or in part. Where the landlord makes such an application the covenant is released to the requested extent if the tenant consents, or if he fails to object, or if he does object but the court decides it is reasonable for the covenant to be released: section 8.

14 These statutory provisions might readily be stultified if the parties to a lease could exclude their operation. In particular, the provision for automatic release of tenant covenants on assignment of a lease would be a weak instrument if it were open to a landlord to provide that the original tenant's contractual liability should continue for the whole term notwithstanding section 5. So the Act, in section 25, enacts a comprehensive anti-avoidance provision.

His Lordship read section 25(1), above.

The words in parenthesis in Avonridge's covenant in clause 6 of each sublease are an 'agreement relating to a tenancy' within the meaning of this section: section 25(4). But does this agreement 'frustrate the operation' of any provision of the Act? That is the key question.

15 The subtenants submit it does. The limited release provisions in sections 6 to 8 were intended to be the sole means whereby an original landlord could obtain a release from the landlord covenants when he assigned the reversion. The parenthetical words in clause 6 would frustrate that statutory purpose if they were allowed to have effect according to their tenor.

16 I am unable to agree. Where I part company with this submission is its statement of the statutory purpose. Sections 5 to 8 are relieving provisions. They are intended to benefit tenants, or landlords, as the case may be. That is their purpose. That is how they are meant to operate. These sections introduced a means, which cannot be ousted, whereby in certain circumstances, without the agreement of the other party, a tenant or landlord can be released from a liability he has assumed. The object of the legislation was that on lawful assignment of a tenancy or reversion, and irrespective of the terms of the tenancy, the tenant or the landlord should have an exit route from his future liabilities. This route should be available in accordance with the statutory provisions.

17 Thus the mischief at which the statute was aimed was the *absence* in practice of any such exit route. Consistently with this the legislation was not intended to close any *other* exit route already open to the parties: in particular, that by agreement their liability could be curtailed from the outset or later released or waived. The possibility that by agreement the parties may limit their liability in this way was not, it seems, perceived as having unfair consequences in practice, even though landlords normally have greater bargaining power than tenants. So there was no call for legislation to exclude the parties' capacity to make such an agreement, ending their liability in circumstances other than those provided in the Act.

18 Section 25 is of course to be interpreted generously, so as to ensure the operation of the Act is not frustrated, either directly or indirectly. But there is nothing in the language or scheme of the Act to suggest the statute was intended to exclude the parties' ability to limit liability under their covenants from the outset in whatever way they may agree. An agreed limitation of this nature does not impinge upon the operation of the statutory provisions.

19 This is so whether the agreed limitation is included in the lease itself or is in a separate document by way of waiver or agreement to release. The legal effect is the same in each case. Whatever its form, an agreed limitation of liability does not impinge upon the operation of the statutory provisions because, as already noted, the statutory provisions are intended to operate to relieve tenants and landlords from a liability which would otherwise exist. They are

not intended to impose a liability which otherwise would be absent. They are not intended to enlarge the liability either of a tenant or landlord. The Act does not compel a landlord to enter into a covenant with his tenant to pay the rent under a headlease. The Act does not compel this, even though it may be eminently reasonable that a landlord should do so. Nor do the statutory restrictions on the circumstances where a landlord can end his liability without his tenant's consent carry any implication that a tenant may not agree to end his landlord's liability in other circumstances. Such an implication would be inconsistent with the underlying scheme of these provisions.

20 This appraisal accords with the thrust of the Law Commission's report. The Commission expressly recognised, in para. 2.17, that the parties to a lease were able to limit their obligations so that their obligations ended on disposal of their interests: 'A lease can, as a matter of bargain, limit the obligations of one or both of the parties, so that they come to an end if the parties transfer their interest in the property. However, this is rarely done.' A similar view is expressed in para. 3.3: the continuing liability of the original parties to leases is a 'matter of contract'. The parties 'are free to vary the normal rule'. This is 'sometimes done, but not frequently'. Nowhere in its report does the commission suggest the parties' freedom to vary the normal rule has given rise to problems and should be curtailed. Had such a fundamental incursion into basic law been intended that would surely have found clear expression in the Act.

21 Nor do the events in this case exemplify a loophole in the Act Parliament cannot have intended. The risks involved were not obscure or concealed. They were evident on the face of the subleases. The sublessees were to pay up-front a capitalised rent for the whole term of the subleases. But clause 6 enabled Avonridge to shake off all its landlord obligations at will. Any competent conveyancer would, or should, have warned the sublessees of the risks, clearly and forcefully.

(v) Authorised guarantee agreements

A landlord consenting to an assignment may impose a condition that the tenant guarantees the performance of the lease covenants by his successor, but only until the following assignment.[346]

LANDLORD AND TENANT (COVENANTS) ACT 1995

16. Tenant guaranteeing performance of covenant by assignee.[347]—(1) Where on an assignment a tenant is to any extent released from a tenant covenant of a tenancy by virtue of this Act ('the relevant covenant'), nothing in this Act (and in particular section 25)[348] shall preclude him from entering into an authorised guarantee agreement with respect to the performance of that covenant by the assignee.

(2) For the purposes of this section an agreement is an authorised guarantee agreement if—

(a) under it the tenant guarantees the performance of the relevant covenant to any extent by the assignee; and

---

[346] Law Committee Report on Privity of Contract and Estate (1988) Law Com No. 174, para. 5(1), (2).

[347] See also s. 17 for the restriction on liability of former tenant or his guarantor for rent or service charge, etc.; s. 19 for their right to an overriding lease; and s. 18 for the restriction on their liability for post-assignment variation; p. 475, above. These sections apply to all tenancies whether created before or after the Act.

[348] P. 491, above.

(b) it is entered into in the circumstances set out in subsection (3); and

(c) its provisions conform with subsections (4) and (5).

(3) Those circumstances are as follows—

(a) by virtue of a covenant against assignment (whether absolute or qualified) the assignment cannot be effected without the consent of the landlord under the tenancy or some other person;[349]

(b) any such consent is given subject to a condition (lawfully imposed) that the tenant is to enter into an agreement guaranteeing the performance of the covenant by the assignee; and

(c) the agreement is entered into by the tenant in pursuance of that condition.

(4) An agreement is not an authorised guarantee agreement to the extent that it purports—

(a) to impose on the tenant any requirement to guarantee in any way the performance of the relevant covenant by any person other than the assignee; or

(b) to impose on the tenant any liability, restriction or other requirement (of whatever nature) in relation to any time after the assignee is released from that covenant by virtue of this Act.

(5) Subject to subsection (4), an authorised guarantee agreement may—

(a) impose on the tenant any liability as sole or principal debtor in respect of any obligation owed by the assignee under the relevant covenant;

(b) impose on the tenant liabilities as guarantor in respect of the assignee's performance of that covenant which are no more onerous than those to which he would be subject in the event of his being liable as sole or principal debtor in respect of any obligation owed by the assignee under that covenant;

(c) require the tenant, in the event of the tenancy assigned by him being disclaimed, to enter into a new tenancy of the premises comprised in the assignment—

(i) whose term expires not later than the term of the tenancy assigned by the tenant, and

(ii) whose tenant covenants are no more onerous than those of that tenancy;

(d) make provision incidental or supplementary to any provision made by virtue of any of paragraphs (a) to (c).

(6) Where a person ('the former tenant') is to any extent released from a covenant of a tenancy by virtue of section 11(2)[350] as from an assignment and the assignor under the assignment enters into an authorised guarantee agreement with the landlord with respect to the performance of that covenant by the assignee under the assignment—

(a) the landlord may require the former tenant to enter into an agreement under which he guarantees, on terms corresponding to those of that authorised guarantee

---

[349] *Wallis Fashion Group Ltd v CGU Life Assurance Ltd* [2000] 2 EGLR 49 (where an assignment of a lease requires the landlord's consent, and the alienation covenant is silent on the specific issue of whether or not he can demand an authorised guarantee agreement, then the landlord can only refuse consent if it is reasonable to do so; Landlord and Tenant Act 1927, s. 19(1), p. 497, below. Therefore a landlord can only impose a condition upon the grant of his consent if that condition is reasonable).

[350] P. 491, above.

agreement, the performance of that covenant by the assignee under the assignment; and

(b)   if its provisions conform with subsections (4) and (5), any such agreement shall be an authorised guarantee agreement for the purposes of this section; and

(c)   in the application of this section in relation to any such agreement—

    (i)   subsections (2)(b) and (c) and (3) shall be omitted, and

    (ii)   any reference to the tenant or to the assignee shall be read as a reference to the former tenant or to the assignee under the assignment.

(7)   For the purposes of subsection (1) it is immaterial that—

    (a)   the tenant has already made an authorised guarantee agreement in respect of a previous assignment by him of the tenancy referred to in that subsection, it having been subsequently revested in him following a disclaimer on behalf of the previous assignee, or

    (b)   the tenancy referred to in that subsection is a new tenancy entered into by the tenant in pursuance of an authorised guarantee agreement;

and in any such case subsections (2) to (5) shall apply accordingly.

(8)   It is hereby declared that the rules of law relating to guarantees (and in particular those relating to the release[351] of sureties) are, subject to its terms applicable in relation to any authorised guarantee agreement.[352]

(vi) Landlord's consent to assignment of tenancy

Section 22 amends the Landlord and Tenant Act 1927 by providing that where a post-1995 lease contains a qualified covenant against assignment (one which permits assignment with the landlord's licence or consent), the parties may agree what conditions shall govern the question of whether the landlord consents to an assignment. These conditions are not capable of being struck down by the court on the ground that they are unreasonable. The amendment only applies to non-agricultural business leases. It is a quid pro quo for the abolition of privity of contract liability.[353]

LANDLORD AND TENANT ACT 1927

19. Provisions as to covenants not to assign, etc., without licence or consent.—(1) In all leases whether made before or after the commencement of this Act containing a covenant condition or agreement against assigning, under-letting, charging or parting with the possession of demised premises or any part thereof without licence or consent, such covenant condition or agreement shall, notwithstanding any express provision to the contrary, be deemed to be subject—

    (a)   to a proviso to the effect that such licence or consent is not to be unreasonably with-held, but this proviso does not preclude the right of the landlord to require payment

---

[351] Subject to the terms of the guarantee, a release occurs where there has been a substantial variation of the tenancy after the date of the guarantee. See *Howard de Walden Estates v Pasta Place* [1995] 1 EGLR 79.

[352] Implied indemnity covenants under LPA 1925, s. 77(1)(*c*), (*d*) and 77(7)(*c*) and LRA 1925, s. 24(1)(b) and (2), p. 473, n. 288, above, have been abolished in respect of post-1995 leases: s. 30(2), Sch. 2.

[353] (1996) 59 MLR 78 at 89 (M. Davey).

of a reasonable sum in respect of any legal or other expenses incurred in connection with such licence or consent; and

(b) (if the lease is for more than forty years, and is made in consideration wholly or partially of the erection, or the substantial improvement, addition or alteration of buildings, and the lessor is not a Government department or local or public authority, or a statutory or public utility company) to a proviso to the effect that in the case of any assignment, under-letting, charging or parting with the possession (whether by the holders of the lease or any under-tenant whether immediate or not) effected more than seven years before the end of the term no consent or licence shall be required, if notice in writing of the transaction is given to the lessor within six months after the transaction is effected.

(1A) Where the landlord and the tenant under a qualifying lease have entered into an agreement specifying for the purposes of this subsection—

(a) any circumstances in which the landlord may withhold his licence or consent to an assignment of the demised premises of any part of them,[354] or

(b) any conditions subject to which any such licence or consent may be granted,

then the landlord—

(i) shall not be regarded as unreasonably withholding his licence or consent to any such assignment if he withholds it on the ground (and it is the case) that any such circumstances exist, and

(ii) if he gives such licence or consent subject to any such conditions, shall not be regarded as giving it subject to unreasonable conditions;

and section 1 of the Landlord and Tenant Act 1988 (qualified duty to consent to assignment etc.) shall have effect subject to the provisions of this subsection.

(1B) Subsection (1A) of this section applies to such an agreement as is mentioned in that subsection—

(a) whether it is contained in the lease or not, and

(b) whether it is made at the time when the lease is granted or at any other time falling before the application for the landlord's licence or consent is made.

(1C) Subsection (1A) shall not, however, apply to any such agreement to the extent that any circumstances or conditions specified in it are framed by reference to any matter falling to be determined by the landlord or by any other person for the purposes of the agreement, unless under the terms of the agreement—

(a) that person's power to determine that matter is required to be exercised reasonably, or

(b) the tenant is given an unrestricted right to have any such determination reviewed by a person independent of both landlord and tenant whose identity is ascertainable by reference to the agreement,

---

[354] *Legends Surf Shops plc v Sun Life Assurance Society plc* [2005] 3 EGLR 43 (whether landlord could insist on personal guarantees in authorised guarantee agreement entered into under Landlord and Tenant (Covenants) Act 1995, s. 16, above, p. 495, above where former tenant in administrative receivership).

and in the latter case the agreement provides for the determination made by any such independent person on the review to be conclusive as to the matter in question.

(1D) In its application to a qualifying lease, subsection (1)(b) of this section shall not have effect in relation to any assignment of the lease.

(1E) In subsections (1A) and (1D) of this section—

(a) 'qualifying lease' means any lease which is a new tenancy for the purposes of section 1 of the Landlord and Tenant (Covenants) Act 1995 other than a residential lease, namely a lease by which a building or part of a building is let wholly or mainly as a single private residence; and

(b) references to assignment include parting with possession on assignment.[355]

---

[355] Sub-sections (1A) to (1E) were added by Landlord and Tenant (Covenants) Act 1995, s. 22. Further duties were imposed on the landlord by Landlord and Tenant Act 1988 (to give consent within a reasonable time, and to prove that refusal of such consent was reasonable). See *International Drilling Fluids Ltd v Louisville Investments (Uxbridge) Ltd* [1986] Ch 513 at 519, per Balcombe LJ; C & B, pp. 258–263.

For the award of exemplary damages where a landlord deliberately tried to prevent assignment in order to procure a surrender from the tenant so as to obtain value of the under-rented property for itself, see *Design Progression Ltd v Thurloe Property Ltd* [2005] 1 WLR 1; [2006] Conv 37 (T. Fancourt).

PART III

EQUITABLE BENEFICIAL INTERESTS IN LAND

6

THE TRUST OF LAND

I. SUCCESSIVE AND CONCURRENT INTERESTS: AN INTRODUCTION

A system of private ownership of property must provide for something more sophisticated than absolute ownership of the property by one person. A property owner needs to be able to do more than own it during his lifetime and pass it on to someone else on his death.

In first place, the freeholder may wish to create *successive interests*; for example, to give the land to his children, subject to an annuity for his widow, or to give a life interest to the widow and a remainder to the children; or to provide, on his son's marriage, a life interest for his son, and after his death for the daughter-in-law and after her death for their children. He may wish to set up a form of family dynasty, such as was popular among the aristocracy in the 17th, 18th and 19th centuries. The law should make possible the satisfaction of an owner's reasonable wishes on these lines.

But a system which allows successive interests in property necessarily raises a number of problems. There is first a question of principle: is it right to allow a land-owner to tie up the property for the future? We have seen that this was addressed through the development of a 'rule against perpetuities' which regulates the period within which future interests can validly be created.[1] But there are other very signifi-cant issues. Who is to manage the property during the period of the working out of the various interests? Above all, who is the person to take the decision to sell the property and to transfer title? And what is to happen, when the land is sold, to the interests of the beneficiaries?

The problem is simplest with a fund of money. The common law never developed a system of limited estates in personalty. But in equity a fund could be vested in trustees, who would receive the income and pay it to the income beneficiary and hand over the capital to the person who was absolutely entitled at the conclusion of the limited interests. Similarly there was no problem in equity with investments. The trustees could buy and sell them, the purchaser taking a good title from the trustees, and the purchase money being added as capital to the trust fund. Chattels can be held in trust; but there has always been doubt as to the forms of limited ownership which could exist in personalty; and heirlooms used to be settled on trusts conforming as far as possible to the devolution of the land with which they were connected.[2] In a trust, it is important to state what powers are to be given to the trustees; powers of management and investment, and the power to sell and to give a good receipt to the purchaser free from the trusts of the settlement. Much of this is now covered by statute.

Successive interests in land provided a special case. The common law system of estates provided for life estates, fees tail, remainders and reversions. When uses and trusts of land developed, equity, generally speaking, followed the law, and allowed similar interests in equity behind a use or a trust. But, when the legal fee simple of land was split up between successive limited owners, there was no provision for the proper management of the land and, above all, no provision for selling. If land were limited to A for life, with remainder to B for life, with remainder to C in fee simple, who would sell the land? The same problem arose if similar limitations were created behind a trust; for, unless special powers were given to the trustees, they could not give a clear title to anyone other than a purchaser of the legal estate for value without notice, because any other purchaser would take the legal estate with notice of the trusts and would be bound by them.[3] Of course, all the legal estate owners in the case of a limita-tion of legal estates, or all the beneficiaries in the case of a trust, could combine to sell.

---

[1] Pp. 49–56, above. Broadly speaking, dispositions are void unless they vest within the period of a life in being plus 21 years, or, if a fixed period of years is chosen, a period not exceeding 80 years, although the Law Commission has proposed a reform of the law on perpetuities. A Bill to give effect to the Law Commission's proposals was introduced on 1 April 2009.

[2] *Shelley v Shelley* (1868) LR 6 Eq 540; *Re Morrison's Settlement* [1974] Ch 326.

[3] P. 13, above.

That might not be difficult where there was a simple limitation, such as one to A for life with remainder to B. But it becomes highly impracticable if there is a long series of limitations, and impossible if the limitations include an entail in a minor or if they create interests which are designed to vest on the happening of some contingencies which have not yet been worked out.[4]

What is needed therefore is a system which meets both these difficulties; which allows a property owner to create future successive and contingent interests in the property and, at the same time, provides for proper management of the fund and the power to sell and to pass a good title to a purchaser free from the trusts affecting the property. The problem is most acute where the capital consists of one single unique piece of property, like a piece of land. How can the interests of the beneficiaries and those of a purchaser be reconciled?

The solution was found by the application of the principle of 'overreaching', a principle by which, on a sale of property which is subject to successive interests, the interests of the beneficiaries leave the property and attach to the purchase money. The interests of the beneficiaries are said to be overreached. The beneficiaries do not lose economically out of the sale. A ton of feathers weighs the same as a ton of lead. A life interest in remainder in £50,000 worth of land is worth exactly the same as the same interest in £50,000; indeed, more valuable if the money is invested more profitably; less valuable, though, if the land proved to be the better investment. The question is one of choice of investment of the family capital.

The two procedures or methods by which successive interests could be achieved before 1997 were the strict settlement and the trust for sale. In the context of family holdings of land, the strict settlement is historically the more significant, because it was in this way that the great families held their ancestral lands. Legislation providing for the application of the overreaching principle to successive interests in land first came in the Settled Land Act 1882. Under the Settled Land Act 1925, which replaced the 1882 Act, where there were successive interests in land the legal estate was vested in the tenant for life (the income beneficiary) and he had the powers of management and of sale of the fee simple; and on such a sale the beneficial interests in the land were overreached and thus transferred from the land to the proceeds of sale.

On the other hand, land held on trust for sale was vested in trustees upon trust to sell and to hold the income until sale and the proceeds of the sale on trust for the beneficiaries according to their interests under the terms of the limitation. Under the doctrine of conversion, by which land subject to a trust for sale was treated in equity as being personalty, the interests of the beneficiaries were from the time of their creation interests in personalty. Overreaching was therefore automatic, but the Law of Property Act 1925 section 2 made express provision for it.[5] The existence of the trust for sale did not mean that the trustees must sell forthwith, for, although they were under a duty to

---

[4] [1972] Duke LJ 517 (W.M. Fratcher); (1977) 42 Missouri LR 355 (R.H. Maudsley).

[5] It makes provision also for overreaching interests prior to the trust for sale where the trustees are either two or more individuals approved or appointed by the court or a trust corporation: LPA 1925, s. 2(2), p. 549, below.

sell, they were given by statute a discretionary power to postpone sale; and they could retain the land under this power as long as they wished. They were also given the same powers of management and sale as the tenant for life in the case of a strict settlement.

The trust for sale before 1997 was thus an alternative method of dealing with successive interests in land. It was more convenient than a strict settlement for various reasons, the most important of which were: land and personalty could be held together, and most family trusts contained both; decisions were taken by a group of persons in a fiduciary position and not by one interested beneficiary; it was equally convenient where there were concurrent as opposed to successive interests; and it proved more flexible and able to accommodate special forms of trusts developed to reduce taxation. Income tax, estate duty (replaced by capital transfer tax in 1974 and by inheritance tax in 1986) and capital gains tax have all played their part in developing the modern law of settlements.[6]

Concurrent interests used to create a similar problem for a purchaser. To get a good title, he had to buy from all the co-owners. This problem was overcome in 1925 by providing that all concurrent interests, other than landholding by trustees, existed only behind a trust for sale which, if not created expressly, was implied as a trust for sale by statute.[7] There could not be more than four trustees of land.[8] So, even if land was beneficially owned by 130 tenants in common, the purchaser bought from not more than four trustees for sale, who passed the title, as with successive interests, free from the beneficial interests of the co-owners. Their interests attached to the purchase money.

Before 1997 all cases of successive or concurrent ownership were thus subject to either a trust for sale or a strict settlement. Conveyancers used the trust for sale almost exclusively, but many titles, especially those deriving from large family landholdings, were still dependent upon the Settled Land Act conveyancing. In the 1980s the Law Commission reviewed the law on successive and concurrent interests, and proposed reforms which were enacted in the Trusts of Land and Appointment of Trustees Act 1996.[9]

Law Commission Working Paper No. 94 on Trusts of Land 1985, paras 4.2, 4.3

4.2 *Successive interests.* The creation of traditional successive interests (e.g. to F for life to S for life to G in Tail)[10] may be less common now than it was when the 1925 legislation was being considered. Changes in social structure and the impact of taxation have made the creation of some elaborate settlements less attractive. However, straightforward settlements are still much used and it is essential that the law provides adequately for their creation. Where successive interests are created, the tenant for life and the remainderman both have interests in the land. To some extent, their interests may conflict, as the tenant for life may wish to maximise what he receives, that is, the income, whereas the remainderman is interested in the security

---

[6] See generally H & M, chap. 9.   [7] Pp. 564–567, below.
[8] TA 1925, s.34.   [9] P. 514, below.
[10] Megarry and Wade, *The Law of Real Property* (5th edn, 1984), p. 410.

and maximisation of the capital which he will eventually receive. Any system must be able to balance these conflicting interests. In addition, the tenant for life, being exclusively entitled to the income, may have a claim to be more closely involved with the management of the property than any other beneficiary of a trust. In making proposals for reform, it is important not to lose sight of one of the main reasons for the present systems within which [if] no one person has complete control, there is a danger that it will be impossible for anyone to deal with the land effectively. The powers that the tenant for life or the trustees for sale now have avoid this problem, and this advantage must be retained.

4.3 *Concurrent interests.* Far more usual than successive interests are concurrent interests. Here are two problems. One is to determine the nature and size of the beneficial interest. The other is to provide a means of settling disputes between beneficiaries as to the use of the property, and its disposition whether by sale, lease, mortgage, etc. Any system must ensure that it is possible for a purchaser to know whether or not the persons with whom he is dealing can give him a good title.

We shall consider one of the problems mentioned by the Law Commission—the determination of the nature and size of the concurrent interests—in chapter 7,[11] together with other matters concerning the nature and validity of successive and concurrent interests in land. In this chapter, however, we consider the *legal framework* within which successive and concurrent interests can now be created—that is, since 1997, through the trust of land. First, however, we shall look briefly at the legal framework which existed before 1997 (the strict settlement and the trust for sale), partly because it helps to appreciate the significance of the reforms of 1996, but also because it is necessary in order to understand cases which were decided under the old law;[12] and also because some of the 'old' law still applies today: although no new strict settlements can be created under the Settled Land Act 1925, the Act still applies to settlements which already existed when the Trusts of Land and Appointment of Trustees Act came into force.[13]

---

[11] Pp. 574–601, below.

[12] E.g. *Binions v Evans* [1972] Ch 359, p. 1102, below, where the agreement to allow the widow of an employee to live in a cottage for the rest of her life was held to create (inadvertently) a settlement under SLA 1925. The courts' approach to occupation licences in a number of cases was influenced by a concern to avoid the consequences of holding that a settlement had been created. See, e.g. *Ungurian v Lesnoff* [1990] Ch 206, esp. at 224; [1990] CLJ 25 (M. Oldham); [1990] Conv 223 (P. Sparkes); [1991] Conv 596 (J. Hill); *Costello v Costello* (1994) 70 P & CR 297; [1994] Conv 391 (M. P. Thompson); *Ivory v Palmer* [1975] ICR 340 at 347 (Cairns LJ: '*Binions v Evans* stretched to the very limit the application of the Settled Land Act'); (1977) 93 LQR 561 (J. A. Hornby); *Dent v Dent* [1996] 1 WLR 683; [1996] All ER Rev 258 (P. J. Clarke). On avoidance of an unintentional creation of a strict settlement in this situation, see *Griffiths v Williams* (1977) 248 EG 947, p. 1061, below; [1978] Conv 250.

[13] For detail of the Settled Land Act 1925, and extracts from cases decided under the Act, see the 8th edn of this book, chap. 6. See also C & B, chaps 4, 11; Gray, paras 7.6.2–7.6.14; M & W, Appendix; MM, pp. 247–279. See also *Harvey, Settlements of Land* (1973). See *Bonfield, Marriage Settlements 1601–1740* (1983); English and Saville, *Strict Settlement* (1983) which contains details of several dynastic settlements of land; and essays in Rubin and Sugarman, *Law, Economy and Society* (1984), pp. 1–123 (D. Sugarman and G.R. Rubin), 124–167 (M.R. Chesterman), 168–191 (E. Spring) and 209–210 (B. English).

II. STRICT SETTLEMENTS AND TRUSTS FOR SALE BEFORE 1997

Law Commission Working Paper No. 94 on Trusts of Land 1985, paras 3.2–3.23, 3.27–3.28[14]

A. *Dual system*

3.2 The following problems are those that arise because, at present, successive interests in land can be created either as settled land under the Settled Land Act 1925 or as interests behind a trust for sale. It has often been suggested that a dual system is unnecessary and that one system for successive interests would be sufficient. Originally the two systems performed different functions.[15] The strict settlement, using combinations of life interests[16] and entailed interests[17] (which before 1926 could exist as legal estates), was intended to keep land within the ownership of a particular family. In many cases the tenant for life would occupy the land. The trust for sale was used either where a sale was actually intended, or where the land concerned was intended to be an investment, to be bought and sold as market conditions demanded, the tenant for life being paid the income from it. By the mid-19th century it was apparent that strict settlements caused difficulty in that, if the settlement was not well drafted, the powers of the tenant for life were too limited to enable the land to be managed properly, and however the settlement was drafted, sale of the land was extremely difficult as no person had the power to convey the fee simple. A series of reforming statutes culminating in the Settled Land Act 1925 increased the powers of the tenant for life and ensured that there was also some person able to convey the fee simple in the land. At the same time the Law of Property Act 1925, s. 1 prevented life interests from existing as legal estates, so that all settlements had to take effect behind a trust. The effect of these reforms has been to remove many of the differences between the two systems of settlement. In either system the land can be sold and the strict settlement is no longer an effective method of keeping land in the family. The remaining differences centre on who makes the decisions with respect to the land. It is arguable that the differences are not sufficient to justify the continuing existence of two systems.

3.3 *Priority given to settled land.* The legislation is so phrased that when successive interests are created, a trust for sale must be expressly adopted (except where imposed by statute); otherwise the Settled Land Act will apply. This means that where trusts of land are created

[14] For other suggested solutions to the problems arising from the pre-1997 dual system of strict settlement and trust for sale, see (1928) 166 LT 45; (1938) 85 LJ News 353 (J.M.L.); (1938) 54 LQR 576 (M.M. Lewis); (1944) 8 Conv (NS) 147 (H. Potter); (1957) CLP 152 (E.H. Scamell); (1961) 24 MLR 123 (G.A. Grove); (1962) CLP 104 (E.C. Ryder).

[15] For a full historical account see Simpson, *An Introduction to the History of Land Law* (1961), pp. 188–194, 218–224. [See also Radcliffe, *Real Property Law* (2nd edn, 1938), pp. 108–109].

[16] [For further details on life interests, see the 8th edn of this book, p. 18; C & B, chap. 15.]

[17] [The entailed interest was used as an essential part of a strict settlement. Land was settled, usually on marriage, to the eldest son for life, with remainder to his son in tail. That entailed interest was limited so that, if the son died without issue, an entailed interest was given to the second son and so on. It became an anachronism, mainly because of taxation, and as from 1 January 1997 TLATA 1996, Sch. 1, para. 5 prevents any attempt to create a new entailed interest. Existing interests are not affected. For further details on entails, see the 8th edn of this book, pp. 13–18; C & B, chap. 14.]

without proper advice it is almost certain that the land will be settled. This is most likely to occur where wills are, as often happens, drawn up without advice. In some cases this will be what the testator would have wanted, but in many cases it will not be and additional expense for the beneficiaries may result because additional documents and a different form of probate are required. If an inadvertent settlement is created by will and the executors do not realise this, problems may be caused for purchasers (see below).

3.4 *Definition of trust for sale.* Inadvertent settlements may arise not through failure to decide which is required but through failure to create a valid trust for sale. The definition of a trust for sale as an immediate binding trust for sale has been criticised.[18] As a definition it is poor because it defines a thing as a particular kind of that thing. The word 'binding' has caused particular problems because a trust should be binding anyway and the courts have considered that it must mean something other than the trustees being under a duty to sell.[19]

3.5 *Rights of residence.* In other cases, settled land has been created inadvertently because a right of residence has been conferred on a person for his or her lifetime. It is not entirely clear that the conferment of such a right was intended to be sufficient to bring the land within the Settled Land Act. The technical question to be decided was whether land 'stands for the time being limited in trust for any persons by way of succession'.[20] However the courts have made it clear that they will treat such land as settled land especially if there is no other way to protect the rights of the life resident.[21] Giving such a person all the powers of disposition and management of a tenant for life has been much criticised. There should be some provision for giving rights of residence during a person's lifetime which do not cause technical complications. This problem is discussed further below.[22]

B. *Making good title*

3.6 If a purchaser of land subject to a trust for sale fails to comply with the provisions of s. 27 of the Law of Property Act 1925, which states that the purchase price must be paid to at least two trustees (or a trust corporation) the conveyance will not be void, although interests under

---

[18] Law of Property Act 1925, s. 205(1)(xxix), and see Megarry and Wade, *The Law of Real Property* (5th edn, 1984), pp. 386–388. [See also C & B, pp. 427–428.]

[19] *Re Parker's Settled Estates* [1928] Ch 247; *Re Ryder and Steadman's Contract* [1927] 2 Ch 62; *Re Norton* [1929] 1 Ch 84; *Re Beaumont Settled Estates* [1937] 2 All ER 353; *Re Sharpe's Deed of Release* [1939] Ch 51.

[20] Settled Land Act 1925, s. 1(1).

[21] *Re Duce and Boots Cash Chemists (Southern) Ltd* [1937] Ch 642; *Bannister v Bannister* [1948] 2 All ER 133; *Binions v Evans* [1972] Ch 359.

[22] [See para. 16.16 of the Working Paper (footnotes omitted):

'Inadvertent settlements fall into two categories. The first are those where the intention is to create some sort of trust or settlement, and the settlor, by failing expressly to subject the land to a trust for sale, brings it within the Settled Land Act 1925. If, as is likely, this is a trust in a will, the executors may not realise the true effect of the provisions and the wrong procedure may be followed, causing problems for subsequent purchasers.... The second type of inadvertent settlement occurs when a person is given the right to reside in a property during his lifetime, and subject to that right the property is conveyed or passes on death to another. At present the result of such an arrangement may be that the land is settled land under the Settled Land Act 1925, and the person with the right of residence is the tenant for life with full powers of disposition and management. This result may be thought to be unsatisfactory, as there was no intention to confer such an extensive interest on the tenant for life. However, these cases should not necessarily be seen as wrongly decided. As Megarry and Wade put it, "it has to be remembered that the deliberate policy of the Act is that the statutory powers must always be available, so that the land is not sterilised, and that these powers cannot be restricted or fettered, whatever the settlor's intentions. This policy may naturally produce unintended results, but that is not necessarily a good reason for excluding a case from the purview of the Act."']

the trust for sale will not be overreached. If a purchaser of settled land fails to comply with the provisions of s. 18 of the Settled Land Act 1925, the conveyance will be void except in so far as it binds the beneficial interest of the tenant for life. In some circumstances a purchaser may be protected by s. 110 of the Settled Land Act, which is discussed in the following paragraph. It is questionable whether it is necessary for the position of a purchaser to vary in this way.

3.7 The drafting of s. 110 of the Settled Land Act 1925 has led to the suggestion that it fails to give purchasers enough protection and that they may have to examine the trust instrument themselves, contrary to the general principles of the Settled Land Act 1925. This is probably a theoretical problem rather than a practical one. A real problem that has arisen is the relationship between s. 110 and s. 18 of the Act. Section 110 is meant to give some protection to a purchaser if he buys in good faith, but under s. 18, if land is settled land, then any unauthorised disposition is void. It is not certain which prevails, nor is it clear whether s. 110 offers any protection where the purchaser does not know that he is dealing with the tenant for life.[23]

3.8 Where settled land is created by will (particularly a home-made one) it is easy for the executors not to realise this and they may, for example, vest the land in trustees rather than in the tenant for life. It may then be difficult for either the tenant for life or the trustees or their successors to make a good title to a later purchaser.[24]

3.9 There is no formal provision for the termination of a trust for sale. This means that purchasers of land which has been subject to a trust for sale may be put in the position of having to investigate the trusts in order to ascertain that the trust for sale has ended.[25]

C. Control by beneficiaries

3.10 In general the beneficiaries of a trust of land are treated no differently from the beneficiaries of a trust of any other kind of property. This may, itself, be the cause of some problems. Land is not like most other kinds of property: each piece is, in principle, unique, and, more importantly, it may be the place where the beneficiaries live, or want to live in the future. Questions of control over the land are therefore particularly important.

3.11 *Those entitled to settled land in remainder.* It is impossible for a remainderman to prevent the sale of the land, unless there is lack of good faith on the part of the tenant for life. This leaves the remainderman in a very weak position because the land may have already been sold before he becomes aware of the tenant for life's intention to sell.[26]

3.12 *Duty to consult.* The trustees of land held on a statutory trust for sale[27] have a duty to consult the beneficiaries.[28] There is no such duty where express trusts for sale are concerned. Even as regards statutory trusts the provision is weak. It only applies 'so far as is practicable'. The trustees only have to give effect to the wishes of the beneficiaries 'so far as consistent with the general interest of the trust' and a purchaser is not affected by the trustees' failure to carry out or comply with the result of any consultation.

3.13 *Delegation.* It has been suggested that the power to delegate the management of land to a tenant for life of land held on trust for sale is inadequate. If the power to delegate is not

---

[23] Compare *Weston v Henshaw* [1950] Ch 510 with *Re Morgan's Lease* [1972] Ch 1. [See also C & B, pp. 995–996.]

[24] As, for example, in *Re Duce and Boots Cash Chemists (Southern) Ltd* [1937] Ch 642.

[25] Except where joint tenants were holding on trust for themselves and there is only one survivor: Law of Property (Joint Tenants) Act 1964.

[26] See, for example, *England v Public Trustee* (1967) 112 SJ 70.

[27] See para. 2.2.

[28] Law of Property Act 1925, s. 26(3) substituted by the Law of Property (Amendment) Act 1926, Sch.

exercised, the tenant for life is left with no control, which may be unsatisfactory if the trust for sale is being used as a substitute for settled land. If the power is exercised, ownership and management are separated, which may be undesirable. The trustees retain the legal interest. If the tenant for life is not in possession, he may not be able to bring an action in his own name to protect the reversion of any property leased. As he is not the covenantee, he cannot sue on the covenants in the lease. It may be that these difficulties do not cause problems in practice as the trustees always take appropriate action, but, in theory at least, they do exist.... In addition it has been said,[29] 'Psychologically in the management of a country estate this duty to act in the name of another seems unsound'. Whether this is true today seems less likely. Ownership and management are commonly separated, for example in limited companies, and we doubt that there is any general issue of principle at stake. Making trustees delegate certain powers in certain situations would minimise the difference between the two systems.

3.14 *Sale subject to consent.* In settled land it is not possible to make the sale of the land or the exercise of other powers subject to the consent of some other person,[30] for example, a remainderman. Making the consent of a beneficiary necessary for the sale of land held on trust for sale does not seem to have caused any problems and a similar provision could be made for settled land.

Specific Settled Land Act problems

3.15 *Complexity.* Perhaps the greatest difficulty of the Settled Land Act 1925 is its sheer complexity. Three different aspects will serve to illustrate this.

   (i) The Act always requires the use of at least two documents, the vesting deed which vests the legal estate in the tenant for life (or whoever is entitled to exercise his powers) and the trust instrument which declares the trusts.[31] If land is acquired after the settlement has been created, a subsidiary vesting deed must be executed vesting the land in the tenant for life (or whoever is entitled to exercise his powers).[32] Hence where there are frequent purchases of land for a settlement, there may be a considerable number of vesting deeds. There are no equivalent provisions for trusts for sale. The deed which vests the land in trustees for sale may also declare the trusts, or there may be two separate documents where that is convenient.[33]

   (ii) The Settled Land Act 1925 does not only provide for the straightforward settlement of a life interest followed by interests in remainder. It also covers a wide range of conditional interests and determinable fees, and land conveyed to infants. Here there is no tenant for life in the proper sense and the Act has to make elaborate provisions giving certain people all the powers of the tenant for life.[34]

   (iii) Because the Act applies in certain circumstances without this being appreciated by the settlor, it can happen that no trustees are appointed by him. Thus a simple gift of land to X for life remainder to Y creates a settlement and it is necessary for

[29] Potter, 'Strict Settlement and Trust for Sale' (1944) 8 Conv (NS) 147, 157.
[30] Settled Land Act 1925, s. 106.   [31] Settled Land Act 1925, ss. 4, 5.
[32] Settled Land Act 1925, s. 10.
[33] Law of Property Act 1925, s. 27(1): the purchaser is not concerned with the trusts.
[34] Settled Land Act 1925, ss. 20–24.

trustees to be appointed. Again this necessitates complex provisions as to who
are to be the trustees where none are appointed.[35]

3.16 *Conflict of interest.* It has been suggested that there is an inherent conflict involved
in the position of the tenant for life. The legal estate and all the powers of dealing with it are
vested in him and under s. 16 of the Settled Land Act 1925 he is a trustee. Yet he is, at the
same time, the principal beneficiary. While it is quite usual for a trustee to be a beneficiary,
given the lack of any other restraints on the tenant's powers, the conflict may become real.
It seems that where there is a conflict of interests, the tenant for life is not treated like an
ordinary trustee. It has been held that the court will not intervene if the tenant for life allows
the estate to become derelict, but only if there is evidence that he has refused to exercise his
powers.[36] Thus the remaindermen may inherit an estate much diminished in value and have
no remedy. Similarly the interests of the remaindermen may be adversely affected by a sale
of the settled land at a low price. Again, they may have no effective remedy[37] as they may
not discover the sale until years after it took place and, even if they could establish a breach
of trust, the tenant for life may be dead and his estate not worth suing. While it is clear that
the courts, recognising the risks arising from conflicts of interest, usually make the purchase
of trust property by a trustee virtually impossible,[38] in one case where the tenant for life
purchased the settled land without the proper procedure being adopted, the sale was simply
allowed to stand.[39]

Trust for sale—specific problems

3.17 *Co-ownership.* The Law of Property Act 1925 imposes a statutory trust for sale wherever land is conveyed to co-owners—whether in equity they are joint tenants or tenants in
common.[40] Thus, wherever a couple buy a house, they become trustees for sale of it although
a sale is probably not what they intend. In 1925, owner-occupation of dwellings was far less
usual than nowadays and, where it did exist, it was less likely that a house would be purchased
in joint names.[41] The co-ownership envisaged by the Law of Property Act would have arisen in
a different context, where, for example, property was left to children in equal shares. In such a
case, a sale at some stage was likely. As far as co-ownership is concerned, a system devised for
one set of social circumstances is being used for very different circumstances.

3.18 *The doctrine of conversion.* The doctrine of conversion states that where land is held
on trust for sale, the interests of the beneficiaries are deemed to be interests in the proceeds of
sale, even before the land has been sold. The doctrine developed during the 18th century.[42] In
the early cases, the nature of the beneficial interests was in question because the law of inheritance differed depending on whether property was real or personal. The doctrine of conversion
meant that land held on trust for sale devolved as personalty. When reform of land law was
being considered, it was the doctrine of conversion that made the trust for sale a useful tool in

---

[35] Settled Land Act 1925, ss. 30–34.   [36] *Re Thornhill's Settlement* [1941] Ch 24.

[37] *England v Public Trustee* (1967) 112 SJ 70.

[38] Pettit, *Equity and the Law of Trusts* (5th edn, 1984), pp. 374–376.

[39] *Re Pennant's Will Trusts* [1970] Ch 75.

[40] Law of Property Act 1925, ss. 34, 36. [On the distinction between joint tenants and tenants in common,
see pp. 563–564, below.]

[41] Co-ownership arises when two or more people rent property, as would have been more usual in 1925,
but most of the problems seem to occur when the co-owners own the fee simple or a long lease.

[42] Lightwood, 'Trusts for Sale' (1927) 3 CLJ 59.

the simplification of conveyancing: since the interests were not in the land anyway, it was easy to provide that a purchaser should take free of them.[43] Now, however, the doctrine of conversion causes problems. To say that a person with an equitable joint tenancy or an equitable tenancy in common has no interest in the house but only an interest in the proceeds of sale, when no sale is contemplated, is wholly artificial. The courts have refused to allow the doctrine of conversion to operate fully in some cases.[44] The position therefore now is that the doctrine of conversion applies for some purposes but not for others, depending on the particular circumstances. This is clearly unsatisfactory.

3.19 *Powers conferred by s. 30 of the Law of Property Act 1925.* Problems have arisen with s. 30 of the Law of Property Act 1925 as to who can apply under the section, the extent of the powers of the court and the factors to be taken into account in exercising the court's discretion. On the face of it, the section only enables an application to be made if the trustee is refusing to sell. However the courts have found ways of protecting beneficiaries who wish to prevent a sale.[45] It also appears that a trustee who has no beneficial interest in the land may be unable to apply, so that the section does not provide a remedy where the trustees cannot agree to a sale.[46]

3.20 While the court is given power to make such order as it thinks fit, it is not certain whether this extends to ordering one co-owner who has sole occupation to pay an occupation rent to the other who is not in occupation. It is probably desirable that they should have power to do so, as this provides a possible solution to the problem that where a sale is refused because of the wishes of one co-owner, the other is deprived of a valuable financial asset.

3.21 A considerable amount of case law exists as to how the discretion should be exercised. Generally the court will look at the purpose for which the trust was created, and see whether the purpose still exists.[47] Particular difficulties have arisen as to the weight to be given to the children's interests,[48] and where one co-owner is bankrupt.[49]

3.22 *Occupation right.* It is not clear whether a tenancy in common confers on beneficiaries as against trustees a right to occupy the land.[50]

3.23 *Creation of tenancy in common.* It has been suggested that a tenancy in common cannot be created informally by e.g. financial contributions, because s. 34(1) of the Law of Property Act states that undivided shares can only be created 'as provided by the Settled Land Act 1925 or as hereinafter mentioned'. The Settled Land Act 1925, s. 36(4) states that undivided shares can only be created under a trust instrument or under the Law of Property Act 1925. This means that only expressly created or statutorily imposed undivided shares can exist. However the courts seem to have accepted the existence of informally created tenancies in common behind a trust for sale. The position could be clarified by statute....

---

[43] See Fourth Report of the Acquisition and Valuation of Land Committee, Cmd. 424, 1919, especially Appendix IV Part I, the Memorandum by B.L. Cherry.

[44] E.g. *Williams & Glyn's Bank v Boland* [1981] AC 487.

[45] See, e.g. *Bull v Bull* [1955] 1 QB 234.

[46] See Law Reform Committee, 23rd Report, para. 3.63.

[47] *Re Buchanan-Wollaston's Conveyance* [1939] Ch 738; *Bull v Bull* [1955] 1 QB 234; *Barclay v Barclay* [1970] 2 QB 677.

[48] Compare *Rawlings v Rawlings* [1964] P 398, 419 and *Burke v Burke* [1974] 1 WLR 1063, 1067.

[49] *Re Holliday* [1981] Ch 405; *Re Lowrie* [1981] 3 All ER 353.

[50] It was accepted in *Bull v Bull* [1955] 1 QB 234 that they did have a right of occupation but this has been criticised. See Crane (1955) 19 Cony (NS) 146. In *Williams & Glyn's Bank v Boland* [1981] AC 487 Lord Wilberforce noted Denning LJ's view in *Bull v Bull* with approval.

G. Bare trusts

3.27   Generally, where two or more people hold interests in land, then either the Settled Land Act will apply or there will be a trust for sale. However, a bare trust is within neither system, and so is to some extent an anomaly. A bare trust exists when the entire beneficial interest is vested in one person and the legal estate in another. The trustee in such a case has no duties other than to obey the beneficial owner, who is, to all intent, the real owner. Such a trust may arise, for example, because land held on trust for several beneficiaries has become vested in one adult beneficiary, or because land is being held by a nominee. A more frequent situation which may involve a bare trust arises where the property of any unincorporated association is held on trust for its members by trustees.[51] Generally bare trusts do not cause problems for purchasers, because either the purchaser is aware of the equitable interest and investigates to ensure the sale is with the consent of the beneficial owners, or he is unaware and takes free of them as a bona fide purchaser of the legal estate for value without notice. However, the overreaching machinery provided by s. 2 of the Law of Property Act 1925 does not apply to bare trusts,[52] and there may be situations where a purchaser fails to obtain a good title.

Summary

3.28   It will be seen from the preceding paragraphs that many of the problems spring from the existence of two systems which can each be used for much the same purpose and yet have major differences in the way they operate. Added to this is the preference that the legislation shows for the creation of settled land, so that land may inadvertently come within the Settled Land Act 1925, even though this is inappropriate. However although it appears at first sight that the legislation governing the two systems covers all possible situations, it has become apparent at this is not so. Bare trusts are not catered for, and lifetime rights of residence have only been made to fit within settled land with difficulty.

III.   THE TRUST OF LAND[53]

In 1996 the first change in the structure of English land law since 1925 was made by the Trusts of Land and Appointment of Trustees Act 1996. The Act applies to trusts of land created before or after the date of its commencement on 1 January 1997. Under it the dual system of strict settlement and trust for sale is replaced by a trust of land which applies to both successive and concurrent interests. Existing strict settlements continue,

---

[51]   *Worthing Rugby Football Club Trustees v Inland Revenue Commissioners* [1985] 1 WLR 409.

[52]   Except where the bare trust has arisen because a trust for sale has ended and the purchaser buying from trustees for sale can assume the trust continues: Law of Property Act 1925, s. 27.

[53]   C & B, chap. 12; Gray, part 7.5; M & W, chap. 12; MM, pp. 283–289; Smith, chap. 16. For commentaries on the Act, see TLATA Bill (House of Lords) *Notes on Clauses*; Whitehouse and Hassall, *Trusts of Land, Trustee Delegation and the Trustee Act 2000* (2nd edn) (a very useful commentary which is referred to throughout this chapter); Barraclough and Matthews, *Trusts of Land and Appointment of Trustees Act* (1996); Kenny and Kenny, *The Trusts of Land and Appointment of Trustees Act 1996* (2nd edn) (with the principal sections of the 1925 legislation as amended, and the Law Commission Report on Trusts of Land 1988 (Law Com No. 181)); Sydenham and Sydenham, *Trusts of Land—The New Law.* See also Emmet, chap. 22; R & R chap. 37; [1996] Conv 401 (A. J. Oakley); (1998) 61 MLR 56 (L. M. Clements).

but no new strict settlements can be created. Existing express trusts for sale, whether of successive or of concurrent interests, also continue, and may still be expressly created so as to come within the wide definition of the trust of land.[54] If, however, trusts of concurrent interests were implied by statute, they are converted into trusts of land. Under the trust of land the legal estate to the land is vested in trustees who are given all the powers of an absolute owner for the purpose of exercising their functions as trustees. The trustees have a power, but not a duty, to sell, and the interests of the beneficiaries are still overreachable on sale, as they were under the previous dual system. The doctrine of conversion is abolished in respect of all trusts for sale, whenever created,[55] and consequently the interests of the beneficiaries under a trust for sale of land are no longer interests in personalty but are interests in land. The Act is another and welcome measure in the long line of measures which over the centuries have sought to develop and simplify the land law; it is an important gloss on the 1925 legislation, and gives to the trustees broad and flexible powers to enable them to manage the land more effectively, and to the beneficiaries more scope in the control of those powers.

A. MEANING OF TRUST OF LAND

'Trust of land' is widely drawn so as to include any trust of property which consists of or includes land; whether created or arising before 1997 or after 1996. It includes a trust for sale: new strict settlements are excluded.[56]

TRUSTS OF LAND AND APPOINTMENT OF TRUSTEES ACT 1996

1. Meaning of 'Trust of Land'.—(1) In this Act—

   (a) 'trust of land' means (subject to subsection (3)) any trust of property which consists of or includes land, and

   (b) 'trustees of land' means trustees of a trust of land.[57]

   (2) The reference in subsection (1)(a) to a trust—

   (a) is to any description of trust (whether express, implied, resulting or constructive), including a trust for sale and a bare trust, and

---

[54] P. 517, below. See (1997) 113 LQR 207 (P. H. Pettit).

[55] Except for a trust for sale created in the will of a testator dying before 1997.

[56] W & H, paras 2.1–2.17.

[57] Trustees are usually appointed by the settlor when creating the trust; in default the court may appoint them. See Trustee Act 1925, ss. 34–43, as amended by TLATA 1996, s. 25(1) Sch. 3, paras 3(9)-(14) and Mental Capacity Act 2005, s. 67, Sch. 6; TLATA 1996 Part II: ss. 19 (appointment and retirement of trustee at instance of beneficiaries); 20 (as amended by Mental Capacity Act 2005, s. 67, Sch. 6: appointment of substitute for trustee who lacks capacity); 21 (supplementary); Trustee Delegation Act 1999, s. 8 (incorporated into TA, s. 36, as (6A)-(6D); appointment of additional trustee by attorney). See generally Maudsley & Burn, *Trusts & Trustees* (7th edn), chap. 13; M & W, paras 11.050–11.064; W & H, paras 3.1–3.33; Law Commission Report on Trustees' Powers and Duties 1999 (Law Com No. 260).

In respect of deaths after 1996, the provisions of Part I of the Act relating to trustees apply to personal representatives, other than ss. 10 (p. 525, below), 11 (p. 526, below) and 14 (p. 532, below): s. 18.

(b)　includes a trust created, or arising, before the commencement of this Act.

(3) The reference to land in subsection (1)(a) does not include land which (despite section 2) is settled land or which is land to which the Universities and College Estates Act 1925 applies.

B. EXCLUSION OF STRICT SETTLEMENTS

TRUSTS OF LAND AND APPOINTMENT OF TRUSTEES ACT 1996

2. Trusts in place of settlements.—(1) No settlement created after the commencement of this Act is a settlement for the purpose of the Settled Land Act 1925; and no settlement shall be deemed to be made under that Act after that commencement.

(2)　Subsection (1) does not apply to a settlement created on the occasion of an alteration in any interest in, or of a person becoming entitled under, a settlement which—

(a)　is in existence at the commencement of this Act, or

(b)　derives from a settlement within paragraph (a) or this paragraph.

(3)　But a settlement created as mentioned in subsection (2) is not a settlement for the purposes of the Settled Land Act 1925 if provision to the effect that it is not is made in the instrument, or any of the instruments, by which it is created.

(4)　Where at any time after the commencement of this Act there is in the case of any settlement which is a settlement for the purposes of the Settled Land Act 1925 no relevant property which is, or is deemed to be, subject to the settlement, the settlement permanently ceases at that time to be a settlement for the purposes of that Act.

In this subsection 'relevant property' means land and personal chattels to which section 67(1) of the Settled Land Act 1925 (heirlooms) applies.

(5)　No land held on charitable, ecclesiastical or public trusts shall be or be deemed to be settled land after the commencement of this Act, even if it was or was deemed to be settled land before that commencement.

(6)　Schedule 1 has effect to make provision consequential on this section (including provision to impose a trust in circumstances in which, apart from this section, there would be a settlement for the purposes of the Settled Land Act 1925 (and there would not otherwise be a trust)).[58]

C. TRUST FOR SALE

(i) Definition

LAW OF PROPERTY ACT 1925

205. General definitions.—(1) In this Act unless the context otherwise requires, the following expressions have the meanings hereby assigned to them respectively, that is to say:—

---

[58] Paras 1 and 2 (minors); 3 (family charges); 4 (charitable, ecclesiastical and public trusts); 5 (entailed interests); 6 (property held on settlement ceasing to exist).

(xxix) 'Trust for sale', in relation to land, means an immediate trust for sale, whether or not exercisable at the request or with the consent of any person; 'trustees for sale' mean the persons (including a personal representative) holding land on trust for sale.

Before 1997 it was necessary to distinguish between a trust for sale and a strict settlement. An interest in succession created a strict settlement unless it satisfied the then definition of a trust for sale which included the word 'binding' between 'immediate' and 'trust'. There must be a trust which imposes on the trustees a duty to sell and not merely a power of sale; the trust for sale must be immediate in that a trust to sell at some future date does not prevent land from being settled land for the time being.[59] It must also be binding. The apparent tautology of this word caused difficulty; trusts are by their very nature binding.[60]

After 1996 it is necessary to discover whether an interest in succession is a trust for sale within the overall definition of a trust of land. To do this it must satisfy the amended definition which excises the word binding (s. 25(2), Sch 4). If it does not satisfy the definition, it still comes within the provisions of the new Act, but if it does, it imposes on the trustees a duty to sell with a mandatory power to postpone sale (under section 4, below).

(ii) Express trusts for sale as trusts of land

Before 1997 section 25 of the Law of Property Act 1925 gave to trustees for sale the power to postpone sale indefinitely, unless a contrary intention was expressed in the trust instrument. After 1996 this power still exists but cannot be excluded by the settlor. The sale can only be postponed if the trustees for sale unanimously decide to exercise the power;[61] if they are not unanimous, then the land must be sold.[62]

Trusts for sale can still be expressly created. It has been suggested that it may be desirable to create an express trust for sale where there is a trust in the residue clause of a will, or where there is a conveyance to co-owners.[63] In any event section 4 of the Trusts of Land and Appointment of Trustees Act 1996 ensures that if a trust for sale is created in ignorance of the new legislation it will be valid under it.

---

[59] See *Re Hanson* [1928] Ch 96; *Bacon v Bacon* [1947] P 151; *Re Herklots' Will Trusts* [1964] 1 WLR 583 (trust for sale subject to X's right to occupy house for life held to be immediate trust for sale subject to X's consent); *Re Nierop's Will Trusts* (23 April 1986, unreported), discussed in *Williams on Wills* (7th edn) pp. 1008, 1174–1178 (trust to sell with consent of beneficiary combined with trust to permit beneficiary to reside while property remains unsold qualifies as trust for sale).

[60] See the 6th edn of this book, pp. 225–229; C & B, pp. 426–428; M & W (5th edn), pp. 386–389; MM, p. 280; Emmet, para. 23.012; *Re Parker's Settled Estates* [1928] Ch 247; cf. *Re Leigh's Settled Estates* [1926] Ch 852. It may be necessary to interpret the word when deciding whether there is a pre-existing strict settlement on 1 January 1997, but this will be very rare.

[61] *Re Mayo* [1943] Ch 302 (where the power to retain required unanimity).

[62] Subject to an order of the court under TLATA 1996, ss. 14 and 15, p. 531, below. Charitable Trustees may act by a majority: *Re Whiteley* [1910] 1 Ch 600 at 607.

[63] W & H, paras 2.26, 2.159, 6.41; Sydenham, *Trusts of Land*, para. 3.8.3; [1998] Conv 84 (R. Mitchell) doubting whether a trust for sale should continue to be used in a will.

Express trusts for sale created before 1997 continue, but are subject to the mandatory power of postponement in section 4(1).

TRUSTS OF LAND AND APPOINTMENT OF TRUSTEES ACT 1996

4. Express trusts for sale as trusts of land.—(1) In the case of every trust for sale of land created by a disposition there is to be implied, despite any provision to the contrary made by the disposition, a power for the trustees to postpone sale of the land; and the trustees are not liable in any way for postponing sale of the land, in the exercise of their discretion, for an indefinite period.

(2) Subsection (1) applies to a trust whether it is created, or arises, before or after the commencement of this Act.

(3) Subsection (1) does not affect any liability incurred by trustees before that commencement.

(iii) Implied trusts for sale as trusts of land

All trusts for sale which are implied by statute, including those arising before 1997, are converted into trusts of land by section 5 (1) of the Trusts of Land and Appointment of Trustees Act 1996. Schedule 2 of the Act identifies these statutory trusts for sale. Statutory provisions have been amended to replace the duty to sell by a power to sell and a power to retain.[64]

TRUSTS OF LAND AND APPOINTMENT OF TRUSTEES ACT 1996

5. Implied trusts for sale as trusts of land.—(1) Schedule 2 has effect in relation to statutory provisions which impose a trust for sale of land in certain circumstances so that in those circumstances there is instead a trust of the land (without a duty to sell).

(2) Section 1 of the Settled Land Act 1925 does not apply to land held on any trust arising by virtue of that Schedule (so that any such land is subject to a trust of land).

Schedule 2 refers to

(a) Mortgaged property held by trustees after redemption barred (LPA 1925, s. 31).

(b) Land purchased by trustees of personal property (LPA 1925, s. 32).

(c) Dispositions to tenants in common (LPA 1925, s. 34, p. 564, below).

(d) Joint tenancies (LPA 1925, s. 36, p. 565, below).

(e) Intestacy (AEA 1925, s. 33).

(f) Reverter of sites (Reverter of Sites Act 1987, s. 1, p. 302, n. 12, above).

---

[64] LPA 1925, s. 35, which set out the meaning of the statutory trusts for sale, is repealed: TLATA 1996, s. 25(2), Sch. 4.

(iv) Doctrine of conversion

Before 1997 the doctrine of conversion applied as soon as a trust for sale came into operation; the interests of the beneficiaries were thus automatically interests in the proceeds of sale of land and not in the land itself. In **Irani Finance Ltd v Singh** [1971] Ch 59 CROSS J said at 80:

The whole purpose of the trust for sale is to make sure, by shifting the equitable interests away from the land and into the proceeds of sale, that a purchaser of the land takes free from the equitable interests. To hold these to be equitable interests in the land itself would be to frustrate this purpose. Even to hold that they have equitable interests in the land for a limited period, namely, until the land is sold, would, we think, be inconsistent with the trust for sale being an 'immediate' trust for sale working an immediate conversion, which is what the Law of Property Act, 1925, envisages (see section 205(1)(xxix)).[65]

But this view gives rise to difficulties and in certain situations it was found undesirable to apply the full logic of the doctrine of conversion.[66] In *Williams & Glyn's Bank Ltd v Boland* [1981] AC 487, p. 203, above, LORD WILBERFORCE said at 507:

To describe the interests of spouses in a house jointly bought to be lived in as a matrimonial home as merely an interest in proceeds of sale, or rents and profits until sale, is just a little unreal.

Section 3 of the Trusts of Land and Appointment of Trustees Act 1996 abolished the doctrine retrospectively in this area, and the interests of beneficiaries under a trust for sale of land are now interests in the land itself.

TRUSTS OF LAND AND APPOINTMENT OF TRUSTEES ACT 1996

3. Abolition of doctrine of conversion.[67]—(1) Where land is held by trustees subject to a trust for sale, the land is not to be regarded as personal property; and where personal property is subject to a trust for sale in order that the trustees may acquire land, the personal property is not to be regarded as land.

(2) Subsection (1) does not apply to a trust created by a will if the testator died before the commencement of this Act.

(3) Subject to that, subsection (1) applies to a trust whether it is created, or arises, before or after that commencement.

---

[65] P. 517, above. This statement was expressly approved and relied upon by Lord Oliver of Aylmerton in *City of London Building Society v Flegg* [1988] AC 54 at 82, p. 551, below.

[66] For analysis of the doctrine and its difficulties, see pp. 292–301 of the 6th edn of this book; C & B, pp. 428–429; M & W, paras 10.029–10.032.

[67] W & H, paras 2.18–2–24. See also TLATA 1996 s. 25(5). The side heading of s. 3 is misleading. The doctrine still subsists, for example in specifically enforceable contracts for the sale of land: (1997) 113 LQR 207 at p. 209 (P. H. Pettit).

D. BARE TRUSTS

Hanbury & Martin, *Modern Equity* (17th edn, 2005), para. 2–034

There is said to be a bare trust when the trustees hold trust property in trust for an adult beneficiary absolutely. In such a situation the beneficiary may call for a conveyance of the legal estate at any time, and the trustees must comply.[68] In the meantime the trustees have no duties to perform and must deal with the trust property in accordance with the instructions of the beneficiary.[69]

Before 1997 bare trusts fell outside the dual system of trust for sale and strict settlement. This caused difficulty, especially in that interests under bare trusts could not be overreached (p. 548, below). After 1996 bare trusts came within the definition of a trust of land (TLATA 1996, s. 1(2)(a), p. 515, above) and interests under them are therefore now overreachable.

IV. FUNCTIONS OF TRUSTEES OF LAND

A. GENERAL POWERS OF TRUSTEES OF LAND

Before 1997 section 28 of the Law of Property Act 1925 gave to trustees for sale 'all the powers of a tenant for life and the trustees of a settlement under the Settled Land Act 1925.' This section is repealed and replaced by section 6 of the Trusts of Land and Appointment of Trustees Act 1996, which applies to all trusts of land whether arising before or after the commencement of the Act. The scope of the new section is much wider than its predecessor and is designed 'to make the scheme of powers as broadly based and as flexible as possible.'[70]

TRUSTS OF LAND AND APPOINTMENT OF TRUSTEES ACT 1996

6. General powers of trustees.—(1) For the purpose of exercising their functions[71] as trustees, the trustees of land have in relation to the land subject to the trust all the powers of an absolute owner.

(2) Where in the case of any land subject to a trust of land each of the beneficiaries interested in the land is a person of full age and capacity who is absolutely entitled to the land, the powers conferred on the trustees by subsection (1) include the power to convey the land to

---

[68] As, indeed, could a multiplicity of beneficiaries, all adult and under no disability; *Saunders v Vautier* (1841) 4 Beav 115.

[69] *Re Cunningham and Frayling* [1891] 2 Ch 567; (1992) 1 JIP 3 (D. Hayton).

[70] Law Commission Report No. 181, paras 10.4, 10.5.

[71] This includes both powers and duties of trustees.

the beneficiaries even though they have not required the trustees to do so; and where land is conveyed by virtue of this subsection—

    (a) the beneficiaries shall do whatever is necessary to secure that it vests in them, and

    (b) if they fail to do so, the court may make an order requiring them to do so.[72]

(3) The trustees of land have power to acquire land under the power conferred by section 8 of the Trustee Act 2000.[73]

(5) In exercising the powers conferred by this section trustees shall have regard to the rights of the beneficiaries.[73a]

(6) The powers conferred by this section shall not be exercised in contravention of, or of any order made in pursuance of, any other enactment or any rule of law or equity.

(7) The reference in subsection (6) to an order includes an order of any court or of the Charity Commission.[74]

(8) Where any enactment other than this section confers on trustees authority to act subject to any restriction, limitation or condition, trustees of land may not exercise the powers conferred by this section to do any act which they are prevented from doing under the other enactment by reason of the restriction, limitation or condition.

(9) The duty of care under section 1 of the Trustee Act 2000 applies to trustees of land when exercising the power conferred by this section.[75]

B. PARTITION BY TRUSTEES OF LAND

TRUSTS OF LAND AND APPOINTMENT OF TRUSTEES ACT 1996

7. Partition by trustees.[76]—(1) The trustees of land may, where beneficiaries of full age are absolutely entitled in undivided shares to land subject to the trust, partition the land, or any part of it, and provide (byway of mortgage or otherwise) for the payment of any equality money.

(2) The trustees shall give effect to any such partition by conveying the partitioned land in severalty (whether or not subject to any legal mortgage created for raising equality money), either absolutely or in trust, in accordance with the rights of those beneficiaries.

(3) Before exercising their powers under subsection (2) the trustees shall obtain the consent of each of those beneficiaries.

(4) Where a share in the land is affected by an incumbrance, the trustees may either give effect to it or provide for its discharge from the property allotted to that share as they think fit.

(5) If a share in the land is absolutely vested in a minor, subsections (1) to (4) apply as if he were of full age, except that the trustees may act on his behalf and retain land or other property representing his share in trust for him.

---

[72] On the difficulties of this subsection, see W & H, paras 2.45–2.51.

[73] As amended by TA 2000, s. 40, Sch. 2, Pt II, para. 45. See s. 17(2) for use by trustees of a trust of proceeds of sale of land.

[73a] [2009] Conv 39 (G. Ferris and G. Battersby).

[74] As amended by Charities Act 2006, s. 75, Sch. 8, para. 182. See *Avis v Turner* [2008] Ch 218 (power to postpone sale in express trust for sale is conferred by s. 4 TLATA, not s. 6(1), so court order to exercise power not subject to restriction in s. 6(6), (7)).

[75] For the duty of care, see p. 524, below.

[76] Replacing LPA 1925, s. 28(3), (4), which with amendments is extended to all trusts of land.

C. EXCLUSION AND RESTRICTION OF POWERS

The powers given under sections 6 and 7 may be excluded or restricted by the disposition creating the trust. They apply to all existing trusts and cannot be excluded. Similarly, they will apply to all implied trusts wherever arising. It is therefore only in express trusts of land created after 1996 that advantage can be taken of section 8.[77]

TRUSTS OF LAND AND APPOINTMENT OF TRUSTEES ACT 1996

8. Exclusion and restriction of powers.—(1) Sections 6 and 7 do not apply in the case of a trust of land created by a disposition in so far as provision to the effect that they do not apply is made by the disposition.

(2) If the disposition creating such a trust makes provision requiring any consent to be obtained to the exercise of any power conferred by section 6 or 7, the power may not be exercised without that consent.[78]

(3) Subsection (1) does not apply in the case of charitable, ecclesiastical or public trusts.[79]

(4) Subsections (1) and (2) have effect subject to any enactment which prohibits or restricts the effect of provision of the description mentioned in them.[80]

D. DELEGATION TO BENEFICIARIES BY TRUSTEES OF LAND COLLECTIVELY

Under section 29 of the Law of Property Act 1925 trustees for sale were empowered to delegate revocably their powers of leasing, accepting surrenders of leases and management to any person of full age for the time being beneficially entitled in possession to the net rents and profits of the land during his life or for any less period. The duty to sell could not be delegated. The trustees were not liable for the acts or defaults of the delegate, but he was, in relation to the exercise of the power by him, deemed to be in the position and to have the duties and liabilities of a trustee.

This section has been repealed by the Trusts of Land and Appointment of Trustees Act 1996,[81] and replaced by a wider provision for delegation by the trustees acting together.[82]

---

[77] W & H, paras 2.68–2.99; [1997] Conv 263 (G. Watt).

[78] For the position of purchasers, see ss. 10, 16(3), pp. 525, 558, below.

[79] This was introduced as an amendment at the Report stage of the Bill to enable these trusts to take advantage of the general powers of trustees of land.

[80] In particular this refers to Pensions Act 1995 s. 35(5) which prevents the powers of occupational pensions scheme trustees being fettered by reference to requirements to obtain the consent of the employer.

[81] S. 25(2), Sch. 4. See W & H, paras 2.72–2.99.

[82] It seems that the power to delegate under s. 9 cannot be excluded: Kenny and Kenny, para. 47–11. For delegation by an individual trustee for a limited period only, see Trustee Act 1925, ss. 25 as substituted by Trustee Delegation Act 1999, s. 5(1). For delegation of general powers by trustees, see TA 2000, Part IV, which creates a new statutory regime. For delegation by trustees of land who are also beneficiaries, see Trustee Delegation Act 1999, ss. 1 and 2. See generally Maudsley & Burn, *Trusts & Trustees* (7th edn), pp. 754–762;

TRUSTS OF LAND AND APPOINTMENT OF TRUSTEES ACT 1996

9. Delegation by trustees.—(1) The trustees of land may, by power of attorney delegate to any beneficiary or beneficiaries of full age and beneficially entitled to an interest in possession in land[83] subject to the trust any of their functions as trustees which relate to the land.[84]

(2) Where trustees purport to delegate to a person by a power of attorney under subsection (1) functions relating to any land and another person in good faith deals with him in relation to the land, he shall be presumed in favour of that other person to have been a person to whom the functions could be delegated unless that other person has knowledge at the time of the transaction that he was not such a person.

And it shall be conclusively presumed in favour of any purchaser whose interest depends on the validity of that transaction that that other person dealt in good faith and did not have such knowledge if that other person makes a statutory declaration to that effect before or within three months after the completion of the purchase.

(3) A power of attorney under subsection (1) shall be given by all the trustees jointly and (unless expressed to be irrevocable and to be given by way of security) may be revoked by any one or more of them; and such a power is revoked by the appointment as a trustee of a person other than those by whom it is given (though not by any of those persons dying or otherwise ceasing to be a trustee).

(4) Where a beneficiary to whom functions are delegated by a power of attorney under subsection (1) ceases to be a person beneficially entitled to an interest in possession in land subject to the trust—

    (a) if the functions are delegated to him alone, the power is revoked,

    (b) if the functions are delegated to him and to other beneficiaries to be exercised by them jointly (but not separately), the power is revoked if each of the other beneficiaries ceases to be so entitled (but otherwise functions exercisable in accordance with the power are so exercisable by the remaining beneficiary or beneficiaries), and

    (c) if the functions are delegated to him and to other beneficiaries to be exercised by them separately (or either separately or jointly), the power is revoked in so far as it relates to him.

(5) A delegation under subsection (1) may be for any period or indefinite.

(6) A power of attorney under subsection (1) cannot be an enduring power of attorney or lasting power of attorney within the meaning of the Mental Capacity Act 2005.[85]

(7) Beneficiaries to whom functions have been delegated under subsection (1) are, in relation to the exercise of the functions, in the same position as trustees (with the same duties and liabilities); but such beneficiaries shall not be regarded as trustees for any other purposes (including, in particular, the purposes of any enactment permitting the delegation of functions by trustees or imposing requirements relating to the payment of capital money).

H & M, paras 20–012—20–021; Law Commission Report on Delegation by Individual Trustees 1994 (Law Com No. 220); Law Commission Report on Trustees' Powers and Duties 1997 (Law Com No. 260).

[83] On the meaning of beneficiary, see s. 22, p. 525, below.

[84] See ss. 6 and 7, pp. 520–521, above.

[85] As amended by Mental Capacity Act 2005, Sch. 6, para. 42(2). On powers of attorney generally, see Cretney and Lush, *Enduring Powers of Attorney* (5th edn).

(8) ...[86]

(9) Neither this section nor the repeal by this Act of section 29 of the Law of Property Act 1925 (which is superseded by this section) affects the operation after the commencement of this Act of any delegation effected before that commencement.

9A. Duties of trustees in connection with delegation etc.[87]—(1) The duty of care under section 1 of the Trustee Act 2000 applies to trustees of land in deciding whether to delegate any of their functions under section 9.

(2) Subsection (3) applies if the trustees of land—

(a) delegate any of their functions under section 9, and

(b) the delegation is not irrevocable.

(3) While the delegation continues, the trustees—

(a) must keep the delegation under review,

(b) if circumstances make it appropriate to do so, must consider whether there is a need to exercise any power of intervention that they have, and

(c) if they consider that there is a need to exercise such a power, must do so.

(4) 'Power of intervention' includes—

(a) a power to give directions to the beneficiary;

(b) a power to revoke the delegation.

(5) The duty of care under section 1 of the 2000 Act applies to trustees in carrying out any duty under subsection (3).

(6) A trustee of land is not liable for any act or default of the beneficiary, or beneficiaries, unless the trustee fails to comply with the duty of care in deciding to delegate any of the trustees' functions under section 9 or in carrying out any duty under subsection (3).

(7) Neither this section nor the repeal of section 9(8) by the Trustee Act 2000 affects the operation after the commencement of this section of any delegation effected before that commencement.

TRUSTEE ACT 2000

1 The duty of care

(1) Whenever the duty under this subsection applies to a trustee, he must exercise such care and skill as is reasonable in the circumstances, having regard in particular—

(a) to any special knowledge or experience that he has or holds himself out as having, and

(b) if he acts as trustee in the course of a business or profession, to any special knowledge or experience that it is reasonable to expect of a person acting in the course of that kind of business or profession.

(2) In this Act the duty under subsection (1) is called 'the duty of care'.[88]

---

[86] Repealed by TA 2000, s. 40(1), (3), Sch. 2, Pt II, para. 46, Sch. 4, Pt II.

[87] As inserted by TA 2000, s. 40(1), Sch. 2, Pt II, para. 47.

[88] For the application of the duty of care, see TA 2000, s,2, Sch. 1; W & H, paras 10.1–10.21; Maudsley & Burn, *Trusts & Trustees* (7th edn), pp. 686–691.

V. BENEFICIARIES UNDER A TRUST OF LAND

Sections 10 to 13 of the Trusts of Land and Appointment of Trustees Act 1996 are mainly concerned with the rights of beneficiaries under a trust of land and with the duties owed to them by their trustees.

A. MEANING OF BENEFICIARY

TRUSTS OF LAND AND APPOINTMENT OF TRUSTEES ACT 1996

22. Meaning of 'beneficiary'.—(1) In this Act 'beneficiary', in relation to a trust, means any person who under the trust has an interest in property subject to the trust (including a person who has such an interest as a trustee or a personal representative).

(2) In this Act references to a beneficiary who is beneficially entitled do not include a beneficiary who has an interest in property subject to the trust only by reason of being a trustee or personal representative.

(3) For the purposes of this Act a person who is a beneficiary only by reason of being an annuitant is not to be regarded as entitled to an interest in possession in land subject to the trust.[89]

B. CONSENTS

Section 10 of the Trusts of Land and Appointment of Trustees Act 1996 is based on section 26 of the Law of Property Act 1925 which has been repealed.[90] Settlors may wish to make the sale of trust land dependent on the consent of the interest in possession beneficiary who will then be able to enjoy the use of the land and so prevent the trustees from selling it over his head and thereby overreaching his interest.

TRUSTS OF LAND AND APPOINTMENT OF TRUSTEES ACT 1996

10. Consents.—(1) If a disposition creating a trust of land requires the consent of more than two persons to the exercise by the trustees of any function relating to the land, the consent of any two of them to the exercise of the function is sufficient in favour of a purchaser.

(2) Subsection (1) does not apply to the exercise of a function by trustees of land held on charitable, ecclesiastical or public trusts.

(3) Where at any time a person whose consent is expressed by a disposition creating a trust of land to be required to the exercise by the trustees of any functions relating to the land is not of full age—

(a) his consent is not, in favour of a purchaser, required to the exercise of the function, but

---

[89] For a detailed analysis, see W & H, paras 4.1–4.8.   [90] S. 25(2), Sch. 4.

(b) the trustees shall obtain the consent of a parent who has parental responsibility for
     him (within the meaning of the Children Act 1989) or of a guardian of his.

In **Re Inns** [1947] Ch 576 there was an application by a widow under the Inheritance
(Family Provision) Act 1938, section 1 for an increased provision from her deceased
husband's very substantial estate. The widow argued that it was the testator's intention
that she should reside during widowhood in a luxurious mansion, 'Springfield', which
was expensive to run and would consume more than the financial provision made for
her. The house was held on trust for sale, but could only be sold with the consent both
of the widow and of the Stevenage Urban District Council, to whom the house was to
be offered, on the widow's remarriage or death, for use as a hospital, with £10,000 in
addition for maintenance and equipment if they accepted the gift.

WYNN-PARRY J refused to hold, on the facts, that the financial provision for the
widow was unreasonable, but at no stage was doubt cast upon the validity of the
requirement of the consent of the widow and of the Council. He said at 582:

After an exhaustive consideration of all the circumstances I come to the conclusion that while, if
I had been sitting in the testator's armchair, I might well have avoided tying up 'Springfield' so
that only the plaintiff's consent to its sale in her lifetime would have been required, and I might
well have provided a somewhat larger fund than the 85,000*l* in view of the size of the estate;
yet, bearing in mind the principles upon which I am directed to proceed by the authorities which
I regard as binding on me, and with which I am respectfully in agreement, I cannot bring myself
to the conclusion that what has been provided is so little as to be unreasonable. From the plaintiff's point of view the provisions regarding 'Springfield' are unfortunate in that neither she nor
the trustees can bring about a sale during her lifetime.

C. CONSULTATION WITH BENEFICIARIES

Section 11 of the Trusts of Land and Appointment of Trustees Act 1996[91] is based on
section 26(3) of the Law of Property Act 1925, which has been repealed, and extends
to express trusts a rule which applied before 1997 to only implied trusts for sale.[92]
It applies to trusts expressly created after 1996 unless excluded by the disposition;
it also applies to implied trusts, whenever arising. As far as pre-1997 express trusts
are concerned, the section does not apply unless it is included by a deed made by the
settlor after 1996. It does not apply to trusts created by will before 1997.

TRUSTS OF LAND AND APPOINTMENT OF TRUSTEES ACT 1996

11. Consultation with beneficiaries.—(1) The trustees of land shall in the exercise of any function relating to land subject to the trust—

(a) so far as practicable, consult the beneficiaries of full age and beneficially entitled to
     an interest in possession in the land, and

---

[91] See W & H, paras 2.107–2.119.   [92] S. 25(2), Sch. 4.

    (b) so far as consistent with the general interest of the trust, give effect to the wishes of those beneficiaries, or (in case of dispute) of the majority (according to the value of their combined interests).[93]

(2) Subsection (1) does not apply—

    (a) in relation to a trust created by a disposition in so far as provision that it does not apply is made by the disposition,

    (b) in relation to a trust created or arising under a will made before the commencement of this Act, or

    (c) in relation to the exercise of the power mentioned in section 6(2).

(3) Subsection (1) does not apply to a trust created before the commencement of this Act by a disposition, or a trust created after that commencement by reference to such a trust, unless provision to the effect that it is to apply is made by a deed executed—

    (a) in a case in which the trust was created by one person and he is of full capacity, by that person, or

    (b) in a case in which the trust was created by more than one person, by such of the persons who created the trust as are alive and of full capacity.

(4) A deed executed for the purposes of subsection (3) is irrevocable.

D. RIGHT TO OCCUPY

Section 12 of the Trusts of Land and Appointment of Trustees Act 1996[94] gives to a beneficiary, who is beneficially entitled to an interest in possession of land, the right to occupy trust land. Section 13 provides that the trustees may exclude, restrict or impose conditions on such occupation.[95]

Before 1997 there were difficulties concerning the occupation by beneficiaries under a trust for sale, especially where the beneficiaries were co-owners under an implied trust. This was due to the doctrine of conversion under which the interests of beneficiaries under a trust for sale were in the proceeds of sale and not in the land itself. As we have seen the courts regarded the doctrine as artificial.[96]

In *Bull v Bull*,[97] for example, a mother and son were equitable tenants in common of residential accommodation and the son was trustee of the legal estate which he held upon an implied trust for sale in favour of his mother and himself. The question was

---

[93] If the trustees fail to consult the beneficiaries it may be a breach of trust; *Re Jones* [1931] 1 Ch 375 at 377 per Bennett J; *Crawley Borough Council v Ure* [1996] QB 13 (notice to quit given to landlord by one joint tenant without consultation with other joint tenant not a 'positive' act for which consultation was necessary, and therefore, not a breach of trust).

[94] [1998] CLJ 123 (D. G. Barnsley).

[95] W & H, paras 2.120–2.138; [1997] Conv 254 (J.G. Ross Martyn).

[96] P. 519, above.

[97] [1955] 1 QB 234; cf. *Barclay v Barclay* [1970] 2 QB 677 (express testamentary trust for sale of bungalow intended to be sold and the proceeds divided). Before 1926 the answer depended very much on the discretion of the trustees: (1955) 19 Conv (NS) 146 at 147 (F. R. Crane).

whether the son could obtain vacant possession against his mother. In holding that the son failed, Lord Denning treated the mother as having an interest in land, and a right to occupy it. The doctrine of conversion has been abolished[98] retrospectively, and the matter is now regulated by sections 12 and 13.

TRUSTS OF LAND AND APPOINTMENT OF TRUSTEES ACT 1996

12. The right to occupy.—(1) A beneficiary who is beneficially entitled to an interest in possession in land subject to a trust of land is entitled by reason of his interest to occupy the land at any time if at that time—

(a) the purposes of the trust include making the land available for his occupation (or for the occupation of beneficiaries of a class of which he is a member or of beneficiaries in general), or

(b) the land is held by the trustees so as to be so available.

(2) Subsection (1) does not confer on a beneficiary a right to occupy land if it is either unavailable or unsuitable for occupation by him.

(3) This section is subject to section 13.

13. Exclusion and restriction of right to occupy.—(1) Where two or more beneficiaries are (or apart from the subsection would be) entitled under section 12 to occupy land, the trustees of land may exclude or restrict the entitlement of any one or more (but not all) of them.

(2) Trustees may not under subsection (1)—

(a) unreasonably exclude any beneficiary's entitlement to occupy land, or

(b) restrict any such entitlement to an unreasonable extent.

(3) The trustees of land may from time to time impose reasonable conditions on any beneficiary in relation to his occupation of land by reason of his entitlement under section 12.

(4) The matters to which trustees are to have regard in exercising the powers conferred by this section include—

(a) the intentions of the person or persons (if any) who created the trust,

(b) the purposes for which the land is held, and

(c) the circumstances and wishes of each of the beneficiaries who is (or apart from any previous exercise by the trustees of those powers would be) entitled to occupy the land under section 12.

(5) The conditions which may be imposed on a beneficiary under subsection (3) include, in particular, conditions requiring him—

(a) to pay any outgoings or expenses in respect of the land, or

(b) to assume any other obligation in relation to the land or to any activity which is or is proposed to be conducted there.

(6) Where the entitlement of any beneficiary to occupy land under section 12 has been excluded or restricted, the conditions which may be imposed on any other beneficiary under subsection (3) include, in particular, conditions requiring him to—

---

[98] TLATA 1996, s. 3; p. 519, above.

(a) make payments by way of compensation to the beneficiary whose entitlement has been excluded or restricted, or

(b) forgo any payment or other benefit to which he would otherwise be entitled under the trust so as to benefit that beneficiary.[99]

(7) The powers conferred on trustees by this section may not be exercised—

(a) so as prevent any person who is in occupation of land (whether or not by reason of an entitlement under section 12) from continuing to occupy the land, or

(b) in a manner likely to result in any such person ceasing to occupy the land,

unless he consents or the court has given approval.

(8) The matters to which the court is to have regard in determining whether to give approval under subsection (7) include the matters mentioned in subsection (4)(a) to (c).

In **Chan Pui Chun v Leung Kam Ho** [2003] 1 FLR 23 the freehold of Hill House, a large four-bedroom family property, was acquired by a company in 1995 and held on trust in the proportions 51:49 for Miss Chan and Mr Leung. The company was also owned by Miss Chan and Mr Leung, in the same proportions. The couple lived at Hill House together until their relationship broke down in 1998 and Miss Chan obtained a non-molestation order against Mr Leung, who left the property. The trial judge rejected Mr Leung's petition for the winding up of the company, and ordered that Hill House be sold but not, without Miss Chan's consent, until the end of the academic term in the summer of 2003, when Miss Chan was due to complete her studies at the University of Surrey (or the earlier cessation of her studies); and he declared that until sale Miss Chan was entitled to occupy Hill House as her residence.

Dismissing Mr Leung's appeal against the judge's decision on Miss Chan's right to occupy, JONATHAN PARKER LJ said at 48:

100 Given the judge's finding that one of the purposes of the trust of Hill House was to provide a home for Miss Chan should her relationship with Mr Leung come to an end, the short issue on this aspect of the case is whether Hill House is 'unsuitable for occupation by [Miss Chan]' within the meaning of s. 12(1) of the TLATA.

101 There is no statutory definition or guidance as to what is meant by 'unsuitable' in this context, and it would be rash indeed to attempt an exhaustive definition or explanation of its meaning. In the context of the present case it is, I think, enough to say that 'suitability' for this purpose must involve a consideration not only of the general nature and physical charac-teristics of the particular property but also a consideration of the personal characteristics, circumstances and requirements of the particular beneficiary. This much is, I think, clear from the fact that the statutory expression is not simply 'unsuitable for occupation' but 'unsuitable for occupation by him', that is to say by the particular beneficiary.

102 In the instant case Mr Leung's complaint, in substance, is that Hill House is too large for Miss Chan's needs and too expensive for her to maintain. However, taking into account that Miss Chan's requirement under the terms of the judge's order (which she has not

---

[99] *French v Barcham* [2009] 1 All ER 145 (ss. 12–15 of TLATA 1996 do not provide exhaustive regime for compensation for exclusion of a beneficiary from occupying land; where s. 13(6) does not apply, court can order payment of compensation in its general equitable jurisdiction).

cross-appealed) is for a right of occupation only until Summer 2003, I agree with the judge that Hill House is not 'unsuitable for occupation by [her]' within the meaning of s. 12(1). In any event I would have taken some persuading that a property which was on any footing suitable for occupation by Miss Chan and Mr Leung whilst they lived together should be regarded as unsuitable for occupation by her alone once Mr Leung had left.

In **Rodway v Landy** [2001] Ch 703, Rodway and Landy were medical practitioners who were the joint owners of a property which they developed as a surgery. They were trustees of land holding the property on a trust of land for themselves as beneficial tenants in common in equal shares. When the practice came to an end, Rodway sought either an order under section 14 of the 1996 Act for the partitioning of the property between them, or an order under section 13 that the parties exercise their powers to exclude or restrict each other's entitlement. The Court of Appeal held that partition was prohibited by the National Health Service Act 1977, but that an order should be made under section 13.

PETER GIBSON LJ said at 712:

31 The main argument of Mr Berry related to section 13 of the 1996 Act. He submitted that the judge erred in concluding that he could make an order excluding or restricting each of the two doctors from a part of the property. This point turns on the construction of the words in parenthesis in section 13(1), '(but not all)'. The judge said of those words:

'The words should not be read in isolation. Section 13 is a limiting provision. It further limits the right of occupation expressly conferred by section 12(1). An exercise of the power so as to exclude or restrict the entitlement of all of the beneficiaries in respect of some part of the land subject to the trust would render section 12(1) nugatory to that extent. The...words therefore prohibit so extensive an exercise of the power. Accordingly, an exercise of the power to exclude or restrict the entitlement to occupation of one of two beneficiaries in relation to part is not offensive to section 12(1) so long as the other beneficiary is entitled to enjoy his right of occupation of that part. There is no ambiguity. The construction merely reflects that every part of a piece of land is unique.'

32 Mr Pearce supported the reasoning and conclusion of the judge. He said that to construe the subsection literally, as Mr Berry urged, would produce an irrational limitation on section 13(1) as it would mean that the trustees can exclude one of two beneficiaries entirely from the occupation of trust property but not limit each of them to occupation of only part of it. Mr Pearce urged that the words 'but not all' mean that the trustees may not exclude or restrict the entitlement of the beneficiaries collectively; after the trustees have exercised their powers the beneficiaries collectively must have rights which are as extensive as those which the beneficiaries collectively had previously. Mr Berry on the other hand submitted that the limitation on the power to exclude or restrict is in terms on the number of beneficiaries who may be excluded or restricted, and it is not related to the land which happens to be the subject of the restriction.

33 I accept that the limitation on the power to exclude or restrict is expressed as a limitation on the number of beneficiaries who may be excluded or restricted. Plainly it would make no sense if there was no beneficiary left entitled to occupy land subject to a trust of land as a result of the exercise of the power under section 13. That is the force of the words "(but not all)". But if an estate consisting of adjoining properties, Blackacre and Whiteacre, was held subject to a trust of land and A and B were entitled to occupy the estate, it would be very surprising if the trustees were not able under section 13 to exclude or restrict B's entitlement to occupy

Blackacre and at the same time to exclude or restrict A's entitlement to occupy Whiteacre. So also I do not see why, in relation to a single building which lends itself to physical partition, the trustees could not exclude or restrict one beneficiary's entitlement to occupy one part and at the same time exclude or restrict the other beneficiary's entitlement to occupy the other part. Each part is land subject to a trust of land and the beneficiaries are entitled to occupy that part until the entitlement of a beneficiary is excluded or restricted by the exercise of the power under section 13. So construed section 3(1) seems to me to make good sense and to provide a useful power which trustees might well wish to exercise in appropriate circumstances so as to be even-handed between beneficiaries. In contrast, I can see no good reason why Parliament should want to confine the trustees to the all or nothing approach urged by Mr Berry. I therefore agree with the conclusion of the judge on this point.

VI. POWERS OF THE COURT

A. GENERAL

Section 14 of the Trusts of Land and Appointment of Trustees Act 1996 gives to the court wide powers to interfere with the trustees' exercise of any of the trust powers, to dispense with any consents or to consult, or to regulate occupation of land by the beneficiaries. Section 15 sets out the matters to which the court must have regard in determining an application under section 14.

The sections apply to all applications whether made before or after the commencement of the Act. In particular, an application may be made by a trustee; an interest in possession beneficiary; a remainderman (whether vested or contingent); a discretionary beneficiary; the secured creditor of a beneficiary; and trustees (and beneficiaries) of a sub-trust (because the 'interest' does not have to be owned beneficially).[100]

There is a considerable body of case law on section 30 of the Law of Property Act 1925, which has been repealed.[101] Those decisions were influenced by the primacy of the trustees' *duty* to sell. The courts invented the doctrine of a secondary or collateral purpose to help them to decide whether that primary purpose could be displaced. They could then exercise their discretion as to whether to make an order for sale or not. As the Law Commission Report said: 'there is something odd about a doctrine whose essential purpose is so obviously the circumvention of an inconvenient position'.[102]

Section 15 puts on a statutory footing the criteria which the courts developed for settling disputes over trusts for sale. The leading cases on section 30 are set out in the sixth edition of this book[103] and are not repeated here except for an extract from *Re*

---

[100] W & H, paras 2.139–2.164. S. 14 also applies in relation to a trust of proceeds of sale of land: s. 17(1).
[101] S. 25(2), Sch. 4.   [102] Law Com No. 181, para. 12.3.
[103] 6th edn, pp. 238–250.

Evers' Trust. The width of section 15 makes it unlikely that much resort will need to be made to them.[104]

In **Re Evers' Trust** [1980] 1 WLR 1327 ORMROD LJ said at 1330:

[W]hen asked to exercise its discretionary powers under section 30 to execute the trust, the court must have regard to its underlying purpose: see *Re Buchanan-Wollaston's Conveyance* [1939] Ch 217, and in this court at p. 738. In that case four adjoining landowners purchased a plot of land to prevent it being built on and held it on trust for sale. They also covenanted with one another that the land would not be dealt with except with the unanimous agreement of the trustees. Subsequently one of them wished to sell, but some of the other trustees objected so the plaintiff applied to the court under section 30 for an order for sale. At first instance, Farwell J refused the order...

His decision was upheld in this court, but on a broader basis, Sir Wilfred Greene MR said, at p, 747:

'....it seems to me that the court of equity, when asked to enforce the trust for sale, whether one created by a settlement or a will or one created by the statute, must look into all the circumstances of the case and consider whether or not, at the particular moment and in the particular circumstances when the application is made to it, it is right and proper that such an order shall be made. In considering a question of that kind, circumstances such as these, the court is bound to look at the contract into which the parties have entered and to ask itself the question whether or not the person applying for execution of the trust for sale is a person whose voice should be allowed to prevail.'

Some 20 years later, in *Jones v Challenger* [1961] 1 QB 176, Devlin LJ reviewed the authorities and affirmed this principle. He said, at p. 181:

'But this simple principle' i.e., that in a trust for sale there is a duty to sell 'cannot prevail where the trust itself or the circumstances in which it was made show that there was a secondary or collateral object besides that of sale. Simonds J, in his judgment in Re Mayo [1943] Ch 302, said that if there were mala fides, the position would be different. If it be not mala fides, it is at any rate wrong and inequitable for one of the parties to the trust to invoke the letter of the trust in order to defeat one of its purposes, whether that purpose be written or unwritten, and the court will not permit it.'

In that case a house had been purchased by a husband and wife jointly as a home. Subsequently, the marriage broke down, the wife left and committed adultery and applied to the court for an order for sale of the property, a leasehold with only a few years to run. The husband continued to live in the house on his own; there were no children. In these circumstances the court decided that the house should be sold. Devlin LJ said, at p. 183:

'In the case we have to consider, the house was acquired as the matrimonial home. That was the purpose of the joint tenancy and, for so long as that purpose was still alive, I think that the right test to be applied would be that in *Re Buchanan-Wollaston's Conveyance* [1939] Ch 738. But with the end of the marriage, that purpose was dissolved and the primacy of the duty to sell was restored.'

TRUSTS OF LAND AND APPOINTMENT OF TRUSTEES ACT 1996

14. Applications for order.—(1) Any person who is a trustee of land or has an interest in property subject to a trust of land may make an application to the court for an order under this section.

---

[104] H & M, p. 297; *Mortgage Corporation v Shaire* [2001] Ch 743, p. 543, below.

(2) On an application for an order under this section the court may make any such order—

(a) relating to the exercise by the trustees of any of their functions (including an order relieving them of any obligation to obtain the consent of, or to consult, any person in connection with the exercise of any of their functions),[105] or

(b) declaring the nature or extent of a person's interest in property subject to the trust, as the court thinks fit.

(3) The court may not under this section make any order as to the appointment or removal of trustees.

(4) The powers conferred on the court by this section are exercisable on an application whether it is made before or after the commencement of this Act.[106]

15. Matters relevant in determining applications.—(1) The matters to which the court is to have regard in determining an application for an order under section 14 include—

(a) the intentions of the person or persons (if any) who created the trust,

(b) the purposes for which the property subject to the trust is held,

(c) the welfare of any minor who occupies or might reasonably be expected to occupy any land subject to the trust as his home, and

(d) the interests of any secured creditor of any beneficiary.

(2) In the case of an application relating to the exercise in relation to any land of the powers conferred on the trustees by section 13,[107] the matters to which the court is to have regard also include the circumstances and wishes of each of the beneficiaries who is (or apart from any previous exercise by the trustees of those powers would be) entitled to occupy the land under section 12.

(3) In the case of any other application, other than one relating to the exercise of the power mentioned in section 6(2)[108], the matters to which the court is to have regard also include the circumstances and wishes of any beneficiaries of full age and entitled to an interest in possession in property subject to the trust or (in case of dispute) of the majority (according to the value of their combined interests).

(4) This section does not apply to an application if section 335A of the Insolvency Act 1986 (which is inserted by Schedule 3 and relates to applications by a trustee of a bankrupt) applies to it.[109]

In **First National Bank Plc v Achampong** [2004] 1 FCR 18[110] Mr and Mrs Achampong were joint proprietors of a house which they mortgaged in favour of the bank to secure a loan for the use of Mr Owusu-Ansah's business in Ghana. In due course Mr Owusu-Ansah defaulted on the loan and the bank sought to enforce the mortgage. The mortgage was held not to be binding on Mrs Achampong by reason of her husband's undue influence. But the bank had an enforceable charge over the

---

[105] *Abbey National Mortgages plc v Powell* (1999) 78 P & CR D16.

[106] S. 14 also applies in relation to a trust of proceeds of sale: TLATA 1996 s. 17(1).

[107] P. 528, above.   [108] P. 520, above.   [109] Below.

[110] [2003] Conv 314 (M. P. Thompson). For other claims under s. 14 by secured creditors for sale of the property, see *Mortgage Corporation v Shaire* [2001] Ch 743, p. 543, below; *Bank of Ireland Home Mortgages Ltd v Bell* [2001] 3 FCR 134 (order for sale); *Edwards v Lloyds TSB Bank plc* [2005] 1 FCR 139 (order for sale, postponed for five years until youngest child reached 18).

husband's share, and sought an order for sale under section 14 of the Trusts of Land and Appointment of Trustees Act 1996. The trial judge refused to make an order for sale, but this was reversed by the Court of Appeal. BLACKBURNE J said at 38:

61 I come then to the particular reason given by the judge in explanation of why he would not have ordered a sale. Although the exercise of a discretion of this kind must turn on the particular facts of the case, I find valuable what was said in *Bank of Ireland Home Mortgages Ltd v Bell* [2001] 3 FCR 134. In that case the husband was found to have forged his wife's signature on various documents pertaining to the mortgage of their matrimonial home. The husband had left the property by the time possession proceedings were brought by the claimant bank following default under the terms of the mortgage. The judge below held that the bank had an equitable charge on the husband's share in the property to secure the sums which it had lent but he refused to order a sale. In coming to that conclusion the judge took into account the fact that the property was purchased as the family home, that it was still occupied by the wife and her son and that the wife was in poor health. He also took into account the fact that there was a second charge. There had also been several years of delay between the commencement of the possession proceedings and the matter coming on for trial. The refusal of the judge to order a sale was the subject of an appeal. Giving the principal judgment, Peter Gibson LJ (with whom Sir Christopher Staughton agreed) held that, as the husband and wife were divorced by the time of the hearing before the judge, the use of the property as a family home, (treating the matter as relevant to s 15(1)(a) or to s 15(1)(b)) had ceased to be operative. He also disregarded as irrelevant the fact that there was a second charge. He then went on to consider the bank's position as an equitable mortgagee of the husband's beneficial share of the property. He said:

'31. Prior to the 1996 Act the courts under s 30 of the Law of Property Act 1925 would order the sale of a matrimonial home at the request of the trustee in bankruptcy of a spouse or at the request of a creditor chargee of a spouse, considering that the creditors' interest should prevail over that of the other spouse and the spouse's family save in exceptional circumstances. The 1996 Act, by requiring the court to have regard to the particular matters specified in s 15, appears to me to have given scope to some change in the court's practice. Nevertheless, a powerful consideration is and ought to be whether the creditor is receiving proper recompense for being kept out of his money, repayment of which is overdue (see *Mortgage Corp v Silkin* [2000] 2 FCR 222). In the present case it is plain that by refusing sale the judge has condemned the bank to go on waiting for its money with no prospect of recovery from Mr and Mrs Bell and with the debt increasing all the time, that debt already exceeding what could be realised on a sale. That seems to me to be very unfair to the bank.

32 Mr de la Rosa also pointed to the bank's delay in the prosecution of the present proceedings, during which time the debt owed to the bank has increased. But it hardly lies in Mrs Bell's mouth to complain, given that she has had the benefit of continuing to occupy the property without paying any interest to the bank, which largely funded the purchase of the property.'

62 So also here. The effect of refusing a sale is to condemn the bank to wait—possibly for many years—until Mrs Achampong should choose to sell before the bank can recover anything. In the meantime its debt continues to increase. (It was £180,000 at the date of the trial as against a value of the property of £195,000.) Nor does it lie with Mrs Achampong to complain of delay since she has had the use of the whole property in the meantime. True it is that, as the judge found, she made a single payment of £13,000 sometime before February 1994 (she refers to the payment in an affidavit that she swore at that time). But that sum can be brought into account on a division of the proceeds following sale.

63 Nor, in my view, is it a consideration of any weight that the bank has not taken steps to recover anything from Mr Achampong or Mr Owusu-Ansah. Those two persons are now in Ghana. There is no evidence as to their wealth or as to the steps open to the bank to pursue them in Ghana with a view to recovering anything from them. Given their default over many years, it is entirely possible that they are substantially without means. It was for Mrs Achampong to adduce evidence to suggest otherwise if she was to place reliance on this as a relevant consideration.

64 It follows that the exercise of discretion by the judge is plainly open to review: he failed to take into account under s 15(1)(d) the bank's position as an unpaid creditor entitled, in the events that have happened, to the whole of Mr Achampong's half share; he wrongly attached weight to the bank's delay in pursuing these proceedings; failing any evidence relevant to the matter, he was wrong to attach any weight to the bank's failure to pursue Mr Achampong and/ or Mr Owusu-Ansah in Ghana.

65 Over and above that, I regard it as plain that an order for sale should be made. Prominent among the considerations which lead to that conclusion is that, unless an order for sale is made, the bank will be kept waiting indefinitely for any payment out of what is, for all practical purposes, its own share of the property. While it is relevant to consider the interests of the infant grandchildren in occupation of the property, it is difficult to attach much if any weight to their position in the absence of any evidence as to how their welfare may be adversely affected if an order for sale is now made. It is for the person who resists an order for sale in reliance on s 15(1)(c) to adduce the relevant evidence. In so far as the Achampongs' intention in creating the trust of the property was to provide themselves with a matrimonial home, and in so far as that was the purpose for which the property was held on trust, that consideration is now spent. Given the many years' absence of contact between Mr and Mrs Achampong, the fact that there has not yet been a divorce cannot disguise the reality that theirs is a marriage which has effectively come to an end. The possibility, therefore, that the property may yet serve again as the matrimonial home can be ignored. In so far as the purpose of the trust—and the intention of the Achampongs in creating it—was to provide a family home and in so far as that is a purpose which goes wider than simply the provision of a matrimonial home, I am unpersuaded that it is a consideration to which much if any weight should be attached. The children of the marriage have long since reached adulthood. One of them is no longer in occupation. It is true that the elder daughter, R, is a person under mental disability and remains in occupation but to what extent that fact is material to her continued occupation of the property and therefore to the exercise of any discretion under s. 14 is not apparent.

66 In all of the circumstances, I would exercise the discretion by ordering a sale of the property to enable the bank to realise its charge over Mr Achampong's beneficial half-share.

In **W v W** [2004] 2 FLR 321 ARDEN LJ rejected the argument that, in exercising his discretion under section 15 of the Trusts of Land and Appointment of Trustees Act 1996 in relation to property which was jointly owned by Mr and Mrs White, the judge was entitled to regard the parties' intentions which had been formed after the trust of land had been created. She said at 327:

22 ... Where more than one person created the trust, the intention for the purposes of s 15(1) (a) must, as I see it, be the intention of all the persons who created the trust and be an intention which they had in common. This is because the subsection speaks of 'the intentions of the person or persons ... who created the trust'. This may be contrasted with the reference in s 15(1)(c) to the welfare of 'any minor'. The use of the definite article and the word 'person' or 'persons' in

subs (1)(a), to my mind, make it clear that the intention referred to in s 15(1)(a) must be the intention of the persons who created the trust, if more than one, in common.

23 The question then remains whether the intention could include intention subsequently come to, as Mr Routley submits. I do not myself consider that this is the correct construction. Parliament has used the word 'intention' which speaks naturally to the intentions of persons prior to the creation of the trust. If that were not its meaning, then it is not clear whether the court should be looking at the parties' intention at the date of the hearing or at some other antecedent point in time and, if so, what date. If Parliament meant the present intention, it would have used some such word as 'wishes' rather than the word 'intention' which implies some statement or opinion as to the future. In all the circumstances, I consider that the appellant's submissions on the point of law on this point are not correct.

B. BANKRUPTCY

Where an application is made by a trustee in bankruptcy under section 14 of the Trusts of Land and Appointment of Trustees Act 1996, the court must take into account the considerations set out in section 335A of the Insolvency Act 1986, which was added to that Act by the 1996 Act.[111] Pre-1997 cases are still relevant when discussing the attitude of the courts to bankruptcy situations.

INSOLVENCY ACT 1986

335A. Rights under trusts of land.—(1) Any application by a trustee of a bankrupt's estate under section 14 of the Trusts of Land and Appointment of Trustees Act 1996 (powers of court in relation to trusts of land) for an order under that section for the sale of land shall be made to the court having jurisdiction in relation to the bankruptcy.

(2) On such an application the court shall make such order as it thinks just and reasonable having regard to —

    (a) the interests of the bankrupt's creditors;

    (b)[112] where the application is made in respect of land which includes a dwelling house which is or has been the home of the bankrupt or the bankrupt's spouse or civil partner or former spouse or former civil partner —

        (i) the conduct of the spouse, civil partner, former spouse or former civil partner, so far as contributing to the bankruptcy,

        (ii) the needs and financial resources of the spouse, civil partner, former spouse or former civil partner, and

        (iii) the needs of any children; and

    (c) all the circumstances of the case other than the needs of the bankrupt.

(3) Where such an application is made after the end of the period of one year beginning with the first vesting under Chapter IV of this Part of the bankrupt's estate in a trustee, the court shall assume, unless the circumstances of the case are exceptional, that the interests of the bankrupt's creditors outweigh all other considerations.

---

[111] TLATA 1996, s. 25(1), Sch. 3, para. 23.
[112] Amended by Civil Partnership Act 2004, Sch. 27, para. 118

(4) The powers conferred on the court by this section are exercisable on an application whether it is made before or after the commencement of this section.

Re Citro
[1991] Ch 142 (CA, **Nourse** and **Bingham LJJ** and **Sir George Waller**)[113]

In 1985 the two Citro brothers, Domenico and Carmine, who ran a garage business as panel beaters and car sprayers, were declared bankrupt. The trustee in bankruptcy of their joint and several estates applied for an order under section 30 of the Law of Property Act 1925 for possession and sale. In each case the house was jointly owned by the bankrupt and his wife in equal shares. Domenico was judicially separated from his wife Mary in December 1984 and she lived in their house with their three children, but Carmine lived in his house together with his wife Josephine and their three children. The youngest child of Domenico was aged 12, and that of Carmine 10. The debts owed by each of the brothers exceeded the value of their interests in their houses.

Hoffmann J made an order for possession and sale, postponed until the youngest child in each case became 16 (i.e. until 1994 and 1995).

Held. (Sir George Waller dissenting) Order confirmed, but period of postponement not to exceed 6 months.

Nourse LJ: In the leading case of *Jones v Challenger* [1961] 1 QB 176 it was held by this court that on an application under section 30 of the Law of Property Act 1925 in relation to property acquired jointly as a matrimonial home neither spouse has a right to demand a sale while that purpose still exists. That is now a settled rule of law, applicable to property owned jointly by joint occupants, whether married or unmarried. But its application depends on the whole of the beneficial interest being vested in the occupants. If one of them has become bankrupt, so that part of the beneficial interest is vested in his or her trustee, there arises a conflict between the interests of the occupants and the statutory obligation of the trustee to realise the bankrupt's assets for the benefit of the creditors.

In a series of bankruptcy decisions relating to matrimonial homes subsequent to *Jones v Challenger* it has been held that the interests of the husband's creditors ought usually to prevail over the interests of the wife and any children and, with one exception, *Re Holliday* [1981] Ch 405, a sale within a short period has invariably been ordered...

Hoffmann J carefully considered the personal circumstances of each wife and her children. He observed that they had very little money coming in and that Mary Citro was not well. In evidence they had both said that their children's education would be upset if they had to move. The judge was clearly concerned, more so perhaps in the case of Mary Citro, that, if the houses had to be sold, the half shares of the proceeds received by the wives would not enable them to find proper accommodation for themselves and their families. He expressed his decision thus:

'The balancing which one is required to do between the interests of the creditors and the interests of the wives and families—who are of course entirely innocent parties—is by no means an easy thing to do. The two interests are not in any sense commensurable. On the one hand, one has the financial interests of the Crown, some banking institutions and a few traders. On the other, one has personal

---

[113] (1991) 107 LQR 177 (S. M. Cretney); [1991] CLJ 45 (J.C. Hall); [1991] Conv 302 (A. M. M. Lawson); (1992) 15 MLR 284 (D. Brown). For discussion and criticism of the paramount status of creditors in proceedings involving recovery of the family home, see [2006] Conv 157 (P. Omar).

and human interests of these two families. It is very hard to see how they can be weighed against each other, except in a way which involves some value judgment on the part of the tribunal.

If one was considering the rights of these two wives to their matrimonial homes in the event of a breakdown of their marriages, I think that it would be accepted that, in so far as the Family Division did not order the interest of the husband to be transferred to the wife, it would be unlikely to make an order for the sale of the house to allow the husband to realise his share until at any rate such time as the youngest child of the marriage had attained the age of 16. It is of course true that the vesting of the husband's share in the trustee brings a new factor into the equation. It requires the interests of the creditors too to be taken into account. Nevertheless the normal practice in the Family Division seems to me a fair indication of the way in which the court might deal with the husband's property rights as property rights, and it is after all to his property rights that the trustee has succeeded. It therefore appears to me that it would be wrong to refuse altogether to make an order for sale. That would be treating the wives as having a permanent right to reside in the houses and to prevent the husband or his trustee from realising their interests. That, in my view, would be inequitable. On the other hand, I think it would be equally wrong to make an immediate order for sale, having regard to the hardship which this would cause to the two families.'

In order to see whether the judge's decision can be supported, it is necessary to give close consideration to the earlier authorities.

His Lordship referred to *Jones v Challenger* [1961] 1 QB 176; *Re Mayo* [1943] Ch 302; *Re Buchanan-Wollaston's Conveyance* [1939] Ch 738; *Re Solomon* [1967] Ch 573; *Boydell v Gillespie* (1970) 216 EG 1505; *Re Hardy's Trust* (1970) Times, 23 October; *Re Turner* [1974] 1 WLR 1556; *Re Densham* [1975] 1 WLR 1519; *Re Bailey* [1977] 1 WLR 278; *Re Holliday* [1981] Ch 405; *Re Lowrie* [1981] 3 All ER 353, p. 541, below; and continued:

The broad effect of these authorities can be summarised as follows. Where a spouse who has a beneficial interest in the matrimonial home has become bankrupt under debts which cannot be paid without the realisation of that interest, the voice of the creditors will usually prevail over the voice of the other spouse and a sale of the property ordered within a short period. The voice of the other spouse will only prevail in exceptional circumstances. No distinction is to be made between a case where the property is still being enjoyed as the matrimonial home and one where it is not.

What then are exceptional circumstances? As the cases show, it is not uncommon for a wife with young children to be faced with eviction in circumstances where the realisation of her beneficial interest will not produce enough to buy a comparable home in the same neighbourhood, or indeed elsewhere. And, if she has to move elsewhere, there may be problems over schooling and so forth. Such circumstances, while engendering a natural sympathy in all who hear of them, cannot be described as exceptional. They are the melancholy consequences of debt and improvidence with which every civilised society has been familiar. It was only in *Re Holliday* that they helped the wife's voice to prevail, and then only, as I believe, because of one special feature of that case. One of the reasons for the decision given by Sir David Cairns was that, it was highly unlikely that postponement of payment of the debts would cause any great hardship to any of the creditors, a matter of which Buckley LJ no doubt took account as well. Although the arithmetic was not fully spelled out in the judgments, the net value of the husband's half share of the beneficial interest in the matrimonial home was about £13,250, against which had to be set debts of about £6,500 or £7,500 as the sum required to obtain a full discharge. Statutory interest at 4 per cent. on £6,500 for five years would have amounted to no more than £1,300 which, when added to the £7,500, would make a total of less than £9,000, well covered by the £13,250. Admittedly, it was detrimental to the creditors to be kept out of a commercial rate of interest and the use of the money during a further period of five years. But if the principal was safe, one can understand that that detriment was not treated as being decisive, even in inflationary times. It must indeed be exceptional for creditors in a bankruptcy to receive 100p In the £ plus statutory interest in full and the passage of years before they do so does not make it less exceptional. On the other hand, without that special feature, I cannot myself see how the circumstances in *Re Holliday* could fairly have been treated as exceptional. I am confirmed in that view by the belief that it would be shared by Balcombe LJ, who in *Harman v Glencross* [1986] Fam 81, 95 said that the decision in *Re Holliday* was very much against the run of the recent authorities. I would not myself have regarded it as an exceptional circumstance that the husband had presented his own petition, even 'as a tactical move'. That was not something of the creditors' choosing and could not fairly have been held against them.[114] I do not say that in other cases there might not be other exceptional circumstances. They must be identified if and when they arise.

If *Re Holliday* is put on one side, are the bankruptcy cases, all of which were decided at first instance or in the Divisional Court in Bankruptcy, consistent with the principles stated in *Jones v Challenger* [1961] 1 QB 176? ...

I am therefore of the opinion that the earlier authorities, as I have summarised them, correctly state the law applicable to the present case. Did Hoffmann J correctly apply it to the facts which were before him? I respectfully think that he did not. First, for the reasons already stated, the personal circumstances of the two wives and their children, although distressing, are not by themselves exceptional. Secondly, I think that the judge erred in fashioning his orders by reference to those which might have been made in the Family Division in a case where bankruptcy had not supervened. That approach, which tends towards treating the home as a source of provision for the children, was effectively disapproved by the earlier and uncontroversial part of the decision of this court in *Re Holliday*. Thirdly, and perhaps most significantly, he did not ask himself the critical question whether a further postponement of payment of their debts would cause hardship to the creditors. It is only necessary to look at the substantial deficiencies referred to earlier in this judgment in order to see that it would. Since then a further 18 months' interest has accrued and the trustee has incurred the costs of these proceedings as well.

In all the circumstances, I think that these cases are clearly distinguishable from *Re Holliday* and ought to have been decided accordingly. Part at least of the reason why they were not was that the points with which we have been concerned were not as fully argued below as they have been here. In particular, a close examination of the figures in order to see whether a postponement would cause increasing hardship to the creditors was not undertaken. This is not to imply any criticism of counsel. It is a characteristic of our system that the higher court often seems partial towards thinking that the important point is the one which was not taken in the lower court.

---

[114] See *Re Lowrie* [1981] 3 All ER 353, p. 541, below, where Walton J said at 355: 'in *Re Holliday*...the petition in bankruptcy had been presented by the husband himself as a tactical move, and quite clearly as a tactical move, to avoid a transfer of property order in favour of his wife, or ex-wife, at a time when no creditors whatsoever were pressing and he was in a position in the course of a year or so out of a very good income to discharge whatever debts he had. He had gone off leaving the wife in the matrimonial home, which was the subject matter of the application, with responsibility for all the children on her own. One can scarcely, I think, imagine a more exceptional set of facts, and the court gave effect to those exceptional facts.'

Finally, I refer to section [335A][115] of the Insolvency Act 1986 which, although it does not apply to either of these cases, will apply to such cases in the future. In [subsection (3)] of that section the court is required, in the circumstances there mentioned, to 'assume, unless the circumstances of the case are exceptional, that the interests of the bankrupt's creditors outweigh all other considerations.' I have no doubt that that section was intended to apply the same test as that which has been evolved in the previous bankruptcy decisions, and it is satisfactory to find that it has....

I would allow both appeals by deleting the provisos for postponement from Hoffmann J's orders and substituting short periods of suspension, the length of which can be discussed with counsel.

(1991) 107 LQR 177 at p. 179 (S. M. Cretney)

The decision of the Court of Appeal is clearly defensible in analytical terms. But it seems inevitable that its effect will be to discourage the exercise of the judicial flexibility which has been found so valuable by the courts in cases involving the family home. *Re Gorman* [1990] 1 WLR 616 provides an instructive recent example of the judicial readiness to be inventive and constructive in cases involving a competition between creditor and family interests which now seems unlikely to be favoured: the Divisional Court indicated that it would be prepared to postpone sale of the former family home (on terms) pending the outcome of legal action by the wife which might furnish her with the funds to buy out the husband's interest. But the court did not decide that it would *impose* such a solution against the wishes of the trustee, and in the light of *Re Citro* it seems difficult to believe that it could now properly do so.

In **Re Mott** [1987] CLY 212, Q had lived in a house for over 40 years with each of her late husbands. She was 70. The house was full of memories and she had done a lot of work on it. She was in poor health which the doctor said would deteriorate if she was forced to move. She and her son, M, had purchased the freehold in 1980 from the local authority. M's creditors were largely the State in the form of the Inland Revenue and the DHSS. M had left home in 1986 and disappeared. In a claim by M's trustee in bankruptcy under section 30 for an order for sale of the house, Q sought postponement of sale until after her death.

Hoffmann J dismissed the trustee's claim. He held that it was necessary to balance the legal and moral claims of the creditors and the mother and to take into account the hardship which the latter would suffer. It would be difficult to imagine a more extreme case of hardship than this one. The creditors should wait until after Q's death.[116]

---

[115] Nourse LJ referred to Insolvency Act 1986, s. 336, which is in part repealed by TLATA 1996, Sch. 4. S. 336 now applies only to occupation orders under FLA 1996, s. 33 in cases of bankruptcy; p. 605, below.

[116] *Judd v Brown* [1998] 2 FLR 360 (cancer); *Re Raval* [1998] 2 FLR 718 (mental illness of wife); *Claughton v Charalambous* [1999] 1 FLR 740 (60-year-old with chronic disease, who had great difficulty in walking in house adapted to her needs); *Re Bremner* [1999] 1 FLR 912; *Re Raval* [1998] 2 FLR 718 (sale postponed for a year to allow accommodation to be found for paranoid schizophrenic with three children); *Nicholls v Lan* [2007] 1 FLR 744 (long-term chronic schizophrenia). See *Re Bennett* [2000] EGCS 41, applying the same test for exceptional circumstances as was applied in pre-1996 Act decisions.

In **Re Lowrie** [1981] 3 All ER 353, the Divisional Court granted an order to the trustee in bankruptcy. WALTON J said at 356:[117]

I think it is desirable to step back for a moment and look at the situation which must in these cases inevitably occur, or at any rate must occur so frequently as to be almost inevitable. The first one is of course that the whole family are going to be rendered homeless. That is not an exceptional circumstance. It is a normal circumstance and is the result, the all too obvious result, of a husband having conducted the financial affairs of the family in a way which has led to bankruptcy. The second result almost invariably is that it is going to be incredibly hard and incredibly bad luck on the co-owner, the wife, who is in most cases a totally innocent person who has done nothing to bring about the bankruptcy. Of course, as against that, one has to realise that she has been enjoying over whatever period it may be the fruits of the debts which the bankrupt has contracted and which debts are not at the moment being paid. So that although it may be very bad luck on her, she at any rate has had some enjoyment of the fruits which led to the bankruptcy.

In **Barca v Mears** [2005] 2 FLR 1[118] NICHOLAS STRAUSS QC held that the special educational needs of the bankrupt's child were not 'exceptional circumstances' to outweigh the creditors' claim for sale of the property. However, at 9 he also considered whether the interpretation of the 'exceptional circumstances' test in *Re Citro* [1991] Ch 142, p. 537, above, and the cases which have followed it, is consistent with the European Convention on Human Rights:[119]

33 ... Mr Barca invokes the European Convention for the Protection of Human Rights and Fundamental Freedoms 1950 (the European Convention). He submits that the deputy registrar failed to take account of his or his son's right to family life, home and privacy, stating that in the 8-year period since he became bankrupt his son had grown to know him as his father and that his right to family life, home and privacy were important aspects of his development. He submits at para 29.4 that 'insolvency legislation in this area is particularly brutal and contrary to the average concept of fundamental freedoms and rights'.

36 Human Rights Act 1998, s. 3(1) provides:

'So far it is possible to do so, primary legislation and subordinate legislation must be read and given effect in a way which is compatible with the Convention rights.'

37 Mr Gibbon submitted, in my view correctly, that where a court considers that a statutory provision, as interpreted before the European Convention became part of English law, is

---

[117] [1982] Conv 374 (A. Sydenham): [1983] Conv 219 (C. Hand).

[118] [2005] Conv 161 (M. Dixon).

[119] See, however, *Hosking v Michaelides* [2006] BPIR 1192 at [70] (Paul Morgan QC: would not have been prepared to hold that s. 335A or 336 of the 1986 Act, construed in accordance with the approach in *Re Citro* [1991] Ch 142, would have been incompatible with Art 8); *Nicholls v Lan* [2007] 1 FLR 744 at [41]-[48], [2007] Conv 78 (M. Pawlowski) (Paul Morgan QC: 'the way in which s. 335A operates in the present case is that the court is required to perform a balancing exercise and to decide what is "just and reasonable" and, amongst the circumstances which are to be taken into account, are the interests of the creditors and the needs of someone like [the wife who jointly owned the property, and who suffered from long-term chronic schizophrenia]. For my part, I do not see that the statutory test, leading to a balancing exercise, is inconsistent with the qualified nature of the rights enshrined in Art 8 and in Art 1 of the First Protocol. Indeed, it might be contended that s. 335A precisely captures what is required by Art 8 and Art 1 of the First Protocol.')

incompatible with the Convention, it should seek to re-interpret the relevant provisions so as to achieve compatibility: only if this is not possible should a court consider granting a declaration of incompatibility...

39 Clearly, in many or perhaps most cases, the sale of a bankrupt's property in accordance with bankruptcy law will be justifiable on the basis that it is necessary to protect the rights of others, namely the creditors, and will not be a breach of the European Convention. Nevertheless, it does seem to me to be questionable whether the narrow approach as to what may be 'exceptional circumstances' adopted in *Re Citro* [1991] Ch 142 is consistent with the Convention. It requires the court to adopt an almost universal rule, which prefers the property rights of the bankrupt's creditors to the property and/or personal rights of third parties, members of his family, who owe the creditors nothing. I think that there is considerable force in what is said by Ms Deborah Rook in *Property Law and Human Rights* (Blackstone Press, 2001), at pp 203–205, to which Mr Gibbon very fairly referred me:

> 'It is arguable that, in some circumstances, [s. 335A(3)] may result in an infringement of Article 8. The mortgagor's partner and children have the right to respect for their home and family life under Article 8 even though they may have no proprietary interest in the house...therefore it is possible that the presumption of sale in s. 335A and the way that the courts have interpreted it, so that in the majority of cases an innocent partner and the children are evicted from the home, violates Convention rights...
>
> The eviction of the family from their home, an event that naturally ensues from the operation of the presumption of sale in s. 335A, could be considered to be an infringement of the right to respect of the home and family life under Article 8 if the presumption is given absolute priority without sufficient consideration being given to the Convention rights of the affected family. Allen[120] observes that:
>
>> "As the law currently stands, the right to respect for family life and the home receives almost no consideration after the one year period. Whether such a strict limitation is compatible with the Convention is doubtful."
>
> ...it may be that the courts, in applying s. 335A...will need to adopt a more sympathetic approach to defining what constitutes 'exceptional circumstances'. If an immediate sale of the property would violate the family's rights under Article 8, the court may be required in compliance with its duty under s. 3 of the HRA 1988 to adopt a broad interpretation of 'exceptional circumstances'...to ensure the compatibility of this legislation with Convention rights.'

40 In particular, it may be incompatible with Convention rights to follow the approach taken by the majority in *Re Citro* [1991] Ch 142, in drawing a distinction between what is exceptional, in the sense of being unusual, and what Nourse LJ refers to as the 'usual melancholy consequences' of a bankruptcy. This approach leads to the conclusion that, however disastrous the consequences may be to family life, if they are of the usual *kind* then they cannot be relied on under s. 335A; they will qualify as 'exceptional' only if they are of an unusual kind, for example where a terminal illness is involved.

41 It seems to me that a shift in emphasis in the interpretation of the statute may be necessary to achieve compatibility with the European Convention. There is nothing in the wording of s. 335A, or the corresponding wording of ss. 336 and 337, to require an interpretation which

---

[120] [T. Allen in 'The Human Rights Act (UK) and Property Law' in *Property and the Constitution* (Hart Publishing, 1999), at p. 163.]

excludes from the ambit of 'exceptional circumstances' cases in which the consequences of the bankruptcy are of the usual kind, but exceptionally severe. Nor is there anything in the wording to require a court to say that a case may not be exceptional, if it is one of the rare cases in which, on the facts, relatively slight loss which the creditors will suffer as a result of the postponement of the sale would be outweighed by disruption, even if of the usual kind, which will be caused in the lives of the bankrupt and his family. Indeed, on one view, this is what the Court of Appeal decided in *Re Holliday* [1981] Ch 405.

42 Thus it may be that, on a reconsideration of the sections in the light of the Convention, they are to be regarded as merely recognising that, in the general run of cases, the creditors' interests will outweigh all other interests, but leaving it open to a court to find that, on a proper consideration of the facts of a particular case, it is one of the exceptional cases in which this proposition is not true. So interpreted, and without the possibly undue bias in favour of the creditors' property interests embodied in the pre-1998 case law, these sections would be compatible with the European Convention.

43 I do not need to reach a conclusion on this in the present case, because, even if this tentative view as to the proper approach to the interpretation of these sections is correct, I would still uphold the deputy registrar's decision on the facts of this case.

C. RELATIONSHIP WITH PRE-1997 CASE LAW

In **Mortgage Corporation v Shaire** [2001] Ch 743[121] the claimant bank, as equitable chargee of the defendant's house, sought possession and sale of it by reason of arrears of payment on the mortgage. In deciding not to make an order until the parties had had an opportunity to consider the consequences of the court's conclusions on the law, NEUBERGER J said at 756:

The question here is: ought I to make an order for sale of the house and, if not, what order ought I to make? Until the 1996 Act came into force on 1 January 1997, property owned by more than one person, not held on a strict settlement, was held on trust for sale, and section 30 of the Law of Property Act 1925 applied. In that connection the law had developed in the following way. In *Re Citro* [1991] Ch 142, 157 Nourse LJ said:

His Lordship read the paragraph 'The broad effect of these authorities' . . . p. 538, above, and continued:

In *Lloyds Bank plc v Byrne* [1993] 1 FLR 369, the Court of Appeal had to consider a number of grounds advanced for distinguishing between a case (such as *Re Citro*) where the trustee in bankruptcy of one of the owners of a beneficial interest in the property wanted to sell and a case (such as *Lloyds Bank plc v Byrne*) where a mortgagee or chargee of one of the parties' beneficial interests wished to sell. Those differences were recorded, at p. 372, including lastly: 'a trustee in bankruptcy is under a statutory duty to realise the assets of the bankrupt whereas there is no such duty upon a chargee under a charging order.' Parker LJ went on to say:

---

[121] [2002] Conv 329 (M. Thompson); [2000] Conv 315 (S. Pascoe); [2001] CLJ 43 (M. Oldham); [2001] All ER Rev 258 (P. J. Clarke).

His Lordship cited Parker LJ at 377, and continued:

Accordingly, there was, in relation to trusts for sale and before the 1996 Act came into force, no difference between the two types of case considered in *Re Citro* and *Lloyds Bank plc v Byrne*. The normal rule in such cases was that, save in exceptional circumstances, the wish of the person wanting the sale, be it a trustee in bankruptcy or a chargee, would prevail, and that the interests of children and families in occupation would be unlikely to prevail. These conclusions were applied in a number of cases at first instance, including *Barclays Bank plc v Hendricks* [1996] 1 FLR 258 (Laddie J) and *Zandfarid v Bank of Credit and Commerce International SA* [1996] 1 WLR 1420 (Jonathan Parker J).

However, trusts for sale and section 30 have now been effectively replaced by the 1996 Act.

His Lordship read sections 14(1) and (2) and 15 and continued:

Two questions of principle have been canvassed. First, as a result of the 1996 Act, has the law, relating to the way in which the court will exercise its power to order a sale at the suit of a chargee of the interest of one of the owners of the beneficial interest in property, changed? In other words, does section 15 change the law from how it had been laid down in *Re Citro* and *Lloyds Bank plc v Byrne?* Secondly, does section 15(3) apply in the present case?

The effect of the 1996 Act

To my mind, for a number of reasons, Mr Asif is correct in his submission on behalf of Mrs Shaire that section 15 has changed the law. First, there is the rather trite point that, if there was no intention to change the law, it is hard to see why Parliament has set out in section 15(2) and, indeed, on one view, section 15(3), the factors which have to be taken into account specifically, albeit not exclusively, when the court is asked to exercise its jurisdiction to order a sale.

Secondly, it is hard to reconcile the contention that Parliament intended to confirm the law as laid down in *Lloyds Bank plc v Byrne* with the fact that, while the interest of a chargee is one of the four specified factors to be taken into account in section 15(1)(d), there is no suggestion that it is to be given any more importance than the interests of the children residing in the house: see section 15 (1)(c). As is clear from the passage I have quoted from the judgment of Nourse LJ in *Re Citro* as applied to a case such as this in light of *Lloyds Bank plc v Byrne,* that would appear to represent a change in the law.

Thirdly, the very name 'trust for sale' and the law as it has been developed by the courts suggest that under the old law, in the absence of a strong reason to the contrary, the court should order sale. Nothing in the language of the new code as found in the 1996 Act supports that approach.

Fourthly, it is clear from the reasons in *Lloyds Bank plc v Byrne,* and indeed the later two first instance cases to which I have referred, that the law, as developed under section 30 of the Law of Property Act 1925, was that the court should adopt precisely the same approach in a case where one of the co-owners was bankrupt (*Re Citro*) and a case where one of the co-owners had charged his interest (*Lloyds Bank plc v Byrne*). It is quite clear that Parliament now considers that a different approach is appropriate in the two cases—compare section 15(2) and section 15(3) of the 1996 Act with section 15(4) and the new section 335A of the Insolvency Act 1986.

Fifthly, an indication from the Court of Appeal that the 1996 Act was intended to change the law is to be found in (an albeit plainly obiter) sentence in the judgment of Peter Gibson LJ in *Bankers Trust Co v Namdar* (unreported) 14 February 1997; Court of Appeal (Civil Division)

Transcript No 349 of 1997. Having come to the conclusion that the wife's appeal against an order for sale had to be refused in light of the reasoning in *Re Citro* and *Lloyds Bank plc v Byrne,* Peter Gibson LJ said: 'It is unfortunate for Mrs Namdar that the very recent Trusts of Land and Appointment of Trustees Act 1996 was not in force at the relevant time'—i.e. at the time of the hearing at first instance. Of course it would be dangerous to build too much on that observation, but it is an indication from the Court of Appeal, and indeed from a former chairman of the Law Commission, as to the perceived effect of the 1996 Act.

Sixthly, the leading textbooks support the view that I have reached. In Megarry & Wade, *The Law of Real Property,* para. 9–064, one finds:

> 'Although the authorities on the law prior to 1997 will therefore continue to provide guidance, the outcome will not in all cases be the same as it would have been under the previous law. This is because the legislation is much more specific as to the matters which a court is required to take into account...'

And in *Emmet on Title,* 19th edn looseleaf, vol. 2, para. 22–035:

> 'Cases decided on pre-1997 law may be disregarded as of little, if any, assistance...because the starting point...was necessarily a trust for sale implied or expressed as a conveyancing device enabling the convenient co-ownership of the property...'

Seventhly, the Law Commission Report which gave rise to the 1996 Act, Transfer of Land, Trusts of Land (1989) (Law Com No. 181), tends to support this view as well. It is fair to say that the Law Commission did not propose a new section in a new Act such as section 15 of the 1996 Act, but a new section 30 of the 1925 Act. It is also fair to say that the terms of the proposed new section 30 were slightly different from those of section 15. However, in my judgment, the way in which the terms of the 1996 Act, and in particular section 15, have been drafted suggests that the Law Commission's proposals were very much in the mind of, and were substantially adopted by, the legislature. In paragraph 12.9 of the report the Law Commission describe the aim as being to 'consolidate *and rationalise*' (emphasis added) the current approach. When commenting on the proposed equivalents of what are now section 15(2) and section 15(3) the Law Commission said, in footnote 143:

> 'Clearly, the terms of these guidelines may influence the exercise of discretion in some way. For example, it may be that the courts' approach to creditors' interests will be altered by the framing of the guideline as to the welfare of children. If the welfare of children is seen as a factor to be considered independently of the beneficiaries' holdings, the courts may be less ready to order the sale of the home than they are at present.'

Finally the Law Commission said, at paragraph 13.6:

> 'Within the new system, beneficiaries will be in a comparatively better position than beneficiaries of current trusts of land. For example, given that the terms governing applications under section 30 will be less restrictive than they are at present, beneficiaries will have greater scope to challenge the decisions of the trustees and generally influence the management of the trust land.'

Eighthly, to put it at its lowest, it does not seem to me unlikely that the legislature intended to relax the fetters on the way in which the court exercised its discretion in cases such as *Re Citro* and *Lloyds Bank plc v Byrne,* and so as to tip the balance somewhat more in favour of families and against banks and other chargees. Although the law under section 30 was clear following *Re Citro* and *Lloyds Bank plc v Byrne,* there were indications of judicial dissatisfaction with the state of the law at that time. Although Bingham LJ agreed with Nourse LJ in *Re Citro,* he expressed, at p. 161F, unhappiness with the result and Sir George Waller's dissatisfaction went so far as led him to dissent: see his judgment, at pp. 161–163. Furthermore, there is a decision of the Court of Appeal in *Abbey National plc v Moss* [1994] 1 FLR 307 which suggests a desire for a new approach.

All these factors, to my mind, when taken together point very strongly to the conclusion that section 15 has changed the law. As a result of section 15, the court has greater flexibility than heretofore, as to how it exercises its jurisdiction on an application for an order for sale on facts such as those in *Re Citro* and *Lloyds Bank plc v Byrne.* There are certain factors which must be taken into account: see section 15(1) and, subject to the next point, section 15(3). There may be other factors in a particular case which the court can, indeed should, take into account. Once the relevant factors to be taken into account have been identified, it is a matter for the court as to what weight to give to each factor in a particular case.

His Lordship referred to *TSB Bank v Marshall* [1998] 2 FLR 769, 771–772, and continued:

A difficult question, having arrived at this conclusion, is the extent to which the old authorities are of assistance, and it is no surprise to find differing views expressed in the two textbooks from which I have quoted. On the one hand, to throw over all the wealth of learning and thought given by so many eminent judges to the problem which is raised on an application for sale of a house where competing interests exist seems somewhat arrogant and possibly rash. On the other hand, where one has concluded that the law has changed in a significant respect so that the court's discretion is significantly less fettered than it was, there are obvious dangers in relying on authorities which proceeded on the basis that the court's discretion was more fettered than it now is. I think it would be wrong to throw over all the earlier cases without paying them any regard. However, they have to be treated with caution, in light of the change in the law, and in many cases they are unlikely to be of great, let alone decisive, assistance.

Section 15(3)

The second question of principle can be dealt with more shortly. The question is whether section 15(3) applies in a case such as this. That turns on the meaning of the words 'In the case of any other application'. Mr Harry for TMC said that those words mean any application which does not fall within subsection (1) or subsection (2) and, as the present application falls within subsection (1), subsection (3) does not apply. Mr Asif for Mrs Shaire contended that the reference to 'any other application' is to any application not falling within subsection (2), and given that the present application falls within subsection (1), subsection (3) applies.

Looking at the matter as one of pure language, either construction appears to me to be acceptable and, if anything, I would tend to favour that preferred by Mr Harry. However, once one looks at the matter more widely in the context of the 1996 Act as a whole, it seems to me clear that Mr Asif is right and subsection (3) does apply to a case such as this. In my judgment, the essential clue is that section 14 is the only section specifically dealing with applications to the court for an order. Many of the other sections are, as I have mentioned, concerned with exercise of powers of duties by trustees, and certain other sections are concerned with the rights of beneficiaries. However, section 14 is the section which deals with the rights of the parties to make applications to the court. If one reads subsection (3) in the way for which Mr Harry contends, it seems to me very difficult to give it any meaning at all in those circumstances, because any application would seem to be governed by section 14 and therefore to fall within subsection (1).

In my judgment, therefore, the position is as follows. When considering any application under the Act, subsection (1) always applies. When considering any application made under the Act relating to section 13, subsection (2) applies. When considering any application other than one made under section 13 or one made under section 6(2), subsection (3) applies. It also seems to me that, bearing in mind the factors which the legislature has said should be taken into account, on any view, when considering an application for sale such as the present, namely the four matters specified in subsection (1), it would be surprising if the legislature intended the factor identified in subsection (3) to be ignored.

An order for sale?

Bearing in mind these conclusions as to the effect of the 1996 Act, ought I to make an order for sale?

His Lordship considered the facts and continued:

An idea which attracts me is that put forward by Mr Lawrence on behalf of the solicitors, and accepted by Mr Harry, if there is no order for sale. This idea is that the house is valued at a specific figure (rather than the range I have mentioned) and that The Mortgage Corporation is effectively taken out by having its equity converted into loan, and Mrs Shaire then has to pay interest on that loan. In my judgment, unless Mrs Shaire is in a position to agree that course and to meet the payments which that course would involve, I would not be prepared to refuse the order for sale. If she is prepared to agree that course and she is in a position to meet the repayments as and when they fall due, then I would be prepared to refuse an order for sale....

I appreciate that this leaves matters slightly up in the air, but I do not believe that I should make an order without a little more information. At the risk of adding further to the time and costs of this case, I would rather make the order on the basis of the parties having an opportunity to consider my conclusions, work out their consequences and, if necessary, argue about their consequences.

VII. PROTECTION OF PURCHASERS

Purchasers are protected by the doctrine of overreaching and also by limitations on powers and consent requirements.

TRUSTS OF LAND AND APPOINTMENTS OF TRUSTEES ACT 1996

23. Other interpretation provisions.—(1) In this Act 'purchaser' has the same meaning as in Part I of the Law of Property Act 1925.[122]

---

[122] 'A person who acquires an interest in or charge on property for money or money's worth; and in reference to a legal estate includes a chargee by way of legal mortgage': LPA 1925 s. 205(1)(xxi).

A. OVERREACHING[123]

The main object of the doctrine is a compromise between, on the one hand, the interest of the public in securing that land held in trust is freely marketable and, on the other hand, the interests of the beneficiaries in preserving their rights under the trust. The overreaching provisions under the Law of Property Act 1925, section 2 (1) were routinely amended by the Trust of Land and Appointment of Trustees Act 1996, and continue to operate.[124] They are improved in that bare trusts are included in the definition of a trust of land by section 1(2)(a) (p. 515, above).

LAW OF PROPERTY ACT 1925

2. **Conveyances overreaching certain equitable interests and powers.**—(1) A conveyance to a purchaser of a legal estate in land shall overreach any equitable interest or power affecting that estate, whether or not he has notice thereof, if— . . .

> (ii) the conveyance is made by trustees of land and the equitable interest or power is at the date of the conveyance capable of being overreached by such trustees under the provisions of subsection (2) of this section or independently of that subsection[125] and the requirements of section 27 of this Act respecting the payment[126] of capital money arising on such a conveyance are complied with;[127] . . .

> (iv) the conveyance is made under an order of the court and the equitable interest or power is bound by such order, and any capital money arising from the transaction is paid into, or in accordance with the order of, the court.

> (1A) An equitable interest in land subject to a trust of land which remains in, or is to revert to, the settlor shall (subject to any contrary intention) be overreached by the conveyance if it would be so overreached were it an interest under the trust.[128]

---

[123] C & B, pp. 447, 997–1000; Gray, paras 7.5.56–7.5.72; M & W, paras 6.052–6.056; MM, pp. 210, 530–535; W & H, paras 1.18–1.29, 6.64. See *City of London Building Society v Flegg* [1988] AC 54, p. 551, below; *Birmingham Midshire's Mortgage Services Ltd v Sabherwal* (1999) 80 P & CR 256, p. 555, below, and for a critical analysis of the statutory provisions on overreaching, see [1990] CLJ 277, at pp. 287–310 (C.J. Harpum); [1998] Conv 168; [2000] Conv 221 (G. Ferris and G. Battersby); [2007] Conv 120 (N. Jackson); W & H, para. 2.175. See also (2003) 119 LQR 94 at p. 125: 'When viewed as a whole the statutory reforms contained in TLATA 1996, TA 2000, and LRA 2002 create a legal environment in which the law of overreaching will continue to operate as a central support to the marketability of land.'

[124] [1997] Conv 81 (N. Hopkins).

[125] *Re Ryder and Steadman's Contract* [1927] 2 Ch 62. The conveyance by the trustees overreaches interests arising *under* the trust by the operation of general equitable principles ('independently of [s.2(2)]'); s. 2(2) provides for the conveyance also to overreach interests which were in existence *before* the creation of the trust of land. The trust of land then becomes 'ad hoc' with additional overreaching powers. See C & B, pp. 997, 1000.

[126] *State Bank of India v Sood* [1997] Ch 276, p. 557, below, (overreaching even when no capital money advanced at time when mortgage was created).

[127] As amended by TLATA 1996, s. 25(1), Sch. 3, para. 4 (2).

[128] As inserted by TLATA 1996, s. 25(1), Sch. 3, para. 4 (2).

(2)[129] Where the legal estate affected is subject to a trust of land, then if at the date of a conveyance made after the commencement of this Act by the trustees, the trustees (whether original or substituted) are either—

 (a) two or more individuals approved or appointed by the court or the successors in office of the individuals so approved or appointed; or

 (b) trust corporation[130]

any equitable interest or power having priority to the trust of land, shall, notwithstanding any stipulation to the contrary, be overreached by the conveyance, and shall, according to its priority, take effect as if created or arising by means of a primary trust affecting the proceeds of sale and the income of the land until sale.

(3) The following equitable interests and powers are excepted from the operation of subsection (2) of this section, namely—

 (i) Any equitable interest protected by a deposit of documents relating to the legal estate affected;

 (ii) The benefit of any covenant or agreement restrictive of the user of land;

 (iii) Any easement, liberty, or privilege over or affecting land and being merely an equitable interest (in this Act referred to as an 'equitable easement');

 (iv) The benefit of any contract (in this Act referred to as an 'estate contract') to convey or create a legal estate, including a contract conferring either expressly or by statutory implication a valid option to purchase, a right of pre-emption, or any other like right;

---

[129] This subsection was amended by LP(A)A 1926, Sch. and TLATA 1996, s. 25(1), Sch. 3, para. 4(2).

[130] Defined in LPA 1925, s. 205 (1) (xxviii) as follows: '"Trust corporation" means the Public Trustee or a corporation either appointed by the court in any particular case to be a trustee or entitled by rules made under subsection (3) of section four of the Public Trustee Act, 1906, to act as custodian trustee.'

Corporations which are entitled under the Public Trustee Rules 1912, r. 30, as substituted by the Public Trustee (Custodian Trustee) Rules 1975 (SI 1975 No. 1189, as amended by SI 1976 No. 836; SI 1981 No. 358; SI 1984 No. 109; SI 1985 No. 132; SI 1987 No. 1891; SI 1994 No. 2519; SI 2002 No. 2469), include 'any corporation constituted under the law of the United Kingdom . . . or of any other Member State of the European Economic Community . . . empowered by its constitution to undertake trust business [and having] one or more places of business in the United Kingdom', and being a company registered in the United Kingdom or another Member State of the European Economic Community 'having a capital (in stock or shares) for the time being issued of not less than £250,000 . . . of which not less than £100,000 . . . has been paid up in cash'.

The definition was extended by LP(A)A 1926, s. 3 to include the 'Treasury Solicitor, the Official Solicitor, and any person holding any other official position prescribed by the Lord Chancellor, and, in relation to the property of a bankrupt and property subject to a deed of arrangement, includes the trustee in bankruptcy and the trustee under the deed respectively, and, in relation to charitable, ecclesiastical and public trusts, also includes any local or public authority so prescribed, and any other corporation constituted under the laws of the United Kingdom or any part thereof which satisfies the Lord Chancellor that it undertakes the administration of any such trusts without remuneration, or that by its constitution it is required to apply the whole of its net income after payment of outgoings for charitable, ecclesiastical or public purposes, and is prohibited from distributing, directly or indirectly, any part thereof by way of profits amongst any of its members, and is authorised by him to act in relation to such trusts as a trust corporation'.

(v) Any equitable interest protected by registration under the Land Charges Act, 1925,[131] other than—

    (a) an annuity within the meaning of Part II of that Act;

    (b) a limited owner's charge or a general equitable charge within the meaning of that Act.

(4) Subject to the protection afforded by this section to the purchaser of a legal estate, nothing contained in this section shall deprive a person entitled to an equitable charge of any of his rights or remedies for enforcing the same.

(5) So far as regards the following interests, created before the commencement of this Act (which accordingly are not within the provisions of the Land Charges Act 1925[132]), namely—

    (a) the benefit of any covenant or agreement restrictive of the user of the land;

    (b) any equitable easement;

    (c) the interest under a puisne mortgage within the meaning of the Land Charges Act, 1925,[133] unless and until acquired under a transfer made after the commencement of this Act;

    (d) the benefit of an estate contract, unless and until the same is acquired under a conveyance made after the commencement of this Act;

a purchaser of a legal estate shall only take subject thereto if he has notice thereof, and the same are not overreached under the provisions contained or in the manner referred to in this section.

27. Purchaser not to be concerned with the trust of the proceeds of sale.—(1) A purchaser of a legal estate from trustees of land shall not be concerned with the trusts affecting the land, the net income of the land or the proceeds of sale of the land whether or not those trusts are declared by the same instrument as that by which the trust of land is created.[134]

(2) Notwithstanding anything to the contrary in the instrument (if any) creating a trust of land or in any trust affecting the net proceeds of sale of the land if it is sold, the proceeds of sale or other capital money shall not be paid to or applied by the direction of fewer than two persons as trustees, except where the trustee is a trust corporation, but this subsection does not affect the right of a sole personal representative as such to give valid receipts for, or direct the application of, proceeds of sale or other capital money, nor, except where capital money arises on the transaction, render it necessary to have more than one trustee.[135]

Whitehouse and Hassall, *Trusts of Land, Trustee Delegation and the Trustee Act 2000* (2nd edn, 2001), para. 6.64[136]

The theoretical basis for overreaching is more confused than ever. The Law of Property Act 1925, s 2(1)(ii) provides for overreaching in the case of trusts of land either under the provisions

---

[131] Now LCA 1972. The annuity referred to in (a) is one created before 1926 and registered in the Register of Annuities which then existed: LCA 1972, Sch. 1.

[132] Now LCA 1972.

[133] Now LCA 1972.

[134] As substituted by TLATA 1996, s. 25(1), Sch. 3, para. 8(a).

[135] As amended by TLATA 1996, s. 25(1), Sch. 3, para. 8(b). Sub-s. 2 was substituted by LP(A)A 1926, s. 7 and Sch. See also TA 1925, s. 14; as amended by TA 2000, S.40, Sch. 2, Pt. II, para. 19.

[136] Footnotes omitted.

of s 2(2) (which is limited to *ad hoc* trusts of land[137]) or 'independently of that sub-section' provided, in both cases, that capital money is paid in accordance with the Law of Property Act 1925, s 27 (i.e. to two trustees or a trust corporation). Prior to 1 January 1997, overreaching outside s 2(2) was sometimes explained in the case of trusts for sale on the basis of the doctrine of conversion. With the abolition of that doctrine in the Trusts of Land and Appointment of Trustees Act 1996, s 3,[138] a new basis has to be found for overreaching in the case of trusts of land which must lie in the power of sale enjoyed by the trustees.

(i) Overreaching and overriding

Where the legal estate in land is held by two trustees, but the beneficial interest is held by at least one person who is not a trustee but who is in actual occupation of the land, a difficult problem arises when the land is sold or mortgaged by the two trustees, and the purchase or mortgage money is paid to them. Can the beneficiary in actual occupation prevent the sale or mortgage without giving his consent; or can the purchaser or mortgagee claim that the overreaching provisions apply and that, by paying the moneys to the two trustees of the legal estate, he can overreach and take free from the beneficial interest? In other words, do the overreaching provisions operate subject to, or in priority to, the provisions of the Land Registration Act[139] under which would allow the beneficiary in actual occupation to assert an overriding interest?

In **City of London Building Society v Flegg** [1988] AC 54 the House of Lords reversed the Court of Appeal [1986] Ch 605 and decided the issue in favour of a mortgagee of registered land. In 1989 the Law Commission in its Report on Overreaching: Beneficiaries (Law Com No. 188) recommended that the interest of an adult beneficiary of full capacity who has a right to occupy trust land and is in actual occupation of it should only be overreached if he consents; in effect reversing the decision of the House of Lords.[140] The recommendation was not followed in the Trusts of Land and Appointment of Trustees Act 1996.

City of London Building Society v Flegg
[1988] AC 54 (HL, **Lords Bridge Of Harwich, Templeman, Mackay of Clashfern, Oliver of Aylmerton** and **Goff of Chieveley**)[141]

Lord Templeman: My Lords, the appellants, City of London Building Society, are the mortgagees under a charge by way of legal mortgage of registered land held at the date of the charge by two trustees upon trust for sale and to stand possessed of the net proceeds of sale and rents and profits until sale upon trust for four tenants in common including the respondents, Mr and Mrs Flegg. The legal charge was entered into by the trustees in breach of trust, although the appellants were unaware of this. The respondents who were in actual occupation of the

---

[137] [See p. 548, n. 125, above.]   [138] [P. 519, above.]

[139] LRA 2002, s. 29(2)(a)(ii), Sch. 3, para. 2, above p. 196.

[140] [1990] CLJ 277 at pp. 311–333 (C. Harpum); (1988) 104 LQR 367 (S. Gardner).

[141] [1987] All ER Rev 149 (P. J. Clarke); (1988) 51 MLR 365 (S. Gardner); [1988] Conv 108 (M. P. Thompson), 141 (P. Sparkes).

mortgaged land claim that the appellants' legal charge is subject to the respondents' overriding interest. The Court of Appeal declined to order the respondents to deliver up possession of the land to the appellants; hence this appeal.

By a conveyance dated 18 October 1977 the land appropriately named Bleak House was conveyed to Mr and Mrs Maxwell-Brown in fee simple upon trust for sale and to stand possessed of the net proceeds of sale and rents and profits until sale upon trust for the Maxwell-Browns as joint tenants. In fact, the purchase price paid by the Maxwell-Browns for Bleak House, amounting to £34,000, had been provided as to £18,000 or more by the respondents who were the parents of Mrs Maxwell-Brown. In consequence and notwithstanding the express trusts set out in the conveyance, Bleak House was held by the Maxwell-Browns on trust for sale and to stand possessed of the net proceeds of sale and rents and profits until sale upon trust for the Maxwell-Browns and the respondents as tenants in common in the proportions in which they had respectively contributed to the purchase price.[142] The respondents were entitled to occupy Bleak House together with the Maxwell-Browns as tenants in common under the trust for sale and all four beneficiaries duly went into occupation.

By a legal charge by way of mortgage dated 8 January 1982 the Maxwell-Browns charged Bleak House to secure £37,500 advanced by the appellants to the Maxwell-Browns. The respondents knew nothing of the legal charge which was granted by the Maxwell-Browns for their own purposes and in breach of trust. The appellants knew nothing of the respondents.

By section 27 of the Law of Property Act 1925 (as amended by the Law of Property (Amendment) Act 1926, Schedule):[143]

'(1) A purchaser of a legal estate from trustees for sale shall not be concerned with the trusts affecting the proceeds of sale of land subject to a trust for sale ... or affecting the rents and profits of the land until sale ... (2) Notwithstanding anything to the contrary in the instrument (if any) creating a trust for sale of land or in the settlement of the net proceeds, the proceeds of sale or other capital money shall not be paid to or applied by the direction of fewer than two persons as trustees for sale, except where the trustee is a trust corporation ...'...

His Lordship read section 28(1) of the Law of Property Act 1925 and section 17 of the Trustee Act 1925, and continued:

Thus the appellants advancing money in good faith to two trustees for sale on the security of a charge by way of legal mortgage of Bleak House were not concerned with the trusts affecting the proceeds of sale of Bleak House or with the propriety of the trustees entering into the legal charge. As a result of the legal charge the interests of the beneficiaries in Bleak House pending sale were transferred to the equity of redemption vested in the Maxwell-Browns and to the sum of £37,500 received by the Maxwell-Browns from the appellants in consideration for the grant of the legal charge. The Maxwell-Browns did not account to the respondents for any part of the sum of £37,500 and defaulted in the performance of their obligations to the appellants under the legal charge. The appellants seek possession of Bleak House with a view to enforcing its security.

The respondents resist the claim of the appellants to possession of Bleak House and rely on section 14 of the Law of Property Act 1925. Sections 27 and 28 of that Act which overreach

---

[142] For the acquisition of a beneficial interest in land by contribution to the purchase price, and the nature of a tenancy in common, see chap. 7, below. After TLATA, the land would be held on a trust of land.

[143] And now amended by TLATA 1996, s. 25(1), Sch. 3, para. 8.

the interests of the respondents under the trust for sale of Bleak House are to be found in Part I of the Act. Section 14 provides:

'This Part of this Act shall not prejudicially affect the interest of any person in possession or in actual occupation of land to which he may be entitled in right of such possession or occupation.'

The respondents were in actual occupation of Bleak House at the date of the legal charge. It is argued that their beneficial interests under the trust for sale were not overreached by the legal charge or that the respondents were entitled to remain in occupation after the legal charge and against the appellants despite the overreaching of their interests.

My Lords, the respondents were entitled to occupy Bleak House by virtue of their beneficial interests in Bleak House and its rents and profits pending the execution of the trust for sale. Their beneficial interests were overreached by the legal charge and were transferred to the equity of redemption held by the Maxwell-Browns and to the sum advanced by the appellants in consideration of the grant of the legal charge and received by the Maxwell-Browns. After the legal charge the respondents were only entitled to continue in occupation of Bleak House by virtue of their beneficial interests in the equity of redemption of Bleak House and that equity of redemption is subject to the right of the appellants as mortgagees to take possession....

It follows that when the legal charge in the present case is registered, the appellants will take free from all the interests of the beneficiaries interested under the trust for sale in the proceeds of sale and rents and profits until sale of Bleak House but subject to any overriding interest.

Section 70(1) of the Land Registration Act 1925[144] defines overriding interests which include:

'(g) The rights of every person in actual occupation of the land or in receipt of the rents and profits thereof, save where inquiry is made of such person and the rights are not disclosed; . . .'

In my view the object of section 70 was to reproduce for registered land the same limitations as section 14 of the Law of Property Act 1925 produced for land whether registered or unregistered. The respondents claim to be entitled to overriding interests because they were in actual occupation of Bleak House on the date of the legal charge. But the interests of the respondents cannot at one and the same time be overreached and overridden and at the same time be overriding interests. The appellants cannot at one and the same time take free from all the interests of the respondents yet at the same time be subject to some of those interests. The right of the respondents to be and remain in actual occupation of Bleak House ceased when the respondents' interests were overreached by the legal charge save in so far as their rights were transferred to the equity of redemption. As persons interested under the trust for sale the respondents had no right to possession as against the appellants and the fact that the respondents were in actual occupation at the date of the legal charge did not create a new right or transfer an old right so as to make the right enforceable against the appellants.

One of the main objects of the legislation of 1925 was to effect a compromise between on the one hand the interests of the public in securing that land held in trust is freely marketable and, on the other hand, the interests of the beneficiaries in preserving their rights under the trusts. By the Settled Land Act 1925 a tenant for life may convey the settled land discharged from all the trusts powers and provisions of the settlement. By the Law of Property Act 1925 trustees for sale may convey land held on trust for sale discharged from the trusts affecting the proceeds

[144] Now LRA 2002, Sch. 3; above, p. 196.

of sale and rents and profits until sale. Under both forms of trust the protection and the only protection of the beneficiaries is that capital money must be paid to at least two trustees or a trust corporation. Section 14 of the Law of Property Act 1925 and section 70 of the Land Registration Act 1925 cannot have been intended to frustrate this compromise and to subject the purchaser to some beneficial interests but not others depending on the waywardness of actual occupation. The Court of Appeal took a different view, largely in reliance on the decision of this House in *Williams & Glyn's Bank Ltd v Boland* [1981] AC 487 [p. 203, above]. In that case the sole proprietor of registered land held the land as sole trustee upon trust for sale and to stand possessed of the net proceeds of sale and rents and profits until sale upon trust for himself and his wife as tenants in common. This House held that the wife's beneficial interest coupled with actual possession by her constituted an overriding interest and that a mortgagee from the husband, despite the concluding words of section 20(1), took subject to the wife's overriding interest. But in that case the interest of the wife was not overreached or overridden because the mortgagee advanced capital moneys to a sole trustee. If the wife's interest had been overreached by the mortgagee advancing capital moneys to two trustees there would have been nothing to justify the wife in remaining in occupation as against the mortgagee. There must be a combination of an interest which justifies continuing occupation plus actual occupation to constitute an overriding interest. Actual occupation is not an interest in itself.

For these reasons and for the reasons to be given by my noble and learned friend, Lord Oliver of Aylmerton, I would allow this appeal and restore the order of Judge Thomas who ordered the respondents to deliver up Bleak House to the appellants.

Lord Oliver of Aylmerton: Considered in the context of a transaction complying with the statutory requirements of the Law of Property Act 1925 the question of the effect of section 70(1) (*g*) of the Land Registration Act 1925 must, in my judgment, be approached by asking first what are the 'rights' of the person in occupation and whether they are, at the material time, subsisting in reference to the land. In the instant case the exercise by the registered proprietors of the powers conferred on trustees for sale by section 28 (1) of the Law of Property Act 1925 had the effect of overreaching the interests of the respondents under the statutory trusts upon which depended their right to continue in occupation of the land. The appellants took free from those trusts (section 27) and were not, in any event, concerned to see that the respondents' consent to the transaction was obtained (section 26). If, then, one asks what were the subsisting rights of the respondents referable to their occupation, the answer must, in my judgment, be that they were rights which, vis-à-vis the appellants, were, eo instante with the creation of the charge, overreached and therefore subsisted only in relation to the equity of redemption. I do not, for my part, find in *Boland's* case anything which compels a contrary conclusion. Granted that the interest of a co-owner pending the execution of the statutory trust for sale is, despite the equitable doctrine of conversion, an interest subsisting in reference to the land the subject matter of the trust and granted also that *Boland's* case establishes that such an interest, although falling within the definition of minor interest and so liable to be overridden by a registered disposition, will, so long as it subsists, be elevated to the status of an overriding interest if there exists also the additional element of occupation by the co-owner, I cannot for my part accept that, once what I may call the parent interest, by which alone the occupation can be justified, has been overreached and thus subordinated to a legal estate properly created by the trustees under their statutory powers, it can, in relation to the proprietor of the legal estate so created, be any longer said to be a right 'for the time being subsisting.' Section 70(1)(*g*) protects only the rights in reference to the land of the occupier whatever they are at the material time—in the instant case the right to enjoy in specie the rents and profits of the land held in trust for him. Once the beneficiary's rights have been shifted from the land to capital moneys in the hands of the trustees, there is no longer an interest in the land to which the occupation can be referred or which it can protect. If the trustees sell in accordance with the statutory provisions and so overreach the beneficial interests in reference to the land, nothing remains to which a right of occupation can attach and the same result must, in my judgment, follow vis-à-vis a chargee by way of legal mortgage so long as the transaction is carried out in the manner prescribed by the Law of Property Act 1925, overreaching the beneficial interests by subordinating them to the estate of the chargee which is no longer 'affected' by them so as to become subject to them on registration pursuant to section 20(1) of the Land Registration Act 1925. In the instant case, therefore, I would for my part, hold that the charge created in favour of the appellants over-reached the beneficial interests of the respondents and that there is nothing in section 70(1)(g) of the Land Registration Act 1925 or in *Boland's* case which has the effect of preserving against the appellants any rights of the respondents to occupy the land by virtue of their beneficial interests in the equity of redemption which remains vested in the trustees.

In **Birmingham Midshires Mortgage Services Ltd v Sabherwal** (2000) 80 P & CR 256,[145] the two sons of Mrs Sabherwal were the registered owners of a house in Gerard's Cross. They had borrowed £225,000 from Midshire's Mortgage Services Ltd secured on the house. Mrs Sabherwal had a significant equitable interest under a common intention constructive trust,[146] or by way of proprietary estoppel[147] (the sons had told their mother that she would always have a roof over her head). She was in actual occupation of the house under section 70(1)(g) of the Land Registration Act 1925. The sons defaulted on the loan.

The question was whether the lender had overreached the equitable interests of Mrs Sabherwal. In holding that it had, the Court of Appeal held that *City London Building Society v Flegg* had not been affected by the Trusts of Land and Appointment of Trustees Act 1996. WALKER LJ said at 261:

22 The judge gave ten reasons for concluding that the decision in *Flegg* has not been affected by the 1996 Act. Since that conclusion is not directly challenged in this court, at any rate on the grounds that the judge considered, it is sufficient to mention three of the most cogent of his reasons. First, the overreaching effect of the legal charges took place when they were executed in July 1990, and cannot be ousted by the coming into force of the 1996 Act over six years later. Second, the 1996 Act contains nothing to exclude the essential overreaching provision contained in section 2(1)(ii) of the Law of Property Act 1925.[148] On the contrary, that provision is amended so as to meet the new terminology of the 1996 Act (see section 25(1) and Schedule 3 paragraph 4(1)) and so is in effect confirmed, with that new terminology, by the 1996 Act. Third, the abolition of the doctrine of conversion (by section 3 of the 1996 Act[149]) is irrelevant for reasons stated by Lord Oliver in *Flegg* (see p. 90G-H)[150]. However, the abolition of that doctrine does explain the amendment of s. 27(1) of the Law of Property Act 1925, on which some reliance has been placed.

---

[145] (2000) 116 LQR 341 (C. Harpum); [2000] Conv 267 (M. Dixon); [2001] Conv 221 (G. Ferris and G. Battersby).

[146] Pp. 573–601, below.   [147] Pp. 1007–1079, below.

[148] P. 548, above.   [149] P. 519, above.   [150] P. 554, above.

23 Instead in this court Mr Marc Beaumont (for Mrs Sabherwal) has in his skeleton argument (in amplification of a very terse notice of appeal) sought to distinguish *Flegg* on two grounds. The first is based on proprietary estoppel. The second is based on Article 8 of the European Convention of Human Rights. The first of these grounds was not argued before the judge but this court has (perhaps over-indulgently) permitted the point to be argued, on the footing that no further findings of fact are required.

24 On the facts of this case, Mrs Sabherwal plainly made a substantial financial contribution to all the properties successively owned by the family. She could rely on a resulting trust and had no need to rely on proprietary estoppel (if and so far as the two are, in the context of the family home, distinct doctrines: see the observations of Sir Nicolas Browne-Wilkinson V-C in *Grant v Edwards* [1986] Ch 638, 656). If she had made no financial contribution, but had nevertheless acted to her detriment in reliance on her sons' promises, she might have obtained (through the medium of estoppel rather than through the medium of a trust) equitable rights of a proprietary nature. Her actual occupation of the house would then have promoted those rights into an overriding interest. That, I think, is not conceded by counsel for the respondents but I assume that to be the case. On that basis, it would have been a remarkable result if those more precarious rights were incapable of being overreached, on a sale by trustees, under section 2(1)(ii) of the Law of Property Act 1925.

25 Mr Beaumont has however contended for that result, citing what Lord Wilberforce said in *Shiloh Spinners v Harding* [1973] AC 691, at 721:

'All this seems to show that there may well be rights, of an equitable character, outside the provisions as to registration and which are incapable of being overreached.'

26 Lord Wilberforce had just before referred to *ER Ives Investment Ltd v High* [1967] 2 QB 379. In that case a boundary dispute between neighbours had been settled by an informal agreement including the grant of a right of way. The agreement about the right of way was never completed by a deed of grant, and was never registered. The Court of Appeal held that it was binding despite the lack of registration. Similarly, *Shiloh Spinners v Harding* was concerned with an equitable right of entry for enforcement of a covenant arising in what Lord Wilberforce called a 'dispute...of a commonplace character between neighbours'.

27 Equitable interests of that character ought not to be overreached, since they are rights which an adjoining owner enjoys over the land itself, regardless of its ownership from time to time. The principle is in my view correctly stated in Megarry and Wade, *The Law of Real Property* 5th edn, p. 409:

'In fact the only examples of such equities likely to occur are commercial (as opposed to family) interests, which it is absurd to speak of overreaching. Two instances are an equitable right of way which is yet not an equitable easement, and an equitable right of entry to secure performance of a covenant, and there are probably others. To overreach such interests is to destroy them...'

28 The footnotes to this passage refer to *ER Ives Investment Ltd v High* and *Shiloh Spinners v Harding* (cases which were cited to the House of Lords in *Flegg*—see especially counsel's argument at p. 63—but are not referred to in any of the speeches of their Lordships). The essential distinction is, as the authors of Megarry and Wade note, between commercial and family interests. An equitable easement or an equitable right of entry cannot sensibly shift from the land affected by it to the proceeds of sale. An equitable interest as a tenant in common can do so, even if accompanied by the promise of a home for life, since the proceeds of sale can be used to acquire another home.

29 Mr Beaumont has also argued that, although in *Grant v Edwards* the Vice-Chancellor regarded interests in the family home created by equitable estoppel or by a constructive trust as closely similar, if not interchangeable, his remarks do not apply to a resulting trust arising from a monetary contribution. This is an area of the law in which the terminology is unfortunately far from uniform, but I do not accept that the Vice-Chancellor's remarks were limited in that way. On the contrary, immediately after his reference to proprietary estoppel he said (see [1986] Ch. at 657H–658A):

30 'Identifiable contributions to the purchase [price] of the house will of course be an important factor in many cases.'

31 Similarly, in *Lloyds Bank v Rosset* [1991] 1 AC 107 Lord Bridge (in a very well-known passage at pp. 132–133) referred to 'direct contributions to the purchase price by [a party] who is not the legal owner', as readily justifying the creation of a constructive trust. Such a trust, however labelled, does not then leave room for a separate interest by way of equitable estoppel: compare the remarks of Morritt LJ in *Lloyds Bank v Carrick* [1996] 4 All ER 630 at p. 639C-E. To do so would cause vast confusion in an area which is already quite difficult enough. The confusion is avoided if what Lord Wilberforce said in *Shiloh Spinners v Harding* is limited, as in my judgment it must be, to some unusual types of equitable interest arising in commercial situations. In this type of family situation, the concepts of trust and equitable estoppel are almost interchangeable, and both are affected in the same way by the statutory mechanism of overreaching, the substance of which is not affected by the 1996 Act.

32 In these circumstances I do not find it necessary to consider how far the judge's findings in this area (which were largely limited to a general acceptance of Mrs Sabherwal's evidence) would establish the necessary conditions for proprietary estoppel. I assume in favour of Mrs Sabherwal that they would do so.

His Lordship held that Article 8 of the Human Rights Act 1988 was of no assistance, on the basis that it was not yet in force, and the fact that its incorporation into domestic law was imminent, in the Human Rights Act 1998, was not a reason to influence the construction of section 2 of the Law of Property Act 1925.

(ii) No advance of capital money

In **State Bank of India v Sood** [1997] Ch 276[151] PETER GIBSON LJ, in holding that the interests of beneficiaries were overreached even when no capital money had been advanced at the time when the mortgage was created, said at 281:

Before I turn to the statutory provisions, I would make a few general observations on overreaching. As is explained by Charles Harpum in his illuminating article, 'Overreaching, Trustees' Powers and the Reform of the 1925 Legislation' [1990] CLJ 277, overreaching is the process whereby existing interests are subordinated to a later interest or estate created pursuant to a trust or power. Mr Harpum arrived at that statement of the true nature of overreaching by a consideration of the effect of the exercise of powers of disposition in a settlement, referring to *Sugden on Powers,* 8th edn. (1861), pp. 482, 483. He argued cogently that a transaction made by a person within the dispositive powers conferred upon him will overreach equitable interests in the property the subject of the disposition, but ultra vires dispositions will not, and the trans-

---

[151] [1997] CLJ 494 (M. Oldham); [1997] Conv 134 (M. P. Thompson).

feree with notice will take the property subject to those interests. Mr Harpum expressed the view that the exercise intra vires of a power of disposition which does not give rise to any capital money, such as an exchange of land, overreaches just as much as a transaction which does. There is every reason to think that the draftsman of the 1925 property legislation fully appreciated the true nature of overreaching. A principal objective of the 1925 property legislation was to simplify conveyancing and the proof of title to land. To this end equitable interests were to be kept off the title to the legal estate and could be overreached on a conveyance to a purchaser who took free of them.

The statutory provision governing overreaching is section 2 of the Law of Property Act 1925 [p. 548, above]: ...

Much though I value the principle of overreaching as having aided the simplification of conveyancing, I cannot pretend that I regard the resulting position in the present case as entirely satisfactory. The safeguard for beneficiaries under the existing legislation is largely limited to having two trustees or a trust corporation where capital money falls to be received. But that is no safeguard at all, as this case has shown, when no capital money is received on and contemporaneously with the conveyance. Further, even when it is received by two trustees as in *City of London Building Society v Flegg* [1986] Ch 605; revsd [1988] AC 54, it might be thought that beneficiaries in occupation are insufficiently protected. Hence the recommendation for reform in the Law Commission's report, 'Transfer of Land, Overreaching: Beneficiaries in Occupation' (1989) (Law Com No 188), that a conveyance should not overreach the interest of a sui juris beneficiary in occupation unless he gives his consent. Mr Harpum in the article to which reference has been made proposed an alternative reform, limiting the power of trustees to mortgage. Whether the legislature will reform the law remains to be seen. I should add for completeness that we were assured by counsel that the recent Trusts of Land and Appointment of Trustees Act 1996 was of no assistance and we have not considered its effect.

B. LIMITATION ON POWERS AND CONSENT REQUIREMENTS

Further protection is given to a purchaser by section 16 of the Trusts of Land and Appointment of Trustees Act 1996. This section only applies to unregistered land.[152]

TRUSTS OF LAND AND APPOINTMENT OF TRUSTEES ACT 1996

16. **Protection of purchasers.**—(1) A purchaser of land which is or has been subject to a trust need not be concerned to see that any requirement imposed on the trustees by section 6(5), 7(3) or 11(1)[153] has been complied with.

  (2) Where—

  (a) trustees of land who convey land which (immediately before it is conveyed) is subject to the trust contravene section 6(6) or (8),[154] but

  (b) the purchaser of the land from the trustees has no actual notice of the contravention,

---

[152] W & H, paras 2.165–2.175.   [153] Pp. 521, 526, above.
[154] P. 521, above.

the contravention does not invalidate the conveyance.

(3) Where the powers of trustees of land are limited by virtue of section 8—

(a) the trustees shall take all reasonable steps to bring the limitation to the notice of any purchaser of the land from them, but

(b) the limitation does not invalidate any conveyance by the trustees to a purchaser who has no actual notice of the limitation.

(4) Where trustees of land convey land which (immediately before it is conveyed) is subject to the trust to persons believed by them to be beneficiaries absolutely entitled to the land under the trust and of full age and capacity—

(a) the trustees shall execute a deed declaring that they are discharged from the trust in relation to that land, and

(b) if they fail to do so, the court may make an order requiring them to do so.

(5) A purchaser of land to which a deed under subsection (4) relates is entitled to assume that, as from the date of the deed, the land is not subject to the trust unless he has actual notice that the trustees were mistaken in their belief that the land was conveyed to beneficiaries absolutely entitled to the land under the trust and of full age and capacity.

(6) Subsections (2) and (3) do not apply to land held on charitable, ecclesiastical or public trusts.

(7) This section does not apply to registered land.

VIII. REGISTERED LAND[155]

Title to land subject to a trust of land must be registered in the name of the trustees (not exceeding four in number), and the purchaser is informed of the necessity to pay capital moneys to at least two trustees or to a trust corporation by entry of a restriction on the register.

If the interests of beneficiaries under a trust of land have not been protected by entry on the register, they may nevertheless be overriding interests under Schedules 1 and 3 of the Land Registration Act 2002.[156] These interests may, however, be overreached.[157]

LAND REGISTRATION ACT 2002

4 When title must be registered

(7) In subsection (1)(a) and (c), references to transfer or grant by way of gift include transfer or grant for the purpose of—

(a) constituting a trust under which the settlor does not retain the whole of the beneficial interest,[158] or

---

[155] C & B, p. 440; M & W, para. 7.078; R & R, chap. 37; [1996] Conv 411 at pp. 427–428 (N. Hopkins).

[156] Pp. 191–196, above.

[157] *City of London Building Society v Flegg* [1988] AC 54, p. 551, above.

[158] R & R, paras 37.001–37.011. Law Commission Report on Land Registration for the Twenty-First Century 2001 (Law Com No. 271), p. 466; '...if S transfers an unregistered estate in land to T1 and T2, to

(b) uniting the bare legal title and the beneficial interest in property held under a trust under which the settlor did not, on constitution, retain the whole of the beneficial interest.

11 Freehold estates

(5) If the proprietor is not entitled to the estate for his own benefit, or not entitled solely for his own benefit, then, as between himself and the persons beneficially entitled to the estate, the estate is vested in him subject to such of their interests as he has notice of.[159]

33 Excluded interests

No notice may be entered in the register in respect of any of the following—

(a) an interest under—

(i) a trust of land, . . .

42 Power of registrar to enter

(1) The registrar may enter a restriction in the register if it appears to him that it is necessary or desirable to do so for the purpose of—

(a) preventing invalidity or unlawfulness in relation to dispositions of a registered estate or charge.

(b) securing that interests which are capable of being overreached on a disposition of a registered estate or charge are overreached, or

(c) protecting a right or claim in relation to a registered estate or charge.

43 Applications

(1) A person may apply to the registrar for the entry of a restriction under section 42(1) if—

(a) he is the relevant registered proprietor, or a person entitled to be registered as such proprietor,

(b) the relevant registered proprietor, or a person entitled to be registered as such proprietor, consents to the application, or

(c) he otherwise has a sufficient interest in the making of the entry.

78 Notice of trust not to affect registrar

The registrar shall not be affected with notice of a trust.

hold on trust of land for S and U in equal shares, that transfer will trigger compulsory registration. However, a transfer by S to T1 and T2 to hold on trust for her as nominee will not trigger compulsory registration. Secondly, a transfer by way of a gift includes a transfer for the purpose of uniting the legal title and a beneficial interest in property held under a trust under which the settlor did not, on constitution, retain the whole of the beneficial interest (see clause [now section] 4(7)(b)). Thus, if T1 and T2 hold an unregistered estate in land on trust for A for life, thereafter to B absolutely, and A dies, so that the trustees hold the land on trust for B absolutely, a transfer of that land by T1 and T2 to B will trigger compulsory registration. However, where T1 and T2 hold on trust for the settlor absolutely, and the land is transferred either to him or to the person entitled to the interest (as for example, under the settlor's will or intestacy), this will not trigger compulsory registration.'

[159] Similarly for leasehold estates: s. 12(5).

LAND REGISTRATION RULES 2003

Persons regarded as having a sufficient interest to apply for a restriction

93. The following persons are to be regarded as included in section 43(1)(c) of the Act—

    (a) any person who has an interest in a registered estate held under a trust of land where a sole proprietor or a survivor of joint proprietors (unless a trust corporation) will not be able to give a valid receipt for capital money, and who is applying for a restriction in Form A to be entered in the register of that registered estate,

    (b) any person who has a sufficient interest in preventing a contravention of section 6(6) or section 6(8) of the Trusts of Land and Appointments of Trustees Act 1996[160] and who is applying for a restriction in order to prevent such a contravention,

    (c) any person who has an interest in a registered estate held under a trust of land where the powers of the trustees are limited by section 8 of the Trusts of Land and Appointment of Trustees Act 1996,[161] and who is applying for a restriction in Form B to be entered in the register of that registered estate, ...

SCHEDULE 4[162]

STANDARD FORMS OF RESTRICTION

Form A (Restriction on dispositions by sole proprietor)

No disposition by a sole proprietor of the registered estate (except a trust corporation) under which capital money arises is to be registered unless authorised by an order of the court.

Form B (Dispositions by trustees—certificate required)

No [disposition *or specify type of disposition*] by the proprietors of the registered estate is to be registered unless one or more of them makes a statutory declaration or statement of truth, or their conveyancer gives a certificate, that the [disposition *or specify type of disposition*] is in accordance with [*specify the disposition creating the trust*] or some variation thereof referred to in the declaration, statement or certificate.

IX. DISCHARGE OF TRUSTS OF LAND

Section 16(4) and (5) makes provision for a new deed of discharge, thereby remedying the defective procedure before 1997. Section 23 of the Law of Property Act has been repealed.

TRUSTS OF LAND AND APPOINTMENT OF TRUSTEES ACT 1996

16. Protection of purchasers.—(4),(5), p. 559, above.

---

[160] P. 521, above.   [161] P. 522, above.
[162] Substituted by LR (Amendment) R 2008, SI 2008 No. 1919, r. 4(6), Sch. 4.

LAND REGISTRATION RULES 2003

Cancellation of a restriction relating to a trust

99. When registering a disposition of a registered estate, the registrar must cancel a restriction entered for the purpose of protecting an interest, right or claim arising under a trust of land if he is satisfied that the registered estate is no longer subject to that trust of land.

QUESTIONS

1. Read again the Law Commission's criticism of the pre-1997 law on strict settlements and trusts for sale (pp. 508–514, above). Did the Trusts of Land and Appointment of Trustees Act 1996 address all those criticisms satisfactorily?

2. Can land be made inalienable under the Trusts of Land and Appointment of Trustees Act 1996? Can a settlor of an express trust of land exclude the power of sale? See TLATA 1996, s. 8(1); p. 522, above; [1997] Conv 263 (G. Watt). Can an argument be made on the basis of decisions on conditions which restrain alienation: *Re Brown* [1954] Ch 39, p. 306, above?

3. What considerations should a settlor have in mind when creating a trust of land under the Act? See Barraclough and Matthews: A Practitioner's Guide to the Trusts of Land and Appointment of Trustees Act 1996, chap. 12, especially pp. 139–140, and Precedents in Appendix 8; Kenny and Kenny, The Trusts of Land and Appointment of Trustees Act 1996, Part II, especially paras 9.1 to 9.5; Sydenham, Trusts of Land—The New Law, pp. 136–138 and Precedents pp. 139–155; W & H, Part IV (Precedents).

4. Is the exercise of powers conferred on trustees of land under section 6 subject to the rule against perpetuities? P & AA 1964, s. 8(1); Emmet, para. 22.022.

5. In view of *City of London Building Society v Flegg* [1988] AC 54, p. 551, above, and *State Bank of India v Sood* [1997] Ch 276, p. 557, above, do you think that overreaching gives sufficient protection to beneficiaries?

6. How far can a strict settlement be reproduced today? See Law Commission Report on Trusts of Land, 1989 (Law Com No. 181), para. 4.5; W & H, paras 2.11–2.17.

7

CONCURRENT INTERESTS[1]

I. JOINT TENANCY AND TENANCY
IN COMMON

In the modern law, the two forms of concurrent interest are the joint tenancy and the tenancy in common.[2] Their essential nature was set out by Blackstone as follows:[3]

The *properties* of a joint estate are derived from its unity, which is fourfold; the unity of *interest*, the unity of *title*, the unity of *time*, and the unity of *possession*: or, in other words, joint-tenants have one and the same interest, accruing by one and the same conveyance, commencing at one and the same time, and held by one and the same undivided possession....

An estate in joint-tenancy may be *severed* and *destroyed*...by destroying any of its constituent unities.

Tenants in *common* are such as hold by several and distinct titles, but by unity of possession... This tenancy therefore happens, where there is an unity of possession merely, but perhaps an entire disunion of interest, of title, and of time.

---

[1] C & B, chap. 13; Gray, parts 7.2–7.4; M & W, paras 11.001–11.032, chap. 13; MM, pp. 303–332; Smith, chaps 11, 15; Thompson, *Co-ownership* (1988); Smith *Plural Ownership* (2005).

[2] For further discussion of the nature and characteristics of different types of co-ownership, and for the pre-1926 law, see C & B, pp. 453–464; Gray, paras 7.4.4–7.4.62; M & W, paras 13.001–13.035, 13.051–13.054, and, on co-parcenary, 5th edn, pp. 456–459; MM, pp. 303–332. The present chapter assumes an understanding of this material.

[3] *Commentaries on the Laws of England*, vol. ii (1766), pp. 180, 185, 191–192.

In other words, joint tenants together form one person in their holding of the land. A consequence of this is that if one of them dies his interest is extinguished and the other joint tenants become entitled to the whole by the right of 'survivorship'—the '*ius accrescendi*'. However, tenants in common, although they own the whole property together and do not own separate physical parts of the land, none the less have separate *shares* in the property (often described as 'undivided shares'), which form part of their separate assets (and therefore pass on their death to their heirs, rather than passing to the other tenants by survivorship).

Co-ownership can be created either as joint tenancy or as tenancy in common. But, as Blackstone indicated, a joint tenancy can become a tenancy in common by *severance*.

II. THE SCHEME OF THE 1925 LEGISLATION

The sections of the 1925 legislation applicable to concurrent interests are a further manifestation of the basic principles of that legislation. They attempt to simplify conveyancing by presenting to the purchaser a single title, however numerous and complicated the beneficial interests are, and by applying the overreaching principle to beneficial interests. In short, this is achieved by providing that the only form of co-ownership that can exist *at law* is a form of unseverable joint tenancy such as trustees hold. This is held on trust, and every form of *beneficial* co-ownership can only exist behind the trust.

Before 1997 co-ownership was governed either by an express trust for sale or by a statutory trust for sale. After 1996 the statutory trust for sale imposed by the 1925 legislation has been modified to become a trust of land, and the statutory trusts (for sale) under section 35 of the Law of Property Act 1925 have been abolished.

TRUSTS OF LAND AND APPOINTMENT OF TRUSTEES ACT 1996

5. Implied trusts for sale as trusts of land. p. 578, above.

LAW OF PROPERTY ACT 1925

1. Legal estates and equitable interests.—(6) A legal estate is not capable of subsisting or of being created in an undivided share in land or of being held by an infant.

34. Effect of future dispositions to tenants in common.—(1) An undivided share in land shall not be capable of being created except as provided by the Settled Land Act, 1925[4] or as hereinafter mentioned.

---

[4] SLA 1925, s. 36(1), (2), p. 566, below

(2) Where, after the commencement of this Act, land is expressed to be conveyed to any persons in undivided shares and those persons are of full age, the conveyance shall (notwithstanding anything to the contrary in this Act) operate as if the land had been expressed to be conveyed to the grantees, or, if there are more than four grantees, to the four first named in the conveyance, as joint tenants in trust for the persons interested in the land.[5]

Provided that, where the conveyance is made by way of mortgage the land shall vest in the grantees or such four of them as aforesaid for a term of years absolute (as provided by this Act) as joint tenants subject to cesser on redemption in like manner as if the mortgage money had belonged to them on a joint account, but without prejudice to the beneficial interests in the mortgage money and interest.

(3) A devise bequest or testamentary appointment, coming into operation after the commencement of this Act, of land to two or more persons in undivided shares shall operate as a devise bequest or appointment of the land to the personal representatives of the testator, and (but without prejudice to the rights and powers of the personal representatives for purposes of administration) in trust for the persons interested in the land.[6]

(3A) In subsections (2) and (3) of this section references to the persons interested in the land include persons interested as trustees or personal representatives (as well as persons beneficially interested).[7]

36. Joint tenancies.[8]—(1) Where a legal estate (not being settled land)[9] is beneficially limited to or held in trust for any persons as joint tenants, the same shall be held in trust,[10] in like manner as if the persons beneficially entitled were tenants in common, but not so as to sever their joint tenancy in equity.

(2) No severance of a joint tenancy of a legal estate, so as to create a tenancy in common in land, shall be permissible, whether by operation of law or otherwise, but this subsection does not affect the right of a joint tenant to release his interest to the other joint tenants, or the right to sever a joint tenancy in an equitable interest whether or not the legal estate is vested in the joint tenants:

Provided that, where a legal estate (not being settled land) is vested in joint tenants beneficially, and any tenant desires to sever the joint tenancy in equity,[11] he shall give to the other joint tenants a notice in writing[12] of such desire or do such other acts or things as would, in the case of personal estate, have been effectual to sever the tenancy in equity, and thereupon the land shall be held in trust on terms which would have been requisite for giving effect to the beneficial interests if there had been an actual severance.[13]

---

[5] As amended by TLATA 1996, s. 5, Sch. 2, para. 3(2).

[6] As amended by TLATA 1996, s. 5, Sch. 2, para. 3(3).

[7] Added by TLATA 1996, s. 5, Sch. 2, para. 3(4).

[8] As to whether beneficial joint tenancies should be abolished, see [1987] Conv 29, 225 (M. P. Thompson) in favour; 273 (A. M. Prichard) against.

[9] The definition of settled land is the same as that in SLA 1925, s. 1; *Re Gaul and Houlston's Contract* [1928] Ch 689.

[10] As amended by TLATA 1996, s. 5, Sch. 2, para. 4(2).

[11] See pp. 567–573, below.

[12] *Re 88 Berkeley Road, NW9* [1971] Ch 648 (notice properly served by recorded delivery, even if not received by addressee); LPA 1925, s. 196(4); (1971) 87 LQR 155; *Kinch v Bullard* [1999] 1 WLR 423 (severance although wife posted notice to husband but destroyed it before he received it); [1999] Conv 60 (M. Percival); [1998] All ER Rev 261 (P. J. Clarke). See also p. 429, n. 209, above.

[13] As amended by TLATA 1996, s. 5, Sch. 2, para. 4(3)(a).

Nothing in this Act affects the right of a survivor of joint tenants, who is solely and beneficially interested, to deal with his legal estate as if it were not held in trust.[14]

37. Rights of husband and wife.—A husband and wife shall, for all purposes of acquisition
of any interest in property, under a disposition made or coming into operation after the commencement of this Act, be treated as two persons.

SETTLED LAND ACT 1925

36. Undivided shares to take effect behind a trust of land.—(1) If and when, after the commencement of this Act, settled land is held in trust for persons entitled in possession under a
trust instrument[15] in undivided shares, the trustees of the settlement (if the settled land is not
already vested in them) may require the estate owner in whom the settled land is vested (but in
the case of a personal representative subject to his rights and powers for purposes of administration), at the cost of the trust estate, to convey the land to them, or assent to the land vesting
in them as joint tenants, and in the meantime the land shall be held on the same trusts as would
have been applicable thereto if it had been so conveyed to or vested in the trustees.

(2) If and when the settled land so held in trust in undivided shares is or becomes vested in the
trustees of the settlement, the land shall be held by them (subject to any incumbrances affecting the settled land which are secured by a legal mortgage, but freed from any incumbrances
affecting the undivided shares or not secured as aforesaid, and from any interests, powers and
charges subsisting under the trust instrument which have priority to the trust for the persons
entitled to the undivided shares) in trust for the persons interested in the land.[16]

(4) An undivided share in land shall not be capable of being created except under a trust
instrument or under the Law of Property Act 1925, and shall then only take effect behind a trust
of land.[17]

(6) In subsections (2) and (3) of this section references to the persons interested in the land
include persons interested as trustees or personal representatives (as well as persons beneficially interested).[18]

Before 1997 the scheme of the Act was to subject to a trust for sale all forms of concurrent ownership except for joint owners taking as tenants for life, in which case the
land remained settled land.[19] The question arose, however, of the position of a form
of concurrent ownership which did not come within the terms of the Law of Property
Act 1925, sections 34 and 36.[20] For example, land conveyed in undivided shares to an
adult and an infant; or where a tenancy in common exists although the land is not
'expressed to be conveyed in undivided shares'.

---

[14] Added by LP(A)A 1926, s. 7 and Sch., and amended by TLATA 1996, s. 5, Sch. 2, para. 4(3)(b). For the
protection given to the purchaser of a legal estate from a surviving joint tenant of unregistered land, see LP
(Joint Tenants) Act 1964, as amended by LP (Miscellaneous Provisions) Act 1994, s. 21(1), para. 3; and LRA
2002, s. 133, Sch. 11, para. 5; [2004] Conv 41 (E. J. Cooke).

[15] For the machinery of a settlement under SLA 1925, see C & B, pp. 403–407.

[16] As amended by TLATA 1996, s. 25(1), Sch. 3, para. 2(11)(a).

[17] Substituted by TLATA 1996, s. 25(1), Sch. 3, para. 2(11)(b).

[18] Substituted by TLATA 1996, s. 25(1), Sch. 3, para. 2(11)(c).

[19] SLA 1925, s. 19(2).

[20] (1945) 9 Conv (NS) 37; (1963) 27 Conv (NS) 51 (B. A. Rudden); *Bull v Bull* [1955] 1 QB 234; *Re Buchanan-
Wollaston's Conveyance* [1939] Ch 217; affd [1939] Ch 238; *Re Kempthorne* [1930] 1 Ch 268.

Since 1996 the gap in the legislation has been plugged. 'Because implied trusts are included within the all embracing definition of a trust of land, these situations are within the Trusts of Land and Appointment of Trustees Act 1996.'[21]

III. SEVERANCE OF JOINT TENANCY[22]

Before 1926 a joint tenancy could be severed—and become a tenancy in common—in a number of ways. Three were stated by PAGE WOOD V-C in *Williams v Hensman* (1861) 1 John & H 546, 557, 70 ER 862, 867, in a passage which is still frequently quoted today:[23]

A joint-tenancy may be severed in three ways: in the first place, an act of any one of the persons interested operating upon his own share may create a severance as to that share.[24] The right of each joint-tenant is a right by survivorship only in the event of no severance having taken place of the share which is claimed under the *jus accrescendi*. Each one is at liberty to dispose of his own interest in such manner as to sever it from the joint fund—losing, of course, at the same time, his own right of survivorship. Secondly, a joint-tenancy may be severed by mutual agreement. And, in the third place, there may be a severance by any course of dealing sufficient to intimate that the interests of all were mutually treated as constituting a tenancy in common. When the severance depends on an inference of this kind without any express act of severance, it will not suffice to rely on an intention, with respect to the particular share, declared only behind the backs of the other persons interested. You must find in this class of cases a course of dealing by which the shares of all the parties to the contest have been effected...

Law of Property Act 1925, s. 36(2) added a new, additional provision for severance by the giving of notice to the other joint tenants.[25] It is still not possible to effect severance by will.[26]

---

21 W & H, para. 2.3.

22 See Law Commission Working Paper: Trusts of Land No. 94 (1988) paras 16.11–16.14; C & B, pp. 457–461, 470–471; Gray, paras 7.4.63–7.4.108; M & W, paras 13.036–13.050; Smith, pp. 289–298; [1995] Conv 105 (L. Tee); [2009] Conv 67 (H. Conway).

23 See, e.g., *Re Draper's Conveyance*, below; *Burgess v Rawnsley*, p. 570, below.

24 E.g. by sale or mortgage or settlement of the share; *First National Securities Ltd v Hegerty* [1985] QB 850 (joint tenancy held to be severed where husband purported to mortgage jointly-owned property by forging wife's signature); *Ahmed v Kendrick and Ahmed* (1987) 56 P & CR 120 (severance where husband sold jointly owned house by forging wife's signature on both contract and registered transfer); cf. *Penn v Bristol and West Building Society* [1995] 2 FLR 938 (no severance where purchaser colluded in forgery by husband joint tenant of his wife's signature on the conveyance); *Monarch Aluminium v Rickman* [1989] CLY 1526 (charging order nisi held to be severance). See also [2000] Conv 208 (L. Fox); [2001] Conv 477 (S. Nield).

For severance by involuntary alienation, as where a joint tenant is adjudicated bankrupt and his interest vests in his trustee in bankruptcy, see *Re Dennis* [1996] Ch 80; [1995] All ER Rev 292 (S. M. Cretney); *Re Gorman* [1990] 1 WLR 616; *Re Pavlou* [1993] 1 WLR 1046; cf. *Re Palmer* [1994] Ch 316 (insolvency administration order); [1995] Conv 68 (M. Haley); [1995] CLJ 52 (L. Tee).

25 *Carr-Glynn v Frearsons* [1999] 2 WLR 1046; (solicitor, who failed to advise 81 year old testatrix promptly to sever joint tenancy in conjunction with execution of her will, held liable to compensate specific legatee for loss suffered thereby); (1999) 115 LQR 201; [1999] Conv 399 (R. Kerridge and A. H. R. Brierley).

26 For severance by homicide, see *Re K* [1985] Ch 85; affd [1986] Ch 180; Maudsley & Burn, *Trusts & Trustees* (7th edn), pp. 302–307.

LAW OF PROPERTY ACT 1925

36. Joint Tenancies.—(1), (2) p. 565, above.

Re Draper's Conveyance[27]
[1969] 1 Ch 486 (ChD, **Plowman J**)

A house was conveyed to a husband and wife as joint tenants. The wife obtained a divorce, and issued a summons under section 17 of the Married Women's Property Act 1882, asking for an order that the house be sold and the proceeds distributed according to the interests of the spouses. The order was made but the husband remained in occupation. The husband died and the question was whether the wife was entitled to the house absolutely by survivorship or whether she and her husband's estate were entitled in equal shares.

Held. The wife held the legal estate on trust for herself and her husband's estate in equal shares.

Plowman J: It is common ground that the answer to the question asked by originating summons in this case depends upon whether a beneficial joint tenancy which subsisted between two persons who were formerly husband and wife in a certain house was severed in the lifetime of the husband... Mr Cooke, on behalf of the defendants, submits that the joint tenancy was severed, and he puts the matter in two ways, either that it was severed by notice in writing, or it was severed by conduct, and in order to explain those submissions I should, I think, refer to section 36(2) of the Law of Property Act 1925....

Mr Cooke, as I say, puts it in two ways: first, he submits that the wife's conduct was such as to effect a severance of the joint tenancy, and in relation to that matter he relies on the summons of 11 February 1966, in the Probate, Divorce and Admiralty Division, coupled with the orders which were made by that court, coupled with the plaintiff's solicitor's letter of 7 June 1966. And he says, either as a result of those three matters or as a result of any of them, the joint tenancy became severed by conduct, and he referred me to the decision of Havers J in *Hawkesley v May* [1956] 1 QB 304. The part of that case which is relevant for present purposes depends upon these facts, which I read from the headnote: 'A settled fund was held by trustees upon trusts under which on attaining the age of 21 the plaintiff and his younger sister became absolutely entitled as joint tenants.' The question was whether that joint tenancy had become severed, and Havers J said:

'The joint tenancy was capable of being severed by the plaintiff on attaining the age of 21. There are a number of ways by which a joint tenancy may be severed. In Williams v Hensman (1861) 1 John & H 546 Page Wood V-C, in the course of his judgment, said: [His Lordship quoted the extract from Page Wood V-C's judgment, above, p. 567].

Havers J continued:

'The first method indicated, namely, an act of any one of the persons interested operating upon his own share, obviously includes a declaration of intention to sever by one party.'

[27] (1968) 84 LQR 462 (PVB).

Then, after referring to *Walmsley v Foxhall* (1870) 40 LJ Ch 28 he said:

'This being the state of the authorities, I hold that on the plaintiff attaining the age of 21 he was entitled to the income of his share of the fund. As regards the severance, I hold that when the sister wrote the letter dated 18 March 1942, in which she said: 'Thank you for your letter of 17th instant with the particulars of the investments. I should like the dividends to be paid into my account at Martins Bank, 208 Kensington High Street' (which was a letter in reply to the first defendant), that was a sufficient act on her part to constitute a severance of the joint tenancy. If I am wrong about that, there clearly was a severance when her share of the trust funds were transferred to her in September 1942.'

So from that case I derive this; a declaration by one of a number of joint tenants of his intention to sever operates as a severance. Mr Cooke also, as I have said, relied upon the notice in writing which under section 36(2) of the Law of Property Act, 1925, is allowed in the case of a joint tenancy in land, although not in personalty, and he submits that the summons to which I have already referred, although not signed, amounted to a notice in writing on the part of the wife that she desired to sever the joint tenancy in equity. I say 'although not signed by the wife or by anybody on her behalf' because there is no requirement in the subsection of a signature.

Dealing with the matter there, and ignoring for a moment certain matters which were submitted by Mr McCulloch, it seems to me that Mr Cooke's submissions are right whether they are based on the new provision in section 36(2) of the Law of Property Act, 1925, or whether they are based on the old law which applied to severing a joint tenancy in the case of a personal estate. It seems to me that that summons, coupled with the affidavit in support of it, clearly evinced an intention on the part of the wife that she wished the property to be sold and the proceeds distributed, a half to her and a half to the husband. And if that is right then it seems to me that that is wholly inconsistent with the notion that a beneficial joint tenancy in that property is to continue, and therefore, apart from these objections to which I will refer in a moment, I feel little doubt that in one way or the other this joint tenancy was severed in equity before the end of February 1966, as a result of the summons which was served on the husband and as a result of what the wife stated in her affidavit in support of the summons.

But then certain matters were submitted to me by Mr McCulloch on behalf of the wife, which I think fall under two heads. In the first place I was referred to certain observations which were made by Lord Denning MR in *Bedson v Bedson* [1965] 2 QB 666. That was a case in which a wife, in September 1964, applied to the County court under section 17 of the Married Women's Property Act 1882, for an order that the property together with the fixtures, fittings, car, stock and goodwill be sold, and the proceeds divided between herself and her husband in equal shares. And then the headnote goes on to state that no matrimonial proceedings had at any relevant date been begun.

But Lord Denning in the course of his judgment had certain things to say about the severance of the joint tenancy in the matrimonial home. He said:

'(3) So long as the house is in the possession of the husband and wife as joint tenants or one of them, there can be no severance of their equitable interests: see section 36(1)(3).' That is a reference to the Law of Property Act 1925. 'Neither of them can sell his or her equitable interest separately. If he or she could do so, it would mean that the purchaser could insist on going into possession himself—with the other spouse there—which is absurd. It would mean also that one of them could, of his own head, destroy the right of survivorship which was the essence of the joint tenancy. That cannot be correct.'

If I may say so, it is not easy to understand what it is in section 36(1) and (3) of the Law of Property Act 1925, on which Lord Denning was relying as authority for the proposition that so long as the house is in the possession of the husband and wife as joint tenants or one of them there can be no severance of their equitable interests.

Then Lord Denning MR added:

'One further point: I am of opinion that, while the husband is in possession of the house, there can be no severance of the joint tenancy. The wife cannot sell her interest separately. In case I am wrong about this, I think we should make an order restraining the wife from doing so. It would be quite intolerable that she should, for instance, be able to sell her interest to her mother and get her to turn him out. The jurisdiction in this behalf is amply covered by *Lee v Lee* [1952] 2 QB 489n, which has been approved by the House of Lords.'

Mr McCulloch points out that in the present case the husband continued in possession until January of 1967 which was some time after the orders of the Divorce court had been made. However, Russell LJ in the same case took a different view about the severance of beneficial joint tenancies. He said:

'I am unable to accept the legal position of Lord Denning MR, that when husband and wife are joint tenants of the legal estate in the matrimonial home and also beneficial joint tenants in respect of it, neither can, so long as one is in possession, sell his or her beneficial interest therein or otherwise sever the beneficial joint tenancy. The proposition is, I think, without the slightest foundation in law or in equity. If anything, it appears to be an attempt to revive to some extent the long defunct tenancy by entireties which, as I have already remarked, was doomed by the Married Women's Property Act, 1882, itself. It may indeed be that either the wife's claim in this case, or the notation in the business accounts of the husband of her interest has long since operated as a severance.'

If I have to choose between those two statements I respectfully express my preference for that of Russell L.J.[28] It is interesting to note that he referred to the possibility that the wife's claim in that case might have operated by itself as a severance, and, as I have already stated, I take the view that in this case the summons issued by the wife in the Divorce Division coupled with the affidavit which she swore in support of that summons did operate to sever her beneficial joint tenancy.[29]

Burgess v Rawnsley
[1975] Ch 429 (CA, **Lord Denning MR, Browne LJ** and **Sir John Pennycuick**)[30]

Lord Denning MR: In 1966 there was a scripture rally in Trafalgar Square. A widower, Mr Honick, went to it. He was about 63. A widow, Mrs Rawnsley, the defendant, also went. She

---

[28] So did CA in *Harris v Goddard* [1983] 1 WLR 1203 at 1208, per Lawton LJ. See also (1966) 82 LQR 29 (R.E.M.); (1976) 40 Conv (NS) 77 (J. F. Garner).

[29] Cf. *Harris v Goddard* [1983] 1 WLR 1203 (a wife's prayer in a divorce petition for a property adjustment order to be made in respect of the former matrimonial home did not operate as severance); [1984] Conv 148 (S. Coneys); *Grindal v Hooper* [1999] EGCS 150 (notice of severance effective, even though not endorsed on conveyance). Whether a unilateral act not amounting to notice under s. 36(2) can effect severance is a matter of dispute; *Burgess v Rawnsley* [1975] Ch 429, below.

[30] (1975) 39 Conv (NS) 443 (F. R. Crane); [1976] CLJ 20 (D. J. Hayton); (1977) 41 Conv (NS) 243 (S. M. Bandali).

was about 60. He went up to her and introduced himself. He was not much to look at. 'He looked like a tramp,' she said. 'He had been picking up fag-ends.' They got on well enough, however, to exchange addresses. His was 36 Queen's Road, Waltham Cross, Hertfordshire. Hers was 74 Downton Avenue, Streatham Hill, London, SW2. Next day he went to her house with a gift for her. It was a rose wrapped in a newspaper. Afterwards their friendship grew apace. She was sorry for him, she said. She smartened him up with better clothes. She had him to meals. She went to his house: he went to hers. They wrote to one another in terms of endearment. We were not shown the letters, but counsel described them as love letters.

A few months later Mr Honick had the opportunity of buying the house where he lived at 36 Queen's Road, Waltham Cross. He had been the tenant of it for some years, but his wife had died and his married daughter had left; so that he was alone there. He talked it over with Mrs Rawnsley. He told her that the owner was willing to sell the house to him for £800. Mrs Rawnsley said that she would go half shares: she would have the upper flat and he the lower flat.

In 1967 they bought the house in their joint names 'as joint tenants', each providing half the purchase price. Mr Honick was minded to marry Mrs Rawnsley, but it was clear that she was not minded to marry him. In fact they did not marry and Mrs Rawnsley did not move into the house. There was evidence of an oral agreement between them in 1968 whereby she agreed to sell her share to him for £750 but she later refused to sell. Mr Honick died and the question was whether his estate was entitled to a half share in the house. In holding that it was, because there had been a severance of the joint tenancy, Lord Denning MR continued:

[W]as there a severance of the beneficial joint tenancy? The judge said:

> 'I hold that there has been a severance of the joint tenancy brought about by the conduct of the defendant in asking £750 for her share which was agreed to.'

In making that statement the judge made a little slip. She did not ask £750. But it was a slip of no importance. The important finding is that there was an agreement that she would sell her share to him for £750. Almost immediately afterwards she went back upon it. Is that conduct sufficient to effect a severance?

Mr Levy submitted that it was not. He relied on the recent decision of Walton J in *Nielson-Jones v Fedden* [1975] Ch 222, given subsequently to the judgment of the judge here. Walton J held that no conduct is sufficient to sever a joint tenancy unless it is irrevocable. Mr Levy said that in the present case the agreement was not in writing. It could not be enforced by specific performance. It was revocable and was in fact revoked by Mrs Rawnsley when she went back on it. So there was, he submitted, no severance.

Walton J founded himself on the decision of Stirling J in *Re Wilks* [1891] 3 Ch 59. He criticised *Hawkesley v May* [1956] 1 QB 304 and *Re Draper's Conveyance* [1969] 1 Ch 486, and said that they were clearly contrary to the existing well-established law. He went back to *Coke upon Littleton*, 189a, 299b and to *Blackstone's Commentaries*. Those old writers were dealing with legal joint tenancies. *Blackstone* said, 8th edn (1778), vol. II, pp. 180, 185:

> 'The properties of a joint estate are derived from its unity, which is fourfold; the unity of interest, the unity of title, the unity of time, and the unity of possession:...an estate in joint tenancy may be severed and destroyed...by destroying any of its constituent unities.'

And he gives instances of how this may be done. Now that is all very well when you are considering how a legal joint tenancy can be severed. But it is of no application today when there can be no severance of a legal joint tenancy; and you are only considering how a beneficial joint tenancy can be severed. The thing to remember today is that equity leans against joint tenants and favours tenancies in common.

Nowadays everyone starts with the judgment of Sir William Page Wood V-C in *Williams v Hensman* (1861) 1 John & H 546, 557, where he said:

'A joint tenancy may be severed in three ways: in the first place, an act of any one of the persons interested operating upon his own share may create a severance as to that share....Secondly, a joint tenancy may be severed by mutual agreement. And, in the third place, there may be a severance by any course of dealing sufficient to intimate that the interests of all were mutually treated as constituting a tenancy in common. When the severance depends on an inference of this kind without any express act of severance, it will not suffice to rely on an intention, with respect to the particular share, declared only behind the backs of the other persons interested. You must find in this class of cases a course of dealing by which the shares of all the parties to the contest have been affected, as happened in the cases of *Wilson v Bell* (1843) Ir 5 Eq R 501 and *Jackson v Jackson* (1804) 9 Ves 591.'

In that passage Page Wood V-C distinguished between severance 'by mutual agreement' and severance by a 'course of dealing.' That shows that a 'course of dealing' need not amount to an agreement, expressed or implied, for severance. It is sufficient if there is a course of dealing in which one party makes clear to the other that he desires that their shares should no longer be held jointly but be held in common. I emphasise that it must be made clear to the other party. That is implicit in the sentence in which Page Wood V-C says:

'it will not suffice to rely on an intention, with respect to the particular share, declared only behind the backs of the other persons interested.'

Similarly it is sufficient if both parties enter on a course of dealing which evinces an intention by both of them that their shares shall henceforth be held in common and not jointly. As appears from the two cases to which Page Wood V-C referred to of *Wilson v Bell* and *Jackson v Jackson*.

I come now to the question of notice. Suppose that one party gives a notice in writing to the other saying that he desires to sever the joint tenancy. Is that sufficient to effect a severance? I think it is.

His Lordship read LPA 1925, section 36(2), p. 565, above, and continued:

The word 'other' is most illuminating. It shows quite plainly that, in the case of personal estate one of the things which is effective in equity to sever a joint tenancy is 'a notice in writing' of a desire to sever. So also in regard to real estate.

Taking this view, I find myself in agreement with Havers J in *Hawkesley v May* [1956] 1 QB 304, 313–314, and of Plowman J in *Re Draper's Conveyance* [1969] 1 Ch 486. I cannot agree with Walton J in *Nielson-Jones v Fedden* [1975] Ch 222 at 234–235 that those cases were wrongly decided. It would be absurd that there should be a difference between real estate and personal estate in this respect. Suppose real estate is held on a joint tenancy on a trust for sale and is sold and converted into personal property. Before sale, it is severable by notice in writing. It would be ridiculous if it could not be severed afterwards in like manner. I look upon section 36(2) as declaratory of the law as to severance by notice and not as a new provision confined to real estate. A joint tenancy in personal estate can be severed by notice just as a joint tenancy in real estate.

His Lordship referred to *Nielson-Jones v Fedden* and *Re Wilks* [1891] 3 Ch 59, and continued:

It remains to apply these principles to the present case. I think there was evidence that Mr Honick and Mrs Rawnsley did come to an agreement that he would buy her share for £750. That agreement was not in writing and it was not specifically enforceable. Yet it was sufficient to effect a severance.[31] Even if there was not any firm agreement but only a course of dealing, it clearly evinced an intention by both parties that the property should henceforth be held in common and not jointly.

On these grounds I would dismiss the appeal.[32]

IV. ESTABLISHING THE BENEFICIAL INTERESTS[33]

Co-ownership inevitably involves a trust. The legal title may be held by one or more trustees; but the beneficial co-owners must in equity hold interests under a trust. If a person claims to have an interest as a co-owner in the land, therefore, he must establish the existence of the trust, and the extent of his beneficial interest.

A. FORMALITIES FOR THE CREATION OF THE TRUST

The trust of land may be declared expressly, or it may be constructive or resulting. If express, it must be evidenced in writing under section 53(1)(*b*) of the Law of Property Act 1925.

The Land Registry recommended wording for the creation of the trust under the Land Registration Act 1925,[34] although it was not compulsory. However, since 1 April 1998,[35] for cases where there is more than one transferee of registered land, the transfer

---

[31] Followed in *Hunter v Babbage* (1994) 69 P & CR 548 (draft agreement); cf. *Edwards v Hastings* [1996] NPC 87 (agreement to sever conditional on sale of family home).

[32] *Cf. Greenfield v Greenfield* (1979) 38 P & CR 570 (conversion of house jointly owned by brothers into two self-contained maisonettes occupied separately held not to be severance by a course of dealing); *Barton v Morris* [1985] 1 WLR 1257 (inclusion of property as a partnership asset in the partnership accounts for tax purposes held not severance by a course of dealing); *Gore and Snell v Carpenter* (1990) 60 P & CR 456 (negotiations between husband and wife with a view to settling claims for ancillary relief in divorce proceedings held not to be severance in absence of a final agreement between them); *Re Denny* (1947) 177 LT 291; *McDowell v Hirschfield* [1992] 2 FLR 126 (onus of proof on party who desires to establish course of dealing).

[33] For further materials, see Maudsley & Burn, *Trusts & Trustees* (7th edn), pp. 322–347.

[34] Practice Advice Leaflet No. 13 Part B3.

[35] LRR 1997, r. 2(2), Sch. 2. See now LRR 2003, r. 206, Sch. 1, as amended by LR (Amendment) R 2008, SI 2008 No. 1919, Sch. 2, para. 1. However, 'the purpose of this is not to give the registrar notice of the trusts

itself contains a form of declaration of trust. For example, in Panel 10 of Form TR 1 for the Transfer of whole of registered title(s), p. 168, above, the parties must indicate (by placing 'X' in the appropriate box) one of the following:

they are to hold the property on trust for themselves as joint tenants
they are to hold the property on trust for themselves as tenants in common in equal shares
they are to hold the property on trust [*Complete as necessary*]

LAW OF PROPERTY ACT 1925

53. Instruments required to be in writing.—(1) Subject to the provisions hereinafter contained with respect to the creation of interests in land by parol—

(*b*) a declaration of trust respecting any land or any interest therein must be manifested and proved by some writing signed by some person who is able to declare such trust or by his will;

(2) This section does not affect the creation or operation of resulting, implied or constructive trusts.

B. FINDING BOTH THE TRUST AND THE EXTENT OF THE BENEFICIAL INTERESTS

Maudsley & Burn's Trusts & Trustees: Cases & Materials (7th edn, 2008), pp. 322–324

When considering the allocation of beneficial interests in the family home it is important to distinguish clearly between issues concerning the identification of such interests and separate issues concerning the extent of such interests.

The principles relating to the beneficial ownership of the family home were reviewed by the House of Lords in *Lloyds Bank plc v Rosset* [1991] 1 AC 107 [below].[36] It was considered that, in the absence of a declaration of trust evidenced in writing [above], there are two ways of acquiring a beneficial interest in the home. The first is to establish that the parties expressed a common intention to share the beneficial interest,[37] followed by detrimental reliance by the claimant which is referable to the common intention.[38] It is this detrimental reliance which makes it unconscionable for the other party to deny the claimant's beneficial interest in the property. Alternatively, the court can *infer* that the parties had a common intention to share

under which the land is held, but simply to enable us to decide whether we need to enter a form A restriction [p. 561, above]. It also serves as a memorandum of the trusts on which the property is held, although details of the trusts will not appear on the register': Land Registry Practice Guide 24 (Private Trusts of Land), para. 5.4. For the use of this form to declare a trust as a joint tenancy, see *Bathurst v Scarborow* [2005] 1 P & CR 4 at [8]–[10], [55].

[36] (1990) 106 LQR 539 (J. Davies); [1990] Conv 314 (M. Thompson), [1990] All ER Rev 138 (S. Cretney); (1991) CLJ 38 (M. Dixon); (1991) 54 MLR 126 (S. Gardner); (1993) 23 *Family Law* 231 (J. Dewar). For the developments of the doctrine before that decision, see the judgment of Lord Walker in *Stack v Dowden* [2007] UKHL 17, [2007] 2 AC 432.

[37] *Grant v Edwards* [1986] Ch 638; *Eves v Eves* [1975] 1 WLR 1338.

[38] *Cox v Jones* [2004] EWHC 1486 (Ch), [2004] 2 FLR 1010.

the beneficial interest. Such an inference can be drawn, it was said, only where the claimant has contributed directly to the purchase price, either initially[39] or by payment of mortgage instalments. It was doubted whether indirect contributions would suffice.[40] Non-financial contributions to the running of the home will not be sufficient to infer a common intention.[41] Direct contributions were regarded as giving rise to a constructive trust, although traditionally such contributions give rise to a presumption of a resulting trust.[42] These financial contributions enable both a common intention to be inferred and establish the detrimental reliance which makes it unconscionable for the other party to deny the claimant's beneficial interest. The practice, prevalent in the 1970s in particular, of recognising a constructive trust simply on the ground of justice and good conscience,[43] has now been rejected.[44]

The application of the law on common-intention constructive trusts has been subject to rigorous criticism, especially in its application to family property disputes.[45] The rejection of the view, expressed in cases before *Lloyds Bank v Rosset*,[46] that an indirect contribution can suffice to establish a proprietary interest in the home without the necessity of finding an express common intention to share, is capable of producing injustice, for example where the wife pays household bills, thereby enabling her husband to pay the mortgage instalments.[47] Some Commonwealth jurisdictions[48] have resolved this problem by legislation[49] or by applying the principles of unconscionability[50] or unjust enrichment,[51] and have rejected the view that domestic duties must be left out of account. A second approach is to invoke the more flexible principles of

---

[39] See, for example, *Parrott v Parkin* [2007] EWHC 210 (Admlty), [2007] 1 Lloyd's Rep 719.

[40] Although it has sometimes been recognised that indirect financial contributions will be enough to infer the common intention to share the beneficial interest if this enables the other party to be able to afford to make mortgage payments: *Le Foe v Le Foe and Woolwich Building Society plc* [2001] 2 FLR 970. It seems that the other party must be aware of the claimant's contributions: *Lightfoot v Lightfoot-Brown* [2005] EWCA Civ 1201, [2005] 2 P and CR 22.

[41] *Lloyds Bank v Rosset* [1991] 1 AC 107, 132 (Lord Bridge) [see p. 576, below]. See also *Buggs v Buggs* [2003] EWHC 1538 (Ch), [2004] WTLR 799; *Mehra v Shah* [2004] EWCA Civ 632.

[42] Later payments of mortgage instalments, without any liability to make them, do not found a presumption of a resulting trust, although a constructive trust can arise: *Curley v Parkes* [2004] EWCA Civ 1515, [2005] 1 P & CR DG 15; *Stack v Dowden* [2007] UKHL 17, [2007] 2 AC 432 [see p. 580, below].

[43] See *Heseltine v Heseltine* [1971] 1 WLR 342; *Hussey v Palmer* [1972] 1 WLR 1286 and *Eves v Eves* [1975] 1 WLR 1338.

[44] See *Grant v Edwards* [1986] Ch 638 at 647 (Nourse LJ). *Eves v Eves* [1975] 1 WLR 1338 was approved by the House of Lords in *Lloyds Bank plc v Rosset* [1991] 1 AC 107 without reference to Lord Denning's approach. But query whether this old practice might be returning in the light of the decision of the House of Lords in *Stack v Dowden* [2007] UKHL 17, [2007] 2 AC 432 [see p. 580, below].

[45] See (1996) LS 325 (N. Glover and P. Todd); (1996) LS 218 (A. Lawson). The Law Commission has now prepared a report on the property rights of those who share homes. [See p. 598, below.] See also *Stack v Dowden* [2007] UKHL 17, [2007] 2 AC 432, para. 34 (Lord Walker), para. 63 (Baroness Hale) [see p. 580, below]; *Abbott v Abbott* [2007] UKPC 53.

[46] *Gissing v Gissing* [1971] AC 886; *Burns v Burns* [1984] Ch 317; *Grant v Edwards* [1986] Ch 638.

[47] Such a contribution may suffice under the 'reasonable expectation' approach in New Zealand: *Lankow v Rose* [1995] 1 NZLR 277.

[48] See (1998) LS 369 (S. Wong).

[49] De Facto Relationships Act 1984 (NSW); (1994) 8 *Trust Law International* 74 (M. Bryan). See also (1999) 19 LS 468 (A. Barlow and C. Lind), who recommend a legislative scheme creating statutory presumptions of co-ownership. See the recommendations of the Law Commission [p. 598, below].

[50] As in Australia: *Muschinski v Dodds* (1985) 160 CLR 583.

[51] As in Canada: *Peter v Beblow* (1993) 101 DLR (4th) 621. See also in Scotland: *Satchwel v McIntosh* 2006 SLT (Sh Ct) 117; *McKenzie v Nuller* 2007 SLT (Sh Ct) 17

proprietary estoppel, where the act of detrimental reliance need not involve expenditure[52] and which does not require a search for an artificial common intention,[53] although it does require there to have been a representation or assurance by the owner of the property that the claimant has an interest in it.[54] The process of assimilating the doctrines of proprietary estoppel and constructive trust has begun, but is not complete.[55] A third view is that the relationship of the parties should itself generate the claim.[56]

The principles laid down in *Lloyds Bank plc v Rosset* have since been examined by the Court of Appeal in *Oxley v Hiscock* [2004] EWCA Civ 546, [2005] Fam 211 [p. 578, below], and reconsidered by the House of Lords in *Stack v Dowden* [2007] UKHL 17, [2007] 2 AC 432 [p. 580, below]. As regards the identification of a beneficial interest, these cases have distinguished between situations where property is registered in the name of one party and where it is registered in the name of both parties. In the former case a common-intention constructive trust needs to be established by means of an express or inferred common intent. Then the beneficial interest must be quantified. In the latter case there is a very strong presumption that the beneficial interest is shared equally and the only relevance of the constructive trust is to determine whether the claimant can establish a larger interest. There is some controversy over whether quantification of the claimant's interest should be achieved by reference to the parties' whole course of conduct, either to determine what would be a fair share, or to determine what share the parties intended. The Court of Appeal in *Oxley v Hiscock* preferred the former approach,[57] focusing on fairness, whereas the House of Lords in *Stack v Dowden* have purported to prefer the latter approach, focusing on intention; see especially Baroness Hale, at para. 61 [p. 587, below]. But even the latter approach requires the court to consider a wide variety of factors.

C. LEGAL ESTATE HELD BY ONE PERSON[58]

In **Lloyds Bank plc v Rosset** [1991] 1 AC 107 Lᴏʀᴅ Bʀɪᴅɢᴇ ᴏꜰ Hᴀʀᴡɪᴄʜ said at 132:

In the course of the argument your Lordships had the benefit of elaborate submissions as to the test to be applied to determine the circumstances in which the sole legal proprietor of a

---

[52] *Greasley v Cooke* [1980] 1 WLR 1306 [p. 1036, below]; *Campbell v Griffin* [2001] EWCA Civ 990, [2001] WTLR 981.

[53] *Gillett v Holt* [2001] Ch 210; *Jennings v Rice* [2002] EWCA Civ 159, [2003] 1 P & CR 100 [p. 1040, below]; [1990] Conv 370 (D. Hayton); (1993) 109 LQR 114 (P. Ferguson) and 485 (D. Hayton); (1993) 3 *Caribbean Law Review* 96 (R. Smith); (2006) 122 LQR 492 (S. Gardner).

[54] *Jennings v Rice* [2002] EWCA Civ 159, [2003] 1 P & CR 100.

[55] *Grant v Edwards* [1986] Ch 638; *Lloyds Bank plc v Rosset* [1991] 1 AC 107; *Stokes v Anderson* [1991] 1 FLR 391; *S v S* [2006] EWHC 2892 (Fam), [2007] 1 FLR 1123; *Stack v Dowden* [2007] UKHL 17, [2007] 2 AC 432, para. 34 (Lord Walker). [On the relationship between proprietary estoppel and constructive trust, see further pp. 1078–1080, below.]

[56] (1993) 109 LQR 263 (S. Gardner).

[57] See also *Midland Bank plc v Cooke* [1995] 4 All ER 562.

[58] See also, after the decision in *Stack v Dowden*: *Abbott v Abbott* [2007] UKPC 53, [2008] 1 FLR 1451; [2007] Conv 456 (M. Dixon), p. 599, below; (2008) 124 LQR 209 (R. Lee) (equal beneficial interest); *Holman v Howes* [2007] EWCA Civ 877; [2008] 1 FLR 1217 (no common intention to share beneficially); *James v Thomas* [2007] EWCA Civ 1212, [2008] 1 FLR 1598 (no common intention to share); *Morris v Morris* [2008] EWCA Civ 257; [2008] Fam Law 521 (no common intention to share); *Parris v Williams* [2008] EWCA Civ 1147, [2009] 1 P & CR 9 (no need for 'bargain' by which claimant had agreed to do something in return for interest; *Lloyds Bank plc v Rosset* applied, *Oxley v Hiscock* and other recent cases not cited), *Webster v Webster* [2008] EWHC 31 (Ch); [2009] 03 EG 102 (CS) (claim for beneficial joint tenancy, but no common intention to share).

dwelling house can properly be held to have become a constructive trustee of a share in the beneficial interest in the house for the benefit of the partner with whom he or she has cohabited in the house as their shared home. Having in this case reached a conclusion on the facts which, although at variance with the views of the courts below, does not seem to depend on any nice legal distinction and with which, I understand, all your Lordships agree, I cannot help doubting whether it would contribute anything to the illumination of the law if I were to attempt an elaborate and exhaustive analysis of the relevant law to add to the many already to be found in the authorities to which our attention was directed in the course of the argument. I do, however, draw attention to one critical distinction which any judge required to resolve a dispute between former partners as to the beneficial interest in the home they formerly shared should always have in the forefront of his mind.

The first and fundamental question which must always be resolved is whether, independently of any inference to be drawn from the conduct of the parties in the course of sharing the house as their home and managing their joint affairs, there has at any time prior to acquisition, or exceptionally at some later date, been any agreement, arrangement or understanding reached between them that the property is to be shared beneficially. The finding of an agreement or arrangement to share in this sense can only, I think, be based on evidence of express discussions between the partners, however imperfectly remembered and however imprecise their terms may have been. Once a finding to this effect is made it will only be necessary for the partner asserting a claim to a beneficial interest against the partner entitled to the legal estate to show that he or she has acted to his or her detriment or significantly altered his or her position in reliance on the agreement in order to give rise to a constructive trust or a proprietary estoppel.

In sharp contrast with this situation is the very different one where there is no evidence to support a finding of an agreement or arrangement to share, however reasonable it might have been for the parties to reach such an arrangement if they had applied their minds to the question, and where the court must rely entirely on the conduct of the parties both as the basis from which to infer a common intention to share the property beneficially and as the conduct relied on to give rise to a constructive trust. In this situation direct contributions to the purchase price by the partner who is not the legal owner, whether initially or by payment of mortgage instalments, will readily justify the inference necessary to the creation of a constructive trust. But, as I read the authorities, it is at least extremely doubtful whether anything less will do.

The leading cases in your Lordships' House are *Pettitt v Pettitt* [1970] AC 777 and *Gissing v Gissing* [1971] AC 886. Both demonstrate situations in the second category to which I have referred and their Lordships discuss at great length the difficulties to which these situations give rise. The effect of these two decisions is very helpfully analysed in the judgment of Lord MacDermott LCJ in *McFarlane v McFarlane* [1972] NI 59.

Outstanding examples on the other hand of cases giving rise to situations in the first category are *Eves v Eves* [1975] 1 WLR 1338 and *Grant v Edwards* [1986] Ch 638. In both these cases, where the parties who had cohabited were unmarried, the female partner had been clearly led by the male partner to believe, when they set up home together, that the property would belong to them jointly. In *Eves v Eves* the male partner had told the female partner that the only reason why the property was to be acquired in his name alone was because she was under 21 and that, but for her age, he would have had the house put into their joint names. He admitted in evidence that this was simply an 'excuse.' Similarly in *Grant v Edwards* the female partner was told by the male partner that the only reason for not acquiring the property in joint names was because she was involved in divorce proceedings and that, if the property were acquired jointly, this might operate to her prejudice in those proceedings. As Nourse LJ put it, at p. 649:

> 'Just as in *Eves v Eves* [1975] 1 WLR 1338, these facts appear to me to raise a clear inference that there was an understanding between the plaintiff and the defendant, or a common intention, that the plaintiff was to have some sort of proprietary interest in the house; otherwise no excuse for not putting her name on to the title would have been needed.'

The subsequent conduct of the female partner in each of these cases, which the court rightly held sufficient to give rise to a constructive trust or proprietary estoppel supporting her claim to an interest in the property, fell far short of such conduct as would by itself have supported the claim in the absence of an express representation by the male partner that she was to have such an interest. It is significant to note that the share to which the female partners in *Eves v Eves* and *Grant v Edwards* were held entitled were one quarter and one half respectively. In no sense could these shares have been regarded as proportionate to what the judge in the instant case described as a 'qualifying contribution' in terms of the indirect contributions to the acquisition or enhancement of the value of the houses made by the female partners.

In **Oxley v Hiscock** [2005] Fam 211 CHADWICK LJ said at 246:

68 I have referred, in the immediately preceding paragraphs, to 'cases of this nature'. By that, I mean cases in which the common features are: (i) the property is bought as a home for a couple who, although not married, intend to live together as man and wife; (ii) each of them makes some financial contribution to the purchase; (iii) the property is purchased in the sole name of one of them; and (iv) there is no express declaration of trust. In those circumstances the first question is whether there is evidence from which to infer a common intention, communicated by each to the other, that each shall have a beneficial share in the property.[59] In many such cases—of which the present is an example—there will have been some discussion between the parties at the time of the purchase which provides the answer to that question. Those are cases within the first of Lord Bridge's categories in *Lloyds Bank plc v Rosset* [1991] 1 AC 107. In other cases—where the evidence is that the matter was not discussed at all—an affirmative answer will readily be inferred from the fact that each has made a financial contribution. Those are cases within Lord Bridge's second category. And, if the answer to the first question is that there was a common intention, communicated to each other, that each should have a beneficial share in the property, then the party who does not become the legal owner will be held to have acted to his or her detriment in making a financial contribution to the purchase in reliance on the common intention.

69 In those circumstances, the second question to be answered in cases of this nature is: 'what is the extent of the parties' respective beneficial interests in the property?' Again, in many such cases, the answer will be provided by evidence of what they said and did at the time

---

59 *Lightfoot v Lightfoot-Brown* [2005] 2 P & CR 22 (repayment of mortgage by one party, not known to the other, was not evidence of common intention). At [27], per Arden LJ: 'Chadwick LJ [in *Oxley v Hiscock*] did not dispense with the requirement for communication of the common intention when determining whether a common intention constructive trust had arisen. Indeed, the concept of communication of common intention has much in common with the manifestation of intention. An intention to share a beneficial interest in property has to be manifested to give to a rival obligation .... The need for communication was only held to be unnecessary in the *Oxley* case in respect to the size of the parties' beneficial interest.' Intention is tested objectively from the other party's perspective: *Gissing v Gissing* [1971] AC 886 at 906.

of the acquisition. But, in a case where there is no evidence of any discussion between them as to the amount of the share which each was to have—and even in a case where the evidence is that there was no discussion on that point—the question still requires an answer. It must now be accepted that (at least in this court and below) the answer is that each is entitled to that share which the court considers fair having regard to the whole course of dealing between them in relation to the property. And, in that context, 'the whole course of dealing between them in relation to the property' includes the arrangements which they make from time to time in order to meet the outgoings (for example, mortgage contributions, council tax and utilities, repairs, insurance and housekeeping) which have to be met if they are to live in the property as their home.[60]

70 As the cases show, the courts have not found it easy to reconcile that final step with a traditional, property-based, approach. It was rejected, in unequivocal terms, by Dillon LJ in *Springette v Defoe* [1992] 2 FLR 388, 393 when he said: 'The court does not as yet sit, as under a palm tree, to exercise a general discretion to do what the man in the street, on a general overview of the case, might regard as fair.' Three strands of reasoning can be identified.

(1) That suggested by Lord Diplock in *Gissing v Gissing* [1971] AC 886, 909D and adopted by Nourse LJ in *Stokes v Anderson* [1991] 1 FLR 391, 399G, 400B-C. The parties are taken to have agreed at the time of the acquisition of the property that their respective shares are not to be quantified then, but are left to be determined when their relationship comes to an end or the property is sold on the basis of what is then fair having regard to the whole course of dealing between them. The court steps in to determine what is fair because, when the time came for that determination, the parties were unable to agree.

(2) That suggested by Waite LJ in *Midland Bank plc v Cooke* [1995] 4 All ER 562, 574D-G. The court undertakes a survey of the whole course of dealing between the parties 'relevant to their ownership and occupation of the property and their sharing of its burdens and advantages' in order to determine 'what proportions the parties must be assumed to have intended [from the outset] for their beneficial ownership'. On that basis the court treats what has taken place while the parties have been living together in the property as evidence of what they intended at the time of the acquisition.

(3) That suggested by Sir Nicolas Browne-Wilkinson V-C in *Grant v Edwards* [1986] Ch 638, 656G-H, 657H and approved by Robert Walker LJ in *Yaxley v Gotts* [2000] Ch 162, 177C-E. The court makes such order as the circumstances require in order to give effect to the beneficial interest in the property of the one party, the existence of which the other party (having the legal title) is estopped from denying. That, I think, is the analysis which underlies the decision of this court in *Drake v Whipp* [1996] 1 FLR 826, 831E-G.

71 For my part, I find the reasoning adopted by this court in *Midland Bank plc v Cooke* to be the least satisfactory of the three strands. It seems to me artificial—and an unnecessary fiction—to attribute to the parties a common intention that the extent of their respective beneficial interests in the property should be fixed as from the time of the acquisition, in circumstances in which all the evidence points to the conclusion that, at the time of the acquisition, they had given no thought to the matter. The same point can be made—although with less

---

[60] *Cox v Jones* [2004] 2 FLR 1010; [2005] Conv 168 (R. Probert) (25% share for partner who contributed nothing to cost of the purchase of house, and a very small amount on works done on it, but forewent income from her practice as barrister, and 'her real contribution was the large amounts of time and energy she put in' during the building works: at [79]).

force—in relation to the reasoning that, at the time of the acquisition, their common intention was that the amount of the respective shares should be left for later determination. But it can be said that, if it were their common intention that each should have some beneficial interest in the property—which is the hypothesis upon which it becomes necessary to answer the second question—then, in the absence of evidence that they gave any thought to the amount of their respective shares, the necessary inference is that they must have intended that question would be answered later on the basis of what was then seen to be fair. But, as I have said, I think that the time has come to accept that there is no difference in outcome, in cases of this nature, whether the true analysis lies in constructive trust or in proprietary estoppel.

D. LEGAL ESTATE HELD BY TWO PERSONS[61]

Stack v Dowden[62]
[2007] 2 AC 432 (**Lords Hoffmann, Hope of Craighead** and **Walker of Gestingthorpe, Baroness Hale of Richmond** and **Lord Neuberger of Abbotsbury**)

In 1983 Mr Stack and Ms Dowden began to live together in a house in Purves Road, London NW10, which Ms Dowden had purchased in her own name. In 1993 she then sold the Purves Road house, and Mr Stack and Ms Dowden purchased 114 Chatsworth Road, London NW2, as the family home, which was conveyed into their joint names. Two-thirds of the purchase price came from Ms Dowden's account and one-third from a mortgage in their joint names, to which they both contributed. The parties separated in 2002. The trial judge ordered that the property be sold and the net proceeds be divided equally between them. Ms Dowden appealed and the Court of Appeal ordered the net proceeds be divided 65 per cent to 35 per cent in her favour. Mr Stack appealed.

Held (Lord Neuberger dissenting on the reasoning). Appeal dismissed.

Lord Hope of Craighead:

2 My Lords, as my noble and learned friend, Baroness Hale of Richmond, whose speech I have had the privilege of reading in draft, indicates, this case is about the property rights of a

---

[61] See also, after the decision in *Stack v Dowden*: *Adekunle v Ritchie* ([2007] 2 P & CR DG20 Leeds County Court, August 17, 2007; discussed as *Ritchie v Ritchie* in [2007] Conv 456 (M. Dixon), p. 600, below; presumption of equal shares rebutted); *Laskar v Laskar* [2008] EWCA Civ 347, [2008] 1 WLR 2695 (presumption of equal shares rebutted: purchase of property primarily as investment, in spite of family relationship: per Neuberger LJ at [17]); [2008] Conv 441 (N. Piska); *Fowler v Barron* [2008] EWCA Civ 377, [2008] 2 FCR 1 (presumption of equal shares not rebutted); [2008] Conv 451 (N. Piska); *Q v Q* [2009] 1 P & CR DG 5 (presumption of equal shares rebutted). Where the legal estate is held by two persons but a *third* person claims to have a beneficial interest, he will have to establish both a trust in his favour and his share, in a similar manner to the cases involving a single legal owner (p. 576, above), since the presumption from the legal title is that he has no beneficial interest; *City of London Building Society v Flegg* [1988] AC 54, p. 551, above.

[62] [2007] CLJ 517 (A. Cloherty and D. Fox); (2007) 123 LQR 511 (W. Swadling); [2007] Conv 352 (M. Dixon), 354 (M. Pawlowski); [2007] All ER Rev 242 (P. J. Clarke); (2008) 71 MLR 120 (N. Piska); [2008] CLJ 265 (Sir Terence Etherton); (2008) 124 LQR 422 (S. Gardner); (2009) 125 LQR 310 (N. Hopkins).

cohabiting couple in a house which they occupied together as their home until the breakdown of their relationship. They have an obvious interest in the determination of their respective property rights in such a valuable asset. But the issue between them is a matter of general public interest too. It has become an increasingly pressing social problem, as house prices rise and more and more people are living together without getting married or entering into a civil partnership. The situation is complicated by the fact that there is no single, or paradigm, set of circumstances. The only feature which these cases have in common is that the problem has not been solved by legislation. The legislation which enables the court to reallocate beneficial interests in the home and other assets following a divorce does not apply to cohabiting couples. Otherwise the circumstances which define relationships between cohabiting couples and their property interests are infinitely various.

3 The key to simplifying the law in this area lies in the identification of the correct starting point. Each case will, of course, turn on its own facts. But law can, and should, provide the right framework. Traditionally, English law has always distinguished between legal ownership in land and its beneficial ownership. The trusts under which the land is held will determine the extent of each party's beneficial ownership. Where the parties have dealt with each other at arms length it makes sense to start from the position that there is a resulting trust according to how much each party contributed. Then there is the question whether the trust is truly a constructive trust. This may be helpful in their case but in others may seem to be a distinctly academic exercise, as my noble and learned friend, Lord Walker of Gestingthorpe, points out. But cohabiting couples are in a different kind of relationship. The place where they live together is their home. Living together is an exercise in give and take, mutual co-operation and compromise. Who pays for what in regard to the home has to be seen in the wider context of their overall relationship. A more practical, down-to-earth, fact-based approach is called for in their case. The framework which the law provides should be simple, and it should be accessible.

4 The cases can be broken down into those where there is a single legal ownership and those where there is joint legal ownership. There must be consistency of approach between these two cases, a point to which my noble and learned friend, Lord Neuberger of Abbotsbury, has drawn our attention. I think that consistency is to be found by deciding where the onus lies if a party wishes to show that the beneficial ownership is different from the legal ownership. I agree with Baroness Hale that this is achieved by taking sole beneficial ownership as the starting point in the first case and by taking joint beneficial ownership as the starting point in the other. In this context joint beneficial ownership means property is assumed to be held by the beneficial owners equally. So in a case of sole legal ownership the onus is on the party who wishes to show that he has any beneficial interest at all, and if so what that interest is. In a case of joint legal ownership it is on the party who wishes to show that the beneficial interests are divided other than equally.

5 The advantage of this approach is that everyone will know where they stand with regard to the property when they enter into their relationship. Parties are, of course, free to enter into whatever bargain they wish and, so long as it is clearly expressed and can be proved, the court will give effect to it. But for the rest the state of the legal title will determine the right starting point. The onus is then on the party who contends that the beneficial interests are divided between them otherwise than as the title shows to demonstrate this on the facts....

11 In a case such as this, where the parties had already been living together for about 18 years and had four children when 114 Chatsworth Road was purchased in joint names and

payments on the mortgage secured on that property were in effect contributed to by each of them equally, there would have been much to be said for adhering to the presumption of English law that the beneficial interests were divided between them equally. But I do not think that it is possible to ignore the fact that the contributions which they made to the purchase of that property were not equal. The relative extent of those contributions provides the best guide as to where their beneficial interests lay, in the absence of compelling evidence that by the end of their relationship they did indeed intend to share the beneficial interests equally. The evidence does not go that far. On the contrary, while they pooled their resources in the running of the household, in larger matters they maintained their financial independence from each other throughout their relationship.

12 The result might have been different if greater weight could have been given to the inclusion in the transfer of the standard-form receipt clause. But English property law does not permit this, for the reasons explained in *Mortgage Corpn v Shaire* [2001] Ch 743, 753. I think that indirect contributions, such as making improvements which added significant value to the property, or a complete pooling of resources in both time and money so that it did not matter who paid for what during their relationship, ought to be taken into account as well as financial contributions made directly towards the purchase of the property. I would endorse Chadwick LJ's view in *Oxley v Hiscock* [2005] Fam 211, para. 69 that regard should be had to the whole course of dealing between them in relation to the property. But the evidence in this case shows that there never was a stage when both parties intended that their beneficial interests in the property should be shared equally. Taking a broad view of the matter, therefore, I agree that the order that the Court of Appeal made provides the fairest result that can be achieved in the circumstances.

Baroness Hale of Richmond:

40 My Lords, the issue before us is the effect of a conveyance into the joint names of a cohabiting couple, but without an explicit declaration of their respective beneficial interests, of a dwelling house which was to become their home. This is, so far as I am aware, the first time that this issue has come before the House, whether the couple be married or, as in this case, unmarried. The principles of law are the same, whether or not the couple are married, although the inferences to be drawn from their conduct may be different: *Bernard v Josephs* [1982] Ch 391, 402, per Griffiths LJ.

How does this problem come about?

41 It may be that, in practice, this is a temporary and transitional problem. It has come about because of developments over the last few decades which would not have been foreseen when the applicable principles and presumptions were first devised. The first development is, of course, the huge expansion in home ownership which has taken place since the Second World War and was given a further boost by the 'right to buy' legislation of the 1980s. Coupled with this has been continuing house price inflation, albeit with occasional interruptions such as occurred at the end of the 1980s. This has meant that it is almost always more advantageous for someone who has contributed to the acquisition of the home to claim a share in its ownership rather than the return of the money contributed, even with interest.

42 Another development has been the recognition in the courts that, to put it at its lowest, the interpretation to be put on the behaviour of people living together in an intimate relationship may be different from the interpretation to be put upon similar behaviour between commercial

men.[63] To put it at its highest, an outcome which might seem just in a purely commercial transaction may appear highly unjust in a transaction between husband and wife or cohabitant and cohabitant. This recognition developed in a series of cases between separating spouses, beginning with *Re Rogers's Question* [1948] 1 All ER 328; *Newgrosh v Newgrosh* (1950) 100 LJ 525; *Jones v Maynard* [1951] Ch 572 and *Rimmer v Rimmer* [1953] 1 QB 63. There was a period during which it was thought that the problem might be solved by resort to the power contained in section 17 of the Married Women's Property Act 1882, in disputes between husband and wife as to the title to or possession of property, to make such order 'as it thinks fit'. The high-water mark of this approach was *Hine v Hine* [1962] 1 WLR 1124, 1127–1128, in which Lord Denning MR held that this discretion 'transcends all rights, legal or equitable'. That section 17 conferred any discretion to interfere with established titles was firmly rejected by this House in *Pettitt v Pettitt* [1970] AC 777. Nevertheless, the opinions in that case and in *Gissing v Gissing* [1971] AC 886 contain vivid illustrations of how difficult it is to apply simple assumptions to the complicated, interdependent and often-changing arrangements made between married couples. As Lord Reid famously put it in *Gissing v Gissing*, at p. 897A, 'It cannot surely depend on who signs which cheques'.

43 As between married couples, the problem has been addressed (if not solved) by the comprehensive redistributive powers in the Matrimonial Causes Act 1973, if the couple divorce, and in the Inheritance (Provision for Family and Dependants) Act 1975, if one of them dies...

44 Inter vivos disputes between unmarried cohabiting couples are still governed by the ordinary law. These disputes have become increasingly visible in recent years as more and more couples live together without marrying. The full picture has recently been painted by the Law Commission in Cohabitation: The Financial Consequences of Relationship Breakdown-A Consultation Paper, (2006) Consultation Paper No. 179, Part 2, and its overview paper, paras 2.3–2.11. For example, the 2001 Census recorded over 10m married couples in England and Wales, with over 7.5m dependent children; but it also recorded over 2m cohabiting couples, with over 1.25m children dependent upon them. This was a 67% increase in cohabitation over the previous ten years and a doubling of the numbers of such households with dependent children. The Government Actuaries Department predicts that the proportion of couples cohabiting will continue to grow, from the present one in six of all couples to one in four by 2031.

46 The history of attempts at law reform is another illustration of the complexity of the problem. Under item 1 of its Eighth Programme of Law Reform (2001) (Law Com No. 274), the Law Commission set out to review 'the law as it relates to the property rights of those who share a home' (the Commission had in fact been working on the problem for some time). This therefore covered 'a broad range of people, including friends and relatives who share a home as

---

[63] Constructive trusts are not restricted to the domestic context: *Banner Homes Group plc v Luff Developments Ltd* [2000] Ch 372, M & B, *Trusts and Trustees* (7th edn.) p. 348 (commercial joint venture parties; an application of the '*Pallant v Morgan* equity' [1953] Ch 43, where 'one of the joint venturers, with the agreement of the others who believe him to be acting for their joint purposes, makes the acquisition [of land] in his own name but subsequently seeks to retain the land for his own benefit, the court will regard him as holding the land on trust for the joint venturers': *Cobbe v Yeoman's Row Management Ltd* [2008] 1 WLR 1752 at [30], per Lord Scott of Foscote); *Lloyd v Pickering* [2004] EWHC 1513, (2004) 154 NLJ 1014 (acquisition of share in a gym business); *Cox v Jones* [2004] 2 FLR 1010 (purchase of an investment property by one of an engaged couple as nominee for the other); [2005] Conv 168. See Gray, para. 7.3.43: 'It is not entirely clear that the relatively recent (and slightly surprising) resurgence of the '*Pallant v Morgan* equity' departs markedly from the traditionally understood constructive trust doctrine of bargain-based detrimental reliance'.

well as unmarried couples and married couples (other than on the breakdown of the marriage)'. It commented that

> 'It is widely accepted that the present law is unduly complex, arbitrary and uncertain in its applica-
> tion. It is ill-suited to determining the property rights of those who, because of the informal nature
> of their relationship, may not have considered their respective entitlements.'

In 2002, however, the commission published Sharing Homes, A Discussion Paper (2002) (Law Com No. 278). Unlike most Law Commission publications, this did not contain even provisional, let alone final, proposals for reform. Its principal conclusion was that:

> 'It is quite simply not possible to devise a statutory scheme for the ascertainment and quantification
> of beneficial interests in the shared home which can operate fairly and evenly across the diversity of
> domestic circumstances which are now to be encountered.' (Para. 1.31.)

While this conclusion is not surprising, its importance for us is that the evolution of the law of property to take account of changing social and economic circumstances will have to come from the courts rather than Parliament.

48 It is fair to assume...that the questions with which the courts are confronted in these cases will continue to be with us for some time to come. Nor will the Commission's proposals provide a solution to the precise question which arises in this case—the effect of a conveyance into joint names without express declaration of the beneficial interests. However, there is some reason to hope that, just as this problem may have arisen because of changes in conveyancing practice over recent decades, it may eventually be resolved in the same way.

49 In the olden days, before registration of title on certain events, including a conveyance on sale, became compulsory all over England and Wales, conveyances of unregistered land into joint names would in practice declare the purchasers' beneficial as well as their legal interests. No one now doubts that such an express declaration of trust is conclusive unless varied by subsequent agreement or affected by proprietary estoppel: see *Goodman v Gallant* [1986] Fam 106. That case also establishes that severance of a beneficial joint tenancy results in a benefi-cial tenancy in common in equal shares. Lord Denning MR's attempt in *Hine v Hine* [1962] 1 WLR 1124, to use section 17 of the Married Women's Property Act 1882 to interfere even with express declarations of trust was firmly rejected by this House in *Pettitt v Pettitt* [1970] AC 777; his suggestion, in *Bedson v Bedson* [1965] 2 QB 666, that severance might not automat-ically lead to a tenancy in common in equal shares was rightly rejected in *Goodman v Gallant* [1986] Fam 106. The effect of such a conveyance is clear, irrespective of why the property was conveyed into joint names and of the parties' later dealings in relation to it.

50 The question with which we are concerned has become apparent with the spread of registration of title. The formalities required for the transfer of registered land were designed to meet the concerns of the Land Registry rather than the parties. The Land Registry is not concerned with the equities. It is concerned with whether the registered proprietor or proprietors can give a good title to a later transferee. This is entirely consistent with the simplification of conveyancing in the 1925 property legislation, which was designed to allow the legal owners of land to pass a good title to bona fide purchasers for value without notice of the equities existing behind the legal title. But it meant that the form of transfer prescribed by the Land Registry did not require, or even give an obvious opportunity to, the transferees to state their beneficial interests as well as their legal title. When this house was bought in 1993, all that the form required was all that the Land Registry needed to know. This was

whether the survivor of joint proprietors was able to give a valid receipt for the capital moneys received on sale: see Form 19(JP) prescribed under rules 98, 109 or 115 of the Land Registration Rules 1925 (SR & O 1925/1093). The version of this form in use from 1995 to 1998 did not even require this; indeed, it did not require execution by the transferee(s) at all but only by the transferor(s).

51 The argument that declaring that the survivor 'can give a valid receipt for capital money arising on a disposition of the land' in itself amounts to an express declaration of a beneficial joint tenancy was rightly rejected by the Court of Appeal in *Harwood v Harwood* [1991] 2 FLR 274 and again in *Huntingford v Hobbs* [1993] 1 FLR 736; see also *Mortgage Corpn v Shaire* [2001] Ch 743. However appealing the proposition might at first sight appear, choosing 'can' rather than 'cannot' on the form is consistent with other intentions. The transferees may hold on trust for a third person or they may intend that, while the survivor can give a good title to a third party without appointing a new trustee, the capital moneys received should be subject to different trusts. Whether the declaration (one way or the other) is some indication of what the parties did intend is another matter, to which I must return.

52 The Land Registry form has since changed. Form TR1,[64] in use from 1 April 1998, provides a box for the transferees to declare whether they are to hold the property on trust for themselves as joint tenants, or on trust for themselves as tenants in common in equal shares, or on some other trusts which are inserted on the form. If this is invariably complied with, the problem confronting us here will eventually disappear. Unfortunately, however, the transfer will be valid whether or not this part of the form is completed. The form itself states that the transferees are only required to execute it 'if the transfer contains transferee's covenants or declarations or contains an application by the transferee (e.g. for a restriction)'. So there may still be transfers of registered land into joint names in which there is no express declaration of the beneficial interests. However desirable such a declaration may be, it is unrealistic, in the consumer context, to expect that it will be executed independently of the forms required to acquire the legal estate. Not only do solicitors and licensed conveyancers compete on price, but more and more people are emboldened to do their own conveyancing. The Land Registry form which has been prescribed since 1998 is to be applauded. If its completion and execution by or on behalf of all joint proprietors were mandatory, the problem we now face would disappear. However, the form might then include an option for those who deliberately preferred not to commit themselves as to the beneficial interests at the outset and to rely on the principles discussed below.

The applicable legal principles

53 I say all this, partly to urge the Land Registry further to review its practice, but mainly to illuminate the factual context in which transfers such as the one with which we are concerned were executed. In what circumstances should it be expected that, independently of the information required by the Land Registry forms, joint transferees would execute a declaration of trust? Is it when they intend that the beneficial interests should be the same as the legal interests or when they intend that they should be different?

54 At first blush, the answer appears obvious. It should only be expected that joint transferees would have spelt out their beneficial interests when they intended them to be different from their legal interests. Otherwise, it should be assumed that equity follows the law and that the

---

[64] See pp. 167, 574, above.

beneficial interests reflect the legal interests in the property. I do not think that this proposition is controversial, even in old fashioned unregistered conveyancing. It has even more force in registered conveyancing in the consumer context.

55 Of course, it is something of an over-simplification. All joint legal owners must hold the land on trust (before the Trusts of Land and Appointment of Trustees Act 1996, there was a debate about whether or not this was always a trust for sale, but that is another matter).[65] Section 53(1)(b) of the Law of Property Act 1925 requires that a declaration of trust respecting any land or any interest therein be manifested and proved by signed writing; but section 53(2) provides that this 'does not affect the creation or operation of resulting, implied or constructive trusts'. The question is, therefore, what are the trusts to be deduced in the circumstances?

56 Just as the starting point where there is sole legal ownership is sole beneficial ownership, the starting point where there is joint legal ownership is joint beneficial ownership. The onus is upon the person seeking to show that the beneficial ownership is different from the legal ownership. So in sole ownership cases it is upon the non-owner to show that he has any interest at all. In joint ownership cases, it is upon the joint owner who claims to have other than a joint beneficial interest.

57 While there is no case in this House establishing this proposition in the consumer context, this is 'Situation A' referred to by Lord Brightman in *Malayan Credit Ltd v Jack Chia-MPH Ltd* [1986] AC 549, 559: 'The lessees at the inception of the lease hold the beneficial interest therein as joint tenants in equity. This will be the case if there are no circumstances which dictate to the contrary.' The issue in that case was whether there were only three quite narrowly defined situations in which the contrary could be found or whether there were other circumstances which could lead to a contrary conclusion. Their Lordships first observed that it was improbable that joint tenancy in equity was intended where joint tenants in law held commercial premises for their separate business purposes. This is a reminder that the parties may not intend survivorship even if they do intend that their shares shall be equal. In many commercial contexts, and no doubt some domestic ones, it will be highly unlikely that the parties intend survivorship with its tontine 'winner takes all' effect. Their Lordships went on to point out that there was no fundamental distinction between buying a lease at a premium with a token rent and taking a lease at a rack rent with no premium. In the latter case the rent is equivalent to the purchase money. This is a reminder that property is often acquired over time, so that payment of mortgage instalments is the equivalent of payment of the purchase price. Finally, their Lordships identified, at p. 561, the features of the case before them which appeared to them 'to point unmistakably towards a tenancy in common in equity, and furthermore towards a tenancy in common in unequal shares'. Amongst these were not only that the parties had paid the refundable deposit, stamp duty, survey fees, rent and service charges in unequal shares, but also that those shares were proportionate to the actual square footage which each of them occupied.

58 The issue as it has been framed before us is whether a conveyance into joint names indicates only that each party is intended to have some beneficial interest but says nothing about the nature and extent of that beneficial interest, or whether a conveyance into joint names establishes a prime facie case of joint and equal beneficial interests until the contrary is shown. For the reasons already stated, at least in the domestic consumer context, a conveyance into joint names indicates both legal and beneficial joint tenancy, unless and until the contrary is proved.

---

[65] See p. 573, above.

59 The question is, how, if at all, is the contrary to be proved? Is the starting point the presumption of resulting trust, under which shares are held in proportion to the parties' financial contributions to the acquisition of the property, unless the contributor or contributors can be shown to have had a contrary intention? Or is it that the contrary can be proved by looking at all the relevant circumstances in order to discern the parties' common intention?

60 ... The search is to ascertain the parties' shared intentions, actual, inferred or imputed, with respect to the property in the light of their whole course of conduct in relation to it.

61 *Oxley v Hiscock* [2005] Fam 211 was, of course, a different case from this. The property had been conveyed into the sole name of one of the cohabitants. The claimant had first to surmount the hurdle of showing that she had any beneficial interest at all, before showing exactly what that interest was. The first could readily be inferred from the fact that each party had made some kind of financial contribution towards the purchase. As to the second, Chadwick LJ said, at para. 69:

> 'in many such cases, the answer will be provided by evidence of what they said and did at the time of the acquisition. But, in a case where there is no evidence of any discussion between them as to the amount of the share which each was to have-and even in a case where the evidence is that there was no discussion on that point-the question still requires an answer. It must now be accepted that (at least in this court and below) the answer is that *each is entitled to that share which the court considers fair having regard to the whole course of dealing between them in relation to the property.* And in that context, 'the whole course of dealing between them in relation to the property' includes the arrangements which they make from time to time in order to meet the outgoings (for example, mortgage contributions, council tax and utilities, repairs, insurance and housekeeping) which have to be met if they are to live in the property as their home.' (Emphasis supplied.)

Oxley v Hiscock has been hailed by Gray & Gray, *Elements of Land Law,* 4th edn, p. 931, para. 10.138, as 'an important breakthrough'. The passage quoted is very similar to the view of the Law Commission in Sharing Homes, A Discussion Paper, para. 4.27 on the quantification of beneficial entitlement:

> 'If the question really is one of the parties' "common intention", we believe that there is much to be said for adopting what has been called a "holistic approach" to quantification, undertaking a survey of the whole course of dealing between the parties and taking account of all conduct which throws light on the question what shares were intended.'

That may be the preferable way of expressing what is essentially the same thought for two reasons. First, it emphasises that the search is still for the result which reflects what the parties must, in the light of their conduct, be taken to have intended. Second, therefore, it does not enable the court to abandon that search in favour of the result which the court itself considers fair. For the court to impose its own view of what is fair upon the situation in which the parties find themselves would be to return to the days before *Pettitt v Pettitt* [1970] AC 777 without even the fig leaf of section 17 of the 1882 Act.

62 Furthermore, although the parties' intentions may change over the course of time, producing what my noble and learned friend, Lord Hoffmann, referred to in the course of argument as an 'ambulatory' constructive trust, at any one time their interests must be the same for all purposes. They cannot at one and the same time intend, for example, a joint tenancy with survivorship should one of them die while they are still together, a tenancy in common in equal shares should they separate on amicable terms after the children have grown up, and a tenancy

in common in unequal shares should they separate on acrimonious terms while the children are still with them.

63   We are not in this case concerned with the first hurdle. There is undoubtedly an argument for saying, as did the Law Commission in Sharing Homes, A Discussion Paper, para. 4.23 that the observations, which were strictly obiter dicta, of Lord Bridge of Harwich in *Lloyds Bank plc v Rosset* [1991] 1 AC 107 have set that hurdle rather too high in certain respects. But that does not concern us now. It is common ground that a conveyance into joint names is sufficient, at least in the vast majority of cases, to surmount the first hurdle. The question is whether, that hurdle surmounted, the approach to quantification should be the same.

64   The majority of cases reported since *Pettitt v Pettitt* [1970] AC 777 and *Gissing v Gissing* [1971] AC 886 have concerned homes conveyed into the name of one party only and it is in that context that the more flexible approach to quantification identified by Chadwick LJ in *Oxley v Hiscock* [2005] Fam 211 has emerged: see, in particular, *Grant v Edwards* [1986] Ch 638, described by Chadwick LJ as 'an important turning point' and referred to with 'obvious approval' in *Lloyds Bank plc v Rosset* [1991] 1 AC 107; *Stokes v Anderson* [1991] 1 FLR 391; *Midland Bank plc v Cooke* [1995] 4 All ER 562 and *Drake v Whipp* [1996] 1 FLR 826.

65   Curiously, it is in the context of homes conveyed into joint names but without an express declaration of trust that the courts have sometimes reverted to the strict application of the principles of the resulting trust: see *Walker v Hall* [1984] FLR 126 and two cases decided by the same court on the same day, S*pringette v Defoe* [1992] 2 FLR 388 and *Huntingford v Hobbs* [1993] 1 FLR 736; but cf *Crossley v Crossley* [2006] 2 FLR 813. However, Chadwick LJ commented in *Oxley v Hiscock* [2005] Fam 211, 235:

> '47. It is, I think, important to an understanding of the reasoning in the judgments in *Springette v Defoe* that each member of this court seems to have thought that when Lord Bridge referred, in *Lloyds Bank plc v Rosset* [1991] 1 AC 107, 132F, to the need to base a "finding of an agreement or arrangement to share in this sense" on "evidence of express discussions between the partners" he was addressing the secondary, or consequential, question—"what was the common intention of the parties as to the extent of their respective beneficial interests"—rather than the primary, or threshold, question—"was there a common intention that each should have a beneficial interest in the property?"...
>
> 48. For the reasons which I have sought to explain, I think that the better view is that, in the passage in Rosset's case [1991] 1 AC 107, 132F., to which both Dillon LJ and Steyn LJ referred in *Springette v Defoe* [see [1992] 2 FLR 388, 393E -F and 395B, agreed with by Sir Christopher Slade at 397G] Lord Bridge was addressing only the primary question—"was there a common intention that each should have a beneficial interest in the property?" He was not addressing the secondary question—"what was the common intention of the parties as to the extent of their respective beneficial interests?" As this court had pointed out in *Grant v Edwards* and *Stokes v Anderson*, the court may well have to supply the answer to that secondary question by inference from their subsequent conduct...'

In the case before us, he observed, at para. 24:

> '... I have not altered my view that, properly understood, the authorities before (and after) *Springette v Defoe* do not support the proposition that, absent discussion between the parties as to the extent of their respective beneficial interests at the time of purchase, it must follow that the presumption of resulting trust is not displaced and the property is necessarily held in beneficial shares proportionate to the respective contributions to the purchase price.'

With these passages I entirely agree. The approach to quantification in cases where the home is conveyed into joint names should certainly be no stricter than the approach to quantification in cases where it has been conveyed into the name of one only. To the extent that *Walker v Hall* [1984] FLR 126; *Springette v Defoe* [1992] 2 FLR 388 and *Huntingford v Hobbs* [1993] 1 FLR 736 hold otherwise, they should not be followed.

66 However, Chadwick LJ went on to say at para. 26, that:

'there is no reason in principle why the approach to the second question—"what is the extent of the parties' respective beneficial interests in the property?"—should be different, in a case where the property is registered in the joint names of cohabitees, from what it would be if the property were registered in the sole name of one of them; although the fact that it has been registered in joint names is, plainly, to be taken into account when having regard "to the whole course of dealing between them in relation to the property".'

But the questions in a joint names case are not simply 'what is the extent of the parties' beneficial interests?' but 'did the parties intend their beneficial interests to be different from their legal interests?' and 'if they did, in what way and to what extent?' There are differences between sole and joint names cases when trying to divine the common intentions or understanding between the parties. I know of no case in which a sole legal owner (there being no declaration of trust) has been held to hold the property on a beneficial joint tenancy. But a court may well hold that joint legal owners (there being no declaration of trust) are also beneficial joint tenants. Another difference is that it will almost always have been a conscious decision to put the house into joint names. Even if the parties have not executed the transfer, they will usually, if not invariably, have executed the contract which precedes it. Committing oneself to spend large sums of money on a place to live is not normally done by accident or without giving it a moment's thought.

67 This is not to say that the parties invariably have a full understanding of the legal effects of their choice: there is recent empirical evidence from a small scale qualitative study to confirm that they do not: see Gillian Douglas, Julia Pearce and Hilary Woodward, 'Dealing with Property Issues on Cohabitation Breakdown' [2007] Fam Law 36. But that is so whether or not there is an express declaration of trust and no one thinks that such a declaration can be overturned, except in cases of fraud or mistake: see para. 49 above. Nor do they always have a completely free choice in the matter. Mortgagees used to insist upon the home being put in the name of the person whom they assumed would be the main breadwinner. Nowadays, they tend to think that it is in their best interests that the home be jointly owned and both parties assume joint and several liability for the mortgage. (It is, of course, a matter of indifference to the mortgagees where the beneficial interests lie.) Here again, this factor does not invalidate the parties' choice if there is an express declaration of trust, nor should it automatically count against it where there is none.

68 The burden will therefore be on the person seeking to show that the parties did intend their beneficial interests to be different from their legal interests, and in what way. This is not a task to be lightly embarked upon. In family disputes, strong feelings are aroused when couples split up. These often lead the parties, honestly but mistakenly, to reinterpret the past in self-exculpatory or vengeful terms. They also lead people to spend far more on the legal battle than is warranted by the sums actually at stake. A full examination of the facts is likely to involve disproportionate costs. In joint names cases it is also unlikely to lead to a different result unless the facts are very unusual. Nor may disputes be confined to the parties themselves. People with an interest in the deceased's estate may well wish to assert that he had a beneficial tenancy in

common. It cannot be the case that all the hundreds of thousands, if not millions, of transfers into joint names using the old forms are vulnerable to challenge in the courts simply because it is likely that the owners contributed unequally to their purchase.

69 In law, 'context is everything' and the domestic context is very different from the commercial world. Each case will turn on its own facts. Many more factors than financial contributions may be relevant to divining the parties' true intentions. These include: any advice or discussions at the time of the transfer which cast light upon their intentions then; the reasons why the home was acquired in their joint names; the reasons why (if it be the case) the survivor was authorised to give a receipt for the capital moneys; the purpose for which the home was acquired; the nature of the parties' relationship; whether they had children for whom they both had responsibility to provide a home; how the purchase was financed, both initially and subsequently; how the parties arranged their finances, whether separately or together or a bit of both; how they discharged the outgoings on the property and their other household expenses. When a couple are joint owners of the home and jointly liable for the mortgage, the inferences to be drawn from who pays for what may be very different from the inferences to be drawn when only one is owner of the home. The arithmetical calculation of how much was paid by each is also likely to be less important. It will be easier to draw the inference that they intended that each should contribute as much to the household as they reasonably could and that they would share the eventual benefit or burden equally. The parties' individual characters and personalities may also be a factor in deciding where their true intentions lay. In the cohabitation context, mercenary considerations may be more to the fore than they would be in marriage, but it should not be assumed that they always take pride of place over natural love and affection. At the end of the day, having taken all this into account, cases in which the joint legal owners are to be taken to have intended that their beneficial interests should be different from their legal interests will be very unusual.

70 This is not, of course, an exhaustive list. There may also be reason to conclude that, whatever the parties' intentions at the outset, these have now changed. An example might be where one party has financed (or constructed himself) an extension or substantial improvement to the property, so that what they have now is significantly different from what they had then.

Applying the law to the facts

86 The starting point is that it is for Ms Dowden to show that the common intention, when taking a conveyance of the house into their joint names or thereafter, was that they should hold the property otherwise than as beneficial joint tenants. Unfortunately, we lack precise findings on many of the factors relevant to answering that question, because the judge addressed himself to 'looking at the parties' entire course of conduct together'. He looked at their relationship rather than the matters which were particularly relevant to their intentions about this property . . . .

87 In some, perhaps many, cases of real domestic partnership, there would be nothing to indicate that a contrary inference should be drawn. However, there are many factors to which Ms Dowden can point to indicate that these parties did have a different common intention. The first, of course, is that on any view she contributed far more to the acquisition of Chatsworth Road than did Mr Stack. There are many different ways of calculating this. The Court of Appeal rejected the judge's view that the Halifax account represented 'joint savings', either at the time of the Purves Road purchase or at the time of the Chatsworth Road purchase. Hence they held that the whole of the purchase price, other than the mortgage loan, had been contributed by

Ms Dowden. She had also contributed more to the capital repayment of that loan, although Mr Stack had made all the payments necessary to keep it going. It is not surprising that the Court of Appeal reached the conclusion that Ms Dowden was entitled to at least the 65% she claimed.

88 On the other hand, there was some evidence that Mr Stack had made payments into the Halifax account before the Purves Road purchase and that he had made payments thereafter which would have enabled Ms Dowden to save more of her income than would otherwise have been possible. This, together with his contributions towards the substantial improvements made to Purves Road, might suffice to give him some interest in the proceeds of sale, although quantifying that share would be very difficult. It might also suffice to give him some lesser interest in the accumulated Halifax account at the time when Chatsworth Road was bought. Again, quantifying that interest would be very difficult. There was certainly little if anything to support the conclusion that these were truly 'joint' savings. But suppose that one apportions the Purves Road proceeds between them in shares of 2 to Ms Dowden and 1 to Mr Stack; the Halifax savings in shares of 3 to her and 1 to him; and shares the mortgage loan equally between them: this would yield total contributions to Chatsworth Road of roughly 64% to 36%. That calculation is, in my view, as generous to Mr Stack as it is possible to be.

89 The fact that it is possible to make two such different calculations on this sort of evidence indicates the pitfalls in an arithmetical approach to ascertaining the parties' intentions. The one thing that can clearly be said is that, when Chatsworth Road was bought, both parties knew that Ms Dowden had contributed far more to the cash paid towards it than had Mr Stack. Furthermore, although they planned that Mr Stack would pay the interest on the loan and premiums on the joint policy, they also planned to reduce the loan as quickly as they could. These are certainly factors which could, in context, support the inference of an intention to share otherwise than equally.

90 The context is supplied by the nature of the parties' conduct and attitudes towards their property and finances. This is not a case in which it can be said that the parties pooled their separate resources, even notionally, for the common good. The only things they ever had in their joint names were Chatsworth Road and the associated endowment policy. Everything else was kept strictly separate. Each made separate savings and investments most of which it was accepted were their own property. It might have been asked, 'why then did they make an exception for Chatsworth Road?' This is the obvious question. The obvious answer, which Ms Dowden has never denied, was that this time it was indeed intended that Mr Stack should have some interest in the property. In the light of all the other evidence, it cannot be conclusive as to what that interest was.

91 There are other aspects to their financial relationship which tell against joint ownership. Chatsworth Road was, of course, to be a home for the parties and their four children. But they undertook separate responsibility for that part of the expenditure which each had agreed to pay. The only regular expenditure to which it is clear that Mr Stack committed himself was the interest and premiums on Chatsworth Road. All other regular commitments in both houses were undertaken by Ms Dowden. Had it been clear that he had undertaken to pay for consumables and child minding, it might have been possible to deduce some sort of commitment that each would do what they could. But Mr Stack's evidence did not even go as far as that.

92 This is, therefore, a very unusual case. There cannot be many unmarried couples who have lived together for as long as this, who have had four children together, and whose affairs have been kept as rigidly separate as this couple's affairs were kept. This is all strongly indicative that

they did not intend their shares, even in the property which was put into both their names, to be equal (still less that they intended a beneficial joint tenancy with the right of survivorship should one of them die before it was severed). Before the Court of Appeal, Ms Dowden contended for a 65% share and in my view she has made good her case for that.

Lord Neuberger of Abbotsbury (dissenting on the reasoning, but concurring in the result):

Beneficial ownership: some general points

98 Where freehold or leasehold property is acquired in the name of two parties, the effect of sections 1, 34, and 36 of the Law of Property Act 1925 is that they must be joint owners of the legal estate: they enjoy equal rights in respect of an undivided title, and survivorship applies. The rules relating to the ownership of the beneficial interest are much less constrained. In general, the parties are free to agree what they want (and if they are joint owners, it is open to either to sever it). If there is a valid declaration of trust, then (subject to any statutory provisions to the contrary) that determines the beneficial ownership. If not, then, in the absence of agreement, the court has to decide the issue.

103 In the present type of case, while the number of unmarried cohabitants has increased very substantially over the past 50 (and even more over the past 20) years, the change has been one of degree, and does not, in my view, justify a departure from established legal principles. I agree with Griffiths LJ (see *Bernard v Josephs* [1982] Ch 391, 402) that the applicable principles are the same whether the parties are married or not, although the nature of the relationship will bear on the inferences to be drawn from their discussions and actions.

104 The Law Commission has considered this topic in the excellent Discussion and Consultation Papers described by Baroness Hale in paras 44 to 47 of her opinion. The fact that the Law Commission has characterised the present state of the law as 'unduly complex, arbitrary and uncertain', does not, in my opinion, justify our changing it. The Discussion Paper refers to the impossibility of devising a scheme 'which can operate fairly and evenly across the diversity of domestic circumstances which are now to be encountered'. This is a warning shot against the courts (as opposed to the legislature) refashioning the law. All the more so bearing in mind that, as Lord Walker says, the Law Commission may soon make specific proposals for change in this area.[66]

105 In other words, the Law Commission's analysis may well justify the legislature changing the law in this field, but it does not support similar intervention by the courts, other than for the purpose of clarification and simplification....

106 In my judgment, it is therefore inappropriate for the law when applied to cases of this sort to depart from the well-established principles laid down over the years. It also seems to me that the law of resulting and constructive trusts is flexible enough to deal with problems such as those thrown up by cases such as this, and it would be a disservice to the important causes of certainty and consistency if we were to hold otherwise. I note that the Court of Appeal's recent decisions in this case and in *Oxley v Hiscock* [2005] Fam 211 (both of which were rightly decided) produced an outcome which would be dictated by a resulting trust solution.

107 Accordingly, while the domestic context can give rise to very different factual considerations from the commercial context, I am unconvinced that this justifies a different approach in principle to the issue of the ownership of the beneficial interest in property held in joint names.

---

[66] The Law Commission published its report *Cohabitation: the Financial Consequences of Relationship Breakdown* (Law Com No. 307) in July 2007, three months after the decision in *Stack v Dowden*. See p. 606, below. The Report discusses *Stack v Dowden* at paras 2.6–2.16 and Appendix A.

In the absence of statutory provisions to the contrary, the same principles should apply to assess the apportionment of the beneficial interest as between legal co-owners, whether in a sexual, platonic, familial, amicable or commercial relationship. In each type of case, one is concerned with the issue of the ownership of the beneficial interest in property held in the names of two people, who have contributed to its acquisition, retention or value.

108 It appears to me helpful for present purposes to consider the issue in a structured way. First, to consider how the beneficial interest is owned at the date of acquisition, which involves identifying the nature and effect of the relevant features of what transpired between the parties up to, and at, the date of acquisition of the property. Then to consider the position at the date of the hearing, which involves identifying the relevant features of what subsequently transpired between the parties, and deciding whether they justify a change in the way in which the beneficial ownership is held. As already explained, I believe that the proper approach to these highly fact-sensitive inquiries should be in accordance with established legal principles and, as far as is consistent with those principles, as simple as possible.

Beneficial ownership on acquisition: where there is no evidence

109 In the absence of any relevant evidence other than the fact that the property, whether a house or a flat, acquired as a home for the legal co-owners is in joint names, the beneficial ownership will also be joint, so that it is held in equal shares. This can be said to result from the maxims that equity follows the law and equality is equity. On a less technical, and some might say more practical, approach, it can also be justified on the basis that any other solution would be arbitrary or capricious.

Beneficial ownership on acquisition: differential contributions

110 Where the only additional relevant evidence to the fact that the property has been acquired in joint names is the extent of each party's contribution to the purchase price, the beneficial ownership at the time of acquisition will be held, in my view, in the same proportions as the contributions to the purchase price. That is the resulting trust solution. The only realistic alternative in such a case would be to adhere to the joint ownership solution. There is an argument to support the view that equal shares should still be the rule in cohabitation cases, on the basis that it may be what many parties may expect if they purchase a home in joint names, even with different contributions. However, I consider that the resulting trust solution is correct in such circumstances.

113 There are also practical reasons for rejecting equality and supporting the resulting trust solution. The property may be bought in joint names for reasons which cast no light on the parties' intentions with regard to beneficial ownership. It may be the solicitor's decision or assumption, the lender's preference for the security of two borrowers, or the happenstance of how the initial contact with the solicitor was made....

114 There is also an important point about consistency of approach with a case where the purchase of a home is in the name of one of the parties. As Baroness Hale observes, where there is no evidence of contributions, joint legal ownership is reflected in a presumption of joint beneficial ownership just as sole legal ownership is reflected in a presumption of sole beneficial ownership. Where there is evidence of the parties' respective contributions to the purchase price (and no other relevant evidence) and one of the parties has contributed X%, the fact that the purchase is in the sole name of the other does not prevent the former owning X% of the beneficial interest on a resulting trust basis. Indeed, it is because of the resulting trust presumption that such ownership arises. It seems to me that consistency suggests that

the party who contributed X% of the purchase price should be entitled to X% (no more and no less) of the beneficial interest in the same way if he is a co-purchaser. The resulting trust presumption arises because it is assumed that neither party intended a gift of any part of his own contribution to the other party. That would seem to me to apply to contributions irrespective of the name or names in which the property concerned is acquired and held, as a matter of both principle and logic.

115 It may be asked why the bigger contributor agreed to the property being taken in joint names, unless he intended joint beneficial ownership. There are four answers to that. The first is that the question sets out to justify what it assumes, namely that, in the absence of any discussion, the parties must have assumed an equal split. Secondly, if the other party was a contributor, he would often want to be a co-owner, and the only way real property can be held in law by two persons is as joint owners. Thirdly, the converse point can be made where a property is acquired in the name of one party: if the other party has contributed to the purchase, his absence from the title is not evidence that he was not intended to have an interest. (In this connection, it seems to me that, where a home is taken in the name of only one party, this is almost as likely to have been a conscious decision as where it is acquired in joint names: where both have contributed to the purchase, it is unlikely that either will have been unaware of the fact that the home was being acquired in the name of only one of them). Fourthly, there are the practical considerations to which I have already alluded.

116 Having said that, the fact that a property is taken in joint names is some evidence that both parties were intended to have some beneficial interest. In that connection, the facts of the present case are not without interest. The parties' previous home in Purves Road was acquired in Ms Dowden's name alone. On the face of it at least, Purves Road was acquired solely with money from Ms Dowden's account or borrowed by her alone (although a small amount may have come indirectly from Mr Stack), so it is not surprising that it was acquired in her sole name. When the house at Chatsworth Road was acquired, Mr Stack directly (and through liability for the mortgage) contributed to its purchase, and it is therefore unsurprising that his name was included on the title. However, for reasons already discussed, as he contributed far less to the purchase than Ms Dowden, it seems wrong to deduce from those bare facts that the parties intended that he should have 50% of the beneficial interest.

122 ...Application of the resulting trust approach in the present case would justify Mr Stack's appeal being dismissed. On the figures summarised by Baroness Hale, Mr Stack could not possibly establish more than a 36% interest in the house as a result of all his contributions. Indeed, on the basis of the evidence, I would put his contribution at around 30%, but, as Ms Dowden is prepared to concede 35%, it is unnecessary to consider that aspect further. Thus, on a resulting trust basis, Mr Stack had no more than a 35% share of the beneficial interest at the date of acquisition.

Beneficial ownership on acquisition: constructive trust

123 Accordingly, in my judgment, where there are unequal contributions, the resulting trust solution is the one to be adopted. However, it is no more than a presumption, albeit an important one....

124 In many cases, there will, in addition to the contributions, be other relevant evidence as at the time of acquisition. Such evidence would often enable the court to deduce an agreement or understanding amounting to an intention as to the basis on which the beneficial interests would be held. Such an intention may be express (although not complying with the requisite

formalities) or inferred, and must normally be supported by some detriment, to justify intervention by equity. It would be in this way that the resulting trust would become rebutted and replaced, or (conceivably) supplemented, by a constructive trust.

125 While an intention may be inferred as well as express, it may not, at least in my opinion, be imputed. That appears to me to be consistent both with normal principles and with the majority view of this House in *Pettitt v Pettitt* [1970] AC 777, as accepted by all but Lord Reid in *Gissing v Gissing* [1971] AC 886, 897H, 898B-D, 900E-G, 901B-D, 904E-F, and reiterated by the Court of Appeal in *Grant v Edwards* [1986] Ch 638, 651F-653A. The distinction between inference and imputation may appear a fine one (and in *Gissing v Gissing* [1971] AC 886, 902G-H, Lord Pearson, who, on a fair reading I think rejected imputation, seems to have equated it with inference), but it is important.

126 An inferred intention is one which is objectively deduced to be the subjective actual intention of the parties, in the light of their actions and statements. An imputed intention is one which is attributed to the parties, even though no such actual intention can be deduced from their actions and statements, and even though they had no such intention. Imputation involves concluding what the parties would have intended, whereas inference involves concluding what they did intend.

127 To impute an intention would not only be wrong in principle and a departure from two decisions of your Lordships' House in this very area, but it also would involve a judge in an exercise which was difficult, subjective and uncertain. (Hence the advantage of the resulting trust presumption). It would be difficult because the judge would be constructing an intention where none existed at the time, and where the parties may well not have been able to agree. It would be subjective for obvious reasons. It would be uncertain because it is unclear whether one considers a hypothetical negotiation between the actual parties, or what reasonable parties would have agreed. The former is more logical, but would redound to the advantage of an unreasonable party. The latter is more attractive, but is inconsistent with the principle, identified by Baroness Hale at para. 61, that the court's view of fairness is not the correct yardstick for determining the parties' shares (and see *Pettitt v Pettitt* [1970] AC 777, 801C-F, 809C-G, 826C).

131 Any assessment of the parties' intentions with regard to the ownership of the beneficial interest by reference to what they said and did must take into account all the circumstances of their relationship, in the same way as the interpretation of a contract must be effected by reference to all the surrounding circumstances. However, that does not mean that all the circumstances of the relationship are of primary or equal relevance to the issue.

132 I am unimpressed, for instance, by the argument that, merely because they have already lived together for a long time sharing all regular outgoings, including those in respect of the previous property they occupied, the parties must intend that the beneficial interest in the home they are acquiring, with differently sized contributions, should be held in equal shares. Particularly where the parties have chosen not to marry, their close and loving relationship does not by any means necessarily imply an intention to share all their assets equally. There is a large difference between sharing outgoings and making a gift of a valuable share in property; outgoings are relatively small regular sums arising out of day-to-day living, but an interest in the home is a capital asset, with a substantial value. I am similarly unconvinced that the ownership of the beneficial interest in a home acquired in joint names is much affected by whether the parties have children at the time of acquisition. While it justifies the obvious inference that it is to be used for the children as well as the parties, it says nothing on its own as to the intended ownership of the beneficial interest.

133 The fact that the parties operated their day-to-day financial affairs through a joint bank account, into which both their wages were paid and from which all family outgoings were paid, could fairly be said to be strong evidence that they intended the sums in that account to be owned equally. Accordingly, it would normally be easy to justify the contention that a home acquired with money from that account (often together with a mortgage in joint names) should be treated as acquired with jointly owned money and therefore as beneficially owned jointly. However, I am unhappy with the suggestion that, because parties share or pool their regular income and outgoings, it can be assumed that they intended that the beneficial interest in their home, acquired in joint names but with significantly different contributions, should be shared equally. There is a substantial difference, in law, in commercial terms, in practice, and almost always in terms of value and importance, between the ownership of a home and the ownership of a bank account or, indeed, furniture, furnishings and other chattels.

134 The fact that the parties keep assets such as bank accounts and financial investments separate and in separate names could be said to indicate that the parties do not intend to pool their resources. But it could equally be said that the fact that they choose, exceptionally, to acquire the home in joint names indicates that it is to be treated differently from their other assets, namely that it is to be jointly owned beneficially. In my view, however, such evidence is again of little value on its own, as it relates to a very different category of assets, in terms of nature and value, from the home they are buying.

135 The factors I have been discussing in the previous three paragraphs will often, however, have some significance. If there is other, possibly contested, evidence which is said to support the contention that the parties intended a different result from that indicated by a resulting trust analysis, those factors may make it easier for the court to accept, or even to interpret, that evidence as justifying such a different result.

136 For instance, the fact that the parties are in a close and loving relationship would render it easier, than in a normal contractual context, to displace the resulting trust solution with, say, an equal division of the beneficial ownership. That is because a departure from the resulting trust solution normally involves a gratuitous transfer of value from one party to the other. Thus, in the present case, if the outcome for which Mr Stack contends applied at the date of acquisition of the property, it would have involved an effectively gratuitous transfer of value equal to at least 15% of the purchase price of the house to him from Ms Dowden. Such a transfer is less unlikely between two parties in a long-term loving relationship than between two commercial entities or even two friends, but that does not mean that the nature of the relationship of itself justifies the inference of such a transfer.

137 In the present case, I consider that there was simply no evidence to justify departing in Mr Stack's favour from the apportionment of the beneficial interest in the house at the date of acquisition indicated by the resulting trust presumption. None of the facts recited in the opinion of Baroness Hale justify such a departure. It is fair to record that Mr Stack did appear to suggest at one point in his evidence that there was some discussion as to the ownership of the house at the time it was acquired, but the judge expressly made no finding in his favour about that, and the Court of Appeal was not invited to do so or to remit it for the judge to make such a finding.

Beneficial ownership: events after the acquisition of the house

138 The fact that the ownership of the beneficial interest in a home is determined at the date of acquisition does not mean that it cannot alter thereafter. My noble and learned friend Lord Hoffmann suggested during argument that the trust which arises at the date of acquisition,

whether resulting or constructive, is of an ambulatory nature. That elegant characterisation does not justify a departure from the application of established legal principles any more than such a departure is justified at the time of acquisition. It seems to me that 'compelling evidence', to use Lord Hope's expression in para. 11, is required before one can infer that, subsequent to the acquisition of the home, the parties intended a change in the shares in which the beneficial ownership is held. Such evidence would normally involve discussions, statements or actions, subsequent to the acquisition, from which an agreement or common understanding as to such a change can properly be inferred....

144 I am unhappy with the formulation of Chadwick LJ in *Oxley v Hiscock* [2005] Fam 211, para. 69, quoted by Baroness Hale at para. 61 of her opinion, namely that the beneficial ownership should be apportioned by reference to what is 'fair having regard to the whole course of dealing between [the parties] in relation to the property'. First, fairness is not the appropriate yardstick. Secondly, the formulation appears to contemplate an imputed intention. Thirdly, 'the whole course of dealing...in relation to the property' is too imprecise, as it gives insufficient guidance as to what is primarily relevant, namely dealings which cast light on the beneficial ownership of the property, and too limited, as all aspects of the relationship could be relevant in providing the context, by reference to which any alleged discussion, statement and actions must be assessed. As already explained, I also disagree with Chadwick LJ's implicit suggestion in the same paragraph that 'the arrangements which [the parties] make with regard to the outgoings' (other than mortgage repayments) are likely to be of primary relevance to the issue of the ownership of the beneficial interest in the home.

145 I am rather more comfortable with the formulation of the Law Commission in Sharing Homes, A Discussion Paper (Law Com No. 278), para. 4.27, also quoted in para. 61 of Baroness Hale's opinion, that the court should 'undertak[e] a survey of the whole course of dealing between the parties...taking account of all conduct which throws light on the question what shares were intended'. It is perhaps inevitable that this formulation begs the difficult questions of what conduct throws light, and what light it throws, as those questions are so fact-sensitive. 'Undertaking a survey of the whole course of dealings between the parties' should not, I think, at least normally, require much detailed or controversial evidence. That is not merely for reasons of practicality and certainty. As already indicated, I would expect almost all of 'the whole course of dealing' to be relevant only as background: it is with actions, discussions and statements which relate to the parties' agreement and understanding as to the ownership of the beneficial interest in the home with which the court should, at least normally, primarily be concerned. Otherwise, the inquiry is likely to be trespassing into what I regard as the forbidden territories of imputed intention and fairness.

146 In other words, where the resulting trust presumption (or indeed any other basis of apportionment) applies at the date of acquisition, I am unpersuaded that (save perhaps in a most unusual case) anything other than subsequent discussions, statements or actions, which can fairly be said to imply a positive intention to depart from that apportionment, will do to justify a change in the way in which the beneficial interest is owned. To say that factors such as a long relationship, children, a joint bank account, and sharing daily outgoings of themselves are enough, or even of potential central importance, appears to me not merely wrong in principle, but a recipe for uncertainty, subjectivity, and a long and expensive examination of facts. It could also be said to be arbitrary, as, if such factors of themselves justify a departure from the original apportionment, I find it hard to see how it could be to anything other than equality. If a departure from the original apportionment was solely based on such factors, it seems to me

that the judge would almost always have to reach an 'all or nothing' decision. Thus, in this case, he would have to ask whether, viewed in the round, the personal and financial characteristics of the relationship between Mr Stack and Ms Dowden, after they acquired the house, justified a change in ownership of the beneficial interest from 35–65 to 50–50, even though nothing they did or said related to the ownership of that interest (save, perhaps, the repayments of the mortgage). In my view, that involves approaching the question in the wrong way. Subject, perhaps, to exceptional cases, whose possibility it would be unrealistic not to acknowledge, an argument for an alteration in the way in which the beneficial interest is held cannot, in my opinion, succeed, unless it can be shown that there was a discussion, statement or action which, viewed in its context, namely the parties' relationship, implied an actual agreement or understanding to effect such an alteration.

[2007] Conv 456 (M. Dixon)

On July 31, 2007, the Law Commission published its long anticipated Report entitled *Cohabitation: The Financial Consequences of Relationship Breakdown.*[67] In a nutshell, this proposes the introduction of a structured judicial discretion to order property adjustment[68] on relationship breakdown for those couples in an intimate (but lawful) relationship, not being married or in civil partnership, provided that certain eligibility criteria are met.[69] The proposed jurisdiction does not give the courts the same wide, sweeping powers as they enjoy in respect of married couples[70] to fundamentally re-assign the parties' wealth; and who can tell what will emerge from the legislative mill (assuming the proposals actually make it that far[71]), but there is little that can be worse than the current litigation-generator that is the law of implied trusts.

The Law Commission's proposed scheme will not catch all situations where there is a dispute about the beneficial ownership of a shared home. Even if the eligibility requirements are set at the modest level proposed by the Law Commission,[72] some unmarried couples will fall outside the scheme, as will disputes concerning the home and a third party (for example, the cases typified by *Lloyds Bank v Rosset*[73]) and those situations where the cohabitants are not in an intimate relationship (e.g. *Abbey National v Stringer,*[74] being mother and son). These types of dispute are not uncommon, especially as more homes are occupied by extended families, and the principles to be applied are those found in *Stack,* as indeed is the case for all claimants until the Law Commission's scheme reaches the statute book. It is no surprise, therefore, that

---

[67] Law Com. Report No. 307 [below, p. 606].

[68] That is, adjustment of the parties' rights of ownership as they appear to be under normal legal principles.

[69] See in general, Report No. 307, Pt 3.

[70] For the sake of brevity, and with apologies for the misnomer, references to marriage, etc. includes civil partnership.

[71] [On 6 March the Government announced that it was postponing its decision on the Law Commission's "very thorough and high quality" report because it was concerned to establish estimates of the financial costs and financial benefits of bringing into effect the Law Commission's recommended scheme. The Government hoped to do so by examining the operation of the Family Law (Scotland) Act 2006: Law Commission, Forty-Second Annual Report, 2007–08, Law Com No. 310, para. 3.68).]

[72] Generally, co-habitants with children, or those without subject to a minimum duration of cohabitation (possibly between 2–5 years).

[73] [1991] 1 AC 107.   [74] [2006] EWCA Civ 338; [2006] Conv 577.

there has already been case law applying *Stack* and, perhaps equally unsurprising, that the judges in these cases found enough in the House of Lords judgments to get them where they wanted to go.

Abbott v Abbott is an appeal to the Judicial Committee of the Privy Council from the Court of Appeal of Antigua and Barbuda[75] and it so happened that the panel of judges giving advice to Her Majesty included three judges that gave leading opinions in *Stack*.[76] The parties were married, but Antigua and Barbuda has no property adjustment legislation for divorcing couples and so ownership of the family home—which was in the sole name of the husband—fell to be decided according to the law of implied trusts. The trial judge had decided on a 50:50 split of the equity, but the Court of Appeal rejected this on the basis that the wife could only claim if she could bring herself within the strict 'acquisition criteria' laid down by Lord Bridge in *Rosset*—namely by reason of an express oral agreement supported by detrimental reliance or direct payments towards the purchase price.[77] Applying this test, the Court of Appeal decided that she was entitled to a much smaller share of the equity based on her actual, financial contribution to the mortgage.[78] The Judicial Committee appeared to have had little trouble in reinstating the award of the trial judge, but not merely because they took a different view of the facts. Rather, Baroness Hale, in delivering the Advice of the Judicial Committee, was at pains to point out that Lord Bridge's analysis in *Rosset* was outdated and ought not to be followed strictly. Times had moved on and, after *Stack*, not only was it 'now clear that the constructive trust is generally the more appropriate tool of analysis in most matrimonial cases',[79] the proper approach was to take an holistic view. Thus, a person could acquire an equitable interest in another's land, at least in a domestic context,[80] under a general enquiry into their common intention, and such intention could be actual, imputed from conduct, or inferred,[81] provided that there was a direct or indirect contribution, in cash or in kind, to the acquisition of the land. It was no longer necessary to find either an express agreement or payments towards the purchase price in order to found a claim. Putting aside the pedantic point that, actually, *Stack* did not decide this (being a case wholly about quantification, not acquisition), it seems that our most senior judges are determined to introduce more flexibility into the law concerning the acquisition of equitable interests and that they have no hesitation in side-stepping Lord Bridge in *Rosset*. Thus, from now on we must look at the claimant's and defendant's conduct in the round, in order to assess each party's contribution to the acquisition of the land.[82] Many will welcome this, remembering

[75] Delivered July 27, 2007. Privy Council Appeal No.142 of 2005.

[76] Baroness Hale (who gave the Advice) and Lords Neuberger and Walker. They were joined by Lords Bingham and Carswell. Conventionally, there are no separate or dissenting opinions in Privy Council cases and it is intriguing that Lord Neuberger is obliged to remain silent in the face of Baroness Hale's repetition of her analysis in *Stack*.

[77] This is the famous dictum where Lord Bridge doubts 'whether anything less will do', a dictum rejected by Lord Walker in *Stack*, at [26], because (apparently) it failed to take account of divergent views in *Gissing v Gissing* [1971] AC 886.

[78] They rejected evidence of an express oral agreement.

[79] Advice, para. 4.

[80] Neither the opinions in *Stack* nor this Advice explains why rules for domestic property should be different from commercial land, a point made forcefully by Lord Neuberger in *Stack*.

[81] Note the use of imputed common intention, that which Lord Neuberger resisted in *Stack*, as did Lord Bridge in *Rosset*, but which Lord Walker in *Stack* now regarded as entirely appropriate.

[82] Probably, these are the factors listed in [69] of Baroness Hale's opinion in *Stack*—even though they were directed to the question of quantification.

Ms Burns,[83] but others might wonder how they are to advise their clients of the likelihood of a successful claim, be they lenders, legal owners, or claimants. Likewise, it is unclear how a trial judge is to separate a course of dealings between the parties which goes to the acquisition of the land (allowable), from a course of conduct which goes to the success of the relationship or simply reflects the normal obligations of everyday life (disallowable). It was just this difficulty that Lord Bridge sought to avoid in *Rosset* by precise, if narrow, criteria. Of course, we all agree that it would be better if the parties had executed a written declaration of equitable ownership at the time of purchase, but that does not mean that the courts should step in and supply the agreement that the parties would have made, or the intention they would have had, had they thought about it at the time. However, it seems that such criticism now carries no weight and *Abbott* confirms what was signposted in *Stack*: a claimant is no longer bound to the rigour of *Rosset*. Times have indeed moved on.

By way of contrast, *Ritchie v Ritchie*[84] is much closer to the facts of *Stack*. The house was conveyed into the joint names of mother and son, with no express declaration of the beneficial interest. Both were liable under a small mortgage, but the mother had contributed a large share by way of a 'right to buy' discount. The mother died and her son claimed the entire equity under the right of survivorship. Of course, this depended on whether they owned the equitable interest also as joint-tenants or whether, as the personal representatives of the mother claimed, as tenants in common in some as yet undetermined shares.[85] It will be remembered that Baroness Hale in *Stack* emphasised that normally, and usually, 'equity would follow the law', so that joint-ownership of the legal title would mean a joint-tenancy of the equitable title (and so survivorship or a 50:50 split if severance had occurred prior to death). Traditionalists—including this author—at least found some comfort in this because it would preserve a measure of certainty for third parties as well as enforcing the curtain principle of land registration. Thus, in *Stack,* much was made of the fact that the circumstances were exceptional and this alone justified the court in looking behind joint-ownership of the legal title and utilising the factors listed in [69] of Baroness Hale's judgment to quantify the equity for each party. Nevertheless, despite the insistence in *Stack* that it should be difficult to subvert a joint-tenancy of the legal title, it was clear that the factors listed in [69] were so wide-ranging that nearly any case could be made 'special'. So it is with *Ritchie* that Judge Behrens decides that the *Stack* principles are not confined to couples in an intimate relationship (this must be correct), but also that the facts of this case are also 'exceptional' because many of the matters raised in [69] in *Stack* are present here.

We should not, of course, build a theory on one case, but the problem with *Stack*—as illustrated by *Ritchie*—is that the House do not explain what makes a case 'exceptional' so as to permit an holistic enquiry into the parties' entire relationship. In *Ritchie,* it is true that, given the parties' actions over the years, it might not be *fair* for the son to claim all the equity by survivorship, as it might not have seemed *fair* that Ms Dowden be limited to half the house in *Stack*. But, it is not at all clear that 'unfairness' equals 'exceptional'. Without a clear idea of what justifies a departure from the normal rule that 'equity follows the law', any claimant can argue that the equitable interest should not be split 50:50 and any judge can agree. In the end,

---

[83] *Burns v Burns* [1984] Ch 317, regarded by the Law Commission as the paradigm of unfairness.

[84] Judge Behrens in the Leeds County Court, August 17, 2007, Case No: 7LS70535 [reported as *Adekunle v Ritchie* [2007] 2 P & CR DG20].

[85] If tenants in common, the claimant's brothers and sisters would succeed to their mother's share under the intestacy rules.

Judge Behrens decided that the son owned less than half of the equity, necessarily under an equitable tenancy in common...[86]

V. RIGHTS OF CO-OWNERS

Once it is established that there is co-ownership of the property, the rights of the co-owners can be examined. We have already seen that the co-ownership must exist either as a beneficial joint tenancy or as a tenancy in common.[87] But that, in either case, it must exist under a trust, which will necessarily be a trust of land. The rights of the co-owners, both amongst themselves and as against the trustee(s), will therefore be governed by the Trusts of Land and Appointment of Trustees Act 1996, which was discussed in detail in chapter 6.

The rights of the beneficial co-owner, who is not also a legal owner,[88] as against *purchasers* of the property will depend upon the circumstances of the sale. If the sale is by two trustees, then the beneficial interests of the co-owners are overreached,[89] even if the co-owners are in actual occupation.[90] Where, however, the legal estate is held at the time of sale by only one trustee[91] the overreaching mechanism does not apply,[92] and the co-owner's rights as against the purchaser depend upon the normal rules of priority of interests. In registered land,[93] assuming that the interest is not protected by an entry on the register,[94] the question is whether the co-owner has an overriding interest under Land Registration Act 2002, Sch. 3, para. 2. Such an interest must be in

[86] A related issue in cases like *Stack* and *Ritchie* is how the equitable interest came to be held as a tenancy in common. A fortiori, when shares are unequal, there must have been a tenancy in common from the time of purchase, because had it once been an equitable joint tenancy, any act of severance would have resulted in a 50:50 split. If the quantification arises under a constructive trust—as we are told it does—this must arise after purchase but somehow relate back to the time of purchase. The constructive trust cannot arise at the time of purchase itself because at that time the parties have had no conduct in relation to the land and neither can have acted unconscionably.

[87] Above, p. 563.

[88] The transfer by the legal owner will transfer to the purchaser all the interest (legal and equitable) of the transferor: LPA 1925, s. 63.

[89] Above, pp. 548–558.

[90] *City of London Building Society v Flegg* [1988] AC 54, p. 551, above.

[91] Unless the trustee is a trust corporation; LPA 1925, s. 27, as amended by TLATA 1996, s. 25(1), Sch. 3, para. 8, p. 550, above. To facilitate a sale under which the purchaser need not concern himself with beneficial interests under a trust of land, a second trustee should therefore be appointed. The other co-owner (e.g. the wife, in a case where the legal title to the land is held only by the husband) would be appropriate, but if there is disagreement, she cannot insist on being appointed. She may, however, as one who has an interest in property subject to a trust of land, apply to the court under section 14 for an order for sale: above, p. 532.

[92] See *Williams & Glyn's Bank Ltd v Boland* [1979] Ch 312 at 330, per Lord Denning MR.

[93] In unregistered land, since the beneficial interest of a co-owner cannot be registered as a land charge under LCA 1972, this still depends upon whether the purchaser is a bona fide purchaser of the legal estate for value without notice: *Kingsnorth Finance Co Ltd v Tizard* [1986] 1 WLR 783, p. 216, above.

[94] LRA 2002, s. 29(2)(a).

the nature of a proprietary interest; and the party claiming it must be in discoverable actual occupation.[95]

VI. RIGHT OF OCCUPATION UNDER FAMILY LAW ACT 1996

A spouse or civil partner has a further means of protection by relying, not upon ownership, but upon the statutory right of occupation given to a spouse or civil partner under the Family Law Act 1996, Part IV, as amended by Civil Partnership Act 2004. This supersedes the Matrimonial Homes Act 1983, which had itself superseded Matrimonial Homes Act 1967.[96] The spouse or civil partner may protect the right against purchasers by registration of a land charge, Class F in the case of unregistered land. With registered land, the right must be protected by entry of a notice. It cannot be an overriding interest, even if the spouse is in actual occupation.[97] In these situations, that is to say, in respect of the statutory protection given to the spouse or civil partner under the Family Law Act 1996, all depends on following the correct procedure for protection. Failure to register or to protect by notice involves the loss of the right against a purchaser. But the loss of that right still leaves open any claim in respect of the spouse or civil partner's beneficial ownership.

FAMILY LAW ACT 1996[98]

30. Rights concerning home where one spouse or civil partner has no estate, etc.—(1) This section applies if—

 (a) one spouse or civil partner ('A') is entitled to occupy a dwelling-house by virtue of

  (i) a beneficial estate or interest or contract; or

  (ii) any enactment giving A the right to remain in occupation; and

 (b) the other spouse or civil partner ('B') is not so entitled.

 (2) Subject to the provisions of this Part, B has the following rights ('home rights')—

  (a) if in occupation, a right not to be evicted or excluded from the dwelling-house or any part of it by A except with the leave of the court given by an order under section 33;

---

[95] See also (under the former provision, LRA 1925, s. 70(1)(g), *Williams & Glyn's Bank Ltd v Boland* [1980] AC 487 at 507, per Lord Wilberforce, p. 203, above.

[96] The Act is based on the Law Commission Report on Domestic Violence and Occupation of the Family Home 1992 (Law Com No. 207). On the matrimonial or civil partnership home in registered land, see R & R, chap. 45.

[97] The difference between a spouse or civil partner who has an equitable interest (protected as an overriding interest: *Williams & Glyn's Bank Ltd v Boland* [1981] AC 487) and one who has only the rights of occupation under the Act is therefore considerable.

[98] As amended by Civil Partnership Act 2004, s. 82, Sch. 9, Pt 1.

(b) if not in occupation, a right with the leave of the court so given to enter into and occupy the dwelling-house.[99]

(3) If B is entitled under this section to occupy a dwelling-house or any part of a dwelling-house, any payment or tender made or other thing done by B in or towards satisfaction of any liability of A in respect of rent, mortgage payments or other outgoings affecting the dwelling-house is, whether or not it is made or done in pursuance of an order under section 40, as good as if made or done by A.

(5) If B—

(a) is entitled under this section to occupy a dwelling-house or any part of a dwelling-house, and

(b) makes any payment in or towards satisfaction of any liability of A in respect of mortgage payments affecting the dwelling-house,

the person to whom the payment is made may treat it as having been made by A, but the fact that that person has treated any such payment as having been so made does not affect any claim of B against A to an interest in the dwelling-house by virtue of the payment.

(6) If B is entitled under this section to occupy a dwelling-house or part of a dwelling-house by reason of an interest of A under a trust, all the provisions of subsections (3) to (5) apply in relation to the trustees as they apply in relation to A.

(7) This section does not apply to a dwelling-house which—

(a) in the case of spouses, has at no time been, and was at no time intended by them to be, a matrimonial home of theirs; and

(b) in the case of civil partners, has at no time been, and was at no time intended by them to be, a civil partnership home of theirs.

(8) B's home rights continue—

(a) only so long as the marriage or civil partnership subsists, except to the extent that an order under section 33(5) otherwise provides; and

(b) only so long as A is entitled as mentioned in subsection (1) to occupy the dwelling-house, except where provision is made by section 31 for those rights to be a charge on an estate or interest in the dwelling-house.

(9) It is hereby declared that a person—

(a) who has an equitable interest in a dwelling-house or in its proceeds of sale, but

(b) is not a person in whom there is vested (whether solely or as joint tenant) a legal estate in fee simple or a legal term of years absolute in the dwelling-house,

is to be treated, only for the purpose of determining whether he has home rights, as not being entitled to occupy the dwelling-house by virtue of that interest.[100]

31. Effect of home rights as charge on dwelling-house.—(1) Subsections (2) and (3) apply if, at any time during a marriage or civil partnership, A is entitled to occupy a dwelling-house by virtue of a beneficial estate or interest.

---

[99] *Watts v Waller* [1973] QB 153 (spouse out of occupation can register before getting leave of court to re-enter); *Barnett v Hassett* [1981] 1 WLR 1385 (spouse having no intention to occupy not permitted to register in attempt to freeze proceeds of intended sale).

[100] For powers of the courts to make occupation orders, see ss. 33–41.

(2) B's home rights are a charge on the estate or interest.

(3) The charge created by subsection (2) has the same priority as if it were an equitable interest created at whichever is the latest of the following dates—

    (a) the date on which A acquires the estate or interest;

    (b) the date of the marriage or of the formation of the civil partnership; and

    (c) 1st January 1968 (the commencement date of the Matrimonial Homes Act 1967).

(4) Subsections (5) and (6) apply if, at any time when B's home rights are a charge on an interest of A under a trust, there are, apart from A or B, no persons, living or unborn, who are or could become beneficiaries under the trust.

(5) The rights are a charge also on the estate or interest of the trustees for A.

(6) The charge created by subsection (5) has the same priority as if it were an equitable interest created (under powers overriding the trusts) on the date when it arises.

(7) In determining for the purposes of subsection (4) whether there are any persons who are not, but could become, beneficiaries under the trust, there is to be disregarded any potential exercise of a general power of appointment exercisable by either or both of A and B alone (whether or not the exercise of it requires the consent of another person).

(8) Even though B's home rights are a charge on an estate or interest in the dwelling-house, those rights are brought to an end by—

    (a) the death of A, or

    (b) the termination (otherwise than by death) of the marriage or civil partnership,

unless the court directs otherwise by an order made under section 33(5).

(9) If—

    (a) B's home rights are a charge on an estate or interest in the dwelling-house, and

    (b) that estate or interest is surrendered to merge in some other estate or interest expectant on it in such circumstances that, but for the merger, the person taking the estate or interest would be bound by the charge,

the surrender has effect subject to the charge and the persons thereafter entitled to the other estate or interest are, for so long as the estate or interest surrendered would have endured if not so surrendered, to be treated for all purposes of this Part as deriving title to the other estate or interest under A or, as the case maybe, under the trustees for A, by virtue of the surrender.

(10) If the title to the legal estate by virtue of which A is entitled to occupy a dwelling-house (including any legal estate held by trustees for A) is registered under the Land Registration Act 2002 or any enactment replaced by that Act—

    (a) registration of a land charge affecting the dwelling-house by virtue of this Part is to be effected by registering a notice under that Act and

    (b) B's home rights are not to be capable of falling within paragraph 2 of Schedule 1 or 3 to that Act.[101]

(12) If—

    (a) B's home rights are a charge on the estate of A or of trustees of A, and

---

[101] As amended by LRA 2002, s. 133, Sch. 11, para. 34(1), (2)(a), (b), i.e. the rights cannot be overriding interests.

(b) that estate is the subject of a mortgage,

then if, after the date of the creation of the mortgage ('the first mortgage'), the charge is registered under section 2 of the Land Charges Act 1972, the charge is, for the purposes of section 94 of the Law of Property Act 1925[102] (which regulates the rights of mortgagees to make further advances ranking in priority to subsequent mortgages), to be deemed to be a mortgage subsequent in date to the first mortgage.

(13) It is hereby declared that a charge under subsection (2) or (5) is not registrable under subsection (10) or under section 2 of the Land Charges Act 1972 unless it is a charge on a legal estate.

54. Dwelling-house subject to mortgage.—(1) In determining for the purposes of this Part whether a person is entitled to occupy a dwelling-house by virtue of an estate or interest, any right to possession of the dwelling-house conferred on a mortgagee of the dwelling-house under or by virtue of his mortgage is to be disregarded.

(2) Subsection (1) applies whether or not the mortgagee is in possession.

SCHEDULE 4

Restriction on registration where spouse entitled to more than one charge

2.—Where one spouse or civil partner is entitled by virtue of section 31 to a registrable charge in respect of each of two or more dwelling-houses, only one of the charges to which that spouse or civil partner is so entitled shall be registered under section 31(10) or under section 2 of the Land Charges Act 1972 at any one time, and if any of those charges is registered under either of those provisions the Chief Land Registrar, on being satisfied that any other of them is so registered, shall cancel the registration of the charge first registered.

Release of matrimonial home rights

5.—(1) A spouse or civil partner entitled to home rights may by a release in writing release those rights or release them as respect part only of the dwelling-house affected by them.[103]

Postponement of priority of charge

6.—A spouse or civil partner entitled by virtue of section 31 to a charge on an estate or interest may agree in writing that any other charge on, or interest in, that estate or interest shall rank in priority to the charge to which that spouse or civil partner is so entitled.

INSOLVENCY ACT 1986

336. Rights of occupation etc. of bankrupt's spouse or civil partner.[104]—(2) Where a spouse or civil partner's home rights under the Act of 1996 are a charge on the estate or interest of the

---

[102] P. 989, below.

[103] *Holmes v H Kennard & Son* (1984) 49 P & CR 202; [1985] Conv 293 (N. S. Price), where purchaser's solicitors were held liable in negligence for failure to obtain release of vendor's wife's right of occupation by correct conveyancing procedure.

[104] As amended by Civil Partnership Act 2004, s. 82, Sch. 9, Pt. 2.

other spouse or civil partner, or of trustees for the other spouse or civil partner, and the other spouse or civil partner is adjudged bankrupt—

    (a)   the charge continues to subsist notwithstanding the bankruptcy and, subject to the provisions of that Act, binds the trustee of the bankrupt's estate and persons deriving title under that trustee, and

    (b)   any application for an order under section 33 of that Act[105] shall be made to the court having jurisdiction in relation to the bankruptcy.

  (4) On such an application as is mentioned in subsection (2) the court shall make such order under section 33 of the Act of 1996 as it thinks just and reasonable having regard to—

    (a)   the interests of the bankrupt's creditors,

    (b)   the conduct of the spouse or former spouse or civil partner or former civil partner, so far as contributing to the bankruptcy,

    (c)   the needs and financial resources of the spouse or former spouse or civil partner or former civil partner,

    (d)   the needs of any children, and

    (e)   all the circumstances of the case other than the needs of the bankrupt.

  (5) Where such an application is made after the end of the period of one year beginning with the first vesting under Chapter IV of this Part of the bankrupt's estate in a trustee, the court shall assume, unless the circumstances of the case are exceptional, that the interests of the bankrupt's creditors outweigh all other considerations.

VII. LAW REFORM

Law Commission Report on Cohabitation: The Financial Consequences of Relationship Breakdown 2007 (Law Com No. 307), paras 1.1–1.3, 1.14–1.21, 2.94, 4.132–4.146[106]

1.1 This Report makes recommendations to Parliament on certain aspects of the law relating to cohabitants. It considers the financial consequences of the ending of cohabiting relationships by separation or death. It follows two years of work by the Law Commission and builds on a Consultation Paper published on 31 May 2006.

1.2 In this Report, we conclude that reform is needed to address inadequacies in the current law. We recommend a new statutory scheme designed specifically for cohabitants on separation. The scheme would apply only to cohabitants who have had children together or who have lived together for a specified number of years.[107] The scheme would not equate cohabitants with married couples or give them equivalent rights. Nor would it provide a new status

---

[105] As amended by TLATA 1996, s. 25(2), Sch. 4; Sch. 8, para. 57(3), (4).

[106] [2008] Conv 197 (D. Hughes, M. Davis and L. Jacklin); (2009) 72 MLR 24 (G. Douglas, J. Pearce and H. Woodward).

[107] Referred to in this Report as a 'minimum duration requirement'.

which cohabitants should sign up to in order to gain new rights. The scheme would apply to all cohabitants who satisfied the eligibility criteria. But it would respect the autonomy of couples by allowing them, subject to necessary protections, to disapply the scheme and make their own arrangements. It would not automatically require parties to share their property with their ex-partners and would not require them to pay maintenance. Instead, the scheme would address particular economic consequences of the contributions made by the parties during the relationship.

1.3 We recognise that these recommendations will be unwelcome to some who, for various reasons, consider that cohabitants should not be granted legal remedies of this sort. Others may feel that the recommendations do not go far enough and that in the twenty-first century cohabitants should be given the same status and the same rights as married couples. Others may disagree with aspects of the technical operation of our recommended scheme. All of these views were expressed during consultation and have been taken into account in forming our recommendations.

THE BACKGROUND TO THE PROJECT

1.14 In July 2002, the Law Commission published a Discussion Paper, Sharing Homes.[108] This paper considered the law relating to the property rights of homesharers. It covered a broad range of relationships, including friends and relatives as well as married and unmarried couples. It focused on the complex legal principles which determine when, and to what extent, a person may claim an interest in property, and sought to formulate a straightforward, more certain scheme for ascertaining and quantifying property rights in the shared home.

1.15 The Commission concluded that it was not feasible to devise a scheme which could operate fairly and evenly across the diversity of contemporary domestic circumstances. It advocated that those who are living together should be encouraged to find out about the legal implications of doing so and to make express written arrangements setting out their intentions.[109]

1.16 However, the Commission also suggested:

'... that further consideration should be given to the adoption, necessarily by legislation, of new legal approaches to personal relationships outside marriage, following the lead given by other jurisdictions (such as France, Australia and New Zealand)'.

These approaches may include such mechanisms as the formal registration of civil partnerships, or, less formally, a power for the court to adjust the legal rights and obligations of individuals who are or have been living together for a defined period or in defined circumstances.[110]

1.17 Since the publication of Sharing Homes, Parliament has offered same-sex couples the opportunity to register their relationships as civil partnerships and thereby to obtain broadly equivalent rights and obligations to those applying to married couples.

1.18 During the passage of the Civil Partnership Bill through Parliament, members of the House of Lords raised questions about the law's treatment of couples and others who live together but who neither marry nor (in the case of same-sex couples) register a civil partnership. Concerns were expressed, amongst other things, about the potential financial hardship

[108] Sharing Homes: A Discussion Paper (2002) Law Com No. 278, available at http://www.lawcom.gov.uk/docs/lc278(1).pdf.

[109] Sharing Homes: A Discussion Paper (2002) Law Com No. 278, para. 1.31(2).

[110] Sharing Homes: A Discussion Paper (2002) Law Com No. 278, Part 6, paras (7) and (8).

suffered by cohabitants on the termination of their relationship owing to the current lack of any coherent legal remedies addressing their financial and property disputes...

TERMS OF REFERENCE

1.19 The Law Commission's Ninth Programme of Law Reform set out the terms of reference for the project, making it clear that the project was not to consider all those who live in the same home. Relationships between blood relatives or 'caring' relationships and 'commercial' relationships (such as landlord and tenant or lodger) were excluded.

1.20 We acknowledged in the Consultation Paper that some would contend that the law relating to these other categories of home-sharers is also in need of reform. We expressed no opinion on the merits of such arguments. However, we took the view that '[a]rguments for wider changes to the law should not prevent us from considering reform for those within our current remit'.[111] That remains our position.

1.21 The home-sharers that this project has considered are those commonly referred to as 'couples', both opposite-sex and same-sex, who live together in intimate relationships.

2.94 We recommend that legislation should create a scheme of general application, whereby cohabiting couples would be entitled to apply for financial relief on separation:[112]

(1) provided they satisfy statutory eligibility criteria;[113]

(2) but not where they had reached an agreement disapplying the statutory scheme ('an opt-out agreement'),[114] in which case the parties' own financial arrangements (if any) would apply.

THE INTERACTION OF THE SCHEME WITH THE LAW OF
IMPLIED TRUSTS AND ESTOPPEL

4.132 Self-evidently, when parties have made contractual arrangements as to what is to happen in the event of separation, those contractual arrangements would be overridden by our recommended scheme, unless the parties had entered into a valid opt-out agreement.[115]

4.133 The parties might also have made arrangements as to the ownership of assets. Property disputes between cohabitants can at present only be resolved using equitable principles developed by the courts over many years. The law relating to implied trusts and the law of estoppel[116] may give a former cohabitant an interest in the other's property or determine the shares in which jointly owned property is held. But some aspects of these areas of law were not designed for relationship breakdown, which is why we are recommending a tailor-made jurisdiction that is sensitive to family situations.

4.134 Our scheme would not abolish implied trusts and estoppel; these principles (which we call the 'general law') would remain important in many contexts.[117] So we have to determine what would happen in cases where it appeared that a claim could be made under both our

---

[111] Cohabitation: The Financial Consequences of Relationship Breakdown (2006) Law Commission Consultation Paper No. 179, para. 1.20, available at http://www.lawcom.gov.uk/docs/cp179.pdf.

[112] [The scheme for financial relief, under which the court would have a structured discretion based on the economic impact of the cohabitation, is discussed in Part 4 of the Report.]

[113] [The eligibility criteria are discussed in Part 3 of the Report.]

[114] [The parties' freedom to opt out is discussed in Part 5 of the Report.]

[115] See Part 5.

[116] See Appendix A. [On implied, constructive and resulting trusts, see earlier in this chapter. On proprietary estoppel, see chap. 12.]

[117] For example, on death, in disputes with third parties and where cohabitants are not eligible under the scheme.

recommended scheme and the general law. Since general law claims arise most frequently in relation to claims to land, typically the formerly shared home, and arise from different kinds of contribution to property, there could be an overlap in a number of cases.

4.135 The few responses to the CP question about the interaction issue[118] were inconclusive, with a number of views expressed. Recent research suggests that practitioners find using the general law in these cases problematic for a number of reasons.[119] We are especially concerned that for parties to plead the new law and the general law together would be a disaster in terms of complexity and costs. It is necessary to recommend a scheme that would replace, rather than merely supplement, the general law in these cases.

Illustrating the interaction problem

4.136 It may help to give an example of the difficulties that might arise if the general law remained relevant. Let us suppose that A and B have bought a house together. They are joint registered proprietors; they contributed one quarter and three-quarters of the deposit respectively, and they continue to make the mortgage payments in those proportions. Later their relationship breaks down and they want to sell the house and divide the proceeds.

4.137 As joint legal owners, A and B hold the house upon trust.[120] They have not executed a declaration of trust,[121] nor have they had any discussion about the proportions in which they own the house.[122] How then is their beneficial interest held? The starting point is that they hold upon trust for themselves as beneficial joint tenants,[123] but B, who has contributed three-quarters of the value of the house, may not be content with this. If B wishes to show that the beneficial interests were different, then B must establish that this is a 'very unusual' case.[124]

4.138 Whether B succeeds will depend upon how A and B's relationship is viewed by the court[125] and in particular the extent to which it appears that they have pooled their resources.

---

[118] CP [Consultation Paper: above, n. 111], para. 6.288.

[119] See G Douglas, J Pearce, H Woodward, *A Failure of Trust: Resolving Property Disputes on Cohabitation Breakdown* (2007), available at http://www.law.cf.ac.uk/researchpapers/papers/1.pdf or http://www.bris.ac.uk/law/research/centres-themes/cohabit/cohabit-rep.pdf (last visited 3 July 2007); see 'Dealing with Property Issues on Cohabitation Breakdown' (2007) 37 *Family Law* 36. The desirability of having an overarching scheme, and the problems created by the multiple applications required by the current law, were also flagged by some solicitors interviewed by R. Tennant, J. Taylor and J. Lewis, *Separating from cohabitation: making arrangements for finances and parenting* (2006) Department for Constitutional Affairs Research Report 7/2006, p. 28.

[120] Law of Property Act 1925, s. 34(2).

[121] Had they done so, that would have been conclusive as to the extent of their beneficial interests: *Goodman v Gallant* [1986] Fam 106; see paras A.10 to A.16 and Appendix A generally on this area of the law. Under our recommended scheme, their express beneficial interests would provide the starting point from which one party might bring a claim under the scheme. In particular, one might argue that the other's share was a retained benefit to the extent that the first had in fact provided more of the purchase price or mortgage payments; such an argument based on mortgage payments would not be tenable where the other had discharged other household bills of equal value.

[122] An expression of common intention, upon which the parties have relied (by investing in the house), will determine the extent of a beneficial interest in property held upon constructive trust following *Lloyds Bank plc v Rosset* [1991] 1 AC 107. The precise status of that principle is unclear following *Stack v Dowden* [2007] UKHL 17, [2007] 2 WLR 831 [p. 580, above], but it is consistent with the House of Lords' view expressed in that case (at [61]) that the court must ascertain 'what the parties must, in view of their conduct, be taken to have intended'.

[123] *Stack v Dowden* [2007] UKHL 17, [2007] 2 WLR 831, at [56].

[124] *Stack v Dowden* [2007] UKHL 17, [2007] 2 WLR 831, at [69]. The House of Lords held in that case that it is not appropriate to use resulting trust reasoning in the domestic context.

[125] See para. 2.8 and following.

The case will probably not be a 'very unusual' one, and it is likely that B will not be able to dis-place the presumption of beneficial joint tenancy under the general law.

4.139 However, if the matter were examined under our recommended scheme, it might be that a different result would be reached. The scheme would not involve the determination of beneficial ownership in property. The court should not consider whether the presumption of joint beneficial ownership should be rebutted. The scheme would require the court to assess whether that presumption left either party with a retained benefit or an economic disadvantage in the event of separation.[126] B's greater financial contribution would point to A's having a retained benefit and, subject to the operation of the discretionary factors, it is likely that A would have to repay that benefit to B.

4.140 If B were able to prove under the general law that the case was unusual and that beneficial ownership should mirror the parties' contributions, then B would have no incentive to invoke our recommended scheme. A, by contrast, might wish to invoke the scheme in order to determine whether the retained benefit might be held to be somewhat smaller in the light of the discretionary factors, and to enable the court to look at other matters and in particular at economic disadvantage.

4.141 It can be seen that the general law governing beneficial entitlement to property might yield, for either party, results different from those generated by our recommended scheme.

Conclusions

4.142 There are two questions to be answered. First, what should be the relationship between the scheme and the general law: which should take priority? And second, given that priority, should it still be possible for litigants to plead both the new scheme and the general law in the alternative, despite the risk of complexity and costs referred to above?

4.143 Taking the first question, it is clear that the law must make priority clear. Our recom-mended scheme and the general law might give similar results in some cases; they would give different results in others. Parties need to know on what basis to negotiate in order to settle their disputes; courts need to know on what basis to make orders for financial relief. It is equally clear that our recommended scheme must 'trump' the general law.

4.144 Once that priority has been determined, it is clear that the second question is deter-mined at least as a matter of logic: even if permitted to do so, the parties would merely waste costs if they brought a concurrent general law claim as between each other, because the general law's attribution of the parties' equitable interests would be superseded by the adjustive powers of the scheme.[127]

4.145 However, even though this is clear as a matter of logic, parties might try to bring alternative claims unless explicitly prevented. Moreover, it is very important that parties—particularly those for whom expense is no object—should be prevented from bringing multiple claims. It is clear from meetings we have had with family law practitioners that this will happen unless the rules make it clear that it must not. Hence our recommendation.[128]

4.146 Our recommendation in this respect would make the interaction between the general law and our scheme no different from that which arises when the MCA[129] is invoked. It is

---

[126] Our scheme would also operate in place of the remedy of equitable accounting: see *Stack v Dowden* [2007] UKHL 17, [2007] 2 WLR 831, at [150]; *Wilcox v Tait* [2006] EWCA Civ 1867.

[127] As it will also adjust the parties' expressly declared beneficial interests; see para. 5.62 and following.

[128] See paras 4.41 and 4.42.

[129] [Matrimonial Causes Act 1973. For similar provisions relating to the breakdown of a civil partner-ship, see Civil Partnership Act 2002, s. 66.]

well-established that in proceedings between separated or divorcing spouses where ancillary relief is available under the MCA, proceedings under the general law are not permitted. The position of civil partners is identical. Nevertheless, the rights of spouses and civil partners under the general law (and those of their creditors) are not otherwise affected and indeed they may need to litigate under the general law where third parties are involved.[130] The position is well-understood by family practitioners.

QUESTIONS

1. In *Stack v Dowden* [2007] 2 AC 432, p. 580, above, do you prefer the approach of the majority (as reflected in Baroness Hale's opinion) or of Lord Neuberger?

2. Should the principles to be applied in determining the existence of a trust of land and the nature of the beneficial interest under the trust, differ according to whether the parties are commercial or non-commercial? See *Stack v Dowden* at [42] (Baroness Hale), [107] (Lord Neuberger); Law Commission Report No. 307, p. 606 above.

3. Make a checklist of the circumstances which are relevant to the court's decision on the nature and quantum of the beneficial interest. How do you assess their relative importance?

4. Does *Stack v Dowden* supersede all the earlier case law on the question of how a constructive trust of the family home is established? Does the decision deal with the question of establishing the existence of the trust in the case of a sole legal owner (the first stage in Chadwick LJ's analysis in *Oxley v Hiscock*, p. 578, above) as well as the quantification of the interest? In other words, after *Stack v Dowden* what is the status of the decisions in *Lloyds Bank plc v Rosset* [1991] 1 AC 107, p. 576, above, and *Oxley v Hiscock* [2005] Fam 211? Consider Baroness Hale in *Stack v Dowden* at [61]; [2008] CLJ 265 at 277 (Sir Terence Etherton); (2008) 124 LQR 422 at 424 (S. Gardner).

5. Consider the difficulties arising from the registrability of Class F land charges in *Wroth v Tyler* [1974] Ch 30; *Watts v Waller* [1973] QB 153; and in *Barnett v Hassett* [1981] 1 WLR 1385. Do you think that registration is a suitable mechanism for the protection of interests of a family character? Cretney, *Principles of Family Law* (8th edn), paras 3.012–3.013; [1974] 38 Conv (NS) 110; (1975) 39 Conv (NS) 78 (D. J. Hayton); [1974] CLP 76 (D. G. Barnsley); [1976] CLP 26 at pp. 31–33, 43–50 (D. J. Hayton).

---

[130] For example, *G v G* (Matrimonial Property: Rights of Extended Family) [2005] EWHC 1560 (Fam), [2006] 1 FLR 62; *TL v ML and others* (Ancillary relief: claim against assets of extended family) [2005] EWHC 2860 (Fam), [2006] 1 FLR 1263. See also issues raised in *Mountney v Treharne* [2002] EWCA Civ 1174, [2003] Ch 135; *Ram v Ram (No 2)* [2004] EWCA Civ 1684, [2005] 2 FLR 75; *Hill v Haines* [2007] EWHC 1012 (Ch), [2007] NPC 58; *X v X (Crown Prosecution Service Intervening)* [2005] EWHC 296 (Fam), [2005] 2 FLR 487; see also CP, paras 6.298 to 6.301 in relation to debt.

PART IV

OTHER LEGAL AND EQUITABLE INTERESTS IN LAND

8

EASEMENTS AND PROFITS
À PRENDRE[1]

I. GENERAL

Easements and profits à prendre are interests entitling their owners to exercise certain rights over the land of another. They may be legal[2] or equitable.[3] They are distinguishable in that a profit entitles its owner to take away something capable of ownership from the servient land, while an easement does not; and also in that a profit may exist 'in gross' (ie, held independently of the ownership of land), while an easement must always be appurtenant to land. Owing to lack of available space, little will be said of profits; or, indeed, of commons.[4]

---

[1] C & B, chap. 18; Gray, part 5; M & W, chaps 27–30; MM, pp. 413–451; Smith, chap. 23; *Gale on Easements* (18th edn, 2008); Sara, *Boundaries and Easements* (4th edn, 2007); Jackson, *Law of Easements and Profits* (1978).

[2] LPA 1925, ss. 1(2), 187.   [3] Pp. 646–649, below.

[4] For registration of commons under Commons Act 2006, see pp. 96–105, above.

Easements and profits play an important role in the regulating the relationship between landowners.[5] We shall see in chapter 9 that covenants play a related role. The Law Commission is in the process of undertaking a significant review of easements, covenants and profits à prendre, and in 2008 published a Consultation Paper making proposals for reform.[6]

Law Commission Consultation Paper on Easements, Covenants and Profits à Prendre 2008 (Consultation Paper No. 186), paras 1.2–1.7

1.2 The majority of the public may be unfamiliar with the interests we are considering even though they facilitate the use of what is many individuals' and businesses' most important asset. The obscure terminology and dry legal complexity of the current law should not hide the fact that easements and covenants remain vitally important in the twenty-first century.

1.3 The law of easements and covenants has practical implications for a large number of landowners. Recent Land Registry figures suggest that at least 65% of freehold titles are subject to one or more easements and 79% are subject to one or more restrictive covenants.[7] These interests can be fundamental to the enjoyment of property. For example, many landowners depend on easements in order to obtain access to their property. Covenants may provide, for example, that a trade or business should not be carried out on, or that no more than one dwelling house should be built upon, a neighbouring plot of land.

1.4 Without the vital role that easements and covenants play in the regulation of the use of land in England and Wales, the full extent to which land can be enjoyed could not be realised. Many properties would be unable to exist fruitfully without rights over neighbouring land. Neighbours' co-operation is, to an extent, based on social convention, but it is supported in the majority of cases by enforceable rights and obligations. This project examines those rights and obligations with the aim of simplifying and improving the current law.

1.5 The significance of the role played by easements and covenants can be demonstrated by reference to current high-profile issues of public policy. The Government's recent Housing Green Paper has set a target of three million new homes by the year 2020.[8] The need for more new homes has arisen because of the growing pressure on existing housing stock where demand outstrips supply. A recent article drew attention to a number of problems with the current law of easements that, it argued, could prevent the development of land for housing.[9] Covenants may also impede land development; the grant of planning permission does not extinguish a

---

[5] Infringement of an easement constitutes the tort of nuisance against the dominant owner, for which the remedies are abatement, injunction or damages. Injunction is the primary judicial remedy, thus ensuring the positive enforcement of the dominant owner's rights over the servient owner's land. See generally C & B, pp. 635–636; Gale, chap. 14; and (for cases relating in particular to infringement of the right to light) p. 730, n. 258, below.

[6] See also pp. 738–741 (easements) and 836–849 (covenants), below.

[7] See Appendix A for a statistical analysis prepared for the Law Commission by Land Registry.

[8] Department for Communities and Local Government, *Homes for the future: more affordable, more sustainable* (2007) Cm 7191.

[9] G Fetherstonhaugh, 'Time to ease out a thorn in the developer's side' (2007) 0747 EG 166. The article instances the case of *Benn v Hardinge* (1993) 66 P & CR 246 which held that a right of way granted in 1818 and never used has nevertheless not been abandoned.

restrictive covenant which may confer upon a landowner an enforceable right to prevent new buildings being erected on neighbouring land.

1.6 However, easements and covenants are also essential to successful land development. Both rights play a vital part in enabling the efficient operation of freehold developments and in preserving the quality of life of people who live there.[10]

1.7 Easements and covenants are therefore capable of both limiting and facilitating the use of land. The balance between providing affordable housing and protecting land from over-development is part of a wider debate in which easements and covenants play a part. But, however these competing interests are resolved, clear, well-designed, modern land law is vitally important in meeting society's needs.

II. NATURE OF EASEMENTS[11]

A. INTRODUCTION

The detailed characteristics of an easement are discussed in the textbooks and need not be repeated here. In short, an easement is a right, appurtenant to one piece of land[12] and exercisable over another piece of land, and capable of forming the subject matter of a grant. Indeed, all easements, other than those created by statute, are either granted expressly or impliedly, or are presumed to have been granted. An easement must be distinguished from a licence in that it is a proprietary interest and must be appurtenant to land; from a lease in that it does not give the owner of the easement any possessory rights over the land of another; from local customary rights in that there cannot be a grant without a capable grantee; from natural rights in that these need no grant; and from a covenant in that it must be a right capable of being granted. Thus rights which are properly licences, leases, customary rights, natural rights or covenants may look very much like easements, but they may be very different. If X, the owner of Whiteacre, tells Y, the owner of Blackacre, that Y's son may enter Whiteacre to collect a lost ball, that is clearly a licence; but if X were to permit the owner of Blackacre to enter Whiteacre at any time for pleasure and recreation, it might create an easement.[13] Again, a letting of a garage on a weekly tenancy is clearly in no sense an easement; but a right to park vehicles on a neighbour's ground without interfering

[10] For example, in securing rights of access to individual plots via private estate roads or regulating the number or type of dwellings that can be erected.

[11] C & B, pp. 586–599; Gray, part 5.1; M & W, paras 27.001–27.042; MM, pp. 413–424; Smith, pp. 482–493; Gale, chap. 1; (1964) 28 Conv (NS) 450 (M. A. Peel).

[12] See (1980) 96 LQR 557 (M. F. Sturley) for criticism of the rule that an easement cannot exist in gross. See also (1982) 98 LQR 279 at p. 305 (S. Gardner).

[13] *Horton v Tidd* (1965) 196 EG 697; *Re Ellenborough Park* [1956] Ch 131, p. 620, below; *Miller v Jackson* [1977] QB 966.

with his user of the land looks more like an easement,[14] and the right to fix a signboard on a neighbour's house can be an easement.[15] Again, local inhabitants of a particular area may have the right to pass across another's land on the way to church,[16] or to dry their nets on someone's land;[17] but these rights rely on custom and not on grant and cannot be easements. Again, every landowner has the right of support from his neighbour to his land in its natural state.[18] A right of support to buildings on land is, however, a right which must be claimed as the result of a grant.[19] A right in the nature of an easement may arise by estoppel, where it would be unconscionable to deny that such a right exists.[20] A covenant not to use land as a fish shop is clearly not an easement; but an arrangement permitting the owner of neighbouring land to walk across it in perpetuity to the road is capable of being an easement. In connection with this comparison between easements and covenants, the anomalous position of the easement of light may be noted.[21] For this easement is more like a negative right; the grantor does not grant the light; he is rather under an obligation not to obstruct it. One can only suppose that in the times of narrow streets, poor lighting and small windows, some way of protecting the access of light to houses in towns was necessary. Until 1848,[22] there was no way of providing that a negative covenant between freeholders could run with the land, and the only way in which a landowner could be protected was by regarding him as the owner of an easement. It seems, however, more natural to look upon that situation as one of covenant—one in which the neighbour is under an obligation not to build, rather than one in which he has granted the landowner a right 'not to have his light obstructed'. Nevertheless it is so treated historically. A similar situation arises in the case of an easement of support.[23] A further anomaly exists in the case of an easement to repair a fence. The general principle is that the servient owner is under no obligation to expend money on the maintenance of any property

---

[14] *Copeland v Greenhalf* [1952] Ch 488, p. 626, below; *London & Blenheim Estates Ltd v Ladbroke Retail Parks Ltd* [1992] 1 WLR 1278, p. 629, below; *Batchelor v Marlow* [2003] 1 WLR 764, p. 630, below; *Moncrieff v Jamieson* [2007] 1 WLR 2620, p. 631, below.

[15] *Re Webb's Lease* [1951] Ch 808, p. 682, below.

[16] *Brocklebank v Thompson* [1903] 2 Ch 344.

[17] *Mercer v Denne* [1905] 2 Ch 538; *Alfred F Beckett Ltd v Lyons* [1967] Ch 449.

[18] *Hunt v Peake* (1860) John 705; *Backhouse v Bonomi* (1861) 9 HL Cas 503; *Midland Bank plc v Bardgrove Property Service Ltd* [1991] 2 EGLR 283; *Holbeck Hall Hotel Ltd v Scarborough Borough Council* [2000] QB 836; [2001] Conv 177 (M. P. Thompson).

[19] *Dalton v Angus* (1881) 6 App Cas 740; *Ray v Fairwa Motors (Barnstaple) Ltd* (1968) 20 P & CR 261.

[20] *ER Ives Investments Ltd v High* [1967] 2 QB 379, p. 1074, below; *Soames-Forsythe Properties Ltd v Tesco Stores Ltd* [1991] EGCS 22 ('full and free right of way on foot only' from supermarket at St Ouen's Centre, Worsley, Manchester, to car park held to include right for customers to use a supermarket trolley on it; a right also arose by estoppel conferring on Tesco a right in the nature of an easement of stacking trolleys on the walkway).

[21] See p. 728, below. Cf. *Hunter v Canary Wharf Ltd* [1997] AC 655 at 708, p. 643, below (no easement for reception of television waves from distant transmitter).

[22] *Tulk v Moxhay* (1848) 2 Ph 774, p. 754, below.

[23] *Dalton v Angus*, n. 19, above.

over which an easement is exercised.²⁴ The dominant owner may enter to effect the necessary repairs.²⁵ Thus the easement of fencing is unusual in that the servient owner is under a duty to take positive steps to maintain the fence, including the expenditure of money.²⁶ There may also be cases where the parties have expressly or impliedly agreed that the servient owner shall bear the burden; as where a local authority, which owned a high-rise block of flats, let them to tenants. Easements of access over the common parts of the building retained by the local authority were implied in favour of the tenants (the dominant owners). And the authority was held liable, on an implied term of the contract, to maintain those parts.²⁷

While the essential characteristics of an easement are reasonably clear, and no right which fails to comply with them can exist as an easement, it is not possible to say that the law will recognise as an easement every right that does comply. An easement can be described rather than defined, and lists of those judicially recognised are collected in the books.²⁸ New ones may arise: 'The category of servitudes and easements must alter and expand with the changes that take place in the circumstances of mankind.'²⁹ Whether or not a new right, complying with the accepted requirements of an easement, will be judicially recognised or not can be difficult to forecast, although the past cases serve as a guide to how the courts would react to claims to new easements.³⁰ Inevitably the cases in this section are a random selection.

²⁴ See *Holden v White* [1982] QB 679 (servient owner owed no duty of care at common law to milkman injured by disintegrating manhole cover on private footpath giving access to terraced house, nor under Occupiers' Liability Act 1957. See now Occupiers' Liability Act 1984, in effect reversing the decision: *Vodden v Gayton* [2001] PIQR P4); cf. *McGeown v Northern Ireland Housing Executive* [1995] 1 AC 233 (public right of way); Gale, paras 1.78–1.85.

²⁵ There is no *general* right. For a statutory right, see Access to Neighbouring Land Act 1992, p. 650, below.

²⁶ *Lawrence v Jenkins* (1873) LR 8 QB 274 (a 'spurious easement'); *Jones v Price* [1965] 2 QB 618; *Crow v Wood* [1971] 1 QB 77, p. 645 below; other rights cannot be easements if they involve expenditure by the servient owner: *Regis Property Co Ltd v Redman* [1956] 2 QB 612 (covenant to supply hot water held not to be an easement so as to pass under LPA 1925, s. 62 being a personal contract to perform services); *Rance v Elvin* (1983) 49 P & CR 65 (right to metered water supply paid for by servient owner held not to be an easement, even though dominant owner agreed to reimburse water charges); (1985) 50 P & CR 9 (CA held that the right was to the uninterrupted passage of water, and not to its supply; it was therefore an easement, and the servient owner was liable in quasi-contract to reimburse); [1985] CLJ 458 (A. J. Waite); *Palmer v Bowman* [2000] 1 WLR 842 (no easement of right by owner of higher land to have water pass by natural flow onto neighbouring lower land); (2000) 150 NLJ 311 (H. W. Wilkinson); [2000] All ER Rev 237 (P. J. Clarke); *Coopind (UK) Ltd v Walton Commercial Group Ltd* [1989] 1 EGLR 241 ('a right to receive a supply of gas' held to extend to right to lay new gas main under service roads retained by lessors); *Duffy v Lamb* (1998) 75 P & CR 364 (right to uninterrupted passage of electricity held to be easement).

²⁷ *Liverpool City Council v Irwin* [1977] AC 239; *King v South Northamptonshire District Council* [1992] 1 EGLR 53; cf. *Duke of Westminster v Guild* [1985] QB 688 (tenant qua dominant owner of right of drainage held to be liable for repairs). See also *Stokes v Mixconcrete (Holdings) Ltd* (1978) 38 P & CR 488.

²⁸ C & B, pp. 592–595; M & W, chap. 20; MM, pp. 443–449; Gale, paras 1.73–1.77.

²⁹ *Dyce v Hay* (1852) 1 Macq 305 at 312–313, per Lord St Leonards.

³⁰ *A-G of Southern Nigeria v John Holt & Co (Liverpool) Ltd* [1915] AC 599; *Miller v Emcer Products Ltd* [1956] Ch 304; (1956) 72 LQR 172 (R.E.M.); *Phipps v Pears* [1965] 1 QB 76; (1964) 80 LQR 318 (R.E.M.), p. 641, below; *Dowty Boulton Paul Ltd v Wolverhampton Corpn (No 2)* [1976] Ch 13.

B. CAPABILITY OF EXISTENCE AS EASEMENT

Hill v Tupper
(1863) 2 H & C 121, 159 ER 51 (Exch, **Pollock CB, Martin** and **Bramwell BB**)

The Company of Proprietors of the Basingstoke Canal Navigation leased premises on the bank of the canal to the plaintiff, a boat proprietor. The lease to the plaintiff purported to give to him, inter alia, 'the sole and exclusive right or liberty to put or use boats on the said canal, and let the same for hire for the purpose of pleasure only'. It was alleged that the defendant, the landlord of an inn adjoining the canal, had interfered with the plaintiff's right by putting boats on the canal. The judge refused an application to nonsuit the plaintiff. A rule *nisi* was obtained to enter a nonsuit.

Held. Rule made absolute. The plaintiff was a licensee only and was not entitled to an easement.

Pollock CB: We are all of opinion that the rule must be absolute to enter the verdict for the defendant on the second plea. After the very full argument which has taken place, I do not think it necessary to assign any other reason for our decision, than that the case of *Ackroyd v Smith* (1850) 10 CB 164 expressly decided that it is not competent to create rights unconnected with the use and enjoyment of land, and annex them to it so as to constitute a property in the grantee. This grant merely operates as a licence or covenant on the part of the grantors, and is binding on them as between themselves and the grantee, but gives him no right of action in his own name for any infringement of the supposed exclusive right. It is argued that, as the owner of an estate may grant a right to cut turves, or to fish or hunt, there is no reason why he may not grant such a right as that now claimed by the plaintiff. The answer is, that the law will not allow it. So the law will not permit the owner of an estate to grant it alternately to his heirs male and heirs female. A new species of incorporeal hereditament cannot be created at the will and pleasure of the owner of property, but he must be content to accept the estate and the right to dispose of it subject to the law as settled by decisions or controlled by act of parliament. A grantor may bind himself by covenant to allow any right he pleases over this property, but he cannot annex to it a new incident, so as to enable the grantee to sue in his own name for an infringement of such a limited right as that now claimed.

(i) Essential characteristics

Re Ellenborough Park
[1956] Ch 131 (ChD, **Danckwerts J** and CA, **Evershed MR, Birkett** and **Romer LJJ**)

In 1855 the White Cross Estate, which included Ellenborough Park, was being developed for building purposes. Purchasers of the several plots surrounding the Park were given in their conveyances certain rights of user over the Park; and for the purposes of the present action it was agreed to take as typical of all these conveyances, one dated 1864 conveying a plot to John Porter. The material part of this conveyance was as follows: 'Together with ... and also full enjoyment at all times hereafter in common with the other persons to whom such easements may be granted of the pleasure ground set out and made in front of the said plot of land…in the centre of the square called Ellenborough Park…but subject to the payment of a fair and just proportion of the costs charges and expenses of keeping in good order and condition the said pleasure ground.' John Porter covenanted to pay a fair proportion of the expenses of the upkeep of the Park, and the vendors covenanted to keep the Park as an ornamental pleasure ground. The Park became vested in the plaintiffs on statutory trusts for sale.

During the Second World War, the Park was requisitioned, and subsequently the War Office paid sums of money in respect of compensation rental and on account of dilapidations. Various questions arose, concerning the rights of the original purchasers and their successors in title to use the Park, and concerning the allocation of compensation money from the War Office. The question was whether the surrounding owners had lost a legal right, for which they would be entitled to be compensated.

Held (affirming Danckwerts J). The right of enjoyment was an easement appurtenant to the plots bought by the original purchasers, and the plaintiffs were therefore entitled to compensation.

Evershed MR: The substantial question in the case, which we have briefly indicated, is one of considerable interest and importance. It is clear from our brief recital of the facts that, if the house owners are now entitled to an enforceable right in respect of the use and enjoyment of Ellenborough Park, that right must have the character and quality of an easement as understood by, and known to, our law. It has, therefore, been necessary for us to consider carefully the qualities and characteristics of easements, and, for such purpose, to look back into the history of that category of incorporeal rights in the development of English real property law. It may be fairly assumed that, in the case of *Duncan v Louch* (1845) 6 QB 904, the Court of Queen's Bench in the year 1845, and particularly Lord Denman CJ, who delivered the first judgment in the court, was of opinion that such a right as the respondent claims was capable of fulfilling the qualifying conditions of an easement. And Buckley J, in the case in 1904 of *Keith v Twentieth Century Club Ltd* (1904) 73 LJ Ch 545, answered certain questions which Byrne J had ordered to be set down to be argued before the court, themselves depending upon the assumption that such a right could exist in law. On the other hand, Farwell J, a judge peculiarly experienced and learned in real property law, on two occasions, namely, in 1903 in the case of *International Tea Stores Co v Hobbs* [1903] 2 Ch 165 at 172, and in 1905 in *A-G v Antrobus* [1905] 2 Ch 188 at 198, used language appearing to treat as axiomatic the proposition, that a right, which should properly be described as a jus spatiandi,[31] was a right excluded by English law, as by Roman law, from the company of servitudes.

The four cases which we have mentioned must be considered hereafter at greater length. But it can be said at once that, with the possible exception of the first, none of them constitutes or involves a direct decision upon the question now before us: and although the existence of gardens surrounded by houses, the owners or occupiers of which enjoy in practice the amenities of the gardens, is a well-known feature of town development throughout the country, no other

---

[31] The right to wander at large over the servient tenement.

case appears to have come before the courts in which the validity of the rights in fact enjoyed in the gardens has ever been tested....[32]

For the purposes of the argument before us, Mr Cross and Mr Goff [counsel for each side] were content to adopt, as correct, the four characteristics formulated in Dr Cheshire's *Modern Real Property* 7th edn, pp. 465[33] et seq. They are (1) there must be a dominant and a servient tenement: (2) an easement must 'accommodate' the dominant tenement: (3) dominant and servient owners must be different persons,[34] and (4) a right over land cannot amount to an easement, unless it is capable of forming the subject-matter of a grant....

We pass, accordingly, to a consideration of the first of Dr Cheshire's conditions—that of the accommodation of the alleged dominant tenements by the rights as we have interpreted them. For it was one of the main submissions by Mr Cross on behalf of the appellant that the right of full enjoyment of the park, granted to the purchaser by the conveyance of 23 December 1864, was insufficiently connected with the enjoyment of the property conveyed, in that it did not subserve some use which was to be made of that property; and that such a right accordingly could not exist in law as an easement. In this part of this argument Mr Cross was invoking a principle which is, in our judgment, of unchallengeable authority, expounded, in somewhat varying language, in many judicial utterances, of which the judgments in *Ackroyd v Smith* (1850) 10 CB 164 are, perhaps, most commonly cited.[35] We think it unnecessary to review the authorities in which the principle has been applied; for the effect of the decisions is stated with accuracy in Dr Cheshire's *Modern Real Property* 7th edn, p. 457. After pointing out that 'one of the fundamental principles concerning easements is that they must be not only appurtenant to a dominant tenement, but also connected with the normal enjoyment of the dominant tenement' and referring to certain citations in support of that proposition the author proceeded: 'We may expand the statement of the principle thus: a right enjoyed by one over the land of another does not possess the status of an easement unless it accommodates and serves the dominant tenement, and is reasonably necessary for the better enjoyment of that tenement, for if it has no necessary connexion therewith, although it confers an advantage upon the owner and renders his ownership of the land more valuable, it is not an easement at all, but a mere contractual right personal to and only enforceable between the two contracting parties.'

His Lordship rejected the argument, based on an observation of Willes J in *Bailey v Stephens* (1862) 12 CB NS 91 to the effect that a right could only exist as an easement if it could benefit only the claimant to the easement and no other person, and continued:

---

[32] Lord Evershed referred to Holdsworth, *Historical Introduction to Land Law* (1927), p. 265.

[33] 17th edn, pp. 587 et seq.

[34] This is not strictly true. A tenant may grant an easement, for a period not exceeding that of his lease, in favour of another tenant of the same landlord; and an easement of light may be so acquired by prescription: *Morgan v Fear* [1907] AC 425; (1949) 13 Conv (NS) 104 (A. K. R. Kiralfy); (1958) 74 LQR 82 (V. T. H. Delany); M & W, para. 27.009.

[35] *Weekly v Wildman* (1698) 1 Ld Raym 405, per Treby CJ; *London & Blenheim Estates Ltd v Ladbroke Retail Parks Ltd* [1994] 1 WLR 31 (right intended as easement and attached to servient tenement before dominant tenement identified held not to be an easement); *Voice v Bell* (1993) 68 P & CR 441. In the USA both easements and profits may be *in gross*. See American Law Institute *Restatement of the Law, Third, Property (Servitudes)* (2000), and generally (1980) 96 LQR 557 (M. F. Sturley), criticising the rule; (1982) 98 LQR at p. 305 (S. Gardner); *Jobson v Record* (1997) 74 P & CR D16 ('a right of way granted for the benefit of a defined area of land may not be used in substance for accommodating another area of land' per Morritt LJ).

Can it be said, then, of the right of full enjoyment of the park in question, which was granted by the conveyance of 23 December 1864, and which, for reasons already given, was, in our view, intended to be annexed to the property conveyed to Mr Porter, that it accommodated and served that property? It is clear that the right did, in some degree, enhance the value of the property, and this consideration cannot be dismissed as wholly irrelevant. It is, of course, a point to be noted, but we agree with Mr Cross's submission that it is in no way decisive of the problem; it is not sufficient to show that the right increased the value of the property conveyed, unless it is also shown that it was connected with the normal enjoyment of that property. It appears to us that the question whether or not this connexion exists is primarily one of fact, and depends largely on the nature of the alleged dominant tenement and the nature of the right granted. As to the former, it was in the contemplation of the parties to the conveyance of 1864 that the property conveyed should be used for residential and not commercial purposes.... As to the nature of the right granted, the conveyance of 1864 shows that the park was to be kept and maintained as a pleasure ground or ornamental garden.... On these facts Mr Cross submitted that the requisite connexion between the right to use the park and the normal enjoyment of the houses which were built around it or near it had not been established. He likened the position to a right granted to the purchaser of a house to use the Zoological Gardens free of charge or to attend Lord's Cricket Ground without payment. Such a right would undoubtedly, he said, increase the value of the property conveyed but could not run with it at law as an easement, because there was no sufficient nexus between the enjoyment of the right and the use of the house. It is probably true, we think, that in neither of Mr Cross's illustrations would the supposed right constitute an easement, for it would be wholly extraneous to, and independent of, the use of a house as a house, namely, as a place in which the householder and his family live and make their home; and it is for this reason that the analogy which Mr Cross sought to establish between his illustrations and the present case cannot, in our opinion, be supported. A much closer analogy, as it seems to us, is the case of a man selling the freehold of part of his house and granting to the purchaser, his heirs and assigns, the right, appurtenant to such part, to use the garden in common with the vendor and his assigns. In such a case, the test of connexion, or accommodation, would be amply satisfied; for just as the use of a garden undoubtedly enhances, and is connected with, the normal enjoyment of the house to which it belongs, so also would the right granted, in the case supposed, be closely connected with the use and enjoyment of the part of the premises sold. Such, we think, is in substance the position in the present case. The park became a communal garden for the benefit and enjoyment of those whose houses adjoined it or were in its close proximity. Its flower beds, lawns and walks were calculated to afford all the amenities which it is the purpose of the garden of a house to provide; and, apart from the fact that these amenities extended to a number of householders, instead of being confined to one (which on this aspect of the case is immaterial), we can see no difference in principle between Ellenborough Park and a garden in the ordinary signification of that word. It is the collective garden of the neighbouring houses, to whose use it was dedicated by the owners of the estate and as such amply satisfied, in our judgment, the requirement of connexion with the dominant tenements to which it is appurtenant. The result is not affected by the circumstance that the right to the park is in this case enjoyed by some few houses which are not immediately fronting on the park. The test for present purposes, no doubt, is that the park should constitute in a real and intelligible sense the garden (albeit the communal garden) of the houses to which its enjoyment is annexed. But we think that the test is satisfied as regards these few neighbouring, though not adjacent, houses. We think that the extension of the right of enjoyment to these few houses does not negative the presence of the necessary 'nexus' between the subject-matter enjoyed and the premises to which the enjoyment is expressed to belong.[36]

Mr Cross referred us to, and to some extent relied upon, *Hill v Tupper*, but in our opinion there is nothing in that case contrary to the view which we have expressed. In that case, the owner of land adjoining a canal was granted the exclusive right to let boats out for hire on the canal. He did so and then sought to restrain a similar activity by a neighbouring landowner. He sought to establish that his grant constituted an easement but failed. Pollock CB said in his judgment: 'It is not competent to create rights unconnected with the use and enjoyment of land, and annex them to it so as to constitute a property in the grantee.' It is clear that what the plaintiff was trying to do was to set up, under the guise of an easement, a monopoly which had no normal connexion with the ordinary use of his land, but which was merely an independent business enterprise. So far from the right claimed subserving or accommodating the land, the land was but a convenient incident to the exercise of the right....

For the reasons which we have stated, we are unable to accept the contention that the right to the full enjoyment of Ellenborough Park fails in limine to qualify as a legal easement for want of the necessary connexion between its enjoyment and the use of the properties comprised in the conveyance of 1864, and in other relevant conveyances.

We turn next to Dr Cheshire's fourth condition for an easement—that the right must be capable of forming the subject-matter of a grant. As we have earlier stated, satisfaction of the condition in the present case depends on a consideration of the questions whether the right conferred is too wide and vague, whether it is inconsistent with the proprietorship or possession of the alleged servient owners, and whether it is a mere right of recreation without utility or benefit.

To the first of these questions the interpretation which we have given to the typical deed provides, in our judgment, the answer; for we have construed the right conferred as being both well defined and commonly understood. In these essential respects the right may be said to be distinct from the indefinite and unregulated privilege which, we think, would ordinarily be understood by the Latin term 'jus spatiandi', a privilege of wandering at will over all and every part of another's field or park, and which, though easily intelligible as the subject-matter of a personal licence, is something substantially different from the subject-matter of the grant in question, namely, the provision for a limited number of houses in a uniform crescent of one single large but private garden.

Our interpretation of the deed also provides, we think, the answer to the second question; for the right conferred no more amounts to a joint occupation of the park with its owners, no more excludes the proprietorship or possession of the latter, than a right of way granted through a passage, or than the use by the public of the gardens of Lincoln's Inn Fields (to take one of our former examples) amount to joint occupation of that garden with the London County Council, or involve an inconsistency with the possession or proprietorship of the council as lessees.

His Lordship referred to *Copeland v Greenhalf* [1952] Ch 488, p. 626, below, discussed the nature of the right claimed in the present case and continued:

As appears from what has been stated earlier, the right to the full enjoyment of Ellenborough Park, which was granted by the 1864 and other relevant conveyances, was, in substance, no more than a right to use the park as a garden in the way in which gardens are commonly used. In a sense, no doubt, such a right includes something of a jus spatiandi, inasmuch as it involves

---

[36] *Todrick v Western National Omnibus Co Ltd* [1934] Ch 561; *Birmingham, Dudley and District Banking Co v Ross* (1888) 38 ChD 295 at 314; *Pugh v Savage* [1970] 2 QB 373 (intervening land between dominant and servient tenements).

the principle of wandering at will round each part of the garden, except of course, such parts as comprise flower beds, or are laid out for some other purpose, which renders walking impossible or unsuitable. We doubt, nevertheless, whether the right to use and enjoy a garden in this manner can with accuracy be said to constitute a mere jus spatiandi. Wandering at large is of the essence of such a right and constitutes the main purpose for which it exists. A private garden, on the other hand, is an attribute of the ordinary enjoyment of the residence to which it is attached, and the right of wandering in it is but one method of enjoying it. On the assumption, however, that the right now in question does constitute a jus spatiandi, or that it is analogous thereto, it becomes necessary to consider whether the right, which is in question in these proceedings, is, for that reason, incapable of ranking in law as an easement.

His Lordship referred to dicta of Farwell J in *International Tea Stores Co v Hobbs* [1903] 2 Ch 165 at 171, and in *A-G v Antrobus* [1905] 2 Ch 188 at 198, 199, 205, which spoke of a jus spatiandi as being a right 'not known to our law'. These statements were obiter and 'cannot be regarded as authoritative'. His Lordship continued:

Duncan v Louch (1845) 6 QB 904, on the other hand, decided more than 100 years ago but not, as we have observed, quoted to Farwell J in either of the two cases which we have cited, is authoritative in favour of the recognition by our law as an easement of a right closely comparable to that now in question which, if it involves in some sense a jus spatiandi, is nevertheless properly annexed and appurtenant to a defined hereditament....

We agree with Danckwerts J in regarding *Duncan v Louch* as being a direct authority in the defendant's favour. It has never, so far as we are aware, been since questioned, and we think it should, in the present case, be followed.

For the reasons which we have stated, Danckwerts J came, in our judgment, to a right conclusion in this case and, accordingly, the appeal must be dismissed.

In **Jackson v Mulvaney** [2003] 1 WLR 360[37] the question was whether a right in common with the owners of the freehold properties surrounding the freehold land shown edged in blue on the plan ('the blue land') to use the blue land as their communal garden was capable of existing as an easement and/or could be acquired by prescription or implied grant. In holding that it could, LATHAM LJ said at 368:

23 As to the fourth characteristic, the Court of Appeal in *Re Ellenborough Park* held that an easement to use land as a communal garden was capable of forming the subject matter of a grant. However, there is no doubt that there is a real difference between a case in which the easement claimed is said to have been the subject matter of an express grant, and one which is said to arise by reason of prescription or under section 62 of the Law of Property Act 1925. In the former case, the issue is simply one of construction of the grant. And the court will undoubtedly lean in favour of the creation of an easement if the intention of the parties was clearly to that end. In the latter case, the court has the more difficult task of assessing the evidence as to alleged use in order to determine whether the claimed right has been established. But if it is clear from that evidence that use has been made of the land for the requisite period which is capable of amounting to an easement, it seems to me that a court should not be deflected from declaring the existence of an easement which can sensibly be formulated by the fact that, of necessity, its parameters may not be so clearly defined as they could be in a deed.

---

[37] [2003] CLJ 571 (M. P. Thompson); Gale, para. 1.69.

24 In my judgment, the findings of fact by the district judge are conclusive of the matter in the claimant's favour. Even though the [servient owners] had not themselves created or maintained the communal garden, the blue land had been used as such ever since the sale of the properties. The fact that they had been content to allow the dominant owners over the years to determine the layout of the garden and to have maintained it themselves does not seem to me to derogate from the conclusion that they have been prepared to set aside this land for the use of the dominant owners as a communal garden. As the district judge himself recognised, this was a potential advantage to the [servient owners] and their predecessors in title at the time that the properties were originally sold.

25 I am therefore satisfied that the facts found by the district judge were sufficient to justify both his and the circuit judge's conclusions that the claimant was entitled to a right to use the blue land as a communal garden along with the other dominant owners.

(ii) Business on dominant tenement

An easement may exist for the purpose of a business carried on on the dominant tenement.

In **Moody v Steggles** (1879) 12 Ch D 261, Harriet Moody, the plaintiff, owned the Grosvenor Arms in Newmarket, which was set back from the High Street down a narrow yard. The defendants' house projected in front of the Grosvenor Arms, making it invisible from the High Street. For some forty years a sign-board advertising the Grosvenor Arms had been affixed to the defendants' house. In granting an injunction to restrain the removal of the sign-board by the defendants, FRY J said at 266:

The next point taken on behalf of the Defendants is this: It is said that the easement in question relates, not to the tenement, but to the business of the occupant of the tenement, and that therefore I cannot tie the easement to the house. It appears to me that the argument is of too refined a nature to prevail, and for this reason, that the house can only be used by an occupant, and that the occupant only uses the house for the business which he pursues, and therefore in some manner (direct or indirect) an easement is more or less connected with the mode in which the occupant of the house uses it.[38]

(iii) Exclusive or joint user[39]

(a) General rule

Copeland v Greenhalf
[1952] Ch 488 (ChD, **Upjohn J**)

The plaintiff was the owner of an orchard and an adjoining house. Access to the orchard from the road was provided by a strip of land of varying width about 150 feet long.

---

[38] *Copeland v Greenhalf,* below; *Henry Ltd v M'Glade* [1926] NI 144 (stationary sandwich-man). See *Hill v Tupper* [1863] 2 H & C 121 at 175, p. 620, above. For a similar issue in relation to restrictive covenants, see *Newton Abbot Co-operative Society v Williamson & Treadgold* [1952] Ch 286, p. 799, below.

[39] Gale, paras 1.54–1.71.

The defendant was a wheelwright whose premises were across the road from the plaintiff's land. The defendant proved that for 50 years he and his father before him had to the plaintiff's knowledge used one side of the plaintiff's strip of land to store and repair vehicles in connection with his business as wheelwright; leaving always room for the plaintiff to have access to the orchard. He claimed a prescriptive right to do so. The plaintiff brought this action to restrain him.

Held. Such a right was not an easement, and the claim amounted to one for beneficial user of the land.

Upjohn J: Mr Horne [for the plaintiff]...says that there are two reasons why this cannot be a valid easement. First, he says that it is uncertain. He says that the court is not in a position to control the exercise of this easement. He relied on *Hill v Tupper* (1863) 2 H & C 121 [p. 620, above], and he referred to the well-known passage in the judgment of Pollock CB, which says: 'A new series of incorporeal hereditament cannot be created at the will and pleasure of the owner of property; but he must be content to accept the estate and the right to dispose of it subject to the law as settled by decisions or controlled by Act of Parliament. A grantor may bind himself by covenant to allow any right he pleases over his property, but he cannot annex to it a new incident, so as to enable the grantee to sue in his own name for an infringement of such a limited right as that now claimed.'

He pressed me, of course, very strongly with the well-known case of *Dyce v Hay* (1852) 1 Macq 305 in the House of Lords, in which the sidenote reads as follows: 'There can be no prescriptive right in the nature of a servitude or easement so large as to preclude the ordinary uses of property by the owner of the lands affected. *Semble,* that where a claim in the nature of a servitude or easement is incapable of judicial control and restriction it cannot be sustained by prescription. It does not follow the rights sustainable by grant are necessarily sustainable by prescription. The law of Scotland agrees with the law of England in holding that the right to village greens and playgrounds stands upon a principle of original dedication to the use of the public. Where new inventions come into use they may have the benefit of servitudes and easements, the law accommodating its practical operation to the varying circumstances of mankind.'...

He contended that there is nothing novel in the business of a wheelwright, but that it is an entirely novel suggestion that a wheelwright or anyone else carrying on trade can have such a right as this. He pointed out the great width of the right claimed: vehicles can be left there for an indefinite time, for years, if necessary; they can be left in a vague and undefined part of the strip, leaving an ill-defined gangway, as it has been called, for the owner of the strip to use in getting to his land. He further pointed out that the defendant is really doing much more than an ordinary wheelwright's business; that he is doing repairs to every form of modern type of vehicle, such as motor lorries, and that that also makes the claim really too uncertain to be enforceable.

Mr Horne's second point is this, that an easement must be for the benefit of the land, and not for a business carried on in connexion with the land....

I think that...the matter is concluded for me by the decision of Fry J in *Moody v Steggles* (1879) 12 ChD 261 [his Lordship quoted the extract from the judgment of Fry J set out at p. 626, above]...I also have in mind that the Judicial Committee in the *Nigerian* case [1915] AC 599 felt no difficulty in principle in holding that there might be an easement in connexion with a right to deposit trade goods.

cerned, I decide that it does not avail the plaintiff; but

holly outside any normal idea of an easement, that is, the right of the owner or the occupier of a dominant tenement over a servient tenement. This claim (to which no closely related authority has been referred to me) really amounts to a claim to a joint user of the land by the defendant. Practically, the defendant is claiming the whole beneficial user of the strip of land on the south-east side of the track there; he can leave as many or as few lorries there as he likes for as long as he likes; he may enter on it by himself, his servants and agents to do repair work thereon. In my judgment, that is not a claim which can be established as an easement. It is virtually a claim to possession of the servient tenement, if necessary to the exclusion of the owner; or, at any rate, to a joint user, and no authority has been cited to me which could justify the conclusion that a right of this wide and undefined nature can be the proper subject-matter of an easement. It seems to me that to succeed, this claim must amount to a successful claim of possession by reason of long adverse possession.[40] I say nothing, of course, as to the creation of such rights by deeds or by covenant; I am dealing solely with the question of a right arising by prescription.

In **Miller v Emcer Products Ltd** [1956] Ch 304[41] premises were demised to a tenant together with the right to use two lavatories on upper floors which were occupied by a third party. One question which arose was whether or not such a right could exist as an easement. As to this ROMER LJ, in a judgment with which Lord Evershed MR and Birkett LJ concurred, said at 316:

In my judgment the right had all the requisite characteristics of an easement. There is no doubt as to what were intended to be the dominant and servient tenements respectively, and the right was appurtenant to the former and calculated to enhance its beneficial use and enjoyment. It is true that during the times when the dominant owner exercised the right, the owner of the servient tenement would be excluded, but this in greater or less degree is a common feature of many easements (for example, rights of way) and does not amount to such an ouster of the servient owner's rights as was held by Upjohn J to be incompatible with a legal easement in *Copeland v Greenhalf* [1952] Ch 488 [p. 626, above].[42] No case precisely in point on this issue was brought to our attention, but the right to use a lavatory is not dissimilar, I think, to the right to use a neighbour's kitchen for washing, the validity of which as an easement was assumed without question in *Heywood v Mallalieu* (1883) 25 ChD 357. No objection can fairly be made based upon uncertainty, and it follows, in my judgment, that the right may properly be regarded as an easement which the lessors were professing to grant for a term of years; and such an easement would rank as an interest in or over land capable of being created at law by virtue of section 1(2) of the Law of Property Act 1925.

In **Grigsby v Melville** [1972] 1 WLR 1355[43] the plaintiff and the defendants were neighbours. The defendants claimed the right to store articles in a cellar beneath the

[40] (1968) 32 Con v (NS) 270 (M. J. Goodman).

[41] (1956) 72 LQR 172 (R.E.M.).

[42] In *Ward v Kirkland* [1967] Ch 194 at 223 a right to enter and maintain a wall was held to be an easement and not to amount to 'the possession or joint possession of part of the [servient] property'.

[43] Affd [1974] 1 WLR 80, when CA held that there was no evidence to support the claim to an easement, and declined to 'embark upon an analysis of the cases'; (1973) 37 Conv (NS) 60 (D. J. Hayton).

plaintiff's drawing room floor. BRIGHTMAN J, in rejecting the claim to an easement of storage, said at 1363:

There are, I think, two issues here: first, whether an easement of unlimited storage within a confined or defined space is capable of existing as a matter of law. Secondly, if so, whether such an easement was reserved in the present case.

His Lordship referred to *Copeland v Greenhalf* [1952] Ch 488, p. 626, above, and continued:

Mr Ainger countered by observing that *Copeland v Greenhalf* was inconsistent with *Wright v Macadam* [1949] 2 KB 744 [p. 665, below], an earlier decision of the Court of Appeal in which it was held that the right of a tenant to store domestic coal in a shed on the landlord's land could exist as an easement for the benefit of the demised premises. I am not convinced that there is any real inconsistency between the two cases. The point of the decision in *Copeland v Greenhalf* was that the right asserted amounted in effect to a claim to the whole beneficial user of the servient tenement and for that reason could not exist as a mere easement. The precise facts in *Wright v Macadam* in this respect are not wholly clear from the report and it is a little difficult to know whether the tenant had exclusive use of the coal shed or of any defined portion of it. To some extent a problem of this sort may be one of degree.

In the case before me, it is, I think, clear that the defendant's claim to an easement would give, to all practical intents and purposes, an exclusive right of user over the whole of the confined space representing the servient tenement. I think I would be at liberty, if necessary, to follow *Copeland v Greenhalf*. I doubt, however, whether I need express any concluded view on this aspect of the case.

His Lordship then held that an easement was not reserved in the present case.[44]

(b) Right to park a vehicle[45]

The question as to whether the right to park a vehicle on the servient tenement can be an easement has arisen in recent years. It has been examined at first instance and in the Court of Appeal,[46] although more recently the House of Lords has cast some doubt on the approach taken in the earlier cases.

In **London & Blenheim Estates Ltd v Ladbroke Retail Parks Ltd** [1992] 1 WLR 1278[47] JUDGE PAUL BAKER QC said at 1287:

The other unreported decision is that of Sir Robert Megarry V-C in *Newman v Jones* (unreported), 22 March 1982. One of the issues was whether the lessees of the flats in a block of

---

[44] *Hanina v Morland* (2000) 97 (47) LSG 41 (use of adjoining roof for entertaining, sunbathing and generally as an extension of living room held to be exclusive user and therefore no easement); *Jackson v Mulvaney* [2003] 1 WLR 360 at 365.

[45] Gale, paras 9.96–9.110.

[46] See also *Pointon York Group plc v Poulton* [2007] 1 P & CR 6 (where easement of parking is established, the right to occupy parking spaces could be 'premises' which were 'occupied' for the purposes of the business on the dominant tenement under Landlord and Tenant Act 1954, s. 23).

[47] Affd [1994] 1 WLR 31; [1994] CLJ 229 (S. Bridge); *Handel v St Stephens Close Ltd* [1994] 1 EGLR 70; (1994) 144 NLJ 579 (H. W. Wilkinson); [1996] 16 LS 51 (P. Luther).

14 flats were entitled to park their cars in the grounds of the block.... The importance of the case for present circumstances resides in the following dicta of Sir Robert Megarry V-C:

'In view of *Wright v Macadam* [1949] 2 KB 744 (which was not cited in *Copeland v Greenhalf* [1952] Ch 488) ... I feel no hesitation in holding that a right for a landowner to park a car anywhere in a defined area nearby is capable of existing as an easement.... An easement may take effect subject to the right of others with a like right, without any guarantee that there will be no competition. In any case, I cannot see why the mere risk of there being not enough space for all to park simultaneously should be a reason for denying that any rights at all exist, though doubtless the limited space available confines the right to one car per flat'—of course, referring to the particular flats in that case....

In the present case the right on its true construction is dependent on the continued existence of car parking facilities for other persons. That leaves the main point under this head, whether the right to park cars can exist at all as an easement. I would not regard it as a valid objection that charges are made, whether for the parking itself or for the general upkeep of the park. The essential question is one of degree. If the right granted in relation to the area over which it is to be exercisable is such that it would leave the servient owner without any reasonable use of his land, whether for parking or anything else, it could not be an easement though it might be some larger or different grant.[48] The rights sought in the present case do not appear to approach anywhere near that degree of invasion of the servient land. If that is so—and I emphasise that I have not gone into the facts—I would regard the right claimed as a valid easement.

In **Batchelor v Marlow** [2003] 1 WLR 764[49] the Court of Appeal considered that a right to park up to six cars on a strip of land on Mondays to Fridays between 8.30 a.m. and 6 p.m., where the land could accommodate only six cars at any one time, was incapable of being an easement. TUCKEY LJ said at 767:

8 [The trial judge] referred to the authorities and accepted that the question he had to answer was one of degree. This followed the approach adopted by Judge Paul Baker QC in *London and Blenheim Estates Ltd v Ladbroke Retail Parks Ltd* [1992] 1 WLR 1278, 1288 [above] who, after reviewing the earlier authorities on car parking, said:

'The essential question is one of degree. If the right granted in relation to the area over which it is to be exercisable is such that it would leave the servient owner without any reasonable use of his land, whether for parking or anything else, it could not be an easement though it might be some larger or different grant.'

9 It was common ground before us that that was the essential question in this case and that there was no authority which provided the answer to it.

15 ... Does an exclusive right to park six cars for 9½ hours every day of the working week leave the plaintiff without any reasonable use of his land, whether for parking or anything else?

16 Miss Williamson [counsel for the plaintiff] emphasised the fact that the right asserted is exclusive of all others, including the plaintiff. Car parking over the whole of the land is highly intrusive because no other use can be made of it when cars are parked on it. In practice it prevents the plaintiff from making any use of his land and makes his ownership of it illusory. Not

---

[48] For example, a lease, for which exclusion possession would be necessary.
[49] [2007] Conv 223 (A. Hill-Smith).

so, said Mr West [counsel for the defendants]. Mathematically the defendants only have use of the land for 47½ hours per week, whereas the plaintiff has 120½ hours. He suggested various uses which the plaintiff could make of the land. He could sell it to the defendants or charge them for using it outside business hours, if that is what they wanted. Outside those hours he could park on the land himself or charge others for doing so. He would be able to concrete over the surface of the land without interfering with the right.

17 I think these suggestions demonstrate the difficulties which Mr West faces. Sale to the defendants would amount to a recognition that the rights they asserted had given them in practice a beneficial interest and no doubt the price would reflect this fact. The plaintiff could of course park himself at night or the weekends but the commercial scope for getting others to pay for doing so must be very limited indeed. I cannot see how the plaintiff would benefit from concreting over the land, although this would certainly enhance the defendants' right.

18 If one asks the simple question: 'Would the plaintiff have any reasonable use of the land for parking?' the answer, I think, must be 'No'. He has no use at all during the whole of the time that parking space is likely to be needed. But if one asks the question whether the plaintiff has any reasonable use of the land for any other purpose, the answer is even clearer. His right to use his land is curtailed altogether for intermittent periods throughout the week. Such a restriction would, I think, make his ownership of the land illusory.

19 I therefore accept Miss Williamson's submissions on this aspect of the case. It follows that I do not think the right found to exist by the deputy judge was capable of being an easement...

Moncrieff v Jamieson[50]
[2007] 1 WLR 2620 (HL, **Lords Hope of Craighead, Scott of Foscote, Rodger of Earlsferry, Mance** and **Neuberger of Abbotsbury**)

The pursuer (i.e., plaintiff[51]) owned the land and a dwelling house on the foreshore at Sandsound on Shetland. There was no access for vehicles to the land, and in 1973 the defender's predecessor in title had granted the pursuer as a servitude[52] the right of access on foot and with vehicles over his land. The land over which this right of access was granted was wide enough for vehicles to turn and to park near to the boundary with the pursuer's land, and the pursuers parked vehicles there until in 1998 the defenders disputed their right to do so. The trial judge declared that the pursuers, as owners of the dominant tenement, were entitled to park vehicles on the defender's servient tenement in the exercise of rights accessory to the servitude right of vehicular

---

[50] [2008] Conv 244 (M. Haley); (2008) 158 NLJ 239 (A. Samuels); Gale, paras 1.68, 9.100–9.103; *Waterman v Boyle* [2009] 10 EG 111 (CS).

[51] This was an appeal from Scotland, where the terminology is 'pursuer' and 'defender' rather than 'plaintiff/claimant' and 'defendant'. For a Scottish perspective on the case, see (2008) 12 Edin LR (K. G. C. Reid).

[52] A *servitude* is in substance the same right of property in Scottish law as an easement in English law. The English law of easements and profits follows closely the Roman law of *servitudes*. Modern legal systems based on the civil law have retained the term 'servitude': e.g. French (*servitude*), Italian (*servitù*), Spanish (*servidumbre*). Servitude is a word that is occasionally adopted by English judges: e.g. *Dalton v Angus & Co* (1881) 6 App Cas 740 at 796, per Lord Selborne; but it is not admitted as a term of art in English law, where the term 'easement' was generally adopted in the common law: 'Our law seems to look at these rights from the stand-point of the person who enjoys them, not from that of the person who suffers by their exercise. They are not "servitudes", they are "easements", "profits", "commodities"': Pollock and Maitland, *History of English Law* (2nd edn), vol. ii, p. 145.

access. The question which fell for decision by the House of Lords was whether a ser-vitude right to park was capable of being constituted as ancillary to a servitude right of vehicular access.

Held. It was so capable.

Lord Hope of Craighead:

22 I doubt whether it is necessary for the purposes of this case to decide whether a right simply to park vehicles on someone else's land can be said to constitute a servitude in its own right, independently of a servitude right of way over that land by means of vehicles. So I would prefer to reserve my opinion on this point. While they did not seek to argue positively that such a servitude right could exist, the pursuers were unwilling to accept the converse proposition for which the defenders contended that it was not possible in the law of Scotland for there to be a servitude of parking. This point does indeed need to be addressed because, as Lord Neuberger of Abbotsbury points out, a right to park as an ancillary to a servitude of access would be diffi-cult to accept if a right to park as a servitude in its own right was in principle unacceptable. It is on the objection in principle, therefore, on which a decision certainly is required in this case, that I wish to concentrate.

Lord Scott of Foscote:

45 My Lords, this is an interesting case raising some very basic questions about the nature of easements/servitudes—and there seems to me no difference relevant to any issue that arises in this case between the common law in England and Wales relating to easements and the com-mon law in Scotland relating to servitudes.... The principle of civiliter, a Scottish law principle which regulates the manner in which a servitude may be exercised (see para. 95 of the opinion of Lord Rodger of Earlsferry) is, if I have understood the principle correctly, equally applicable, although not so named, under English law and requires the dominant owner, the owner entitled to exercise a servitudal right over the land of his neighbour, to exercise the right reasonably and without undue interference with the servient owner's enjoyment of his own land. The converse of this principle is that an interference by the servient owner with the dominant owner's exercise of the servitude will not be an actionable interference unless it prevents the dominant owner from making a reasonable use of the servitude. Thus, for example, the erection by the servient owner of a building that encroached by, say, one foot on to a ten-foot wide domestic driveway would not constitute an actionable interference with a right of way over the driveway: see *Pettey v Parsons* [1914] 2 Ch 653 and *Celsteel Ltd v Alton House Holdings Ltd* [1985] 1 WLR 204. These principles are well exemplified by the English case of *Saint v Jenner* [1973] Ch 275, where a dominant owner had been exercising his vehicular right of way over a domestic drive by driving at excessive speeds. This unreasonable use, a use not consistent with the principle of civiliter, entitled the servient owner to erect speed bumps along the drive but did not justify the erection of speed bumps of such severity that a motor car moving at, say, ten to 15 mph would be unable to cross the bumps without the bumps striking the car's undercarriage. So the servient owner was held to be entitled to erect speed bumps but was required to reduce slightly the severity of the bumps he had erected. As in *Saint v Jenner,* both the manner of exercise by the pursuers of their rights over the servient land and the steps that could lawfully be taken by the defenders that might appear to interfere with those rights are subject to the principle of civiliter, a principle that, as it seems to me, limits the pursuers' use of the servient land to a reasonable use but enables the defenders, subject only to an obligation not to interfere with that reasonable use, to make whatever use they wish of their servient land.

47 It is convenient to start with the question whether a servitudal right to park appurtenant to some identifiable dominant land, i.e. a right in rem and not simply a contractual right, is recognised by law. In my opinion there should be no doubt that it is and, if there is any such doubt, that doubt should be now dispelled. I can see no reason in principle, subject to a few qualifications, why any right of limited use of the land of a neighbour that is of its nature of benefit to the dominant land and its owners from time to time should not be capable of being created as a servitudal right in rem appurtenant to the dominant land: see *Gale on Easements*, 17th edn (2002), para. 1–35.[53] An essential qualification of the above stated proposition, a qualification that I would derive from the all-important civiliter principle, is that the right must be such that a reasonable use thereof by the owner of the dominant land would not be inconsistent with the beneficial ownership of the servient land by the servient owner. I must later examine the so-called 'ouster' principle, the principle which, it is said, prevents the creation of a servitude if the servitude contended for would prevent any reasonable use being made of the servient land, and some of the authorities relating to that principle. To the extent, however, that the 'ouster' principle is asserting that a servitude must not be inconsistent with the continued beneficial ownership of the servient land by the servient owner, I would unreservedly accept it. If, for example, the nature of the purported servitude were to place the dominant owner in such occupation of the servient land as to bar the servient owner from possession or control of the land I would find it very difficult to accept that the right could constitute a servitude. An express grant of such a right might be construed as a grant of the fee simple (see per Lopes LJ in *Reilly v Booth* (1890) 44 Ch D 12, 26) or might be construed as the grant of a contractual licence, but I do not as at present advised see how it could be the grant of a servitude. A second necessary qualification to the proposition aforestated would be that the grant of a right that required some positive action to be undertaken by the owner of the servient land in order to enable the right to be enjoyed by the grantee could not, in my opinion, be a servitude. Thus the grant of a right of way over a driveway cannot place on the servient owner the obligation to keep the driveway in repair: see *Jones v Pritchard* [1908] 1 Ch 630, 637. The dominant owner would be entitled, although not obliged, as a right ancillary to his right of way to do such repairs to the driveway as were necessary or desirable. On the other hand I doubt whether the grant of a right to use a neighbour's swimming pool could ever qualify as a servitude. The grantor, the swimming pool owner, would be under no obligation to keep the pool full of water and the grantee would be in no position to fill it if the grantor chose not to do so. The right to use the pool would be no more than an in personam contractual right at best. There may be other qualifications than the two I have mentioned but I can think of none that could oppose the recognition as an acceptable servitude of a right to park in convenient proximity to the dominant land....

54 It has been argued that the rights of parking claimed by the pursuers in respect of the pink land [a small portion of land, marked in pink on the plans before the court, identified as most suitable for car parking] deprive the defenders of any reasonable use of that land, are therefore inconsistent with their ownership of the pink land and should not be recognised as servitudal rights in rem that can bind them and their successors in title. This is the so-called 'ouster' principle to which I have already referred. There are conflicting decisions and dicta regarding the 'ouster' principle. In *Dyce v Hay* 1 Macq 305 a prescriptive right for the public at large to use a strip of land for the purpose of recreation was claimed. The case was a Scottish one that reached this House where Lord St Leonards LC said that the right claimed was one that 'cannot

---

[53] See now Gale (18th edn, 2008), para. 1.36.

be maintained' and 'ought not to be maintained'. The sidenote to the report records that 'There can be no prescriptive right in the nature of a servitude or easement so large as to preclude the ordinary uses of property by the owner of the lands affected'. However, the right claimed was a public right not a servitude. But in any event, in my opinion, the proposition stated by the sidenote is unhelpful. Every servitude or easement will bar some ordinary use of the servient land. For example, a right of way prevents all manner of ordinary uses of the land over which the road passes. The servient owner cannot plough up the road. He cannot grow cabbages on it or use it for basketball practice. A viaduct carrying water across the servient land to the dominant land will prevent the same things. Every servitude prevents any use of the servient land, whether ordinary or otherwise, that would interfere with the reasonable exercise of the servitude. There will always be some such use that is prevented. Bearing in mind that any servitude that can be granted can be acquired by prescription and that *Dyce v Hay* was a case about public rights, not about private law servitudes, the proposition as stated in the sidenote tells us nothing about the essential nature of servitudes. In *Attorney-General of Southern Nigeria v John Holt & Co (Liverpool) Ltd* [1915] AC 599, a case in which the right to use servient land for the purpose of storage was claimed, Lord Shaw of Dunfermline, giving the judgment of the Privy Council, said, at p. 617, that: 'there is nothing in the purposes for which the easement is claimed inconsistent in principle with a right of easement as such.'

55 In *Wright v Macadam* [1949] 2 KB 744 [p. 665, below], the Court of Appeal had to consider whether the right to use a coal shed could exist as an easement and held that it could: see per Jenkins LJ, at p. 752. It has been suggested that the case may have turned on whether the claimant had sole use of the coal shed, but it is difficult to see any difference in principle between a case in which the dominant owner has sole use of a patch of ground for storage purposes, e g a coal shed, and a case in which the dominant owner is the only user of a strip of road for access purposes or of a viaduct for the passage of water. Sole user, as a concept, is quite different from, and fundamentally inferior to, exclusive possession. Sole use of a coal shed for the storage of coal does not prevent the servient owner from using the shed for any purposes of his own that do not interfere with the dominant owner's reasonable use for the storage of coal. The dominant owner entitled to a servitude of way or for the passage of water along a viaduct does not have possession of the land over which the road or the viaduct passes. If the coal shed door had been locked with only the dominant owner possessing a key and entry by the servient owner barred, so that the dominant owner would have been in possession and control of the shed, I would have regarded it as arguable that the right granted was inconsistent with the servient owner's ownership and inconsistent with the nature of a servitude or an easement. But sole use for a limited purpose is not, in my opinion, inconsistent with the servient owner's retention of possession and control or inconsistent with the nature of an easement. This conclusion is supported by Lord Evershed MR's remarks in *In Re Ellenborough Park* [1956] Ch 131, 176 where the issue was whether the right to use a communal garden could take effect as an easement. He said that:

> 'the right conferred no more amounts to a joint occupation of the park with its owners, no more excludes the proprietorship or possession of the latter, than a right of way granted through a passage, or than the use by the public of the gardens of Lincoln's Inn Fields ... amount to joint occupation of that garden with the London County Council, or involve an inconsistency with the possession or proprietorship of the council as lessees.'

56 *Copeland v Greenhalf* [1952] Ch 488 [p. 626, above], a case that goes the other way, was a case in which a prescriptive easement to use a strip of land by the side of a private roadway for

depositing vehicles and for other purposes connected with a wheelwright's business had been claimed. Upjohn J, at p. 498, rejected the claim on the ground that:

'Practically, the defendant is claiming the whole beneficial user of the strip of land... It is virtually a claim to possession of the servient tenement, if necessary to the exclusion of the owner...'

There may be arguments as to whether the facts of the case justified those remarks but, for my part, I would accept that if they did Upjohn J was right to reject the easement claim and to require the defendant, if he was to succeed in resisting the plaintiff's claim to remove him from the land, to establish a title by adverse possession.

57 It has often been commented that *Wright v Macadam* was not cited to Upjohn J and the possible inconsistency between the two cases was addressed by Judge Paul Baker QC in *London & Blenheim Estates Ltd v Ladbroke Retail Parks Ltd* [1992] 1 WLR 1278 [above, p. 629] where a right of parking had been claimed. He commented, at p. 1286, that the question whether the right to park that had been claimed was consistent with the nature of an easement was one of degree: 'A small coal shed in a large property is one thing. The exclusive use of a large part of the alleged servient tenement is another.' I think, with respect, that this attempt to reconcile the two authorities was addressing the wrong point. The servient land in relation to a servitude or easement is surely the land over which the servitude or easement is enjoyed, not the totality of the surrounding land of which the servient owner happens to be the owner. If there is an easement of way over a 100-yard roadway on a 1,000-acre estate, or an easement to use for storage a small shed on the estate access to which is gained via the 100-yard roadway, it would be fairly meaningless in relation to either easement to speak of the whole estate as the servient land. Would the right of way and the storage right fail to qualify as easements if the whole estate bar the actual land over which the roadway ran and on which the shed stood, with or without a narrow surrounding strip, were sold? How could it be open to the servient owner to destroy easements by such a stratagem? In my opinion such a stratagem would fail. It would fail because the servient land was never the whole estate but was the land over which the roadway ran and on which the shed stood. Provided the servient land was land of which the servient owner was in possession, the rights of way and of storage would continue, in my opinion, to qualify as easements.

58 As to the right to park and the 'ouster' objection, Sir Robert Megarry V-C in *Newman v Jones* (unreported), 22 March 1982, a case concerning the right of lessees of a block of 14 flats to park in the grounds of the block, said: 'I feel no hesitation in holding that a right for a land-owner to park a car anywhere in a defined area is capable of existing as an easement.' But Judge Paul Baker QC in the *London & Blenheim Estates* case [1992] 1 WLR 1278 formulated, and the Court of Appeal in *Batchelor v Marlow* [2003] 1 WLR 764 applied, a test that disqualified the right to park from existing as an easement if (per Judge Paul Baker QC):

'the right granted in relation to the area over which it is to be exercisable is such that it would leave the servient owner without any reasonable use of his land, whether for parking or anything else...'

In *Batchelor v Marlow* Tuckey LJ posed the question, at p. 768:

'Does an exclusive right to park six cars for 9½ hours every day of the working week leave the plaintiff without any reasonable use of his land, whether for parking or anything else?'

and gave the answer that:

'[The plaintiff's] right to use his land is curtailed altogether for intermittent periods throughout the week. Such a restriction would, I think, make his ownership of the land illusory.'

For that reason the Court of Appeal rejected the claim to a prescriptive easement to park the six cars for the period mentioned.

59 In my respectful opinion the test formulated in the *London & Blenheim Estates* case and applied by the Court of Appeal in *Batchelor v Marlow*, a test that would reject the claim to an easement if its exercise would leave the servient owner with no 'reasonable use' to which he could put the servient land, needs some qualification. It is impossible to assert that there would be no use that could be made by an owner of land over which he had granted parking rights. He could, for example, build above or under the parking area. He could place advertising hoardings on the walls. Other possible uses can be conjured up. And by what yardstick is it to be decided whether the residual uses of the servient land available to its owner are 'reasonable' or suffi-cient to save his ownership from being 'illusory'? It is not the uncertainty of the test that, in my opinion, is the main problem. It is the test itself. I do not see why a landowner should not grant rights of a servitudal character over his land to any extent that he wishes. The claim in *Batchelor v Marlow* for an easement to park cars was a prescriptive claim based on over 20 years of that use of the strip of land. There is no difference between the characteristics of an easement that can be acquired by grant and the characteristics of an easement that can be acquired by pre-scription. If an easement can be created by grant it can be acquired by prescription and I can think of no reason why, if an area of land can accommodate nine cars, the owner of the land should not grant an easement to park nine cars on the land. The servient owner would remain the owner of the land and in possession and control of it. The dominant owner would have the right to station up to nine cars there and, of course, to have access to his nine cars. How could it be said that the law would recognise an easement allowing the dominant owner to park five cars or six or seven or eight but not nine? I would, for my part, reject the test that asks whether the servient owner is left with any reasonable use of his land, and substitute for it a test which asks whether the servient owner retains possession and, subject to the reasonable exercise of the right in question, control of the servient land.

60 If, which as at present advised I regard as doubtful, *Batchelor v Marlow* was correctly decided,[54] I can see some force in the defenders' arguments regarding the pink land. The use that the servient owner can still make of the pink land, if two cars are parked there, is very limited. But it is the servient owner, not the pursuers, who is in possession and control of the pink land and entitled to remain so. The pursuers are entitled to do nothing with the pink land other than park vehicles on it, while the defenders are entitled to do what they like with the pink land provided they do not interfere with the pursuers' right to park two cars there. For the reasons I have given I regard the 'ouster' principle as inapplicable to this case.

Lord Mance:

102 ...If, as I consider, a right to park can exist as impliedly ancillary to an express ser-vitude right of access over property retained, I find it difficult to think that it cannot exist as an independent servitude over the property retained when this is impliedly necessary for the convenient and comfortable enjoyment of the property disposed of. However, it is not I think necessary for me to express a final view on this.

---

[54] Gale, para. 9.102, n. 266: 'unless and until *Batchelor v Marlow* is overruled, courts inferior to the House of Lords will be bound to follow it, unless it can be distinguished', e.g. on the ground that it was a claim to an easement by prescription, or account was there not taken of the sort of concurrent uses open to the servient owner mentioned by Lord Scott in *Moncrieff v Jamieson*.

Lord Neuberger of Abbotsbury:

134 On behalf of the defenders, it was contended that the right to park a motor vehicle cannot, as a matter of law, be a servitude.... The fundamental point relied on to justify the contention that a right to park cannot, as a matter of law, be a servitude is that it would involve 'the partial, or total, exclusion of [the servient] proprietor': see para. 3.50 of Cusine & Paisley, *Servitudes and Rights of Way*. In my judgment, if a right to park a vehicle cannot, for this reason, be a servitude, then there is considerable force in the contention that, for the same reason, it cannot be claimed as a property (as opposed to a personal) right, whether implied or ancillary to a servitude. In other words, if the principle identified in para. 3.50 of Cusine & Paisley does indeed prevent a right being a servitude, binding on successors of the grantor, then there is force in the contention that it also would prevent a right from being ancillary to a servitude, binding on such successors. I am prepared to assume in the defenders' favour, without deciding, that that contention is correct.

135 The decision of Upjohn J in *Copeland v Greenhalf* [1952] Ch 488 has been relied on in England to support the contention that the right to park cannot be an easement. In that case, Upjohn J held that the right claimed in that case could not be an easement because 'Practically, the defendant is claiming the whole beneficial user' of the land in question: see at p. 498. This is consistent with what Lopes LJ said in *Reilly v Booth* (1890) 44 ChD 12, 26, namely that an easement could not give 'exclusive and unrestricted use of a piece of land'. Similarly in *Grigsby v Melville* [1972] 1 WLR 1355 [p. 628, above], Brightman J intimated that he considered, without having to decide, that an effectively exclusive right to use a cellar for storage could not have been an easement.

136 At least on the basis of the authorities to which we have been referred, the case law of England (which is more fully discussed in paras 54–58 of Lord Scott's opinion) and of Scotland seem to me, at least so far, to have marched together on this issue. Not only is *Copeland v Greenhalf* one of the cases cited in this connection by Cusine & Paisley, para. 3.50, but in that case Upjohn J relied on a Scottish case, *Dyce v Hay* 1 Macq 305, to support his conclusion. (However, given the differences between the principles governing land law in the two jurisdictions, and in particular the existence in Scots law of feudal conditions and real burdens, referred to by Lord Hope and unknown in English law, it would not be safe, in my view, to assume that the law on this issue in the two jurisdictions will necessarily be the same in every respect).

137 In my judgment, the grant of a right to park a single vehicle anywhere on a servient tenement which is large enough to hold, say, twenty vehicles, must be capable of being a servitude or an easement. In such a case, there is no specific place where the vehicle is to be parked, so that there is no specific area from which the servient owner can be said to be excluded. In this connection I agree with the view expressed in *Gale on Easements*, paras 9–73 and 9–74,[55] supported as it is by the unreported decision of Sir Robert Megarry V-C in *Newman v Jones* (unreported), 22 March 1982, that provided, of course, there is a dominant tenement to which the right is appurtenant, there is 'no reason in principle why a right to park a car somewhere in the defined area should not be capable of being an easement'.

---

[55] 17th edn, 2002. See now 18th edn, 2008, paras 9.96–9.110 for a discussion of this question in the light of *Moncrieff v Jamieson*.

138 It was on this basis that Judge Paul Baker QC held that the right to park granted in *London & Blenheim Estates Ltd v Ladbroke Retail Parks Ltd* was a valid easement. He said, at p. 1286, that

> 'The matter must be one of degree. A small coal shed in a large property is one thing. The exclusive use of a large part of the alleged servient tenement is another'.

A somewhat similar test was applied in *Batchelor v Marlow*, where the Court of Appeal held that a right to park vehicles for 9½ hours a day was not an easement because it left 'the servient owner without any reasonable use of his land whether for parking or anything else', and that it thereby rendered 'his ownership of the land illusory'.

139 Accordingly, it seems to me that, on the pursuers' case, a right to park could only be prevented from being a servitude or an easement if it resulted in the servient owner either being effectively excluded from the whole of the land in question or being left without any reasonable use of that land. If the right to park a vehicle in an area that can hold 20 vehicles is capable of being a servitude or an easement, then it would logically follow that the same conclusion should apply to an area that can hold two vehicles. On that basis, it can be said to be somewhat contrary to common sense that the arrangement is debarred from being a servitude or an easement simply because the parties have chosen to identify a precise space in the area, over which the right is to be exercised, and the space is just big enough to hold the vehicle. Also, presumably on the pursuers' case, such a right would indeed be capable of being a servitude or an easement if the servient owner had the right to change the location of the precise space within the area from time to time.

140 At least as at present advised, I am not satisfied that a right is prevented from being a servitude or an easement simply because the right granted would involve the servient owner being effectively excluded from the property. In this connection, the Privy Council in *Attorney-General of Southern Nigeria v John Holt & Co (Liverpool) Ltd* [1915] AC 599, 617 appears to have held that a right to store materials on land could be an easement although it involved the dominant owner enjoying an 'exclusive' right to enjoy the property concerned. Citing *Dyce v Hay* in support, the Privy Council immediately went on to observe that, in considering arguments as to whether a right could be an easement 'The law must adapt itself to the conditions of modern society and trade'. Further, the Court of Appeal in *Wright v Macadam* [1949] 2 KB 744 held that an apparently exclusive right to store coal in a small shed was capable of being an easement. Neither case was cited to Upjohn J in *Copeland v Greenhalf*.

141 There are also Australian cases which support the notion that a right could be an easement even if the servient owner was thereby excluded from the land concerned: see for instance *Mercantile General Life Reinsurance Co v Permanent Trustee Australia Ltd* (1988) 4 BPR 9534, and per Handley JA (who described parking as 'a form of storage') in *Wilcox v Richardson* (1997) 8 BPR 15,491.

142 Further, as Lord Rodger pointed out during argument in this case, a right of aqueduct (or water rights) or a right of drainage is often granted over a specific route, so that that route may often be the full extent of the servient tenement. In such a case, the servient owner is effectively excluded from the whole of his tenement, yet such a right has always been assumed to be capable of constituting a valid servitude or easement: see the discussions at paras 3.80 (aqueduct) and 3.82 (drainage) of Cusine & Paisley, and paras 6-49–6-57 (drainage) and 6-71–6-72 (water rights) of *Gale on Easements*.

143 Accordingly, I see considerable force in the views expressed by Lord Scott in paras 57 and 59 of his opinion, to the effect that a right can be an easement notwithstanding that the

dominant owner effectively enjoys exclusive occupation, on the basis that the essential requirement is that the servient owner retains possession and control. If that were the right test, then
it seems likely that *Batchelor v Marlow* was wrongly decided. However, unless it is necessary to
decide the point to dispose of this appeal, I consider that it would be dangerous to try and identify degree of ouster is required to disqualify a right from constituting a servitude or easement,
given the very limited argument your Lordships have received on the topic.

144 As I have mentioned, there are a number of cases which can be said to support the
approach of the Court of Appeal in *Batchelor v Marlow*, although it may be possible to distinguish them. The point does not appear to be settled in Australia: see the difference of opinion
in the recent case *White v Betalli* [2007] NSWCA 243. I am also concerned that, if we were
unconditionally to suggest that exclusion of the servient owner from occupation, as opposed to
possession, would not of itself be enough to prevent a right from being an easement, it might
lead to unexpected consequences or difficulties which have not been explored in argument in
this case. Thus, if the right to park a vehicle in a one-vehicle space can be an easement, it may be
hard to justify an effectively exclusive right to store any material not being an easement, which
could be said to lead to the logical conclusion that an occupational licence should constitute an
interest in land.

Law Commission Consultation Paper on Easements, Covenants and Profits à Prendre 2008 (Consultation Paper No. 186), paras 3.45–3.52

3.45 The House of Lords has recently considered the operation of the ouster principle in
Moncrieff v Jamieson.[56] While the decision is important, it cannot be said to have determined
the issues conclusively. First, as an appeal from the Court of Session, the applicable law was that
of Scotland, not England and Wales. Secondly, the central question in the case was whether an
expressly granted right of way included (as an ancillary right) the right to park on the servient land.
Thirdly, the right claimed was not a right to park on a space large enough for only one vehicle.

3.46 Lord Scott doubted whether the test of 'degree', expounded by H.H. Judge Baker QC
in *London & Blenheim* and applied by the Court of Appeal in *Batchelor v Marlow*,[57] was appropriate, not only because of its uncertainty and difficulty in application but also because of its
focus.[58] He believed that it should be rejected, and replaced with a test which asks:

'... whether the servient owner retains possession and, subject to the reasonable exercise of the right
in question, control of the servient land.'[59]

3.47 With respect, we are not convinced that this test is particularly helpful.[60] In particular,
we are not sure how it is possible to determine whether a servient owner has retained 'control'
of the servient land over which the right is being exercised. In *Moncrieff v Jamieson*, Lord
Neuberger expressed reservations with Lord Scott's formulation:

'... if we were unconditionally to suggest that exclusion of the servient owner from occupation, as
opposed to possession, would not of itself be enough to prevent a right from being an easement, it

---

56 [2007] UKHL 42, [2007] 1 WLR 2620 [p. 631, above; and see Gale, para. 9.102.].
57 [2001] EWCA 1051, [2003] 1 WLR 764 [p. 630, above].
58 [2007] UKHL 42 at [57].   59 Above, at [59].
60 [Cf. Gale, para. 9.103: 'the present editors cannot see why it should not be [helpful].']

might lead to unexpected consequences or difficulties which have not been explored in argument in this case. Thus, if the right to park a vehicle in a one-vehicle space can be an easement, it may be hard to justify an effectively exclusive right to store any material not being an easement, which could be said to lead to the logical conclusion that an occupational licence should constitute an interest in land.'[61]

3.48 If we return to first principles, we can see that there are two grounds for the case that a right which confers exclusive possession of the servient land should not be capable of taking effect as an easement. First, as previously argued, the grant of exclusive possession involves something qualitatively different from the conferral of a lesser interest over the land of another, and it should not therefore be capable of taking effect as an easement. Secondly, it is essential to maintain a clear line of demarcation between leases and other interests in land. If the distinction were to be drawn only with reference to the parties' intentions with regard to the right being granted (that is, whether they considered it to be, and referred to it, as one or the other), the principle laid down in *Street v Mountford*[62] would be entirely circumvented.[63]

3.49 We currently believe that the best approach is to consider the scope and extent of the right that is created, and to ask whether it purports to confer a right with the essential characteristics of an easement. The question should be 'What can the dominant owner do?', rather than 'What can the servient owner not do?'.[64] The right must therefore be clearly defined, or (particularly relevant where it is an implied or prescriptive easement) at least capable of clear definition, and it must be limited in its scope; it should not involve the unrestricted use of the servient land. This takes us back to *Copeland v Greenhalf*[65] where Mr Justice Upjohn concluded that 'a right of this wide and undefined nature' could not be an easement.

3.50 We consider that this approach would provide a satisfactory resolution of the current state of the authorities. The right to receive water through a pipe, the right to store particular materials, the right to lay and to retain a pipe; all would be capable of taking effect as easements as they are sufficiently clear and limited in their scope. The 'exclusive possession' question should not arise, save and in so far as it can be contended that the interest arising is a lease rather than an easement.

3.51 As far as parking is concerned, we believe that this approach would justify the recognition of easements to park vehicles even though the effect of exercise of the right is seriously to restrict the use to which the servient land could be put. Only where the grant creates a lease rather than an easement would the right to park fail to have its intended effect, in which case the grantee would obtain a greater property interest.

3.52 The operation of these principles can be illustrated as follows:

(1) A allows B to park her car on any space in his car park. B's right would be clear and limited enough in its scope to comprise an easement.

(2) A allows B to park her car on a designated space in his car park, and only on that space. B's right has been clearly defined, and it is limited in scope: all B can do on the space is park her car. Again, this right could take effect as an easement.

---

[61] Above, at [144]. The concept of an 'occupational licence' is itself unclear. To confer a right to occupy, which does not amount to exclusive possession, cannot give rise to a lease. However, it may give rise to another interest, including an easement: see *Gale on Easements* (17th edn, 2002), para. 1–53.

[62] [1985] AC 809 [p. 383, above].   [63] The principle is set out at 3.35 above.

[64] Luther, 'Easements and Exclusive Possession' (1996) 16 Legal Studies 51.

[65] [Above, p. 626].

(3) A allows B to park her car in A's garage, and A provides B with a key so that she can secure the garage. B is not entitled to do anything in A's garage except to park her car. This right could also take effect as an easement, as it is sufficiently well-defined and limited in its scope: it is a right to park and no more. Depending on the circumstances, however, the arrangement may involve the grant of exclusive possession to B for a term at a rent, in which case it will take effect as a lease rather than an easement.

(iv) Negativity

In **Phipps v Pears** [1965] 1 QB 76,[66] the question was whether a right to make use of a neighbour's house as protection from the weather could exist as an easement.

Two houses, Nos. 14 and 16 Market St., Warwick, were owned by a single owner. No. 16 was rebuilt, 'with its flank wall flat up against the old wall of No. 14,' the two walls not being bonded together. No. 16 was sold and then No. 14. No. 14 was demolished, and the flank wall of No. 16 was exposed to the weather, and damage resulted.

The owner of No. 16 argued that a right to protection passed to him on the purchase of No. 16 by virtue of Law of Property Act 1925, section 62, p. 664, below.

On the question whether such a right could exist as an easement, LORD DENNING MR said at 82:

There are two kinds of easements known to the law: positive easements, such as a right of way, which give the owner of land *a right himself to do something* on or to his neighbour's land: and negative easements, such as a right of light, which gives him *a right to stop his neighbour doing something* on his (the neighbour's) own land. The right of support does not fall neatly into either category. It seems in some way to partake of the nature of a positive easement rather than a negative easement. The one building, by its weight, exerts a thrust, not only downwards, but also sideways on to the adjoining building or the adjoining land, and is thus doing something to the neighbour's land, exerting a thrust on it, see *Dalton v Angus* (1881) 6 App Cas 740, 793, per Lord Selborne LC. But a right to protection from the weather (if it exists) is entirely negative. It is a right to stop your neighbour pulling down his own house. Seeing that it is a negative easement, it must be looked at with caution. Because the law has been very chary of creating any new negative easements.

His Lordship referred to the fact that the law recognised no easement to a view: *Bland v Mosely* (1587) cited in 9 Co Rep at 58a; nor to the passage of air through an undefined channel to the sails of a windmill[67] and continued:

The reason underlying these instances is that if such an easement were to be permitted, it would unduly restrict your neighbour in his enjoyment of his own land. It would hamper legitimate development, see *Dalton v Angus* per Lord Blackburn (1881) 6 App Cas 740 at 824. Likewise here, if we were to stop a man pulling down his house, we would put a brake on desirable improvement. Every man is entitled to pull down his house if he likes. If it exposes your house to

---

[66] Criticised (1964) 80 LQR 318 (R.E.M.); 27 MLR 614; (1965) 28 MLR 264 (H. W. Wilkinson); supported in (1964) 27 MLR 768 (J. F. Garner).

[67] *Webb v Bird* (1861) 10 CBNS 268; *Hunter v Canary Wharf Ltd* [1997] AC 655, p. 643, below.

the weather, that is your misfortune. It is no wrong on his part. Likewise every man is entitled to cut down his trees if he likes, even if it leaves you without shelter from the wind or shade from the sun, see the decision of the Master of the Rolls in Ireland in *Cochrane v Verner* (1895) 29 ILT 571. There is no such easement known to the law as an easement to be protected from the weather. The only way for an owner to protect himself is by getting a covenant from his neighbour that he will not pull down his house or cut down his trees. Such a covenant would be binding on him in contract: and it would be enforceable on any successor who took with notice[68] of it. But it would not be binding on one who took without notice.[69]

(1964) 80 LQR 321 (R. E. Megarry)

Finally, there seems to be at least one field in which the decision [*Phipps v Pears*] may cause difficulty, namely, that of freehold flats and maisonettes. If A sells the upper part of his house to B, the conveyance may well provide for the grant of easements of support by A to B, and for the reservation of easements of shelter and protection by A against B: see, e.g. George, *The Sale of Flats* (2nd edn, 1959), pp. 27,128. *Phipps v Pears* now seems to mean that the reservation by A creates no easement, and that B's successors in title will not be bound by it. Yet it would be most unsatisfactory to be compelled to hold that although A's successors in title may not remove the support from B's flat, B's successors in title may freely remove any or all of their flat and leave A's flat at the mercy of the elements. Even though a right 'to protection from the weather', *totidem verbis,* may well be too indefinite to be an easement, it is still questionable why such a right, if sufficiently and clearly defined in its ambit by the instrument granting it, should be refused recognition as an easement, and left to more complex and less potent means of enforcement such as covenants of indemnity and the doctrine of *Halsall v Brizell* [1957] Ch 169 [p. 748, below]. In recent years many new rights have been accepted as easements, not least the right to use a lavatory: see *Miller v Emcer Products Ltd* [1956] Ch 304 [p. 628, above]. Is the law of easements not ample enough to match bodily relief with protection from the elements?[70]

---

[68] Notice is no longer the test. A successor is bound by a restrictive covenant in *registered* land if it the covenant is noted on the register of title to the servient property; or, in *unregistered* land if it is registered as a land charge, class D(ii): p. 760, below.

[69] Cf. *Rees v Skerrett* [2000] 1 WLR 1541 (where the adjacent buildings were *not* free-standing; on demolition right of support was infringed: at [15]; there was also breach of the duty of care to take steps to waterproof wall after demolition: at [27]). The case would now have been governed by the Party Wall etc. Act 1996: at [34]; [2002] Conv 237 (T. H. Wu). In *Sedgwick Forbes Bland Payne Group Ltd v Regional Properties Ltd* (1979) 257 EG 64 at 70, it was suggested that a right to protection against the weather by a *roof* might be an easement, thereby limiting *Phipps v Pears* to an easement of protection against the weather in the vertical plane. On party-walls generally, see C & B, p. 480; M & W, paras 30.040–30.045; Gale, paras 11.01 to 11.33; Bickford-Smith and Sydenham, *Party Walls Law and Practice* (2nd edn, 2004). The Party Wall etc. Act 1996 which extends to England and Wales repealed London Building Acts (Amendment) Act 1939 as from 1 July 1997, which only applied to London; *Roadrunner Properties Ltd v Dean* [2004] 1 EGLR 73. For liability for failure to weather proof party-wall where there is a right of support, see *Bradburn v Lindsay* [1983] 2 All ER 408 (servient owner held liable in negligence for infestation of dominant tenement by dry rot, and in nuisance for loss of support to, and consequent exposure of, the side of the dominant tenement to rot and decay); [1984] Conv 54 (P. Jackson). See also *Brace v South East Regional Housing Association Ltd* (1984) 270 EG 1286; [1987] Conv 47 (A. J. Waite), *Tollemache & Cobbold Breweries Ltd v Reynolds* (1983) 268 EG 52 (fire damage); (1984) 269 EG 200 (C. M. Brand and D. W. Williams).

[70] Many of the difficulties can be overcome by suitably drawn restrictive covenants. See p. 750, below.

Hunter v Canary Wharf Ltd
[1997] AC 655 (HL, **Lords Goff of Chieveley, Lloyd of Berwick, Hoffmann, Cooke of Thorndon** and **Hope of Craighead**)

Lord Hoffmann: Canary Wharf is part of the old West India Docks which straddle the neck of land formed where the Thames doubles back on itself between Limehouse Reach and Blackwall Reach. That part of the river used to be a thriving port. Thousands of people who worked in the docks or on the ships lived nearby in Limehouse and Poplar to the north and the Isle of Dogs to the south. But container transport and motorways made the London docks obsolete. By the mid-1970s they had largely been abandoned. The land along the river lay derelict.

[In 1981 the Secretary of State designated the London docklands as an urban development area, and planning permission was granted.]

The local residents complain that the construction of the Canary Wharf Tower and the Limehouse Link Road caused them serious disturbance and inconvenience. First, the construction of the road caused a great deal of dust in the air which settled upon their homes and gardens. If they opened their windows, everything in the room was soon covered in a layer of dust. If they hung out the washing in the garden it became dirty again.[71] Secondly, the Canary Wharf Tower interfered with television reception. The great metal-clad tower stood between the BBC transmitter at Crystal Palace in south London and a swathe of houses, mainly in Poplar to the north of Canary Wharf, which lay in the building's electromagnetic shadow. The effect was that many houses could not receive television at all. In others the quality of the signal was impaired. This state of affairs continued until April 1991, when the BBC brought a relay transmitter into service. Between July 1991 and August 1992 the residents had their aerials aligned to the new transmitter and the problem was thereby solved....

   In the television action, the plaintiffs complain that Canary Wharf Tower has diminished the amenity of their houses by interfering with television reception. In *Bridlington Relay Ltd v Yorkshire Electricity Board* [1965] Ch 436, 447, Buckley J said, tentatively and obiter:

> 'For myself, however, I do not think that it can at present be said that the ability to receive television free from occasional, even if recurrent and severe, electrical interference is so important a part of an ordinary householder's enjoyment of his property that such interference should be regarded as a legal nuisance, particularly, perhaps, if such interference affects only one of the available alternative programmes.'

The judge was plainly not laying down a general rule that interference with television can never be an actionable nuisance. In principle I do not see why in an appropriate case it should not. *Bridlington Relay* was a case of alleged interference by electromagnetic radiation from high tension electric cables. The Court of Appeal left open the question of whether interference of such a kind could be actionable and so would I.

   In this case, however, the defendants say that the type of interference alleged, namely by the erection of a building between the plaintiffs' homes and the Crystal Palace transmitter, cannot as a matter of law constitute an actionable nuisance. This is not by virtue of anything peculiar to television. It applies equally to interference with the passage of light or air or radio signals

---

[71] HL held that an action in private nuisance can only be brought in respect of acts directed against the enjoyment of rights over land, so that, generally only a person with an interest in land can sue; 'Many of the plaintiffs [in the dust action] had no proprietary interest in land at all': per Lord Hoffmann at 702.

or to the obstruction of a view. The general principle is that at common law anyone may build whatever he likes upon his land. If the effect is to interfere with the light, air or view of his neighbour, that is his misfortune. The owner's right to build can be restrained only by covenant or the acquisition (by grant or prescription) of an easement of light or air for the benefit of windows or apertures on adjoining land.

That such has until now been the law of England seems to me indisputable. A right to an uninterrupted prospect cannot be acquired even by prescription: *Aldred's Case,* 9 Co Rep. 57b. The same is true of a right to the uninterrupted flow of undefined air to a chimney: *Bryant v Lefever* (1879) 4 CPD 172.[72] In the absence of an easement, there is no right to light. In *Bury v Pope* (1588) 1 Cro Eliz 118 the owner of land was held entitled to erect a house against his neighbour's windows even though they had enjoyed light for over 30 years. Reporting the case, Sir George Croke succinctly noted the ratio decidendi in terms which might have had in mind Canary Wharf: 'Nota, Cujus est solum, ejus est summitas usque ad coelum. Temp. Ed. 1.'[73]

The circumstances in which this principle should be subject to limitations in favour of neighbours was considered by the House of Lords in *Dalton v Angus* (1881) 6 App Cas 740. By that time it was well established that a neighbour could prescribe for a right of light which would restrict his neighbour's freedom to build. The Prescription Act 1832 [p. 728, below] had fixed the period for the acquisition of such an easement at 20 years. As Willes J pointed out in *Webb v Bird* (1861) 10 CB (NS) 268, 285, prescription for an easement of light was anomalous. In the normal case of prescription, the dominant owner will have been doing something for the period of prescription (such as using a footpath) which the servient owner could have stopped. But one cannot stop a neighbour from erecting a building with windows. Nevertheless, they will after 20 years acquire an easement of light. In *Dalton v Angus* the House of Lords decided that, in like fashion, the owner of a building could prescribe for an easement of support from neighbouring land. On the other hand, it was well settled that one could not prescribe for a right to an uninterrupted view or to a flow of air otherwise through a defined aperture or channel. Lord Blackburn considered how these cases were to be distinguished. He said, at p. 824, that allowing the prescription of a right to a view would impose a burden 'on a very large and indefinite area.' Rights of light, air and support were strictly a matter between immediate neighbours. The building entitled to support, the windows entitled to light and the apertures entitled to air would be plain and obvious. The restrictions on the freedom of the person erecting the building would be limited and precise.

In the absence of agreement, therefore, the English common law allows the rights of a landowner to build as he pleases to be restricted only in carefully limited cases and then only after the period of prescription has elapsed. In this case there is no claim to an easement of television

---

[72] In *Cable v Bryant* [1908] 1 Ch 259, it was held that an easement could exist which entitled the dominant owner to the access of air through a defined aperture (a ventilator), although there was no defined channel across the servient tenement through which the air flowed. See also *Harris v De Pinna* (1886) 33 ChD 238. The right may arise under the doctrine of non-derogation from grant: *Aldin v Latimer, Clark, Muirhead & Co* [1894] 2 Ch 437; *Chartered Trust plc v Davies* [1997] 2 EGLR 83. On the doctrine generally, see C & B, pp. 231–232 (in the context of leasehold covenants), 607–608 (easements); Gale, paras 1.77, 3.32–3.52; (1964) 80 LQR 244 (D. W. Elliott); (1965) 81 LQR 28 (M. A. Peel); *Johnston & Sons Ltd v Holland* [1988] 1 EGLR 264 at 267–268, per Nicholls LJ: 'The expression "derogation from grant" conjures up images of parchment and sealing wax, of copperplate handwriting and fusty title deeds. But the principle is not based on some ancient technicality of real property… it is a principle which merely embodies in a legal maxim a rule of common honesty'; *Romulus Trading Co Ltd v Comet Properties Ltd* [1996] 2 EGLR 70.

[73] 'The owner of land owns it up as far as heaven.' The Canary Wharf tower is 800 feet tall.

by prescription. And in any event, on the reasoning in *Dalton v Angus* I do not think that such an easement can exist. The extent to which a building may interfere with television reception is far from obvious. Nor is its potential effect limited to immediate neighbours. The number of plaintiffs in the television action [690] is itself enough to demonstrate how large a burden would be imposed on anyone wishing to erect a tall building.

Once again we must consider whether modern conditions require these well established principles to be modified. . . .

On the one hand, therefore, we have a rule of common law which, absent easements, entitles an owner of land to build what he likes upon his land. It has stood for many centuries. If an exception were to be created for large buildings which interfere with television reception, the developers would be exposed to legal action by an indeterminate number of plaintiffs, each claiming compensation in a relatively modest amount. Defending such actions, whatever their merits or demerits, would hardly be cost-effective. The compensation and legal fees would form an unpredictable additional cost of the building. On the other hand, the plaintiffs will ordinarily have been able to make their complaints at the planning stage of the development and, if necessary, secure whatever conditions were necessary to prove them with an alternative source of television signals. The interference in such a case is not likely to last very long because there is no technical difficulty about the solution. In my view the case for a change in the law is not made out.

I would therefore agree with the Court of Appeal on this point and dismiss the plaintiffs' appeal in the television action.

(v) Expenditure by servient owner

In **Crow v Wood** [1971] 1 QB 77[74] the parties farmed land adjoining a large sheep moor in the North Riding of Yorkshire. Each had the right to allow his sheep to stray on the moor. The defendant's sheep trespassed on the plaintiff's land by passing through the plaintiff's fence, which had not been repaired since 1966. There was no arrangement between the parties as to fencing, but the defendant claimed that he was entitled to an easement requiring the plaintiff to maintain the fence. Such an easement, if it existed, passed to the defendant under Law of Property Act 1925, section 62. LORD DENNING MR said at 84:

The question is, therefore, whether a right to have a fence or wall kept in repair is a right which is capable of being granted by law. I think it is because it is in the nature of an easement. It is not an easement strictly so called because it involves the servient owner in the expenditure of money. It was described by Gale [*Easements* (11th edn, 1932), p. 432] as a 'spurious kind of easement'. But it has been treated in practice by the courts as being an easement. Professor Glanville Williams on *Liability for Animals* (1939), says, at p. 209: 'If we put aside these questions of theory and turn to the practice of the courts, there seems to be little doubt that fencing is an easement.' In *Jones v Price* [1965] 2 QB 618 at 633, Willmer LJ said: 'It is clear that a right to require the owner of adjoining land to keep the boundary fence in repair is a right which the law will recognise as a quasi-easement.' Diplock LJ, at 639, points out that it is a right of such a nature that it can be acquired by prescription which imports that it lies in grant, for prescription rests on a presumed grant.

---

[74] See also *Liverpool City Council v Irwin* [1977] AC 239.

It seems to me that it is now sufficiently established—or at any rate, if not established hith-erto, we should now declare—that a right to have your neighbour keep up the fences is a right in the nature of an easement which is capable of being granted by law so as to run with the land and to be binding on successors. It is a right which lies in grant and is of such a nature that it can pass under section 62 of the Law of Property Act 1925.'[75]

QUESTIONS

1. Having read the cases on the nature of easements, can you set out any guide-lines to help a court decide whether or not a right which complies with the accepted requirements of an easement is to be recognised judicially? See C & B, pp. 595–597; *Dowty Boulton Paul Ltd v Wolverhampton Corpn (No. 2)* [1976] Ch 13 at 23, per Russell LJ: 'A tendency in the past to freeze the cat-egories of easements has been overtaken by the defrosting operation in *Re Ellenborough Park* [1956] Ch 131'.

2. Is it, and should it be, easier to establish that a right satisfies the *Ellenborough Park* criteria for acceptance as an easement in the case of an express grant than in a claim to an easement by prescription? See *Jackson v Mulvaney* [2003] 1 WLR 360 at [23], p. 625, above; *Batchelor v Marlow* [2003] 1 WLR 764 at [4]-[6].

3. Can there be an easement to park a car in a single garage? See *Moncrieff v Jamieson* [2007] 1 WLR 2620, p. 631, above; Gale, paras 9.96–9.110; Law Commission Consultation Paper on Easements, Covenants and Profits à Prendre 2008 (Consultation Paper No. 186), para. 3.52, p. 640, above.

C. LEGAL AND EQUITABLE EASEMENTS. ENFORCEABILITY BY AND AGAINST THIRD PARTIES

LAW OF PROPERTY ACT 1925

1. Legal estates and equitable interests.[76]—(2) The only interests or charges in or over land which are capable of subsisting or of being conveyed or created at law are—

(a) An easement, right, or privilege in or over land for an interest equivalent to an estate in fee simple absolute in possession or a term of years absolute...

(3) All other estates, interests, and charges in or over land take effect as equitable interests.

2. Conveyances overreaching certain equitable interests and powers.—(3) The following equit-able interests and powers are excepted from the operation of subsection (2) of this section,[77] namely—

---

[75] An easement of fencing may also be acquired (i) as an easement by prescription: *Lawrence v Jenkins* (1873) LR 8 QB 274; *Jones v Price* [1965] 2 QB 618; (ii) by custom: *Egerton v Harding* [1975] QB 62.
[76] See also p. 13, above.   [77] I.e., from the effect of overreaching: see p. 548, above.

(iii) Any easement, liberty, or privilege over or affecting land and being merely an equitable interest (in this Act referred to as an 'equitable easement').

4. Creation and disposition of equitable interests.—(1) Interests in land validly created or arising after the commencement of this Act, which are not capable of subsisting as legal estates, shall take effect as equitable interests...

52. Conveyances to be by deed.—(1) All conveyances of land or of any interest therein are void for the purpose of conveying or creating a legal estate unless made by deed.

187. Legal easements.—(1) Where an easement, right or privilege for a legal estate is created, it shall enure for the benefit of the land to which it is intended to be annexed.[78]

LAND CHARGES ACT 1972

2. Register of land charges.—(4) Class C (iv), p. 66, above.

(5) Class D (iii), p. 67, above.

Land Registration Act 2002

27 Dispositions required to be registered

(1) If a disposition of a registered estate or registered charge is required to be completed by registration, it does not operate at law until the relevant registration requirements are met.

(2) In the case of a registered estate, the following are the dispositions which are required to be completed by registration—

(d) the express grant or reservation of an interest of a kind falling within section 1(2)(a) of the Law of Property Act 1925, other than one which is capable of being registered under the Commons Registration Act 1965...

(7) In subsection (2)(d), the reference to express grant does not include grant as a result of the operation of section 62 of the Law of Property Act 1925.[79]

SCHEDULE 3

UNREGISTERED INTERESTS WHICH OVERRIDE REGISTERED DISPOSITIONS

Easements and profits a prendre

3 (1) A legal easement..., except for an easement...which at the time of the disposition—

(a) is not within the actual knowledge of the person to whom the disposition is made, and

---

[78] *Wall v Collins* [2007] Ch 390 (easement granted for benefit of a 999-year lease not necessarily extinguished when tenant purchased freehold: 'An easement must be appurtenant to a dominant tenement, but not necessarily to any particular interest for the time being. Thus for example the 1925 Act provides that a legal easement may be created for the equivalent of a freehold interest, or for an interest "equivalent to...a term of years absolute": section 1(2)(a). In the latter case, there is nothing to suggest that an easement for a term of years has to be attached to a leasehold interest of equivalent duration. All that matters is that the grantee has an interest at least co-extensive with the period of the easement. (The same distinction seems to me implicit in section 187, which provides that any easement "shall enure for the benefit of *the land* to which it is intended to be annexed": section 187(1). Notwithstanding the wide definition of "land" in other parts of the 1925 Act (section 205(ix)), the context appears to direct attention to the dominant tenement as such, rather than any particular type of interest in it)': per Carnwath LJ at [15]).

[79] For LPA 1925 s. 62, see p. 663, below.

(b) would not have been obvious on a reasonably careful inspection of the land over which the easement or profit is exercisable.

(2) The exception in sub-paragraph (1) does not apply if the person entitled to the easement or profit proves that it has been exercised in the period of one year ending with the day of the disposition.

An easement is capable of being a legal interest if it (a) complies with Law of Property Act 1925 section 1(2)(a) and is held for 'an interest equivalent to an estate in fee simple absolute in possession or a term of years absolute', (b) is created either by statute, deed or prescription, and (c) in registered land has satisfied the requirements for registration. Registration requirements are that a notice of the interest must be entered on the register of the servient land;[80] and if the interest is for the benefit of a registered dominant tenement, the registered proprietor must be entered on the register as its proprietor.[81] An easement which fails to satisfy either (a) or (b) is not a legal, but an equitable, interest, e.g., if it is for the life of the grantee or created by an equitable owner.

The distinction between a legal easement and an equitable easement affects its enforceability against third parties (typically, a purchaser of the servient tenement). In *unregistered* land, a legal easement will bind a purchaser of the servient tenement; an equitable easement is registrable, if created after 1925, as a Land Charge Class D(iii), or, if it is granted informally or is the subject of a contract to grant an easement, as an estate contract Class C(iv).[82] In spite of some earlier views to the contrary,[83] it is now settled that the definition of an equitable easement (which is defined in section 2(3)(iii) of the Law of Property Act 1925, above, as 'any easement, liberty,[84] or privilege over or affecting land and being merely an equitable interest') is to be construed narrowly. This excludes such informal equitable rights as an equitable right of re-entry,[85] or any rights arising in equity by reason of proprietary estoppel or the doctrine of mutual benefit and burden.[86] These rights are therefore not registrable as land charges, and their enforcement against third parties in unregistered land depends solely on the doctrine of notice.[87]

---

[80] In the case of first registration the registrar will enter a notice on the register of the servient land.

[81] LRA 2002, Sch. 2, para. 7. See also LRA 2002, s. 13; LRR 2003, r. 73A, inserted by LR (Amendment) Rules 2008 (SI 2008 No. 1919), Sch. 1, para. 24. 'Obviously this cannot be done when the easement or profit is for the benefit of an estate in unregistered land. Nor can it be done in respect of an easement that is granted for the benefit of a lease that was not capable of registration when it was granted.' H & B para. 8.13, n. 8.

[82] *McManus v Cooke* (1887) 35 ChD 681 (easement); *Mason v Clarke* [1955] AC 778 (profit à prendre); *Lowe v JW Ashmore Ltd* [1971] Ch 545 at 557–558 (profit à prendre).

[83] (1935) 15 Bell Yard 18 (G. Cross); see also (1948) 12 Conv (NS) 202 (J. F. Garner).

[84] The definition in LCA 1972, s. 2(5) substitutes the word 'right' for 'liberty'.

[85] *Shiloh Spinners Ltd v Harding* [1973] AC 691, p. 68, above.

[86] *ER Ives Investment Ltd v High* [1967] 2 QB 379, p. 1073, below; followed in *Poster v Slough Estates Ltd* [1969] 1 Ch 495 (right of entry to remove fixtures at end of lease); (1937) 53 LQR 259 (C. V. Davidge); (1969) 33 Conv (NS) 135 (P. Jackson). See also *Lewisham Borough Council v Maloney* [1948] 1 KB 50 (requisitioning authority's right to possession).

[87] P. 58, above. Report of the Committee on Land Charges 1956 (Cmnd 9825), para. 16 suggested that Class D (iii) might be abolished. Law Commission Report on Land Charges affecting Unregistered Land

In *registered* land,[88] the express grant of a legal easement must have been completed by registration (failing which it takes effect only as an equitable interest). However, easements which have been created by implied grant are not required to be registered, but they will normally be an overriding interest under Land Registration Act 2002, Schedule 3, paragraph 3.[89] However, under the provisions of that paragraph, it will not override if the purchaser did not have actual notice of it, and it would not have been obvious on a reasonably careful inspection of the land—in substance, if he did not have actual or constructive notice of it—unless the easement has in fact been exercised during the year before the disposition to the purchaser. However, an equitable easement is not an overriding interest under paragraph 3, and so if it is to bind a purchaser of the servient tenement it must be protected by a notice on the register, or by the dominant owner's discoverable actual occupation of the servient tenement under Land Registration Act 2002, Schedule 3, paragraph 2.[90] However, normally the dominant owner will not be in actual occupation of the servient tenement, and so an equitable easement will bind only if it is noted on the register.

III. ACQUISITION OF EASEMENTS[91]

Easements, like any other incorporeal hereditaments,[92] lie in grant at common law—that is, they must be created by a *deed of grant*. They could not, like corporeal hereditaments, pass by 'livery of seisin'—that is, by simply putting the recipient in possession of the property. Situations could arise, however, in which it was felt that the landowner should have an easement, but he could show no express grant. The common law, true to the basic rule that easements lie in grant, developed rules whereby the grant could be *implied* in a deed conveying land but making no mention of the easement, or could be *presumed* where there was no deed at all; this latter case deals with what is more commonly called prescription. As has been seen, an easement may also be granted in equity, where the requirements of either substance or form for the creation of an easement at common law are not satisfied.

1969 (Law Com No. 18, HC 125), para. 65, recommended its retention. Registrations in that class were then running at an annual rate of 2,500–3,500; there were 689 registrations during the years 1995–1996.

[88] Under LRA 1925 easements and profits à prendre enjoyed a privileged position: under section 70(1)(a), p. 182, above, legal easements and profits à prendre were overriding interests, as were equitable easements and profits à prendre.

[89] R & R, paras 17.022–17.027, chap. 36; H & B, paras 8.12–8.14; Law Commission Report on Land Registration for the Twenty-First Century 2001 (Law Com No. 217), paras 4.24–4.26. For a critical analysis, see [2002] Conv 304 (P. Kenny).

[90] P. 196, above.

[91] C & B, pp. 600–628; Gray, paras 5.2.1–5.2.86; M & W, chap. 28; MM, pp. 424–441; Smith, pp. 493–514; Gale, Part II. For the creation of an easement through the doctrine of proprietary estoppel, see *Crabb v Arun DC* [1976] Ch 179, p. 1051, below.

[92] See *Willies-Williams v National Trust* (1993) 65 P & CR 359 at 361, per Hoffmann LJ.

And, on occasion, statutes have been passed specifically creating easements between adjoining owners; the common example of this type of statute is an Inclosure Act which distributes among individual owners land which had been subject to rights of common and created certain easements among these owners.[93] Modern examples of easements created by statute are to be found in local Acts of Parliament. Statutory rights similar to easements are also created by general Acts and are sometimes called statutory easements.[94]

A landowner may acquire an easement to enter upon his neighbour's land in order to carry out maintenance work to his own property.[95] The Access to Neighbouring Land Act 1992[96] enables him to obtain an order of the court if the neighbour refuses access where an easement has not been acquired.

ACCESS TO NEIGHBOURING LAND ACT 1992

1. Access orders.—(1) A person—

    (a) who, for the purpose of carrying outworks to any land[97] (the 'dominant land'), desires to enter upon any adjoining or adjacent land (the 'servient land'), and

    (b) who needs, but does not have, the consent of some other person to that entry,

may make an application to the court for an order under this section ('an access order') against that other person.

(2) On an application under this section, the court shall make an access order if, and only if, it is satisfied—

    (a) that the works are reasonably necessary for the preservation of the whole or any part of the dominant land; and

    (b) that they cannot be carried out, or would be substantially more difficult to carry out, without entry upon the servient land;

but this subsection is subject to subsection (3) below.

(3) The court shall not make an access order in any case where it is satisfied that, were it to make such an order—

    (a) the respondent or any other person would suffer interference with, or disturbance of, his use or enjoyment of the servient land, or

    (b) the respondent, or any other person (whether of full age or capacity or not) in occupation of the whole or any part of the servient land, would suffer hardship,

---

93 For example, *Adeane v Mortlock* (1839) 5 Bing NC 236.

94 Gale, paras 1.119–1.128; (1956) 20 Conv (NS) 208 (J. F. Garner).

95 *Ward v Kirkland* [1967] Ch 194; p. 628, n. 42, above.

96 The Act is based on the Law Commission Report on Rights of Access to Neighbouring Land 1985 (Law Com No. 151, Cmnd 9692). The Act had a chequered history: [1992] 26 EG 136 (J. Adams). It came into force on 31 January 1993. In unregistered land an access order is registrable as a writ or order under LCA 1972, s. 6(1) (d), and is regarded as a pending land action under s. 5(1). If the land is registered, the order is registrable by way of notice under LRA 2002, and cannot be an overriding interest: Access to Neighbouring Land Act 1992, s. 5(5), amended by LRA 2002, s. 133, Sch. 11, para. 26(4). See Gale, paras 11.41–11.69.

97 Land does not include a highway; s. 8(3); but does include a party wall; *Dean v Walker* (1996) 73 P & CR 366.

to such a degree by reason of the entry (notwithstanding any requirement of this Act or any term or condition that may be imposed under it) that it would be unreasonable to make the order.

A. ACQUISITION BY EXPRESS GRANT OR RESERVATION[98]

(i) At law

Coke (Co Litt 9a)

And here is implyed a division of fee, or inheritance, viz, into corporeall,...and incorporeall (which lie in grant, and cannot passe by livery, but by deede, as advowsons, commons &c., and of some is called haereditas incorporata, and, by the delivery of the deede, the freehold, and inheritance of such inheritance, as doth lie in grant, doth passe) comprehended in this word grant. And the deed of incorporeate inheritances doth equall the livery of corporeate.

LAW OF PROPERTY ACT 1925

52. Conveyances to be by deed.—(1) p. 42, above.[99]

65. Reservation of legal estates.—(1) A reservation of a legal estate shall operate at law without any execution of the conveyance by the grantee of the legal estate out of which the reservation is made, or any regrant by him, so as to create the legal estate reserved, and so as to vest the same in possession in the person (whether being the grantor or not) for whose benefit the reservation is made.

(2) A conveyance of a legal estate expressed to be made subject to another legal estate not in existence immediately before the date of the conveyance, shall operate as a reservation, unless a contrary intention appears.[100]

(3) This section applies only to reservations made after the commencement of this Act.

In **St Edmundsbury and Ipswich Diocesan Board of Finance v Clark (No 2)** [1975] 1 WLR 468 the question arose whether on the reservation of an easement by a vendor the terms of the reservation were, in case of doubt, to be construed against the vendor or against the purchaser. The Court of Appeal held that it should be construed against the purchaser, as on a re-grant. SIR JOHN PENNYCUICK said at 477:

Second, is the maxim 'omnia praesumuntur contra proferentem' applicable against the vendor or against the purchaser where there is a conveyance subject to the reservation of a new right of way? In view of the full discussion of this question by Megarry J, and of the fact that we do not agree with his conclusion, we think it right to deal fairly fully with it. But it is necessary to

---

[98] C & B, pp. 601–603; Gray, paras 5.2.4–5.2.14; M & W, paras 28.005–28.007; MM, pp. 425–427; Gale, paras 3.04–3.14.

[99] The creation of a licence by a deed does not convert it into an easement: *IDC Group Ltd v Clark* [1992] 1 EGLR 187 (deed purporting to 'grant licence and consent' to the use of a fire escape).

[100] *Wiles v Banks* (1983) 50 P & CR 80 (conveyance 'subject to a right of way').

make clear that this presumption can only come into play if the court finds itself unable on the material before it to reach a sure conclusion on the construction of a reservation. The presumption is not itself a factor to be taken into account in reaching the conclusion. In the present case we have indeed reached a sure conclusion, and on this footing the presumption never comes into play, so that the view which we are about to express upon it is not necessary to the decision of the present case.

The point turns upon the true construction of section 65(1) of the Law of Property Act 1925.

His Lordship read the section and continued:

Formerly, the law was that on a conveyance with words merely reserving an easement, the easement was held to be created, provided that the purchaser executed the conveyance, without the necessity for words of regrant. The law treated the language of the reservation as having the same effect as would the language of regrant though there was not in terms a regrant, and in those circumstances regarded the purchaser as the proferens for present purposes. This was a relaxation of the strict requirements for the creation of an easement. (An easement could be created without execution by the purchaser of a conveyance by reference to the Statute of Uses, once section 62 of the Conveyancing Act 1881 removed the technical objection that that statute could not operate to create an easement. This method disappeared with the repeal of the Statute of Uses in the 1925 property legislation...)

Section 65 must be read in the light, therefore, of two aspects of the preceding law. First: that previously the law was sufficiently relaxed from its prima facie stringency to permit the language of mere reservation to have the effect of a regrant though it was not in truth a regrant by its language. Second: that for this purpose the purchaser must execute the conveyance if an easement was to be created; that is to say, although a regrant in terms was not required. Against that background, are the words in section 65 'without... any regrant by' the purchaser to be regarded as altering the law so that the purchaser is no longer to be regarded as the relevant proferens? Or are they to be regarded as merely maintaining for the avoidance of doubt the situation that had been already reached by the development of the law, viz. that mere words of reservation could be regarded as having the same effect as would the language of regrant though without there being in terms any purported regrant by the purchaser? We would, apart from authority, construe the words in the latter sense, so that the only relevant change in the law is the absence of the requirement that the purchaser should execute the conveyance. We read the section as if it were in effect saying that whereas an easement could be created by mere words of reservation without any words of regrant by the purchaser, provided that the purchaser executes the conveyance, hereafter the easement can be created by mere words of reservation without any words of regrant by the purchaser even if he does not execute the conveyance: it is not to be said that in the latter event the previous relaxation of the strict law has disappeared, so that the language of the conveyance must be more than the mere language of reservation. It will be observed that that view keeps in line, on the relevant point, a post-1925 conveyance executed by the purchaser, which is apparently not touched by section 65, and one which is executed by him.

The above is our view apart from authority. What then of authority? We start with the fact that Sir Benjamin Cherry, architect of the 1925 property legislation, made no reference to this suggested change of principle in the law in the first edition of Wolstenholme and

Cherry's *Conveyancing Statutes* after the 1925 property legislation. Further, in more than one case since 1925, judges of high authority took it for granted that the old principle still prevails: see *Bulstrode v Lambert* [1953] 1 WLR 1064, per Upjohn J at 1068; *Mason v Clarke* [1954] 1 QB 460, in the Court of Appeal, per Denning LJ at 467 and in the House of Lords per Lord Simmonds [1955] AC 778 at 786. In these cases the contrary was not argued and the judicial statements are not of binding authority. But in *Johnstone v Holdway* [1963] 1 QB 601 in the Court of Appeal, Upjohn LJ, giving the judgment of the court, not only in terms re-stated the old principle but made it part of the ratio decidendi of his judgment. He said, at 612:

> 'that the exception and reservation of the mines and minerals was to the vendor, that is the legal owner, but the exception and reservation of the right of way was to the company, the equitable owner. If the reservation of a right of way operated strictly as a reservation, then, as the company only had an equitable title, it would seem that only an equitable easement could have been reserved. But it is clear that an exception and reservation of a right of way in fact operates by way of regrant by the purchaser to his vendor and the question, therefore, is whether as a matter of construction the purchaser granted to the company a legal easement or an equitable easement'

The opposing view was expressed by Megarry J in *Cordell v Second Clanfield Properties Ltd* [1969] 2 Ch 9 (upon motion and without being referred to *Johnstone v Holdway*) and in the present case (after a full review of the authorities, including *Johnstone v Holdway*). He distinguishes *Johnstone v Holdway* as a decision based on mistake and states his own conclusion in the following words [1973] 1 WLR 1572 at 1591:

> 'The fair and natural meaning of section 65(1) seems to me to be that if a vendor reserves an easement, the reservation is to be effective at law without any actual or notional regrant by the purchaser, and so without the consequences that flow from any regrant. At common law, the rule that a reservation of an easement was to be construed against the purchaser depended solely upon the notional regrant. Apart from that, the words of reservation, being the words of the vendor, would be construed against the vendor in accordance with the general principle stated in Norton on Deeds, 2nd edn (1928), just as an exception or a reservation of a rent would; it was the fiction of a regrant which made reservations of easements stand out of line with exceptions and reservations in the strict sense. With the statutory abolition of the fictitious regrant, reservations of easements fall into line with the broad and sensible approach that it is for him who wishes to retain something for himself to see that there is an adequate statement of what it is that he seeks to retain; and if after considering all the circumstances of the case there remains any real doubt as to the ambit of the right reserved, then that doubt should be resolved against the vendor. Accordingly, in this case I hold that the words "subject also to a right of way over the land coloured red on the said plan to and from St Botolph's Church" in the 1945 conveyance should, if their meaning is not otherwise resolved, be construed against the church authorities and so in favour of Mr Clark.'

We see much force in this reasoning. But we find it impossible to accept Megarry J's analysis of the decision in *Johnstone v Holdway*. We are not prepared to infer from the report that experienced and responsible counsel misrepresented the terms of section 65 to the court and that the judge based his decision on the terms of the section as so misrepresented. It follows that the decision in *Johnstone v Holdway* is binding upon this court and that we ought to follow it.

Law Commission Consultation Paper on Easements, Covenants and Profits à Prendre 2008 (Consultation Paper No. 186), paras 4.20–4.23

4.20 Doubts have been expressed over the correctness of the Court of Appeal decision in the *St Edmundsbury* case.[101] It has not been followed in Australia,[102] and the Northern Ireland Land Law Working Group have recommended that, for the purposes of interpretation, 'a reservation should not be treated as taking effect by way of re-grant'.[103]

4.21 In our view, the *St Edmundsbury* rule is quite illogical. The vendor decides what land he is going to sell, and what restrictions and qualifications are to be made, and it should therefore be the responsibility of the vendor to make the terms of the transaction clear. One would therefore expect the terms of any rights reserved in favour of the vendor to be interpreted, in cases of ambiguity, against him or her. The vendor should certainly not be allowed to benefit from ambiguity and thereby to increase the burden on the servient land. What has been said in relation to the Scots law should be of equal application south of the border:

> 'If ambiguous drafting will be construed *contra proferentem*, this will tend to favour an expansive grant of the servitude and militate against the established rule favouring freedom of property from restrictions. It is submitted that the latter rule will always prevail to the effect that ambiguity is always interpreted in a manner which is least burdensome to the servient tenement.'[104]

4.22 Moreover, the decision of the Court of Appeal in *St Edmundsbury* leads to inconsistency. In particular, its application is in stark contrast with the approach taken towards implied reservation of easements. An implied reservation will, as it contradicts the express terms of the instrument, be on the face of it a derogation from the grant.[105] It is a well-established rule that there is a duty to make any reservation expressly in the grant and that therefore no easements will normally be implied in favour of a grantor.[106] It seems counter-intuitive that while there is little scope for courts to imply a reservation in the first place, where there is an express reservation, the courts will interpret it more favourably towards the person making the reservation that it would towards a person making an express grant.

4.23 We have therefore taken the provisional view that the *St Edmundsbury* rule should no longer apply where there is an express reservation of an easement. We do not consider that this necessitates repeal of section 65(1) of the Law of Property Act 1925.[107]

---

[101] Megarry and Wade, *The Law of Real Property* (6th edn, 2000), para. 18–094; K. Gray and S. F. Gray, *Elements of Land Law* (4th edn, 2005), para. 8.198.

[102] A. Bradbrook and M. Neave, *Easements and Restrictive Covenants in Australia* (1981), pp. 53–54; *Yip v Frolich & Frolich* [2004] SASC 287.

[103] Office of Law Reform, *The Final Report of the Land Law Working Group*, vol. 1, para. 2.5.32.

[104] J. Cusine and R. R. M. Paisley, *Servitudes and Rights of Way* (1998), para. 14.47.

[105] *Chaffe v Kingsley* (2000) 79 P & CR 404, 417, by Jonathan Parker J; *Holaw (470) Ltd v Stockton Estates Ltd* (2001) 81 P & CR 29 at [82], by Neuberger J.

[106] *Wheeldon v Burrows* (1879) 12 Ch D 31, 49; *Re Webb's Lease* [1951] 1 Ch 808 at 828; *Holaw (470) Ltd v Stockton Estates Ltd* (2001) 81 P & CR 29 at [82]. There are two exceptions to this rule (easements of necessity, and easements of intended use), but in either case there is a heavy burden of proof on the person claiming the benefit of an implied reservation.

[107] This is because we would be following the interpretation of s. 65(1) advanced by Megarry J at first instance in *St Edmundsbury*: see para. 4.18 above.

(ii) In equity

An agreement in writing[108] for valuable consideration to grant an easement or a profit à prendre is a contract which equity will specifically enforce. Equity looks on that as done which ought to be done and such an agreement operates as a grant in equity of an easement under the doctrine of *Walsh v Lonsdale*.[109] As in the case of an agreement for a lease, equity will construe an informal grant (that is, a grant which is not contained in a deed) as a contract to grant an easement, and therefore as the creation of an equitable easement.[110]

(iii) Registration

Under the Land Registration Act 2002 legal easements and profits à prendre which are expressly granted or reserved are registrable dispositions and do not take effect at law until they are registered.[111] An easement or profit à prendre which arises as a result of the operation of section 62 of the Law of Property Act 1925 (p. 664, below) is not an express grant (section 27(7), p. 647, above).

B. ACQUISITION BY IMPLIED GRANT OR RESERVATION[112]

When the owner of land grants part of it, or certain interests in part of it, to another person, there will be implied into the grant of the land, in appropriate circumstances (i) certain rights in favour of the grantee exercisable over the land retained (implied grant), and (ii) certain rights in favour of the grantor over the land granted (implied reservation). These rights are rights in the nature of easements, but which could not be easements before the grant because all the land was under single ownership. These two cases—implied grant and implied reservation—are treated differently and must be dealt with separately.

(i) Easements implied in favour of the grantee

(a) The common law rule

Consistently with the principle that a grantor must not derogate from his grant,[113] the law readily implies easements in favour of the grantee. The rule has been laid down

---

[108] Such a contract, being an agreement for a disposition of an interest in land, is required to be in writing: LP(MP)A 1989, s. 2, p. 18, above.

[109] (1882) 21 ChD 9; p. 30, above.

[110] See also *McManus v Cooke* (1887) 35 ChD 681; *May v Belleville* [1905] 2 Ch 605; *Mason v Clarke* [1955] AC 778 (profit à prendre), p. 32, n. 86, above.

[111] P. 647, above. Profits in gross (i.e. where there is no dominant land to which the profit is appurtenant) are registrable with a separate title (LRA 2002, s. 3(1)(a), p. 131, above).

[112] C & B, pp. 607–613; Gray, paras 5.2.20–5.2.56; M & W, paras 28.008–28.027; MM, pp. 427–430; Smith, pp. 494–506; Gale, paras 3.17–3.163; Farrand, *Contract and Conveyance* (2nd edn), pp. 382–390.

[113] P. 644, n. 72, above. *Ward v Kirkland* [1967] Ch 194 at 226–227; *Sovmots Investments Ltd v Secretary of State for the Environment* [1979] AC 144 at 165, per Lord Wilberforce, p. 673, below.

in an obiter dictum in *Wheeldon v Burrows*, which has subsequently been accepted universally as a correct statement of the law, to the effect that in a grant of land there may be implied in favour of the grantee those rights in the nature of easements which (1) are 'continuous and apparent' or 'in other words all those easements which are necessary to the reasonable enjoyment of the property granted' and (2) have been and are, at the time of the grant, used by the grantor for the benefit of the part granted. Easements of necessity without which the property could not be enjoyed at all and easements which were clearly within the common intention of the parties[114] will also be implied in favour of the grantee.

The doctrine of *Wheeldon v Burrows* has been shorn of much of its importance by section 62 of the Law of Property Act 1925. But it still remains available wherever, for one reason or another, a claimant cannot rely on section 62.[115] It always operates subject to the terms of the contract or conveyance,[116] and to the circumstances existing at the date of the grant.

Under *Wheeldon v Burrows* an easement is implied into the grant of the land. If the grant is of the fee simple or a term of years absolute by deed, the easement will be an implied grant by deed, and so will be a legal easement.[117] But if the grant is only by contract, and so takes effect only as a grant in equity under the doctrine of *Walsh v Lonsdale*[118] the easement can also be only equitable.

Wheeldon v Burrows
(1879) 12 ChD 31 (CA, **Thesiger, James** and **Baggallay LJJ**)

Of land owned in 1875 by one Tetley, part was sold in January 1876 to the plaintiff's husband, William Wheeldon. Another part was sold in February 1876 to the

---

[114] *Pwllbach Colliery Co Ltd v Woodman* [1915] AC 634; *Keewatin Water Power Co Ltd v Lake of the Woods Milling Co Ltd* [1930] AC 640; *Wong v Beaumont Trust Ltd* [1965] 1 QB 173, p. 660, below; *Nickerson v Barraclough* [1981] Ch 426, p. 680, n. 193, below; *Manjang v Drammeh* (1990) 61 P & CR 194 (PC held no easement of necessity where available access by water across the River Gambia 'albeit perhaps less convenient than access across *terra firma*'); [1992] CLJ 220 (C. Harpum); *Stafford v Lee* (1992) 65 P & CR 172 (common intention implied by reference to conveyancing plan); *Mobil Oil Co v Birmingham City Council* [2002] 2 P & CR 186.

[115] See pp. 663–664, below.

[116] This may be expressed by a condition of sale; see *Selby District Council v Samuel Smith Old Brewery (Tadcaster) Ltd* (2000) 80 P & CR 466, where Peter Gibson LJ said at 474: 'The rule in *Wheeldon v Burrows* only operates to the extent that it is not inconsistent with the intention of the parties which may be inferred from the circumstances.' For doubt as to whether the contrary intention should only be sought in the words used in the conveyancing documents, see Emmet, para. 17.058, citing *Millman v Ellis* (1995) 71 P & CR 158. For a similar issue in relation to LPA 1925, s. 62, p. 664, below, see *Squarey v Harris-Smith* (1981) 42 P & CR 118 (where a standard condition that the purchaser should not acquire any rights which would restrict the free use of the vendor's other land for building was held to negative the operation of s. 62); cf. *Lyme Valley Squash Club Ltd v Newcastle under Lyme Borough Council* [1985] 2 All ER 405, in which *Squarey v Harris-Smith* was not cited, and the opposite conclusion was reached; [1985] Conv 243. See also *William Hill (Southern) Ltd v Cabras Ltd* [1987] 1 EGLR 37; *Pretoria Warehousing Co Ltd v Shelton* [1993] EGCS 120; [1996] Conv 238 (A. Dowling); *Millman v Ellis*, above (grant of narrower easement not necessarily a contrary intention); [1995] Conv 346 (J. West).

[117] It will comply with LPA 1925, s. 1(2)(a), p. 646, above, as to content, and LPA 1925, 52(1), p. 647, above as to formality. In registered land an implied grant does not have to be completed by registration in order to be a legal easement: p. 649, above.

[118] P. 29, above.

defendant; on this part there was a shed containing, and lighted by, three windows which overlooked the plaintiff's land. In 1878 the plaintiff, then the widow and devisee of William Wheeldon, erected hoardings near the edge of her land facing the defendant's shed for the purpose of ascertaining her right to exclude the light from the shed. The defendant, claiming an easement of light, knocked down the hoardings, and this action was brought for trespass.

Held. The defendant had no right to knock down the hoardings because no right to the access of light to the windows of the shed had been reserved by Tetley on the sale of the land to the plaintiff's husband.

Thesiger LJ: We have had a considerable number of cases cited to us, and out of them I think that two propositions may be stated as what I may call the general rules governing cases of this kind. The first of these rules is, that on the grant by the owner of a tenement of part of that tenement as it is then used and enjoyed, there will pass to the grantee all those continuous[119] and apparent easements (by which, of course, I mean *quasi* easements), or, in other words, all those easements which are necessary to the reasonable enjoyment of the property granted, and which have been and are at the time of the grant used by the owners of the entirety for the benefit of the part granted. The second proposition is that, if the grantor intends to reserve any right over the tenement granted, it is his duty to reserve it expressly in the grant. Those are the general rules governing cases of this kind, but the second of those rules is subject to certain exceptions. One of those exceptions is the well-known exception which attaches to cases of what are called ways of necessity; and I do not dispute for a moment that there may be, and probably are, certain other exceptions, to which I shall refer before I close my observations upon this case.

Both of the general rules which I have mentioned are founded upon a maxim which is as well established by authority as it is consonant to reason and common sense, viz., that a grantor shall not derogate from his grant. It has been argued before us that there is no distinction between what has been called an implied grant and what is attempted to be established under the name of an implied reservation; and that such a distinction between the implied grant and the implied reservation is a mere modern invention and one which runs contrary, not only to the general practice upon which land has been bought and sold for a considerable time, but also to authorities which are said to be clear and distinct upon the matter. So far, however, from that distinction being one which was laid down for the first time by and which is to be attributed to Lord Westbury in *Suffield v Brown* (1864) 4 De GJ & Sm 185, it appears to me that it has existed almost as far back as we can trace the law upon the subject; and I think it right, as the case is one of considerable importance, not merely as regards the parties, but as regards vendors and purchasers of land generally, that I should go with some little particularity into what I may term the leading cases upon the subject.

... These cases in no way support the proposition for which the Appellant in this case contends; but, on the contrary, support the propositions that in the case of a grant you may imply a grant of such continuous and apparent easements or such easements as are necessary to the

---

[119] C & B, pp. 610–611; M & W, para. 28.016; MM, pp. 428–430; Gale, para. 3.53; Farrand (2nd edn), pp. 383–384; *Polden v Bastard* (1865) LR 1 QB 156; *Hansford v Jago* [1921] 1 Ch 322; *Millman v Ellis*, above (driveway and lay-by both covered with unbroken and undivided layer of tarmac held to be continuous and apparent); cf. Maugham J in *Borman v Griffith* [1930] 1 Ch 493, p. 420, above; *Ward v Kirkland* [1967] Ch 194 at 224–225, per Ungoed-Thomas J, citing with approval Cheshire, *Modern Law of Real Property* (9th edn), p. 468.

reasonable enjoyment of the property conveyed, and have in fact been enjoyed during the unity of ownership, but that, with the exception which I have referred to of easements of necessity, you cannot imply a similar reservation in favour of the grantor of land.[120]

In **Ward v Kirkland** [1967] Ch 194 UNGOED-THOMAS J referred to the discrepancy in the first and last paragraphs of Thesiger LJ's judgment in *Wheeldon v Burrows*.[121] Of the first paragraph he said at 224:

There, it might appear that the words 'in other words' in that passage would indicate that the requirement, 'which are necessary to the reasonable enjoyment of the property granted', and the earlier words, 'continuous and apparent easements', refer to the same easements.

Of the last paragraph he said:

Reading that passage on its own, on first impression, it would appear that the 'easements which are necessary to the reasonable enjoyment of the property conveyed' might be a separate class from 'continuous and apparent easements.'... It has been suggested that perhaps the 'easements necessary to the reasonable enjoyment of the property conveyed' might refer to negative easements.... I understand that there is no case in which positive easements which are not 'continuous and apparent' have been held to come within the doctrine of *Wheeldon v Burrows*.... The words 'continuous and apparent' seem to be directed to there being on the servient tenement a feature which would be seen on inspection and which is neither transitory nor intermittent, for example, drains, paths, as contrasted with the bowsprits of ships overhanging a piece of land.[122]

In **Kent v Kavanagh** [2007] Ch 1[123] the Court of Appeal considered the application of the rule in *Wheeldon v Burrows* to the case where the grantor conveys the freehold to a tenant holding under a long lease who exercises his statutory right to call for the freehold under the Leasehold Reform Act 1967. The Court held that the statutory obligation to convey did not of itself exclude the operation of the rule, but that the rule was inapplicable in a case where land, although in common ownership, was not also in common occupation. For such a case, the appropriate mechanism for the implied grant of easements was section 62 of the Law of Property Act 1925, below pp. 663–679, rather than the rule in *Wheeldon v Burrows*. CHADWICK LJ said at 19:

Does the rule in Wheeldon v Burrows have any application to a conveyance on enfranchisement?

36 The first ground of appeal is that the principle which has become known as 'the rule in *Wheeldon v Burrows*' can have no application to a conveyance executed to give effect to the obligation imposed by section 8(1) of the 1967 Act. It is said, correctly, that the principle is based on the proposition that a man does not intend to derogate from his grant. As Lord Wilberforce observed in the consolidated appeals in *Sovmots Investments Ltd v Secretary of*

---

[120] *Aldridge v Wright* [1929] 2 KB 117; *Suffield v Brown* (1864) 4 De GJ & Sm 185; *Borman v Griffith*, above.

[121] See also *Squarey v Harris-Smith* (1981) 42 P & CR 118 at 124, per Oliver LJ; *Wheeler v J J Saunders Ltd* [1996] Ch 19, at 30, per Peter Gibson LJ; [1995] Conv 239 (M. P. Thompson); [1995] All ER Rev 311 (P. J. Clarke).

[122] (1967) 83 LQR 240 (A. W. B. Simpson).   [123] [2006] All ER Rev 252 (P. J. Clarke).

State for the Environment [1979] AC 144 [p. 673, below] at 168: 'He cannot grant or agree to grant land and at the same time deny to his grantee what is at the time of the grant obviously necessary for its reasonable enjoyment.' Put shortly, it is said that an intention not to derogate from grant cannot be imputed to a landlord whose obligation to convey the freehold is founded on an agreement which was imposed upon him by statute. There is no basis upon which to impute to an involuntary transferor an intention to grant any larger or further rights than those the statute expressly requires.

37 At first sight the submission finds support in the speeches of four of the members of the House of Lords in the *Sovmots* appeals. Lord Wilberforce rejected the submission that the rule in *Wheeldon v Burrows* could apply in a case where the conveyance was made pursuant to a compulsory purchase order [1979] AC 144, 168–169:

'To apply this to a case where a public authority is taking from an owner his land without his will is to stand the rule on its head: it means substituting for the intention of a reasonable voluntary grantor the unilateral, opposed, intention of the acquirer.'

Lord Edmund-Davies took the same view. After setting out the familiar passage in the judgment of Thesiger LJ in *Wheeldon v Burrows* 12 Ch D 31, 49, he said [1979] AC 144, 175:

'The basis of such propositions is, as Lord Parker of Waddington stressed in *Pwllbach Colliery Co Ltd v Woodman* [1915] AC 624, 646, that, 'The law will readily imply the grant or reservation of such easements as may be necessary to give effect to the common intention of the parties to a grant of real property...' But there is no common intention between an acquiring authority and the party whose property is compulsorily taken from him, and the very basis of implied grants of easements is accordingly absent.'

Lord Keith of Kinkel (with whose speech Lord Fraser of Tullybelton agreed in all respects) expressed the view, at p. 183ɢ , that both the rule in *Wheeldon v Burrows* and the provisions of section 62 of the 1925 Act had 'no place in compulsory purchase'.

38 It is important to keep in mind, however, that the statutory scheme for giving effect to a compulsory purchase order—formerly in the Acquisition of Land (Authorisation Procedure) Act 1946 and now found in the Acquisition of Land Act 1981—is not the same as that for giving effect to the right to enfranchise under the 1967 Act. In particular, there is nothing in the compulsory purchase legislation comparable to the provisions of section 5(3) of the 1967 Act:

'In the event of any default by the landlord or the tenant in carrying out the obligations arising from [a tenant's notice served under section 5(1)], the other of them shall have the like rights and remedies as in the case of a contract freely entered into.'

Nor is there anything in the compulsory purchase legislation comparable to the provisions of section 22(2) of the 1967 Act, to which I have already referred:

'the rights and obligations of all parties in relation to...matters arising in giving effect to [a tenant's notice]...subject to or in the absence of provision made by any such regulations [made by statutory instrument under that section]...shall be as nearly as may be the same as in the case of a contract for sale...freely negotiated between the parties.'

As Lord Denning MR observed in *Byrnlea Property Investments Ltd v Ramsay* [1969] 2 QB 253, 263: 'Once the notice is given, both parties are bound just as they are by an ordinary contract.'

39 For my part, I would reject the submission that the reasoning in the *Sovmots* appeal compels the conclusion that the rule in *Wheeldon v Burrows* can have no application to a convey-ance executed to give effect to the obligation imposed by section 8(1) of the 1967 Act....

43 The two propositions which, together, comprise the rule (or rules) in *Wheeldon v Burrows* are confined, in their application, to cases in which, by reason of the conveyance (or lease), land formerly in common ownership ceases to be owned by the same person. It is in cases of that nature that, in order to give effect to what must be taken to be the common intention of the grantor and the grantee, the conveyance (or lease) will operate as a grant (for the benefit of the land conveyed) of such easements over the land retained by the grantor as are necessary to the reasonable enjoyment of the land conveyed. But, because the principle is founded on the common intention of the parties, the easements necessary to the reasonable enjoyment of the land conveyed are those which reflect (and, following separation of ownership, are needed to give effect to) the use and enjoyment of the land conveyed at the time of the conveyance and while that land and the retained land were in the common ownership of the grantor.

44 It is necessary to ask how far either of the two propositions which Thesiger LJ identified in *Wheeldon v Burrows* can have any application in a case where, at the time of the conveyance, the land conveyed and the land retained, although in common ownership, were not in common occupation. In particular, can either of the two propositions have any application where the land conveyed was occupied by a tenant holding under a lease from the common owner. Assuming, for the moment, that the land is not conveyed to the tenant, there are, of course, two distinct questions: (i) what easements over the retained land pass with the conveyance of the freehold and (ii) what easements are reserved out of the land conveyed for the benefit of the retained land. The rights of the tenant over the land retained; and the rights of the grantor (as owner of the land retained) over the land held under the lease are unaffected by the conveyance. Prima facie, those rights will depend on the terms of the lease—but may include rights which passed to the tenant under the first rule in *Wheeldon v Burrows* when the lease was granted.

45 In the absence of an express grant, the answer to the first of those questions—what ease-ments over the retained land pass with the conveyance of the freehold—turns, as it seems to me, not on any application of the first rule in *Wheeldon v Burrows* but on the operation of section 62 of the Law of Property Act 1925 [p. 664, below]. Under section 62 a conveyance of land operates to convey with the land 'all . . . ways . . . easements, rights, and advantages whatsoever, appertaining or reputed to appertain to the land . . . or, at the time of conveyance, demised . . . or enjoyed with . . . the land'. I can see no reason why those words are not apt to convey, with the freehold, rights of way over the retained land which are, at the time of the conveyance, enjoyed by the tenant in occupation of the land conveyed. For my part, I find that analysis more attractive than one which relies upon the first rule in *Wheeldon v Burrows*. It seems to me an unnecessary and artificial construct to hold that the grantor, as common owner and the landlord of the land conveyed, is himself using the rights over the retained land which his tenant enjoys under the lease.

Wong v Beaumont Property Trust Ltd
[1965] 1 QB 173 (CA, **Lord Denning MR, Pearson** and **Salmon LJJ**)

In 1957, three cellars in Exeter were let to one Blackaby who covenanted to use the premises as a popular restaurant and to control all smells and odours accord-ing to health regulations and so as not to become a nuisance. To comply with these undertakings, it was necessary to construct a ventilation duct fixed to the outside wall of the landlords' premises. This was not realised by the parties at the time, and no duct was built.

In 1961 the plaintiff bought the remainder of the lease and developed the premises into a highly successful Chinese restaurant. The smells and odours caused the Midland Bank, who occupied the floor above, to complain and the public health inspector required the duct to be built. The defendants, assignees in 1962 of the original landlords, refused to allow the work to be done, and the plaintiff asked for a declaration of entitlement and damages.

Held. Declaration that the plaintiff was entitled to an easement as an easement of necessity.

Lord Denning MR: The question is: Has the plaintiff a right to put up this duct without the landlords' consent? If he is to have any right at all, it must be by way of easement and not merely byway of implied contract. He is not the original lessee, nor are the defendants the original lessors. Each is a successor in title. As between them, a right of this kind, if it exists at all, must be by way of an easement. In particular, an easement of necessity. The law on the matter was stated by Lord Parker of Waddington in *Pwllbach Colliery Co Ltd v Woodman* [1915] AC 634, where he said at 646, omitting immaterial words, 'The law will readily imply the grant or reservation of such easements as may be necessary to give effect to the common intention of the parties to a grant of real property, with reference to the manner or purposes in and for which the land granted... is to be used. But it is essential for this purpose that the parties should intend that the subject of the grant... should be used in some definite and particular manner. It is not enough that the subject of the grant... should be intended to be used in a manner which may or may not involve this definite and particular use.' That is the principle which underlies all easements of necessity. If you go back to Rolle's Abridgment you will find it stated in this way: 'If I have a field inclosed by my own land on all sides, and I alien this close to another, he shall have a way to this close over my land, as incident to the grant; for otherwise he cannot have any benefit by the grant.'

I would apply those principles here. Here was the grant of a lease to the lessee for the very purpose of carrying on a restaurant business. It was to be a popular restaurant, and it was to be developed and extended. There was a covenant not to cause any nuisance; and to control and eliminate all smells; and to comply with the Food Hygiene Regulations. That was 'a definite and particular manner' in which the business had to be conducted. It could not be carried on in that manner at all unless a ventilation system was installed by a duct of this kind. In these circumstances it seems to me that, if the business is to be carried on at all—if, in the words of Rolle's Abridgment, the lessee is to 'have any benefit by the grant' at all—he must of necessity be able to put a ventilation duct up the wall. It may be that in Blackaby's time it would not have needed such a large duct as is now needed in the plaintiff's time. But nevertheless a duct of some kind would have had to be put up the wall. The plaintiff may need a bigger one. But that does not matter. A man who has a right to an easement can use it in any proper way, so long as he does not substantially increase the burden on the servient tenement. In this case a bigger duct will not substantially increase the burden.

There is one point in which this case goes further than the earlier cases which have been cited. It is this. It was not realised by the parties, at the time of the lease, that this duct would be necessary. But it was in fact necessary from the very beginning. That seems to me sufficient to bring the principle into play. In order to use this place as a restaurant, there must be implied an easement, by the necessity of the case, to carry a duct up this wall. The county court judge so held. He granted a declaration. I agree with him.[124]

In **Barry v Hasseldine** [1952] Ch 835 DANCKWERTS J said at 839:

In my opinion, however, if the grantee has no access to the property which is sold and conveyed to him except over the grantor's land or over the land of some person or persons whom he cannot compel to give him any legal right of way, common sense demands that a way of necessity should be implied, so as to confer on the grantee a right of way, for the purposes for which the land is conveyed, over the land of the grantor; and it is no answer to say that a permissive method of approach was in fact enjoyed, at the time of the grant, over the land of some person other than the grantor because that permissive method of approach may be determined on the following day, thereby leaving the grantee with no lawful method of approaching the land which he has purchased.

Law Commission Consultation Paper on Easements, Covenants and Profits à Prendre 2008 (Consultation Paper No. 186), paras 4.61–4.64

4.61 The following three requirements must be satisfied in order for there to be an implied grant under the rule [in *Wheeldon v Burrows*]:

(1) The right must be 'continuous and apparent'. This is taken to mean that it is 'seen on inspection' and 'is neither transitory nor intermittent'.[125]

(2) The right must be necessary to the reasonable enjoyment of the property granted. Necessity is not as narrowly interpreted as it is in the context of easements of necessity.[126] The question is whether the right will contribute to the enjoyment of the property for the purpose for which it was transferred.[127]

(3) At the time of the grant the quasi-easement was being used by the common owner for the benefit of the part granted.

4.62 It should further be noted that:

(1) The rule can only grant as easements rights that are capable of fulfilling the requirements of an easement.[128] It cannot transform rights that do not satisfy the necessary characteristics into easements.

(2) The estate transferred may be legal or equitable. If an easement is implied, it will assume the same status as the estate that was transferred and to which it pertains. For example, if the estate transferred was an equitable lease, the easement will be equitable too.

---

[124] *MRA Engineering Ltd v Trimster Co Ltd* (1987) 56 P& CR 1 (no easement of necessity because access on foot was 'merely difficult and inconvenient'; land was not inaccessible or useless without right of way claimed).

[125] *Ward v Kirkland* [1967] Ch 194, 225 [p. 658, above], by Ungoed-Thomas J.

[126] See para. 4.81 below.

[127] It has not been authoritatively determined whether these first two requirements are cumulative, alternative or synonymous. The general consensus taken from the decided case law is that they are cumulative: see, for example, *Sovmots Investments Ltd v Secretary for State for the Environment* [1979] AC 144 [p. 673, below].

[128] *Re Ellenborough Park* [1956] Ch 131 [p. 620, above].

(3) The transfer of the land from the common owner may be a sale, a devise or a gift. It does not therefore have to be for value. However, it must be voluntary.[129]

4.63 Implied easements arising from the rule in *Wheeldon v Burrows* are based on the doctrine of non-derogation from grant.[130] Where there is an obvious right being exercised prior to the disposal of part, it will be presumptively assumed that there should be a grant to use it.[131] As a result, it is said that the express grant of a more limited right in the conveyance will not be sufficient to exclude the implication of a *Wheeldon v Burrows* easement....

4.64 Where it can be shown that the parties to a transaction did not intend that a right should pass, the rule in *Wheeldon v Burrows* will not apply, even where all the other requirements for an implied grant have been satisfied.[132] However, contrary intention will only preclude the grant of the easement if it is manifest from the documents that transfer the land.[133] Contrary intention can be evidenced by express words or deduced by implication from the language used.[134]

> ## QUESTION
>
> Is there a difference between an easement of necessity, and an easement which is 'necessary to give effect to the common intention of the parties?' If there is a difference, is it relevant in either case that the parties did not realise that the necessity existed? See (1964) 80 LQR 322–323 (R. E. Megarry) and pp. 679–686; below; *Horn v Hiscock* (1972) 223 EG 1437 at 1441; *Nickerson v Barraclough* [1980] Ch 325 at 332.

(b) Law of Property Act 1925, section 62

The Law of Property Act 1925, section 62 (replacing the Conveyancing Act 1881, section 6), has taken over much of the area formerly governed by the rule in *Wheeldon v Burrows*, p. 656, above. Its application is wider, in that the right need not be 'continuous and apparent'[135] nor 'necessary for the reasonable enjoyment of the property granted';[136] it also applies to profits à prendre.[137] On the other hand, it does not

---

[129] See, for example, *Sovmots Investments Ltd v Secretary of State for the Environment* [1979] AC 144 (no application where compulsory purchase).

[130] See, for example, *Browne v Flower* [1911] 1 Ch 219.

[131] *Millman v Ellis* (1996) 71 P & CR 158.

[132] *Wheeler v J J Saunders Ltd* [1996] Ch 19.

[133] *Borman v Griffith* [1930] 1 Ch 493, 499.

[134] *Millman v Ellis* (1996) 71 P & CR 158. For instance, in *Squarey v Harris-Smith* (1981) 42 P & CR 118, a right of way was not implied under the rule in *Wheeldon v Burrows* because the lease contained a condition of sale which provided that when the property adjoined another, a purchaser of the property should not become entitled to any easement 'which would restrict or interfere with the free use of [the] other land...'.

[135] *Ward v Kirkland* [1967] Ch 194 (right to enter farmyard to maintain a wall held to be not continuous and apparent, but to be an easement created under s. 62).

[136] *Goldberg v Edwards* [1950] Ch 247, p. 668, below.

[137] *Polden v Bastard* (1865) LR 1 QB 156; *White v Williams* [1922] 1 KB 727; *White v Taylor (No 2)* [1969] 1 Ch 160; *Anderson v Bostock* [1976] Ch 312; *Re Yateley Common, Hampshire* [1977] 1 WLR 840 at 850; *Re Broxhead Common, Whitehill, Hampshire* (1977) 33 P & CR 451.

apply where the dominant owner obtains his interest without a conveyance executed as a deed (as by will or under contract).[138] Until the recent decision of the Court of Appeal in *P & S Platt Ltd v Crouch* [2004] 1 P & CR 18, p. 675, below, it was also held that section 62 did not apply where there was no diversity of occupation of the two tenements before the grant.[139]

Under section 62 an easement is implied into the grant of the land. Since the section applies only where there is a deed into which the easement is implied (or where there is a grant of the legal estate in the land which can be effected without a deed[140]), the easement will be a legal easement.[141]

LAW OF PROPERTY ACT 1925

62. General words implied in conveyances.[142]—(1) A conveyance of land shall be deemed to include and shall by virtue of this Act operate to convey, with the land, all buildings, erections, fixtures, commons, hedges, ditches, fences, ways, waters, watercourses, liberties, privileges, easements, rights, and advantages whatsoever, appertaining or reputed to appertain to the land, or any part thereof, or, at the time of conveyance,[143] demised, occupied, or enjoyed with[144] or reputed or known as part or parcel of or appurtenant to the land or any part thereof.

(2) A conveyance of land, having houses or other buildings thereon, shall be deemed to include and shall by virtue of this Act operate to convey, with the land, houses, or other buildings, all outhouses, erections, fixtures, cellars, areas, courts, courtyards, cisterns, sewers, gutters, drains, ways, passages, lights, watercourses, liberties, privileges, easements, rights, and advantages whatsoever, appertaining or reputed to appertain to the land, houses, or other buildings conveyed, or any of them, or any part thereof, or, at the time of conveyance, demised, occupied, or enjoyed with,[145] or reputed or known as part or parcel of or appurtenant to, the land, houses, or other buildings conveyed, or any of them, or any part thereof.

---

[138] *Borman v Griffith* [1930] 1 Ch 493, p. 420, above; *Schwann v Cotton* [1916] 2 Ch 459; *Horn v Hiscock* (1972) 223 EG 1437.

[139] *Long v Gowlett* [1923] 2 Ch 177, p. 670, below; *Ward v Kirkland* [1967] Ch 194; *Sovmots Investments Ltd v Secretary of State for the Environment* [1979] AC 144, p. 673, below.

[140] *Wright v Macadam* [1949] 2 KB 744 at 746–748, p. 665, below (legal lease not exceeding three years not required to be in writing or by deed by virtue of s. 54(2) LPA 1925).

[141] It will comply with LPA 1925, s. 1(2)(a), p. 646, above, as to content, and LPA 1925, 52(1), p. 647, above as to formality. In registered land a grant implied by s. 62 does not have to be completed by registration in order to be a legal easement: p. 649, above.

[142] (1966) 30 Conv (NS) 340 (P. Jackson). See also LPA 1925, s. 63 (all estate clause implied), p. 466, n. 278.

[143] This section is not concerned with future rights: *Nickerson v Barraclough* [1981] Ch 426; *Payne v Inwood* (1996) 74 P & CR 42 ('section 62 cannot create new rights where there has been no actual enjoyment of a facility by the owner or occupier of the dominant tenement over the servient tenement', at 47, per Roch LJ); [1997] Conv 453 (M. P. Thompson). The right must be exercised at the date of the conveyance: *Penn v Wilkins* (1974) 236 EG 203 (passage of sewage, which ceased many years before conveyance, not covered by s. 62).

[144] This is not synonymous with user: *Re Yateley Common, Hampshire*, above; *MRA Engineering Ltd v Trimster Co Ltd* (1987) 56 P & CR 1, p. 662, n. 124, above (rights of access granted to an existing tenant held not to pass under s. 62 on sale of freehold after surrender of the lease); *Re St. Clements, Leigh-on-Sea* [1988] 1 WLR 720.

[145] *Commission for New Towns v JJ Gallagher Ltd* [2003] 2 P & CR 24 ('enjoyed with' and 'appurtenant' refer to incorporeal hereditaments, such as easements, and not to physical property; land cannot be appurtenant to other land: citing *Lister v Pickford* (1865) 34 Beav 576 at 580).

(4) This section applies only if and as far as a contrary intention is not expressed in the conveyance, and has effect subject to the terms of the conveyance and to the provisions therein contained.[146]

(6) This section applies to conveyances made after the thirty-first day of December, eighteen hundred and eighty-one.

1. Licence into easement

Wright v Macadam[147]
[1949] 2 KB 744 (CA, **Tucker**, **Jenkins** and **Singleton LJJ**)

In 1940, the defendant let a top floor flat at 13 Mount Ararat Road, Richmond, to Mrs Wright for one week. After the expiration of that time Mrs Wright continued in occupation by virtue of the Rent Acts.

In 1941, the defendant gave Mrs Wright permission to use a shed in the garden for the storage of coal, and this permission was exercised.

In 1943, the defendant granted a new one-year tenancy of the premises with an additional room to Mrs Wright and her daughter by a document[148] which made no reference to the use of the shed. The Wrights enjoyed the use of the shed until 1947 when the defendant suggested that 1s. 6d. a week should be paid for its use. They refused, and were denied the use of the shed. This action was brought for an injunction to restrain interference with their use of it and for £10 in damages.

Held. The right to use the coalshed passed to the Wrights as an easement under section 62 of the Law of Property Act 1925 on the grant of the tenancy in 1943.

Jenkins LJ: The plaintiffs claimed an injunction to restrain the defendant from trespassing or otherwise interfering with their lawful use of the coal shed, a declaration that their tenancy of the flat included the right to use the coal shed, and damages limited to 10*l*. I may mention that, as matters stand at present, the last of those claims appears to be the only relevant one, inasmuch as we were informed in the course of the hearing that the defendant has in fact pulled down the coal shed. The question, therefore, is simply this: whether the plaintiffs, as tenants of the top floor flat at 13, Mount Ararat Road, were entitled to the use of the coal shed in question. It is argued for the plaintiffs that they were so entitled, by virtue of section 62 of the Law of Property Act 1925, which is the section replacing the old section 6 of the Conveyancing and Law of Property Act 1881, and providing by statute the general words which it was formerly customary to insert in full in the parcels of conveyances and other dispositions of land. The plaintiffs claim that this section covers the case. The defendant, on the other hand, claims that, although the coal shed was admittedly used, it was used under no sufficiently definite arrangement; that it was used purely as a matter of personal licence and precariously; and that the arrangement under which it was used could not be said to confer a right in any way appurtenant to the flat, but was an arrangement of a kind to which section 62 of the Act had no application.

---

[146] See p. 656, n. 116, above.

[147] (1950) 66 LQR 302 (R. E. M.). Followed in *Graham v Philcox* [1984] QB 747, p. 715, below.

[148] As the grant of a lease for not more than three years, the grant did not need to be by deed (or, indeed, even a written document): LPA 1925, s. 54(2).

His Lordship came to the conclusion that the tenancy agreement, being sufficient by virtue of the Law of Property Act 1925, section 52, 54, to pass a legal estate, was a 'conveyance' within the meaning given to that term in section 205(1)(ii). There was therefore a 'conveyance of land' within the meaning of section 62(1). He continued:

The question in the present case, therefore, is whether the right to use the coal shed was at the date of the letting of 28 August 1943 a liberty, privilege, easement, right or advantage appertaining or reputed to appertain, to the land, or any part thereof, or, at the time of the conveyance, demised, occupied or enjoyed with the land—that is the flat—or any part thereof. It is enough for the plaintiffs' purposes if they can bring the right claimed within the widest part of the sub-section—that is to say, if they can show that the right was at the time of the material letting demised, occupied or enjoyed with the flat or any part thereof.

The predecessor of section 62 of the Act of 1925, in the shape of section 6 of the Act of 1881 has been the subject of a good deal of judicial discussion, and I think the effect of the cases can be thus summarised. First, the section is not confined to rights which, as a matter of law, were so annexed or appurtenant to the property conveyed at the time of the conveyance as to make them actual legally enforceable rights. Thus, on the severance of a piece of land in common ownership, the quasi easements de facto enjoyed in respect of it by one part of the land over another will pass although, of course, as a matter of law, no man can have a right appendant or appurtenant to one part of his property exercisable by him over the other part of his property.[149] Secondly, the right, in order to pass, need not be one to which the owner or occupier for the time being of the land has had what may be described as a permanent title. A right enjoyed merely by permission is enough. The leading authority for that proposition is the case of *International Tea Stores Co v Hobbs* [1903] 2 Ch 165.[150] That was a decision of Sir George Farwell as a judge of first instance. It was a case in which the defendant, who owned two houses, let one of them for business purposes and there had been a practice of giving permission to the successive managers of the property to let to pass and re-pass with their servants and so forth across a yard which was part of the property and remained in the defendant's occupation. The part of the property which had been let was later sold to the tenants, nothing being said in the conveyance about the right of way. The purchasers claimed to exercise the right of way by virtue of section 6 of the Act of 1881. That claim was disputed, and the point was taken that it could not be a right which would pass under the implied general words inasmuch as it was only precariously enjoyed. The learned judge held that the fact that the way was permissive only was irrelevant for this purpose, and that by virtue of section 6 of the Act of 1881 the grant included a corresponding right of way in fee simple. Dealing with the question of licence or permission, the learned judge said this: 'Unless I am prepared to say that in no case can a tenant obtain under the Conveyancing Act 1881 a right of way unless he has enjoyed it as of right, I must hold in this case that the fact of licence makes no difference. In all these cases the right of way must be either licensed or unlicensed. If it is unlicensed it would be at least as cogent an argument to say, "True you went there, but it was precarious, because I could have sent a man to stop you or stopped you myself any day." If it is by licence, it is precarious, of course, in the sense that the licence, being ex hypothesi revocable, might be revoked at any time; but if there be degrees of precariousness, the latter is less precarious than the former. But, in my opinion,

---

[149] Cf. *Long v Gowlett* [1923] 2 Ch 177, p. 670, below.
[150] See the remarks of Cross J in *Green v Ashco Horticulturist Ltd* [1966] 1 WLR 889 at 896- 897; *Ward v Kirkland* [1967] Ch 194; [1998] Conv 115 (L. Tee).

precariousness has nothing to do with this sort of case, where a privilege which is by its nature known to the law—namely, a right of way—has been in fact enjoyed. Lord Coleridge's argument was founded upon a misconception of a judgment of mine in *Burrows v Lang* [1901] 2 Ch 502, where I was using the argument of precariousness to show that the right which was desired to be enjoyed there was one which was unknown to the law—namely, to take water if and whenever the defendant chose to put water into a particular pond; such a right does not exist at law; but a right of way is well known to the law.'

His Lordship referred also to *Lewis v Meredith* [1913] 1 Ch 571 and *White v Williams* [1922] 1 KB 727 and continued:

There is, therefore, ample authority for the proposition that a right in fact enjoyed with property will pass on a conveyance of the property by virtue of the grant to be read into it under section 62, even although down to the date of the conveyance the right was exercised by permission only, and therefore was in that sense precarious.

The next proposition deducible from the cases is the one laid down in *Burrows v Lang,* which has been referred to in some of the passages I have already read. It is that the right in question must be a right known to the law.... For the purposes of section 62, it is only necessary that the right should be one capable of being granted at law, or, in other words, a right known to the law. If it is a right of that description it matters not, as the *International Tea Stores* case [1903] 2 Ch 165 shows, that it has been in fact enjoyed by permission only. The reason for that is clear, for, on the assumption that the right is included or imported into the parcels of the conveyance by virtue of section 62, the grant under the conveyance supplies what one may call the defect in title, and substitutes a new title based on the grant.

His Lordship also referred to *Birmingham & Dudley District Banking Co v Ross* (1888) 38 ChD 295 and continued:

I think those are all the cases to which I can usefully refer, and applying the principles deducible from them to the present case one finds, I think, this. First of all, on the evidence the coal shed was used by Mrs Wright by the permission of Mr Macadam, but *International Tea Stores Co v Hobbs* shows that that does not prevent section 62 from applying, because permissive as the right may have been it was in fact enjoyed.

Next, the right was, as I understand it, a right to use the coal shed in question for the purpose of storing such coal as might be required for the domestic purposes of the flat. In my judgment that is a right or easement which the law will clearly recognise,[151] and it is a right or easement of a kind which could readily be included in a lease or conveyance by the insertion of appropriate words in the parcels. This, therefore, is not a case in which a title to a right unknown to the law is claimed by virtue of section 62. Nor is it a case in which it can be said to have been in the contemplation of the parties that the enjoyment of the right should be purely temporary.[152] No

---

[151] On easements of storage, cf. *Copeland v Greenhalf* [1952] Ch 488, p. 626, above; *Grigsby v Melville* [1972] 1 WLR 1355, p. 628, above.

[152] In *Hair v Gillman* (2000) 80 P & CR 108 (right to park car which could be withdrawn at any time held to be within s. 62) Chadwick LJ identified at 114 'the distinction between a right that is temporary, in the sense that it is merely precarious, so that it can be withdrawn at any time, and a right that is temporary in the sense that, to the knowledge of the parties, it will only be capable of being enjoyed for some limited period because of the nature of the property over which it is to be enjoyed'. Only the former can become an easement under s. 62.

limit was set as to the time during which the coal shed could continue to be used. Mr Macadam simply gave his permission; that permission was acted on; and the use of the coal shed in fact went on down to 28 August 1943, and thereafter down to 1947. Therefore, applying to the facts of the present case the principles which seem to be deducible from the authorities, the conclusion to which I have come is that the right to use the coal shed was at the date of the letting of 28 August 1943 a right enjoyed with the top floor flat within the meaning of section 62 of the Law of Property Act 1925, with the result that (as no contrary intention was expressed in the document) the right in question must be regarded as having passed by virtue of that letting, just as it would have passed if it had been mentioned in express terms in cl. 1, which sets out the subject-matter of the lease....

For these reasons I would allow the appeal and direct that, inasmuch as the coal shed is now no longer in existence, judgment should be entered for the plaintiffs for the sum of damages claimed.

Tucker LJ: The result is that the defendant, through his act of kindness in allowing this lady to use the coalshed, is probably now a wiser man, and I may perhaps regret that the decision in this case may tend to discourage landlords from acts of kindness to their tenants. But there it is: that is the law.

Goldberg v Edwards
[1950] Ch 247 (CA, **Evershed MR, Cohen** and **Asquith LJJ**)

The first defendant was the owner of a house at Salford and of an annexe consisting of two storeys at the rear. The annexe could be reached by an uncovered passage to the East of the house, and this approach had always been used by the tenants previous to the plaintiffs. During the course of the negotiations with the plaintiffs, Isadore Goldberg and Barnett Sewelson, for the letting of the annexe, the first defendant agreed to give a personal privilege to the plaintiffs to use another approach to the annexe which led through the front door of the house, and to use the letter box in that door.

On 13 January 1947, an oral agreement for a lease of the annexe to the plaintiffs was reached, and they went into possession on 18 January 1947. On 10 July 1947, the first defendant, pursuant to this agreement, demised the annexe to the plaintiffs 'with the appurtenances' for two years from 18 January 1947 with an option to renew for a further two. From the time of taking possession the plaintiffs took privileges beyond those given to them, but the first defendant was held by the Vice-Chancellor of the County Palatine Court of Lancaster to have consented to such acts for the period of time during which she should be in possession of the house.

In January 1949, the first defendant agreed to let the house to the second defendant who went into possession and obstructed the plaintiffs in the enjoyment of these privileges. The action was to restrain interference with the use of the passage through the front door to the annexe by the plaintiffs, their servants and agents.

Held (reversing in part the Vice-Chancellor of the County Palatine). The plaintiffs were entitled to the right of way because it was a right appertaining to their premises on 10 July 1947, the date of the lease; but not to the other privileges.

Evershed MR: The substance of the judge's finding is clearly this: he found that there was a sharp and substantial distinction between the privilege to the two plaintiffs themselves to go to and from the annexe through the front door, on the one hand, and all the other privileges on the other. [His Lordship quoted from the judge's judgment and continued:] The passage just read seems to me consistent only with the view that in the Vice-Chancellor's opinion the privilege given to the plaintiff tenants was intended to be one which otherwise was capable of annexation to the demised property and therefore capable of being caught by section 62 of the Law of Property Act 1925....

The claim of the plaintiffs...has been based on two grounds: first, implied grant, apart altogether from section 62 of the Law of Property Act 1925, and secondly section 62. In my judgment, the first ground cannot be sustained.

His Lordship explained that the use of the front door and passage was not 'necessary for the reasonable or convenient enjoyment' of the annexe, and a grant could not therefore be implied, and continued:

I therefore reject the argument based on implied grant, and turn to section 62.

The various rights here claimed are these: first, a right for the plaintiffs personally to pass through the front door and along the passage of the house.... Secondly, a right to maintain a signboard and an electric bell; thirdly, as a necessary corollary to that, a right for the plaintiff's customers to use the front door and passage; and, fourthly, a right to use it for the passage of goods.... It is plain, in my view, that these rights, other than the plaintiffs' personal right of passage, were not within the language of section 62 so as to be covered by the demise to them.

That leaves only the personal right.... Having regard to his judgment, I think that I am bound to regard the view of the judge as having been that, in contra-distinction to the other rights, it was intended to be something which the plaintiffs should enjoy qua lessees during the term of the demise, though it should not be enjoyed by their servants, workmen or any other persons with their authority. Therefore, I think, to quote Jenkins LJ, in the recent case of *Wright v Macadam* [1949] 2 KB 744 at 752 [p. 665, above]: 'It is a right or easement of a kind which could be readily included in a lease or conveyance by the insertion of appropriate words in the parcels.' What those would be I will state later, because, in the view which I take, it is necessary to see that the injunction or declaration to which the plaintiffs may be entitled is properly formulated.

Wright v Macadam was decided after the Vice-Chancellor gave judgment in this case.... The present privilege is in some ways indeed not dissimilar to that which in *Wright v Macadam* was held to be covered by section 62, namely, a privilege for the tenant to use a shed for storing her coal. I therefore think that, if the right which I have defined was one which was being enjoyed at the time of the conveyance, it is covered by section 62.

That therefore leaves the final point: what is the 'time of conveyance' within the meaning of section 62, subsections 1 and 2? The arrangement about this use of the passage appears to have been made at various dates, the last of which was January 13, 1947. The plaintiffs went into occupation of the annexe on January 18, 1947. The fitting of the bell and signboard took place after that. Several months passed (why, I know not, and it is quite immaterial) before the lease was executed on July 10, 1947, though the term was expressed to run from January 18. It is plain that before July 10 there was no written instrument whatever. Possession may no doubt have been attributable to an oral agreement of which, having regard to the position, specific performance might have been granted; but I fail to find any instrument in writing within the meaning of section 62 before the lease of July 10. It seems to me, therefore, that the phrase 'at the time of conveyance' must mean in this case July 10. I am unable to accept the view that one should construe that as meaning at the time when the terms granted by the lease is stated to have begun. On July 10, 1947, under the privilege granted, this right of ingress and egress was being enjoyed in fact. As I have held, though it is limited to the lessees themselves and does not extend to other persons, it would be capable of formulation and incorporation as a term of the lease, and it is, in my judgment, covered by section 62. To that extent, therefore, but to that limited extent only, the plaintiffs are entitled to succeed.

2. Nature of right

In **Phipps v Pears** [1965] 1 QB 76, p. 641, above, LORD DENNING MR, after holding that a right to protection from the weather could not exist as an easement, added at 84:

There is a further point. It was said that when the owner...conveyed No. 16 to Helena Field, the plaintiff's predecessor, there was implied in the conveyance all the general words of section 62 of the Law of Property Act 1925. The conveyance included all 'easements, rights and advantages whatsoever appertaining or reputed to appertain to the land'. On the conveyance of No. 16, Market Street, to the plaintiff's predecessor, there passed to him all these 'advantages' appertaining to No. 16. One of these advantages, it was said, was the benefit of having the old No. 14 there as a protection from the weather. I do not think this argument avails the plaintiff for the simple reason that, in order for section 62 to apply, the right or advantage must be one which is known to the law, in this sense, that it is capable of being granted at law so as to be binding on all successors in title, even those who take without notice, see *Wright v Macadam* [1949] 2 KB 744 [p. 665, above]. A fine view, or an expanse open to the winds, may be an 'advantage' to a house but it would not pass under section 62. Whereas a right to use a coal shed or to go along a passage would pass under section 62. The reason being that these last are rights known to the law, whereas the others are not. A right to protection from the weather is not a right known to the law. It does not therefore pass under section 62.

3. Diversity of occupation

Until recently it has been said that section 62 only applies, unlike the rule in *Wheeldon v Burrows*, if there has been a 'diversity of occupation' before the sale or lease; that is to say that the section does not apply where a person who has been both owner and occupier of adjoining premises sells or leases one of them. A number of problems would arise if the exercise of general rights of ownership by the common owner and occupier over the part to be sold were treated as 'rights and advantages' so as to give the purchaser an easement in respect of such of them as were capable of existing as easements. However, in *P & S Platt Ltd v Crouch*, p. 675, below, the Court of Appeal has held that section 62 can operate to create an easement where there is no prior diversity of occupation of the dominant and servient tenements, where the easement is continuous and apparent— that is, where there is a physically visible separation of the use of the dominant and servient tenements, even though they are owned and occupied by the same person.

In **Long v Gowlett** [1923] 2 Ch 177,[153] Mrs Nichols, the owner of land adjoining the River Granta at Linton, Cambridgeshire, sold the land in two lots by contempor-

---

[153] See also *Ward v Kirkland* [1967] Ch 194 at 227–231, p. 628, n. 42, above; *Kent v Kavanagh* [2007] Ch 1, p. 658, above.

aneous sales to two purchasers; Lot 1 to Gowlett and Lot 2 to Long's predecessor in title. The common owner had been accustomed to go from Lot 1, on which Hadstock Mill stood, to Lot 2 higher up the river, to repair the river bank and cut weeds therefrom, so as to ensure a free flow of water downstream to the Mill. Gowlett, the owner of Lot 1, claimed that an easement to enter Lot 2 to repair and cut had been created in his favour by the conveyance of 1909 under section 6 Conveyancing Act 1881 (now section 62 Law of Property Act 1925). Long sought an injunction and damages for trespass. In rejecting Gowlett's claim, SARGANT J said at 199:

And on these facts it is contended for the defendant that this constituted a 'privilege ease-ment right or advantage' over or in relation to Lot 2, which at the time of the conveyance was occupied or enjoyed with Lot 1; and accordingly, that this advantage passed to the defendant by virtue of the express words of the sub-section as included in the conveyance by virtue of the statute. The argument is not based in any way on the existence of any continuous and apparent easement existing over Lot 2 in favour of Lot 1; indeed, any such claim would be incompatible with the evidence, which clearly established that there was no defined way at all along the south bank. The claim is founded upon there having been a statutory introduction into the conveyance to the defendant of words equivalent to or identical with those either expressly contained or statutorily introduced in the corresponding conveyances in such cases as *James v Plant* (1836) 4 Ad & El 749; *Watts v Kelson* (1870) 6 Ch App 166; *Bayley v Great Western Rly Co* (1884) 26 ChD 434; and *White v Williams* [1922] 1 KB 727.

It is, therefore, necessary for the purpose of dealing with the matter on this footing to con-sider whether, during the common ownership and occupation of Lot 1 and Lot 2 by Mr Nichols and his widow, and therefore at the date of the conveyance, there was a 'privilege, easement, right or advantage' of the kind now claimed, which can properly be said to have been 'demised, occupied or enjoyed' with Lot 1 over Lot 2. It is very difficult to see how this can have been the case. No doubt the common owner and occupier did in fact repair the bank of Lot 2, and cut the weeds there; and no doubt also this repair and cutting would enure not solely for the benefit of Lot 2 (which comprised, amongst other things, a lawn tennis court), so as to prevent its being flooded, but also and very likely to a greater extent for the benefit of Lot 1. But there is nothing to indicate that the acts done on Lot 2 were done otherwise than in the course of the ownership and occupation of Lot 2, or that they were byway of using a 'privilege, easement or advantage' over Lot 2 in connection with Lot 1. The common owner and occupier of Whiteacre and Blackacre may in fact use Blackacre as an alternative and more convenient method of communication between Whiteacre and a neighbouring village. But it has never been held, and would I think be contrary to principle to hold, that (in default of there being a made road over Blackacre forming a continuous and apparent means of communication) a sale and conveyance of Whiteacre alone would carry a right to pass over Blackacre in the same way in which the common owner had been accustomed to pass. As it seems to me, in order that there may be a 'privilege, easement or advantage' enjoyed with Whiteacre over Blackacre so as to pass under the statute, there must be something done on Blackacre not due to or comprehended within the general rights of an occupying owner of Blackacre, but of such a nature that it is attribut-able to a privilege, easement, right or advantage, however precarious, which arises out of the ownership or occupation of Whiteacre, altogether apart from the ownership or occupation of Blackacre. And it is difficult to see how, when there is a common ownership of both Whiteacre and Blackacre, there can be any such relationship between the two closes as (apart from the case of continuous and apparent easements or that of a way of necessity) would be necessary to create a 'privilege, easement, right or advantage' within the words of section 6, subsection 2, of the statute. For this purpose it would seem that there must be some diversity of ownership or occupation of the two closes sufficient to refer the act or acts relied on not to mere occupying ownership, but to some advantage or privilege (however far short of a legal right) attaching to the owner or occupier of Whiteacre as such and de facto exercised over Blackacre. Let me illustrate my meaning from the latest case on the subject—namely, *White v Williams* [1922] 1 KB 727....

Mr Greene for the defendant was challenged to produce from the very many cases in which, on a conveyance of Whiteacre, an easement over Blackacre has been held to pass under the statutory words or their equivalent, a single case in which both the closes in question had been in common ownership and occupation, or in which there had not been an actual enjoyment over Blackacre on the part of an owner or occupier of Whiteacre who was not the owner and occupier of Blackacre. And neither from among the cases cited to me, nor from any other case in the books, was he able (with one solitary exception) to produce such a case as required. The exception, however, is one of high authority—namely, that of *Broomfield v Williams* [1897] 1 Ch 602—and it is necessary to examine it with some attention.[154]

In that case the common owner of a house and of adjoining land over which light had in fact been received through the windows of the house, sold and conveyed the house by a conveyance after the date of the Conveyancing Act 1881, but retained the adjoining land. It was held by the Court of Appeal that, although the retained land was marked on the plan on the conveyance as 'building land', the vendor was not at liberty subsequently to build on the retained land so as to interfere substantially with the access of light to the windows of the house. A. L. Smith LJ, it is true, based his judgment solely on the principle that the grantor was not entitled to derogate from his grant; and this was quite sufficient to support the actual decision. But the other two members of the Court relied mainly, if not exclusively, on the express words of section 6, subsection 2, of the Act; and the decision is, therefore, undoubtedly binding on me with regard to the access of light, and also with regard to any other 'privilege, easement, right or advantage' that is on the same footing as 'light.'

But such an easement or advantage as is now claimed is, in my judgment, very different from light, or a right to light. The access of light to a window over adjoining land is a physical fact plainly visible to any one buying a house. It is extremely similar to a continuous and apparent easement. It is mentioned in the subsection in the midst of a number of physical features ending with the word 'watercourses'; and the special position of light to an existing window as compared with other easements is fully recognised in the Prescription Act, which makes the acquisition of an easement of light depend on the enjoyment of the light simpliciter, and not, as in the case of other easements, on enjoyment as of right. The fact, therefore, that the inclusion of light in the subject matter of conveyance in section 6, subsection 2, has been held to entitle the grantee to the light coming to an existing window, does not necessarily involve the further inclusion of imperceptible rights or advantages, corresponding with intermittent practice or user as between two tenements of the common owner and occupier of both. Such an intermittent and non-apparent user or practice stands, in my judgment, on a completely different footing from the visible access of light to an existing window.

---

[154] See *Payne v Inwood* (1996) 74 P & CR 42 at 48–51, per Roch LJ.

The importance of such a distinction is specially obvious in a case like the present, where there is a contemporaneous sale by a common owner to two separate purchasers of adjoining lots completely divided by a physical boundary. If the contention of the defendant is correct, it would be necessary in any such case for the purchaser to inquire how the common owner and occupier had been accustomed to make use of each close in connection with the other. Would the plaintiff, for instance, in this case be entitled, as against the defendant, to an alternative way over Lot 1 to reach Lot 2, because while both lots were in common ownership and occupation, it was the practice of Mr and Mrs Nichols by way of Lot 1 to repair the south bank of Lot 2? Any number of similar puzzles would arise, if the law were as the defendant would have it. The fact that the common owner and occupier sells two adjoining closes separately is, in my mind, a negation of the intention to preserve access between them: compare such a case as *Midland Rly Co v Gribble* [1895] 2 Ch 827.

The only two exceptions to this rule appear to be those of ways of necessity and of continuous and apparent easements. Had the general words of section 6, subsection 2, any such effect as is suggested by the defendant—and it must be remembered that these words were not new, but represented conveyancing practice for many years previously—it is difficult, if not impossible, to understand how there have not been numerous cases in which, on a severance of two closes, a subsisting practice by the common owner and occupier of both has not been given effect to by way of legal easement as a result of general words of this kind.

In **Sovmots Investments Ltd v Secretary of State for the Environment** [1979] AC 144[155] the House of Lords considered both the rule in *Wheeldon v Burrows* and section 62. The London Borough of Camden made a compulsory purchase order to acquire 36 residential maisonettes in Centre Point. The question was whether certain rights over and in respect of other parts of Centre Point, without which the maisonettes could not be used as housing accommodation, passed on the convey-ance; and whether, if they did not pass, the Borough had power to make a compul-sory purchase order to acquire the maisonettes which, without the additional rights, could not be used for housing purposes. In quashing the order, LORD WILBERFORCE said at 168:[156]

The main argument before the inspector and in the courts below was that in this case and under the compulsory purchase order as made no specific power to require the creation of ancillary rights was necessary because these would pass to the acquiring authority under either, or both, of the first rule in *Wheeldon v Burrows* (1879) 12 ChD 31 ('the rule') or of section 62 of the Law of Property Act 1925. Under the rule (I apologise for the reminder but the expression of the rule is important)

'on the grant by the owner of a tenement of part of that tenement *as it is then used and enjoyed*, there will pass to the grantee all those continuous and apparent easements (by which, of course, I mean quasi-easements), or, in other words, all those easements which are necessary to the reasonable enjoyment of the property granted, and *which have been and are at the time of the grant used* by the owners of the entirety for the benefit of the part granted' (see per Thesiger LJ at 49, my emphasis).

---

[155] (1977) 41 Conv (NS) 415; [1979] Conv 113 (C. Harpum); [1978] Conv 449 (P. Smith); 127 NLJ 695 (H. W. Wilkinson).

[156] See also at 175–176, per Lord Edmund-Davies.

Under section 62 a conveyance of land operates to convey with the land all ways, water-courses, liberties, privileges, easements, rights and advantages whatsoever, appertaining or reputed to appertain to the land, or any part thereof, or, at the time of conveyance, demised, occupied or enjoyed with, or reputed or known as part or parcel of or appurtenant to the land or any part thereof.

My Lords, there are very comprehensive expressions here, but it does not take much analysis to see that they have no relevance to the situation under consideration.

The rule is a rule of intention, based on the proposition that a man may not derogate from his grant. He cannot grant or agree to grant land and at the same time deny to his grantee what is at the time of the grant obviously necessary for its reasonable enjoyment. To apply this to a case where a public authority is taking from an owner his land without his will is to stand the rule on its head: it means substituting for the intention of a reasonable voluntary grantor the unilateral, opposed, intention of the acquirer.[157]

Moreover, and this point is relevant to a later argument, the words I have underlined[158] show that for the rule to apply there must be actual, and apparent, use and enjoyment at the time of the grant. But no such use or enjoyment had, at Centre Point, taken place at all.

Equally, section 62 does not fit this case. The reason is that when land is under one ownership one cannot speak in any intelligible sense of rights, or privileges, or easements being exercised over one part for the benefit of another. Whatever the owner does, he does as owner and until a separation occurs, of ownership or at least of occupation, the condition for the existence of rights, etc., does not exist: see *Bolton v Bolton* (1879) 11 ChD 968, 970 per Fry J and *Long v Gowlett* [1923] 2 Ch 177, 189, 198, in my opinion a correct decision.[159]

A separation of ownership, in a case like the present, will arise on conveyance of one of the parts (e.g. the maisonettes), but this separation cannot be projected back to the stage of the compulsory purchase order so as, by anticipation to bring into existence rights not existing in fact.

[1978] Conv 449, at pp. 454–455 (P. Smith)

In fact there is a considerable body of authority against [*Long v Gowlett*], both academic and precedent based, none of which was seriously considered by the House of Lords. There is no need to consider it in any detail as most readers will be aware of it.[160] The first limitation namely that section 62 has no ambit where there is no diversity of occupation, does not stand up to precedent for a start. In *Broomfield v Williams*[161] the Court of Appeal made no such limitation as suggested by Sargant J in *Long v Gowlett* and Lord Wilberforce and Lord Edmund-Davies

---

[157] This argument does not apply where the grantor conveys the freehold to a tenant holding under a long lease who exercises his statutory right to call for the freehold under the Leasehold Reform Act 1967: *Kent v Kavanagh* [2007] Ch 1, p. 658, above.

[158] As printed in italics.

[159] See *Ward v Kirkland* [1967] Ch 194 at 227–231; *Wright v Macadam* [1949] 2 KB 744 at 748; *Squarey v Harris-Smith* (1981) 42 P & CR 118 at 129, per Oliver LJ.

[160] For starters Jackson (1966) 30 Conv (NS) 342–348 and thence Jackson, *The Law of Easements and Profits*, pp. 97–103; Megarry and Wade, *The Law of Easements and Profits*, pp. 97–103; Megarry and Wade, *The Law of Real Property* (4th edn), pp. 835, n. 47 and 837–838; Farrand, *Contract and Conveyance* (2nd edn), pp. 384–386; *Emmet*, p. 515; Barnsley, *Conveyancing Law and Practice*, pp. 484–485 (perhaps?); and *Gale on Easements* (14th edn), pp. 125–126. The last book is particularly significant as the 13th edn of that book supported *Long v Gowlett* but was changed after Professor Jackson's article above.

[161] [1897] 1 Ch 602.

in the *Sovmots case.* With respect to Lord Edmund-Davies and to Mr Harpum,[162] merely to state easements of light are different from other easements does not explain why section 62, apparently very widely drawn, applies to those easements and not to others when there is no diversity of occupation. There is absolutely nothing in the section to justify such a limitation. Furthermore the objection that the rights etc. do not exist at the relevant time, ignores the substantial body of case law where section 62 has turned a precarious right into a full legal easement....[163]

The real problem now is what is left after *Sovmots*? It appears that one of the major opponents of the limitations imposed by the case is prepared to concede it now,[164] but is such resignation necessary? Only two of the five law lords considered the point, no argument was addressed to them on the point and no cases cited.

In **P & S Platt Ltd v Crouch** [2004] 1 P & CR 18 the defendants owned a hotel, a house in the grounds of the hotel, and a separate plot of land (called Noosa Sound) adjacent to the Norfolk Broads where river moorings were used for the benefit of the hotel guests. Signs at the river side made clear that the moorings were for the use of hotel guests only, and the hotel's website advertised the availability of the moorings. The claimant purchased the hotel, but not the other properties, but claimed that it had acquired the right to the moorings, for the benefit of the hotel, as an easement. Holding that there was an easement by virtue of section 62 of the Law of Property Act 1925 PETER GIBSON LJ said at 244:

1 English law has long recognised that a conveyance by a grantor of part of his property carries with it certain rights over the retained land which are not expressly conveyed by the conveyance. Because of the common ownership of the property such rights cannot have been easements prior to the conveyance. Under the rule in *Wheeldon v Burrows* (1879) 12 ChD 31 on the conveyance there pass to the grantee as easements all quasi-easements over the land retained which were continuous and apparent, necessary for the reasonable enjoyment of the land conveyed and were at the time of the conveyance used by the grantor for the benefit of the land conveyed. Somewhat similar but more extensive in effect is section 62 of the Law of Property Act 1925, replacing section 6 of the Conveyancing Act 1881, and designed to make it unnecessary to set out the full effect of every conveyance....

2 This appeal gives rise to the question whether on a transfer by vendors of part of their property, certain quasi-easements over the retained property became legal easements by the operation of section 62....

42 To my mind the evidence is clear that the rights in question did appertain to and were reputed to appertain to and were enjoyed with the hotel, being part of the hotel business and advertised as such and enjoyed by the hotel guests. The rights were continuous and apparent, and so it matters not that prior to the sale of the hotel there was no prior diversity of occupation of the dominant and servient tenancies. Accordingly, I reach the conclusion that section 62 operated to convert the rights into full easements...

---

[162] (1977) 41 Conv (NS) 415.

[163] See e.g. *Wright v Macadam* [1949] 2 KB 744; *Goldberg v Edwards* [1950] Ch 247 and *International Tea Stores v Hobbs* [1903] 2 Ch 165. None of these cases featured in the *Sovmots* case.

[164] See Jackson, *Law of Easements and Profits*, p. 100.

LONGMORE LJ said at 256:

57 The only document relevantly evidencing the genesis and aim of the contract for the sale of the hotel is the 'Particulars of Sale'. Those particulars said nothing about the riverside moorings as such but did make it clear that the hotel was being offered as a going concern making good profits on a specified turnover. In not untypical estate agents' language the particulars also said:

> 'The attraction of the Broads for leisure activities is hard to understate; it is a Mecca for activities such as boating, walking, fishing and for those interested in nature and it is this that provide the main driving force for the business.'

58 The natural implication from this is that those visiting the hotel by boat have been and will be able to moor their boats in the vicinity of the Hotel. In this I only reiterate the conclusion of the judge in para. [43] of his judgment where he said that the assets of the business, on any objective consideration, included advertising signs on Noosa Sound and the availability of moorings for use by patrons of the hotel.

59 I am, therefore, satisfied that the rights claimed by the claimants were 'continuous' and 'apparent' rights which passed under the conveyance to them pursuant to section 62 of the Law of Property Act 1925, see Megarry and Wade, *Law of Real Property*, 6th edn (2000), para. 18–114.

Law Commission Consultation Paper on Easements, Covenants and Profits à Prendre 2008 (Consultation Paper No. 186), paras 4.69–4.71, 4.73–4.78, 4.102–4.104

4.69 The statutory predecessor of [section 62 of the Law of Property Act 1925], section 6 of the Conveyancing Act 1881, was initially viewed as a 'word-saving' device, taking away the need painstakingly to enumerate in conveyances all the rights that were to pass with the land. Since the early twentieth century the provision has been given a wider interpretation, by also transforming precarious benefits, merely enjoyed by licence of the owner prior to the conveyance, into permanent property rights.[165] Section 62 often takes effect 'automatically' without an appreciation of its effect by the parties to the conveyance.

4.70 The following conditions must be fulfilled for section 62 to operate:

(1) the right must have been exercised over land retained by the grantor;[166]

(2) the right must have been appurtenant to or "enjoyed with" the quasidominant tenement;[167]

(3) the right must have already been enjoyed "at the time of the conveyance";[168] and

---

[165] *International Tea Stores Ltd v Hobbs* [1903] 2 Ch 165; *Wright v Macadam* [1949] 2 KB 744.

[166] *Nickerson v Barraclough* [1981] Ch 426.

[167] 'Enjoyed with' is defined by reference to the factual user of the land: *International Tea Stores Co v Hobbs* [1903] 2 Ch 165.

[168] This refers to the date of the completion of the conveyance, not the date of exchange of contracts nor the date of commencement of the lease (*Goldberg v Edwards* [1950] Ch 247). The court will look at a reasonable period of time before the conveyance to determine this (*Green v Ashco Horticulturist Ltd* [1966] 1 WLR 889). In *Costagliola v English* (1969) 210 EG 1425 it was held that a right could still be transferred under s. 62 if the period during which it had not been used amounted to less than a year.

(4) the conveyance must be of a legal estate.[169]

4.71 However, the operation of the section is subject to the following important limitations:

(1) the right in question must be capable of being an easement;[170]

(2) the grant must be within the competence of the grantor;[171]

(3) the user must not be excessively personal,[172] excessively precarious,[173] merely temporary[174] or a 'mere memory';[175] and

(4) the section applies only in so far as a contrary intention is not expressed in the conveyance.[176]

4.73 We consider that section 62 suffers from a number of serious defects. The principal problem is that it transforms precarious interests, such as licences, into property rights. This transformative aspect of the provision has been adversely commented upon by both judges[177] and scholars.[178]

4.74 As was noted in the report leading to the Land Registration Act 2002, section 62 'tends to operate without an appreciation of its effect by the parties to the conveyance'.[179] If they do not understand how it works, or even that it will apply, the parties do not take section 62 into account when negotiating the transfer of land. In addition, section 62 can only be excluded expressly. This means that the section will be excluded only by those properly advised, so it primarily acts as a trap for the unwary.

4.75 There are further difficulties with section 62. The extent of its operation is not entirely clear. In particular, there has been considerable debate as to whether it is necessary that prior to the conveyance there was a diversity of ownership or occupation as between the dominant

---

[169] LPA 1925, s. 205(1)(ii). This includes the grant of a (legal) lease, but not an agreement for lease: see *Borman v Griffith* [1930] 1 Ch 493, and para. 4.63 above.

[170] *Regis Property Co Ltd v Redman* [1956] 2 QB 612.

[171] *Quicke v Chapman* [1903] 1 Ch 659.

[172] *Goldberg v Edwards* [1950] Ch 247 [p. 668, above].

[173] *Green v Ashco Horticulturist Ltd* [1966] 2 All ER 232.

[174] *Wright v Macadam* [1949] 2 KB 744 [p. 665, above].

[175] *Penn v Wilkins* (1974) 236 EG 203.

[176] LPA 1925, s. 62(4). Any intention to exclude must be clear and in the past there has been a strict interpretation of when and how the section is excluded (*Gregg v Richards* [1926] Ch 521). Although this approach may have softened more recently, particularly where the section would create an injustice (*Selby District Council v Samuel Smith Old Brewery (Tadcaster) Ltd* (2000) 80 P & CR 466), it would appear that only those who have been properly advised can be confident the section is effectively excluded. The Law Society's 4th edn of the Standard Conditions of Sale (Standard Condition 3.4) excludes s. 62 as standard only in so far as it relates to rights to light and air. For all other easements, including rights of way, the conditions allow s. 62 to operate in favour of the purchaser.

[177] See, for example, *Hair v Gillman* (2000) 80 P & CR 108, 116, by Chadwick LJ; *Commission for the New Towns v Gallagher* [2002] EWHC 2668, (2003) 2 P & CR 24 at [61] by Neuberger J; in *Dewsbury v Davies* (unreported, Court of Appeal, 21 May 1992) Fox LJ said that it 'seems a rather odd result that a section whose purpose was to shorten conveyances should have the effect of turning....a permissive and precarious right into a revocable easement'.

[178] See L. Tee, 'Metamorphoses and Section 62 of the Law of Property Act 1925' [1998] 62 *The Conveyancer and Property Lawyer* 115; Megarry and Wade, *The Law of Real Property* (6th edn, 2000), para. 18–111.

[179] Law Com No. 271, para. 4.25.

and servient lands.[180] The better view now seems to be that, subject to two exceptions,[181] there must have been such a diversity, on the basis that:

'…when land is under one ownership one cannot speak in any intelligible sense of rights, or privileges, or easements being exercised over one part for the benefit of another. Whatever the owner does, he does as owner and, until a separation occurs, of ownership or at least of occupation, the condition for the existence of rights, etc., does not exist.'[182]

4.76   The effect is that the operation of section 62 and the rule in *Wheeldon v Burrows* tend to be mutually exclusive. *Wheeldon v Burrows* applies to quasi-easements being exercised by a common owner over one part of his or her land for the benefit of another. Section 62 appears generally not to be effective unless there is diversity of ownership or occupation as between the dominant and servient lands.

4.77   However, the precise relationship between section 62 and *Wheeldon v Burrows* remains doubtful and uncertain:

'There is a considerable overlap between s.62 and the *Wheeldon* rule and it is sometimes difficult to discern why only one or the other of them was relied on in a particular case.'[183]

4.78   In general terms, it is easier to succeed under section 62 than the rule in *Wheeldon v Burrows* as there is no need to prove either that the right was continuous and apparent[184] or that it was necessary for the reasonable enjoyment of the property conveyed. However, as a counsel of prudence, it is often sensible to base a claim on both methods of implication in the alternative.[185] Moreover, in the absence of a 'conveyance' triggering section 62, the rule in *Wheeldon v Burrows* may be the only recourse available to the claimant to the easement.[186]

4.102   …We would like to make a provisional proposal for one reform…That is, the removal of the transformative effect of section 62 of the Law of Property Act 1925. As we have noted,[187] aside from the ambiguity of the provision, section 62 suffers from a problem of principle. The provision often operates in circumstances where the parties would not necessarily expect an easement to be granted.

4.103   We do not propose any abrogation of the useful 'word-saving' function performed by section 62, and for that reason we do not consider that it should be repealed.

---

[180]   *Long v Gowlett* [1923] 2 Ch 177 [p. 670, above]; *Sovmots Investments Ltd v Secretary of State for the Environment* [1979] AC 144 [p. 673, above]; C. Harpum, 'Easements and Centre Point: Old Problems resolved in a Novel Setting' [1977] Conv 415; P. Smith, 'Centre Point: Faulty Towers with Shaky Foundations' [1978] Conv 449; C Harpum, '*Long v Gowlett*: A Strong Fortress' [1979] Conv 113.

[181]   The general exception relates to rights which were 'continuous and apparent' at the time of the conveyance: *P & S Platt v Crouch* [2003] EWCA Civ 1110, [2004] 1 P & CR 18 [p. 675, above]. Quasi-easements of light will also pass: *Watts v Kelson* (1870) 6 Ch App 166.

[182]   *Sovmots Investments Ltd v Secretary of State for the Environment* [1979] AC 144, 169, by Lord Wilberforce.

[183]   *Hillman v Rogers* [1997] NPC 183, by Robert Walker LJ.

[184]   Save where there was no diversity of ownership or occupation prior to the conveyance: see para. 4.61 above.

[185]   *Wheeler v JJ Saunders Ltd* [1996] Ch 19 has been cited as a case which lost on the rule in *Wheeldon v Burrows* but may have succeeded on s. 62: see Thompson [1995] 59 Conv 239.

[186]   See e.g. *Borman v Griffith* [1930] 1 Ch 493, summarised at para. 4.63 above: s. 62 could not operate, as an agreement for a lease does not comprise a 'conveyance'.

[187]   See para. 4.74 above.

4.104 We provisionally propose that section 62 of the Law of Property Act 1925 should no longer operate to transform precarious benefits, enjoyed with the owner's licence or consent, into legal easements on a conveyance of the dominant estate.

QUESTIONS

1. Is there good reason in particular or authority for requiring a diversity of occupation for the operation of section 62? What bearing does the *Sovmots* case have on the matter? What is the current state of the law, given that neither *Long v Gowlett* nor *Sovmots* were cited in *P & S Platt Ltd v Crouch* and the Court of Appeal there did not discuss the arguments and authorities in favour of a requirement of diversity of occupation? And is there justification for applying a different rule to easements of light?

   See Gale, paras 3.129–3.134; [1978] Conv 449 (P. Smith); Gray, para. 5.2.50; M & W, para. 28.025.

2. Is there good reason for differentiating in this respect between the operation of the rule in *Wheeldon v Burrows* and the Law of Property Act 1925, section 62? See Jenkins LJ in *Wright v Macadam* [1949] 2 KB 744, p. 665, above; C & B, pp. 610–612; Gray, para. 5.2.43 M & W, paras 28.028–28.031; MM, pp, 429–430; Smith, pp. 504–506; Jackson, *Law of Easements and Profits*, pp. 100–103. Notice that the decision in *P & S Platt Ltd v Crouch* applies one of the criteria for the application of the rule in *Wheeldon v Burrows* ('continuous and apparent') without the further requirement that the right be necessary for the reasonable enjoyment of the dominant tenement.

3. Should the 'transformative effect' of section 62 be abolished? See Law Commission Consultation Paper on Easements, Covenants and Profits à Prendre 2008 (Consultation Paper No. 186), paras 4.102–4.104.

4. How far should the law on the implied acquisition of easements be reformed? Would a test based simply on the intention of the parties be preferable? See Law Commission Consultation Paper on Easements, Covenants and Profits à Prendre 2008, paras 4.36–4.150.

(ii) Easements implied in favour of the grantor

Generally, any rights which a grantor wishes to enjoy as easements in favour of the land he retains, and exercisable over the land sold, must be expressly reserved[188] or regranted. Otherwise he may not derogate from his grant.[189] In exceptional cases, however, easements will be implied in his favour. These are easements of necessity,[190] and maybe (*a*) 'an easement without which the property retained cannot be used at

---

[188] LPA 1925, s. 65, p. 651, above.   [189] (1964) 80 LQR 244 (D. W. Elliott).

[190] See *Nickerson v Barraclough* [1980] Ch 325 at 332. Where access to retained land could be obtained only over the property granted or by destruction of a physical barrier on the retained land (a building) the continued existence of which was obviously contemplated by the parties, the retained land was to be regarded as landlocked: *Sweet v Sommer* [2004] 4 All ER 288, affd on other grounds [2005] EWCA Civ 227.

all, and not one merely necessary to the reasonable enjoyment of that property',[191] and (b) an easement which is required to carry out the common intention of the parties.[192] These are usually easements of support, and such easements can only be claimed when the intention is clear.[193] In each case the right which the grantor can claim is the minimum necessary to comply with the rule under which it is claimed.

Corporation of London v Riggs
(1880) 13 ChD 798 (ChD, Jessel MR)

In 1887, Heathcote, the owner of land in Essex, conveyed part of this land to London Corporation who declared that they would hold the land conveyed as an open space for ever. This land completely encircled a close of about two acres called Barn Hoppet which was owned also by Heathcote, and had been used up to that time for agricultural purposes only. No easements in favour of Barn Hoppet were reserved in the conveyance of the other land to London Corporation. In 1879 Riggs entered into possession of Barn Hoppet as tenant, and he made preparations for the erection of a house and of other buildings for the sale of refreshments to the public. The plaintiffs claimed a declaration that Riggs' right of way of necessity was limited to purposes sufficient to the use of Barn Hoppet for agricultural purposes only; and an injunction and damages. The action was tried on demurrer.

Held. The defendant's right of way was limited to the purposes for which it was used in 1877.

Jessel MR: I am afraid that, whatever I may call my decision, it will, in effect, be making law, which I never have any desire to do; but I cannot find that the point is covered by any decided case, or even appears to have been discussed in any decided case. The only satisfaction I have in deciding the point is this, that it will in all probability be carried to a higher Court, and it will be for that Court to make the law, or, as we say, declare the law, and not for me.

The real question I have to decide is this—whether, on a grant of land wholly surrounding a close, the implied grant, or re-grant, of a right of way by the grantee to the grantor to enable him to get to the reserved, or excepted, or inclosed close, is a grant of a general right of way for all purposes, or only a grant of a right of way for the purpose of the enjoyment of the reserved or excepted close in its then state.

There is, as I have said, no distinct authority on the question. It seems to me to have been laid down in very early times—and I have looked into a great number of cases, and among others several black-letter cases[194]—that the right to a way of necessity is an exception to the

---

[191] *Union Lighterage Co v London Graving Dock Co* [1902] 2 Ch 557 at 573; *Pinnington v Galland* (1853) 9 Exch 1; *Deacon v South Eastern Rly Co* (1889) 61 LT 377; *Midland Rly Co v Miles* (1886) 33 ChD 632.

[192] *Richards v Rose* (1853) 9 Exch 218; *Shubrook v Tufnell* (1882) 46 LT 886; *Re Webb's Lease* [1951] Ch 808, p. 682, below.

[193] See *Nickerson v Barraclough* [1981] Ch 426 (where CA, reversing Megarry V-C, held that 'the doctrine of way of necessity is not founded upon public policy at all but upon an implication from the circumstances' (per Brightman LJ at 440); and so if the grant implied by way of construction was negated by an express contrary provision in the conveyance, no grant could be implied by the court under a rule of public policy, for example, against land being rendered unusable by being landlocked); [1981] Conv 442 (L. Crabb).

[194] 'The black-letter books are described by Sir William Holdsworth (*A History of the English Law*, 4th edn (1936), vol. 2 p. 525) as being printed editions of the Year Books, which were early case notes created from

ordinary rule that a man shall not derogate from his own grant, and that the man who grants the surrounding land is in very much the same position as regards the right of way to the reserved close as if he had granted the close, retaining the surrounding land. In both cases there is what is called a way of necessity; and the way of necessity, according to the old rules of pleading, must have been pleaded as a grant, or, where the close is reserved, as it is here, as a re-grant. . . .

Well, now, if we try the case on principle—treating this right of way as an exception to the rule—ought it to be treated as a larger exception than the necessity of the case warrants? That of course brings us back to the question, What does the necessity of the case require? The object of implying the re-grant, as stated by the older Judges, was that if you did not give the owner of the reserved close some right of way or other, he could neither use nor occupy the reserved close, nor derive any benefit from it. But what is the extent of the benefit he is to have? Is he entitled to say, I have reserved to myself more than that which enables me to enjoy it as it is as the time of the grant? And if that is the true rule, that he is not to have more than necessity requires, as distinguished from what convenience may require, it appears to me that the right of way must be limited to that which is necessary at the time of the grant; that is, he is supposed to take a re-grant to himself of such a right of way as will enable him to enjoy the reserved thing as it is.

That appears to me to be the meaning of a right of way of necessity. If you imply more, you reserve to him not only that which enables him to enjoy the thing he has reserved as it is, but that which enables him to enjoy it in the same way and to the same extent as if he reserved a general right of way for all purposes: that is—as in the case I have before me—a man who reserves two acres of arable land in the middle of a large piece of land is to be entitled to cover the reserved land with houses, and call on his grantee to allow him to make a wide metalled road up to it. I do not think that is a fair meaning of a way of necessity: I think it must be limited by the necessity at the time of the grant; and that the man who does not take the pains to secure an actual grant of a right of way for all purposes is not entitled to be put in a better position than to be able to enjoy that which he had at the time the grant was made. I am not aware of any other principle on which this case can be decided.

I may be met by the objection that a way of necessity must mean something more than what I have stated, because, where the grant is of the inclosed piece, the grantee is entitled to use the land for all purposes, and should therefore be entitled to a right of way commensurate with his right of enjoyment. But there again the grantee has not taken from the grantor any express grant of a right of way: and all he can be entitled to ask is a right to enable him to enjoy the property granted to him as it was granted to him. It does not appear to me that the grant of the property gives any greater right. But even if it did, the principle applicable to the grantee is not quite the same as the principle applicable to the grantor: and it might be that the grantee obtains a larger way of necessity—though I do not think he does—than the grantor does under the implied re-grant.

I am afraid that I am laying down the law for the first time—that I am for the first time declaring the law; but it is a matter of necessity from which I cannot escape.

The demurrer must, therefore, be overruled, with costs.

the reign of Edward I to Henry VIII. It seems likely "black-letter cases" were those taken from the black-letter books. The black-letter books are now thought not to be an accurate transcription of the Year Book manuscripts; at p. 530 is quoted F W Maitland who was of the view that "of mere, sheer nonsense those old black-letter books are but too full": YB 1, 2 Ed II (SS), xxi': *Adealon International Proprietary Ltd v Merton LBC* [2007] 1 WLR 1898, p. 685, below, at [12], per Carnwath LJ.

Re Webb's Lease
[1951] Ch 808 (CA, Evershed MR, Jenkins and Morris LJJ)

The defendant (the landlord) was head lessee of a three storey building. He occupied the ground floor for his own business as a butcher, and leased the upper two storeys to the plaintiff (the tenant). The first letting was in 1939 for three years; the tenant remained in occupation until 1949 when he was granted a 21 year lease. Throughout all this time one side of the building contained an advertisement for the defendant's business, and another side (the west wall) one for Bryant and May's matches, both of which covered all or part of the external walls of the upper two storeys. None of the leases made any reservation of the right of the landlord to use the outer walls of the demised premises for this purpose. In 1950, the tenants began to make enquiries concerning the landlord's right so to use the walls and finally issued this summons to determine the question.

Held (reversing Danckwerts J). Without express reservation, the landlord had no right to claim the easement in question.

Jenkins LJ: The matter therefore stands thus: The landlord did not include in the provisions of the lease as executed any reservation of advertising rights over any part of the outer walls; but, at the date of the lease, the advertisements now in dispute were in their present positions on the walls and plainly to be seen. Moreover, they had existed in their present positions continuously since before the commencement of the tenant's original tenancy in 1939; and the tenant never objected to their presence at any time during his original tenancy, or at the time of the granting of the lease of August 11, 1949, or thereafter until January 1950. There is no evidence that either party ever even mentioned the subject of the advertisements to the other during the whole of this period of more than ten years.

This being in substance the whole of the available facts, the question is whether on those bare facts without more, the court can and ought as a matter of law to imply in favour of the landlord a reservation during the term of twenty-one years granted by the lease of August 11, 1949, of advertising rights over the outer walls demised, at all events to the extent required to enable him to maintain the existing advertisements and to retain for his own benefit any periodical payments receivable from the Borough Billposting Co. in respect of the site of the 'Brymay' poster.

As to the law applicable to the case, it is not disputed that as a general rule a grantor, whether by way of conveyance or lease, of part of a hereditament in his ownership, cannot claim any easement over the part granted for the benefit of the part retained, unless it is expressly reserved out of the grant. See (for instance) *Suffield v Brown* (1864) 4 De GJ & Sm 185; *Crossley & Sons Ltd v Lightowler* (1867) LR 2 Ch App 478; *Wheeldon v Burrows* (1879) 12 ChD 31 [p. 656, above].

There are, however, certain exceptions to the general rule. Two well-established exceptions relate to easements of necessity and mutual easements such as rights of support between adjacent buildings. But it is recognised in the authorities that these two specific exceptions do not exhaust the list, which is indeed incapable of exhaustive statement, as the circumstances of any particular case may be such as to raise a necessary inference that the common intention of the parties must have been to reserve some easement to the grantor, or such as to preclude the grantee from denying the right consistently with good faith, and there appears to be no doubt that where circumstances such as these are clearly established the court will imply the appropriate reservation.

His Lordship quoted from the judgment of Thesiger LJ, in *Wheeldon v Burrows,* p. 656, above, and referred to *Russell v Watts* (1885) 10 App Cas 590, *Aldridge v Wright* [1929] 2 KB 117 and *Liddiard v Waldron* [1934] 1 KB 435, and continued:

The most comprehensive statement of the area of potential exceptions is probably that contained in the speech of Lord Parker in *Pwllbach Colliery Co Ltd v Woodman* [1915] AC 634 at 646, where his Lordship, after referring to the exception with respect to easements of necessity, said this:

'The second class of cases in which easements may impliedly be created depends not upon the terms of the grant itself, but upon the circumstances under which the grant was made. The law will readily imply the grant or reservation of such easements as may be necessary to give effect to the common intention of the parties to a grant of real property, with reference to the manner or purposes in and for which the land granted or some land retained by the grantor is to be used. See *Jones v Pritchard* [1908] 1 Ch 630, and *Lyttleton Times Co Ltd v Warners Ltd* [1907] AC 476. But it is essential for this purpose that the parties should intend that the subject of the grant or the land retained by the grantor should be used in some definite and particular manner. It is not enough that the subject of the grant or the land retained should be intended to be used in a manner which may or may not involve this definite and particular use.'...

The question is whether the circumstances of the case as proved in evidence are such as to raise a necessary inference that the common intention of the parties was to reserve to the landlord during the twenty-one years' term some, and if so what, rights in regard to the display of advertisements over the outer walls of the demised premises, or such as to preclude the tenant from denying the implied reservation to the landlord of some such rights consistently with good faith.

That question must be approached with the following principles in mind: (i) If the landlord intended to reserve any such rights over the demised premises it was his duty to reserve them expressly in the lease of August 11, 1949 (*Wheeldon v Burrows* (1879) 12 ChD 31); (ii) The landlord having failed in this duty, the onus was upon him to establish the facts to prove, and prove clearly, that his case was an exception to the rule (*Aldridge v Wright* [1929] 2 KB 117); (iii) The mere fact that the tenant knew at the date of the lease of August 11, 1949 that the landlord was using the outer walls of the demised premises for the display of the advertisements in question did not suffice to absolve the landlord from his duty of expressly reserving any rights in respect of them he intended to claim, or to take the case out of the general rule: see *Suffield v Brown* (1864) 4 De GJ & Sm 185; *Crossley & Sons Ltd v Lightowler* (1867) LR 2 Ch App 478.

Applying these principles to the present case, I ask myself whether the landlord has on the meagre facts proved discharged the onus which lies upon him of proving it an exception to the general rule. He can, so far as I can see, derive no assistance from the passage quoted above from Lord Parker's speech in the *Pwllbach Colliery Case* [1915] AC 634 at 646. It might, I suppose, be said to have been in the contemplation of the parties that the landlord would continue to use the ground floor of the premises for the purposes of his business as a butcher and provision merchant, but it cannot in my view be contended that the maintenance during the term of the lease of his advertisement over the door was a necessary incident of the user so contemplated. This applies a fortiori to the 'Brymay' advertisement, the display of which on the outer wall of the demised premises by the Borough Billposting Company as licensees of the landlord was so far as I can see not related in any way to the use or occupation of the ground floor for the existing or any other purpose. The transaction with the Borough Billposting Company was simply a hiring out for reward of part of an outer wall of the demised premises for use as an advertising or billposting site or station.

The mere fact that the tenant knew of the presence of the advertisements at the date when the lease of August 11, 1949 was granted being, as stated above, beside the point, nothing is left beyond the bare circumstance that the advertisements were not only present at the date of the grant but had been continuously present without objection by the tenant since the commencement of his original tenancy in 1939. Does this circumstance suffice to raise a necessary inference of an intention common to both parties at the date of the lease that the landlord should have reserved to him the right to maintain these advertisements throughout the twenty-one years' term thereby granted? I cannot see that it does. The most that can be said is that the facts are consistent with such a common intention. But that will not do. The landlord must surely show at least that the facts are not reasonably consistent with any other explanation. Here he manifestly fails....

In short, I can hold nothing more established by the facts proved than permissive user of the outer walls by the landlord for the display of the advertisements during the original tenancy and thereafter from the granting of the lease until the tenant's objection in January 1950; with nothing approaching grounds for inferring, as a matter of necessary inference, an intention common to both parties that such permissive user should be converted by the lease into a reservation to the landlord of equivalent rights throughout the twenty-one years' term thereby granted.

In **Peckham v Ellison** (2000) 79 P & CR 276, CAZALET J, in holding that there was an implied reservation of a right of way in favour of No. 16 Kirklands over No. 15, said at 278:[195]

In the mid-1940s, Preston Council built a housing estate in Chipping, Preston, which included, at the end of a cul-de-sac, a row of four terraced houses—Nos 15, 16, 17 and 18 Kirklands. I shall refer to them by their numbers. Facing the front of the properties they are numbered consecutively from 15 on the right to 18 on the left. The defendants own and occupy No. 15, which is the end of terrace property. The plaintiffs own No. 16 which adjoins No. 15 on one side and No. 17 on the other. The plaintiffs claim a right of way ('the claimed right of way'), for all purposes around the side and across the rear of the defendants' house, that claimed right of way providing a means of access to the rear of the plaintiff's house. The four houses were occupied from the late 1940s by council tenants until the 'right to buy' provisions of the Housing Act 1980 came into force. Subsequently each house was bought by its tenant....

I do not accept that the judge applied the wrong test. In my view, his findings demonstrated a necessary inference of an intention common to both parties that the council should have a right of way reserved to it over No. 15 for the benefit of No. 16. Furthermore, although the judge indicated that the grounds for dismissing the appeal might constitute an extension to the exceptions to the rule in *Wheeldon v Burrows* I consider that the judge's decision came fully

---

[195] Citing with approval at 285 Cheshire and Burn, *Modern Law of Real Property* (15th edn), p. 538, para. (ii); (2000) 150 NLJ (H. W. Wilkinson); cf. *Chaffe v Kingsley* (1999) 79 P & CR 404; *Holaw (470) Ltd v Stockton Estates Ltd* (2001) 81 P & CR 404.

within the formula laid down by Jenkins LJ in *Re Webb's Lease,* and did not constitute a new exception to that rule.

I would also add, having considered the facts of the different cases in the line of authorities cited, that this case is clearly an exceptional one, not least (i) because of the grantees' acknowledged belief that the claimed right of way existed over the servient tenement, (ii) that such claims to the right of way had in fact been exercised for more than 30 years, (iii) that the vendor Miss Rich, of the servient tenement (No. 15) disclosed to the defendants in the pre-contract enquiries in regard to the sale in 1993 of No. 15 to the defendants the existence of the claimed right of way, (iv) that following the defendants moving into No. 15 the claimed right of way was used by the plaintiffs for more than 10 months, (v) that there was evidence that other properties on the estate enjoyed 'mirror' rights and (vi) that the judge found that the grantor (the council) under the later conveyance of No. 16 had mistakenly omitted properly to deal with rights of way.

HIRST LJ said at 298:

I entirely agree and only wish to stress that, in my judgment the upholding of an implied reservation is, on the special facts of this case fully in line with the established authorities and is in no sense an extension let alone a relaxation, of the very stringent tests there laid down.

In **Adealon International Proprietary Ltd v Merton LBC** [2007] 1 WLR 1898 the Court of Appeal held that the reservation of an easement of access was not implied by necessity where the land was granted to an associated party and the grantor could at that time expect to be able to enjoy rights of access. CARNWATH LJ said at 1903:

10 A good starting point is Lord Oliver of Aylmerton's succinct statement of the principle in the Privy Council in *Manjang v Drammeh* (1990) 61 P & CR 194, 196–197:

'It seems hardly necessary to state the essentials for the implication of such an easement. There has to be found, first, a common owner of a legal estate in two plots of land. It has, secondly, to be established that access between one of those plots and the public highway can be obtained only over the other plot. Thirdly, there has to be found a disposition of one of the plots without any specific grant or reservation of a right of access. Given these conditions, it may be possible as a matter of construction of the relevant grant (see *Nickerson v Barraclough* [1981] Ch 426) to imply the reservation of an easement of necessity.'

11 As that passage confirms, the principle is one of implication from the circumstances of a grant of land, not (as suggested in some of the earlier cases and in academic writings: see e.g. A. J. Bradbrook, 'Access to Landlocked Land: A Comparative Study of Legal Solutions' (1983) 10 Syd L Rev 39) a freestanding rule of public policy. This was settled by this court in *Nickerson v Barraclough* [1981] Ch 426 where Buckley LJ summarised the correct approach, at p. 447:

'In my judgment the law relating to ways of necessity rests not upon a basis of public policy but upon the implication to be drawn from the fact that unless some way is implied, a parcel of land will be inaccessible. From that fact the implication arises that the parties must have intended that some way giving access to the land should have been granted... Public policy may inhibit the parties from carrying their intention into effect, but I cannot see how public policy can have a bearing upon what their intention was. In my judgment, that must be ascertained in accordance with the ordinary principles of construction, the language used and relevant admissible evidence of surrounding circumstances.'

12 The classic case of an easement of necessity is where the land of one party to a grant is entirely surrounded by that of the other. As between the two of them, it is not difficult to infer that the landlocked property, whether of the grantor or the grantee, was intended to have some form of access over the surrounding land. That was explained by Sir George Jessel MR in *London Corpn v Riggs* (1880) 13 Ch D 798, 805–806 [p. 680, above]...

13 So much is uncontroversial. But as one moves away from that simple, bipartite model, to one in which the surrounding land is shared with strangers to the grant, the issues become more complex. Where there is a realistic possibility of alternative access over the land of third parties, the case for an easement of necessity is much less clear.

14 In particular, in that situation there is no reason in my view to assume that the same rule should apply to grantor and grantee. In this context the presumption of non-derogation from grant works in favour of the grantee, but against the grantor. Further, the grantee may also be able to rely on other forms of implied right, not available to the grantor: see generally Megarry & Wade, *Law of Real Property*, 6th edn (2000), paras 18–097ff. As is said at para. 18–097:

> 'The general rule...is that a grant is construed in favour of the grantee. Therefore normally no easements will be implied in favour of a grantor; if he wishes to reserve any easements he must do so expressly.'

Conversely, at para. 18–101: 'In favour of a grantee easements are implied much more readily, on the principle that a grant must be construed in the amplest rather than in the narrowest way.'

15 This contrast can be seen clearly in the leading statement of the applicable law by Thesiger LJ in *Wheeldon v Burrows* (1879) 12 Ch D 31, 49: [his Lordship quoted the 'two propositions' of the rule in *Wheeldon v Burrows*, above, p. 656].

16 This distinction becomes particularly relevant when considering the possibilities of alternative access over land of third parties. In the case of the grantee, the application of the presumption should in principle be unaffected by such possibilities. The grantee's normal expectation is that access, if not otherwise available will be allowed as an incident to the grant, and thus that it will be provided by the grantor over land within his control. Where the roles are reversed, the grantor has no equivalent expectation. On the contrary the presumption is that any rights he requires over the land transferred will have been expressly reserved in the grant, and the burden lies on the grantor to establish an exception. To that issue the existence of other realistic possibilities of access, even if not legally enforceable at the time of the grant, is clearly relevant.

C. ACQUISITION BY PRESUMED GRANT, OR PRESCRIPTION[196]

There are three different methods of acquisition of easements and profits by prescription: at common law; under the doctrine of 'lost modern grant', and by statute (Prescription Act 1832).

---

[196] C & B, pp. 613–628; Gray, paras 5.2.55–5.2.81; M & W, paras 28.032–28.080; MM, pp. 430–441; Smith, pp. 506–514; Gale, chap. 4; (1975) 38 MLR 641 (S. Anderson).

(i) Prescription at common law: time immemorial

In **Bryant v Foot** (1867) LR 2 QB 161,[197] the question was whether the rector of Horton, Buckinghamshire, could establish a claim based on long user, to a fee of 13 shillings for marriages performed in the parish church. User was proved since 1808, but there was no evidence prior to that time.

Cockburn CJ, Mellor and Lush (Blackburn J dissenting) held that the size of the fee made it impossible to believe that it existed in the time of Richard I. The presumption of immemorial legal existence which arose from user within living memory was rebutted. In discussing the methods of proof of immemorial user, COCKBURN CJ said at 179:

The law of England ever has been and still is, in respect of prescriptive rights, in a most unsatisfactory state. The common law admitted of no prescription in the matter of real estate, or of any franchise which was matter of record, as not lying in grant. In respect of things incorporeal, lying in grant, it admitted of a species of prescription, not upon the ground that possession or enjoyment for a given period gave an indefeasible right, but on the assumption, when possession or enjoyment had been carried back as far as living memory would go, that a grant had once existed which had since been lost.

Practically speaking, by means of this presumption prescriptive rights were established in respect of matters which lay in grant. Protection, in respect of real estates, after continued and peaceable enjoyment, was effected, not by the law being that after possession for a given number of years the right of property should be absolutely acquired, but by the indirect contrivance of debarring the adverse claimant from the benefit of the procedure by which alone his right could be established. And here again our ancestors, instead of fixing a given number of years as the period within which legal proceedings to recover real property must be resorted to, had recourse to the singular expedient of making the period of limitation run from particular events or dates. From the time of Henry I to that of Henry III, on a writ of right, the time within which a descent must be shewn was the time of King Henry I (Co Litt 114b). In the 20th year of Henry III, by the Statute of Merton (c. 8) the date was altered to the time of Henry II. Writs of mort d'ancestor were limited to the time of the last return of King John into England; writs of novel disseisin to the time of the King's first crossing the sea into Gascony. In the previous reign, according to Glanville (Lib 13, c. 33), the disseisin must have been since the last voyage of King Henry II into Normandy. So that the time necessary to bar a claim varied materially at different epochs. Thus matters remained till the 3 Edw I (Stat West 1 c. 39), when, as all lawyers are aware, the time within which a writ of right might be brought was limited to cases in which the seisin of the ancestor was since the time of King Richard I, which was construed to mean the beginning of that king's reign (2 Inst 238), a period of not less than eighty-six years. The legislature having thus adopted the reign of Richard I as the date from which the limitation in a real action was to run, the courts of law adopted it as the period to which, in all matters of prescription or custom, legal memory, which till then had been confined to the time to which living memory could go back, should thenceforth be required to extend. Thus the law remained for two centuries and a half, by which time the limitation imposed in respect of actions to recover real property having long become inoperative to bar claims which had their origin posterior to

---

[197] *Duke of Norfolk v Arbuthnot* (1880) 5 CPD 390 (no prescription in respect of church built about 1380).

the time of Richard I, and having therefore ceased practically to afford any protection against antiquated claims, the legislature, in 32nd of Henry VIII (c. 2), again interfered, and on this occasion, instead of dating the period of limitation from some particular event or date, took the wiser course of prescribing a fixed number of years as the limit within which a suit should be entertained. The legislature having thus altered the period within which rights to real estate could be asserted by parties out of possession, the courts on this occasion omitted to follow the analogy of the recent statute as fixing the date from which legal memory was to commence, as they had done on the passing of the statute of the 3 Edw I, and adhered in all that related to prescription or custom to the previously established standard. It was of course impossible that as time went on the adoption of a fixed epoch, as the time from which legal memory was to run, should not be attended by grievous inconvenience and hardship. Possession, however long, enjoyment, however uninterrupted, afford no protection against stale and obsolete claims, or the assertion of long abandoned rights. And as parliament failed to intervene to amend the law, the judges set their ingenuity to work, by fictions and presumptions, to atone for the supineness of the legislature, and to amend, so far as in them lay, the law, which I cannot think they were bound to administer as they found it. They first laid down the somewhat startling rule that from the usage of a lifetime the presumption arose that a similar usage had existed from a remote antiquity. Next, as it could not but happen that, in the case of many private rights, especially in that of easements, which had a more recent origin, such a presumption was impossible, judicial astuteness to support possession and enjoyment, which the law ought to have invested with the character of rights, had recourse to the questionable theory of lost grants. Juries were first told that from user, during living memory, or even during twenty years, they might presume a lost grant or deed; next they were recommended to make such presumption; and lastly, as the final consummation of judicial legislation, it was held that a jury should be told, not only that they might, but also that they were bound to presume the existence of such a lost grant, although neither judge nor jury, nor any one else, had the shadow of a belief that any such instrument had ever really existed. In this manner the courts have endeavoured to supply the deficiency of the law in the matter of rights acquired by possession and enjoyment. When the doctrine of presumptions had proceeded far towards its development, the legislature at length interfered, and in respect of real property and of certain specified easements, fixed certain periods of possession or enjoyment as establishing presumptive rights. But with regard to all prescriptions or customs not provided for by statutory enactment the law remains as before.[198]

In advising the House of Lords in **Dalton v Angus** (1881) 6 App Cas 740 at 773–774, where a claim to an easement of support for a building based upon 27 years' user was upheld, FRY J, in a famous passage, based the doctrine of prescription upon acquiescence.

But leaving such technical questions aside, I prefer to observe that, in my opinion, the whole law of prescription and the whole law which governs the presumption or inference of a grant or covenant rest upon acquiescence. The Courts and the Judges have had recourse to various expedients for quieting the possession of persons in the exercise of rights which have not been resisted by the persons against whom they are exercised, but in all cases it appears to me that acquiescence and nothing else is the principle upon which these expedients rest. It becomes

---

[198] See *R v Oxfordshire County Council, ex p Sunningwell Parish Council* [2000] 1 AC 335 at 349–353, per Lord Hoffmann.

then of the highest importance to consider of what ingredients acquiescence consists. In many cases, as, for instance, in the case of that acquiescence which creates a right of way, it will be found to involve, 1st, the doing of some act by one man upon the land of another; 2ndly, the absence of right to do that act in the person doing it; 3rdly, the knowledge of the person affected by it that the act is done; 4thly, the power of the person affected by the act to prevent such act either by act on his part or by action in the Courts; and lastly, the abstinence by him from any such interference for such a length of time as renders it reasonable for the Courts to say that he shall not afterwards interfere to stop the act being done. In some other cases, as, for example, in the case of lights, some of these ingredients are wanting; but I cannot imagine any case of acquiescence in which there is not shewn to be in the servient owner: 1, a knowledge of the acts done; 2, a power in him to stop the acts or to sue in respect of them; and 3, an abstinence on his part from the exercise of such power. That such is the nature of acquiescence and that such is the ground upon which presumptions or inferences of grant or covenant may be made appears to me to be plain both from reason, from maxim, and from the cases.

As regards the reason of the case, it is plain good sense to hold that a man who can stop an asserted right, or a continued user, and does not do so for a long time, may be told that he has lost his right by his delay and his negligence, and every presumption should therefore be made to quiet a possession thus acquired and enjoyed by the tacit consent of the sufferer. But there is no sense in binding a man by an enjoyment he cannot prevent, or quieting a possession which he could never disturb.

(ii) User as of right[199]

Gardner v Hodgson's Kingston Brewery Co Ltd
[1903] AC 229 (HL, **Earl of Halsbury LC** and **Lords Ashbourne, Macnaghten, Davey, Robertson** and **Lindley**)

For some 70 or 80 years, the owners of the plaintiff's house had been accustomed to use a way from their stable across the yard of the defendant's inn to reach a road. The user was open and uninterrupted, but, for a long period, and certainly since 1855, an annual payment of 15 shillings had been made.

[199] M & W, para. 28.035, n. 200: '*Solomon v Mystery of Vintners* (1859) 4 H & N 585 at 602 (common law prescription); *Sturges v Bridgman* (1879) 11 ChD 852 at 863 (lost modern grant); *Tickle v Brown* (1836) 4 Ad & El 369 at 382 (prescription under the Prescription Act 1832; and see ss. 1, 2).' See also [1998] Conv 442 at p. 448 (E. Simpson). Illegal user prevents prescription: *Neaverson v Peterborough Rural District Council* [1902] 1 Ch 557; *George Legge & Son Ltd v Wenlock Corporation* [1939] AC 204, 222. Cf., however, where user would not have been illegal if the landowner had consented to it: *Bakewell Management Ltd v Brandwood* [2004] 2 AC 519 (driving over common land without lawful authority under LPA 1925, s. 193(4)), thus rendering s. 68 of the Countryside and Rights of Way Act 2000 otiose: [2004] Conv 67 (C. McNall); (2004) 148 SJ 455 (S. Bickford-Smith and C. Lamont); [2004] All ER Rev 240 (P. J. Clarke). It was 'the landowner's unfettered power of dispensing from criminal liability, exercisable at his own discretion and if he thinks fit for his own private profit, which is the key to the disposal of this appeal', per Lord Walker of Gestingthorpe at [60]. Cf., however, *Williams v Sandy Lane (Chester) Ltd* [2007] 1 EGLR 10 at [50], per Chadwick LJ: 'It is no answer to a prescriptive claim to assert that the user upon which the claimant relies is unlawful. Public policy does not prevent conduct which is unlawful (in the sense that it is tortious or in breach of contract) or which is illegal (in a criminal sense) from leading to the acquisition of property rights—see the observations of Lord Scott of Foscote in *Bakewell Management Ltd v Brandwood* [2004] UKHL 14, [46]; [2004] 2 AC 519, 544'; [2007] Conv 161.

The plaintiff claimed a declaration that she was entitled to a right of way.

Held. No claim could be made under the Prescription Act or under the doctrine of lost modern grant because the user, being by permission, was not 'as of right'.

Lord Lindley: The plaintiff's statement of claim is so drawn as to entitle her to succeed if she can bring herself within the Prescription Act, or failing that, if the facts warrant the presumption of a lost grant. Cozens-Hardy J considered that she was entitled to succeed under the Prescription Act; but that if not, a lost grant in her favour ought to be presumed. It is necessary to consider both of these methods of establishing her right; for the Prescription Act has not taken away any of the modes of claiming easements which existed before that Act was passed: see *Aynsley v Glover* (1875) 10 Ch App 283.

I will take the Prescription Act first. Section 2 is the important section, and the last part of it is relied upon by the plaintiff. To bring herself within this enactment she must prove that she and her predecessors in title have enjoyed the way in question 'claiming right thereto' without interruption for forty years. The difficulty is raised by the words 'claiming right thereto', and by the payment of the 15s. a year. I understand the words 'claiming right thereto' and the equivalent words 'as of right', which occur in section 5, to have the same meaning as the older expression nec vi, nec clam, nec precario. A temporary permission, although often renewed, would prevent an enjoyment from being 'as of right'; but a permanent, irrevocable permission attributable to a lost grant would not have the same effect. The common law doctrine is that all prescription presupposes a grant. But if the grant is proved and its terms are known, prescription has no place.

A title by prescription can be established by long peaceable open enjoyment only; but in order that it may be so established the enjoyment must be inconsistent with any other reasonable inference than that it has been as of right in the sense above explained. This, I think, is the proper inference to be drawn from the authorities discussed in the Court below. If the enjoyment is equally consistent with two reasonable inferences, enjoyment as of right is not established; and this, I think, is the real truth in the present case.[200]

The enjoyment is equally open to explanation in one of two ways, namely, by a lost grant of a right of way in consideration of a rent-charge on the plaintiff's land of 15s. a year, or by a succession of yearly licences not, perhaps, expressed every year, but implied and assumed and paid for.[201]

In **Mills v Silver** [1991] Ch 271[202] the defendants purchased in 1985 a hill farm in Herefordshire to which the only access was along a track on the plaintiff's adjoining land. A previous occupier of the hill farm had used the track sporadically between 1922 and 1981 when it was dry enough to be passable. No express grant or permission was ever given for the use although it was known to and acquiesced in by the then owners of the land. From 1981 until the defendants purchased the farm in 1985, very little use of the track occurred. In 1987 the defendants put down between 600 and 700 tons of stone along the length of the track in order to make it passable in all weathers.

---

[200] *Smith v Brudenell-Bruce* [2002] 2 P & CR 4.
[201] *Monmouth Canal Co v Harford* (1834) 1 Cr M & R 614; *Diment v NH Foot Ltd* [1974] 1 WLR 1427 (agent's knowledge); *Patel v WH Smith (Eziot) Ltd* [1987] 1 WLR 853.
[202] [1992] CLJ 222 (C. Harpum).

The plaintiffs sought an injunction to restrain the defendants from using the track with vehicles and damages for trespass for the laying of the stone. The defendants claimed a prescriptive right of way over the track and the right to repair it. The Court of Appeal held (1) that a right of way for vehicles had been sufficiently continuous to warrant the implication of a lost modern grant; mere tolerance by the owners of the land over which the track passed would not defeat such a claim; and (2) that the defendants were entitled to repair but not to improve it. The laying of the stone road went far beyond repair and damages of £8,175 were awarded.

PARKER LJ said at 287:

In *Sturges v Bridgman* (1879) 11 ChD 852, 863, Thesiger LJ giving the judgment of the court said:

> 'the law governing the acquisition of easements by user stands thus: Consent or acquiescence of the owner of the servient tenement lies at the root of prescription, and of the fiction of a lost grant, and hence the acts or user, which go to the proof of either the one or the other, must be, in the language of the civil law, nec vi, nec clam, nec precario; for a man cannot, as a general rule, be said to consent to or acquiesce in the acquisition by his neighbour of an easement through an enjoyment of which he has no knowledge, actual or constructive, or which he contests and endeavours to interrupt, or which he temporarily licenses.'

This passage is in my judgment of prime importance in the determination of the present appeal for it makes plain (i) that consent or acquiescence to the user asserted as giving rise to the easement is an essential ingredient of the acquisition of the easement and (ii) that it is the nature of the acts of user which has to be examined in order to see whether the easement is established.

Unless the acts of user are of the requisite character, consent or acquiescence is irrelevant. If they are then consent or acquiescence is essential.

In *Hollins v Verney* (1884) 13 QBD 304, 315, Lindley LJ giving the judgment of the court said:

> 'no actual user can be sufficient to satisfy the statute, unless during the whole of the statutory term... the user is enough at any rate to carry to the mind of a reasonable person who is in possession of the servient tenement, the fact that a continuous right to enjoyment is being asserted, and ought to be resisted if such right is not recognised, and if resistance to it is intended.'

This shows clearly that the crucial matter for consideration is whether for the necessary period the use is such as to bring home to the mind of a reasonable person that a continuous right of enjoyment is being asserted. If it is and the owner of the allegedly servient tenement knows or must be taken to know of it and does nothing about it the right is established. It is no answer for him to say, 'I "tolerated" it.' If he does nothing he will be taken to have recognised the right and not intended to resist it. He will have consented to it or acquiesced in it.

For the plaintiffs it was submitted that this apparently simple position had been altered or modified by later cases. I do not consider that it has. Certainly there are statements in speeches in the House of Lords and the judgments of this court in later cases which might appear to suggest that a claim will be defeated if there are two possible explanations of the situation or if it is not shown that the user is against the will of the owner or if the user has been 'tolerated.' Such statements, however, were in my judgment not statements of principle but statements relating to the particular facts of the cases under consideration.

I instance but one of such cases by way of example, namely, *Gardner v Hodgson's Kingston Brewery Co Ltd* [1903] AC 229 [above]. In that case the owner of a house had for more than 40 years used a cart way from his stables through the yard of an adjoining inn. He paid 15s. a year to the owners of the yard but there was no conclusive evidence as to the origin of this payment. The owners of the yard contended that the payment was for rent or for a series of annual licences. The owner of the house contended that it was more probably a perpetual payment attached to some original grant of the alleged right of way. The observations in their Lordship's speeches must therefore be considered in the light of these facts and contentions....

His Lordship referred to the speech of Lord Lindley at 239, p. 690, above, and continued:

In my judgment that passage is of no assistance to the plaintiffs. There being one of two possible explanations of the annual payment of 15s. one of which would and the other of which would not establish the easement claimed and the plaintiff being unable to prove which was the correct one, she simply failed to make out the case.

The statement made must be related to the facts and cannot be regarded as a statement of principle for if it were no one could as it seems to me ever establish an easement by prescription or by the fiction of lost modern grant.

On examination none of the other cases cited, in my judgment, detract from the principles so clearly stated in *Sturges v Bridgman* and *Hollins v Verney*. The true approach is to determine the character of the acts of user or enjoyment relied on. If they are sufficient to amount to an assertion of a continuous right, continue for the requisite period, are actually or presumptively known to the owner of the servient tenement and such owner does nothing that is sufficient, as May LJ said in *Goldsmith v Burrow Construction Ltd* [(1987) Times, 31 July]:

> 'I agree with Mr Mowbray's submission that it is not merely a question of the servient owner saying 'I could have locked the gate and therefore there was no permission.' The fact in this case is that he did lock the gate.'

Every servient owner can always say, until it is too late: 'I could have stopped it.' That is not enough.

I add only this, that any statement that the enjoyment must be against the will of the servient owner cannot mean more than 'without objection by the servient owner.' If it did, a claimant would have to prove that the right was contested and thereby defeat his own claim.

Davies v Du Paver [1953] 1 QB 184, p. 701, below.

In **Healey v Hawkins** [1968] 1 WLR 1967 the question arose of the effect of initial oral permission on user for the 20 year period under the Prescription Act 1832. GOFF J held that the user which was permissive in origin did not so continue and thus prevent the defendant from acquiring an easement of way. He said at 1973:

In principle it seems to me that once permission has been given, the user must remain permissive and not be capable of ripening into a right save where the permission is oral and the user has continued for 40 or 60 years, unless and until, having been given for a limited period only, it expires or, being general, it is revoked, or there is a change in circumstances from which revocation may fairly be implied. Moreover, *Gaved v Martyn* (1865) 19 CBNS 732 appears to me to be a decision expressly in point and in accordance with the conclusion in Megarry and Wade [(3rd edn, 1966), p. 850, para. 4(iii)]. In that case, oral permission had been given to use an artificial watercourse, and a successor who did not claim under the original licensee and who had no actual knowledge of permission having been given continued to exercise the privilege, but in circumstances which ought to, or might, have put him on inquiry, and the court held that there was evidence and, as Byles J at 747 thought, abundant evidence, on which the jury could find, as it had done, that the user even by the new occupier remained permissive.

Of course, when the user has continued for 40 or 60 years a prior parol consent affords no answer, because it is excluded by the express terms of section 2 of the Prescription Act, but, even so, permission given during the period will defeat the claimant because it negatives user as of right. That is, in my judgment, the explanation of the distinction drawn by the House of Lords in *Gardner v Hodgson's Kingston Brewery* [1903] AC 229 between antecedent and current parol consents.[203]

In **Odey v Barber** [2008] Ch 175[204] SILBER J held that the *unsolicited* permission to the user of a track precluded the acquisition of an easement of way under the doctrine of lost modern grant. He said at 192, para. 74:

I find the reasoning in *O'Mara v Gascoigne* 9 BPR 16,349 compelling and I consider that the law is that an unsolicited permission to use the track prevents a right of way arising under the doctrine of lost modern grant because: (a) in the words of Lord Lindley in the *Gardner* case [1903] AC 229, 239 [p. 690, above], 'if the grant is proved... prescription has no place'; (b) as Lord Hoffmann explained in *R v Oxfordshire County Council, ex p Sunningwell Parish Council* [2000] 1 AC 335, 350, that juries were instructed that 'if there was no evidence *absolutely inconsistent* with there having been immemorial user or a lost modern grant, they not merely could but should find the prescriptive right established'. An unsolicited grant of permission would preclude such a permission being granted; (c) no authority has been put forward to show that any court has decided a case on the basis that there is a crucial difference between an unsolicited grant of permission and a solicited grant of permission. In other words, there is no decision which runs contrary to the decision in the *O'Mara* case and states that an unsolicited grant of permission prevents an easement arising; (d) in none of the authorities relied on by the claimant in this case is there a statement that unsolicited grants of permission should be treated differently from solicited grants of permission; and (e) there is no logical reason for deciding that unsolicited grants of permission should be disregarded in the way contended for by Miss Bleasdale because as Lord Hoffmann reminded us in the *Sunningwell* case [2000] 1 AC 335, 350, that user for the 20-year period has to be without 'the licence of the owner'. So an unsolicited grant of permission is a licence of the owner.

(iii) User in fee simple[205]

In **Kilgour v Gaddes** [1904] 1 KB 457, a dispute arose between two neighbouring tenants of Sir James Graham in connection with the use of a pump which was situated on the land occupied by the plaintiff. The defendant and his predecessors in title had used the pump for forty years before the action was brought.

---

[203] *Jones v Price and Morgan* (1992) 64 P & CR 404 (claim defeated by 40-year user which continued on common understanding that the user was, and continued, by permission).

[204] [2007] All ER Rev 258 (P. J. Clarke).

[205] *Pugh v Savage* [1970] 2 QB 373; *Davis v Whitby* [1973] 1 WLR 629; *Simmons v Dobson* [1991] 1 WLR 720, p. 695, below (lost modern grant).

The Court of Appeal held that there was no prescriptive right to use the pump. COLLINS MR said at 460:

The question in this case is whether, as between two persons who are termors of different tenements, a right of way to a pump has been acquired by prescription for the owner of one of the tenements over the other tenement under section 2 of the Prescription Act 1832. I say a right for the owner, for it appears to me clear that under the section the right cannot be acquired merely by a tenant as against a tenant, but must be acquired by the owner of the fee in one of the tenements as against the owner of the fee in the other. Here the respective tenants of the so-called dominant and servient tenements hold under the same landlord; and, if the proposition be correct that a prescriptive right of way under section 2 of the Act must be acquired by the owner of the fee in one of the tenements as against the owner of the fee in the other, then in this case the defendant's contention would involve the result that the tenant of one of the tenements has acquired for his landlord a right of way over the landlord's own land; which is impossible and inconsistent with the essential notion of a right by prescription, namely, that the right is acquired by the owner of land over land belonging to another owner. I limit what I am saying to such an easement as a right of way, because questions with regard to the easements of light stand on a different footing, and depend on the provisions of section 3 of the Act.[206] ... The learned Chief Baron [Palles] said in *Timmons v Hewitt* (1888) 22 LR Ir 627: '... If I am asked how it is consistent with the Prescription Act, I answer that such user and enjoyment is not as of right within the meaning of the 2nd section. It is a user by a termor, who, if he acquire the right, must acquire it as incident to the land of which he is termor, and thus for the benefit of his reversioner. Such user cannot be as of right, unless a reversioner can in law by user acquire a right against himself.' That reasoning appears to me conclusive of the present case. There was a long discussion in the course of the argument as to the possibility of a termor under one landlord acquiring for his landlord an easement by user over land in the occupation of a termor under another landlord, and as to whether an easement in such a case could be acquired, unless and until the user had continued for the period of three years after the determination of the term in the servient tenement without interference by the reversioner.[207] That no doubt raises an interesting question, which appears to have been decided in Ireland in the case of *Beggan v M'Donald* (1877) 2 LR IR 560, contrary to the view expressed in this country in *Bright v Walker* (1834) 1 Cr M & R 211 and also in *Wheaton v Maple & Co* [1893] 3 Ch 48, in neither of which cases, however, was it necessary actually to decide the point. That question, however, is not the question raised in the present case. ...

In the case of *Wheaton v Maple & Co* the view which I am expressing was very clearly stated by Lindley LJ in his judgment. He dealt first with the question of the possibility of acquiring an easement as against a tenant of land by a presumption of a lost grant as follows: 'I am not aware of any authority for presuming, as a matter of law, a lost grant by a lessee for years in the case of ordinary easements, or a lost covenant by such a person not to interrupt in the case of light, and I am certainly not prepared to introduce another fiction to support a claim to a novel prescriptive right. The whole theory of prescription at common law is against presuming any grant or covenant not to interrupt, by or with any one except an owner in fee. A right claimed by prescription must be claimed as appendant or appurtenant to land, and not as annexed to it for a term of years. Although, therefore, a grant by a lessee of the Crown, commensurate with his lease, might be inferred as a fact, if there was evidence to justify the inference, there is no legal presumption, as distinguished from an inference in fact, in favour of such a grant. This view of

---

[206] P. 728, below.   [207] Prescription Act 1832, s. 8, p. 700, below.

the common law is in entire accordance with *Bright v Walker* where this doctrine of presumption is carefully examined.' He was there dealing with the question of an implied grant...

In **Simmons v Dobson** [1991] 1 WLR 720[208] the freeholder of two adjoining properties in Smallbrook Lane, Leigh, retained one and leased the other. Subsequently the lease was assigned to the plaintiff and the retained property leased to the defendants. At all material times the fee simple of both properties was vested in the same person. The defendants blocked a passageway along two sides of their land which the plaintiff used to reach the road from the rear of his garden. The plaintiff claimed a right of way under the doctrine of lost modern grant.

In rejecting the claim, Fox LJ said at 724:

I take the view that, as a matter of authority, it is established that one tenant cannot acquire an easement by prescription at common law against another tenant holding under the same landlord. The position is, I think, the same in relation to section 2 of the Prescription Act 1832. The purpose of that section is to shorten the period required by common law prescription to 20 years prior to the bringing of the action....

What we are concerned with here is neither common law prescription strictly so called nor a claim under the Prescription Act 1832 but a claim based on the lost modern grant doctrine. The question is whether the restrictive rule as to prescription by and against leaseholders applies to cases of lost modern grant.

In terms of practicalities, it is difficult to see if one were starting from scratch that there is serious objection to leaseholders prescribing against each other for the duration of their limited interests (but it has to be said that to introduce such a rule retrospectively now could affect what were hitherto bought and sold as clear titles). And, as Mr Vickers says, in a modern, urban situation it is hard to see why two householders on one side of the street should be able to prescribe for easements against each other's land because each holds in fee simple while on the other side of the street one leaseholder under the residue of a 999-year lease can for 20 years or more walk along a path at the back of his neighbour's garden (also held on a long lease) without acquiring any rights in respect thereof. That, however, is the way the law has gone in England. The point about long leaseholds held of the same landlord was recognised by Scrutton LJ in the passage in *Derry v Sanders* [1919] 1 KB 223, 237, to which I have referred, where he regarded the law as clear.

His Lordship referred to *Wheaton v Maple & Co* [1893] 3 Ch 48, 63 per Lindley LJ and *Kilgour v Gaddes* [1904] 1 KB 457, 465 per Collins MR, and continued:

While, therefore, there appears to be no case which directly decides that there can be no lost modern grant by or to a person who owns a lesser estate than the fee, the dicta are to the contrary and are very strong and of long standing. I take them to represent settled law. I should mention for completeness that the law in Ireland has gone the other way: *Flynn v Harte* [1913] 2 IR 322 and *Tallon v Ennis* [1937] IR 549.

As to any departure from that state of the law, there are, I think, difficulties of principle. It is clear that common law prescription and prescription under the Act of 1832 are, as a matter of decision, not available by or to owners of less estates than the fee. Lost modern grant is merely

---

[208] Criticised [1992] Conv 167 (P. Sparkes); [1992] CLJ 222 (C. Harpum), following (1958) 74 LQR 82 (V. T. H. Delany).

a form of common law prescription. It is based upon a fiction which was designed to meet, and did meet, a particular problem. It would, I think, be anomalous to extend the fiction further by departure, in relation to lost modern grant, from the fundamental principle of common law prescription referred to by Lindley LJ.

In **Williams v Sandy Lane (Chester) Ltd** [2007] 1 EGLR 10[209] Chadwick LJ set out at [24] the circumstances in which the owner of the dominant tenement could acquire by prescription an easement against the freeholder who granted a lease of the servient tenement:

In my view it is possible to derive from the decision of this court in *Pugh v Savage* [1970] 2 QB 373 the following principles applicable to cases where the servient land is, or has been, subject to a tenancy. First, in a case where the grant of the tenancy of the servient land predates the user by or on behalf of the owner of the dominant land, it is necessary to ask whether, notwithstanding the tenancy, the freehold owner of the servient land could take steps to prevent user during the tenancy. The answer to that question is likely to turn on the terms of the tenancy. Secondly, if (notwithstanding the tenancy) the owner of the servient land could take steps to prevent the user, then it is necessary to ask whether (and, if so, when) the freehold owner had knowledge (actual or imputed) of that user by the owner of the dominant land. The fact that the freehold owner of the servient land was out of possession when the user began and throughout the term of the tenancy may well lead to the conclusion that knowledge of that user should not be imputed. But if, on the facts, the owner of the servient land does have knowledge of the user and could (notwithstanding the tenancy) take steps to prevent that user, but does not do so, then prima facie acquiescence will be established. Thirdly, in a case where user of the servient land by the owner of the dominant land began before the grant of the tenancy, it is necessary to ask whether the freehold owner of the servient land had knowledge (actual or imputed) at or before the date of the grant. If so, then it is likely to be immaterial whether the terms of the tenancy are such that the owner of the servient land could (or could not) take steps to prevent that user. That is because if (with knowledge of the user) the owner of the servient land grants a tenancy of that land on terms which put it out of his power to prevent that user, he can properly be said to have acquiesced in it. Fourthly, if the owner of the servient land did not have knowledge of the user at the date of the grant, then the position is the same as it would be if the grant had pre-dated the user. It is necessary to ask whether (notwithstanding the tenancy) the freehold owner can take steps to prevent the user; and, if so, whether (and if so when) the owner had knowledge of the user.

(iv) The doctrine of lost modern grant[210]

Hulbert v Dale
[1909] 2 Ch 570 (ChD, **Joyce J**; CA, **Cozens-Hardy MR**, **Fletcher Moulton** and **Farwell LJJ**)

By an Inclosure Award of 1804, a 'private carriage road of the width of thirty feet' over Crown Farm (now owned by the plaintiff) was allotted to the predecessor in title of

---

[209] [2007] Conv 161.
[210] Holdsworth, vol. vii, pp. 347–349; *Healey v Hawkins* [1968] 1 WLR 1967, p. 692, above (grant of right of way presumed); *Oakley v Boston* [1976] QB 270 (incumbent of glebe land is capable grantor with consent

the defendant's lessor, owner of Fishmore Farm. The road was never made, and trees grew and buildings were built on the intended site. However, the defendant and his predecessor in title or occupation had, since 1804, uninterruptedly used a private road running across the plaintiff's farm, parallel to the site of the awarded road and some 100 yards from it.

There had been unity of possession of the two farms from 1889 to 1905, while they were in the occupation of the same tenant.

The plaintiff brought this action for an injunction to restrain the defendant from using the road.

Held (affirming Joyce J). A lost grant of a right of way should be presumed.

Joyce J: There was a considerable conflict of evidence in the case, but, upon the whole, the result to my mind is that I come to the conclusion, and find as a fact, that for a period as far back as living memory extends the owners and occupiers for the time being of Fishmore Farm have openly and without interruption had an unquestioned user until quite recently, when the dispute arose, of the now disputed road, and I should have held such user to have been as of right (or by persons claiming a right thereto) but for the circumstance that during the period between the years 1889 and 1905 there was unity of possession (not of ownership) of the two farms, Fishmore and Crown Farms, both being in the occupation of the same tenant or tenants.

This being so, the defendant could not make good any claim to a right of way along the disputed road by prescription under the 2nd section of the Prescription Act. Nor could he, I think, have succeeded upon a claim by prescription at common law, because I consider it to be tolerably plain, for various reasons, that the existence of the right of way claimed, if it does exist, originated and commenced at a date long subsequent to the reign of King Richard I—in fact very little more than one hundred years ago. The defendant, therefore, has to base his claim upon the existence of a grant not produced, and he contends that it is a case for presuming a grant, now lost, of the right to use the disputed road.

I must say that it seems to me that if ever there was a case in which some such presumption ought to be made, this is the case. For I am tolerably certain that the owners and occupiers of Fishmore Farm have had the use of the disputed road without interruption and with the full knowledge of the occupiers, and presumably of the owners, of Crown Farm, who have acquiesced in such use possibly because of the existence of the right of the awarded way, which right, if enforced, would have been much more disadvantageous to Crown Farm than the user of the disputed road by the owners and occupiers of Fishmore Farm.

In **Tehidy Minerals Ltd v Norman** [1971] 2 QB 528 the defendants proved that they were accustomed to graze Tawna Down, Cardinham, Cornwall, from 19 January 1920 to 6 October 1941, a period of 21 years, eight and a half months. In holding that they had acquired a profit à prendre under the doctrine of lost modern grant, BUCKLEY LJ,

of Ecclesiastical Commissioners); *Ward (Helston) Ltd v Kerrier District Council* (1981) 42 P & CR 412 (grant of right of way presumed); *Mills v Silver* [1991] Ch 271, p. 690, above; *Simmons v Dobson* [1991] 1 WLR 720, p. 695, above; *Bowring Services Ltd v Scottish Widows' Fund & Life Assurance Society* [1995] 1 EGLR 158 (presumption failed because of custom of City of London that a man may rebuild upon ancient foundations to what height he pleases); *Smith v Brudenell-Bruce* [2002] 2 P & CR 4.

delivering the judgment of the Court of Appeal (Salmon, Sachs and Buckley LJJ), said at 547:

The question is whether on the facts of this case enjoyment of this grazing for a period of upwards of 20 years preceding October 6, 1941 permits or requires us to presume that such enjoyment was had by virtue of grants made after January 19, 1920, but before October 6, 1921 (being 20 years before October 6, 1941), and subsequently lost, and whether we ought to act on such a presumption.[211]

His Lordship then analysed the judgments in *Angus v Dalton* (1877) 3 QBD 85, (1878) 4 QBD 162, (1881) 6 App Cas 740: the 'celebrated case, which in the course of its history enjoyed the attention of no less than 18 judges and members of the House of Lords, perhaps embodies a greater variety of judicial opinion than any other leading case', and continued:

In our judgment *Angus v Dalton* decides that, where there has been upwards of 20 years' uninterrupted enjoyment of an easement, such enjoyment having the necessary qualities to fulfil the requirements of prescription, then unless, for some reason such as incapacity on the part of the person or persons who might at some time before the commencement of the 20-year period have made a grant, the existence of such a grant is impossible, the law will adopt a legal fiction that such a grant was made, in spite of any direct evidence that no such grant was in fact made.

If this legal fiction is not to be displaced by direct evidence that no grant was made, it would be strange if it could be displaced by circumstantial evidence leading to the same conclusion, and in our judgment it must follow that circumstantial evidence tending to negative the existence of a grant (other than evidence establishing impossibility) should not be permitted to displace the fiction. Precisely the same reasoning must, we think, apply to a presumed lost grant of a profit à prendre as to an easement.

In the present case, if we are to presume lost grants, we must do so in respect of each of the four farms, Higher and Lower Hill, Cabilla and Pinsla Park. Each of the presumed grants must be supposed to have been made between January 20, 1920 and October 5, 1921, and to have been since lost in circumstances of which no one now has any recollection. This combination of circumstances seems to us to be exceedingly improbable, and we feel sympathy for the view expressed by Farwell J in *A-G v Simpson* [1901] 2 Ch 671 at 698:

'It cannot be the duty of a judge to presume a grant of the non-existence of which he is convinced, nor can he be constrained to hold that such a grant is reasonably possible within the meaning of the authorities.'

In view, however, of the decision in *Angus v Dalton* we consider that it is not open to us in the present case to follow this line.[212]

---

[211] CA rejected an argument that, as the Prescription Act 1832 lays down longer periods for prescription in respect of profits than in respect of easements, so by analogy a longer period of enjoyment should be required in the case of a profit than in the case of an easement to support the prescription.

[212] *Bridle v Ruby* [1989] QB 169 (mistaken belief of dominant owner and predecessors in title that a right of way had been reserved over servient tenement held not to rebut presumption of lost modern grant arising from 22 years' user). See too *Thomas W. Ward Ltd v Alexander Bruce (Grays) Ltd* [1959] 2 Lloyd's Rep 472, where Harman LJ also reviewed *Earl de la Warr v Miles* (1881) 17 ChD 535 and *Chamber*

(v) Prescription Act 1832[213]

PRESCRIPTION ACT 1832

Whereas the expression 'time immemorial, or time whereof the memory of man runneth not to the contrary,' is now by the Law of England in many cases considered to include and denote the whole period of time from the Reign of King Richard the First, whereby the title to matters that have been long enjoyed is sometimes defeated by shewing the commencement of such enjoyment, which is in many cases productive of inconvenience and injustice.

1. Claims to right of common[214] **and other profits à prendre, not to be defeated after thirty years enjoyment by shewing the commencement; after sixty years enjoyment the right to be absolute, unless had by consent or agreement.**—No claim which may be lawfully made at the common law, by custom, prescription, or grant, to any right of common or other profit or benefit to be taken and enjoyed from or upon any land of our sovereign lord the King, or any land being parcel of the duchy of Lancaster or of the duchy of Cornwall, or of any ecclesiastical or lay person, or body corporate, except such matters and things as are herein specially provided for, and except tithes, rent, and services, shall, where such right, profit, or benefit shall have been actually taken and enjoyed by any person claiming right thereto without interruption for the full period of thirty years, be defeated or destroyed by showing only that such right, profit, or benefit was first taken or enjoyed at any time prior to such period of thirty years, but nevertheless such claim may be defeated in any other way by which the same is now liable to be defeated; and when such right, profit, or benefit shall have been so taken and enjoyed as aforesaid for the full period of sixty years, the right thereto shall be deemed absolute and indefeasible, unless it shall appear that the same was taken and enjoyed by some consent or agreement expressly made or given for that purpose by deed or writing.

2. In claims of right of way or other easements the periods to be twenty years and forty years.—No claim which may be lawfully made at the common law, by custom, prescription, or grant, to any way or other easement, or to any watercourse, or the use of any water, to be enjoyed or derived upon, over, or from any land or water of our said lord the King, or being parcel of the duchy of Lancaster or of the duchy of Cornwall, or being the property of any ecclesiastical or lay person, or body corporate, when such way or other matter as herein last before mentioned shall have been actually enjoyed by any person claiming right thereto without interruption for the full period of twenty years, shall be defeated or destroyed by showing only that such way or other matter was first enjoyed at any time prior to such period of twenty years, but nevertheless such claim may be defeated in any other way by which the same is now liable to be defeated; and where such way or other matter as herein last before mentioned shall have been so enjoyed as aforesaid for the full period of forty years, the right thereto shall be deemed absolute and indefeasible, unless it shall appear that the same was

Colliery Co v Hopwood (1886) 32 ChD 549; *Hamilton v Joyce* [1984] 3 NSWLR 279; [1986] Conv 356 (A. H. Hudson).

[213] 'One of the worst drafted Acts on the Statute Book': Law Reform Committee Report on Acquisition of Easements and Profits by Prescription (1966) Cmnd 3100. For the history of prescription, see Holdsworth, vol. vii, pp. 343 et seq.; Simpson, *A History of the Land Law* (2nd edn), pp. 266–269; Underhill, *Century of Law Reform*, p. 308.

[214] P. 96, above.

enjoyed by some consent or agreement expressly given or made for that purpose by deed or writing.[215]

4. Before mentioned periods to be deemed those next before suits.[216]—Each of the respective periods of years herein-before mentioned shall be deemed and taken to be the period next before some suit or action wherein the claim or matter to which such period may relate shall have been or shall be brought into question; and no act or other matter shall be deemed to be an interruption, within the meaning of this statute, unless the same shall have been or shall be submitted to or acquiesced in for one year after the party interrupted shall have had or shall have notice thereof, and of the person making or authorising the same to be made.[217]

7. Proviso for infants, &c.—Provided also, that the time during which any person otherwise capable of resisting any claim to any of the matters before mentioned shall have been or shall be an infant, idiot, non compos mentis,[218] feme covert, or tenant for life, or during which any action or suit shall have been pending, and which shall have been diligently prosecuted, until abated by the death of any party or parties thereto, shall be excluded in the computation of the periods herein-before mentioned, except only in cases where the right or claim is hereby declared to be absolute and indefeasible.

8. What time to be excluded in computing the term of forty years appointed by this Act.— Provided always, that when any land or water upon, over, or from which any such way or other convenient[219] watercourse or use of water shall have been or shall be enjoyed or derived hath been or shall be held under or by virtue of any term of life, or any term of years[220] exceeding three years from the granting thereof, the time of the enjoyment of any such way or other matter as herein last before mentioned, during the continuance of such term, shall be excluded in the computation of the said period of forty years, in case the claim shall within three years next after the end or sooner determination of such term be resisted by any person entitled to any reversion expectant on the determination thereof.

In **Gardner v Hodgson's Kingston Brewery Co Ltd** [1903] AC 229, p. 689, above, LORD MACNAGHTEN said at 236:

I rather doubt whether the scope and effect of the Prescription Act have been always rightly apprehended. The Act was passed, as its preamble declares, for the purposes of getting rid of

---

[215] Even a 40-year period of user could be defeated by showing that it was ultra vires the owner of the servient tenement to grant the easement claimed because the opening words of s. 2 ('no claim which may be lawfully made') control the whole section: *Housden v Conservators of Wimbledon and Putney Commons* [2008] 1 WLR 1172 (CA, obiter; but the decision in *Staffordshire and Worcestershire Canal Navigation v Birmingham Canal Navigations* (1866) LR 1 HL 254 is binding to this effect: Mummery LJ at [66]); [2009] CLJ 40 (S. Bridge).

[216] Prescriptive claims to rights of common are not to be defeated by reason of interruptions due to requisition of the common land by a Government Department, or to inability to exercise a right to graze animals for reasons of animal health: Commons Registration Act 1965, s. 16. See Rights of Light Act 1959, s. 3(6), p. 734, below.

[217] *Newnham v Willison* (1987) 56 P & CR 8 (interruption lasting more than a year before action brought); [1989] Conv 357 (J. E. Martin).

[218] Modern statutes refer to a person suffering a 'mental disorder': Mental Health Act 1983, s. 1; and to a lack of capacity: Mental Capacity Act 2005: see C & B, pp. 919–920. However, s. 7 Prescription Act 1832 remains unamended.

[219] Probably a misprint for 'easement': *Wright v Williams* (1836) Tyr & Gr 375 at 390; *Laird v Briggs* (1881) 19 ChD 22 at 33.

[220] *Palk v Shinner* (1852) 18 QB 568.

the inconvenience and injustice arising from the meaning which the law of England attached to the expressions 'time immemorial' and 'time whereof the memory of man runneth not to the contrary'. The law as it stood put an intolerable strain on the consciences of judges and jurymen. The Act was an Act 'for shortening the time of prescription in certain cases'. And really it did nothing more. A person who claims a right of way and invokes the protection of the Act must claim 'as of right'. But when the way in question has been used without interruption, as defined in the Act, for forty years 'as of right'—whether the claimant is really entitled of right or not—the claim cannot be defeated except by shewing that the right claimed was enjoyed 'by some consent or agreement expressly given or made for that purpose by deed or writing'. No parol consent will do. I fail to understand how that provision helps the appellant. The respondents do not set up a parol consent given before the period of forty years. They rely on the acknowledgment and recognition of their dominion over the property—their right to grant or withhold the grant of the way in question—involved in and evidenced by the annual payment accompanying the use of the way, and they point out that no other reasonable explanation of that payment is forthcoming.

(a) Interruption

In **Davies v Du Paver** [1953] 1 QB 184 a dispute arose over the question whether the plaintiff had acquired a right (profit) by prescription based upon 60 years' user to pasture sheep upon the defendant's land. Two main questions arose:

(i) The defendant in August 1950 completed a fence which excluded the sheep in spite of the plaintiff's vigorous protests. No further action was taken until the writ was issued in September 1951, and the defendant argued that the user was interrupted for more than a year.

(ii) During the first 55 of the 60 years during which user was proved, the defendant's land (servient tenement) had been in the possession of lessees.

The Court of Appeal (Birkett and Morris LJJ, Singleton LJ, dissenting) held that:

(i) there was no interruption within the Act, but

(ii) the plaintiff failed to show that the defendant had the knowledge or means of knowledge of the user and the power to object to it.

On the first point, MORRIS LJ said at 206:

The first point raised by the defendant is that there was a fatal interruption of the enjoyment by the plaintiff of his alleged rights of pasturage. In the notice of appeal this contention is formulated on the basis that there was no evidence that Mr Davies 'had asserted his alleged rights or protested at the interruption of his alleged rights of pasturage' between August 1, 1950 and September 28, 1951, and 'that accordingly the judge was wrong in law in holding that the plaintiff Davies did not acquiesce in, or submit to, any interruption which had continued for more than one year'. This language raises the question as to the meaning of an 'assertion of rights or of a protest'. But the real question is not whether there was an assertion of rights or a protest during some period, but whether there was in this case a submission or an acquiescence. It is provided by the Prescription Act 1832, that no act or other matter is deemed to be an interruption within the meaning of the Act unless submitted to, or acquiesced in, for one year after the party interrupted has notice of the interruption and of the person making it or authorising it to be made.

There is no doubt that there was an actual interruption for more than a year before September 27, 1951. The question is whether there was acquiescence in such interruption or submission to it lasting for one year. This is, in my judgment, a question of fact. If a case were being tried with a jury it would be a question for the jury to determine: see *Bennison v Cartwright* (1864) 5 B & S 1....

The fence was completed on August 9. Could it be said that the plaintiff had submitted to, or acquiesced in, the existence of the fence by that date? Having regard to the events that had happened, and to the correspondence, I would have thought, had it been for me to decide this question of fact, that the answer would be in the negative. The parties were breathing fury on each side of a newly erected fence. Could it be said that the challenging protests of the plaintiff must, as the August days passed, be deemed to have signified nothing, and that his former claims and assertions should be regarded as supplanted by submission and acquiescence? As time went by, it might well be that silence and inaction could be interpreted as submission or acquiescence. But the date when submission or acquiescence begins must be determined as a question of fact, having regard to all the circumstances. Had there been a beginning by January 1, 1951, or by December 1, 1950, or by November 1, 1950? These are all questions of fact. Unless it is held that there was submission or acquiescence by September 27, 1950, there would not be a period of one year. The judge referred to *Glover v Coleman* (1874) LR 10 CP 108, and stated: 'On the evidence I hold that neither of the plaintiffs submitted to or acquiesced in the interruption.' This was a finding of fact which the judge was, in my view, entitled to make, and accordingly I consider that the first submission fails.[221]

On the second point, the court appears to have treated the question of the knowledge or means of knowledge of the user as being a matter related to user as of right. BIRKETT LJ said at 206:

I see no evidence on which the judge could find that the common knowledge extended to the servient owner, or any evidence that the servient owner had the means of knowledge. It is on this ground that I would allow the appeal, for the claim 'as of right' cannot in these circumstances be established.

The user, as the judge found, was common knowledge; the defendant was unaware because he was the lessor, not in possession. The question should then be, it is submitted, not whether the user was as of right, but whether it was in fee simple. The answer to that question would be that, in the case of 40 years' user for easements under the Prescription Act (60 years for profits), the fact that the servient tenement was in the occupation of a tenant for years was immaterial—unless the period of user under the tenancy was excluded under the special defence provided by section 8.[222]

(b) User as of right is necessary for prescription under either period

Gardner v Hodgson's Kingston Brewery Co Ltd [1903] AC 229, p. 689, above.

---

[221] Cf. *Dance v Triplow* [1992] 1 EGLR 190 (where 'the plaintiffs failed to prove both their unwillingness to tolerate the interruption and some word or act making that clear to the defendant', per Glidewell LJ); [1992] Conv 197 (J. Martin).

[222] *Wright v Williams* (1836) 1 M & W 77 (not cited); (1956) 72 LQR 32 (R.E.M.). Compare *Kilgour v Gaddes* [1904] 1 KB 457, p. 693, above, where both tenements were owned by the same landlord.

Healey v Hawkins [1968] 1 WLR 1967, p. 692, above.

In **Union Lighterage Co v London Graving Dock Co** [1902] 2 Ch 557, one question was whether the defendants could prescribe for an easement in respect of underwater support of a wharf, none of the metal supports except two nuts showing above the surface. The Court of Appeal (Romer and Stirling LJJ, Vaughan Williams LJ dissenting) held that there could be no prescription as the user was secret. ROMER LJ said at 570:

Now, on principle, it appears to me that a prescriptive right to an easement over a man's land should only be acquired when the enjoyment has been open—that is to say, of such a character that an ordinary owner of the land, diligent in the protection of his interests, would have, or must be taken to have, a reasonable opportunity of becoming aware of that enjoyment. And I think on the balance of authority that the principle has been recognised as the law, and ought to be followed by us.[223]

(c) Next before action brought

Hyman v Van Den Bergh
[1908] 1 Ch 167 (CA, **Cozens-Hardy MR, Fletcher Moulton** and **Farwell LJJ**)

In 1877, Cox, a former tenant of the plaintiff, built a cowshed with eight windows overlooking land subsequently purchased by the defendant. In 1896 and 1898, the defendant obstructed the windows by boards but these were quickly removed by the plaintiff. On 18 January 1899, Cox wrote a letter agreeing to pay 1 shilling per annum for the use of the light. In 1906, Cox left, and a dispute arose between the parties as to the right to the light.

Held. The plaintiff was not entitled to an easement although 22 years' uninterrupted user had been enjoyed before the permission was given.

Cozens-Hardy MR: It is often asserted that an absolute right is obtained to access of light by reason merely of twenty years' undisturbed enjoyment, but I think this statement is too wide. Lord Macnaghten in *Colls v Home and Colonial Stores* [1904] AC 179 at 189, after referring to certain 'expressions not perhaps sufficiently guarded' which are to be found in the judgment in the House of Lords in *Tapling v Jones* (1865) 11 HL Cas 290, said: 'In that case Lord Westbury, Lord Cranworth, and Lord Chelmsford all assumed that a period of twenty years' enjoyment of the access and use of light to a building creates an absolute and indefeasible right immediately on the expiration of the period of twenty years. No doubt section 3 says so in terms, but section 4 must be read in connection with section 3; and if the two sections are read together it will be seen that the period is not a period in gross, but a period next before some suit or action wherein the claim or matter to which such period may relate shall have been or shall be brought into question. Unless and until the claim or matter is thus brought into question, no absolute or indefeasible right can arise under the Act. There is what has been described as an inchoate right. The owner of the dominant tenement after twenty years' uninterrupted enjoyment is in a position to avail himself of the Act if his claim is brought into

---

[223] *Barney v BP Truckstops Ltd* [1995] NPC 5.

question. But in the meantime, however long the enjoyment may have been, his right is just the same, as the origin of his right is just the same, as if the Act had never been passed. No title is as yet acquired under the Act. This point seems to have been much discussed shortly after the Act was passed. It was finally settled in a series of cases at common law, beginning, I think, with *Wright v Williams* (1836) 1 M & W 77, and including *Richards v Fry* (1837) 7 Ad & El 698 and *Cooper v Hubbuck* (1862) 12 CB NS 456.' If this is to be regarded as a decision upon sections 3 and 4, it is of course binding upon us. If, however, it is to be regarded only as a dictum of Lord Macnaghten, I desire respectfully to say that I agree with it, and I accept it as an accurate statement of the law.

It only remains to apply the law to the facts of the present case. No action was brought by the plaintiff or any other person until the present action was commenced on July 11, 1906. The only material period to be considered is the period of twenty years prior to that date. No evidence as to what was the condition of the windows prior to that date can be regarded. Now during that period there was undoubtedly the actual enjoyment of light through the windows in question, but at the end of 1898 the windows were for a short time obstructed by the defendant. The then tenant in occupation having a doubt whether a right to light could be established, and being desirous of avoiding litigation, signed and addressed to the defendant the letter of 18 January 1899; thereupon the boards were removed, and the lights were thenceforth actually enjoyed. Under these circumstances I think it is clear that the light was enjoyed by 'consent or agreement' expressly made or given for that purpose by writing. It is true that it was made or given, not to or with the freeholder, but to or with the tenant in occupation. The tenant in occupation was the proper person to make such agreement or to obtain such consent as the section requires. In my view it is a fallacy to say that the freeholder had an absolute right which his lessee ought not to be permitted to defeat. In truth he had only an inchoate right which never became an absolute and indefeasible right.

Hulbert v Dale [1909] 2 Ch 570, p. 696, above.

In **Reilly v Orange** [1955] 2 QB 112 neighbouring owners in 1934 came to an agreement whereby the defendant could use a way over the plaintiff's land until the defendant should construct a way of his own; this he did in 1953. In December 1953 the plaintiff purported to terminate the defendant's right to use the way, and began proceedings for this purpose; the defendant counterclaimed for a declaration that, by reason of his user for over 19 years, he was entitled to an easement.

The Court of Appeal (Singleton, Jenkins and Morris LJJ) affirmed the county court judge in finding for the plaintiff. JENKINS LJ said at 116:

Mr Blease, for the defendant, very properly admits that for the purpose of this appeal he must accept the deputy judge's finding as to the nature and terms of the agreement, but he says that notwithstanding this he is entitled to succeed. He says that on two grounds: (1) that he has had 20 years' uninterrupted enjoyment of the right claimed, as required by the Prescription Act 1832; (2) that although the right he claims had its origin in the agreement of 1934, and although that agreement, as found by the deputy judge, would only give him a right to use the drive for domestic purposes, and only until such time as he made a drive of his own, that permission did not prevent the 20 years' user on which he relies from establishing his right under the Prescription Act 1832. The second of those points can only arise if Mr Blease is entitled to succeed on the first....

Mr Blease's argument on this part of the case is of this nature: he says that what must be shown is 20 years' uninterrupted user, and that, according to section 4, no act or matter counts as an interruption unless the same shall have been or shall be submitted to or acquiesced in for one year. It follows, says Mr Blease, that inasmuch as in this case over 19 years' user down to the commencement of the action is proved, the defendant's right is made good inasmuch as there could be no interruption acquiesced in for one year between the date of the commencement of the action and the completion of the full period of 20 years.

In support of that proposition he referred us to the well-known case of *Flight v Thomas* (1841) 8 Cl & Fin 231. In that case: 'A. had the free access of light and air through a window of his house for nineteen years and 330 days, and B. then raised a wall which obstructed the light, and the obstruction was submitted to only for 35 days, when A. brought an action to remove it.' It was held: 'that the right of action was complete; that the twenty years' enjoyment was to be reckoned from the commencement of the enjoyment to the time of bringing the action; and that an interruption of the enjoyment, in whatever period of the twenty years it may happen, cannot be deemed an interruption within the meaning of the Act, unless it is acquiesced in for a whole year.'

Mr Blease seeks to apply that to the present case in this way: he says that the commencement of the action constituted an interruption, and that, inasmuch as the action was not commenced until after the alleged easement had been enjoyed for more than 19 years, the interruption so constituted could not last for the required period of one year, so that his title was complete at the time of action brought. In my view that argument cannot prevail. What the Prescription Act requires, as appears from the combined effect of section 2 and section 4, is the full period of 20 years, being 'the period next before some suit or action wherein the claim or matter to which such period may relate shall have been or shall be brought into question.' The commencement of the suit or action in my view is clearly not an interruption within the meaning of section 4, but is the event marking the date down to which the requisite period of user must be shown. What must be shown is a full 20 years reckoned down to the date of action brought. That must be an uninterrupted period, but in considering whether it is an uninterrupted period or not, interruptions not acquiesced in for at least a year are not to be counted as interruptions.

In **Davis v Whitby** [1974] Ch 186 (CA, Lord Denning MR, Stamp and Orr LJJ), STAMP LJ said at 192:

[A]s the point is a somewhat novel one, I will express my views in my own words. The basis of prescription, as Lord Denning MR has pointed out, is that if long enjoyment of a right is shown, the courts will strive to uphold the right by presuming that it had a lawful origin. Here, the owner of no. 51 (which, for the purpose of convenience, I will call 'the dominant tenement') has for upwards of 30 years enjoyed access from the rear of his house over no. 49 (which I will call 'the servient tenement'). During the first 15 years it was enjoyed over one path, and during the second period of over 15 years it was enjoyed partly over that path and partly over a substituted path. Viewed as the exercise of a right to pass and re-pass over the servient tenement, it has been enjoyed for upwards of 30 years, which is more than a sufficiently long period for it to be presumed that the right had a lawful origin. Viewed as a right so to pass and re-pass over a specified path, it has not. The question, as I see it, is which is the right way of looking at it. What happened was that in 1950 the new track or path over the back garden of the servient owner's house was established; but, using it, the dominant owner still used, as he had formerly done, the path at the side of the servient owner's house. Was the dominant owner then using the new way as of right and as of the same right as formerly? I think he was. In substance, what was enjoyed as well before as after 1950 was access by the dominant owner to the back of his little house from the road in front of the terrace along the side of the servient owner's premises and across his back garden.

On the facts of this case, the use of the substituted route is, in my judgment, to be considered as substantially an exercise of the right claimed and enjoyed for the whole period of 30 years. It is not as though the servient owner had said: 'I will stop up the way you have been using over these last 15 years, but you may have a new defined way over a wholly different part of my land', a situation about which I will say nothing.

I had at one time thought that the point taken that the agreement of 1950 by the servient owner amounted to a consent by him which interrupted the enjoyment as of right and so made the user 'precario' was a good point.[224] But I accept Mr Gidley Scott's submission that what was agreed in 1950 did not involve a simple consent to the user given by the owner of the dominant tenement, but is more consistent (as I think Burgess V-C thought) with the existence of a claim of right by the dominant owner settled by the servient owner affording a route less disadvantageous to him than a path crossing the middle of his garden; and I do not think that it was a case of consent, but rather of compromise.

I would, for these reasons, dismiss the appeal.

(vi) Proposals for reform of the law of prescription[225]

Law Commission Consultation Paper on Easements, Covenants and Profits à Prendre 2008 (Consultation Paper No. 186), paras 4.167–4.183, 4.194–4.196, 4.221–4.222

4.167 In 1971, the Court of Appeal stated:

> 'The co-existence of three separate methods of prescribing is, in our view, anomalous and undesirable, for it results in much unnecessary complication and confusion. We hope that it may be possible for the Legislature to effect a long-overdue simplification in this branch of the law.'[226]

4.168 We concur with this analysis and consider that the defects of the current law are clear. There is no discernible need for three concurrent systems of prescriptive acquisition.

---

[224] *Rafique v Trustees of the Walton Estate* (1992) 65 P & CR 356; [1994] Conv 196 at pp. 207–210 (H. Wallace).

[225] Gale, para. 4.131. See *Housden v Conservators of Wimbledon and Putney Commons* [2008] 1 WLR 1172 at [72], per Mummery LJ: 'I wish the Law Commission well in its deliberations. It is better equipped than the courts to recommend improvements in this area of the law, though prescription is low down in the priorities for law reform. Nevertheless, the rapid expansion of home ownership, the increasing pressures on land available for development and the almost universal reliance on cars for travel outside the city all mean that the need for a simpler law of prescription has become of more rather than less concern. The experience of the courts is that bitter and unaffordable neighbour disputes sometimes stem from claims to user of a way as a means of access to, and for parking close by, a private house, and from complaints of increased and excessive user of an existing access'. For further criticism of the role of prescription in the creation of easements in the modern law see [2007] Conv 133 (F. Burns); S. Bridge, *Prescriptive Acquisition of Easements: Abolition or Reform?* in Cooke (ed.) *Modern Studies in Property Law*, vol. 3, p. 3.

[226] *Tehidy Minerals Ltd v Norman* [1971] 2 QB 528, 543, by Buckley LJ.

Common law prescription is effectively obsolete. Lost modern grant, although archaic, remains important in practice. As there is no requirement that the prescriptive period of use be that period immediately 'before action brought', lost modern grant may often be easier to establish than prescription under the 1832 Act. The co-existence of three systems leads inevitably to complicated proceedings as claimants argue their case in the alternative to maximise their chances of success. As a result, it is sometimes difficult to discern from the decided cases which ground formed the basis of a successful claim. We are compelled to question whether such an unsatisfactory legal framework should have any part to play in the twenty-first century.

4.169 Whichever method of prescription is used, the easement obtained by the successful claimant is likely to be a legal easement. As with implied creation, the lack of any reference to the interest in the documents of title makes it difficult for a purchaser to discover the existence of the rights over the land being acquired. This may result in a purchaser of land being bound by an easement that has not been used for many years[227] and the existence of which is not apparent from an inspection of the land. While the purchaser may have a claim in damages against the vendor of the land on the implied covenants for title,[228] this may be an inadequate substitute for the land free of the incumbrance.

4.170 The prescriptive acquisition of easements may give rise to other practical difficulties. It is often more difficult to determine the precise nature and extent of a right that has been acquired by prescription than if it has been expressly granted or reserved. Its nature and extent must necessarily be ascertained only by reference to the actual use over the prescriptive period. For a person (such as a purchaser of the burdened land) who has no knowledge of the relevant history, it will be difficult to contest the evidence in support of the prescriptive claim given by neighbours who may have lived in the vicinity throughout the period.

4.171 Finally, the current law is unsatisfactory as it is based on a fiction of grant. Reliance on this fiction, to such an extent that a court is even obliged to disregard clear evidence that no interest was ever granted in favour of the dominant land, cannot be justified and is difficult to explain to lay persons who are affected by its operation.

Options for reform

4.172 There are three options which require consideration:

(1) do nothing;

(2) abolish prescriptive acquisition with prospective effect; and

(3) introduce a new statutory regime with a single method of prescriptive acquisition.

4.173 In our view the first option is not desirable. The case for doing something with the current mixture of uncertainty, duplication and overlap is quite overwhelming....

4.174 We provisionally propose that the current law of prescriptive acquisition of easements (that is, at common law, by lost modern grant and under the Prescription Act 1832) be abolished with prospective effect.

---

[227] Those easements which were overriding before the LRA 2002 came into force (13 October 2003) will retain their overriding status indefinitely: LRA 2002, Sch. 12, para. 9.

[228] Assuming that full title guarantee is given: see Law of Property (Miscellaneous Provisions) Act 1994, s. 3(1). Even if s. 3(1) is applicable, the vendor may not be liable if he or she did not know of the right and could not reasonably have done so. If an easement or profit has not been asserted for many years, but is then claimed pursuant to lost modern grant, this could be the case.

Outright abolition

4.175 The question of abolition is not by any means new. Forty years ago, the Law Reform Committee, albeit by a slender majority, recommended the abolition of the prescriptive acquisition of easements and profits. It could be argued that the case for abolition in 2008 is, if anything, stronger than it was in 1966.

4.176 The arguments of principle in favour of abolition of prescriptive acquisition of easements[229] can be summarised as follows:

(1) Prescription allows the claimant to get something for nothing. The owner of the servient land is not compensated for the acquisition of the right by the owner of the dominant land.

(2) Prescription may penalise altruism. The claim may well originate from the servient owner's 'good neighbourly' attitude, making no complaint about the claimant's assertiveness.

(3) Prescription may sometimes operate disproportionately. The claimant may 'deserve' some recognition of the expectations which have arisen from the servient owner's acquiescence. But should this always result in the conferment of a property right which may be equivalent in duration to a fee simple absolute in possession?

4.177 Whilst these arguments provide a case for outright abolition, they must be considered in light of the function that prescription serves and whether the gap left by abolition would be sufficiently served by existing legal or equitable principles.

4.178 We consider that a useful starting point is to ask what function the law of prescriptive acquisition currently serves. The overwhelming argument in favour of the retention of prescription is that the law—the legal position—should reflect and recognise the fact of long use. In 1879, Mr Justice Fry stated that '[w]here there has been a long enjoyment of property in a particular manner it is the habit, and, in my view, the duty, of the Court so far as it lawfully can, to clothe the fact with right'.[230] More recently in *R v Oxfordshire County Council, ex parte Sunningwell Parish Council* Lord Hoffmann asserted:

'Any legal system must have rules of prescription which prevent the disturbance of long-established de facto enjoyment.'[231]

4.179 It may be that for many years a person who is now claiming an easement has used adjacent land in a particular way, and the owner of that land has stood by and not objected to his or her actions. The issue of the lawfulness of the claimant's conduct may only arise sometime much later. It may be unconscionable in such circumstances for the owner of the servient land, who has failed to take any action, to be able to prevent the claimant, or the claimant's successors in title, from using it. In the words of the Law Reform Committee in 1966:

'If it is accepted that a *status quo* of long standing ought to be given legal recognition, prescription has not outlived its usefulness.'[232]

---

[229] We set out our provisional proposals for the reform of the prescriptive acquisition of profits in Part 6 below.

[230] *Moody v Steggles* (1879) LR 12 Ch D 261, 265.

[231] *R v Oxfordshire County Council ex parte Sunningwell Parish Council* [2000] 1 AC 335.

[232] Acquisition of Easements and Profits by Prescription: Fourteenth Report (1966) Law Reform Committee, Cmnd 3100, para. 38(d).

4.180 Long use has always been recognised as giving rise to beliefs or expectations in relation to land that ought to be protected on the basis of security of possession and utility.[233] There are a number of examples of the utility of prescription. Prescription performs the useful function of saving landowners from the consequences of a failure to grant or reserve easements expressly. In some cases, the landowner would have a remedy in negligence against the solicitor or other conveyancer responsible for the problem which has come to light. In other cases, particularly where the error happened some time ago, such a remedy may not be viable. However, irrespective of the availability of a remedy in negligence, it seems to us that where the parties have clearly proceeded for some considerable time on the basis that rights exist and may be exercised, it may be just and reasonable for the court to recognise those rights.

4.181 Claimants rarely set out deliberately to acquire an easement by long use; they much more frequently believe or assume that they are entitled to an easement. Although it is not necessary that it do so, this belief may have induced the purchase of, or the expenditure of money upon, the dominant land. Abolition of prescription without replacement could lead to a situation where landowners mistakenly believe that they are entitled to an easement and use the land accordingly. In these circumstances, the land would be being used in a way which is not reflected on the register or recognised outside it.

4.182 Finally, and most importantly, prescription recognises the fact that land is a social resource, in that it cannot be utilised without the co-operation of neighbouring landowners. Neighbouring landowners, to varying degrees, rely on one another for rights of access, drainage, support, and water. In many cases co-operation between neighbouring landowners is regulated through legal instruments and informal arrangements. However, there will always remain cases where reliance on one's neighbour is entirely unregulated and may have occurred for a substantial period of time. In such circumstances there is an arguable case for clothing the user with legal right.

4.183 We therefore do not currently consider that outright abolition of prescriptive acquisition is desirable. Prescription plays a useful residual role, ensuring that long use is recognised as a legal interest binding upon the owners of servient land.

A new statutory scheme for prescriptive acquisition

4.194 In this section, we give the brief outline of a possible statutory scheme for the acquisition of easements by long use. It is a scheme which has been devised to apply where titles to the dominant and servient estates are registered. We recognise the necessity to make provisions to deal with prescriptive easements where one or both titles are not yet registered, and we deal with this issue below.[234]

4.195 The basis of acquisition would be the long use of the servient land by the owner of the dominant land, and in that respect it would bear some similarity to the existing law. In determining what does not count as long use, the question would be whether the use by the

---

[233] See, for example, J. Getzler, 'Roman and English Prescription for Incorporeal Property' in J. Getzler (ed.), *Rationalizing Property, Equity and Trusts: Essays in Honour of Edward Burn* (2003); J. Bentham, *Principles of the Civil Code* (1802), Part 1 and ch 1 of Part 2; H. Maine, *Ancient Law* (1861), chap. 8; and J. Mill, *Principles of Political Economy with Some of their Applications to Social Philosophy* (1871), Book 2. Consider also G. Hegel, *Philosophy of Right* (1821) §64.

[234] As the law currently stands, title to *unregistered* land can normally be acquired by 12 years' adverse possession (Limitation Act 1980, s. 15(1) [p. 249, above]). This will change if our proposals on limitation of actions are carried forward, and the limitation period is reduced to 10 years: Limitation of Actions (2001) Law Com No. 270, para. 4.135.

claimant has been by force, by stealth or by licence. If any of those questions were answered in the affirmative, the claim would fail. Unlike the existing law, we see no need for any past grant to be presumed.

4.196 The essential components of a successful claim would therefore be:

(1) 'qualifying use' by the claimant;

(2) for the duration of the prescriptive period; and

(3) registration.

4.221 We provisionally propose:

(1) that it should be possible to claim an easement by prescription on proof of 20 years' continuous qualifying use;

(2) that qualifying use shall continue to within 12 months of application being made to the registrar for entry of a notice on the register of title;

(3) that qualifying use shall be use without force, without stealth and without consent; and

(4) that qualifying use shall not be use which is contrary to law, unless such use can be rendered lawful by the dispensation of the servient owner.

4.222 Under our proposed scheme, the easement would not come into being until the claimant applied successfully to Land Registry for the right to be noted as appurtenant to the claimant's title. The registry would not be confirming the existence of a right that had already been acquired, but would be declaring that, in view of the use to which the servient land has been put for the requisite duration, the claimant should now be entitled to an easement over that land. That easement would take effect as a legal easement on being entered on the register of the dominant land. The registrar would then, in accordance with its current practice, enter a notice on the register of the servient land.

> ## QUESTION
>
> Consider the arguments for and against the abolition of the acquisition of easements by prescription. Is it necessary or appropriate for the same rules or principles to apply to the acquisition of easements by prescription and the acquisition of the title to land by adverse possession?

IV. CONTENT OF EASEMENTS[235]

After establishing that an easement has been created, questions can still arise as to its content and extent. Such questions often relate to changes in the neighbourhood and, in connection with rights of way, to changes in methods of transportation. The principles applicable vary with the mode of creation of the easement.

---

[235] C & B, pp. 628–631; Smith, pp. 514–517. As to easements of light, see p. 728, below. As to rights of way, see Gray, paras 5.1.79–5.1.88; M & W, paras 30.001–30.009 Gale, paras 9.03–9.69.

A. EASEMENTS CREATED BY EXPRESS GRANT

The extent of an easement is dependent upon the proper construction of the deed of grant. This is dependent upon the circumstances surrounding its execution, and they may be sufficient to restrict an apparently unlimited grant.

In **Williams v James** (1867) LR 2 CP 577 WILLES J said at 581:

The distinction between a grant and prescription is obvious. In the case of proving a right by prescription the user of the right is the only evidence. In the case of a grant the language of the instrument can be referred to, and it is of course for the Court to construe that language; and in the absence of any clear indication of the intention of the parties, the maxim that a grant must be construed most strongly against the grantor must be applied.

In **White v Grand Hotel, Eastbourne, Ltd** [1913] 1 Ch 113,[236] an unrestricted right of way to a public road granted to the owner of a private house was held not to be limited to the circumstances existing at the time of the grant. When the private house became the Grand Hotel, Eastbourne, the owners of the hotel were entitled to a right of way for the general purposes of the hotel.

In **Kain v Norfolk** [1949] Ch 163, the rector of Bradwell had conveyed to a purchaser in 1919 land adjoining the rectory, together with a grant of the 'right at all times hereafter with or without horses carts and agricultural machines and implements to go pass and repass' over a strip of land within the rectory grounds.

A sand and gravel pit was later opened, and substantial traffic of lorries carrying sand developed. The question was whether such user was within the terms of the grant of the easement. Jenkins J, relying on *White v Grand Hotel, Eastbourne, Ltd,* held that it was.

In **Bulstrode v Lambert** [1953] 1 WLR 1064,[237] a reservation in the conveyance by the plaintiff's predecessor in title to the defendant's predecessor in title in 1944 had been made of a right of way as follows—'reserving unto the vendor his tenants and workmen and others authorised by him the right to pass and repass with or without vehicles over and along the land coloured brown on the...plan for the purpose of obtaining access to the building at the rear of the said premises and known as the auction mart.'

At the date of the conveyance the route to the auction mart (coloured brown) was obstructed and could not be used by large vans. The obstructions were removed, and, on occasions when a better route was too crowded, the plaintiff made use of the route

---

[236] *United Land Co v Great Eastern Rly Co* (1875) 10 Ch App 586; *Robinson v Bailey* [1948] 2 All ER 791 (right of way to building plot held to include business user); *Jalnarne Ltd v Ridewood* (1989) 61 P & CR 143 (right of way held to permit its use by juggernaut lorries and customers in vans and cars for access to dominant tenements subsequently used for motorcar dealing, frozen food business and snooker club with bar); *Hamble Parish Council v Haggard* [1992] 1 WLR 122; *Brooks v Young* [2008] 3 EGLR 26.

[237] *McIlraith v Grady* [1968] 1 QB 468 (a right 'to pass and repass through over and along' included a right for vehicles to stop for a reasonable time to load and unload).

with furniture vans and pantechnicons for bringing goods to the mart. The defendant objected on the ground that the parked pantechnicons interfered with his business as a cafe and car hire proprietor, but Upjohn J held that the plaintiff could use the way with pantechnicons which could park as long as was necessary for loading and unloading, this being an incident of a right of way.[238]

Keefe v Amor
[1965] 1 QB 334 (CA, **Sellers, Davies** and **Russell LJJ**)

The plaintiff was the owner of one (No. 1) of two semi-detached houses whose only outlet to the road was a strip of land to the rear. This land and the other house (No. 2) were owned by the defendant.

The plaintiff's parents had bought No. 1 in 1930 from the previous owner of both houses and the conveyance contained an express grant of a right of way in the following terms: 'Together also with a right of way over the land shown and coloured brown on the plan hereto annexed the purchasers paying a fair proportion in common with the adjoining owners of the cost of keeping the said way in good repair and condition subject to the liability of contributing (in common with the adjoining owners) to the upkeep and repair of the wall on the west side of the said right of way shown and marked with a T on the plan drawn hereon.'

At the date of the transfer there was at the frontage to the highway a continuous wall, except for a gap four feet six inches wide between two brick pillars. Inside, a gravelled strip eight feet wide led to a doorway three feet wide to the plaintiff's property and to a gap some seven feet wide leading to the remainder of the defendant's property. In 1962 the defendant widened the entrance from the highway to about seven feet six inches wide by rehanging the original gate and hanging another, three feet wide, alongside, which she kept locked, claiming the right so to do. The plaintiff sought a declaration that she was entitled to a right of way for all purposes, including vehicular traffic, over the whole of the strip of land coloured brown and an injunction to restrain the defendant from interfering with her reasonable enjoyment of this right.

The defendant contended that, in accordance with the circumstances existing at the time of the grant, the right of way was a footway only, or, at most, for such use as the four feet six inch gap permitted.

Held. On the proper construction of the grant, the right of way included user by vehicular traffic.

Russell LJ: What were the circumstances and the condition of the property at the time of the grant? The inward end of the 'brown strip' abutted on the boundary wall of the plaintiff's

---

[238] Cf. *London and Suburban Land and Building Co (Holdings) Ltd v Carey* (1991) 62 P & CR 480 (express grant of a right of way to commercial premises did not imply a right to unload from the access way onto the dominant tenement); *CP Holdings v Dugdale Real Property* [1998] NPC 97 (unrestricted right of way over disused railway line; servient owner reopening line held not able to lower level crossing thereby causing temporary but lengthy queues); *Nationwide Building Society v James Beauchamp* [2001] 3 EGLR 6 (grant of right of way includes ancillary rights to make grant effective).

property, No. 1—presumably a wall belonging to No. 1—in which was a doorway about three feet wide. Down one side of the 'brown strip' was the wall referred to in the transfer. Down the other side was a hedge, which, at the inward end, left a gap of some seven feet or so, which afforded access between the 'brown strip' and No. 2. At the highway frontage of the 'brown strip' was a wall between the ends of the hedge and the other wall, continuous except for the gap of about four feet six inches between two 14-inch-square brick pillars suitable for a gateway; and from this gateway to the inward end of the 'brown strip' was a gravelled strip appreciably wider than the gateway, with some kind of edging of tiles, and on each side beyond that edging were garden beds and bushes, though apparently not much kept up. In appearance it looked like a footpath rather than a roadway. During the tenancy of the plaintiff's parents (which had lasted since 1903), there did not appear to have been any vehicular use of the 'brown strip' by them.

Bearing all those matters in mind, do they lead to the conclusion that the grant was of a footway only, or alternatively, if the grant was of a vehicular way, then that it was one limited as to the dimensions of the vehicle in the manner I have indicated? For myself, I think not. It is argued that that view, which I have just expressed, means that the plaintiff's parents could, had they been so minded, immediately after the transfer have insisted on the four feet six inch wide gap being widened, by pulling down a post and a part of the wall, if the vendor refused to do so, so as to enable a motor car, if they so wished, to come right up to their property, to enter and leave, and it is said that this surely would not have been a situation intended by the parties at the time of the grant. But there are several aspects of the transfer which I think lead to the conclusion that the greater right was intended.

First and foremost, the right of way was expressed to be over the strip whose whole 20-feet width was coloured brown. It would have been perfectly simple to define it more narrowly if that had been intended, or, of course, to define it as a footway, or as a right of way to and from the then existing gateway. Moreover, the fact that the whole 20-feet width was regarded as available if necessary for the exercise of the right is stressed by the reference to the wall marked with a 'T' as being 'on the west side of the said right of way', showing that the whole of the 20-feet strip was being referred to as the right of way. Why (I ask myself) should the whole width be regarded as being available, if necessary, for the use as a right of way, if all that was intended was the restricted right suggested by the defendant?

I further observe that there was no obligation imposed to contribute to the upkeep of the frontage wall and, further, that an express grant of the footway alone would have been quite superfluous in the circumstances. I refer, of course, to the history of previous user; and, whether one speaks of it as a way of necessity or whether one speaks of it, as I think more correctly, as a grant which would have been implied having regard to the pre-existing user, in either event an express grant in 1930 was technically a superfluity.

Finally I would add that an obligation to pay a fair proportion of the cost of keeping the way in good repair and condition is at least unusual if all that was envisaged was the impact of human feet.

The county court judge decided against the defendant because he felt himself bound so to do by the decision of Upjohn J in *Bulstrode v Lambert* [1953] 1 WLR 1064 [p. 711, above]. In that case there was at the time of the grant a gateway and an overhead bar which would have limited the size of vehicles having access to the auction room premises and prevented the entry of furniture vans or pantechnicons. Nevertheless, in the judge's view that did not restrict the scope of the grant. I do not myself think that that case is conclusive of the present case, because the terms of the grant in that case were very particular, though I think that it is of use in approaching the alternative contention (which, if I may say so, was certainly not Mr Poole's favourite of the two contentions), namely, the small-vehicle right.

Perhaps it would be desirable to stress what I have said by quoting from the judgment in that case where the judge says: 'I am unable to accept that submission. Here is a perfectly plain, unambiguous reservation for "the vendor, his tenants and workmen"—there is no limitation whatever upon the vehicles—"over and along the land coloured brown" on the plan. Pausing there, in my judgment the true effect of those words, that there is a right of way over and along the land coloured brown, cannot be affected by the circumstance that at the date of the grant there was this gate and bar across. The words of the grant are plain and unambiguous, and in my judgment the plaintiff plainly has a right over the whole of the yard coloured brown, and not merely a right to enter through the gates some six feet in width. Not only that: he has a right to enter it with vehicles. That must mean vehicles of any size appropriate to go down the yard, and as the yard is at no stage, until the garage is reached, less than eleven feet wide, there seems to be no reason why a pantechnicon should not use that yard.'

The part that I have quoted there shows that there were particular considerations in the language of the grant in the *Bulstrode* case which are absent from the present case; and for my part I would not have thought that the judge was necessarily bound, simply as a result of that decision, to conclude that in the present case there was more than a footpath. However, as I say, I differ in the end from the conclusion at which, but for the *Bulstrode* decision, the judge would have arrived. . . .

I would remark that it is sometimes thought that the grant of a right of way in respect of every part of a defined area involves the proposition that the grantee can object to anything on any part of the area which would obstruct passage over that part. This is a wrong understanding of the law. Assuming a right of way of a particular quality over an area of land, it will extend to every part of that area, as a matter, at least, of theory. But a right of way is not a right absolutely to restrict user of the area by the owner thereof. The grantee of the right could only object to such activities of the owner of the land, including retention of obstruction, as substantially interfered with the use of the land in such exercise of the defined right as for the time being is reasonably required.[239] (I am, of course, talking now about private rights of way.)

This proposition is exemplified by the decision of this court in *Dyer v Mousley,* (1962) unreported Transcript No. 315, where the dominant owner asserted the right to clear and level the whole of the strip dedicated to the right of way, at a time when there was no need to do so for the current requirement of the dominant tenant.

For those reasons, in my judgment, this appeal fails.

In **Jelbert v Davis** [1968] 1 WLR 589[240] the plaintiff, in a conveyance of agricultural land to him in 1961, was granted 'a right of way at all times and for all purposes

---

[239] See *Celsteel Ltd v Alton House Holdings Ltd* [1985] 1 WLR 204 (interference with driving in forwards and reversing out of a garage held to be substantial); *West v Sharp* (1999) 79 P & CR 327; *B & Q Plc v Liverpool and Lancashire Properties Ltd* [2001] 1 EGLR 92 at 96G: 'the test of an actionable interference is not whether what the grantee is left with is reasonable, but whether his insistence upon being able to continue the use of the whole of what he contracted for is reasonable': (per Blackburne J).

[240] *Hanover Trust Co Ltd v Eastern Counties Leather Group Ltd* (2000) 25 July, CA, unreported (grant to purchase of rights to be exercisable over retained land of vendor 'in common with the vendor and all persons authorised by it' held expressly to contemplate that vendor might grant further rights over that land in favour of third parties.

over the driveway retained by the vendor leading to the main road in common with all other persons having the like right'. In 1966 he obtained planning permission to use part of the land as a tourist and caravan site for up to 200 caravans or tents. The defendants, two neighbouring landowners, objected to the proposed use of the driveway for caravan traffic and put up notices warning off caravans and campers. The plaintiff sued for nuisance and slander of title, and the defendants counter-claimed for an injunction to restrain the plaintiff from using the driveway for access to the caravan site. The Court of Appeal held that the plaintiff was entitled to use the driveway for caravans, but not so as to cause substantial interference with its use by the defendants: the user by 200 caravans was excessive. DANCKWERTS LJ said at 597:

On the authorities, it is plain that the easement so granted is in such wide terms that the use by the plaintiff of it for caravans is permissible; but it is an easement which on its terms is a right which is to be used 'in common with all other persons having the like right'. That includes the defendants. A use of the right of way which is so excessive that it renders the rights of such other persons practically impossible, therefore, is not justified. The difficulty is to fix the limit in respect of such use. The test must be whether the interference is so substantial as to interfere with the rights of other persons in an unreasonable manner. It cannot be right that the others should be swamped by the traffic created by the plaintiff so as to amount to a legal nuisance. It is impossible to quantify this in figures, particularly as the problem relates to the future. These people are neighbours and share the right of way and there must be give and take and accom-modation. Time will show what is practicable, and in the interests of both parties a practical solution must be found or a deadlock will result.[241]

In **Graham v Philcox** [1984] QB 747[242] M, who owned a large house and garden and a coach house at the rear in High Rocks Lane, Tunbridge Wells, let the first floor flat of the coach house in 1960 to B for five years together with a right of way for all purposes over the entrance drive to the house and thence along the side of the garden as far as the coach house. In 1963 B assigned his lease to D who later became a statutory tenant under the Rent Act. In 1975 M's executors conveyed the freehold of the entire coach house to W, subject to D's tenancy of the first floor flat. Nothing was said in the con-veyance about the means of access.

In June 1977 M's executors conveyed to the defendants, Mr and Mrs Philcox, the freehold of that part of the retained land over which the right of way had been granted in the lease of 1960. Finally in November 1970, W's interest in the coach house was conveyed to the plaintiffs, Mr and Mrs Graham, subject to D's tenancy. D later sur-rendered his tenancy to the plaintiffs who then occupied the whole coach house as their residence. The defendants refused to allow the plaintiffs to continue to use the right of way.

---

[241] *Rosling v Pinnegar* (1986) 54 P & CR 124 (access to Hammerwood Park, near East Grinstead, built by Latrobe, American architect of the White House); cf. *National Trust v White* [1987] 1 WLR 907 (access to Figsbury Ring, near Salisbury); *White v Richards* (1993) 68 P & CR 105 (track not intended to carry jug-gernauts); *Gardner v Davis* [1998] PLSCS 219 (extent of sewage easement unreasonable).

[242] [1985] Conv 60 (P. Todd); [1985] CLJ 15 (S. Tromans).

The Court of Appeal, following *Wright v Macadam* [1949] 2 KB 744 p. 665, above, held that, when the coach house was conveyed in 1925, the right of way had passed under LPA 1925, s. 62(2) to the plaintiffs' predecessor in title. PURCHAS LJ said at 760:

It was certainly an easement, right or advantage '*reputed to appertain to the first floor flat*' and was enjoyed with that part 'of *the* land, houses or other buildings conveyed.' I can find nothing in the wording of section 62(2) of the Act to indicate that the 'land conveyed' cannot include land subject to a lease or an adverse right of occupation by a tenant protected by statute. The easement, right or advantage is enjoyed with and appertains to the land, not to the statutory right of occupation.

The Court of Appeal further held that the alteration of the dominant tenement by the enlargement of the first floor flat of the coach house into one dwelling did not affect the existence of the right of way. MAY LJ said at 755:

Mr Godfrey's principal submission was that as the dominant tenement for the benefit of which the way is now claimed, namely the coach house, is not the same as and is indeed greater than the dominant tenement for the benefit of which the way was originally granted, namely only the upper flat in the coach house, therefore the plaintiffs cannot use that way now when the coach house is now one dwelling and the original two flats which it comprised have been combined into one... Mr Godfrey submitted further that if one substantially alters a dominant tenement, an easement therefore enjoyed with it can no longer be used, because by the alterations one has increased the burden of the use on the servient tenement. The easement is consequently lost, or at least suspended temporarily: thus in the present case the plaintiffs must accept that they cannot enforce their use of the disputed right of way for so long as the coach house remains one dwelling...

In none of the judgments in any of the cases to which Mr Godfrey referred us is there suggestion that a mere alteration of a dominant tenement to which a right of way may be appurtenant is sufficient to extinguish it, or indeed to affect the entitlement to its use unless as the result of that alteration the extent of the user is thereby increased.

In my opinion, therefore, the mere alteration of the coach house into one dwelling cannot have had any effect upon the existence of the right of way. It should be borne in mind that there was no evidence whatever before the judge that the actual or anticipated user by the plaintiffs of the way was in any way excessive, either in quantity or quality.

Further, I do not think that on this issue any real distinction can be drawn between the instant case on the one hand and *Wright v Macadam* on the other. In the latter case also the right for which the plaintiffs contended had, at the date of the conveyance relied on for the purposes of section 62(2), been enjoyed by the occupier of only part of the whole premises in respect of which the continued enjoyment of the right was claimed in the action.[243]

In **St. Edmundsbury and Ipswich Diocesan Board of Finance v Clark (No 2)** [1975] 1 WLR 468 land, including the former rectory of St Botolph's Church, Iken, in Suffolk, was sold and conveyed in 1945 by the church authorities to the defendant. It then

---

[243] *Mills v Silver* [1991] Ch 271 p. 690, above (grantee of prescriptive right of way entitled to repair but not to improve it; improvement would increase burden on servient tenement).

wholly surrounded the church and churchyard. Access from the village to the church porch was by Church Lane (a narrow public highway) which then became a path 100 yards long leading to the church porch. The first third of the path ('the disputed strip') crossed the rectory grounds, and the remainder ('the church path') was within the churchyard and church property. The first 7 yards of the disputed strip could be used by vehicles for access from the lane to a driveway, leading to the rectory. The remainder ('the chestnut path') was not wider than 4 feet 6 inches and was a derelict gravel and sandy path covered with leaves. At the end of the chestnut path on the defendant's land was a gate between two gateposts, standing no more than 4 feet apart. There was no evidence that the path was used by vehicles before 1946.

On 31 December 1945 the land was conveyed to the defendant 'subject to a right of way over the land coloured red on the said plan to and from St Botolph's Church'. The question was whether the right of way reserved by the church authorities was a right exercisable on foot only, or with vehicles also.

The Court of Appeal, construing the language of the conveyance in the light of all the surrounding circumstances, decided that it was a right of footway only. In explaining the correct approach in these matters, SIR JOHN PENNYCUICK said at 476:

What is the proper approach upon the construction of a conveyance containing the reservation of a right of way? We feel no doubt that the proper approach is that upon which the court construes all documents; that is to say, one must construe the document according to the natural meaning of the words contained in the document as a whole, read in the light of surrounding circumstances.

A similar approach is adopted in the identification of the dominant tenement. In **Johnstone v Holdway** [1963] 1 QB 601 George Horace Johnstone agreed in 1936 to sell land to the Trewithin Estates Company, but no conveyance was executed. In 1948 Trewithin Estates Company sold part of the land to Henry Bosustow, whereupon Johnstone as trustee and the company as beneficial owner conveyed it to Bosustow. The conveyance excepted and reserved to the company and its successors in title 'a right of way at all times and for all purposes (including quarrying)' over the land conveyed from a point on its north-western boundary to a point on its south-eastern boundary. The conveyance failed to specify any dominant tenement for the right of way, but it was meant to be the quarry, retained as part of their land by the company. The plaintiffs, as successors in title of the company, claimed a right of way against the successors in title of Bosustow.

In holding that the plaintiffs were entitled to a legal easement, UPJOHN LJ said at 609:

Mr Seward, for the defendant...submits that it is essential to the valid creation of every easement that the dominant tenement must be defined in the deed itself and that no extrinsic evidence is admissible to define it.... But the question we have to determine is whether that is essential to the validity of the easement or whether it is permissible to identify the dominant tenement by inferences from facts and circumstances which must have been known to the parties at the time of the conveyance....

In our judgment, it is a question of the construction of the deed creating a right of way as to what is the dominant tenement for the benefit of which the right of way is granted and to which the right of way is appurtenant. In construing the deed the court is entitled to have evidence of all material facts at the time of the execution of the deed, so as to place the court in the situation of the parties.... It seems to us perfectly plain that in this case the dominant tenement was the land and quarry.[244]

B. EASEMENTS CREATED BY IMPLIED GRANT

As explained above[245] the rules for the creation of easements by implied grant vary with the question whether the easement is claimed by the grantor or grantee.

Easements implied in favour of the grantor are limited to cases of necessity or to cases where the intention of the parties is clear.[246] Easements of necessity are strictly limited to the circumstances of the necessity.

In the case of easements implied in favour of the grantee—where they are 'continuous and apparent', 'necessary for the reasonable enjoyment of the property granted', or where the common intention of the parties was clear—there seems to be little authority on the question of the extent of the easement. If tested at the time of the conveyance, no difficulty arises, for the same rules as govern implication will govern extent. But difficulties may arise if the matter is tested at a time when circumstances have changed. If, for example, a narrow track is sufficient to establish that a right of way is 'continuous and apparent' in a conveyance of 1880, will this cover travellers on foot, horseback, by car or by lorry? The cases on easements by express grant would suggest that the extent of the easement will develop as circumstances change and that limitations will only be imposed where such a restriction is clearly justified.[247]

---

[244] See p. 651, above. (1963) 79 LQR 182 (R.E.M.); *Shannon Ltd v Venner Ltd* [1965] Ch 682; *Bracewell v Appleby* [1975] 1 All ER 993 (right to pass over close A to reach close B held to be not usable as access to close C lying beyond close B), following *Harris v Flower* (1904) 74 LJ Ch 127; (1975) 39 Conv (NS) 277 (F. R. Crane); *Nickerson v Barraclough* [1980] Ch 325 at 336 (such a right held to be usable as access where close B is itself used as access to close C at time of grant); *Jobson v Record* (1997) 75 P & CR 375; *Peacock v Custins* [2001] 1 WLR 1815; *Das v Linden Mews Ltd* (2003) 2 P & CR 58; [2003] Conv 127 (E. Paton and G. Seabourne); *Massey v Boulden* [2003] 1 WLR 1792; *Macepark (Whittlebury) Ltd v Sargeant* [2003] 1 WLR 2284; *Scott v Martin* [1987] 1 WLR 841 (plan used to explain 'private road'); *Hamble Parish Council v Haggard* [1992] 1 WLR 122 ('I have to put myself into the shoes of the notional judge visiting the site with the conveyance in one hand and gazing about him to identify on the ground those features which would enable him to ascertain the extent of the dominant land', per Millett J at 130). See also *Minor v Groves* (1997) 80 P & CR 136 (dominant owner limited in user to extend with right of way; occasional technical trespasses caused by side of vehicles intruding into airspace of servient tenement did not give rise to a right over it).

[245] Pp. 655–656, above.

[246] *London Corpn v Riggs* (1880) 13 ChD 798, p. 680, above; *Nickerson v Barraclough* [1981] Ch 426; *Re Webb's Lease* [1951] Ch 808, p. 682, above.

[247] See, however, *Milner's Safe Co Ltd v Great Northern and City Rly Co* [1907] 1 Ch 208; *Stafford v Lee* (1992) 65 P & CR 172.

C. EASEMENTS ACQUIRED BY PRESCRIPTION

Easements acquired by prescription are dependent upon user and their content is limited by the user proved. Small adjustments are allowed. Whether a variation is a new form of user or an extended example of that proved may be a difficult question.

British Railways Board v Glass
[1965] Ch 538 (CA, **Lord Denning MR, Harman** and **Davies LJJ**)

In 1847 the Wilts, Somerset and Weymouth Railway, predecessors in title to the plaintiffs, constructed a railway line near a farm owned by X, the defendant's predecessor in title, and through a field owned by X, and through a field also owned by him but occupied by a tenant Y. They purchased part of this field, and the conveyance contained the following proviso (inter alia): 'Save and except that the...company and their successors shall and will at all times hereafter allow unto...my heirs and assigns at all times...a right of crossing the...railway to the extent of twelve feet in width on the level thereof with all manner of cattle to and from one part of the land...to the other part...severed by the...railway.' To provide for this right of way, the company constructed a level crossing. For many years prior to 1942 one of the fields near the crossing, formerly owned by X and occupied by Z (called the 'blue land') was used for campers and caravanners and in 1942 there were six caravans established on the site. Since then the numbers had grown, and the traffic of vehicles and people over the crossing substantially increased. The plaintiffs brought this action to limit the user of the crossing.

It was conceded that (i) the right of way was not limited to linking the separated parts of the field previously occupied by Y, but linked the farm occupied by Z (which included the 'blue land') with the severed part of that field and with a highway beyond, and (ii) the way was not limited to foot passengers or cattle, but extended to vehicles.

Two main questions arose:

(i)   Whether the grant of the right of way covered the traffic of the caravanners;

(ii)   Whether, if not covered by the grant, there was a prescriptive right for all the caravanners, the defendant admitting a prescriptive right since 1942 for 6 caravanners.

Held (affirming Ungoed-Thomas J; Lord Denning MR dissenting).

(i)   The right of way was general and not limited to agricultural purposes in the contemplation of the parties to the conveyance;

(ii)   A prescriptive right had been acquired for the use of the crossing by the caravanners, the increase in number of caravanners since 1942 not being an excessive user.

The construction of the express grant of the right of way was influenced by the fact that the conveyance of 1847 was stated to be in compensation for, inter alia, the right to have certain 'accommodation works' carried out by the railway company in pursuance of their duties under the Railways Clauses Consolidation Act 1845, section 68. It was argued that the right of way should not be more extensive than the company's duty in respect of the 'accommodation works', for it was an exception to them, and should therefore be limited to agricultural or domestic purposes and those in the contemplation of the parties in 1847. The Court of Appeal (Lord Denning MR dissenting), as stated above, rejected this argument.[248] The present extracts from the judgments are limited to the issue of prescription.

Lord Denning MR (dissenting): *The Prescriptive Right.* The defendant says that alternatively he obtained a right by prescription. The judge found that for 20 years before the action, from 1942 to 1962, there had been six caravans on the site permanently, but that there had been 10 or 11 there at times from 1942 to 1945 and thereafter, and increased to 28 or 29 immediately before the issue of the writ. It is clear that by prescription there is a right of way for six caravans. But is there a right for 28 or 29 caravans?

It is quite clear that, when you acquire a right of way by prescription, you are not entitled to change the character of your land so as substantially to increase or alter the burden upon the servient tenement. If you have a right of way for your pasture land, you cannot turn it into a manufactory and claim a right of way for the purposes of the factory. If you have a right of way by prescription for one house, you cannot build two more houses on the land and claim a right of way for the purposes of those houses also. I think this rule is not confined to the character of the property. It extends also to the intensity of the user. If you use your land for years as a caravan site for six caravans and thereby gain a prescriptive right over a level crossing, you are not thereby entitled to put 30 caravans on the site and claim a right for those 30. As Baggallay JA said in *Wimbledon and Putney Commons Conservators v Dixon* (1875) 1 ChD 362 at 374, 'You must neither increase the burden on the servient tenement nor substantially change the nature of the user.' This seems to me good sense. It would be very wrong that, because the plaintiffs have been so tolerant as to allow the occupants of six caravans to use the crossing, in consequence they are thereby to be saddled with the use of 30 caravans. Trains would be obstructed and delayed. Dangers would abound. After all, prescription is a presumed grant. No such grant for 30 caravans could ever be presumed from user for six.

On this part of the case, counsel for the defendant made a technical point. He said that the defendant had a prescriptive right to a 'caravan site' and so phrased it in his defence: and that in the reply the plaintiffs had admitted that the field had been used 'as a caravan site' since 1938. He says that, by this admission, the plaintiffs are debarred from saying that the defendant had a prescriptive right only for six caravans, and that the defendant has a right for as many caravans as the site will hold. I regard this as special pleading of the worst description. The facts and issues before the court are plain enough: and no one has been in the least misled by this verbal nicety. I would decide this case on the facts found, and I hold that the defendant had no prescriptive right to use the crossing for more than six caravans.

We were told that the local authority have taken steps to deal with this caravan site. They have exercised their statutory powers to see that it is gradually removed. All the caravans should

---

[248] For a similar construction of s. 68, see *TRH Sampson Associates Ltd v British Railway Board* [1983] 1 WLR 170 (owner of dominant tenement held entitled to alter user of bridge provided no increased burden on servient tenement).

be gone by 1966. That is satisfactory, in a way. But I do not see why the local authority should be forced to do this: or to pay compensation to the defendant. I think the plaintiffs are entitled to come to the court and ask for protection on their own account. I think they are entitled to restrain the defendant from putting this greatly increased burden on the crossing.

I would allow the appeal and grant a declaration and injunction as asked in the notice of appeal.

Harman LJ: It appeared from the evidence that before the last war there were three caravans and a tent dwelling permanently situated upon the 'blue land', and that this number increased after the war began, when the Admiralty moved some of its departments to Bath, to six permanent caravans and five more that came and went, and there was a further increase in the spring of 1942 after the first bombs fell on Bath, and that after the war there were further increases from time to time until shortly before the writ was issued the number of caravans had increased to 29 and it was of this burden that the plaintiffs not unnaturally complained. All the caravanners and those who visited them, and their suppliers, had no access to the blue land save over the level crossing.

This part of the case has become largely academic because the local planning authority has, by exercise of its statutory powers, ordered the gradual clearance of the site from caravans. At the date of the hearing in the court below the number had been reduced to 16 and will be reduced to none by the end of the year 1966 or thereabouts. Nevertheless the judge considered the state of things when the writ was issued, and rightly so, and he came to the conclusion that the plaintiffs could not complain of the state of things as it then existed. He reached this conclusion upon the admissions appearing upon the face of the pleadings. The plaintiffs admitted that the 'blue land' was used 'as a caravan site', that is to say, the whole of the 'blue land' and not merely such portions of it as had in fact been the standings of caravans. I understand that in fact there were no such permanent standings, but that caravans coming and going occupied any part of the field they chose. The prescriptive claim was not made in the right of individual caravans, which would have been a claim by individual caravanners, but by the defendant as the owner of the whole of the 'blue land' and on the footing that it constituted 'the caravan site'. It may be regrettable that this part of the case should turn on a point of pleading, as this to some extent has, but I do not think the judge could have come to his conclusion upon any other footing. The fact is that this expression 'caravan site' has only recently come into prominence, and it was not perhaps fully appreciated until the recent decision of this court in *Biss v Smallburgh RDC* [1965] Ch 335 that it ought not to be used in a loose way. In that case a large area, which varied at various stages of the action from 70-odd acres to three or four, was claimed as being a 'caravan site', but the court came to the conclusion that there was no caravan site at all within the meaning of that phrase in the Caravan Sites and Control of Development Act 1960, that the mere casual placing of caravans here and there on a large area did not constitute that area a 'caravan site'. So here, if the plaintiffs had not admitted that the 'blue land' constituted a 'caravan site', the defendant might have been in great difficulty in defining the area of the site. He was relieved of that difficulty by the pleadings and his case was that, admitting the whole 'blue land' to be 'a caravan site', the mere increase from, say, 10 to 29 caravans did not constitute such an increase in the burden of the prescriptive right as was a legitimate subject of complaint by the plaintiffs. The leading case on this subject is *Williams v James* (1867) LR 2 CP 577. The headnote reads: 'The defendant being entitled by immemorial user to a right of way over the plaintiff's land from field N, used the way for the purpose of carting from field N some hay stacked there, which had been grown partly there and partly on land adjoining. The jury found in effect that the defendant in so doing had used the way bona fide, and for the ordinary and reasonable use of field N as a field: *Held,* that the mere fact that some of the hay had not been grown on field N did not make the carrying of it over the plaintiff's land an excess in the user of the right of way.' Bovill CJ says this at 580: 'In all cases of this kind which depend upon user the right acquired must be measured by the extent of the enjoyment which is proved. When a right of way to a piece of land is proved, then that is, unless something appears to the contrary, a right of way for all purposes according to the ordinary and reasonable use to which that land might be applied at the time of the supposed grant. Such a right cannot be increased so as to affect the servient tenement by imposing upon it any additional burthen. It is also clear, according to the authorities, that where a person has a right of way over one piece of land to another piece of land, he can only use such right in order to reach the latter place. He cannot use it for the purpose of going elsewhere.' Willes J says this at 582: 'I agree with the argument of Mr Jelf that in cases like this, where a way has to be proved by user, you cannot extend the purposes for which the way may be used, or for which it might be reasonably inferred that parties would have intended it to be used. The land in this case was a field in the country, and apparently only used for rustic purposes. To be a legitimate user of the right of way, it must be used for the enjoyment of the nine acre field, and not colourably for other closes. I quite agree also with the argument that the right of way can only be used for the field in its ordinary use as a field. The right could not be used for a manufactory built upon the field. The use must be the reasonable use for the purposes of the land in the condition in which it was while the user took place.'

Applying that to the present case, you must do what the judge did, namely, base your conclusion on a consideration of what must have been the supposed contents of the lost grant on which the prescription rests. If this be supposed to be a grant of the right to use the 'blue land' as 'a caravan site', then it is clear that a mere increase in the numbers of the caravans using the site is not an excessive user of the right. A right to use a way for this purpose or that has never been to my knowledge limited to a right to use the way so many times a day or for such and such a number of vehicles so long as the dominant tenement does not change its identity. If there be a radical change in the character of the dominant tenement, then the prescriptive right will not extend to it in that condition. The obvious example is a change of a small dwelling-house to a large hotel, but there has been no change of that character according to the facts found in this case. The caravan site never became a highly organised town of caravans with fixed standings and roads and all the paraphernalia attendant on such a place and in my opinion the judge was right in holding that there had been so such increase in the burden of the easement as to justify the plaintiffs in seeking as they did by injunction to restrict the user to three caravans or six or to prevent its use as what in the statement of claim is called 'a caravan camp or site.'

I, accordingly, hold the judge was right in both branches of the case and that the appeal should be dismissed.

Davies LJ: If any prescriptive right has been acquired, it has been acquired not by any one or more caravans but by the 'blue land' as dominant tenement. And it is not easy to contemplate an express grant of a right of way in respect of a specified or limited number of caravans. The 'blue land' is still being used as a caravan site. Its use as such has been intensified. But there has been no alteration in the nature of its use . . .

So here, once it is admitted, as it has been admitted, that the 'blue land' as 'a caravan site' acquired by prescription a right of way, it does not seem to me that the plaintiffs can prevent a mere increase in the number of caravans upon the site and the consequent increase in the use of the right of way. An increase in the number of caravans on the site is quite a different thing from the erection of a number of new houses, though no doubt from the point of view of the servient tenement the effect is somewhat similar.

(1965) 81 LQR, at p. 18 (R. E. Megarry)

Two cases that were not cited provide a little assistance on the point. First, in *Lock v Abercester Ltd* [1939] Ch 861, the dominant owners had to rely on user for the prescriptive period mainly for horse-drawn vehicles delivering goods to the dominant tenement, a house previously used as a rectory. Within the last few years these owners had begun to keep cows, pigs and chickens on the land held with the house, and motor-vehicles brought the food stuffs for these animals as well as other goods. Despite this additional burden on the way, Bennett J held that the way established by prescription was wide enough to cover this user. The main point of the case was, of course, the question whether user by horse-drawn vehicles authorised enjoyment by horseless vehicles; but the element of the recent increase in agricultural user was mentioned in the judgment.

Secondly, there is *Cowling v Higginson* (1838) 4 M & W 245. This raised the question of the validity of a claim to a right of way for all purposes where the user proved was for a variety of purposes though not for every conceivable purpose. If the right were to be measured by the *de facto* user, then such a claim would fail; for the right would be 'confined to the identical carriages that have previously been used upon the road, and would not warrant even the slightest alteration in the carriage or the loading, or the purpose for which it was used': *Cowling v Higginson* (1838) 4 M & W at 254, per Parke B. On this footing, there might be 'a right to carry corn and manure, though not coals' (at 253). And so it was laid down that 'If a way has been used for several purposes, there may be a ground for inferring that there is a right of way for all purposes' (at 256, per Lord Abinger CB). As Parke B said during the argument, if the dominant owners 'shew that they have used [the way] time out of mind, for all the purposes that they wanted, it would seem to me to give them a general right' (at 252). If user for a limited number of purposes can be generalised into a right to use for all purposes, it would be remarkable if on a claim to use the way for one purpose only there were to be imposed a strict quantitative restriction to the amount of use for that purpose during the prescriptive period. In the end, the point seems to come down to the difference between quantity and quality. It may well be that a change in quantity may be so vast as to amount to a change in quality; but short of such extremities, the distinction seems valid.

In **Woodhouse & Co Ltd v Kirkland (Derby) Ltd** [1970] 1 WLR 1185 PLOWMAN J held that a considerable increase in the number of customers using a right of way was 'a mere increase in user and not a user of a different kind or for a different purpose'.[249]

In **Giles v County Building Contractors (Hertford) Ltd** (1971) 22 P & CR 978, BRIGHTMAN J referred to Harman LJ in *British Railways Board v Glass* [1965] Ch 583 at 562, p. 719, above and said at 987:

The important expressions, to my mind, are 'change of identity' and 'radical change in character'. In my view, the use of the convent site for the erection of seven modern dwelling units

---

[249] See also *Cargill v Gotts* [1981] 1 WLR 441 (drawing of extra water from neighbour's millpond for agricultural purposes held to be mere increase in user, but not exercisable without licence under Water Resources Act 1963, s. 24(1)). Cf. *Ward (Helston) Ltd v Kerrier District Council* (1981) 42 P & CR 412 (right of way for use in connection with slaughter house not extended to cartage of materials for house building).

in place of the two existing houses, cannot properly be described as 'changing the identity' or 'radically changing the character' of the convent site. I think it is evolution rather than mutation.

Atwood v Bovis Homes Ltd
[2001] Ch 379 (ChD, **Neuberger** J)[250]

The defendant was the registered proprietor of agricultural land in the Isle of Sheppey. It had a prescriptive right to drain surface water through the land of the plaintiffs. In 1998 the defendant began an extensive development on its land of 1,000 houses, a shopping centre, community facilities, hospital and school and associated infrastructure. The plaintiffs sought a declaration that the easement of drainage was no longer exercisable, since the defendant's land had undergone a radical alteration irrespective of the fact that there would be no material increase in the volume of water discharged.

Held. The easement of drainage remained enforceable

Neuberger J: The issue in the present proceedings is one of some potential general significance in relation to the law of easements, and in particular to the extent of an easement acquired by prescription...

The issue

Is an easement of drainage acquired by prescription still exercisable over the servient tenement (i.e. the plaintiffs' land) following a radical alteration (i.e. from fields used for agricultural purposes to a substantial residential development with associated commercial, community and infrastructure aspects) to the dominant tenement (i.e. the defendant's land) even where the alterations will have no material effect on the volume or rate of discharge of water over the servient tenement?

At first sight, it may be thought that the question should be resolved in the defendant's favour, once it is accepted that the ditches on the plaintiffs' land, burdened with the defendant's right to discharge water from its land by virtue of use and enjoyment over a substantial period, will not have that burden in any way increased or altered because of the change, however radical it may be, to the nature and use of the defendant's land. After all, the plaintiffs are only concerned with the drainage of water over their land and, if the volume passing through the ditches in their land is unaffected by any change in the defendant's land, why should they have any cause for complaint? They may object to the development of, and consequent change of use to, the defendant's land. They may wish to cash in on the profit which the defendant may make from that development. However, such matters are extraneous to the question of drainage. The essential point is that neither the plaintiffs nor their land will be detrimentally affected by the change of use and development of the defendant's land so far as water drainage is concerned. That, in essence, is the argument of Mr Martin Rodger, who appears on behalf of the defendant.

However, Mr Rodney Stewart Smith, who represents the plaintiffs, contends that, as is frequently the case with easements, the law is not as simple or commonsensical as that. His case is

---

[250] [2000] All ER Rev 238 (P. J. Clarke); (2001) 151 NLJ 1307 (H. W. Wilkinson). See also *McAdams Homes Ltd v Robinson* [2005] 1 P & CR 30 at [50], per Neuberger LJ (easement of drainage implied under the rule in *Wheeldon v Burrows*; there should be little difference between easements by prescription and implied easements as regards changes of user: at [22]); Gale, paras 1.133–1.135.

that, on the basis of a number of authorities, it is clear that an easement of drainage which has been acquired by prescription will be lost, or at least incapable of lawful enjoyment, if and so long, as there is a radical change in the use or nature of the dominant tenement.

The authorities relied on by the plaintiffs

His Lordship referred to *Williams v James* (1867) LR 2 CP 577; *Wimbledon and Putney Commons Conservators v Dixon* (1875) 1 ChD 362; *British Railways Board v Glass* [1965] Ch 538, p. 719, above; *Loder v Gaden* (unreported 28 July 1999); and *Cargill v Gotts* [1981] 1 WLR 441, and continued:

The principles ... derived from the cases

I would summarise the points to be derived from these cases as follows.

1 The only case where the question at issue was whether a change in the nature of use (as opposed to intensification of the existing use) of the dominant tenement could destroy or result in an impermissible enjoyment of a right of way obtained by prescription was *Wimbledon and Putney Commons Conservators v Dixon.*

2 Not only in the decision in the *Wimbledon* case (binding on me as a decision of the Court of Appeal) but in other cases, it has been stated or assumed to be right that a substantial change in the nature of the use of the dominant tenement will result in the right to use the way, obtained by prescription, being either destroyed or impermissible.

3 There is a dispute between the parties in relation to the observations of the Court of Appeal in the *Wimbledon* case, and indeed in the other cases, as to the proper analysis of those observations. Is the principle that a radical alteration in the use or nature of the dominant tenement of itself puts an end to, or renders impermissible any use of, the right of way? This is what I shall call the 'strict rule'. Alternatively, is the rule more flexible, namely, that a radical change in the use or nature of a dominant tenement will lead to such a conclusion, unless the change is such that it will not result in any significant increase in the quantum, or of any significant alteration in the nature, of the use of the way from that enjoyed in relation to the original use of the way. By 'quantum' I mean frequency of usage, and by 'nature' I mean, for instance, lorries, motor cars, pedestrians, bicycles and so on.

4 In that connection, observations which one sees in the cases, whether part of the ratio (as in the *Wimbledon* case) or included as the obiter observations (as in *Williams v James* and *British Railways Board v Glass*), relating to a change from a field to a factory, from a house to a hotel or from a field to a house building site, do not seem to me to be decisive. They all carry with them the understandable assumption that the changes would involve an increase in the quantum of the user and/or a change in the nature of the user of the way resulting from the change in the use of the dominant tenement.

5 The advantage of the flexible rule is that it can be said to be in accordance with commercial common sense as discussed above. Why should the owner of the servient tenement, in that capacity, care about a change of use to the dominant tenement, however radical, if it can be shown that it makes no difference to the quantum or nature of the use of the way? It could be said to be contrary to common sense that, if a right of way has been obtained by prescription in favour of a building being used as a hotel, the right to use the way would be lost if the owner of the dominant tenement changed the use to a house and could demonstrate that it was inconceivable that anything other than a diminution in the quantum of the use will arise and that there will be no change in the nature of the use.

6 The advantage of the strict rule is that it leads to a relative degree of certainty. It might be asked how one could predict the extent of the future likely use of the way following a change of use of the dominant tenement. For instance, what would be the position if the radical change of use was itself changed or subsequently intensified? It might also be asked, is one to compare the projected use of the way following the change of use of the dominant tenement with the historic actual use of the way, or with what might have been the maximum permitted use of the way in relation to the original use of the dominant tenement?

7 I would tentatively suggest that the rule may be that, if there is a subsequent radical change in the use of the dominant tenement, a right of way acquired by prescription can only continue to be used in connection with the dominant tenement if the court can be satisfied that the change cannot result in the use of the way being greater in quantum or different in character from that which it was for any continuous period of 20 or 40 years during the period of use of the way in connection with the original use of the dominant tenement. (For completeness, I should explain that the periods of 20 or 40 years are selected on the basis of the periods necessary to obtain an easement, be it a right of way or other easement, by prescription.) The onus would be on the owner of the dominant tenement, and would, I suspect, normally be difficult to satisfy in relation to a right of way.

8 It should be added, however, that the strict rule can be justified on an additional ground to that of certainty. I have in mind the reasoning of Harman LJ in *British Railways Board v Glass,* to which I have not so far referred. This is to the effect that a prescriptive right of way involves a fictional grant, and one should presume that this fictional grant is related to, indeed limited to, the type of use to which the dominant tenement was put at the time the right was acquired.

9 Whichever of the two rules is correct, it is clear that a prescriptive right of way arises from a fictional grant. Whether the flexible rule or the strict rule applies, it is accepted by both parties that the general purpose of the rule is to ensure that the owner of the dominant tenement does not use the way for a purpose, or to a degree, not contemplated by the fictional grant.

Application of the principles in this case

I turn now to consideration of the application of these principles, so far as one can identify them, to the present case.

1 It is clear to my mind that there are principles to be derived from the right of way cases which apply equally to all easements. The law of easements relates to a particular category of rights, and there will be principles which apply to all types of rights within that category. That is demonstrated by the decision in *Cargill v Gotts,* where the principles in the right of way cases were applied to a different easement.

2 However, to my mind equally self-evidently, while there will be general principles applicable to all easements to be derived from the right of way cases, there will also be principles applicable more specifically to rights of way, which do not, at least necessarily, apply to all other types of easements.

3 Thus, on any view, a change of use of a building in the dominant tenement, however radical and far-reaching that change may be, cannot result in an easement of support acquired by prescription against an adjoining building being lost. A change from a house to a hotel, assuming that it will result, as it apparently will, in the loss of a right of way acquired by prescription in favour of the building, would not, at least in the absence of very special facts, result in the building losing its right of support acquired by prescription from the adjoining building. In such a case one would expect the right of support to continue and to be exercisable, at least unless

there was a change in the structure or use of the building on the dominant tenement which substantially increased the burden on the servient tenement. That, indeed, appears to be the law: *Lloyds Bank Ltd v Dalton* [1942] Ch 466....

4 Although the easement in *Cargill v Gotts* had obvious similarities to the easement in the present case, in that it involved water, there are important differences. First, like a right of way, the easement in *Cargill's* case involved the owner of the dominant tenement going onto the servient tenement, and indeed stopping on the servient tenement with large vehicles: see the observations of Templeman LJ at p. 448E. Secondly, *Cargill's* case involved the abstraction of water from the servient tenement, not merely the running off of water over the servient tenement.

5 If what I have called the flexible rule in relation to rights of way is correct, then the defendant clearly succeeds here. There would be no change in the volume of the water discharging from the defendant's land over the plaintiffs' land, and, therefore, whether one looks at the quantum of water or the manner of its discharge, there is no change.

6 If, however, the strict rule applies to rights of way, then I accept that the position is more difficult, but in the end it does not cause me to reach a different conclusion.

It seems to me that, in relation to the point at issue between the parties, the easement in the present case is very different from a right of way. The change of use of the dominant tenement would not increase the quantum of water coming on to the dominant tenement. It would not therefore, by any means, automatically be expected to alter the quantum of water passing from the dominant tenement to the servient tenement, and would most certainly not alter the nature of what passes from the dominant tenement to the servient tenement....

Conclusion

In the event, therefore, I propose to determine this issue in favour of the defendant. In reaching this conclusion, I have not relied on cases which were referred to me involving express grants of easements. While nothing in those cases has caused me to doubt the conclusion that I have reached, I think it is safer to rest my reasoning on authorities dealing with easements acquired by prescription.[251]

> **QUESTION**
>
> A landlord granted to his tenant a right of way 'at all times and for all purposes' over a roadway leading to the tenant's factory. The landlord then started to build over the roadway and planned to construct a long bridge or tunnel through which the tenant could have access to the factory. Although this would not affect the roadway itself, the freedom of manoeuvre, during loading and unloading from the tenant's vehicles, would be restricted, both vertically and laterally. Is the tenant entitled to an injunction to restrain the landlord from building in such a way as to restrict his freedom to load and unload as he had been accustomed to do? See *VT Engineering Ltd v Richard Barland & Co Ltd* (1968) 19 P & CR 890; *Hayns v Secretary of State for the Environment* (1977) 36 P & CR 317.

[251] For a similar approach where an easement of drainage was created by implied grant under LPA 1925, s. 62, see *McAdams Homes Ltd v Robinson* [2005] 1 P & CR 30.

V. EASEMENT OF LIGHT[252]

The rules relating to the acquisition of easements of light by prescription, and the extent of such rights, are sufficiently distinct to warrant separate discussion.

A. PRESCRIPTION ACT 1832

PRESCRIPTION ACT 1832

3. Claim to the use of light enjoyed for 20 years.—When the access and use of light to and for any dwelling house, workshop, or other building[253] shall have been actually enjoyed therewith for the full period of twenty years without interruption, the right thereto shall be deemed absolute and indefeasible, any local usage or custom to the contrary notwithstanding,[254] unless it shall appear that the same was enjoyed by some consent or agreement expressly made or given for that purpose by deed or writing.[255]

Colls v Home and Colonial Stores Ltd
[1904] AC 179 (HL, **Earl of Halsbury LC, Lords Macnaghten, Davey, Robertson** and **Lindley**)

The Home and Colonial Stores were the lessees of a building in Shoreditch where they carried on their business. They brought an action for an injunction against Colls to restrain him from building on the opposite side of the road. Joyce J found as a fact that, even after the erection of the building, the Home and Colonial Stores premises would be 'well and sufficiently lighted for all ordinary purposes of occupancy as a place of business'. Joyce J refused an injunction and was reversed by the Court of Appeal.

Held (reversing the Court of Appeal). Injunction refused.

Lord Lindley: The language of section 3 of the Prescription Act shews that in order to acquire a right to a light there must be—(1) Access and use of light, not access alone. Access here is understood to refer to free passage of light over the servient tenement (see per Fry LJ, in *Scott v*

---

[252] C & B, pp. 624–626; Gray, paras 5.1.91–5.1.94; M & W, paras 28.073–28.080, 30.010–30.018; MM, pp. 439–441, 445–446; Gale, paras 4.23–4.42, chap. 7; Bickford-Smith and Francis, *Rights of Light: The Modern Law* (2nd edn, 2007); Ellis, *Rights to Light* (1989).

[253] *Allen v Greenwood* [1980] Ch 119, p. 731, below (greenhouse); *Carr-Saunders v Dick McNeil Associates Ltd* [1986] 1 WLR 922 (dominant owner's right was for access of light to building as a whole and not to any particular room; therefore there was a right to light to windows of rooms produced by sub-division).

[254] *Bowring Services Ltd v Scottish Widows' Fund & Life Assurance* [1995] 1 EGLR 158 (custom of City of London).

[255] The consent or agreement need not refer expressly to light; 'the phrase "expressly made or given for that purpose" can be satisfied by an express provision in the relevant document which, on its true construction according to normal principles, has the effect of rendering the enjoyment of light permissive or consensual, or capable of being terminated or interfered with by the adjoining owner, and is therefore inconsistent with the enjoyment becoming absolute and indefeasible after 20 years': *RHJ Ltd v FT Pattern (Holdings) Ltd* [2008] Ch 341 at [44], per Lloyd LJ.

Pape (1886) 31 ChD at 575, and per Kay J in *Cooper v Straker* (1888) 40 ChD at 26). (2) Such access and use must be to and for some dwelling-house, workshop, or other building (as to which see *Harris v De Pinna* (1886) 33 ChD 238). (3) Such access and use must be actually enjoyed therewith. (4) Such enjoyment must be without interruption for twenty years. (5) If all these are proved, the right to the access and use of light so enjoyed becomes absolute and indefeasible, unless it can be explained by some deed or writing.

Pausing here for a moment, it will be observed that the statute does not in terms confer a right to light, but rather assumes its acquisition by use and enjoyment, and declares it to be 'absolute and indefeasible'.

Again, your Lordships will observe that nothing is said about enjoyment as of right; and notwithstanding section 5 of the Act,[256] which refers to enjoyment as of right, it was early decided that as regards light claimed under section 3 enjoyment as of right need not be alleged or proved, and that the right, whatever it may be, is acquired by twenty years' use and enjoyment without interruption and without written consent: see *Truscott v Merchant Taylors' Co* (1856) 11 Exch 855 and *Frewen v Phillips* (1861) 11 CBNS 449; *Simper v Foley* (1862) 2 John & H 555 and *Harbridge v Warwick* (1849) 3 Exch 557. This was not so under the old law.

As regards use and enjoyment, there are some instructive decisions on unfinished and uninhabited houses, and on windows kept closed by shutters. These decisions shew that a right to light may be acquired in respect of a house which has stood for twenty years without being occupied or even finished so as to be fit for occupation; and that the fact that shutters have been closed for some months at a time does not prevent the acquisition of a right to light through the windows: see *Courtauld v Legh* (1869) LR 4 Exch 126; *Cooper v Straker* (1888) 40 ChD 21; *Collis v Laugher* [1894] 3 Ch 659; *Smith v Baxter* [1900] 2 Ch 138.

These decisions did not, however, turn upon or settle with any precision the amount of light to which a right is acquired by twenty years' user. Nor is the statute clear upon this point....

The doctrine laid down in *Back v Stacey* (1826) 2 C & P 465, as I understand it, is the same as that laid down, although in somewhat different language, by the Court of Appeal in *Kelk v Pearson* (1871) 6 Ch App 809 and *City of London Brewery Co v Tennant* (1873) 9 Ch App 212, and must, I think, be taken as finally established and as good sound law, which your Lordships should adopt, notwithstanding the observations in the Irish case of *Mackey v Scottish Widows' Fund Assurance Society* (1877) IR 11 Eq 541. That doctrine, as stated in *City of London Brewery Co v Tennant,* is that generally speaking an owner of ancient lights is entitled to sufficient light according to the ordinary notions of mankind for the comfortable use and enjoyment of his house as a dwelling-house, if it is a dwelling-house, or for the beneficial use and occupation of the house if it is a warehouse, a shop, or other place of business: see (1873) 9 Ch App at 217. The expressions 'the ordinary notions of mankind', 'comfortable use and enjoyment', and 'beneficial use and occupation' introduce elements of uncertainty; but similar uncertainty has always existed and exists still in all cases of nuisance, and in this country an obstruction of light has commonly been regarded as a nuisance, although the right to light has been regarded as a peculiar kind of easement....

The expression 'right to light' is sanctioned by the Prescription Act, and is convenient; but its use is apt to lead to error and to forgetfulness of the burden thrown on the servient tenement. This burden, however, ought never to be lost sight of in considering the extent of the right claimed in respect of the dominant tenement.

---

[256] P. 690, above.

But the adoption of the more flexible standard of comfort and convenience has introduced difficulties of a serious nature, especially when dealing with places of business, and it is not surprising that different views on this subject should have been taken, and that the decisions upon it should be inconsistent with each other....

There is no rule of law that if a person has 45 degrees of unobstructed light through a particular window left to him he cannot maintain an action for a nuisance caused by diminishing the light which formerly came through that window: *Theed v Debenham* (1876) 2 ChD 165.[257] But experience shews that it is, generally speaking, a fair working rule to consider that no substantial injury is done to him where an angle of 45 degrees is left to him, especially if there is good light from other directions as well. The late Lord Justice Cotton pointed this out in *Ecclesiastical Commissioners for England v Kino* (1880) 14 ChD 213 at 228; see also *Parker v First Avenue Hotel Co* (1883) 24 ChD 282.

As regards light from other quarters, such light cannot be disregarded; for, as pointed out by James V-C, in the *Dyers' Co v King* (1870) LR 9 Eq 438, the light from other quarters, and the light the obstruction of which is complained of, may be so much in excess of what is protected by law as to render the interference complained of non-actionable. I apprehend, however, that light to which a right has not been acquired by grant or prescription, and of which the plaintiff may be deprived at any time, ought not to be taken into account. (See the case just cited.)

The purpose for which a person may desire to use a particular room or building in future does not either enlarge or diminish the easement which he has acquired. If he chooses in future to use a well-lighted room or building for a lumber-room for which little light is required, he does not lose his right to use the same room or building for some other purpose for which more light is required. *Aynsley v Glover* (1875) 10 Ch App 283 is in accordance with this view. But if a room or building has been so built as to be badly lighted, the owner or occupier cannot by enlarging the windows or altering the purpose for which he uses it increase the burden on the servient tenement. *Martin v Goble* (1808) 1 Camp 320, where a malthouse was turned into a workhouse, may, I think, be upheld on this principle; and the observations of Wood V-C on *Martin v Goble* in *Dent v Auction Mart Co* (1866) LR 2 Eq 238 support this view....

Coming now to the present case, I am clearly of opinion that no injunction, and certainly no mandatory injunction, ought to have been granted. Joyce J was asked for an injunction and he refused it, and, in my opinion, quite rightly. He came to the conclusion that although there would be a sensible diminution of light and some inconvenience to the plaintiffs, yet they had not established by twenty years' user a right to all the light which they had had, and that the obstruction complained of would not amount to an actionable nuisance, and so infringe the plaintiff's right. The Court of Appeal, taking a different view of the amount of light to which the plaintiffs were entitled, reversed this decision, and ordered a partial demolition of the buildings erected by the defendants. For the reasons already given, I have come to the conclusion that this was wrong.[258]

---

[257] Nor is there a rule of law that if half a room at table height is receiving one or more lumens the room as a whole is adequately lit: *Ough v King* [1967] 1 WLR 1547; *Frogmore Developments Ltd v Shirayama Shokusan Ltd* [2000] 1 EGLR 121 (grant of right to 'the free and unobstructed passage of light and air to the premises at all times' held to entitle grantee only to a degree of light which satisfies the test in *Colls v Home and Colonial Stores*).

[258] See *Pugh v Howells* (1984) 48 P & CR 298 (mandatory injunction granted); *Blue Town Investments Ltd v Higgs and Hill plc* [1990] 1 WLR 696; *Marine and General Mutual Life Assurance Society v St. James' Real Estate Co Ltd* [1991] 2 EGLR 178 (measure of damages); *Voyce v Voyce* (1991) 62 P & CR 290 (right of light enforceable against equitable owner); *Deakins v Hookings* [1994] 1 EGLR 190; (1994) 144 NLJ 875

In **Allen v Greenwood** [1980] Ch 119[259] the plaintiffs were the owners of 13 Woodtop Avenue, Rochdale, in which there was a greenhouse. After the greenhouse had been in use as an ordinary domestic greenhouse for more than 20 years, the defendants erected a fence on their adjoining property. This left sufficient light in the greenhouse for working in it, but insufficient for growing plants ('tomatoes, geraniums, stocks, antirrhinums, various kinds of marigold, zinnias, violets, pansy—the red ones that are rather tender'). The plaintiffs brought an action for injunctions to restrain the defendants from causing a nuisance by diminution of the access of the light to the greenhouse.

In reversing the decision of Blackett-Ord V-C and granting the injunctions, the Court of Appeal (Buckley, Orr and Goff LJJ) held that the light required for the normal use of a greenhouse is ordinary, and also that a right to a specially high degree of light may be acquired by prescription. The Court rejected 'an overriding argument' that 'in any event one can only prescribe a right to light, whether ordinary or special in degree, for purposes of illumination, not a right to the direct rays of the sun, or to heat, or to other beneficial properties from the sun's rays'. GOFF LJ said at 132:

In my judgment, therefore, the crux of this case at the end of the day is the overriding argument, which I must now consider.

The defendants argue on this as follows. (1) In *Colls'* case [1904] AC 179 [p. 728, above] the House of Lords was seeking to limit, or restrict, the extent of the right to light, so as to prevent undue restrictions on the development or improvement of surrounding land or buildings, and the court should be very chary of any extension of the right. (2) Although the standards prescribed by the speeches in *Colls'* case are expressed in terms susceptible of a wider interpretation, in their context they must be taken as referring to illumination only. (3) In all cases, at least since *Colls*, the right to light has been tested or measured in terms of illumination only. They refer, for example, to Mr Waldram's calculations and the theory of the 'grumble point:' see *Charles Semon & Co Ltd v Bradford Corpn* [1922] 2 Ch 737, 746–747, and to *Hortons' Estate Ltd v James Beattie Ltd* [1927] 1 Ch 75, where the question was whether the extent of the right to light should vary according to locality, and Russell J said, at 78: 'The human eye requires as much light for comfortable reading and sewing in Darlington Street, Wolverhampton, as in Mayfair.' Mr Maddocks on the defendants' behalf, in his supporting argument, referred also to *Warren v Brown* [1900] 2 QB 722, 725, where the test was stated to be 'all ordinary purposes of inhabitancy or business,' and to the test applied by the Court of Appeal in *Ough v King* [1967]

(H. W. Wilkinson); *Midtown Ltd v City of London Real Property Co Ltd* [2005] 1 EGLR 65 (injunction refused); *Regan v Paul Properties DPF No 1 Ltd* [2007] Ch 135 (injunction granted); [2007] Conv 175 (P. Chynoweth); (2006) 156 NLJ 1868 (A. Craig); [2007] All ER Rev 256 (P. J. Clarke); *Tamares (Vincent Square) Ltd v Fairpoint Properties (Vincent Square) Ltd* [2007] 1 WLR 2148 (injunction would be oppressive and unjust), *Tamares (Vincent Square) Ltd v Fairpoint Properties (Vincent Square) Ltd (No. 2)* [2007] 1 WLR 2167 (assessment of damages in lieu of injunction: 'the court needs to consider whether the "deal feels right"', per Moss QC at [22]); [2007] 14 EG 103 (S. Murdoch); *Forsyth-Grant v Allen* [2008] 27 EG 118 (damages awarded on basis of actual loss caused by infringement of right; account of profits by respondent developer refused).

[259] [1979] Conv 298 (F. R. Crane); [1984] Conv 408 (A. H. Hudson); Conv Prec 19–32. See also *Carr-Saunders v Dick McNeil Associates Ltd* [1986] 1 WLR 922, p. 728, n. 253, above.

1 WLR 1657, ordinary notions of contemporary mankind. These, however, I think, are at best neutral and possibly tell the other way, since a greenhouse is perfectly normal and ordinary in private gardens.... (6) In reality or in substance the injury here is not deprivation of light, but of heat or other energising properties of the sun and it is the plant life and not the human beings who are deprived.

I do not think this last point is in any case wholly accurate, as plants need light as well as heat, but it seems to me, with all respect to Blackett-Ord V-C and to counsel, to lead to an absurd conclusion. It cannot, I think, be right to say that there is no nuisance because one can see to go in and out of a greenhouse and to pot plants which will not flourish, and to pick fruit which cannot properly be developed and ripened, still less because one can see to read a book.

The plaintiffs answer all this simply by submitting that they are entitled, by virtue of their prescriptive right to light, to all the benefits of the light, including the rays of the sun. Warmth, they say, is an inseparable product of daylight, and they stress the absurd conclusion which I have already mentioned, to which the contrary argument inevitably leads. This reply commends itself to me, and I adopt it.

So the overriding argument, in my judgment, does not prevail, and for the reasons I have already given the plaintiffs are right, both on their primary and their alternative case, and I would allow this appeal....

I desire, however, to add one important safeguarding proviso to this judgment. On other facts, particularly where one has solar heating (although that may not arise for some years) it may be possible and right to separate the heat, or some other property of the sun, from its light, and in such a case a different result might be reached. I leave that entirely open for decision when it arises. My judgment in this case is based upon the fact that this was a perfectly ordinary greenhouse, being used in a perfectly normal and ordinary manner, which user has, by the defendants' acts, been rendered substantially less beneficial than it was throughout the period of upwards of 20 years before action brought, and if necessary upon the fact that all this was known to the defendants and their predecessors for the whole of the relevant time.

In **Morgan v Fear** [1907] AC 425, it was held that a tenant could, by 20 years' enjoyment of access to light from neighbouring land in the occupation of another tenant of the same landlord, prescribe for an easement of light under section 3. The House of Lords relied upon established authority, and LORD LOREBURN LC said at 428:

The question ... is whether a right can be acquired by a termor over land held by another termor under the same reversion, by virtue of section 3 of the Prescription Act. This has been decided in the affirmative as long ago as 1861, in *Frewen v Phillips* (1861) 11 CB NS 449, and the same view was expressly indicated in *Mitchell v Cantrill* (1887) 37 ChD 56. I think it is accurate to say that that rule of law has been acted upon for forty-six years. I cannot advise your Lordships to disturb so well settled a rule.

Prescription is in favour of the fee simple owner, and even in the case of an easement of light, there cannot be prescription in favour of a leaseholder.[260]

---

[260] *Wheaton v Maple & Co* [1893] 3 Ch 48.

QUESTIONS

Why can prescription not operate in favour of a leasehold estate? Compare
  Morgan v Fear [1907] AC 425;
  Kilgour v Gaddes [1904] 1 KB 457, p. 693, above;
  Wheaton v Maple & Co [1893] 3 Ch 48;
  Simmons v Dobson [1991] 1 WLR 720, p. 695, above.

B. RIGHTS OF LIGHT ACT 1959

RIGHTS OF LIGHT ACT 1959[261]

2. Registration of notice in lieu of obstruction of access of light.—(1) For the purpose of preventing the access and use of light from being taken to be enjoyed without interruption, any person who is an owner of land (in this and the next following section referred to as 'the servient land') over which light passes to a dwelling-house, workshop or other building (in this and the next following section referred to as 'the dominant building') may apply to the local authority in whose area the dominant building is situated for the registration of a notice under this section.[262]

3. Effect of registered notice and proceedings relating thereto.—(1) Where, in pursuance of an application made in accordance with the last preceding section, a notice is registered thereunder, then, for the purpose of determining whether any person is entitled (by virtue of the Prescription Act, 1832, or otherwise) to a right to the access of light to the dominant building across the servient land, the access of light to that building across that land shall be treated as obstructed to the same extent, and with the like consequences, as if an opaque structure, of the dimensions specified in the application.—

  (a) had, on the date of registration of the notice, been erected in the position on the servient land specified in the application, and had been so erected by the person who made the application, and

  (b) had remained in that position during the period for which the notice has effect and had been removed at the end of that period.

  (2) For the purposes of this section a notice registered under the last preceding section shall be taken to have effect until either—

  (a) the registration is cancelled, or

---

[261] This is based on recommendations in the Report of the Committee on Rights of Light (1958 Comnd 473); [1959] CLJ 182 (H. W. R. Wade). See *Hawker v Tomalin* (1969) 20 P & CR 550 at 551, per Harman LJ.

[262] Lands Tribunal Rules 1996 (SI 1996 No. 1002), Part VI; Lands Tribunal Fees Rules 1996 (SI 1996 No. 1021); Local Land Charges Rules 1977 (SI 1977 No. 985), r. 10. The application must be accompanied by a certificate from the Lands Tribunal. 938 definitive and 211 temporary certificates were issued between 1959 and 1980; see (1978) 122 SJ 515, 534; (1981) 259 EG 123 (W. A. Greene).

(b) the period of one year beginning with the date of registration of the notice expires, or

(c) in the case of a notice registered in pursuance of an application accompanied by a certificate issued under paragraph (b) of subsection (3) of the last preceding section, the period specified in the certificate expires without such a further certificate as is mentioned in paragraph (c) of subsection (5) of that section having before the end of that period been lodged with the local authority,[263]

and shall cease to have effect on the occurrence of any of those events.

(3) Subject to the following provisions of this section, any person who, if such a structure as is mentioned in subsection (1) of this section had been erected as therein mentioned, would have had a right of action in any court in respect of that structure, on the grounds that he was entitled to a right to the access of light to the dominant building across the servient land, and that the said right was infringed by that structure, shall have the like right of action in that court in respect of the registration of a notice under the last preceding section:

Provided that an action shall not be begun by virtue of this subsection after the notice in question has ceased to have effect.

(4) Where, at any time during the period for which a notice registered under the last preceding section has effect, the circumstances are such that, if the access of light to the dominant building had been enjoyed continuously from a date one year earlier than the date on which the enjoyment thereof in fact began, a person would have had a right of action in any court by virtue of the last preceding subsection in respect of the registration of the notice, that person shall have the like right of action in that court by virtue of this subsection in respect of the registration of the notice.

(6) For the purposes of section four of the Prescription Act, 1832 (under which a period of enjoyment of any of the rights to which that Act applies is not to be treated as interrupted except by a matter submitted to or acquiesced in for one year after notice thereof)—

(a) as from the date of registration of a notice under the last preceding section, all persons interested in the dominant building or any part thereof shall be deemed to have notice of the registration thereof and of the person on whose application it was registered;

(b) until such time as an action is brought by virtue of subsection (3) or subsection (4) of this section in respect of the registration of a notice under the last preceding section, all persons interested in the dominant building or any part thereof shall be deemed to acquiesce in the obstruction which, in accordance with subsection (1) of this section, is to be treated as resulting from the registration of the notice;

(c) as from the date on which such an action is brought, no person shall be treated as submitting to or acquiescing in that obstruction:

Provided that if, in any such action, the court decides against the claim of the plaintiff, the court may direct that the preceding provisions of this subsection shall apply in relation to the notice as if that action had not been brought.

---

[263] *Bowring Services Ltd v Scottish Widows' Fund & Life Assurance Society* [1995] 1 EGLR 158 (calculation of date from which time runs).

VI. EXTINGUISHMENT[264]

Easements and profits may be extinguished by statute (e.g. under an Inclosure Act or the Town and Country Planning Act 1990[265] or, in the case of a profit à prendre, as a result of failure to register under the Commons Act 2006[266]), by release, express or implied, and by unity of both ownership and possession.

A. IMPLIED RELEASE. ABANDONMENT[267]

In **Tehidy Minerals Ltd v Norman** [1971] 2 QB 528 BUCKLEY LJ said at 553:

Abandonment of an easement or of a profit à prendre can only, we think, be treated as having taken place where the person entitled to it has demonstrated a fixed intention never at any time thereafter to assert the right himself or to attempt to transmit it to anyone else.

The difficulty of proving that an easement or profit à prendre has been released by abandonment because it has not been exercised for many years has been lessened by LRA 2002, Schedule 3, paragraph 3, p. 647, above, since legal easements and profits which are not discoverable on a reasonably careful inspection of the land, and which have not been exercised in the last year before the disposition to a purchaser, do not constitute overriding interests and so will not bind the purchaser.[268]

In **Huckvale v Aegean Hotels Ltd** (1989) 58 P & CR 163,[269] the Court of Appeal considered a novel claim that an easement can be extinguished by its ceasing to accommodate the dominant tenement. In granting an interlocutory injunction, SLADE J said at 173:

In the absence of evidence of proof of abandonment, the court should be slow to hold that an easement has been extinguished by frustration, unless the evidence shows clearly that

---

[264] C & B, pp. 636–640; Gray, paras 5.2.87–5.2.96; M & W, paras 29.007–29.014; MM, pp. 441–443; Smith, pp. 517–519; Gale, chap. 12.

[265] S. 236. See also HA 1985, s. 295(1)-(3); New Towns Act 1981, s. 19, as amended by Telecommunications Act 1984, s. 109(1), Sch. 4, para. 79(3); *R v City of London Council, ex p. Mystery of the Barbers of London* (1996) 73 P & CR 59. Cf. *Jones v Cleanthi* [2001] 1 WLR 1604 (extinguishment of easement by fire precaution works required by s. 352 HA 1985); [2007] L & T Rev 75 (J. Summers); [2007] All ER Rev 259 (P. J. Clarke).

[266] P. 97, above.

[267] *Gotobed v Pridmore* (1971) 217 EG 759; *Benn v Harding* (1992) 66 P & CR 246 (no abandonment in spite of 175 years of non-user); *Bosomworth v Faber* (1995) 69 P & CR 288; *Snell & Prideaux Ltd v Dutton Mirrors Ltd* [1995] 1 EGLR 259; [1995] Conv 291 (C. J. Davis); *CDC2020 plc v Ferreira* [2005] 3 EGLR 15 (abandonment); (2005) 155 SJ 969 (A. Rosenthal); *Walker v Bridgewood* [2006] NSWSC 149, discussed in [2007] Conv 87 (H. Conway).

[268] See H & B, para. 11.16; Law Commission Report on Land Registration for the Twenty-First Century (Law Com No. 271), paras 8.65, 8.72.

[269] [1990] Conv 292 (G. Kodilinye).

because of a change of circumstances since the date of the original grant there is no practical possibility of its ever again benefiting the dominant tenement in the matter contemplated by that grant.[270]

Moore v Rawson[271]
(1824) 3 B & C 332, 107 ER 756 (Ct of KB, **Abbott CJ, Bayley, Holroyd** and **Littledale JJ**)

The plaintiff's predecessor in title enjoyed easements of light and air in respect of certain windows in a wall of his house. He pulled down this wall and built another wall without any windows. Fourteen years later the defendant erected a building opposite to the plaintiff's blank wall. After another three years the plaintiff opened a window in the blank wall in the place of one of the old windows, and then brought an action for obstruction.

Held. The plaintiff failed, because he had abandoned his rights.

Holroyd J: It appears that the former owner of the plaintiff's premises at one time was entitled to the house with the windows, so that the light coming to those windows over the adjoining land could not be obstructed by the owner of that land. I think, however, that the right acquired by the enjoyment of the light, continued no longer than the existence of the thing itself in respect of which the party had the right of enjoyment; I mean the house with the windows; when the house and the windows were destroyed by his own act, the right which he had in respect of them was also extinguished. If, indeed, at the time when he pulled the house down, he had intimated his intention of rebuilding it, the right would not then have been destroyed with the house. If he had done some act to shew that he intended to build another in its place, then the new house, when built, would in effect have been a continuation of the old house, and the rights attached to the old house would have continued. If a man has a right of common attached to his mill, or right of turbary attached to his house, if he pulls down the mill or the house, the right of common or of turbary will prima facie cease. If he shew an intention to build another mill or another house, his right continues. But if he pulls down the house or the mill without shewing any intention to make a similar use of the land, and after a long period of time has elapsed, builds a house or mill corresponding to that which he pulls down, that is not the renovation of the old house or mill, but the creation of a new thing, and the rights which he had in respect of the old house or mill, do not in my opinion attach to the new one. In this case, I think, the building of a blank wall is a stronger circumstance to shew that he had no intention to continue the enjoyment of his light than if he had merely pulled down the house. In that case he might have intended to substitute something in its place. Here, he does in fact substitute quite a different thing, a wall without windows. There is not only nothing to shew that he meant to renovate the house so as to make it a continuance of the old house, but he actually builds a new house different from the old one, thereby shewing that he did not mean to renovate the old

---

[270] The onus of proof lies fairly and squarely on the person who alleges abandonment, and the onus is a very heavy one: *Re Yateley Common, Hampshire* [1977] 1 WLR 840 at 845.

[271] *Crossley & Sons Ltd v Lightowler* (1867) 2 Ch App 478; *Cook v Bath Corpn* (1868) LR 6 Eq 177; *Ecclesiastical Comrs for England v Kino* (1880) 14 ChD 213; *Swan v Sinclair* [1924] 1 Ch 254; affd [1925] AC 227; *Re Yateley Common, Hampshire*, above.

house. It seems to me, therefore, that the right is not renewed as it would have been, if, when he pulled down the old house, he had shewn an intention to rebuild it within a reasonable time, although he did not do so eo instanti.[272]

B. UNITY OF OWNERSHIP AND POSSESSION

Unity of both ownership and possession may cause extinguishment.[273] 'An unity of possession merely suspends; there must be an unity of ownership to destroy a prescriptive right'.[274] Similarly unity of ownership without unity of possession does not suffice; the easement continues until there is also unity of possession.[275] If an easement is extinguished, it may nevertheless be re-created under the doctrine of *Wheeldon v Burrows*[276] if the land is later severed into its original parts.

In **Richardson v Graham** [1908] 1 KB 39, BUCKLEY LJ said at 44.[277]

On 29 March 1906, the plaintiffs were entitled to a leasehold interest for a term of years in the dominant tenement. The reversion in the dominant tenement was in one Eadie. The dominant tenement enjoyed over the servient tenement which was vested in the defendant a prescriptive right to ancient light acquired by user for more than twenty years. On 29 March 1906, Eadie conveyed to the defendant the reversion in the dominant tenement. It is said that the effect of that conveyance was to destroy the easement of ancient light; that is to say, that by acts done by the plaintiffs' lessor and by the owner of the servient tenement the rights enjoyed by the plaintiffs were destroyed.

In my opinion that is not the law. It is inconsistent with reason, with good sense, and with authority....

It is perfectly plain on the authorities that if in this case the two tenements had belonged throughout, not to different owners, but to one owner, but the circumstances were such that a lessee of the dominant tenement had acquired a prescriptive right against the servient tenement, the right would have been good as against all the world. It is said, however, that this case is different because there was not a common owner of the dominant and servient tenement during the whole period, but common ownership of the two tenements arose after the right to light had been acquired. This seems to me an extravagant proposition.

---

[272] On implied rights to make alterations to the servient tenement, see *Greenwich Healthcare National Health Service Trust v London and Quadrant Housing Trust* [1998] 1 WLR 1749.

[273] *Buckby v Coles* (1814) 5 Taunt 311 (easement); *Tyrringham's Case* (1584) 4 Co Rep 36b at 38a (profit à prendre).

[274] *Canham v Fisk* (1831) 2 Cr & J 126, per Bayley B.

[275] *Richardson v Graham* [1908] 1 KB 39.

[276] P. 656, above. But (subject to the decision in *P & S Platt Ltd v Crouch* [2004] 1 P & CR 18, p. 675, above) not under LPA 1925, s. 62, since there would be no diversity of occupation.

[277] This was a case on the easement of light, but, in principle, the rule should apply generally. Cf. *Buckby v Coles*, above, at 315, 316; M & W, para. 29.014, n. 75.

VII. LAW REFORM

Law Commission Consultation Paper on Easements, Covenants and Profits à Prendre 2008 (Consultation Paper No. 186), paras 1.14, 1.16, 1.20, 16.4–16.30[278]

Background to the project

1.14 The law of easements has never been subject to a comprehensive review. Although the Law Commission has given some preliminary consideration to the question of reforming the law of easements, notably in its 1971 Working Paper on Appurtenant Rights,[279] it has never made any recommendations for reform.[280]

1.16 The Commission's consideration of previous reform work in this area, and its comparative research on other systems of law around the world, have been extremely illuminating. We have viewed this material critically. In particular, one cannot ignore the effect of different cultures and legal systems on the specific areas of overseas law. Our review of previous work relating to this jurisdiction has had to take account of the wide-ranging reforms introduced by the Land Registration Act 2002 and the implementation of the Human Rights Act 1998, both of which set parameters within which any modern reform of land law must take effect.

1.20 What is now required is a detailed review of the law of easements, profits and covenants as a whole. We should emphasise that the case for reform is widely acknowledged. The current edition of *Gale on Easements* contains the following passage in its preface:

> 'If one stands back from the detail...it cannot be denied that there is much that is unsatisfactory about the law of easements. In essence, easements can sometimes be acquired too easily (light and support by prescription, any easement by mistake under section 62 of the Law of Property Act 1925), are too difficult to detect (because they are overriding interests and not required to be entered on the register) and are impossible to get rid of or to modify (there being in this jurisdiction no equivalent to section 84 of the Law of Property Act 1925 which enables the discharge or modification of restrictive covenants). And there is the Prescription Act.'[281]

PART 16

LIST OF PROVISIONAL PROPOSALS AND CONSULTATION QUESTIONS

Characteristics of an easement

16.4 Our provisional view is that the current requirement that an easement be attached to a dominant estate in the land serves an important purpose and should be retained. We do not believe that easements in gross should be recognised as interests in land. Do consultees agree? If they do not agree, could they explain what kinds of right they believe should be permitted by law to be created in gross?

---

[278] [2008] Conv 269 (M. Dixon). A final report and draft Bill is planned for July 2010: Law Commission, Tenth Programme of Law Reform 2008 (Law Com No. 311), para. 3.2.

[279] Transfer of Land: Appurtenant Rights (1971) Law Commission Working Paper No. 36.

[280] But note the Law Reform Committee's recommendations for the reform of the law of prescription: Acquisition of Easements and Profits by Prescription: Fourteenth Report (1966) Cmnd 3100.

[281] *Gale on Easements* (17th edn, 2002), p. vi (footnotes omitted).

16.5 We consider that the basic requirements that an easement accommodate and serve the land and that it has some nexus with the dominant land serve an important purpose and should be retained. We invite the views of consultees as to whether there should be any modification of these basic requirements.

16.6 We provisionally propose that in order to comprise an easement:

(1) the right must be clearly defined, or be capable of clear definition, and it must be limited in its scope such that it does not involve the unrestricted use of the servient land; and

(2) the right must not be a lease or tenancy, but the fact that the dominant owner obtains exclusive possession of the servient land should not, without more, preclude the right from being an easement.

16.7 We provisionally propose that where the benefit and burden of an easement is registered, there should be no requirement for the owners to be different persons, provided that the dominant and servient estates in land are registered with separate title numbers.

Creation of easements

16.8 We provisionally propose that an easement which is expressly reserved in the terms of a conveyance should not be interpreted in cases of ambiguity in favour of the person making the reservation.

16.9 We invite the views of consultees as to whether it should be possible for parties to create short-form easements by reference to a prescribed form of words. Where the prescribed form of words is used, a fuller description of the substance of the easement would be implied into the instrument creating the right.

16.10 We invite the views of consultees as to which easements should be so dealt with and the extent to which parties should be free to vary the terms of short-form easements.

16.11 We provisionally propose that in determining whether an easement should be implied, it should not be material whether the easement would take effect by grant or by reservation. In either case, the person alleging that there is an easement should be required to establish it.

16.12 We provisionally propose that section 62 of the Law of Property Act 1925 should no longer operate to transform precarious benefits, enjoyed with the owner's licence or consent, into legal easements on a conveyance of the dominant estate. Do consultees agree?

16.13 We invite the views of consultees as to whether it should be provided that the doctrine of non-derogation from grant should not give rise to the implied acquisition of an easement. If consultees are aware of circumstances in which the doctrine continues to have residual value, could they let us know?

16.14 We invite consultees' views on the following:

(1) Whether they consider that the current rules whereby easements may be acquired by implied grant or reservation are in need of reform.

(2) Whether they consider that it would be appropriate to replace the current rules (a) with an approach based upon ascertaining the actual intentions of the parties; or (b) with an approach based upon a set of presumptions which would arise from the circumstances.

(3) Whether they consider that it would appropriate to replace the current rules with a single rule based on what is necessary for the reasonable use of the land.

16.15 We invite consultees' views as to whether it would be desirable to put the rules of implication into statutory form.

16.16 We provisionally propose that the current law of prescriptive acquisition of easements (that is, at common law, by lost modern grant and under the Prescription Act 1832) be abolished with prospective effect.

16.17 We invite the views of consultees as to:

(1) whether prescriptive acquisition of easements should be abolished without replacement;

(2) whether certain easements (such as negative easements) should no longer be capable of prescriptive acquisition, and, if so, which; and

(3) whether existing principles (for example, proprietary estoppel) sufficiently serve the function of prescriptive acquisition.

16.18 We provisionally propose:

(1) that it should be possible to claim an easement by prescription on proof of 20 years' continuous qualifying use;

(2) that qualifying use shall continue to within 12 months of application being made to the registrar for entry of a notice on the register of title;

(3) that qualifying use shall be use without force, without stealth and without consent; and

(4) that qualifying use shall not be use which is contrary to law, unless such use can be rendered lawful by the dispensation of the servient owner.

16.19 We invite consultees' views as to whether prescriptive acquisition of easements should only be possible in relation to land the title to which is registered following service of an application on the servient owner.

16.20 We invite consultees' views as to whether the registration of a prescriptive easement should be automatic or subject to the servient owner's veto.

16.21 We invite the views of consultees as to whether the rule that easements may only be acquired by prescription by or against the absolute owners of the dominant and servient lands should be relaxed, and if so in what circumstances.

16.22 We invite the views of consultees as to whether adverse possessors should be treated any differently from others who claim an easement by prescription.

16.23 We invite the views of consultees on the issue of the capacity of both servient and dominant owners.

16.24 We invite the views of consultees on the appropriate approach to be adopted in relation to prescriptive claims over land the title to which is not registered.

Extinguishment of easements

16.25 We provisionally propose that, where title to land is registered and an easement or profit has been entered on the register of the servient title, it should not be capable of extinguishment by reason of abandonment.

16.26 We provisionally propose that, where title to land is not registered or title is registered but an easement or profit has not been entered on the register of the servient title, it should be capable of extinguishment by abandonment, and that where it has not been exercised for a specified continuous period a presumption of abandonment should arise.

16.27 We provisionally propose that excessive use of an easement should be held to have occurred where:

(1) the dominant land is altered in such a way that it undergoes a radical change in character or a change in identity; and

(2) the changed use of the dominant land will lead to a substantial increase or alteration in the burden over the servient land.

16.28 We provisionally propose that where the court is satisfied that use of an easement is excessive, it may:

(1) extinguish the easement;

(2) suspend the easement on terms;

(3) where the excessive use can be severed, order that the excessive use should cease but permit the easement to be otherwise exercised; or

(4) award damages in substitution for any of the above.

16.29 We provisionally propose that, where land which originally comprised the dominant land is added to in such a way that the easement affecting the servient land may also serve the additional land, the question of whether use may be made for the benefit of the additional land should depend upon whether the use to be made of the easement is excessive as defined above.

16.30 We provisionally propose that where an easement is attached to a leasehold estate, the easement should be automatically extinguished on termination of that estate. We invite the views of consultees on this proposal, and in particular whether there should be any qualifications or restrictions on the operation of this principle.

9

COVENANTS BETWEEN FREEHOLDERS[1]

I. INTRODUCTION

In this chapter we consider the enforceability of a covenant entered into by the owner of land in favour of the owner of neighbouring land—a covenant which is generally undertaken in order to preserve or enhance the saleable value or residential amenities of the land which benefits from the covenant. Such a covenant is binding in contract between the original parties. But the question is whether and when it may be enforced between persons who were not original parties to the covenant. In considering this, two main distinctions must be made. First, different rules apply to the 'running' of the benefit and the 'running' of the burden. And, secondly, in connection both with the burden and the benefit, the rules of common law are different from those of equity. This is most marked in connection with the running of the burden, where the decision in equity of *Tulk v Moxhay* in 1848[2] provided the basis of the modern doctrine.

---

[1] C & B, chap. 19; Gray, parts 3.3, 3.4; M & W, chap. 32; MM, pp. 453–473; Smith, chap. 24; Preston & Newsom, *Restrictive Covenants Affecting Freehold Land* (9th edn, 1998); Scamell, *Land Covenants* (1996); Francis, *Restrictive Covenants and Freehold Land: A Practical Guide* (2nd edn, 2005); Elphinstone, *Covenants Affecting Land* (1946); Farrand (2nd edn), pp. 404–427; Maitland, *Equity* (2nd edn), pp. 162–178. For an historical account, see Simpson, *History of the Land Law* (2nd edn, 1986), pp. 116–118, 140–141, 256–260.

[2] (1848) 2 Ph 774, p. 754, below.

The common law rules for the running of the benefit are still applicable, but they have been further developed in equity[3] and by statute.[4] The burden and the benefit will be considered separately.

The common law rules for the running of the benefit are ancient. As with every case of a covenant running at common law, the covenant ran with the estate of the covenantee and not with the land,[5] and it was necessary for the assignee of the covenantee to show that he had the same legal estate as the original covenantee.[6] Equity, both with the benefit and the burden, developed a different concept of a covenant running with the land, and avoided the requirement that the assignee of the covenantee or covenantor should hold the same estate as his assignor.[7]

These factors have to be considered when the question is whether or not an assignee of the covenantee can sue. He may be able to do so under the common law rules alone, as where there is no servient land;[8] or he may have to rely on the further developments in equity and under statute.[9]

As indicated, the rules relating to the running of the burden of a covenant between freeholders are almost exclusively equitable. The origin of the rule is the equitable principle that a person cannot come to property with knowledge that a contract affecting the property is in existence and then ignore it. But there has been much development from the general principle in the case of restrictive covenants affecting land.[10] It is not in the general interest to allow burdens to be attached to land unless there is some corresponding benefit to be protected. And a covenant enforceable between adjoining freeholders is now looked upon as an interest which imposes a burden on one piece of land and confers a benefit on another; as something in the nature of an equitable negative easement.[11] Moreover, although the original principle by which the burden of a restrictive covenant could bind the successor in title of the covenantor was that the successor came to the land with notice of the covenant, it should be noted from that, since 1926, the enforceability of the burden of a freehold covenant against a successor does not depend upon the doctrine of notice, but upon whether it has been registered.

This branch of equity grew with the great era of suburban development in the 19th century; control was in the hands of individual landowners. But, since the 1930s, this type of control has been largely superseded by public control in the hands of planning

---

[3] See p. 777, below.

[4] LPA 1925, s. 78, p. 783, below. See also Contracts (Rights of Third Parties) Act 1999, p. 772, below.

[5] For covenants in leases, see pp. 462 ff et seq., above.

[6] See p. 773, below; *Smith and Snipes Hall Farm Ltd v River Douglas Catchment Board* [1949] 2 KB 500.

[7] See p. 777, below; *Tichbone v Weir* (1892) 67 LT 735; *Re Nisbet and Potts' Contract* [1906] 1 Ch 386.

[8] *The Prior's Case* (1368) YB 42 Edw 3, fo 3A, pl. 14, discussed under *Spencer's Case* (1583) 5 Co Rep 16a; Smith's *Leading Cases* (13th edn, 1929), vol. I, pp. 51, 65, 73; *Smith and Snipes Hall Farm Ltd v River Douglas Catchment Board*, above, per Tucker LJ at 506.

[9] LPA 1925, s. 78(1); *Federated Homes Ltd v Mill Lodge Properties Ltd* [1980] 1 WLR 594, p. 783, below; *Crest Nicholson Residential (South Ltd v McAlister)* [2004] 1 WLR 2409, p. 790, below.

[10] For the operation of this principle in the case of chattels, see CFF, pp. 593–598; Treitel, pp. 656–663.

[11] *London and South Western Rly Co v Gomm* (1882) 20 ChD 562, p. 758, below; *LCC v Allen* [1914] 3 KB 642, p. 755, below; *Formby v Barker* [1903] 2 Ch 539, p. 756, below; *Re Nisbet and Potts' Contract* [1906] 1 Ch 386, p. 759, below.

authorities exercised in the public interest.[12] The development or change of user of land may now only be carried out after planning permission has been obtained. Public planning control has thus overtaken the earlier method, both in influence and complexity. But the law relating to covenants between freeholders is still operative. The two methods of control are sometimes complementary, sometimes contrary. They are cumulative, and a purchaser must satisfy himself in respect of both forms of restriction.[13]

It has always been clear that no covenant will run with the land unless it 'touches and concerns' the land—that is, 'it must either affect the land as regards mode of occupation, or it must be such as *per se*, and not merely from collateral circumstances, affects the value of the land'.[14] This requirement exists also in connection with covenants between landlord and tenant, and has been discussed in that connection.[15] An additional point of importance here is the view current before 1926 that the Real Property Act 1845, section 5 (under which the benefit of a covenant in an indenture may be given to a person who was not a party to the indenture) applied only to cases of covenants which ran with the land.[16] This section is now repealed and replaced by Law of Property Act 1925, section 56, which has been said to be free from such restriction. The question whether a particular covenant touches and concerns the land is, therefore, not material in deciding whether the benefit of it can be given to a person not a party to it; it is material in deciding whether the benefit of the covenant so given will run with the land of the person to whom it was given. Similarly, if the claimant can establish that he is the beneficiary of a covenant under the Contracts (Rights of Third Parties) Act 1999,[17] he need not also show that the covenant touches and concerns the land because he can has a direct contractual right to enforce it. However, if the

---

[12] TCPA 1990; Planning (Listed Buildings and Conservation Areas) Act 1990; Planning (Hazardous Substances) Act 1990; Planning (Consequential Provisions) Act 1990; Land Compensation Acts 1961, 1973; Compulsory Purchase Act 1965; Planning and Compensation Act 1991; Acquisition of Land Act 1981; Planning and Compulsory Purchase Act 2004; Planning and Energy Act 2008; Planning Act 2008; C & B, chaps 29, 30; Gray, part 11; pp. 833–836, below.

[13] (1964) 28 Conv (NS) 190 (A. R. Mellows).

[14] *Rogers v Hosegood* [1900] 2 Ch 388 at 395; p. 780, below. In *Whitgift Homes Ltd v Stocks* [2001] EWCA Civ 1732, [2001] 49 EGCS 130 at [8] Parker LJ preferred the expression 'relates to the land' to the 'old expression' of touch and concern. The Law Commission in its Consultation Paper on Easements, Covenants and Profits à Prendre 2008 (Consultation Paper No. 186, para. 8.80) also proposes that a Land Obligation (its proposed replacement for covenants) must '"relate to" or be for the benefit of' dominant land.

[15] See pp. 463, 482, above. The position in connection with covenants between freeholders is not exactly the same, for in this situation there are two pieces of land involved. Preston & Newsom, paras 2.30 to 2.38; *Rogers v Hosegood*, n. 14, above; *Formby v Barker* [1903] 2 Ch 539 at 554; *Dyson v Forster* [1909] AC 98; *Smith and Snipes Hall Farm Ltd v River Douglas Catchment Board* [1949] 2 KB 500 at 506, p. 774, below; *Newton Abbot Co-operative Society Ltd v Williamson and Treadgold Ltd* [1952] Ch 286, p. 799, below; *Federated Homes Ltd v Mill Lodge Properties Ltd* [1980] 1 WLR 594, p. 783, below. The distinction is not kept clear by Lindley LJ in *Austerberry v Oldham Corpn* (1885) 29 ChD 750 at 781.

[16] *Kelsey v Dodd* (1881) 52 LJ Ch 34 at 39; *Forster v Elvet Colliery Co Ltd* [1908] 1 KB 629; affd sub nom *Dyson v Foster* [1909] AC 98; *Westhoughton UDC v Wigan Coal and Iron Co Ltd* [1919] 1 Ch 159; *Re Ecclesiastical Comrs for England's Conveyance* [1936] Ch 430, p. 765, below; *Amsprop Trading Ltd v Harris Distribution Ltd* [1997] 1 WLR 1025, p. 769, below.

[17] Pp. 771–772, below.

defendant is not the original covenantor, but is only subject to the burden of the covenant under the doctrine of *Tulk v Moxhay*, the claimant must show that the covenant touches and concerns the land, since that is a prerequisite of the running of the burden of the covenant in equity.[18]

This branch of the law is particularly concerned with covenants between freeholders. Covenants between landlord and tenant have already been discussed, and are governed by rules of their own. Where, however, a covenant between landlord and tenant is not enforceable under those special rules, it may, nevertheless, be enforceable under the rules discussed in this section where they are applicable.[19]

Finally, it will be seen that the law relating to the passing of the benefit of restrictive covenants has become difficult and technical. But there is a tendency now to escape from many of the technicalities. This is shown by recent decisions in the context of annexation of the benefit of a covenant to the land of the covenantee,[20] and also in connection with schemes of development.[21] 'The tendency is…to assimilate the law of covenants to the law of easements, where no formalities are required for establishing the right as appurtenant to the dominant tenement'.[22] This policy was a feature of the Law Commission Report in 1984 on the Law of Positive and Restrictive Covenants,[23] although in its latest proposals the Law Commission has rejected the assimilation of easements and covenants, whilst still proposing reform of the law of covenants which is designed to produce a consistency in the regimes governing easements and covenants.[24]

II. THE BURDEN[25]

A. COMMON LAW

(i) *The general rule*

The general rule is that the burden of a covenant affecting land does not run with the land at common law. This is a basic principle, the existence of which has necessitated the development in equity of the doctrine of restrictive covenants. The rule is one of

---

[18] P. 750, below.

[19] *Hall v Ewin* (1887) 37 ChD 74, p. 751, n. 57, below; *Patman v Harland* (1881) 17 ChD 353, p. 461, above.

[20] *Federated Homes Ltd v Mill Lodge Properties Ltd*, above; *Roake v Chadha* above.

[21] *Re Dolphin's Conveyance* [1970] Ch 654, p. 811, below. The enforceability of obligations in respect of freehold flats is now possible under the Commonhold and Leasehold Reform Act 2002, p. 750, below.

[22] (1972 B) 31 CLJ 157 at 163 (H. W. R. Wade).

[23] Law Commission Report on the Law of Positive and Restrictive Covenants 1984 (Law Com No. 127).

[24] Law Commission Consultation Paper on Easements, Covenants and Profits à Prendre 2008 (Consultation Paper No. 186), esp. paras 2.12–2.13 and Part 15; pp. 836–849, below.

[25] C & B, pp. 662–674; Gray, paras 3.3.24–3.3.38, 3.4.9–3.4.33, 3.4.70–3.4.72; M & W, paras 32.017–32.055; MM, pp. 462–471; Smith, pp. 521–524, 526–531.

the many results of the wider principle of privity of contract, that a person may neither sue upon nor be made liable under a contract unless he is a party to it. If, for instance, A sold Whiteacre, part of his land, to B who covenanted with A to lay out pleasure gardens on Whiteacre, A could sue B at law for damages if B refused to perform the covenant; but if B sold or gave the land to C, C could not be made liable on the covenant, because he was not a party to it. This is a matter of the greatest importance because, apart from cases in which specific performance will be decreed, equity only interferes, as will be seen, where the covenant is 'restrictive'. Positive covenants are therefore not enforceable by an action for damages against an assignee of the covenantor.

It is questionable whether the policy behind such a rule is satisfactory, for it often has the effect of leaving a covenantee without a remedy. The matter was considered in 1965 by the Wilberforce Committee which recommended that, subject to certain conditions, the burden of positive covenants should run, and again in 1984 by the Law Commission on the wider topic of both Positive and Restrictive Covenants.[26] The latest proposals of the Law Commission also favour a new regime under which the burden of positive covenants can run.[27] The rule does not exist in such absolute form in most of the United States.[28] It is, however, possible in England to effect the observance of a positive covenant in other ways.[29]

Rhone v Stephens
[1994] 2 AC 310 (HL, **Lords Templeman, Oliver of Aylmerton, Woolf, Lloyd of Berwick** and **Nolan**)[30]

Walford House and Walford Cottage were in common ownership until 1990 when Walford Cottage was sold. The vendor covenanted to keep the common roof which covered part of Walford Cottage in wind and water tight condition. The question arose whether the covenant was enforceable against the owners of Walford House.

Held. The covenant was not enforceable.

Lord Templeman: In the *Austerberry* case (1885) 29 ChD 750 the owners of a site of a road covenanted that they and their successors in title would make the road and keep it in repair. The road was sold to the defendants and it was held that the repair covenant could not be enforced against them...

---

[26] Report of the Committee on Positive Covenants Affecting Land (1965) Cmnd 2719; Law Commission Report on Restrictive Covenants 1967 (Law Com No. 11); Law Commission Report on Positive and Restrictive Covenants 1984 (Law Com No. 127). See also (1972 B) 31 CLJ 157 (H. W. R. Wade).

[27] Law Commission Consultation Paper on Easements, Covenants and Profits à Prendre 2008 (Consultation Paper No. 186), pp. 836–849, below.

[28] Clark, *Real Covenants* (2nd edn, 1947), pp. 231–232; (1943) 52 Yale LJ 699; (1945) 30 Cornell LQ 378; American Restatement (1944) Property: vol. 5, Servitudes, chap. 45.

[29] P. 747, below. *Brewster v Kitchell* (1698) 12 Mod Rep 166 at 169; *Morland v Cook* (1868) LR 6 Eq 252; *Aspden v Seddon* (1876) 1 Ex D 496; *Austerberry v Oldham Corpn* (1885) 29 ChD 750 per Lindley LJ at 781; *South Eastern Rly Co v Associated Portland Cement Manufacturers (1900) Ltd* [1910] 1 Ch 12; *Westhoughton UDC v Wigan Coal and Iron Co Ltd* [1919] 1 Ch 159; *Halsall v Brizell* [1957] Ch 169, p. 748, below; (1954) 18 Conv (NS) 558–564 (E. H. Scamell); Preston & Newsom, paras 3.01–3.04.

[30] [1994] Conv 477 (J. Snape); (1994) 110 LQR 346 (N. P. Gravels); [1994] All ER Rev (P. J. Clarke); [1995] CLJ 60 (S. Gardner).

For over 100 years it has been clear and accepted law that equity will enforce negative covenants against freehold land but has no power to enforce positive covenants against successors in title of the land. To enforce a positive covenant would be to enforce a personal obligation against a person who has not covenanted. To enforce negative covenants is only to treat the land as subject to a restriction.

Mr Munby, who argued the appeal persuasively on behalf of the plaintiffs, referred to an article by Professor Sir William Wade [1972 B] CLJ 157 and other articles in which the present state of the law is subjected to severe criticism. In 1965 a report by a committee appointed by the Lord Chancellor and under the chairmanship of Lord Wilberforce, the Report of the Committee on Positive Covenants Affecting Land (1965) (Cmnd 2719), referred to difficulties caused by the decision in the *Austerberry* case and recommended legislation to provide that positive covenants which relate to the use of land and are intended to benefit specified other land should run with the land. The Law Commission published on 5 July 1971 Working Paper No. 36 in which the present law on positive rights was described as being illogical, uncertain, incomplete and inflexible. The Law Commission Report on Transfer of Land (1984) (Law Com 127) (HC 201) laid before Parliament in 1965 made recommendations for the reform of the law relating to positive and restrictive obligations and submitted a draft Bill for that purpose. Nothing has been done.

In these circumstances your Lordships were invited to overrule the decision of the Court of Appeal in the *Austerberry* case. To do so would destroy the distinction between law and equity and to convert the rule of equity into a rule of notice. It is plain from the articles, reports and papers to which we were referred that judicial legislation to overrule the *Austerberry* case would create a number of difficulties, anomalies and uncertainties and affect the rights and liabilities of people who have for over 100 years bought and sold land in the knowledge, imparted at an elementary stage to every student of the law of real property, that positive covenants, affecting freehold land are not directly enforceable except against the original covenantor. Parliamentary legislation to deal with the decision in the *Austerberry* case would require careful consideration of the consequences. Moreover, experience with leasehold tenure where positive covenants are enforceable by virtue of privity of estate has demonstrated that social injustice can be caused by logic. Parliament was obliged to intervene to prevent tenants losing their homes and being saddled with the costs of restoring to their original glory buildings which had languished through wars and economic depression for exactly 99 years.[31]

(ii) Methods of circumvention

A number of current techniques and devices by which lawyers attempt to surmount or circumvent the difficulties of enforcing positive covenants are listed in the Report of the Committee on Positive Covenants Affecting Land.[32] They are:

(i)   To lease land instead of selling it and to rely upon the enforceability of covenants between landlord and tenant.[33]

[31] The burden of a positive covenant was held by Macnaghten J (following the dicta in *Austerberry v Oldham Corpn*) not to run at law with the land of the covenantor in *E and G C Ltd v Bate* (1935) 79 LJ 203.

[32] (1965) Cmnd 2719. The quotations in (ii), (iii) and (iv) are from para. 8 of the Report. See also Law Commission Report on Positive and Restrictive Covenants 1984 (Law Com No. 127), paras 3.19–3.42; Farrand (2nd edn), pp. 422–427; George and George, *The Sale of Flats* (5th edn, 1984), pp. 76–89; (1973) 37 Conv (NS) 194 (A. M. Prichard).

[33] See pp. 462 ff, above.

(ii) Chains of Indemnity Covenants. A covenant could be taken by each successive purchaser and liability on the covenant will exist down the line of purchasers. 'But in practice this device sooner or later becomes ineffective, either in consequence of the death or disappearance of the original covenantor, or because a break occurs in the chain of indemnities.'[34]

(iii) Covenants against sale of registered land without the developer's consent.[35] 'Where the title to plots on a newly developed estate is going to be registered and the developer is interested in the continuing observance of the covenants, he can insert a covenant in the original conveyances that the plot shall not be sold without his consent. He can then enter a restriction in the register to ensure compliance with the covenant and can refuse to give his consent to any sale under which the purchaser does not assume the appropriate positive obligations.'

(iv) The doctrine of *Halsall v Brizell.* 'In some cases a positive covenant can be enforced in practice by the operation of the maxim *qui sentit commodum sentire debet et onus.* This obliges a person who wishes to take advantage of a service or facility (e.g. a road or drains) to comply with any corresponding obligation to contribute to the cost of providing or maintaining it (*Halsall v Brizell* [1957] Ch 169). The maxim cannot, however, be invoked where the burdened owner does not enjoy any service or facility to which his obligations attach or has no sufficient interest in the continuance of these benefits'.[36]

In **Thamesmead Town Ltd v Allotey** [1998] 3 EGLR 97 PETER GIBSON LJ explained the limits of the doctrine at 99:

'The reasoning of Lord Templeman [in *Rhone v Stephens*] suggests that there are two requirements for the enforceability of a positive covenant against a successor in title to the covenantor. The first is that the condition of discharging the burden must be relevant to the exercise of the rights that enable the benefit to be obtained. In *Rhone v Stephens* the mutual obligation of support was unrelated to and independent of the covenant to maintain the roof. The second

---

[34] See *Radford v De Froberville* [1977] 1 WLR 1262; *TRW Steering Systems Ltd v North Properties Ltd* (1993) 69 P & CR 265.

[35] LRA 2002, s. 40, p. 175, above.

[36] (1957) 73 LQR 154 (R.E.M.); [1957] CLJ 35 (H. W. R. Wade); (1957) 21 Conv (NS) 160 (F. R. Crane); *E R Ives Investment Ltd v High* [1967] 2 QB 379, p. 1073, below; *Montague v Long* (1972) 24 P & CR 240; *Four Oakes Estate Ltd v Hadley* [1986] LS Gaz R 2326 (no benefit to which burden could be attached); *Law Debenture Trust Corporation plc v Urial Caspian Oil Corporation Ltd* [1993] 1 WLR 148; *Rhone v Stephens* (1993) 67 P & CR 9 (CA) (doctrine not invoked where benefit technical or minimal). For a detailed discussion of the doctrine, see *Tito v Waddell (No 2)* [1977] Ch 106 at 289–311, where Megarry V-C held at 303 that it covered not merely successors in title but also 'anybody whose connection with the transaction creating the benefit and burden is sufficient to show that he has some claim to the benefit whether or not he has a valid title to it'. See also (1977) 41 Conv (NS) 432–435 (F. R. Crane); [1985] Conv 12 (E. P. Aughterson); [1998] CLJ 523 (C. J. David); Emmet, para. 19.018.

In *Rhone v Stephens* [1994] 2 AC 310, p. 746, above, Lord Templeman said at 322: 'The condition must be relevant to the exercise of the right…The owners of Walford House could not in theory or practice be deprived of the benefit of the mutual rights of support if they failed to repair the roof'.

is that the successors in title must have the opportunity to choose whether to take the benefit or, having taken it, to renounce it, even if only in theory, and thereby to escape the burden and that the successors in title can be deprived of the benefit if they fail to assume the burden.'

(v) Easement of fencing.[37]

(vi) On some occasions on which a long leasehold is converted into a freehold. Two statutes give such a right to a tenant:

(a) The Law of Property Act 1925, section 153,[38] which provides for certain long leases[39] to be enlarged into freeholds, and for the freehold to be subject 'to all the same covenants...as the term would have been subject to if it had not been so enlarged'.

(b) The Leasehold Reform Act 1967 permits the tenant of a leasehold house[40] held on a long tenancy at a low rent, which he has occupied as his residence for three years, to acquire the freehold on fair terms and free from incumbrances, but 'Burdens...in respect of the upkeep or regulation for the benefit of any locality of any land, building, structure, works, ways or watercourse[41] shall not be treated as incumbrances for purposes of this Part of this Act, but any conveyance executed to give effect to this section shall be made subject thereto...'.[42]

(vii) Certain statutory powers which entitle Local Authorities to impose positive obligations on land and to enforce them upon successive owners.[43]

In addition to the methods of circumvention set out in the Report of the Committee on Positive Covenants Affecting Land there are other possibilities:

(viii) Rentcharge. The creation of a rentcharge to secure the payment of money or contribution to the maintenance of property.[44] This method of enforcing a positive covenant was preserved by the Rentcharges Act 1977.[45]

---

[37] *Jones v Price* [1965] 2 QB 618; *Crow v Wood* [1971] 1 QB 77, p. 645, above.

[38] As amended by TLATA 1996, s. 25(1), Sch. 3, para. 16.

[39] Restricted to those: (i) which were originally created for at least 300 years of which not less than 200 years is unexpired; (ii) in which no rent or money value is payable; (iii) which are not liable to be determined by re-entry for condition broken; (1958) 22 Conv (NS) 101 (T. P. D. Taylor).

[40] See C & B, pp. 364–370.

[41] This clearly includes provisions of the type found in *Halsall v Brizell* [1957] Ch 169.

[42] S. 8(3). There is an exception in the case of rentcharges: s. 11. For restrictive covenants, see s. 10(4)(a).

[43] TCPA 1990, ss. 71–72, and 106. Section 106 was due to be replaced by the new scheme of 'planning contribution' under Planning and Compulsory Purchase Act 2004, s. 46, but that section was never brought into force and was repealed by Planning Act 2008, s. 225, Sch. 13, para. 1; Highways Act 1980, s. 35; Local Government (Miscellaneous Provisions) Act 1982, s. 33, and various Private Acts.

[44] *Morland v Cook* (1868) LR 6 Eq 252; *Austerberry v Oldham Corpn* (1885) 29 ChD 750 at 782.

[45] Ss. 2(3)(c), (4), (5) (creation of 'estate rentcharges'); *Orchard Trading Estate Management Ltd v Johnson Security Ltd* [2002] 2 EGLR 1. See C & B, pp. 706–707; M & W, para. 31.017; George and George, pp. 82–89.

(ix) Right of re-entry. A right of re-entry may be reserved exercisable on events which amount to the breach of a positive covenant.[46] This right of re-entry runs with the land, but is subject to the rule against perpetuities.[47]

(x) Under the Commonhold and Leasehold Reform Act 2002 the burden of a positive covenant may run by statute as between the unit-holders of commonhold land.[48] The rights and duties, as between the unit-holders themselves and as between the unit-holders and the Commonhold association, are specified in a Commonhold Community Statement. By section 16(1) a right or duty conferred or imposed by a Commonhold Community Statement 'shall affect a new unit-holder in the same way as it affected the former unit-holder'.[49] This at a stroke does away with the problem of the enforceability of obligations in respect of freehold flats. 'That is a lacuna which has bedevilled conveyancing law and led to the ugly and varied leasehold structures which are a feature of our conveyancing landscape.'[50]

B. EQUITY

It was held in the leading case of *Tulk v Moxhay* in 1848[51] that the purchaser of land with notice of a restrictive covenant affecting it would be restrained from using the land in away inconsistent with that covenant. The vendor, who takes from a purchaser a covenant which restricts the way in which the land can be used, was said to be entitled in appropriate circumstances to an injunction restraining improper use of the land, not only against the original covenantor, but also against other parties coming to the land.[52] This right to an injunction is of course an equitable right, and is

---

[46] *Shiloh Spinners Ltd v Harding* [1973] AC 691, p. 68, above. The possibility of relief against forfeiture reduces its effectiveness as a device.

[47] (1950) 14 Conv (NS) 350 at pp. 354–357 (S. M. Tolson). Legal rentcharges and rights of entry are registrable dispositions: LRA 2002, s. 27(2)(c), Sch. 2, para. 6. Law Commission Report on Land Registration for the Twenty-First Century (Law Com No. 271), paras 3.18, 4.27. H & B, paras 8.2, 8.17–8.21.

[48] Pp. 309–322, above.

[49] 'Former unit-holder' means a person from whom a commonhold unit has been transferred'; and 'new unit-holder' means a person to whom a commonhold unit is transferred' (s. 16(4)).

[50] Current Law Statutes 2002, chap. 15; commentary by P. H. Kenny on s. 16.

[51] (1848) 2 Ph 774; following Lord Cottenham's earlier decision in *Mann v Stephens* (1846) 15 Sim 377.

[52] The court has power to grant damages in lieu of an injunction under Supreme Court Act 1981, s. 50 (formerly Chancery Amendment Act 1858, s. 2). See *Sefton v Tophams Ltd* [1965] Ch 1140; *Baxter v Four Oaks Properties Ltd* [1965] Ch 816; *Wrotham Park Estate Co v Parkside Homes Ltd* [1974] 1 WLR 798; *Surrey County Council v Bredero Homes Ltd* [1993] 1 WLR 1361; [1996] Conv 457 (N. S. Price); [1994] Conv 110 (T. Ingram); *Jaggard v Sawyer* [1995] 1 WLR 269; [1995] Conv 141 (T. Ingram); *Amec Developments Ltd v Jury's Hotel Management (UK) Ltd* (2001) 82 P & CR 286; *Small v Oliver & Saunders (Developments) Ltd* [2006] 3 EGLR 141; *Forsyth-Grant v Allen* [2008] 2 EGLR 16. On remedies for breach of restrictive covenants generally, see C & B, pp. 690–693; Gray, paras 3.4.73–3.4.81; [1996] Conv 329 (J. Martin); Preston & Newsom, chap. 8 (injunctions, including damages in lieu of injunction at paras 8–11 to 8–19) and 9 (declarations). The Supreme Court Act 1981 will be known as the Senior Courts Act 1981 under Constitutional Reform Act 2005, Sch. 11, para. 1, once the latter Act is brought into force.

never enforceable against bona fide purchasers of the legal estate in the land for value without notice of the covenant,[53] but it can be enforced against all other persons. The burden of such a covenant is then said to run with the land in equity. However, as has already been noted, it is important to remember that, since 1926, the enforceability of the burden of a freehold covenant against a successor no longer depends upon the equitable doctrine of notice, but upon whether it has been registered.

The conditions on which the burden of a covenant will run with the land are established in the cases leading from *Tulk v Moxhay,* and these cases show that the basic principle on which such covenants are enforced has changed since 1848. *Tulk v Moxhay* was decided on the general equitable ground that it was contrary to conscience that a person should come to land with notice of a covenant affecting it, and act in a way inconsistent with the covenant. And this principle was applied in a number of subsequent cases.[54] It soon became clear, however, that such a policy would result in the imposition of burdens on land without there being any corresponding interest in the plaintiff which required protection. The end of the 19th century saw the change of emphasis.[55] There must be an intent that the burden of the covenant should run with the land.[56] There must also be land benefited by the covenant, and the plaintiff must show that he has an interest in that land[57] the identity of which is 'easily ascertainable'

On the jurisdiction of the Court of Chancery to award damages before the 1858 Act, see (1992) 108 LQR 652 (P. M. McDermott).

[53] *Pilcher v Rawlins* (1872) 7 Ch App 259, p. 60, above.

[54] *Luker v Dennis* (1877) 7 ChD 227; *Catt v Tourle* (1869) 4 Ch App 654; *Millbourn v Lyons* [1914] 2 Ch 231; *Clegg v Hands* (1890) 44 ChD 503; *De Mattos v Gibson* (1859) 4 De G & J 276; *Western v MacDermott* (1866) 2 Ch App 72; *Lord Strathcona Ss Co Ltd v Dominion Coal Co Ltd* [1926] AC 108.

[55] *London and South Western Rly Co v Gomm* (1882) 20 ChD 562.

[56] This intent may be clear from the nature of the covenant or by virtue of LPA 1925, s. 79, which will apply unless a contrary intention is shown: *Re Royal Victoria Pavilion (Ramsgate)* [1961] Ch 581; *Tophams Ltd v Earl of Sefton* [1967] 1 AC 50 at 73, 81; *Morrells of Oxford Ltd v Oxford United Football Club* [2001] Ch 459.

[57] *Formby v Barker* [1903] 2 Ch 539, p. 756, below; *LCC v Allen* [1914] 3 KB 642, p. 755, below; *Millbourn v Lyons* [1914] 2 Ch 231; *Kelly v Barrett* [1924] 2 Ch 379; *Re Ballard's Conveyance* [1937] Ch 473; *Tophams Ltd v Earl of Sefton* [1967] 1 AC 50 at 81, per Lord Wilberforce ('under what I am content for present purposes to take as accepted doctrine'). For statutory exceptions to this rule (some of which are no longer in force), see National Trust Act 1937, s. 8; *Gee v National Trust* [1966] 1 WLR 170 at 174; Green Belt (London and Home Counties) Act 1938, s. 22; Water Industry Act 1991, s. 164(3); National Parks and Access to the Countryside Act 1949, s. 16(4); Forestry Act 1967, s. 5(2); Endowments and Glebe Measure 1976, s. 22; Ancient Monuments and Archaeological Areas Act 1979, s. 17(5); Wildlife and Countryside Act 1981, s. 39(3); Local Government (Miscellaneous Provisions) Act 1982, s. 33; HA 1985, s. 609; TCPA 1990, s. 106, as amended by Planning and Compensation Act 1991, s. 12 (for possible replacement of this, see p. 749, n. 43, above); *Re Martin's Application* (1988) 57 P & CR 119; and a number of local authorities have power under local Acts. See also *Governors of the Peabody Donation Fund v London Residuary Body* (1987) 55 P & CR 355 (Artisans and Labourers Dwellings Improvements Act 1875, s. 9, 'a valuable site in Covent Garden'). There are further exceptions in the cases of (i) schemes of development, p. 809, below; (ii) the landlord's reversion on a tenancy; *Hall v Ewin* (1887) 37 ChD 74; *Teape v Douse* (1905) 92 LT 319; (iii) the mortgagee's interest in the land: *Regent Oil Co Ltd v J A Gregory (Hatch End) Ltd* [1966] Ch 402, following *John Bros Abergarw Brewery Co v Holmes* [1900] 1 Ch 188. On the question whether a covenant to restrain the pursuance of a non-noxious trade so as to avoid competition with the plaintiff can benefit the plaintiff's land, see *Wilkes v Spooner* [1911] 2 KB 473 at 485; *Newton Abbot Co-operative Society Ltd v Williamson and Treadgold Ltd* [1952] Ch 286, p. 799, below; *Re Royal Victoria Pavilion (Ramsgate)* [1961] Ch 581.

from the instrument containing the covenant.[58] On the question of benefit, the court does not apply its own standard, but takes a decision on expert evidence presented to it.[59] The onus is on the defendant to show that a covenant does not benefit the land,[60] either originally, or at the date of the action. 'This means that if there were possible opinions either way, the defendant will still fail unless he can show that the opinion that the covenant benefits the land could not reasonably be held.'[61] The benefit of such a covenant then becomes associated with a piece of land in the way that an easement is appurtenant to the dominant tenement; and the phraseology of the law of easements is introduced into the law of restrictive covenants.[62]

The doctrine of *Tulk v Moxhay* is applicable only to restrictive covenants; covenants, that is, which are negative in substance, even though positive in form: indeed, the covenant in *Tulk v Moxhay* itself was positive in form. But the boundary between those that are, and those that are not, negative in substance is not always easy to draw,[63] for almost every positive covenant can, in some sense, be regarded negatively. Moreover, it is difficult to see any inherent distinction between negative and positive covenants so far as enforceability is concerned.[64] In some situations, such as a covenant to supply water to land in a waterless area, the economic and moral reasons for enforcing positive covenants are just as strong as in the case of negative covenants. The jurisdiction, however, is exclusively equitable, and is limited to the situations which are susceptible to equitable remedies. The Report on Positive Covenants Affecting Land emphasised the inconvenience of the present law (under which the burden of positive covenants does not run) to adjoining owners of land and especially to owners of divided buildings and blocks of flats.[65] This has been remedied by the Commonhold and Leasehold Reform Act 2002 where there is freehold ownership of buildings divided into flats or other units.[66]

However, the burden of a positive covenant does not run in equity any more than it runs at law. Such covenants may, as we have seen,[67] be enforceable on other grounds,

---

[58] *Marquess of Zetland v Driver* [1939] Ch 1 at 8; *Crest Nicholson Residential (South) Ltd v McAllister* [2004] 1 WLR 2409 at [33].

[59] *Marten v Flight Refuelling Ltd* [1962] Ch 115 at 137; *Earl of Leicester v Wells-next-the-Sea UDC* [1973] Ch 110; *Wrotham Park Estate Co Ltd v Parkside Homes Ltd* [1974] 1 WLR 798.

[60] *Wrotham Park Estate Co Ltd v Parkside Homes Ltd*, above, at 808; *Dano Ltd v Earl Cadogan* [2003] 12 EG 128 (CS); affd [2004] 1 P & CR 13.

[61] (1974) JPL at p. 133 (G. H. Newsom).

[62] Per Jessel MR in *London and South Western Rly Co v Gomm*, quoted at p. 758, below.

[63] *Bridges v Harrow London Borough Council* (1981) 260 EG 284 at 288 (covenant to retain trees in hedgerow held to be probably negative in substance); *Bedwell Park Land Quarry Company v Hertfordshire County Council* [1993] JPL 349 ('It is hard to think of an obligation which was more positive in substance as well as in form').

[64] Positive and negative undertakings may be contained in a single covenant, but 'there cannot be any doctrine of contagious proximity whereby the presence of the positive inhibits the enforcement of the neighbouring negative'; *Shepherd Homes Ltd v Sandham (No. 2)* [1971] 1 WLR 1062 at 1067, per Megarry J; Preston & Newsom, paras 3–06 to 3–11.

[65] See Law Commission Report on Restrictive Covenants 1961 (Law Com No. 11); Law Commission Report on Positive and Restrictive Covenants 1984 (Law Com No. 127), paras 4.3–4.6.

[66] Pp. 309–322, above.   [67] See p. 747, above.

and will, if the Law Commission's latest proposals[68] for the reform of the law of covenants are adopted, be enforceable subject to certain conditions. In the early days of the *Tulk v Moxhay* doctrine, equity made gallant attempts to enforce some positive covenants by issuing an injunction restraining the defendant from omitting to perform the undertaking.[69] This development, not surprisingly, was brought to an abrupt halt five years later in *Haywood v Brunswick Permanent Benefit Building Society* (1881) 8 QBD 403. It is, however, of interest in demonstrating the crucial importance of the scope of equitable remedies in the development of the doctrine of *Tulk v Moxhay*.[70]

The burden of a covenant enforceable in equity under this doctrine is, unlike covenants between landlord and tenant, a burden on the land, and not on the estate held by the defendant.[71] Thus it is not necessary to show that the defendant holds the estate which the covenantor held; for the defendant is bound merely by coming to the land, whether as squatter, tenant at will, underlessee—as anyone indeed, other than one who takes free of equitable burdens on the land. For covenants entered into before 1926, this meant that the burden of a restrictive covenant which fulfilled the criteria of the doctrine of *Tulk v Moxhay* was binding on all except a bona fide purchaser of the legal estate for value without notice.[72] Now the enforceability against the successor of the covenantor depends on registration. In unregistered land, provision is made in section 2(5) of the Land Charges Act 1972 for the registration, as a land charge Class D(ii), of a restrictive covenant made after 1925 otherwise than between lessor and lessee;[73] and such registration, in accordance with the usual rules, is notice to all the world.[74] In registered land a restrictive covenant may be protected by the entry of a notice under Land Registration Act 2002, s. 33(c), so as to bind a purchaser for value of

[68] Law Commission Consultation Paper on Easements, Covenants and Profits à Prendre 2008 (Consultation Paper No. 186); pp. 836–849, below.

[69] *Morland v Cook* (1868) LR 6 Eq 252; *Cook v Chilcott* (1876) 3 ChD 694, which was expressly disapproved in *Haywood v Brunswick Permanent Benefit Building Society* (1881) 8 QBD 403; *Hall v Ewin* (1887) 37 ChD 74. In *Andrew v Aitken* (1882) 22 ChD 218 at 220 Fry J suggested that, in the case of a covenant to build, the covenantor and his assigns might be called upon to allow the covenantee to enter and carry out the work.

[70] [1981] Conv 55 (C. D. Bell); [1983] Conv 29 (R. Griffith); 327 (C. D. Bell).

[71] *Tichborne v Weir* (1892) 67 LT 735; *Re Nisbet and Potts' Contract* [1905] 1 Ch 391; affd [1906] 1 Ch 386, p. 759, below; *Mander v Falcke* [1891] 2 Ch 554.

[72] *Pilcher v Rawlins* (1872) 7 Ch App 259; *Wilkes v Spooner* [1911] 2 KB 473.

[73] This exception has been interpreted widely in both LCA 1925 and the LRA 1925 so as to exclude the protection of a restrictive covenant relating to *other* land of the lessor. LRA 2002 has changed this by excepting a restrictive covenant between lessor and lessee so far as relating to the demised premises; s. 33(c). The result is that a restrictive covenant relating to other land of the lessor can now be protected by the entry of a notice; *Oceanic Village Ltd v United Attractions Ltd* [2000] Ch 234 (registered land); [2000] CLJ 451 (S. Bridges); [2001] All ER Rev 240 (P. J. Clarke). See also *Newman v Real Estate Debenture Corpn Ltd and Flower Decorations Ltd* [1940] 1 All ER 131 at 149–150; *Dartstone Ltd v Cleveland Petroleum Co Ltd* [1969] 1 WLR 1807; (1956) 20 Conv (NS) 370 (R. G. Rowley).

[74] LPA 1925, s. 198(1), p. 64, above. Positive and negative covenants entered into with a local authority, a Minister of the Crown or Government Department (otherwise than as between landlord and tenant) are registrable as local land charges: LLCA 1975, ss. 1, 2, p. 88, above.

For the duty of a solicitor to advise a purchaser on the nature and effect of a restrictive covenant, see *Bittlestone v Keegan Williams* [1997] EGCS 8.

the registered estate under s. 29.[75] It cannot be an overriding interest.[76] An entry of the covenant on the register merely binds the purchaser if the covenant otherwise satisfies the requirements of the doctrine of *Tulk v Moxhay*: it does not of itself mean that the covenant is necessarily enforceable against the servient land.[77]

(i) *The doctrine of Tulk v Moxhay*

Tulk v Moxhay
(1848) 2 Ph 774, 41 ER 1143 (Lord Cottenham LC)

In 1808, the plaintiff sold a vacant piece of land in Leicester Square to Elms, who covenanted for himself his heirs and assigns with the plaintiff his heirs and assigns that the purchaser would 'at all times thereafter at his...own costs...keep and maintain the said piece of ground...in an open state, uncovered with any buildings, in neat and ornamental order...' The piece of land passed by 'divers mesne conveyances into the hands of the defendant' whose conveyance did not contain any such covenant, but who admitted that he had notice of the covenant in the deed of 1808. The defendant threatened to build on the land in contravention of the covenant. An injunction was granted by Lord Langdale, the Master of the Rolls. On a motion to discharge that order:

Held. The plaintiff was entitled to an injunction to restrain a breach of the covenant by the defendant.[78]

Lord Cottenham LC: That this Court has jurisdiction to enforce a contract between the owner of land and his neighbour purchasing a part of it, that the latter shall either use or abstain from using the land purchased in a particular way, is what I never knew disputed. Here there is no question about the contract: the owner of certain houses in the square sells the land adjoining, with a covenant from the purchaser not to use it for any other purpose than as a square garden. And it is now contended, not that the vendee could violate that contract, but that he might sell

---

[75] P. 170, above; R & R, paras 9.018–9.021. No provision is made by LRA 2002 for recording the benefit of a restrictive covenant on the register of the dominant tenement: H & B, para. 25.13; R & R, para. 42.019.01; nor for making entries relating to positive covenants since the burden does not run with the land. In practice, however, positive covenants are often intermixed with restrictive covenants, and where this occurs they are not edited out of the restrictive covenant entry.

[76] The burden of a restrictive covenant is not a category of overriding interest under LRA 2002, Sch. 3; and the beneficiary of the covenant will not be in actual occupation of the burdened land so as to give rise to an overriding interest under para. 2 of Sch. 3.

[77] *Hodges v Jones* [1935] Ch 657 at 671, per Luxmoore J; *Cator v Newton* [1940] 1 KB 415. If the restrictive covenant was protected under LCA 1972 before first registration, it will become unenforceable if no notice is entered on first registration: *Freer v Unwins Ltd* [1976] Ch 288; (1976) 40 Conv (NS) 304 (F. R. Crane); (1977) 41 Conv (NS) 1; (1976) 35 CLJ 211 (D. Hayton); (1976) 92 LQR 338 (R. J. Smith); (1976) 126 NLJ 523 (S. M. Cretney). See (1984) 81 LSG 1723, where Chief Land Registrar states that on first registration he does not normally inquire whether a covenant has become void for non-registration under LCA 1925; R & R, para. 9.020.

[78] For the continued enforceability of the covenant, see *R v Westminster City Council and London Electricity Board* (1989) 59 P & CR 51, where Simon Brown J describes Leicester Square as 'one of London's ornaments'.

the piece of land, and that the purchaser from him may violate it without this Court having any power to interfere. If that were so, it would be impossible for an owner of land to sell part of it without incurring the risk of rendering what he retains worthless. It is said that, the covenant being one which does not run with the land, this Court cannot enforce it; but the question is, not whether the covenant runs with the land, but whether a party shall be permitted to use the land in a manner inconsistent with the contract entered into by his vendor, and with notice of which he purchased. Of course, the price would be affected by the covenant, and nothing could be more inequitable than that the original purchaser should be able to sell the property the next day for a greater price, in consideration of the assignee being allowed to escape from the liability which he had himself undertaken.

That the question does not depend upon whether the covenant runs with the land is evident from this, that if there was a mere agreement and no covenant, this Court would enforce it against a party purchasing with notice of it; for if an equity is attached to the property by the owner, no one purchasing with notice of that equity can stand in a different situation from the party from whom he purchased....

I think the cases cited before the Vice-Chancellor and this decision of the Master of the Rolls perfectly right, and, therefore, that this motion must be refused, with costs.

(ii) *The necessity for benefited land*

London County Council v Allen
[1914] 3 KB 642 (CA, **Buckley** and **Kennedy LJJ** and **Scrutton J**)

In 1906, the defendant, M. J. Allen, a builder, applied to the L.C.C. for their permission to lay out certain land of which Allen was in possession under an option to purchase. He was treated in the Court of Appeal as if he were the owner. The L.C.C. gave permission subject to a condition that Allen would enter into a covenant not to build upon part of the land which was needed for the continuation of certain proposed streets. By a deed of 1907, Allen covenanted 'for himself, his heirs and assigns, and other the persons claiming under him, and so far as practicable to bind the land and hereditaments herein mentioned into whosesoever hands the same may come' that he would not place any erection on the land, and that he would give notice of this covenant in every document dealing with the land.

The land was conveyed to Allen in 1908; and part mortgaged to Willcocks who, in 1911, conveyed it on redemption, with M. J. Allen's concurrence, to Emily Allen, M. J. Allen's wife. Emily Allen built three houses on the plot, and mortgaged it to Norris.

The question was whether the covenant was binding on Emily Allen and Norris.

Held. Not binding, because the plaintiffs held no land for the benefit of which the covenant was taken.

Scrutton J: The question then is whether it is essential to the doctrine of *Tulk v Moxhay* that the covenantee should have at the time of the creation of the covenant, and afterwards, land for the benefit of which the covenant is created, in order that the burden of the covenant may bind assigns of the land to which it relates.

His Lordship then reviewed the authorities, and referred to *Haywood v Brunswick Permanent Benefit Building Society* (1881) 8 QBD 403, *De Mattos v Gibson* (1858) 4 De G & J 276; *Luker v Dennis* (1877) 7 ChD 227; *London and South Western Rly Co v Gomm* (1882) 20 ChD 562; *Clegg v Hands* (1890) 44 ChD 503, and *Catt v Tourle* (1869) 4 Ch App 654, and continued:

I think the result of this long chain of authorities is that, whereas in my view, at the time of *Tulk v Moxhay* and for at least twenty years afterwards, the plaintiffs in this case would have succeeded against an assign on the ground that the assign had notice of the covenant, since *Formby v Barker* [1903] 2 Ch 539; *Re Nisbet and Potts' Contract* [1905] 1 Ch 391; *affd.* [1906] 1 Ch 386 and *Millbourn v Lyons* [1914] 1 Ch 34; *affd.* [1914] 2 Ch 231, three decisions of the Court of Appeal, the plaintiffs must fail on the ground that they have never had any land for the benefit of which this 'equitable interest analogous to a negative easement' could be created, and therefore cannot sue a person who bought the land with knowledge that there was a restrictive covenant as to its use, which he proceeds to disregard, because he is not privy to the contract. I think the learned editors of Dart on *Vendors and Purchasers* (7th edn), vol. ii, p. 769, are justified by the present state of the authorities in saying that 'the question of notice to the purchaser has nothing whatever to do with the question whether the covenant binds him, except in so far as the absence of notice may enable him to raise the plea of purchaser for valuable consideration without notice'. If the covenant does not run with the land in law, its benefit can only be asserted against an assign of the land burdened, if the covenant was made for the benefit of certain land, all or some of which remains in the possession of the covenantee or his assign, suing to enforce the covenant...I regard it as very regrettable that a public body should be prevented from enforcing a restriction on the use of property imposed for the public benefit against persons who bought the property knowing of the restriction, by the apparently immaterial circumstance that the public body does not own any land in the immediate neighbourhood. But, after a careful consideration of the authorities, I am forced to the view that the later decisions of this court compel me so to hold.[79]

In my opinion, therefore, the demurrer of Mr Norris and of Mrs Allen succeeds. This action against Mr Norris must be dismissed with costs. I regret that I do not see my way to depriving Mrs Allen of her costs, as, whatever may be her equitable rights, I am not at all favourably impressed with her conduct as a good citizen.

Formby v Barker
[1903] 2 Ch 539 (CA, **Vaughan Williams, Romer** and **Stirling LJJ**)

In 1868, R. H. Formby sold all the land owned by him in Formby, Lancashire, to the Mutual Land Company Ltd, subject to various covenants restricting the user of the land. The defendant was an assignee of the company of part of the land, and took with notice of the covenants. R. H. Formby died in 1884, and letters of administration with the will annexed were granted to his widow, the plaintiff, to whom he had given all his property by his will. In 1902, the defendant began to erect certain shops which were alleged to be in breach of the covenant.

---

[79] For exceptions to this rule, see p. 751, n. 57, above, especially the statutory exceptions in favour of local authorities; Francis, *Restrictive Covenants and Freehold Land: A Practical Guide* (2nd edn, 2005), chap. 10.

Held (affirming Hall V-C of the County Palatine of Lancaster).

(i)   The building of the shops was not a breach of the covenant.

(ii) Even if it were, the plaintiff, having no land capable of benefiting, was unable to maintain the action.

Vaughan Williams LJ: The plaintiff sues in her individual capacity and also as administratrix with the will annexed of R. H. Formby deceased.

His Lordship held that, on its proper construction, the covenant had not been broken by the defendant, and continued:

This view really puts an end to the plaintiff's case. But, as another defence was raised and was discussed by the learned Vice-Chancellor, I think it right to deal with that point also.

The learned Vice-Chancellor expressed an opinion that, even if the plaintiff's construction of the covenant was right, and there had been a breach of the covenant, nevertheless the plaintiff was not entitled to sue—that is, was not entitled to sue either as personal representative of R. H. Formby or as residuary devisee under his will....

Before dealing with the question of the plaintiff's right to sue, I wish to point out that that which R. H. Formby conveyed was his whole estate, and that he had no contiguous estate which would be benefited by the covenant in question. Moreover, there is in the deed no re-entry clause under which the vendor could go in as of his old estate, or, indeed, as of any estate....

It becomes necessary, therefore, to ascertain whether the principle of *Tulk v Moxhay* applies to a case in which the vendor sells his whole estate. I have not been able to find any case in which, after the sale of the whole of an estate in land, the benefit of a restrictive covenant has been enforced by injunction against an assignee of the purchaser at the instance of a plaintiff having no land retained by the vendor, although there are cases in which restrictive covenants seem to have been enforced at the instance of plaintiffs, other than the vendor, for the benefit of whose land it appears from the terms of the covenant, or can be inferred from surrounding circumstances, that the covenant was intended to operate. In all other cases the restrictive covenant would seem to be a mere personal covenant collateral to the conveyance. It is a covenant which cannot run with the land, either at law or in equity, and therefore the burden of the covenant cannot be enforced against an assignee of the purchaser.

In **Re Gadd's Land Transfer** [1966] Ch 56, Buckley J held that the retention only of a road to the land burdened by the covenant was sufficient to enable the covenantee to enforce a restrictive covenant. BUCKLEY J said at 67:

The question must, I think, be what is the impact of the covenants on the owner of Bridle Lane in respect of its occupation or enjoyment of that property.... If the use of the pink land is to be changed from agricultural use to use as a building estate of that kind, there will be a great increase in the traffic over the right-of-way. Now the increase in the traffic over the right-of-way must inevitably mean that the maintenance of the roadway will become a more burdensome expense than otherwise it would be....

If the cost of maintaining Bridle Lane became very much heavier than at present because of a great increase in the traffic over the road, it seems to me that there would be a risk that cannot be regarded as non-existent that the frontagers may not all be able to honour their obligations to contribute towards the cost of maintenance. I cannot suppose that that risk is negligible....

Moreover, I think there is substance in the suggestion that if the lane is not kept in a proper state of repair there will be a risk that the road will be taken over by the local authority and the defendant company would thereby be deprived of some element of its ownership in the road.

Now it may be that this road is not a readily saleable asset, but it is not, I think, inconceivable that the residents in the road under certain circumstances would want themselves to acquire the road from the defendant company with a view to preserving it as their private road. If the burden of maintaining the road were to be made substantially more onerous than it is at present owing to an increase of traffic, the likelihood of the defendant company being able to dispose of this asset in any such way as that would, I think, decrease. These may not be very substantial interests or benefits which result to the defendant company from possible enforcement of the restrictive covenants, but nevertheless I do not think they are wholly negligible; I do not think they are matters that the court ought to disregard and I think they are matters of sufficient significance to justify the view that the capacity to enforce the covenants is a matter which does affect the defendant company in its position as owner of Bridle Lane.

(iii) The nature of a restrictive covenant

In **London and South Western Rly Company v Gomm** (1882) 20 ChD 562,[80] Sir George Jessel MR described the doctrine of *Tulk v Moxhay* as follows, at p. 583:

The doctrine of that case, rightly considered, appears to me to be either an extension in equity of the doctrine of *Spencer's Case* to another line of cases, or else an extension in equity of the doctrine of negative easements; such, for instance, as a right to the access of light, which prevents the owner of the servient tenement from building so as to obstruct the light. The covenant in *Tulk v Moxhay* was affirmative in its terms, but was held by the Court to imply a negative. Where there is a negative covenant expressed or implied, as, for instance, not to build so as to obstruct a view, or not to use a piece of land otherwise than as a garden, the Court interferes on one or other of the above grounds. This is an equitable doctrine, establishing an exception to the rules of Common Law which did not treat such a covenant as running with the land, and it does not matter whether it proceeds on analogy to a covenant running with the land or on analogy to an easement.

In other words, the doctrine of *Spencer's Case* was to apply so as to impose liability between parties, between whom there was no privity of estate; or the concept of a negative easement was to be extended in equity to cover the burden imposed, not by grant but by covenant, upon one piece of land for the benefit of another piece of land. The latter is the better analogy; for, under *Spencer's Case*, as with all covenants running with land at common law, the covenant ran with the estate and not with the land. A restrictive covenant under the doctrine of *Tulk v Moxhay*, like an easement, runs with the land, and not with the estate.

---

[80] (1971) 87 LQR 539 (D. J. Hayton). See *Spencer's Case* (1583) 5 Co Rep 16a, p. 465, above.

Tichborne v Weir
(1892) 67 LT 735 (CA, Lord **Esher MR, Bowen** and **Kay LJJ**)

The plaintiff's predecessor in title was seised of a house in fee simple. In 1802 she leased it to Baxter for eighty-nine years. The lease contained a covenant to repair. Baxter made an equitable mortgage of the premises to Giraud, and Giraud entered on the premises in 1836. In 1836 Baxter disappeared, and Giraud remained in occupation of the premises till 1876. During that period he paid the rent reserved in Baxter's lease to the lessor. In 1876 Giraud purported to assign the lease to the defendant. The defendant entered and paid the rent till the term ended in 1891. He then delivered up possession to the plaintiff. The plaintiff sought to make him liable on the covenant to repair, but the Court of Appeal held that he was not liable.

The Real Property Limitation Act 1833 had barred the action and extinguished the right of Baxter; but it had not vested Baxter's lease in Giraud. The covenant to repair would run with the lease on an assignment; but neither Giraud nor the defendant had taken Baxter's lease and the defendant was not bound by the covenant to repair.[81]

To the argument that he was estopped by the payment of rent from denying that he had taken Baxter's estate, it was said that such payment estopped him from disputing the title of the plaintiff, but it did not estop him from denying that he was bound by the terms of the lease. It estopped him from denying that he was a lessee: it did not estop him from denying that he was the holder of Baxter's lease.[82]

Re Nisbet and Potts' Contract
[1905] 1 Ch 391 (Ch D, **Farwell J**); [1906] 1 Ch 386
(CA, **Sir Richard Henn Collins MR, Romer** and **Cozens-Hardy LJJ**)

A summons was taken out by Potts asking for a declaration that Nisbet, the vendor under a contract of sale, failed to produce a good title.

Nisbet had purchased in 1901 from X and Y who had themselves purchased in 1890 from Headde, whose title was based upon occupation since 1878. Nisbet agreed to accept a title commencing at that date. Restrictive covenants had been imposed on the land in 1867 and 1872; Nisbet knew nothing of these but would have discovered them if he had insisted on a forty years' title.[83]

On Potts' complaint that Nisbet was unable to produce a good title because of the restrictive covenants, Nisbet replied:

(i)   that he had purchased without notice; and

(ii) that, in any case, covenants would not be binding upon a title acquired by adverse possession.

---

[81] See especially Kay LJ at 737, p. 272, above.

[82] Much of this account of *Tichborne v Weir* is taken from Holdsworth, *Historical Introduction to the Land Law* (1927), pp. 286–287.

[83] The period of commencement of title which a purchaser could then require. It was reduced to 30 years by LPA 1925, s. 44(1), and then to 15 years by LPA 1969, s. 23, p. 57, above.

Farwell J, affirmed by the Court of Appeal, held that a party had constructive notice of all that he would have ascertained if he had made proper enquiries and searched back for forty years; and also that the restrictive covenants were an equitable burden on the land, and were not terminated by the adverse possession. He said at 396:

Covenants restricting the enjoyment of land, except of course as between the contracting parties and those privy to the contract, are not enforceable by anything in the nature of action or suit founded on contract. Such actions and suits alike depend on privity of contract, and no possession of the land coupled with notice of the covenants can avail to create such privity: *Cox v Bishop* (1857) 8 DM & G 815. But if the covenant be negative, so as to restrict the mode of use and enjoyment of the land, then there is called into existence an equity attached to the property of such a nature that it is annexed to and runs with it in equity: *Tulk v Moxhay*. This equity, although created by covenant or contract, cannot be sued on as such, but stands on the same footing with, and is completely analogous to, an equitable charge on real estate created by some predecessor in title of the present owner of the land charged.

(iv) Registration

(a) Unregistered land

Land Charges Act 1972

2.—The register of land charges.—(1) If a charge on or obligation affecting land falls into one of the classes described in this section, it may be registered in the register of land charges as a land charge of that class.

(5) A Class D land charge is any of the following (not being a local land charge), namely—

(ii) a restrictive covenant;

and for this purpose—

(ii) a restrictive covenant is a covenant or agreement (other than a covenant or agreement between a lessor and a lessee) restrictive of the user of land and entered into on or after 1st January 1926...

(b) Registered land

Land Registration Act 2002

28 **Basic rule**: p. 170, above
29 **Effect of registered dispositions: estates**: p. 170, above

QUESTION

K Ltd, a garage company which owned the site of a garage, mortgaged it to E, and entered into a 'solus' agreement, under which it undertook to sell E's petrol only; and to extract similar undertakings from any person to whom it might sell the garage.

I H purchased all the sharers in K Ltd, and took a conveyance of the site of the garage, with the intention of breaking the provision relating to the sale of the petrol. They did so. E owned no land capable of benefiting. E sues for an injunction, joining K Ltd and I H as defendants. What result? See *Esso Petroleum Co Ltd v Kingswood Motors (Addlestone) Ltd* [1974] QB 142.

C. LAW OF PROPERTY ACT 1925, SECTION 79[84]

In **Rhone v Stephens** [1994] 2 AC 310, p. 746, above, LORD TEMPLEMAN said at 321:

Mr Munby submitted that the decision in the *Austerberry* case (1885) 29 Ch D 750 had been reversed remarkably but unremarked by section 79 of the Law of Property Act 1925 which, so far as material, provides:

'(1) A covenant relating to any land of a covenantor or capable of being bound by him, shall unless a contrary intention is expressed, be deemed to be made by the covenantor on behalf of himself, his successors in title and the persons deriving title under him or them, and, subject as aforesaid, shall have effect as if such successors and other persons were expressed...'

This provision has always been regarded as intended to remove conveyancing difficulties with regard to the form of covenants and to make it unnecessary to refer to successors in title. A similar provision relating to the benefit of covenants is to be found in section 78 of the Act of 1925. In *Smith and Snipes Hall Farm Ltd v River Douglas Catchment Board* [1949] 2 KB 500, [p. 774, below], followed in *Williams v Unit Construction Co Ltd* (1951) 19 Conv (NS) 262 [p. 776, below], it was held by the Court of Appeal that section 78 of the Act of 1925 had the effect of making the benefit of positive covenants run with the land. Without casting any doubt on those long standing decisions I do not consider that it follows that section 79 of the Act of 1925 had the corresponding effect of making the burden of positive covenants run with the land. In *Jones v Price* [1965] 2 QB 618, 633 Willmer LJ repeated that: 'a covenant to perform positive acts... is not one the burden of which runs with the land so as to bind the successors in title of the covenantor: see *Austerberry v Oldham Corporation.*'

In *Sefton v Tophams Ltd* [1967] 1 AC 50, 73, 81, Lord Upjohn and Lord Wilberforce stated that section 79 of the Law of Property Act 1925 does not have the effect of causing covenants to run with the land. Finally, in *Federated Homes Ltd v Mill Lodge Properties Ltd* [1980] 1 WLR 594, 605–606 [p. 783, below]. Brightman J referred to the authorities on section 78 of the Act of 1925 and said that: 'Section 79, in my view, involves quite different considerations and I do not think that it provides a helpful analogy.'[85]

---

[84] P. 466, above; [2000] Conv 377 (L. Tee).

[85] See the laconic 'No' given as an answer by Sir Benjamin Cherry in his *Lectures on the New Property Acts* (1926), p. 131, to the question 'Is the case of *Austerberry v Corporation of Oldham* overruled by s. 79 of the Law of Property Act?'

Unlike section 78,[86] section 79 contains the words 'unless a contrary intention is expressed'. In **Re Royal Victoria Pavilion, Ramsgate** [1961] Ch 581 PENNYCUICK J considered a covenant which began 'The vendors hereby covenant with the purchasers that they the vendors will…'. He said at 589:

[H]ere it is contended that no contrary intention is expressed in the conveyance… and that, therefore, the covenant in clause 5 must be deemed to be made by Thanet Theatrical on behalf of itself and its successors in title. If the words 'unless the contrary intention is expressed' in section 79 mean: unless the instrument contains express provision to the contrary, this contention would, I think, be unanswerable. But it seems to me the words 'unless a contrary intention is expressed' mean rather: unless an indication to the contrary is to be found in the instrument, and that such an indication may be sufficiently contained in the wording and context of the instrument even though the instrument contains no provision expressly excluding successors in title from its operation. It can hardly be the intention of the section that a covenant which, on its natural construction, is manifestly intended to be personal only, must be construed as running with the land merely because the contrary is not expressly provided….

So here, although the covenant contains no express provision to the effect that it is not made on behalf of successors in title, it does, as it seems to me, contain sufficient indication to this effect.[87]

In **Lynnthorpe Enterprises Ltd v Sidney Smith (Chelsea) Ltd** [1990] 1 EGLR 148,[88] WARNER J said at 152:

Mr Fenwick's main submission on this part of the case was that section 79 did not apply because at the time when the deed of 1986 was entered into the assignment to Lynnthorpe had not taken place, and indeed might never take place, so that Lynnthorpe had no land and was capable of binding no land to which the covenant related….

It seems to me that, in truth, I am faced here with a simple question of construction of section 79 itself. It is plain from the terms of the deed of 1986 that, at the time it was executed, the parties to it contemplated that the lease would be assigned to Lynnthorpe, though it might not be. Lynnthorpe thereby entered into a covenant that was to take effect if and when the lease was assigned to it. Is it to be held that the land comprised in the lease was not 'capable of being bound' by Lynnthorpe in that event? To answer that question in the affirmative would, to my mind, be to place an unwarrantable restriction on the meaning of those words in the section. Parliament, by referring in the section to 'any land of a covenantor or capable of being bound by him' has evinced an intention that the land need not belong to the covenantor at the time of the covenant. Otherwise, the words 'or capable of being bound by him' add nothing. I therefore hold that section 79 does apply here.

---

[86] P. 466, above. See, however, *Roake v Chadha* [1984] 1 WLR 40, p. 787, below.

[87] Followed in *Morrells of Oxford Ltd v Oxford United Football Club* [2001] Ch 459 (covenant not to permit sale or consumption either on or off the premises of intoxicating liquors contained no reference to successors in title, whereas another covenant did: held that the first covenant was intended to be personal and s. 79 did not apply).

[88] Upheld by CA [1990] 2 EGLR 131; see Staughton LJ at 134. See *Crest Nicholson Residential (South) Ltd v McAllister* [2004] 1 WLR 2409 at paras 41–44, where Chadwick LJ expressed the view that s. 78 did not contain the words 'unless a contrary intention is expressed' because 'it did not need to'.

III. THE BENEFIT[89]

A. ENFORCING THE COVENANT AS AN ORIGINAL BENEFICIARY

There are two situations where a person may be able to enforce the covenant as an original beneficiary of it, even though he is not the direct covenantee.

(i) Section 56 of the Law of Property Act 1925

The effect of this section, when it applies, is to make into a covenantee a person claiming the benefit of the covenant, even though he was not a party to the instrument in which the covenant was contained. However, its operation is limited.

LAW OF PROPERTY ACT 1925

56. Persons taking who are not parties and as to indentures.—(1) A person may take an immediate or other interest in land or other property, or the benefit of any condition, right of entry, covenant or agreement over or respecting land or other property, although he may not be named as a party to the conveyance or other instrument.

In **Beswick v Beswick** [1968] AC 58, LORD UPJOHN said at 102:

Section 56 of the Law of Property Act 1925 has a long history behind it. Section 56 replaced section 5 of the Real Property Act 1845, which amended some very ancient law relating to indentures inter partes, so I shall start by stating the common law on the subject.

The rule was that a grantee or covenantee, though named as such in an indenture under seal expressed to be made inter partes, could not take an *immediate* interest as grantee nor the benefit of a covenant as covenantee unless named as a party to the indenture. This rule, as the authorities I shall quote show, applied not only to real estate but to personal grants and covenants.

But how narrow this rule was, but equally, how well understood, will also be shown by those authorities.

His Lordship referred to *Scudamore v Vandenstene* (1587) 2 Co Inst 673; *Cooker v Child* (1673) 2 Lev 74; *Berkeley v Hardy* (1826) 5 B & C 355 and continued:

In *Forster v Elvet Colliery Co Ltd* [1908] 1 KB 629, 639 Farwell LJ pointed out that the old rule of law still holds good that no one can sue on a covenant in an indenture who is not mentioned as a party to it, except so far as it had been altered by the Real Property Act 1845. Substituting a reference to section 56 for the Act of 1845 that statement, I suppose, is still true.

---

[89] C & B, pp. 674–690; Gray, paras 3.3.5–3.3.23, 3.4.34–3.4.69; M & W, paras 32.004–32.016, 32.056–32.080; MM, pp. 454–461; Smith, pp. 524–526, 531–540; [1938] CLJ 339 (S. J. Bailey); (1971) 82 LQR 539 (D. J. Hayton); (1982) 2 LS 53 (D. J. Hurst); (1982) 98 LQR 279 (S. Gardner).

In 1844 Parliament abrogated this rule by section 11 of the Transfer of Property Act 1844, which enacted:

'That it shall not be necessary in any case to have a deed indented; and that any person, not being a party to any deed, may take an immediate benefit under it in the same manner as he might under a deed poll.'

For whatever reason, this short workmanlike section, which plainly applied to all covenants whether relating to realty or personal grants or covenants, never had any operation, for it was repealed by the Real Property Act 1845, and replaced by section 5 of that Act in these terms:

'That, under an indenture, executed after October 1, 1845, an immediate estate or interest, in any tenements or hereditaments, and the benefit of a condition or covenant, respecting any tenements or hereditaments, may be taken, although the taker thereof be not named a party to the same indenture; ...'

No one has ever suggested that that section was intended to do more than supplant the old common law rule relating to indentures inter partes in relation to realty.

Then came the great changes in the law of real property; the Law of Property Act 1922, and the Law of Property (Amendment) Act 1924. The researches of counsel have not revealed any amendment in those Acts to section 5 of the Act of 1845. The Law of Property Act 1925 was a consolidation Act consolidating those and many earlier Acts. It repealed section 5 of the Act of 1845 and replaced it by section 56(1).

Since a person who takes advantage of section 56 is treated as an original covenantee, it is essential that he should be in existence and identifiable at the time when the covenant was made; the section cannot be used to give the benefit of a covenant to future purchasers, for they could not be made covenantees.[90] Indeed, no enactment is needed to guard the interests of future purchasers, for they can obtain the benefit of existing covenants by virtue of the rules of annexation, or express assignment of the benefit of the covenant.[91] The person who would suffer, apart from section 56 or the existence of a scheme of development,[92] is the owner of adjoining land which needs protection from the covenant and which may have been sold to an earlier purchaser of the land sold off in plots by a common vendor.

Assume that X owns a piece of land, Blackacre, which he is selling off in plots, in circumstances which do not give rise to the existence of a scheme of development. Plot 1 is bought by A, who covenants, in terms appropriate to annex the benefit of the covenant to each and every part of the land retained by X, not to use the premises as a fish shop; plot 2 is bought by B who gives a similar covenant, and similarly plot 3 by C. B opens a fish shop. X of course can sue as covenantee; C will be able to sue as being the purchaser of land to which the benefit of the covenant is annexed; but A will

---

[90] *Smith and Snipes Hall Farm Ltd v River Douglas Catchment Board*, p. 774, below. See also *Pinemain Ltd v Welbeck International Ltd* (1984) 272 EG 1166 (benefit of covenant to sue surety on contract of guarantee not within s. 56, since plaintiffs were not identifiable when covenant was made); *Re Distributors and Warehousing Ltd* [1986] 1 EGLR 90, per Walton J; cf. *Wiles v Banks* (1983) 50 P & CR 80 (plaintiff identifiable).

[91] Below, pp. 773–777, 779–808.   [92] For schemes of development, see p. 809, below.

not, for the benefit of B's covenant, being given later, was not annexed to the piece of land which he bought. Later purchasers, in other words, can sue earlier purchasers; earlier purchasers cannot sue later. Earlier purchasers can be given the right to sue by section 56. The safe way to do so is to draft the later covenants in such a way as to purport to covenant expressly with 'A, his heirs and assigns, successors in title, owners for the time being of (plot 1) land adjoining the premises now sold.' Some cases require that the benefit could only be taken by a person 'to whom that...instrument purports to grant something or with whom some agreement or covenant is purported to be made'.[93] This view that the covenant must purport to be made with A and not merely for the benefit of A, has been followed by Neuberger J in *Amsprop Trading Ltd v Harris Distribution Ltd*.[94] Further A may be able to enforce the covenant in his own right under the Contracts (Rights of Third Parties) Act 1999, if there is either a term to that effect or if the contract purports to confer a benefit on him.[95]

Re Ecclesiastical Commissioners for England's Conveyance
[1936] Ch 430 (ChD, **Luxmoore J**)

An originating summons was brought under section 84(2) Law of Property Act 1925,[96] to decide whether West Heath House, in the ownership of the applicants, was bound by any, and if so, what, restrictive covenants. The applicants were successors in title of one Gotto who purchased in 1887 from the Ecclesiastical Commissioners giving the following covenant:

'The said Henry Gainsford Gotto doth hereby...covenant with the said Ecclesiastical Commissioners and their successors' (in such a way as to annex the benefit of the covenant to the land retained by the vendor) 'and also as a separate covenant with their assigns owners for the time being of land adjoining or adjacent to the said land hereby conveyed in manner following, that is to say:' A number of covenants followed.

Some of the defendants were successors in title to land adjoining or adjacent to the applicants' house and which had been bought from the Ecclesiastical Commissioners before the conveyance of 1887. It was as to the position of these defendants that the main issue in the case arose.

Held. The owners of adjacent and adjoining lands and their successors in title were able to enforce the covenants although they or their predecessors in title were not parties to the conveyance of 1887.

Luxmoore J: The questions to be determined are: (1) were any restrictions imposed on West Heath House before or by the conveyance of April 21, 1887; (2) were such restrictions imposed for the benefit of any, and what other hereditaments; and (3) who are the persons, if any, now entitled to the benefit of such restrictive covenants? It is not contended by any of the parties

---

[93] *White v Bijou Mansions Ltd* [1937] Ch 610 at 625; affd [1938] Ch 351, p. 767, below; *Re Ecclesiastical Comrs for England's Conveyance* [1936] Ch 430, below.
[94] [1997] 1 WLR 1025, p. 769, below.
[95] P. 772, below.   [96] See p. 822, below.

that West Heath House forms part of a larger estate which has been subjected to what is usually referred to as a building scheme, and it is quite plain that there is not sufficient evidence on which it could be argued with any hope of success that such a scheme existed. . . .

Having ascertained that restrictive covenants were imposed in respect of the West Heath House property and that the form of the covenants is such as to make the burden of them run with the land, it is necessary to consider whether they were imposed for the benefit of any and what other hereditaments. For it is well settled that, apart from any building scheme, restrictive covenants may be enforced if they are expressed in the original deed to be for the benefit of a particular parcel or particular parcels of land, either expressly mentioned or clearly identified in the deed containing the original covenants. It was argued on behalf of the applicants that the right to enforce such covenants is limited to the original covenantees and their successors in title—the right in the case of the successors in title being limited to those whose land was the property of the original covenantees at the date when the covenants were imposed. It was also argued that the right to enforce the covenants did not extend to any owners of land who were neither express assignees of the benefit of the covenants, nor successors in title of the original covenantees in respect to land acquired by such successors from the Ecclesiastical Commissioners subsequent to the date of the deed by which the covenants were imposed. I think these arguments failed to give due consideration to the provisions of section 5 of the Real Property Act 1845, as repealed and re-enacted by section 56 of the Law of Property Act 1925. Section 5 of the Act of 1845 provides that under an indenture, executed after October 1, 1845, the benefit of a condition or covenant respecting any tenements or hereditaments may be taken, although the taker thereof be not named as a party to the indenture. In the case of *Forster v Elvet Colliery Co Ltd* [1908] 1 KB 629, it was held that the condition or covenant referred to in the section must, in order to be enforceable by a person not a party to the deed, be one the benefit of which runs with the land of the person seeking to enforce it. The actual decision was upheld in the House of Lords under the name *Dyson v Forster* [1909] AC 98, 102, but Lord Macnaghten expressed doubt whether the section ought to be so restricted. He refrained however from resolving the doubt, because he agreed with the view that the covenants in the particular case ran with the land and it was therefore unnecessary to do so.

The alteration which has been made in the verbiage of section 5 of the 1845 Act by section 56 of the 1925 Act, has not in my opinion affected the position so as to limit the right of a person not a party to the deed to enforce covenants affecting land to those which run with the land. The material words are as follows: 'A person may take . . . the benefit of any condition, . . . covenant or agreement . . . respecting land or other property, although he may not be named as a party to the conveyance or other instrument.' It seems to me that the effect of these words is to enlarge the scope of the earlier words, for it extends the rights of a person not a party to a deed to covenants affecting every kind of property personal as well as real. So far as every species of personal property other than leasehold is concerned it is obvious that the covenants to be enforced cannot be restricted to those running with the property, for there are no such covenants. What it is necessary to consider is the true construction of the conveyance of April 21, 1887, in order to ascertain whether any persons, not parties thereto, are described therein as the covenantees, and whether such covenants are expressed to affect any and what hereditaments. To determine what is the true construction of that document it is necessary to consider the surrounding circumstances as they existed at the date when it was executed.

His Lordship then examined the circumstances existing at the date of execution of the deed and concluded that the covenants were enforceable by the original covenantees, and persons deriving title under them; that the original covenantees need not have been parties to the conveyance of 1887; but that such persons could only enforce the covenant if they held land adjoining or adjacent to the applicants' house.[97]

White v Bijou Mansions Ltd
[1937] Ch 610, affd [1938] Ch 351 (**Simonds J**, ChD)
(CA, **Sir Wilfrid Greene MR, Luxmoore** and **Farwell JJ**)

The owners of the Shaftesbury House Estate conveyed part of it in 1887 to James Israel Fellows. Fellows covenanted that he would build a dwelling house for a certain sum and would use it only as a private dwelling house or as a residence and place of practice of a medical man. The vendors covenanted that every building lease or future sale should include covenants from the lessee or purchaser with the builders imposing similar restrictions on the use of the land, though certain parts were to be permitted to be used as shops. The plaintiff was the successor in title to Fellows.

In 1890, a nearby plot was conveyed to Nicholson, who covenanted for himself, his heirs, executors, administrators and assigns with the intent to bind himself and his successors in title and the owner for the time being of the property thereby conveyed with the vendors, their heirs and assigns, that the piece of land thereby conveyed should be used for the purpose of a private dwelling house only. This plot was later conveyed to Miss Plumbly who, in 1935, leased it to two ladies for a term of 28 years; the lease contained a covenant that no part of the demised premises would be used for any purpose other than a private dwelling house or for private suites or flats. The lease was in due course assigned to the defendants who used the house for flatlets. The action was for an injunction to restrain a breach of covenant.

Held (by Simonds J and the Court of Appeal). The plaintiff was not entitled to the benefit of the covenant given by Nicholson in the conveyance of 1890.

Simonds J (in the court of first instance): . . . Then the question arises: Can the plaintiff here enforce that covenant? I turn to look at it once more. There are covenants entered into in the year 1890, the first with the Davidsons, the second with the Daws, and they are covenants which are not annexed to any particular parcel of land. They are covenants entered into four years after the plaintiff acquired the title to his land. They are covenants the benefit of which has not, expressly or by implication, or in any manner whatsoever, been assigned to the plaintiff, and it appears to me to be quite impossible, apart from any building scheme or from the special statutory provision to which I shall presently refer, that the plaintiff can avail himself of this covenant and enforce it. There is here no question of a building scheme. . . .

It remains to consider the only other ground on which, as it appears to me, Mr Grant can possibly rest his case. He claims that he is entitled to enforce this covenant, entered into on May 2, 1890, on the ground that either under section 5 of the Real Property Act 1845, or under section 56 of the Law of Property Act 1925, that right is conferred on him. In the view which I take of both these sections it is unnecessary for me to consider whether he is in any way entitled to

---

[97] Followed in *Re Shaw's Application* (1994) 68 P & CR 591 (purchaser covenanted '*with* the vendor').

call in aid section 56 of the Act of 1925, with regard to covenants or agreements contained in a deed executed in 1890. It is necessary for me to say something about the earlier section before I come to consider the later section.

Section 5 of the Real Property Act 1845, which was, as its title suggests, an Act to amend the law of real property, was aimed at remedying certain mischiefs in the state of the common law as it then was. There was a highly technical and artificial rule that by an indenture, as distinguished from a deed poll, an immediate interest in land could not be granted in favour of a grantee unless that grantee was a party to the deed. That mischief this section was designed to remedy. Further, there was the defect, as it was supposed, in the common law, that a person could not take advantage of a covenant in a deed unless he was a party to the deed. Be it observed that the Act of 1845 dealt with real property. This section was confined to the case of an indenture, and of an immediate interest created by that indenture, for it was never the law that an estate in remainder could not be validly granted in favour of a grantee if he were not a party. Indeed the common form of settlement then for centuries in vogue had limited estates in remainder not only to persons not parties to the deed but to persons not yet in existence.

His Lordship read section 5 and continued:

I think the important aspect of that section for my present purpose is this. It appears to me to be quite plain that the section has a limited operation. It is intended to confer a benefit only on those persons to whom the deed purports to grant an estate or interest or those persons with whom there purports to be a covenant or agreement. It is impossible, in my view, to regard this section as creating a benefit in favour of any persons who may like to avail themselves of it and say: 'It we can take advantage of this it will be for our benefit.' It seems to me clear that this section was intended merely to provide that A.B., the grantee under a deed, might take an immediate interest although he was not a party, and similarly that A.B., with whom the covenant was purported to be made by the deed, should be able to avail himself of it although he was not a party to the deed, and in the few cases which have arisen under this section since 1845—and there appear to be very few—it will be found in every case where it has been applied that it has been in favour of a person who although not a party to the deed was a person to or with whom a grant or covenant purported to be made. That was the position under the Act of 1845.

I now turn to consider section 56 of the Act of 1925, which, it is said, however inaptly, takes the place of the earlier section.

His Lordship read subsection 1 and continued:

I think many difficulties may well arise on that section which do not fall to me today to solve. It appears to one at once that, so far as any other than an immediate interest in land is concerned the section is superfluous, because a person always could take another interest in land though not a party. It is at least a question how far such a provision is necessary at all in the case of personalty. Without deciding it, I should be disposed to think that equitable estates even in land were not subject to the old artificial rule and it is very doubtful if an interest in personalty was ever so subject. However that may be, for the purposes of the present case I think I am only concerned with one aspect of this question. Just as under section 5 of the Act of 1845 only that person could call it in aid who, although not a party, yet was a grantee or covenantee, so under section 56 of this Act only that person can call it in aid who, although not named as a party to the conveyance or other instrument, is yet a person to whom that conveyance or other instrument purports to grant some thing or with whom some agreement or covenant is purported to be made. To give it any other meaning appears to me to open the door to claims or assertion of rights which cannot have been contemplated by the Legislature, for if that be not the limitation which must be imposed on this section, it appears to me that there is no limit and it will be open to anybody to come into court and say: 'Here is a covenant which if enforced will redound to my advantage, therefore I claim the benefit of the section. I claim that this covenant or condition is one which should be enforced in my favour because it is for my benefit, whether intended for my benefit or not intended for my benefit would not appear to matter.' I cannot give to the section any such meaning as that. I interpret it as a section which can be called in aid only by a person in whose favour the grant purports to be made or with whom the covenant or agreement purports to be made.[98] If that is so, whether the plaintiff's claim arises under the earlier or the later Act, he cannot sue on it in this Court because he is not a person who, under the deed of 1890, can point to any grant or any covenant purported to be made to or with him. That is the construction which I place on section 56, with the result that the plaintiff's claim must fail.

In the Court of Appeal, where Simonds J's decision was upheld, SIR WILFRID GREENE MR said at 365:

Whatever else section 56 may mean, it is, I think, confined to cases where the person seeking to take advantage of it is a person within the benefit of the covenant in question, if I may use that phrase. The mere fact that somebody comes along and says: 'It would be useful to me if I could enforce that covenant' does not make him a person entitled to enforce it under section 56. Before he can enforce it he must be a person who falls within the scope and benefit of the covenant according to the true construction of the document in question.

In **Amsprop Trading Ltd v Harris Distribution Ltd** [1997] 1 WLR 1025, clause 3(4) of an underlease contained a covenant, expressed to be made by the tenants with the landlords, to repair the demised premises. Clause 3(7) required the tenants to permit the superior landlords or the landlords to enter to view the state of the premises, and clause 3(8) provided that the tenant would remedy defects identified in a notice issued by the superior landlords or the landlords, and that 'if the tenants shall fail to comply with the requirements of such notice as aforesaid [it] shall be lawful for the superior landlords and the landlords...or their [agents] to enter upon the...premises to execute such works as may be necessary to comply with the same and in the event of the superior landlords or the landlords so entering the...premises and carrying out such works to pay their costs and expenses of executing such works...on demand as liquidated damages...'. NEUBERGER J held that the successor in title of the original superior landlords could not enforce the covenant against the tenant and its assignee, because the covenant did not to purport to be made with the superior landlords, even though they were named as persons for whose benefit the covenant was made). He said at 1030:

In the present case, the covenants in clause 3 of the underlease are expressed to be made with 'the landlords,' which means Keddie and, at least where the context admits, its 'successors in title and assigns.' Amsprop, Keddie's own landlord, clearly does not fall within that expression.

---

[98] Similarly per Crossman J in *Re Foster* [1938] 3 All ER 357 at 365; per Dillon J in *Lyus v Prowsa Developments Ltd* [1982] 1 WLR 1044 at 1049.

Accordingly, it seems to me that the plaintiff's argument on this point faces a substantial hurdle, in that the parties to the underlease have expressly agreed that the covenants of the 'tenants' are with 'the landlords' and no one else is mentioned as a person for whose benefit the covenants are made.

However, clause 3(7) and (8) of the underlease are covenants which, in terms, state that the first defendant will do certain things which could be said to benefit 'the superior landlords:' the first defendant will permit them to enter in order to inspect, to view, to leave notice, and to carry out works and will also reimburse them the cost of the works. These rights, it is contended, were clearly meant to be for the benefit of the superior landlords, and therefore, even in light of the observations in *Beswick v Beswick* [1968] AC 58 [p. 763, above], may be enforced directly by the superior landlords, by virtue of section 56. I do not accept that argument for three reasons.

First, it seems to me that the provisions of clause 3(7) and (8) of the underlease, even in so far as they relate to the superior landlords, operate perfectly satisfactorily if they are treated as imposing obligations which can be enforced only by 'the landlords' against 'the tenants.'...

Secondly, in light of the observations in *Beswick v Beswick*, to which I have referred, I consider that, particularly in a case, such as clause 3 of the underlease, where the identity of the covenantee is clear and unambiguous, section 56 does not operate to confer the benefit of the covenant on a party who is not within the ambit of the expressly identified covenantee. Only two cases have been cited to me which call that view into question.

The first is the decision of the Court of Appeal in *Drive Yourself Hire Co. (London) Ltd v Strutt* [1954] 1 QB 250.... The decision and reasoning of Denning LJ are inconsistent with my conclusion, but I consider that the whole of this judgment, in so far as it was based on section 56, cannot be regarded as authority in light of the observations in *Beswick v Beswick* [1968] AC 58, to which I have referred. This point is of some significance, because it appears that the editors of at least one of the two leading textbooks on the law of landlord and tenant consider that at least some of the observations of Denning LJ in *Strutt's* case as to the effect of section 56 survive: see Hill & Redman's *Law of Landlord and Tenant*, 18th edn, vol. 1, paras 2587–2590, note 10. Woodfall's *Landlord and Tenant*, 28th edn, vol. 1, para. 11.123 is more circumspect. The point is of some importance, not only in relation to the type of covenant with which I am here concerned, but also in connection with the type of covenant before the court in *Strutt's* case, namely a covenant in an underlease against alienation without the consent of the landlord or the superior landlord. The reasoning of Denning LJ, based on section 56, led him to conclude that the superior landlord could effectively enforce the requirement for consent contractually against the subtenant provided the underlease contained a proviso as between landlord and tenant that the tenant would not assign without the superior landlord's consent. I do not consider that this view can survive the reasoning of the majority of the House of Lords in *Beswick v Beswick* [1968] AC 58, particularly in light of the approval therein of the reasoning of Simonds J in *White v Bijou Mansions Ltd* [1937] Ch 610 [p. 767, above].

The other case which might be said to be inconsistent with the conclusion I have reached is the recent decision of Judge Marder QC in *Re Shaw's Application* (1994) 68 P & CR 591. To my mind, he decided that case on the basis of reading observations of Sir Wilfrid Greene MR in *White v Bijou Mansions Ltd* [1938] Ch 351 [p. 767, above] (upholding the decision of Simonds J) out of context. In my opinion, the observations of Sir Wilfrid Greene MR were intended to have the same effect as the observations of Simonds J, and that view is supported by the fact that they are both cited as having the same effect by Lord Reid and Lord Guest and, inferentially, Lord Pearce in *Beswick v Beswick* [1968] AC 58, 75A-D, 86B-C, 94B.

Mr Cant relied on *Stromdale & Ball Ltd v Burden* [1952] Ch 223 and *Wiles v Banks* (1984) 50 P & CR 80. I consider that both these decisions are distinguishable on two grounds. First, the court was in each case concerned with whether a purported grant to a person who was not a party to the deed could be enforced by that person; in the present case, as I have mentioned, I am concerned with the covenant, and not a grant. Second, it appears that in neither case was the covenantee expressly identified (in such a way as to exclude the person who is seeking to enforce the covenant).

I consider that the ambit of section 56 is accurately summarised in Megarry and Wade, p. 763:

'The true aim of section 56 seems to be not to allow the third party to sue on a contract merely because it is made for his benefit; the contract must purport to be made *with* him. Just as, under the first part of the section, a person cannot benefit by conveyance unless it purports to be made *to* him (as grantee), so he cannot benefit by a covenant which does not purport to be made *with* him (as covenantee).'

(See also the notes to section 56(1) in Wolstenholme and Cherry's *Conveyancing Statutes*, 13th edn (1972), vol. 1, p. 133.)

Quite apart from this, I agree with Miss Judith Jackson in her submission that the observations of Dillon J in *Lyus v Prowsa Developments Ltd* [1982] 1 WLR 1044, 1049C-E are consistent with the view I have formed. Indeed, I accept her submission that, if I were to decide this point in favour of the plaintiff, my decision would be inconsistent with the conclusion of Dillon J in the passage I have referred to in *Lyus's* case.

His Lordship's third reason was based on the interpretation of the terms of the lease which indicated that the superior landlords were not to have direct rights of enforcement of clauses 3(7) and (8).

In the event, therefore, I consider that it would not be open to Amsprop to enforce the covenants contained in clause 3(7) and (8) directly against the first defendant, even though there is express reference to 'the superior landlords' in those two sub-clauses. From this it must follow that it would not be open to Amsprop to enforce the covenants contained in clause 3(7) and (22) of the underlease, because there is not even any reference to 'the superior landlords' in those two sub-clauses. It must also follow that the plaintiff cannot enforce any of these covenants in these proceedings.

(ii) Contracts (Rights of Third Parties) Act 1999

The Contracts (Rights of Third Parties) Act 1999 has provided an exception to the doctrine of privity of contract.[99] Under the Act, which only applies to contracts

---

[99] On the Act generally, see Emmet, paras 2.091–2.095, 19.004; Blundell Lectures 25th Anniversary Series 2000: The Contracts (Rights of Third Parties) Act 1999 and Its Implications for Property Transactions (A. Burrows and C. Harpum); (1999) 143 SJ 1082 (S. Bright and P. J. G. Williams); [2001] CLJ 353 (N. Andrews); (2004) 120 LQR 292 (R. Stevens); Treitel, pp. 691–708. CFF, pp. 588–593.

entered into on and after 11 May 2000,[100] a third party may be able to enforce in his own right a term of the contract and obtain the remedies that would have been available to him in an action for breach of contract if he had been a party to the contract. As far as land law is concerned, it is relevant in the area of the passing of the benefit of positive and restrictive covenants;[101] and may also be useful in enabling a licensor and a purchaser from him to include a term in their contract which will enable the licensee to enforce his licence against the purchaser.[102]

CONTRACTS (RIGHTS OF THIRD PARTIES) ACT 1999

1. **Right of third party to enforce contractual term.**—(1) Subject to the provisions of this Act, a person who is not a party to a contract (a 'third party') may in his own right enforce a term of the contract if—

    (a) the contract expressly provides that he may, or

    (b) subject to subsection (2), the term purports to confer a benefit on him.

(2) Subsection (1)(b) does not apply if on a proper construction of the contract it appears that the parties did not intend the term to be enforceable by the third party.

(3) The third party must be expressly identified in the contract by name, as a member of a class or as answering a particular description but need not be in existence when the contract is entered into.

(4) This section does not confer a right on a third party to enforce a term of a contract otherwise than subject to and in accordance with any other relevant terms of the contract.[103]

(5) For the purpose of exercising his right to enforce a term of the contract, there shall be available to the third party any remedy that would have been available to him in an action for breach of contract if he had been a party to the contract (and the rules relating to damages, injunctions, specific performance and other relief shall apply accordingly).

In so far as the Act applies to the enforcement of a freehold covenant at common law, there are three observations to make. First, such phrases as 'successors in title' bring the covenant within section 1(3), enabling them to sue directly the original covenantor on the covenant. In this respect the Act is broader than section 56 of the Law of Property Act 1925, above, which requires the beneficiary to be in existence and identifiable at the time when the covenant is made. Secondly, being a contractual and not a land law right, there is no need to satisfy the common law requirement of touching and concerning the land and of a legal estate to be benefited. Thirdly, however, it will only be rarely necessary to invoke the 1999 Act, since in most cases the width of section 78(1) of the Law of Property Act 1925 will suffice to annex to the land the benefit of a covenant which touches and concerns the land of the covenantee.[104]

---

[100] It was possible for parties to contract into it six months before 11 May 2000: s. 10(3).

[101] Since it only allows for the *benefit* of a term to be enforced by a third party, the Act does not affect the rules relating to the running of the burden of a covenant.

[102] P. 1101, n. 204, below.

[103] The parties may therefore contract out of the Act. For subsequent variation or rescission of the contract, see s. 2. On clauses to deal with aspects of the Act, see Conv. Prec. 19-B9.

[104] Pp. 773 (common law) and 783 (equity), below.

B. ENFORCING THE COVENANT AS
A SUCCESSOR AT COMMON LAW

(i) The benefit may run with the land

It has long been held that the benefit of a covenant will run with the land at law in certain circumstances.[105] The rule is thought to have its origin in the old warranties for title which were enforceable not only by the covenantee, but also by his heirs and, later, by assigns; if the warranty were broken, the warrantor would be liable in some cases to provide lands of equal value, in other cases to pay damages.[106] The conditions which are necessary for the benefit of a covenant to run with the land at law are a matter of some doubt, owing to the paucity of modern authority; it is clear however that the covenant will run if the following conditions are complied with.[107]

(i) The covenant must touch and concern the land of the covenantee.[108] It may do this even though the covenantor is a stranger to the land, and there is no servient tenement to be bound by the covenant.[109]

(ii) There must be an intention that the benefit should run with the land owned by the covenantee at the date of the covenant.[110]

(iii) The covenant must have been entered into with the owner of the legal estate in the land to be benefited.[111]

(iv) Before 1926, it was necessary for a person seeking to enforce the covenant to have the same legal estate in the land as the original covenantee,[112] but it has been held that section 78(1) of the Law of Property Act 1925 excludes this last requirement.[113] It may be that the wide interpretation given to that section in *Federated Homes Ltd v Mill Lodge Properties Ltd*[114] will have the effect of

---

[105] *The Prior's Case* (1368) YB 42 Edw 3, fo 3A pl 14; *Smith's Leading Cases* (13th edn, 1929), vol. i, pp. 51, 65, 73.

[106] Simpson, *A History of the Land Law* (2nd edn, 1986), pp. 140–141.

[107] Much of this section is based on (1954) 18 Conv (NS) 546 (E. H. Scamell). It is also sometimes said that the land to be benefited must be expressly identified by the deed containing the covenant. However, there appears to be no authority for this, and if it is a requirement, it is weakened by the operation of the maxim 'id certum est quod certum reddi potest': *Smith and Snipes Hall Farm Ltd v River Douglas Catchment Board* [1949] 2 KB 500 at 508, 517, below.

[108] See p. 744, n. 15, above.

[109] *The Prior's Case,* see n. 105, above; *Smith and Snipes Hall Farm Ltd v River Douglas Catchment Board* [1949] 2 KB 500; and for cases where there is a servient tenement which would not be bound by the covenant, see *Sharp v Waterhouse* (1857) 7 E & B 816; *Shayler v Woolf* [1946] Ch 320.

[110] *Rogers v Hosegood* [1900] 2 Ch 388 at 396; *Shayler v Woolf* [1946] Ch 320; *Smith and Snipes Hall Farm Ltd v River Douglas Catchment Board,* above, at 506.

[111] Co Litt 385a; *Webb v Russell* (1789) 3 Term Rep 393; cf. *Rogers v Hosegood* [1900] 2 Ch 388.

[112] *Westhoughton UDC v Wigan Coal and Iron Co Ltd* [1919] 1 Ch 159.

[113] *Smith and Snipes Hall Farm Ltd v River Douglas Catchment Board,* above.

[114] [1980] 1 WLR 594, where, however, the defendant was the original covenantor and so the enforceability of the covenant did not depend upon *Tulk v Moxhay,* but the application of the equitable

excluding some of the others as well. This was a case dealing with the running of the benefit in equity, which is the context in which the question usually arises because the burdened land will commonly have also been assigned and so the enforceability of the burden depends upon the application (in equity) of the doctrine of *Tulk v Moxhay*.

The common law rules continue to apply in cases not covered by equity, as, for example, where there is no land upon which the burden of the covenant is imposed.[115]

Smith and Snipes Hall Farm Ltd v River Douglas Catchment Board[116]
[1949] 2 KB 500 (CA, **Tucker, Somervell** and **Denning LJJ**)

The defendant Board was the Drainage Authority for a part of Lancashire. In 1938 the Board covenanted under seal with the freehold owners of land within that area that in consideration of the Board's widening, deepening and making good the banks of the Eller Brook, taking control of the Brook and maintaining for all time the work when it was completed, the landowners would contribute to the cost.

In 1940, Mrs Ellen Smith, one of the owners, sold her land, expressly with the benefit of the covenant, to the first plaintiff, John Bruce Smith, who leased it to the second plaintiff under a yearly tenancy. Owing to the faulty work of the defendants, the brook broke its banks, and flooded the land of the plaintiffs. They brought this action in tort and for breach of contract.

Held (reversing Morris J [1948] WN 414). Both plaintiffs could succeed under the contract.[117]

Tucker LJ [having held that the defendants were in breach of the contract and that such breach caused the damage]: . . . It remains to consider whether, in these circumstances, the plaintiffs, or either of them, can sue in respect of this breach. It is said for the defendants that the benefit of the covenant does not run with the land so as to bind a stranger who has not and never had an interest in the land to be benefited and there being no servient tenement to bear the burden. Further, it is contended that such a covenant must by the terms of the deed in which it is contained relate to some specific parcel of land, the precise extent and situation of which can be identified by reference to the deed alone. It is first necessary to ascertain from the deed that the covenant is one which 'touches or concerns' the land, that is, it must either affect the land as regards mode of occupation, or it must be such as per se, and not merely from collateral circumstances, affects the value of the land, and it must then be shown that it was the intention

---

rules was necessary because the plaintiff had taken an assignment of part only of the land from the original covenantee; see pp. 783, 796, below.

[115] See p. 755, above.   [116] See (1981) 97 LQR 32, at pp. 43–47 (G. H. Newsom).

[117] The action in tort did not therefore arise for decision and no decision was reached on that point. The plaintiffs would have found it necessary to distinguish the House of Lords case of *East Suffolk Rivers Catchment Board v Kent* [1941] AC 74, on which see Markesinis and Deakin's *Tort Law* (6th edn, 2008), pp. 209, 406–410.

of the parties that the benefit thereof should run with the land. In this case the deed shews that its object was to improve the drainage of land liable to flooding and prevent future flooding. The location of the land is described as situate between the Leeds and Liverpool Canal and the River Douglas and adjoining the Eller Brook. In return for lump sum payments the board covenants to do certain work to the banks of the Eller Brook, one of such banks being in fact situate upon and forming part of the plaintiffs' lands, and to maintain for all time the work when completed. In my view the language of the deed satisfies both tests. It affects the value of the land per se and converts it from flooded meadows to land suitable for agriculture, and shows an intention that the benefit of the obligation to maintain shall attach thereto into whosesoever hands the lands shall come.

With regard to the covenantor being a stranger the case of *The Prior* is referred to in *Spencer's* case, in these words: 'In the case of a grandfather, father and two sons, the grandfather being seised of the manor of D, whereof a chapel was parcel: a prior with the assent of his convent, by deed covenanted for him and his successors, with the grandfather and his heirs that he and his convent would sing all the week in his chapel, parcel of the said manor, for the lords of the said manor and his servants, etc.; the grandfather did enfeoff one of the manor in fee, who gave it to the younger son and his wife in tail; and it was adjudged that the tenants in tail, as terre-tenants (for the elder brother was heir), should have an action of covenant against the prior, for the covenant is to do a thing which is annexed to the chapel, which is within the manor, and so annexed to the manor, as it is there said.' ...

In *Rogers v Hosegood* [1900] 2 Ch 388, 395, Farwell J, in a passage where he refers, amongst others, to *The Prior's* case—and I quote from Farwell J's judgment because, although this case went to the Court of Appeal, his judgment was approved, and the Court of Appeal had to deal with a rather different point—after stating what are the requirements in order that the covenant may run with the land, proceeds: 'It is not contended that the covenants in question in this case have not the first characteristic, but it is said that they fail in the second. I am of opinion that they possess both. Adopting the definition of Bayley J in *Congleton Corpn v Pattison* (1808) 10 East 130, 135, the covenant must either affect the land as regards mode of occupation, or it must be such as per se, and not merely from collateral circumstances, affects the value of the land. It is to my mind obvious that the value of Sir J Millais's land is directly increased by the covenants in question. If authority is needed, I would refer to *Mann v Stephens* (1846) 15 Sim 377, a case very similar to the present; *Vyvyan v Arthur* (1823) 1 B & C 410; *The Prior's* case; *Fleetwood v Hull* (1889) 23 QBD 35; *White v Southend Hotel Co* [1897] 1 Ch 767. I see no difficulty in holding that the benefit of a covenant runs with the land of the covenantee, while the burden of the same covenant does not run with the land of the covenantor.'

In this state of the authorities it seems clear, despite some dicta tending to the contrary view, that such a covenant if it runs with the land is binding on the covenantor though a mere stranger, and that this point will not avail the defendant board. As to the requirement that the deed containing the covenant must expressly identify the particular land to be benefited, no authority was cited to us and in the absence of such authority I can see no valid reason why the maxim 'Id certum est quod certum reddi potest' should not apply, so as to make admissible extrinsic evidence to prove the extent and situation of the lands of the respective land owners adjoining the Eller Brook situate between the Leeds and Liverpool Canal and the River Douglas.

... I have accordingly arrived at the conclusion that the covenant by the board in the agreement of 25 April 1938 is one which runs with the land referred to therein, which land is capable of identification, and that it is binding on the defendant board; and, further, that by virtue of section 78 of the Law of Property Act 1925,[118] it can be enforced at the suit of the covenantee and her successors in title and the persons deriving title under her or them, so that both the plaintiff Smith and the plaintiff company can sue in respect of the damage resulting to their respective interests therein by reason of the defendants' breach of covenant.

Denning LJ: The law on this subject was fully expounded by Mr Smith in his note in *Spencer's* case which has always been regarded as authoritative. Such covenants [made with the owner of the land to which they relate] are clearly intended, and usually expressed, to be for the benefit of whomsoever should be the owner of the land for the time being; and at common law each successive owner has a sufficient interest to sue because he holds the same estate as the original owner. The reason which Lord Coke gave for this rule is the reason which underlies the whole of the principle now under consideration. He said in his work upon Littleton that it was 'to give damages to the party grieved'. If a successor in title were not allowed to sue it would mean that the covenantor could break his contract with impunity, for it is clear that the original owner, after he has parted with the land, could recover no more than nominal damages for any breach that occurred thereafter. It was always held, however, at common law that, in order that a successor in title should be entitled to sue, he must be of the same estate as the original owner. That alone was a sufficient interest to entitle him to enforce the contract. The covenant was supposed to be made for the benefit of the owner and his successors in title, and not for the benefit of anyone else. This limitation, however, was, as is pointed out in Smith's Leading Cases, capable of being 'productive of very serious and disagreeable consequences', and it has been removed by section 78 of the Law of Property Act 1925, which provides that a covenant relating to any land of the covenantee shall be deemed to be made with the covenantee and his successors in title, 'and the persons deriving title under him or them' and shall have effect as if such successors 'and other persons' were expressed.

The covenant of the catchment board in this case clearly relates to the land of the covenantees. It was a covenant to do work on the land for the benefit of the land. By the statute, therefore, it is to be deemed to be made, not only with the original owner, but also with the purchasers of the land and their tenants as if they were expressed. Now if they were expressed, it would be clear that the covenant was made for their benefit; and they clearly have sufficient interest to entitle them to enforce it because they have suffered the damage. The result is that the plaintiffs come within the principle whereby a person interested can sue on a contract expressly made for his benefit.

In **Williams v Unit Construction Co Ltd**[119] the question again arose whether section 78 of the Law of Property Act 1925[120] allowed the benefit of a restrictive covenant to pass at law in favour of persons who did not hold the same legal estate as the original covenantee. Counsel argued that a decision to that effect could only be taken by a court which was prepared also to hold that section 79 would have the same effect upon the burden; in other words, to hold that, since 1925, 'successors in title and persons deriving title under him or them' would be bound by the burden of the covenant. The Court of Appeal declined to express a view on the effect of section 79[121] upon the

---

[118] P. 783, below.
[119] Unreported, but discussed in (1955) 19 Conv (NS) 262 (W. L. Blease).
[120] See p. 783, above.   [121] On the application of s. 79, see p. 761, above.

burden—the point not being before the court—and followed *Smith and Snipes Hall Farm Ltd v River Douglas Catchment Board.*

Similarly, in **Federated Homes Ltd v Mill Lodge Properties Ltd** [1980] 1 WLR 594 Brightman LJ said at 606:

We were referred to observations in the speeches of Lord Upjohn and Lord Wilberforce in *Sefton v Tophams Ltd* [1967] 1 AC 50, 73 and 81, to the effect that section 79 ... achieved no more than the introduction of statutory shorthand into the drafting of covenants. Section 79, in my view, involves quite different considerations and I do not think that it provides a helpful analogy.[122]

(ii) Enforcing the covenant as assignee

If the benefit of the covenant is not annexed to the land at common law, it may be transferred by assignment. To be effective at law, an assignment must be in writing, and express notice in writing must be given to the covenantor.

LAW OF PROPERTY ACT 1925

136. Legal assignments of things in action.—(1) Any absolute assignment by writing under the hand of the assignor (not purporting to be byway of charge only) of any debt or other legal thing in action, of which express notice in writing has been given to the debtor ... is effectual in law (subject to equities having priority over the right of the assignee) to pass and transfer from the date of such notice—

(a) the legal right to such debt or thing in action;

(b) all legal and other remedies for the same; and

(c) the power to give a good discharge for the same without the concurrence of the assignor ...

C. ENFORCING THE COVENANT AS A SUCCESSOR IN EQUITY

We have seen that the benefit of a covenant would run at law in certain circumstances. But there are some situations outside the limits of the common law where the benefit would run in equity. Generally, equity follows the law, and this development is probably an elucidation of the rules of common law, rather than a separate contribution of equity.[123]

The situations in which the equitable rules must be observed are these:

(i)   where the claimant or the original covenantee was an equitable owner;[124]

---

[122] The case held that s. 78 effected an annexation of the benefit of the covenant in equity; p. 783, below. See also M & W, para. 32.013; W & C vol. i, 162–163; (1956) 20 Conv (NS) 43, 52 (D. W. Elliott); [1972 B] CLJ 157 at pp. 171–175 (H. W. R. Wade); Emmet, para. 19.006.

[123] (1938) 6 CLJ 339 (S. J. Bailey).

[124] *Fairclough v Marshall* (1878) 4 Ex D 37; *Rogers v Hosegood* [1900] 2 Ch 388 (a mortgagor before 1926), p. 780, below.

(ii)   (subject to section 78 of the Law of Property Act 1925) where the claimant does not have the same legal estate as the covenantee;[125]

(iii) where the servient land has been assigned, and enforcement depends on the doctrine of *Tulk v Moxhay*;[126]

(iv)   where the claimant relies upon an express assignment of the benefit of the covenant without compliance with the requirements of section 136 of the Law of Property Act 1925;[127]

(v)   where the claimant takes an assignment of part of the land only, for 'at law, the benefit could not be assigned in pieces. It would have to be assigned as a whole or not at all',[128]

(vi)   where the claimant relies upon his land being part of a scheme of development.

A purchaser of land may show that the benefit of a restrictive covenant has passed to him in one of three ways.

In **Re Pinewood Estate, Farnborough** [1958] Ch 280[129] WYNN-PARRY J, said at 284:

I propose first to consider whether there is in existence what is known as a building scheme affecting this area of land which is clearly ascertained; because, if there is an existing building scheme, fulfilling the conditions laid down by Parker J in *Elliston v Reacher* [1908] 2 Ch 374; affd. [1908] 2 Ch 665 [p. 809, below], then the respondent and the other persons interested will have the benefit of the covenants in the deed...

His Lordship considered the evidence and concluded that there was no building scheme in existence.

It is admitted by Mr Newsom that she could claim the benefit of the restrictive covenants if it could be shown either that the benefit had been annexed by proper words of annexation, or that there was a complete chain of assignments of the benefit of the covenants; but it is conceded on behalf of the respondent that there are no words of annexation, and it is conceded that the chain is not complete. In those circumstances, what the respondent says is that she is entitled to the benefit of the restrictive provisions because it is a deed which shows clearly by its language an intention that the parties should be mutually bound by the restrictions, and that that element of mutuality is enough to carry the benefit of the restrictive stipulations. That means that they

---

[125] *The Prior's Case* (1368) YB 42 Edw 3, fo 3A pl 14; *Smith's Leading Cases* (13th edn, 1929), vol. i, pp. 51, 65, 73. S. 78 LPA 1925 removes this limitation for covenants entered into after 1925: *Smith and Snipes Hall Farm Ltd v River Douglas Catchment Board* [1949] 2 KB 500, p. 774, above.

[126] *Renals v Cowlishaw* (1878) 9 ChD 125, p. 782, below; *Re Union of London and Smith's Bank Ltd's Conveyance, Miles v Easter* [1933] Ch 611, per Romer J at 630, p. 798, below; *Marten v Flight Refuelling Ltd* [1962] Ch 115, p. 803, below.

[127] *Re Union of London and Smith's Bank Ltd's Conveyance, Miles v Easter*, above; *Newton Abbot Co-operative Society Ltd v Williamson and Treadgold Ltd* [1952] Ch 286, p. 799, below; *Stilwell v Blackman* [1968] Ch 508.

[128] *Re Union of London and Smith's Bank Ltd's Conveyance*, above, at 630 per Romer LJ; *Federated Homes Ltd v Mill Lodge Properties Ltd* [1980] 1 WLR 594, p. 783, below.

[129] [1957] CLJ 146 (H. W. R. Wade).

are endeavouring to set up a further method by which the benefit of restrictive stipulations can be transferred....

The real question is: Is there a fourth class at all? The first class is the *Elliston v Reacher* type of case; the second consists of cases where there are proper words of annexation; the third consists of cases where there is a continuous chain of express assignments. But is there a fourth class?...

But I can find no authority, certainly none was cited to me, which establishes the fourth class suggested. In my opinion, therefore, it is not open either to the respondent or to anybody else upon this line of reasoning to rely on these restrictive covenants.

(i) By annexation

Whether or not the benefit of a restrictive covenant has been annexed to the land of the covenantee depends upon the intention of the parties, as construed from the language of the conveyance.[130] If such an intention is manifested, the benefit of the covenant is notionally annexed to the land to be benefited; and the benefit of the covenant then passes automatically on an assignment of the covenantee's land.

This situation is contrasted with a covenant whose terms fail to manifest such an intention. The benefit of such a covenant is available, by the contract, to the covenantee; but is only available to successors in title of the covenantee if the benefit of the covenant has been expressly assigned at the time of the conveyance; and, in the case of a series of assignments of the land, it is necessary to show that there has been a similar 'chain of assignments' of the benefit of the covenant.

The leading cases illustrating these rules were *Rogers v Hosegood* [1900] 2 Ch 388, where annexation was achieved; and *Renals v Cowlishaw* [1878] 9 ChD 125, where it failed. Describing the methods of annexation, GREENE LJ said in *Drake v Gray* [1936] Ch 451 at 466:

There are two familiar methods of indicating in a covenant of this kind the land in respect of which the benefit is to enure. One is to describe the character in which the covenantee receives the covenant. That is the form which is adopted here, a covenant with so and so, owners or owner for the time being of whatever the land may be. Another method is to state by means of an appropriate declaration that the covenant is taken 'for the benefit of' whatever the lands may be.[131]

The language which succeeded in effecting an annexation in *Rogers v Hosegood* was in this form: 'with intent that the covenants...might enure for the benefit of the [vendors]...their heirs and assigns and others claiming under them to all or any of their lands adjoining or near to the said premises.' It has never been suggested that this precise form of words is necessary; what is needed is a manifestation of an intention to annex. Would annexation be effected if the covenant were made in the following form?

---

[130] See *Re MCA East Ltd* [2003] 1 P & CR 9.
[131] The relevant date for identifying the benefited land is that of transfer not registration: *Mellon v Sinclair* [1996] CL January 560.

'With the covenantee and his successors in title (including the owners and occupiers for the time being of the land of the covenantee intended to be benefited) and the persons deriving title under him or them'? If such a covenant would be effective to annex the benefit of the covenant, annexation would appear to be effected in every case; for, by section 78 of the Law of Property Act 1925, every covenant 'relating to the land of the covenantee' shall be deemed to be made in that form—that is, section 78 implies into the conveyance words which are sufficient to annex the benefit of the covenant to the land. And the problem of determining whether the express language of the conveyance is sufficient to manifest an intention to annex then disappears. That is the decision in *Federated Homes Ltd v Mill Lodge Properties Ltd* [1980] 1 WLR 594, p. 783, below.[132]

(a) Construction of the instrument

Rogers v Hosegood

[1900] 2 Ch 388 (Ch D, **Farwell J**; affd, CA, **Lord Alverstone MR, Rigby** and **Collins LJJ**)

Four partners, carrying on business as builders, were the owners in fee simple, subject to a mortgage, of land at Palace Gate, Kensington. One plot was sold in 1869 to the Duke of Bedford who entered into a covenant 'with intent that the covenants... might so far as possible bind the premises thereby conveyed and every part thereof and might enure to the benefit of [the vendors]... their heirs and assigns and others claiming under them to all or any of their lands adjoining or near to the said premises'... that 'no more than one messuage or dwelling house... should at any one time be erected or be standing on the... plot...'. In 1872, a nearby plot was sold, and in 1873 conveyed to Sir John Millais, who had no knowledge of the covenant given by the Duke. Successors in title of the Duke by purchase proposed, in breach of the restrictive covenant, to erect, on this and adjoining plots, a large building which was to be occupied as residential flats. Among various actions, the trustees of the will of Sir John Millais claimed an injunction to restrain the defendants from erecting the block of flats.

Held. The plaintiffs were entitled to enforce the covenant.

Collins LJ (reading the judgment of the court): This case raises questions of some difficulty, but we are of opinion that the decision of Farwell J is right, and ought to be affirmed.... The real and only difficulty arises on the question—whether the benefit of the covenants has passed to the assigns of Sir John Millais as owners of the plot purchased by him on March 25, 1873, there

---

[132] There is no suggestion of a wide construction of s. 78 in Sir Benjamin Cherry's book (Wolstenholme and Cherry's *Conveyancing Statutes* (11th edn, 1925)). See also the 30th Anniversary Blundell Lecture (27 June 2005), where Neuberger LJ, whilst noting that the decision in *Crest Nicholson Residential (South) Ltd v McAllister* [2004] 1 WLR 2409, p. 790, below, confirms that *Federated Homes* is authority for the wider construction, which renders the law much simpler and clearer, said that 'there do seem to be pretty formidable arguments... for doubting the correctness of the decision in *Federated Homes*', especially the failure to repeat in s. 78 the annexation formulae in the two preceding sections, ss. 76 and 77: [1982] JPL 295; (1982) 98 LQR 202 (G. H. Newsom and E.H.B.).

being no evidence that he knew of these covenants when he bought.[133] Here, again, the difficulty is narrowed, because by express declaration on the face of the conveyances of 1869 the benefit of the two covenants in question was intended for all or any of the vendor's lands near to or adjoining the plot sold, and therefore for (among others) the plot of land acquired by Sir John Millais, and that they 'touched and concerned' that land within the meaning of those words so as to run with the land at law we do not doubt. Therefore, but for a technical difficulty which was not raised before Farwell J, we should agree with him that the benefit of the covenants in question was annexed to and passed to Sir John Millais by the conveyance of the land which he bought in 1873. A difficulty, however, in giving effect to this view arises from the fact that the covenants in question in the deeds of May and July 1869 were made with the mortgagors only, and therefore in contemplation of law were made with strangers to the land: *Webb v Russell* (1789) 3 Term Rep 393, to which, therefore, the benefit did not become annexed. That a court of equity, however, would not regard such an objection as defeating the intention of the parties to the covenant is clear; and, therefore, when the covenant was clearly made for the benefit of certain land with a person who, in the contemplation of such a court was the true owner of it, it would be regarded as annexed to and running with that land, just as it would have been at law but for the technical difficulty....

These observations [referring to observations of Jessel MR in *London and South Western Rly Co v Gomm* (1882) 20 ChD 562, 583] which are just as applicable to the benefit reserved as to the burden imposed, shew that in equity, just as at law, the first point to be determined is whether the covenant or contract in its inception binds the land. If it does, it is then capable of passing with the land to subsequent assignees... of the land. The benefit may be annexed to one plot and the burden to another, and when this has been once clearly done, the benefit and the burden pass to the respective assignees, subject, in the case of the burden, to proof that the legal estate, if acquired, has been acquired with notice of the covenant....

His Lordship then referred to *Renals v Cowlishaw* (1878) 9 ChD 125, 130, below and *Child v Douglas* (1854) Kay 560, 571.

These authorities establish the proposition that, when the benefit has been once clearly annexed to one piece of land, it passes by assignment of that land, and may be said to run with it, in contemplation as well of equity as of law, without proof of special bargain or representation on the assignment. In such a case it runs, not because the conscience of either party is affected, but because the purchaser has bought something which inhered in or was annexed to the land bought. This is the reason why, in dealing with the burden, the purchaser's conscience is not affected by notice of covenants which were part of the original bargain or on the first sale, but were merely personal and collateral, while it is affected by notice of those which touch and concern the land. The covenant must be one that is capable of running with the land before the question of the purchaser's conscience and the equity affecting it can come into discussion. When, as in *Renals v Cowlishaw*, there is no indication in the original conveyance, or in the circumstances attending it, that the burden of the restrictive covenant is imposed for the benefit of the land reserved, or any particular part of it, then it becomes necessary to examine the circumstances under which any part of the land reserved is sold, in order to see whether a benefit, not originally annexed to it, has become annexed to it on the sale, so that the purchaser is deemed to have

---

[133] See *R v Westminster City Council and London Electricity Board* (1989) 59 P & CR 51 (benefit described as 'a hidden treasure in the hands of the present owner (whoever he may be) of Tulk's retained land').

bought it with the land, and this can hardly be the case when the purchaser did not know of the existence of the restrictive covenant. But when, as here, it has been once annexed to the land reserved, then it is not necessary to spell an intention out of surrounding facts, such as the existence of a building scheme, statements at auctions, and such like circumstances, and the presumption must be that it passes on a sale of that land, unless there is something to rebut it, and the purchaser's ignorance of the existence of the covenant does not defeat the presumption. We can find nothing in the conveyance to Sir John Millais in any degree inconsistent with the intention to pass to him the benefit already annexed to the land sold to him. We are of opinion, therefore, that Sir John Millais's assigns are entitled to enforce the restrictive covenant against the defendant, and that his appeal must be dismissed.

In **J Sainsbury plc v Enfield London Borough Council** [1989] 1 WLR 590,[134] where there was no reference in the covenant either to the covenantee's land or to his successors in title other than his assigns, MORRITT J held that 'the intention must be manifested in the conveyance in which the covenant was contained when construed in the light of the surrounding circumstances, including any necessary implication in the conveyance from those surrounding circumstances.' He rejected a claim that 'such intention may be inferred from surrounding circumstances which fall short of those which necessitate an implication in the conveyance itself.'

Rogers v Hosegood is to be contrasted with **Renals v Cowlishaw** (1878) 9 ChD 125, the difference turning on the language of the covenant. In *Renals v Cowlishaw* trustees sold lands to a purchaser who covenanted 'for himself, his heirs, executors and administrators' with the trustees 'their heirs, executors, administrators, and assigns' that he would not use the lands in certain ways. The lands purchased were later sold to other purchasers who took with notice of the covenant. And the trustees later sold their retained land to the plaintiffs, no mention being made of the covenant in this conveyance.

The question was whether the benefit of the covenant had passed to the plaintiffs. Hall V-C (affirmed by the Court of Appeal (1879) 11 ChD 866) held that it had not. There was no building scheme, no express assignment of the benefit of the covenant; and the language of the covenant was inadequate to annex the benefit of the covenant to the plaintiffs' land.

The modern practice is to draft the covenant so as to manifest an intention to annex the benefit of the covenant to the land retained by the vendor; unless the vendor wishes to retain the power to choose which of his later purchasers shall be given the benefit (by expressly assigning it[135]). Correct drafting may no longer be important, however,

---

134 P. 786, n. 140, below. [1991] Conv 52 (S. Goulding). See also *Shropshire County Council v Edwards* (1982) 46 P & CR 270, where Judge Rubin held that, on the construction of a covenant made in 1908, the benefit had been annexed: *R v Westminster City Council and London Electricity Board* (1989) 59 P & CR 51, p. 754, n. 78.

135 *Marquess of Zetland v Driver* [1937] Ch 651; [1939] Ch 1; *Federated Homes Ltd v Mill Lodge Properties Ltd* [1980] 1 WLR 594 at 606, per Brightman LJ; *Roake v Chadha* [1984] 1 WLR 40, p. 787, below; *Crest Nicholson Residential (South) Ltd v McAllister* [2004] 1 WLR 2409.

because it has been held that section 78 of the Law of Property Act 1925 supplies the words necessary to effect annexation.[136]

(b) Law of Property Act 1925, section 78

LAW OF PROPERTY ACT 1925

78. Benefit of covenants relating to land.—(1) A covenant relating to any land of the covenantee shall be deemed to be made with the covenantee and his successors in title and the persons deriving title under him or them, and shall have effect as if such successors and other persons were expressed.

For the purposes of this subsection in connexion with covenants restrictive of the user of land 'successors in title' shall be deemed to include the owners and occupiers for the time being of the land of the covenantee intended to be benefited.

(2) This section applies to covenants made after the commencement of this Act, but the repeal of section fifty-eight of the Conveyancing Act, 1881, does not affect the operation of covenants to which that section applied.

Federated Homes Ltd v Mill Lodge Properties Ltd
[1980] 1 WLR 594 (CA, **Megaw, Browne** and **Brightman LJJ**)[137]

Mackenzie Hill Ltd owned land which was to be the subject of a large development in Newport Pagnell in Buckinghamshire. Planning permission was obtained in 1970, and was valid for 3 years. The building programme was phased, and was subject to restrictions upon the overall density of the number of houses to be built on the area. The present litigation arises out of sales by Mackenzie Hill Ltd of three parts of the land; the blue, the red and the green.

The blue land was sold to Mill Lodge Properties Ltd, the defendant company, subject to various conditions, the one relevant for present purposes being the following covenant:

'The Purchaser hereby covenants with the Vendor that... (iv) in carrying out the development of the "blue" land the Purchaser shall not build at a greater density than a total of 300 dwellings so as not to reduce the number of units which the Vendor might eventually erect on the retained land under the existing planning consent.'

The red and green lands were also sold, and the plaintiff company eventually became the owner of each. It will be seen that the terms of the covenant were not such as, from the express language of the covenant, to annex the benefit of the covenant to the land of the covenantee under the rule in *Rogers v Hosegood*. There was, however, a complete chain of assignments of the benefit of the covenant, through the various purchasers to the plaintiff, in the case of the *green* land. But not in the case of the red land.

---

[136] *Federated Homes Ltd v Mill Lodge Properties Ltd,* below.
[137] [1980] JPL 371; (1981) 97 LQR 32; JPL 149; (1982) 98 LQR 202 (G. H. Newsom); (1980) 43 MLR 445 (D. J. Hayton); 130 NLJ 531 (T. Bailey); (1982) 2 LS (D. J. Hurst); C & B, pp. 680–683, esp. nn. 131, 135; M & W, paras 32.063–32.064; *Robins v Berkeley Homes (Kent) Ltd* [1996] EGCS 75.

The question was whether the plaintiffs could sue to restrain the breach of the defendants' covenant relating to building density.

Held. The plaintiff company was entitled to the benefit of the covenant in respect of the *green* land by reason of the completed chain of assignments; in respect of the *red* land, because section 78(1) had the effect of annexing the benefit of the covenant to all or any part of the land of the covenantee.

Brightman LJ: In September 1978, after much prevarication on the part of Mill Lodge, the plaintiff issued a writ to restrain Mill Lodge from building on the blue land at a greater density than a total of 300 dwellings in breach, it was alleged, of clause 5(iv) of the Mill Lodge conveyance. The defences raised by Mill Lodge so far as relied upon in this appeal were as follows: (1) the covenant in clause 5(iv) was said to be personal to Mackenzie Hill so that the benefit thereof was incapable of assignment to the plaintiff; (2) alternatively, it was said that the covenant became spent when the 1970 planning permission became void at the end of the three-year period; and (3) it was said that, if the covenant was assignable and was not spent, then the benefit had not become vested in the plaintiff by assignment or otherwise.

That, in broad effect, was now the defence was pleaded so far as relevant for present purposes. In a reserved judgment Mr Mills held that the covenant was not personal to Mackenzie Hill and was not spent when the original planning permission lapsed. As regards the transmission of the benefit of the covenant, he held that the benefit was not annexed to the red and the green land, so that it did not automatically pass upon conveyances of the red and the green land. However, he found, as was clearly the fact, that there was an unbroken chain of assignments between transferor and transferee of the green land, so that the benefit of the covenant was now vested, by reason of such assignments, in the plaintiff as the present owner of the green land. There was no such unbroken chain of assignments in the case of the red land; but the judge considered that section 62 of the Law of Property Act 1925, which implies general words into a conveyance of land, was apt to carry the benefit of the covenant from U.D.T. Properties Ltd., the previous assignee of such benefit, to the plaintiff when the registered transfer in its favour was made.[138] The defence, therefore, failed. The judge rejected a submission that damages would be the proper remedy. He granted an injunction against building in excess of the permitted density and gave liberty to apply for a mandatory injunction.

I deal first with the question of construction, upon which two issues arise: whether the covenant was personal to Mackenzie Hill, and whether it is spent.

His Lordship decided that the covenant was not personal to Mackenzie Hill; nor was the covenant 'spent' by the lapse of the planning permission in 1973.

Having reached the conclusion that the restrictive covenant was capable of assignment and is not spent, I turn to the question whether the benefit has safely reached the hands of the plaintiff. The green land has no problem, owing to the unbroken chain of assignments. I am disposed to think that is sufficient to entitle the plaintiff to relief, and that the plaintiff's right to relief would be no greater at the present time if it were held that it also had the benefit of the covenant in its capacity as owner of the red land. However, the judge dealt with both areas of land and I propose to do the same.

---

[138] See *Roake v Chadha* [1984] 1 WLR 40 at 47, p. 787, below.

An express assignment of the benefit of a covenant is not necessary if the benefit of the covenant is annexed to the land. In that event, the benefit will pass automatically on a conveyance of the land, without express mention, because it is annexed to the land and runs with it. So the issue of annexation is logically the next to be considered....

In my judgment the benefit of this covenant was annexed to the retained land, and I think that this is a consequence of section 78 of the Act of 1925....

His Lordship read this section and continued:

Mr Price submitted that there were three possible views about section 78. One view, which he described as 'the orthodox view' hitherto held, is that it is merely a statutory shorthand for reducing the length of legal documents. A second view, which was the one that Mr Price was inclined to place in the forefront of his argument, is that the section only applies, or at any rate only achieves annexation, when the land intended to be benefited is signified in the document by express words or necessary implication as the intended beneficiary of the covenant.[139] A third view is that the section applies if the covenant in fact touches and concerns the land of the covenantee, whether that be gleaned from the document itself or from evidence outside the document.

For myself, I reject the narrowest interpretation of section 78, the supposed orthodox view, which seems to me to fly in the face of the wording of the section. Before I express my reasons I will say that I do not find it necessary to choose between the second and third views because, in my opinion, this covenant relates to land of the covenantee on either interpretation of section 78. Clause 5(iv) shows clearly that the covenant is for the protection of the retained land and that land is described in clause 2 as 'any adjoining or adjacent property retained by the vendor.' This formulation is sufficient for annexation purposes: see *Rogers v Hosegood* [1900] 2 Ch 388 [p. 780, above].

There is in my judgment no doubt that this covenant 'related to the land of the covenantee,' or, to use the old-fashioned expression, that it touched and concerned the land, even if Mr Price is correct in his submission that the document must show an intention to benefit identified land. The result of such application is that one must read clause 5(iv) as if it were written: 'The purchaser hereby covenants with the vendor and its successors in title and the persons deriving title under it or them, including the owners and occupiers for the time being of the retained land, that in carrying out the development of the blue land the purchaser shall not build at a greater density than a total 300 dwellings so as not to reduce, etc.' I leave out of consideration section 79 as unnecessary to be considered in this context, since Mill Lodge is the original covenantor.

The first point to notice about section 78 (1) is that the wording is significantly different from the wording of its predecessor section 58(1) of the Conveyancing Act 1881. The distinction is underlined by section 78(2), which applies section 78(1) only to covenants made after the commencement of the Act. Section 58(1) of the Act of 1881 did not include the covenantee's successors in title or persons deriving title under him or them, or the owner or occupiers for the time being of the land of the covenantee intended to be benefited. The section was confined, in

---

[139] See *Bridges v Harrow London Borough Council* (1981) 260 EG 284, where Stuart-Smith J held that, even if this second and stricter view were preferable, the plaintiff failed as there was no such signification in the document; [1982] Conv 313 (F. Webb). Cf. *Crest Nicholson Residential (South) Ltd v McAllister* [2004] 1 WLR 2409, p. 790, below, at paras 43–44, per Chadwick LJ, where CA applied the second view.

relation to realty, to the covenantee, his heirs and assigns, words which suggest a more limited scope of operation than is found in section 78.[140]

If, as the language of section 78 implies a covenant relating to land which is restrictive of the user thereof is enforceable at the suit of (1) a successor in title of the covenantee, (2) a person deriving title under the covenantee or under his successors in title, and (3) the owner or occupier of the land intended to be benefited by the covenant, it must, in my view, follow that the covenant runs with the land, because ex hypothesi every successor in title to the land, every derivative proprietor of the land and every other owner and occupier has a right by statute to the covenant. In other words, if the condition precedent of section 78 is satisfied— that is to say, there existed a covenant which touches and concerns the land of the covenantee—that covenant runs with the land for the benefit of his successors in title, persons deriving title under him or them and other owners and occupiers.

This approach to section 78 has been advocated by distinguished textbook writers; see Dr Radcliffe's article 'Some Problems of the Law Relating to Restrictive Covenants' (1941) 57 LQR 203, Professor Wade's article, 'Covenants—A Broad and Reasonable View' and the apt cross-heading 'What is wrong with section 78?' [1972B] CLJ 151, 171, and Megarry and Wade, *The Law of Real Property,* 4th edn (1975), p. 764. Counsel pointed out to us that the fourth edition of Megarry and Wade indicates a change of mind on this topic since the third edition.

Although the section does not seem to have been extensively used in the course of argument in this type of case, the construction of section 78 which appeals to me appears to be consistent with at least two cases decided in this court. The first is *Smith and Snipes Hall Farm Ltd v River Douglas Catchment Board* [1949] 2 KB 500 [p. 774, above]. In that case an agreement was made in April 1938 between certain landowners and the catchment board under which the catchment board undertook to make good the banks of a certain brook and to maintain the same, and the landowners undertook to contribute towards the cost. In 1940 the first plaintiff took a conveyance from one of the landowners of a part of the land together with an express assignment of the benefit of the agreement. In 1944 the second plaintiff took a tenancy of that land without any express assignment of the benefit of the agreement. In 1946 the brook burst its banks and the land owned by the first plaintiff and tenanted by the second plaintiff was inundated. The two important points are that the agreement was not expressed to be for the benefit of the landowner's successors in title; and there was no assignment of the benefit of the agreement in favour of the second plaintiff, the tenant. In reliance, as I understand the case, upon section 78 of the Act of 1925, it was held that the second plaintiff was entitled to sue the catchment board for damages for breach of the agreement. It seems to me that that conclusion can only have been reached on the basis that section 78 had the effect of causing the benefit of the agreement to run with the land so as to be capable of being sued upon by the tenant.

The other case, *Williams v Unit Construction Co Ltd* (unreported in the usual series of law reports but fully set out in 19 Conveyancer 262 [p. 776, above]), was decided by this court in 1951. There a company had acquired a building estate and had underleased four plots to Cubbin for 999 years. The underlessors arranged for the defendant company to build houses on the four plots. The defendant covenanted with Cubbin to keep the adjacent road in repair until adopted.

---

140 In *J Sainsbury plc v Enfield London Borough Council* [1989] 1 WLR 590, Morritt J held that the benefit of a covenant made in 1894 was not annexed by s. 58 of the Conveyancing and Law of Property Act 1881.

Cubbin granted a weekly tenancy of one house to the plaintiff without any express assignment of the benefit of the covenant. The plaintiff was injured owing to the disrepair of the road. She was held entitled to recover damages from the defendant for breach of the covenant.

We were referred to observations in the speeches of Lord Upjohn and Lord Wilberforce in *Sefton v Tophams Ltd* [1967] 1 AC 50, 73 and 81, to the effect that section 79 of the Act of 1925, relating to the burden of covenants, achieved no more than the introduction of statutory shorthand into the drafting of covenants. Section 79, in my view, involves quite different considerations and I do not think that it provides a helpful analogy.

It was suggested by Mr Price that, if this covenant ought to be read as enuring for the benefit of the retained land, it should be read as enuring only for the benefit of the retained land as a whole and not for the benefit of every part of it; with the apparent result that there is no annexation of the benefit to a part of the retained land when any severance takes place. He referred us to a passage in *Re Union of London and Smith's Bank Ltd's Conveyance* [1933] Ch 611, 628 [p. 798, below], which I do not think it is necessary for me to read....

I find the idea of the annexation of a covenant to the whole of the land but not to a part of it a difficult conception fully to grasp....[The discussion of this question is postponed to section (d), p. 796, below].

In the end, I come to the conclusion that section 78 of the Law of Property Act 1925 caused the benefit of the restrictive covenant in question to run with the red land and therefore to be annexed to it, with the result that the plaintiff is able to enforce the covenant against Mill Lodge, not only in its capacity as owner of the green land, but also in its capacity as owner of the red land.

For these reasons I think that the judge reached the correct view on the right of the plaintiff to enforce the covenant, although in part he arrived there by a different route.

In **Roake v Chadha** [1984] 1 WLR 40[141] a part of the Sudbury Court Estate in North Wembley was sold and conveyed to Wembley (C and W) Land Co Ltd, who then proceeded to lay out the land in lots and sell them off, using a standard form of transfer. In April 1934 William Lambert purchased one plot, No 4, Audrey Gardens, and covenanted not to erect any building on the plot apart from one private dwelling-house. The covenant contained the words 'so as to bind (so far as practicable) the land hereby transferred into whosesoever hands the same may come... but so that this covenant shall not enure for the benefit of any owner or subsequent purchaser of any part of the vendors' Sudbury Court Estate at Wembley unless the benefit of this covenant shall be expressly assigned.'

The defendant was the successor in title to William Lambert, and was proposing to erect an additional house on his plot. The plaintiffs were successors in title to Wembley (C & W) Land Co Ltd; they had subsequently purchased neighbouring plots, but had not had the benefit of the covenant expressly assigned to them.

---

[141] [1984] Conv 68 (P. N. Todd); [1983] All ER Rev 231 (P. J. Clarke). The decision was approved by CA in *Crest Nicholson Residential (South) Ltd v McAllister* [2004] 1 WLR 2409 at paras 37–42. See also *Mahon v Sims* [2005] 3 EGLR 67 (requirement that covenantor obtain consent of 'the Transferor' before carrying out work; on construction, this was not personal to the original transferor, but referred to successor in title for the time being under s. 78 LPA 1925); cf. *City Inn (Jersey) Ltd v Ten Trinity Square Ltd* [2008] EWCA Civ 156, [2008] 1 P & CR DG22 (on construction, 'Transferor' was personal to original transferor).

In holding that the plaintiffs were not entitled to an injunction restraining the defendant from building the additional house, Judge Paul Baker QC said at 43:

From these facts, which are not in dispute the plaintiffs contend that the benefit of the covenant of No 4, Audrey Gardens has become annexed to each of the plots respectively owned by them. Alternatively, it is contended that the benefit has passed under the general words of section 62 of the Law of Property Act 1925.

As to annexation, Mr Walter, appearing for the plaintiffs, conceded that the express terms of the covenant appeared to exclude annexation, and there was no suggestion that the case fell within the category known as building schemes. Mr Walter, however, in an interesting argument submitted that annexation had come about through the operation of section 78 of the Law of Property Act, as interpreted in *Federated Homes Ltd v Mill Lodge Properties Ltd* [1980] 1 WLR 594 [p. 783, above], a Court of Appeal decision. I can summarise his argument by the following four points.

(1) The covenant was a covenant relating to the land of the covenantee.

(2) Section 78(1) of the Law of Property Act 1925 provides, as regards such covenants relating to land that they are deemed:

'to be made with the covenantee and his successors in title and the persons deriving title under him or them, and shall have effect as if such successors and other persons were expressed. For the purposes of this subsection in connection with covenants restrictive of the user of land "successors in title" shall be deemed to include the owners and occupiers for the time being of the land of the covenantee intended to be benefited.'

(3) In the *Federated Homes* case it was held that by virtue of section 78(1) the benefit of a covenant relating to land retained by the covenantee ran with that land and was annexed to it and to every part of it.

(4) The provisions of section 78, unlike those of section 79 relating to the burden of the covenant, cannot be excluded by the expression of a contrary intention. Section 79 reads:

His Honour read the section, and continued:

Unlike section 78, which had a counterpart in section 58 of the Conveyancing Act 1881, section 79 was a new section in 1925. The important point to which attention is called is 'unless a contrary intention is expressed,' in section 79. There is no corresponding expression in section 78. Those are the main points of the argument.

I have no difficulty in accepting that the covenant in the standard form of the 1934 transfer is a covenant relating to the retained land of the covenantee, that is to say, Wembley (C & W) Land Co Ltd, and that therefore section 78 comes into play. It is the third and fourth points which have given rise to the argument in this case.

I must begin, therefore, by examining the *Federated Homes* case.... The plaintiff became clearly entitled to the relief sought in right of the green land.

Mr Henty, for the defendant in the present case, has argued that accordingly the Court of Appeal's judgments in relation to the red land were obiter. I am unable to accept this view of the effect of the judgments. As it seems to me, the status of the covenant in relation to both pieces of land—the red and the green—was in issue in the case. If the defendant in subsequent proceedings had sought to challenge the validity of the covenant in relation to the red land, he could, as I would see it, be met by a plea of issue estoppel and consequently the principle underlying the court's conclusion cannot be regarded as obiter.[142] That principle I take from the following passage in the judgment of Brightman LJ, at p. 605:

> 'If, as the language of section 78 implies, a covenant relating to land which is restrictive of the user thereof is enforceable at the suit of (1) a successor in title of the covenantee, (2) a person deriving title under the covenantee or under his successors in title, and (3) the owner or occupier of the land intended to be benefited by the covenant, it must, in my view, follow that the covenant runs with the land, because ex hypothesi every successor in title to the land, every derivative proprietor of the land and every other owner and occupier has a right by statute to the covenant. In other words, if the condition precedent of section 78 is satisfied—that is to say, there exists a covenant which touches and concerns the land of the covenantee—that covenant runs with the land for the benefit of his successors in title, persons deriving title under him or them and other owners and occupiers.'

That seems to be the essential point of the decision. Mr Henty made a frontal attack on this use of section 78, which he reinforced by reference to an article by Mr G. H. Newsom QC in (1981) 97 LQR 32 which is critical of the decision. The main lines of attack are (1) that the conclusion overlooks the legislative history of section 78 which it is said shows that it has a narrower purpose than is claimed and does not in itself bring about annexation; (2) this narrower purpose has been accepted in relation to the corresponding section 79 (relation to burden) by Lord Upjohn and Lord Wilberforce in *Sefton v Tophams Ltd* [1967] 1 AC 50, 73, 81. Further, it is said by way of argument sub silentio that in a number of cases, notably *Marquess of Zetland v Driver* [1939] Ch 1 and *Re Jeff's Transfer (No. 2)* [1966] 1 WLR 841, that the argument could have been used to good effect but was not deployed.

Now, all this is very interesting, and the views of Mr Newsom are entitled to very great respect seeing that until his recent retirement he was a practitioner of long experience who had made a special study of this branch of the law. He has written a valuable monograph on it. All the same, despite Mr Henty's blandishments, I am not going to succumb to the temptation of joining in any such discussion. Sitting here as a judge of the Chancery Division, I do not consider it to be my place either to criticise or to defend the decisions of the Court of Appeal. I conceive it my clear duty to accept the decision of the Court of Appeal as binding on me and apply it as best I can to the facts I find here.

Mr Walter's method of applying it is simplicity itself. The *Federated Homes* case shows that section 78 of the Act of 1925 brings about annexation, and that the operation of the section cannot be excluded by a contrary intention. As I have indicated, he supports this last point by reference to section 79, which is expressed to operate 'unless a contrary intention is expressed,' a qualification which, as we have already noticed, is absent from section 78. Mr Walter could not suggest any reason of policy why section 78 should be mandatory, unlike, for example, section 146 of the Act of 1925, which deals with restrictions on the right to forfeiture of leases and which, by an express provision 'has effect notwithstanding any stipulation to the contrary.'

I am thus far from satisfied that section 78 has the mandatory operation which Mr Walter claimed for it. But if one accepts that it is not subject to a contrary intention, I do not consider that it has the effect of annexing the benefit of the covenant in each and every case irrespective

---

[142] In *Allen v Veranne Builders Ltd* [1988] EGCS 2 Browne-Wilkinson V-C also held that it was the ratio of CA's decision.

of the other express terms of the covenant. I notice that Brightman LJ in the *Federated Homes* case did not go so far as that, for he said, at p. 606:

'I find the idea of the annexation of a covenant to the whole of the land but not to a part of it a difficult conception fully to grasp. I can understand that a covenantee may expressly or by neces-sary implication retain the benefit of a covenant wholly under his own control, so that the benefit will not pass unless the covenantee chooses to assign; but I would have thought, if the benefit of a covenant is, on a proper construction of a document, annexed to the land, prima facie it is annexed to every part thereof, unless the contrary clearly appears'.

So at least in some circumstances Brightman LJ is considering that despite section 78 the benefit may be retained and not pass or be annexed to and run with land. In this connection, I was also referred by Mr Henty to *Elphinstone's Covenants Affecting Land* (1946), p. 17, where it is said in a footnote:

'but it is thought that, as a covenant must be construed as a whole, the court would give due effect to words excluding or modifying the operation of the section...'

The true position as I see it is that even where a covenant is deemed to be made with suc-cessors in title as section 78 requires, one still has to construe the covenant as a whole to see whether the benefit of the covenant is annexed. Where one finds, as in the *Federated Homes* case, the covenant is not qualified in any way, annexation may be readily inferred; but where, as in the present case, it is expressly provided:

'this covenant shall not enure for the benefit of any owner or subsequent purchaser of any part of the vendor's Sudbury Court Estate at Wembley unless the benefit of this covenant shall be expressly assigned...'

One cannot just ignore these words. One may not be able to exclude the operation of the sec-tion in widening the range of the covenantees, but one has to consider the covenant as a whole to determine its true effect. When one does that, then it seems to me that the answer is plain and in my judgment the benefit was not annexed. That is giving full weight to both the statute in force and also what is already there in the covenant.

His Honour then considered the alternative claim based on LPA 1925, s. 62 (see p. 808, below) and concluded:

I thus conclude overall that the plaintiffs have failed to show that they are entitled to the benefit of the covenant in relation to their respective properties.'

In **Crest Nicholson Residential (South) Ltd v McAlister** [2004] 1 WLR 2409[143] Chadwick LJ said at 2420:

29 It is clear that the court approached the question of annexation in the *Federated Homes* case [1980] 1 WLR 594 on the basis that the density covenant was taken for the benefit of retained land which could be identified in the 1971 conveyance. Brightman LJ expressed his conclusion in these terms, at p. 605:

---

[143] [2004] Conv 507 (J. Howell); [2004] All ER Rev 244 (P. J. Clarke); [2005] Conv 2 (P. Kenny). See also *Sugarman v Porter* [2006] 2 P & CR 14 (wording of covenant, which made clear that benefit of covenant lasted only as long as covenantee retained land unsold, displaced statutory annexation of s. 78 LPA 1925).

'If, as the language of section 78 implies, a covenant relating to land which is restrictive of the user thereof is enforceable at the suit of (1) a successor in title of the covenantee, (2) a person deriving title under the covenantee or under his successors in title, and (3) the owner or occupier of the land intended to be benefited by the covenant, it must, in my view, follow that the covenant runs with the land, because ex hypothesi every successor in title to the land, every derivative proprietor of the land and every other owner and occupier has a right by statute to the covenant. In other words, if the condition precedent of section 78 is satisfied—that is to say, there exists a covenant which touches and concerns the land of the covenantee—that covenant runs with the land for the benefit of his successors in title, persons deriving title under him or them and other owners and occupiers.'

There is, in effect, statutory annexation of the benefit of the covenant to '*the land intended to be benefited by the covenant*'. The words which I have emphasised, which are incorporated by Brightman LJ in the passage which I have just cited, are derived, of course, from section 78(1):

'For the purposes of this subsection... "successors in title" shall be deemed to include the owners and occupiers for the time being of the land of the covenantee intended to be benefited.'

30 The decision of this court in the *Federated Homes* case leaves open the question whether section 78 of the 1925 Act only effects annexation when the land intended to be benefited is described in the instrument itself (by express words or necessary implication, albeit that it may be necessary to have regard to evidence outside the document fully to identify that land) or whether it is enough that it can be shown, from evidence wholly outside the document, that the covenant does in fact touch and concern land of the covenantee which can be identified.

31 It is clear from Brightman LJ's reference in the *Federated Homes* case [1980] 1 WLR 594, 604c–g to *Rogers v Hosegood* [1900] 2 Ch 388 that it is sufficient for the conveyance to describe the land intended to be benefited in terms which enable it to be identified from other evidence. In *Rogers v Hosegood* the covenant was given for the benefit of the vendors, their heirs and assigns 'and others claiming under them to all or any of their lands adjoining or near to the' premises conveyed. The Court of Appeal held that to be a sufficient description, at pp. 403–404...

32 The question left open in the *Federated Homes* case had, I think, already been answered in the judgment of this court in *Marquess of Zetland v Driver* [1939] Ch 1, a decision not cited in the *Federated Homes* case. The applicable principles were restated in the following passage, at pp. 7–8:

'Covenants restricting the user of land imposed by a vendor upon a sale fall into three classes: (i) covenants imposed by the vendor for his own benefit; (ii) covenants imposed by the vendor as owner of other land, of which that sold formed a part, and intended to protect or benefit the unsold land; and (iii) covenants imposed by a vendor upon a sale of land to various purchasers who are intended mutually to enjoy the benefit of and be bound by the covenants: *Osborne v Bradley* [1903] 2 Ch 446, 450. Covenants of the first class are personal to the vendor and enforceable by him alone unless expressly assigned by him. Covenants of the second class are said to run with the land and are enforceable without express assignment by the owner for the time being of the land for the benefit of which they were imposed. Covenants of the third class are most usually found in sales under building scheme, although not strictly confined to such sales. It is not suggested that the present covenant falls within this class. Nor will it assist the appellant if it falls within the first class, since he was not the original covenantee or an express assignee from him. If, therefore, the appellant is entitled to sue on this covenant it must fall within the second class above mentioned. Such covenants can only be validly imposed if they comply with certain conditions. Firstly, they must be negative covenants... Secondly, the covenant must be one that touches or concerns the land, by which is meant that it must be imposed for the benefit or to enhance the value of the land retained by the vendor or some part of it, and no such covenant can ever be imposed if the sale comprises the whole of the vendor's land... Thirdly, *the land which is intended to be benefited must be so defined as to be easily ascertainable* , and the fact that the covenant is imposed for the benefit of that particular land should be stated in the conveyance and the persons or the class of persons entitled to enforce it. The fact that the benefit of the covenant is not intended to pass to all persons into whose hands the unsold land may come is not objectionable so long as the class of persons intended to have the benefit of the covenant is clearly defined.' (Emphasis added.)

33 In its later decision in the *Federated Homes* case this court held that the provisions of section 78 of the 1925 Act had made it unnecessary to state, in the conveyance, that the covenant was to be enforceable by persons deriving title under the covenantee or under his successors in title and the owner or occupier of the land intended to be benefited, or that the covenant was to run with the land intended to be benefited; but there is nothing in that case which suggests that it is no longer necessary that the land which is intended to be benefited should be so defined that it is easily ascertainable. In my view, that requirement, identified in *Marquess of Zetland v Driver* remains a necessary condition for annexation.

34 There are, I think, good reasons for that requirement. A restrictive covenant affecting land will not be enforceable in equity against a purchaser who acquires a legal estate in that land for value without notice of the covenant. A restrictive covenant imposed in an instrument made after 1925 is registrable as a land charge under class D(ii): section 10(1) of the Land Charges Act 1925 and, now, section 2(5) of the Land Charges Act 1972. If the title is registered, protection is effected by entering notice of the restrictive covenant on the register: section 50 of the Land Registration Act 1925 and, now, section 11 of the Land Registration Act 2002. Where practicable the notice shall be by reference to the instrument by which the covenant is imposed and a copy or abstract of that instrument shall be filed at the registry: section 50(1) of the Land Registration Act 1925 and section 3(5) of the Land Charges Act 1972. It is obviously desirable that a purchaser of land burdened with a restrictive covenant should be able not only to ascertain, by inspection of the entries on the relevant register, that the land is so burdened, but also to ascertain the land for which the benefit of the covenant was taken-so that he can identify who can enforce the covenant. That latter object is achieved if the land which is intended to be benefited is defined in the instrument so as to be easily ascertainable. To require a purchaser of land burdened with a restrictive covenant, but where the land for the benefit of which the covenant was taken is not described in the instrument, to make inquiries as to what (if any) land the original covenantee retained at the time of the conveyance and what (if any) of that retained land the covenant did, or might have, 'touched and concerned' would be oppressive. It must be kept in mind that (as in the present case) the time at which the enforceability of the covenant becomes an issue may be long after the date of the instrument by which it was imposed....

37 To my mind, the decision in *Marquess of Zetland v Driver* goes much of the way to answer a second question which this court did not need to address in the *Federated Homes* case [1980] 1 WLR 594: whether the effect of the section 78 of the Law of Property Act 1925 is displaced by a contrary intention manifested in the instrument itself. But that question was addressed, specifically, in *Roake v Chadha* [1984] 1 WLR 40, to which I now turn....

41 I respectfully agree [with Judge Paul Baker QC in *Roake v Chadha*, p. 787, above], first, that it is impossible to identify any reason of policy why a covenantor should not, by

express words, be entitled to limit the scope of the obligation which he is undertaking; nor why a covenantee should not be able to accept a covenant for his own benefit on terms that the benefit does not pass automatically to all those to whom he sells on parts of his retained land. As Brightman LJ pointed out, in the passage cited by Judge Paul Baker QC, a developer who is selling off land in lots might well want to retain the benefit of a building restriction under his own control. Where, as in *Roake v Chadha* and the present case, development land is sold off in plots without imposing a building scheme, it seems to me very likely that the developer will wish to retain exclusive power to give or withhold consent to a modification or relaxation of a restriction on building which he imposes on each purchaser; unfettered by the need to obtain the consent of every subsequent purchaser to whom (after imposing the covenant) he has sold off other plots on the development land. I can see no reason why, if original covenantor and covenantee make clear their mutual intention in that respect, the legislature should wish to prevent effect being given to that intention.

42 Second, it is important to keep in mind that, for the purposes of its application to restrictive covenants—which is the context in which this question arises where neither of the parties to the dispute were, themselves, party to the instrument imposing the covenant or express assignees of the benefit of the covenant—section 78 of the 1925 Act defines 'successors in title' as the owners and occupiers of the time being *of the land of the covenantee intended to be benefited*. In a case where the parties to the instrument make clear their intention that land retained by the covenantee at the time of the conveyance effected by the transfer is to have the benefit of the covenant only for so long as it continues to be in the ownership of the original covenantee, and not after it has been sold on by the original covenantee—unless the benefit of the covenant is expressly assigned to the new owner—*the land of the covenantee intended to be benefited* is identified by the instrument as (i) so much of the retained land as from time to time has not been sold off by the original covenantee and (ii) so much of the retained land as has been sold off with the benefit of an express assignment, but as not including (iii) so much of the land as has been sold off without the benefit of an express assignment. I agree with the judge in *Roake v Chadha* that, in such a case, it is possible to give full effect to the statute and to the terms of the covenant.

43 This approach to section 78 of the 1925 Act provides, as it seems to me, the answer to the question why, if the legislature did not intend to distinguish between the effect of section 78 (mandatory) and the effect of section 79 (subject to contrary intention), it did not include the words 'unless a contrary intention is expressed' in the first of those sections. The answer is that it did not need to. The qualification 'subject to contrary intention' is implicit in the definition of 'successors in title' which appears in section 78(1); that is the effect of the words 'the land of the covenantee intended to be benefited'. If the terms in which the covenant is imposed show—as they did in *Marquess of Zetland v Driver* and in *Roake v Chadha*—that the land of the covenantee intended to be benefited does not include land which may subsequently be sold off by the original covenantee in circumstances where (at the time of that subsequent sale) there is no express assignment of the benefit of the covenant, then the owners and occupiers of the land sold off in those circumstances are not 'owners and occupiers for the time being of the land of the covenantee intended to be benefited'; and so are not 'successors in title' of the original covenantee for the purposes of section 78(1) in its application to covenants restrictive of the user of land.

44 By contrast, the definition of 'successors in title' for the purposes of section 79(1) appears in subsection (2) of that section: 'the owners and occupiers for the time being of *such*

land'. In that context 'such land' means 'any land of a covenantor or capable of being bound by him [to which the covenant relates].' The counterpart in section 79 of 'land of the covenantee intended to be benefited' (in section 78(1)) is 'such land'. 'Such land' in that context means the land referred to in section 79(1); that is to say 'any land of a covenantor or capable of being bound by him'. But section 79(1) imposes two qualifications; (i) the land must be land to which the covenant relates and (ii) there must be no expression of contrary intention. The section could, perhaps, have described the land as 'land of the covenantor (or capable of being bound by him) intended to be burdened'. But the effect would have been the same. If the parties did not intend that land, burdened while in the ownership of the covenantor, should continue to be subject to the burden in hands of his successors (or some of his successors), they could say so. On a true analysis there is no difference in treatment in the two sections. There is a difference in the drafting technique used to achieve the same substantive result. That may well simply reflect the legislative history of the two sections. Section 78(1) of the 1925 Act re-enacted section 58 of the Conveyancing and Law of Property Act 1881 as applied by section 96(3) of the Law of Property Act 1922 and amended by section 3 of, and paragraph 11 of Schedule 3 to, the Law of Property (Amendment) Act 1924. Section 79 was a new provision, first introduced in the 1925 Act.

(c) Annexation to the whole of the covenantee's land

The covenantee may enforce the covenant against the covenantor or his assigns, so long as the covenantee has some land capable of benefiting. But, when the question concerns the annexation of the benefit of the covenant to the dominant land, so as to make the benefit run with the land on a conveyance, it has been held that this can only be done at law or in equity, if substantially the whole of the 'dominant' land is capable of benefiting; it is not possible for the court to effect a severance and allow the covenant to be annexed to such land as is capable of benefiting.[144]

The difficulty, however, disappears if the covenant is correctly drafted, so as to show an intention to annex the benefit to the whole or *any part or parts of* the estate, for the benefit will then be annexed to such parts as are in fact benefited.[145] It has been held that the court will hear evidence as to the capability of the land to be benefited by the covenant,[146] and that the burden of proof is on the defendant to show that it does not do so, either originally, or at the date of the action.[147]

(d) Annexation to part of the covenantee's land

Even if the whole of the dominant land is capable of benefiting, and if the benefit of the covenant is annexed to the whole, it has usually been held that the benefit of the

---

[144] *Re Ballard's Conveyance* [1937] Ch 473; 57 LQR at p. 210 (G. R. Y. Radcliffe); Elphinstone, *Covenants Affecting Land* (1946), p. 60; *Marten v Flight Refuelling Ltd* [1962] Ch 115 at 137, p. 803, below.

[145] *Marquess of Zetland v Driver* [1937] Ch 651; (1941) 57 LQR 203 (G. R. Y. Radcliffe).

[146] *Marten v Flight Refuelling Ltd*, above; *Earl of Leicester v Wells-next-the Sea UDC* [1973] Ch 110 (expert evidence admitted to show that a covenant restricting 19 acres afforded 'great benefit and much needed protection to the Holkham Estate as a whole', i.e. to 32,000 acres). In *Re Ballard's Conveyance*, above, no evidence was offered to show benefit to the dominant land as a whole.

[147] *Wrotham Park Estate Co Ltd v Parkside Homes Ltd* [1974] 1 WLR 798; *Cryer v Scott Bros (Sunbury) Ltd* (1986) 55 P & CR 183.

covenant will only run in favour of the purchaser of a *part* of the land, if he can show that the benefit was annexed to the part which he purchased, or to each portion of the whole.

For instance, A, the owner of a large property, sells part of it to Y and takes a covenant that no public house shall be opened on it. This covenant is annexed to A's land. Later A sells part of the dominant land to B. If B seeks to enforce the covenant by virtue of its annexation to A's land, he must prove that its benefit was annexed to each and every part of those lands or to the very part bought by him.[148]

In **Drake v Gray** [1936] Ch 451[149] the Court of Appeal (Slesser, Romer and Greene LJJ) held that a covenant taken with the other parties to the deed…'and other the owners or owner for the time being of the remaining hereditaments so agreed to be partitioned' operated to annex the covenant to each portion of the land, so as to allow the benefit of the covenant to run with each portion of the partitioned land.

SLESSER LJ said at 461:

I recognize, and I accept entirely, what was said by this Court in *Re Union of London and Smith's Bank Ltd's Conveyance, Miles v Easter* [1933] Ch 611 [p. 798, below], that it must be shown that the benefit was intended to enure to each portion of the land, and it is true that it has been held that the use of the words 'or any part thereof' may be apt for that purpose; but I cannot read that case as meaning that those words, and those words only, are the sole means by which a conveyance may show that the benefit was intended to enure to each portion. In this case, the intention, as gathered from the documents and the recital of the whole history of the case, is clear that the benefit of the covenant was to enure to the owner of any part of the remaining hereditaments, and as the plaintiff was such an owner, the learned judge was right in the conclusion to which he came.

In **Re Selwyn's Conveyance** [1967] Ch 674 GOFF J held that a covenant 'for the protection of the adjoining or neighbouring land part of or lately part of the Selwyn Estate' was sufficient to annex the benefit to separate parts of the land.

In **Russell v Archdale** [1964] Ch 38[150] BUCKLEY J held that a restrictive covenant 'to benefit and protect the vendor's adjoining and neighbouring land' was annexed to that land as a whole, but that the plaintiff, a subsequent purchaser of only part of that land, was not entitled to rely on the annexation. He said at 45:

The next question which was debated was whether this annexation was an annexation to the whole of the land referred to by the words 'adjoining and neighbouring land' or to each and every part of it, and in that connection I was referred by Mr Arnold to the decision of the Court of Appeal in *Drake v Gray*. That was relied upon as authority for the proposition that where one finds annexation by general words such as 'for the benefit of the vendor's remaining land' or,

---

[148] C & B, p. 684; Preston & Newsom, paras 2–20 to 2–26. In *Griffiths v Band* (1974) 29 P & CR 243 at 246, Goulding J referred to 'this somewhat muddy corner of legal history.'

[149] *Reid v Bickerstaff* [1909] 2 Ch 305.

[150] (1962) 78 LQR 334, 482 (R.E.M.); affd CA (Lord Denning MR dissenting) (1962) Times, 1 December, where only the issue of acquiescence is discussed.

such as we have in the present case, 'adjoining and neighbouring land', the proper interpretation is to construe that as a reference to each and every part of the land which falls within the
description....

In the course of his judgment, Romer LJ said at 465: 'Most of the cases that have come before
the court have been cases where a covenant has been entered into by a vendor for the benefit of,
say, the A.B. estate for the time being. There, of course, no intention is shown that the benefit
should enure for any particular part of the estate; but where one finds not "the land coloured
yellow" or "the estate" or "the field named so-and-so" or anything of that kind, but "the lands
retained by the vendor", it appears to me that there is a sufficient indication that the benefit of
the covenant enures to every one of the lands retained by the vendor, and if a plaintiff in a subsequent action to enforce a covenant can say: "I am the owner of a piece of land that belonged to
the vendor at the time of the conveyance", he is entitled to enforce the covenant.'...

No doubt every case of this kind, being one of construction, must be determined on the facts
and the actual language used, but with the utmost respect to Romer LJ, I cannot see that the
mere fact that the land intended to be benefited was described by such an expression as 'the land
retained by the vendor' is sufficient to enable the court to come to the conclusion that the covenant is intended to benefit each and every part of that land. This observation of Romer LJ was,
I think, clearly obiter dictum, ... and in my judgment that authority does not assist the plaintiffs
to say that the benefit of the covenant is annexed to each and every part of what is described by
the conveyance as 'the adjoining and neighbouring land of the vendor'. That being so, I think it
must follow that the plaintiffs cannot, merely by reason of annexation of this covenant to the
'adjoining and neighbouring land of the vendor' in the conveyance of 1938 and the fact that they
have acquired part only of that land, enforce the covenant.[151]

In **Federated Homes v Mill Lodge Properties Ltd** [1980] 1 WLR 594, p. 783, above,
Brightman LJ said at 606:

It was suggested by Mr Price that, if this covenant ought to be read as enuring for the benefit of
the retained land, it should be read as enuring only for the benefit of the retained land as a whole
and not for the benefit of every part of it; with the apparent result that there is no annexation
of the benefit to a part of the retained land when any severance takes place. He referred us to a
passage in *Re Union of London and Smith's Bank Ltd's Conveyance* [1933] Ch 611, 628, which
I do not think it is necessary for me to read.

The problem is alluded to in Megarry and Wade, *The Law of Real Property*, 4th edn, p. 763.

'In drafting restrictive covenants it is therefore desirable to annex them to the covenantee's land
'or any part or parts thereof'. An additional reason for using this form of words is that, if there is no
indication to the contrary, the benefit may be held to be annexed only to the whole of the covenantee's
land, so that it will not pass with portions of it disposed of separately. But even without such words
the court may find that the covenant is intended to benefit any part of the retained land; and small

---

[151] Similarly in *Re Jeff's Transfer* (No 2) [1966] 1 WLR 841 ('for the benefit of the remainder of the
Chorleywood Estate (Loudwater) belonging to the vendor'); *Stilwell v Blackman* [1968] Ch 508 ('to benefit
and protect the adjoining property of the vendor'). The Law Commission Consultation Paper on Easements,
Covenants and Profits à Prendre 2008 (Consultation Paper No. 186), para. 10.44, p. 848, below, proposes
that on a sub-division of the benefited land the benefit of a Land Obligation (their proposed replacement
for covenants) should run with each and every part of the benefited land unless it does not 'relate to', or
benefit, that part of the land, or the sub-division increases the scope of obligations, or a contrary intention is
expressed. See also Victoria Property Law Act 1958, s. 79A.

indications may suffice, since the rule that presumes annexation to the whole only is arbitrary and inconvenient. In principle it conflicts with the rule for assignments, which allows a benefit annexed to the whole to be assigned with part, and it also conflicts with the corresponding rule for easements.'

I find the idea of the annexation of a covenant to the whole of the land but not to a part of it a difficult conception fully to grasp. I can understand that a covenantee may expressly or by necessary implication retain the benefit of a covenant wholly under his own control, so that the benefit will not pass unless the covenantee chooses to assign; but I would have thought, if the benefit of a covenant is, on a proper construction of a document, annexed to the land, prima facie it is annexed to every part thereof, unless the contrary clearly appears. It is difficult to see how this court can have reached its decision in *Williams v Unit Construction Co Ltd,* 19 Conveyancer 262, unless this is right. The covenant was, by inference, annexed to every part of the land and not merely to the whole, because it will be recalled that the plaintiff was a tenant of only one of the four houses which had the benefit of the covenant.

There is also this observation by Romer LJ in *Drake v Gray* [1936] Ch 451, 465. He was dealing with the enuring of the benefit of a restrictive covenant and he said:

His Lordship quoted Romer LJ's dictum set out at p. 796, above, and continued:

In the instant case the judge in the course of his judgment appears to have dismissed the notion that any individual plot-holder would be entitled, even by assignment, to have the benefit of the covenant that I have been considering. I express no view about that. I only say this, that I am not convinced that his conclusion on the point is correct. I say no more about it.[152]

(ii) By express assignment

If the benefit of a restrictive covenant is not annexed to the land of the covenantee, an assignee must show that the benefit passed to him by express assignment of the benefit at the time of the conveyance. Such express assignment will be necessary in fewer cases in the future if, on the authority of *Federated Homes Ltd v Mill Lodge Properties Ltd* [1980] 1 WLR 594, p. 783, above, annexation is held to be effected by section 78 of the Law of Property Act 1925. Cases requiring express assignment can, however still arise; as where there is express provision to the effect that express assignment of the benefit of the covenant shall be required,[153] or where there is no identification in the conveyance of the land to be benefited.[154] Further, the benefit of a covenant passes under the 'general words' of section 62 of the Law of Property Act 1925, but only if there has already been annexation or assignment.[155]

---

[152] See *Allen v Veranne Builders Ltd* [1988] EGCS 2, where Sir Nicolas Browne-Wilkinson V-C said: 'To my mind there is everything to suggest an intention to annex it to each and every part. We are not here dealing with an old-fashioned country gentleman's landed estate, where it might well be that there would be an intention to annex the benefit to the whole of the estate. In the present case we are dealing with a development estate, the whole of which was intended to be disposed of. I can see nothing in the case to suggest that one should depart from the general presumption as laid down by the Court of Appeal.'

[153] *Marquess of Zetland v Driver* [1937] Ch 651; *Roake v Chadha* [1984] 1 WLR 40, p. 787, above.

[154] *Newton Abbot Co-operative Society v Williamson and Treadgold Ltd* [1952] Ch 286, p. 799, below. But see *Federated Homes Ltd v Mill Lodge Properties Ltd,* above, at 604, per Brightman LJ.

[155] P. 808, n. 182, below; *Federated Homes Ltd v Mill Lodge Properties Ltd,* above, at 601.

Preston & Newsom, *Restrictive Covenants Affecting Freehold Land* (9th edn, 1998), para. 2–40.

Where the defendant is the original covenantor, he is liable at law. Against him the original covenantee can succeed at common law in an ordinary action on the covenant. Further, a plaintiff who is the express assignee of the benefit of the covenant can succeed against the original covenantor in an action at law governed by the ordinary action rules as to the assignment of a chose in action.[156] But 'at law the benefit could not be assigned in pieces. It would have to be assigned as a whole or not at all.'[157] The plaintiff must therefore rely upon an equitable title even as against the original covenantor if the benefit of the covenant has been assigned 'in pieces.' And, more importantly, he must always rely on an equitable title against a defendant who is not the original covenantor (or his personal representative). For the burden of a covenant never runs at law and a successor of the covenantor is liable only in equity, under the rule in *Tulk v Moxhay*.[158] Requiring the assistance of equity, against a defendant who is liable in equity only or because the plaintiff's own title depends upon equity, a plaintiff must therefore show that he is within the special rules laid down by equity for establishing whether a title by express assignment can be relied upon. Accordingly the assignment may be expressed as taking effect in equity.[159]

(a) Contemporaneous with conveyance

It has long been clear that it was possible in equity to assign expressly the benefit of a restrictive covenant on the sale of the land of the covenantee.[160] Such assignment must be contemporaneous with the conveyance; if once the covenant becomes separated from the land to be benefited, it ceases to be operative.[161] It was not, however, until 1952 that it was authoritatively held that the benefit would pass in this way.[162] And this decision has been criticised.[163]

In **Re Union of London and Smith's Bank Ltd's Conveyance, Miles v Easter** [1933] Ch 611,[164] ROMER LJ referred to *Renals v Cowlishaw* (1878) 9 ChD 125 and *Rogers v Hosegood* [1900] 2 Ch 388, p. 780, above and said at 629:

In neither of these cases, therefore, did it become necessary for the Court to inquire into the circumstances in which an express assignee of the benefit of a covenant that does not run with the land is entitled to enforce it. In the present case, however, it is necessary to do so, inasmuch

---

[156] LPA 1925, s. 136 [p. 777, above].

[157] *Miles v Easter* [1933] Ch 611 per Romer LJ at 630.

[158] (1848) 2 Ph 774 [p. 754, above].

[159] *Newton Abbot Co-operative Society v Williamson and Treadgold Ltd* [1952] Ch 286.

[160] *Renals v Cowlishaw* (1878) 9 ChD 125; *Ives v Brown* [1919] 2 Ch 314; *Lord Northbourne v Johnston & Son* [1922] 2 Ch 309; *Chambers v Randall* [1923] 1 Ch 149; *Re Union of London and Smith's Bank Ltd's Conveyance, Miles v Easter* [1933] Ch 611; *Re Rutherford's Conveyance* [1938] Ch 396; (1948) 6 CLJ 339 (S. J. Bailey); (1952) 68 LQR 353 (Sir Lancelot Elphinstone). The assignment may be to a lessee; *South Eastern Rly Co v Associated Portland Cement Manufacturers (1900) Ltd* [1910] 1 Ch 12.

[161] *Chambers v Randall*, above; *Re Union of London and Smith's Bank Ltd's Conveyance, Miles v Easter*, above; cf. *Lord Northbourne v Johnston*, above; *Newton Abbot Co-operative Society Ltd v Williamson and Treadgold Ltd* [1952] Ch 286, p. 799, below.

[162] *Newton Abbot Co-operative Society Ltd v Williamson and Treadgold Ltd*, above.

[163] (1952) 68 LQR 353 (Sir Lancelot Elphinstone).

[164] (1933) 49 LQR 483 (H. A. Hollond).

as the defendants claim to be the express assignees of the benefit of the restrictive covenants contained in the deeds of 23 October 1908 and 11 May 1909.

Now it may be conceded that the benefit of a covenant entered into with the covenantee or his assigns is assignable. The use of the word 'assigns' indicates this: see Williams on *Personal Property*, 18th edn p. 33. But it by no means follows that the assignee of a restrictive covenant affecting land of the covenantor is entitled to enforce it against an assign of that land. For the burden of the covenant did not run with the land at law, and is only enforceable against a purchaser with notice by reason of the equitable doctrine that is usually referred to as the rule in *Tulk v Moxhay*. It was open, therefore, to the Courts of Equity to prescribe the particular class of assignees of the covenant to whom they should concede the benefit of the rule. This they have done, and in doing so have included within the class persons to whom the benefit of the covenant could not have been assigned at law. For at law the benefit could not be assigned in pieces. It would have to be assigned as a whole or not at all. And yet in equity the right to enforce the covenant can in certain circumstances be assigned by the covenantee from time to time to one person after another. Who then are the assignees of the covenant that are entitled to enforce it? The answer to this question is to be found in several authorities which it now becomes necessary to consider.

His Lordship referred to *Formby v Barker* [1903] 2 Ch 539, p. 756, above and *London County Council v Allen* [1914] 3 KB 642, p. 755, above, and continued:

It is plain, however, from these and other cases, and notably that of *Renals v Cowlishaw* (1878) 9 ChD 125 [p. 782, above], that if the restrictive covenant be taken not merely for some personal purpose or object of the vendor, but for the benefit of some other land of his in the sense that it would enable him to dispose of that land to greater advantage, the covenant, though not annexed to such land so as to run with any part of it, may be enforced against an assignee of the covenantor taking with notice, both by the covenantee and by persons to whom the benefit of such covenant has been assigned, subject however to certain conditions. In the first place, the 'other land' must be land that is capable of being benefited by the covenant—otherwise it would be impossible to infer that the object of the covenant was to enable the vendor to dispose of his land to greater advantage. In the next place, this land must be 'ascertainable' or 'certain', to use the words of Romer and Scrutton LJJ, respectively. For, although the Court will readily infer the intention to benefit the other land of the vendor where the existence and situation of such land are indicated in the conveyance or have been otherwise shown with reasonable certainty, it is impossible to do so from vague references in the conveyance or in other documents laid before the Court as to the existence of other lands of the vendor, the extent and situation of which are undefined. In the third place, the covenant cannot be enforced by the covenantee against an assign of the purchaser after the covenantee has parted with the whole of his land....

Newton Abbot Co-operative Society Ltd v Williamson and Treadgold Ltd
[1952] Ch 286[165] (ChD, **Upjohn J**)

In 1923, Mrs Mardon, who was owner of premises known as Devonia, in Fore St., Bovey Tracey, on which she carried on business as an ironmonger, conveyed property on the other side of the street to a purchaser who covenanted not to use if for the

---

[165] (1952) 68 LQR 353 (Sir Lancelot Elphinstone).

business of an ironmonger. There was no indication in the conveyance of the land to be benefited, but Mrs Mardon's address was given as Devonia.

In 1941, Mrs Mardon died, having left Devonia in her will to her son Leonard Soper Mardon.

In 1947, the purchasers of the property opposite Devonia sold it to the defendants.

In 1948, Leonard Soper Mardon assigned the ironmongery business to Bovey Tracey Co-operative Society (which later amalgamated with the plaintiffs) together with the benefit of the restrictive covenant, and granted them a lease of Devonia for 21 years.

In 1950, the defendants began to expose articles of ironmongery for sale in breach of the restrictive covenant.

Held. The plaintiffs were entitled to an injunction. The covenant touched and concerned the land and had been validly assigned.

Upjohn J: The sole issue before me is whether the plaintiffs are entitled to the benefit of the restrictive covenant, and, if so, whether they are entitled to enforce it against the defendants.

I will deal with the first point first. Mr Binney on behalf of the plaintiffs submitted first that the benefit of the restrictive covenant was annexed to Devonia so as to pass with the assignment of Devonia in equity without any express mention in that subsequent assignment; in other words, that the covenant runs with the land. Alternatively, he said that the plaintiffs are the express assigns of the benefit of the covenant, and as such are entitled to enforce it. In this difficult branch of the law one thing in my judgment is clear, namely, that in order to annex the benefit of a restrictive covenant to land, so that it runs with the land without express assignment on a subsequent assignment of the land, the land for the benefit of which it is taken must be clearly identified in the conveyance creating the covenant.

His Lordship referred on this point to *Renals v Cowlishaw* (1878) 9 ChD 125, p. 782, above, *Re Union of London and Smith's Bank Ltd's Conveyance, Miles v Easter* (1933) Ch 611, p. 798, above, and came to the conclusion that the land for the benefit of which the covenant was taken was not sufficiently identified by the conveyance to annex the benefit of it to the land.

I turn then to his second submission, namely, that the plaintiffs are express assigns of the benefit of the restrictive covenant. Mr Bowles, on behalf of the defendants, contends that, even if it be assumed that his submission (with which I shall deal later) that the covenant was not taken for the benefit of Devonia, but of the business carried on thereat, is wrong, and the covenant was taken by Mrs Mardon for the benefit of Devonia to enable her to dispose of it to better advantage, yet there is no complete chain of assignments vesting the benefit in the plaintiffs. He says that there was never any assignment of the benefit of the covenant by the executors of Mrs Mardon to Leonard Soper Mardon and therefore he was not in a position to assign the benefit of the covenant to the plaintiffs' predecessors in title. He relied on *Ives v Brown* [1919] 2 Ch 314 and *Lord Northbourne v Johnston & Son* [1922] 2 Ch 309.

In my judgment those authorities do not support his contention. The position as I see it was this: On the footing that the restrictive covenant was not annexed to the land so as to run with it, the benefit of the covenant is capable of passing by operation of law as well as by express assignment and formed part of Mrs Mardon's personal estate on her death: see *Ives v Brown*.

It was not suggested that there was any implied assent to the assignment of the benefit of the covenant to the residuary legatee, but in my judgment, when her estate was duly wound up and administered, and this case has been argued before me on the footing that that happened many years ago, the benefit of the covenant was held by the executors as bare trustees for the residuary legatee, Leonard Soper Mardon, who was himself one of the executors. He therefore became entitled to the benefit of this restrictive covenant in equity and, in my judgment, he was entitled to assign the benefit in equity on an assignment of Devonia. No doubt had the covenant been assigned to him by the executors, he could also have assigned it at law. That this is the position is, in my judgment, made clear by the . . . judgment of Sargant J in *Lord Northbourne v Johnston & Son . . .* [166]

The second main question was whether the defendants are liable to have the covenant enforced against them. This was Mr Bowles' main defence in this action and he says that the restrictive covenant was not taken for the benefit of Devonia, and he puts his case in this way: First, he says that in any event this was not taken for the benefit of any land, but was a covenant with Mrs Mardon personally, solely for the benefit of her business. Secondly, he says that in order that an express assign of the benefit may sue an assignee of the burden of the covenant there must be some reference in the conveyance creating that covenant to the land for the benefit of which it was taken. . . .

His Lordship came to the conclusion that the covenant was taken for the benefit of Devonia, and continued:

Mr Bowles' second point was that, in order that the benefit of the covenant may be assignable, the land for which the benefit of the covenant is taken must in some way be referred to in the conveyance creating the covenant, and I was naturally pressed with the headnote in *Re Union of London and Smith's Bank Ltd's Conveyance, Miles v Easter* [1933] Ch 611, which reads as follows: 'Where on a sale otherwise than under a building scheme a restrictive covenant is taken, the benefit of which is not on the sale annexed to the land retained by the covenantee so as to run with it, an assign of the covenantee's retained land cannot enforce the covenant against an assign (taking with notice) of the covenantor unless he can show (i) that the covenant was taken for the benefit of ascertainable land of the covenantee capable of being benefited by the covenant, and (ii) that he (the covenantee's assign) is an express assign of the benefit of the covenant', and with the following passage in the judgment of Bennett J at 625: 'In my judgment, in order that an express assignee of a covenant restricting the user of land may be able to enforce that covenant against the owner of the land burdened with the covenant, he must be able to satisfy the court of two things. The first is that it was a covenant entered into for the benefit or protection of land owned by the covenantee at the date of the covenant. Otherwise it is a covenant in gross, and unenforceable except as between the parties to the covenant; see *Formby v Barker* [1903] 2 Ch 539 [p. 756, above]. Secondly, the assignee must be able to satisfy the court that the deed containing the covenant defines or contains something to define the property for the benefit of which the covenant was entered into: see James LJ in *Renals v Cowlishaw* (1879) 11 ChD at 866.'

With all respect to the statement of the judge, I am unable to agree that where a person is suing as an assign of the benefit of the covenant there must necessarily be something in the deed

---

[166] See *Marten v Flight Refuelling Ltd* [1962] Ch 115 at 140, where Wilberforce J relied upon Sargant J's reasoning; *Earl of Leicester v Wells-next-the-Sea UDC* [1973] Ch 110 (special executors of settled land held to be bare trustees of benefit of restrictive covenant for beneficiary under SLA 1925, s. 7(1)).

containing the covenant to define the land for the benefit of which the covenant was entered into. In the first place, the passage in the judgment of James LJ in *Renals v Cowlishaw,* which I have already read, on which the judge relied, does not in my judgment support the statement of the law for which it was cited. In *Renals v Cowlishaw* there was no express assignment of the benefit of the restrictive covenant (see the statement of fact in the report in the court below); and when James LJ says that to enable an assign to take the benefit of restrictive covenants there must be something in the deed to define the property for the benefit of which they were entered into, he is, I think, dealing with the case where it is contended that the benefit of the covenant has been annexed to the land so as to run with the land. When he uses the word 'assign' he is using the word as meaning an assign of the land and not an assign of the benefit of the covenant. Secondly, the views expressed by Bennett J appear to me to be inconsistent with the views expressed in some of the earlier decisions. I do not propose to cite them, but I refer to the following observations on the law on this point, namely, the observations of Collins LJ, delivering the judgment of the Court of Appeal in *Rogers v Hosegood* [1900] 2 Ch at 407, those of Vaughan Williams LJ in *Formby v Barker* [1903] 2 Ch at 551; and to the observations of Cozens-Hardy MR in *Reid v Bickerstaff* [1909] 2 Ch at 319, 325; and to the words of Buckley LJ in the same case. Finally, in *Re Union of London and Smith's Bank Ltd's Conveyance, Miles v Easter* [1933] Ch at 628, 631, Romer LJ, reading the judgment of the Court of Appeal, having considered the cases where the benefit of the covenant is annexed to land so as to run without express mention, says: 'In all other cases the purchaser will not acquire the benefit of the covenant unless that benefit be expressly assigned to him—or to use the words of the Vice-Chancellor, "it must appear that the benefit of the covenant was part of the subject-matter of the purchase".'

His Lordship then cited the paragraph from Romer LJ's judgment set out on p. 799, above, and continued:

In my judgment, therefore, the problem which I have to consider is this: First, when Mrs Mardon took the covenant in 1923, did she retain other lands capable of being benefited by the covenant? The answer is plainly yes. Secondly, was such land 'ascertainable' or 'certain' in this sense that the existence and situation of the land must be indicated in the conveyance or otherwise shown with reasonable certainty?

Apart from the fact that Mrs Mardon is described as of Devonia, there is nothing in the conveyance of 1923 to define the land for the benefit of which the restrictive covenant was taken, and I do not think that carries one very far; but, for the reasons I have given, I am, in my judgment, entitled to look at the attendant circumstances to see if the land to be benefited is shown 'otherwise' with reasonable certainty. That is a question of fact and, on the admitted facts, bearing in mind the close juxtaposition of Devonia and the defendants' premises, in my view the only reasonable inference to draw from the circumstances at the time of the conveyance of 1923 was that Mrs Mardon took the covenant restrictive of the user of the defendants' premises for the benefit of her own business of ironmonger and of her property Devonia where at all material times she was carrying on that business, which last-mentioned fact must have been apparent to the purchasers in 1923.

I should perhaps mention that at the date of her death, Mrs Mardon owned other property in Fore Street, but counsel on neither side founded any argument on that circumstance.

It follows, therefore, in my judgment, that Mrs Mardon could on any subsequent sale of her land Devonia, if she chose, as part of the transaction of sale, assign the benefit of the covenant so as to enable the purchaser from her and his assignees of the land and covenant to enforce it against an owner of the defendants' premises taking with notice, and her legatee, Leonard Soper Mardon, was in no worse position. I do not regard the fact that he assigned the covenant In the deed containing the assignment of the business as affecting the matter. I say nothing as to the position when the plaintiffs' lease expires so that their estate in Devonia comes to an end, nor whether Leonard Soper Mardon, having apparently assigned away the entire benefit of the covenant, will then be in any position further to enforce it.

Mr Bowles took one further point. He submitted that a covenant restrictive of business could not be annexed to land, unless it was a covenant not to carry on a business so as to be a nuisance or annoyance to an adjoining occupier, but he cited no authority for that proposition and, in my judgment, it cannot be maintained: see *Nicoll v Fenning* (1881) 19 ChD 258.

Accordingly, in my judgment, the plaintiffs are entitled to succeed in this action and to an injunction...

Marten v Flight Refuelling Ltd [1962] Ch 115[167] raised again, inter alia, the questions (a) of the enforceability of the benefit of a covenant when the identity of the land to be benefited could be shown by the use of extrinsic evidence but was not defined in the conveyance itself; and (b) of the devolution of the benefit of a covenant through personal representatives.

In 1943 Mrs Marten, the first plaintiff, was an infant tenant in tail of the Crichel estate, a large agricultural estate in Dorset of about 7,500 acres. In that year, the second plaintiffs, who were then holding the estate in trust for Mrs Marten as special executors under the Settled Land Act 1925, conveyed to Harding in fee simple Crook Farm of some 562 acres of which 200 acres had been requisitioned by the Air Ministry for the establishment of an aerodrome. Harding covenanted with the vendors and their successors in title that no part of the land conveyed nor any building thereon should thereafter be used for any purposes other than agricultural purposes. This covenant was registered in 1943 under Land Charges Act 1925, section 10(1),[168] as a land charge Class D(ii).

In 1947 the Air Ministry permitted the first defendants, Flight Refuelling Ltd, to occupy the aerodrome. In 1950 Mrs Marten attained her majority and disentailed; the second plaintiffs assented to the vesting in her of the fee simple, but the assent did not mention the covenant. In 1958 the Air Ministry compulsorily purchased most of the land still occupied by Flight Refuelling Ltd from Harding's executors. The plaintiffs claimed a declaration that they were entitled to the benefit of the covenant and an injunction to restrain Flight Refuelling Ltd from using the land for industrial purposes.

WILBERFORCE J held, inter alia, that the plaintiffs were entitled to the benefit of the covenant and to an injunction to restrain the company from undertaking industrial activities beyond those necessary for Air Ministry purposes. He said at 129:

First, are the plaintiffs, or is one of them, entitled to the benefit of the restrictive covenant? This involves several subsidiary questions, namely (a) whether the covenant was entered into

---

[167] This is not a case involving annexation or express assignment: (1972) 36 Conv (NS) 20 (E. C. Ryder).
[168] Now LCA 1972, s. 2(5).

for the benefit of any land of the covenantee; (b) whether that land is sufficiently defined or ascertainable by permissible inference or evidence; (c) whether that land is, or was, capable of being benefited by the covenant; (d) whether, since the first plaintiff is not the express assignee of the covenant, the action can be brought by the second plaintiff or by the two plaintiffs jointly.

(a) and (b) This would appear to be a simple point... However, an elaborate argument was addressed to me by the defendants to support a contention that the benefit of the covenant was not available to the plaintiffs. The conveyance, it was said, does not 'annex' the benefit of the covenant to any land so that it would pass automatically on a conveyance of the land to a purchaser. Further, it does not indicate that it was made for the benefit of any land, and even supposing that it was so made, it does not identify or provide any material upon which to identify what that land is.

It is, however, well established by the authorities that the benefit of restrictive covenants can pass to persons other than the original covenantee, even in the absence of annexation, provided that certain conditions are fulfilled. There is, however, dispute as to the nature of these conditions.

The defendants' contentions are, first, that there must appear from the terms of the deed itself an intention to benefit some land, and, secondly, that the precise land to be benefited must also be stated in the deed, or at least must be capable of ascertainment from the terms of the deed by evidence which is admissible in accordance with the normal rules of interpretation of documents. They rely principally on *Re Union of London and Smith's Bank Ltd's Conveyance, Miles v Easter* [1933] Ch 611, and submit that the decision of Upjohn J in *Newton Abbot Cooperative Society Ltd v Williamson and Treadgold Ltd* [1952] Ch 286, [p. 799, above], which appears to admit parole evidence for the purpose of identifying the land to be benefited, goes too far.

His Lordship referred to *Re Union of London and Smith's Bank Ltd's Conveyance, Miles v Easter*; *Formby v Barker* [1903] 2 Ch 539, p. 756, above; *Lord Northbourne v Johnston & Son* [1922] 2 Ch 309, and *Newton Abbot Co-operative Society Ltd v Williamson and Treadgold Ltd*, and, referring to the last, continued:

This decision was attacked by the Attorney-General in a lively argument, and I was invited not to follow it. Of course, it relates to its own special facts, and no doubt I could leave it on one side. But I see nothing in it contrary to the principles which appear to be securely laid down. Here were two shops in common ownership facing each other in the same street, one of them, Devonia, an ironmonger's shop. The shops opposite are sold with a covenant against carrying on an ironmonger's business. What could be more obvious than that the covenant was intended for the protection or benefit of the vendor's property Devonia? To have rejected such a conclusion would, I venture to think, have involved not only an injustice, but a departure from common sense. So far from declining the authority of his case, I welcome it as a useful guide. But it is only a guide, and I must ultimately reach my conclusion on the facts of the present case....

On these facts I consider that I should come to the conclusion that the covenant was taken for the benefit of land of the vendors, that land being the Crichel estate. In doing so I do not, so it seems to me, go outside such surrounding or attendant circumstances as in accordance with the authorities, it is legitimate for the court to take into account. A decision based on the mere wording of clause 2 of the conveyance would, in my judgment be unduly narrow and indeed technical, and would go far to undermine the usefulness of the rule which equity courts have evolved that the benefit of restrictive covenants may be capable of passing to assigns of the 'dominant' land or of the covenant in cases other than those of annexation. I would add two observations: first, the rules in *Miles v Easter* properly relate to cases where the covenant is sought to be enforced by an assign from the original covenantee. In this case, however, the second plaintiff is the original covenantee and the first plaintiff is the person for whose benefit in equity the covenant was taken. To that important extent the plaintiffs' case is stronger than that of the defendant in *Miles v Easter*. Secondly, in holding that the covenant was for the benefit of the Crichel estate, I mean the Crichel estate as a whole, as a single agricultural estate which it was and is, and I express no opinion whether it enures for the benefit of each and every part, for example, if parts are separately sold off. That is not a question which arises in this case.

There remain certain specific arguments which were put forward, and I must shortly deal with them....

It was said that unless the identity of the land to be benefited was clearly stated in, or directly ascertainable from, the conveyance, a purchaser would be placed in an impossible position: he would never know by whom the covenant could be enforced, or whether it was enforceable at all.[169] I am not impressed by this objection: the original covenantee is ascertainable from the document—and moreover appears on or can be ascertained from the land charges register.[170] In a case where the covenant is sought to be enforced by an assign from him, such assign must always prove his right to sue, whether by virtue of annexation, by devolution, by assignment of the benefit of the covenant. The plaintiff may also (as in *Tulk v Moxhay*) have to show that he retains property for whose benefit the covenant was imposed. These are matters which arise in all cases where restrictive covenants are sought to be enforced otherwise than as between the original parties, and I see no greater difficulty in dealing with them in cases such as the present....

Question (c): Was the land capable of being benefited by the covenant? On this point, as on those last dealt with, the answer would appear to be simple. If an owner of land, on selling part of it, thinks fit to impose a restriction on user, and the restriction was imposed for the purpose of benefiting the land retained, the court would normally assume that it is capable of doing so. There might, of course, be exceptional cases where the covenant was on the face of it taken capriciously or not bona fide, but a covenant taken by the owner of an agricultural estate not to use a sold-off portion for other than agricultural purposes could hardly fall within either of these categories. As Sargant J said in *Lord Northbourne v Johnston & Son* [1922] 2 Ch 309, 319: 'Benefit or detriment is often a question of opinion on which there may be the greatest divergence of view, and the greatest difficulty in arriving at a clear conclusion.' Why, indeed, should the court seek to substitute its own standard for those of the parties—and on what basis can it do so? However, much argument was devoted to this point, and evidence was called as to it. These I must consider.

---

[169] (1952) 68 LQR 353, 361.

[170] The position is rather more complex. Land charges are registered against the name of the estate owner whose estate is to be affected: that is against the name of the covenantor. A search will not reveal the name of the covenantee, nor a description of the land. The name and address of the original covenantee will be known to the Land Registry, for they would have been stated on the original application to register, and they may be ascertained by an application for an office copy of an entry in the register on Form K19, Land Charges Rules 1974. That will in most cases be sufficient to identify the benefited land; but often only with the assistance of extrinsic evidence.

First it was said that a mere examination of the figures showed that the covenant could not benefit the estate: the Crichel estate extends in some 7,500 acres, and it was asked how such a covenant could benefit the estate as a whole. In my view, there is no such manifest impossibility about this. I have already referred to the character of the estate, and I can well imagine that, for the owner of it, whether he wished to retain it in his family or to sell it as a whole, it might be of very real benefit to be able to preserve a former outlying portion from development. This seems to me to be a question of fact to be determined on the evidence: and I note that when a similar argument was placed before the court in *Re Ballard's Conveyance* [1937] Ch 473, Clauson J, while accepting it in the absence of evidence, showed it to be his opinion that evidence could have been called. . . .

Question (d): Can the action be brought by the first plaintiffs or by the two plaintiffs jointly? I can deal with this point quite shortly. The second plaintiff is the original covenantee, and the first plaintiff is the person for whose benefit in equity the covenant was made. Taken together, the plaintiffs represent the whole legal and equitable interest in the covenant. The matter appears, therefore, to be completely covered by the judgment of Sargant J in *Lord Northbourne v Johnston & Son*, the reasoning of which I adopt. So much was not really contested by the Attorney-General, who, however, reserved the right to challenge that judgment should this case go to a higher court.

P. V. Baker, 'The Benefit of Restrictive Covenants' (1968) 84 LQR 22 at p. 29

From the principles outlined above, and especially from the analogy of easements, we should expect the right to go along automatically with the benefited or dominant land, and, indeed, this happens where the benefit has been annexed by the original covenant.[171] There is, however, a complicating factor as not every restrictive covenant is initially annexed, and in these cases the covenantee has the option of annexing it to the land or allowing it to lapse. As it cannot exist as a separate piece of property like a profit in gross, there seems to be no justification in principle for requiring it to be passed by a succession of assignments parallel with the assignment of the benefited land, for this is still treating it as either a covenant which is only enforceable as such against the covenantor, or as existing in gross. If the original express covenantor is still the owner of the burdened land, the benefit of the covenant could be assigned separately and then ultimately annexed, but if the burdened land has passed it is annexation or nothing, for it is a piece of property which is an adjunct of the benefited land. In other words, express assignment is delayed annexation. One puts together the deed containing the original covenant and the subsequent conveyance of the benefited land. The original covenant in these cases does not have to indicate the benefited land,[172] but that deficiency is naturally supplied by the subsequent conveyance of it. Building schemes go still further since the annexation is effected by facts which are not necessarily or wholly indicated in the conveyance. . . .

The proposition that an express assignment of the benefit of covenant annexes it to the land so that it will thereafter pass to future owners without express assignment is supported by

---

[171] *Rogers v Hosegood* [1900] 2 Ch 388; and see *Lawrence v South County Freeholds Ltd* [1939] Ch 656 at 680 ('a hidden treasure').

[172] *Newton Abbot Co-operative Society Ltd v Williamson and Treadgold Ltd* [1952] Ch 286.

dicta in older cases[173] and by some writers.[174] It is, however, repudiated by others, expressly[175] or by implication,[176] and in one recent case it was assumed, though not decided, that a chain of assignments was necessary.[177] Until *Stilwell v Blackman*[178] there was no decision which was inconsistent with the proposition, but it must follow that if express assignment operates as a mode of annexation, it is necessarily excluded where annexation has already occurred. Nevertheless, as we have seen, it was decided that annexation did not preclude the passing of the benefit by express assignment.

To the learned judge it was 'a question of construction whether or not express assignment is excluded by annexation'. There was, he said, nothing to interfere with the ordinary principles of contract so that, for example, the covenant could in express terms provide that either annexation or express assignment should be the only method of passing the benefit, or 'since they do not operate against each other, and if there were any advantage in so doing, by both methods simultaneously'.[179] Reference was then made to the dicta in *Renals v Cowlishaw*[180] which supported the proposition that on express assignment the benefit became automatically annexed, but it was thought that these words were not directed to the question of the simultaneous application of both methods of passing the benefit, 'or, indeed, even to the recognition that this question arose'. Nor was it clear 'whether, if there were such automatic annexation, it is suggested that the annexation would be merely to the whole, or also to each and every part of the land passing to the assignee of the covenant'. Ungoed-Thomas J expressed his final conclusion that 'there is no reason either in contract or in the relevant principles of equity why an express assignment of the benefit of a covenant with the passing of land should automatically operate exclusively, as an annexation of the covenant to the land (whether to the whole or to any part of it).'[181]

The reason, it is respectfully suggested, for such automatic annexation, is that when the burdened land passes from the covenantor, one leaves the realm of contract and enters that of property. The question then ceases to be exclusively a matter of what the original parties may or may not have agreed, but what incidents the law will allow. When one finds that the benefit of the covenant cannot exist by itself but only alongside the ownership of the benefited land, convenience suggests that it should be annexed to that land and not require a chain of assignments parallel with the conveyances of the land. Further, if the arguments in the earlier part of this article are accepted, the assignment of the benefit of the covenant by the covenantee would prima facie annex that benefit to each and every part of the land comprised in that benefit.

[173] *Renals v Cowlishaw* (1878) 9 ChD 125 at 130, 131 (affd (1879) 11 ChD 866); *Rogers v Hosegood* [1900] 2 Ch 388 at 408; *Reid v Bickerstaff* [1909] 2 Ch 305 at 320.
[174] Megarry & Wade's *Law of Real Property* (3rd edn, 1966), p. 771; M. Bowles [1962] JPL 234; S. J. Bailey (1938) 6 CLJ 339 at 360, 361.
[175] Preston and Newsom [4th edn, 1967], p. 33, n. 4, relying on a dictum of Romer LJ in *Re Union of London and Smiths' Bank Ltd's Conveyance* [1933] Ch 611 at 631.
[176] Cheshire's *Modern Law of Real Property* (10th edn, 1967), p. 546, relying on another dictum of Romer LJ at p. 630 of the case last cited, but this was dealing with concurrent assignments of different parts of the benefited land by the original covenantee.
[177] *Re Pinewood Estate, Farnborough* [1958] Ch 280, criticised H. W. R. Wade [1957] CLJ 146. [See also *Federated Homes Ltd v Mill Lodge Properties Ltd* [1980] 1 WLR 594 at 603 where John Mills QC said: 'I am not satisfied or prepared to hold that there is any such thing as "delayed annexation by assignment" to which the covenantor is not party or privy.']
[178] [[1968] Ch 508]. [179] [[1968] Ch 508 at 525].
[180] [See n. 173, above.] [181] [At 526.]

(b) Law of Property Act 1925, section 62

In **Roake v Chadha** [1984] 1 WLR 40, p. 787, above, Judge Paul Baker QC said at 46:

I must now turn to the alternative argument of the plaintiffs based on section 62 of the Law of Property Act 1925. This argument is directed to the conveyances or transfers conveying the alleged benefited land to the predecessors of the plaintiffs, and ultimately to the respective plaintiffs themselves. In each of these transfers, so I am prepared to assume, there is to be implied the general words of section 62 of the Act of 1925:

His Honour read sub-s. (1), p. 664, above, and continued:

The argument is that the benefit of the covenant contained in the original transfer to the predecessor of the defendants, William Lambert, was carried by the words 'rights and advantages whatsoever appertaining or reputed to appertain to the land, or any part thereof.' It seems an argument on these lines was accepted by Mr John Mills QC, the deputy judge who gave the decision at first instance in the *Federated Homes* case [1980] 1 WLR 594 [p. 783, above], but I have not seen it, and so cannot comment on it. The proposition now contended for is not a new one. In *Rogers v Hosegood* [1900] 2 Ch 388, it was similarly put forward as an alternative argument to an argument based on annexation. In that case however it was decided that the benefit of the covenant was annexed so that the point on section 6 of the Conveyancing Act 1881, the forerunner of section 62 of the Law of Property Act 1925, did not have to be decided. Nevertheless, Farwell J, sitting in the Chancery Division, said, at 398:

> 'It is not necessary for me to determine whether the benefit of the covenants would pass under the general words to which I have referred above, if such covenants did not run with the land. If they are not in fact annexed to the land, it may well be that the right to sue thereon cannot be said to belong, or be reputed to belong, thereto; but I express no final opinion on this point.'

In the Court of Appeal the point was canvassed in argument but not referred to in the judgment of the court, which was given by Collins LJ.

In the present case, the covenant in terms precludes the benefit passing unless it is expressly assigned. That being so, as it seems to me, it is not a right 'appertaining or reputed to appertain' to land within the meaning of section 62 of the Law of Property Act 1925. As to whether the benefit of a covenant not annexed can ever pass under section 62, I share the doubts of Farwell J. Mr Henty suggested—and there may well be something in this—that the rights referred to in section 62 are confined to legal rights rather than equitable rights which the benefit of restrictive covenants is. But again I place it on construction. It cannot be described as a right appertaining or reputed to appertain to land when the terms of the covenant itself would seem to indicate, or indicates, to be the opposite.[182]

---

[182] See also (1971) 87 LQR 539 at p. 570 (D. J. Hayton); *Shropshire County Council v Edwards* (1982) 46 P & CR 270 at 279, where Judge Rubin 'decided to remain silent on this highly debatable point under section 62, since a determination was not necessary.' See also *Kumar v Dunning* [1989] QB 193, where Sir Nicolas Browne-Wilkinson V-C said at 198: 'A right under covenant cannot appertain to the land unless the benefit is in some way annexed to the land. If the benefit of a covenant passes under s. 62 even if not annexed to the land, the whole modern law of restrictive covenants would have been established on an erroneous basis.'

(iii) Scheme of development[183]

The necessity to show either express annexation or express assignment of the benefit of a restrictive covenant is avoided if the circumstances surrounding a series of sales indicate an intention that all the purchasers should be bound by restrictive covenants, and that each should be able to enforce them against the others. In such circumstances there is a scheme of development. There is created a sort of 'local law'[184] among the purchasers, disregarding the ordinary rules of contract and covenants and permitting mutual enforcement. 'The major theoretical difficulties', says Megarry J,[185] 'based on the law of covenant seem to me to disappear when instead there is an equity created by circumstances which is independent of contractual obligation'. The same principle applies where there is a letting scheme for individual flats in a single building under which the intention is that each lessee should have the benefit of restrictive covenants relating to the common user of the property.[186]

The test for the existence of a scheme of development has been modified in the past 40 years; the emphasis has changed from a position in which specific requirements need to be observed to one in which there must be a defined area and 'the existence of the common interest and the common intention actually expressed in the conveyances themselves.'[187]

In **Elliston v Reacher** [1908] 2 Ch 374,[188] PARKER J said at 384:

I pass, therefore, to the consideration of the question whether the plaintiffs can enforce these restrictive covenants. In my judgment, in order to bring the principles of *Renals v Cowlishaw* (1878) 9 ChD 125 and *Spicer v Martin* (1888) 14 App Cas 12 into operation it must be proved (1) that both the plaintiffs and defendants derive title under a common vendor; (2) that previously to selling the lands to which the plaintiffs and defendants are respectively entitled, the vendor laid out his estate, or a defined portion thereof (including the lands purchased by the plaintiffs and defendants respectively), for sale in lots subject to restrictions intended to be

---

[183] For the history of the development of the present doctrine, see *Whatman v Gibson* (1838) 9 Sim 196; *Coles v Sims* (1854) 5 De GM & G 1; *Sidney v Clarkson* (1865) 35 Beav 118; *Western v MacDermott* (1866) 2 Ch App 72; *Renals v Cowlishaw* (1878) 9 ChD 125; *Gaskin v Balls* (1879) 13 ChD 324; *Nottingham Patent Brick and Tile Co v Butler* (1885) 15 QBD 261; on appeal (1886) 16 QBD 778; *Collins v Castle* (1887) 36 ChD 243; *Spicer v Martin* (1888) 14 App Cas 12; *Mackenzie v Childers* (1889) 43 ChD 265; *White v Bijou Mansions Ltd* [1938] Ch 351. For successful schemes, see *Baxter v Four Oaks Properties Ltd* [1965] Ch 816, p. 811, below; *Re Dolphin's Conveyance* [1970] Ch 654, p. 811, below; *Eagling v Gardner* [1970] 2 All ER 838; *Brunner v Greenslade* [1971] Ch 993; *Texaco Antilles Ltd v Kernochan* [1973] AC 609; *Re 6, 8, 10 and 12 Elm Avenue, New Milton* [1984] 1 WLR 1398; cf. *Lund v Taylor* (1975) 31 P & CR 167, p. 814, below, especially Stamp LJ at 176; *Kingsbury v LW Anderson Ltd* (1979) 40 P & CR 136, p. 815, n. 199, below; *Allen v Veranne Builders Ltd* [1988] EGCS 2; *Emile Elias & Co Ltd v Pine Groves Ltd* [1993] 1 WLR 305. This is in marked contrast to the usual fate of schemes during the previous four decades; Preston & Newsom, paras 2–53 to 2–83.
On schemes of development in registered land, see R & R, chap. 21.

[184] *Reid v Bickerstaff* [1909] 2 Ch 305 at 319; *Re Dolphin's Conveyance* [1970] Ch 654 at 663, per Stamp J.

[185] *Brunner v Greenslade* [1971] Ch 993 at 1005.

[186] *Spicer v Martin* (1888) 14 App Cas 13; extended in *Williams v Kiley* [2003] 1 EGLR 46 to competing traders holding leases within a single development.

[187] *Re Dolphin's Conveyance*, above, at 664; *Lund v Taylor*, above, at 178.

[188] Affirmed by CA [1908] 2 Ch 665.

imposed on all the lots, and which, though varying in details as to particular lots, are consistent and consistent only with some general scheme of development;[189] (3) that these restrictions were intended by the common vendor to be and were for the benefit of all the lots intended to be sold,[190] whether or not they were also intended to be and were for the benefit of other land retained by the vendor;[191] and (4) that both the plaintiffs and the defendants, or their predecessors in title, purchased their lots from the common vendor upon the footing that the restrictions subject to which the purchases were made were to enure for the benefit of the other lots included in the general scheme whether or not they were also to enure for the benefit of other lands retained by the vendors. If these four points[192] be established, I think that the plaintiffs would in equity be entitled to enforce the restrictive covenants entered into by the defendants or their predecessors with the common vendor irrespective of the dates of the respective purchases. I may observe, with reference to the third point, that the vendor's object in imposing the restrictions must in general be gathered from all the circumstances of the case, including in particular the nature of the restrictions. If a general observance of the restrictions is in fact calculated to enhance the values[193] of the several lots offered for sale, it is an easy inference that the vendor intended the restrictions to be for the benefit of all the lots, even though he might retain other land the value of which might be similarly enhanced, for a vendor may naturally be expected to aim at obtaining the highest possible price for his land. Further, if the first three points be established, the fourth point may readily be inferred, provided the purchasers have notice of the facts involved in the three first points; but if the purchaser purchases in ignorance of any material part of those facts, it would be difficult, if not impossible, to establish the fourth point.... It is, I think, enough to say, using Lord Macnaghten's words in *Spicer v Martin* (1888) 14 App Cas 12, that where the four points I have mentioned are established, the community of interest imports in equity the reciprocity of obligation which is in fact contemplated by each at the time of his own purchase.

A further requirement was added in **Reid v Bickerstaff** [1909] 2 Ch 305, where Cozens-Hardy MR said at 319:

In my opinion there must be a defined area within which the scheme is operative. Reciprocity is the foundation of the idea of a scheme. A purchaser of one parcel cannot be subject to an implied obligation to purchasers of an undefined and unknown area. He must know both the extent of his burden and the extent of his benefit. Not only must the area be defined, but the obligations

---

[189] See *Jackson v Bishop* (1979) 48 P & CR 57 (developer held liable for breach of covenant of title and negligence where there was a double conveyance due to inaccurate plans of neighbouring plots).

[190] 'The mere fact that the covenant is not expressly stated to be for the benefit of the plot holders is in no sense decisive....I do not think that it is inconsistent with the existence of a scheme of development that the vendor retains his right to exempt part of the [Wildernesse] Estate from stipulations': *Allen v Veranne Builders Ltd*, above, n. 183, per Sir Nicolas Browne-Wilkinson V-C.

[191] The reservation to the vendor of the right to sell land free from the restriction is of little force either for or against the existence of a building scheme: *Re Wembley Park Estate Co Ltd's Transfer* [1968] Ch 491 at 498; *Eagling v Gardner* [1970] 2 All ER 838.

[192] 'They are in summary, first, common title, second, setting out of lots, third, an intention to be for the benefit of all lots, and, fourth, purchase by the parties or their predecessors upon that footing': *Briggs v McCusker* [1996] 2 EGLR 197 at 199, per Judge Rich QC.

[193] 'Enhancement in value...does not mean merely monetary enhancement, but also enhancement of the ambiance in which the residents live': *Allen v Veranne Builders Ltd*, above, n. 183.

to be imposed within that area must be defined.[194] Those obligations need not be identical. For example, there may be houses of a certain value in one part and houses of a different value in another part. A building scheme is not created by the mere fact that the owner of an estate sells it in lots and takes varying covenants from various purchasers. There must be notice to the various purchasers of what I may venture to call the local law imposed by the vendors upon a definite area.[195]

In **Baxter v Four Oaks Properties Ltd** [1965] Ch 816 there was no evidence that the common vendor 'laid out the part of his estate…in plots before beginning to sell it off. He appeared to have sold plots, of the size which purchasers wished to take, to purchasers as they came along'. Cross J held that there was a scheme, having found sufficient evidence of an intention to create mutually binding covenants, although Parker J's second requirement was not observed.

Re Dolphin's Conveyance
[1970] Ch 654 (ChD, Stamp J)[196]

The Selly Hill Estate, of some 30 acres near Birmingham, became vested in fee simple in Ann and Mary Dolphin as tenants in common. In 1871 they sold off four parcels, and each purchaser entered into a restrictive covenant with them that only detached dwelling houses, each of at least one-quarter acre, should be built on the land. The vendors covenanted to procure similar covenants from subsequent purchasers of any other part of the estate. Ann Dolphin died in 1873, leaving by will her interest in the unsold part of the estate to her nephew, John Watts. In 1876 John became owner in fee simple in possession when Mary Dolphin made a deed of gift to him of her share. He then sold off the remainder of the estate in six parcels, in each case taking a restrictive covenant, and, except for the last parcel, giving a covenant to procure similar covenants from subsequent purchasers.

In 1969 part of the estate was purchased by Birmingham Corporation, whose predecessor in title had purchased part in 1871 from Ann and Mary, and part in 1877 from John. The Corporation wished to build in breach of the covenants, of which it had notice. It sought a declaration that the land was no longer subject to them, and argued that there was no building scheme, since there was no common vendor, and no lotted plan prior to the sales.

Held. There was a scheme, and the covenants were binding.

---

[194] It is not necessary that the covenants entered into should benefit only the defined area: *Allen v Veranne Builders Ltd*, above, n. 183.

[195] See also Buckley LJ at 323; cited with approval by PC in *Jamaica Mutual Life Assurance Society v Hillsborough Ltd* [1989] 1 WLR 1101 (no reciprocity: no building scheme); *Torbay Hotel Ltd v Jenkins* [1927] 2 Ch 225 at 240, per Clauson J; *Emile Elias & Co Ltd v Pine Groves Ltd* [1993] 1 WLR 305 at 310, per Lord Browne-Wilkinson; *Whitgift Homes Ltd v Stocks* [2001] EWCA (Civ) 1732, [2001] 48 EGCS 130 (no defined area within which scheme intended to operate; but land sufficiently identified for the purposes of annexation under LPA 1925, s. 78).

[196] (1970) 86 LQR 445 (P. V. B.); 117 SJ 798 (G. H. Newsom). For the modification of these covenants under LPA 1925, s. 84, see *Re Farmiloe's Application* (1983) 48 P & CR 317, p. 828, n. 256, below.

Stamp J: As Cross J pointed out in the course of the judgment in *Baxter v Four Oaks Properties Ltd* [1965] Ch 816...the intention that the several purchasers from a common vendor shall have the benefit of the restrictive covenants imposed on each of them, may be evidenced by the existence of a deed of mutual covenant to which all the several purchasers are to be parties.[197] That common intention may also be evidenced by, or inferred from, the circumstances attending the sales: the existence of what has often been referred to in the authorities as a building scheme. I have been referred to a considerable number of authorities where the court has had to consider whether there were, or were not, present in the particular case those facts from which a building scheme—and, therefore, the common intention to lay down a local law involving reciprocal rights and obligations between the several purchasers—could properly be inferred. In *Elliston v Reacher* [1908] 2 Ch 374, 384, Parker J laid down the necessary concomitants of such a scheme.

What has been argued before me is that here there is neither a deed of mutual covenant nor a building scheme. In the latter connection, it is pointed out that there was not a common vendor, for the parcels were sold off, first by the Dolphins and then by Watts. Nor, prior to the sales, had the vendor laid out the estate, or a defined portion of it, for sale in lots. Therefore, so it is urged, there were not present the factors which, on the authority of *Elliston v Reacher* [1908] 2 Ch 374 [p. 809, above], are necessary before one can find the existence of a building scheme.

In my judgment, these submissions are not well-founded. To hold that only where you find the necessary concomitants of a building scheme or a deed of mutual covenant can you give effect to the common intention found in the conveyances themselves, would, in my judgment, be to ignore the wider principle on which the building scheme cases are founded and to fly in the face of other authority of which the clearest and most recent is *Baxter v Four Oaks Properties Ltd* [1965] Ch 816. The building scheme cases stem, as I understand the law, from the wider rule that if there be found the common intention and the common interest referred to by Cross J at 825 in *Baxter v Four Oaks Properties Ltd* the court will give effect to it, and are but an extension and example of that rule. Hall V-C remarked in his judgment in *Renals v Cowlishaw* (1878) 9 ChD 125, 129:

> 'This right exists not only where the several parties execute a mutual deed of covenant, but wherever a mutual contract can be sufficiently established. A purchaser may also be entitled to the benefit of a restrictive covenant entered into with his vendor by another or others where his vendor has contracted with him that he shall be the assign of it, that is, have the benefit of the covenant. And such contract need not be express, but may be collected from the transaction of sale and purchase.'

That passage was quoted, with approval, by Lord Macnaghten in *Spicer Martin* (1889) 14 App Cas 12, 24. (I ought perhaps to mention that the word 'contract' in the last sentence I have quoted was substituted for the word 'covenant' in the errata in the volume of the reports in which *Renals v Cowlishaw* is reported.) Moreover, where deeds of mutual covenant have fallen to be considered, effect has been given not to the deed of mutual covenant itself as such but to the intention evidenced by its existence. *Baxter v Four Oaks Properties Ltd* is such a case. As Parker J in *Elliston v Reacher* [1908] 2 Ch 374, 384 pointed out in a passage quoted by Cross J in *Baxter v Four Oaks Properties Ltd* at 826, the equity arising out of the establishment of the four points which he mentioned as the necessary concomitants of a building scheme has been sometimes explained by the implication of mutual contracts between the various

---

[197] See, for example, *Price v Bouch* (1986) 53 P & CR 257 (co-operative scheme on part of 53 Victorian tradesmen in Northumberland).

purchasers and sometimes by the implication of a contract between each purchaser and the common vendor, that each purchaser is to have the benefit of all the covenants by the other purchasers, so that each purchaser is in equity an assign of the benefit of those covenants; but the implication of mutual contracts is not always a satisfactory explanation. Parker J in *Elliston v Reacher*...points out that a prior purchaser may be dead or incapable of contracting at the time of a subsequent purchase, and that in any event it is unlikely that the prior and subsequent purchasers are ever brought into personal relationship, and yet the equity may exist between them.

There is not, therefore, in my judgment, a dichotomy between the cases where effect has been given to the common intention inferred from the existence of the concomitants of a building scheme and those where effect has been given to the intention evidenced by the existence of a deed of covenant. Each class of case, in my judgment, depends upon a wider principle. Here the equity, in my judgment, arises not by the effect of an implication derived from the existence of the four points specified by Parker J in *Elliston v Reacher* at 384, or by the implication derived from the existence of a deed of mutual covenant, but by the existence of the common interest and the common intention actually expressed in the conveyances themselves.

In *Nottingham Patent Brick and Tile Co v Butler* (1885) 15 QBD 261 at 268, Wills J, in a passage which I find illuminating and which was referred to with approval in the Court of Appeal (1886) 16 QBD 778, put the matter thus:

'The principle which appears to me to be deducible from the cases is that where the same vendor selling to several persons plots of land, parts of a larger property, exacts from each of them covenants imposing restrictions on the use of the plots sold without putting himself under any corresponding obligation, it is a question of fact whether the restrictions are merely matters of agreement between the vendor himself and his vendees, imposed for his own benefit and protection, or are meant by him and understood by the buyers to be for the common advantage of the several purchasers. If the restrictive covenants are simply for the benefit of the vendor, purchasers of other plots of land from the vendor cannot claim to take advantage of them. If they are meant for the common advantage of a set of purchasers, such purchasers and their assigns may enforce them inter se for their own benefit. Where, for instance, the purchasers from the common vendor have not known of the existence of the covenants, that is a strong, if not a conclusive, circumstance to shew that there was no intention that they should enure to their benefit. Such was the case in *Keates v Lyon* (1869) 4 Ch App 218; *Master v Hansard* (1876) 4 ChD 718; and *Renals v Cowlishaw* (1879) 11 ChD 886. But it is in all cases a question of intention at the time when the partition of the land took place, to be gathered, as every other question of fact, from any circumstances which can throw light upon what the intention was: *Renals v Cowlishaw*. One circumstance which has always been held to be cogent evidence of an intention that the covenants shall be for the common benefit of the purchasers is that the several lots have been laid out for sale as building lots, as in *Mann v Stephens* (1846) 15 Sim 377; *Western v MacDermott* (1866) 2 Ch App 72; *Coles v Sims* (1853) Kay 56, 5 De GM & G 1; or, as it has been sometimes said, that there has been "a building scheme": *Renals v Cowlishaw* (1879) 11 ChD 866 at 867.'

I can approach the matter in another way. The conveyances of the several parts of the estate taking the form they do, and evidencing the same intention as is found in a deed of mutual covenant, I equate those conveyances with the deed of mutual covenant considered by Cross J in *Baxter v Four Oaks Properties Ltd* [1965] Ch 816—the deed which he did not treat for the purposes of his judgment as itself bringing all the successive purchasers and persons claiming through them into contractual relations one with the other, but as showing the common intention. So equating them, I follow what I conceive to be the ratio decidendi of *Baxter v Four Oaks*

Properties Ltd and give effect to that intention by holding that the restrictive covenants are enforceable by the successors in title of each of the original covenantors against any of them who purchased with notice of those restrictions.

In **Lund v Taylor** (1975) 31 P & CR 167,[198] the Court of Appeal (Russell and Stamp LJJ and Sir John Pennycuick) held that no scheme of development could be inferred. Stamp LJ (delivering the judgment of the Court) said at 176:

Because there was no extrinsic evidence, nor anything in his own conveyance to show a purchaser that there was a scheme relating to a defined area or that Tellings [the vendors], if they did, intended that stipulations should be imposed in respect of each part of that area, he could not on the authority of *Reid v Bickerstaff*[1909] 2 Ch 305 be subject to an implied obligation to the other purchasers. On this ground alone the action must in our opinion fail. Whatever scheme involving reciprocal rights and obligations Tellings may have sought to establish, the necessary evidence that the several purchasers intended to be bound by a scheme or local law under which they were to have reciprocal rights and obligations is lacking. The difficulties of the plaintiffs in this regard are perhaps emphasised when one observes that whatever inference you may draw from the conveyances there is nothing in them from which a purchaser could draw the inference that Tellings intended to confer on a purchaser a right to prevent Tellings from dealing as they thought fit—e.g. by the erection of a block of flats—with the unplotted part of the estate. . . .

Because it was submitted that in recent times the courts, in determining whether the necessary ingredients of a building scheme or local law are shown to have existed, have adopted what was called a more liberal approach than was formerly the case it is right that we should refer to the two cases relied upon in support of that submission. They are *Baxter v Four Oaks Properties Ltd*[1965] Ch 816 and *Re Dolphin's Conveyance*[1970] Ch 654. In both those cases it had been submitted that in order to establish a building scheme the requirements laid down by Parker J in *Elliston v Reacher*[1908] 2 Ch 374 must be satisfied. One of those requirements was, and we quote Parker J's judgment, that:

> 'in order to bring the principles of *Renals v Cowlishaw and Spicer v Martin* into operation it must be proved . . . (2) that previously to selling the lands to which the plaintiffs and defendants are respectively entitled the vendor laid out his estate or a defined portion thereof (including the land purchased by the plaintiffs and defendants respectively) for sale in lots subject to restrictions intended to be imposed on all the lots. . . .'

In his judgment in *Baxter v Four Oaks Properties Ltd* Cross J rejected the condition that the defined estate should have been laid out for sale in lots. He pointed out that *Elliston v Reacher* was not a case in which there was direct evidence afforded by the execution of a deed of mutual covenant that the parties intended a building scheme but *whether one could properly infer that intention in all the circumstances.* Cross J took the view, also adopted in *Re Dolphin's Conveyance,* that Mr Justice Parker was not intending to lay down that the fact that the common vendor did not bind himself to sell off the defined area to which the local law was to apply in lots of any particular size but proposed to sell off parcels of various sizes according to the requirements of the various purchasers must, as a matter of law, preclude the court from giving effect to a clearly proved intention that the purchasers were to have rights *inter se* to enforce the provisions of the local law over the area.

---

[198] *Harlow v Hartog* (1977) 245 EG 140 (no scheme of development due to no estate plan).

In *Re Dolphin's Conveyance,* in which the *Baxter v Four Oaks* case was followed, the area over which the scheme or local law was to extend was specified and the intention that the purchasers were to have rights *inter se* to enforce the stipulations of the local law was, so the judge thought, expressed clearly in every conveyance. The stipulations which each purchaser covenanted to observe in the several conveyances were identical[199] and the first and every subsequent conveyance by the vendor contained a covenant by him, in effect, to obtain a covenant from every other purchaser to observe them; a useless series of covenants except upon the basis that all could enforce them. It would, no doubt, have been better if the draftsman of the conveyances in that case had added the words 'to the intent that the covenants by the purchasers shall be mutually enforceable' and if a plan had been attached showing the area affected by the scheme; but the judge found a sufficient indication of that intention and a sufficient identification of that area.

No doubt the last mentioned two cases are authorities for the proposition that Mr Justice Parker, in the well known passage of his judgment in *Elliston v Reacher,* did not intend to lay down that the fact that the common vendor did not bind himself to sell off the defined area to which the local law was to apply in lots of any particular size was fatal to the creation of a local law over that area, but rather that if the vendor has done so you have one of the necessary ingredients from which the creation of the local law may be inferred. And where you find that all those concerned—the vendor and the several purchasers—have by the effect of the documents they have executed evidenced the intention to create such a local law over a defined area those cases are authority for saying that the court may give effect to that intention. But we find nothing in those cases indicating that the conditions from which a 'building scheme' may be inferred from the facts are any different than was formerly the case.

In the instant case the creation of a building scheme cannot for the reasons we have given be inferred; and there is absent from the deeds themselves that clear evidence of intention to create reciprocal rights and obligations over a defined area which was found in *Baxter v Four Oaks Properties Ltd* and in the *Dolphin's Conveyance* cases.

We allow the appeal.

Preston & Newsom, *Restrictive Covenants Affecting Freehold Land* (9th edn, 1998), paras 2-71–2-73, 2-75

The final requirement is, as we have seen, that there shall be sufficient evidence to establish the intention that the purchasers of the lots shall have mutual rights and obligations. Or, as it was put by Stamp J in *Dolphin's* case[200] there must be shown to be 'a common intention to lay down a local law involving reciprocal rights and obligations.' Where that is so the purchasers and their successors 'all have a common interest in maintaining the restriction. This community of interest necessarily ... requires and imports reciprocity of obligation.'[201] This requirement is undoubtedly essential.[202]

The intention can be found in the deed, but extrinsic evidence is admissible and is frequently relied upon. If the scheme of local law is modern, the common vendor may be called to give

---

[199] In *Kingsbury v L W Anderson Ltd* (1979) 40 P & CR 136, the scheme failed where covenants imposed on some plots were expressed to be by way of indemnity only, and on others by way of absolute covenant.

[200] [1970] Ch 654, 662, 663.

[201] *Spicer v Martin* (1888) 14 App. Cas. 12, 25, per Lord Macnaghten.

[202] *Jamaica Life Mutual Assurance Society v Hillsborough* [1989] 1 WLR 1101.

evidence of his own intention.[203] Evidence may also be given by someone who was closely involved with the transactions of the common vendor.[204] In the Lands Tribunal a common vendor has given evidence himself on at least one occasion.[205] Where a scheme is old, there may well be no documents at all except the formal conveyancing instruments, and often only a few of them. The proportion of conveyancing documents that survive varies enormously. In *Dolphin's* case [[1970] Ch 654] almost all of them had been found, though nothing else survived. In the *Wembley Park* case [[1968] Ch 491] a great many conveyancing instruments were in evidence. In the *Texaco* case [[1973] AC 609], where the estate was of some 500 lots, only four conveyances were put in and one of them was of about 300 lots expressed to be subject to no restrictions at all. Nevertheless the scheme was upheld. On the other hand in *White v Bijou Mansions Ltd*[206] Lord Greene MR commented adversely on the fact that only two conveyances were available, and the scheme was not upheld. In *Baxter's* case [[1965] Ch 816] the intention of mutuality was evidenced by a deed of mutual covenant.

In regard to the extrinsic evidence, where it survives, a lotted plan is one of the ingredients from which the creation of a local law may be inferred,[207] as would auction particulars specifying a scheme.[208] The same would no doubt be true of a set of particulars and conditions of sale showing that all the lots were to be taken subject to the relevant paragraphs of a set of standard stipulations. A print of a common form of contract or of conveyance would point in the same direction, though the mere fact that the conveyances are broadly in a common form is not by itself enough.[209] The actual evidence in *Elliston v Reacher* itself is always worth study, if one has to consider a case in which extrinsic evidence is going to be important. In that case Parker J said 'If a general observance of the restrictions is in fact calculated to enhance the value of the several lots offered for sale, it is an easy *inference* that the vendor intended the restrictions to be for the benefit of all.'[210] Likewise, in *White v Bijou Mansions Ltd*[211] Lord Greene MR said that 'an auction sale with provisions for each purchaser to give the same covenants is strong evidence of the intention'. Such contemporaneous, extrinsic evidence is essential where the deeds merely prove the existence of a common vendor and the existence of common covenants. These alone are not enough to prove the requisite intention.[212] Evidence of subsequent acts, such as a deed of release executed by all plot owners, will rarely be sufficient unless the contents of such a deed unequivocally point to the alleged earlier mutual intention.[213]

To conclude this review of the principles underlying the doctrine of schemes, two requirements are essential and are universally insisted upon, namely (i) that the area shall be defined; (ii) that the purchasers from the person who creates the scheme shall purchase on the footing that all purchasers shall be mutually bound by, and mutually entitled to enforce, a defined set of

---

[203] *Kelly v Battershell* [1949] 2 All ER 830, 839, per Cohen LJ.

[204] *Page v Kings Parade Properties Ltd* (1967) 20 P & CR 710; evidence was given by the conveyancing managing clerk of the solicitors for the alleged common vendor.

[205] *Re Emery's Application* (1956) 8 P & CR 113; this evidence was accepted as a substitute for a lotted plan.

[206] [1938] Ch 351.   [207] *Lund v Taylor* (1975) 31 P & CR 167 [p. 814, above].

[208] See *Re Birmingham & District Land Co. and Allday* [1893] 1 Ch 342.

[209] *Re Wembley Park Estate Co Ltd's Transfer* [1968] Ch 491.

[210] Such value is not confined to monetary enhancement: per Browne-Wilkinson V-C, *Allen v Veranne Builders Ltd* [1988] EGCS 2.

[211] [1938] Ch 351.

[212] *Re Wembley Park Estate Co Ltd's Transfer* [1968] Ch 491; *Jamaica Mutual Life Assurance Society v Hillsborough Ltd* [1989] 1 WLR 1101, PC.

[213] *Emile Elias & Co Ltd v Pine Groves Ltd* [1993] 1 WLR 305, PC.

restrictions (varying no doubt to some extent as between lots). A common vendor is usual, but there may be cases in which the purpose of this requirement can be met by some other state of the title. A covenant is probably necessary and a lotted map probably is a great help; but again the purposes which these requirements serve can perhaps be fulfilled in other ways. None of these elements is necessarily decisive in itself or even in combination if the scheme fails for want of either of the two essentials. . . .

Elliston v Reacher appeared to have put the doctrine into something like a final shape, and during the next 60 years schemes were always discussed in terms of the judgment of Parker J in that case. But in retrospect it now seems clear that that judgment was treated too narrowly as defining what came to be known as the rule in *Elliston v Reacher*. This rule was applied with great precision. Thus in *Lawrence v South County Freeholds Ltd*[214] Simonds J described the doctrine as 'this very artificial branch of the law,' and alleged schemes were held to fail in a remarkable number of cases.[215] Some of these decisions were indeed highly artificial and at least two of the cases (*Re Pinewood Estate, Farnborough* and *Page v Kings Parade Properties Ltd*) might very well be decided otherwise today. Between *Elliston v Reacher* in 1908 and *Baxter v Four Oaks Properties Ltd* in 1965 there appear to be only two reported cases in which schemes were upheld. One of them was *Bell v Norman C Ashton Ltd*[216] in 1956, a freehold case noted above, and the other was a leasehold scheme in *Newman v Real Estate Debenture Corpn.*[217] Of this last case Cohen LJ said in *Kelly v Battershell*[218] that it is 'the high-water mark of cases where a scheme can be inferred.'

Since *Baxter's* case, the courts have been prepared to approach the question of a scheme more broadly[219] appealing to *Renals v Cowlishaw* and *Spicer v Martin* rather than to *Elliston v Reacher*. Although the alleged schemes failed to be upheld in the *Wembley Park* case,[220] and in *Lund v Taylor Ltd*,[221] these decisions were based on the fundamental ground that there was no defined area.[222] In *Baxter's* case itself and also in *Dolphin's* case schemes were upheld notwithstanding the absence of lotting, and in the *Texaco* case notwithstanding a considerable scarcity of evidence. The doctrine of schemes, which had become very fragile through excessive

[214] [1939] Ch 656, 674.

[215] See *Reid v Bickerstaff* [1909] 2 Ch 305; *Willé v St. John* [1910] 1 Ch 84, 325; *Browne v Flower* [1911] 1 Ch 219; *Torbay Hotel Ltd v Jenkins* [1927] 2 Ch 225; *Ridley v Lee* [1935] Ch 591; *White v Bijou Mansions Ltd* [1938] Ch 351; *Lawrence v South County Freeholds Ltd* [1939] Ch 656; *Re Pinewood Estate, Farnborough* [1958] Ch 280; *Page v Kings Parade Properties Ltd* (1967) 20 P & CR 710; *Re Wembley Park Estate Co Ltd's Transfer* [1968] Ch 491.

[216] (1956) 7 P & CR 359.

[217] [1940] 1 All ER 131. A leasehold scheme was assumed for the purposes of the decision in *Pearce v Maryon-Wilson* [1935] Ch 188.

[218] [1949] 2 All ER 830, 842.

[219] But, curiously, in *Eagling v Gardner* (1970) 21 P & CR 723, decided six weeks after *Dolphin's* case, neither that case nor *Baxter's* case seems to have been cited, and the decision of the learned judge was founded entirely upon *Elliston v Reacher*.

[220] If *Federated Homes Ltd v Mill Lodge Properties Ltd* [1980] 1 WLR 594 [p. 783, above] was correctly decided the *Wembley Park* case must have been decided wrongly. For, though there was no scheme, the covenants must have been annexed to the land which the common vendor retained at the date of his conveyance to the applicants' predecessor in title. Thus an order under LPA 1925, s. 84(2) declaring the covenants unenforceable cannot have been right.

[221] (1975) 31 P & CR 167.

[222] In the latter case an indication against a scheme was found in the fact that these were provisions requiring the common vendor's consent for such things as lopping trees after the estate was fully developed.

reliance on *Elliston v Reacher,* has been given new vitality by the appeal to the principles of the earlier decisions. Nevertheless the limits to what can be enforced as a scheme are set by the two fundamental requirements upon which the court always insists.

QUESTIONS

1. Why have the strict technicalities which grew up in relation to restrictive covenants been relaxed in favour of a general rule based on the intention of the parties? See *Re Dolphin's Conveyance* [1970] Ch 654, p. 811, above; *Brunner v Greenslade* [1971] Ch 993; *Lund v Taylor* (1975) 31 P & CR 167, p. 814, above; [1972B] CLJ 157 (H. W. R. Wade).

2. Are restrictive covenants in schemes of development registrable? (1928) 78 LJ 39 (J.M.L.); (1933) 77 SJ 550; (1950) 20 Conv (NS) 370 (R. G. Rowley); Emmet, para. 19.042; Farrand (2nd edn), pp. 420–421; Barnsley, pp. 388–389; Preston & Newsom, paras 2–80 to 2–83; *Freer v Unwins Ltd* [1976] Ch 288, p. 754, n. 77, above.

3. Which of the three views of the construction of LPA 1925, s. 78, as set out in the *Federated Homes* case [1980] 1 WLR 594 at 604 (p. 785, above) do you prefer? See *Crest Nicholson Residential (South) Ltd v McAllister* [2004] 1 WLR 2409, paras 43–44, p. 793–794, above; the articles at p. 783, n. 137; and [1972 B] CLJ 151 (H. W. R. Wade).

IV. DISCHARGE AND MODIFICATION[223]

A. THE POSITION AT COMMON LAW

(i) Change in character of neighbourhood. Non-enforcement

Chatsworth Estates Co v Fewell[224]
[1931] 1 Ch 224 (ChD, **Farwell J**)

The predecessors in title of the plaintiffs, owners of Compton Place, Eastbourne, had sold land to the predecessors in title of the defendant subject to various covenants, of which the defendant had notice when he purchased, one of which was that he would not use the land 'otherwise than as a private dwelling house'. The land was on the sea front at Eastbourne, and various owners of adjoining land, which had also been

---

[223] C & B, pp. 693–701; Gray, paras 3.4.83–3.4.97; M & W, paras 32.083–32.093; MM, pp. 472–473; Preston & Newsom, chap. 12; Francis, *Restrictive Covenants and Freehold Land* (2nd edn, 2005), chap. 16; Scamell, *Land Covenants,* chaps 11–21; (1986) 48 MLR 195 (P. Polden).

[224] (1948) 92 SJ 570.

purchased subject to the same covenant from the predecessors in title of the plaintiffs, had, with their consent, used the land for a school, for flats, and in three cases where the circumstances were exceptional for boarding houses. The defendant opened a guest house called Bella Vista; his attention was drawn to the covenant, and he was given an opportunity to apply under section 84 of the Law of Property Act 1925 for the modification of the covenant. He did nothing and this action was for an injunction and damages. The defendant admitted the breach and contended that the covenants were not enforceable for two reasons:

(i)   by reason of the change in the general character of the neighbourhood, whereby the object of those covenants had completely disappeared.

(ii) by reason of the fact that this change had been brought about by the acts and omissions of the plaintiffs and their predecessors in title.

Held. The plaintiffs were entitled to an injunction.

Farwell J: Nothing can be said against the defendant's conduct of his establishment except that it is a breach of covenant. That being so ought I to refuse the plaintiffs relief?

The defendant's first ground of defence is that there has been such a complete change in the character of the neighbourhood, apart from the plaintiff's acts or omissions, that the covenants are now unenforceable. But to succeed on that ground the defendant must show that there has been so complete a change in the character of the neighbourhood that there is no longer any value left in the covenants at all. A man who has covenants for the protection of his property cannot be deprived of his rights thereunder merely by the acts or omissions of other persons unless those acts or omissions bring about such a state of affairs as to render the covenants valueless, so that an action to enforce them would be unmeritorious, not bona fide at all, and merely brought for some ulterior purposes. It is quite impossible here to say that there has been so complete a change in the character of this neighbourhood as to render the covenants valueless to the plaintiffs. Whether right or wrong the plaintiffs are bringing this action bona fide to protect their property, and it is hopeless to say that the change in the character of the neighbourhood is so complete that it would be useless for me to give them any relief.

The defendant really relied on the acts and omissions of the plaintiffs and their predecessors as a bar to equitable relief. Now the plaintiffs are not unduly insistent on the observance of these covenants in this sense, that they do not conduct inquisitorial examinations into their neighbours' lives, and do not make it their business to find out very carefully exactly what is being done, unless the matter is brought to their notice, either by complaints of other inhabitants, or by seeing some board or advertisement. I cannot think that plaintiffs lose their rights merely because they treat their neighbours with consideration. They are doing what they think sufficient to preserve the character of the neighbourhood. Whether they do enough is another matter, but I am quite satisfied that they are not intending, by their acts or omissions, to permit this area to be turned into anything other than a mainly residential area. There is no doubt however that they have permitted breaches of covenant in several cases where houses have been turned into flats, they have permitted at least four houses to be carried on as boarding houses or hotels, and they have not prevented—in some cases because they did not know of them—some half a dozen other houses being used as boarding houses or guest houses.

There are still however a very large number of private dwelling houses in the area, and I am satisfied that while the use of Bella Vista as a guest house or boarding house may not at the moment cause any actual damage to Compton Place or its owners, there is a prospect of damage in the future if the defendant is allowed to continue to use Bella Vista in that way, because it might well lead to many other houses being so used which would undoubtedly damnify the owners of Compton Place, especially if they develop the park and grounds as intended. In that way it will certainly be detrimental to the plaintiffs to permit Bella Vista to be used as a guest house. But whether they are entitled to relief depends on the exact effect of their past acts and omissions.

Now, as stated in many authorities, the principle upon which this equitable doctrine rests is that the plaintiffs are not entitled to relief if it would be inequitable to the defendant to grant it. In some of the cases it is said that the plaintiffs by their acts and omissions have impliedly waived performance of the covenants. In other cases it is said that the plaintiffs, having acquiesced in past breaches, cannot now enforce the covenants. It is in all cases a question of degree. It is in many ways analogous to the doctrine of estoppel, and I think it is a fair test to treat it in that way and ask, 'Have the plaintiffs by their acts and omissions represented to the defendant that the covenants are no longer enforceable and that he is therefore entitled to use his house as a guest house?'[225]

(ii) Unity of seisin

In **Texaco Antilles Ltd v Kernochan** [1973] AC 609, LORD CROSS OF CHELSEA, giving the judgment of the Privy Council, said at 624:

Their Lordships now turn to the 'unity of seisin' point which was the main ground upon which the appellants founded their contention that the restrictions were not binding on them. As stated above from 12 January 1942 until 12 November 1951, Chapmans Ltd owned both the lots now owned by the respondents and also the lots now owned by the appellants. As soon as the two sets of lots came into the same hands it became impossible for any action to enforce the covenants to be brought by the owner of one set against the owner of the other since he was the same person and that fact, so the argument runs, put an end to the restrictions so far as concerned the relations of the two sets of lots inter se.... The point of law which arises for consideration is therefore whether in a case where there is nothing in the conveyance putting an end to the unity of seisin or in the surrounding circumstances to indicate that the restrictions in the scheme are no longer to apply as between the owners of the lots previously in common ownership the fact that they have been in common ownership puts an end to the restrictions so far as concerns the relations of subsequent owners for the time being of that part of the estate inter se so that if the common owner of those lots wished them to apply after the severance he would have to reimpose them as fresh restrictions under a sub-scheme relating to them. It would their

---

[225] See also *Westripp v Baldock* [1939] 1 All ER 279; *Shaw v Applegate* [1977] 1 WLR 970, where an injunction was refused against the original covenantor on grounds of acquiescence, but damages were awarded. Buckley LJ said at 978: 'The real test, I think, must be whether upon the facts of the particular case, the situation has become such that it would be dishonest or unconscionable for the plaintiff, or the person having the right sought to be enforced, to continue to seek to enforce it'; *Gafford v Graham* (1998) 77 P & CR 73; *A-G of Hong Kong v Fairfax Ltd* [1997] 1 WLR 149 (covenant in 999-year Crown lease abandoned); *Harris v Williams-Wynne* [2006] 2 P & CR 27.

Lordships think be somewhat unfortunate if this was the law.... It is no doubt true that if the restrictions in question exist simply for the mutual benefit of two adjoining properties and both those properties are bought by one man the restrictions will automatically come to an end[226] and will not revive on a subsequent severance unless the common owner then recreates them. But their Lordships cannot see that it follows from this that if a number of people agree that the area covered by all their properties shall be subject to a 'local law' the provisions of which shall be enforceable by any owner for the time being of any part against any other owner and the whole area has never at any time come into common ownership an action by one owner of a part against another owner of a part must fail if it can be shown that both parts were either at the inception of the scheme or at any time subsequently in common ownership. The view which their Lordships favour is supported by dicta of Sir H. H. Cozens-Hardy MR in *Elliston v Reacher* [1908] 2 Ch 665, 673 and of Simonds J in *Lawrence v South County Freeholds Ltd* [1939] Ch 656, 677–683, but at the time when this case was heard by the Court of Appeal there was no decision on the point. Subsequently, however, in *Brunner v Greenslade* [1971] Ch 993, which raised the point, Megarry J followed those dicta. The appellants submitted that his decision was wrong but in their Lordships' view it was right.

B. LAW OF PROPERTY ACT 1925, SECTION 84[227]

Under section 84(2) the court may be asked to declare whether land is affected by a restrictive covenant, and under section 84(1) the Lands Tribunal[228] has power in its discretion to modify or discharge such a covenant. Section 84 was substantially amended by Law of Property Act 1969, section 28, extending the powers of the Lands Tribunal to cover a situation where a restrictive covenant which prevents some reasonable use of land confers no substantial benefit on anyone or is contrary to the public interest. Compensation may be ordered in some cases.[229]

---

[226] *Re Tiltwood, Sussex* [1978] Ch 269; (1980) 54 ALJ 156 (G. M. Bates); (1982) 56 ALJ 587 (A. A. Preece); *Re Victoria Recreation Ground, Portslade's Application* (1979) 41 P & CR 119; *Re MCA East Ltd* [2003] 1 P & CR 9.

[227] See also HA 1985, s. 610(1), (2); *Josephine Trust Ltd v Champagne* [1963] 2 QB 160; *Lawntown Ltd v Camenzuli* [2008] 1 WLR 2656; [2008] Conv 328 (J. Morgan); TCPA 1990 ss. 106, 237; Local Government Act 1972, ss. 120(3), 124(2); *R v City of London Council, ex p Master Governors and Commonality of the Mystery of the Barbers of London* [1996] 2 EGLR 128. For possible replacement of TCPA 1990, s. 106, see p. 749, n. 43, above.

[228] See the Lands Tribunal website, www.landstribunal.gov.uk, for information about the Tribunal and up to date copies of the Land Tribunals Rules and Practice Directions. Applications made to the Tribunal under s. 84 are noted in Current Law and in the Journal of Planning and Environment Law. Some are recorded in P & CR, EGLR and the EG. Condensed reports of all applications from 1974–1979 appeared in Lands Tribunal Cases, and decisions since 2000 can be found on the Lands Tribunal website. The address of the Lands Tribunal is Procession House, 55 Ludgate Hill, London EC4. See also Law Commission Report on Land, Valuation and Housing Tribunals 2003 (Law Com No. 281).

[229] For an unsuccessful application to the European Commission of Human Rights (No. 1074/84) on the ground that the Northern Ireland equivalent of s. 84 violated the ECHR, see [1986] Conv 124 (N. Dawson). As to whether s. 84 is compatible with HRA 1998, see Rook, *Property Law and Human Rights*, pp. 208–211.

LAW OF PROPERTY ACT 1925

84. Power to discharge or modify restrictive covenants affecting land.—(1) The Lands Tribunal shall (without prejudice to any concurrent jurisdiction of the court) have power from time to time, on the application of any person interested in any freehold land affected by any restriction[230] arising under covenant[231] or otherwise as to the user thereof or the building thereon,[232] by order wholly or partially to discharge or modify any such restriction[233] on being satisfied[234]

    (a) that by reason of changes in the character of the property or the neighbourhood[235] or other circumstances of the case[236] which the Lands Tribunal may deem material, the restriction ought to be deemed obsolete; or

   (aa) that (in a case falling within subsection (1A) below) the continued existence thereof would impede some reasonable user of the land for public or private purposes[237] or, as the case may be, would unless modified so impede such user;[238] or

    (b) that the persons of full age and capacity for the time being or from time to time entitled to the benefit of the restriction, whether in respect of estates in fee simple or any lesser estates or interests in the property to which the benefit of the restriction is annexed, have agreed, either expressly or by implication,[239] by their acts or omissions, to the same being discharged or modified; or

---

[230] The covenant must be restrictive, not positive: *Blumenthal v Church Commissioners for England* [2005] 1 EGLR 78.

[231] The covenant may be personal only: *Shepherd Homes Ltd v Sandham (No 2)* [1971] 1 WLR 1062; *Gilbert v Spoor* [1983] Ch 27.

[232] *Re Milius's Application* (1995) 70 P & CR 427 (restriction on disposal may not be a restriction on user or building).

[233] *Re Kentwood Properties Ltd's Application* [1987] JPL 137 (discretion to modify not exercised where there had been a 'flagrant, cynical and continuing breach of covenant').

[234] There is a greater presumption that a restriction under a building scheme will be upheld; and a greater burden of proof on the applicant: *Re Lee's Application* (1996) 72 P & CR 439.

[235] *Keith v Texaco Ltd* (1977) 34 P & CR 249 (coming of oil industry to Aberdeenshire); *Re Bradley Clare Estates Ltd's Application* (1987) 55 P & CR 126; *Re Quaffers Ltd's Application* (1988) 56 P & CR 142 (advent of motorway network); *Re North's Application* (1997) 75 P & CR 117 (change in neighbourhood not material; house in Winkfield, Berkshire, retained attractive semi-rural character despite infilling).

[236] *Re Cox's Application* [1985] JPL 564 (covenant requiring occupiers of extension of house in East Sussex to be domestic staff employed for service in the house held obsolete); *Re Beechwood Homes Ltd's Application* [1994] 2 EGLR 178 (covenant requiring any building to be approved by vendors held not obsolete, even though vendors had altered pattern of development and had disappeared from the scene); *Re Kalsi's Application* (1993) 66 P & CR 313; *Re Wards Construction (Medway) Ltd's Application* (1994) 67 P & CR 379 (green field area now an infill site); *Re Kennet Properties Application* [1996] 1 EGLR 163 (original purpose of unimpeded views across each neighbour's land no longer possible due to housing development), *Re Nichols' Application* [1997] 1 EGLR 144; *Re Marcello Developments Ltd's Application* [2002] RVR 146 (frontage and building line restrictions obsolete); *Re Davies' Application* [2001] 1 EGLR 111; *Re Broomhead's Application* [2003] 2 EGLR 157 (purpose of covenant to control development and extract premium on release held not to be obsolete).

[237] See *Stannard v Issa* [1987] AC 175, where PC construed a similar but not identical paragraph under the Restrictive Covenants (Discharge and Modification) Act (No. 2 of 1960) of Jamaica, s. 3(1).

[238] *Shephard v Turner* [2006] 2 P & CR 28 at [58], per Carnwath LJ ('The general purpose [of para. (aa)] is to facilitate the development and use of land in the public interest, having regard to the development plan and the pattern of permissions in the area. The section seeks to provide a fair balance between the needs of development in the area, public and private, and the protection of private contractual rights.').

[239] *Re Memvale Securities Ltd's Application* (1975) 233 EG 689; *Re Fettishaw's Application (No. 2)* (1973) 27 P & CR 292; *Re University of Westminster's Application* (1999) 78 P & CR 82.

(c) that the proposed discharge or modification will not injure the persons entitled to the benefit of the restriction,[240]

and an order discharging or modifying a restriction under this subsection may direct the applicant to pay to any person entitled to the benefit of the restriction such sum by way of consideration[241] as the Tribunal may think it just to award under one, but not both, of the following heads, that is to say, either—

(i) a sum to make up for any loss or disadvantage suffered by that person in consequence of the discharge or modification; or

(ii) a sum to make up for any effect which the restriction had, at the time when it was imposed, in reducing the consideration then received for the land affected by it.

(1A) Subsection (1)(aa) above authorises the discharge or modification of a restriction by reference to its impeding some reasonable user of land in any case in which the Lands Tribunal is satisfied that the restriction, in impeding that user, either—

(a) does not secure to persons entitled to the benefit of it any practical benefits of substantial value or advantage to them; or

(b) is contrary to the public interest;

and that money will be an adequate compensation for the loss or disadvantage (if any) which any such person will suffer from the discharge or modification.

(1B) In determining whether a case is one falling within subsection (1A) above, and in determining whether (in any such case or otherwise) a restriction ought to be discharged or modified, the Lands Tribunal shall take into account the development plan[242] and any declared or ascertainable pattern for the grant or refusal of planning permission in the relevant areas, as well as the period at which and context in which the restriction was created or imposed and any other material circumstances.

(1C) It is hereby declared that the power conferred by this section to modify a restriction includes power to add such further provisions restricting the user of or the building on the land affected as appear to the Lands Tribunal to be reasonable in view of the relaxation of the existing provisions, and as may be accepted by the applicant; and the Lands Tribunal may accordingly refuse to modify a restriction without some such addition.[243]

(2) The court shall have power on the application of any person interested—

(a) to declare whether or not in any particular case any freehold land is, or would in any given event be, affected by a restriction imposed by any instrument; or

(b) to declare what, upon the true construction of any instrument purporting to impose a restriction, is the nature and extent of the restriction thereby imposed

---

[240] *Re Forestmere Properties Ltd's Application* (1980) 41 P & CR 390 ('replacement of one eyesore (Odeon cinema) by another could hardly be said to be an improvement'); *Re Bailey's Application* (1981) 42 P & CR 108 ('quaint rural backwater' not to be changed into riding school with attendant manure and noise including sound of human voice); *Re Livingstones' Application* (1982) 47 P & CR 462 ('eyesore' carport). *Re Severn Trent Water Ltd's Application* (1993) 67 P & CR 236 (site for sewage disposal works to become leisure centre).

[241] In *SJC Construction Co Ltd v Sutton London Borough Council* (1975) 29 P & CR 322, Stephenson LJ said, arguendo, that 'consideration' was probably a mis-print for 'compensation'.

[242] *Re Kennet Properties' Application* [1996] 1 EGLR 163.

[243] *Re Patten Ltd's Application* (1975) 31 P & CR 180; *Re Dransfield's Application* (1975) 31 P & CR 192; *Re Kershaw's Application* (1975) 31 P & CR 187; *Re Banks Application* (1976) 33 P & CR 138; *Re Forestmere Properties Ltd's Application* (1980) 41 P & CR 390; *Re Austin's Application* (1980) 42 P & CR 102; *Re Shah and Shah's Application* (1991) 62 P & CR 450.

and whether the same is, or would in any given event be, enforceable and if so by whom.[244]

Neither subsections (7) and (11) of this section nor, unless the contrary is expressed, any later enactment providing for this section not to apply to any restrictions shall affect the operation of this subsection or the operation for purposes of this subsection of any other provisions of this section.

(3) The Lands Tribunal shall, before making any order under this section, direct such enquiries, if any, to be made of any government department or local authority, and such notices, if any, whether by way of advertisement or otherwise, to be given to such of the persons who appear to be entitled to the benefit of the restriction intended to be discharged, modified, or dealt with as, having regard to any enquiries, notices, or other proceedings previously made, given or taken, the Lands Tribunal may think fit.

(3A) On an application to the Lands Tribunal under this section the Lands Tribunal shall give any necessary directions as to the persons who are or are not to be admitted (as appearing to be entitled to the benefit of the restriction) to oppose the application, and no appeal shall lie against any such direction; but rules under the Lands Tribunal Act 1949 shall make provision[245] whereby, in cases in which there arises on such an application (whether or not in connection with the admission of persons to oppose) any such question as is referred to in subsection (2)(a) or (b) of this section, the proceedings on the application can and, if the rules so provide, shall be suspended to enable the decision of the court to be obtained on that question by an application under that subsection, or by means of a case stated by the Lands Tribunal, or otherwise, as may be provided by those rules or by rules of court.

(5) Any order made under this section shall be binding on all persons, whether ascertained or of full age or capacity or not, then entitled or thereafter capable of becoming entitled to the benefit of any restriction, which is thereby discharged, modified or dealt with, and whether such persons are parties to the proceedings or have been served with notice or not.

(7) This section applies to restrictions whether subsisting at the commencement of this Act or imposed thereafter, but this section does not apply where the restriction was imposed on the occasion of a disposition made gratuitously or for a nominal consideration for public purposes.

(8) This section applies whether the land affected by the restrictions is registered or not.[246]

(9) Where any proceedings by action or otherwise are taken to enforce a restrictive covenant, any person against whom the proceedings are taken, may in such proceedings apply to the court for an order giving leave to apply to the Lands Tribunal under this section, and staying the proceedings in the meantime.[247]

(12) Where a term of more than forty years is created in land (whether before or after the commencement of this Act) this section shall, after the expiration of twenty-five years of the term, apply to restrictions affecting such leasehold land in like manner as it would have applied had the land been freehold:

Provided that this subsection shall not apply to mining leases.

---

[244] Lands Tribunal Rules 1996, r. 16; *In The Girls' Day School Trust (1872) Application* [2002] 2 EGLR 89.
[245] Lands Tribunal Rules 1996 (SI 1996 No. 1002); Lands Tribunal (Amendment) Rules 1997 (SI 1997 No. 1965), 1998 (SI 1998 No. 22), 2003 (SI 2003 No. 2945), 2006 (SI 2006 No. 880); Lands Tribunal (Fees) Rules 1996 (SI 1996 No. 1021); Lands Tribunal Fees (Amendment) Rules 2002 (SI 2002 No. 770); Scamell, chap. 21. Lands Tribunal Practice Directions are available on the Lands Tribunal website, n. 228, above.
[246] As amended by LRA 2002, ss. 133, Sch. 11, para. 2(1), (5), Sch. 13.
[247] *Luckies v Simons* [2003] 2 P & CR 30.

In **Ridley v Taylor** [1965] 1 WLR 611, HARMAN LJ said at 617:

Section 84(1) of the Law of Property Act 1925 primarily applies to restrictions on freehold land, but by subsection (12), as amended by the Landlord and Tenant Act 1954, is made applicable to restrictions affecting leasehold land where a term of more than 40 years is created by the lease of which more than 25 years have expired. It seems to me that it should be more difficult to persuade the court to exercise its discretion in leasehold than in freehold cases.[248] In the latter the court is relaxing in favour of a freeholder's own land restrictions entered into for the benefit of persons owning other land. In the former the land in question is the property of the covenantee who is prima facie entitled to preserve the character of his reversion. Section 84 cases usually arise between the assigns of both the benefit and the burden of the covenant, and one may suppose that the section was designed with a view to cases within the doctrine of Tulk v Moxhay, but there is nothing in the language of the section to limit the power of the court to a case where the lessee is not himself bound by contract, and I do not feel able to say that such a covenant cannot be modified under the section, although it seems to me that the court should be slow to relieve an applicant of covenants which he himself has entered into. Were it otherwise, it would be easy to avoid the effect of the section by an assignment. It is to be observed that what is to be discharged or modified is not the covenant, but any restriction under the covenant, and it was suggested that this would leave direct contractual liability untouched. This would produce an extraordinary result in a case where the restriction was modified in favour of an assign if the covenantee could still sue the original covenantor in damages on his contractual liability although he had parted with all interest in the property. I cannot but think that the covenant must, where an order is made, be treated in all respects as modified or discharged.

H. W. Wilkinson, 'Covenant 'Impeding Some Reasonable User' (1979) 129 NLJ 523[249]

In Re Bass Ltd's Application (1973) 26 P & CR 156, the Tribunal (J S Daniel QC) accepted the submission of counsel, Graham Eyre QC, that the questions which properly arose [under subsection (1)(aa)] were:

1 Is the proposed user reasonable?
2 Do the covenants impede that user?
3 Does impeding the proposed user secure practical benefits to the objectors?
4 If yes, are those benefits of substantial value or advantage?
5 Is impeding the proposed user contrary to the public interest?
6 If no, would money be an adequate compensation?
7 If yes, would money be an adequate compensation?

In considering questions 3 to 7 inclusive, regard must be had to the planning context, by subsection (1B).

The questions will be discussed in the order of formulation.

---

[248] 'Since 1950, something over a dozen of these cases [under s. 84(12)] have appeared in the Property, Planning and Compensation Reports and in about two-thirds of them the lessee has succeeded': Preston & Newsom, para. 10–21. See, e.g., Re Briarwoods Estates Ltd (1979) 39 P & CR 419; Re EMI (Social Centres) Ltd's Application (1979) 39 P & CR 421; Re Forestmere Properties Ltd's Application (1980) 41 P & CR 390.

[249] See further (2000) 150 NLJ 1525, 1623 (H. W. Wilkinson).

1. *Is the proposed user reasonable?*

In the *Bass* case (1973) the applicants sought the modification of a covenant in order to allow them to use some of their land for the loading and unloading of 228 articulated lorries daily—a 'trunker park'. There had been objections from over 200 nearby house owners. The Tribunal considered that the purpose of the restriction was to make a '*cordon sanitaire* of residential buildings masking any new industrial development'. The applicants already had planning permission for the development and the Tribunal said that 'planning permissions are very persuasive in this connection' though it must not be thought that the question of reasonable user 'could always be concluded in the affirmative by the production of a planning permission'. Partly because of the need for businesses in the area to be provided with communications it was held that the proposed user was reasonable.

The first hurdle is not usually difficult for an applicant to surmount. It is not easy for an objector to establish that there is anything unreasonable about a wish to build houses or flats or to extend a legitimate business enterprise. The requirement of reasonableness was satisfied in all the following cases (though not all the applications eventually succeeded):

Re John Twiname Ltd's Application (1971) 23 P & CR 413; covenant imposed in 1924 not to build within 200 feet of a mansion house, The Towers, which was now four habitations and had two pairs of semi-detached houses in its grounds. A proposal to build three pairs of semis and three detached houses within 200 feet of the house was held to be reasonable.

Re Beardsley's Application (1972) 25 P & CR 233; covenant imposed in 1922 forbade the building of more than two private residences on the site. A proposed development of 12 flats, each with a garage, was held to be reasonable.

Re Carter's Application (1973) 25 P & CR 542; infilling with a second house of conventional design in keeping with the other houses on the site held to be reasonable although there was a covenant against putting more than one dwelling house on the plot.

Re Osborn's and Easton's Application [(1978) 38 P & CR 251]; restrictions were imposed on two sites in 1913 to ensure that not more than one house was put on to each plot. A proposal to erect two blocks of flats to make 20 flats on one and 12 on the other was held reasonable.[250]

2. *Do the covenants impede that user?*

If the applicant did not consider that the covenant impeded or was likely to impede his proposed development he would not make the application under section 84(1) and if the objector did not feel that the covenant impeded the user he would not object. An affirmative answer to question 2 will almost invariably follow an affirmative answer to question 1. If there is doubt about whether any land is affected by a restriction, or about the nature and extent of the restriction the appropriate procedure is to apply for construction of the restriction, under section 84(2).

3. *Does impeding the proposed user secure practical benefits to the objectors?*

The following decisions may help to give meaning to the phrase 'practical benefits'. The statute is silent on the matter.

[250] [See also *Re Manxguard Ltd's Application* [1982] JPL 521 (restriction imposed in 1862 on use of building in Saltburn-by-the-Sea as a public house modified to convert it into Victorian style inn); *Re Hextall's Application* (2000) 79 P & CR 82 (development for social housing and open space purposes held to be reasonable user).]

(a) Loss of privacy and view

A proposed block of flats would have had a 'devastating effect' on the amenities and value of a house as the house's principal rooms would face it and be overlooked by it, *Re Mercian Housing Society's Application* (1971) 23 P & CR 116.

Gardens of existing houses would be overlooked by two proposed houses. One garden could be screened to some extent by a hawthorn hedge but as the Tribunal said, a hawthorn is a poor substitute for a covenant, *Re Gossip's Application* (1972) 25 P & CR 215.[251]

(b) Increase in density

Covenants allowed one house per acre, the proposal was to put 32 houses into four acres. It was held that this would be alien to the character of the area, 'it is not merely the arithmetic of the density which matters, but the general effect on the amenity of the area', *Re Collins' Application* (1974) 30 P & CR 527.[252]

A proposal to build ten houses on backland where covenants would allow none was refused. It would otherwise result in objectors finding 'dumped virtually on their back doors a group of houses with no apparent visual relationship with their own properties', *Re Patten Ltd's Application* (1975) 31 P & CR 180.

(c) Other loss of amenity

A proposed block of 12 flats would deprive the objectors of space, quiet, light and some sunlight, *Re Ward's Construction (Medway) Ltd's Application* (1973) 25 P & CR 223; another proposal would deprive objectors of 'peace and quiet and the feeling of openness which the restriction gave them', *Re Davies' Application* (1971) 25 P & CR 115. Both applications failed.[253]

A local authority which had granted planning permission for six flats in a two-storey block objected validly that the block would injure the view from an old people's dwelling which they proposed to erect on the dominant land, *Re SJC Construction Co Ltd's Application* (1974) 28 P & CR 200.

---

[251] [See also *Re Bank's Application* (1976) 33 P & CR 138 ('direct view of the sea is of immense value'); *Re Bovis Homes Southern Ltd's Application* [1981] JPL 368 (beauty and aesthetic and historic interest of National Trust house and its setting); *Gilbert v Spoor* [1983] Ch 27 (resplendent view over Tyne valley from road *adjacent to* objector's land); [1984] Conv 429 (P. Polden); *Re Burr's Application* [1987] JPL 137 (amenities of a high class development); *Stannard v Issa* [1987] AC 175 ('the privacy and quietude of an enclave of single dwellings in large gardens is going to be adversely affected by the introduction on adjoining lands of no less than 40 additional families', per Lord Oliver of Aylmerton at 196); *Re Bushell's Application* (1987) 54 P & CR 386 (particularly fine landscape view at Wimbledon 'very unusual so near the centre of London'); *Re Purnell's Application* (1987) 55 P & CR 133 (large garden providing privacy in Orpington, Kent); *Re William's Application* (1987) 55 P & CR 400 (sense of spaciousness; preventing nuisance of building works); *Re Whiting's Application* (1988) 58 P & CR 321 (natural beauty of Howley, Gloucestershire); *Re Tarhale Ltd's Application* (1990) 60 P & CR 368 (preventing intolerable nuisance during construction work); *Re Hopcraft's Application* (1993) 66 P & CR 475 (pleasant open area to remain open); *Re Heydeshire's Application* (1993) 67 P & CR 93; *Dobbin v Redpath* [2007] 4 All ER 465 (in the case of covenants within a building scheme there is a different approach to application of s. 84(1) discretion, although not a 'presumption' against modification); *Duffield v Gandy* [2008] EWCA Civ 379, [2008] 2 P & CR D16 (privacy to be protected against erection of a bungalow and from use of an adjoining part of property as a garden ancillary to occupation of the bungalow).]

[252] [*Re Diggens Application* [2001] 2 EGLR 163 (practical benefits secured by density restriction were preservation of view, privacy, seclusion and sense of spaciousness and tranquillity in semi-rural atmosphere).]

[253] [*Re Ballamy's Application* [1977] JPL 456 ('enjoyment of evening sunshine in the sun-lounge').]

Increased traffic, noise, fumes, vibration, dirt and the risk of accidents were important factors against the applicants in *Re Bass* (1973).[254]

(d) Loss of value

Loss of amenity will often cause loss of value but the fact that it does not is not a reason for
holding that the covenant does not secure a practical advantage. In *Re Collins* (1974) it was
not disputed that the proposed development would not reduce the market value of existing
houses. Nevertheless it was accepted as important that the objectors regarded the restrictions
as having substantial advantage, some having bought their houses in reliance on them. Indeed in
Re Munday's Application (1954) 7 P & CR 130 (a claim to declare a covenant obsolete) it was
likely that a successful application would increase the value of the objectors' property by giving
it a potential commercial user. The claim failed however as it was clear that the personal tastes
of the objectors would be adversely affected if the covenant was lifted.[255]

(e) 'Thin end of the wedge' argument

It can be a relevant consideration that the proposal, though not particularly harmful in itself,
must be rejected in case it gives rise to similar proposals which would succeed because the
first had done so, and which would cumulatively be disadvantageous. In *Re Gossip* (1972) the
applicant had converted two houses into flats in breach of covenant and now wished to build
two further houses in their gardens. He argued that there had already been some breaches of
covenant by other house-owners by conversions of single houses into flats but the Tribunal considered that these breaches had been minimal whereas a modification might be the 'thin end of
the wedge' for a considerable change in the amenities and character of the neighbourhood. The
recent case of *Re Osborn* (1979) illustrates this consideration along with several others. The
applicants wished to erect two three-storey blocks of flats on a large estate of eight-bedroomed
houses. Sixty-three owners of such houses objected. It was held that if the applications were
granted it would set an undesirable precedent for other developments on the estate, particularly
as there was much profit in such developments. Other important considerations were that the
building would be out of place in a high value, low density, single house estate; that the flats
would be visually injurious there; and that the traffic noise generated by the greater numbers of
people would be injurious.

The validity of the 'thin end of the wedge' argument is not universally accepted. In *Re Forgac's
Application* (1976) 32 P & CR 464, Mr J H Emlyn-Jones FRICS in his judgment quoted what
he said in *Re Gaffney's Application* (1973, unreported, LP/21/1973) to the effect that if a
modification is in itself unlikely to cause injury it should not be refused on the ground that later
applications might do so. They should each be looked at on the merits when they arise and should
then be rejected if need be.[256]

---

[254] [See also *Re Crest Homes plc's Application* (1983) 48 P & CR 309 (proposal to build twelve houses to
replace neglected Edgware Lawn Tennis Club would cause undesirable increase in housing density and
change area from semi-rural to urban); *Re Lake's Application* [1984] JPL 887 (proposal to erect split-level
house in Lyme Regis would be design out of character with surroundings); *Re Sheehy's Application* (1992)
63 P & CR 95 (moral obligation undertaken by the St. Aubyn Discretionary Trustees to maintain a scheme
of covenants within the Devonport Estate, where cost of administration exceeded total rental income, held
to be of practical benefit); *Re Azfar's Application* [2002] 1 P & CR 215 (adverse impact from traffic, parking,
access to neighbouring properties and unsightliness of large extension).]

[255] [*Re H and H Ltd's Application* [1987] JPL 452 (10% reduction in value of objectors' properties).]

[256] [See also *Re Chapman's Application* (1980) 42 P & CR 114; *Re Farmiloe's Application* (1983) 48 P & CR
317; *Re Love's and Love's Application* (1993) 67 P & CR 101; *Re Solarfilms (Sales) Ltd's Application* (1993) 67 P

4. *Are the benefits secured by the restrictions of substantial value or advantage to the objectors?*

The use of the words 'value or advantage' in harness was said by the Tribunal in *Re Bass* (1973) to indicate that pecuniary values are not the only things to be considered in this context and *Re Collins* (1974) and *Re Munday* (1953) support this.[257] However, the benefits secured must be substantial. In *Re Dransfield's Application* (1975) 31 P & CR 192 the objector, in seeking to uphold a covenant made by the applicant himself only 20 years earlier, claimed that the proposed house would obstruct the view from the rear windows of his house and from the first floor terrace where he frequently entertained guests. It was held that the restriction which prevented building did not secure a substantial benefit to him and that £1,000 was adequate compensation in money terms.[258]

5. *Is it contrary to the public interest to impede the proposed user?*

In *Re Collins* (1974) the Tribunal said that for an application to succeed on the ground of public interest 'it must be shown that that interest is so important and immediate as to justify the serious interference with private rights and the sanctity of contract.' Applications based on this ground seem to have a high rate of failure. We will examine three of the lines of approach which have been used.[259]

(a) Shortage of accommodation

In *Re New Ideal Homes Ltd's Application* [1978] JPL 632 a covenant linked with planning permission allowed 79 houses to be build on a plot of land. The applicants asked for the covenant to be modified only four years after they had entered into it, to permit 150 houses to be built there. They claimed that the 1973/4 property collapse has made it uneconomic to build at such a low density and that the covenant was against the public interest in preventing them from satisfying the great need for housing locally. The Tribunal held that the restriction was not against the public interest merely because there was a housing need but modified it, on

& CR 110; *Re Page's Application* (1995) 71 P & CR 440; *Re Snaith and Dolding's Application* (1995) 71 P & CR 104 ('erection of this house could materially alter the context in which further applications would be considered'). *Re Churchill's Application* (1994) LP/45/94; *Re Hunt's Application* (1996) 73 P & CR 126. *McMorris v Brown* [1998] 3 WLR 971, especially at 978, per Lord Cooke of Thorndon, citing this note; *Shephard v Turner* [2006] 2 P & CR 28 at [29] ('thin end of the wedge' argument relevant but the issues it raises are ones of fact not law, so limited scope for challenge on appeal).]

[257] [*Re Matcham's Application* [1981] JPL 431 (house built on tranquil site because of wife's severe migraine); *Re Heydeshire's Application* (1993) 67 P & CR 93 (right to build within set limit, provided no one else had done so, held not a practical benefit); *Re Willis' Application* [1997] 2 EGLR 185 (bed and breakfast accommodation wholly compatible with surrounding residential area): cf. *Re Pennington's Application* [2002] RVR 271 (bed and breakfast accommodation would result in reduction of value of adjoining properties and loss of privacy).]

[258] [On the meaning of 'substantial' see *Re Gaffney's Application* (1974) 35 P & CR 440.]

[259] [*Re Lloyd's and Lloyd's Application* (1993) 66 P & CR 112 (covenant modified to permit house to be used as community care home for ten psychiatric patients: government policy favoured their rehabilitation in the community); *Re Fisher of Gimson (Builders) Ltd's Application* (1992) 65 P & CR 312 (risk of demolition of important housing accommodation against public interest; £6,000 compensation); cf. *O'Reilly's Application* (1993) 66 P & CR 485; *Re Hounslow and Ealing London Borough Council's Application* (1995) 71 P & CR 100 (part of ground floor of mansion to be used as horticultural training centre); *Re Bromor Properties Ltd's Application* (1995) 70 P & CR 569; *Re Milius's Application* (1995) 70 P & CR 427 (restriction adopted by local authority pursuant to lawful policy approved by Parliament held not contrary to public interest).]

payment of compensation, because it did not secure practical benefits of substantial value to the objecting local authority.

Similarly in *Re Osborn* (1979) the Tribunal held that although it was government policy to encourage high density development, that did not mean that all low density development was against the public interest and that it ought to be replaced by high density development. In *Re Beardsley* (1972) an acute shortage of building land in a given area was held not of itself to prove that a restriction was contrary to the public interest; the question was to be considered in a wider context, having regard especially to the planning considerations mentioned in section 84(1B).[260]

(b) Existence of planning permission

It has been argued in several cases that where the local planning authority has granted planning permission a restriction which prevents the development from proceeding must be contrary to the public interest. That argument was firmly dealt with in *Re Bass* (1973) where the Tribunal said, 'a planning permission only says, in effect, that a proposal will be allowed; it implies perhaps that such a proposal will not be a bad thing but it does not necessarily imply that it will be positively a good thing and in the public interest, and that failure of the proposal to materialise would be positively bad. Many planning permissions have got through by the skin of their teeth'.

The Tribunal will resist attempts to turn the proceedings into a planning enquiry, by the introduction of miscellaneous documents concerning the planning of the vicinity or of wider areas. In *Re Collins* (1974) it refused to consider any documents save those which had been published, subjected to public enquiry and approved by the Minister, such as the approved town map or development plan.[261]

---

[260] [*Re Beech's Application* (1990) 59 P & CR 502 (residential enclave in predominantly commercial setting).]

[261] [See also *Re Beecham Group Ltd's Application* (1980) 41 P & CR 369 (refusal to differ from 'very carefully reasoned decision' of Secretary of State granting planning permission on appeal from inspector); *Gilbert v Spoor* [1983] Ch 27 ('The subsection does not make planning decisions decisive', per Eveleigh LJ at 34). *Re Hextall's Application* (2000) 79 P & CR 382 (planning permission is strongly persuasive); *Re Diggen's Application* (No 2) [2001] 2 EGLR 163.

Under TCPA 1990, s. 106 (replacing TCPA 1971, s. 52), a local authority has power to regulate land use by agreement. Such an agreement is within LP (Miscellaneous Provisions) Act 1989, s. 2; p. 18, above. *Jelson Ltd v Derby County Council* [1999] 3 EGLR 91; [1999] Conv 379 (J.E.A.). See Current Law Statutes TCPA 1990, s. 106, annotated by M. Grant, paras 8.299 to 8.302. For possible replacement of TCPA 1990, s. 106, see p. 749, n. 43, above.

The authority is said to hold the benefit of the covenant as 'custodian of the public interest': *Re Abbey Homesteads (Developments) Ltd's Application* [1986] 1 EGLR 24; *Re Martin's Application* (1988) 57 P & CR 119, especially at 125, p. 832, below, per Fox LJ; *Re Houdret & Co Ltd's Application* (1989) 58 P & CR 310; *Re Jones' and White & Co's Application* (1989) 58 P & CR 512; *Re Quartley's Application* (1989) 58 P & CR 518; *Re Beech's Application* (1989), above; [1990] Conv 455 (N. D. M. Parry); *Re Wallace's Application* (1993) 66 P & CR 124; *Re Hopcraft's Application* (1993) 66 P & CR 475 (storage of touring caravans refused); *Re Bromor Properties Ltd's Application* (1995) 70 P & CR 569. *J. A. Pye (Oxford) Ltd v South Gloucestershire District Council* [2001] EGCS 47. For successful modifications, see *Re Cox's Application* (1985) 51 P & CR 335; *Re Towner's and Goddard's Application* (1989) 58 P & CR 316 (tennis-court with chain link fencing); *Re Barclays Bank plc's Application* (1990) 60 P & CR 354 (discharge in favour of mortgagee); *Re Poulton's Application* (1992) 65 P & CR 319 (extension of bungalow in Metropolitan Green Belt); *Re O'Reilly's Application* (1993) 66 P & CR 485 (user for car parking modified only to allow erection of six houses on payment of £11,000 compensation); *Re Williamson's Application* (1994) 68 P & CR 384 (granny annexe as a separate dwelling);

(c) Economic advantages

In *Re Bass* (1973) it was said that the company had a need to expand its trunker park because mergers and rationalisations within the company required it to reorganise its distribution system. The Tribunal said that this was not an irrelevant factor but that it must be set against other questions, such as amenity; 'the proposition that this operation is in the public interest is strange indeed unless the public interest is to be equated to the economic benefits to this particular part of the beer trade'.

A case where the public interest argument succeeded was *Re SJC Construction Co Ltd* (1975). Here £47,000 worth of building work on flats had been done with planning permission from the local authority when the same authority issued a writ to enforce restrictive covenants which would have prevented the building of the flats. Modification of the covenant to permit them to be built was allowed because: planning permission existed, the adverse effect on the dominant land would not be serious, there was a scarcity of building land in the area, the work already done would otherwise have been wasted, the applicants had gone ahead in good faith, and substantial compensation would be paid by them.

6 and 7. *Would money be an adequate compensation to the objector?*

It was emphasised by Lord Evershed MR in *Re Ghey and Galton's Application* [1957] 2 QB 650 that section 84 does not enable the court to expropriate objectors merely because an applicant may have put forward a worthy enterprise (in that case a proposal to turn a large house into a convalescent home). When modification is allowed money, in some cases coupled with a restriction on the development, must be capable of being an adequate compensation.

In *Re Carter* (1973) views of the sea from four dominant houses would have been impaired by a proposed bungalow. Sums of £200, £200 and £100 were awarded to three owners but nothing to the fourth as his loss was too small to be compensated. In addition an offer by the applicant to excavate so as to make the bungalow roof 2½ feet lower than originally intended was accepted and was made a condition of the modification order. *Re Bank's Application* (1976) 33 P & CR 138 is a similar case but there compensation of £2,000 was ordered to be paid to each objector before the development was begun. In *Re Patten Ltd's Application* (1975) 31 P & CR 180 a proposed development often houses which would have caused overcrowding was allowed on payment of up to £750 compensation to objectors and the reduction of the number of houses to seven.[262]

It might be thought that all compensation payments must in the nature of things be modest because large awards would indicate that the application should have been refused. This is not necessarily so. In *Re New Ideal Homes* (1978) an agreed sum of £51,000 was awarded, representing the reduction in purchase money which had been allowed because of the covenant when it was imposed. By section 84(1) the Tribunal can award compensation either (a) for the loss or disadvantage suffered from the discharge or modification or (b) for making up for

---

Re Bewick's Application (1996) 73 P & CR 240; *Re Caton's Application* [1999] 3 EGLR 121 (change in planning policy did not render restriction obsolete).]

[262] [See also *Re Edwards' Application* (1983) 47 P & CR 458 (restriction modified to enable house in Mold, North Wales, to be used as a general village store, for 'groceries, sweets, tobacco, cigarettes, cigars, soft drinks, ice cream, newspapers, trinkets, haberdashery, gardening utensils and supplies, tools, nuts and bolts', subject to payment of £500 as compensation to objector for loss of amenity); *Re Shah and Shah's Application* (1991) 62 P & CR 450 (restriction impeding nursing home user so small as to warrant monetary compensation only of £23,000); *Re Cornick's Application* (1994) 69 P & CR 726 (jam factory).]

any effect the restriction had when it was imposed in reducing the consideration then received for the burdened land. In the *SJC Construction* case (1974) compensation was awarded so as to share the development value of the burdened land equally between the applicant and the objector. This decision purported to follow in principle *Wrotham Park Estate Co v Parkside Homes Ltd* (1973) 27 P & CR 296 where the compensation was calculated by taking 5 per cent of the profit made by the developer who had broken a layout covenant. The basis of the award in the *SJC* case was upheld on appeal at (1975) 29 P & CR 322.[263]

In **Re Martin's Application** (1988) 57 P & CR 119, Fox LJ said at 125:

In my view, the applicants' contention is wrong in so far as it suggests that the granting of planning permission by the Secretary of State necessarily involves the result that the Lands Tribunal must discharge the covenant. The granting of planning permission is, it seems to me, merely a circumstance which the Lands Tribunal can and should take into account when exercising its jurisdiction under section 84. To give the grant of planning permission a wider effect is, I think, destructive of the express statutory jurisdiction conferred by section 84. It is for the Tribunal to make up its own mind whether the requirements of section 84 are satisfied.... All the facts of the case have to be examined by the Lands Tribunal. There is nothing in the Town and Country Planning Acts 1962 or 1971[264] which suggests that these are intended to interfere in any way with the jurisdiction of the Lands Tribunal under section 84.

Law Commission Consultation Paper on Easements, Covenants and Profits à Prendre 2008 (Consultation Paper No. 186), paras 16.88–16.94[265]

16.88 We provisionally propose that the statutory jurisdiction to discharge or modify restrictions on land contained in section 84(1) of the Law of Property Act 1925 should be extended to include:

(1) easements;

(2) profits; and

---

[263] [*Re London Borough of Islington's Application* [1986] JPL 214 (covenant forbidding use of land in Islington 'except for open space', purchased from Greater London Council who remitted half of the purchase price, discharged on repayment of that half with adjustments for inflation).

Loss of bargaining power is not a proper head of compensation: *Stockport Metropolitan Borough Council Alwiyah Developments* (1986) 52 P & CR 278; *Re Bennett's and Tamarlin Ltd's Application* (1987) 54 P & CR 378 (loss of ability to extract money for agreeing to modification of restriction not a benefit); cf. *Re Quaffers Ltd's Application* (1988) 56 P & CR 142 (loss of competition advantage); *Winter v Traditional & Contemporary Contracts Ltd* [2008] 3 EG 180 at [26]-[28], per Carnwath LJ (the test is not the 'negotiated share approach ... [which] is well recognised in civil proceedings for breach of restrictive covenants.... compensation under section 84 is based on the impact of the development on the objectors, not on the loss of the opportunity to extract a share of the development value. Short of intervention by the House of Lords, or the legislature, it is too late to turn the clock back). *Re Jillas' Application* [2000] 23 EG 147 (covenant modified to allow for extension of house; £10,000 compensation with adjustment for inflation); (2000) 150 NLJ 1523 (H. W. Wilkinson; *Re Davies' Application* [2001] 1 EGLR 111 (£2,000).]

[264] Or 1990.

[265] For the detailed discussion relating to these proposals, and other aspects of s. 84 LPA 1925, see Part 14 of the Consultation Paper.

(3) Land Obligations.[266]

16.89 We invite the views of consultees as to whether they consider that there should be a jurisdiction to discharge and modify each of the above interests.

16.90 We provisionally propose that:

(1) the Tribunal in exercising its jurisdiction should seek to give effect to the 'purpose' for which the restriction or other interest in land was imposed; and

(2) the Tribunal should be able to discharge or modify where it is satisfied of one of the statutory grounds and where it is reasonable in all the circumstances to discharge or modify the restriction or interest.

16.91 We provisionally propose that it should be a ground for discharge or modification that the discharge or modification:

(1) would not cause substantial injury to the person entitled to the benefit of the restriction or other interest in land; or

(2) would enable the land to be put to a use that is in the public interest and that could not reasonably be accommodated on other land; and

(3) that in either case money would provide adequate compensation to the person entitled to the benefit of the restriction or other interest in land.

16.92 We provisionally propose that obsoleteness should cease to be a ground for discharge or modification.

16.93 We provisionally propose that where a number of persons are entitled to the benefit of a restriction or any other interest within the ambit of section 84, it should not be necessary for the applicant to establish that the ground or grounds for discharge or modification relied upon apply to each and every one of the persons entitled.

16.94 We provisionally propose that the Lands Tribunal should have the power to add new restrictions on the discharge or modification of a restrictive covenant, easement or profit, if the Tribunal considers it reasonable in view of the relaxation of the existing provisions and if the applicant agrees.

V. PUBLIC PLANNING CONTROL[267]

Tulk v Moxhay was decided in 1848 and the doctrine to which it gave rise was one of the bases for control of land use by private landowners during the suburban expansion of the 19th century. Together with leasehold and reciprocal positive freehold covenants (and, to a lesser extent, easements), it is fundamental to all private planning. Such private control can however only have a limited effect. It can only be effective where a landowner is in control of a considerable area of undeveloped land, and has the foresight to devise a suitable system of obligations at a time when demand for the development of that land is beginning to be felt—when that land is 'ripe for development'. It

---

[266] For the Law Commission's provisional proposals to reform the law of covenants and thereby create a new category of 'Land Obligation', see pp. 836–849, below.

[267] C & B, chaps 29, 30; Gray, part 11; M & W, paras 32.094–32.095; MM, pp. 569–580.

also requires constant vigilance and determination to enforce the covenants over an indefinite period of time at the discretion of a succession of private owners who are not in anyway responsible to the public, legally or politically, for ensuring that the policy is carried out or even that the controls actually imposed are desirable. And so, in spite of the many excellent schemes of residential development carried out under freehold and leasehold covenants in the more spacious suburbs of many large and small towns, including seaside resorts, spas and 'garden cities,'[268] a system of public control of the use and development of land had to be introduced.

The principal planning statute, which consolidates the previous statutes from the Town and Country Planning Acts of 1947 onwards, is the Town and Country Planning Act 1990, as further refined by the Planning and Compulsory Purchase Act 2004 and (when it comes into force) the Planning Act 2008. Planning control is administered by a system of central and local authorities. The central authority is now the Department for Communities and Local Government. The Secretary of State for that Department, and the Minister for Housing and Planning within the Department, do not usually administer planning control directly but are responsible for planning policy. Appeals from decisions of local planning authorities are made to the Secretary of State, but are normally determined by the Planning Inspectorate although the Secretary of State may 'recover' appeals for direct decision, usually because the proposed development is large or controversial.[269] Detailed administration is in the hands of the local planning authorities, which are county and district councils. The former are 'county planning authorities', concerned chiefly with strategic matters; the latter are 'district planning authorities', concerned normally with the routine business of planning control. In Greater London; the Metropolitan Counties and unitary council areas, there is a one-tier system i.e., a single local planning authority for each.

Private planning thus co-exists side by side with the public control of the use and development of land. A purchaser of land must not only satisfy himself about the existence of private covenants that may bind the land which he is buying, but he must also investigate its planning aspect.

In 1979 the Royal Commission on Legal Services put forward the idea that all, or nearly all, existing and future restrictive covenants should become totally unenforceable except as between the original parties. In 1984 the Law Commission rejected this view.

Law Commission Report on The Law of Positive and Restrictive Covenants 1984 (Law Com No. 127), paras 2.5–2.7

2.5 Planning law may overlap to some extent with restrictive covenants, but we do not believe that it has removed the need for them. Perhaps especially in residential property developments,

---

[268] See Burke, *Towns in the Making* (1971).

[269] Around 27,000 appeals are made each year: in 2007, 110 appeals were determined by the Secretary of State: see written ministerial statement, Hansard HC vol. 478 col. 43WS (30 Jun 2008), where the Secretary of State's current policy for the recovery of appeals is set out.

restrictive covenants commonly regulate many things for which planning law would not cater—and do so for the mutual benefit of the residents and with the aim of preserving the character and standard of the development as a whole. Nor does it seem to us that these things are confined, as the Royal Commission suggested they might be, to matters affecting privacy. Powerful support for this view is to be found in this extract from the preface to the sixth edition of Preston & Newsom's *Restrictive Covenants Affecting Freehold Land:*

> 'One thing that is abundantly plain is that there is no prospect whatever that restrictive covenants will become unnecessary and that their place will be taken by the planning laws. For planning standards are still too often below the standards imposed by restrictive covenants. Thus in *Re Bass Ltd's Application*[270] the Lands Tribunal held that the suggested modification would inflict upon the persons entitled to the benefit of the restriction noise, fumes, vibrations, dirt and the risk of accidents: these proposals had received planning permission. Again, in the *Wrotham Park* case [1974] 1 WLR 798, it was the local authority itself which, having bought the land for a very small sum, put it up for sale and received £90,000 on the basis that it was to be built upon, thereby destroying an open space which the owners of surrounding houses valued and which had been deliberately created by the original covenantee.'

It is also true that certain changes of use and building operations to which an adjoining resident might reasonably and justifiably object do not require planning permission at all.

2.6 It might perhaps be argued that the answer lies not in preserving the power to impose private restrictions but in extending the ambit of planning law. We think it unrealistic, however, to expect planning authorities to concern themselves with all the detailed matters for which restrictive covenants now commonly make provision. Indeed a Past President of the Royal Town Planning Institute[271] has expressed the view that: 'It puts planning authorities under unreasonable pressure if they are expected to safeguard the interests of adjoining owners.' It must also be remembered that restrictive covenants may be used to serve purposes which are private and individual and for which planning law would not cater however far it was extended.

2.7 It must also be remembered that planning restrictions, even if they are wholly adequate to the needs of adjoining owners, are enforceable only by the planning authorities. Most owners would wish to have the power of enforcement in their own hands.

The statutes on Town and Country Planning[272] and Compulsory Purchase and Compensation of Land[273] and books dealing with them must be consulted before a

---

[270] (1973) 26 P & CR 156. There have been other cases in which the Lands Tribunal has refused to modify covenants so as to allow development for which planning permission has already been obtained—e.g., *Re M Howard (Mitcham) Ltd's Application* (1956) 7 P & CR 219; *Re Sloggetts (Properties) Ltd's Application* (1952) 7 P & CR 78. See pp. 830, 832, above.

[271] Sir John Boynton, in an address in 1978 to a joint conference of The Law Society, the Bar Council and the Royal Institution of Chartered Surveyors.

[272] TCPA 1990; Planning (Listed Buildings and Conservation Areas) Act 1990; Planning (Hazardous Substances) Act 1990; Planning (Consequential Provisions) Act 1990; Planning and Compensation Act 1991, Part I; Planning and Compulsory Purchase Act 2004 (Parts 1–7); Planning Act 2008; *Encyclopedia of Planning Law and Practice;* Telling and Duxbury, *Planning Law and Procedure* (13th edn, 2005); Moore, *A Practical Approach to Planning Law* (10th edn, 2007). On the impact of ECHR on planning law, see Rook, *Property Law and Human Rights,* section 8.10; Allen, *Property Law and the Human Rights Act* 1998, chap. 7.

[273] Compulsory Purchase Act 1965; Acquisition of Land Act 1981; Compulsory Purchase (Vesting Declarations) Act 1980; Land Compensation Acts 1961 and 1973; Planning and Compensation Act 1991, Part III; Planning and Compulsory Purchase Act 2004 (Part 8); Planning Act 2008, ss. 122–134. *Encyclopedia*

working knowledge of the law of control of land can be obtained; but lack of space forbids their treatment here.[274]

VI. LAW REFORM

The Law Commission is currently considering not only whether (and, if so, how) the law of covenants should be reformed, but also whether any reform should go so far as to assimilate the law of covenants with the law of easements and profits à prendre.

Law Commission Consultation Paper on Easements, Covenants and Profits à Prendre 2008 (Consultation Paper No. 186), paras 1.21, 2.1–2.14, 7.67–7.80, 8.13, 9.3–9.21, 9.38, 9.41, 9.43, 10.9–10.10, 10.26, 10.31, 10.44, 15.1–15.2[275]

1.21 ...It is possible to identify the following main defects in the law governing covenants:[276]

(1) The burden of positive covenants does not run so as to bind successors in title of the covenantor. Such devices as are available to circumvent this rule are complex and insufficiently comprehensive.[277]

---

of *Compulsory Purchase and Compensation;* Denyer-Green, *Compulsory Purchase and Compensation* (8th edn, 2005). On the impact of ECHR on the law relating to compulsory purchase, see Rook, *Property Law and Human Rights,* section 8.9; Allen, *Property Law and the Human Rights Act 1998*, chap. 6.

For proposed reform of compulsory purchase, see Law Commission Consultation Papers in 2002: Towards a Compulsory Purchase Code: (1) Compensation (Law Com No. 165); (2) Procedure (Law Com No. 169), which are the bases for Law Commission Reports on Towards a Compulsory Purchase Code (1) (2003) (Law Com No. 286) and (2) (2004) (Law Com No. 291). However, the Government decided in 2005 not to make any further reforms in this area: ODPM: Government Response to Law Commission Report: Towards a Compulsory Purchase Code (December 2005), para. 29.

[274] See C & B, chaps 29 and 30.

[275] [2008] Conv 270 (M. Dixon). A final report and draft Bill is planned for July 2010: Law Commission, Tenth Programme of Law Reform 2008 (Law Com No. 311), para. 3.2. See also the proposals relating to easements: p. 738–741, above. For earlier proposals, see Wilberforce Committee Report on Positive Covenants 1965 (Cmnd 2719); Law Commission Report on Restrictive Covenants 1967 (Law Com No. 11) and its Working Paper on Rights Appurtenant to Land 1971 (No. 36); Second Report of the Conveyancing Committee: Conveyancing Simplifications 1985, paras 4.52–4.57, 7.21–7.22; Law Commission Report on the Law of Positive and Restrictive Covenants 1984 (Law Com No. 127); [1984] JPL 222, 317, 401, 485 (S. B. Odell); 134 NLJ 459, 481 (H. W. Wilkinson); (1984) 47 MLR 566 (P. Polden); Law Commission Report on Obsolete Restrictive Covenants 1991 (Law Com No. 201).

See A New Property Law Act, drafted by the Law Commission of New Zealand (Law Com Report No. 29) which proposes that the burden of both negative and positive covenants should run with the land if they relate to the subject matter of the land and are noted on the register; [1994] Conv 428 (H. W. Wilkinson).

[276] [For more detailed discussion by the Law Commission of these defects, see paras 7.36–7.45.]

[277] This problem was highlighted by the House of Lords' decision in *Rhone v Stephens* [1994] 2 AC 310 [p. 746, above].

(2) The burden of a restrictive covenant can run in equity under the doctrine of *Tulk v Moxhay*,[278] but only if certain complex and technical conditions are met.

(3) The benefit of a restrictive covenant can run at law and in equity, but according to rules which are different, and which are possibly even more complicated than the rules for the running of the burden.[279]

(4) There is no requirement that the instrument creating the covenant should describe the benefited land with sufficient clarity to enable its identification without extrinsic evidence.[280]

(5) There is no requirement to enter the benefit of a covenant on the register of title to the dominant land.

(6) The contractual liability, which exists between the original parties to a covenant, persists despite changes in ownership of the land. It is therefore possible for a covenant to be enforced against the original covenantor even though he or she has disposed of the land.

WHY WE ARE DEALING WITH EASEMENTS, PROFITS AND COVENANTS TOGETHER

2.1 We have commented above that this is a substantial project. The reason for this is that it covers a range of distinct rights, all of which have elements that are in need of reform. It is a premise of the project that the interaction between, and the essential nature of, the separate rights require detailed consideration. This includes the question of whether it remains necessary to have separate types of right at all. These questions will be considered in detail in Part 15. In this short Part, we set out our general approach and explain our reasons for dealing with these rights as part of a single project while keeping their treatment distinct.

Ways in which the rights are similar

2.2 Easements, covenants and profits are all rights enjoyed by one party relating to the land of another. They are limited rights, falling short of rights of ownership or possession.

2.3 Easements and covenants are functionally similar in terms of the role they play in controlling the enjoyment and development of land over time. The two rights are complementary, each comprising an important tool for facilitating and controlling the use of land. In some cases, parties will be able to achieve the same result by means either of a negative easement or a restrictive covenant.[281]

2.4 Given this functional similarity, contemporaneous and consistent reform of all three types of interest might considerably simplify and rationalise the law. Further, it might give rise to inconsistencies and potential anomalies if the reform of one right were considered without taking into account the reform of the others. While, as discussed below, we have taken the provisional view that the reform of these rights should be treated individually,[282] we consider that

---

[278] [1843–60] All ER Rep 9 [p. 754, above].

[279] [Pp. 773, 777, above.] [280] [Pp. 801–802, above.]

[281] For example, access to light through a window could be protected on a sale of part either by the reservation of an easement of light or by the creation of a restrictive covenant preventing the neighbour from building above a certain height.

[282] See Part 15 below.

any reforms must also be consistent in terms of policy.[283] This is best achieved by considering them together as part of a single project.

Ways in which the rights are distinct

2.5 Easements and profits are both 'incorporeal hereditaments'; that is, they belong to a defined list of rights recognised by the law of property as being, like land itself, a species of 'real property' to which the rules of land law apply. If created expressly, such rights should be granted by deed.[284] Once created and registered, they are binding against the whole world.

2.6 All easements, and some profits, are appurtenant (that is to say, attached) to a dominant estate in land. That is, once created for the benefit of an estate in land, they attach to that estate for the benefit of all those who subsequently become entitled to it. As a result, if A buys land that has the benefit of an easement—such as a right of way over B's neighbouring land—A will be automatically entitled to exercise that right of way without any need to negotiate further with B. B will be obliged, like everyone else, not to interfere with A's exercise of the right even if B is not the person who originally granted it.

2.7 By contrast, covenants have their origin in the law of contract. Having been created expressly by agreement, the terms of that agreement define the nature and scope of the rights. In line with the doctrine of privity of contract, the starting point for these rights is that they will only affect parties to the particular contract and no one else. There are three exceptions to this principle in relation to covenants affecting land.

2.8 First, covenants between landlord and tenant in their capacity as such are subject to special rules and these rules are outside the scope of this project.

2.9 Secondly, it is a long-standing rule of law that the benefit of a covenant affecting land may, in some circumstances, be 'annexed' to an estate in that land.[285] This means that, where the requirements for annexation are met, subsequent owners of that estate are automatically entitled to enforce the covenant. To this extent, a covenant may behave like an interest appurtenant to an estate in land. This is one of a number of acknowledged situations where the doctrine of privity of contract is limited in its application to the benefit of an agreement.[286]

2.10 Finally, and most significantly, the rule in *Tulk v Moxhay* holds that the burden of a restrictive covenant affecting land is sometimes capable of binding in equity third parties who subsequently acquire an interest in the land. This constitutes a rare exception to the rule that the burden of an agreement can only bind the original parties.[287] In effect, it means that restrictive covenants to which the rule in *Tulk v Moxhay* applies can be enforced against third party purchasers, a characteristic normally associated only with property rights.

2.11 In this sense, *Tulk v Moxhay* partially blurs the distinction between easements and profits on the one hand and restrictive covenants affecting land on the other. However, it has

---

283 For example, the approach to registration.

284 In order to take effect as legal interests: Law of Property Act 1925, s. 52. They can also be granted by written instrument, provided that the instrument complies with the Law of Property (Miscellaneous Provisions) Act 1989, s. 2; however, they would only take effect as equitable interests. [See pp. 29–34, above.]

285 [Pp. 773, 779, above.]

286 Others not relating specifically to land include contracts to which the Contract (Rights of Third Parties) Act 1999 applies and contracts relating to the bailment of goods.

287 In *Taddy & Co v Sterious & Co* [1904] 1 Ch 354, it was held by Swinfen Eady J at 358 that the principle in *Tulk v Moxhay* was limited to restrictive covenants affecting land only: 'Conditions of this kind do not run with goods, and cannot be imposed upon them'.

not assimilated them. Unlike easements and profits, covenants remain rights created only by contract and freely defined by the parties.[288] Cases subsequent to *Tulk v Moxhay* have reflected this tension between the contractual nature of covenants and their proprietary effect; they affirm the proprietary effect but subject it to a number of complex limitations the total effect of which is difficult to justify.[289] It is arguable that some of these difficult rules spring from the discomfort of the courts with the apparent contradiction inherent in the concept of covenants that behave like property rights. This is visible in the fact that, for instance, the cases affirming the rule that *Tulk v Moxhay* does not apply to positive covenants have drawn on the language of privity of contract to justify the distinction.[290]

OUR PROVISIONAL APPROACH TO REFORM

2.12 As we have explained, easements, profits and covenants are clearly distinct under the current law, yet to some extent all can be used to achieve similar ends. We have taken the provisional view that the distinction between easements, profits and covenants is valuable and should be retained.[291] Although we therefore reject the complete assimilation of these interests, we believe that we should not limit ourselves to an entirely piecemeal, ameliorative approach that only addresses specific problems within the existing law. There is scope for rationalisation across the different categories of interest.

2.13 Our overarching aim is to have a law of easements, covenants and profits that is as coherent and clear as possible. There should, so far as practicable, be consistency within and between these three types of rights relating to land. Overlapping and alternative doctrines should be rationalised or eradicated wherever possible. We also aim to standardise certain key principles governing easements, profits and covenants. For instance, we provisionally propose in Part 14 that there should be a single jurisdiction to govern the discharge and modification of all three types of interest under an expanded section 84 of the Law of Property Act 1925.[292]

2.14 We consider that there is a need for fundamental reform of covenants affecting land, and we provisionally propose the replacement of such covenants with a new interest in land: the Land Obligation.[293] As suggested above, many of the flaws in the current law of covenants may be explained by the fundamental tension between the contractual nature of the rights and the proprietary effect introduced by *Tulk v Moxhay*. It is obvious from the subsequent expansion of the law of restrictive covenants[294] that there is a significant demand for parties to be able to attach freely negotiated rights and obligations to their land.[295] Rather than eliminating the contradiction by returning the law of covenants affecting land to its contractual roots, we

---

[288] Subject to the principle that, in order for the benefit or the burden to run, they must 'touch and concern' or be for the benefit of the land in some way. For the touch and concern requirement, see paras 8.68 to 8.80 below.

[289] See paras 7.9 to 7.58 [of the Report].

[290] For example Lord Templeman in *Rhone v Stephens* [1994] 2 AC 310 at 318: 'Equity cannot compel an owner to comply with a positive covenant entered into by his predecessors in title without flatly contradicting the common law rule that a person cannot be made liable upon a contract unless he was a party to it'.

[291] See Part 15 [of the Report].   [292] [P. 821, above.]

[293] See Parts 7 to 12 [of the Report].

[294] As well as the proliferation of devices enabling parties to circumvent the rule that the burden of a positive covenant does not run with the land: see paras 7.46 to 7.58 [of the Report; and pp. 747, above].

[295] For the desirability of retaining the proprietary effect of restrictive covenants see paras 7.34 to 7.35 [of the Report].

consider that it is preferable to resolve it by creating a new category of property interest that performs this function.

The case for Land Obligations

7.67 The Law Commission recommended comprehensive reform of the law of covenants in 1984,[296] drawing upon the easement analogy to construct a new interest to be known as the land obligation, which would replace both restrictive and positive covenants.[297]

7.68 The 1984 scheme of land obligations would permit both negative and positive obligations to be imposed on one piece of land for the benefit of other land, and be enforceable by or on behalf of the owners for the time being of the dominant land. This would depart from the principle currently applicable to restrictive and positive covenants (which remain enforceable between the original parties even after they have parted with the land) in accordance with the logic that the interest attaches to the ownership of the benefited and burdened lands.

7.69 Parties intending to create a land obligation running with the land would be required to label it expressly as a 'land obligation'. There would therefore be no doubt as to whether the positive or negative obligation was intended to run with the land. The highly technical rules determining whether the benefit and burden of covenants pass with the land would disappear.

7.70 The proposed land obligation would normally subsist as a legal interest in land. It would be enforceable by legal remedies including an action for damages at common law. It would also be enforceable by equitable remedies such as an injunction (including a mandatory injunction).[298]

7.71 The name 'land obligation' was chosen 'because the things in question are obligations, and because they are capable of subsisting only for the benefit of, and as a burden on, pieces of land'.[299] We retain this terminology for the purposes of this Consultation Paper as we feel it best describes the type of interest under consideration. However, we use the capitalised term 'Land Obligation' to distinguish our proposals from the 1984 scheme of land obligations, which differ in a number of important respects.[300]

7.72 Although the 1984 Report adopted the single term 'land obligation', it was considered necessary to formulate different principles in relation to positive and restrictive obligations. For instance, the range of persons liable to comply with a positive obligation (for example to repair the premises) should be narrower than those liable to comply with a restrictive obligation.[301] The scheme was designed to cater both for the simple case of two neighbouring landowners and the more complicated cases involving property development. The 1984 Report accordingly made a distinction between 'neighbour obligations' and 'development obligations'.[302] We examine this in greater detail in Part 8.

---

[296] [Law Commission Report on the Law of Positive and Restrictive Covenants 1984 (Law Com No. 127).]

[297] The 1984 Report, para. 4.22.   [298] The 1984 Report, para. 13.9.

[299] The 1984 Report, para. 4.22.

[300] The term 'land obligations' has been used on a number of different occasions to mean different things. For example, the 1971 Working Paper on Appurtenant Rights' concept of land obligations included easements and profits [Law Commission Working Paper No. 36]. These interests were not included within the 1984 scheme of land obligations, and they are not included within our current proposals for Land Obligations.

[301] The 1984 Report, para. 4.25.

[302] A drawback of the 1984 Report, however, was the absence of any provision specifying when neighbour or development obligations should be used.

7.73 If reform of the law of covenants is supported, one option would be to adopt the principal recommendation of the 1984 Report to replace the current law of covenants with land obligations (based on the easement analogy) but to review and amend the details of the 1984 scheme to take account of developments in property law. However, it is important first to ask the question whether reform on this scale is necessary.

7.74 It could be argued that the law should simply be amended to allow positive covenants to run with the land, without reforming the law of restrictive covenants. In 1984, the Law Commission strongly rejected the idea of making recommendations designed solely to ensure that the burden of positive covenants in future ran with the burdened land, and to leave the law of restrictive covenants entirely alone.[303] The Commission was confident that the law of positive covenants was 'in urgent need of radical reform' and, in the context of a project designed to achieve this, concluded that it would not be possible for the law of restrictive covenants to remain unchanged.[304] Nor could the law of covenants.[305] This remains the case today for the following reasons:[306]

(1) Positive covenants demand a legal regime which is different in fundamental respects to that which currently applies to restrictive covenants. For example:[307]

   (a) A smaller class of persons should be bound by a positive covenant than a restrictive covenant. This is because positive covenants require action to be taken and that action may be burdensome and expensive.[308] It would be inappropriate, for example, if a weekly tenant of the burdened land became liable to perform a positive covenant to erect and maintain a costly sea wall. By contrast, the owner of any interest, however small, in the burdened land is bound to observe a restrictive covenant.[309] This is as it should be, because a restrictive covenant requires people merely to refrain from doing the specified thing.

   (b) The burden of a restrictive covenant runs only in equity, so that equitable remedies alone are available for its enforcement. This may not greatly matter in the case of a restrictive covenant because the remedy most often sought will be the equitable remedy of an injunction, possibly with damages in lieu. But legal remedies must be available for positive covenants because the idea of enforcing a simple covenant to pay money by means of equitable remedies is wholly artificial.[310]

---

[303] The 1984 Report, para. 4.14.

[304] The 1984 Report, para. 4.16. The Law Commission were of the opinion that the law of restrictive covenants was also in need of reform, but they acknowledged that 'opinions may possibly differ as to the gravity of its defects and the degree of priority which should be given to its improvement'.

[305] The 1984 Report, para. 4.18.

[306] The 1984 Report. paras 4.18 to 4.19.

[307] These examples were set out in the 1984 Report, para. 4.17.

[308] As the Wilberforce Report recognised in 1965: Report of the Committee on Positive Covenants Affecting Land (1965) Cmnd 2719, paras 19 to 21.

[309] This is subject to rules about registration of the burden.

[310] The 1984 Report suggested that the normal remedy for breach of a covenant to carry out works must be damages at law. The Report further pointed out that legal remedies will only be available if the burden runs at law and it can only do that if it amounts to a legal (not an equitable) interest in land. The law of restrictive covenants is therefore fundamentally unsuitable: see para. 4.17. This was also recognised by the Wilberforce Report in 1965. Report of the Committee on Positive Covenants Affecting Land (1965) Cmnd 2719, para. 18.

(2) Since a new legal regime would have to be created for positive covenants, it would not be right to reproduce in that regime the serious incidental faults which beset the law of restrictive covenants.[311] Any new legal regime for positive covenants would be different from and, in a number of important ways, simpler and more logical than, the existing law of restrictive covenants.

(3) It would be inconsistent to leave two separate and different regimes, one markedly inferior to the other, governing two legal entities (positive and restrictive covenants) which ought in any rational system of law to be conceptually the same.[312]

7.75 This leads us to the provisional conclusion that, if reform of the law of positive covenants is supported, we must also reform the law of restrictive covenants.

7.76 Our current view is that it is highly desirable to take steps to render certain positive covenants enforceable against successors in title. If the purpose of permitting positive burdens to run with the land is to enable the owner for the time being of the benefited land to enforce the obligation against the owner for the time being of the burdened land, a model based on contract does not appear to us to be the most suitable option. A contractual model would obscure the proprietary nature of the right and create unnecessary problems that would have to be dealt with by more complex rules and exceptions. Even if a method were to be developed to enable the burden of a covenant to run with the land at law, the covenant would remain enforceable as between the original contracting parties after they had parted with the land. To deal with this, one option would be to apply to covenants an approach similar to that developed in the Landlord and Tenant (Covenants) Act 1995. This additional layer of complexity would be unnecessary if, like an easement, the positive obligation attached to the ownership of the benefited and burdened estates in the land.

7.77 We currently believe that the law of restrictive covenants, the defects of which we have already identified, is itself also in need of reform.

7.78 If it is accepted that it is necessary to reform either the law of positive covenants[313] or both the law of positive covenants and the law of restrictive covenants, then the case for entirely replacing them with a new legislative regime appears to us to be extremely strong.

7.79 We provisionally propose:

(1) that there should be reform of the law of positive covenants;

(2) that there should be reform of the law of restrictive covenants; and

(3) that there should be a new legislative scheme of Land Obligations to govern the future use and enforcement of positive and restrictive obligations.

---

[311] The example given at para. 4.18 of the 1984 Report is as follows:

...we should not wish the new regime to reproduce the rule that the covenant remained enforceable as between the original contracting parties after they had parted with their lands; and we should wish to recommend a new rule whereby clear descriptions of the benefited and burdened lands had to be given in the creating instrument. Our views on these matters fully correspond, again, with those of the... [Report of the Committee on Positive Covenants Affecting Land (1965) Cmnd 2719] paras 15 and 18. We should wish also to eliminate the complexities and uncertainties to which we have referred earlier.

[312] For example, 'there would be great confusion and complexity if developers had to create two different kinds of scheme—development schemes for positive covenants under the new law, and building schemes for restrictive covenants under the old—and allow them to operate side by side': the 1984 Report, para. 4.36.

[313] This is because, as we explain above, if consultees agree that reform of the law of positive covenants is necessary, we consider that the law of restrictive covenants must also be reformed.

Do consultees agree?

7.80 We invite consultees' views as to whether, in the alternative, it would be possible to achieve the necessary reforms by simply amending the current law of positive and restrictive covenants.

LAND OBLIGATION CHARACTERISTICS

8.13 We provisionally propose that a Land Obligation should have the following characteristics:[314]

(1) A Land Obligation could be a restrictive obligation (imposing a restriction on the doing of some act on the burdened land) or a positive obligation (such as an obligation to carry out works or provide services).

(2) A Land Obligation would have to be expressly labelled as a 'Land Obligation' in the instrument creating it.

(3) A Land Obligation could only be created expressly over registered title.

(4) The express creation of a Land Obligation would require the execution of an instrument in prescribed form:

(a) containing a plan clearly identifying all land benefiting from and burdened by the Land Obligation; and

(b) identifying the benefited and burdened estates in land for each Land Obligation.

(5) The creation of a Land Obligation capable of comprising a legal interest would have to be completed by registration of the interest in the register for the benefited land and a notice of the interest entered in the register for the burdened land. A Land Obligation would not operate at law until these registration requirements were met.

(6) A Land Obligation could subsist as a legal or as an equitable interest in land, but would normally subsist as a legal interest in land.

(7) A Land Obligation would have to have a dominant and a servient tenement (that is, there should be separate benefited and burdened estates in the land).

(8) The benefit of a Land Obligation would be appurtenant to the benefiting estate in the dominant land. The burden of a Land Obligation would attach to the burdened estate in the servient land.

(9) A Land Obligation would have to 'relate to' or be for the benefit of dominant land.

(10) There would have to be separate title numbers for the benefited and burdened estates, but there would be no need for the benefited and burdened estates in the land to be owned and possessed by different persons.

(11) A Land Obligation could be enforced by legal remedies (such as damages) and by equitable remedies (such as an injunction or specific performance).

(12) Subject to certain defined exceptions, it would no longer be possible to create new covenants which run with the land where the title to that land is registered.

---

[314] [For further discussion of the characteristics, and the Law Commission's reasoning, see paras 8.15–8.113.]

THE RUNNING OF THE BENEFIT AND WHO CAN ENFORCE

Land Obligations: the easement analogy

9.3 The 1984 Report recommended that the benefit of a neighbour obligation should, like an easement, be appurtenant to the dominant land and run with it on that basis.[315] The 1984 Report refined the phrase 'appurtenant to the dominant land' by explaining:

> Although easements are spoken of as being appurtenant to the dominant land, it is really more accurate to speak of them as being appurtenant to a particular estate in that land. If this estate is the fee simple, as is normally the case, the distinction is in a sense academic, but in other cases it may be important. If for example, an easement is granted solely to a lessee of the dominant land, it is appurtenant only to his leasehold estate: it is not appurtenant to any superior estate and no superior estate owner can benefit from it.[316]

9.4 We understand it to be accepted orthodoxy that easements are appurtenant to an estate in the dominant land.[317] We consider that the benefit of a Land Obligation should be appurtenant to an estate in the dominant land and run with it on that basis. The estate concerned would be identified in the Land Obligation deed.

9.5 We provisionally propose that a Land Obligation would be appurtenant to an estate in the dominant land ('the benefited estate').

9.6 We consider that a person seeking to enforce a Land Obligation would be required to show that:

(1) at the time of enforcement he or she has the benefit of a Land Obligation; and

(2) there is a breach of the Land Obligation.

9.7 The benefit of a Land Obligation should pass automatically on a disposition of the estate to which it is appurtenant.[318] Following the easement analogy, we consider that the benefit of a Land Obligation should also pass if the disposition is of some lesser estate granted out of the one to which the Land Obligation is appurtenant.[319] For example, if the Land Obligation is appurtenant to the freehold estate and the freehold owner grants a lease out of his estate, the benefit of the Land Obligation should pass to the tenant in the same way.

9.8 However, we consider that it should be possible for a Land Obligation, on any such disposition, to be expressly 'held back' and so excluded from the disposition.[320] This means that if, for example, the landlord of a benefited estate does not wish the tenant to enjoy the benefit of a Land Obligation, the landlord may expressly exclude that benefit in the lease. In the alternative, if the disposition is a disposition of the whole of the dominant land for the estate to which the

---

[315] The 1984 Report, para. 10.2.   [316] The 1984 Report, para. 10.3.

[317] See for example Ruoff and Roper which states "easements and profits à prendre are incorporeal hereditaments being property rights exercisable over the land (or more accurately the estate) of another person": Ruoff and Roper, *Registered Conveyancing* (Release 36, 2007), para. 36.001. Contrast the suggestion made by the Court of Appeal in *Wall v Collins* [2007] EWCA Civ 724, [2007] Ch 390 [p. 647, n. 78, above] that an easement must be appurtenant to a dominant tenement, but not necessarily to a particular interest in that dominant tenement: see paras 5.80 and following above. It should be noted that the fact situation which arose in *Wall v Collins* could not arise for Land Obligations, as the legal estate to be benefited by the Land Obligation will be clear from the title number of the dominant tenement on which the Land Obligation is required to be registered.

[318] It is in the nature of appurtenant interests that such rights pass automatically under the common law: *Godwin v Schweppes* [1902] 1 Ch 926, 932. This will remain the case, even though LPA 1925, s. 62, will not apply to Land Obligations.

[319] *Skull v Glenister* (1864) CB (NS) 81.

[320] See the 1984 Report, para. 10.4 for the easement analogy.

Land Obligation is appurtenant, this would amount to extinction of the Land Obligation. This is because an appurtenant interest cannot exist on its own.

9.9 We set out the general principle relating to the passing of the benefit below and deal, more particularly, with the circumstances in which the benefit of a Land Obligation will pass with a part of the benefiting estate on a sub-division in Part 10.

9.10 Subject to our proposals on sub-division, we provisionally propose that the benefit of a Land Obligation should pass to any person who:

(1) is a successor in title of the original owner of the benefited estate or any part of it; or

(2) who has an estate derived out of the benefited estate or any part of it;

unless express provision has been made for the benefit of the Land Obligation not to pass.

THE RUNNING OF THE BURDEN AND WHO SHOULD BE BOUND

9.11 Taking the law of easements as an analogy, we consider that the burden of a Land Obligation should attach to the burdened estate in the servient land and run with it on that basis.[321] However, it is necessary to distinguish between two types of Land Obligation to answer the question of who should be bound by it: positive and reciprocal payment obligations on the one hand and restrictive obligations on the other.

Positive and reciprocal payment obligations

9.12 As the 1984 Report put it, 'positive obligations...[require] the expenditure of money. It is therefore inappropriate that all those with an interest, however small, in the servient land should be liable to perform a positive obligation'.[322] Why, for example, should a periodic tenant be obliged to replace the roof of the property at the request of the neighbouring freeholder? The responsibility should surely be that of the tenant's landlord.

9.13 This reasoning led the Law Commission in 1984, in common with other law reform bodies,[323] to recommend limiting the range of persons against whom positive obligations can be enforced. It was important to strike a balance. The class of those bound 'must comprise a sufficient range of substantial 'targets' to make the obligations real and valuable from the point of dominant owners; but it must not include anyone whom it would be unfair to burden with their performance'.[324]

9.14 The Commission therefore recommended that the class potentially bound by a positive or reciprocal payment obligation should include only:[325]

(1) those with a freehold interest in the servient land or any part of it, provided they have a right to possession;[326]

---

[321] Unlike the current law of covenants, the original creator of a Land Obligation will not remain bound by it once he or she has parted with all interest in the burdened land.

[322] The 1984 Report, para. 4.25.

[323] New Zealand Property Law and Equity Committee, *Positive Covenants Affecting Land* (1985), para. 28(a); Ontario Law Reform Commission, *Covenants Affecting Freehold Land* (1989), pp. 124 to 128; New South Wales Land Titles Office, *Review of the Law of Positive Covenants Affecting Freehold Land* (1994), paras 6.22 to 6.31; American Law Institute, *Restatement (Third) Of Property: Servitudes* (2000), vol. 2, pp. 16 to 26; Report on Real Burdens (2000) Scot Law Com 181, paras 4.31 to 4.38.

[324] The 1984 Report, para. 11.8.

[325] The 1984 Report, paras 11.9 to 11.13. This recommendation was subject to the exceptions set out at paras 11.14 to 11.15 of the Report. We discuss possible exceptions to who should be bound by a Land Obligation at paras 9.45 to 9.48 [of this Report].

[326] The 1984 Report, para. 11.10 explains that: 'A right to possession is not to be confused with a right to occupy. Thus "possession" includes receipt of rents and profits, so a freeholder does not cease to have a

(2) those who have long leases (terms of more than 21 years) of the servient land or any part of it, provided they have a right to possession;

(3) mortgagees of the servient land or any part of it;[327] and

(4) owners of the burdened estate which do not fall within any of the above three categories, where that interest is clearly intended to be bound.[328]

9.15 The Scottish Law Reform Commission has recently examined this issue in the context of real burdens and has adopted a different approach. They recommended that positive covenants should only be enforceable against the owner of the burdened property.[329] They reasoned:

> If a person possesses under a long lease, or a liferent, there is an argument that expenditure of an income nature—routine maintenance, cleaning, gardening and the like—should be recoverable directly from him rather than from the owner. The law reform bodies which have considered this issue in other jurisdictions have usually concluded that lessees holding on long leases should be liable for some or all affirmative burdens. On balance, however, we do not support this solution. The most important thing is to have a clear rule. The parties can then make appropriate adjustments by contract.[330]

9.16 As a Land Obligation can be created by a leasehold owner with registered title, it would not be possible to provide that positive and reciprocal payment obligations would only be enforceable against the owner of an estate in fee simple. We could, however, (as an alternative to the 1984 approach) limit enforcement against the owner for the time being of the original burdened estate.

9.17 If it was considered that owners of lesser estates derived from the burdened estate should also be bound, there is a further option. We could provide that anyone having an estate greater than a certain number of years[331] should also be bound by a positive or reciprocal payment obligation. However, this may not be appropriate where there is only one year or even one day remaining on the term of the derivative estate.[332] This could be dealt with by providing that the class of those who should be bound by a positive or reciprocal payment obligation should encompass any person who:

(1) is a successor in title of the original owner of the burdened estate; or

right to possession merely because he has leased the property to a tenant. But the limitation we propose does have the effect of excluding cases where the interest is one in remainder or in reversion. If, for example, the servient land is settled on A for life and then to B absolutely, B has technically a freehold interest, but during A's lifetime it does not entitle him to possession and we do not think he should be bound by a land obligation because he has it'.

[327] The 1984 Report, para. 12.8 suggested that a mortgagee should not be liable for a contravention of a land obligation unless, at the relevant time, he or she has actually taken possession of the land or has appointed a receiver.

[328] This was a residual category and was intended to catch, for example, the case of a tenant with a 20-year lease entering into an obligation to carry out works. As a Land Obligation would not bind the owners of any interests superior to the tenant, unless it bound his interest it would not bind anyone at all.

[329] Report on Real Burdens (2000) Scot Law Com No 181, para. 4.38.

[330] Para. 4.32. The Scottish Law Commission goes on to emphasise the desirability of retaining the current legal position.

[331] Perhaps 21 years or more. We seek consultees' views on what minimum unexpired term they believe would be most suitable below.

[332] See for example *Scottish Mutual Assurance plc v Jardine Public Relations Ltd* [1999] EGCS 43.

(2) has an estate derived from the burdened estate provided that it has more than a certain number of years (perhaps 21 years or more)[333] unexpired.

9.18 We deal with the circumstances in which the burden of a Land Obligation will pass with a part of the burdened estate in Part 10.

9.19 We provisionally propose that a Land Obligation would attach to an estate in the servient land ('the burdened estate').

9.20 We invite the views of consultees on the following three alternatives for the class of persons who should be bound by a positive obligation or a reciprocal payment obligation:

(1) Option 1: Should the class encompass:

    (a) those with a freehold interest in the servient land or any part of it, provided they have a right to possession;

    (b) those who have long leases (terms of more than 21 years) of the servient land or any part of it, provided they have a right to possession;

    (c) mortgagees of the servient land or any part of it; or

    (d) owners of the burdened estate which do not fall within any of the above three categories, where the interest is clearly intended to be bound?

(2) Option 2: Should the class be restricted to the owner for the time being of the burdened estate or any part of it? Or

(3) Option 3: Should the class encompass:

    (a) the owner for the time being of the burdened estate or any part of it; and

    (b) any person who has an estate derived out of the burdened estate or any part of it for a term of which at least a certain number of years are unexpired at the time of enforcement?

We invite consultees' views on what minimum unexpired term they believe would be most appropriate.

9.21 We invite consultees to state whether they consider that any other persons with interests in or derived out of the burdened estate should be bound by a positive obligation or a reciprocal payment obligation, and if so which persons.

WHO SHOULD BE LIABLE?

9.38 Finally, after determining the question of who, at any given time would be bound by a Land Obligation, we need to ascertain who would be liable for a particular contravention of the Land Obligation. In dealing with this question, it is necessary to distinguish once again between different types of Land Obligation.[334]

Restrictive obligations

9.41 We provisionally propose that a restrictive obligation should be enforceable against any person bound by it in respect of any conduct by that person which amounts to doing the prohibited act (or to permitting or suffering it to be done by another person).

---

[333] A dividing line of 21 years is well recognised in property law. See for example, the Landlord and Tenant Act 1954, Part I, and the Leasehold Reform Act 1967.

[334] [In the case of continuing breaches, both old and new owners would be liable: para. 9.44. A mortgagee would not be liable if it has not taken possession nor appointed a receiver: para. 9.46; and the scope of liability could be extended by the terms of the instrument creating the Land Obligation: para. 9.47.]

Positive and reciprocal payment obligations

9.43 We provisionally propose that a positive or reciprocal payment obligation should be enforceable, in respect of any breach, against every person bound by the obligation at the time when the breach occurs.

10.9 We provisionally propose that Land Obligations should be capable of variation and extinguishment:

(1) expressly; and

(2) by operation of statute.

10.10 We provisionally propose that Land Obligations should be automatically extinguished on the termination of the estate in land to which they are attached.

10.26 We provisionally propose that on a sub-division of the servient land, the burden of a positive or reciprocal payment obligation should run with each and every part of the land. The owners of each part bound by the obligation would therefore be jointly and severally liable in the event of a breach of the Land Obligation.

10.31 We provisionally propose that on a sub-division of the servient land, the burden of a restrictive obligation should run with each and every part of the land.

10.44 We provisionally propose that on sub-division of the benefited land, the benefit of a Land Obligation should run with each and every part of it unless:

(1) the Land Obligation does not 'relate to' or benefit that part of the dominant land;

(2) the sub-division increases the scope of the obligations owed by the burdened owner to an extent beyond that contemplated in the Land Obligation deed; or

(3) express provision has been made for the benefit of the Land Obligation not to pass.

15.1 The outcome of our provisional proposals would be to offer the following types of right:

Easements

(1) Positive: a right to make use of a neighbour's land, such as to walk or drive across it or to install and use a drain.

(2) Negative: a right to receive something from a neighbour's land without that neighbour obstructing or interfering with it. Currently, only four negative easements are recognised in law: a right of support of buildings from land (or from buildings), a right to receive light through a defined aperture, a right to receive air through a defined channel and a right to receive a flow of water in an artificial stream.[335]

Profits appurtenant

(3) A right to take products of natural growth from the land of another (such as fish, turf or timber).[336]

---

[335] See *Gale on Easements* (17th edn, 2002), para. 1–01.

[336] Profits are also capable of existing in gross. For the purposes of this Part we discuss profits appurtenant to land only.

Land Obligations

(4) Positive:[337] an obligation on the servient owner to do something or to pay towards the cost of doing something, such as building a wall, or maintaining a building.

(5) Restrictive: an obligation on the servient owner not to do something, such as build on the land, or use a building as retail premises.

15.2 These interests are all property rights burdening land for the benefit of other land. As such, they have certain fundamental characteristics in common. However, despite these similarities, we have taken the provisional view that the distinction between the three types of interest should be maintained. We consider that reclassification or fusion of these interests would be inappropriate.[338]

QUESTION

Do you agree with the Law Commission that the assimilation of easements and covenants into a single, unified category of interest in land is undesirable? Law Commission Report on the Law of Positive and Restrictive Covenants 1984 (Law Com No. 127); Law Commission Consultation Paper on Easements, Covenants and Profits à Prendre 2008 (Consultation Paper No. 186), Part 15.

---

[337] Land obligations of a positive nature include positive obligations and reciprocal payment obligations.

[338] For a different approach see the American Law Institute, *Restatement (Third) Of Property: Servitudes* (2000) which comprehensively reconsidered and unified the law governing the broad equivalent to easements, profits and covenants.

10

MORTGAGES[1]

---

[1] C & B, chap. 21; Gray, parts 6.1–6.5; M & W, chaps 24–26; MM, chap. 13; Smith, chap. 25. See generally Coote, *Law of Mortgages* (9th edn, 1927); Cousins, *Law of Mortgages* (2nd edn, 2001), chap. 22; Fisher and Lightwood, *Law of Mortgage* (12th edn, 2006); *Snell's Equity* (31st edn), Part VII; Waldock, *Law of Mortgage* (2nd edn, 1950); (1978) 94 LQR 571 (P. Jackson); *Council of Mortgage Lenders Handbook* (2nd edn, 2002, revised from time to time: the up-to-date version is available on the CML website, www.cml.org.uk) The Code of Mortgage Lending Practice, a voluntary code followed by lenders (from 1 July 1997) and mortgage intermediaries (from 31 April 1998) in their relations with personal customers in the United Kingdom, ceased to apply from 31 October 2004, and was superseded by the Mortgages: Conduct of Business requirements published by the Financial Services Authority as statutory regulator of the mortgage industry; n. 10, below. See also American Law Institute, *Restatement of the Law, Property 3d, Mortgages* (1997).

I. INTRODUCTION

The mortgage transaction has, throughout its history, been a collection of contradictions. Maitland described it as 'one long suppressio veri and suggestio falsi'.[2] Before 1926, the usual form of mortgage of a fee simple was by conveyance of that fee simple subject to an undertaking by the mortgagee to reconvey on payment, at a stated time in the future, of all moneys due; mortgages of leaseholds were by assignment of the leasehold or by sub-demise. After 1925,[3] mortgages of freeholds could no longer be made by a transfer of the freehold, nor could mortgages of leaseholds be made by the assignment of the leasehold term itself. Rather, a legal mortgage of freehold could be made only by way of demise (that is, by granting a long lease to the mortgagee, which would determine on payment of all moneys due) and mortgages of leaseholds by sub-demise; or, in either case, by a new form of mortgage instrument: the *charge by deed expressed to be by way of legal mortgage* in accordance with section 87(1) of the Law of Property Act 1925. The legal charge was a much simpler form of mortgage, and the mortgage by demise or sub-demise became obsolescent and in 2003, in relation to mortgages of registered land, finally became formally obsolete.[4] Statutory provision for the creation of charges by way of legal mortgage at last made it possible for a mortgage transaction to appear to be what it really is—the charging of property as security for the repayment of a loan. The historical practice of conveying an estate in land to the mortgagee had hidden the true nature of the transaction, and had made it necessary for Courts of Chancery to make great exertions to prevent the mortgagee from using the property as something more than a security for the debt.

The legal mortgage before 1926, and even thereafter the mortgage by demise or sub-demise, were drafted so as to appear to give the mortgagee something more than a security; they provided for the conveyance to the mortgagee of a legal estate in the land (the fee simple or a term of years) subject to reconveyance, or for cesser of the demise respectively, on repayment of all sums due at a time in the future. This was usually six months ahead, although in most cases there was no intention on the part of either party that the payment should be made by that date. If the payment was not made on the due date, the mortgagor's legal right was then lost and the only protection that he received was from equity; he was given an equitable right to redeem, and this right was held by a series of cases to be absolute and inviolable.[5] In accordance with the proviso for redemption given by the mortgagee, the mortgagor has a legal, or contractual, right to redeem and to obtain a reconveyance of the property; and by virtue of his right to

---

[2] Maitland, *Equity* (2nd edn), p. 182; Simpson, *A History of the Land Law* (2nd edn, 1986), pp. 141–143, 242–247. In *Samuel v Jarrah & Wood Paving Corpn Ltd* [1904] AC 323 at 326, Lord Macnaghten said: 'No one...by the light of nature ever understood an English mortgage of real estate.' See also *National Westminster Bank v Kitch* (1996) 74 P & CR 98 at 101 (writ issued for sums due on two overdrawn accounts secured by mortgage held not to be a 'mortgage action').

[3] LPA 1925, ss. 85(1) (freeholds), 86(1) (leaseholds), p. 856, below.

[4] LRA 2002, s. 23(1), p. 860, below.   [5] See pp. 869 ff, below.

obtain specific performance of the mortgagee's covenant to reconvey, equity considered him to be the owner of the land subject to the mortgage. Equity's insistence upon the inviolability of the mortgagor's right to redeem, even after his contractual right had ended, led to the creation of an equitable right to redeem; and equity's willingness to enforce this right at any time on payment of all sums due meant that he continued to be the owner in equity subject to the mortgage. The equitable interest which he owns is called the Equity of Redemption; and just as, centuries earlier, equitable estates in land became proprietary by the protection given by equity to the cestui que use against everyone except the bona fide purchaser of the legal estate for value without notice,[6] so also the equity of redemption was regarded as a proprietary interest which could be bought, sold, mortgaged and pass to the Crown as bona vacantia.[7]

The interest which the mortgagee acquires is a real and not merely a personal security, which prevails against the general body of creditors in the event of the mortgagor's bankruptcy. He is not only a creditor of the mortgagor; he is a secured creditor. As long as the mortgaged property remains worth as much as the debt, the mortgagee will receive payment in full; but if it falls in value and becomes worth less than the debt—in modern parlance, the mortgagor has 'negative equity'—the mortgagee will only be a secured creditor to the extent of its value, and he must prove in the mortgagor's bankruptcy with the unsecured creditors for the remainder of the debt.

Traditionally, Courts of Equity have looked upon a mortgage transaction as one in which the terms were likely to be dictated by the mortgagee. In early days the mortgagor was at a disadvantage in that he was in need of money and must take it on the mortgagee's terms; it was a lender's market. And, while the law followed the maxim 'caveat emptor' in the affairs of merchants and trade, equity not surprisingly took a different view in the case of mortgages. The fact that mortgagors were, in the early days, often members of great families and mortgagees were professional money lenders no doubt contributed to some extent to the development. A consideration of the changed position of borrowers and lenders in the capitalist society of the present day will suggest that the old cases should be accepted with some reserve. The cases on this subject show a continual struggle between the principle of binding precedent and the requirements of a changing society; they can only be understood with this in mind. Those which were decided about the turn of the twentieth century do not create the principle they apply. That litigation was a challenge to the validity of the principle laid down in earlier centuries, but generally it succeeded only in re-affirming the old principles; it was not until 1914[8] that substantial progress was made.

The problem at the present day is the extent to which these old rules still hold good. A modern mortgage of land is very commonly a transaction between an individual house-buyer and a bank, building society or other institutional lender,[9] or forms part of a development project embarked upon by property financiers. The individual

---

[6] See p. 58, above.

[7] *Re Sir Thomas Spencer Wells* [1933] Ch 29, p. 868, below.

[8] *Kreglinger v New Patagonia Meat and Cold Storage Co Ltd* [1914] AC 25, p. 890, below.

[9] Lord Diplock in *Pettitt v Pettitt* [1970] AC 777 at 824 referred to 'a real-property-mortgaged-to-a-building-society-owning democracy'. For the two main types of mortgage, the endowment mortgage

borrower is generally protected from unfair pressure by the high standards set by banks and building societies as well as by competition within, and regulation[10] of, the mortgage industry and also by special statutory safeguards[11] and the general law of contract[12] and the criminal law.[13] Business borrowers are also, of course, protected by some of these same safeguards, but in general terms can be expected to look after themselves. One may therefore doubt whether the historical concerns of the Courts of Equity, designed to provide special protection to mortgagors, find a place in the modern mortgage market.

When a borrower falls into arrears with his payments, a bank or building society does all it can to avoid repossession, but if it has to take action to enforce the security, difficult social questions arise. The mortgagor has given as security, not an investment, but his home. And a mortgagor who has defaulted with one lender will have difficulty in borrowing money from another. Most of the litigation is in respect of applications for possession.[14] The mortgagee is, in law, entitled to possession 'before the ink is dry on the mortgage.'[15] A bank or building society will not go into possession without a court order; but it will go into possession before sale in order to be able to give vacant possession to a purchaser. Applications for possession are thus usually a preliminary to sale by the mortgagee. It is in this context that questions arise at the present day concerning the mortgagor's need for protection, and mortgagors of dwelling houses have had statutory protection since 1970.[16] In recent years there has been a very strong housing market, with a correspondingly strong market for mortgages. This is reflected

and the instalment or repayment mortgage, see p. 855, n. 19, below. For the idea that there should be a *Eurohypothec*—a common mortgage for Europe—see [2005] Conv 32 (S. Nasarre-Aznar).

[10] The Financial Services Authority is the regulator responsible for the authorisation and regulation of mortgage lending and mortgage advice business in the UK under Financial Services and Markets Act 2000. A regulated mortgage contract is a loan to an individual or trustees, secured by a first legal mortgage on land of which at least 40% of that land is used, or is intended to be used, as or in connection with a dwelling by the borrower or (in the case of credit provided to trustees) by an individual who is a beneficiary of the trust, or by a related person: Financial Services and Markets Act 2000 (Regulated Activities) Order 2001 (SI 2001 No. 544), art. 61 (3) as substituted by Financial Services and Markets Act 2000 (Regulated Activities) (Amendment) Order 2001 (SI 2001 No. 3544), art. 8. This includes business loans to customers under a regulated mortgage contract. The detailed provisions for regulation are set out in the FSA's *Mortgages: Conduct of Business* (MCOB), which can be viewed on the FSA website: www.fsa.gov.uk. Regulation of Financial Services (Land Transactions) Act 2005 amended Financial Services and Markets Act 2000 to bring Islamic mortgages within the regulatory framework; [2005] 34 EG 107 (M. Rutter). For the principles of Islamic banking and finance, see Kettell, *Introduction to Islamic Banking and Finance*; Schoon, *Islamic Banking and Finance*.

[11] Consumer Credit Act 1974, p. 921, below; Administration of Justice Act 1970, s. 36, p. 935, below.

[12] *Barclays Bank plc v O'Brien* [1994] 1 AC 180, p. 900, below; *Royal Bank of Scotland v Etridge (No 2)* [2002] 2 AC 773, p. 902, below (undue influence and misrepresentation); *Multiservice Bookbinding Ltd v Marden* [1979] Ch 84, p. 894, below (unconscionable bargains). Unfair Terms in Consumer Contracts Regs 1999 (SI 1999 No. 3159) also apply to mortgages.

[13] On mortgage fraud, see Clarke, *Mortgage Fraud* (1991); Osborn, *Mortgage Fraud* (1995); [1993] Conv 181 (H. W. Wilkinson). Theft (Amendment) Act 1996 created two new offences by inserting s. 15A (obtaining a money transfer by deception) and 24A (dishonestly retaining a wrongful credit) into Theft Act 1968. See Law Commission Report Offences of Dishonesty: Money Transfers (1996) Law Com No 243. S. 15A was repealed and replaced by Fraud Act 2006.

[14] See p. 930, below.

[15] Per Harman J, in *Four-Maids Ltd v Dudley Marshall (Properties) Ltd* [1957] Ch 317 at 320, p. 929, below.

[16] Administration of Justice Act 1970, s. 36, p. 935, below.

in the Office of National Statistics 2008 report, set out below. However, during 2008 there was a downturn in the housing market, with falls in house prices and a significant reduction in the availability of credit through banks and building societies, as the United Kingdom economy entered a period of recession.[17] This means that, in the short term, the mortgage market is much less certain and predictable, although we are likely to see an increase in the number of mortgagors who are unable to meet their mortgage debts as they fall due and therefore a corresponding increase in bank and building society repossessions.[18]

Office of National Statistics Social Trends 38 (2008 edn), pp. 146–148

In 2006 the average price paid for a dwelling in the UK was £192,648, an increase of around 6 per cent from 2005.... This was almost three times the average dwelling price compared with 1995, when it was £66,786....

In recent years steep increases in house prices have made affordability a particular concern for first-time buyers. Between 1996 and 2006 average prices paid by first-time buyers in the UK rose by around 200 per cent (not adjusting for inflation). The average price paid by first-time buyers in the UK in 2006 was £145,970, 3 per cent higher than in 2005.... The average price paid by former owner-occupiers rose by 14 per cent to £239,042 over the same period, but this larger increase will have been compensated for by an increase in the price of the house they sold. In 2006 the average deposit paid by first-time buyers in the UK represented 16 per cent of the purchase price. This proportion has been falling steadily since 2003 when it peaked at 23 per cent. This may in part reflect recent trends for mortgage lenders to offer loans at higher multiples of incomes (on average three times annual income in 2006) and repayment terms over longer periods than the traditional 25 years. These mortgage terms have the effect of increasing the amount first-time buyers are able to borrow whilst lowering typical monthly repayments. This helps to compensate for the increase in the average income of first-time buyers falling behind the increase in average dwelling prices since the mid-1990s. Between 1996 and 2006 the average declared income of first-time buyers increased by 106 per cent to reach £41,000.... Declared income is the income against which the mortgage was obtained and could include one income or joint incomes but is not necessarily the same as household income (as the mortgage could be secured against only one income in households where more than one person is earning).

Many people who plan to buy a home live in private rented accommodation. In England in 2006/07, the most common reasons for not yet buying a home, given by those who expected to buy eventually, were that they could not afford the property they liked (62 per cent) or they

[17] The Bank of England publishes monthly statistics on lending. The Monetary and Financial Statistics, November 2008, Table A5.4 shows that in the six months to October 2008 the value of loans secured on dwellings which were approved by banks and building societies was just under £100m, and a total of 226,000 loans were approved for house purchase, compared with £196m of loans secured on dwellings, and 704,000 loans approved for house purchase, for the same period in 2007.

[18] On 3 December 2008 the Government announced a Homeowner Mortgage Support Scheme, designed to enable households that experience a significant and temporary loss of income as a result of the economic downturn to defer a proportion of the interest payments on their mortgage for up to two years. The Government will guarantee the deferred interest payments in return for the banks' participation in the scheme.

could not afford the deposit (60 per cent)....In 2006/07 half of those who expected to buy a home eventually had concerns that it might be difficult to keep up mortgage repayments compared with just over one-third (36 per cent) in 2005/06. A further half felt that they would not get a mortgage and that their job was not secure enough to buy a home yet. Other common reasons for not yet buying were related to concerns over finance and job security. Sixteen per cent expected to buy within the next year and a further 18 per cent in one to two years' time.

Private renters who did not expect to buy their own property gave more reasons for not being able to do so than those who did expect to buy in the future. The most common reason given was that they would not get a mortgage (78 per cent) with 75 per cent concerned that it might be difficult to keep up the repayments, a 19 per cent increase since 2005/06.

Housing costs constitute a substantial proportion of household budgets. In 2005/06 the average monthly mortgage payment of owner-occupier households in England was £530.00, representing 20 per cent of average household disposable income. This compared with a peak of 27 per cent in 1990, during a period of high mortgage interest rates, and a low of 16 per cent in 1996. For first time buyers mortgage payments comprised 22 per cent of monthly income in 2006 compared with 28 per cent in 1990 and 17 per cent in 1996. These data include both interest only and repayment mortgages.[19]

The proportion of monthly household income used to pay mortgages varied according to levels of household income. Owner-occupier households with the lowest incomes spent a far higher proportion of their monthly disposable income on mortgage payments than any other. In 2005/06 owner-occupier households in England with a monthly disposable income of less than £1,000 spent an average 39 per cent of it on mortgage payments....In contrast, households with a monthly disposable income of £4,000 or more spent an average 14 per cent of it on mortgage payments. One-third of households in this income group made monthly mortgage payments of £1,000 or more. This was at least three times the proportion of those in any other income group.

For most owner-occupiers their home represents their most valuable financial asset.... Releasing equity from the value of a home can be a relatively inexpensive and convenient way of borrowing money.[20] In 2005/06 it was reported that almost 5 per cent (656,000) of

[19] ['Those buying a home can choose from a variety of different types of mortgage, the most common being repayment and interest-only. With repayment mortgages the debt and the interest are both repaid during the life of the mortgage (usually 25 years). Around 81 per cent of all new mortgages were standard repayment mortgages in 2002. Interest-only mortgages, which include endowment policies, ISAs (individual savings accounts) and personal pensions, account for the bulk of other mortgages. Since the late 1980s there has been a decrease in the popularity of endowment mortgages because of the possibility that investments may not grow fast enough to repay the capital borrowed. In 1988, 83 per cent of new mortgages for house purchase were endowment mortgages but by 2002 this had fallen to 5 per cent. The proportion of fixed (as opposed to variable) rate mortgages is markedly lower in the United Kingdom than in many other countries. Research published by the Council of Mortgage Lenders in July 2002 suggested that flexible mortgages are accounting for a rapidly growing share of the mortgage market. Flexible mortgages allow people to pay off some of the loan early through overpayments and lump sum investments, and to borrow funds back by withdrawing lump sums': Office of National Statistics, Social Trends 34 (2004 edn), pp. 162–163.]

[20] [Very significant increases in property values in recent decades have made it particularly attractive for home owners to release capital in this way; several banks and building societies now offer "equity release schemes", one form of which involves the provision of a capital sum (often up to 50% of the market value of the home) or a regular income payment, secured on a 'lifetime mortgage' intended to be called in only on the death of the borrower, thus giving the borrower the freedom to release some of the capital value of his major asset during his lifetime—at the expense of those who would otherwise inherit on his death. The total value of lifetime mortgages outstanding at the end of 2006 was £6.6 billion: CML Press Release 1 February 2007.]

owner-occupiers in England had withdrawn equity from their home within the previous three years. The average amount released by each homeowner was £33,300. Home improvements or renovations was the most common reason for withdrawing equity (56 per cent), followed by paying off debts (29 per cent) and buying new goods for the property (15 per cent). Those who withdrew more than £20,000 were far more likely than those withdrawing less to use the proceeds towards financing the purchase of another property for themselves in the UK (10 per cent compared with 2 per cent), or to invest or save (17 per cent compared with 8 per cent). The most common methods of equity release borrowing were to increase the size of the current mortgage through a further advance or top-up (used in 33 per cent of cases) or to remortgage the current home (used in 27 per cent of cases).

II. METHODS OF CREATION

A. LEGAL MORTGAGES AND LEGAL CHARGES[21]

(i) Unregistered land

Since 1926 it has not been possible to create a legal mortgage by the transfer to the mortgagee of the legal estate which is to be mortgaged. A mortgage of unregistered land must be made by demise (or sub-demise), or by a charge by deed expressed to be by way of legal mortgage.

LAW OF PROPERTY ACT 1925

85. Mode of mortgaging freeholds.—(1) A mortgage of an estate in fee simple shall only be capable of being effected at law either by a demise for a term of years absolute, subject to a provision for cesser on redemption, or by a charge by deed expressed to be by way of legal mortgage:

Provided that a first mortgagee shall have the same right to the possession of documents as if his security included the fee simple.

(2) Any purported conveyance of an estate in fee simple by way of mortgage made after the commencement of this Act shall (to the extent of estate of the mortgagor) operate as a demise of the land to the mortgagee for a term of years absolute, without impeachment for waste, but subject to cesser on redemption, in manner following, namely:—

(a) A first or only mortgagee shall take a term of three thousand years from the date of the mortgage;

(b) A second or subsequent mortgagee shall take a term (commencing from the date of the mortgage) one day longer than the term vested in the first or other mortgagee whose security ranks immediately before that of such second or subsequent mortgagee; ...

---

[21] C & B, pp. 725–729; Gray, paras 6.1.7–6.1.16; M & W, paras 24.006–24.038; MM, pp. 491–503; Smith, pp. 549–550; Waldock, pp. 19–43; Fisher and Lightwood, chap. 2.

(3) Subsection (2) does not apply to registered land, but, subject to that, this section applies whether or not the land is registered land and whether or not the mortgage is expressed to be made by way of trust for sale or otherwise.[22]

86. Mode of mortgaging leaseholds.—(1) A mortgage of a term of years absolute shall only be capable of being effected at law either by a subdemise for a term of years absolute, less by one day at least than the term vested in the mortgagor, and subject to a provision for cesser on redemption, or by a charge by deed expressed to be by way of legal mortgage; and where a licence to subdemise by way of mortgage is required, such licence shall not be unreasonably refused:[23]

Provided that a first mortgagee shall have the same right to the possession of documents as if his security had been effected by assignment.

(2) Any purported assignment of a term of years absolute by way of mortgage made after the commencement of this Act shall (to the extent of the estate of the mortgagor) operate as a subdemise of the leasehold land to the mortgagee for a term of years absolute, but subject to cesser on redemption, in manner following, namely:—

    (a) The term to be taken by a first or only mortgagee shall be ten days less than the term expressed to be assigned;

    (b) The term to be taken by a second or subsequent mortgagee shall be one day longer than the term vested in the first or other mortgagee whose security ranks immediately before that of the second or subsequent mortgagee, if the length of the last mentioned term permits, and in any case for a term less by one day at least than the term expressed to be assigned: ...

(3) Subsection (2) does not apply to registered land, but, subject to that, this section applies whether or not the land is registered land and whether or not the mortgage is made by way of sub-mortgage of a term of years absolute, or is expressed to be by way of trust for sale or otherwise.[24]

87. Charges by way of legal mortgage.—(1) Where a legal mortgage of land is created by a charge by deed expressed[25] to be by way of legal mortgage, the mortgagee shall have the same protection, powers and remedies (including the right to take proceedings to obtain possession from the occupiers and the persons in receipt of rents and profits, or any of them) as if—

    (a) where the mortgage is a mortgage of an estate in fee simple, a mortgage term of three thousand years without impeachment of waste had been thereby created in favour of the mortgagee; and

    (b) where the mortgage is a mortgage of a term of years absolute, a sub-term less by one day than the term vested in the mortgagor had been thereby created in favour of the mortgagee....

---

[22] As substituted by LRA 2002, s. 133, Sch. 11, para. 2(1), (6).

[23] A charge probably dispenses with the need for a licence: *Gentle v Faulkner* [1900] 2 QB 267; *Matthews v Smallwood* [1910] 1 Ch 777; *Grand Junction Co Ltd v Bates* [1954] 2 QB 160, p. 859, n. 29, below.

[24] As substituted by LRA 2002, s. 133, Sch. 11, para. 2(1), (7).

[25] Such a statement is not required in the case of registered land: *Cityland and Property (Holdings) Ltd v Dabrah* [1968] Ch 166.

(4) Subsection (1) of this section shall not be taken to be affected by section 23(1)(a) of the Land Registration Act 2002 (under which owner's powers in relation to a registered estate do not include power to mortgage by demise or sub-demise).[26]

The Law of Property Act 1925, Schedule 5, gave the following simple form of legal charge:[27]

CHARGE BY WAY OF LEGAL MORTGAGE

This Legal Charge is made [&c.] between A. of [&c.] of the one part and B. of [&c.] of the other part.

[Recite the title of A. to the freeholds or leaseholds in the Schedule and agreement for the loan by B.]

Now in consideration of the sum of... pounds now paid by B. to A. (the receipt &c.) this Deed witnesseth as follows:-

1. A. hereby covenants with B. to pay [*Add the requisite covenant to pay principal and interest*].

2. A. as Beneficial Owner[28] hereby charges by way of legal mortgage All and Singular the property mentioned in the Schedule hereto with the payment to B. of the principal money, interest, and other money hereby covenanted to be paid by A.

3. [*Add covenant to insure buildings and any other provisions desired.*]

In witness [&c.] [*Add Schedule*].

In **Regent Oil Co Ltd v JA Gregory (Hatch End) Ltd** [1966] Ch 402 HARMAN LJ said at 431:

In my opinion, the new charge by way of legal mortgage created by section 87 was intended to be a substitute in all respects for a mortgage by demise, and anything which would be good in the one is good in the other. It would indeed be a trap if the rights of the mortgagee depended on whether his charge were created in one way or the other. Support for this view is to be found in *Grand Junction Co Ltd v Bates* [1954] 2 QB 160; I read from the judgment of Upjohn J at 168:

'My approach to the problem is this: A charge by way of legal mortgage, as I have already said, was introduced as a conveyancing device by the Law of Property Act 1925, with a view to simplifying conveyancing, and it would be pity to introduce subtle differences between one way of creating a charge and another way of creating a charge unless the words of the Act so required. It may be that there is a difference with regard to obtaining consent of the landlord to the charge, though that depends on the construction of the lease; but in any event that is no reason for making another difference between the two forms of creating a security, unless the Act so requires.'

---

[26] Inserted by LRA 2002, s. 133, Sch. 11, para. 2(1), (8).

[27] LPA 1925, s. 206, Sch. 5, Form No. 1; this was repealed in 2004: Statute Law (Repeals) Act 2004, s. 1 (1), Sch. 1, Part 12. Forms of statutory legal charge are also provided by LPA 1925, s. 117, Sch. 4, Forms 1 and 4, but these are in practice rarely used: Emmet, para. 25.010. This precedent gives the flavour of the simplicity of a legal charge, although in practice legal charges take a more expanded form, containing further appropriate covenants by the borrower. For a fuller precedent, see *Encyclopaedia of Forms and Precedents*, vol. 28, Form 2.

[28] The words 'as beneficial owner' were designed to imply certain covenants; since 30 June 1995 the appropriate wording is 'with full title guarantee': LP(MP)A 1994: C & B, pp. 967–969.

It was there held that the chargee by way of legal mortgage had a right to claim relief against forfeiture just as if he had been a mortgagee by sub-demise.

In **Weg Motors Ltd v Hales** [1962] Ch 49, DONOVAN LJ said at 77:

The section does not create even a notional term of years in the mortgagee but simply defines what protection, powers and remedies the mortgagee is to have.[29]

(ii) Registered land[30]

Under the Land Registration Act 2002[31] a registered proprietor may exercise owner's powers in relation to a registered charge. These are set out in section 23(1)-(3), below. The main change is that since the Act came into force in 2003 it has no longer been possible to create a mortgage of registered land by demise or sub-demise.

Compulsory first registration was introduced by the Land Registration Act 1997 for the 'creation of a protected first legal mortgage': see now Land Registration Act 2002, section 4(1)(g) and (8), below. A charge of registered land is a disposition and must be completed by registration, but does not operate at law until the relevant registration requirements have been met: section 27(1), Schedule 2, paragraphs 8–11, below. If the requirement of registration is not complied with, the creation becomes void as regards the creation of a legal estate, and has effect as 'a contract made for valuable consideration to create the legal estate': section 7(1), (2), p. 135, above. This is an equitable interest and needs protection by a notice or actual occupation.

Land and charge certificates ceased to have any legal significance when the 2002 Act came into force. Instead, the Land Registry now issues an official copy showing the entries which exist on the register.

LAND REGISTRATION ACT 2002

4 When title must be registered

(1) The requirement of registration applies on the occurrence of any of the following events—

(g) the creation of a protected first legal mortgage of a qualifying estate.

---

[29] See also *Grand Junction Co Ltd v Bates* [1954] 2 QB 160 at 168, where it was said that a tenant who charges his lease is probably not in breach of a covenant against sub-letting without the landlord's consent. Nor does a chargee have a term so as to effect a transfer to him under LPA 1925, s. 115: *Cumberland Court (Brighton) Ltd v Taylor* [1964] Ch 29; nor is it necessary to serve upon a chargee a notice under LPA 1925, s. 146, p. 429, above; nor under Leasehold Property (Repairs) Act 1938, p. 448, above; *Church Comrs for England v Ve-Ri-Best Manufacturing Ltd* [1957] 1 QB 238; *Ushers Brewery v PS King & Co (Finance) Ltd* (1969) 212 EG 787; *Thompson v Salah* [1972] 1 All ER 530; *Edwards v Marshall-Lee* (1975) 235 EG 901; W & C, vol. i., 177–178.

[30] For provision for the creation of legal charges in electronic form using the Land Registry electronic communications network, see LRA 2002, ss. 91, 92, p. 226, above; Land Registration (Electronic Conveyancing) Rules 2008 (SI 2008 No. 1750).

[31] LRR 2003, Part 9; R & R, chap. 27; H & B, chap. 12; Law Commission Report on Land Registration for the Twenty-First Century 2001 (Law Com No. 271), paras 4.29–4.30, Part VII.

(8) For the purposes of subsection (1)(g)—

    (a) a legal mortgage is protected if it takes effect on its creation as a mortgage to be protected by the deposit of documents relating to the mortgaged estate, and

    (b) a first legal mortgage is one which, on its creation, ranks in priority ahead of any other mortgages then affecting the mortgaged estate.

23 Owner's powers

(1) Owner's powers in relation to a registered estate consist of—

    (a) power to make a disposition of any kind permitted by the general law in relation to an interest of that description, other than a mortgage by demise or sub-demise, and

    (b) power to charge the estate at law with the payment of money.

(2) Owner's powers in relation to a registered charge consist of—

    (a) power to make a disposition of any kind permitted by the general law in relation to an interest of that description, other than a legal sub-mortgage, and

    (b) power to charge at law with the payment of money indebtedness secured by the registered charge.

(3) In subsection (2)(a), 'legal sub-mortgage' means—

    (a) a transfer by way of mortgage,

    (b) a sub-mortgage by sub-demise, and

    (c) a charge by way of legal mortgage.

27 Dispositions required to be registered

(1) If a disposition of a registered estate or registered charge is required to be completed by registration, it does not operate at law until the relevant registration requirements are met.

(2) In the case of a registered estate, the following are the dispositions which are required to be completed by registration—

    (f) the grant of a legal charge.

(3) In the case of a registered charge, the following are the dispositions which are required to be completed by registration—

    (a) a transfer, and

    (b) the grant of a sub-charge.

(4) Schedule 2 to this Act (which deals with the relevant registration requirements) has effect.

51 Effect of completion by registration

On completion of the relevant registration requirements, a charge created by means of a registrable disposition of a registered estate has effect, if it would not otherwise do so, as a charge by deed by way of legal mortgage.

52 Protection of disponees

(1) Subject to any entry in the register to the contrary, the proprietor of a registered charge is to be taken to have, in relation to the property subject to the charge, the powers of disposition conferred by law on the owner of a legal mortgage.

(2) Subsection (1) has effect only for the purpose of preventing the title of a disponee being questioned (and so does not affect the lawfulness of a disposition).

53 Powers as sub-chargee

The registered proprietor of a sub-charge has, in relation to the property subject to the principal charge or any intermediate charge, the same powers as a sub-chargor.

132 General interpretation

(1) In this Act

'charge' means any mortgage, charge or lien for securing money or money's worth;

'registered charge' means a charge the title to which is entered on the register;

'sub-charge' means a change under section 23(2)(b).

SCHEDULE 2
REGISTRABLE DISPOSITIONS: REGISTRATION REQUIREMENTS

PART 1
REGISTERED ESTATES

Creation of legal charge

8 In the case of the creation of a charge, the chargee, or his successor in title, must be entered in the register as the proprietor of the charge.

PART 2
REGISTERED CHARGES

Introductory

9 This Part deals with the registration requirements relating to those dispositions of registered charges which are required to be completed by registration.

Transfer

10 In the case of a transfer, the transferee, or his successor in title, must be entered in the register as the proprietor.

Creation of sub-charge

11 In the case of the creation of a sub-charge, the sub-chargee, or his successor in title, must be entered in the register as the proprietor of the sub-charge.

LAND REGISTRATION RULES 2003

Form of charge of registered estate

103. A legal charge of a registered estate may be made in Form CH1.[32]

---

[32] Form CH1 is set out in LRR 2003, Sch. 1, as substituted by LR (Amendment) R 2008 (SI 2008 No. 1919), r. 11, Sch. 2, and is reproduced on pp. 862–863. In practice, many institutional lenders will have their own form of charge which will have been approved by the Land Registry: H & B, para. 12.14; Land Registry Practice Guide 30, *Approval of Mortgage Documentation* (March 2003).

Land Registry
Legal charge of a registered estate

This form should be accompanied by either Form AP1 or Form FR1

If you need more room than is provided for in a panel, and your software allows, you can expand any panel in the form. Alternatively use continuation sheet CS and attach it to this form.

'Conveyancer' is a term used in this form. It is defined in rule 217(1) of the Land Registration Rules 2003 and includes, among others, solicitor, licensed conveyancer and fellow of the Institute of Legal Executives.

Leave blank if not yet registered.	1	Title number(s) of the property:
Insert address including postcode (if any) or other description of the property, for example 'land adjoining 2 Acacia Avenue'.	2	Property:
	3	Date:
Give full name(s).	4	Borrower:
Complete as appropriate where the borrower is a company.		For UK incorporated companies/LLPs Registered number of company or limited liability partnership including any prefix: For overseas companies (a) Territory of incorporation: (b) Registered number in England and Wales including any prefix:
Give full name(s).	5	Lender for entry in the register:
Complete as appropriate where the lender is a company. Also, for an overseas company, unless an arrangement with Land Registry exists, lodge either a certificate in Form 7 in Schedule 3 to the Land Registration Rules 2003 or a certified copy of the constitution in English or Welsh, or other evidence permitted by rule 183 of the Land Registration Rules 2003.		For UK incorporated companies/LLPs Registered number of company or limited liability partnership including any prefix: For overseas companies (a) Territory of incorporation: (b) Registered number in England and Wales including any prefix:
Each proprietor may give up to three addresses for service, one of which must be a postal address whether or not in the UK (including the postcode, if any). The others can be any combination of a postal address, a UK DX box number or an electronic address.	6	Lender's intended address(es) for service for entry in the register:

Place 'X' in any box that applies.	7	The borrower with
		☐ full title guarantee
Add any modifications.		☐ limited title guarantee
		charges the property by way of legal mortgage as security for the payment of the sums detailed in panel 9
Place 'X' in the appropriate box(es).	8	☐ The lender is under an obligation to make further advances and applies for the obligation to be entered in the register
You must set out the wording of the restriction in full.		☐ The borrower applies to enter the following standard form of restriction in the proprietorship register of the registered estate:
Standard forms of restriction are set out in Schedule 4 to the Land Registration Rules 2003.		
Insert details of the sums to be paid (amount and dates) and so on.	9	Additional provisions
The borrower must execute this charge as a deed using the space opposite. If there is more than one borrower, all must execute. Forms of execution are given in Schedule 9 to the Land Registration Rules 2003. If a note to an obligation to make further advances has been applied for in panel 8 this document must be signed by the lender or its conveyancer.	10	Execution

Cheshire and Burn's Modern Law of Real Property (17th edn, 2006), p. 725

The modern law of mortgages cannot...be understood without the perspective of history. The registered proprietor today has the power to make any disposition of his estate—including mortgaging it—*except* for the mortgage by demise or sub-demise.[33] To comprehend this, it is necessary to understand the general powers of mortgaging which are still contained in the Law of Property Act 1925. But the principles of mortgages contained in that Act are themselves a development of the pre-1926 law of mortgages and have to be understood in that light. Although the Land Registration Act 2002 has prohibited the creation of mortgages by demise, the form of mortgage which is retained as the universal method of mortgaging registered land—the legal charge—is itself defined in the Law of Property Act 1925, for the purposes of registered land as much as unregistered land,[34] as giving the mortgagee the same protection, powers and remedies as if it had been a mortgage by demise. The 2002 Act does not therefore break with history: the theory of a demise underpins the present day law.

B. EQUITABLE MORTGAGES AND EQUITABLE CHARGES[35]

(i) Unregistered land

(a) Mortgage of an equitable interest

This is created by assigning the equitable interest to the mortgagee with a proviso for reassignment on redemption. The assignment, if not made by will, must satisfy the requirements of section 53(1)(c) of the Law of Property Act 1925.[36]

(b) Contract to create a legal mortgage

Under the doctrine of *Walsh v Lonsdale*[37] a contract to create a legal mortgage (or an imperfect legal mortgage) is treated in Equity as an actual mortgage, as long as it satisfies the formality requirements for a valid contract for the disposition of an interest in land under section 2 of the Law of Property (Miscellaneous Provisions) Act 1989.[38]

(c) Deposit of title deeds

It used to be held, following the case of *Russel v Russel*[39] in 1783 a deposit of title deeds, with the intention that the depositee shall hold them as a security, created an

---

[33] LRA 2002, s. 23 (1).

[34] LPA 1925, s. 87 (4), inserted by LRA 2002, s. 133, Sch. 11, para. 2 (1), (8), reinforces this by providing that it is not affected by the removal of the registered owner's power to mortgage by demise.

[35] C & B, pp. 729–734; Gray, paras 6.1.19–6.1.29; M & W, paras 24.039–24.042; MM, pp. 499–501; Smith, pp. 549–550; Cousins, chap. 5; Waldock, pp. 43–59, 136–139; Fisher and Lightwood, chap. 3.

[36] See p. 47, above.   [37] (1882) 21 ChD 9, pp. 29–34, above.

[38] See p. 18, above.

[39] (1783) 1 Bro CC 269; *Dixon v Muckleston* (1872) 8 Ch App 155; *Re Wallis and Simmonds (Builders) Ltd* [1974] 1 WLR 391; *Thames Guaranty Ltd v Campbell* [1985] QB 210 (deposit of title deeds (land certificate)

equitable mortgage of the land. This was because such a deposit was construed as a contract to create a mortgage. Before 1989 no formalities were necessary, because the deposit ranked as an act of part performance.[40] Under section 2 of the Law of Property (Miscellaneous Provisions) Act 1989, however, that doctrine ceased to apply. Equitable mortgages by deposit must now satisfy the requirements of that section.[41] In practice, however, it has been usual for a memorandum of the agreement to accompany the deposit, and, if it is desired to enable the mortgagee to pass a legal estate on sale, the mortgagor will execute a deed and insert in it a power of attorney or a declaration of trust, or both.[42]

(d) Equitable charge

This arises where property is charged in equity with the payment of a debt or some other obligation. In **Matthews v Goodday** (1861) 31 LJ Ch 282, KINDERSLEY V-C said at 282:

Suppose a man signed a written contract, by which he simply agreed that he thereby charged his real estate with £500 to A, what would be the effect of it? It would be no agreement to give a legal mortgage, but a security by which he equitably charged his land with the payment of a sum of money.[43]

An equitable charge does not have to satisfy section 2 of the Law of Property (Miscellaneous Provisions) Act 1989. It involves the *creation* of a security rather than an *agreement to create a* legal charge. Nor does it have to satisfy section 53(1) (c) of the Law of Property Act 1925,[44] since it is the creation of a new interest and not the disposition of an existing interest. Its validity depends on section 53(1)(a) of the Law of Property Act 1925, which requires the writing to be signed by the chargor only.[45]

---

to secure a debt by one joint tenant without consent of the other joint tenant not effective to create equitable charge of the jointly owned land; but it may create a charge of the equitable interest to the depositor, if the deposit amounts to an act of severance, p. 567, above); *First National Securities Ltd v Hegerty* [1985] QB 850, p. 567, n. 24, above.

[40] LPA 1925, s. 40, p. 17, above.

[41] *United Bank of Kuwait v Sahib* [1997] Ch 107 ('The clear intention of section 2...is to introduce certainty in relation to contracts for the disposition of interests in land where uncertainty existed before', per Phillips LJ at 387); (1997) 113 LQR 533 (M. Robinson). For the liability of a solicitor for failing to advise (even before *Kuwait*) that the mortgage was required to satisfy s. 2, see *Dean v Allin & Watts* [2001] 2 Lloyd's Rep 249.

[42] See p. 950, below. The right to create this kind of equitable mortgage was saved by LPA 1925, s. 13. The mortgagee could retain the deeds until he was paid, but had no separate legal lien: *Re Molton Finance Ltd* [1968] Ch 325; see also *Capital Finance Co Ltd v Stokes* [1969] 1 Ch 261 at 278.

[43] See *Swiss Bank Corpn v Lloyds Bank Ltd* [1982] AC 584 at 594–595, per Buckley LJ; *Thames Guaranty Ltd v Campbell*, above; *First National Securities Ltd v Hegerty*, above; *Re Cosslett (Contractors) Ltd* [1998] 2 WLR 131; *Edwards v Lloyds Bank plc* [2005] 1 FCR 139 (wife's signature forged).

[44] P. 47, above; *Kinane v Mackie-Conteh* [2005] EWCA Civ 45, [2005] 2 P & CR DG3.

[45] Emmet, para. 25.218. If there is no writing to satisfy s. 53(1)(a) the charge may still take effect under a constructive trust (s. 53(2)): *Kinane v Mackie-Conteh*, above.

(ii) Registered land

Law Commission Report on Land Registration for the Twenty-First Century 2001 (Law Com No. 271), paras 7.9–7.10.

Equitable charges

7.9 The Bill has nothing specific to say about equitable charges. A registered proprietor may create them to the extent permitted by the general law under his or her owner's powers. They may also arise in other ways, as where a creditor obtains a charging order over the land of a registered proprietor.[46]

7.10 The fact that the Bill says nothing about such charges is important for one specific reason. In the Consultative Document,[47] we recommended that the statutory power[48] to create a lien over registered land by depositing the land certificate as security should be abolished. Our reasoning was as follows. Such charges operated by analogy with the mortgage by deposit of title deeds in unregistered land. However, in *United Bank of Kuwait Plc v Sahib*,[49] the Court of Appeal held that the basis for mortgages by deposit of title deeds was the doctrine of part performance that had been abolished by the Law of Property (Miscellaneous Provisions) Act 1989.[50] Such mortgages were only valid if they complied with the formal requirements for contracts laid down in that Act. The decision rendered obsolete the power to create a lien by the deposit of a land certificate.... The Bill therefore contains nothing replicating the power.[51]

C. CHARGING ORDERS[52]

The court has powers under the Charging Orders Act 1979 to impose a charge on the land of a judgment debtor to secure the payment of his judgment debt. Such a charge has the same effect as 'an equitable charge created by the debtor by writing under his hand.'[53]

CHARGING ORDERS ACT 1979

1. Charging orders.—(1) Where, under a judgment or order of the High Court or a county court, a person (the 'debtor') is required to pay a sum of money to another person (the 'creditor') then, for the purpose of enforcing that judgment or order, the appropriate court may

---

[46] Such a charge takes effect as 'an equitable charge created by the debtor by writing under his hand': Charging Orders Act 1979, s. 3(4).

[47] Law Com No. 254, paras 9.8–9.11.

[48] Found in Land Registration Act 1925, s. 66.

[49] [1997] Ch 107; explained in Law Com No. 254, para. 9.9.　　　[50] Section 2.

[51] [Furthermore, under LRA 2002, land certificates are no longer issued by the Land Registry, p. 859, above.]

[52] C & B, p. 734; Gray, paras 6.1.31–6.1.41; M & W, paras 13.078–13.080; Smith, pp. 548–549; Walker and Buckley, *Charging Orders Against Land* (2nd edn).

[53] Charging Orders Act 1979, s. 3(4). This does not include the right to possession: *Yorkshire Bank Finance Ltd v Mulhall* [2008] 50 EG 74.

make an order in accordance with the provisions of this Act imposing on any such property of the debtor as may be specified in the order a charge for securing the payment of any money due or to become due under the judgment or order.

(5) In deciding whether to make a charging order the court shall consider all the circumstances of the case and, in particular, any evidence before it as to—

(a) the personal circumstances of the debtor, and

(b) whether any other creditor of the debtor would be likely to be unduly prejudiced by the making of the order.

2. Property which may be charged.—(1) Subject to subsection (3) below, a charge may be imposed by a charging order only on—

(a) any interest held by the debtor beneficially—

(i) in any asset of a kind mentioned in subsection (2) below, or

(ii) under any trust;[54] or

(b) any interest held by a person as trustee of a trust ('the trust'), if the interest is in such an asset or is an interest under another trust and—

(i) the judgment or order in respect of which a charge is to be imposed was made against that person as trustee of the trust, or

(ii) the whole beneficial interest under the trust is held by the debtor unencumbered and for his own benefit, or

(iii) in a case where there are two or more debtors all of whom are liable to the creditor for the same debt, they together hold the whole beneficial interest under the trust unencumbered and for their own benefit.

(2) The assets referred to in subsection (1) above are—

(a) land

(b) securities of any of the following kinds—

(i) government stock,

(ii) stock of any body (other than a building society) incorporated within England and Wales,

(iii) stock of any body incorporated outside England and Wales or of any state or territory outside the United Kingdom, being stock registered in a register kept at any place within England and Wales,

(iv) units of any unit trust in respect of which a register of the unit holders is kept at any place within England and Wales, or

(c) funds in court.

---

[54] *Ladup Ltd v Williams & Glyn's Bank plc* [1985] 1 WLR 851; *Clark v Chief Land Registrar* [1994] Ch 370. If a charging order is obtained over land which is subject to a trust of land, the judgment creditor may then apply to the court under TLATA 1996, s. 14, p. 532, above, for an order for sale of the property. See *Mortgage Corpn v Shaire* [2001] Ch 743 at 756–761, per Neuberger J (under TLATA 1996 the interest of the charge, unlike that of the trustee in bankruptcy, is only one factor to be taken into account in deciding whether to order sale, thus changing the position which formerly applied in cases such as *Lloyds Bank plc v Byrne* [1993] 1 FLR 369). A sample form of order for sale following a charging order is set out in Appendix A to CPR, PD73.

(3) In any case where a charge is imposed by a charging order on any interest in an asset of a kind mentioned in paragraph (*b*) or (*c*) of subsection (2) above, the court making the order may provide for the charge to extend to any interest or dividend payable in respect of the asset.

3. Provisions supplementing sections 1 and 2.—(2) The Land Charges Act 1972 and the Land Registration Act 2002[55] shall apply in relation to charging orders as they apply in relation to other orders or writs issued or made for the purpose of enforcing judgments.

Where the interest affected by the order is a beneficial interest under a trust of land, the interest can be overreached on sale,[56] and there is no provision for registration in unregistered land;[57] in registered land the order should be protected by a restriction.[58] All other charging orders should be protected by registration under the Land Charges Act 1972[59] (in the case of unregistered land) or by a notice on the register of the debtor's title[60] (in the case of registered land).

III. THE EQUITY OF REDEMPTION

In **Casborne v Scarfe** (1738) 1 Atk 603, 26 ER 377, Lord HARDWICKE LC said at 605, at 379:

An equity of redemption has always been considered as an estate in the land, for it may be devised, granted, or entailed with remainders, and such cannot be considered as a mere right only, but such an estate whereof there may be a seisin; the person therefore entitled to the equity of redemption is considered as the owner of the land. . . .

The interest of the land must be somewhere, and cannot be in abeyance, but it is not in the mortgagee, and therefore must remain in the mortgagor.

In **Re Sir Thomas Spencer Wells** [1933] Ch 29, the question was whether the Crown could claim, as bona vacantia, the equity of redemption of property owned by a company on its dissolution and not disposed of in its winding up. The property was leasehold land, and at the time of the dissolution, the rents received from it were insufficient to cover the interest on the mortgage money. The liquidator concluded that the equity of redemption was of no value. After a considerable time, the rents increased and were greater than the interest due on the mortgage to which the plaintiffs, as mortgagees, were entitled. All arrears of interest were paid off; the equity of redemption thus became of value. It was claimed by the plaintiffs on the ground that they were the legal owners of the term of years and that, the mortgagor having ceased to exist, no one was entitled to redeem. The Court of Appeal held that the equity of redemption was a proprietary

---

[55] As amended by LRA 2002, s. 133, Sch. 11, para. 15.
[56] For overreaching, see p. 548, above.
[57] LCA 1972, s. 6 (1A), inserted by TLATA 1996, s. 25 (1), Sch. 3, para. 12(1), (3).
[58] LRR 2003, r. 91, Sch. 4 (form K).
[59] S. 6 (register of writs and orders affecting land).   [60] LRA 2002, s. 32.

interest which had never passed to the mortgagees. The Crown was therefore entitled to claim the equity of redemption as bona vacantia.[61] LAWRENCE LJ said at 52:

The position of a mortgagee of land whether freehold or leasehold is well established. In equity the right of the mortgagee is limited to the money secured and he holds the land only as security for his money, therefore although he has the legal estate in the land, yet in equity he has a mere charge for the amount due to him. In equity the mortgagor is regarded as the owner of the mortgaged land subject only to the mortgagee's charge, and the mortgagor's equity of redemption is treated as an equitable estate in the land of the same nature as other equitable estates. Moreover no agreement between the parties that the mortgage should not be redeemable has any effect in equity, and any attempt to fetter the equity of redemption with any other condition than the payment of the money secured is null and void.

It follows from this relationship between mortgagor and mortgagee that it would be just as unconscionable for a mortgagee to set up a claim to hold the land comprised in his mortgage free from the equity of redemption as it would be for a trustee to set up a claim to retain the trust property in his hands for his own use. Consequently the reasoning which has induced the Court to hold that a trustee cannot on failure of the trusts set up his legal title so as to defeat the Crown's claim to bona vacantia applies with equal force to a mortgagee of leaseholds where the mortgagor, being an individual, has died intestate without next of kin or, being a company, has been dissolved; in neither case will the mortgagee be permitted to set up his legal estate in the term so as to defeat the Crown's equity of redemption any more than he would have been permitted to set up that title to defeat the mortgagor's equity of redemption had the mortgagor still been in existence.

IV. PROTECTION OF THE MORTGAGOR[62]

A. PROTECTION IN EQUITY: 'ONCE A MORTGAGE, ALWAYS A MORTGAGE'

Equity insists that unfair advantage shall not be taken of the mortgagor. It will be seen that mortgagors have been subjected to schemes which attempt to take away the right

---

[61] On bona vacantia, see Ing, *Bona Vacantia* (2nd edn); Halsbury's Laws of England, vol. 12(1), paras 231–241.

[62] C & B, pp. 721–722, 735–760; Gray, part 6.2; M & W, paras 24.017–24.018, 24.022, 25.084–25.139; MM, pp. 520–526; Smith, pp. 561–569; Cousins, chap. 17; Waldock, pp. 170–223; Fisher and Lightwood, para. 1.9, chap. 47. For a mortgagor's action in negligence against (a) his solicitor where he enters into a mortgage as a result of the solicitor's failure to give proper advice, see *Forster v Outred & Co* [1982] 1 WLR 86; *Mortgage Express v Bowerman* [1996] 2 All ER 836 (duty of solicitor acting for mortgagor and sub-purchaser to inform mortgagor of price increase); *National Home Loans Corpn plc v Giffen Couch & Archer* [1998] 1 WLR 207 (solicitor acting for both mortgagor and mortgagee under a duty to inform mortgagee of mortgagor's default in previous mortgage); (b) the mortgagee's surveyor on whose negligent report he relied, see *Smith v Eric S Bush* [1990] 1 AC 831; [1989] Conv 359 (C. Francis); [1989] CLJ 306 (W. V. H. Rogers); (1989) 105 LQR 511 (D. Allen); (1989) 52 MLR 841 (T. Kaye); *Midland Bank v Cox McQueen* [1999] 1 FLR

to redeem by providing that the mortgagee may purchase the mortgaged property, or that the mortgagor shall not be permitted to redeem it for a certain period of time, or that, even after redemption, certain advantages shall still be enjoyed by the mortgagee. The rules which equity has laid down have been developed during the centuries, and have been summarised in the words: 'Once a mortgage, always a mortgage.'[63] However, since the beginning of the twentieth century the courts have expressed dissatisfaction with the absolute nature of these rules of equity, and have sought in certain contexts to soften them.

(i) Option to purchase the mortgaged property

Where a transaction is, on its proper construction, a mortgage, any provisions inserted for the advantage of the mortgagee which are inconsistent with the nature of a mortgage are void. This has been applied in particular in relation to provisions contained within a mortgage which purport to allow the mortgagee to take a transfer of the mortgaged property, since the grant of such an option puts it outside the power of the mortgagee to recover the unencumbered property on payment of the full mortgage debt.

Samuel v Jarrah Timber and Wood Paving Corporation Ltd[64]
[1904] AC 323 (HL, Earl of Halsbury LC, Lords Macnaghten and Lindley)

First mortgage debenture stock of £30,000 was mortgaged to Samuel to secure an advance of £5,000 at 6 per cent. The principal was to become payable with interest at thirty days' notice on either side; and the mortgagee, Samuel, was given 'the option to purchase the whole or any part of such stock at 40 per cent. at any time within twelve months'. Within that period Samuel claimed to exercise this option in respect

---

1002 (solicitor not liable for loss caused by forged signature of wife executing charge); *Nationwide Building Society v Goodwin Harte* [1999] Lloyd's Rep PN 338 (breach of contract and fiduciary duty). On the duties of a solicitor acting for both mortgagor and mortgagee, see Solicitors' Code of Conduct 2007, rr. 3.16–3.22; and (c) a valuer: *South Australian Asset Management Corpn v York Montague Ltd* (the *Banque Bruxelles* case) [1997] AC 191 (extent of liability of valuer who provided mortgagee with negligent overvaluation, where mortgagee would not have lent if it had received careful valuation); (1997) 113 LQR 1 (J. Stapleton); [1997] CLJ 19 (J. O'Sullivan); *Nykredit Mortgage Bank plc v Edward Erdman Group Ltd (No 2)* [1997] 1 WLR 1627; Cartwright, *Misrepresentation, Mistake and Non-disclosure* (2nd edn), para. 6.41; *Oates v Anthony Pitman & Co* (1998) 76 P & CR 490; *Platform Homes Ltd v Oyston Shipways Ltd* [1996] 2 EGLR 110, per Jacob J ('valuation is an art not a science, but it is not astrology'); on appeal [2002] 2 AC 190 (imprudent lending policy can constitute contributory negligence under LR (Contributory Negligence) Act 1945, s. 1 when loan made in reliance on negligent valuation); *United Bank of Kuwait v Prudential Property Services Ltd* [1994] 30 EG 103 (criteria for valuation; contributory negligence of mortgagee in making advance); RICS Valuation Standards (6th edn, 2008).

63 *Seton v Slade* (1802) 7 Ves 265, 273, per Lord Eldon LC.

64 Followed in *Lewis v Frank Love Ltd* [1961] 1 WLR 261; (1961) 77 LQR 163 (P. V. Baker); *Re Supreme Court Registrar to Alexander Dawson Inc* [1976] 1 NZLR 615; cf. *Pye v Ambrose* [1994] NPC 53 (obligation to repay only arose when option no longer exercisable); *Jones v Morgan* [2002] 1 EGLR 125, p. 872, below. See also *Salt v Marquess of Northampton* [1892] AC 1, discussed by Lord Davey in *Noakes & Co Ltd v Rice* [1902] AC 24, p. 887, below.

of the whole stock. The Company claimed to redeem and to have a declaration that the option was illegal and void.

Held (affirming the Court of Appeal [1903] 2 Ch 1). The option was void, and the Company was entitled to redeem.

Earl of Halsbury LC: My Lords, I regret that the state of the authorities leaves me no alternative other than to affirm the judgment of Kekewich J and the Court of Appeal. A perfectly fair bargain made between two parties to it, each of whom was quite sensible of what they were doing, is not to be performed because at the same time a mortgage arrangement was made between them. If a day had intervened between the two parts of the arrangement, the part of the bargain which the appellant claims to be performed would have been perfectly good and capable of being enforced; but a line of authorities going back for more than a century has decided that such an arrangement as that which was here arrived at is contrary to a principle of equity, the sense or reason of which I am not able to appreciate, and very reluctantly I am compelled to acquiesce in the judgments appealed from.

Lord Macnaghten: In *Vernon v Bethell* (1762) 2 Eden 110, 113, however, Northington LC (then Lord Henley) laid down the law broadly in the following terms: 'This Court, as a Court of conscience, is very jealous of persons taking securities for a loan and converting such securities into purchases. And therefore I take it to be an established rule that a mortgagee can never provide at the time of making the loan for any event or condition on which the equity of redemption shall be discharged and the conveyance absolute. And there is great reason and justice in this rule, for necessitous men are not, truly speaking, free men, but to answer a present exigency will submit to any terms that the crafty may impose upon them.'

This doctrine, described by Lord Henley as an established rule nearly 150 years ago, has never, so far as I can discover, been departed from since or questioned in any reported case. It is, I believe, universally accepted by text-writers of authority. Speaking for myself, I should not be sorry if your Lordships could see your way to modify it so as to prevent its being used as a means of evading a fair bargain come to between persons dealing at arms' length and negotiating on equal terms. The directors of a trading company in search of financial assistance are certainly in a very different position from that of an impecunious landowner in the toils of a crafty money-lender. At the same time I quite feel the difficulty of interfering with any rule that has prevailed so long, and I am not prepared to differ from the conclusion at which the Court of Appeal has arrived.

In **Reeve v Lisle** [1902] AC 461 property was mortgaged to secure a loan of money. At a later date it was agreed between the parties to the mortgage that, if within five years the mortgagees should elect to enter into partnership with the mortgagors, they should be entitled to do so on the terms, inter alia, that the mortgagors should be relieved of the liability to repay the loan and that a ship (which was part of the security) should be transferred free from the mortgage for the purposes of the partnership. The House of Lords (Earl of Halsbury LC, and Lords Macnaghten, Brampton and Lindley) construed these two transactions as being separate and independent, and held that the agreement was binding on the mortgagor.[65]

---

[65] See *Alec Lobb (Garages) Ltd v Total Oil Great Britain Ltd* [1983] 1 WLR 87 (sale and 51-year leaseback of part of property entered into between mortgagor and mortgagee after date of mortgage held valid under mortgage rules, but reversed in CA [1985] 1 WLR 173 as being void for restraint of trade).

(1903) 13 LQR 359 (Sir Frederick Pollock)

The doctrine of 'clogging' threatens to become an intolerable nuisance—an interference with the freedom of the subject. It was a useful enough doctrine in a primitive and more technical age when ignorant people were often entrapped into oppressive bargains, but today it is an anachronism and might with advantage be jettisoned. Instead the Courts have taken to emphasizing the doctrine in all its original crudity. It was open to them a few years since to have moulded the doctrine to meet the changing conditions of modern life, and to have confined redress to cases where there was something oppressive or unconscionable in the bargain to make this the test, as it was the origin of the doctrine; but the Courts have preferred to adhere to technicality and an unprogressive judicial policy. The decision of the Court of Appeal in *Jarrah Timber and Wood Paving Corpn v Samuel* [1903] 2 Ch 1 was inevitable after *Noakes & Co Ltd v Rice* [1902] AC 24 [p. 887, below]; but see to what a conclusion it leads. A company with a board of directors composed of experienced men of business, advised by a competent solicitor, after it has invited a loan and settled considered terms is supposed to be the victim of some oppression at the hands of the mortgagee, because it has given the mortgagee an option of purchasing the mortgaged property at a certain price, and is permitted by the Court to repudiate its own bargain deliberately entered into in its own interests—surely a proceeding more unconscionable than anything involved in the so-called 'clogging', if there is any such thing as sanctity in contracts. Alas! for the cobwebs of technicality which lawyers are so fond of spinning, and which so often shut out the daylight of common sense.[66]

In **Jones v Morgan** [2002] 1 EGLR 125,[67] the Court of Appeal followed the House of Lords decision in *Samuel v Jarrah Timber and Wood Paving Corporation Ltd.*

Two brothers, William and John Morgan, owned Vauxhall Farm in the Vale of Glamorgan. In June 1994 they mortgaged it to Mr Jones, a retired investment broker for £105,000, in order to develop it as a nursing home. This was however insufficient to fund the development.

In June 1997 a new agreement was made between the broker and Mr Jones under which part of the land was to be sold to a neighbouring farmer. The proceeds of sale were to be used to discharge the mortgage loan, and by clause (2) the brothers were to transfer to Mr Jones 'a one half share or interest in the legal estate'. Mr Jones sought specific performance of the 1997 agreement.

The Court of Appeal, in refusing specific performance, held that:

(i)   the 1997 agreement was neither an unconscionable bargain[68] nor procured by duress;

---

[66] See (1985) Real Property Probate and Trust Journal 821 (L. C. Prebble and D. W. Cartwright); (1986–86) 60 St John's Law Review 452 (J. L. Light).

For legislation in the USA removing the mortgagee's option from the purview of the doctrine of clogs, see Uniform Land Security Interest Act 1986, para. 211; New York General Obligations Law 1986, para. 5.334; California Civil Code (1984), para. 2906; cited 60 St John's Law Review at pp. 492–497.

[67] [2001] Conv 500 (M. P. Thompson).

[68] 'Although the bargain evidenced by clause 2 of the 1997 agreement may be seen as unwise or improvident, it does not seem to me to be so harsh and oppressive as to make it self-evident that no competent solicitor could have advised his client to enter into it; or would have been obliged to withdraw if, against his advice, the client was determined to proceed with the transaction.... The real vice underlying clause 2, as it

(ii) (by a majority: Lord Phillips MR and Chadwick LJ) the 1997 agreement was a
     clog on the equity of redemption.

CHADWICK LJ said at p. 134:

69 The judge was correct to reject the proposition that a mortgagee could never take an interest in the mortgaged property by an agreement made after the mortgage had been granted: see
Reeve v Lisle [1902] AC 461 [p. 871, above]. But he was not correct to hold that there were no
circumstances in which the principle which prevents a mortgagee from stipulating for an interest in the mortgaged property at the time of the mortgage could have application to stipulation
agreed subsequently. The question, in each case, is whether the arrangement made after the
mortgage has been granted is 'in substance and in fact subsequent to and independent of the
original bargain': see the observations of Vaughan Williams LJ in that case, at [1901] 1 Ch 53,
71. It is, to my mind, clear that the House of Lords would not have reached the decision which
they did in *Reeve v Lisle* if they had not been satisfied that the Court of Appeal were correct to
hold, on the facts, that the July 1898 agreement was independent of the June mortgage.

70 A related point has arisen, more recently, in *Lewis v Frank Love Ltd* [1961] 1 All ER
446. In that case, the plaintiff, who was indebted to mortgagees under a mortgage on which
judgment had been recovered, agreed with the defendants that it would pay off the existing
mortgagees and take a transfer of the existing mortgage, upon making an advance of a small
additional sum and upon terms that they would have an option to purchase part of the mortgaged property on condition that they did not require repayment of the principal for a period
of two years. The small additional sum was never advanced. The defendant sought to exercise
its option, and the plaintiff claimed that the option was invalid as a clog. Plowman J explained
the point at pp. 451H–I:

> 'It was argued by counsel for the defendants that the doctrine of a clog on the equity does not apply
> where the clog is not imposed as part of the original mortgage transaction, and that there had not
> heretofore been a case in which the doctrine had been applied where the transaction in question was
> a transfer of an existing mortgage and not the original mortgage itself. It is agreed that there is not,
> in the reports, any such case. But in my view the principles on which the courts have held that a clog
> on the equity of redemption is void apply just as much to a transfer of a mortgage which is arranged
> between the mortgagor and the transferees, where one of the terms of that arrangement is that
> the transferees in return for parting with their money shall have an option to purchase part of the
> mortgaged property.'

71 In my view, the principle which prevents a mortgagee from stipulating for an interest in
the mortgaged property at the time of the mortgage does have application in the circumstances
of the present case, notwithstanding that the stipulation was contained in the 1997 agreement
rather than in the 1994 mortgage. There are two reasons that lead me to that conclusion. First,
it seems to me artificial to regard the 1997 agreement as being, in substance, independent of

---

seems to me, was not that the concept of a half share in the development value was necessarily oppressive;
the real vice (if any) lay in a failure to think through what the financial consequences of a clause in that form
might be. It is in that respect that Mr Morgan could be expected to rely on his solicitor.... As [the judge]
put it: "Mr Will Morgan is naïve, trusting and unbusinesslike and no match for an astute businessman like
Mr Tudor Jones." But it is for a solicitor to advise the naïve, trusting or the unbusinesslike in their dealings
with the more astute. In such a case the client relies on the solicitor to protect his interests': per Chadwick
LJ at [40].

the 1994 mortgage transaction. It is, I think, important to have in mind that the genesis of clause 2 of the 1997 agreement was the assurance given to the appellant on 6 June 1994. The judge took the view that that assurance was spent when Mr Will Morgan abandoned the plan to develop the farmhouse at West Hall Farm as a nursing home. Whether or not that would be correct if the assurance were otherwise enforceable as a contract, the true position was that the appellant sought, and the respondents were content to concede, the inclusion of clause 2 in the 1997 agreement because that gave effect, in the context of the new plan to develop the farmhouse as residential flats, to the understanding that had been reached in 1994. It was, throughout, the intention of the parties to the mortgage transaction that the appellant should have a share of the development. The 1997 agreement sought to give effect to that intention.

72 Second, the 1997 agreement constituted a variation of the contractual terms upon which the respondents were entitled to redeem the mortgaged property. Prior to that agreement, the position was that they were entitled to redeem the mortgage upon payment off of the whole of the principal and interest then secured. On redemption they would get back the whole of the mortgaged property free from any encumbrance created by, or at the time of, the mortgage. The effect of the 1997 agreement was that they were entitled to redeem part of the mortgaged property, that is to say, the part that was to be sold to Mr Lougher, on payment of an amount equal to the price which they were to receive from the purchaser, and they were entitled to redeem the remainder of the mortgaged property, that is to say the retained lands, on payment of an amount equal to the balance of the principal and interest then outstanding, and further interest accruing thereafter. In substance, the effect of the 1997 agreement was to convert what had been a single, indivisible, mortgage loan into two distinct mortgage loans. It seems to me that there is no reason why the principle which prevents a mortgagee from stipulating for an interest in the mortgaged property should not apply to a transaction that has that effect. Plainly, the principle would apply if the transaction in 1997 had taken the form of a payment off of the whole of the secured loan, a discharge of the existing mortgage, and a relending of the difference between the amount of the secured loan and the moneys to be received from the purchaser upon the security of a mortgage of the retained lands. Although different in form, the 1997 transaction was identical in substance.

73 For those reasons, I am satisfied that the judge was wrong to reject the contention, advanced in argument before him (although not in the respondents' pleaded defence), that clause 2 was repugnant to the mortgage transaction into which the parties had entered.

LORD PHILLIPS MR said at p. 136:

86 This appeal turns on the question of whether clause 2 of the 1997 agreement is unenforceable as a clog on the equity of redemption of a mortgage. That question I have found far from easy because (i) the doctrine of a clog on the equity of redemption is, so it seems to me, an appendix to our law that no longer serves a useful purpose and would be better excised; and (ii) the nature of the 1997 agreement and the circumstances in which it was concluded are neither clear nor satisfactory...

92 The position, following the repeal of the usury laws, is that there is now no rule in equity that precludes a lender from stipulating for any collateral advantage, provided that the stipulation is not (i) unfair or unconscionable, (ii) in the nature of a penalty clogging the equity of redemption or (iii) inconsistent with or repugnant to the right to redeem—see *Kreglinger v New Patagonia Meat and Cold Storage Company Limited* [1914] AC 25, 61 [p. 890, below].

93 The 1997 agreement varied the loan and the mortgage that secured it, but did not alter the nature of the contract. It was, in effect, a refinancing agreement. Clause 2 was inserted as an integral part of the refinancing agreement. It was not part of a collateral contract.

94 The facts of this case are analogous to those of *Lewis v Frank Love Ltd* [1961] 1 All ER 446. I endorse the conclusion of Chadwick LJ that clause 2 constituted a clog on the equity of redemption of the mortgaged property and was, in consequence, void.

PILL LJ (dissenting) said at p. 135:

80 The 1997 agreement was, in my judgment, neither in substance a rearrangement of the 1994 mortgage nor in substance a fresh mortgage loan. Being a commercial agreement made in the circumstances described, the doctrine of clog on the equity of redemption does not extend to render it unenforceable.

81 The effect of this conclusion is not to cast doubt upon the decision in *Lewis v Frank Love Ltd*. Chadwick LJ has set out the statement of principle made by Plowman J at p. 451 in *Lewis*. It is not in issue in this case. The transfer of the mortgage in that case was subsequent to the original mortgage transaction but was plainly a mortgage transaction between the mortgagor and transferee.

In **Warnborough Ltd v Garmite Ltd** [2003] EWCA Civ 1544, [2004] 1 P & CR DG 8, Warnborough sold property to Garmite in 1996, leaving the purchase price outstanding as a loan secured on the property, but at the same time Garmite granted Warnborough an option to repurchase the property in the event of it defaulting on the loan. In 1999, after Garmite had fallen into arrears with the loan payments, the parties entered into a further compromise agreement, involving both the execution by Garmite of a supplemental legal charge over the property and the grant by Garmite in favour of Warnborough of a further option to purchase the property. The trial judge held that the options to purchase were invalid on the ground that they amounted to a clog on Garmite's equity of redemption. The Court of Appeal reversed this, and remitted the case for decision on further evidence at trial. Evidence was required to determine the substance of the transaction: if it was a sale and not a mortgage, the options would not be a clog on the equity of redemption. JONATHAN PARKER LJ said:

42 As long ago as the beginning of the last century, the origins and rationale of the principle that an option to purchase mortgaged property granted at the same time as the mortgage constitutes a 'clog' on the borrower's equity of redemption and is accordingly unenforceable were already regarded by the House of Lords as obscure.

His Lordship discussed *Samuel v Jarrah Timber and Wood Paving Corporation Ltd* [1904] AC 323, p. 870, above, and continued:

50 The following comments can, I think, fairly be made on the above extracts from the judgments of their Lordships in *Samuel v Jarrah*. In the first place, none of their Lordships expressed any enthusiasm for the rule, at least in its application to an option to purchase entered into contemporaneously with a mortgage; and Lords Halsbury and Macnaghten viewed it with positive distaste, in so far as it operated to strike down a fair commercial bargain freely negotiated on equal terms between parties who knew what they were doing. Secondly, both Lord Macnaghten

and Lord Lindley regarded the relevant question as being whether or not the option fell to be characterised as a term of the loan: i.e. in the words of Lord Lindley, 'What is the true nature of [the] agreement?' Thirdly, both their Lordships treated that question as primarily one of fact.

51 In *Davies v Chamberlain* (1909) 26 TLR 138 there was an agreement for the sale of land which the parties considered to be ripe for profitable working. It was agreed that part of the purchase price would be left outstanding for a period of five years. It was further agreed that the vendor would have the option of contributing one third of the capital of any company which the parties might form for the working of the land, and that in the event of the purchaser failing to grant that option within two years after completion of the sale the purchaser would pay the vendor an additional £5,000. The purchase was completed and a company was formed for the purpose of working the land. However, the purchaser failed to give the vendor an opportunity to contribute to its capital. The vendor claimed the additional £5,000 under the agreement. The purchaser contended that the option term constituted a 'clog' and was accordingly unenforceable, and hence that he was not liable to pay the additional £5000.

52. The Court of Appeal, affirming the decision of Pickford J at first instance, held that the option term was not a 'clog' on the ground that in substance it formed part of the agreement to purchase. In a short judgment, with which Fletcher Moulton and Farwell LJJ agreed, Cozens-Hardy MR said (and I quote from the report at p.139):

'...that he had had to consider more than once the question of clogging the equity of redemption, but that doctrine entirely depended on its being a bargain by the mortgagee *in his relation as mortgagee towards the mortgagor, and it had nothing to do with a bargain which a vendor made in dealing with his own property*.... On the agreement it was impossible to say that this bargain to pay £5,000 was *a term of the mortgage*.' (Emphasis supplied.)

53 *Davies v Chamberlain* is thus an example of a case in which, on an examination of the transaction, it was held that the true nature of the agreement was that of sale and purchase, and that the option was not to be characterised as a term of the mortgage.

54 The next relevant authority is *Kreglinger v New Patagonia Meat and Cold Storage Co Ltd* [1914] AC 25 [p. 890, below]... In that case, Viscount Haldane LC (at p. 35) identified the origin of the jurisdiction as being 'merely a special application of a more general power to relieve against penalties and to mould them into mere securities'. He continued:

'My Lords, this was the origin of the jurisdiction which we are now considering, and it is important to bear that origin in mind. For the end to accomplish which the jurisdiction has evolved ought to govern and limit its exercise by equity judges. *That end has always been to ascertain, by parol evidence if need be, the real nature and substance of the transaction, and if it turned out to be in truth one of mortgage simply, to place it on that footing. It was, in ordinary cases, only where there was conduct which the Court of Chancery regarded as unconscientious that it interfered with freedom of contract.... The equity judges looked, not at what was technically the form, but at what was really the substance of transactions, and confined the application of their rules to cases in which they thought that in its substance the transaction was oppressive.*' (Emphasis supplied.)

55 Later in his judgment Lord Haldane returned to this theme, saying (at pp. 36–40):

'The principle was thus in early days limited in its application to the accomplishment of the end which was held to justify interference of equity with freedom of contract. It did not go further.... [I]t did not apply to cases which were only apparently or technically within it but *in reality something more than cases of mortgage*.... [I]t is inconsistent with the objects for which they were established that these rules should crystallize into technical language so rigid that the letter can defeat the underlying spirit and purpose. Their application must correspond with the practical necessities of the time.... [T]he question in the present case is whether the right to redeem has been interfered with. And this must...depend on the answer to a question which is primarily one of fact. What was the true character of the transaction?.... The question is not one of form but of substance, and *it can be answered in each case only by looking at all the circumstances,* and not by mere reliance on some abstract principle, or upon the dicta which have fallen obiter from judges in other and different cases.... For each case forms a real precedent only in so far as it affirms a principle, the relevancy of which in other cases turns on *the true character of the particular transaction, and to that extent on circumstances*.... What is vital in the appeal now under consideration is to classify accurately the transaction between the parties.' (Emphasis supplied.)

56 I should perhaps record that in concluding that the stipulation for the option of pre-emption in Kreglinger did not form part of the mortgage transaction, Lord Haldane laid considerable emphasis on the fact that the security in question was a floating charge, a factor which is not, of course, present in the instant case.

57 Lord Mersey, in the course of his judgment (at p.46), famously compared the rule with:

'...an unruly dog, which, if not securely chained to its own kennel, is prone to wander into places where it ought not to be.'

58 He concluded that to introduce the rule into the case:

'...would give effect to no equity and would defeat justice.'

His Lordship discussed the opinion of Lord Parker of Waddington in *Kreglinger*, pp. 893–894, below, and continued:

69 Thus, in *Kreglinger* their Lordships adopted the same approach as that of Lords Macnaghten and Lindley in *Samuel v Jarrah* in addressing the question whether the relevant transaction was in substance one of mortgage and in answering that question by reference to the parties' intentions as gathered from all the circumstances.

70 In *Lewis v Frank Love Ltd* [1961] 1 All ER 446, Plowman J reviewed the authorities and held that the transaction in question in that case was in substance a mortgage. He accordingly held that the option was unenforceable.

71 The final authority I should mention is *Jones v Morgan* [2001] EWCA Civ 995 [p. 872, above]. I mention it only to record the observation of Lord Phillips MR (in paragraph 86) that:

'...the doctrine of a clog on the equity of redemption is, so it seems to me, an appendix to our law which no longer serves a useful purpose and would be better excised.'

72 In the light of the authorities to which I have referred, it has to be accepted that the 'unruly dog' is still alive (although one might perhaps reasonably expect its venerable age to inhibit it from straying too far or too often from its kennel); and that however desirable an appendectomy might be thought to be, no such relieving operation has as yet been carried out....

73 That said, it is in my judgment glaringly clear from the authorities that the mere fact that, contemporaneously with the grant of a mortgage over his property, the mortgagor grants the mortgagee an option to purchase the property does no more than raise the question whether

the rule against 'clogs' applies: it does not begin to answer that question. As has been said over and over again in the authorities, in order to answer that question the court has to look at the 'substance' of the transaction in question: in other words, to inquire as to the true nature of the bargain which the parties have made. To do that, the court examines all the circumstances, with the assistance of oral evidence if necessary.

74 Against that background of authority, I return to the instant case.

75 In relation to the First Option, Garmite invites the court to conclude, by reference only to the bare transaction documents, that if the action went to trial the court would be bound to conclude that the First Option is a 'clog'. With all respect to the deputy judge, that seems to me to be an invitation which the court cannot possibly accept, for the reasons expressed so cogently by the Master in his judgment. Indeed, as I ventured to suggest in argument, it seems to me that if any party were in a position to seek to summary judgment by reference only to the transaction documents it would be Warnborough and not Garmite.

76 Although it would clearly not be appropriate to attempt to lay down any absolute rule, it does seem to me that where the option to purchase which is sought to be challenged as a 'clog' is granted against the background of a sale of the property by the grantee of the option, as owner of the property, to the grantor for a price which is to be left outstanding on mortgage, there must be a very strong likelihood that, on an examination of all the circumstances, the court will conclude, as it did in *Davies v Chamberlain*, that the substance of the transaction is one of sale and purchase and not one of mortgage. At all events, if one is limited to a consideration of only the bare transaction documents (as we have been) that seems to me to be the provisional conclusion to which they point. On the face of the transaction documents (and leaving aside any other factor) to describe the sale as 'incidental' to the loan seems to me . . . to turn the transaction completely on its head.

At the later trial the judge held that the transaction was one of sale and purchase, and therefore valid: [2007] 1 P & CR 2.

(ii) Contractual postponement of the right to redeem

This section deals with cases in which the mortgagor covenants to postpone redemption for a substantial length of time. The situations cover a wide range between two extremes. On the one hand are cases in which the mortgagee, solely for his own benefit, insists on the postponement of redemption for so long a time that the security is virtually irredeemable. On the other hand are cases in which a fair business transaction includes, at the request of the mortgagor, a term postponing redemption for a certain period of time, and the mortgagor, finding that interest rates have gone down, seeks to make use of these rules to escape from his bargain.

It used to be said that a postponement was valid if it were for a reasonable time. It is clear, however, since the *Knightsbridge case*,[69] that this is not the proper test, whether 'reasonableness' is judged in terms of mere length of time or in terms of all the circumstances of the case. Sir Wilfrid Greene MR laid down the test in that case as follows:[70]

---

[69] *Knightsbridge Estates Trust Ltd v Byrne* [1939] Ch 441; affd [1940] AC 613, p. 882, below.

[70] [1939] Ch 441 at 457.

Equity does not reform mortgage transactions because they are unreasonable. It is concerned to see two things—one that the essential requirements of a mortgage transaction are observed, and the other than oppressive or unconscionable terms are not enforced.

With the second requirement no one could quarrel; it is possible, however, that the first may some day be held to be too wide. In that case, the mortgagor covenanted not to redeem a mortgage of freehold land for 40 years, and the covenant was held valid. There was no suggestion of hardship or oppression. An interesting situation would have arisen if the property mortgaged had been a 41-year lease;[71] assuming again that there was no hardship or oppression, the conflict between *Fairclough v Swan Brewery Co Ltd* [1912] AC 565, p. 881, below and *Santley v Wilde* [1899] 2 Ch 474, below, would then have to be resolved, and there is much to be said for the view that a business transaction of that nature ought to be upheld.

Cases falling within the present section should be distinguished from those dealt with in the next. The next section deals with cases where an advantage still remains to the mortgagee after redemption. Failure to appreciate this distinction has caused most of the misunderstanding of *Santley v Wilde*. The criticism which that case received in the House of Lords,[72] and particularly from Lord Davey, was directed against it on the assumption that it concerned a collateral advantage existing after redemption. It is clear, however, from the judgment of the case itself, that Lord Lindley treated it as a case of contractual postponement.

(a) Mortgage of leasehold

Santley v Wilde[73]
[1899] 2 Ch 474 (CA, **Lindley MR**, **Sir F. H. Jeune** and **Romer LJ**, reversing **Byrne J** [1899] 1 Ch 747)

The plaintiff, as sub-lessee of a theatre, had the option to take over the head lease on payment of £2,000. She arranged to borrow this money from the defendant Wilde, and mortgaged to him her sub-lease as security. The mortgage provided that the mortgagor should repay the capital by instalments under an arrangement which was not challenged, and that she should 'during the residue of the term...notwithstanding that all principal moneys and interest may have been paid...pay...a sum equal to one-third part of the clear net profit rent or rents to be derived' from the lease. The proviso for cesser provided that the mortgage should determine on payment of the principal sum and interest, 'and all other the moneys hereinbefore covenanted...to be paid'. After certain payments had fallen into arrear, the plaintiff, on payment of all arrears, and on tender of the outstanding principal, interest and costs, claimed a declaration that she was entitled to redeem on payment of principal, interest and costs and that so far as the

---

71   See the question on p. 885, below.
72   Especially in *Noakes & Co Ltd v Rice* [1902] AC 24 at 33, p. 888, below.
73   It was the view of Dr J. H. C. Morris that 'the transaction was not in essence one of mortgage, but a partnership agreement to share in the profits of the theatre', and therefore valid on that ground: Waldock, p. 187.

mortgage deed provided for payment of a share of the rents and profits or precluded her from redeeming on payment of principal and interest, it was invalid.

Held. The plaintiff could not redeem except by observing all the covenants for which her property was given as security, including the covenant to pay the profits.

Lindley MR: The question raised on this appeal is extremely important: I do not profess to be able to decide it on any principle which will be in harmony with all the cases; but it appears to me that the true principle running through them is not very difficult to discover, and I think that it can be applied so as to do justice in this case and in all other cases on the subject that may arise. The principle is this: a mortgage is a conveyance of land or an assignment of chattels as a security for the payment of a debt or the discharge of some other obligation for which it is given. This is the idea of a mortgage: and the security is redeemable on the payment or discharge of such debt or obligation, any provision to the contrary notwithstanding. That, in my opinion, is the law. Any provision inserted to prevent redemption on payment or performance of the debt or obligation for which the security was given is what is meant by a clog or fetter on the equity of redemption and is therefore void.... A 'clog' or 'fetter' is something which is inconsistent with the idea of 'security': a clog or fetter is in the nature of a repugnant condition. If I convey land in fee subject to a condition forbidding alienation, that is a repugnant condition. If I give a mortgage on a condition that I shall not redeem, that is a repugnant condition. The Courts of Equity have fought for years to maintain the doctrine that a security is redeemable. But when and under what circumstances? On the performance of the obligation for which it was given. If the obligation is the payment of a debt, the security is redeemable on the payment of that debt. That, in my opinion, is the true principle applicable to the cases, and that is what is meant when it is said there must not be any clog or fetter on the equity of redemption. If so, this mortgage has no clog or fetter at all. Of course, the debt or obligation may be impeachable for fraud, oppression, or over-reaching: there the obligation is tainted to that extent and is invalid. But, putting such cases out of the question, when you get a security for a debt or obligation, that security can be redeemed the moment the debt or obligation is paid or performed, but on no other terms.

Now, let us see what the contract here is. It is not suggested that there has been fraud or undue influence or over-reaching or hard bargaining. Here is a lady who has a lease, of which there are ten years to run, subject to a rent and covenants. She wants to carry on a theatre, and she wants to borrow a sum of 2,000*l* for the purpose. What is the security she offers? The security of the lease is probably absolutely insufficient. A security of that sort, unless it is kept up for the ten years, is very shaky. The lender took that view. He says, 'I will lend you the money, and you may have five years in which to pay it; and you shall pay me a sum equal to one-third part of the net profits to be derived from any underleases'. What is the lender's position? It is obvious that his security depends not only on the solvency of the lady, but also on the success of the theatre. This is the kind of security proposed, and the lender says he will lend upon that. Accordingly the 2,000*l* is lent, and the mortgagor by her security covenants to repay the money by instalments; the deed then further goes on as follows:

His Lordship read the second testatum and covenant by the mortgagor for payment to the mortgagee of one-third of the net profit rents to be derived from any underleases or undertenancies, and also the provision for redemption: and continued:

That means that this lease is granted or assigned by the mortgagor to the mortgagee as security not only for the payment of the 2,000*l* and interest, but also for the payment of the one-third of the net profit rents to the end of the term. If I am right in the principle which I have laid down, that does not clog the right of redemption upon the performance of the obligation for which the security was given. That is the nature of the transaction, and the good sense of it.

But it is said that is not good law. Those, however, who say so lose sight of the true principle underlying the expression that there must be no clog or fetter on the equity of redemption. The plaintiff says, 'I will pay off the balance of the 2,000*l* and interest, and you will give me back the lease, and this is the end of my obligation.' But the mortgagee says, 'No; that is not the bargain: you cannot redeem on those terms. On the contrary, you may pay me the 2,000*l* and interest, but if you do, you must also pay the one-third profit rents'. On principle that is right: it follows from what I have said. That is the bargain, and there has been no oppression, and there is no reasonable legal ground for relieving this lady.

Fairclough v Swan Brewery Co Ltd
[1912] AC 565 (PC, **Lords Macnaghten, Atkinson, Shaw of Dunfermline** and **Mersey**)

The appellant was lessee of a hotel owned by the respondent brewery. He executed a mortgage of his lease (of which 17½ years remained) for £500 which contained a clause precluding him from redeeming the mortgage during the remainder of his term less six weeks, and from purchasing beer from any person other than the respondent brewery during the continuance of the mortgage. On the appellant's offering to redeem and claiming to be free to purchase beer elsewhere, the respondent brewery brought this action in the Supreme Court of Western Australia for damages for breach of covenant and an injunction to restrain further breaches. The appellant argued that the covenant was void on the ground, inter alia, that it was a clog on his equity of redemption, and claimed that he was entitled to redeem. On appeal to the Privy Council:

Held. The covenant was void and the appellant was entitled to redeem.

Lord Macnaghten: The arguments of counsel ranged over a very wide field.[74] But the real point is a narrow one. It depends upon a doctrine of equity, which is not open to question.

'There is', as Kindersley V-C said in *Gossip v Wright* (1863) 32 LJ Ch 648, 653, 'no doubt that the broad rule is this: that the Court will not allow the right of redemption in any way to be hampered or crippled in that which the parties intended to be a security either by any contemporaneous instrument with the deed in question, or by anything which this Court would regard as a simultaneous arrangement or part of the same transaction.' The rule in comparatively recent times was unsettled by certain decisions in the Court of Chancery in England which seem to have misled the learned judges in the Full Court. But it is now firmly established by the House of Lords that the old rule still prevails and that equity will not permit any device or contrivance being part of the mortgage transaction or contemporaneous with it to prevent or impede redemption. The learned counsel on behalf of the respondents admitted, as he was bound to admit, that a mortgage cannot be made irredeemable. That is plainly forbidden. Is there any difference between forbidding redemption and permitting it, if the permission be a mere pretence? Here the provision for redemption is nugatory.... For all practical purposes this

---

[74] Restraint of trade was also pleaded, at p. 566.

mortgage is irredeemable. It was obviously meant to be irredeemable. It was made irredeemable in and by the mortgage itself.

(b) Mortgage of freehold

Knightsbridge Estates Trust Ltd v Byrne
[1939] Ch 441 (CA, Sir Wilfrid Greene MR, Scott and Farwell LJJ)

The plaintiff company was the owner of certain freehold property in London which had been mortgaged at 6½ per cent. Wishing to pay off their mortgage, they asked the defendants for a loan of £310,000 at 5¼ per cent repayable over forty years. The defendants agreed to make this loan, repayment to be made by half-yearly instalments over forty years. The deed so provided, and in it the defendant mortgagees undertook, if the instalments were promptly paid, not to require repayment in any other way.

The plaintiffs claimed, less than six years later, that they were entitled to redeem on payment of all principal, interest and costs, on the ground that, in so far as the term prevented them from redeeming on making such payments, it was illegal and void as a clog on their right to redeem and that it rendered the mortgage irredeemable for an undue length of time.

Held (reversing Luxmoore J [1938] Ch 741). The plaintiffs were bound by the agreement and could only redeem in accordance with its terms.

Sir Wilfrid Greene MR: We will deal first with the arguments originally presented on behalf of the respondents. The first argument was that the postponement of the contractual right to redeem for forty years was void in itself, in other words, that the making of such an agreement between mortgagor and mortgagee was prohibited by a rule of equity. It was not contended that a provision in a mortgage deed making the mortgage irredeemable for a period of years is necessarily void. The argument was that such a period must be a 'reasonable' one, and it was said that the period in the present case was an unreasonable one by reason merely of its length. This argument was not the one accepted by the learned judge.

Now an argument such as this requires the closest scrutiny, for, if it is correct, it means that an agreement made between two competent parties, acting under expert advice and presumably knowing their own business best, is one which the law forbids them to make upon the ground that it is not 'reasonable'. If we were satisfied that the rule of equity was what it is said to be, we should be bound to give effect to it. But in the absence of compelling authority we are not prepared to say that such an agreement cannot lawfully be made. A decision to that effect would, in our view, involve an unjustified interference with the freedom of business men to enter into agreements best suited to their interests and would impose upon them a test of 'reasonableness' laid down by the Courts without reference to the business realities of the case.

It is important to remember what those realities were. The respondents are a private company and do not enjoy the facilities for raising money by a public issue possessed by public companies. They were the owners of a large and valuable block of property, and so far as we know they had no other assets. The property was subject to a mortgage at a high rate of interest and this mortgage was liable to be called in at any time. In these circumstances the respondents were, when the negotiations began, desirous of obtaining for themselves two advantages: (1) a reduction in the rate of interest, (2) the right to repay the mortgage moneys by instalments spread over a long period of years. The desirability of obtaining these terms from a business point of view is manifest, and it is not to be assumed that these respondents were actuated by anything but pure considerations of business in seeking to obtain them. The sum involved was a very large one, and the length of the period over which the instalments were spread is to be considered with reference to this fact. In the circumstances it was the most natural thing in the world that the respondents should address themselves to a body desirous of obtaining a long term investment for its money. The resulting agreement was a commercial agreement between two important corporations experienced in such matters, and has none of the features of an oppressive bargain where the borrower is at the mercy of an unscrupulous lender. In transactions of this kind it is notorious that there is competition among the large insurance companies and other bodies having large funds to invest, and we are not prepared to view the agreement made as anything but a proper business transaction.

But it is said not only that the period of postponement must be a reasonable one, but that in judging the 'reasonableness' of the period the considerations which we have mentioned cannot be regarded; that the Court is bound to judge 'reasonableness' by a consideration of the terms of the mortgage deed itself and without regard to extraneous matters. In the absence of clear authority we emphatically decline to consider a question of 'reasonableness' from a standpoint so unreal. To hold that the law is to tell business men what is reasonable in such circumstances and to refuse to take into account the business considerations involved, would bring the law into disrepute. Fortunately we do not find ourselves forced to come to any such conclusion. . . .

Assuming therefore, without in any way deciding, that the period during which the contractual right of redemption is postponed must be a 'reasonable' one (a question which we will not proceed to examine), we are of the opinion that the respondents have failed to establish (and the burden is on them) that there is anything unreasonable in the mere extension of the period for forty years in the circumstances of the present case.

But in our opinion the proposition that a postponement of the contractual right of redemption is only permissible for a 'reasonable' time is not well-founded. Such a postponement is not properly described as a clog on the equity of redemption, since it is concerned with the contractual right to redeem. It is indisputable that any provision which hampers redemption after the contractual date for redemption has passed will not be permitted. Further, it is undoubtedly true to say that a right of redemption is a necessary element in a mortgage transaction, and consequently that, where the contractual right of redemption is illusory, equity will grant relief by allowing redemption. This was the point in the case of *Fairclough v Swan Brewery Co Ltd* [1912] AC 565. . . .

Moreover, equity may give relief against contractual terms in a mortgage transaction if they are oppressive or unconscionable, and in deciding whether or not a particular transaction falls within this category the length of time for which the contractual right to redeem is postponed may well be an important consideration. In the present case no question of this kind was or could have been raised.

But equity does not reform mortgage transactions because they are unreasonable. It is concerned to see two things—one that the essential requirements of a mortgage transaction are observed, and the other that oppressive or unconscionable terms are not enforced. Subject to this, it does not, in our opinion, interfere. The question therefore arises whether, in a case where the right of redemption is real and not illusory and there is nothing oppressive or unconscionable in the transaction, there is something in a postponement of the contractual right to redeem, such as we have in the present case, that is inconsistent with the essential requirements of a mortgage transaction? Apart from authority the answer to this question would, in our opinion, be clearly in the negative. Any other answer would place an unfortunate restriction on the liberty of contract of competent parties who are at arm's length—in the present case it would have operated to prevent the respondents obtaining financial terms which for obvious reasons they themselves considered to be most desirable. It would, moreover, lead to highly inequitable results. The remedy sought by the respondents and the only remedy which is said to be open to them is the establishment of a right to redeem at any time on the ground that the postponement of the contractual right to redeem is void. They do not and could not suggest that the contract as a contract is affected, and the result would accordingly be that whereas the respondents would have had from the first the right to redeem at any time, the appellants would have had no right to require payment otherwise than by the specified instalments. Such an outcome to a bargain entered into by business people negotiating at arm's length would indeed be unfortunate, and we should require clear authority before coming to such a conclusion....

The second ground upon which the respondents endeavoured to support the judgment of the Court below was that the postponement of the contractual right to redeem for a period of forty years offended the rule against perpetuities and was therefore invalid. The learned judge decided against the respondents on this question and in our judgment rightly....

This decision was affirmed on appeal to the House of Lords [1940] AC 613, on the ground that the mortgage was a debenture within the meaning of the Companies Act 1929, section 380 and, as such and by virtue of section 74 of that Act,[75] not invalid by reason of postponement of the date for redemption. No views were expressed in the House of Lords on the reasoning of the Court of Appeal.

(c) Misleading maxims

In **Kreglinger v New Patagonia Meat and Cold Storage Co Ltd** [1914] AC 25, Lord PARKER said at 53:

My Lords, I desire, in connection with what I have just said, to add a few words on the maxims in which attempts have been made to sum up the equitable principles applicable to mortgage transactions. I refer to the maxims, 'Once a mortgage, always a mortgage', or, 'A mortgage cannot be made irredeemable'. Such maxims, however convenient, afford little assistance where the Court has to deal with a new or doubtful case. They obviously beg the question, always of great importance, whether the particular transaction which the Court has to consider is, in fact, a mortgage or not, and if they be acted on without a careful consideration of the equitable considerations on which they are based, can only, like Bacon's idols of the market place,[76] lead to misconception and error.

We will suppose that money is advanced to a company repayable at the expiration of fifteen years, not an unusual period, and that the company by way of security subdemises (as is often the case) to trustees for the lenders a number of leaseholds, some of which are held for terms less than fifteen years. It would, in my opinion, be a serious error to argue that this was an

---

75 Now CA 2006, ss. 738, 739 respectively.

76 'For the benefit of those who, like myself, can boast only a passing acquaintance with the works of Francis Bacon, it may be helpful to explain that in using the expression 'Idols of the Market Place' Bacon was referring to fallacies which result from a confusing use of words or descriptions': per Jonathan Parker LJ, *Warnborough Ltd v Garmite Ltd* [2003] EWCA Civ 1544, [2004] 1 P & CR DG8, above, p. 875, at [64].

attempt to make an irredeemable mortgage. There would be the same error in objecting on the like ground to a mortgage of leaseholds to secure an annuity for a period exceeding the term of the lease. If the mortgage is irredeemable at all, this arises from the nature of the property mortgaged, and not from any penal or repugnant stipulation on the part of the mortgagee, and the maxim properly understood is in no way infringed.'

QUESTION

X owned a 99-year lease in Blackacre. He wished to raise £100,000 in order to develop the land. His calculations showed that once the buildings were erected— estimated at 5 years—the income from the land would allow him to pay interest on the loan at 8 per cent and repay £1,000 of the capital each year. As the capital outstanding and thus the interest payable each year was reduced, a sum, increasing annually, would be available for himself. His expectation was that interest rates would rise.

With this plan in mind, he suggested to Y that he borrow £100,000 at 8 per cent, the capital repayable at the rate of £1,000 per annum starting five years hence, and £2,000 per annum in the last six years of the lease. Y agreed, saying that the repayment of capital was longer delayed than he wished, but that he was happy to help X.

Interest rates then declined to 6½ per cent. X claimed to be entitled to pay off the capital forthwith, on the ground that the terms of the mortgage made it irredeemable and therefore void.

Will he succeed? What assistance could Y obtain from (a) *Knightsbridge Estates Trust Ltd v Byrne*, or (b) *Santley v Wilde*?

(iii) Collateral advantages

The cases in this section show how modifications were made during the twentieth century to the strict rule that an advantage or benefit collateral to the mortgage and in favour of the mortgagee is void in so far as it is to continue after redemption. A covenant is collateral where an obligation is placed on the mortgagor which is independent of that for the performance of which the land is charged. *Biggs v Hoddinott* [1898] 2 Ch 307 held that such a collateral advantage was valid if it was to exist only until redemption; but covenants drafted so as to exist beyond redemption were struck down in *Noakes & Co Ltd v Rice* [1902] AC 24 and *Bradley v Carritt* [1903] AC 253, even though in the latter case the covenant was not of such a type that it could in any circumstances 'run with' the property mortgaged. Inevitably the situation arose in which the strict application of this rule was not consistent with contemporary business requirements; and the speeches of Lords Haldane and Parker in *Kreglinger v New Patagonia Meat and Cold Storage Co Ltd* [1914] AC 25[77] show that the law has managed to conform both to the requirements of the day and to the precedents and rules of earlier times.

---

[77] See *Cityland and Property (Holdings) Ltd v Dabrah* [1968] Ch 166, p. 895, below.

The most common method of reconciling the *Kreglinger* case with *Noakes & Co Ltd v Rice* and *Bradley v Carritt,* is to construe the covenant to sell the skins in the *Kreglinger* case as being a 'contract, contained in the same document as constituted the security, but in substance independent of it.'[78] Once it is so construed it must stand or fall on its own merits. It is difficult to see why a commercial contract, which is in itself valid, should become void because it is recorded in the same document as a mortgage. Where it can be construed as separate from the mortgage, the position is that if it were entered into on Monday and the mortgage on Tuesday,[79] the two are separate and incapable of affecting each other. It has already been seen that a covenant to do something other than repay principal, interest and costs may be part of the obligation for the performance of which the mortgage is given to secure; and a covenant of this type is not a 'collateral advantage' and cannot be affected by these rules.[80] Whether or not a contract is (i) part of the mortgage security, as in *Santley v Wilde,* (ii) entirely independent of the mortgage transaction, as in the *Kreglinger* case, or (iii) part of the mortgage transaction without being part of the security, as in *Noakes & Co Ltd v Rice* and *Bradley v Carritt,* is a question of construction in each particular case. If the contract is of types (i) or (ii), it is not affected by the rules relating to collateral advantages. If it is of type (iii), which is in its nature between types (i) and (ii), then it is subjected to the authority of the cases declaring collateral advantages to be void. The selection of the correct category for any particular contract is a question for the court in each particular case, but the way is at least open now to the courts to permit the enforcement of bona fide business deals by construing them as falling outside the authority of *Noakes & Co Ltd v Rice* and *Bradley v Carritt.*

(a) Ending with redemption

Biggs v Hoddinott
[1898] 2 Ch 307 (CA, **Lindley MR, Chitty** and **Collins LJJ**)

On 18 March 1896, the defendant Hoddinott, the owner of a public house, mortgaged it to Biggs, a brewer. The deed contained an undertaking by Hoddinott that during the continuance of the mortgage he would deal with only the plaintiff in his purchase of certain liquor; an undertaking by the plaintiff that during the continuance of the mortgage he would supply such liquor at the scheduled prices; and a provision that redemption should not take place, nor should the money be called in, for five years. About two years later, the defendant ceased to purchase liquor from the plaintiff who brought this action for an injunction, and the defendant claimed to be entitled to redeem the mortgage. Romer J granted an injunction and refused to allow the defendant to redeem. On appeal on the question of the issue of the injunction.

---

[78] Per Lord Haldane at 41; *Re Petrol Filling Station, Vauxhall Bridge Road, London* (1968) 20 P & CR 1, p. 898, below.

[79] See Lord Halsbury in *Samuel v Jarrah Timber and Wood Paving Corpn Ltd* [1904] AC 323, p. 870, above.

[80] Because it does not continue after redemption: *Santley v Wilde* [1899] 2 Ch 474, p. 879, above.

Held. The covenant tying the public house during the continuance of the mortgage was valid.

Lindley MR: We have listened to a very ingenious and learned argument with the view of inducing us under pressure to lay down a proposition of law which would be very unfortunate for business men. The proposition contended for comes to this—that while two people are engaged in a mortgage transaction they cannot enter into any other transaction with each other which can possibly benefit the mortgagee, and that any such transaction must be before or after the mortgage and be independent of it, so that it cannot be said that the mortgagee got any additional benefit from the mortgage transaction. Mr Farwell did not attempt to uphold this on any rational principle, but relied on authority. Of course, we must follow settled authorities whether we like them or not; but do they support this proposition? *Jennings v Ward* (1705) 2 Vern 520 was the first case relied upon. That was a redemption suit, and the stipulation which was in question seriously interfered with the redemption of the mortgaged property, and the Master of the Rolls (Sir J Trevor) decreed redemption without regard to that stipulation. He is reported to have said: 'A man shall not have interest for his money, and a collateral advantage besides for the loan of it, or clog the redemption with any by-agreement.' That has been understood as meaning exactly what was said, without regard to the circumstances of the case, and has found its way into the textbooks as establishing that a mortgagee cannot have principal, interests, and costs, and also some collateral advantage. But that supposed rule has been departed from again and again. Take the case of West India mortgages: it has been repeatedly decided that the mortgagee, if not in possession, may stipulate that he shall be appointed consignee. The proposition stated in *Jennings v Ward* is too wide. If properly guarded it is good law and good sense. A mortgage is regarded as a security for money, and the mortgagor can always redeem on payment of principal, interest, and costs; and no bargain preventing such redemption is valid, nor will unconscionable bargains be enforced. There is no case where collateral advantages have been disallowed which does not come under one of these two heads. To say that to require such a covenant as that now in question is unconscionable is asking us to lay down a proposition which would shock any business man, and we are not driven to it by authority....

(b) Existing after redemption

Noakes & Co Ltd v Rice
[1902] AC 24 (HL, **Earl of Halsbury LC, Lords Macnaghten, Shand, Davey, Brampton, Robertson** and **Lindley**)

Rice, the plaintiff, purchased in 1897 the lease of a public house; the lease was to expire in 1923. Before this purchase, Noakes and Co, brewers, were mortgagees of the house and advanced money to Rice to enable him to purchase the leasehold premises which were mortgaged to them as security for the loan. Both this and the prior mortgage included a covenant, 'so as to charge the premises into whosesoever possession the same may come...and to the further intent that the obligation of this covenant may run with the land' that the mortgagor would not, during the continuance of the lease, 'whether any principal moneys or interest shall or shall not be owning' under the mortgage, use any liquor that had not been purchased from Noakes & Co. Provision was made for payment of liquidated damages in case of breach.

Rice now wished to pay off the loan and claimed to redeem the property free from
the covenant tying the house.

Held. On payment of all that was due, the plaintiff could recover the property free
from the tie.

Lord Davey: My Lords, there are three doctrines of the Courts of Equity in this country which
have been referred to in the course of the argument in this case. The first doctrine to which
I refer is expressed in the maxim, 'Once a mortgage always a mortgage.' The second is that the
mortgagee shall not reserve to himself any collateral advantage outside the mortgage contract;
and the third is that a provision or stipulation which will have the effect of clogging or fettering
the equity of redemption is void.

My Lords, the first maxim presents no difficulty: it is only another way of saying that a
mortgage cannot be made irredeemable, and that a provision to that effect is void. In the case
of *Salt v Marquess of Northampton* [1892] AC 1 the question was whether a certain life policy,
the premiums on which were charged against the mortgagor, was comprised in the mortgage
security. That question having been decided in the affirmative, it was declared to be redeemable, notwithstanding an express provision to the contrary contained in the deed.

My Lords, the second doctrine to which I refer, namely that the mortgagee shall not reserve
to himself any collateral advantage outside the mortgage contract, was established long ago
when the usury laws were in force. The Court of Equity went beyond the usury laws, and set its
face against every transaction which tended to usury. It therefore declared void every stipulation by a mortgagee for a collateral advantage which made his total remuneration for the loan
indirectly exceed the legal interest. I think it will be found that every case under this head of
equity was decided either on this ground, or on the ground that the bargain was oppressive and
unconscionable. The abolition of the usury laws[81] has made an alteration in the view the Court
should take on this subject, and I agree that a collateral advantage may now be stipulated for by
a mortgage, provided that no unfair advantage be taken by the mortgagee which would render
it void or voidable, according to the general principles of equity, and provided that it does not
offend against the third doctrine. On these grounds I think the case of *Biggs v Hoddinott* [1898]
2 Ch 307 in the Court of Appeal was rightly decided.

The third doctrine to which I have referred is really a corollary from the first, and it might
be expressed in this form: Once a mortgage always a mortgage and nothing but a mortgage.
The meaning of that is that the mortgagee shall not make any stipulation which will prevent a
mortgagor, who has paid principal, interest, and costs, from getting back his mortgaged property in the condition in which he parted with it. I do not dissent from the opinion expressed by
my noble and learned friend opposite (Lord Lindley), when Master of the Rolls, in the case of
Santley v Wilde [1899] 2 Ch 474. He says: 'A clog or fetter is something which is inconsistent
with the idea of security; a clog or fetter is in the nature of a repugnant condition.' But I ask,
'security' for what? I think it must be security for the principal, interest, and costs, and, I will
add, for any advantages in the nature of increased interest or remuneration for the loan which
the mortgagee has validly stipulated for during the continuance of the mortgage. There are
two elements in the conception of a mortgage: first, security for the money advanced; and,
secondly, remuneration for the use of the money. When the mortgage is paid off the security is
at an end, and, as the mortgagee is no longer kept out of his money, the remuneration to him

---

[81] The usury laws were repealed in 1854: Usury Laws Repeal Act 1854. See further C & B, pp. 740–741.

for the use of his money is also at an end. I confess I should have decided the case of *Santley v Wilde* differently from the way in which it was dealt with in the Court of Appeal. After the payment of principal and interest, and everything which had become payable up to the date of redemption, the property in that case remained charged with the payment to the mortgagee of one-third share of the profits, and the stipulation to that effect should, I think, have been held to be a clog or fetter on the right to redeem. The principle is this—that a mortgage must not be converted into something else; and when once you come to the conclusion that a stipulation for the benefit of the mortgagee is part of the mortgage transaction, it is but part of his security, and necessarily comes to an end on the payment off of the loan. In my opinion, every yearly or other recurring payment stipulated for by the mortgagee should be held to be in the nature of interest, and no more payable after the principal is paid off than interest would be. I apprehend a man could not stipulate for the continuance of payment of interest after the principal is paid, and I do not think he can stipulate for any other recurring payment such as a share of profits. Any stipulation to that effect, would, in my opinion be void as a clog or fetter on the equity of redemption.

Lord Lindley: The conclusion thus arrived at is not inconsistent with *Santley v Wilde* on which the appellants so strongly rely. Some of your Lordships think that case went too far. I do not think so myself; but I will not trouble your Lordships with its details, which were complicated. The principle on which the Court of Appeal decided the case was, I still think, sound. Whether it was properly applied in that case is now of no importance. I believe the true principle applicable to these cases to be that expounded by the Court of Appeal in *Biggs v Hoddinott* and *Santley v Wilde*. That principle is perfectly consistent with a real pledge and with the maxim 'Once a mortgage always a mortgage'; but it will not render valid the covenant which your Lordships have to consider in the present case.

In **Bradley v Carritt** [1903] AC 253, one Bradley, who was the owner of a controlling number of shares in the Sephinjuri Bheel Tea Company, mortgaged them to Carritt, a tea broker, who wished to become the sole broker for the sale of the company's teas. By a written agreement, Bradley undertook, in clause 4, to use his 'best endeavours to secure that [Carritt, the plaintiff] shall always hereafter have the sale of all the company's teas as broker; and, in the event of any of the company's teas being sold otherwise than through' Carritt, to pay to him the commission which he would have earned if they had been sold through him. After the mortgage was paid off, the shares were again mortgaged to a different mortgagee, who took advantage of his voting-power to oust the plaintiff from his position as broker of the company. Carritt sued to recover, as damages for breach of contract, the amount of the commission.

By a bare majority, Lords MACNAGHTEN, DAVEY and ROBERTSON, with Lords SHAND and LINDLEY dissenting, the House of Lords reversed Bigham J and the Court of Appeal and held that the covenant was void as a clog on the equity of redemption, and that no action therefore lay.

The covenant was one that on its terms continued after redemption. The main question was whether or not it was a clog on the equity of redemption. It differed in this respect from the covenant in *Noakes v Rice* [1902] AC 24, for the covenant in that case was one that directly affected the property mortgaged; the mortgagor, having mortgaged a free house, would on redemption have received back a tied house. In this case, however, the covenant did not run with the tea shares; as Lord LINDLEY said at 276:

Clause 4 in no way fetters the right to redeem, nor obstructs the mortgagor in the practical exercise of that right, or of the use or enjoyment of his shares when he gets them back. He can then do what he likes with them, free from all control by the mortgagee.

However, Lord DAVEY said at 268:

Can it be said that the mortgagee does not retain a hold upon the shares which form the mortgaged property, or that the mortgagor has full redemption of it, when the latter is not free to exercise an important right in such manner as he may think most conducive to his own interests?.... Again, the appellant could not part with or otherwise deal with his shares without losing the influence in the company's counsels which might enable him to secure the performance of the first part of the agreement, or running a serious risk of liability under the second part.

The speeches show again the different views of Lords Lindley and Davey upon the principles involved in the question of collateral advantages in particular and of the protection of the mortgagor in general.

Kreglinger v New Patagonia Meat and Cold Storage Co Ltd
[1914] AC 25 (HL, **Viscount Haldane LC, Earl of Halsbury, Lords Atkinson, Mersey** and **Parker of Waddington**)

The appellants, a firm of woolbrokers agreed to lend £10,000 to the respondents, a firm of meat packers. Provided that all interest was paid punctually and all the terms of the agreement observed, the appellants agreed not to call in the principal for five years, but the respondents were at liberty to pay off the loan whenever they wished. The loan was secured by a floating charge[82] on the respondents' undertaking. Clause 8 of the agreement provided in sub-clause (A) that the respondents would not, for a period of five years, 'sell any sheepskins to any person...other than the lenders so long as the lenders are willing to purchase the same at a price equal to the best price...offered...by any...other person...'. Sub-clause (C) provided that the respondent company 'will pay to the lenders a commission of one per cent upon the sale price of all sheepskins sold by the company' to anyone other than the lenders.

After a few months over two years the respondents paid off the loan in accordance with the terms of the agreement, and disputed the right of the appellants to exercise

---

[82] This, though a charge upon the assets for the time being, does not prevent a company from dealing with its property in the ordinary course of business, but it does so when the chargee takes steps, such as by the appointment of a receiver, to crystallise the security. For the characteristics of the charge, see *Re Yorkshire Woolcombers Association Ltd* [1903] 2 Ch 284 at 295, per Romer J; *Re Spectrum Plus Ltd* [2005] 2 AC 680; and for crystallisation of a charge: see *Re Woodroffes (Musical Instruments) Ltd* [1986] Ch 366; *Re Brightlife Ltd* [1987] Ch 200; (1976) 40 Conv (NS) 397 (J. H. Farrar); [1988] CLJ 213 (E. Ferran); *William Gaskell Group v Highley (Nos 1, 2 and 3)* [1993] BCC 200. See generally [1994] CLJ 81 (S. Worthington); *Re Cosslett (Contractors) Ltd* [1998] Ch 495.

their option to purchase the sheepskins. The appellants brought an action for an injunction to restrain the sale of sheepskins to other persons.

Held (reversing Swinfen Eady J and the Court of Appeal (Cozens-Hardy MR, Buckley and Kennedy LJJ) (1913) 29 TLR 393; 464). Appellants entitled to an injunction.

Viscount Haldane LC: My Lords, the respondents have now, as they were entitled to do under the agreement, paid off the loan. They claim that such payment has put an end to the option of the appellants to buy the respondents' sheepskins. Under the terms of the agreement this option, as I have already stated, will, if it is valid, continue operative until August 24, 1915. What the respondents say is that the stipulation is one that restricts their freedom in conducting the undertaking or business which is the subject of the floating charge; that it was consequently of the nature of a clog on their right to redeem and invalid; and that, whether it clogged the right to redeem or was in the nature of a collateral advantage, it was not intended and could not be made to endure after redemption. The appellants, on the other hand, say that the stipulation in question was one of a kind usual in business, and that it was in the nature not of a clog but of a collateral bargain outside the actual loan, which they only agreed to make in order to obtain the option itself. They further say that even if the option could be regarded as within the doctrine of equity which forbids the clogging of the right to redeem, that doctrine does not in a case such as this extend to a floating charge....

My Lords, before I refer to the decisions of this House which the Courts below have considered to cover the case, I will state what I conceive to be the broad principles which must govern it.

The reason for which a Court of Equity will set aside the legal title of a mortgagee and compel him to reconvey the land on being paid principal, interest and costs is a very old one....

The principle was... in the early days limited in its application to the accomplishment of the end which was held to justify interference of equity with freedom of contract. It did not go further. As established it was expressed in three ways. The most general of these was that if the transaction was once found to be a mortgage, it must be treated as always remaining a mortgage and nothing but a mortgage. That the substance of the transaction must be looked to in applying this doctrine and that it did not apply to cases which were only apparently or technically within it but were in reality something more than cases of mortgage, *Howard v Harris* (1683) 1 Vern 33 and other authorities shew. It was only a different application of the paramount doctrine to lay it down in the form of a second rule that a mortgagee should not stipulate for a collateral advantage which would make his remuneration for the loan exceed a proper rate of interest. The Legislature during a long period placed restrictions on the rate of interest which could legally be exacted. But equity went beyond the limits of the statutes which limited the interest, and was ready to interfere with any usurious stipulation in a mortgage. In so doing it was influenced by the public policy of the time. That policy has now changed, and the Acts which limited the rate of interest have been repealed. The result is that a collateral advantage may now be stipulated for by the mortgagee provided that he has not acted unfairly or oppressively, and provided that the bargain does not conflict with the third form of the principle. That is that a mortgage... cannot be made irredeemable, and that any stipulation which restricts or clogs the equity of redemption is void. It is obvious that the reason for the doctrine in this form is the same as that which gave rise to the other forms. It is simply an assertion in a different way of the principle that once a mortgage always a mortgage and nothing else.

My Lords, the rules I have stated have now been applied by Courts of Equity for nearly three centuries, and the books are full of illustrations of their application. But what I have pointed out shews that it is inconsistent with the objects for which they were established that these rules should crystallize into technical language so rigid that the letter can defeat the underlying spirit and purpose. Their application must correspond with the practical necessities of the time. The rule as to collateral advantages, for example, has been much modified by the repeal of the usury laws[83] and by the recognition of modern varieties of commercial bargaining....

His Lordship referred to *Biggs v Hoddinott* [1899] 2 Ch 307 and to the dictum of Trevor MR in *Jennings v Ward* (1705) 2 Vern 520 and continued:

Unless such a bargain is unconscionable it is now good. But none the less the other and wider principle remains unshaken, that it is the essence of a mortgage that in the eye of a Court of Equity it should be a mere security for money, and that no bargain can be validly made which will prevent the mortgagor from redeeming on payment of what is due including principal, interest, and costs. He may stipulate that he will not pay off his debt, and so redeem the mortgage, for a fixed period. But whenever a right to redeem arises out of the doctrine of equity, he is precluded from fettering it. This principle has become an integral part of our system of jurisprudence and must be faithfully adhered to.

My Lords, the question in the present case is whether the right to redeem has been interfered with. And this must, for the reasons to which I have adverted in considering the history of the doctrine of equity, depend on the answer to a question which is primarily one of fact. What was the true character of the transaction? Did the appellants make a bargain such that the right to redeem was cut down, or did they simply stipulate for a collateral undertaking, outside and clear of the mortgage, which would give them an exclusive option of purchase of the sheepskins of the respondents? The question is in my opinion not whether the two contracts were made at the same moment and evidenced by the same instrument, but whether they were in substance a single and undivided contract or two distinct contracts. Putting aside for the moment consider-ations turning on the character of the floating charge, such an option no doubt affects the free-dom of the respondents in carrying on their business even after the mortgage has been paid off. But so might other arrangements which would be plainly collateral, an agreement, for example, to take permanently into the firm a new partner as a condition of obtaining fresh capital in the form of a loan. The question is one not of form but of substance, and it can be answered in each case by looking at all the circumstances, and not by mere reliance on some abstract principle, or upon the dicta which have fallen obiter from judges in other and different cases....

My Lords, if in the case before the House your Lordships arrive at the conclusion that the agreement for an option to purchase the respondents' sheepskins was not in substance a fet-ter on the exercise of their right to redeem, but was in the nature of a collateral bargain the entering into which was a preliminary and separable condition of the loan, the decided cases cease to present any great difficulty. In questions of this kind the binding force of previous decisions, unless the facts are indistinguishable, depends on whether they establish a principle. To follow previous authorities, so far as they lay down principles, is essential if the law is to be preserved from becoming unsettled and vague. In this respect the previous decisions of a Court of co-ordinate jurisdiction are more binding in a system of jurisprudence such as ours than in systems where the paramount authority is that of a code. But when a previous case has not

---

[83] Above, p. 888, n. 81.

laid down any new principle but has merely decided that a particular set of facts illustrates an existing rule, there are few more fertile sources of fallacy than to search in it for what is simply resemblance in circumstances, and to erect a previous decision into a governing precedent merely on this account. To look for anything except the principle established or recognised by previous decisions is really to weaken and not to strengthen the importance of precedent....

It is not, in my opinion, conclusive in favour of the appellants that the security assumed the form of a floating charge. A floating charge is not the less a pledge because of its floating character, and a contract which fetters the right to redeem on which equity insists as regards all contracts of loan and security ought on principle to be set aside as readily in the case of a floating security as in any other case. But it is material that such a floating charge, in the absence of bargain to the contrary effect, permits the assets to be dealt with freely by the mortgagor until the charge becomes enforceable.... No doubt it is the fact that on redemption the respondents will not get back their business as free from obligation as it was before the date of the security. But that may well be because outside the security and consistently with its terms there was a contemporaneous but collateral contract, contained in the same document as constituted the security, but in substance independent of it. If it was the intention of the parties, as I think it was, to enter into this contract as a condition of the respondents getting their advance, I know no reason either in morals or in equity which ought to prevent this intention from being left to have its effect. What was to be capable of redemption was an undertaking which was deliberately left to be freely changed in its details by ordinary business transactions with which the mortgage was not to interfere. Had the charge not been a floating one, it might have been more difficult to give effect to this intention.

His Lordship referred to *Noakes & Co Ltd v Rice* [1902] AC 24, p. 887, above, where 'this difficulty is illustrated' and to *Bradley v Carritt* [1903] AC 253, p. 889, above, and continued:

[The decision in *Bradley v Carritt*] certainly cannot, in my opinion, be taken as authoritatively laying down that the mere circumstances that after redemption the property redeemed may not, as the result of some bargain made at the time of the mortgage, be in the same condition as it was before that time, is conclusive against the validity of that bargain. To render it invalid the bargain must, when its substance is examined, turn out to have formed part of the terms of the mortgage and to have really cut down a true right of redemption. I think that the tendency of recent decisions has been to lay undue stress on the letter of the principle which limits the jurisdiction of equity in setting aside contracts. The origin and reason of the principle ought, as I have already said, to be kept steadily in view in applying it to fresh cases. There appears to me to have grown up a tendency to look at the letter rather than the spirit of the doctrine. The true view is, I think, that judges ought in this kind of jurisdiction to proceed cautiously, and to bear in mind the real reasons which have led Courts of Equity to insist on the free right to redeem and the limits within which the purpose of the rule ought to confine its scope. I cannot but think that the validity of the bargain in such cases as *Bradley v Carritt* and *Santley v Wilde* [1899] 2 Ch 474 [p. 879, above], might have been made free from serious question if the parties had chosen to seek what would have been substantially the same result in a different form....

Lord Parker of Waddington: My Lords, the defendants in this case are appealing to the equitable jurisdiction of the Court for relief from a contract which they admit to be fair and reasonable and of which they have already enjoyed the full advantage. Their title to relief is based on some equity which they say is inherent in all transactions in the nature of a mortgage. They can state no intelligible principle underlying this alleged equity, but contend that your Lordships are bound by authority. That the Court should be asked in the exercise of its equitable jurisdiction to assist in so inequitable a proceeding as the repudiation of a fair and reasonable bargain is somewhat startling, and makes it necessary to examine the point of view from which Courts of Equity have always regarded mortgage transactions....

My Lords, after the most careful consideration of the authorities I think it is open to this House to hold, and I invite your Lordships to hold, that there is now no rule in equity which precludes a mortgagee, whether the mortgage be made upon the occasion of a loan or otherwise, from stipulating for any collateral advantage, provided such collateral advantage is not either (1) unfair and unconscionable, or (2) in the nature of a penalty clogging the equity of redemption, or (3) inconsistent with or repugnant to the contractual and equitable right to redeem.

In the present case it is clear from the evidence, if not from the agreement of 24 August 1910 itself, that the nature of the transaction was as follows: The defendant company wanted to borrow 10,000*l*, and the plaintiffs desired to obtain an option of purchase over any sheepskins the defendants might have for sale during a period of five years. The plaintiffs agreed to lend the money in consideration of obtaining this option, and the defendant company agreed to give the option in consideration of obtaining the loan. The loan was to carry interest at 6 per cent per annum, and was not to be called in by the plaintiffs for a specified period. The defendant company, however, might pay it off at any time. It was to be secured by a floating charge over the defendant company's undertaking. The option was to continue for five years, whether the loan was paid off or otherwise, and if the plaintiffs did not exercise their option as to any of the defendant company's skins, a commission on the sale of such skins was in certain events payable to the plaintiffs.

I doubt whether, even before the repeal of the usury laws, this perfectly fair and businesslike transaction would have been considered a mortgage within any equitable rule or maxim relating to mortgages. The only possible way of deciding whether a transaction is a mortgage within any such rule or maxim is by reference to the intention of the parties. It never was intended by the parties that if the defendant company exercised their right to pay off the loan they should get rid of the option. The option was not in the nature of a penalty, nor was it nor could it ever become inconsistent with or repugnant to any other part of the real bargain within any such rule or maxim. The same is true of the commission payable on the sale of skins as to which the option was not exercised. Under these circumstances it seems to me that the bargain must stand and that the plaintiffs are entitled to the relief they claim.[84]

In **Multiservice Bookbinding Ltd v Marden** [1979] Ch 84[85] the plaintiffs in September 1966 charged their business premises to the defendant as security for a loan of £36,000, in order to purchase new premises in North London. The defendant was only willing to lend the money if he could be safeguarded against a decline in the purchasing power of sterling. The terms of the mortgage, which was created with solicitors' advice, were that (i) interest be payable at 2 per cent above bank rate on the full capital sum for the duration of the mortgage (ii) arrears of interest be capitalised after 21 days (thus

---

[84] (1944) 60 LQR 191 (G. L. Williams).
[85] [1978] Conv 346 (H. W. Wilkinson); 432 (D. W. Williams); and for an economist's view (1981) 131 NLJ 4 (R. A. Bowles). The Consumer Credit Act 1974, p. 921, below, was not applicable because the mortgagor was a body corporate.

providing for interest on interest) (iii) the loan be neither called in nor redeemed for 10 years, and (iv) the value of the capital and interest be index-linked to the Swiss franc ('the Swiss franc uplift' clause 6).

In September 1966 the Swiss franc was just over 12 to the pound but in October 1976, when a redemption statement was prepared, it had fallen to just over 4. The total capital repayment was £87,588, as against £36,000 lent, and the total interest due was £45,380 (£31,051 basic plus £14,329 uplift). The average rate of interest over the ten years would have been 16.01 per cent. On the other hand, the book value of the mortgaged property had more than doubled, and the plaintiff company's 'growth had been considerable.'

The plaintiffs took out a summons to determine how far the terms of the mortgage were enforceable. BROWNE-WILKINSON J held that all terms were valid. Having decided that an index-linked money obligation is not contrary to public policy, his Lordship continued at 109:

I have dealt with these authorities [*Kreglinger v New Patagonia Meat and Cold Storage Co Ltd* [1914] AC 25, p. 890, above; *Knightsbridge Estates Trust Ltd v Byrne* [1939] Ch 441, p. 882, above; *Biggs v Hoddinott* [1898] 2 Ch 307, p. 886, above; *Davis v Symons* [1934] Ch 442] at some length because the sheet anchor of Mr Nugee's argument, that mere unreasonableness is sufficient to invalidate a stipulation, is the use of the word 'unreasonable' by Goff J in *Cityland and Property (Holdings) Ltd v Dabrah* [1968] Ch 166. In that case the plaintiff company was the freehold owner of a house of which the defendant had been the tenant for 11 years. His lease expired and the plaintiff company sold the freehold to him for £3,500, of which the defendant paid £600 in cash and the balance of £2,900 was left by the plaintiff company on mortgage. The mortgage was in unusual terms in that it contained simply a covenant to pay, by instalments, the sum of £4,553, that is to say, a premium of 57 per cent over the sum advanced. No explanation was given as to what this premium represented. The defendant defaulted in paying his instalments after only one year, and the plaintiff was seeking to enforce his security for the full sum of £4,553 less payments actually made. Not surprisingly Goff J refused to permit this on the grounds that the excess over £2,900 was an unlawful premium. Bearing in mind the relative strength of lender and borrower, the size of the premium and the lack of any explanation or justification for it, the premium in that case was unconscionable and oppressive. . . .

I therefore approach the second point on the basis that, in order to be freed from the necessity to comply with all the terms of the mortgage, the plaintiffs must show that the bargain, or some of its terms, was unfair and unconscionable: it is not enough to show that, in the eyes of the court, it was unreasonable. In my judgment a bargain cannot be unfair and unconscionable unless one of the parties to it has imposed the objectionable terms in a morally reprehensible manner, that is to say, in a way which affects his conscience.

The classic example of an unconscionable bargain is where advantage has been taken of a young, inexperienced or ignorant person to introduce a term which no sensible well-advised person or party would have accepted. But I do not think the categories of unconscionable bargains are limited: the court can and should intervene where a bargain has been procured by unfair means.

Mr Nugee submitted that a borrower was, in the normal case, in an unequal bargaining position vis-à-vis the lender and that the care taken by the courts of equity to protect borrowers—to which Lord Parker referred in the passage I have quoted[86]—was reflected in a general rule that, except in the case of two large equally powerful institutions, any unreasonable term would be 'unconscionable' within Lord Parker's test. I cannot accept this. In my judgment there is no such special rule applicable to contracts of loan which requires one to treat a bargain as having been unfairly made even where it is demonstrated that no unfair advantage has been taken of the borrower. No decision illustrating Mr Nugee's principle was cited. However, if, as in the *Cityland* case, there is an unusual or unreasonable stipulation the reason for which is not explained, it may well be that in the absence of any explanation, the court will assume that unfair advantage has been taken of the borrower. In considering all the facts, it will often be the case that the borrower's need for the money was far more pressing than the lender's need to lend: if this proves to be the case, then circumstances exist in which an unfair advantage could have been taken. It does not necessarily follow that what could have been done has been done: whether or not an unfair advantage has in fact been taken depends on the facts of each case.

Applying those principles to this case, first I do not think it is right to treat the 'Swiss franc uplift' element in the capital-repayments as being in any sense a premium or collateral advantage. In my judgment a lender of money is entitled to insure that he is repaid the real value of his loan and if he introduces a term which so provides, he is not stipulating for anything beyond the repayment of principal. I do not think equity would have struck down clause 6 as a collateral advantage even before the repeal of the usury laws....

Secondly, considering the mortgage bargain as a whole, in my judgment there was no great inequality of bargaining power as between the plaintiffs and the defendant. The plaintiff company was a small but prosperous company in need of cash to enable it to expand: if it did not like the terms offered it could have refused them without being made insolvent or, as in the *Cityland* case, losing its home. The defendant had £40,000 to lend, but only, as he explained to the plaintiffs, if its real value was preserved. The defendant is not a professional moneylender and there is no evidence of any sharp practice of any kind by him. The borrowers were represented by independent solicitors of repute. Therefore the background does not give rise to any presupposition that the defendant took an unfair advantage of the plaintiffs.

Mr Nugee's main case is based on the terms of the mortgage itself. He points to the facts that (1) the defendant's principal and interest is fully inflation proofed (2) that interest is payable at two per cent above minimum lending rate and (3) that interest is payable on the whole £36,000 throughout the term of the loan. He says that although any one of these provisions by itself might not be objectionable, when all these are joint in one mortgage they are together 'unfair and unconscionable'. He adds further subsidiary points, amongst them that it is impossible to know the sum required for redemption when notice to redeem has to be given; that interest is payable in advance; that no days of grace were allowed for paying the instalments of capital and any expenses incurred by the lender are charged on the property and therefore under clause 6 subject to the Swiss franc uplift even though incurred long after 1966. He also contends that if there were capitalised arrears of interest, the Swiss franc uplift would be applied twice: once when the arrears are capitalised and again when the capitalised sum is paid: in my opinion this is not the true construction of the mortgage.

However, Mr Nugee's other points amount to a formidable list and if it were relevant I would be of the view that the terms were unreasonable judged by the standards which the court would adopt if it had to settle the terms of a mortgage. In particular I consider that it was unreasonable

---

[86] *Kreglinger v New Patagonia Meat and Cold Storage Co Ltd* [1914] AC 25 at 49–50, 54–56.

both for the debt to be inflation proofed by reference to the Swiss franc and at the same time to provide for a rate of interest two per cent above bank rate—a rate which reflects at least in part the unstable state of the pound sterling. On top of this interest on the whole sum advanced was to be paid throughout the term. The defendant made a hard bargain. But the test is not reasonableness. The parties made a bargain which the plaintiffs, who are businessmen, went into with their eyes open, with the benefit of independent advice, without any compelling necessity to accept a loan on these terms and without any sharp practice by the defendant. I cannot see that there was anything unfair or oppressive or morally reprehensible in such a bargain entered into in such circumstances. The need for the defendant to invest his money in a way which preserved its real purchasing power provides an adequate explanation of all the terms of the mortgage.[87]

In **De Beers Consolidated Mines Ltd v British South Africa Co** [1912] AC 52, a company agreed to grant a perpetual licence for mining diamonds on its land, and later mortgaged the land to the licensee. The House of Lords held that after redemption the agreement to grant the licence still bound the company. This was so even though the agreement for the licence expressly contemplated the later mortgage, since the two transactions were substantially independent of each other. When the property was mortgaged, 'it had already been burdened and encumbered with the prior obligation, superior to the mortgage security, to grant the licence' (at 66, per Lord ATKINSON). The licence was not a clog on the equity of redemption, 'because when the redemption took place everything which had been charged was restored to the mortgagor' (at 73, per Earl LOREBURN LC).

The problem has also arisen in connection with the distribution of petroleum products through tied garages. In general terms, the garage proprietor undertakes to deal only in the products of a particular oil company. The oil company undertakes to supply the products and to allow a special rebate. Sometimes the oil company advances money to the garage proprietor, and in such a case the mortgage of the garage will include an undertaking to observe the terms of the agreement during the continuance of the mortgage.

A garage proprietor who wishes to pay off the mortgage before the due date and to be free of its provisions may attack its validity on two grounds. First, on the ground of the doctrine, previously discussed, which protects a mortgagor against oppression. Secondly, on the ground that the agreement is void as being in restraint of trade. This second ground is a matter for the law of contract and its details must be sought elsewhere.[88] We should, however, note here an argument that the doctrine of restraint of

---

[87] A building society has power to make an index-linked mortgage: *Nationwide Building Society v Registry of Friendly Societies* [1983] 1 WLR 1226 (decided under Building Societies Act 1962, ss. 1, 4). See also Building Societies Act 1986, ss. 10 (10), 11 (2) (repealed by Building Societies Act 1997, s. 12 (1)), 9A (inserted by Building Societies Act 1997, s. 10). See also *Boustany v Piggott* (1995) 69 P & CR 288, where PC set aside a lease on the grounds that it was an unconscionable bargain; *Commercial Bank of Australia Ltd v Amadio* (1983) 46 ALR 402; [1996] Conv 454 (M. Pawlowski); *Jones v Morgan* [2002] 1 EGLR 125, p. 872, above, at 129–130.

[88] CFF, pp. 517–537; Treitel, paras 11.056–11.098; (1969) 85 LQR 229 (J. D. Heydon); Heydon, *Restraint of Trade Doctrine* (1971), chaps. 3, 9; Jefferson, *Restraint of Trade* (1997).

As to the possible impact of Art. 85 of the Treaty of Rome (now Art. 81 of the Treaty of Amsterdam) on solus agreements, see *Delimitis v Henninger Bräu A-G* [1991] ECR I–935; *Passmore v Morland plc* [1999] 3 All

trade has no application to mortgages; that the mortgagor, being especially protected by equity, has equity's protection but no other. As would be expected, this argument has not been accepted.[89]

Thus a mortgage is open to attack on both grounds. The two grounds must be kept distinct, for different evidence is relevant to each, and different rules are applicable; and, following the doctrine of the *Kreglinger case*, the court may consider whether an operation is properly construed as a single transaction or as two separate transactions; one being a mortgage which is governed by the doctrine here discussed, and the other being a commercial agreement which is dealt with under the doctrine of restraint of trade.

Re Petrol Filling Station, Vauxhall Bridge Road London
(1968) 20 P & CR 1 (ChD, **Ungoed-Thomas J**)

The plaintiffs were owners of a petrol filling station, and entered into a twenty-year contract on 9 April 1956 with the defendants, whereby the plaintiffs agreed to sell only the defendants' products, and were entitled to a rebate on the price in addition to the usual commission.

On 1 November 1956 the plaintiffs mortgaged their garage to the defendants in consideration of a loan which was required for the modernisation of the premises. The mortgage deed:

(1) provided for the repayment of the loan over nineteen years;

(2) gave the defendants (the mortgagees) a right of pre-emption over the premises during the continuance of the mortgage;

(3) provided that the term of the contract of 9 April 1956 tying the petrol station should remain in force during the continuance of the mortgage.

The question was whether the plaintiffs were entitled to redeem, and to be free of the restrictions contained in the contract and the mortgage.

Held. The plaintiffs were bound by the terms of the mortgage.

Ungoed-Thomas J: It is common ground that the ties in the November agreement are, in accordance with its express provisions, limited to the continuance of the security and that, therefore, on redemption they cease to operate and no question of clog can arise with regard to them. It is also common ground that the ties contained in the sales agreement are capable of constituting a clog on an equity of redemption if they are (and I purposely use vague words)

ER 1005 (tie void only during period of invalidity); *Courage Ltd v Crehan* [2002] QB 507 (European Court of Justice); *Crehan v Inntrepreneur Pub Co* [2004] 3 EGLR 128 (damages awarded to tenant; reversed on different grounds [2007] 1 AC 333).

[89] *Esso Petroleum Co Ltd v Harper's Garage (Stourport) Ltd* [1968] AC 269, per Lord Wilberforce at 342; *Alec Lobb (Garages) Ltd v Total Oil Great Britain Ltd* [1985] 1 WLR 173, p. 871, n. 65, above; [1985] Conv 141 (P. Todd); *Plummer v Tibsco Ltd* [2002] 1 EGLR 29 (option to renew lease of public house subject to purchase of minimum quantity of liquor from landlord held void).

sufficiently connected with it. Therefore, the only question for my decision becomes whether the ties imposed by the sales agreement of April are sufficiently connected with the equity of redemption of the legal charge of November as to constitute a clog upon it. . . .

If, in accordance with my view, the plaintiffs executed the sales agreement without there being any contract with regard to the loan, then it seems to me to follow that the sales agreement and the legal charge were what they appear on their face to be, namely, two separate contracts. Such a conclusion would be in line with the reliance, based on *De Beer's Consolidated Mines Ltd v British South Africa Co* [1912] AC 52 [p. 897, above] on the British South Africa Company's obligation to grant the licence being absolute and immediate and their granting of the mortgage being optional. This distinction in that case was relied on as itself establishing that there were two contracts, one with regard to the licence and one with regard to the mortgage, and not one contract comprehending them both.

Secondly, even if there were, contrary to my view, a binding contract with regard to the loan and with regard to the sales agreement before or at the time of the sales agreement, the question would still remain whether they constituted one or two contracts. Having regard to authorities and the evidence, which I have already considered, including the commercial nature of the ties in the sales agreement, it seems to me that at its highest the defendants' agreement to lend 'in return for the plaintiffs' agreeing to enter into a petrol sales agreement' as stated by Mr Pugh, was, in the words of Lord Haldane in the *Kreglinger case* [1914] AC 25, 'in consideration of being given' a petrol sales agreement, which was 'a collateral bargain the entering into which was a preliminary and separable condition of the loan.'

Thirdly, even if there were one contract, as the plaintiffs contend, I, for my part, if I were driven to it, would conclude that that contract comprehending the sales agreement and the agreement to lend on the legal charge was not in its 'real nature and substance', as a whole, a mortgage transaction, nor, to use Lord Haldane's words, 'a mere mortgage', and so falls outside the doctrine of once a mortgage always a mortgage, of which the clog on the equity of redemption is an emanation. I again quote Lord Haldane, where he said, at 37:

> 'That the substance of the transaction must be looked to in applying this doctrine and that it did not apply to cases which were only apparently or technically within it but were in reality something more than cases of mortgage'.

If there were the one contract, as the plaintiffs say, then it was 'something more than' a mortgage—it was a commercial transaction, of which the mortgage formed part, leaving at any rate the sales agreement part of the transaction with the sales agreement ties outside the ambit of the other part of the transaction, namely, the mortgage, altogether. As I have indicated, the effect on the ties specified in the document of legal charge if those ties were expressed to endure beyond redemption, does not arise.

My conclusion, therefore, is that the defendants succeed on the issue before me.

B. UNDUE INFLUENCE, MISREPRESENTATION AND THIRD PARTIES

A mortgagor may be protected through the application of the general principles of the law of contract. For example, a mortgage may be set aside for duress, undue influence[90] or misrepresentation[91] exercised against the mortgagor; or as an 'unconscionable bargain'.[92] In a significant number of cases, where a mortgage was given to secure not the mortgagor's own borrowings or business activities but those of another family member, the mortgagor has sought to have the mortgage set aside on the basis of undue influence, sometimes on the basis that the mortgagee himself exerted undue influence on him,[93] but more often the claim is of undue influence or misrepresentation exerted by the third party for whose benefit the mortgage was entered into: commonly the husband, for whom the wife has agreed to mortgage her interest in the family home. The House of Lords set out the principles to be applied in such a case in *Barclays Bank plc v O'Brien* [1994] 1 AC 180, below, and further clarified and refined the approach in *Royal Bank of Scotland plc v Etridge (No 2)* [2002] 2 AC 773, p. 902, below.

(i) The O'Brien Rule

In **Barclays Bank plc v O'Brien** [1994] 1 AC 180 the House of Lords considered whether a bank was entitled to enforce against a wife an obligation to secure a debt owed by her husband to the bank, where the wife had been induced to stand as surety for her husband's debt by his undue influence or misrepresentation. Lord BROWNE-WILKINSON said at 191:

Up to this point I have been considering the right of a claimant wife to set aside a transaction as against the wrongdoing husband when the transaction has been procured by his undue influence. But in surety cases the decisive question is whether the claimant wife can set aside the transaction, not against the wrongdoing husband, but against the creditor bank. Of course, if the wrongdoing husband is acting as agent for the creditor bank in obtaining the surety from the wife, the creditor will be fixed with the wrongdoing of its

[90] On duress and undue influence, see CFF, pp. 383–403; Treitel, chap. 10. On the relationship between the doctrine and unconscionability, see (1997) 113 LQR 10 (H. Tjio); [1997] CLJ 71 (E. O'Dell); (1998) 114 LQR 479 (D. Capper).

[91] On misrepresentation, see CFF, pp. 330–383; Treitel, chap. 9; Cartwright, *Misrepresentation, Mistake and Non-disclosure* (2nd edn), esp. chap. 4.

[92] On 'unconscionable bargains', see *Multiservice Bookbinding Ltd v Marden* [1979] Ch 84, p. 894, above; CFF, pp. 385–386; Treitel, paras 10.039–10.041.

[93] See, in particular, *Lloyds Bank Ltd v Bundy* [1975] QB 326 (undue influence presumed where assistant bank manager obtained mortgage guaranteeing £10,000 on property worth only £11,000 from client's aged father to support client's failing company, visiting him at home in presence of his family to obtain his signature on forms already filled in, without leaving them for him to consider or giving him the opportunity of taking independent advice: he 'crossed the line': at 347, per Sir Eric Sachs); *National Westminster Bank plc v Morgan* [1985] AC 686 (mortgage by wife to support husband's business not entered into under undue influence, even though signed on visit by bank manager to their home, where the 'atmosphere . . . was plainly tense. Mr Morgan was in and out of the room, "hovering around." ': at 701, per Lord Scarman. 'A relationship of banker and customer may become one in which the banker acquires a dominating influence. If he does and a manifestly disadvantageous transaction is proved, there would then be room for the court to presume that it resulted from the exercise of undue influence': ibid, at 707. But the manager did not 'cross the line', nor was the transaction unfair to the wife).

own agent and the surety contract can be set aside as against the creditor. Apart from this, if the creditor bank has notice, actual or constructive, of the undue influence exercised by the husband (and consequentially of the wife's equity to set aside the transaction) the creditor will take subject to that equity and the wife can set aside the transaction against the creditor (albeit a purchaser for value) as well as against the husband: see *Bainbrigge v Browne* (1881) 18 ChD 188 and *Bank of Credit and Commerce International SA v Aboody* [1990] 1 QB 923, 973. . . .

A wife who has been induced to stand as a surety for her husband's debts by his undue influence, misrepresentation or some other legal wrong has an equity as against him to set aside that transaction. Under the ordinary principles of equity, her right to set aside that transaction will be enforceable against third parties (e.g. against a creditor) if either the husband was acting as the third party's agent or the third party had actual or constructive notice of the facts giving rise to her equity. Although there may be cases where, without artificiality, it can properly be held that the husband was acting as the agent of the creditor in procuring the wife to stand as surety, such cases will be of very rare occurrence. The key to the problem is to identify the circumstances in which the creditor will be taken to have had notice of the wife's equity to set aside the transaction.

The doctrine of notice lies at the heart of equity. Given that there are two innocent parties, each enjoying rights, the earlier right prevails against the later right if the acquirer of the later right knows of the earlier right (actual notice) or would have discovered it had he taken proper steps (constructive notice). In particular, if the party asserting that he takes free of the earlier rights of another knows of certain facts which put him on inquiry as to the possible existence of the rights of that other and he fails to make such inquiry or take such other steps as are reasonable to verify whether such earlier right does or does not exist, he will have constructive notice of the earlier right and take subject to it. Therefore where a wife has agreed to stand surety for her husband's debts as a result of undue influence or misrepresentation, the creditor will take subject to the wife's equity to set aside the transaction if the circumstances are such as to put the creditor on inquiry as to the circumstances in which she agreed to stand surety. . . .

Therefore in my judgment a creditor is put on inquiry when a wife offers to stand surety for her husband's debts by the combination of two factors: (a) the transaction is on its face not to the financial advantage of the wife; and (b) there is a substantial risk in transactions of that kind that, in procuring the wife to act as surety, the husband has committed a legal or equitable wrong that entitles the wife to set aside the transaction.

It follows that unless the creditor who is put on inquiry takes reasonable steps to satisfy himself that the wife's agreement to stand surety has been properly obtained, the creditor will have constructive notice of the wife's rights.

His Lordship then set out the guidelines as to what reasonable steps a bank has to take in order to avoid being fixed by constructive notice. These principles are not limited to transactions involving husband and wife, but apply to all other cases where there is an emotional relationship between cohabitees.

In *Royal Bank of Scotland v Etridge (No 2)* the House of Lords refined the approach to this problem and set new detailed guidelines for its solution.

Royal Bank of Scotland plc v Etridge (No 2)[94]
[2002] 2 AC 773 (HL, **Lords Bingham of Cornhill, Nicholls of Birkenhead, Clyde, Hobhouse of Woodborough** and **Scott of Foscote**).

Lord Bingham of Cornhill:

2 The transactions which give rise to these appeals are commonplace but of great social and economic importance. It is important that a wife (or anyone in a like position) should not charge her interest in the matrimonial home to secure the borrowing of her husband (or anyone in a like position) without fully understanding the nature and effect of the proposed transaction and that the decision is hers, to agree or not to agree. It is important that lenders should feel able to advance money, in run-of-the-mill cases with no abnormal features, on the security of the wife's interest in the matrimonial home in reasonable confidence that, if appropriate procedures have been followed in obtaining the security, it will be enforceable if the need for enforcement arises. The law must afford both parties a measure of protection. It cannot prescribe a code which will be proof against error, misunderstanding or mishap. But it can indicate minimum requirements which, if met, will reduce the risk of error, misunderstanding or mishap to an acceptable level. The paramount need in this important field is that these minimum requirements should be clear, simple and practically operable.

Lord Nicholls of Birkenhead:

5 My Lords, before your Lordships' House are appeals in eight cases. Each case arises out of a transaction in which a wife charged her interest in her home in favour of a bank as security for her husband's indebtedness or the indebtedness of a company through which he carried on business. The wife later asserted she signed the charge under the undue influence of her husband. In *Barclays Bank plc v O'Brien* [1994] 1 AC 180 your Lordship enunciated the principles applicable in this type of case. Since then, many cases have come before the courts, testing the implications of the *O'Brien* decision in a variety of different factual situations. Seven of the present appeals are of this character. In each case the bank sought to enforce the charge signed by the wife. The bank claimed an order for possession of the matrimonial home. The wife raised a defence that the bank was on notice that her concurrence in the transaction had been procured by her husband's undue influence. The eighth appeal concerns a claim by a wife for damages from a solicitor who advised her before she entered into a guarantee obligation of this character.

Undue influence

6 The issues raised by these appeals make it necessary to go back to first principles. Undue influence is one of the grounds of relief developed by the courts of equity as a court of conscience. The objective is to ensure that the influence of one person over another is not abused. . . .

8 Equity identified broadly two forms of unacceptable conduct. The first comprises overt acts of improper pressure or coercion such as unlawful threats. Today there is much overlap with the principle of duress as this principle has subsequently developed. The second form arises out of a relationship between two persons where one has acquired over another a measure of influence, or ascendancy, of which the ascendant person then takes unfair advantage. An example from the 19th century, when much of this law developed, is a case where an impoverished father

---

[94] [2002] Conv 174 (M. P. Thompson); [2002] CLJ 229 (M. Oldham); (2002) 65 MLR 435 (R. Bigwood); (2002) 118 LQR 337 (D. O'Sullivan); [2001] All ER Rev 254 (P. J. Clarke); Emmet, paras 25.049–25.079.

prevailed upon his inexperienced children to charge their reversionary interests under their parents' marriage settlement with payment of his mortgage debts: see *Bainbrigge v Browne* (1881) 18 ChD 188.

9 In cases of this latter nature the influence one person has over another provides scope for misuse without any specific overt acts of persuasion. The relationship between two individuals may be such that, without more, one of them is disposed to agree a course of action proposed by the other. Typically this occurs when one person places trust in another to look after his affairs and interests, and the latter betrays this trust by preferring his own interests. He abuses the influence he has acquired.

His Lordship referred to *Allcard v Skinner* (1882) 36 ChD 145, 181 and *Zamet v Hyman* [1961] 1 WLR 1442, 1444–1445, and continued:

10 The law has long recognised the need to prevent abuse of influence in these 'relationship' cases despite the absence of evidence of overt acts of persuasive conduct. The types of relationship, such as parent and child, in which this principle falls to be applied cannot be listed exhaustively. Relationships are infinitely various. Sir Guenter Treitel QC has rightly noted that the question is whether one party has reposed sufficient trust and confidence in the other, rather than whether the relationship between the parties belong to a particular type: see Treitel, *The Law of Contract*, 10th edn (1999), pp. 380–381. For example, the relation of banker and customer will not normally meet this criterion, but exceptionally it may: see *National Westminster Bank plc v Morgan* [1985] AC 686, 707–709.

11 Even this test is not comprehensive. The principle is not confined to cases of abuse of trust and confidence. It also includes, for instance, cases where a vulnerable person has been exploited. Indeed, there is no single touchstone for determining whether the principle is applicable. Several expressions have been used to an endeavour to encapsulate the essence: trust and confidence, reliance, dependence or vulnerability on the one hand and ascendancy, domination or control on the other. None of these descriptions is perfect. None is all embracing. Each has its proper place.

12 In *CIBC Mortgages plc v Pitt* [1994] 1 AC 200 your Lordships' House decided that in cases of undue influence disadvantage is not a necessary ingredient of the cause of action. It is not essential that the transaction should be disadvantageous to the pressurised or influenced person, either in financial terms or in any other way....

Burden of proof and presumptions

13 Whether a transaction was brought about by the exercise of undue influence is a question of fact. Here, as elsewhere, the general principle is that he who asserts a wrong has been committed must prove it. The burden of proving an allegation of undue influence rests upon the person who claims to have been wronged. This is the general rule. The evidence required to discharge the burden of proof depends on the nature of the alleged undue influence, the personality of the parties, their relationship, the extent to which the transaction cannot readily be accounted for by the ordinary motives of ordinary persons in that relationship, and all the circumstances of the case.

14 Proof that the complainant placed trust and confidence in the other party in relation to the management of the complainant's financial affairs, coupled with a transaction which calls for explanation, will normally be sufficient, failing satisfactory evidence to the contrary, to discharge the burden of proof. On proof of these two matters the stage is set for the court

to infer that, in the absence of a satisfactory explanation, the transaction can only have been procured by undue influence.

His Lordship referred to *Bainbrigge v Browne* (1881) 18 ChD 188 and *National Westminster Bank plc v Morgan* [1985] AC 686, and continued:

16 Generations of equity lawyers have conventionally described this situation as one in which a presumption of undue influence arises. This use of the term 'presumption' is descriptive of a shift in the evidential onus on a question of fact. When a plaintiff succeeds by this route he does so because he has succeeded in establishing a case of undue influence. The court has drawn appropriate inferences of fact upon a balanced consideration of the whole of the evidence at the end of a trial in which the burden of proof rested upon the plaintiff. The use, in the course of the trial, of the forensic tool of a shift in the evidential burden of proof should not be permitted to obscure the overall position. These cases are the equitable counterpart of common law cases where the principle of res ipsa loquitur is invoked. There is a rebuttable evidential presumption of undue influence....

18 The evidential presumption discussed above is to be distinguished sharply from a different form of presumption which arises in some cases. The law has adopted a sternly protective attitude towards certain types of relationship in which one party acquires influence over another who is vulnerable and dependent and where, moreover, substantial gifts by the influenced or vulnerable person are not normally to be expected. Examples of relationships within this special class are parent and child, guardian and ward, trustee and beneficiary, solicitor and client, and medical adviser and patient. In these cases the law presumes, irrebuttably, that one party had influence over the other. The complainant need not prove he actually reposed trust and confidence in the other party. It is sufficient for him to prove the existence of the type of relationship.

19 It is now well established that husband and wife is not one of the relationships to which this latter principle applies. In *Yerkey v Jones* (1939) 63 CLR 649, 675 Dixon J explained the reason, ...

Independent advice

20 Proof that the complainant received advice from a third party before entering into the impugned transaction is one of the matters a court takes into account when weighing all the evidence. The weight, or importance, to be attached to such advice depends on all the circumstances. In the normal course, advice from a solicitor or other outside adviser can be expected to bring home to a complainant a proper understanding of what he or she is about to do. But a person may understand fully the implications of a proposed transaction, for instance, a substantial gift, and yet still be acting under the undue influence of another. Proof of outside advice does not, of itself, necessarily show that the subsequent completion of the transaction was free from the exercise of undue influence. Whether it will be proper to infer that outside advice had an emancipating effect, so that the transaction was not brought about by the exercise of undue influence, is a question of fact to be decided having regard to all the evidence in the case.

Manifest disadvantage

21 As already noted, there are two prerequisites to the evidential shift in the burden of proof from the complainant to the other party. First, that the complainant reposed trust and confidence in the other party, or the other party acquired ascendancy over the complainant. Second, that the transaction is not readily explicable by the relationship of the parties.

22 Lindley LJ summarised this second prerequisite in the leading authority of *Allcard v Skinner* (1882) 36 ChD 145, where the donor parted with almost all her property. Lindley LJ pointed out that where a gift of a small amount is made to a person standing in a confidential relationship to the donor, some proof of the exercise of the influence of the donee must be given. The mere existence of the influence is not enough. He continued, at p. 185, 'But if the gift is so large as not to be reasonably accounted for on the ground of friendship, relationship, charity, or other ordinary motives on which ordinary men act, the burden is upon the donee to support the gift.' In *Bank of Montreal v Stuart* [1911] AC 120, 137 Lord Macnaghten used the phrase 'immoderate and irrational' to describe this concept....

26 [In *National Westminster Bank plc v Morgan* at 703–707] Lord Scarman attached the label 'manifest disadvantage' to this second ingredient necessary to raise the presumption. This label has been causing difficulty. It may be apt enough when applied to straightforward transactions such as a substantial gift or a sale at an undervalue. But experience has now shown that this expression can give rise to misunderstanding. The label is being understood and applied in a way which does not accord with the meaning intended by Lord Scarman, its originator.

27 The problem has arisen in the context of wives guaranteeing payment of their husband's business debts. In recent years judge after judge has grappled with the baffling question whether a wife's guarantee of her husband's bank overdraft, together with a charge on her share of the matrimonial home, was a transaction manifestly to her disadvantage.

28 In a narrow sense, such a transaction plainly ('manifestly') is disadvantageous to the wife. She undertakes a serious financial obligation, and in return she personally receives nothing. But that would be to take an unrealistically blinkered view of such a transaction. Unlike the relationship of solicitor and client or medical adviser and patient, in the case of husband and wife there are inherent reasons why such a transaction may well be for her benefit. Ordinarily, the fortunes of husband and wife are bound up together. If the husband's business is the source of the family income, the wife has a lively interest in doing what she can to support the business. A wife's affection and self-interest run hand-in-hand in inclining her to join with her husband in charging the matrimonial home, usually a jointly-owned asset, to obtain the financial facilities needed by the business. The finance may be needed to start a new business, or expand a promising business, or rescue an ailing business.

29 Which, then, is the correct approach to adopt in deciding whether a transaction is disadvantageous to the wife: the narrow approach, or the wider approach? The answer is neither. The answer lies in discarding a label which gives rise to this sort of ambiguity. The better approach is to adhere more directly to the test outlined by Lindley LJ in *Allcard v Skinner,* and adopted by Lord Scarman in *National Westminster Bank plc v Morgan,* in the passages I have cited.

30 I return to husband and wife cases. I do not think that, in the ordinary course, a guarantee of the character I have mentioned is to be regarded as a transaction which, failing proof to the contrary, is explicable only on the basis that it has been procured by the exercise of undue influence by the husband. Wives frequently enter into such transactions. There are good and sufficient reasons why they are willing to do so, despite the risks involved for them and their families. They may be enthusiastic. They may not. They may be less optimistic than their husbands about the prospects of the husbands' businesses. They may be anxious, perhaps exceedingly so. But this is a far cry from saying that such transactions as a class are to be regarded as prima facie evidence of the exercise of undue influence by husbands.

31 I have emphasised the phrase 'in the ordinary course'. There will be cases where a wife's signature of a guarantee or a charge of her share in the matrimonial home does call for explanation. Nothing I have said above is directed at such a case.

A cautionary note

32 I add a cautionary note, prompted by some of the first instance judgments in the cases
currently being considered by the House. It concerns the general approach to be adopted by
a court when considering whether a wife's guarantee of her husband's bank overdraft was
procured by her husband's due influence. Undue influence has a connotation of impropriety.
In the eye of the law, undue influence means that influence has been misused. Statements or
conduct by a husband which do not pass beyond the bounds of what may be expected of a reasonable husband in the circumstances should not, without more, be castigated as undue influence.
Similarly, when a husband is forecasting the future of his business, and expressing his hopes
or fears, a degree of hyperbole may be only natural. Courts should not too readily treat such
exaggerations as misstatements.

33 Inaccurate explanations of a proposed transaction are a different matter. So are cases
where a husband, in whom a wife has reposed trust and confidence for the management of their
financial affairs, prefers his interests to hers and makes a choice for both of them on that footing. Such a husband abuses the influence he has. He fails to discharge the obligation of candour
and fairness he owes a wife who is looking to him to make the major financial decisions.

The complainant and third parties: suretyship transactions

34 The problem considered in *O'Brien's* case and raised by the present appeals is of comparatively recent origin. It arises out of the substantial growth in home ownership over the last 30
or 40 years and, as part of that development, the great increase in the number of homes owned
jointly by husbands and wives. More than two-thirds of householders in the United Kingdom
now own their own homes. For most home-owning couples, their homes are their most valuable
asset. They must surely be free, if they so wish, to use this asset as a means of raising money,
whether for the purpose of the husband's business, or for any other purpose. Their home is their
property. The law should not restrict them in the use they may make of it. Bank finance is in fact
by far the most important source of external capital for small businesses with fewer than ten
employees. These businesses comprise about 95% of all businesses in the country, responsible
for nearly one-third of all employment. Finance raised by second mortgages on the principal's
home is a significant source of capital for the start-up of small businesses.

35 If the freedom of home-owners to make economic use of their homes is not to be frustrated, a bank must be able to have confidence that a wife's signature of the necessary guarantee and charge will be as binding upon her as is the signature of anyone else on documents which
he or she may sign. Otherwise banks will not be willing to lend money on the security of a jointly
owned house or flat.

36 At the same time, the high degree of trust and confidence and emotional interdependence
which normally characterises a marriage relationship provides scope for abuse. One party may
take advantage of the other's vulnerability. Unhappily, such abuse does occur. Further, it is all
too easy for a husband, anxious or even desperate for bank finance, to misstate the position
in some particular or to mislead the wife, wittingly or unwittingly, in some other way. The law
would be seriously defective if it did not recognise these realities.

37 In *O'Brien's* case this House decided where the balance should be held between these
competing interests. On the one side, there is the need to protect a wife against a husband's
undue influence. On the other side, there is the need for the bank to be able to have reasonable confidence in the strength of its security. Otherwise it would not provide the required
money. The problem lies in finding the course best designed to protect wives in a minority of

cases without unreasonably hampering the giving and taking of security. The House produced a practical solution. The House decided what are the steps a bank should take to ensure it is not affected by any claim the wife may have that her signature of the documents was procured by the undue influence or other wrong of her husband. Like every compromise, the outcome falls short of achieving in full the objectives of either of the two competing interests. In particular, the steps required of banks will not guarantee that, in future, wives will not be subjected to undue influence or misled when standing as sureties. Short of prohibiting this type of suretyship transaction altogether, there is no way of achieving that result, desirable although it is. What passes between a husband and wife in this regard in the privacy of their own home is not capable of regulation or investigation as a prelude to the wife entering into a suretyship transaction.

38 The jurisprudential route by which the House reached its conclusion in *O'Brien's* case has attracted criticism from some commentators. It has been said to involve artificiality and thereby create uncertainty in the law. I must first consider this criticism. In the ordinary course a bank which takes a guarantee security from the wife of its customer will be altogether ignorant of any undue influence the customer may have exercised in order to secure the wife's concurrence. In *O'Brien* Lord Browne-Wilkinson prayed in aid the doctrine of constructive notice [p. 901, above]. In circumstances he identified, a creditor is put on inquiry. When that is so, the creditor 'will have constructive notice of the wife's rights' unless the creditor takes reasonable steps to satisfy himself that the wife's agreement to stand surety has been properly obtained: see [1994] 1 AC 180, 196.

39 Lord Browne-Wilkinson would be the first to recognise this is not a conventional use of the equitable concept of constructive notice. The traditional use of this concept concerns the circumstances in which a transferee of property who acquires a legal estate from a transferor with a defective title may nonetheless obtain a good title, that is, a better title than the transferor had. That is not the present case. The bank acquires its charge from the wife, and there is nothing wrong with her title to her share of the matrimonial home. The transferor wife is seeking to resile from the very transaction she entered into with the bank, on the ground that her apparent consent was procured by the undue influence or other misconduct, such as misrepresentation, of a third party (her husband). She is seeking to set aside her contract of guarantee and, with it, the charge she gave to the bank.

40 The traditional view of equity in this tripartite situation seems to be that a person in the position of the wife will only be relieved of her bargain if the other party to the transaction (the bank, in the present instance) was privy to the conduct which led to the wife's entry into the transaction. Knowledge is required: see *Cobbett v Brock* (1855) 20 Beav 524, 528, 531, per Sir John Romilly MR, *Kempson v Ashbee* (1874) LR 10 Ch App 15, 21, per James LJ, and *Bainbrigge v Browne* 18 ChD 188, 197, per Fry J. The law imposes no obligation on one party to a transaction to check whether the other party's concurrence was obtained by undue influence. But *O'Brien* has introduced into the law the concept that, in certain circumstances, a party to a contract may lose the benefit of his contract, entered into in good faith, if he ought to have known that the other's concurrence had been procured by the misconduct of a third party.

41 There is a further respect in which *O'Brien* departed from conventional concepts. Traditionally, a person is deemed to have notice (that is, he has 'constructive' notice) of a prior right when he does not actually know of it but would have learned of it had he made the requisite inquiries. A purchaser will be treated as having constructive notice of all that a reasonably prudent purchaser would have discovered. In the present type of case, the steps a bank is required to take, lest it have constructive notice that the wife's concurrence was procured improperly by

her husband, do not consist of making inquiries. Rather, *O'Brien* envisages that the steps taken by the bank will reduce, or even eliminate, the risk of the wife entering into the transaction under any misapprehension or as a result of undue influence by her husband. The steps are not concerned to discover whether the wife has been wronged by her husband in this way. The steps are concerned to minimise the risk that such a wrong may be committed.

42 These novelties do not point to the conclusion that the decision of this House in *O'Brien* is leading the law astray. Lord Browne-Wilkinson acknowledged he might be extending the law: see at 197; Some development was sorely needed. The law had to find a way of giving wives a reasonable measure of protection, without adding unreasonably to the expense involved in entering into guarantee transactions of the type under consideration. The protection had to extend also to any misrepresentations made by a husband to his wife. In a situation where there is a substantial risk the husband may exercise his influence improperly regarding the provision of security for his business debts, there is an increased risk that explanations of the transaction given by him to his wife may be misleadingly incomplete or even inaccurate.

43 The route selected in *O'Brien* ought not to have an unsettling effect on established principles of contract. *O'Brien* concerned suretyship transactions. These are tripartite transactions. They involve the debtor as well as the creditor and the guarantor. The guarantor enters into the transaction at the request of the debtor. The guarantor assumes obligations. On the face of the transaction the guarantor usually receives no benefit in return, unless the guarantee is being given on a commercial basis. Leaving aside cases where the relationship between the surety and the debtor is commercial, a guarantee transaction is one-sided so far as the guarantor is concerned. The creditor knows this. Thus the decision in *O'Brien* is directed at a class of contracts which has special features of its own. That said, I must at a later stage in this speech return to the question of the wider implications of the *O'Brien* decision.

The threshold: when the bank is put on inquiry

44 In *O'Brien* the House considered the circumstances in which a bank, or other creditor, is 'put on inquiry'. Strictly this is a misnomer. As already noted, a bank is not required to make inquiries. But it will be convenient to use the terminology which has now become accepted in this context. The House set a low level for the threshold which must be crossed before a bank is put on inquiry. For practical reasons the level is set much lower than is required to satisfy a court that, failing contrary evidence, the court may infer that the transaction was procured by undue influence. Lord Browne-Wilkinson said at 196:

> 'Therefore in my judgment a creditor is put on inquiry when a wife offers to stand surety for her husband's debts by the combination of two factors: (a) the transaction is on its face not to the financial advantage of the wife; and (b) there is a substantial risk in transactions of that kind that, in procuring the wife to act as surety, the husband has committed a legal or equitable wrong that entitles the wife to set aside the transaction.'

In my view, this passage, read in context, is to be taken to mean, quite simply, that a bank is put on inquiry whenever a wife offers to stand surety for her husband's debts.

45 The Court of Appeal, comprising Stuart-Smith, Millett and Morritt LJJ, interpreted this passage more restrictively. The threshold, the court said, is somewhat higher. Where condition (a) is satisfied, the bank is put on inquiry if, but only if, the bank is aware that the parties are cohabiting or that the particular surety places implicit trust and confidence in the principal debtor in relation to her financial affairs: see *Royal Bank of Scotland plc v Etridge (No 2)* [1998] 4 All ER 705, 719.

46 I respectfully disagree. I do not read (a) and (b) as factual conditions which must be proved in each case before a bank is put on inquiry. I do not understand Lord Browne-Wilkinson to have been saying that, in husband and wife cases, whether the bank is put on inquiry depends on its state of knowledge of the parties' marriage, or of the degree of trust and confidence the particular wife places in her husband in relation to her financial affairs. That would leave banks in a state of considerable uncertainty in a situation where it is important they should know clearly where they stand. The test should be simple and clear and easy to apply in a wide range of circumstances. I read (a) and (b) as Lord Browne-Wilkinson's broad explanation of the reason why a creditor is put on inquiry when a wife offers to stand surety for her husband's debts. These are the two factors which, taken together, constitute the underlying rationale.

47 The position is likewise if the husband stands surety for his wife's debts. Similarly, in the case of unmarried couples, whether heterosexual or homosexual, where the bank is aware of the relationship: see Lord Browne-Wilkinson in *O'Brien's* case, at p. 198. Cohabitation is not essential. The Court of Appeal rightly so decided in *Massey v Midland Bank plc* [1995] 1 All ER 929: see Steyn LJ, at p. 933.

48 As to the type of transactions where a bank is put on inquiry, the case where a wife becomes surety for her husband's debts is, in this context, a straightforward case. The bank is put on inquiry. On the other side of the line is the case where money is being advanced, or has been advanced, to husband and wife jointly. In such a case the bank is not put on inquiry, unless the bank is aware the loan is being made for the husband's purposes, as distinct from their joint purposes. That was decided in *CIBC Mortgages plc v Pitt* [1994] 1 AC 200.[95]

49 Less clear cut is the case where the wife becomes surety for the debts of a company whose shares are held by her and her husband. Her shareholding may be nominal, or she may have a minority shareholding or an equal shareholding with her husband. In my view the bank is put on inquiry in such cases, even when the wife is a director or secretary of the company. Such cases cannot be equated with joint loans. The shareholding interests, and the identity of the directors, are not a reliable guide to the identity of the persons who actually have the conduct of the company's business.

The steps a bank should take

50 The principal area of controversy on these appeals concerns the steps a bank should take when it has been put on inquiry. In *O'Brien,* at 196–197, Lord Browne-Wilkinson said that a bank can reasonably be expected to take steps to bring home to the wife the risk she is running by standing as surety and to advise her to take independent advice. That test is applicable to past transactions. All the cases now before your Lordships' House fall into this category. For the future a bank satisfies these requirements if it insists that the wife attend a private meeting with a representative of the bank at which she is told of the extent of her liability as surety, warned of the risk she is running and urged to take independent legal advice. In exceptional cases the bank, to be safe, has to insist that the wife is separately advised.

---

[95] *Chater v Mortgage Agency Services Number Two Ltd* [2004] 1 P & CR 4 (the bank was not put on inquiry as to any equitable wrong. The transaction would have appeared to the bank as perfectly ordinary: it was a joint application for a joint loan by a mother and son living in the same house. The mere fact that the application was by a mother and son, and that is was the mother's house that was to be the security for the loan, was not enough. There was nothing to indicate the loan was solely for the purposes of the son's business. The bank did not know the true purpose of the loan, and was under no obligation to discover that. Even if the bank had known that the advance was for the son alone, there were many reasons why a mother might justifiably wish to help her son financially, without there being any unfair pressure on her to do so.)

51 The practice of the banks involved in the present cases, and it seems reasonable to assume this is the practice of banks generally, is not to have a private meeting with the wife. Nor do the banks themselves take any other steps to bring home to the wife the risk she is running. This has continued to be the practice since the decision in *O'Brien's* case. Banks consider they would stand to lose more than they would gain by holding a private meeting with the wife. They are, apparently, unwilling to assume the responsibility of advising the wife at such a meeting. Instead, the banking practice remains, as before, that in general the bank requires a wife to seek legal advice. The bank seeks written confirmation from a solicitor that he has explained the nature and effect of the documents to the wife.[96]

52 Many of the difficulties which have arisen in the present cases stem from serious deficiencies, or alleged deficiencies, in the quality of the legal advice given to the wives. I say 'alleged', because three of the appeals before your Lordships' House have not proceeded beyond the interlocutory stage. The banks successfully applied for summary judgment. In these cases the wife's allegations, made in affidavit form, have not been tested by cross-examination. On behalf of the wives it has been submitted that under the current practice the legal advice is often perfunctory in the extreme and, further, that everyone, including the banks, knows this. Independent legal advice is a fiction. The system is a charade. In practice it provides little or no protection for a wife who is under a misapprehension about the risks involved or who is being coerced into signing. She may not even know the present state of her husband's indebtedness.

53 My Lords, it is plainly neither desirable nor practicable that banks should be required to attempt to discover for themselves whether a wife's consent is being procured by the exercise of undue influence of her husband. This is not a step the banks should be expected to take. Nor, further, is it desirable or practicable that banks should be expected to insist on confirmation from a solicitor that the solicitor has satisfied himself that the wife's consent has not been procured by undue influence. As already noted, the circumstances in which banks are put on inquiry are extremely wide. They embrace every case where a wife is entering into a suretyship transaction in respect of her husband's debts. Many, if not most, wives would be understandably outraged by having to respond to the sort of questioning which would be appropriate before a responsible solicitor could give such a confirmation. In any event, solicitors are not equipped to carry out such an exercise in any really worthwhile way, and they will usually lack the necessary materials. Moreover, the legal costs involved, which would inevitably fall on the husband who is seeking financial assistance from the bank, would be substantial. To require such an intrusive, inconclusive and expensive exercise in every case would be an altogether disproportionate response to the need to protect those cases, presumably a small minority, where a wife is being wronged.

54 The furthest a bank can be expected to go is to take reasonable steps to satisfy itself that the wife has had brought home to her, in a meaningful way, the practical implications of the proposed transaction. This does not wholly eliminate the risk of undue influence or misrepresentation. But it does mean that a wife enters into a transaction with her eyes open so far as the basic elements of the transaction are concerned.

55 This is the point at which, in the *O'Brien* case, the House decided that the balance between the competing interests should be held. A bank may itself provide the necessary information directly to the wife. Indeed, it is best equipped to do so. But banks are not following that course. Ought they to be obliged to do so in every case? I do not think Lord Browne-Wilkinson so stated in *O'Brien*. I do not understand him to have said that a personal meeting was the only way a

---

[96] See [2001] Conv 229 at 237–238, 241–243 (M. Pawlowski and S. Greer).

bank could discharge its obligation to bring home to the wife the risks she is running. It seems to me that, provided a suitable alternative is available, banks ought not to be compelled to take this course. Their reasons for not wishing to hold a personal meeting are understandable. Commonly, when a bank seeks to enforce a security provided by a customer, it is met with a defence based on assurances alleged to have been given orally by a branch manager at an earlier stage: that the bank would continue to support the business, that the bank would not call in its loan, and so forth. Lengthy litigation ensues. Sometimes the allegations prove to be well founded, sometimes not. Banks are concerned to avoid the prospect of similar litigation which would arise in guarantee cases if they were to adopt a practice of holding a meeting with a wife at which the bank's representative would explain the proposed guarantee transaction. It is not unreasonable for the banks to prefer that this task should be undertaken by an independent legal adviser.

56 I shall return later to the steps a bank should take when it follows this course. Suffice to say, these steps, together with advice from a solicitor acting for the wife, ought to provide the substance of the protection which *O'Brien* intended a wife should have. Ordinarily it will be reasonable that a bank should be able to rely upon confirmation from a solicitor, acting for the wife, that he has advised the wife appropriately.

57 The position will be otherwise if the bank knows that the solicitor has not duly advised the wife or, I would add, if the bank knows facts from which it ought to have realised that the wife has not received the appropriate advice. In such circumstances the bank will proceed at its own risk.

The content of the legal advice

58 In *Royal Bank of Scotland plc v Etridge (No 2)* [1998] 4 All ER 705, 715, para. 19, the Court of Appeal set out its views of the duties of a solicitor in this context:[97]

> 'A solicitor who is instructed to advise a person who may be subject to the undue influence of another must bear in mind that it is not sufficient that she understands the nature and effect of the transaction if she is so affected by the influence of the other that she cannot make an independent decision of her own. It is not sufficient to explain the documentation and ensure she understands the nature of the transaction and wishes to carry it out: see *Powell v Powell* [1900] 1 Ch 243, 247, approved in *Wright v Carter* [1903] 1 Ch 27. His duty is to satisfy himself that his client is free from improper influence, and the first step must be to ascertain whether it is one into which she could sensibly be advised to enter if free from such influence. If he is not so satisfied it is his duty to advise her not to enter into it, and to refuse to act further for her in the implementation of the transaction if she persists. In this event, while the contents of his advice must remain confidential, he should inform the other parties (including the bank) that he has seen his client and given her certain advice, and that as a result he has declined to act for her any further. He must in any event advise her that she is under no obligation to enter into the transaction at all and, if she still wishes to do so, that she is not bound to accept the terms of any document which has been put before her: see *Credit Lyonnais Bank Nederland NV v Burch* [1997] 1 All ER 144.'

59 I am unable to accept this as an accurate formulation of a solicitor's duties in cases such as those now under consideration. In some respects it goes much too far. The observations of

---

[97] 'An experienced legal executive in a firm with a conveyancing practice is well able to give full and adequate advice as to the contents and effect of a straightforward legal charge': per Lord Scott of Foscote at [292].

Farwell J in *Powell v Powell* [1900] 1 Ch 243, 247, should not be pressed unduly widely. *Powell v Powell* was a case where strong moral pressure was applied by a stepmother to a girl who was only just 21. She was regarded as not really capable of dealing irrevocably with her parent or guardian in the matter of a substantial settlement. Farwell J's observations cannot be regarded as of general application in all cases where a solicitor is giving advice to a person who may have been subject to undue influence.

60 More pertinently, in *Re Coomber* [1911] 1 Ch 723, 730, Fletcher Moulton LJ summarised the general rules applicable to cases of persons who are competent to form an opinion of their own:

> 'All that is necessary is that some independent person, free from any taint of the relationship, or of the consideration of interest which would affect the act, should put clearly before the person what are the nature and the consequences of the act. It is for adult persons of competent mind to decide whether they will do an act, and I do not think that independent and competent advice means independent and competent approval. It simply means that the advice shall be removed entirely from the suspected atmosphere; and that from the clear language of an independent mind, they should know precisely what they are doing.'

61 Thus, in the present type of case it is not for the solicitor to veto the transaction by declining to confirm to the bank that he has explained the documents to the wife and the risks she is taking upon herself. If the solicitor considers the transaction is not in the wife's best interests, he will give reasoned advice to the wife to that effect. But at the end of the day the decision on whether to proceed is the decision of the client, nor the solicitor. A wife is not to be precluded from entering into a financially unwise transaction if, for her own reasons, she wishes to do so.

62 That is the general rule. There may, of course, be exceptional circumstances where it is glaringly obvious that the wife is being grievously wronged. In such a case the solicitor should decline to act further. In *Wright v Carter* [1903] 1 Ch 27, 57–58, Stirling LJ approved Farwell J's observations in *Powell v Powell* [1900] 1 Ch 243, 247. But he did so by reference to the extreme example of a poor man divesting himself of all his property in favour of his solicitor.

63 In *Royal Bank of Scotland plc v Etridge (No 2)* [1998] 4 All ER 705, 722, para. 49, the Court of Appeal said that if the transaction is 'one into which no competent solicitor could properly advise the wife to enter', the availability of legal advice is insufficient to avoid the bank being fixed with constructive notice. It follows from the views expressed above that I am unable to agree with the Court of Appeal on this point.

64 I turn to consider the scope of the responsibilities of a solicitor who is advising the wife. In identifying what are the solicitor's responsibilities the starting point must always be the solicitor's retainer. What has he been retained to do? As a general proposition, the scope of a solicitor's duties is dictated by the terms, whether express or implied, of his retainer. In the type of case now under consideration the relevant retainer stems from the bank's concern to receive confirmation from the solicitor that, in short, the solicitor has brought home to the wife the risks involved in the proposed transaction. As a first step the solicitor will need to explain to the wife the purpose for which he has become involved at all. He should explain that, should it ever become necessary, the bank will rely upon his involvement to counter any suggestion that the wife was overborne by her husband or that she did not properly understand the implications of the transaction. The solicitor will need to obtain confirmation from the wife that she wishes

him to act for her in the matter and to advise her on the legal and practical implications of the proposed transaction.[98]

65 When an instruction to this effect is forthcoming, the content of the advice required from a solicitor before giving the confirmation sought by the bank will, inevitably, depend upon the circumstances of the case. Typically, the advice a solicitor can be expected to give should cover the following matters as the core minimum. (1) He will need to explain the nature of the documents and the practical consequences these will have for the wife if she signs them. She could lose her home if her husband's business does not prosper. Her home may be her only substantial asset, as well as the family's home. She could be made bankrupt. (2) He will need to point out the seriousness of the risks involved. The wife should be told the purpose of the proposed new facility, the amount and principal terms of the new facility, and that the bank might increase the amount of the facility, or change its terms, or grant a new facility, without reference to her. She should be told the amount of her liability under her guarantee. The solicitor should discuss the wife's financial means, including her understanding of the value of the property being charged. The solicitor should discuss whether the wife or her husband has any other assets out of which repayment could be made if the husband's business should fail. These matters are relevant to the seriousness of the risks involved. (3) The solicitor will need to state clearly that the wife has a choice. The decision is hers and hers alone. Explanation of the choice facing the wife will call for some discussion of the present financial position, including the amount of the husband's present indebtedness, and the amount of his current overdraft facility. (4) The solicitor should check whether the wife wishes to proceed. She should be asked whether she is content that the solicitor should write to the bank confirming he has explained to her the nature of the documents and the practical implications they may have for her, or whether, for instance, she would prefer him to negotiate with the bank on the terms of the transaction. Matters for negotiation could include the sequence in which the various securities will be called upon or a specific or lower limit to her liabilities. The solicitor should not give any confirmation to the bank without the wife's authority.

66 The solicitor's discussion with the wife should take place at a face-to-face meeting, in the absence of the husband. It goes without saying that the solicitor's explanations should be couched in suitably non-technical language. It also goes without saying that the solicitor's task is an important one. It is not a formality.

67 The solicitor should obtain from the bank any information he needs. If the bank fails for any reason to provide information requested by the solicitor, the solicitor should decline to provide the confirmation sought by the bank.

68 As already noted, the advice which a solicitor can be expected to give must depend on the particular facts of the case. But I have set out this 'core minimum' in some detail, because the quality of the legal advice is the most disturbing feature of some of the present appeals. The perfunctory nature of the advice may well be largely due to a failure by some solicitors to understand what is required in these cases.

Independent advice

69 I turn next to the much-vexed question whether the solicitor advising the wife must act for the wife alone. Or, at the very least, the solicitor must not act for the husband or the bank in

---

[98] Lord Scott said at [168]: 'Knowledge by a bank that a solicitor is acting for a surety wife does not, without more, justify the bank in assuming that the solicitor's instructions extend to advising her about the nature and effect of the transaction'. See *UCB Corporate Services Ltd v Williams* [2003] 1 P & CR 12.

the current transaction save in a wholly ministerial capacity, such as carrying out conveyancing formalities or supervising the execution of documents and witnessing signatures. Commonly, in practice, the solicitor advising the wife will be the solicitor acting also for her husband either in the particular transaction or generally.

70 The first point to note is that this question cannot be answered by reference to reported decisions. The steps a bank must take once it is put on inquiry, if it is to avoid having constructive notice of the wife's rights, are not the subject of exposition in earlier authority. This is a novel situation, created by the *O'Brien* decision.

71 Next, a simple and clear rule is needed, preferably of well nigh universal application. In some cases a bank deals directly with a husband and wife and has to take the initiative in requiring the wife to obtain legal advice. In other cases, a bank may deal throughout with solicitors already acting for the husband and wife. *Bank of Baroda v Rayarel* [1995] 2 FLR 376 is an example of the latter type of case. It would not be satisfactory to attempt to draw a distinction along these lines. Any such distinction would lack a principled base. Inevitably, in practice, the distinction would disintegrate in confusion.

72 Thirdly, here again, a balancing exercise is called for. Some features point in one direction, others in the opposite direction. Factors favouring the need for the solicitor to act for the wife alone include the following. Sometimes a wife may be inhibited in discussion with a solicitor who is also acting for the husband or whose main client is the husband. This occurred in *Banco Exterior International v Mann* [1995] 1 All ER 936: see the finding of the judge, at p. 941F-G. Sometimes a solicitor whose main client is the husband may not, in practice, give the same single-minded attention to the wife's position as would a solicitor acting solely for the wife. Her interests may rank lower in the solicitor's scale of priorities, perhaps unconsciously, than the interests of the husband. Instances of incompetent advice, or worse, which have come before the court might perhaps be less likely to recur if a solicitor were instructed to act for the wife alone and gave advice solely to her. As a matter of general understanding, independent advice would suggest that the solicitor should not be acting in the same transaction for the person who, if there is any undue influence, is the source of that influence.

73 The contrary view is that the solicitor may also act for the husband or the bank, provided the solicitor is satisfied that this is in the wife's best interests and satisfied also that this will not give rise to any conflicts of duty or interest. The principal factors favouring this approach are as follows. A requirement that a wife should receive advice from a solicitor acting solely for her will frequently add significantly to the legal costs. Sometimes a wife will be happier to be advised by a family solicitor known to her than by a complete stranger. Sometimes a solicitor who knows both husband and wife and their histories will be better placed to advise than a solicitor who is a complete stranger.

74 In my view, overall the latter factors are more weighty than the former. The advantages attendant upon the employment of a solicitor acting solely for the wife do not justify the additional expense this would involve for the husband. When accepting instructions to advise the wife the solicitor assumes responsibilities directly to her, both at law and professionally. These duties, and this is central to the reasoning on this point, are owed to the wife alone. In advising the wife the solicitor is acting for the wife alone. He is concerned only with her interests. I emphasise, therefore, that in every case the solicitor must consider carefully whether there is any conflict of duty or interest and, more widely, whether it would be in the best interests of the wife for him to accept instructions from her. If he decides to accept instructions, his assumption of legal and professional responsibilities to her ought, in the ordinary course of

things, to provide sufficient assurance that he will give the requisite advice fully, carefully and conscientiously. Especially so, now that the nature of the advice called for has been clarified. If at any stage the solicitor becomes concerned that there is a real risk that other interests or duties may inhibit his advice to the wife he must cease to act for her.

Agency

75 No system ever works perfectly. There will always be cases where things go wrong, sometimes seriously wrong. The next question concerns the position when a solicitor has accepted instructions to advise a wife but he fails to do so properly. He fails to give her the advice needed to bring home to her the practical implications of her standing as surety. What then? The wife has a remedy in damages against the negligent solicitor. But what is the position of the bank who proceeded in the belief that the wife had been given the necessary advice?

76 Mr Sher contended that, depending on the facts, the solicitor should be regarded as the agent of the bank. Commonly, what happens is that the bank asks the solicitor acting for the husband to undertake the conveyancing formalities on behalf of the bank. The bank also asks the solicitor to undertake the further task of explaining the nature and effect of the documents to the wife, and then confirming to the bank that he has done so. In carrying out these requested tasks, it was submitted, the solicitor is acting for the bank. The bank requires the solicitor to advise the wife, not for her benefit, but for the benefit and protection of the bank. Any deficiencies in the advice given to the wife should be attributed to the bank. In this regard, it was submitted, the solicitor's knowledge is to be imputed to the bank. A certificate furnished by the solicitor to the bank should not prejudice the position of the wife when, as happened in several cases, the contents of the certificate are untrue. If the solicitor has not given the wife any advice, her rights should not be diminished by the solicitor telling the bank that she has been fully advised.

77 I cannot accept this analysis. Confirmation from the solicitor that he has advised the wife is one of the bank's preconditions for completion of the transaction. But it is central to this arrangement that in advising the wife the solicitor is acting for the wife and no one else. The bank does not have, and is intended not to have, any knowledge of or control over the advice the solicitor gives the wife. The solicitor is not accountable to the bank for the advice he gives to the wife. To impute to the bank knowledge of what passed between the solicitor and the wife would contradict this essential feature of the arrangement. The mere fact that, for its own purposes, the bank asked the solicitor to advise the wife does not make the solicitor the bank's agent in giving that advice.

78 In the ordinary case, therefore, deficiencies in the advice given are a matter between the wife and her solicitor. The bank is entitled to proceed on the assumption that a solicitor advising the wife has done his job properly. I have already mentioned what is the bank's position if it knows this is not so, or if it knows facts from which it ought to have realised this is not so.

Obtaining the solicitor's confirmation

79 I now return to the steps a bank should take when it has been put on inquiry and for its protection is looking to the fact that the wife has been advised independently by a solicitor.

(1) One of the unsatisfactory features in some of the cases is the late stage at which the wife first became involved in the transaction. In practice she had no opportunity to express a view on the identity of the solicitor who advised her. She did not even know that the purpose for which the solicitor was giving her advice was to enable him to send, on her behalf, the protective confirmation sought by the bank. Usually the solicitor acted for both husband and wife.

Since the bank is looking for its protection to legal advice given to the wife by a solicitor who, in this respect, is acting solely for her, I consider the bank should take steps to check *directly with the wife* the name of the solicitor she wishes to act for her. To this end, in future the bank should communicate directly with the wife, informing her that for its own protection it will require written confirmation from a solicitor, acting for her, to the effect that the solicitor has fully explained to her the nature of the documents and the practical implications they will have for her. She should be told that the purpose of this requirement is that thereafter she should not be able to dispute she is legally bound by the documents once she has signed them. She should be asked to nominate a solicitor whom she is willing to instruct to advise her, separately from her husband, and act for her in giving the necessary confirmation to the bank. She should be told that, if she wishes, the solicitor may be the same solicitor as is acting for her husband in the transaction. If a solicitor is already acting for the husband and the wife, she should be asked whether she would prefer that a different solicitor should act for her regarding the bank's requirement for confirmation from a solicitor.

The bank should not proceed with the transaction until it has received an appropriate response directly from the wife.

(2) Representatives of the bank are likely to have a much better picture of the husband's financial affairs than the solicitor. If the bank is not willing to undertake the task of explanation itself, the bank must provide the solicitor with the financial information he needs for this purpose. Accordingly it should become routine practice for banks, if relying on confirmation from a solicitor for their protection, to send to the solicitor the necessary financial information. What is required must depend on the facts of the case. Ordinarily this will include information on the purpose for which the proposed new facility has been requested, the current amount of the husband's indebtedness, the amount of his current overdraft facility, and the amount and terms of any new facility. If the bank's request for security arose from a written application by the husband for a facility, a copy of the application should be sent to the solicitor. The bank will, of course, need first to obtain the consent of its customer to this circulation of confidential information. If this consent is not forthcoming the transaction will not be able to proceed.

(3) Exceptionally there may be a case where the bank believes or suspects that the wife has been misled by her husband or is not entering into the transaction of her own free will. If such a case occurs the bank must inform the wife's solicitors of the facts giving rise to its belief or suspicion.

(4) The bank should in every case obtain from the wife's solicitor a written confirmation to the effect mentioned above.

80 These steps will be applicable to future transactions. In respect of past transactions, the bank will ordinarily be regarded as having discharged its obligations if a solicitor who was acting for the wife in the transaction gave the bank confirmation to the effect that he had brought home to the wife the risks she was running by standing as surety.[99]

The creditor's disclosure obligation

81 It is a well-established principle that, stated shortly, a creditor is obliged to disclose to a guarantor any unusual feature of the contract between the creditor and the debtor which makes it materially different in a potentially disadvantageous respect from what the guarantor might

---

[99] *Royal Bank of Scotland v Hill* [2002] EWCA Civ 1081, [2003] 1 P & CR DG7; *National Westminster Bank plc v Amin* [2002] 1 FLR 735; [2002] Conv 499 (M. Haley); *First National Bank plc v Achampong* [2004] 1 FCR 18; [2003] Conv 314 (M. P. Thompson). On prospective overruling, see (2004) 120 LQR 7 (Arden LJ).

naturally expect. The precise ambit of this disclosure obligation remains unclear. A useful summary of the authorities appears in O'Donovan & Phillips, *The Modern Contract of Guarantee,* 3rd edn (1996), pp. 122–130. It is not necessary to pursue these difficult matters in this case. It is sufficient for me to say that, contrary to submissions made, the need to provide protection for wives who are standing as sureties does not point to a need to re-visit the scope of this disclosure principle. Wives require a different form of protection. They need a full and clear explanation of the risks involved. Typically, the risks will be risks any surety would expect. The protection needed by wives differs from, and goes beyond, the disclosure of information. The *O'Brien* principle is intended to provide this protection.

A wider principle

82 Before turning to the particular cases I must make a general comment on the *O'Brien* principle. As noted by Professor Peter Birks QC, the decision in *O'Brien* has to be seen as the progenitor of a wider principle: see 'The Burden on the Bank', in *Restitution and Banking Law,* edited by Francis Rose (1998), at p. 195. This calls for explanation. In the *O'Brien* case the House was concerned with formulating a fair and practical solution to problems occurring when a creditor obtains a security from a guarantor whose sexual relationship with the debtor gives rise to a heightened risk of undue influence. But the law does not regard sexual relationships as standing in some special category of their own so far as undue influence is concerned. Sexual relationships are no more than one type of relationship in which an individual may acquire influence over another individual. The *O'Brien* decision cannot sensibly be regarded as confined to sexual relationships, although these are likely to be its main field of application at present. What is appropriate for sexual relationships ought, in principle, to be appropriate also for other relationships where trust and confidence are likely to exist.

83 The courts have already recognised this. Further application, or development, of the *O'Brien* principle has already taken place. In *Credit Lyonnais Bank Nederland NV v Burch* [1997] 1 All ER 144 the same principle was applied where the relationship was employer and employee. Miss Burch was a junior employee in a company. She was neither a shareholder nor a director. She provided security to the bank for the company's overdraft. She entered into a guarantee of unlimited amount, and gave the bank a second charge over her flat. Nourse LJ, at p. 146, said the relationship 'may broadly be said to fall under [*O'Brien*]'. The Court of Appeal held that the bank was put on inquiry. It knew the facts from which the existence of a relationship of trust and confidence between Miss Burch and Mr Pelosi, the owner of the company, could be inferred.

84 The crucially important question raised by this wider application of the *O'Brien* principle concerns the circumstances which will put a bank on inquiry. A bank is put on inquiry whenever a wife stands as surety for her husband's debs. It is sufficient that the bank knows of the husband-wife relationship. That bare fact is enough. The bank must then take reasonable steps to bring home to the wife the risks involved. What, then, of other relationships where there is an increased risk of undue influence, such as parent and child? It is enough that the bank knows of the relationship? For reasons already discussed in relation to husbands and wives, a bank cannot be expected to probe the emotional relationship between two individuals, whoever they may be. Nor is it desirable that a bank should attempt this. Take the case where a father puts forward his daughter as a surety for his business overdraft. A bank should not be called upon to evaluate highly personal matters such as the degree of trust and confidence existing between the father and his daughter, with the bank put on inquiry in one case and not in another. As with

wives, so with daughters, whether a bank is put on inquiry should not depend on the degree of trust and confidence the particular daughter places in her father in relation to financial matters. Moreover, as with wives, so with other relationships, the test of what puts a bank on inquiry should be simple, clear and easy to apply in wifely varying circumstances. This suggests that, in the case of a father and daughter, knowledge by the bank of the relationship of father and daughter should suffice to put the bank on inquiry. When the bank knows of the relationship, it must then take reasonable steps to ensure the daughter knows what she is letting herself into.

85   The relationship of parent and child is one of the relationships where the law irrebuttably presumes the existence of trust and confidence. Rightly, this has already been rejected as the boundary of the *O'Brien* principle. *O'Brien* was a husband-wife case. The responsibilities of creditors were enunciated in a case where the law makes no presumption of the existence of trust and confidence.

86   But the law cannot stop at this point, with banks on inquiry only in cases where the debtor and guarantor have a sexual relationship or the relationship is one where the law presumes the existence of trust and confidence. That would be an arbitrary boundary, and the law has already moved beyond this, in the decision in *Burch*. As noted earlier, the reality of life is that relationships in which undue influence can be exercised are infinitely various. They cannot be exhaustively defined. Nor is it possible to produce a comprehensive list of relationships where there is a substantial risk of the exercise of undue influence, all others being excluded from the ambit of the *O'Brien* principle. Human affairs do not lend themselves to categorisations of this sort. The older generation of a family may exercise undue influence over a younger member, as in parent-child cases such as *Bainbrigge v Browne* 18 ChD 188 and *Powell v Powell* [1900] 1 Ch 243. Sometimes it is the other way round, as with a nephew and his elderly aunt in *Inche Noriah v Shaik Allie Bin Omar* [1929] AC 127. An employer may take advantage of his employee, as in *Credit Lyonnais Bank Nederland NV v Burch* [1997] 1 All ER 144. But it may be the other way round, with an employee taking advantage of her employer, as happened with the secretary-companion and her elderly employer in *Re Craig* [1971] Ch 95. The list could go on.

87   These considerations point forcibly to the conclusion that there is no rational cut-off point, with certain types of relationship being susceptible to the *O'Brien* principle and others not. Further, if a bank is not to be required to evaluate the extent to which its customer has influence over a proposed guarantor, the only practical way forward is to regard banks as 'put on inquiry' in every case where the relationship between the surety and the debtor is non-commercial,[100] the creditor must always take reasonable steps to bring home to the individual guarantor the risks he is running by standing as surety. As a measure of protection, this is valuable. But, in all conscience, it is a modest burden for banks and other lenders. It is no more than is reasonably to be expected of a creditor who is taking a guarantee from an individual. If the bank or other creditor does not take these steps, it is deemed to have notice of any claim the guarantor may have that the transaction was procured by undue influence or misrepresentation on the part of the debtor.

---

[100] *Leeder v Stevens* [2005] EWCA Civ 50 (where CA assumed that the presumption applies to a relationship between fiancé and fiancée and by analogy between a man and a woman who were not engaged but had talked about getting married); (2005) 121 LQR 567 N. Enonchong); *Turkey v Awadh* [2005] 2 P & CR 29 (father and his daughter and son-in-law); *Watson v Huber* [2005] All ER(D) 156 (March) (half-sisters); *Hughes v Hughes* [2005] 1 FCR 679 (loving relationship between mother and son); (2005) 155 NLJ 1579.

88 Different considerations apply where the relationship between the debtor and guarantor is commercial, as where a guarantor is being paid a fee, or a company is guaranteeing the debts of another company in the same group. Those engaged in business can be regarded as capable of looking after themselves and understanding the risks involved in the giving of guarantees.

89 By the decisions of this House in *O'Brien* and the Court of Appeal in *Credit Lyonnais Bank Nederland NV v Burch* [1997] 1 All ER 144, English law has taken its first strides in the development of some such general principle. It is a workable principle. It is also simple, coherent and eminently desirable. I venture to think this is the way the law is moving, and should continue to move. Equity, it is said, is not past the age of child-bearing. In the present context the equitable concept of being 'put on inquiry' is the parent of a principle of general application, a principle which imposes no more than a modest obligation on banks and other creditors. The existence of this obligation in all non-commercial cases does not go beyond the reasonable requirements of the present times. In future, banks and other creditors should regulate their affairs accordingly.

Lord Scott of Foscote:

Summary

191 My Lords I think, given the regrettable length of this opinion, I should try and summarise my views about the principles that apply and the practice that should be followed in surety wife cases.

(1) The issue as between the surety wife and the lender bank is whether the bank may rely on the apparent consent of the wife to the suretyship transaction.

(2) If the bank knows that the surety wife's consent to the transaction has been procured by undue influence or misrepresentation, or if it has shut its eyes to the likelihood that that was so, it may not rely on her apparent consent.

(3) If the wife's consent has in fact been procured by undue influence or misrepresentation, the bank may not rely on her apparent consent unless it has good reason to believe that she understands the nature and effect of the transaction.

(4) Unless the case has some special feature, the bank's knowledge that a solicitor is acting for the wife and has advised her about the nature and effect of the transaction will provide a good reason for the purposes of (3) above. That will also be so if the bank has a reasonable belief that a solicitor is acting for her and has so advised her. Written confirmation by a solicitor acting for the wife that he has so advised her will entitle the bank to hold that reasonable belief.

(5) So, too, a sufficient explanation of the nature and effect of the transaction given by a senior bank official would constitute good reason for the purposes of (3) above.

(6) If there are any facts known to the bank which increase the inherent risk that the wife's consent to the transaction may have been procured by the husband's undue influence or misrepresentation, it may be necessary for the bank to be satisfied that the wife has received advice about the transaction from a solicitor independent of the husband before the bank can reasonably rely on the wife's apparent consent.

(7) If the bank has not taken reasonable steps to satisfy itself that the wife understands the nature and effect of the transaction, the wife will, subject to such matters as delay, acquiescence, change of position etc., be able to set aside the transaction if her consent was in fact procured by undue influence or misrepresentation.

(8) Subject to special instructions or special circumstances, the duty of a solicitor instructed to act for a wife proposing to stand as surety, or to give security, for her husband's debts is to try and make sure that she understands the nature and effect of the transaction.

(9) In all surety wife cases the bank should disclose to the surety wife, or to the solicitor acting for her, the amount of the existing indebtedness of the principal debtor to the bank and the amount of the proposed new loan or drawing facility.

(10) Subject to (9) above, a creditor has no greater duty of disclosure to a surety wife than to any other intending surety.

192 I am in full agreement with the analysis of the applicable principles of law and with the conclusions expressed in the opinion of my noble and learned friend, Lord Nicholls of Birkenhead. I believe the analysis I have sought to give in this opinion and my conclusions are consistent with them.[101]

(ii) The rule in Scotland

In **Smith v Governor and Company of the Bank of Scotland** 1997 SLT 1061, the House of Lords (Lords Goff of Chieveley, Jauncey of Tullichettle, Lloyd of Berwick, Hoffmann and Clyde) held that 'the development of the law which was achieved in *Barclays Bank plc v O'Brien* should be extended to Scotland'. Lord CLYDE said at 1068:

It was not disputed that effect could be given in Scotland to the decision in *O'Brien* by the use of the concept of constructive notice... But it seems to me preferable to recognise the element of good faith which is required of the creditor on the constitution of a contract of cautionary and find there a proper basis for decision. The law already recognises, as I have sought to explain, that there may arise a duty of disclosure to a potential cautioner in certain circumstances. As a part of that same good faith which lies behind that duty it seems to me reasonable to accept that there should also be a duty in particular circumstances to give the potential cautioner certain advice. Thus in circumstances where the creditor should reasonably suspect that there may be factors bearing on the participation of the cautioner which might undermine the validity of the contract through his or her intimate relationship with the debtor the duty would arise and would have to be fulfilled if the creditor is not to be prevented from later enforcing the contract. Such a duty does not alter the existing law regarding the duty, or the absence of a duty, to make representations. Nor does it carry with it a duty of investigation. This is simply a duty arising out of the good faith of the contract to give advice.[102]

---

[101] On relief for the surety, see *TSB Bank plc v Camfield* [1995] 1 WLR 430 (wife entitled to have charge set aside in toto; bank can be in no better position than husband); (1995) 111 LQR 555 (P. Ferguson); [1996] RLR 21 (L. Proksch); followed in *Bank Melli Iran v Samadi-Rad* [1995] 2 FLR 367; *Castle Phillips Finance v Piddington* [1995] 1 FLR 783 (subrogation). Cf. *Midland Bank plc v Greene* (1995) 27 HLR 350 (set aside on terms); *Dunbar Bank plc v Nadeem* [1998] 3 All ER 876 (wife would have had to pay half to bank, if there had been undue influence); *Barclays Bank plc v Caplan* (1997) 78 P & CR 153 (wife succeeds in transaction in respect of which bank failed to see that she had independent advice, but bank held able to sever transactions in respect of which she did receive such advice).

[102] Lord Jauncey concurred with reservations; (1998) 114 LQR 17 (C. E. F. Rickett).

> **QUESTION**
>
> How has *Royal Bank of Scotland v Etridge (No 2)* changed the positions of
>
> (a) the mortgagor husband;
>
> (b) the mortgagor's surety wife;
>
> (c) the bank; and
>
> (d) the solicitor acting for the wife?
>
> Are their positions better or worse?

C. CONSUMER CREDIT ACT 1974[103]

The Consumer Credit Act gives the court a wide power to make orders in connection with credit agreements where the relationship between the creditor and the debtor arising out of the agreement is 'unfair'. This will include consumer mortgage agreements, although not land mortgages which are regulated by the Financial Services Authority under the Financial Services and Markets Act 2000.[104]

CONSUMER CREDIT ACT 1974[105]

140A Unfair relationships between creditors and debtors.—(1) The court may make an order under section 140B in connection with a credit agreement if it determines that the relationship between the creditor and the debtor arising out of the agreement (or the agreement taken with any related agreement) is unfair to the debtor because of one or more of the following—

(a) any of the terms of the agreement or of any related agreement;

(b) the way in which the creditor has exercised or enforced any of his rights under the agreement or any related agreement;

(c) any other thing done (or not done) by, or on behalf of, the creditor (either before or after the making of the agreement or any related agreement).

(2) In deciding whether to make a determination under this section the court shall have regard to all matters it thinks relevant (including matters relating to the creditor and matters relating to the debtor).

---

[103] Gray, paras 6.2.49–6.2.53; M & W, paras 25.117–25.119; Lomnicka, *Encyclopedia of Consumer Credit Law*; Goode, *Consumer Credit Law and Practice*; Fisher and Lightwood, chap. 20 (the amendments made by Consumer Credit Act 2006 are discussed in the first supplement).

[104] Consumer Credit Act 1974, s. 16(6C), n. 106, below. For regulated mortgages, see p. 853, n. 10, above.

[105] Ss. 140A-140C were inserted with effect from 6 April 2007 by Consumer Credit Act 2006, ss. 19–21, to replace earlier provisions set out in Consumer Credit Act 1974, s. 137–140 by which the courts had power to 're-open' a credit agreement if the credit bargain was 'extortionate'—i.e., either if the payments to be made under it were 'grossly exorbitant' or if it 'otherwise grossly contravenes ordinary principles of fair dealing' (s. 138(1)). For discussion of the old provisions, see C & B, pp. 745–748; and for criticism of the old provisions and proposals for reform, see Unjust Credit Transactions: Report by the Director General of Fair Trading (1991), paras 1.7, 1.9 and 3.9, set out in the 8th edn of this book at pp. 850–851.

(3) For the purposes of this section the court shall (except to the extent that it is not appropriate to do so) treat anything done (or not done) by, or on behalf of, or in relation to, an associate or a former associate of the creditor as if done (or not done) by, or on behalf of, or in relation to, the creditor.

(4) A determination may be made under this section in relation to a relationship notwithstanding that the relationship may have ended.

(5) An order under section 140B shall not be made in connection with a credit agreement which is an exempt agreement by virtue of section 16(6C).[106]

140B Powers of court in relation to unfair relationships.—(1) An order under this section in connection with a credit agreement may do one or more of the following—

(a) require the creditor, or any associate or former associate of his, to repay (in whole or in part) any sum paid by the debtor or by a surety by virtue of the agreement or any related agreement (whether paid to the creditor, the associate or the former associate or to any other person);

(b) require the creditor, or any associate or former associate of his, to do or not to do (or to cease doing) anything specified in the order in connection with the agreement or any related agreement;

(c) reduce or discharge any sum payable by the debtor or by a surety by virtue of the agreement or any related agreement;

(d) direct the return to a surety of any property provided by him for the purposes of a security;

(e) otherwise set aside (in whole or in part) any duty imposed on the debtor or on a surety by virtue of the agreement or any related agreement;

(f) alter the terms of the agreement or of any related agreement;

(g) direct accounts to be taken, or (in Scotland) an accounting to be made, between any persons.

(2) An order under this section may be made in connection with a credit agreement only—

(a) on an application made by the debtor or by a surety;

(b) at the instance of the debtor or a surety in any proceedings in any court to which the debtor and the creditor are parties, being proceedings to enforce the agreement or any related agreement; or

(c) at the instance of the debtor or a surety in any other proceedings in any court where the amount paid or payable under the agreement or any related agreement is relevant.

(3) An order under this section may be made notwithstanding that its effect is to place on the creditor, or any associate or former associate of his, a burden in respect of an advantage enjoyed by another person.

---

[106] S. 16(6C): 'This Act does not regulate a consumer credit agreement if—

(a) it is secured by a land mortgage and entering into the agreement as lender is a regulated activity for the purposes of the Financial Services and Markets Act 2000; or

(b) it is or forms part of a regulated home purchase plan and entering into the agreement as home purchase provider is a regulated activity for the purposes of that Act.'

(9) If, in any such proceedings, the debtor or a surety alleges that the relationship between the creditor and the debtor is unfair to the debtor, it is for the creditor to prove to the contrary

140C Interpretation of ss. 140A and 140B.—(1) In this section and in sections 140A and 140B 'credit agreement' means any agreement between an individual (the 'debtor') and any other person (the 'creditor') by which the creditor provides the debtor with credit of any amount.

(4) References in sections 140A and 140B to an agreement related to a credit agreement (the 'main agreement') are references to—

(a) a credit agreement consolidated by the main agreement;

(b) a linked transaction in relation to the main agreement or to a credit agreement within paragraph (a);

(c) a security provided in relation to the main agreement, to a credit agreement within paragraph (a) or to a linked transaction within paragraph (b).

D. UNFAIR TERMS IN CONSUMER CONTRACTS REGULATIONS 1999

Cheshire and Burn's Modern Law of Real Property (17th edn, 2006), p. 748

The Unfair Terms in Consumer Contracts Regulations 1999[107] apply to mortgages entered into by consumers[108]—that is, where the mortgagor is a natural person acting for purposes which are outside his trade, business or profession.[109] An unfair term is not binding on the consumer, but the contract continues to bind the parties if it is capable of continuing in existence without the unfair term[110]—and so the court has the power to strike out just the unfair clause. A term which has not been individually negotiated is regarded as unfair if, contrary to the requirement of good faith, it causes a significant imbalance in the parties' rights and obligations arising under the contract, to the detriment of the consumer.[111]

---

[107] SI 1999 No. 2083 implementing Council Directive 93/13/EEC, and replacing Unfair Terms in Consumer Contracts Regulations 1994. The Law Commission has proposed the replacement of the Regulations and the Unfair Contract Terms Act 1977 with a single unified legislative regime, which would continue to maintain the control on unfair contract terms in land contracts (including mortgages) in favour of a consumer: Law Com No. 292 (2005), Cm 6464, paras 3.80, 5.76.

[108] *Falco Finance Ltd v Michael Gough* (1999) 17 Tr LR 526 (terms providing for (i) higher interest rate payable in case of single default; (ii) flat rate of interest; and (iii) 6-month deferment of redemption of mortgage all unfair within 1994 Regulations, n. 107, above); (1999) 143 SJ 572 (C. Banks); Emmet, paras 25.143–148; [1995] CLJ 235 (J. Beatson); (1995) 111 LQR 655 (S. Bright and C. Bright); (1999) 115 LQR 360 (S. Bright); (2000) 4 L & T Rev 38 (J. Holbrook). On the Regulations see generally Lawson, *Exclusion Clauses and Unfair Contract Terms*. [See also *Evans v Cherry Tree Finance Ltd* [2008] EWCA Civ 331 (borrower who took out loan on property which was partly residential and partly commercial was a 'consumer' for purposes of the Regulations).]

[109] Unfair Terms in Consumer Contracts Regulations 1999, reg. 3 (1).   [110] Ibid., reg. 8.

[111] Ibid., reg. 5 (1). An 'indicative and non-exhaustive list of terms which *may* be regarded as unfair' is set out in Sch. 2. The list is drafted with contracts of sale or supply of goods in mind, and is not aimed at the terms normally found in a mortgage, but includes such things as (para. 1 (j), (k), (l)) the power to increase

QUESTIONS

1. X Co wishes to lend money on mortgage to Y Co to enable Y Co to acquire land and to develop it. X Co requires interest on the loan and an option to purchase the developed site within the next ten years. Advise X Co on the difficulties which arise from the cases on

   (a) option to purchase; and

   (b) collateral advantages.

   See articles on p. 872, n. 66, above.

2. A mortgagee wishes to ensure prompt payment of interest by the mortgagor. How would you draft the clause in the mortgage deed? See *Dunlop Pneumatic Tyre Co Ltd v New Garage and Motor Co Ltd* [1915] AC 79; *Wallingford v Mutual Society and Official Liquidator* (1880) 5 App Cas 685; *Union Bank of London v Ingram* (1880) 16 Ch D 53; *Swingcastle Ltd v Alastair Gibson* [1991] 2 AC 223.

V. STATUTORY PROVISIONS AFFECTING THE RIGHTS OF THE MORTGAGOR[112]

LAW OF PROPERTY ACT 1925

91. Sale of mortgaged property in action for redemption or foreclosure.—(1) Any person entitled to redeem mortgaged property may have a judgment or order for sale instead of for redemption in an action brought by him either for redemption alone, or for sale alone, or for sale or redemption in the alternative.[113]

(2) In any action, whether for foreclosure, or for redemption, or for sale, or for the raising and payment in any manner of mortgage money, the court, on the request of the mortgagee, or of any person interested either in the mortgage money or in the right of redemption,[114] and, notwithstanding that—

---

the price or change other terms unilaterally—but with specific exception (para. 2 (b), (c) and (d)) for interest rate fluctuations in contracts of financial services, as long as the supplier is required to notify the consumer, and the consumer has the right to dissolve the contract; and lawful price indexation clauses, so it appears that an index-linked mortgage [p. 897, n. 87, above] would not normally be unfair within the meaning of the Regulations. On the application of the test (as set out in the 1994 Regulations: n. 107, above) to an unsecured credit agreement regulated under CCA 1974, see *Director General of Fair Trading v First National Bank plc* [2002] 1 AC 481. A term of the mortgage which might appear unfair might, on proper construction, be limited: *Paragon Finance plc v Pender* [2005] 1 WLR 3412 (increase by mortgagee in rate of interest; whether breach of implied obligation not to exercise variation right improperly); leave to appeal to HL refused [2006] 1 WLR 398.

[112] C & B, pp. 760–762; MM, pp. 520–526.

[113] He is apparently entitled to such an order as of right: *Clarke v Pannell* (1884) 29 SJ 147.

[114] *Palk v Mortgage Services Funding plc* [1993] Ch 330, p. 965, below (mortgagor).

(a) any other person dissents; or

(b) the mortgagee or any person so interested does not appear in the action;

and without allowing any time for redemption or for payment of any mortgage money, may direct a sale of the mortgaged property, on such terms as it thinks fit, including the deposit in court of a reasonable sum fixed by the court to meet the expenses of sale and to secure performance of the terms.[115]

95. Obligation to transfer instead of re-conveying, and as to right to take possession.—(1) Where a mortgagor is entitled to redeem, then subject to compliance with the terms on compliance with which he would be entitled to require a reconveyance or surrender, he shall be entitled to require the mortgagee, instead of re-conveying or surrendering, to assign the mortgage debt and convey the mortgaged property to any third person, as the mortgagor directs; and the mortgagee shall be bound to assign and convey accordingly.

(2) The rights conferred by this section belong to and are capable of being enforced by each incumbrancer, or by the mortgagor, notwithstanding any intermediate incumbrance; but a requisition of an incumbrancer prevails over a requisition of the mortgagor, and, as between incumbrancers, a requisition of a prior incumbrancer prevails over a requisition of a subsequent incumbrancer.

(3) The foregoing provisions of this section do not apply in the case of a mortgagee being or having been in possession.

(4) Nothing in this Act affects prejudicially the right of a mortgagee of land whether or not his charge is secured by a legal term of years absolute to take possession of the land, but the taking of possession by the mortgagee does not convert any legal estate of the mortgagor into an equitable interest.

(5) This section applies to mortgages made either before or after the commencement of this Act, and takes effect notwithstanding any stipulation to the contrary.

96. Regulations respecting inspection, production and delivery of documents, and priorities.—(1) A mortgagor, as long as his right to redeem subsists, shall be entitled from time to time, at reasonable times, on his request, and at his own cost, and on payment of the mortgagee's costs and expenses in this behalf, to inspect and make copies or abstracts of or extracts from the documents of title relating to the mortgaged property in the custody or power of the mortgagee.

This subsection applies to mortgages made after the thirty-first day of December, eighteen hundred and eighty-one, and takes effect notwithstanding any stipulation to the contrary.

98. Actions for possession by mortgagors.—(1) A mortgagor for the time being entitled to the possession or receipt of the rents and profits of any land, as to which the mortgagee has not given notice of his intention to take possession or to enter into the receipt of the rents and profits thereof, may sue for such possession, or for the recovery of such rents or profits, or to prevent or recover damages in respect of any trespass or other wrong relative thereto, in his own name only, unless the cause of action arises upon a lease or other contract made by him jointly with any other person.

(2) This section does not prejudice the power of a mortgagor independently of this section to take proceedings in his own name only, either in right of any legal estate vested in him or otherwise.

---

[115] *Twentieth Century Banking Corpn Ltd v Wilkinson* [1977] Ch 99; *Arab Bank plc v Mercantile Holdings Ltd* [1994] Ch 71.

(3) This section applies whether the mortgage was made before or after the commencement of this Act.

VI. RIGHTS COMMON TO
MORTGAGOR AND MORTGAGEE[116]

LAW OF PROPERTY ACT 1925

91. **Sale of mortgaged property in action for redemption or foreclosure.**—p. 924, above.

99. **Leasing powers of mortgagor and mortgagee in possession.**—(1) A mortgagor of land while in possession shall, as against every incumbrancer, have power to make from time to time any such lease of the mortgaged land, or any part thereof, as is by this section authorised.

(2) A mortgagee of land while in possession shall, as against all prior incumbrancers, if any, and as against the mortgagor, have power to make from time to time any such lease as aforesaid.

(3) The leases which this section authorises are –

(i) agricultural or occupation leases for any term not exceeding twenty-one years, or, in the case of a mortgage made after the commencement of this Act, fifty years; and

(ii) building leases for any term not exceeding ninety-nine years, or, in the case of a mortgage made after the commencement of this Act, nine hundred and ninety-nine years.[117]

(5) Every lease shall be made to take effect in possession not later than twelve months after its date.

(6) Every such lease shall reserve the best rent that can reasonably be obtained; regard being had to the circumstances of the case, but without any fine being taken.

(7) Every such lease shall contain a covenant by the lessee for payment of the rent, and a condition of re-entry on the rent not being paid within a time therein specified not exceeding thirty days.

(8) A counterpart of every such lease shall be executed by the lessee and delivered to the lessor, of which execution and delivery the execution of the lease by the lessor shall, in favour of the lessee and all persons deriving title under him, be sufficient evidence.

(11) In case of a lease by the mortgagor, he shall, within one month after making the lease, deliver to the mortgagee, or, where there are more than one, to the mortgagee first in priority, a counterpart of the lease duly executed by the lessee, but the lessee shall not be concerned to see that this provision is complied with.

(13) Subject to subsection 13A below,[118] this section applies only if and as far as a contrary intention is not expressed by the mortgagor and mortgagee in the mortgage deed, or otherwise

---

[116] C & B, pp. 760–762; M & W, paras 25.071–25.083; MM, pp. 518–520.
[117] For further details, see sub-ss. (9), (10).
[118] Inserted by Agricultural Tenancies Act 1995, s. 31(2).

in writing, and has effect subject to the terms of the mortgage deed or of any such writing and to the provisions therein contained.[119]

(14) The mortgagor and mortgagee may, by agreement in writing, whether or not contained in the mortgage deed, reserve to or confer on the mortgagor or the mortgagee, or both, any further or other powers of leasing or having reference to leasing; and any further or other powers so reserved or conferred shall be exercisable, as far as may be, as if they were conferred by this Act, and with all the like incidents, effects, and consequences: ...

100. Powers of mortgagor and mortgagee in possession to accept surrenders of leases.—(1) For the purpose only of enabling a lease authorised under the last preceding section, or under any agreement made pursuant to that section, or by the mortgage deed (in this section referred to as an authorised lease) to be granted, a mortgagor of land while in possession shall, as against every incumbrancer, have, by virtue of this Act, power to accept from time to time a surrender of any lease of the mortgaged land or any part thereof comprised in the lease, with or without an exception of or in respect of all or any of the mines and minerals therein, and, on a surrender of the lease so far as it comprises part only of the land or mines and minerals leased, the rent may be apportioned.

(2) For the same purpose, a mortgagee of land while in possession shall, as against all prior or other incumbrancers, if any, and as against the mortgagor, have, by virtue of this Act, power to accept from time to time any such surrender as aforesaid.

(5) No surrender shall, by virtue of this section, be rendered valid unless:—

(a) An authorised lease is granted of the whole of the land or mines and minerals comprised in the surrender to take effect in possession immediately or within one month after the date of the surrender; and

(b) The term certain or other interest granted by the new lease is not less in duration than the unexpired term or interest which would have been subsisting under the original lease if that lease had not been surrendered; and

(c) Where the whole of the land mines and minerals originally leased has been surrendered, the rent reserved by the new lease is not less than the rent which would have been payable under the original lease if it had not been surrendered; or where part only of the land or mines and minerals has been surrendered, the aggregate rents respectively remaining payable or reserved under the original lease and new lease are not less than the rent which would have been payable under the original lease if no partial surrender had been accepted.

(7) This section applies only if and as far as a contrary intention is not expressed by the mortgagor and mortgagee in the mortgage deed, or otherwise in writing, and shall have effect subject to the terms of the mortgage deed or of any such writing and to the provisions therein contained.

---

[119] There is no implied term that the mortgagee must act reasonably in considering an application to let; nor that consent should not be unreasonably withheld; *Citibank International plc v Kessler* [1999] Lloyd's Rep. Bank 123; cf. LTA 1927, s. 19(1), p. 497, above; nor is the mortgagee under a duty in equity properly to consider any request for permission: *Starling v Lloyds TSB Bank Ltd* [2000] 1 EGLR 101 (in extreme circumstances there might be scope for a complaint of bad faith).

VII. RIGHTS AND REMEDIES OF THE MORTGAGEE[120]

A. ACTION ON THE PERSONAL COVENANT

The mortgage deed contains an express covenant whereby the mortgagor covenants to repay the principal sum and interest. Once the payment is due,[121] the mortgagee can sue on this personal covenant for the recovery of the principal sum and any interest that may be in arrear, and can have the judgment satisfied out of any property belonging to the mortgagor, though it is not comprised in the mortgage. Further, the mortgagor remains liable on the covenant to the mortgagee, even though he has transferred his interest in the mortgaged property.[122] He usually takes a covenant of indemnity from the transferee.[123]

B. POSSESSION OF THE MORTGAGED PREMISES[124]

(i) Right to enter

LAW OF PROPERTY ACT 1925

95. Obligation to transfer instead of reconveying, and as to right to take possession.—(4), p. 925, above.

---

[120] C & B, pp. 762–784; Gray, parts 6.3, 6.4; M & W, paras 25.002–25.070; MM, pp. 501–518; Smith, pp. 569–589; Cousins, chap. 16; Waldock, pp. 224–295; Fisher and Lightwood, Part V. The mortgagee's remedies are cumulative: *Rudge v Richens* (1873) LR 8 CP 358 (mortgagee, after exercising power of sale, may sue for balance on personal covenant); *Gordon Grant & Co Ltd v FL Boos* [1926] AC 781 (purchase of land (by leave) at auction and re-sale at a large profit still leaves personal action for balance not found at the auction sale); *Refuge Assurance Co Ltd v Pearlberg* [1938] Ch 687 (a mortgagee in possession is not prevented from appointing a receiver). See also *Alliance and Leicester plc v Slayford* [2001] 1 All ER (Comm) 1; [2002] Conv 53 (M. P. Thompson). Foreclosure however puts an end to other remedies.

Where there are successive mortgages on the same property, the mortgagor is not entitled to require the satisfaction of the debts in the original order, if both mortgagees agree to vary the priority of the mortgages without the mortgagor's consent: *Cheah Theam Swee v Equiticorp Finance Group Ltd* [1992] 1 AC 472.

For the mortgagee's action in the tort of deceit against a surveyor who overvalued the property, see *Cheshire Building Society v Dunlop Haywards (DHL) Ltd* [2008] EWHC 51 (Comm); [2008] 4 EG 169 (CS).

[121] The date at which the mortgagor becomes liable to pay is a question of construction of the deed. An action to recover the principal sum is barred unless it is brought within 12 years from the date when the right to receive the money accrued: Limitation Act 1980, s. 20(1): C & B, pp. 763–764; *Wilkinson v West Bromwich Building Society* [2005] 1 WLR 2303; [2005] Conv 566 (T. Prime); [2005] All ER Rev 267 (P. J. Clarke); *Gotham v Doodes* [2007] 1 WLR 86.

[122] *Kinnaird v Trollope* (1888) 39 ChD 636.

[123] A transferee for value is under an implied obligation to indemnify: *Bridgman v Daw* (1891) 40 WR 253.

[124] C & B, pp. 764–768; Gray, paras 6.3.21–6.3.35, 6.4.13–6.4.40; M & W, paras 25.024–25.035; MM, pp. 506–511; Smith, pp. 570–581; Cousins, paras 16.22–16.40; Fisher and Lightwood, chap. 29; [1979] Conv

Four-Maids Ltd v Dudley Marshall (Properties) Ltd
[1957] Ch 317 (ChD, **Harman J**)[125]

The legal charge provided that, if the interest payments were made punctually, the principal would not be called in for some 2 years 10 months. Six months after the loan was made interest was late and the lender called in the principal. Arrears of interest were then paid, but the lender claimed the whole sums due and took out an originating summons asking for possession.

Held. The mortgagee was entitled to possession.

Harman J: This is an originating summons for possession.... This subject is one which is constantly being agitated in this court. I have had my attention called to some observations I made on it recently in *Hughes v Waite* [1957] 1 WLR 713, and even more recently in *Alliance Perpetual Building Society v Belrum Investments Ltd* [1957] 1 WLR 720, which came before me on an application to commit the editor of the 'Daily Mail' for comments on a mortgagee's action for possession of a sort exactly similar to the present. The comments and, indeed, the arguments of counsel for the newspaper showed an entire misapprehension of what an originating summons for possession is about. They all assumed that it involved some kind of default on the part of the mortgagor, but I said there, and I repeat now, that the right of the mortgagee to possession in the absence of some contract has nothing to do with default on the part of the mortgagor. The mortgagee may go into possession before the ink is dry on the mortgage unless there is something in the contract, express or by implication,[126] whereby he has contracted himself out of that right. He has the right because he has a legal term of years in the property or its statutory equivalent. If there is an attornment clause, he must give notice. If there is a provision that, so long as certain payments are made, he will not go into possession, then he has contracted himself out of his rights. Apart from that, possession is a matter of course.

[An application for possession] has become a very fashionable form of relief because, owing to the conditions now prevailing, if it is desired to realize a security by sale, vacant possession is almost essential. Where, therefore, the mortgagor is in occupation, a summons for possession is taken out, and no other relief is sought, and where the mortgagee is in a position to exercise his power of sale, that is all the help he requires from the court....

The mortgagor said here that his default was of a very small order. So it was. If this were a case where there was discretion in the matter, I should feel that it was a hard case. But the mortgagor has entered into a contract with the mortgagee, and the mortgagee asks for his rights under the contract, and this court, in my judgment, has no power to refuse him those rights.

(NS) 266 (R. J. Smith); [1983] Conv 293 (A. Clarke); [1997] LS 483 (M. Haley); [1998] LS 279 (M. Dixon); Report of the Committee on the Enforcement of Judgment Debts 1969 (Cmnd 3909), paras 1363–1427. As to the rights of an equitable mortgagee to possession, see M & W, paras 25.046–25.048; (1955) 71 LQR 204 (H. W. R. Wade).

[125] (1957) 73 LQR 300 (R.E.M.); *Birmingham Citizens' Permanent Building Society v Caunt* [1962] Ch 883, p. 931, below; *Alnwick RDC v Taylor* [1966] Ch 355.

[126] See *Esso Petroleum Co Ltd v Alstonbridge Properties Ltd* [1975] 1 WLR 1474; *Western Bank Ltd v Schindler* [1977] Ch 1.

(ii) Liability of mortgagee in possession

It is possible for the mortgagee to take possession for the purpose of receiving the income of the property. It is more usual, however, to appoint a receiver[127] if the object is to make up income in arrear, for a mortgagee in possession is made to account not only for what he has received, but also for what he could, by prudent management, have received.

White v City of London Brewery Co
(1889) 42 ChD 237 (CA, **Lord Esher MR, Cotton** and **Fry LJJ**)

In 1868, the plaintiff, a publican, mortgaged his public house to the defendants in return for a loan. In 1869, when the plaintiff's financial affairs were in a serious condition, the defendants exercised their right to take possession, and leased the premises to a tenant who covenanted to purchase his ale, beer and porter from the defendants.

In 1879, the defendants sold the property, took what they claimed was due to them under the mortgage debt and paid the surplus to second mortgagees. The plaintiff, acting in the interests of the second mortgagees, brought this action for an account of what was due to the defendants. One question which arose was whether the defendants were chargeable, not merely with the rent which they received from their tenants, but with the rent which they would have obtained if the premises had been let free from the covenant to purchase ale, etc., from the defendants.

Held. The defendants were chargeable with the rent which they would have obtained if the tenant had not been so restricted, but not with the profit which they made by the sale of beer, etc., to the tenant.

Cotton LJ: A mortgagee in possession must account for the rents which, but for his wilful default, he would have received. The plaintiff says that if he fails as to the brewers' profits yet he ought to have a larger sum in respect of the rents which the mortgagees would, but for their wilful default, have received.... The learned Judge has allowed an addition of £20 a year from 19 August 1874, down to the date of the sale, in addition to the rent obtained by the mortgagees.

His Lordship considered the evidence relating to the rent for which the public house could have been let, and continued:

The evidence on that question is of a somewhat doubtful character, but I think the plaintiff has not established that more should be given him than what the learned Judge has allowed, viz. £20 a year, which comes altogether, as the Master of the Rolls has said, to £100.[128]

(iii) Relief of mortgagor against mortgagee's claim for possession

Contract and statute apart, a legal mortgagee's right to possession of the mortgaged property cannot be defeated by a cross-claim on the part of the mortgagor, even if it

---

127 See p. 972, below.
128 See also *Hughes v Williams* (1806) 12 Ves 493; *Nelson v Booth* (1858) 3 De G & J 119; *Wrigley v Gill* [1905] 1 Ch 241; (1979) 129 NLJ 334 (H. E. Markson); [1982] Conv 345 at pp. 346–348 (J. E. Stannard).

is both liquidated and admitted, and even if it exceeds the amount of the mortgage arrears.[129]

(a) At common law

In **Mobil Oil Co Ltd v Rawlinson** (1981) 43 P & CR 221, Rawlinson was the owner of the equity of redemption in respect of Heathfield Garage, North Petherton in Somerset. The mortgage on the petrol station secured a loan from, and also all sums due to, the defendants under a supply agreement. When Rawlinson fell into arrears, the plaintiffs sought possession of the filling station. Rawlinson sought to counterclaim and set off against the arrears sums alleged to be due to him from the defendants under the supply agreement. The Master made an order for possession, subject to a proviso that it was not to be enforced, if Rawlinson paid £8,000 into court within 14 days. In holding that the proviso should be deleted, Nourse J said at 224:

Before 1936 a mortgagee who was only asking for possession had to commence his proceedings in the Queen's Bench Division. That was because possession alone could not be sought by summons in the Chancery Division. But in 1936, RSC, Ord. 55, r. 5A was amended so as to make that possible. The Chancery judges of the time issued a practice direction which said, amongst other things, that when possession was sought and the defendant was in arrear with any instalments due under the mortgage or charge and the master was of the opinion that the defendant ought to be given an opportunity to pay off the arrears, the master might adjourn the summons on such terms as he thought fit. The direction caused confusion. It led to a general view among the Chancery masters, no doubt assisted by the benevolent attitude which the legislature had by then assumed towards tenants faced with eviction by their landlords, that they had a discretion to adjourn a legal mortgagee's application for possession, at any rate in instalment cases, against the wishes of the mortgagee in order to enable the mortgagor to catch up on instalment arrears; and, inferentially, a right, if he did so, to continue to deny the mortgagee possession notwithstanding that on the default the whole of the mortgage money had become and thereafter remained repayable. By the end of the 1950s it had become necessary for the Chancery judges of a later generation to reassert the legal mortgagee's right to possession. In the van of the movement was Harman J, although even he subscribed to the view that the practice direction had qualified the right in the case of an instalment mortgage: see *Four-Maids Ltd v Dudley Marshall (Properties) Ltd* [1957] Ch 317 at 321 [p. 929, above].

In 1961 the whole question was fully argued and considered in *Birmingham Citizens Permanent Building Society v Caunt* [1962] Ch 883, and it is on Russell J's judgment in that case that the foregoing summary of the earlier history is based. I well remember that decision and the general view of the profession that it had settled once and for all the limited extent of the court's power to adjourn a legal mortgagee's application for possession. The rule in regard to instalment mortgages, and a fortiori in regard to ordinary mortgages, was stated by Russell J at the end of his judgment, in the following terms at 912:

'Accordingly, in my judgment, where (as here) the legal mortgagee under an instalment mortgage under which by reason of default the whole money has become payable, is entitled to possession, the court has no jurisdiction to decline the order or to adjourn the hearing whether on terms of keeping up payments or paying arrears, if the mortgagee cannot be persuaded to agree to this course. To this

---

[129] *Midland Bank plc v McGrath* [1996] EGCS 61.

the *sole exception* is that the application may be adjourned for a short time to afford to the mortgagor a chance of paying off the mortgagee in full or otherwise satisfying him; but this should not be
done if there is no reasonable prospect of this occurring. When I say the sole exception, I do not, of
course, intend to exclude adjournments which in the ordinary course of procedure may be desirable
in circumstances such as temporary inability of a party to attend, and so forth.'

The reason for the exception is that the court has never allowed a mortgagee to enforce his
rights under the mortgage in the face of a concrete offer by the mortgagor to redeem.

Since then the court has twice been given additional powers of adjournment in cases
where the mortgaged property consists of or includes a dwellinghouse: see section 36 of the
Administration of Justice Act 1970 and section 8 of the Administration of Justice Act 1973. But
the general rule continues to apply to other types of property, for example commercial premises
of the kind with which the present case is concerned....[130]

I am prepared to assume in the defendant's favour that the amount of his cross-claims
exceeds the amount of the mortgage debt. I say at once that I regard that as an assumption of
extremely doubtful validity—on the Master's estimate there is a shortfall of about £8,000—but
I will make it nonetheless. However, I find it impossible to make any distinction between this
case and *Samuel Keller (Holdings) Ltd v Martins Bank Ltd* [1971] 1 WLR 43. Megarry J's
statement of the principle at 47–48i which was expressly approved by the Court of Appeal, is
in entirely general terms. The principle is that a mortgagor cannot unilaterally appropriate
the amount of a cross-claim, even if it is both liquidated and admitted, and a fortiori if it is
unliquidated or not admitted, in discharge of the mortgage debt. On that footing the origin and
nature of the cross-claim and its relationship to the mortgage debt are wholly irrelevant.

In the circumstances this case must be approached on the footing that when the matter came
before the Master there were substantial arrears outstanding. Consistently with the general
rule established in *Birmingham Citizens Permanent Building Society v Caunt* he ought then to
have made an unconditional order for possession, unless of course he was satisfied that there
was a reasonable prospect of the defendant's paying the arrears in full, not into court but to
the plaintiffs, or otherwise satisfying the plaintiffs, in which case he should have adjourned the
application for a short time....

I do not intend to suggest that there may not be other circumstances in which the court will
refuse a mortgagee possession on terms that the mortgagor pays the full amount of the mortgage debt into court. A number of other possibilities are mentioned in the passage in Fisher
and Lightwood's *Law of Mortgage* (9th edn 1977) p. 325 which I have already read. Without
attempting to decide any point which does not arise for decision in the present case, I will only
say that it seems to me that that course could only be adopted in the case where there was a
substantial question as to the existence or enforceability of the right to possession, for example
where it was claimed that the mortgage was void for illegality or that the mortgagee was in
some way estopped from asserting his right. It appears probable that *Lido Investments Ltd v
Hale* (1971) 219 EG 715 is a case which falls within the former category.[131]

---

[130] *Cheltenham and Gloucester plc v Krausz* [1997] 1 WLR 1558 at 1561, p. 965, below.

[131] *Citibank Trust Ltd v Ayivor* [1987] 1 WLR 1157 (right to possession not affected where mortgagor's counterclaim for damages greater than arrears due under mortgage); *First National Bank plc v Syed*
[1991] 2 All ER 250; (1991) 141 NLJ 793 (H. W. Wilkinson); (1994) 110 LQR 221 (N. Hickman); *National
Westminster Bank plc v Skelton* [1993] 1 WLR 72n; *Ashley Guarantee plc v Zacaria* [1993] 1 WLR 62 (no
distinction in principle where mortgagor is principal debtor and where he is only guarantor); [1993] All
ER Rev 253 (P. J. Clarke); *Midland Bank Co plc v McGrath* [1996] EGCS 61. See Derham, *Set-Off* (3rd edn,
2003), para. 4.93.

(b) In equity

Quennell v Maltby

[1979] 1 WLR 318 (CA, **Lord Denning MR, Bridge** and **Templeman LJJ**)[132]

Quennell, who owned a large house in Lewes, Sussex, worth more than £30,000, mortgaged it to Barclays Bank Ltd to secure a loan of £2,500. The mortgage deed prohibited the creation of a tenancy without the bank's consent. In breach of that covenant Quennell let the house to the defendants who became statutory tenants protected by the Rent Act 1977. This tenancy was binding on Quennell but not on the bank.[133]

Quennell, who wanted to sell the house with vacant possession, asked the bank to bring an action for possession against the defendants. On the bank's refusal, Quennell's wife then paid off the mortgage debt, took a transfer of the mortgage from the bank and claimed possession against the defendants as mortgagee.

Held (reversing the County Court judge). The wife was not entitled to an order for possession.

Lord Denning MR: [The decision of the judge], if right, opens the way to widespread evasion of the Rent Acts. If the owner of a house wishes to obtain vacant possession, all he has to do is charge it to the bank for a small sum. Then grant a new tenancy without telling the bank. Then get his wife to pay off the bank and take a transfer. Then get the wife to sue for possession.

That indeed was what happened here. In October 1977, when Mr Quennell went to the bank, he told them about the tenancies. They said that they did not intend to take proceedings. So he got Mrs Quennell to do it. In evidence, she said:

'I paid £2,500. This was for my husband. I took the charge to make the debt to his bank less onerous. I was aware he wanted to obtain possession of the house to sell it. I merely paid off the charge. These proceedings have been brought to get possession to sell.'

So the objective is plain. It was not to enforce the security or to obtain repayment or anything of that kind. It was in order to get possession of the house and to overcome the protection of the Rent Acts.

Is that permissible? It seems to me that this is one of those cases where equity steps in to mitigate the rigour of the law. Long years ago it did the same when it invented the equity of redemption. As is said in *Snell's Principles of Equity,* 27th edn (1973), p. 376:

'The courts of equity left the legal effect of the transaction unaltered but declared it to be unreasonable and against conscience that the mortgagee should retain as owner for his own benefit what was intended as a mere security.'

---

[132] (1979) 129 NLJ 624 (H. W. Wilkinson); 38 CLJ 257 (R. A. Pearce).

[133] *Dudley and District Benefit Building Society v Emerson* [1949] Ch 707; *Sadiq v Hussain* (1997) 73 P & CR D44.

Section 98 of the Rent Act 1977 prohibits the court from ordering possession of a dwelling house subject to a statutory tenancy unless certain criteria are met: it does not prohibit a prior mortgagee with title paramount from recovering possession (i) from a protected contractual tenant: *Dudley and District Benefit Building Society v Emerson,* above; (ii) from a statutory tenant: *Britannia Building Society v Earl* [1990] 1 WLR 422; [1990] Conv 450 (S. Bridge); but it does prohibit a mortgagee in all cases where the tenancy predates the mortgagee's mortgage: *Woolwich Building Society v Dickman* [1996] 3 All ER 204; [1996] All ER Rev 254 (P. J. Clarke); 279 (P.H. Pettit); cf. *Barclays Bank plc v Zaroovabli* [1997] Ch 321 (tenancy predated registration but not grant of bank's charge); (1997) 113 LQR 390 (M. Robinson).

So here in modern times equity can step in so as to prevent a mortgagee, or a transferee from him, from getting possession of a house contrary to the justice of the case. A mortgagee will be restrained from getting possession except when it is sought bona fide and reasonably for the purpose of enforcing the security and then only subject to such conditions as the court thinks fit to impose. When the bank itself or a building society lends the money, then it may well be right to allow the mortgagee to obtain possession when the borrower is in default. But so long as the interest is paid and there is nothing outstanding, equity has ample power to restrain any unjust use of the right to possession.

It is plain that in this transaction Mr and Mrs Quennell had an ulterior motive. It was not done to enforce the security or due payment of the principal or interest. It was done for the purpose of getting possession of the house in order to resell it at a profit. It was done so as to avoid the protection which the Rent Acts afford to tenants in their occupation. If Mr Quennell himself had sought to evict the tenants, he would not be allowed to do so. He could not say the tenancies were void. He would be estopped from saying so. They certainly would be protected against him. Are they protected against his wife now that she is the transferee of the charge? In my opinion they are protected. For this simple reason, she is not seeking possession for the purpose of enforcing the loan or the interest or anything of that kind. She is doing it simply for an ulterior purpose of getting possession of the house, contrary to the intention of Parliament as expressed in the Rent Acts.

On that simple ground it seems to me that this action fails and it should be dismissed. The legal right to possession is not to be enforced when it is sought for an ulterior motive. I would on this account allow the appeal and dismiss the action for possession.[134]

Bridge LJ: I entirely agree. The situation arising in this case is one, it seems to me, in which the court is not only entitled but bound to look behind the formal legal relationship between the parties to see what is the true substance of the matter. Once one does that, on the facts of this case it is as plain as a pikestaff that the purpose of the bringing of these proceedings via Mrs Quennell is not for her own benefit to protect or enforce the security which she holds as the transferee of the legal charge but for the benefit of her husband as mortgagor to enable him to sell the property with the benefit of vacant possession. In substance she is suing as his agent. That being so, it seems to me inevitably to follow that she can be in no better position in these proceedings than her husband would be if they had been brought in his name. If they had been brought in his name, it is clear that the defendants would have had an unanswerable defence under the Rent Acts.

I agree that the appeal should be allowed.[135]

(c) By statute

Since 1970 there has been a statutory exception to the Draconian rule in *Four-Maids Ltd v Dudley Marshall Properties Ltd* [1957] Ch 317, p. 929, above in favour of the mortgagor. The additional powers can be exercised by the court whether or not the mortgagor is in default[136] and whether the loan is by way of an instalment or endowment mortgage.[137]

---

[134] Followed in *Albany Home Loans Ltd v Massey* [1997] 2 All ER 609; *Abbey National v Tufts* [1999] 2 FLR 399.

[135] Templeman LJ delivered a judgment concurring with Bridge LJ.

[136] *Western Bank Ltd v Schindler* [1977] Ch 1.

[137] *Governor and Co of the Bank of Scotland v Grimes* [1985] QB 1179, p. 943, below.

1. Administration of Justice Act 1970, s. 36

ADMINISTRATION OF JUSTICE ACT 1970

36. Additional powers of court in action by mortgagee for possession of dwelling-house.—(1) Where the mortgagee under a mortgage of land which consists of or includes a dwelling-house brings an action[138] in which he claims possession of the mortgaged property, not being an action for foreclosure in which a claim for possession of the mortgaged property is also made, the court may exercise any of the powers conferred on it by subsection (2) below if it appears to the court that in the event of its exercising the power the mortgagor is likely to be able within a reasonable period[139] to pay any sums due under the mortgage or to remedy a default consisting of a breach of any other obligation arising under or by virtue of the mortgage.

(2) The court—

    (a) may adjourn the proceedings,[140] or

    (b) on giving judgment, or making an order, for delivery of possession of the mortgaged property, or at any time before the execution of such judgment or order, may—

        (i) stay or suspend execution of the judgment or order,[141] or

        (ii) postpone the date for delivery of possession,

    for such period or periods as the court thinks reasonable.[142]

(3) Any such adjournment, stay, suspension or postponement as is referred to in subsection (2) above may be made subject to such conditions with regard to payment by the mortgagor of any sum secured by the mortgage or the remedying of any default as the court thinks fit.

(4) The court may from time to time vary or revoke any condition imposed by virtue of this section.

38A.[143] This part of this Act shall not apply to a mortgage securing an agreement which is a regulated agreement within the meaning of the Consumer Credit Act 1974.[144]

---

[138] The proceedings are normally taken in the county court: CPR, r. 55.3.

[139] *Royal Trust Co of Canada v Markham* [1975] 1 WLR 1416 (an order for suspension must be for a fixed 'period'; and the mortgagor must provide evidence that he is 'likely to be able to pay'); *Cheltenham and Gloucester Building Society v Norgan* [1996] 1 WLR 343, p. 945, below; *Bristol and West Building Society v Ellis* (1996) 73 P & CR 158, p. 947, below.

[140] *Albany Homes Ltd v Massey* (1997) 73 P & CR 509 (joint mortgagors in default; order for possession made against husband alone; in absence of undertaking by mortgagee not to enforce the order, proceedings should be adjourned with liberty to restore if wife was ordered out or left).

[141] *Target Homes Loans Ltd v Clothier* (1992) 25 HLR 48 (three months' postponement; mortgagor had better prospect of achieving earlier sale if in possession); [1993] Conv 62 (J. Martin).

[142] *National Provincial Building Society v Ahmed* [1995] 2 EGLR 127 at 129; *Cheltenham and Gloucester Building Society v Obi* (1994) 28 HLR 22 (after mortgagee has obtained possession order, court cannot suspend effect of order unless the order itself can be set aside); *Cheltenham and Gloucester Building Society v Grattidge* (1993) 25 HLR 454; *Cheltenham and Gloucester Building Society v Johnson* (1996) 73 P & CR 293 (when a mortgagee is entitled to a money judgment, this may be suspended on same terms as, and in line with, the possession order itself). For the inter-relation between s. 36(1) and LPA 1925, s. 91(2), p. 924, above, see *Cheltenham and Gloucester plc v Krausz* [1997] 1 WLR 1558, p. 965, below.

[143] Added by Consumer Credit Act 1974, s. 192, Sch. 4, para. 30.

[144] Where one spouse has defaulted on the mortgage of a dwelling-house, and the mortgagee brings an action for possession, the other spouse may be entitled to be made a party to the action: Family Law Act 1996, s. 56.

39. Interpretation of Part IV.—(1) In this Part of this Act—

'dwelling-house' includes any building or part thereof which is used as a dwelling;

'mortgage' includes a charge and 'mortgagor' and 'mortgagee' shall be construed accordingly;

'mortgagor' and 'mortgagee' includes any person deriving title under the original mortgagor or mortgagee.[145]

(2) The fact that part of the premises comprised in a dwelling-house is used as a shop or office or for business, trade or professional purposes shall not prevent the dwelling-house from being a dwelling-house for the purposes of this Part of this Act.[146]

In **Ropaigealach v Barclays Bank plc** [2000] QB 263[147] the question arose whether the common law right of a mortgagee to take possession of the premises without a court order had been abrogated by section 36 of the Administration of Justice Act 1970. In holding that it had not, CHADWICK LJ said at 271:

The section is expressed to apply where a mortgagee brings an action in which he claims possession of the mortgaged property. Where the conditions in subsection (1) are satisfied the court is given powers, by subsection (2), which may fairly be described as procedural—in the sense that they are only capable of being exercised in the context of existing proceedings in which a claim for possession is made. But, it is said, Parliament could not have intended that the protection against ejectment which the section was plainly intended to give to mortgagors in respect of their homes should be capable of being circumvented by a mortgagee who resorted to self-help; that is to say, by a mortgagee who obtained possession by entry without the assistance of the court. Accordingly, so it is contended, the section must be construed in such a way as to make it unlawful for a mortgagee to take possession of a dwelling house except under an order of the court. It never became clear in argument how, by any interpretation of the words actually used, that result could be achieved; but that objection was brushed aside as unduly technical. What mattered, it was said, was that the court should give effect to the purpose of which the section was plainly enacted....

I find it impossible to be satisfied that Parliament must have intended, when enacting section 36 of the Act of 1970, that the mortgagee's common law right to take possession by virtue of his estate should only be exercisable with the assistance of the court. In my view, the only conclusion as to parliamentary intention that this court can properly reach is that which can be derived from the circumstances in which the section was enacted, the statutory context in which it appears and the language which was used. All point in the same direction. Parliament was concerned with the problem which had arisen following *Birmingham Citizens Permanent Building Society v Caunt* [1962] Ch 883; it intended to restore the position to what it had been thought to be before that decision; and it did not address its mind to the question whether the mortgagor required protection against the mortgagee who took possession without the

---

[145] *Britannia Building Society v Earl* [1990] 1 WLR 422 (statutory tenant of mortgagor whose tenancy was not binding on mortgagee, p. 933, n. 133, above, was not such a person and court had no jurisdiction to adjourn proceedings); (1990) 140 NLJ 823 (H. W. Wilkinson).

[146] The relevant date for determining whether premises consist of a dwelling-house is the date when the mortgagee brings an action for possession: *Royal Bank of Scotland v Miller* [2002] QB 255.

[147] Leave to appeal to HL was refused: [2000] 1 WLR 1034; [1999] Conv 263 (A. Dunn); [1999] CLJ 281 (M. Dixon); [1999] All ER Rev 226 (P. J. Clarke).

assistance of the court. It is impossible to be sure what course Parliament would have thought it appropriate to adopt, in 1970, if it had identified and addressed that question. It is impossible to be sure that Parliament did not intend (or would not have intended, if it had addressed its mind to the question) to leave the position as it was in that regard. It is not irrelevant that, at the date at which the Act of 1970 was enacted, the mortgagor who was in occupation had the protection—subsequently replaced in a different and, perhaps, more limited form by section 6 of the Criminal Law Act 1977—afforded by the Forcible Entry Acts 1381–1623 [p. 422, above]. It is because it is impossible to be sure that Parliament cannot have intended to leave the position as it was—but must have intended that the mortgagee should only be entitled to exercise his common law right to possession with the assistance of the court—that it cannot be appropriate to embark on an investigation whether the words which have been used are capable of some other construction than that which they naturally bear.

In **Horsham Properties Group Ltd v Clark** [2009] 1 P & CR 8 Briggs J held that the mortgagee's power of sale without first obtaining a court order for possession, or an order for sale, did not infringe the mortgagor's rights under the European Convention of Human Rights.[148] He said at 115:

7 There is no relevant dispute of fact. In particular, Ms Beech accepts that (i) she and Mr Clark were in arrears with their mortgage payments; (ii) the mortgage money had become due within the meaning of section 101(1)(iii) of the LPA;[149] (iii) the mortgage contained the requisite power, in addition to section 101, for GMAC [the mortgagee] to appoint receivers; and (iv) the mortgage contained the requisite power enabling the receivers to sell the property [to Horsham] free from the rights of the defendants as mortgagors.

8 Further, Ms Beech acknowledges that, prior to the coming into force of the Human Rights Act 1998 (the 1998 Act), she would have had no defence to Horsham's claim for possession. In particular, and having regard to the implications of the decision of the Court of Appeal in *Ropaigealach v Barclays Bank plc* [2000] QB 263 [p. 936, above], Ms Victoria Williams, who appeared for Ms Beech, sensibly acknowledged that the traditional (pre-1998 Act) understanding of the relationship between section 101 of the LPA and section 36 of the Administration of Justice Act 1970 (section 36) enabled a mortgagee to sell without seeking a court order permitting it to do so, and enabled a purchaser from the mortgagee to obtain possession without thereby triggering the court's powers to adjourn the proceedings to stay or suspend execution of a judgment for possession or to postpone the date for the delivery of possession in circumstances where it appears that the mortgagor is likely to be able, within a reasonable period, to pay any sums due under the mortgage or remedy any other default or breach of obligation.

9 The essence of Ms Beech's defence is that the traditional understanding which I have described is not compatible with the Convention rights of residential mortgagors. The statutory framework would, so Ms Williams submits, be compatible only if either:

(i) section 101 was construed as requiring a mortgagee first to obtain a court order for possession or to make an application for an order permitting sale, and giving the court on such an application a discretion similar to that conferred by section 36 ; or

[148] For a different analysis, see Rook, *Property Law and Human Rights*, pp. 199–203.
[149] P. 951, below.

(ii) section 36 was construed so as to confer upon the court the discretionary powers to adjourn or suspend the making of a possession order where the application was made, not by the mortgagee, but by the mortgagee's purchaser.

14 Ms Williams usefully identified four issues or, as she put it, hurdles for her client to surmount. They are as follows:

(i) did the sale of the Property by the receivers deprive Ms Beech of one of her possessions in such a way as to engage A1FP [Article 1 of the First Protocol to the Convention]?;

(ii) if so, can the conditions imposed for a lawful deprivation of possessions by A1FP be satisfied otherwise than by subjecting the mortgagee's power of sale in section 101 to a prior application to the court for permission, at which the court is vested with a discretion to adjourn or stay broadly equivalent to that conferred in possession cases by section 36;

(iii) if not, is it possible for section 101 to be read and/or given effect in such a way as to require the mortgagee to make such an application before selling the mortgaged property;

(iv) if not, should there be a declaration of incompatibility.

23 Turning directly to issue one, A1FP in its English translation is as follows:

'Every natural or legal person is entitled to the peaceful enjoyment of his possessions. No one shall be deprived of his possessions except in the public interest and subject to the conditions provided for by law and by the general principles of international law.

The preceding provisions shall not, however, in any way impair the right of a State to enforce such laws as it deems necessary to control the use of property in accordance with the general interest or to secure the payment of taxes or other contributions or penalties.'

24 Ms Williams submitted that Ms Beech's loss of her rights as co-owner of the property or, as I would prefer to put it, her share in the equity of redemption, amounted to being deprived of a possession of hers within the meaning of the second sentence of the first paragraph of A1FP. She acknowledged, in the light of relevant authority, that it was incumbent upon Ms Beech to show first that the rights that she lost fell within the meaning of 'possessions' and secondly that she lost them by virtue of some form of state intervention, rather than purely as the result of the terms of her private bargain with GMAC.

25 I have no difficulty in concluding that Ms Beech's share in the equity of redemption in relation to the property was a 'possession', a widely defined expression which may include purely statutory rights in relation to property, such as the result to renew a business tenancy under Part II of the Landlord and Tenant Act 1954: see *Pennycook v Shaws (EAL) Ltd* [2004] Ch 296 at 310–311 per Arden LJ, in [35]. It is the second of those requirements which constituted the issue most keenly debated before me.

31 Attractively though Ms Williams' submissions were presented, I have not been persuaded by them. In my judgment the correct analysis is as follows.

32 First, Ms Beech lost her equity of redemption in the property by virtue of the contract for sale which ensued from the receivers' placing of the property in the auction. In this respect, they enjoyed no statutory power to sell the property free from the mortgage. Although section 101(1)(iii) confers on a mortgagee a statutory power to appoint receivers, such receivers are given no statutory power of sale.

33 The result is that Ms Beech lost her equity of redemption by virtue of the exercise of powers conferred purely by contract. By the time the receivers transferred the property to Coastal on completion as agents for GMAC, which may well have been, or been deemed to be, the exercise of a statutory power, Ms Beech had already lost her equity of redemption. It follows that, on a strict analysis of the particular facts of the present case, Ms Beech lost her equity of redemption without any state intervention.

34 I do not however rest my conclusion upon that narrow ground, not least because it would leave open at least the possibility that on only slightly different facts, such as for example a contract for sale by the receivers expressly as agents for GMAC under its statutory powers, a different result might have ensued. That the outcome of this important question should turn on such technicalities is both unattractive and, in my judgment, unrealistic. Even if GMAC had sold (both by way of contract and on completion) purely in exercise of its statutory powers, I consider that there would still have been no relevant deprivation of possessions within the meaning of A1FP.

35 My primary reason for that conclusion is that section 101 serves to implement rather than override the private bargain between mortgagor and mortgagee. As I have described, its history, going back to 1860, is that it supplies a convenient power of sale out of court to mortgagees in substitution for the parties having (as they routinely did before 1860) to spell out such a power in every legal mortgage. It is in substance a form of conveyancing shorthand designed to implement the ordinary expectations of mortgagors and mortgagees while reducing the costs and delays of conveyancing. Far from overriding the parties' private bargain, as in the case of the Consumer Credit Act 1974 reviewed in *Wilson v First County Trust Ltd* [2004] 1 AC 816, it implements and gives effect to it. It is in that respect nothing to the point that the modern facilities of photocopiers and word processors enable the parties to modern mortgages to spell out private powers which overlap or replace the convenient statutory powers in section 101.

36 Furthermore, all the statutory powers in section 101 are expressed to be subject to contrary intention. Section 101(4) provides that:

> 'This section applies only if and as far as a contrary intention is not expressed in the mortgage deed, and has effect subject to the terms of the mortgage deed and to the provisions therein contained.'

That sub-section on its own demonstrates that section 101 serves rather than overrides the parties' bargain. It is in my judgment as far removed from the concept of state intervention into private rights through overriding legislation, which lies behind A1FP, as it is possible for legislation to get. It is neither rigid, arbitrary nor discriminatory, and its effect is not only apparent on the face of section 101, but (in the present case) spelt out in terms in the mortgage itself. It therefore has none of the characteristics which led to the Court of Appeal in *Pennycook*, or for that matter Lord Nicholls (albeit without the support of his brethren) in *Wilson*, to characterise the relevant statutory provisions as giving rise to a deprivation of possessions within the meaning of A1FP.

37 Furthermore, the case that section 101 engages A1FP gains nothing from the undoubted fact that the exercise by a mortgagee of a power of sale under section 101, without first obtaining possession, will probably be a necessary and sufficient preliminary to the easy obtaining of possession by the purchaser, who will, after the sale, properly be able to characterise the mortgagor, if still in possession, as a trespasser. As was pointed out in *Ropaigealach* the continued occupation of mortgaged property by the mortgagor once the ink is dry on the mortgage is,

subject to statutory intervention or contractual restraint, at the mercy of the mortgagee, which has an immediate right to possession by virtue of its estate in the property. In the present case, as is typical with most modern residential mortgages, the mortgagor's right of occupation is better than that because the taking of possession by the mortgagee is usually expressed contractually to be dependent upon the mortgagor's prior default.

39 There is, finally, nothing in my judgment in Ms Williams' point that section 101(3) requires privately created powers of sale to be treated as if contained in the Act. That piece of unusual statutory ingenuity was no doubt designed to ensure that the provisions in section 104, designed to protect the title of purchasers from mortgagees, could not be circumvented by nit-picking arguments that a particular sale was achieved by the exercise by a contractual rather than a statutory power. It does not, however, begin to detract from the substance of the statutory power as the servant rather than the overriding master of the parties' bargain.

40 It follows in my judgment that Ms Beech's case under A1FP falls at the first of Ms Williams' hurdles. The exercise of a statutory power of sale under section 101 after a relevant default by the mortgagor is not a deprivation of possessions within the meaning of A1FP and, *a fortiori*, the exercise by receivers appointed and acting under purely contractual powers in overriding Miss Beech's equity of redemption by contracting to sell the Property cannot be either.

41 I leave for another occasion the more difficult question whether a sale in breach of the terms of a mortgage (for example in the absence of any default by the mortgagor), relied upon by the purchaser under section 104(2)(a) might engage A1FP. In such a case the sale would overreach the mortgagor's equity of redemption without any justification, as between the parties to the mortgage, and leave the mortgagor to a remedy in damages against the mortgagee. If the need for the purchaser to rely upon section 104 engaged A1FP, the question might arise whether it was justified by the public interest in affording certainty of title in real property transactions. In the present case, by contrast, it is common ground that Ms Beech was in default, so that, as between her and GMAC, the latter was entitled to sell, and the claimant therefore has no need to rely upon section 104.

42 That is, on Ms Williams' eminently sensible concessions, sufficient to determine the case against Ms Beech. None the less, for completeness, and because a higher court might take a different view as to the interpretation of A1FP on the meaning of deprivation of possessions, I shall briefly state what my conclusions would have been on the remaining issues, had Ms Beech surmounted the first hurdle of demonstrating that A1FP was engaged.

43 The second question is whether any supposed deprivation of possessions constituted by a mortgagee's sale out of court without first obtaining a court order for possession is justified in the public interest....

44 In my judgment, any deprivation of possession constituted by the exercise by a mortgagee of its powers under section 101 of the LPA after a relevant default by the mortgagor is justified in the public interest, and requires no case-by-case exercise of a proportionality discretion by the court, for the following reasons. First, it reflects the bargain habitually drawn between mortgagors and mortgagees for nearly 200 years, in which the ability of a mortgagee to sell the property offered as a security without having to go to court has been identified as a central and essential aspect of the security necessarily to be provided if substantial property-based secured lending is to be available at affordable rates of interest. That it is in the public interest that property buyers and owners should be able to obtain lending for that purpose can hardly be open to doubt, even if the loan-to-value ratios at which it has recently become possible have now become a matter of controversy.

45 Secondly, I am bound by the decision of the Court of Appeal in *Ropaigealach* (*supra*) to conclude that there was no wider policy behind section 36 of the 1970 Act than to put back what the courts had shortly before taken away, namely a discretion to stay or adjourn proceedings for possession, triggered only where the mortgagee considered it necessary or appropriate to go to court in the first place....

47 As to issues three and four, if I had concluded that the ability of a mortgagee to sell the mortgaged property without first obtaining possession, or an order of the court, both engaged and contravened A1FP, I would not have concluded that any construction of section 101, however purposive, could have led to the recognition of a statutory requirement first to seek a court order permitting sale. That would override the central purpose of section 101 and its statutory predecessors, namely to give the mortgagee the ability to realise its security over the mortgaged property without having to go to court. It would apply to all forms of mortgage by deed, regardless of the nature of the property offered as security, an enormous class of which mortgages of residential homes form only a subset. I would have accordingly had been obliged to make a declaration of incompatibility...

2. Administration of Justice Act 1973, s. 8

ADMINISTRATION OF JUSTICE ACT 1973

8. Extension of powers of court in action by mortgagee of dwelling-house.—(1) Where by a mortgage of land which consists of or includes a dwelling-house, or by any agreement between the mortgagee under such a mortgage and the mortgagor, the mortgagor is entitled or is to be permitted to pay the principal sum secured by instalments or otherwise to defer payment of it in whole or in part, but provision is also made for earlier payment in the event of any default by the mortgagor or of a demand by the mortgagee or otherwise, then for purposes of section 36 of the Administration of Justice Act 1970 (under which a court has power to delay giving a mortgagee possession of the mortgaged property so as to allow the mortgagor a reasonable time to pay any sums due under the mortgage) a court may treat as due under the mortgage on account of the principal sum secured and of interest on it only such amounts as the mortgagor would have expected to be required to pay if there had been no such provision for earlier payment.[150]

(2) A court shall not exercise by virtue of subsection (1) above the powers conferred by section 36 of the Administration of Justice Act 1970 unless it appears to the court not only that the mortgagor is likely to be able within a reasonable period to pay any amounts regarded (in accordance with subsection (1) above) as due on account of the principal sum secured, together with the interest on those amounts, but also that he is likely to be able by the end of that period to pay any further amounts that he would have expected to be required to pay by then on account of that sum and of interest on it if there had been no such provision as is referred to in subsection (1) above for earlier payment.

(3) Where subsection (1) above would apply to an action in which a mortgagee only claimed possession of the mortgaged property, and the mortgagee brings an action for foreclosure (with or without also claiming possession of the property), then section 36 of the Administration of

---

[150] Reversing the effect of *Halifax Building Society v Clark* [1973] Ch 307; but the grant of the statutory concession was unnecessary: *First Middlesbrough Trading and Mortgage Co Ltd v Cunningham* (1974) 28 P & CR 69; (1973) 37 Conv (NS) 213; (1974) 38 Conv (NS) 309. See *Centrax Trustees Ltd v Ross* [1979] 2 All ER 952; [1979] Conv 371 (F. R. Crane); *Habib Bank Ltd v Tailor* [1982] 1 WLR 1218, below; *Governor and Co of the Bank of Scotland v Grimes* [1985] QB 1179, p. 943, below; *Royal Bank of Scotland v Miller* [2002] QB 257.

Justice Act 1970 together with subsections (1) and (2) above shall apply as they would apply if it were an action in which the mortgagee only claimed possession of the mortgaged property, except that—

   (a) section 36(2)(b) shall apply only in relation to any claim for possession....

   (4) For purposes of this section the expressions 'dwelling-house', 'mortgage', 'mortgagee' and 'mortgagor' shall be construed in the same way as for the purposes of Part IV of the Administration of Justice Act 1970.

Habib Bank Ltd v Tailor
[1982] 1 WLR 1218 (CA, **Cumming-Bruce, Dunn** and **Oliver LJJ**)[151]

Tailor mortgaged his dwelling-house, 142 Walton Avenue, Harrow, to Habib Bank Ltd to secure an overdraft of up to £6,000. He covenanted to pay, on demand in writing, all moneys which might become owing to the bank. When Tailor exceeded the overdraft limit, the bank made a written demand for the whole sum owing for principal, interest and bank charges, and later began proceedings for possession. The sum owing was £7,212, and there was no likelihood of Tailor being able to repay the whole sum within a reasonable period.

The question was whether Administration of Justice Act 1973, s. 8 applied, so as to bring into operation Administration of Justice Act 1970, s. 36.

Held (reversing the County Court judge). The Acts did not apply.

Oliver LJ: The reasoning by which the judge arrived at his conclusion that the section applied was that he was referred to a decision of Goulding J in *Centrax Trustees Ltd v Ross* [1979] 2 All ER 952. It was a case in which there was a mortgage with a fixed date for repayment six months ahead of the date of the mortgage, the classic case in effect of the old type of fixed mortgage where the legal date for redemption is fixed at six months after the date of the execution of the mortgage, but there was a clear intention from other provisions in the mortgage, notably the provision for the payment of interest (which was clearly envisaged as extending beyond the period of six months limited for the repayment of the principal) which indicated that the common intention of the parties was that the mortgage would be allowed to stay out indefinitely and that the mortgagor would be entitled to defer payment of the principal sum beyond the date fixed so long as he paid interest on that principal sum....

His Lordship quoted from the judgment of Goulding J at 955 and continued:

He goes on to hold that the section applied in that case.

   That of course was a very different case from the instant case. It was a case where there was a fixed date for repayment of the principal sum and it was a case where it was quite clearly intended that the actual payment of the principal sum should be deferred beyond that fixed date. And it was a case also where, if default was made in payment of interest, the mortgage contained a provision for calling in the whole sum.

   Mr Wilmers, who appears for the bank in this case, has forcibly submitted that the reasoning of that case cannot apply here. In my judgment he is right in making that submission. I say nothing about the correctness of the decision in the *Centrax Trustees* case on the construction of the

---

[151] [1983] Conv 80 (P. H. Kenny); [1982] All ER Rev 177 (P. J. Clarke); [1984] Conv 91 (S. Tromans).

section. It is indeed difficult, I think, to escape from the conclusion that the section did apply to that case, even though I, for myself, rather question whether it was intended by the legislature to do so. But the instant case is really quite a different case. As Mr Wilmers pointed out, and indeed as was pointed out by Goulding J in the *Centrax Trustees* case, there are two necessary conditions for the application of the section: first, either the mortgage itself or some agreement made under it must have the effect that—I will quote only the relevant words—'the mortgagor...is to be permitted...otherwise to defer payment of' the principal sum 'in whole or in part'; secondly, provision must be made in the mortgage or agreement 'for earlier payment in the event of any default by the mortgagor or of a demand by the mortgagee or otherwise.' Mr Wilmers's first submission is that there is no permission to defer payment. As he points out, this is a simple case of a bank mortgage to secure an overdraft. It is quite clear on the authorities that in these circumstances the money is not capable of being sued for by the bank until demand has been made. Indeed, the mortgage itself so provides, because it is to secure the moneys covenanted to be paid and the moneys are covenanted to be paid on demand having been made in writing. This nowhere more clearly appears than from *Lloyds Bank Ltd v Margolis* [1954] 1 WLR 644. I think it is only necessary to read briefly from the judgment of Upjohn J at 649....

When one looks at the charge in the instant case, one asks immediately: 'Where is the agreement to be found that the mortgagor is to be permitted otherwise to defer payment of the principal?' because, by definition, the principal does not become due, and cannot be sued for by the bank, until a written demand has been made. Deferment, I think, involves the deferment of payment after it has become due, and quite clearly in this case there appears to me to be no provision, either in the agreement between the parties or in the mortgage itself, by which, on any realistic construction, it can be said that payment by the customer was to be 'deferred,' or that the customer was permitted to 'defer' payment. Mr Cutting has in fact submitted that every case where the principal money does not become payable immediately the mortgage is executed is a case where the mortgagor is entitled to defer payment. That is a submission which I find is impossible to accept.

It seems to me that the defendant's case on the application of section 8 fails at that point, but it also fails, I think, on the other condition, too, because, as Mr Wilmers pointed out, the section requires that provision must be made for earlier payment, and one has to ask oneself: 'Earlier than what?' In the instant case the payment was not due until the demand was made, and there is no provision for any payment earlier than that. It is the demand itself which makes the payment due.

For both those reasons, it seems to me that this is clearly a case where section 8 cannot apply to this mortgage, and that really concludes the case. I think it unnecessary to elaborate the matter further. If there had been some reasonable prospect of the defendant repaying the whole of the principal sum, then no doubt it would have been appropriate for the judge to have remitted the matter back to the registrar for a determination of whether he should exercise his power under section 36(2) of the Act of 1970 to adjourn the proceedings or to postpone the date for the delivery of possession, but that, as Mr Cutting accepts, does not arise. Section 8 does not apply. There is then no further room for the operation of the discretion under section 36, and accordingly in my judgment the decision of the judge must be reversed and the decision of the deputy registrar restored. I would therefore allow the appeal.

In **Governor and Company of the Bank of Scotland v Grimes** [1985] QB 1179, the defendants borrowed from the plaintiffs £15,015 in order to purchase 26 Guppy

Street, Swindon. The loan was secured by an endowment mortgage[152] which provided for repayment of the principal sum at the end of 25 years, with interest payable by monthly instalments, and for the principal sum and accrued interest to be payable immediately in the case of default.

The defendants defaulted on the payments of interest, and the endowment policy lapsed. On the bank's summons for the payment of interest due and an order for possession, the County Court judge held that there was no deferred repayment of capital within section 8 of the Administration of Justice Act 1973, and that he could not exercise his discretion to postpone possession under section 36 of the 1970 Act.

In allowing the appeal, Sir John ARNOLD P said at 1187:

In certain circumstances the provisions of section 36 are amended and controlled by section 8 of the Administration of Justice Act 1973, and the principal issue in this case is whether that amendment and control extends to the present case.

His Lordship read section 8 and continued:

What that effects in substance is an omission of the obligation for expedited payment which is to be found in the default clause for the purpose of the application of section 36 as a matter of the discretion of the court.

We have considered, and have been assisted by counsel, in the task of giving some meaning to the words 'or is to be permitted' following the word 'entitled' in that subsection, but we have been wholly unable to come to any conclusion as to any possible meaning of that phrase. It must have been included for some purpose, but what that purpose is, for my part at least, I find myself wholly unable to determine. If it is something which is short of a contractual obligation or a contractual right which is there intended to be referred to, the words 'is to be' are peculiarly unsuitable. If it is something distinct from being entitled, then what it is is wholly obscure. But I do not think much turns on that in the present case; it is the presence of so impenetrable a phrase which makes one think that one has to be very careful in construing this section to feel oneself free to give effect to the general tenor of the language in a purposive way so as to make it fit in with the general intention which is evidently exhibited and the context of section 36 in the Administration of Justice Act 1970 in which it has to be read rather than to be bound by a literal meaning of the language used which would not have the purposive effect which seems to be desired. There is no doubt whatever that section 36 of the Act of 1970 applies to such a case as this. It is not made any the less to apply because this is a case in which there is a fixed period for payment of the mortgage principal as a whole rather than an instalment arrangement. One might expect that in a suitable case in which that was the situation, for the purpose of effecting the mitigation which was evidently intended by section 8 of the Administration of Justice Act 1973, the two situations would be equated.

The construction which appealed to the judge was that a deferred payment was a payment which the payer was required to make under one provision of the bargain, but which he was

---

[152] In an endowment mortgage, an endowment assurance policy is taken out at the same time as the money is borrowed; only interest payments are made by the mortgagor during the life of the mortgage, the outstanding debt being repaid when the policy matures. Cf. an instalment or repayment mortgage, where the debt is paid off by monthly instalments at a rate which covers payment of interest and repayment of capital, so that the capital is paid off over an agreed period of time, for example 25 years.

entitled to have deferred under another provision of the bargain, so that, unless there was to be found an obligation to make the payment in question at some time earlier than the date of postponement of that obligation to be found in the relevant other provisions, section 8 of the Administration of Justice 1973 could not be made to apply....

Habib Bank Ltd v Tailor [1982] 1 WLR 1218 [p. 942, above] was a case in which what was before the court was a charge to secure an ordinary banking overdraft so that the subject matter of the debt was one which was due immediately upon the making of an unconditional demand. That is a rather different case, at least socially, in regard to the purpose of this legislation, from the present case where what is primarily in question is a mortgage of a fixed sum for a fixed term. I do not find anything in Habib Bank Ltd v Tailor which prevents this court giving to the conception of 'deferred payment' a definition which includes any case in which there is a stated period before the end of which payment does not require to be made which extends into a defined future, and it seems to me that that condition is satisfied by the language of the agreement which, in its extended interpretation, which is not in dispute, is imported by the language 'period of loan 25 years.' It seems to be, therefore, that it can without doing violence to the language of the section and by way of giving effect and purpose to this section, be construed in that way so that there is, thus looked at, a provision here for deferred payment to be found in the agreement. There is no question but that there is also a provision for earlier payment in the event of any default, because that is to be found in clause 4 of the agreement. It seems to me, therefore, that this is a case in which section 8 of the Administration of Justice Act 1973 applies to modify and control the language of section 36 of the Administration of Justice Act 1970 and for that reason I would allow the appeal.

GRIFFITHS LJ said at 1190:

It seems to me that it would be highly improbable that Parliament would intend such relief to apply only to instalment mortgages taken out with a building society and not to apply to the alternative and increasingly popular form of finance by loan from a bank, backed by an endowment policy. I am satisfied, for the reasons given by Sir John Arnold P that the wording 'or otherwise to defer payment of it in whole or in part' are deliberately inserted to cover this second type of mortgage transaction where there is no obligation to repay the capital until the end of the term of the loan.[153]

3. Reasonable period

In **Cheltenham and Gloucester Building Society v Norgan** [1996] 1 WLR 343,[154] the Court of Appeal set out the considerations which are likely to be relevant when a reasonable period has to be established for the purposes of section 36 of the Administration of Justice Act 1970. WAITE LJ said at 345:

The rights of mortgagees to take possession of a dwelling house, whether by virtue of their legal estate in the land or in fulfilment of some express term of the mortgage operating in the event of default or arrears, have for many years been moderated by statutory powers giving

---

[153] *Royal Bank of Scotland plc v Miller* [2002] QB 255 (mortgage repayable at end of fixed period was a provision for deferred payment).

[154] (1996) 146 NLJ 252 (H. W. Wilkinson); [1996] Conv 118 (M. P. Thompson); (1996) 112 LQR 553 (J. Morgan); [1996] All ER Rev 260 (P. J. Clarke); *Household Mortgage Corporation plc v Pringle* (1998) 30 HLR 250 (duration of mortgage 25 years with 17 years outstanding).

the court discretion to suspend possession orders on appropriate terms. The mortgage to which this appeal relates is a term mortgage—that is to say a charge under which no instalments of capital are repayable and the whole principal debt remains outstanding until a specified date in the future, with the mortgagor being liable in the meantime for instalments of interest only. The appellant mortgagor fell into arrears with her interest payments. Thereupon, under the terms of the mortgage, the whole mortgage debt became immediately repayable. The mortgagee sought and obtained a possession order, execution of which was suspended by a series of orders on terms as to payment of current interest instalments and payment-off of arrears with which the mortgagor made strenuous efforts to comply, but without success, so that she remained in default, both under the terms of the mortgage and the terms of the suspension....

In the present plight of the housing market possession cases play a major part in the case-load for the county courts. That is particularly true of the district judges, who deal with those cases in such numbers that they develop a 'feel' for them and have achieved an excellent disposal record. It is not surprising that they have found it convenient to adopt a relatively short period of years as the rough rule of thumb which aids a just determination of the 'reasonable period' for the purposes of section 36 of the Act of 1970 and section 8 of the Act of 1973. Nevertheless, although I would not go quite so far with Mr Croally as to say it should be an 'assumption,' it does seem to me that the logic and spirit of the legislation require, especially in cases where the parties are proceeding under arrangements such as those reflection in the CML statement,[155] that the court should take as its starting point the full term of the mortgage and pose at the outset the question: 'Would it be possible for the mortgagor to maintain payment-off of the arrears by instalments over that period?'

EVANS LJ said at 357:

In conclusion, a practical summary of our judgments may be helpful in future cases. Drawing on the above and on the judgment of Waite LJ, the following considerations are likely to be relevant when a 'reasonable period' has to be established for the purposes of section 36 of the Act of 1970. (a) How much can the borrower reasonably afford to pay, both now and in the future? (b) If the borrower has a temporary difficulty in meeting his obligations, how long is the difficulty likely to last? (c) What was the reason for the arrears which have accumulated? (d) How much remains of the original term? (e) What are the relevant contractual terms, and what type of mortgage is it, i.e. when is the principal due to be repaid? (f) Is it a case where the court should exercise its power to disregard accelerated payment provisions (section 8 of the Act of 1973)? (g) Is it reasonable to expect the lender, in the circumstances of the particular case, to recoup the arrears of interest (1) over the whole of the original term, or (2) within a shorter period, or even (3) within a longer period, i.e. by extending the repayment period? Is it reasonable to expect the lender to capitalise the interest or not? (h) Are there any reasons affecting the security which should influence the length of the period for payment? In the light of the answers to the above, the court can proceed to exercise its overall discretion, taking account also of any further factors which may arise in the particular case.

[155] Council of Mortgage Lenders Statement of Current Practice (February 1995) dealing with 'Alleviating Arrears Problems'. Under this lenders can help borrowers by lengthening the term of a repayment loan; changing from an endowment mortgage to a repayment or interest-only mortgage; deferment of part of the interest where there is a temporary shortfall of income; capitalisation of interest; and ensuring that borrowers are aware of social security benefits.

In **Bristol and West Building Society v Ellis** (1996) 73 P & CR 158,[156] AULD LJ said at 161:

In the absence of unusual circumstances and where discharge of all arrears by periodic payments is proposed, the outstanding period of the mortgage, whether term or repayment, is the starting point in determining the reasonableness of the period for payment of sums due under a mortgage. See *Cheltenham & Gloucester Building Society v Norgan.*

However, that convenient starting point is not available to a mortgagor who cannot discharge the arrears by periodic payments and whose only prospect of repaying the entire mortgage loan and accrued and accruing interest is from the sale of the property. In such a case the only general guidance is that the reasonableness of the period is a matter for the court in the circumstances of the case. See *Royal Trust Co of Canada v Markham* [1975] 1 WLR 1416 and *National & Provincial Building Society v Lloyd* [1996] 1 All ER 630.

The prospect of settling the mortgage debt, including arrears of principal and/or interest, by sale of the property raises a number of questions on the reasonableness of any period which a court may consider allowing for the purpose.

The critical matters are, of course, the adequacy of the property as a security for the debt and the length of the period necessary to achieve a sale. There should be evidence, or at least some informal material (see *Cheltenham & Gloucester Building Society v Grant* (1994) 26 HLR 703), before the court of the likelihood of a sale the proceeds of which will be discharge of the debt and of the period within which such a sale is likely to be achieved. If the court is satisfied on both counts and that the necessary period for sale is reasonable, it should, if it decides to suspend the order for possession, identify the period in its order.

The instinct of the courts in determining a reasonable period for this purpose seems to have been to adopt the common law approach before the 1970 Act, see *Birmingham Citizens Permanent Building Society v Caunt* [1962] Ch 883 [p. 931, above], of fixing on a 'short' period. See *Target Home Loans Ltd v Clothier* [1994] 1 All ER 439. However, in *Markham* neither the county court judge nor the Court of Appeal considered what, in the circumstances of that case, might have been a reasonable period. The defendants had called no evidence and the judge had not fixed any period in his order. The Court of Appeal contented itself with ruling that he should have fixed a period, but only after hearing evidence on the matter. In *Clothier,* the Court of Appeal, on the strength of evidence before it, but not before the county court judge, made an order for possession, suspending it for three months.

In *Lloyd*, Neill LJ, with whom Bennet J agreed, after reviewing the above authorities, held that the word 'reasonable' in the statute should not necessarily be equated with 'short'; what was a reasonable period was 'a question for the court in the individual case'. He said:

'... if there were, in a hypothetical case, clear evidence that the completion of the sale of a property, perhaps by piecemeal disposal, could take place in six or nine months or even a year, I see no reason why a court could not come to the conclusion in the exercise of its discretion under the two sections that, to use the words of the section "the mortgagor [was] likely to be able within a reasonable period to pay any sums due under the mortgage". The question of a "reasonable period" would be a question for the court in the individual case'.[157]

---

[156] [1998] Conv 125 (M. P. Thompson).

[157] *National Home Loans Corp plc v Yaxley* (1997) 73 P & CR D41 (hope of successful litigation by mortgagor against mortgagee for breach of duty not relevant to discharge of liability to pay); (1997) 147 NLJ 459 (N. Madge).

For postponement to enable sale to take place, see *National & Provincial Building Society v Lloyd* [1996] 1 All ER 630 (sale by part disposals). For retention by mortgagor while mortgagee sells, see

4. Civil Procedure Rules: Pre-Action Protocol

A mortgagee's exercise of his right to possession through possession proceedings can also be regulated by the Civil Procedure Rules. A new Pre-Action Protocol was introduced on 19 November 2008, which applies to all residential mortgages and is designed to provide further protection to the mortgagor.

Pre-Action Protocol for Possession Claims based on Mortgage or Home Purchase Plan Arrears in Respect of Residential Property[158]

1 Preamble

1.1 This Protocol describes the behaviour the court will normally expect of the parties prior to the start of a possession claim...

1.2 This Protocol does not alter the parties' rights and obligations.

1.3 It is in the interests of the parties that mortgage payments or payments under home purchase plans are made promptly and that difficulties are resolved wherever possible without court proceedings. However in some cases an order for possession may be in the interest of both the lender and the borrower.

2 Aims

2.1 The aims of this Protocol are to –

(1) ensure that a lender or home purchase plan provider (in this Protocol collectively referred to as 'the lender') and a borrower or home purchase plan customer (in this Protocol collectively referred to as 'the borrower') act fairly and reasonably with each other in resolving any matter concerning mortgage or home purchase plan arrears; and

(2) encourage more pre-action contact between the lender and the borrower in an effort to seek agreement between the parties, and where this cannot be reached, to enable efficient use of the court's time and resources.

5 Initial contact and provision of information

5.2 The parties should take all reasonable steps to discuss with each other, or their representatives, the cause of the arrears, the borrower's financial circumstances and proposals for repayment of the arrears (see 7.1). For example, parties should consider whether the causes of

---

Target Homes Loans Ltd v Clothier [1994] 1 All ER 439 (three months' postponement; mortgagor had better prospect of achieving earlier sale if in possession); [1993] Conv 62 (J. Martin); *Cheltenham & Gloucester plc v Booker* (1996) 73 P & CR 412 at 415 per Millett LJ (possible if mortgagor's presence will not depress sale price, and mortgagor will complete sale and give up possession to purchaser on completion).

[158] (2009) 106(2) LSG 18 (C. Atkinson), 24 (P. Jolly); [2008] Conv. 474 (M. Dixon, discussing the draft Protocol). The court may take into account compliance or non-compliance with an applicable protocol when giving directions for the management of proceedings (see CPR rr.3.1(4), (5), 3.9(e)) and when making orders for costs (see CPR r. 44.3(5)(a)).

the arrears are temporary or long term and whether the borrower may be able to pay the arrears in a reasonable time.

5.3 The lender should advise the borrower to make early contact with the housing department of the borrower's Local Authority and, should, where necessary, refer the borrower to appropriate sources of independent debt advice.

5.4 The lender should consider a reasonable request from the borrower to change the date of regular payment (within the same payment period) or the method by which payment is made. The lender should either agree to such a request or, where it refuses such a request, it should, within a reasonable period of time, give the borrower a written explanation of its reasons for the refusal.

5.5 The lender should respond promptly to any proposal for payment made by the borrower. If the lender does not agree to such a proposal it should give reasons in writing to the borrower within 10 business days of the proposal.

5.6 If the lender submits a proposal for payment, the borrower should be given a reasonable period of time in which to consider such proposals. The lender should set out the proposal in sufficient detail to enable the borrower to understand the implications of the proposal.

5.7 If the borrower fails to comply with an agreement, the lender should warn the borrower, by giving the borrower 15 business days notice in writing, of its intention to start a possession claim unless the borrower remedies the breach in the agreement.

6 Postponing the start of a possession claim

6.1 A lender should consider not starting a possession claim for mortgage arrears where the borrower can demonstrate to the lender that the borrower has –

(1) submitted a claim to an insurer under a mortgage payment protection policy and has provided all the evidence required to process a claim;

(2) a reasonable expectation of eligibility for payment from the insurer; and

(3) an ability to pay a mortgage instalment not covered by the insurance.

6.2 If a borrower can demonstrate that reasonable steps have been or will be taken to market the property at an appropriate price in accordance with reasonable professional advice, the lender should consider postponing starting a possession claim. The borrower must continue to take all reasonable steps actively to market the property where the lender has agreed to postpone starting a possession claim.

7 Alternative dispute resolution

7.1 The court takes the view that starting a possession claim is usually a last resort and that such a claim should not normally be started when a settlement is still actively being explored. Discussion between the parties may include options such as:

(1) extending the term of the mortgage;

(2) changing the type of a mortgage;

(3) deferring payment of interest due under the mortgage; or

(4) capitalising the arrears.

QUESTIONS

1. How would you have decided *Quennell v Maltby* [1979] 1 WLR 318, p. 933, above?

2. Should possession be no longer a *right* of the mortgagee but only a *remedy* available in particular defined circumstances? See [2008] Conv 474 at 480 (M. Dixon).

C. POWERS TO GRANT AND ACCEPT
SURRENDERS OF LEASES

LAW OF PROPERTY ACT 1925

99. Leasing powers of mortgagor and mortgagee in possession.—p. 926, above.

100. Powers of mortgagor and mortgagee in possession to accept surrenders of leases.— p. 927, above.

D. SALE, INSURANCE, APPOINTMENT OF RECEIVER,
CUTTING AND SELLING OF TIMBER

LAW OF PROPERTY ACT 1925

101. Powers incident to estate or interest of mortgagee.—(1) A mortgagee, where the mortgage is made by deed, shall, by virtue of this Act, have the following powers, to the like extent as if they had been in terms conferred by the mortgage deed, but not further (namely):—

(i) A power, when the mortgage money has become due,[159] to sell, or to concur with any other person in selling, the mortgaged property, or any part thereof, either subject to prior charges or not,[160] and either together or in lots, by public auction or by private contract, subject to such conditions respecting title, or evidence of title, or other matter, as the mortgagee thinks fit, with power to vary any contract for sale, and to buy in at an auction, or to rescind any contract for sale, and to re-sell, without being answerable for any loss occasioned thereby; and

(ii) A power, at any time after the date of the mortgage deed, to insure[161] and keep insured against loss or damage by fire any building, or any effects or property of an insurable nature, whether affixed to the freehold or not, being or forming part of

---

[159] I.e., as soon as the contractual date for redemption has passed. If the mortgage money is payable by instalments the power of sale arises as soon as any instalment is in arrear: *Payne v Cardiff RDC* [1932] 1 KB 241; cf. *Twentieth Century Banking Corpn Ltd v Wilkinson* [1977] Ch 99 (where interest was in arrear but capital not yet due: held no power of sale). See also AJA 1973, s. 8, p. 941, above.

[160] *Kaolim Private Ltd v United Overseas Land Ltd* [1983] 1 WLR 472 at 476, per Lord Brightman.

[161] *Colonial Mutual General Insurance Co Ltd v ANZ Banking Group (New Zealand) Ltd* [1995] 1 WLR 1140. For amount and application of insurance money, see LPA 1925, s. 108.

the property which or an estate or interest wherein is mortgaged, and the premiums paid for any such insurance shall be a charge on the mortgaged property or estate or interest, in addition to the mortgage money, and with the same priority, and with interest at the same rate, as the mortgage money; and

(iii) A power, when the mortgage money has become due, to appoint a receiver of the income of the mortgaged property, or any part thereof; or, if the mortgaged property consists of an interest in income, or of a rentcharge or an annual or other periodical sum, a receiver of that property or any part thereof; and

(iv) A power, while the mortgagee is in possession, to cut and sell timber and other trees ripe for cutting, and not planted or left standing for shelter or ornament, or to contract for any such cutting and sale, to be completed within any time not exceeding twelve months from the making of the contract.

(1A) Subsection (1)(i) is subject to section 21 of the Commonhold and Leasehold Reform Act 2002 (no disposition of part-units).[162]

(3) The provisions of this Act relating to the foregoing powers, comprised either in this section, or in any other section regulating the exercise of those powers, may be varied or extended by the mortgage deed, and, as so varied and extended, shall, as far as may be, operate in the like manner and with all the like incidents, effects, and consequences, as if such variations or extensions were contained in this Act.

(4) This section applies only if and as far as a contrary intention is not expressed in the mortgage deed, and has effect subject to the terms of the mortgage deed and to the provisions therein contained.

(i) Sale[163]

(a) Legal mortgagee

LAW OF PROPERTY ACT 1925

101. Powers incident to estate or interest of mortgage.—(1) (i) p. 950, above.

103. Regulation of exercise of power of sale.—A mortgagee shall not exercise the power of sale conferred by this Act unless and until—

(i) Notice requiring payment of the mortgage money has been served on the mortgagor or one of two or more mortgagors, and default has been made in payment of the mortgage money, or of part thereof, for three months after such service; or

(ii) Some interest under the mortgage is in arrear and unpaid for two months after becoming due; or

---

[162] Inserted by CLRA 2002, Sch. 5, para. 2. See p. 318, above.

[163] C & B, pp. 769–775; Gray, paras 6.4.41–6.4.81; M & W paras 25.013–25.023; MM, pp. 504–506; Smith, pp. 581–589; Cousins, paras 16.53–16.80; Fisher and Lightwood, chap. 30; (1976) 73 LSG 92, 654; (1977) 74 LSG 493 (H. E. Markson). For a detailed analysis of the mortgagee's power of sale, see (1995) 46 NILQ 182 (P. Devonshire); and *Silven Properties v Royal Bank of Scotland plc* [2004] 1 WLR 997 at [13]–[20], p. 962, below, per Lightman J. See also *Horsham Properties Group Ltd v Clark* [2009] 1 P & CR 8, p. 937, above (exercise of power of sale without first obtaining a court order for possession, or an order for sale, did not infringe the mortgagor's rights under ECHR).

(iii) There has been a breach of some provision contained in the mortgage deed or in this Act, or in an enactment replaced by this Act, and on the part of the mortgagor, or of some person concurring in making the mortgage, to be observed or performed, other than and besides a covenant for payment of the mortgage money or interest thereon.

104. Conveyance on sale.—(1) A mortgagee exercising the power of sale conferred by this Act shall have power, by deed, to convey the property sold, for such estate and interest therein as he is by this Act authorised to sell or convey or may be the subject of the mortgage, freed from all estates, interests, and rights to which the mortgage has priority, but subject to all estates, interests, and rights which have priority to the mortgage.[164]

(2) Where a conveyance is made in exercise of the power of sale conferred by this Act, or any enactment replaced by this Act, the title of the purchaser shall not be impeachable on the ground—

(a) that no case had arisen to authorise the sale; or

(b) that due notice was not given; or

(c) where the mortgage is made after the commencement of this Act, that leave of the court, when so required, was not obtained,[165] or

(d) whether the mortgage was made before or after such commencement, that the power was otherwise improperly or irregularly exercised;

and a purchaser is not, either before or on conveyance, concerned to see or inquire whether a case has arisen to authorise the sale, or due notice has been given, or the power is otherwise properly and regularly exercised;[166] but any person damnified by an unauthorised, or improper, or irregular exercise of the power shall have his remedy in damages against the person exercising the power.

(3) A conveyance on sale by a mortgagee, made after the commencement of this Act, shall be deemed to have been made in exercise of the power of sale conferred by this Act unless a contrary intention appears.

105. Application of proceeds of sale.—The money which is received by the mortgagee, arising from the sale, after discharge of prior incumbrances to which the sale is not made subject, if any, or after payment into court under this Act of a sum to meet any prior incumbrance, shall be held by him in trust to be applied by him, first, in payment of all costs, charges, and expenses properly incurred by him as incident to the sale or any attempted sale, or otherwise; and secondly, in discharge of the mortgage money, interest, and costs, and other money, if any, due under the

---

[164] Cf. LPA 1925, s. 2(1)(iii), p. 548, above.

[165] See LPA 1925, s. 110, as amended by Insolvency Act 1985, s. 222, Sch. 10, Part III (mortgagor a bankrupt and mortgage executed after 1925); (1944) 5 Conv YB, pp. 70–71.

[166] *Bailey v Barnes* [1894] 1 Ch 25 at 30, per Stirling J. If, however, he 'becomes aware…of any facts showing that the power of sale is not exercisable, or that there is some impropriety in the sale, then, in my judgment, he gets no good title on taking the conveyance'; *Lord Waring v London and Manchester Assurance Co Ltd* [1935] Ch 310 at 318, per Crossman J; *Jenkins v Jones* (1860) 2 Giff 99; *Selwyn v Garfit* (1888) 38 ChD 273; *Price Bros (Somerford) Ltd v J Kelly Homes (Stoke-on-Trent) Ltd* [1975] 1 WLR 1512; *Northern Developments (Holdings) Ltd v UDT Securities Ltd* [1976] 1 WLR 1230; *Forsyth v Blundell* (1973) 129 CLR 477; *Pasquarella v National Australia Finance Ltd* [1987] 1 NZLR 312; [1988] Conv 317; [1989] Conv 412 (S. Robinson); *Corbett v Halifax Building Society* [2003] 1 WLR 964.

mortgage; and the residue of the money so received shall be paid to the person entitled to the mortgaged property,[167] or authorised to give receipts for the proceeds of the sale thereof.

106. Provisions as to exercise of power of sale.—(1) The power of sale conferred by this Act may be exercised by any person for the time being entitled to receive and give a discharge for the mortgage money.

(2) The power of sale conferred by this Act does not affect the right of foreclosure.

(4) At any time after the power of sale conferred by this Act has become exercisable, the person entitled to exercise the power may demand and recover from any person, other than a person having in the mortgaged property an estate, interest, or right in priority to the mortgage, all the deeds and documents relating to the property, or to the title thereto, which a purchaser under the power of sale would be entitled to demand and recover from him.[168]

88. Realisation of freehold mortgages.—(1) Where an estate in fee simple has been mortgaged by the creation of a term of years absolute limited thereout or by a charge by way of legal mortgage and the mortgagee sells under his statutory or express power of sale—

(a) the conveyance by him shall operate to vest in the purchaser the fee simple in the land conveyed subject to any legal mortgage having priority to the mortgage in right of which the sale is made and to any money thereby secured, and thereupon;

(b) the mortgage term or the charge by way of legal mortgage and any subsequent mortgage term or charges shall merge or be extinguished as respects the land conveyed;

and such conveyance may, as respects the fee simple, be made in the name of the estate owner in whom it is vested.

89. Realisation of leasehold mortgages.—(1) Where a term of years absolute has been mortgaged by the creation of another term of years absolute limited thereout or by a charge by way of legal mortgage and the mortgagee sells under his statutory or express power of sale,—

(a) the conveyance by him shall operate to convey to the purchaser not only the mortgage term, if any, but also (unless expressly excepted with the leave of the court)[169] the leasehold reversion affected by the mortgage, subject to any legal mortgage having priority to the mortgage in right of which the sale is made and to any money thereby secured, and thereupon;

---

[167] M & W point out (para. 25.010, n. 138) that these words literally refer to the purchaser; 'but plainly the phrase must be read as "to the person who immediately before the sale was entitled to the mortgaged property"' and this of course includes other mortgagees. But if the rights of the mortgagor and other encumbrances have become extinguished by lapse of time (Limitation Act 1980, s. 16, p. 260, above) the mortgagee may keep all the purchase money himself: *Young v Clarey* [1948], Ch 191. See also *Halifax Building Society v Thomas* [1996] Ch 217 (mortgagee to pay surplus proceeds of sale to Crown Prosecution Service which had obtained a confiscation order in respect of fraudulent mortgagor's interest in sale proceeds).

[168] In unregistered land, the first mortgagee is entitled also to the custody of the title deeds: LPA 1925, ss. 85(1), 86(1), p. 856, above; on redemption by the mortgagor, the mortgagee must deliver the deeds to him, unless he has notice of a later mortgage, when he must deliver them to the mortgagee next in order of priority of whom he has notice. In this context, registration is not notice: LPA 1925, s. 96(2) as amended by LP(A)A 1926, Sch. In registered land there are no longer documents of title: the mortgagee's title, and his practical ability to exercise his power of sale, depends upon his registration of the charge: p. 859, above.

[169] This may be done to prevent the purchaser becoming liable upon the covenants in the lease.

(b) the mortgage term, or the charge by way of legal mortgage and any subsequent
mortgage term or charge, shall merge in such leasehold reversion or be extinguished
unless excepted as aforesaid;

and such conveyance may, as respects the leasehold reversion, be made in the name of the estate
owner in whom it is vested.

Where a licence to assign is required on a sale by a mortgagee, such licence shall not be
unreasonably refused.

2. Conveyances overreaching certain equitable interests and powers.—(1)(iii): p. 548,
above.

1. Effect of mortgagee's contract to sell

In **Lord Waring v London and Manchester Assurance Co Ltd** [1935] Ch 310, the
mortgagee had contracted to sell the property for £186,000. The mortgagor, who was
negotiating elsewhere for a loan (on a mortgage of the property) of £200,000, sought
an injunction to stop the sale.

CROSSMAN J refused, and said at 317:

If, before the date of the contract, the plaintiff had tendered the principal with interest and
costs, or had paid it into Court in proceedings, then, if the company had continued to take
steps to enter into a contract for sale, or had purported to do so, the plaintiff would, in my
opinion, have been entitled to an injunction restraining it from doing so. After a contract has
been entered into, however, it is, in my judgment, perfectly clear (subject to what has been said
to me today) that the mortgagee (in the present case, the company) can be restrained from
completing only on the ground that he has not acted in good faith and that the sale is therefore
liable to be set aside. Counsel for the plaintiff, who has argued the case most excellently,
submitted that, notwithstanding that the company exercised its power of sale by entering into
the contract, the plaintiff's equity of redemption has not been extinguished, as there has been
no completion by conveyance, and that, pending completion, the plaintiff is still entitled to
redeem, that is, to have the property reconveyed to him on payment of principal, interest, and
costs. Counsel is relying, to some extent, on the provisions of the Law of Property Act 1925,
which creates a statutory power of sale. In my judgment, section 101 of that Act, which gives
to a mortgagee power to sell the mortgaged property, is perfectly clear, and means that the
mortgagee has power to sell out and out, by private contract or by auction, and subsequently
to complete by conveyance; and the power to sell is, I think, a power by selling to bind the mortgagor. If that were not so, the extraordinary result would follow that every purchaser from a
mortgagee would, in effect, be getting a conditional contract liable at any time to be set aside
by the mortgagor's coming in and paying the principal, interest and costs. Such a result would
make it impossible for a mortgagee, in the ordinary course of events, to sell unless he was in
a position to promise that completion should take place immediately or on the day after the
contract, and there would have to be a rush for completion in order to defeat a possible claim
by the mortgagor.

It seems to me impossible seriously to suggest that the mortgagor's equity of redemption
remains in force pending completion of the sale by conveyance.[170]

---

[170] Followed in *Property and Bloodstock Ltd v Emerton* [1968] Ch 94; *National and Provincial
Building Society v Ahmed* [1995] 2 EGLR 127; *Corbett v Halifax Building Society* [2003] 1 WLR 964. For

2. Duty of mortgagee to obtain the true market value, or the best price reasonably obtainable

Parker Tweedale v Dunbar Bank plc[171]
[1991] Ch 12 (CA, **Purchas and Nourse LJJ** and **Sir Michael Kerr**)

The plaintiff and his wife purchased Ditchford Hill Farm, Fosseway, Moreton-in-Marsh, with the aid of a mortgage from Dunbar Bank Plc. The wife was sole legal owner and mortgagor; the plaintiff had a beneficial interest in the farm and occupied it as a licensee. In 1988 the mortgagee, in the exercise of its power of sale under the mortgage, sold the farm, with the wife's consent, for £575,000. It had been valued by estate agents at between £380,000 and £450,000. A week later it was resold to another developer for £700,000.

The plaintiff brought an action against the Bank claiming that it was in breach of a duty to take reasonable care to obtain a proper price.

Held. The plaintiff failed:

(i)   The Bank did not owe him a duty of care.

(ii) On the evidence £575,000 was a proper price.

Nourse LJ: In this case a husband claims that a mortgagee, in exercising its power of sale over joint property of which his wife was the sole legal owner and mortgagor, owed him an independent duty to take reasonable care to obtain a proper price. He also claims that the mortgagee did not take reasonable care and did not obtain a proper price. Peter Gibson J decided both issues in favour of the mortgagee and the husband has now appealed to this court....

It was settled by the decision of this court in *Cuckmere Brick Co Ltd v Mutual Finance Ltd* [1971] Ch 949 that a mortgagee, although he may exercise his power of sale at any time of his own choice, owes the mortgagor a duty to take reasonable care to obtain a proper price for the mortgaged property at that time. But there is no support, either in the authorities or on principle, for the proposition that where the mortgagor is a trustee, even a bare trustee, of the mortgaged property, a like duty is owed to a beneficiary under the trust of whose interest the mortgagee has notice.

In seeking to support that proposition the plaintiff relied on the decision of this court in *Jarrett v Barclays Bank Ltd* [1947] Ch 187. For reasons which were stated by Peter Gibson J and need not be repeated here, that case does not assist him. He also relied on the following passage in the judgment of Salmon LJ in *Cuckmere Brick Co Ltd v Mutual Finance Ltd* [1971] Ch 949, 966.

---

the effect of a contract of sale by the mortgagor upon the mortgagee's powers, see *Duke v Robson* [1973] 1 WLR 267.

[171] [1990] Conv 431 (L. Bentley). HL Appellate Committee refused leave to appeal: [1991] Ch 12 at 25. In *Bishop v Bonham* [1988] 1 WLR 742, Slade LJ said at 752: 'The duty of care imposed on a selling mortgagee, by what I may call the *Cuckmere* principle, is essentially in the nature of an obligation implied by law, and as such is, in my judgment, undoubtedly capable of being excluded by agreement. The exclusion clause must be construed strictly'; *Mercantile Credit Co v Clarke* (1995) 71 P & CR D18 (agreement of mortgagor to a lower sale price); *Raja Lloyds v TSB Bank plc* (2001) 82 P & CR 191 (the duty being in equity, mortgagor's claim statute barred after six years under Limitation Act 1980, s. 8); [2001] Conv 421 (L. McMurtry).

'Approaching the matter first of all on principle, it is to be observed that if the sale yields a surplus over the amount owed under the mortgage, the mortgagee holds this surplus in trust for the mort-gagor. If the sale shows a deficiency, the mortgagor has to make it good out of his own pocket. The mortgagor is vitally affected by the result of the sale but its preparation and conduct is left entirely in the hands of the mortgagee. The proximity between them could scarcely be closer. Surely they are "neighbours." Given that the power of sale is for the benefit of the mortgagee and that he is entitled to choose the moment to sell which suits him[172] it would be strange indeed if he were under no legal obligation to take reasonable care to obtain what I call the true market value at the date of the sale.'

This reference to 'neighbours' has enabled the plaintiff to argue that the duty is owed to all those who are within the neighbourhood principle; i.e., to adapt the words of Lord Atkin,[173] to all persons who are so closely and directly affected by the sale that the mortgagee ought reasonably to have them in contemplation as being so affected when he is directing his mind to the sale. Further support for the application of the neighbourhood principle in this context can be gained from the judgment of Lord Denning MR in *Standard Chartered Bank Ltd v Walker* [1982] 1 WLR 1410, 1415 where it was held that the duty to take reasonable care to obtain a proper price was owed to a surety for the mortgage debt as well as to the mortgagor himself.

In my respectful opinion it is both unnecessary and confusing for the duties owed by a mort-gagee to the mortgagor and the surety, if there is one, to be expressed in terms of the tort of negligence. The authorities which were considered in the careful judgments of this court in *Cuckmere Brick Co Ltd v Mutual Finance Ltd* [1971] Ch 949 demonstrate that the duty owed by the mortgagee to the mortgagor was recognised by equity as arising out of the particular relationship between them. Thus Salmon LJ himself said, at 967:

'It would seem, therefore, that many years before the modern development of the law of negligence, the courts of equity had laid down a doctrine in relation to mortgages which is entirely consonant with the general principles later evolved by the common law.'

The duty owed to the surety arises in the same way. In *China and South Sea Bank Ltd v Tan Soon Gin (alias George Tan)* [1990] 1 AC 536 [p. 958, below], Lord Templeman, in delivering

---

172 *China and South Sea Bank Ltd v Tan Soon Gin (alias George Tan)* [1990] 1 AC 536 at 545, p. 958, below, per Lord Templeman; *Countrywide Banking Corpn v Robinson* [1991] 1 NZLR 75; *Tse Kwong Lam v Wong Chit Sen* [1983] 1 WLR 1349, p. 960, below. Cf. *Standard Chartered Bank Ltd v Walker* [1982] 1 WLR 1410 where Lord Denning MR said at 1415: 'There are several dicta to the effect that the mortgagee can choose his own time for the sale, but I do not think this means that he can sell at the worst possible time. It is at least arguable that, in choosing the time, he must exercise a reasonable degree of care'. See also *Predeth v Castle Phillips Finance Co Ltd* [1986] 2 EGLR 144 (where CA accepted the judge's finding that the exercise of reasonable care required mortgagee to expose uninhabitable bungalow at Alton in Hampshire to the market for approximately three months); *Palk v Mortgage Services Funding plc* [1993] Ch 330, p. 965, below, where Sir Donald Nicholls V-C said at 338: 'If the mortgagee sells the property, he cannot sell hastily at a knock-down price sufficient to pay off his debt'; *Downsview Nominees Ltd v First City Corpn Ltd* [1993] AC 295; [1993] Conv 401 (R. Grantham); *Meftah v Lloyds TSB Bank plc* [2001] 2 All ER (Comm) 741 (timing of sale is for mortgagee; if there is urgency 'the necessity of exposure to the market must be evaluated in the light of the circumstances', per Lawrence Collins J at 745); *Silven Properties v Royal Bank of Scotland plc* [2004] 1 WLR 997, p. 962, below (mortgagee under no duty to postpone sale until after further pursuit of application for planning permission or grant of a lease, even though outcome of either course might increase value of property); *Bell v Long* [2008] 2 BCLC 706 (receiver entitled to see four properties as a single portfolio rather than waiting for possible sale of individual properties).

173 *Donoghue v Stevenson* [1932] AC 562, 580.

the judgment of the Privy Council, having pointed out that the surety in that case admitted that the moneys secured by the guarantee were due, continued at 543:

'But the surety claims that the creditor owed the surety a duty to exercise the power of sale conferred by the mortgage and in that case the liability of the surety under the guarantee would either have been eliminated or very much reduced. The Court of Appeal [in Hong Kong] sought to find such a duty in the tort of negligence but the tort of negligence has not yet subsumed all torts and does not supplant the principles of equity or contradict contractual promises... Equity intervenes to protect a surety.'

Once it is recognised that the duty owed by the mortgagee to the mortgagor arises out of the particular relationship between them, it is readily apparent that there is no warrant for extending its scope so as to include a beneficiary or beneficiaries under a trust of which the mortgagor is the trustee. The correctness of that view was fully established in the clear and compelling argument of Mr Lloyd, who drew particular attention to the rights and duties of the trustee to protect the trust property against dissipation or depreciation in value and the impracticabilities and potential rights of double recovery inherent in giving the beneficiary an additional right to sue the mortgagee, a right which is in any event unnecessary.

The only exception for which Mr Lloyd allowed was the special case where the trustee has unreasonably refused to sue on behalf of the trust or has committed some other breach of his duties to the beneficiaries, e.g., by consenting to an improvident sale, which disables or disqualifies him from acting on behalf of the trust. In such a case the beneficiary is permitted to sue on behalf of the trust. This exception is established by a series of authorities, some of which were recently considered by the Privy Council in *Hayim v Citibank NA* [1987] AC 730. In delivering the judgment of their Lordships, Lord Templeman said, at 748:

'These authorities demonstrate that a beneficiary has no cause of action against a third party save in special circumstances which embrace a failure, excusable or inexcusable, by the trustees in the performance of the duty owed by the trustees to the beneficiary in the trust estate.'

It is important to emphasise that when a beneficiary sues under the exception he does so in right of the trust and in the room of the trustee. He does not enforce a right reciprocal to some duty owed directly to him by the third party.[174]

---

[174] See also *Palmer v Barclays Bank Ltd* (1971) 23 P & CR 30; *Johnson v Ribbins* (1975) 235 EG 757; *Waltham Forest London Borough v Webb* (1974) 232 EG 461; *Bank of Cyprus (London) Ltd v Gill* [1980] 2 Lloyd's Rep 51; (1981) 25 NLJ 249 (H. E. Markson); *Norwich General Trust v Grierson* [1984] CLY 2306 (mortgagee held liable for diminution of purchase price due to his negligence in allowing premises to deteriorate between date of taking possession and date of sale); *Garland v Ralph Ray & Ransom* (1984) 271 EG 106, 197 (action by mortgagor against mortgagee's valuer for negligent marketing technique and valuation); *Predeth v Castle Phillips Finance Co Ltd* [1986] 2 EGLR 144 (action by mortgagee against surveyor instructed to provide 'crash-sale' valuation); [1986] Conv 442 (M. P. Thompson); *AIB Finance Co Ltd v Debtors* [1997] 4 All ER 677 (security included good will of business carried on on mortgaged property; held duty on mortgagee to ensure that on sale value of the combined asset was maximised); *Struggles v Lloyds TSB plc* [2000] EGCS 17 (for a quarry to be sold for the best possible price, it should be exposed to the market for 6 to 12 months to enable investigations to be made of both mineral and waste-fill potential); *Skipton Building Society v Stott* [2000] 2 All ER 779 (guarantor liable for difference between amount owed under guarantee and market value of premises at date of sale); *Michael v Miller* [2004] 2 EGLR 151 ('bracket' or margin of error approach for assessing whether mortgagee in breach of duty).

In **China and South Sea Bank Ltd v Tan Soon Gin (alias George Tan)** [1990] 1 AC
536 the appellant creditor advanced $30,000,000 to Carrian Holdings Ltd. The loan
was secured by a mortgage of shares in Carrian Holdings Ltd and by a guarantee by
the respondent. At the time of the loan the shares were worth $60,000,000, at the time
of default $30,000,000, and at the time of the action nothing. The Court of Appeal
of Hong Kong held that it was arguable that the surety's liability was extinguished
or reduced by creditor's breach of a duty in not selling the shares. The Privy Council
rejected this view, and Lord TEMPLEMAN said at 543:

The surety does not and cannot impugn the validity of the provisions of the guarantee and
admits that the moneys claimed by the creditor are due in accordance with the express terms
of the guarantee. But the surety claims that the creditor owed the surety a duty to exercise the
power of sale conferred by the mortgage and in that case the liability of the surety under the
guarantee would either have been eliminated or very much reduced. The Court of Appeal sought
to find such a duty in the tort of negligence but the tort of negligence has not yet subsumed all
torts and does not supplant the principles of equity or contradict contractual promises or complement the remedy of judicial review or supplement statutory rights.[175]

   Equity intervenes to protect a surety. In *Watts v Shuttleworth* (1860) 5 H & N 235 the
creditor had covenanted to insure mortgaged goods and failed to insure. A surety was released.
Pollock CB said, at 247–248:

   'The substantial question in the case is, whether the omission to insure discharges the defendant, the
   surety. The rule upon the subject seems to be that if the person guaranteed does any act injurious to
   the surety, or inconsistent with his rights, or if he omits to do any act which his duty enjoins him to do,
   and the omission proves injurious to the surety, the latter will be discharged . . . the rights of a surety
   depend rather on principles of equity than upon the actual contract.'

His Lordship referred to *Wulff v Jay* (1872) LR 7 QB 756, and continued:

In the present case . . . the creditor had three sources of repayment. The creditor could sue the
debtor, sell the mortgage securities or sue the surety. All these remedies could be exercised
at any time or times simultaneously or contemporaneously or successively or not at all. If the
creditor chose to sue the surety and not pursue any other remedy, the creditor on being paid in
full was bound to assign the mortgaged securities to the surety. If the creditor chose to exercise
his power of sale over the mortgaged security he must sell for the current market value but the
creditor must decide in his own interest if and when he should sell. The creditor does not become
a trustee of the mortgaged securities and the power of sale for the surety unless and until the
creditor is paid in full and the surety, having paid the whole of the debt is entitled to a transfer
of the mortgaged securities to procure recovery of the whole or part of the sum he has paid to
the creditor.
   The creditor is not obliged to do anything. If the creditor does nothing and the debtor declines
into bankruptcy the mortgaged securities become valueless and the surety decamps abroad,
the creditor loses his money. If disaster strikes the debtor and the mortgaged securities but
the surety remains capable of repaying the debt then the creditor loses nothing. The surety
contracts to pay if the debtor does not pay and the surety is bound by his contract. If the surety,

---

[175] See *Murphy v Brentwood District Council* [1991] 1 AC 398 on the restrictive approach of HL to a remedy in negligence for economic loss. See generally *Winfield and Jolowicz on Tort* (17th edn), chap. 5.

perhaps less indolent or less well protected than the creditor, is worried that the mortgaged securities may decline in value then the surety may request the creditor to sell and if the creditor remains idle then the surety may bustle about, pay off the debt, take over the benefit of the securities and sell them. No creditor could carry on the business of lending if he could become liable to a mortgagor and to a surety or to either of them for a decline in value of mortgaged property, unless the creditor was personally responsible for the decline. Applying the rule as specified by Pollock CB in *Watts v Shuttleworth* at 247, it appears to their Lordships that in the present case the creditor did not act injurious to the surety, did not act inconsistent with the rights of the surety and the creditor did not omit any act which his duty enjoined him to do. The creditor was not under a duty to exercise his power of sale over the mortgaged securities at any particular time or at all.

Their Lordships will humbly advise Her Majesty that this appeal should be allowed.

L. Bently, 'Mortgagee's Duties on Sale—No Place for Tort?' [1990] Conv 431 at p. 439

At first glance *Parker-Tweedale* looks very much as if it is a backward step in terms of protection for borrowers. Such a view fits well with arguments about the decline of the courts' willingness to grant protection to individuals (at the expense of lenders) from that seen in the 1970s and early 1980s.[176] However, in terms of changing developments in legal doctrine it places the mortgagor's rights on much safer ground than they would be if based on the shifting sands of liability in negligence. It is important to remember that recent developments have revealed that the role of tort is not quite as all-encompassing as it at one time seemed. In particular it is now clear that tortious duties will rarely be held to exist with respect to economic loss. The *Parker-Tweedale* approach is solid because it rests on principle—namely that prior to the Judicature Acts all mortgage actions would have taken place in Chancery, and that to apply tort principles to any of these relationships represents a 'fusion fallacy.'[177] It also has the advantage of simplicity and avoids difficult questions concerning the overlapping of tort and equity. In the current climate this is the most solid basis for the duty—that is until the Law Commission makes its final recommendations.[178] It would be useful if the Commission recommended an exhaustive list of the parties covered by any such duty.

3. Sale by mortgagee to self

It has long been the rule that in exercising the power of sale a 'mortgagee cannot sell to himself, either alone or with others, nor to a trustee for himself, nor to anyone employed by him to conduct the sale. A sale by a person to himself is no sale at all.'[179]

---

[176] Particularly, the retreat from *William & Glyn's Bank v Boland* [1981] AC 487 evidenced in cases such as *City of London Building Society v Flegg* [1988] AC 54, and *Abbey National Building Society v Cann* [1990] 1 All ER 1085.

[177] E.g. Meagher, Gummow & Lehane, *Equity: Doctrine and Remedies* (2nd edn, 1984), para. 230, at p. 51; Hayton & Marshall, *Cases and Commentary on the Law of Trusts* (8th edn), at p. 9, n. 42; Tyler (1981) 55 ALJ at p. 568.

[178] [See Law Commission Report on Land Mortgages 1991 (Law Com No. 204), para. 7.23, p. 995, below.]

[179] *Farrar v Farrars Ltd* (1888) 40 ChD 395 at 409, per Lindley LJ; *Martinson v Clowes* (1882) 21 ChD 857 (purchase by secretary of building society mortgage); *Williams v Wellingborough Borough Council* [1975] 1

But there is no hard and fast rule that a mortgagee may not sell to a company in which he is interested.[180]

Tse Kwong Lam v Wong Chit Sen
[1983] 1 WLR 1349 (PC, Lords Fraser of Tullybelton, Brandon of Oakbrook, Brightman and Templeman and Sir John Megaw)[181]

In 1963 the appellant mortgagor constructed a large building, containing shops, offices and flats at Kowloon in Hong Kong. He financed it by a loan from the respondent to whom he mortgaged the building.

In 1966 the appellant fell into arrears and the outstanding mortgage debt was $HK 1.4 m. The respondent arranged for the building to be sold at public auction on 24 June. A few days before the auction, the respondent and his wife, as directors of a company, of which they and their children were the sole shareholders, held a directors' meeting at which they resolved that the wife should bid for the property on behalf of the company up to a price of $HK 1.2 m. At the auction, which was attended by some 30–40 people, the respondent informed the auctioneer that $HK 1.2 m. was the reserve price; and at that price the wife, who was the sole bidder, purchased the property for the company.

In an action by the respondent in 1966, the appellant counter-claimed that the sale should be set aside on the ground that it had been improper and at an undervalue. This counter-claim was not pursued to judgment until 1979.

Held.

(1) The respondent had failed to show that he had taken reasonable steps to obtain the best price reasonably obtainable.

(2) By reason of his inexcusable delay, the appellant was not entitled to have the sale set aside but only to damages.

Lord Templeman: In the view of this Board on authority and on principle there is no hard and fast rule that a mortgagee may not sell to a company in which he is interested. The mortgagee and the company seeking to uphold the transaction must show that the sale was in good faith and that the mortgagee took reasonable precautions to obtain the best price reasonably obtainable at the time.[182] The mortgagee is not however bound to postpone the sale in the hope of obtaining a better price or to adopt a piecemeal method of sale which could only be carried out over a substantial period or at some risk of loss. This view of the matter is consistent with the decision of the House of Lords in *York Buildings Co v Mackenzie* (1795) 3 Pat 378....

WLR 1327 ('a see-through dress of a sale', at 1329, per Russell LJ: the decision itself was reversed by Housing Act 1980, s. 112 for the benefit of existing local authority mortgagees).

180 *Tse Kwong Lam v Wong Chit Sen,* below; *Bradford & Bingley plc v Ross* [2005] EWCA Civ 394, (2005) Times 3 May (mortgagee failed to disclose to the court its sale of mortgaged property to a 'closely connected company'; mortgagor entitled to retrial, but not to have judgment set aside as abuse of process).

181 [1984] Conv 143 (P. Jackson); [1983] All ER Rev 57 (D. D. Prentice).

182 *Downsview Nominees Ltd v First City Corpn Ltd* [1993] AC 295, where Lord Templeman said at 312, 'Powers must be exercised in good faith for the purpose of obtaining repayment'; *Caricom Cinemas Ltd v Republic Bank Ltd* [2003] UKPC 2.

In the present case in which the mortgagee held a large beneficial interest in the shares of the purchasing company, was a director of the company, and was entirely responsible for financing the company, the other shareholders being his wife and children, the sale must be closely examined and a heavy onus lies on the mortgagee to show that in all respects he acted fairly to the borrower and used his best endeavours to obtain the best price reasonably obtainable for the mortgaged property.

His Lordship referred to *Hodson v Deans* [1903] 2 Ch 647; *Kennedy v De Trafford* [1897] AC 180; *McHugh v Union Bank of Canada* [1913] AC 299; and *Cuckmere Brick Co Ltd v Mutual Finance Ltd* [1971] Ch 949, and continued:

In the result their Lordships consider that in the present case the company was not debarred from purchasing the mortgaged property but, in view of the close relationship between the company and the mortgagee and in view in particular of the conflict of duty and interest to which the mortgagee was subject, the sale to the company for $1.2 m. can only be supported if the mortgagee proves that he took reasonable precautions to obtain the best price reasonably obtainable at the time of sale.

On behalf of the mortgagee it was submitted that all reasonable steps were taken when the mortgagee, with adequate advertisement, sold the property at a properly conducted auction to the highest bidder. The submission assumes that such an auction must produce the best price reasonably obtainable or, as Salmon LJ expressed the test, the true market value. But the price obtained at any particular auction may be less than the price obtainable by private treaty and may depend on the steps taken to encourage bidders to attend. An auction which only produces one bid is not necessarily an indication that the true market value has been achieved....

The mortgagee could have consulted estate agents about the method of sale and about the method of securing the best price. At the very least he could have consulted an estate agent about the level of the reserve price. The auctioneer was not informed of the reserve price until immediately before the auction and in evidence he very properly declined to comment on the reserve because he had not valued the property. This confirms the impression that the auctioneers were not instructed to do more than put the property under the hammer, a procedure which may be appropriate to the sale of second-hand furniture but is not necessarily conducive to the attainment of the best price for freehold or leasehold property. It was not of course in the interests of the company that enthusiasm for the sale should be stimulated or that the reserve should be settled by anyone other than the mortgagee. The reserve of $1.2 m. was fixed by the mortgagee and was the price at which he advised and intended that the company should purchase. The mortgagee was a property investor and speculator. The company was his family company and he held shares in and financed the company. The mortgagee would not have advised the company to bid $1.2 m. for the property unless he thought that was an advantageous price for the company to pay....

At the trial and on this appeal the mortgagee adopted the attitude that a mortgagee exercising his power of sale is entitled to secure the mortgaged property for a company in which he is interested at a price advised by the mortgagee provided that the property is properly advertised and sold by auction. A decision to this effect would expose borrowers to greater perils than those to which they are now subject as a result of decisions which enable a mortgagee to choose the date of the exercise of his powers. A mortgagee who wishes to secure the mortgaged property for a company in which he is interested ought to show that he protected the interests of the borrower by taking expert advice as to the method of sale, as to the steps which ought reasonably to be taken to make the sale a success and as to the amount of the reserve. There was no difficulty in obtaining such advice orally and in writing and no good reason why a mortgagee, concerned to act fairly towards his borrower, should fail or neglect to obtain or act upon such advice in all respects as if the mortgagee were desirous of realising the best price reasonably obtainable at the date of the sale for property belonging to the mortgagee himself.

Where a mortgagee fails to satisfy the court that he took all reasonable steps to obtain the best price reasonably obtainable and that his company bought at the best price, the court will, as a general rule, set aside the sale and restore to the borrower the equity of redemption of which he has been unjustly deprived. But the borrower will be left to his remedy in damages against the mortgagee for the failure of the mortgagee to secure the best price if it will be inequitable as between the borrower and the purchaser for the sale to be set aside. In the present case...the mortgagee and the company submit that the delay on the part of the borrower in pursuing his counterclaim has rendered it unjust for the building to be restored to the borrower....

The borrower has...been guilty of inexcusable delay in prosecuting his counterclaim.

His Lordship reviewed the evidence, and continued:

The borrower by his delay achieved a favourable position; if the property decreased in value he could either abandon his action or seek damages in setting aside the sale. If the property increased in value he could persist with his claim to set aside the sale. In the circumstances the Board consider that the borrower is not[183] entitled to the alternative remedy of damages. That was the view taken by the trial judge.

The measure of damages must be the difference between the best price reasonably obtainable on June 24, 1966, and the price of $1.2 m. paid by the company.

4. Summary

In **Silven Properties Ltd v Royal Bank of Scotland** [2004] 1 WLR 997, the appellants brought a claim for damages, contending that the respondents had sold the properties at an undervalue in breach of their duties to the appellants. They did not dispute that the prices obtained had been the best reasonably obtainable for the properties in their then current condition. Instead, they agued that the properties should not have been sold in that state, but had been under a duty to pursue planning applications for development of the properties and to proceed with the grant of leases, deferring sale until these goals had been achieved. In holding that the appellants failed, LIGHTMAN J (giving the judgment of the Court) said at 1003:

13 A mortgagee has no duty at any time to exercise his powers as mortgagee to sell, to take possession or to appoint a receiver and preserve the security or its value or to realise his security. He is entitled to remain totally passive. If the mortgagee takes possession, he becomes the manager of the charged property: see *Kendle v Melsom* (1998) 93 CLR 46, 64 (High Court of Australia). He thereby assumes a duty to take reasonable care of the property secured: see *Downsview Nominees Ltd v First City Corporation Ltd (No 1)* [1993] AC 295, 315A, per Lord Templeman; and this requires him to be active in protecting and exploiting the security, maximising the return, but without taking undue risks: see *Palk v Mortgage Services Funding plc* [1993] Ch 330, 338A, per Sir Donald Nicholls V-C.

---

183 The word 'not' is correctly omitted in [1983] 3 All ER 54 at 64.

14 A mortgagee 'is not a trustee of the power of sale for the mortgagor'. This time-honoured expression can be traced back at least as far as Sir George Jessel MR in *Nash v Eads* (1880) 25 SJ 95. In default of provision to the contrary in the mortgage, the power is conferred upon the mortgagee by way of bargain by the mortgagor for his own benefit and he has an unfettered discretion to sell when he likes to achieve repayment of the debt which he is owed: see *Cuckmere Brick Co v Mutual Finance Ltd* [1971] Ch 949, 969G [p. 955, above]. A mortgagee is at all times free to consult his own interests alone as to whether and when to exercise his power of sale. The most recent authoritative restatement of this principle is to be found in *Raja v Austin Gray* [2003] 1 EGLR 91, 96, para. 59, per Peter Gibson LJ. The mortgagee's decision is not constrained by reason of the fact that the exercise or non-exercise of the power will occasion loss or damage to the mortgagor: see *China & South Sea Bank Ltd v Tan Soon Gin (alias George Tan)* [1990] 1 AC 536 [p. 958 above]. It does not matter that the time may be unpropitious and that, by waiting a higher price could be obtained: he is not bound to postpone in the hope of obtaining a better price: see *Tse Kwong Lam v Wong Chit Sen* [1983] 1 WLR 1349, 1355B.

15 The claimants contend that a mortgagee is not entitled to ignore the fact that a short delay might result in a higher price. For this purpose, they rely upon certain obiter dicta of Lord Denning MR in *Standard Chartered Bank Ltd v Walker* [1982] 1 WLR 1410, 1415G-H, 1416A. The mortgagee in that case, having obtained insufficient funds on the sale at auction of the property charged to recover the sum secured, applied for summary judgment against the mortgagor for that sum. The mortgagor resisted the application, alleging that the mortgagee had sold at an undervalue on a variety of grounds one of which was that the sale took place at the wrong time of year. The Court of Appeal gave the mortgagor leave to defend on the ground that there was an arguable case that the sale had been negligently handled. It was common ground in that case that a mortgagee can choose his own time for sale: see Fox LJ, at p. 1418F-G. Lord Denning MR accepted that there were dicta to this effect, but added that he did not think that this meant that the mortgagee could sell at the worst possible moment and that it was at least arguable that in choosing the time he must exercise a reasonable degree of care. The view expressed by Lord Denning cannot stand with the later authorities to which we have referred and which state quite categorically that the mortgagee is under no such duty of care to the mortgagor in respect of the timing of a sale and can act in his own interests in deciding whether and when he should exercise his power of sale.

16 The mortgagee is entitled to sell the mortgaged property as it is. He is under no obligation to improve it or to increase its value. There is no obligation to take any such pre-marketing steps to increase the value of the property, as is suggested by the claimants.

His Lordship referred to *McHugh v Union Bank of Canada* [1913] AC 299 and continued:

17 The mortgagee is free (in his own interest as well as that of the mortgagor) to investigate whether and how he can 'unlock' the potential for an increase in value of the property mortgaged (e.g. by an application for planning permission or the grant of a lease), and indeed (going further) he can proceed with such an application or grant. But he is likewise free at any time to halt his efforts and proceed instead immediately with a sale. By commencing on this path, the mortgagee does not in any way preclude himself from calling a halt at will: he does not assume any such obligation of care to the mortgagor in respect of its continuance as the claimants contend. If however the mortgagee is to seek to charge to the mortgagor the costs of the exercise that he has undertaken of obtaining planning permission or a lessee, subject to any applicable

terms of the mortgage, the mortgagee may be entitled to do so only if he acted reasonably in incurring those costs and fairly balanced the costs of the exercise against the potential benefits taking fully into account the possibility that he might at any moment 'pull the plug' on these efforts and the consequences for the mortgagor if he did so.

18 If the mortgagor requires protection in any of these respects, whether by imposing further duties on the mortgagee or limitations on his rights and powers, he must insist upon them when the bargain is made and upon the inclusion of protective provisions in the mortgage. In the absence of such protective provisions, the mortgagee is entitled to rest on the terms of the mortgage and (save where statute otherwise requires) the court must give effect to them. The one method available to the mortgagor to prevent the mortgagee exercising the rights conferred upon him by the mortgage is to redeem the mortgage. If he redeems, there can be no need or justification for recourse by the mortgagee to the power of sale to achieve repayment of the debt due to him secured by the mortgage.

19 When and if the mortgagee does exercise the power of sale, he comes under a duty in equity (and not tort) to the mortgagor (and all others interested in the equity of redemption) to take reasonable precautions to obtain 'the fair' or 'the true market' value of, or the 'proper price' for, the mortgaged property at the date of the sale, and not (as the claimants submitted) the date of the decision to sell. If the period of time between the dates of the decision to sell and of the sale is short, there may be no difference in value between the two dates and indeed in many (if not most) cases this may be readily assumed. But where there is a period of delay, the difference in date could prove significant. The mortgagee is not entitled to act in a way that unfairly prejudices the mortgagor by selling hastily at a knock-down price sufficient to pay off his debt: *Palk v Mortgage Services Funding plc* [1993] Ch 330, 337–338, per Sir Donald Nicholls V-C. He must take proper care whether by fairly and properly exposing the property to the market or otherwise to obtain the best price reasonably obtainable at the date of sale. The remedy for breach of this equitable duty is not common law damages, but an order that the mortgagee account to the mortgagor and all others interested in the equity of redemption, not just for what he actually received, but for what he should have received: see *Standard Chartered Bank Ltd v Walker* [1982] 1 WLR 1410, 1416B.

20 In our judgment there can accordingly be no duty on the part of a mortgagee, as suggested by the claimants, to postpone exercising the power of sale until after the further pursuit (let alone the outcome) of an application for planning permission or the grant of a lease of the mortgaged property, though the outcome of the application and the effect of the grant of the lease may be to increase the market value of the mortgaged property and price obtained on sale. A mortgagee is entitled to sell the property in the condition in which it stands without investing money or time in increasing its likely sale value. He is entitled to discontinue efforts already undertaken to increase the likely sale value in favour of such a sale. A mortgagee is under a duty to take reasonable care to obtain a sale price that reflects the added value available on the grant of planning permission and the grant of a lease of a vacant property and (as a means of achieving this end) to ensure that the potential is brought to the notice of prospective purchasers and, accordingly, taken into account in their offers: see *Cuckmere*. But that is the limit of his duty.

5. Discretion of court to order sale at request of mortgagor

Under section 91(2) of the Law of Property Act 1925 the court has discretion to order a sale at the request of the mortgagor. This may be of significant help to a mortgagor with negative equity, but the court will only order a sale where an application has been made by the mortgagor before the mortgagee has obtained a warrant for possession.

LAW OF PROPERTY ACT 1925

91. Sale of mortgaged property in action for redemption or foreclosure.—(2) p. 924, above.

In **Palk v Mortgage Services Funding plc** [1993] Ch 330[184] Mr and Mrs Palk borrowed £300,000 from Mortgage Services Funding plc on a joint mortgage in 1990. Mr Palk's business failed and he went bankrupt; Mrs Palk remained liable. In 1991 when £360,000 was needed for redemption, the Palks negotiated a sale for £283,000. They wished to sell the house in order to stop interest continuing to accrue on the debt, but the mortgagees wished to take possession of the house and to let it on a short-term lease and then sell when the market improved.

In holding that the court had a discretion under section 91(2) of the Law of Property Act 1925 to order a sale at a depressed market price, even against the wishes of the mortgagee, Sir Donald NICHOLLS V-C said at 340:

Section 91(2) gives the court a discretion in wide terms. The discretion is unfettered. It can be exercised at any time. Self-evidently, in exercising that power the court will have due regard to the interests of all concerned. The court will act judicially. But it cannot be right that the court should decline to exercise the power if the consequence will be manifest unfairness.

In my view this is a case in which a sale should be directed even though there will be a deficiency. It is just and equitable to order a sale because otherwise unfairness and injustice will follow. I can summarise the four factors which combine to produce this result. First, there is a substantial income shortfall: the rental under the proposed letting would fall significantly short of the interest Mrs Palk would save if the house were sold. Second, the only prospect of recoupment of the shortfall lies in the hope that there will be a substantial rise in house prices generally. This is not a case where sale is being postponed for a reason specific to this property: for example, pending the outcome of an application for planning permission for development. Following on from this, third, on the scanty evidence before the court the likelihood of Mrs Palk suffering increased loss if the company's plan proceeds is so high as to make the plan oppressive to her. Her liability is open-ended and will increase indefinitely. This risk of increased loss to her under her repayment obligation far outweighs the prospect of any gain the company may make from its proposed realisation scheme for the house. The one is unacceptably disproportionate to the other. Fourth, directing a sale will not preclude the mortgagee from having the opportunity to wait and see what happens to house prices. The mortgagee can buy the property. A mortgagee cannot buy property from itself, but here the sale is directed by the court; it is not a sale by a mortgagee in exercise of its own power of sale.

In **Cheltenham and Gloucester plc v Krausz** [1997] 1 WLR 1558[185] the mortgagors of 8 Springhill, Clapton, London E5, had fallen into arrears with their mortgage.

---

[184] [1993] Conv 59 (J. Martin); (1993) 143 NLJ 448 (H. W. Wilkinson); *Barrett v Halifax Building Society* (1985) 28 HLR 634; *Polonski v Lloyds Bank Mortgages Ltd* (1999) 31 HLR 721; Emmet, para. 25.101.

[185] [1998] Conv 223 (A. Kenny); [1998] LS 279 (M. Dixon); approved in *Albany Home Loans v Massey* (1997) 73 P & CR 509 at 513, per Schiemann LJ, referring to a similar requirement by Lord Templeman

The mortgagee obtained an order for possession of the property and on four occasions warrants for possession were issued. Each time the warrant was discharged after agreement between the parties and on each occasion the mortgagors defaulted on the agreement. A fifth warrant was issued and had fallen due for execution when the mortgagors arranged a sale of the property to the M. Y. A. Charitable Trust. They applied to the County Court for an order suspending the warrant for possession pending an application to the High Court for an order that the property be sold under section 91(2) of the Law of Property Act 1925. The mortgagees resisted the application because the mortgage debt, which had increased from £58,300 in January 1987 to some £83,000 in 1995, far exceeded the sale price of £65,000, which the mortgagees believed to be based on an underestimation of the value of the property. The judge granted the order.

In allowing the appeal, PHILLIPS LJ said at 1561:

The law

This appeal requires consideration of the interrelationship of two areas of the law relating to the mortgage of a dwelling-house: (1) the circumstances in which the mortgagor is entitled to an order for the sale of the mortgaged property: (2) the circumstances in which the court has jurisdiction to suspend entry into possession of the dwelling-house by the mortgagee.

Mortgagor's right of sale

His Lordship read section 91 of the Law of Property Act 1925, p. 924, above, and continued:

The origin and history of these provisions are described by Sir Donald Nicholls V-C in *Palk v Mortgage Services Funding plc* [1993] Ch 330, 335, [p. 965, above]. Sir Donald Nicholls V-C also cited the statement of Jessel MR in *Union Bank of London v Ingram* (1882) 20 Ch D 463, 464 about the essentially identical provisions of section 25(2) of the Conveyancing Act 1881;

'The Act is a remedial act, one effect of it being to allow a mortgagor whose property is worth more than the mortgage-money, but who cannot raise it, to obtain a sale and get the benefit of the surplus.'

Until *Palk's* case it was the practice of the Chancery court only to entertain an application for sale by the mortgagor if the proceeds of sale were expected to be sufficient to discharge the entirety of the mortgage debt. In such circumstances the mortgagor might initiate proceedings by bringing an action for sale under section 91(1), or, if the mortgagee sought to foreclose, the mortgagor could apply for an order for sale in place of foreclosure. The practice thus reflected the heading to section 91: 'Sale of mortgaged property in action for redemption or foreclosure'.

Palk's case established, for the first time, that the court has power under section 91(2) to make an order for sale on the application of a mortgagor, notwithstanding that the proceeds of sale will be insufficient to discharge the mortgage debt. In *Palk's* case the mortgagees had obtained an order for possession with the intention, not of proceeding to sell the property but of waiting in the hope that the market might improve. The mortgagor was anxious that the

in *Downsview Nominees Ltd v First City Corpn Ltd* [1993] AC 295 at 312; and to European Convention on Human Rights, art. 8.

property should be sold so that the proceeds would reduce the mortgage debt, on which interest was accruing at an alarming rate. The Court of Appeal held that, as the mortgagees could buy the property themselves if they wished to speculate on an increase in the value, in the interests of fairness the property should be sold.

In *Palk's* case the mortgagor had initially applied for an order for sale to the Eastbourne County Court. It is not clear on what basis that court entertained the claim, for the jurisdiction of the county court to make an order for sale is limited to cases where the value of the property does not exceed £30,000. It also appears from the judgment in the Court of Appeal that the mortgagees obtained an order for possession which was suspended pending the result of their application. It is not clear which court made the order for possession, or which court suspended that order. What does seem clear is that no challenge was made of the jurisdiction to suspend the possession order.

In *Palk's* case the issue was simply whether or not the property should be sold. No issue arose as to the terms on which it should be sold. As to that matter, section 91(2) empowers the court to direct a sale 'on such terms as it thinks fit'. In cases before *Palk's* case, where the proceeds of sale were likely to exceed the mortgage debt, the court was prepared to entrust the sale to the mortgagor on the basis that the mortgagor had a keener interest than the mortgagee in obtaining the best price. We have not been referred to any case, however, where there was a contest between the mortgagee and the mortgagor as to who should have conduct of the sale.

Barrett v Halifax Building Society (1995) 28 HLR 634 marks the next development in this area of the law, and one which demonstrates the importance of the present appeal. In that case the plaintiffs had mortgaged their home and then defaulted on their repayment obligations. The situation was one of negative equity—the mortgage debt substantially exceeded the value of their home. On 6 August 1992 the mortgagees obtained a possession order, with a view to exercising their power of sale. There were numerous suspensions of this order to give the plaintiffs a chance to discharge the instalment arrears. What then occurred was explained by the judge, at p. 636:

> 'On 6 March 1995 there was a further suspension of the order for the purpose of leaving [the] mortgagors in possession of the property themselves to find a buyer notwithstanding that there was a deficit over the sum secured so that the property would be on the market, lived in and without it becoming known to the market that it was subject to a forced sale, thereby increasing the realisations available to discharge at least part of the amount due.'

The plaintiffs then applied to the Chancery court for an order for sale pursuant to section 91 of the Act of 1925. By the time that their action came on for hearing they had negotiated a sale of the property, subject to contract. They sought an order that they be permitted to proceed with that sale and to remain in possession until completion. The judge summarised the evidence on which they relied, at p. 637:

> 'The evidence of the plaintiffs, including the expert evidence of a valuer, is that it is a recognised feature of today's property market that where a mortgagee obtains possession of property and sells in the exercise of its power of sale it is able to obtain a price which is usually not as good as the price which might have been obtained by the mortgagor had the mortgagor remained in possession and the fact of the forced sale not become apparent. It is also the plaintiffs' evidence that if the mortgagee building society were to take over the sale or were now to obtain possession and proceed to sell itself there would be likely to be a delay of some months at least before a fresh purchaser could be found and a sale completed.'

The mortgagees resisted the order sought. They did not contend that they would be able to obtain a better price but urged that if the sale went ahead it would break their established policy not to permit borrowers with negative equity themselves to conduct the sale of their property without also at the same time making proposals for the repayment of any resulting deficit. The judge held that this was not a material circumstance which he ought to take into account when exercising his discretion. He held, at p. 640:

> 'I am left, therefore, with a case [in] which, on the evidence before me, there is no discernible advan-
> tage to the building society in refusing to allow this sale to complete, whereas there is an obvious
> advantage to the mortgagors to complete their proposed sale at what is accepted as the best price
> that is likely to be obtainable in the current market.'

He proceeded to grant the plaintiffs the order that they sought. Just as in *Palk's* case the report does not suggest that in *Barrett's* case any challenge was made by the mortgagees to the order suspending possession pending the plaintiff's action to the Chancery court.

The consequences of the procedure followed in *Barrett's* case appear to me to be far reaching. In any case in which there is negative equity it will be open to the mortgagor to resist an order for possession on the ground that he wishes to obtain a better price by remaining in possession and selling the property himself. In not every case will the primary motive for such an application be the wish to obtain a better price than that which the mortgagee is likely to obtain on a forced sale. Often the mortgagor will be anxious to postpone for as long as possible the evil day when he has to leave his home. This court has ample experience of hopeless applications for leave to appeal against possession orders designed to achieve just that end. There will be a danger, if the mortgagee does not obtain possession, that the mortgagor will delay the realisation of the property by seeking too high a price, or deliberately procrastinating on completion. At present there is a simple procedure for seeking possession in the county court and the issue tends to be whether there are arrears and whether the mortgagor is likely to be able to discharge these in a reasonable time. If possession is to be suspended whenever this appears reasonable in order to give mortgagors the opportunity to sell the property themselves, the courts are going to have to enter into an area of difficult factual inquiry in order to decide in the individual case whether or not this course will be to the common benefit of mortgagor and mortgagee. Furthermore there will be obvious practical difficulties for mortgagees in monitoring the negotiations of mortgagors who are permitted time to market their properties. For these reasons it seems to me that the procedure followed and the decision reached in the *Barrett* case tend fundamentally to undermine the value of the mortgagee's entitlement to possession. Having touched on the implications of the issue raised in this case I turn to consider whether, in law, the county court has jurisdiction to suspend possession in such circumstances.

Suspension of possession

The right of the mortgagee to enter into possession of the mortgaged property was one which the common law protected strictly. The position was accurately stated by Russell J in *Birmingham Citizens Permanent Building Society v Caunt* [1962] Ch 883, 912:

> 'Accordingly, in my judgment, where (as here) the legal mortgagee under an instalment mortgage
> under which by reason of default the whole money has become payable, is entitled to possession, the
> court has no jurisdiction to decline the order or to adjourn the hearing whether on terms of keeping up
> payments or paying arrears, if the mortgagee cannot be persuaded to agree to this course. To this the
> *sole exception* is that the application may be adjourned for a short time to afford to the mortgagor

a chance of paying off the mortgagee in full or otherwise satisfying him; but this should not be done if there is no reasonable prospect of this occurring. When I say the sole exception, I do not, of course, intend to exclude adjournments which in the ordinary course of procedure may be desirable in circumstances such as a temporary inability of a party to attend, and so forth.'

The rigours of the common law in this respect were mitigated by section 36 of the Administration of Justice Act 1970. . . .

His Lordship read the section, p. 935, above, and continued:

It seems likely that the draftsman of this section intended to confer on the court power to suspend possession where the mortgagor was in a position to pay arrears of instalments within a reasonable period. He overlooked the fact that most mortgages provide for the principal to become immediately payable if instalments are in arrears. It was held in *Halifax Building Society v Clark* [1973] Ch 307 that in that event, the court was only given power to suspend if it appeared that the mortgagor would be able within a reasonable time to repay the total mortgage debt. To reverse the effect of this decision section 36 was amended by section 8(1) of the Administration of Justice 1973. . . .

His Lordship read section 8(1), p. 941, above, and continued:

The effect of section 36, as amended, on the power to suspend possession is as follows. (1) The power can be exercised to enable the mortgagor to pay off instalment arrears due under the mortgage agreement from sources other than the sale of the mortgaged property, but (2) if the mortgagor intends to sell the mortgaged property to provide the source of payment, the court must be satisfied that the proceeds will be sufficient to discharge the entirety of the mortgage debt: see *Royal Trust Co of Canada v Markham* [1975] 1 WLR 1416; *National and Provincial Building Society v Lloyd* [1996] 1 All ER 630.

Before the decision in *Palk's* case it seemed that section 36 of the Act of 1970 and section 91 of the Act of 1925 were complementary. An application under section 91 of the Act of 1925 would only be contemplated where the proceeds of the sale were expected to exceed the mortgage debt. In these circumstances section 36 gave the court the power to suspend possession in order to enable an application for sale under section 91 to be made. It is, however, quite clear that section 36 does not empower the court to suspend possession in order to permit the mortgagor to sell the mortgaged premises where the proceeds of sale will not suffice to discharge the mortgage debt, unless of course, other funds will be available to the mortgagor to make up the shortfall. A mortgagor seeking relief in the circumstances of *Palk's* case is thus unable to invoke any statutory power to suspend the mortgagee's right to possession . . .

In *Royal Trust Co of Canada v Markham* Sir John Pennycuick, when delivering the leading judgment of this court, cited with approval the passage from the judgment of Russell J in *Birmingham Citizens Permanent Building Society v Caunt* which I myself have cited above. He then said, at p. 1420:

'A characteristic instance in which that sole exception is applicable is where the mortgagor has entered or is about to enter into a contract for the sale of the property at a price which will enable the mortgage to be paid off in full. . . . So, as the law stood before 1970, the mortgagee had a right, subject only to that one exception mentioned by Russell J, to possession, and it was not in the power of the court to refuse him possession.'

Megaw LJ added, at pp. 1423–1424:

'There was, as I think is clear, no power, before the enactment of section 36 of the Administration of Justice Act 1970, for a court to grant a stay or suspension of execution of an order for possession in a mortgagee's action, such as the present one, based on default in payment or breach of other obligations. Therefore, if there be such power to suspend or stay the execution of the order for possession, it can come only from the provisions of section 36 of the Act of 1970 as amended by section 8 of the Administration of Justice Act 1973.'

In my judgment the very specific delimitation of the power given by section 36 makes it clear that the legislature did not intend that the court should have any wider jurisdiction to curtail the mortgagee's right to possession. That right enables the mortgagee to exercise his power of sale in the manner he chooses and in the confidence that he can offer a purchaser vacant possession. Section 36 circumscribes that right where the proceeds of the sale are likely to discharge the mortgage debt. It does not do so where the mortgage debt will not be fully discharged, and it is in those circumstances that the mortgagee's rights are of particular importance.

I recognise the principle of the inherent jurisdiction of the court, as explained by Lord Morris in *Connelly v Director of Public Prosecutions* [1964] AC 1254, but I question whether that principle can justify the court in exercising its power to order a sale of mortgaged property under section 91 in circumstances where the mortgagee is seeking to enter into possession in order to sell property in which there is negative equity and where the sole object with which the mortgagor seeks that order is to prevent the mortgagee exercising his right to possession so that the mortgagor can negotiate his own sale while in possession. Even if one assumes that the Chancery court has power to order sale of mortgaged property on terms that displace the mortgagee's right to possession, I do not consider that it follows from this that the county court, as part of its inherent jurisdiction, can properly suspend an order or warrant for possession in order to enable a mortgagor to apply to the High Court for an order under section 91. It seems to me incumbent on the mortgagor to seek from the High Court any relief which that court is empowered to give before the possession warrant takes place.

In the present case the judge purported in 1995 to suspend a warrant for possession that was properly issued pursuant to an order for possession made in 1991. For the reasons I have given I consider that he had no jurisdiction to make such an order and this appeal should be allowed.

Millett LJ: I have had the advantage of reading in draft the judgment of Phillips LJ with which I am in full agreement. *Palk v Mortgage Services Funding plc* was a case in which the mortgagee had no wish to realise its security in the foreseeable future, whether by sale or foreclosure. It established that in such a case the mortgagor might obtain an order for sale even though the proceeds of sale would be insufficient to discharge the mortgage debt. It does not support the making of such an order where the mortgagee is taking active steps to obtain possession and enforce its security by sale. Still less does it support the giving of the conduct of the sale to the mortgagor in a case where there is negative equity, so that it is the mortgagee who is likely to have the greater incentive to obtain the best price and the quickest sale. Both these steps were taken in *Barrett v Halifax Building Society*. I have serious doubt whether that case was rightly decided. In fairness to the judge it should be said that it does not appear to have been argued as a matter of principle; the mortgagor's application was resisted on purely pragmatic grounds, and somewhat feeble ones at that. For the reasons given by Phillips LJ I agree that this appeal should be allowed.

QUESTIONS

1. What restrictions, if any, should be placed on the time at which the mortgagee exercises his power of sale?

2. A mortgagor defaults and then contracts to sell the mortgaged property to X. X's rights under the contract are protected by registration. The mortgagee, under the statutory power of sale, contracts to sell the property to Y. Can X succeed in a claim for specific performance against the mortgagor and for an injunction against the mortgagee? See *Duke v Robson* [1973] 1 WLR 267; (1973) 27 Conv (NS) 210 (F. R. Crane); Law Commission Report on Land Mortgages 1991 (Law Com No. 204), paras 7.16–7.19, p. 995, below.

(b) Equitable mortgagee

LAW OF PROPERTY ACT 1925

90. Realisation of equitable charges by the court.—(1) Where an order for sale is made by the court in reference to an equitable mortgage on land (not secured by a legal term of years absolute or by a charge by way of legal mortgage) the court may, in favour of a purchaser, make a vesting order conveying the land or may appoint a person to convey the land or create and vest in the mortgagee a legal term of years absolute to enable him to carry out the sale, as the case may require, in like manner as if the mortgage had been created by deed by way of legal mortgage pursuant to this Act, but without prejudice to any incumbrance having priority to the equitable mortgage unless the incumbrancer consents to the sale.

(2) This section applies to equitable mortgages made or arising before or after the commencement of this Act, but not to a mortgage which has been overreached under the powers conferred by this Act or otherwise.

In the case of an equitable mortgage, the mortgagee has no inherent power of sale.[186] If he wishes to sell, he must apply to the court under Law of Property Act 1925, section 91(2), p. 924, above. The mortgagee's statutory power of sale becomes available if the mortgage is made by deed, and equitable mortgages are commonly accompanied by a memorandum executed as a deed. Such a power, however, covers only 'the mortgaged property'[187]—that is the equitable interest. In order to give the mortgagee power to sell the legal estate, the deed often includes a power of attorney,[188] or a declaration of trust, or both.

In **Re White Rose Cottage** [1965] Ch 940 one question was whether a sale by the mortgagor (the Kamerun company) and the bank (an equitable mortgagee) gave a title free from or subject to an equitable charge in favour of a later equitable chargee. The Court of Appeal construed the sale as one by the mortgagor with the concurrence of the

---

[186] C & B, pp. 782–783; Gray, para. 6.4.94; M & W, paras 25.043–25.045; MM, p. 513.

[187] LPA 1925, s. 101(1)(i).   [188] Powers of Attorney Act 1971, ss. 4(1), 5(3).

mortgagee, and the title which passed was therefore that held by the mortgagor and the purchaser took subject to the later charge.

A different construction had been placed upon the sale by Wilberforce J at first instance [1964] Ch 483; he treated it as being a sale by an equitable mortgagee.

The mortgagor had executed a memorandum under seal 'in the usual form for effecting a charge to secure [an] advance. It was stated that the documents of title had been deposited as security for the money due. The liability under the charge was not to exceed £50,000. The Kamerun company gave an undertaking to execute a legal charge or mortgage on request and agreed to hold the property as trustee for executing such a charge, the bank having power to appoint a new trustee in the place of the Kamerun company at any time. An irrevocable power of attorney was given to the bank so that the bank, in the name and on behalf of the Kamerun company, could vest the legal estate in the property in any purchaser or other person in exercise of the statutory powers conferred on mortgagees free and discharged from all rights of redemption'.

Both judgments of the Court of Appeal (Lord Denning MR and Harman LJ, with Salmon LJ agreeing with both) expressed the view that, if they had construed the sale, as Wilberforce J did, as being a sale by an equitable mortgagee under a power of sale, the legal estate would have passed; and by virtue of Law of Property Act 1925, section 104(1), would have passed to the purchaser free from the subsequent charge. HARMAN LJ said at 955:

In other words, I think that an equitable mortgagee under a deed in the terms of the memo-randum...can by virtue of the power of attorney contained in it convey to a purchaser the legal estate in the mortgaged property without first going through the form of calling for the execution by the mortgagor of a legal mortgage.

LORD DENNING MR said at 951:

Wilberforce J has held that that conveyance was an exercise by the bank of their statutory power of sale as mortgagees; and that selling as mortgagees they were entitled to sell the prop-erty freed from all charges subsequent to their own. If this be the correct construction of the conveyance, I would agree with him.

His Lordship referred to Law of Property Act 1925, section 104(1) and continued:

The subject of the mortgage here was the property itself, both the legal and equitable estate in it: and I see no reason why an equitable mortgagee, exercising his power of sale, should not be able to convey the legal estate.[189]

(ii) Appointment of receiver[190]

LAW OF PROPERTY ACT 1925

101. Powers incident to estate or interest of mortgagee.—(1) (iii), p. 951, above.

---

[189] See W & C, vol. i., 212, where this view is doubted.

[190] C & B, pp. 768–769; Gray, paras 6.4.10–6.4.12; M & W, paras 25.036–25.040; MM, pp. 511–513; Smith, p. 589; Fisher and Lightwood, chap. 28.

109. Appointment, powers, remuneration and duties of receiver.—(1) A mortgagee entitled to appoint a receiver under the power in that behalf conferred by this Act shall not appoint a receiver until he has become entitled to exercise the power of sale conferred by this Act, but may then, by writing under his hand, appoint such person as he thinks fit to be receiver.

(2) A receiver appointed under the powers conferred by this Act, or any enactment replaced by this Act, shall be deemed to be the agent of the mortgagor;[191] and the mortgagor shall be solely responsible for the receiver's acts or defaults unless the mortgage deed otherwise provides.[192]

(4) A person paying money to the receiver shall not be concerned to inquire whether any case has happened to authorise the receiver to act.

(8) Subject to the provisions of this Act as to the application of insurance money,[193] the receiver shall apply all money received by him as follows, namely:

    (i) In discharge of all rents, taxes,[194] rates, and outgoings whatever affecting the mortgaged property; and

    (ii) In keeping down all annual sums or other payments, and the interest on all principal sums, having priority to the mortgage in right whereof he is receiver; and

    (iii) In payment of his commission,[195] and of the premiums on fire, life or other insurances, if any, properly payable under the mortgage deed or under this Act, and the cost of executing necessary or proper repairs directed in writing by the mortgagee; and

    (iv) In payment of the interest accruing due in respect of any principal money due under the mortgage; and

    (v) In or towards discharge of the principal money if so directed in writing by the mortgagee;

and shall pay the residue, if any, of the money received by him to the person who, but for the possession of the receiver, would have been entitled to receive the income of which he is appointed receiver, or who is otherwise entitled to the mortgaged property.[196]

---

[191] For the peculiar incidents of the agency, see *Silven Properties Ltd v Royal Bank of Scotland plc* [2004] 1 WLR 997 at [21]–[29], per Lightman J.

[192] *Chatsworth Properties Ltd v Effiom* [1971] 1 WLR 144; *Standard Chartered Bank Ltd v Walker* [1982] 1 WLR 1410; *American Express International Banking Corpn v Hurley* [1985] 3 All ER 564 (mortgagee responsible for what receiver does as his agent, but not responsible for what he does as mortgagor's agent, unless the mortgagee directs or interferes with receiver's activities); *Shamji v Johnson Matthey Bankers Ltd* [1991] BCLC 36 (mortgagee owes no duty of care to mortgagor or guarantor in deciding whether or not to appoint a receiver); *Lever Finance Ltd v Trustee of the Property of Needleman and Kreutzer* [1956] Ch 375 (receipt by receiver as agent of mortgagor does not create tenancy by estoppel binding on mortgagee): *Mann v Nijar* (2000) 32 HLR 223.

[193] LPA 1925, s. 108.

[194] *Sargent v Customs & Excise Comrs* [1993] EGCS 182 (VAT).

[195] *Marshall v Cottingham* [1982] Ch 82.

[196] A receiver, when managing the mortgaged property owes not only a duty of good faith to the mortgagor and anyone else with an interest in the equity of redemption, but also a duty to manage the property with due diligence; *Medforth v Blake* [2000] Ch 86; [1999] Conv 434 (A. Kenny); [2000] CLJ 31 (L. S. Sealy); [1999] All ER Rev 227 (P. J. Clarke).

E. RESTITUTION

The law of restitution may provide a remedy for the mortgagee. In **Goss v Chilcott** [1996] AC 788, Lord GOFF OF CHIEVELEY said at 792:

This appeal is concerned with an action brought by the plaintiff (as liquidator of a finance company, Central Acceptance Ltd) to recover from the defendants, Mr and Mrs Goss, the amount of an advance made by the company to the defendants which was secured by a mortgage over their property. (For the purposes of this appeal, their Lordships will for convenience treat the action as having been brought by the company itself.) The mortgage instrument was subsequently altered by a solicitor, Mr Haddon, in circumstances in which, on the authority of a line of cases stretching back to *Pigot's Case* (1614) 11 Co. Rep. 26b, the effect was that (as is now accepted) the defendants were discharged from liability under the instrument from the date of the alteration; and the central question in the case has been on what basis, if any, in these circumstances the company is entitled to recover the amount of the advance from the defendants....

From the beginning, the defendants were under an obligation to repay the advance once it had been paid to them or to their order; and this obligation was of course unaffected by the fact that they had allowed the money to be paid over to Mr Haddon. The effect of the alteration of the mortgage instrument was that their contractual obligation to repay the money was discharged; but they had nevertheless been enriched by the receipt of the money, and prima facie were liable in restitution to restore it. They had however allowed the money to be paid over to Mr Haddon in circumstances in which, as they well knew, the money would nevertheless have to be repaid to the company. They had, therefore, in allowing the money to be paid to Mr Haddon, deliberately taken the risk that he would be unable to repay the money, in which event they themselves would have to repay it without recourse to him. Since any action by them against Mr Haddon would now be fruitless they are seeking, by invoking the defence of change of position, to shift that loss onto the company. This, in their Lordships' opinion, they cannot do. The fact that they cannot now obtain reimbursement from Mr Haddon does not, in the circumstances of the present case, render it inequitable for them to be required to make restitution to the company in respect of the enrichment which they have received at the company's expense.[197]

F. FORECLOSURE[198]

LAW OF PROPERTY ACT 1925

88. Realisation of freehold mortgages.—(2) Where any such mortgagee obtains an order for foreclosure absolute, the order shall operate to vest the fee simple in him (subject to any legal mortgage having priority to the mortgage in right of which the foreclosure is obtained and to

---

[197] The defence of change of position on the basis that the defendants had allowed the money to be paid to the solicitor was rejected; Goff and Jones, *The Law of Restitution* (7th edn), paras 19–007—19–008. See also *Portman Building Society v Harmyn Taylor Neck* [1998] 4 All ER 202 (mortgagee's loss arising from mistake induced by solicitor: no restitution because solicitor not enriched).

[198] C & B, pp. 775–777; Gray, paras 6.4.88–6.4.92; M & W, paras 25.006–25.012; MM, pp. 502–504; Smith, p. 569–570; Cousins, paras 16.89–16.106; Fisher and Lightwood, chap. 32; (1978) LS Gaz 447; (1979) 129 NLJ

any money thereby secured), and thereupon the mortgage term, if any, shall thereby be merged in the fee simple, and any subsequent mortgage term or charge by way of legal mortgage bound by the order shall thereupon be extinguished.

89. Realisation of leasehold mortgages.—(2) Where any such mortgagee obtains an order for foreclosure absolute, the order shall, unless it otherwise provides, operate (without giving rise to a forfeiture for want of a licence to assign) to vest the leasehold reversion affected by the mortgage and any subsequent mortgage term in him, subject to any legal mortgage having priority to the mortgage in right of which the foreclosure is obtained and to any money thereby secured, and thereupon the mortgage term and any subsequent mortgage term or charge by way of legal mortgage bound by the order shall, subject to any express provision to the contrary contained in the order, merge in such leasehold reversion or be extinguished.

The mortgagee or any person interested may ask the court[199] to order a sale instead of foreclosure: Law of Property Act 1925, section 91(2).[200]

In **Campbell v Holyland** (1877) 7 ChD 166, Blakely mortgaged a reversionary interest in a trust fund to Campbell and died insolvent. A foreclosure decree was made in 1876 ordering payment of the money by 4 January 1877. Blakely's administrator, Holyland, transferred the equity of redemption to X and Y who negotiated for the purchase of the interest of the mortgagee, Campbell; and failed to pay on 4 January 1877 because they thought, incorrectly, that they had purchased the interest. They discovered subsequently that Campbell had sold his interest on 3 January to Ford, who was aware of the negotiations to sell to X and Y. The foreclosure decree was made absolute.

In March 1877, X and Y's executors moved to reopen the foreclosure decree, and JESSEL MR allowed them to do so. He said at 171:

I have no doubt that I ought to make the order asked for.

The question in dispute is really whether a mortgagor can be allowed to redeem after an order of foreclosure absolute, and I think, on looking at the authorities, that no Chancellor or Vice-Chancellor has ever laid down that any special circumstances are essential to enable a mortgagor to redeem in such a case.

Now what is the principle? The principle in a Court of Equity has always been that, though a mortgage is in form an absolute conveyance when the condition is broken, in equity it is always security; and it must be remembered that the doctrine arose at the time when mortgages were made in the form of conditional conveyance, the condition being that if the money was not paid at the day, the estate should become the estate of the mortgagee; that was the contract between

---

33 (H. E. Markson), 225 (C. M. Pepper); (1981) 260 EG 899 (D. Brahams). On a revival in its popularity as a remedy, see Report of Committee on Enforcement of Judgment Debts 1969 (Cmnd 1309), para. 1360; on its rarity, see *Palk v Mortgage Services Funding plc* [1993] Ch 330 at 336; and on its commercial use, see *Lloyds and Scottish Trusts Ltd v Britten* (1982) 44 P & CR 249. For registration requirements for foreclosure in registered land, see LRR 2003, r. 112.

199 The jurisdiction of the Chancery Division in respect of foreclosure actions was not affected by the introduction of CPR Part 55, p. 935, n. 138, above. CPR PD4 provides for the forms of order for foreclosure nisi (N299) and foreclosure absolute (N309) of a legal mortgage of land.

200 P. 924, above. For the inter-relation between the two remedies, see *Twentieth Century Banking Corpn Ltd v Wilkinson* [1977] Ch 99.

the parties; yet Courts of Equity interfered with actual contract to this extent, by saying there was a paramount intention that the estate should be security, and that the mortgage money should be debt; and they gave relief in the shape of redemption on that principle. Of course that would lead, and did lead, to this inconvenience, that even when the mortgagor was not willing to redeem, the mortgagee could not sell or deal with the estate as his own, and to remedy that inconvenience the practice of bringing a foreclosure suit was adopted, by which a mortgagee was entitled to call on the mortgagor to redeem within a certain time, under penalty of losing the right of redemption. In that foreclosure suit the Court made various orders—interim orders fixing a time for payment of the money—and at last there came the final order which was called foreclosure absolute, that is, in form, that the mortgagor should not be allowed to redeem at all; but it was form only, just as the original deed was form only; for the Courts of Equity soon decided that, notwithstanding the form of that order, they would after that order allow the mortgagor to redeem. That is, although the order of foreclosure absolute appeared to be a final order of the Court, it was not so, but the mortgagee still remained liable to be treated as mortgagee and the mortgagor still retained a claim to be treated as mortgagor, subject to the discretion of the Court. Therefore everybody who took an order for foreclosure absolute knew that there was still a discretion in the Court to allow the mortgagor to redeem.

Under what circumstances that discretion should be exercised is quite another matter. The mortgagee had a right to deal with an estate acquired under foreclosure absolute the day after he acquired it; but he knew perfectly well that there might be circumstances to entitle the mortgagor to redeem, and everybody buying the estate from a mortgagee who merely acquired a title under such an order was considered to have the same knowledge, namely, that the estate might be taken away from him by the exercise, not of a capricious discretion, but of a judicial discretion by the Court of Equity which had made the order.

That being so, on what terms is that judicial discretion to be exercised? It has been said by the highest authority that it is impossible to say *a priori* what are the terms. They must depend upon the circumstances of each case.... In the first place the mortgagor must come, as it is said, promptly; that is, within a reasonable time. He is not to let the mortgagee deal with the estate as his own—if it is a landed estate, the mortgagee being in possession of it and using it—and then without any special reason come and say, 'Now I will redeem'. He cannot do that; he must come within a reasonable time. What is a reasonable time? You must have regard to the nature of the property. As has been stated in more than one of the cases, where the estate is an estate in land in possession—where the mortgagee takes it in possession and deals with it and alters the property, and so on—the mortgagor must come more quickly than where it is an estate in reversion, as to which the mortgagee can do nothing except sell it. So that you must have regard to the nature of the estate in ascertaining what is to be considered reasonable time.

Then, again, was the mortgagee[201] entitled to redeem, but by some accident unable to redeem? Did he expect to get the money from a quarter from which he might reasonably hope to obtain it, and was he disappointed at the last moment? Was it a very large sum, and did he require a considerable time to raise it elsewhere? All those things must be considered in determining what is a reasonable time.

Then an element for consideration has always been the nature of the property as regards value.[202] For instance, if an estate were worth £50,000, and had been foreclosed for a mortgage

---

[201] Presumably 'mortgagor' was intended here.

[202] *Lancashire and Yorkshire Reversionary Interest Co v Crowe* (1970) 114 SJ 435 (foreclosure decree made absolute in respect of mortgage of reversionary interest; and re-opened after the interest fell into possession on life tenant's death. The sum due was £3,000 and the fund £6,100). This is a very rare case in the modern

debt of £5,000, the man who came to redeem that estate would have a longer time than where the estate was worth £5,100, and he was foreclosed for £5,000. But not only is there money value, but there may be other considerations. It may be an old family estate or a chattel, or picture, which possesses a special value for the mortgagor, but which possesses not the same value for other people; or it may be, as has happened in this instance, that the property, though a reversionary interest in the funds, is of special value to both the litigants: it may possess not merely a positive money value, but a peculiar value having regard to the nature of the title and other incidents, so that you cannot set an actual money value upon it. In fact, that is the real history of this contest, for the property does not appear to be of much more money value— though it is of some more— than the original amount of the mortgage. All this must be taken into consideration.

Then it is said you must not interfere against purchasers. As I have already explained, there are purchasers and purchasers. If the purchaser buys a freehold estate in possession after the lapse of a considerable time from the order of foreclosure absolute, with no notice of any extraneous circumstances which would induce the Court to interfere, I for one should decline to interfere with such a title as that; but if the purchaser bought the estate within twenty-four hours after the foreclosure absolute, and with notice of the fact that it was of much greater value than the amount of the mortgage debt, is it to be supposed that a Court of Equity would listen to the contention of such a purchaser that he ought not to be interfered with? He must be taken to know the general law that an order for foreclosure may be opened under proper circumstances and under a proper exercise of discretion by the Court; and if the mortgagor in that case came the week after, is it to be supposed a Court of Equity would so stultify itself as to say that a title so acquired would stand in the way? I am of opinion it would not.

Now I come to the circumstances of this case, and I must say they are very strong in favour of opening the foreclosure....

The present purchaser, Mr Ford, being very desirous to acquire the property for a collateral object[203]—I am not saying a wrong object, but a collateral object—had, before the time for foreclosure absolute had arrived, entered into a contract with the mortgagee to buy it. He was not a purchaser coming in even the day after foreclosure, but a purchaser coming in before foreclosure, and at that time of course he knew the property was redeemable. He bought a property certainly redeemable, for the day for redemption had not even arrived. That is the kind of purchase I am dealing with. He was aware on the day of redemption that it was not from unwillingness to redeem that the mortgagor failed to pay the money, but because the mortgagor was under the belief that he had acquired a right to take the property on paying less than the mortgage money, by reason of a contract of purchase with the mortgagee....

I am of opinion...that such a sale as this ought to have no weight whatever, and that under the circumstances the mortgagor is entitled to open the foreclosure on the usual terms, that is, on payment of principal, interest, and costs.

In **Kinnaird v Trollope** (1888) 39 ChD 636, STIRLING J said at 642:

Where a mortgagee has obtained a decree for foreclosure absolute he may still sue the mortgagor on the covenant for payment of the mortgage debt provided he retains the mortgaged property in his possession, but (as is laid down by Lord Langdale in *Lockhart v Hardy* (1846) 9 Beav

---

law. There appears to be no case reported in the Law Reports since the beginning of the 20th century in which a foreclosure was re-opened, the last such case in which a claim to re-open was made being *Pennington v Cayley* [1912] 2 Ch 236.

[203] To obtain the property for Blakely's widow.

349 at 355) by so suing he gives the mortgagor a new right of redemption, notwithstanding the foreclosure, and the mortgagor may file a bill to redeem. If, however, the mortgagee has sold the mortgaged property, a Court of Equity will interfere to restrain an action on the covenant.[204]

G. CONSOLIDATION[205]

If the same mortgagor has mortgaged more than one property to the same mortgagee, and if one of the properties so mortgaged is worth less than the debt for the repayment of which it has been charged as security, it is in the mortgagor's interest to redeem the other properties but not that one. The courts of Equity, however, took the view that the mortgagor is asking a favour in being allowed to redeem any property after the contractual date for redemption has passed, and, in accordance with the maxim: 'He who comes to Equity must do Equity', the mortgagor may be prevented from redeeming one mortgage without redeeming others. In other words, the mortgagee has a right in certain circumstances to consolidate the various mortgages against the mortgagor. However, in mortgages made after 1881, the mortgagee's right to consolidate must be expressly reserved in the various deeds, or at least in one of them.

LAW OF PROPERTY ACT 1925

93. Restriction on consolidation of mortgages.—(1) A mortgagor seeking to redeem any one mortgage is entitled to do so without paying any money due under any separate mortgage made by him, or by any person through whom he claims, solely on property other than that comprised in the mortgage which he seeks to redeem.

This subsection applies only if and as far as a contrary intention is not expressed in the mortgage deeds or one of them.

(2) This section does not apply where all the mortgages were made before the first day of January, eighteen hundred and eighty two.[206]

(3) Save as aforesaid, nothing in this Act, in reference to mortgages, affects any right of consolidation or renders inoperative a stipulation in relation to any mortgage made before or after the commencement of this Act reserving a right to consolidate.

Pledge v White
[1896] AC 187 (HL, **Lords Halsbury LC, Watson** and **Davey**)

There were mortgages on seven different properties; the properties will be referred to as Nos. 1–7. They were mortgaged by James Banks to various mortgagees between 1863 and 1866.

---

[204] Followed in *Lloyds and Scottish Trust Ltd v Britten* (1982) 44 P & CR 249 (guarantor of mortgagor likewise held not suable).

[205] C & B, pp. 779–782; M & W, paras 25.055–25.069; MM, pp. 515–518; Waldock, pp. 284–295; Cousins, chap. 24; Fisher and Lightwood, chap. 46. As to whether the right amounts to a general equitable charge within LCA 1972, s. 2(4), Class C(iii), see (1948) 92 SJ 736; W & C, vol. 1, 189. For registered land, see LRA 2002, s. 57; LRR 2003, r. 110, under which a right of consolidation may be entered on the register.

[206] This provision is re-enactment of Conveyancing Act 1881, s. 17.

In 1866 James Banks the mortgagor made a second mortgage of Nos. 4–7 to Brockman: and in 1868 a third mortgage of these properties and a second mortgage of Nos. 1–3 to Brockman and Harrison. In 1885, Brockman and Harrison assigned their equities of redemption in all 7 properties to Pledge, the appellant.

Between 1871 and 1890, Brockman became the transferee of all the first mortgages except that on No. 3.[207] He died in 1877, and in 1890 his executors, the respondents, took an assignment of the first mortgage on No. 3.

In 1890 the appellant claimed to redeem No. 2 alone. The respondents refused to allow him to do so without redeeming the other six.

Held. The mortgagee was entitled to consolidate.

Lord Halsbury LC: My Lords, I have had an opportunity of considering the judgment prepared by my noble and learned friend (Lord Davey) and I am not prepared to dissent from it. I use that form of expression because I confess I lament the conclusion to which it has been found necessary to come, although I believe the strict principle upon which it rests is founded in our law at present, and in dealing with a technical system it is better to adhere to a principle when once established, than to create greater confusion by dissenting from it. I think the principle laid down in *Vint v Padget* (1858) 2 De G & J 611 has been so firmly established now by authority in our technical system, that I feel more mischief would be done by dissenting from it, than by acquiescing in it....

Lord Davey: The question for your Lordships' decision is whether the respondents have the right of consolidation which they claim, notwithstanding that the mortgages which it is sought to consolidate were not united in title with the mortgage sought to be redeemed until after the assignment of the equity of redemption to the present appellant's predecessors in title....

The equitable rule as to the consolidation of mortgages is not one of those doctrines of the Court of Chancery which has met with general approbation—at any rate as regards its later development. Originally it may have been a right of a mortgagee holding two separate mortgages on estates of the same mortgagor which have become absolute estates at law against the mortgagor and debtor personally to refuse to be redeemed as regards one estate without having his other debt also paid. But it has long been settled that the right of consolidation may be exercised by the transferee of the mortgages as well as by the original mortgagee, and may be exercised in respect of equitable mortgages as well as by a mortgagee holding the legal estate absolute at law; and on the other hand, that it may be asserted against the assignee of an equity of redemption from the mortgagor as well as against the mortgagor himself...

The case of *Vint v Padget* came before Stuart V-C in the first instance, whose judgment may be referred to as shewing how entirely that experienced judge considered the point to be settled. 'In accepting', he says, 'by way of security the equity of redemption of two separate estates, Mr Lee deliberately incurred the risk of their uniting in one hand, and when that union has taken place there is only one single debt, and in order to redeem he must pay off both mortgages, each of which affects the entirety of both estates.'

His Lordship referred to *Bovey v Skipwich* (1671) 1 Cas in Ch 201; *Titley v Davies* (1743) 2 Y & C Ch Cas 399; *Selby v Pomfret* (1861) 3 De G F & J 595; *Beevor v Luck* (1867) LR

---

[207] The facts as given by Lord Davey do not explain how Brockman obtained the mortgages on Nos. 6 and 7.

4 Eq 537; *White v Hillacre* (1839) 3 Y & C Ex 597; *Harter v Colman* (1882) 19 ChD 630; *Jennings v Jordan* (1881) 6 App Cas 698, and continued:

It appears to me, my Lords, that an assignee of two or more equities of redemption from one mortgagor stands in a widely different position from the assignee of one equity only. He knows, or has the opportunity of knowing, what are the mortgages subject to which he has purchased the property, and he knows that they may become united by transfer in one hand. If the doctrine of consolidation be once admitted it appears to me not unreasonable to hold that a person in such a position occupies the place of the mortgagor or assignor to him towards the holders of the mortgages, subject to which he has purchased, although it may be unreasonable to hold that he can be affected by the transfer to such holders of mortgages to other persons by the same mortgagor on property which he has not purchased, and with the equity of redemption of which he has no concern. He does not investigate the title to such other property and cannot know in the latter case to what mortgages the property is subject. If your Lordships affirm the decree now under appeal, the doctrine of consolidation will be confined within at least intelligible limits. It will be applicable where at the date when redemption is sought all the mortgages are united in one hand and redeemable by the same person, or where after that state of things has once existed the equities of redemption have become separated.[208] If the purchaser of two or more equities of redemption desires to prevent consolidation, he has it in his power to redeem any one mortgage before consolidation takes place; but if for his own convenience he delays doing so, he runs the same risk as his assignor ran of the mortgages becoming united by transfer in one hand.

I am of opinion that the application of the doctrine of consolidation to a case like the present has been too long considered part of the equitable jurisprudence of this country to be altered at the present time, and it is not so unreasonable as to demand a reversal of it by this House.

I move, therefore, that this appeal be dismissed with costs.

In **Cummins v Fletcher** (1880) 14 Ch D 699, the trustees of a building society, who were mortgagees of two properties, refused to allow a bank, the second mortgagee of one of the properties, to redeem it, without also redeeming the other. All payments due under the first mortgage were up to date, but those on the second were in arrears.

The Court of Appeal (James, Cotton and Thesiger LJJ, reversing Hall V-C) refused to allow the building society to consolidate, on the ground that consolidation arose only where the mortgagor was in default and was asking a favour of the Court of Equity. JAMES LJ said at 708:

The whole doctrine of consolidation, whatever may have been the particular circumstances under which it has been applied to different cases, arises from the power of the Court of Equity to put its own price upon its own interference as a matter of equitable consideration in favour of any suitor.

A further reason, mentioned by the court, was that the mortgagors were not the same in the two mortgages. In the first mortgage, the mortgagor was Vaugham and in the second Vaugham and Neesham, partners. This point was not necessary for the decision.

---

[208] It will not apply where the equities of redemption separated before the mortgages became united in one hand: *Harter v Colman* (1882) 19 ChD 630.

In **Hughes v Britannia Permanent Building Society** [1906] 2 Ch 607, A in 1894 mortgaged Blackacre to the defendants, the mortgage providing that A should not be entitled to redeem without paying all the moneys due by A to the defendants under any other mortgage.

A then mortgaged Whiteacre to the defendants, and gave a second mortgage to the plaintiffs, the defendants having notice of this mortgage; A subsequently mortgaged two separate properties to the defendants.

The plaintiffs claimed to redeem Whiteacre, and the question was whether the defendants could consolidate against the plaintiffs all their mortgages or only those made before the second mortgage of Whiteacre to the plaintiffs.

KEKEWICH J held that the defendants could consolidate against the plaintiffs the mortgages on Blackacre and Whiteacre, but not those on the other properties. The mortgagor, by his express contract, would have been compelled to submit to consolidation of all the properties; and the plaintiffs would have been in the same position if the defendants, at the time of the later mortgages, had not had notice of the second mortgage on Whiteacre to the plaintiffs.[209]

VIII. DISCHARGE OF MORTGAGES[210]

A. UNREGISTERED LAND

LAW OF PROPERTY ACT 1925

115. Reconveyances of mortgages by endorsed receipts.—(1) A receipt endorsed on, written at the foot of, or annexed to, a mortgage for all money thereby secured, which states the name of the person who pays the money and is executed by the chargee by way of legal mortgage or the person in whom the mortgaged property is vested and who is legally entitled to give a receipt for the mortgage money shall operate, without any reconveyance, surrender, or release—

   (a) Where a mortgage takes effect by demise or subdemise, as a surrender of the term, so as to determine the term or merge the same in the reversion immediately expectant thereon;

   (b) Where the mortgage does not take effect by demise or subdemise, as a reconveyance thereof to the extent of the interest which is the subject matter of the mortgage, to the person who immediately before the execution of the receipt was entitled to the equity of redemption;

and in either case, as a discharge of the mortgaged property from all principal money and interest secured by, and from all claims under the mortgage, but without prejudice to any term

---

[209] See also *Andrews v City Permanent Benefit Building Society* (1881) 44 LT 641.

[210] C & B, pp. 756–759; Gray, para. 6.1.18; M & W, paras 25.150–25.154; MM, pp. 529–530; Cousins, Part VIII; Fisher and Lightwood, Part VIII.

or other interests which is paramount to the estate or interest of the mortgagee or other person in whom the mortgaged property was vested.[211]

(2) Provided that, where by the receipt the money appears to have been paid by a person who is not entitled to the immediate equity of redemption, the receipt shall operate as if the benefit of the mortgage had by deed been transferred to him; unless—

(a) it is otherwise expressly provided; or

(b) the mortgage is paid off out of capital money, or other money in the hands of a personal representative or trustee properly applicable for the discharge of the mortgage, and it is not expressly provided that the receipt is to operate as a transfer.

(3) Nothing in this section confers on a mortgagor a right to keep alive a mortgage paid off by him, so as to affect prejudicially any subsequent incumbrancer; and where there is no right to keep the mortgage alive, the receipt does not operate as a transfer.[212]

(4) This section does not affect the right of any person to require a reassignment, surrender, release, or transfer to be executed in lieu of a receipt.

(8) This section applies to the discharge of a charge by way of legal mortgage, and to the discharge of a mortgage, whether made by way of statutory mortgage or not, executed before or after the commencement of this Act, but only as respects discharges effected after such commencement.

(10) This section does not apply to the discharge of a registered charge within the meaning of the Land Registration Act 2002.[213]

116. Cesser of mortgage terms.—Without prejudice to the right of a tenant for life or other person having only a limited interest in the equity of redemption to require a mortgage to be kept alive by transfer or otherwise, a mortgage term shall, when the money secured by the mortgage has been discharged, become a satisfied term and shall cease.[214]

B. REGISTERED LAND[215]

LAND REGISTRATION RULES 2003

Discharges and releases of registered charges

114.—(1) Subject to rule 115, a discharge of a registered charge must be in Form DS1.

(2) Subject to rule 115, a release of part of the registered estate in a registered title from a registered charge must be in Form DS3.

(3) Any discharge or release in Form DS1 or DS3 must be executed as a deed or authenticated in such other manner as the registrar may approve.

---

[211] A building society may use either a reconveyance or a special statutory receipt: Building Societies Act 1986, Sch. 4, para. 2.

[212] *Otter v Lord Vaux* (1856) 6 De GM & G 638; *Parkash v Irani Finance Ltd* [1970] Ch 101.

[213] As amended by LRA 2002, s. 133, Sch. 11, para. 2(1), (11).

[214] *Edwards v Marshall-Lee* (1975) 235 EG 901 (vacating receipt on a legal charge not complying with s. 115 held a valid discharge); (1976) 40 Conv (NS) 102.

[215] See generally Land Registry Practice Guide 31: Discharge of Charges (revised 2008), which contains in the appendix copies of the prescribed forms; H & B, paras 12.86–12.107.

(4) Notwithstanding paragraphs (1) and (2) and rule 115, the registrar is entitled to accept and act upon any other proof of satisfaction of a charge that he may regard as sufficient.

Discharges and releases of registered charges in electronic form[216]

115.—(1) During the currency of a notice given under Schedule 2 and subject to and in accordance with the limitations contained in such notice, notification of—

(a) the discharge of, or

(b) the release of part of a registered estate in a registered title from a registered charge may be delivered to the registrar in electronic form.

(2) Notification of discharge or release of part given in accordance with paragraph (1) shall be regarded as having the same effect as a discharge in Form DS1, or a release of part in Form DS3, as appropriate, executed in accordance with rule 114 by or on behalf the person who has delivered it to the registrar.

IX. PRIORITY OF MORTGAGES[217]

Very substantial alterations were made by the legislation of 1925 to the rules concerning the priority of mortgages. The rules which were in force before 1926 are of importance as there are still circumstances in which they may apply.[218] However, the detail of the pre-1926 rules must be found elsewhere.[219]

A. BEFORE 1926

Radcliffe, *Real Property Law* (2nd edn, 1938), pp. 228–231

Priorities

The doctrine of consolidation[220] deals with the situation which arises where the same mortgagor has mortgaged a number of different properties. Problems regarding the priorities of mortgages arise when the mortgagor has created several mortgages on the same property, and the value of the property is insufficient to discharge them all.

---

[216] See Land Registry Practice Guide 31: Discharge of Charges, section 8: Form e-DS1, a new form of electronic discharge.

[217] C & B, pp. 784–808; Gray, part 6.5; M & W, chap. 26; MM, pp. 530–546; Cousins, chap. 18; Waldock, pp. 381–435; Fisher and Lightwood, Part VI; (1949) 7 CLJ 243 (R. E. Megarry).

[218] C & B, pp. 804–807: the pre-1926 rules relating to priorities as between mortgagees of an equitable interest in pure personalty (the rule in *Dearle v Hall* (1823) 3 Russ 1, under which priority depended upon the order in which the trustees had received notice from the mortgagees) was extended by LPA 1925, s. 137(1) to mortgages of *all* equitable interests, realty being put on the same footing as personalty; and the rules that existed before 1926 with regard to the nature of the notice still hold good, except that by s. 137(3) a notice given otherwise than in writing in respect of any dealing with an equitable interest in real or personal property shall not affect the priority of competing claims of purchasers or mortgagees.

[219] C & B, pp. 784–794; For the cases, see the 8th edn of this book, pp. 904–915.

[220] [Pp. 978–981, above.]

Under the law as it stood prior to January 1st, 1926, the general rule was that the legal mortgagee ranked first, and all equitable incumbrancers ranked after him in the order in which their securities were created. But this general rule was liable to be disturbed, as regards the legal mortgagee, by his being postponed in certain circumstances to prior, and even to subsequent, equitable incumbrances, and as regards the equitable incumbrancers by the doctrine of tacking.

Circumstances in which a legal mortgagee was postponed to an equitable mortgagee

(a) A legal mortgagee could only claim to be preferred to a prior equitable incumbrancer on the ground that he was a purchaser for value of the legal estate without notice of the equity. Consequently he took subject to any equitable charge of which he had notice, actual or constructive, when he advanced his money. An equitable mortgagee by deposit of title-deeds almost invariably ranked in front of a subsequent legal mortgage, for the possession of the title-deeds was clear notice to all the world of the existence of the equitable mortgage.[221]

(b) A prior legal mortgagee could be postponed to subsequent equitable incumbrancers upon four different grounds:

(i) By agreement. It often happens, particularly in cases of mortgages of property which is being developed for building, that it is to the mutual advantage of the mortgagor and legal mortgagee that the mortgagor should raise further money to be spent on the mortgaged premises, but that the legal mortgagee is not in a position to make any further advances. In such circumstances the parties would arrange for an advance from an equitable mortgagee upon terms that his charge should rank in front of the legal mortgage. Such an equitable mortgagee would require that the title-deeds should be handed over to him.

(ii) By estoppel. A principal is always estopped from asserting against third parties, who deal with his agent, that the agent has exceeded his ostensible authority, and contravened instructions given to him by the principal, but not disclosed to the third party. Accordingly, if the legal mortgagee handed over the title-deeds to the mortgagor, in order that the mortgagor should raise £1,000 by equitable mortgage to rank in front of the legal mortgage, and the mortgagor raised £2,000, the legal mortgagee was estopped from contesting the right of the equitable mortgagee to rank first for his whole advance.[222]

(iii) By collusion or fraud. A fortiori if the action of the legal mortgagee in handing over the title-deeds to the mortgagor was tainted by a collusive and fraudulent intent to deceive a fresh incumbrancer by leading him to think that he was getting a first mortgage, the legal mortgagee was postponed.

(iv) By gross negligence on the part of the legal mortgagee in failing to obtain possession of the title-deeds when he made his advance, so that the mortgagor was enabled to impose upon a subsequent incumbrancer by representing the premises as unencumbered.[223]

---

[221] *Oliver v Hinton* [1899] 2 Ch 264. In that case the person postponed to the prior equitable mortgagee was a person who had bought the premises, not a legal mortgagee, but the same principle applies to all purchasers of legal estates, whether by mortgage or sale. See also the instructive and interesting case of *Jared v Clements* [1902] 2 Ch 39 and in CA, [1903] 1 Ch 428.

[222] *Perry Herrick v Atwood* (1857) 2 De G & J 21.

[223] *Walker v Linom* [1907] 2 Ch 104.

No amount of negligence, however gross, on the part of the legal mortgagee, in the custody of the title-deeds, when once he had got them, was sufficient, apart from estoppel or fraud, to postpone him to a subsequent equitable incumbrancer.[224]

Tacking

The doctrine of tacking...was but another instance of the superiority of the legal mortgagee to equitable mortgagees. Just as a legal mortgagee had priority over prior equitable incumbrances of which he had no notice, so if, after making his first advance, he made a subsequent advance to the mortgagor, he was entitled to join his two advances together, and to claim priority for both of them over any intervening equitable incumbrancer, who had advanced his money between the dates of the first and second advance, always provided that the legal mortgagee, at the time when he made the second advance, had no notice, actual or constructive, of the intervening equity.

This proviso was insisted upon so strictly that the legal mortgagee was not permitted to tack a second advance as against an intervening equity of which he had notice, even though he was bound by the terms of the mortgage to make the second advance when required to do so by the mortgagor.[225]

Equitable mortgagees who advanced their money subject to a prior legal mortgage, invariably protected themselves against the danger of the legal mortgagee tacking a subsequent advance by giving him notice of their mortgage. Notice to one of two or more mortgagees who are joint tenants is notice to them all.[226]

From the tacking of further advances by a legal mortgagee the doctrine of tacking was extended to cover the case where a third or subsequent equitable mortgagee, on discovering the existence of prior equitable mortgages, of which he had no notice when he advanced his money, bought up the legal mortgage and tacked his equitable mortgage to it. Thus, suppose a property mortgaged first to A by legal mortgage for £1,000, then to B by equitable mortgage for £500, and then to C by equitable mortgage for £500. If C, when he advanced his £500, had no notice of B's mortgage, and could, on discovering its existence, buy up A's mortgage, he could insist upon being paid £1,500 before B got anything. The legal estate in such a case was said to be *tabula in naufragio* or a plank in a shipwreck.[227]

While the doctrine of tacking originated in the superiority of the legal to the equitable estate, the right of tacking further advances could be exercised even by an equitable incumbrancer, provided he had as between himself and the other incumbrancer a better right to the legal estate.[228] The possession of the title-deeds was one of the circumstances which gave an equitable incumbrancer such a better right. Thus a banker, accepting a deposit of title-deeds from a customer to secure present and future advances, could tack the future advances to the original debt as against any intervening incumbrancer of whom he had no notice.[229] But an equitable incumbrancer could not tack against an intervening incumbrancer who was himself a purchaser for value of the legal estate without notice.

224 *Northern Fire Insurance Co v Whipp* (1864) 26 ChD 482.
225 *West v Williams* [1899] 1 Ch 132.
226 *Freeman v Laing* [1899] 2 Ch 355.
227 *Taylor v Russell* [1892] AC 244.
228 Coote, *Mortgages* (9th edn), p. 1242 et seq.
229 *Wormald v Maitland* (1866) 35 LJ Ch 69.

B. AFTER 1925

(i) Unregistered land

(a) Mortgages of legal estates

The system of priority of mortgages which is in operation at the present day is the creation of the legislation of 1925. The paucity of litigation on the subject suggests that the system has, on the whole, worked reasonably well; though it may be due more to the considerable rise in land prices than to the merits of the system. It is however open to certain theoretical objections which are fully explained elsewhere. No more will be attempted here than to give the statutory enactments on which the system is based.

LAW OF PROPERTY ACT 1925

13. Effect of possession of documents.—This Act shall not prejudicially affect the right or interest of any person arising out of or consequent on the possession by him of any documents relating to a legal estate in land, nor affect any question arising out of or consequent upon any omission to obtain or any other absence of possession by any person of any documents relating to a legal estate in land.

97. Priorities as between puisne mortgages.—Every mortgage affecting a legal estate in land made after the commencement of this Act, whether legal or equitable (not being a mortgage protected by the deposit of documents relating to the legal estate affected) shall rank according to its date of registration as a land charge pursuant to the Land Charges Act 1925.[230]

This section does not apply to mortgages or charges to which the Land Charges Act 1972 does not apply by virtue of section 14(3) of that Act (which excludes certain land charges created by instruments necessitating registration under the Land Registration Act 2002),[231] or to mortgages or charges of registered land[232] ...

199. Restrictions on constructive notice.—(1)(i) p. 80, above.

LAND CHARGES ACT 1972

2. The register of land charges.—(4) Class C, p. 66, above.[233]

4. Effect of land charges and protection of purchasers.—(5) p. 71, above.

17. Interpretation.—(1) p. 72, above.

(b) Mortgages by companies

LAND CHARGES ACT 1972

3. Registration of land charges.—(7) and (8), p. 93, above.

---

230 Now LCA 1972.   231 As substituted by LRA 2002, s. 133, Sch. 11, para. 2(1), (10).
232 As amended by LCA 1972, s. 18(1), Sch. 3, para. 1, as substituted by LRA 1997, s. 4(1), Sch. 1, para. 3.
233 As to whether a protected equitable mortgage is registrable as an estate contract (Class C (iv)), see C & B, pp. 796–797; Waldock, pp. 425–428; [1940] CLJ pp. 250–251 (R. E. Megarry); (1962) 26 Conv (NS), pp. 446–449 (R. G. Rowley); Williams, *Contract of Sale of Land*, p. 247; Fairest, *Mortgages* (2nd edn), pp. 133–136; Fisher and Lightwood, para. 4.4.

COMPANIES ACT 2006

(c) Mortgages of equitable interests

LAW OF PROPERTY ACT 1925

137. Dealings with life interests, reversions and other equitable interests.—(1) The law applicable to dealings with equitable things in action which regulates the priority of competing interests therein, shall, as respects dealings with equitable interests in land, capital money, and securities representing capital money effected after the commencement of this Act, apply to and regulate the priority of competing interests therein.[234]

This subsection applies whether or not the money or securities are in court.

(2) (i) In the case of a dealing with an equitable interest in settled land, capital money or securities representing capital money, the persons to be served with notice of the dealing shall be the trustees of the settlement; and where the equitable interest is created by a derivative or subsidiary settlement, the persons to be served with notice shall be the trustees of that settlement.

(ii) In the case of a dealing with an equitable interest in land subject to a trust of land, or the proceeds of the sale of such land, the persons to be served with notice shall be the trustees.[235]

(iii) In any other case the person to be served with notice of a dealing with an equitable interest in land shall be the estate owner of the land affected.

The persons on whom notice is served pursuant to this subsection shall be affected thereby in the same manner as if they had been trustees of personal property out of which the equitable interest was created or arose.

This subsection does not apply where the money or securities are in court.

(3) A notice, otherwise than in writing, given to, or received by, a trustee after the commencement of this Act as respects any dealing with an equitable interest in real or personal property, shall not affect the priority of competing claims of purchasers in that equitable interest.

(4) Where, as respects any dealing with an equitable interest in real or personal property—

(a) the trustees are not persons to whom a valid notice of the dealing can be given; or

(b) there are no trustees to whom a notice can be given; or

(c) for any other reason a valid notice cannot be served, or cannot be served without unreasonable cost or delay;

a purchaser may at his own cost require that—

(i) a memorandum of the dealing be endorsed, written on or permanently annexed to the instrument creating the trust;

---

[234] For an analysis of the section, see [1993] Conv 22 (J. Howell).
[235] As amended by TLATA 1996, s. 25(1), Sch. 3, para. 4(15).

(ii) the instrument be produced to him by the person having the possession or custody thereof to prove that a sufficient memorandum has been placed thereon or annexed thereto.

Such memorandum shall, as respects priorities, operate in like manner as if notice in writing of the dealing had been given to trustees duly qualified to receive the notice at the time when the memorandum is placed on or annexed to the instrument creating the trust.

(5) Where the property affected is settled land, the memorandum shall be placed on or annexed to the trust instrument and not the vesting instrument.

Where the property affected is land held subject to a trust of land,[236] the memorandum shall be placed on or annexed to the instrument whereby the equitable interest is created.

(6) Where the trust is created by statute or by operation of law, or in any other case where there is no instrument whereby the trusts are declared, the instrument under which the equitable interest is acquired or which is evidence of the devolution thereof shall, for the purposes of this section, be deemed the instrument creating the trust.

In particular, where the trust arises by reason of an intestacy, the letters of administration or probate in force when the dealing was effected shall be deemed such instrument.

(7) Nothing in this section affects any priority acquired before the commencement of this Act.

(8) Where a notice in writing of a dealing with an equitable interest in real or personal property has been served on a trustee under this section, the trustees from time to time of the property affected shall be entitled to the custody of the notice, and the notice shall be delivered to them by any person who for the time being may have the custody thereof; and subject to the payment of costs, any person interested in the equitable interest may require production of the notice.

(9) The liability of the estate owner of the legal estate affected to produce documents and furnish information to persons entitled to equitable interests therein shall correspond to the liability of a trustee for sale to produce documents and furnish information to persons entitled to equitable interests in the proceeds of sale of the land.[237]

(ii) Registered land

Where there are registered charges on the same registered estate, they rank in priority as between themselves in the order shown on the register.[238] This was provided both by the Land Registration Act 1925 in section 29, and now by the Land Registration Act 2002 in section 48 (below) and by the Land Registration Rules 2003, rules 101–102. The priority of equitable charges, however, depends upon the general rules of priority under sections 28–30 of the Land Registration Act 2002, pp. 170–171, above, where the order of priority is determined by the order in which the charges are created.

---

236 As amended by TLATA 1996, s. 25(1), Sch. 3, para. 4(15).

237 This undermines *Low v Bouverie* [1891] 3 Ch 82. For the power to nominate a trust corporation to receive notices, see LPA 1925, s. 138: Law Reform Committee 23rd Report (The Powers and Duties of Trustees) 1982 (Cmnd 8733), paras 2.17–2.24.

238 R & R, paras 27.008–27.009. Law Commission Report on Land Registration in the Twenty-First Century 2001 (Law Com No. 271), paras 7.13–7.17; H & B, para. 12.48.

The order of priority may be varied by agreement between the chargees: LRR 2003, r. 102(1), below; or by estoppel: *Scottish & Newcastle Plc v Lancashire Mortgage Corp Ltd* [2007] EWCA Civ 684, [2007] NPC 84.

For the priority of overriding statutory charges, such as the charge in favour of the Legal Services Commission under Access to Justice Act 1999, s. 10(7), see LRA 2002, s. 50; LRR 2003, rr. 105–106; H & B, paras 12.51–12.58.

LAND REGISTRATION ACT 2002

48 Registered charges

(1) Registered charges on the same registered estate, or on the same registered charge, are to be taken to rank as between themselves in the order shown in the register.

(2) Rules may make provision about—

(a) how the priority of registered charges as between themselves is to be shown in the register, and

(b) applications for registration of the priority of registered charges as between themselves.

LAND REGISTRATION RULES 2003

How ranking of registered charges as between themselves to be shown on register

101. Subject to any entry in the individual register to the contrary, for the purpose of section 48(1) of the Act the order in which registered charges are entered in an individual register shows the order in which the registered charges rank as between themselves.

Alteration of priority of registered charges

102.—(1) An application to alter the priority of registered charges, as between themselves, must be made by or with the consent of the proprietor or a person entitled to be registered as the proprietor of any registered charge whose priority is adversely affected by the alteration, but no such consent is required from a person who has executed the instrument which alters the priority of the charges.

(2) The registrar may accept a conveyancer's certificate confirming that the conveyancer holds any necessary consents.

(3) The registrar must make an entry in the register in such terms as the registrar considers appropriate to give effect to the application.

C. TACKING AND FURTHER ADVANCES[239]

(i) Unregistered land

LAW OF PROPERTY ACT 1925

94. Tacking and further advances.—(1) After the commencement of this Act, a prior mortgagee shall have a right to make further advances to rank in priority to subsequent mortgages (whether legal or equitable)—

(a) if an arrangement has been made to that effect with the subsequent mortgagees; or

---

[239] C & B, pp. 789–791, 802–804, 807–808; Gray, paras 6.5.19–6.5.21; M & W, paras 26.050–26.069, 26.073; MM, pp. 530, 542–544. On tacking generally see *MacMillan Inc v Bishopsgate Trust (No. 3)* [1995] 1 WLR 978 at 1002–1005, per Millett J. The doctrine is of reduced importance after 1925. For tacking before 1926, see p. 985, above.

(b) if he had no notice of such subsequent mortgages at the time when the further advance was made by him; or

(c) whether or not he had such notice as aforesaid, where the mortgage imposes an obligation on him to make such further advances.

This subsection applies whether or not the prior mortgage was made expressly for securing further advances.

(2) In relating to the making of further advances after the commencement of this Act a mortgagee shall not be deemed to have notice of a mortgage merely by reason that it was registered as a land charge . . . if it was not so registered at the time when the original mortgage was created[240] or when the last search (if any) by or on behalf of the mortgagee was made, whichever last happened.

This subsection only applies where the prior mortgage was made expressly for securing a current account or other further advances.[241]

(3) Save in regard to the making of further advances as aforesaid, the right to tack is hereby abolished:

Provided that nothing in this Act shall affect any priority acquired before the commencement of this Act by tacking, or in respect of further advances made without notice of a subsequent incumbrance or by arrangement with the subsequent incumbrancer.

(4) This section applies to mortgages of land made before or after the commencement of this Act, but not to charges on registered land.[242]

(ii) Registered land

There was no equivalent statutory code under the Land Registration Act 1925 which applied to tacking and further advances in relation to charges over registered land. 'The applicable law prior to the implementation of the LRA 1925 comprised the old common law rules of tacking that had been abolished in relation to unregistered land with a partial statutory gloss'.[243]

A statutory code is now set out in section 49 of the Land Registration Act 2002.[244] This contains a new provision in subsection (4) under which an agreement may be registered for the maximum amount secured by a charge. This will give the chargee priority over any later registered charges for the original loan and any further advances up to the maximum amount specified.

LAND REGISTRATION ACT 2002

49 Tacking and further advances

(1) The proprietor of a registered charge may make a further advance on the security of the charge ranking in priority to a subsequent charge if he has not received from the subsequent chargee notice of the creation of the subsequent charge.

---

[240] As substituted by LP(A) A 1926, s. 7 and Sch.   [241] (1958) 22 Conv (NS) 44 (R. G. Rowley).

[242] As amended by LRA 2002, s. 133, Sch. 11, para. 2(1), (9).

[243] H & B, para. 12.61; R & R, paras 27.014–27.015. See LRA 1925, s. 3.

[244] H & B paras 12.60–12.78; LRR 2002, rr. 107, 108, 109. Law Commission Report on Land Registration for the Twenty-First Century 2001 (Law Com No. 271), paras 7.18–7.41.

(2) Notice given for the purposes of subsection (1) shall be treated as received at the time when, in accordance with rules, it ought to have been received.

(3) The proprietor of a registered charge may also make a further advance on the security of the charge ranking in priority to a subsequent charge if—

(a) the advance is made in pursuance of an obligation, and

(b) at the time of the creation of the subsequent charge the obligation was entered in the register in accordance with rules.

(4) The proprietor of a registered charge may also make a further advance on the security of the charge ranking in priority to a subsequent charge if—

(a) the parties to the prior charge have agreed a maximum amount for which the charge is security, and

(b) at the time of the creation of the subsequent charge the agreement was entered in the register in accordance with rules.

(5) Rules may—

(a) disapply subsection (4) in relation to charges of a description specified in the rules, or

(b) provide for the application of that subsection to be subject, in the case of charges of a description so specified, to compliance with such conditions as may be so specified.

(6) Except as provided by this section, tacking in relation to a charge over registered land is only possible with the agreement of the subsequent chargee.

X. LAW REFORM

A. LAW COMMISSION REPORT ON LAND MORTGAGES 1991

Law Commission Report on Land Mortgages 1991 (Law Com No. 204), paras 10.2–10.17, 10.28–10.32, 10.35, 10.37–10.52, 10.55–10.62[245]

The new mortgages

10.2 All existing methods of consensually mortgaging or charging interests in land should be abolished and replaced by new forms of mortgage (the formal land mortgage and the informal

---

[245] Appendix A of the Report contains a draft Bill. See [1992] Conv 69 (H. W. Wilkinson); (1992) 136 SJ 267, 292 (G. Frost). In March 1989 the Law Commission's Conveyancing Standing Committee published a consultation document suggesting the use of a new form of mortgage called a flexi-mortgage as a means of avoiding chains, cutting out delays and defeating gazumping. Its unique feature is that for a limited time it gives the borrower the right to extend the period of the mortgage on a property he is buying and increase the amount he borrows to cover the cost of an overlapping sale and purchase. Payments under his old mortgage are suspended. This allows the house-owner to agree to buy a new property before selling his own by

land mortgage) the attributes of which would be expressly defined by statute, and which would be the only permissible methods of mortgaging any interest in land, whether legal or equitable. (Paras 2.20 to 2.30)

10.3 In principle, the rights, powers, duties and obligations of mortgagor and mortgagee under a land mortgage should be such as are appropriate for making the mortgaged property security for the performance of the mortgagor's obligations. (Paras 3.2 and 6.1 to 6.3)

Variable and overriding provisions

10.4 The statutory provisions defining the rights, powers, duties and obligations of the parties to a land mortgage should be categorised as either 'variable' or 'overriding'. Variable provisions should be variable or excludable, either directly by an express term of the mortgage or indirectly by necessary implication from any express term. Overriding provisions should apply notwithstanding any provision to the contrary contained in the mortgage or in any other instrument.[246] Any provision of a mortgagee or any other instrument should be void to the extent that it (i) purports to impose a liability which has the effect of allowing the mortgagee to escape or mitigate the consequences of an overriding provision, or to be reimbursed the consequences of complying with it or (ii) has the effect of preventing or discouraging the mortgagor or any other person from enforcing or taking advantage of an overriding provision. (Para. 3.3)

Requirement of good faith

10.5 The rights, remedies and powers of a mortgagee under a land mortgage should be expressly stated to be exercisable only in good faith and for the purposes of protecting or enforcing the security. This should apply to all the mortgagee's rights, remedies and powers, whether derived from statute, contract, or elsewhere. (Para. 3.4)

Creation of formal land mortgage

10.6 A formal land mortgage should not be valid unless made by deed, whether the property mortgaged is a legal estate or an equitable interest. No particular form of words should be necessary in order for it to be a valid formal land mortgage, provided the words used demonstrate an intention to make the mortgaged property security for performance of the mortgagor's obligations. As an additional requirement where the mortgagor's title to all or part of the mortgaged property is registered at H. M. Land Registry, the mortgage should not qualify as a formal land mortgage unless it is substantively registered against that title. (Paras 3.5 to 3.8)

Informal land mortgage

10.7 Informal mortgages should be recognised, to the extent that any purported consensual security over an interest in land that does not constitute a formal land mortgage but would, in the present law, give rise to an equitable mortgage or charge, should take effect as an informal land mortgage, provided the formal requirements for the creation of an informal land mortgage (para. 10.9 below) are satisfied. (Paras 3.6, 3.9, and 3.10)

10.8 A mortgagee under an informal land mortgage should have no right to enforce the security, nor to take any other action in relation to the mortgaged property, but should have a right to have the mortgage perfected by having a formal land mortgage granted to it. In the

---

incurring only a small increase in mortgage interest and without increasing his capital repayments (Law Com No. 190), para. 2.2.

[246] [For a summary of the overriding provisions, see para. 5.8 of the Report.]

case of a protected mortgage (para. 10.16 below) the mortgagee should not be allowed to have the mortgage perfected without a court order; in all other cases a mortgagee who was able to procure perfection of the mortgage without recourse to the court (for example, by use of a power of attorney) should be entitled to do so. (Paras 3.11 to 3.13 and 5.12)

10.9 An informal land mortgage should not be valid unless it is made by deed or it satisfies requirements equivalent to those set out in section 2 of the Law of Property (Miscellaneous Provisions) Act 1989,[247] that is unless it is in writing signed by or on behalf of the parties to it and incorporating (either directly, or indirectly by reference to another document) all the terms expressly agreed between the parties. (Paras 3.14 to 3.17)

All other consensual securities void

10.10 Any purported security interest that does not constitute a formal land mortgage or an informal land mortgage should be void (in the sense that, whilst the purported mortgagor remains personally liable to pay the debt or discharge the liabilities incurred, the purported mortgagee acquires no interest in the property and no right of recourse to it). This should not apply to non-consensual charges (that is, equitable charges arising by operation of law, statutory charges and liens): these are not affected by our recommendations. (Para. 2.6)

Protection and Priority

10.11 Where the mortgagor's title to the mortgaged property is registered at H. M. Land Registry, a formal land mortgage of that property should be substantively registrable. Unless and until registered it should take effect as an informal land mortgage. Once registered, it would constitute a registered charge for the purposes of the Land Registration Acts 1925 to 1988.[248] As such, its priority would depend on the date of its registration. (Paras 3.18 to 3.19; Schedule 1, paras 9–15)

10.12 An informal land mortgage of a legal estate in registered land should be protectable by notice where the informal land mortgage is acknowledged by the registered proprietor. Otherwise, it should be protectable by caution. Protection by notice of deposit and notice of intended deposit should be abolished. The priority of informal land mortgages protected by notice or caution should, for the present, continue to be governed by the rules applicable to the priority of minor interests in the present law. (Paras 3.20 and 3.21)

10.13 Formal and informal land mortgages of commercial equitable interests in registered land should be protectable by entry of notice or caution, but for the present, protection and priority of trust equitable interests should continue to be governed by the rule in *Dearle v Hall*.[249] (Paras 3.22 to 3.29)

10.14 In unregistered land all formal land mortgages of a legal estate or a commercial equitable interest should be registrable as Class C(i) land charges, and all informal land mortgages of a legal estate or a commercial equitable interest should be registrable as Class C(iii) land charges.[250] Formal and informal mortgages of trust equitable interests should continue to be governed by the rule in *Dearle v Hall* (Paras 3.30 to 3.33)

10.15 Section 4(5) of the Land Charges Act 1972 should be amended to remove the possibility of insoluble priority circles arising where there are successive mortgages of the same property. (Para. 3.34)

---

[247] [P. 18, above.]

[248] [The references in the Report to registered land must now be read in the light of LRA 2002.]

[249] [P. 983, n. 218, above.]   [250] [P. 66, above.]

Protected mortgages

10.16 There should be a class of protected mortgage consisting of all formal and informal land mortgages of any interest in land which includes a dwelling-house except those where either (a) the mortgagor is a body corporate, or (b) enforcement of the mortgage would not affect the occupation of the dwelling-house or (c) the dwelling-house is occupied under a service tenancy. (Part IV)

Standardisation

10.17 The front page of a protected mortgage should be in a form to be prescribed by regulations.... (Paras 5.1 to 5.11)

Rights and duties during the security

Interest rates

10.28 In all protected mortgages, a provision that purports to increase the rate of interest payable on default should be void. In all other mortgages, such a provision should be challengeable only under the general law relating to penalties or under the new general statutory jurisdiction to set aside or vary mortgage terms described in Part VIII of this Report. (Paras 6.33 and 6.34)

10.29 In the case of all mortgages, the court should have jurisdiction to vary interest rates under the new general statutory jurisdiction described in Part VIII of this Report if the mortgage has become challengeable as a result of a variation of or failure to vary the rate of interest payable, even if under the mortgage the mortgagee is fully entitled to vary or not vary interest rates as it chooses. (Para. 6.36)

10.30 In the case of protected mortgages, the court should also be entitled to alter the interest rate payable, if satisfied by the mortgagor that the mortgagee has unreasonably varied or failed to vary the interest rate payable under the mortgage. In order to assess whether a variation or failure to vary is unreasonable, the court should be required to have particular regard to whether the difference between the rate complained of and the current market rate charged for loans made in equivalent circumstances is substantially greater than the difference between the rate originally charged and the then market rate. The Office of Fair Trading should have power to exempt specified lenders from these provisions. (Paras 6.35 to 6.41)

Redemption

10.31 The equitable right to redeem the property free from the mortgage after the contractual redemption date by paying and discharging all obligations under it should apply to formal and informal mortgages as it applies to all other mortgages and charges. (para. 6.42)

10.32 In protected mortgages, any term of the mortgage which postpones the mortgagor's right to redeem should be void, unless the property includes non-residential premises. If it includes non-residential property, or the mortgage is not protected, then a postponement of the right to redeem should be challengeable only under the new general statutory jurisdiction described in Part VIII of this Report. (Para. 6.43(a))

Consolidation

10.35 In relation to all land mortgages the right to consolidate should be abolished. (Para. 6.44)

Enforcement of the Security

Sale

10.37 It should be a variable implied term of all formal land mortgages that the mortgagee has power to sell the mortgagor's interest in the mortgaged property, free from the mortgagee's own mortgage and from subsequent mortgages and other interests to which the mortgage has priority, but subject to all prior mortgages and interests taking priority over the mortgage. The power should not be exercisable unless a specified 'enforceable event' has occurred and is still operative. This restriction on the exercise of the power of sale should be overriding and should also apply to the statutory power of sale varied or replaced by any contractual provisions. (Paras 7.5 to 7.10)

10.38 If the mortgage is a protected mortgage, the mortgagee should not be entitled to exercise the power of sale without leave of the court. (Paras 7.14 to 7.15)

10.39 In addition in the case of protected mortgages, before exercising the power of sale the mortgagee should first have served on the mortgagor an enforcement notice in prescribed form specifying the enforceable event on which the mortgagee relies and the action (if any) to be taken by the mortgagor to remedy any default. The enforcement notice should also explain the consequences of default and how to obtain help and advice. Once the mortgagor has taken the action required by the notice, or the enforceable event is no longer operative for some other reason, the power of sale should not be exercisable. (Paras 7.11 to 7.13)

10.40 If the mortgagee exercises the power of sale after having been notified that the mortgagor has contracted to sell to someone else, the mortgagee should be liable to indemnify the mortgagor for any sum the mortgagor becomes liable to pay to a third party by reason of being unable to complete his sale contract. This should not apply if the mortgagee contracted to sell before receiving notice of the mortgagor's sale contract, or if it was reasonable for the mortgagee to sell, either because the mortgagor's contract was for sale at a price insufficient to pay off the mortgagee in full, and the mortgagee was able to sell at a higher price than the mortgagor's price, or because the mortgagor's sale was not completed within a reasonable time or because of some other reason. (Paras 7.16 to 7.19)

10.41 A purchaser from a mortgagee purporting to sell in exercise of the power of sale should get a good title, provided there is a valid formal land mortgage and the purchaser is in good faith, unless the purchaser has notice that the power of sale is not exercisable or that the exercise is improper for some other reason. Notice should include constructive notice. (Paras 7.20 and 7.21)

10.42 A mortgagee under a formal land mortgage should be entitled to exercise the power of sale by selling the property to itself, provided leave of the court is first obtained. The court should not grant leave unless satisfied that sale to the mortgagee is the most advantageous method of realising the security. (Paras 7.22 and 7.27)

10.43 A mortgagee and a receiver appointed under a formal land mortgage should have an overriding duty (owed to the mortgagor, to any guarantors of the mortgagor, and to any subsequent mortgagees) to take reasonable care to ensure that on a sale the price is the best price that can reasonably be obtained. (Para. 7.23)

10.44 After paying off prior encumbrances, the mortgagee should hold the proceeds of sale on trust to be applied first in payment of the costs of sale, secondly in paying off everything due under the mortgage, and thirdly to be paid to the person next entitled (that is the subsequent encumbrancers or, if none, the mortgagor). (Para. 7.25)

Foreclosure

10.45 The remedy of foreclosure should be abolished. (Paras 7.26 and 7.27)

Possession

10.46 In all formal land mortgages there should be an implied overriding provision that the mortgagee is entitled to take possession of the mortgaged property when it is reasonably necessary to do so to enable the property to be sold pursuant to the mortgagee's power of sale. Once in possession the mortgagee should be under an overriding duty to sell as quickly as is consonant with the duty to take reasonable care to ensure that on sale the price is the best price that can reasonably be obtained. (Paras 7.28 to 7.30)

10.47 In protected mortgages the mortgagee should not be entitled to possession without serving an enforcement notice and obtaining a court order. The court making an order for possession should have discretion to order that interest payable under the mortgage should cease to accrue twelve weeks (or such other period as the court thinks fit) after the execution of the order for possession. Similar provisions should apply if the mortgagor leaves voluntarily in response to a demand for possession from the mortgagee. In both cases the mortgagee should be free to apply to the court for an extension of time at any stage. The Secretary of State should have power by order to vary the period of twelve weeks. (Paras 7.31 to 7.35)

10.48 In formal land mortgages which are not protected, the mortgagee should also have a right to take possession of the property when it is reasonably necessary to do so in order to preserve its value. Once in possession, the mortgagee should be entitled to remain there only for so long as is reasonable, given that the purpose of being there is to preserve the value of the property. (Para. 7.36(a) and (b))

10.49 A mortgagee under a protected mortgage should have no right to take possession of the property for the purpose of preserving its value unless the property includes non-residential property. If non-residential property is included the mortgagee should be entitled to apply to the court for possession for this purpose: the court should be entitled to make an order affecting the non-residential part only on the same grounds as if it were a non-protected mortgage, but should not be entitled to make an order affecting the residential part unless satisfied that it would not otherwise be possible to preserve the value of the property. The court making an order for possession for this purpose should have the same discretion to order that interest should cease to accrue as if possession was for sale, and the same should apply if the mortgagor leaves voluntarily in response to a demand for possession from the mortgagee. (Para. 7.36(c), (d) and (e))

10.50 A mortgagee who is in possession, for whatever purpose, should have a duty to repair (para. 10.22 above) and a liability to account. The liability to account should not apply during a period when interest has ceased to accrue. (Paras 6.14 and 7.37 to 7.38)

Appointment of a receiver

10.51 It should be a variable implied term of a formal land mortgage that the mortgagee should have power to appoint a receiver of the income of the property who should be the agent of the mortgagor. (Paras 7.39 to 7.41)

10.52 The power should be exercisable only in circumstances in which the power of sale would be exercisable.... (Para. 7.42)

Jurisdiction of the court on enforcement

10.55 In the case of a formal land mortgage which is not protected if a mortgagee applies to the court for an order to enforce or protect the security, the court should have no specific powers to delay or withhold the remedy requested once the mortgagee has established that the right to take the appropriate action is available and has become exercisable. (Paras 7.48 and 7.49)

10.56 On an application by a mortgagee to protect or enforce a protected mortgage, or for payment of sums due under a protected mortgage, the court should have powers equivalent to those currently applicable to residential mortgages by virtue of Part IV of the Administration of Justice Act 1970,[251] and the Consumer Credit Act 1974. In addition, it should have power to order the mortgagee to accept re-scheduled payments in some circumstances, and it should be allowed to consider whether any of the terms of the mortgage ought to be set aside or varied. It should not have power to refuse or delay an enforcement order on the ground that a tenant of the mortgagor whose tenancy is not binding on the mortgagee has offered to pay all sums due under the mortgage, nor should it have power to order that the mortgagor's interest should be transferred to such a tenant. (Paras 7.48 to 7.59)

Jurisdiction to set aside or vary terms of the mortgage

10.57 There should be a new statutory jurisdiction for the court to set aside or vary terms of a land mortgage. The new jurisdiction should be in addition to the court's general law powers to set aside terms or bargains on grounds such as fraud, mistake, rectification, estoppel, undue influence, or restraint of trade. The equitable jurisdiction to set aside a term of a land mortgage which constitutes a clog or fetter on the equity of redemption should be abolished in so far as it relates to land mortgages, and the extortionate credit bargain provisions of the Consumer Credit Act 1974 should be amended so that they no longer apply to credit bargains secured by a land mortgage. (Paras 8.1 to 8.4 and 8.8)

10.58 Under the new jurisdiction the court should have power to set aside or vary any term of a mortgage with a view to doing justice between the parties if (a) principles of fair dealing were contravened when the mortgage was granted, or (b) the effect of the terms of the mortgage is that the mortgagee now has rights substantially greater than or different from those necessary to make the property adequate security for the liabilities secured by the mortgage, or (c) the mortgage requires payments to be made which are exorbitant, or (d) the mortgage includes a postponement of the right to redeem. (Paras 8.4 and 8.5)[252]

10.59 In deciding whether to exercise its powers on grounds (b) or (d) the court should discount the fact that the terms were freely negotiated between the parties, but in such circumstances should have a discretion to order the mortgagor to compensate the mortgagee. Otherwise, the powers the court should have under the new jurisdiction, and the factors it ought to take into account should be analogous to those now contained in the extortionate credit bargain provisions of the Consumer Credit Act 1974. (Paras 8.6 to 8.8)

Miscellaneous matters

Tacking of further advances

10.60 Section 94 of the Law of Property Act 1925 should be amended to make it clear (a) that registration of a later mortgage under the Companies Act 1989 does not constitute notice of it to an earlier mortgagee seeking to tack advances made after the creation of the later mortgage, and (b) that a mortgagee who is under an obligation to make further advances remains entitled to rely on section 94 despite any default by the mortgagor releasing the mortgagee from the obligation. (Paras 9.3 to 9.4)

10.61 It should be made clear in section 30 of the Land Registration Act 1925 that where it is noted on the register that a charge contains an obligation to make further advances, subsequent charges that are unregistered, as well as those that are registered, will take subject to any such further advances made. (Para. 9.5)

---

[251] P. 935, above.

[252] [The Consumer Credit Act 1974 was amended by Consumer Credit Act 2006, although the reform was more limited than that proposed here: p. 921, n. 105, above.]

Land mortgages and the Consumer Credit Act 1974

10.62 The Consumer Credit Act 1974 should continue to apply to land mortgages in so far as it regulates the carrying on of mortgage lending business, but no longer apply in so far as it regulates form and content of mortgages and their enforcement. (Para. 9.6)

In 1998 the Government decided not to implement the Report due to lack of support, and invited the Law Commission to reconsider its proposals: Law Commission Thirty-Third Annual Report (Law Com No. 258), para. 1.10. The invitation was to return to the topic when the Commission's then current work on land registration was finished, but there has not yet been a proposal from the Commission to work further on it.

B. LIMITATION OF ACTIONS

The Law Commission Report on Limitation of Actions 2001 (Law Com No. 270) made recommendations on limitation and claims relating to mortgages and other charges.[253]

Law Commission Report on Limitation of Actions 2001 (Law Com No. 270), pp. 201, 204, 213–214

Part VI Summary of Recommendations

When should time start to run?

(1) The primary limitation period should start to run from the 'date of knowledge' rather than, for example, the date the cause of action accrues (Paragraph 3.7, Draft Bill, Cl 1(1)).

How long should the primary limitation period be?

(15) The primary limitation period applying under the core regime should be three years. (Paragraph 3.98, Draft Bill, Cl 1(1)).

The long-stop limitation period

(16) A claim, other than in respect of a personal injury, should be subject to a long-stop limitation period of ten years. (Paragraph 3.101, Draft Bill, Cl 1(2)).

(18) The long-stop limitation period should, as a general rule, start to run from the date on which the cause of action accrues... (Paragraph 3.113, Draft Bill, Cl 3).

Application of the core regime

(69) The primary limitation period should not apply to claims to enforce a mortgage or charge over land; and the long-stop limitation period should apply to claims to enforce a mortgage or charge over land, running from the date on which the mortgagee's or chargee's right to enforce the mortgage or charge accrues (Paragraph 4.166, Draft Bill, Cl 15(2)).

---

[253] The Report is accompanied by a draft Bill. For further recommendations contained in the Report, see pp. 273–278, above.

(70) Claims to enforce a mortgage or charge over personal property should be subject to the core regime (Paragraph 4.169).

(71) The primary limitation period should not apply to claims to enforce a mortgage or charge over both land and personal property; and the long-stop limitation period should apply to claims to enforce a mortgage or charge over land and personal property, running from the date on which the mortgagee's or chargee's right to enforce the mortgage or charge, *vis-à-vis* the land, accrues (Paragraph 4.173, Draft Bill, Cl 15(2), (9)).

(72) Only the long-stop limitation period should apply to claims to enforce an obligation secured by a mortgage or charge by suing on the covenant to repay. (Paragraph 4.177, Draft Bill, Cl 15(2)(b)).

(73) Where a mortgage or charge comprises a future interest or a life insurance policy, the limitation period applying to claims to enforce the mortgage or charge should not begin to run until the future interest determines or the life insurance policy matures. (Paragraph 4.181, Draft Bill, Cl 15(4)).

(74) Where a prior mortgagee is in possession of the property which is subject to the mortgage, the limitation period applicable to a claim by the subsequent mortgagee to recover arrears of interest (or damages in lieu) should (if necessary) be extended so that it does not end before the date one year after the prior mortgagee ceases to be in possession. (Paragraph 4.184, Draft Bill, Cl 15(3)).

(75) The limitation period applying to foreclosure proceedings should be suspended during the period that the mortgagee is in possession of the mortgaged property. (Paragraph 4.185, Draft Bill, Cl 15(5)).

(76) No limitation period should apply to claims by the mortgagor to redeem a mortgage over land. (Paragraph 4.189, Draft Bill, Cl 15(1)).

(77) Claims to redeem mortgaged personal property should not be subject to a limitation period. (Paragraph 4.194, Draft Bill, Cl 15(1)).

(78) The expiry of the limitation period applying to claims to enforce a mortgage should extinguish the claimant's interest in the mortgaged property. (Paragraph 4.196, Draft Bill, Cl 15(6)).

In July 2002 the Government accepted in principle the recommendations in the Report, although time was not found for its implementation, and in 2007 the Government announced a further consultation on the implementation of the Law Commission's recommendations.[254]

---

[254] Law Commission Annual Report 2007–2008 (Law Com No. 310), paras 3.26–3.27. The general regime governing limitation of actions was substantially modified in relation to registered land by LRA 2002; pp. 279–287, above. There is no change to the position of *mortgagors* in possession: the mortgagee's rights to possession or foreclosure as against the mortgagor in possession remain subject to the limitation provisions of LA 1980. The provisions of LA 1980 are however disapplied in relation to the *mortgagee* in possession: LRA 2002, s. 96, p. 282, above; Law Commission Report of Land Registration for the Twenty-First Century, 2001 (Law Com No. 271), paras 14.12–14.18.

11

EQUITIES, PROPRIETARY
ESTOPPEL AND LICENCES

I. INTRODUCTION

In the preceding chapters we have discussed those estates and interest in land that are recognised as subsisting at law or in equity. In this chapter we consider certain claims relating to land, or to the use of land, which do not have the same established proprietary characteristics as an estate or interest in land.

An 'equity' (often referred to as a 'mere equity') is the right to an equitable remedy which is ancillary to a right in property (such as the vendor's right to rescission of the transfer of land for misrepresentation or undue influence, or rectification of the terms of a lease for mistake, or the right to re-open the foreclosure of mortgaged property), and where the remedy, if granted, would change the property rights. As we shall see, although an equity is not recognised as having the same nature as an equitable interest in the land, it still has proprietary characteristics since the acquisition of the property can in certain circumstances carry with it the burden of the equity—that is, the person who acquires the property may find that his rights are liable to be changed by the court granting the equitable remedy in question. Equities are considered in section II, below. A particularly significant form of equity is the equity which arises by virtue of the doctrine of proprietary estoppel. This will be considered in some detail in section III.

A licence, by contrast, is the right to the use or occupation of land which does not of itself grant the licensee any estate or interest in the land. On the other hand, licences can be given in circumstances where the licensee's right to the land is protected not only against the licensor but sometimes even against a successor in title to the licensor's estate in the land. In such cases the effect of a licence appears to be proprietary. We shall consider the essential nature of a licence, and the different circumstances in which the licensor's rights under the licence are protected against both the licensor and his successors, in section IV.

II. MERE EQUITIES[1]

A. NATURE OF AN EQUITY

Snell's Equity (21st edn, 2005), para. 2.05

Equitable interests must be distinguished from 'mere equities'.[2] It is difficult to define these with clarity.[3] It is typically said that an equitable interest is an actual right of property, such as an interest under a trust,[4] a mere equity is not a right of property but a right, usually of a procedural nature, which is ancillary to some right of property, and which limits or qualifies it in some way.[5] Thus, mere equities include the right to have a transaction set aside for fraud,[6] misrepresentation[7] or undue influence,[8] to claim a remedy arising from a proprietary estoppel,[9] or to have a document rectified for mistake, as by inserting a repairing covenant.[10]

The distinction between equitable interests and mere equities is slight since even mere equities show some of the features of a right of property. They may bind successors in title of the property to which they relate, provided that their priority has been protected over the disposition to the successor in title.[11] For avoidance of doubt, the Land Registration Act 2002

---

[1] C & B, pp. 812–814; M & W, paras 8.012–8.013; MM, pp. 60–61; Smith, pp. 28–30, 212–213.

[2] See *Shiloh Spinners v Harding* [1973] AC 691 at 721, referring to this passage.

[3] See A. R. Everton (1976) 40 Conv (NS) 209 for a valiant attempt.

[4] *Cave v Cave* (1880) 15 ChD 639.

[5] See *National Provincial Bank Ltd v Ainsworth* [1965] AC 1175 at 1238, 1254 [p. 1002, below]; *Malory Enterprises v Cheshire Homes Ltd* [2002] Ch 216, 232; and see generally (1955) 71 LQR 480; V. T. H. Delaney (1957) 21 Conv (NS) 195.

[6] *Ernest v Vivian* (1863) 33 LJ Ch 513; and see *Latec Investments Ltd v Hotel Terrigal Pty Ltd* (1965) 113 CLR 265.

[7] See *Bristol & West Building Society v Mothew* [1998] Ch 1 at 22.

[8] See *Bainbrigge v Brown* (1881) 18 ChD 188.

[9] See *Inwards v Baker* [1965] 2 QB 29 [p. 1049, below].

[10] *Smith v Jones* [1954] 1 WLR 1089.

[11] *Blacklocks v JB Developments (Godalming) Ltd* [1982] Ch 183; *Malory Enterprises v Cheshire Homes Ltd* [2002] Ch 216 (treating the right to rectify a document or to alter the land register as overriding interests

explicitly so provides in relation to registered land.[12] A mere equity is in some cases capable of alienation, provided that the person to whom it is assigned is also entitled to the right of property to which the equity is ancillary. So an equity to rectify a document or the land register may be enforced by a successor in title of the property to which it relates.[13] An equity to set aside a transaction procured in breach of the rules on self-dealing or fair-dealing by fiduciaries may also be enforced as an incident of the property conveyed to the successor in title.[14]

The main distinction appears in the different effect of the doctrine of the purchaser without notice on the priority of each kind of right.[15] But even this distinction is no longer relevant to dispositions of registered land, where the statutory rules of priority draw no distinction between equitable interests and mere equities.[16]

In **National Provincial Bank Ltd v Ainsworth** [1965] AC 1175 the House of Lords held that a wife's right of occupation of the matrimonial home did not constitute an interest in the land capable of enforcement against a third party.[17] Rejecting the argument that the wife had an 'equity' which gave her a property right, LORD UPJOHN said at 1236:

The deserted wife's right is said...to be a licence coupled with an equity. In the words of Lord Denning MR in the Court of Appeal [1964] Ch 665, 686: 'The wife has no tenancy. She has no legal estate or equitable interest in the land. All that she has is a licence. But not a bare licence. She has a licence coupled with an equity. I mean an 'equity' as distinguished from an equitable interest.' Then after referring to *Westminster Bank Ltd v Lee* [1956] Ch 7 he continued at 686: 'It is an equity which the court will enforce against any successor except a purchaser for value without notice.'

The wife is asserting rights over the land of another and in respect of which she has no beneficial ownership. Nevertheless, she claims to enforce her rights against an assignee of her husband, the owner. How, as a matter of principle, can she do this?

First (I am still dealing with the general law), mere exclusive occupation is by itself not sufficient to establish such a right. It all depends on what her rights are; of course it may

---

under LRA 1925, s. 70(1)(*g*); and see now LRA 2002, Sch. 3, para. 2 [p. 196, above]); *El Ajou v Dollar Land Holdings plc* [1993] 3 All ER 717; reversed on other grounds [1994] 2 All ER 685 (equity to rescind transaction for fraud); *Inwards v Baker* [1965] 2 QB 29 (proprietary estoppel). Contrast *Smith v Jones* [1954] 1 WLR 1089 (equity to rectify document does not bind *bona fide* purchaser for value without notice of unregistered land).

[12] LRA 2002, s. 116 [p. 1006, below].

[13] *Boots the Chemist Ltd v Street* (1983) 268 EG 817; *Berkeley Leisure Group Ltd v Williamson* [1996] EGCS 18 (relying on LPA 1925, s. 63(1)).

[14] *Stump v Gaby* (1852) 2 De GM & G 623; *Dickinson v Burrell* (1866) LR 1 Eq 337. See below, para. 7–120 *et seq. Semble* a bare right of rescission may not be assigned separately from the property to which it relates as this might savour of maintenance or champerty: see below, para. 3–36 *et seq.* A right to rescind a contract for fraud may be enforced by an assignee of the original representee only [if] he first rescinds the contract between himself and the representee so that all the parties are restored to their original position: *Edinburgh United Breweries Ltd v Molleson* [1894] AC 96; *Gross v Lewis Hillman Ltd* [1970] Ch 445.

[15] See below, para. 4–27.

[16] LRA 2002, s. 116 [p. 1006, below].

[17] The spouse's right of occupation was later given statutory protection by Matrimonial Homes Act 1967, now Family Law Act 1996, s. 30, and extended also to civil partners by Civil Partnership Act 2004: pp. 602–606, above.

be sufficient, e.g., if the wife is a lessee who thereby necessarily has an interest in the land. Secondly, notice to a purchaser that the wife is in occupation as a deserted wife (assuming contrary to my opinion that such a right is capable of reasonable definition) is not per se sufficient. The general observations of Knight Bruce LJ in *De Mattos v Gibson* (1858) 4 De G & J 276, 282 with regard to the obligations imposed by mere notice of a covenant cannot be applied to the law of real property (see *London County Council v Allen* [1914] 3 KB 642, 658 [p. 755, above]). Furthermore, the necessity for notice is to get rid of the effect of the legal estate; notice itself does not create the right. To create a right over the land of another that right must (apart from statute) create a burden on the land, i.e., an equitable estate or interest in the land. All this was pointed out in the closely analogous case of restrictive covenants by Farwell J in *Re Nisbet and Potts Contract* [1905] 1 Ch 391, 397, 398 [p. 759, above] in a very full judgment reviewing the earlier authorities which though at first instance has always been accepted as authoritatively stating the law. So in principle, in my opinion, to create a right over the land of another that right must in contemplation of law be such that it creates a legal or equitable estate or interest in that land and notice of something though relating to land which falls short of an estate or interest is insufficient. There are no doubt many cases where judges have said the purchaser 'takes subject to all equities' but they meant 'equitable interests.' Such, in my opinion, were the cases of *Jones v Smith* (1841) 1 Hare 43, 60 and *Barnhart v Greenshields* (1853) 9 Moo. PCC 18. This, I think, is quite clear from the case of *Reeves v Pope* [1914] 2 KB 284. See the interjection of Buckley LJ at 286 and the judgment of Lord Reading CJ at 288, 289. An equity to which a subsequent purchaser is subject must create an interest in the land. As Professor Crane has pointed out in an interesting article in The Conveyancer and Property Lawyer, Vol. 19 (NS), p. 343 at p. 346: 'Beneficial interests under trusts, equitable mortgages, vendors' liens, restrictive covenants and estate contracts are all equitable interests.' No lesser interests have been held to be sufficient. A mere 'equity' used in contradistinction to an 'equitable interest' but as a phrase denoting a right which in some circumstances may bind successors is a word of limited application and, like the learned editors of Snell, 25th edition, at p. 18, I shall attempt no definition of that phrase. It was illustrated in the case before me of *Westminster Bank Ltd v Lee* [1956] Ch 7, where I was constrained in the then state of the authorities to assume that a mere equity might bind successors, yet being at most a mere equity, even subsequent equitable encumbrancers, contrary to the usual rule, could plead purchaser for value without notice. But, my Lords, freed from the fetters which there bound me, I myself cannot see how it is possible for a 'mere equity' to bind a purchaser unless such an equity is ancillary to or dependent upon an equitable estate or interest in the land. As Mr Megarry has pointed out in the Law Quarterly Review, Vol. 71, at p. 482, the reason why a mere equity can be defeated by a subsequent purchaser of an equitable estate for value without notice is that the entire equitable estate passes and it is not encumbered or burdened by a mere equity of which he has no notice. For example, a purchaser takes subject to the rights of a tenant in possession whatever they may be. If he sees a document under which the tenant holds, that is sufficient unless he knows, or possibly in some circumstances is put on inquiry to discover, that the tenant has in addition a mere equity, e.g., a right to rectify the document. If the purchaser knows that, he knows that the document does not correctly describe the estate or interest of the tenant in the land and he takes subject to that estate or interest, whatever it may be. But a mere 'equity' naked and alone is, in my opinion, incapable of binding successors in title even with notice; it is personal to the parties.

B. PROPRIETARY CHARACTERISTICS OF EQUITIES

Cartwright, *Misrepresentation, Mistake and Non-Disclosure* (2nd edn, 2006), para. 4.10

The 'equity to rescind'; property rights before rescission. The fact that a contract was induced by misrepresentation does not prevent the transfer of legal property rights in goods delivered or land transferred pursuant to the (voidable) contract: on rescission of the contract the representee therefore obtains a revesting of the property.[18] The position as regards the *equitable* property rights in the goods delivered or land transferred has however been the subject of some controversy. A representee who has a right to the remedy of rescission under the rules set out later in this chapter is said to have an *equity to rescind*. Some authorities[19] hold that the representee retains an equitable interest in the property, but others[20] deny this and hold that the whole property passes under the contract and that the equity to rescind does not constitute a retained right of property for the representee.

It may be possible to reconcile the cases by accepting that the equity to rescind does not give rise to a full equitable interest in the transferred property of the kind which would arise if, for example, the representee transferred the legal title to be held on trust for himself; but

[18] *Stevenson v Newnham* (1853) 13 CB 285 at 302–303; 138 ER 1208 at 1215–1216. For the means by which the revesting of property is effected, see below, para. 4.11. The revesting of legal title in the case of rescission of a contract of sale induced by fraudulent misrepresentation is well established; but for the view that this is a misinterpretation of the old authorities, and incorrect in principle, see W. Swadling, 'Rescission, Property, and the Common Law' (2005) 121 LQR 123.

[19] E.g. *Stump v Gaby* (1852) 2 De GM & G 623 at 630; 42 ER 1015 at 1018; *Gresley v Mousley* (1859) 4 De G & J 78 at 93; 45 ER 31 at 37; *Melbourne Banking Corp Ltd v Brougham* (1882) 7 App Cas 307, PC, at 311; J. Mowbray, L. Tucker, N. Le Poidevin and E. Simpson, *Lewin on Trusts* (17th edn, 2000), para. 3.39. Such a position has also been taken in the context of contracts voidable on grounds other than misrepresentation; e.g. in *Re Garnett* (1886) 33 ChD 300, CA, at 306 Lindley LJ held that the setting aside of a release by a residuary legatee of her rights under a will, which was entered into without independent advice and in ignorance of the value of the rights in question, 'confers no new title. It removes an impediment to the enjoyment of a pre-existing title'. And in the context of a contract voidable for undue influence, Cotton LJ suggested that the transferor of property could recover 'on the ground that it was property the beneficial interest in which she had never effectually parted with': *Allcard v Skinner* (1887) 36 ChD 145, CA, at 172. In Australia, see *Daly v Sydney Stock Exchange Ltd* (1986) 160 CLR 371, HCA, at 388–389 (duty of disclosure arising out of fiduciary relationship; it 'may be that ... [the transferor] had an equitable interest in the property from the beginning', but the transferee does not hold as constructive trustee as long as the contract stands); *Latec Investments Ltd v Hotel Terrigal Pty Ltd* (1965) 113 CLR 265, HCA, at 282–284, 290–291. The reasoning behind the idea that a voidable contract gives rise to a continuing equitable interest appears to be similar to the principle that a contract to transfer an interest in land creates an equitable interest where a court would grant specific performance of the contract to order the interest to be conveyed: an operation of the maxim that 'Equity looks on that as done which ought to be done': *Walsh v Lonsdale* (1882) 21 Ch D 9, CA [p. 30, above]; Snell, para. 5.25; cf. *Stump v Gaby*, above; R. Chambers, *Resulting Trusts*, pp. 174–175. However the cases are not exactly parallel because in the case of rescission for misrepresentation the right to rescind does not (apart from Misrepresentation Act, s. 2(2), below, para. 4.61) depend on the exercise of the court's discretion; and it is a right which the representee can choose whether to exercise, not a right which the court can presume should be exercised.

[20] *Clough v London and North Western Railway Co.* (1871) LR 7 Exch. 26 at 32, 34; *Bristol and West Building Society v Mothew* [1998] Ch 1, CA, at 22; *Barclays Bank Plc v Boulter* [1999] 1 WLR 1919, HL, at 1925; *Twinsectra Ltd v Yardley* [1999] Lloyd's Rep Bank 438, CA, at 461–462 (reversed on different grounds [2002] UKHL 12, [2002] 2 AC 164); Snell, para. 13.15.

that after the transfer the representee retains rights which can be recognised as proprietary for some purposes.[21] The retained rights can be disposed of *inter vivos*[22] or by will[23] so that the recipient can invoke the right to rescission and therefore recover the full property rights. And where registered land is transferred under a voidable contract the transferor's equity to rescind has effect from the time the equity arises—that is, from the time of the transfer and therefore before rescission is effected—as an interest capable of binding successors to the registered title.[24]

However, it is clear that the transferee of property under a voidable contract does not hold the property as trustee during the period before the contract is rescinded, nor does he have fiduciary duties to the transferor in respect of his use of the property.[25] And the equity to rescind is not treated as equivalent to an equitable interest when the issue is whether a later purchaser

---

[21] *Latec Investments Ltd v Hotel Terrigal Pty Ltd*, above, n. 19 at 291; *Blacklocks v JB Developments (Godalming) Ltd* [1982] Ch 183 at 196; *Lewin on Trusts*, above, n. 19, para. 7–29. For a most thorough discussion, see S. Worthington, 'The Proprietary Consequences of Rescission' [2002] RLR 28 (the classical model 'suggests that the claimant has a mere equity prior to rescission, but that after rescission legal or equitable title to the underlying property revests in the respective parties. The model is supported by precedent, consistent with legal doctrine, and suited to commercial and public goals': at 67). For a different view, that the transferee of property under a voidable contract holds the recoverable property under a resulting trust, see R. Chambers, *Resulting Trusts*, chap. 7.

[22] *Dickinson v Burrell* (1866) LR 1 Eq 337; *Gross v Lewis Hillman Ltd* [1970] Ch 445, CA, at 460–461; *Melbourne Banking Corporation Ltd v Brougham*, above, n. 19.

[23] *Stump v Gaby*, above, n. 19; *Gresley v Mousley*, above, n. 19.

[24] Land Registration Act 2002, s. 116(b) [p. 1006, below], which is declared 'for the avoidance of doubt' and applies to 'a mere equity', including the equity to rescind. A registered disponee who gives valuable consideration will take free of the equity unless it is protected by entry of a notice in the register, or as an overriding interest: ibid, s. 29; see E. H. Burn and J. Cartwright, *Cheshire and Burn's Modern Law of Real Property* (17th edn, 2006), pp. 812–814. Before the 2002 Act it had already been held that an equity had the quality of a 'right' capable of constituting an overriding interest and therefore binding a purchaser under Land Registration Act 1925, s. 70(1)(*g*) (rights of person in actual occupation of the land or in receipt of rents and profits: see now Land Registration Act 2002, Sch. 3, para. 2; *Cheshire and Burn's Modern Law of Real Property*, p. 980); *Blacklocks v JB Developments (Godalming) Ltd*, above, n. 21 (equity to rectify, rather than to rescind; but at 195–196 Judge Mervyn Davies used rescission cases interchangeably with cases involving rectification); *Nurdin & Peacock Plc v Ramsden & Co. Ltd* [1999] 1 EGLR 119 at 124–126; [1999] Conv. 421 (S. Pascoe). The point was left open by the Court of Appeal in *Collings v Lee* [2001] 2 All ER 332 at 338. Statements by Lord Upjohn and Lord Wilberforce in *National Provincial Bank Ltd v Ainsworth* [1965] AC 1175, HL, at 1238, 1254 [p. 1002, above] appeared to deny that an equity to rescind could bind a purchaser of the land. The earlier statement (obiter) of Upjohn J in *Smith v Jones* [1954] 1 WLR 1089 at 1091 that the equity to rectify did not bind a purchaser of unregistered land can be read as saying not that the equity does not have proprietary characteristics, but that the rules of notice operative in unregistered land would not apply to hold a purchaser bound by such an equity.

[25] *Lonrho Plc v Fayed (No. 2)* [1992] 1 WLR 1 at 11 (transferee of shares under contract voidable for fraud has no duty to transferor in respect of use of the shareholding for mounting takeover bid for the remaining shares); *Daly v Sydney Stock Exchange Ltd*, above, n. 19 at 389; and in relation to the payment of money under a voidable contract, see *Shalson v Russo* [2003] EWHC 1637; [2005] Ch 281 at [108] (Rimer J, distinguishing at [109]-[111] and [118] contrary dicta of Lord Browne-Wilkinson in *Westdeutsche Landesbank Girozentrale v Islington LBC* [1996] AC 669 at 715–6, and of Bingham J in *Neste Oy v Lloyds Bank Plc* [1983] 2 Lloyd's Rep 658 at 665–6). Cf. *Collings v Lee*, above, n. 24 at 337 (equitable interest retained where transferors did not intend to transfer property, but transferee acquired transfer of legal estate without their knowledge and consent and in breach of his fiduciary duty to them).

takes priority over the earlier rights.[26] But an equity to rescind will bind the transferee's trustee in bankruptcy.[27]

(i) Unregistered land

In unregistered land a mere equity is less potent than an equitable interest. Not only is it not binding on the bona fide purchaser of a legal estate in the land, it is not even binding on a bona fide purchaser of an *equitable* interest for value without notice.[28]

In **Phillips v Phillips** (1861) 4 De GF & J 208, 45 ER 1164, LORD WESTBURY when speaking of the occasions on which the ordinary rules of priority in point of time among claimants in equity would be disturbed by the doctrine of the bona fide purchaser, said at 218, at 1167:

Thirdly, where there are circumstances that give rise to an equity as distinguished from an equitable estate—as for example, an equity to set aside a deed for fraud, or to correct it for mistake—and the purchaser under the instrument maintains the plea of purchaser for valuable consideration without notice, the court will not interfere.

(ii) Registered land

In registered land, however, an equity is given the same priority as an equitable interest, and will therefore bind a transferee of the land except a disponee for valuable consideration where the equity has not been protected, either by entry of a notice in the register, or as an overriding interest by the beneficiary being in discoverable actual occupation of the land.

Land Registration Act 2002

116 Proprietary estoppel and mere equities

It is hereby declared for the avoidance of doubt[29] that, in relation to registered land . . . —

> (b) a mere equity,

---

[26] *Phillips v Phillips* (1862) 4 De GF & J 208 at 218; 45 ER 1164 at 1167 [below]. The rule is that, where equities are equal, the earlier in time prevails; but the purchaser of an equitable interest takes priority over an earlier equity to rescind. In *Latec Investments Ltd v Hotel Terrigal Pty Ltd*, above, n. 19 at 286 Taylor J suggested that, rather than the equity to rescind being of a lesser right than an equitable interest, the result might follow because a representee requires 'the assistance of a court of equity to remove an impediment to his title as a preliminary to asserting his interest.' However, the exercise of the right to rescind for misrepresentation is not dependent upon a court order: below, para. 4.18. In *registered* land an equity now has the same priority as an equitable interest: Land Registration Act 2002, s. 116(b); above, n. 24.

[27] *Re Eastgate* [1905] 1 KB 465. Where however, *money* is transferred under a voidable contract no proprietary rights are retained and therefore the representee has no priority in the representee's bankruptcy: *Re Goldcorp Exchange Ltd* [1995] 1 AC 74, PC, at 102–103; below, para. 4.11.

[28] For the general rules of notice (and notice constituted by registration under the Land Charges Act 1972) in unregistered land, see pp. 58–84, above.

[29] For the position before the 2002 Act, see the cases discussed at n. 24, above

has effect from the time the equity arises as an interest capable of binding successors in title (subject to the rules about the effect of dispositions on priority[30]).

III. PROPRIETARY ESTOPPEL[31]

The basic principle of the doctrine of estoppel is that a person who makes, by words or conduct, a representation to another, intending that other to act on it, and the other does so act to his detriment, will not be allowed subsequently to take a position inconsistently with the representation. Different forms of estoppel have been recognised at common law and in equity.[32] At common law, the representation had to be one of existing fact.[33] The estoppel acted as a rule of evidence. The representor could not subsequently allege, in dealings with the representee, that the facts were different from those represented. The estoppel did not however give rise to any independent cause of action.

The doctrine was widened in equity so as to cover a representation, not only of fact, but of intention, or a promise. This is promissory estoppel; which became well known through *Central London Property Trust Ltd v High Trees House Ltd* [1947] KB 130, and was firmly established in later years. Promissory estoppel also gives negative protection only, and is not a cause of action—or, as it is often put, promissory estoppel can be used only as a 'shield' and not as a 'sword'.[34]

The last half of the twentieth century saw a remarkable growth of the doctrine of proprietary estoppel. The doctrine deals with the equities arising out of a situation where one party (A) makes a representation or promise to another party (B) to the effect that B has or shall have an interest in, or right over, A's property, or acquiesces

[30] For the rules governing priority of interests on disposition of the land, see LRA 2002, ss. 28–30 and Sch. 3; pp. 166–220, above.

[31] C & B, pp. 814–824; Gray, part 9.2; M & W, chap. 16; MM, pp. 69, 483–489; Smith, chap. 10; H & M, pp. 893–909; Cooke, *The Modern Law of Estoppel* (2000); Pawlowski, *The Doctrine of Proprietary Estoppel* (1996); Spencer Bower and Turner, *Estoppel by Representation* (4th edn, 2004) passim, and especially chap. 12; Wilken and Villiers, *The Law of Waiver, Variation and Estoppel* (2nd edn, 2002), chap. 11; Snell, chap. 10; [1983] CLJ 257 (M. P. Thompson); [1988] Conv 346 (P. T. Evans); (1994) 14 LS 147 (S. Baughen); (1995) 58 MLR 637 (G. Battersby); (1997) 17 LS 258 (E. Cooke); Sir Christopher Slade, *The Informal Creation of Interests in Land* (1984) Child & Co Oxford Lecture; Finn, *Essays in Equity* (1985), pp. 59–94; J. Cartwright in *Rationalizing Property, Equity and Trusts: Essays in Honour of Edward Burn* (ed. Getzler), chap. 3. See also, on particular aspects of proprietary estoppel in relation to licences for the use or occupation of land, further articles cited at p. 1107, n. 208, below.

[32] C & B, pp. 815–816; Cooke, *The Modern Law of Estoppel*.

[33] *Jorden v Money* (1854) 5 HL Cas 185.

[34] *Combe v Combe* [1951] 2 KB 215; *Baird Textiles Holdings Ltd v Marks and Spencer plc* [2002] 1 All ER (Comm) 737 at [55]. By contrast, promissory estoppel has been used to found a cause of action to remedy the non-performance of a promise unsupported by consideration—as a 'sword'—in the law of the United States: American Law Institute, *Restatement of the Law (2d), Contracts* (1981), para. 90; and Australia: *Waltons Stores (Interstate) Ltd v Maher* (1988) 164 CLR 387; (1988) 104 LQR 362 (A. Duthie). See generally Treitel, para. 3.093.

in B's mistaken belief that he has or shall have such an interest or right. If A intends B to act in reliance to his detriment on the representation, promise or mistaken belief, and B does so act in reliance, an equity is said to arise, which may prevent (estop) A from asserting his own strict legal rights to his property. B will have the right to seek a remedy from the court to protect this equity, and the remedy may sometimes even give effect to B's expectations by granting him the interest in A's land which A led him to believe he had or would acquire. Thus, unlike other estoppels, this doctrine may create a claim, and an entitlement to property rights in or over land: it can be used as a 'sword'.[35]

A. DEVELOPMENT OF PROPRIETARY ESTOPPEL

The modern doctrine of proprietary estoppel can be traced to nineteenth century cases, and in particular to *Ramsden v Dyson* (1866) LR 1 HL 129 and *Willmott v Barber* (1880) 15 ChD 96. In the latter case Fry J specified the detailed requirements in what have come to be called 'the five probanda'. In more recent years, however, the principle in *Ramsden v Dyson* has been expressed in much broader terms, emphasising both the element of 'unconscionability' in the defendant's conduct which gives rise to the equity against him,[36] and the scope of the court's discretion in determining the existence and scope of the equity—that the court must look at the case 'in the round'.[37]

In **Crabb v Arun District Council** [1976] Ch 179, p. 1050, below, SCARMAN LJ said at 193:

In the course of an interesting addition to his submissions this morning, Mr Lightman cited *Ramsden v Dyson* (1866) LR 1 HL 129, 142, to support his proposition that in order to establish an equity by estoppel there must be a belief by the plaintiff in the existence of a right created or encouraged by the words or actions of the defendant. With respect, I do not think that that is today a correct statement of the law. I think the law has developed so that today it is to be considered as correctly stated by Lord Kingsdown in his dissenting speech in *Ramsden v Dyson*. Like Lord Denning MR, I think that the point of dissent in *Ramsden v Dyson* was not on the law but on the facts. Lord Kingsdown's speech, in so far as it dealt with propositions of law, has been often considered, and recently followed by this court in *Inwards v Baker* [1965] 2 QB 29 [p. 1049, below]. So what is the effect of looking to Lord Kingsdown's speech for a statement of the law? Lord Kingsdown said at 170:

'The rule of law applicable to the case appears to me to be this: If a man, under a verbal agreement with a landlord for a certain interest in land, or, what amounts to the same thing, *under an expectation, created or encouraged by the landlord,'*—my italics—'that he shall have a certain interest, takes possession of such land, with the consent of the landlord, and upon the faith of such promise or

---

[35] For a comparison of proprietary estoppel and promissory estoppel, see Treitel, paras 3.142–3.145.
[36] [2008] Conv 401 (H. Delaney and D Ryan).
[37] *Gillett v Holt* [2001] Ch 210, p. 1010, below.

expectation, with the knowledge of the landlord, and without objection by him, lays out money upon the land, a court of equity will compel the landlord to give effect to such promise or expectation.'

That statement of the law is put into the language of landlord and tenant because it was a landlord and tenant situation with which Lord Kingsdown was concerned;[38] but it has been accepted as of general application. While *Ramsden v Dyson* may properly be considered as the modern starting-point of the law of equitable estoppel, it was analysed and spelt out in a judgment of Fry J in 1880 in *Willmott v Barber* (1880) 15 ChD 96, a decision to which Pennycuick V-C referred in his judgment. I agree with Pennycuick V-C in thinking that the passage from Fry J's judgment, from p. 105, is a valuable guide as to the matters of fact which have to be established in order that a plaintiff may establish this particular equity. Moreover, Mr Lightman for the defendants sought to make a submission in reliance upon the judgment. Fry J said, at pp. 105–106:

> 'It has been said that the acquiescence which will deprive a man of his legal rights must amount to fraud, and in my view that is an abbreviated statement of a very true proposition. A man is not to be deprived of his legal rights unless he has acted in such a way as would make it fraudulent for him to set up those rights. What, then, are the elements or requisites necessary to constitute fraud of that description? In the first place the plaintiff must have made a mistake as to his legal rights. Secondly, the plaintiff must have expended some money or must have done some act (not necessarily upon the defendant's land) on the faith of his mistaken belief. Thirdly, the defendant, the possessor of the legal right, must know of the existence of his own right which is inconsistent with the right claimed by the plaintiff. If he does not know of it he is in the same position as the plaintiff, and the doctrine of acquiescence is founded upon conduct with a knowledge of your legal rights. Fourthly, the defendant, the possessor of the legal right, must know of the plaintiff's mistaken belief of his rights. If he does not, there is nothing which calls upon him to assert his own rights. Lastly,'—'if I may digress, this is the important element as far as this appeal is concerned—'the defendant, the possessor of the legal right, must have encouraged the plaintiff in his expenditure of money or in the other acts which he has done, either directly or by abstaining from asserting his legal right.'

Mr Lightman, in the course of an interesting and vigorous submission, drew the attention of the court to the necessity of finding something akin to fraud before the equity sought by the plaintiff could be established. 'Fraud' was a word often in the mouths of those robust judges who adorned the bench in the 19th century. It is less often in the mouths of the more wary judicial spirits today who sit upon the bench. But it is clear that whether one uses the word 'fraud' or not, the plaintiff has to establish as a fact that the defendant, by setting up his right, is taking advantage of him in a way which is unconscionable, inequitable or unjust. It is to be observed from the passage that I have quoted from the judgment of Fry J, that the fraud or injustice alleged does not take place during the course of negotiation, but only when the defendant decides to refuse to allow the plaintiff to set up his claim against the defendants' undoubted right. The fraud, if it be such, arises after the event, when the defendant seeks by relying on his right to defeat the expectation which he by his conduct encouraged the plaintiff to have. There need not be anything fraudulent or unjust in the conduct of the actual negotiations—the conduct of the transaction by the defendants.

---

[38] The modern doctrine is a development of earlier cases which had dealt almost exclusively with situations in which a landlord encouraged the occupier of his land to believe that the latter held under a lease: *Huning v Ferrers* (1710) Gilb Ch 85; *Stiles v Cowper* (1748) 3 Atk 692; *East India Co v Vincent* (1740) 2 Atk 83; *Jackson v Cator* (1800) 5 Ves 688.

The court therefore cannot find an equity established unless it is prepared to go as far as to say that it would be unconscionable and unjust to allow the defendants to set up their undoubted rights against the claim being made by the plaintiff.

In **Taylors Fashions Ltd v Liverpool Victoria Trustees Co Ltd** (1979) [1982] QB 133n, p. 1012, below, OLIVER J said at 151:

[T]he more recent cases indicate, in my judgment, that the application of the *Ramsden v Dyson* principle—whether you call it proprietary estoppel, estoppel by acquiescence or estoppel by encouragement is really immaterial—requires a very much broader approach which is directed rather at ascertaining whether, in particular individual circumstances, it would be unconscionable for a party to be permitted to deny that which, knowingly, or unknowingly, he has allowed or encouraged another to assume to his detriment than to inquiring whether the circumstances can be fitted within the confines of some preconceived formula serving as a universal yardstick for every form of unconscionable behaviour.[39]

The effect of this approach is that the courts now regard the five probanda no longer as rigid criteria to be satisfied, but as being 'guidelines, which will probably prove to be the necessary and essential guidelines, to assist the court to decide the question whether it is unconscionable for the plaintiffs to assert their legal rights by taking advantage of the defendant'.[40] Oliver J had suggested at 146 that the five probanda might be necessary where the defendant has done no positive act, and merely 'stands by without protest'.

In **Gillett v Holt** [2001] Ch 210, ROBERT WALKER LJ followed the approach of Oliver J and emphasised that unconscionable conduct underpins all the elements of the doctrine. He said, at 225, that:

the doctrine of proprietary estoppel cannot be treated as subdivided into three or four water-tight compartments.... Moreover the fundamental principle that equity is concerned to prevent unconscionable conduct permeates all the elements of the doctrine. In the end the court must look at the matter in the round.

However, in **Cobbe v Yeoman's Row Management Ltd** [2008] 1 WLR 1752, p. 1021, below, the House of Lords warned against relying on a broad test of unconscionability without focusing on the necessary elements of the estoppel—and in particular the

---

[39] Approved by Oliver LJ in *Habib Bank Ltd v Habib Bank AG Zurich* [1981] 1 WLR 1265 at 1285; (1981) 97 LQR 513; *Pridean Ltd v Forest Taverns Ltd* (1998) 75 P & CR 447.

For recent illustrations of this broader approach by PC, see *Lim Teng Huan v Ang Swee Chuan* [1992] 1 WLR 113, p. 1060, below; *Lloyds Bank plc v Carrick* [1996] 4 All ER 630; *Elitestone Ltd v Morris* (1995) 73 P & CR 259; cf. *Matharu v Matharu* (1994) 68 P & CR 93, where majority of CA somewhat liberally applied the five probanda; (1995) 58 MLR 412 (P. Milne); *Jones v Stones* [1999] 1 WLR 1739 (no acquiescence where delay in complaining about acts of trespass in using wall to place flower pots thereon and to support an oil tank). See also the approval of the probanda in *Kammins Ballrooms Co Ltd v Zenith Investments (Torquay) Ltd* [1971] AC 850 at 884, per Lord Diplock, and their application in detail by Jonathan Parker QC in *Combes v Smith* [1986] 1 WLR 808.

[40] *Swallow Securities Ltd v Isenberg* [1985] 1 EGLR 132 at 134, per Cumming-Bruce LJ (no evidence to induce in the defendant an expectation that she had legal rights more extensive than was in fact the case).

need for the claimant to show that he believed that he had, or would have, an interest in the land. LORD WALKER OF GESTINGTHORPE said at 1775:[41]

46 My Lords, equitable estoppel is a flexible doctrine which the court can use, in appropriate circumstances, to prevent injustice caused by the vagaries and inconstancy of human nature. But it is not a sort of joker or wild card to be used whenever the court disapproves of the conduct of a litigant who seems to have the law on his side. Flexible though it is, the doctrine must be formulated and applied in a disciplined and principled way. Certainty is important in property transactions. As Deane J said in the High Court of Australia in *Muschinski v Dodds* (1985) 160 CLR 583, 615–616,

> 'Under the law of [Australia]—as, I venture to think, under the present law of England—proprietary rights fall to be governed by principles of law and not by some mix of judicial discretion, subjective views about which party "ought to win" and "the formless void" of individual moral opinion...' (references omitted).

58 In *Taylors Fashions* Oliver J analysed the authorities in a masterly way (with the assistance of two Chancery silks who were later to become Law Lords[42]) and put this part of the law back on the right track. He pointed out that the five probanda (including the defendant's knowledge of his own title, and of the claimant's mistake as to title) are relevant only to cases of unilateral mistake, where the defendant's only encouragement to the claimant has been passive non-intervention: see at p. 147. Oliver J discussed *Ramsden v Dyson* at some length and followed the preference shown by the Privy Council in *Plimmer's* case for Lord Kingsdown's analysis rather than Lord Cranworth's: see at pp 148–151.

59 Towards the end of his judgment Oliver J made some important general observations, at pp 151–152:

His Lordship quoted the extract from the judgment of Oliver J, set out above, and continued:

This passage certainly favours a broad or unified approach to equitable estoppel. But it is emphatically not a licence for abandoning careful analysis for unprincipled and subjective judicial opinion. It is worth noting that on this part of the case Oliver J analysed over 20 authorities spanning more than two centuries.

And LORD SCOTT OF FOSCOTE said at 1762:

16 ... My Lords, unconscionability of conduct may well lead to a remedy but, in my opinion, proprietary estoppel cannot be the route to it unless the ingredients for a proprietary estoppel

---

[41] See also *Taylor v Dickens* [1998] 1 FLR 806 at 820, per Judge Weeks QC: 'there is no equitable jurisdiction to hold a person to a promise simply because the court thinks it unfair, unconscionable or morally objectionable for him to go back on it. If there were such a jurisdiction, one might as well forget the law of contract and issue every civil judge with a portable palm tree. The days of justice varying with the size of the Lord Chancellor's foot would have returned'; (2006) 122 LQR 492 at 512 (S. Gardner: 'overall, this discretion cannot be sufficiently reconciled with the Rule of Law: it involves an unacceptable degree of rule by men (the individual judges), not laws. The reasons for this are, however, fully capable of repair'); *Knowles v Knowles* [2008] UKPC 30 at [27], per Sir Henry Brooke ('While recourse to the doctrine of estoppel provides a welcome means of effecting justice when the facts demand it, it is equally important that the courts do not penalise those who through acts of kindness simply allow other members of their family to inhabit their property rent free').

[42] Richard Scott QC [later Lord Scott of Foscote], for Taylors Fashions Ltd; and Peter Millett QC [later Lord Millett], for Liverpool Victoria Trustees Co Ltd and Liverpool Victoria Friendly Society.

are present. These ingredients should include, in principle, a proprietary claim[43] made by a claimant and an answer to that claim based on some fact, or some point of mixed fact and law, that the person against whom the claim is made can be estopped from asserting. To treat a 'proprietary estoppel equity' as requiring neither a proprietary claim by the claimant nor an estoppel against the defendant but simply unconscionable behaviour is, in my respectful opinion, a recipe for confusion.

B. ESTABLISHING THE EQUITY

(i) General principles

Taylors Fashions Ltd v Liverpool Victoria Trustees Co Ltd
Old & Campbell Ltd v Liverpool Victoria Friendly Society
[1982] QB 133n (ChD, **Oliver J**)

The first plaintiffs (Taylors) sought to exercise an option to renew a lease, granted in 1948, of commercial premises at No 22 Westover Road, Bournemouth. The option had not been registered as a Class C(iv) Land Charge under the Land Charges Act 1925, and, following *Beesly v Hallwood Estates Ltd* [1960] 1 WLR 549, p. 67, n. 234, above, was void as against the defendants. The question was whether the defendants were estopped from asserting their strict legal rights against Taylors, who had spent some £12,000 on improving the premises, including the installation of a lift, in the expectation that the option would be enforceable. The defendants acquiesced in the works carried out by Taylors, and at the time did not suspect that they might have any reason for challenging the validity of the option. The fourth of Fry J's five probanda (see p. 1009, above) was therefore not fulfilled.

The second plaintiffs (Olds) had been granted a lease in 1949 of No 21 (adjacent to Taylors' premises), and a further lease in 1963 of No 20. The 1949 lease contained a clause permitting the defendants to determine that lease, if Taylors did not exercise their option in regard to No 22. The 1963 lease contained in Clause 4 an option enabling Olds to renew, if Taylors in fact exercised their option.

Held. Taylors were not entitled to obtain a renewal of their lease, but the defendants were estopped from denying that Olds were entitled to exercise their option.

Oliver J: The points which arise for decision, therefore, are these. (1) Is Taylors' option, as the defendants claim and as the plaintiffs contest, void against the defendants for want of registration? (2) If it is, are the defendants estopped as against Taylors from relying upon this ground of invalidity having regard to the expenditure by Taylors made with the defendants' concurrence in

---

[43] In *Western Fish Products v Penwith District Council* [1981] 2 All ER 204, Megaw LJ said at 218: 'We know of no case, and none has been cited to us, in which the principle set out in *Ramsden v Dyson* and *Crabb v Arun District Council* has been applied otherwise than to rights and interests created in and over land. It may extend to other forms of property. See Lord Denning MR in *Moorgate Mercantile Co Ltd v Twitchings* [1976] QB 225 at 242. In our judgment there is no good reason for extending the principle further.' See also *Re Basham* [1986] 1 WLR 1498 (future property; representor's residuary estate).

1959 and 1960? (3) If the option is indeed unenforceable against the defendants, has it never-theless been 'exercised' for the purposes of the break and renewal clauses in the lease to Olds? (4) If it has not, are the defendants estopped as against Olds from relying upon the invalidity of an option which their own grants assert to be subsisting?

His Lordship considered the first point, concluded that he must follow the decision of Buckley J in *Beesly v Hallwood Estates Ltd* [1960] 1 WLR 549,[44] and continued:

I approach the case, therefore, on the footing that, whatever the parties may have thought, the option was in fact void as against the defendants (although of course still contractually binding as between the original parties) from the moment when they completed their purchase. This brings me to the second and fourth questions which I have postulated above. As regards the general principles applicable I can treat the two questions together, although there are certain circumstances peculiar to Olds and some additional arguments of law in their case to which I shall have to refer later on. The starting point of both Mr Scott's and Mr Essayan's argu-ments on estoppel is the same and was expressed by Mr Essayan in the following proposition: if A under an expectation created or encouraged by B that A shall have a certain interest in land, thereafter, on the faith of such expectation and with the knowledge of B and without objection by him, acts to his detriment in connection with such land, a Court of Equity will compel B to give effect to such expectation. This is a formulation which Mr Millett accepts but subject to one important qualification, namely that at the time when he created and encouraged the expectation and (I think that he would also say) at the time when he permitted the detriment to be incurred (if those two points of time are different) B not only knows of A's expectation but must be aware of his true rights and that he was under no existing obligation to grant the interest.

This is the principal point upon which the parties divide. Mr Scott and Mr Essayan contend that what the court has to look at in relation to the party alleged to be estopped is only his con-duct and its result, and not—or, at any rate, not necessarily—his state of mind. It then has to ask whether what that party is now seeking to do is unconscionable. Mr Millett contends that it is an essential feature of this particular equitable doctrine that the party alleged to be estopped must, before the assertion of his strict rights can be considered unconscionable, be aware both of what his strict rights were and of the fact that the other party is acting in the belief that they will not be enforced against him.

The point is a critical one in the instant case and it is one upon which the authorities appear at first sight to be divided. The starting point is *Ramsden v Dyson* (1866) LR 1 HL 129 where a tenant under a tenancy at will had built upon the land in the belief that he would be entitled to demand a long lease. The majority in the House of Lords held that he would not, but Lord Kingsdown dissented on the facts. There was no—or certainly no overt—disagreement between their Lordships as to the applicable principle, but it was stated differently by Lord Cranworth LC and Lord Kingsdown and the real question is how far Lord Cranworth was purporting to make an exhaustive exposition of principle and how far what he stated as the appropriate conditions for its application are to be treated, as it were, as being subsumed sub silentio in the speech of Lord Kingsdown. Lord Cranworth expressed it thus, at 140–141:

'If a stranger begins to build on my land supposing it to be his own, and I, perceiving his mistake, abstain from setting him right, and leave him to persevere in his error, a court of equity will not allow

---

[44] Approved by CA in *Phillips v Mobil Oil Co Ltd* [1989] 1 WLR 888.

me afterwards to assert my title to the land on which he had expended money on the supposition that the land was his own. It considers that, when I saw the mistake into which he had fallen, it was my duty to be active and to state my adverse title; and that it would be dishonest in me to remain wilfully passive on such an occasion, in order afterwards to profit by the mistake which I might have prevented. But it will be observed that to raise such an equity two things are required, first, that the person expending the money supposes himself to be building on his own land; and, secondly, that the real owner at the time of the expenditure knows that the land belongs to him and not to the person expending the money in the belief that he is the owner. For if a stranger builds on my land knowing it to be mine, there is no principle of equity which would prevent my claiming the land with the benefit of all the expenditure made on it. There would be nothing in my conduct, active or passive, making it inequitable in me to assert my legal rights.'

So here, clearly stated, is the criterion upon which Mr Millett relies. Lord Kingsdown stated the matter differently and rather more broadly although in the narrower context of landlord and tenant. He says, at 170:

'The rule of law applicable to the case appears to me to be this: If a man, under a verbal agreement with a landlord for a certain interest in land, or, what amounts to the same thing, under an expectation, created or encouraged by the landlord, that he shall have a certain interest, takes possession of such land, with the consent of the landlord, and upon the faith of such promise or expectation, with the knowledge of the landlord, and without objection by him, lays out money upon the land, a court of equity will compel the landlord to give effect to such promise or expectation. This was the principle of the decision in *Gregory v Mighell* (1811) 18 Ves 328, and as I conceive, is open to no doubt.'

So here, there is no specific requirement, at any rate in terms, that the landlord should know or intend that the expectation which he has created or encouraged is one to which he is under no obligation to give effect.

Mr Millett does not—nor could he in the light of the authorities—dispute the principle. What he contends is that even if (which he contests) this is a case where the defendants could be said to have encouraged the plaintiffs' expectations—and that it is not necessarily the same as having encouraged or acquiesced in the expenditure—the principle has no application to a case where, at the time when the expectation was encouraged, both parties were acting under a mistake of law as to their rights.

There is, he submits, a clear distinction between cases of proprietary estoppel or estoppel by acquiescence on the one hand and promissory estoppel or estoppel by representation (whether express or by conduct) on the other. In the latter case, the court looks at the knowledge of the party who has acted and the effect upon him of his having acted. The state of mind of the promissor or representor (except to the extent of knowing, either actually or inferentially, that his promise or representation is likely to be acted upon) is largely irrelevant. In the former case, however, it is essential, Mr Millett submits, to show that the party alleged to have encouraged or acquiesced in the other party's belief himself knew the true position, for if he did not there can be nothing unconscionable in his subsequently seeking to rely upon it. Mr Millett concedes that there may be cases which straddle this convenient dichotomy—cases which can be put either as cases of encouragement or proprietary estoppel on Lord Kingsdown's principle or as estoppel by representation, express or implied. But, he submits, the party alleging the estoppel must, whichever way he elects to put his case or even if he runs them as alternatives, demonstrate the presence of all the essential ingredients of whatever type of estoppel he relies on. He cannot manufacture a third and new hybrid type of estoppel by an eclectic application of some of the ingredients of each. So, if he wishes to put his case as one of estoppel by representation, he must, for instance, show an unequivocal representation of existing fact. Equally, if he wants to rely upon the circumstances of the case as raising a proprietary estoppel arising from acquiescence in his having acted upon an erroneous supposition of his legal rights, then he must accept the burden of showing that the error was known to the other party.

So far as proprietary estoppel or estoppel by acquiescence is concerned, he supports his submission by reference to the frequently cited judgment of Fry J in *Willmott v Barber* (1880) 15 ChD 96, which contains what are described as the five 'probanda'. The actual case was one where what was alleged was a waiver by acquiescence. A lease contained a covenant against assigning, subletting or parting with possession without the lessor's consent and the lessee had let a sublessee into possession of part of the land under an agreement with him which entitled him to occupy that part for the whole term and conferred an option to purchase the remaining land for the balance of the term outstanding when the option was exercised. The sublessee built on the land and the head landlord was aware that he was in possession and was expending money. It was, however, proved that he did not then know that his consent was required to a subletting or assignment. The question arose between the sublessee and the head landlord when the sublessee tried to exercise his option over the remaining land and found himself met with the response that the head landlord refused consent to the assignment. The case was, on Fry J's finding of fact, one simply of acquiescence by standing by and what was being argued was that the landlord was estopped by his knowledge of the plaintiff's expenditure on the part of the land of which the plaintiff *was* in possession from withholding his consent to an assignment of that part of which he was not. It having been found as a fact that the landlord did not, at the time of the plaintiff's expenditure, know about the covenant against assignment and that there was nothing in what had passed between them to suggest either that the landlord was aware that the plaintiff was labouring under the belief that no consent was necessary or to encourage that belief, Fry J dismissed the plaintiff's claim. It has to be borne in mind, however, in reading the judgment, that this was a pure acquiescence case where what was relied on was a waiver of the landlord's rights by standing by without protest. It was a case of mere silence where what had to be established by the plaintiff was some duty in the landlord to speak. The passage from the judgment in *Willmott v Barber* most frequently cited is where Fry J says, at 105–106:

His Lordship cited the passage set out at p. 1009, above, and continued:

Mr Millett's submission is that when one applies these five probanda to the facts of the instant case it will readily be seen that they are not all complied with. In particular, Mr Millett submits, the fourth probandum involves two essential elements, viz., (i) knowledge by the possessor of the legal right of the other party's belief; and (ii) knowledge that that belief is mistaken. In the instant case the defendants were not aware of their inconsistent right to treat the option as void and equally they could not, thus, have been aware that the plaintiff's belief in the validity of the option was a mistaken belief. The alternative approach via estoppel by representation is not, he submits, open to the plaintiffs in this case because so far as Taylors were concerned the defendants made no representation to them at all and so far as Olds were concerned the representation of the continuing validity of the option, if there was one at all, was a representation of law.

Now, convenient and attractive as I find Mr Millett's submissions as a matter of argument. I am not at all sure that so orderly and tidy a theory is really deducible from the authorities— certainly from the more recent authorities, which seem to me to support a much wider equitable jurisdiction to interfere in cases where the assertion of strict legal rights is found by the court to be unconscionable. It may well be (although I think that this must now be considered open to doubt) that the strict *Willmott v Barber* probanda are applicable as necessary requirements in those cases where all that has happened is that the party alleged to be estopped has stood by without protest while his rights have been infringed. It is suggested in Spencer Bower and Turner, *Estoppel by Representation,* 3rd edn (1977), para. 290 that acquiescence, in its strict sense, is merely an instance of estoppel by representation and this derives some support from the judgment of the Court of Appeal in *De Bussche v Alt* (1878) 8 ChD 286, 314. If that is a correct analysis then, in a case of mere passivity, it is readily intelligible that there must be shown a duty to speak, protest or interfere which cannot normally arise in the absence of knowledge or at least a suspicion of the true position. Thus for a landowner to stand by while a neighbour lays drains in land which the landowner does not believe that he owns (*Armstrong v Sheppard & Short Ltd* [1959] 2 QB 384) or for a remainderman not to protest at a lease by a tenant for life which he believes he has no right to challenge (*Svenson v Payne* (1945) 71 CLR 531) does not create an estoppel. Again, where what is relied on is a waiver by acquiescence, as in *Willmott v Barber* itself, the five probanda are no doubt appropriate. There is, however, no doubt that there are judicial pronouncements of high authority which appear to support as essential the application of all the five probanda over the broader field covering all cases generally classified as estoppel by 'encouragement' or 'acquiescence': see, for instance, the speech of Lord Diplock in *Kammins Ballrooms Co Ltd v Zenith Investments (Torquay) Ltd* [1971] AC 850, 884.

Mr Scott submits, however, that it is historically wrong to treat these probanda as holy writ and to restrict equitable interference only to those cases which can be confined within the strait-jacket of some fixed rule governing the circumstances in which, and in which alone, the court will find that a party is behaving unconscionably. Whilst accepting that the five probanda may form an appropriate test in cases of silent acquiescence, he submits that the authorities do not support the absolute necessity for compliance with all five probanda, and, in particular, the requirement of knowledge on the part of the party estopped that the other party's belief is a mistaken belief, in cases where the conduct relied on has gone beyond mere silence and amounts to active encouragement. In Lord Kingsdown's example in *Ramsden v Dyson,* for instance, there is no room for the literal application of the probanda, for the circumstances there postulated do not presuppose a 'mistake' on anybody's part, but merely the fostering of an expectation in the minds of *both* parties at the time but from which, once it has been acted upon, it would be unconscionable to permit the landlord to depart. As Scarman LJ pointed out in *Crabb v Arun District Council* [1976] Ch 179 [p. 1008, above], the 'fraud' in these cases is not to be found in the transaction itself but in the subsequent attempt to go back upon the basic assumptions which underlay it.

His Lordship considered *Stiles v Cowper* (1748) 3 Atk 692; *Jackson v Cator* (1800) 5 Ves 688; *Gregory v Mighell* (1811) 18 Ves 328; *Plimmer v Wellington Corpn* (1884) 9 App Cas 699, p. 1065, below; *Sarat Chunder Dey v Gopal Chunder Laha* (1892) 19 LR Ind App 203; *Craine v Colonial Mutual Fire Insurance Co Ltd* (1920) 28 CLR 305; *Re Eaves* [1940] Ch 109; *Hopgood v Brown* [1955] 1 WLR 213; *Electrolux Ltd v Electric Ltd* (1953) 71 RPC 23, and continued:

Furthermore the more recent cases indicate, in my judgment, that the application of the *Ramsden v Dyson* principle—whether you call it proprietary estoppel, estoppel by acquiescence or estoppel by encouragement is really immaterial—requires a very much broader approach which is directed rather at ascertaining whether, in particular individual circumstances, it would be unconscionable for a party to be permitted to deny that which, knowingly, or unknowingly, he has allowed or encouraged another to assume to his detriment than to inquiring whether the circumstances can be fitted within the confines of some preconceived formula serving as a universal yardstick for every form of unconscionable behaviour.

So regarded, knowledge of the true position by the party alleged to be estopped, becomes merely one of the relevant factors—it may even be a determining factor in certain cases—in the overall inquiry. This approach, so it seems to me, appears very clearly from the authorities to which I am about to refer. In *Inwards v Baker* [1965] 2 QB 29 [p. 1049, below], there was no mistaken belief on either side. Each knew the state of the title, but the defendant had been led to expect that he would get an interest in the land on which he had built and, indeed, the overwhelming probability is that that was indeed the father's intention at the time. But it was not mere promissory estoppel, which could merely be used as a defence, for, as Lord Denning MR said, at 37, 'it is for the court to say in what way the equity can be satisfied.' The principle was expressed very broadly both by Lord Denning MR and by Danckwerts LJ. Lord Denning said at 37:

'But it seems to me, from *Plimmer's* case, 9 App Cas 699, 713–714 in particular, that the equity aris-ing from the expenditure on land need not fail "merely on the ground that the interest to be secured has not been expressly indicated...the court must look at the circumstances in each case to decide in what way the equity can be satisfied."'

And a little further down he said:

'All that is necessary is that the licensee should, at the request or with the encouragement of the landlord, have spent the money in the expectation of being allowed to stay there. If so, the court will not allow that expectation to be defeated where it would be inequitable so to do.'

And Danckwerts LJ said, at 38:

'It seems to me that this is one of the cases of an equity created by estoppel, or equitable estoppel, as it is sometimes called, by which the person who has made the expenditure is induced by the expect-ation of obtaining protection, and equity protects him so that an injustice may not be perpetrated.'

An even more striking example is *ER Ives Investment Ltd v High* [1967] 2 QB 379 [p. 1074, below]. Here again, there does not appear to have been any question of the persons who had acquiesced in the defendant's expenditure having known that his belief that he had an enforce-able right of way was mistaken. Indeed, at the stage when the expenditure took place, both sides seem to have shared the belief that the agreement between them created effective rights. Nevertheless the successor in title to the acquiescing party was held to be estopped. Lord Denning MR said, at 394–395:

'The right arises out of the expense incurred by Mr High in building his garage, as it is now, with access only over the yard: and the Wrights standing by and acquiescing in it, knowing that he believed he had a right of way over the yard. By so doing the Wrights created in Mr High's mind a reasonable expectation that his access over the yard would not be disturbed. That gives rise to an "equity arising out of acquiescence." It is available not only against the Wrights but also their successors in title. The court will not allow that expectation to be defeated when it would be inequitable to do so. It is for the court in each case to decide in what way the equity can be satisfied...'

It should be mentioned that the Wrights themselves clearly also believed that Mr High had a right of way, because when they came to sell, they sold expressly subject to it. So, once again, there is an example of the doctrine of estoppel by acquiescence being applied without regard to the question of whether the acquiescing party knew that the belief of the other party in his supposed rights was erroneous.

Mr Scott and Mr Essayan have also drawn my attention to the Privy Council decision in *Bank Negara Indonesia v Hoalim* (1973) 2 MLJ 3 where again, it seems that the misconception of the legal position which gave rise to the assurance creating the estoppel seems to have been shared by both parties. This is, however, rather a case of promissory estoppel than of the application of the *Ramsden v Dyson* principle. More nearly in point is *Crabb v Arun District Council* [1976] Ch 179 [p. 1050, below], where the plaintiff had altered his legal position in the expectation, encouraged by the defendants, that he would have a certain access to a road. Now there was no mistake here. Each party knew that the road was vested in the defendants and each knew that no formal grant had been made. Indeed I cannot see why in considering whether the defendants were behaving unconscionably, it should have made the slightest difference to the result if, at the time when the plaintiff was encouraged to open his access to the road, the defendants had thought that they were bound to grant it. The fact was that he had been encouraged to alter his position irrevocably to his detriment on the faith of a belief, which was known to and encouraged by the defendants, that he was going to be given a particular right of access—a belief which, for all that appears, the defendants probably shared at that time.

The particularly interesting features of the case in the context of the present dispute are, first, the virtual equation of promissory estoppel and proprietary estoppel or estoppel by acquiescence as mere facets of the same principle and secondly the very broad approach of both Lord Denning MR and Scarman LJ, both of whom emphasised the flexibility of the equitable doctrine. It is, however, worth noting that Scarman LJ adopted and applied the five probanda in *Willmott v Barber*, which he described as 'a valuable guide.' He considered that those probanda were satisfied and it is particularly relevant here to note again the fourth one—namely that the defendant, the possessor of the legal right, must know of the plaintiff's mistaken belief. If Scarman LJ had interpreted this as meaning—as Mr Millett submits that it does mean—that the defendant must know not only of the plaintiffs belief but also that it was mistaken, then he could not, I think, have come to the conclusion that this probandum was satisfied, for it seems clear from Lord Denning's recital of the facts that, up to the critical moment when the plaintiff acted, *both* parties thought that there *was* a firm assurance of access. The defendants had, indeed, even erected a gate at their own expense to give effect to it. What gave rise to the necessity for the court to intervene was the defendant's attempt to go back on this subsequently when they fell out with the plaintiff. I infer therefore that Scarman LJ must have construed this probandum in the sense which Mr Scott and Mr Essayan urge upon me, namely that the defendant must know merely of the plaintiff's belief which, in the event, turns out to be mistaken.

Finally, there ought to be mentioned the most recent reference to the five probanda which is to be found in *Shaw v Applegate* [1977] 1 WLR 970. That was a case where the plea of estoppel by acquiescence failed on appeal, but it is significant that two members of the court expressed serious doubt whether it was necessary in every case of acquiescence to satisfy the five probanda. Buckley LJ said at 977–978:

'As I understand that passage' and there he is referring to the passage from the judgment of Fry J in *Willmott v Barber* to which I have already referred, 'what the judge is there saying is that where a man has got a legal right—as the plaintiffs have in the present case, being legal assignees of the benefit of the covenant binding the defendant—acquiescence on their part will not deprive them of that legal right unless it is of such a nature and in such circumstances that it would really be dishonest or unconscionable of the plaintiffs to set up that right after what was occurred. Whether in order to reach that stage of affairs it is really necessary to comply strictly with all five tests there set out by Fry J may, I think, still be open to doubt, although no doubt if all those five tests were satisfied there would be shown to be a state of affairs in which it would be dishonest or unconscionable for the owner of the right to insist upon it. In *Electrolux Ltd v Electric Ltd* (1953) 71 RPC 23 Sir Raymond Evershed MR said, at 33: "I confess that I have found some difficulty—or should find some difficulty if it were necessary to make up my mind and express a view whether all five requisites which Fry J stated in *Willmott v Barber must* be present in every case in which it is said that the plaintiff will be deprived of his right to succeed in an action on the ground of acquiescence. All cases (and this is a trite but useful observation to repeat) must be read in the light of the facts of the particular case." So I do not, as at present advised, think it is clear that it is essential to find all the five tests set out by Fry J literally applicable and satisfied in any particular case. The real test, I think, must be whether upon the facts of the particular case the situation has become such that it would be dishonest or unconscionable for the plaintiff, or the person having the right sought to be enforced, to continue to seek to enforce it.'

And Goff LJ referred again to the judgment in *Willmott v Barber* and said, at 980:

'But for my part, I share the doubt entertained by Sir Raymond Evershed MR in the *Electrolux* case, whether it is necessary in all cases to establish the five tests which are laid down by Fry J, and I agree that the test is whether, in the circumstances, it has become unconscionable for the plaintiff to rely upon his legal right.'

So here, once again, is the Court of Appeal asserting the broad test of whether in the circumstances the conduct complained of is unconscionable without the necessity of forcing those incumbrances[45] into a Procrustean bed constructed from some unalterable criteria.

The matter was expressed by Lord Denning MR in *Moorgate Mercantile Co Ltd v Twitchings* [1976] QB 225, 241 as follows:

'Estoppel is not a rule of evidence. It is not a cause of action. It is a principle of justice and of equity. It comes to this: when a man, by his words or conduct, has led another to believe in a particular state of affairs, he will not be allowed to go back on it when it would be unjust or inequitable for him to do so. Dixon J put it in these words: "The principle upon which estoppel in pais is founded is that the law should not permit an unjust departure by a party from an assumption of fact which he has caused another party to adopt or accept for the purpose of their legal relations." Sir Owen said so in 1937 in *Grundt v Great Boulder Proprietary Gold Mines Ltd* (1937) 59 CLR 641, 674. In 1947 after the *High Trees* case (*Central London Property Trust Ltd v High Trees House Ltd* [1947] KB 130), I had some correspondence with Sir Owen about it: and I think I may say that he would not limit the principle to an assumption of fact, but would extend it, as I would, to include an assumption of fact or law, present or future. At any rate, it applies to an assumption of ownership or absence of ownership. This gives rise to what may be called proprietary estoppel. There are many cases where the true owner of goods or of land had led another to believe that he is not the owner, or, at any rate, is not claiming an interest therein, or that there is no objection to what the other is doing. In such cases it has been held repeatedly that the owner is not to be allowed to go back on what he has led the other to believe. So much so that his own title to the property, be it land or goods, has been held to be limited or extinguished, and new rights and interests have been created therein. And this operates by reason of his conduct—what he has led the other to believe—even though he never intended it.'

---

[45] Presumably 'circumstances' is intended.

The inquiry which I have to make therefore, as it seems to me, is simply whether, in all the circumstances of this case, it was unconscionable for the defendants to seek to take advantage of the mistake which, at the material time, everybody shared, and, in approaching that, I must consider the cases of the two plaintiffs separately because it may be that quite different considerations apply to each.

So far as Taylors are concerned there seem to me to be two difficulties in counsel's way. In the first place, whilst it is, no doubt, true that at that time when the work of putting in the lift was commenced with the defendants' knowledge and co-operation—co-operation at least, to the extent of entering into discussions with regard to the siting of the lift—all parties shared the common belief that there was a valid and enforceable option, it is difficult to see how that belief had been in any way created or encouraged by the defendants.... So far as acquiescence pure and simple is concerned the defendants could not lawfully object to the work and could be under no duty to Taylors to communicate that which they did not know themselves, namely that the non-registration of the option rendered it unenforceable. So far as encouragement is concerned, it is not in my judgment possible fairly to say that the mere presence of the defendants' representative at a site meeting 'encouraged' Taylors in their belief that the option was valid. No doubt it did nothing to discourage such a belief, but their representative would, I venture to think, have been present even if Taylors had already made up their minds that the option was not going to be exercised....

The second difficulty in Mr Scott's way seems to me to be this. The work which was carried out was work which was referable to the unexpired term which Taylors then held and was no doubt undertaken with a view to making the premises more attractive and convenient for customers of the business which, after all, was going to be carried on for another 18 years before any question of exercising the option even arose. By that time, the initial expense would long since have been written off by normal depreciation. Taylors believed that the option was a valid option—that is to say that they had, potentially, a longer term than they had in fact. But what is there to indicate that the work was undertaken 'on the faith of that belief rather than merely 'in' that belief?

His Lordship referred to Lord Eldon LC in *Dann v Spurrier* (1802) 7 Ves 231, 235–236; and Lord Hardwicke LC in *A-G v Balliol College, Oxford* (1744) 9 Mod Rep 407, 411, and continued:

It is conceivable that Taylors might not have done the work, although I find it difficult to believe that they would have contemplated operating a ladies' store on three floors in a fashionable Bournemouth shopping centre for 18 years without the convenience of a lift. It is conceivable that, if they had known the true position, they might have sought to re-negotiate a fresh option with the defendants rather than rely upon their rights under the Landlord and Tenant Act 1954. But what Mr Taylor was unable to say was that they would not have done the work if they had not thought that option was available, much less that the defendants were or must have been aware that they would not have done it.

Whilst, therefore, it may not seem very admirable for the defendants to avail themselves of a technicality which runs counter to the common assumption entertained by all the parties to the transaction, that is what the law permits them to do; and I cannot find, in the circumstances of this case, and even given the flexibility of the equitable principles, that Taylors have discharged the burden of showing that it is dishonest or unconscionable for them to do so. I must, therefore, dismiss Taylors' claim for specific performance of the option, although I do so with some regret.

Turning now to the case of Olds, the position appears to me to be very different....

Mr Essayan puts his case... upon the *Ramsden v Dyson* principle. Here Olds were encouraged by the defendants to alter their legal position irrevocably upon the faith of the belief or expectation, of which the defendants knew and which they themselves fostered by the terms of the lease, that they would be getting a term which was to be cut down only upon a particular supposition, namely that Taylors would be either unwilling or would disentitle themselves from exercising their option.

But it is, I think, unnecessary for Mr Essayan to rely solely upon the transaction in 1949. The 1963 transaction presents an even clearer picture, because Olds were encouraged by the defendants to expend a very large sum on the premises and to take a lease of the adjoining premises, upon the faith of the expectation, encouraged by the defendants that they would be entitled to renew in a particular event which, whether it was probable or not, Olds were at least invited to believe was possible. That they acted upon that supposition cannot I think be doubted. One has only to refer to Mr Old's statement in the correspondence leading up to the lease that 'this is no 14-year project.' Nor, equally, can it be doubted that the defendants were aware of, and indeed, shared that supposition. Again, I do not think that it really matters whether the case is put as one of estoppel by acquiescence or of estoppel by representation. Clause 4 of the 1963 lease, in its entirety, is without sense except on the footing that the reference to the tenants of the neighbouring premises known as no. 22 Westover Road exercising 'their option to have granted to them by the landlords,' i.e., by the defendants, 'a further term' is construed as a reference to an option between those tenants and the defendants subsisting and still capable of being exercised at the date of the lease. On any other footing the clause never could have any sphere of operation at all....

It would, in my judgment, be most inequitable that the defendants, having put forward Taylors' option as a valid option in two documents, under each of which they are the grantors, and having encouraged Olds to incur expenditure and to alter their position irrevocably by taking additional premises on the faith of that supposition, should now be permitted to resile and to assert, as they do, that they are and were all along entitled to frustrate the expectation which they themselves created and that the right which they themselves stated to exist did not, at any material time, have any existence in fact....

In the result, therefore, the claim of Taylors for specific performance must be dismissed and there will be in favour of Olds a declaration as regards the non-operation of the break clause in the 1949 lease and a decree of specific performance of the renewal option in the 1963 lease.

(ii) Proprietary estoppel in the House of Lords: right refused

Cobbe v Yeoman's Row Management Ltd

[2008] 1 WLR 1752 (HL, **Lords Hoffmann, Scott of Foscote, Walker of Gestingthorpe, Brown of Eaton-under-Heywood** and **Mance**)[46]

The owner of a building and a developer reached an oral agreement in principle under which the developer would obtain planning permission to develop the property, and the property would then be transferred to him for development and later sale and distribution of the profits between the parties. No contract was ever finalised. The

---

[46] [2008] LMCLQ 449 (B. McFarlane and A Robertson); (2008) 158 NLJ 1171 (M. Dowden), 1629 (K. Chambers). See also pp. 26–27, above.

developer obtained the planning permission, and sought to enforce the agreement. The trial judge held that the claimant was entitled to a lien for 50% of the increase in value of the property in consequence of the grant of planning permission, by way of satisfaction of an equity arising under the doctrine of proprietary estoppel. This was affirmed by the Court of Appeal. On appeal to the House of Lords:

Held. The developer had no interest in the property on the basis of either proprietary estoppel or constructive trust. However, he was entitled to a quantum meruit[47] for the value of his services which the defendant knew he was not providing gratuitously.

Lord Scott of Foscote:

14 Both the judge and the Court of Appeal regarded the relief granted as justified on the basis of proprietary estoppel. I respectfully disagree. The remedy to which, on the facts as found by the judge, Mr Cobbe is entitled can, in my opinion, be described neither as based on an estoppel nor as proprietary in character. There are several important authorities to which I want to refer but I want first to consider as a matter of principle the nature of a proprietary estoppel. An 'estoppel' bars the object of it from asserting some fact or facts, or, sometimes, something that is a mixture of fact and law, that stands in the way of some right claimed by the person entitled to the benefit of the estoppel. The estoppel becomes a 'proprietary' estoppel—a sub-species of a 'promissory' estoppel—if the right claimed is a proprietary right, usually a right to or over land but, in principle, equally available in relation to chattels or choses in action. So, what is the fact or facts, or the matter of mixed fact and law, that, in the present case, the defendant company is said to be barred from asserting? And what is the proprietary right claimed by Mr Cobbe that the facts and matters it is barred from asserting might otherwise defeat?

15 The pleadings do not answer these questions. The terms of the oral 'agreement in principle', the second agreement, relied on by Mr Cobbe are pleaded but it is accepted that there remained still for negotiation other terms. The second agreement was, contractually, an incomplete agreement. The terms that had already been agreed were regarded by the parties as being 'binding in honour', but it follows that the parties knew they were not legally binding. So what is it that the defendant company is estopped from asserting or from denying? It cannot be said to be estopped from asserting that the second agreement was unenforceable for want of writing, for Mr Cobbe does not claim that it was enforceable; nor from denying that the second agreement covered all the terms that needed to be agreed between the parties, for Mr Cobbe does not claim that it did; nor from denying that, pre-18 March 2004, Mr Cobbe had acquired any proprietary interest in the property, for he has never alleged that he had. And what proprietary claim was Mr Cobbe making that an estoppel was necessary to protect? His originally pleaded claim to specific performance of the second agreement was abandoned at a very early stage in the trial (see para. 8 above) and the proprietary claims that remained were claims that the defendant company held the property on trust for itself and Mr Cobbe. These remaining proprietary claims were presumably based on the proposition that a constructive trust of the property, with appropriate beneficial interests for the defendant company and Mr Cobbe, should, by reason of the unconscionable conduct of Mrs Lisle-Mainwaring, be imposed on the property. I must examine that proposition when dealing with constructive trust as a possible

---

[47] I.e., a personal claim based on unjust enrichment. See Anson, pp. 649–652; Goff & Jones, *Law of Restitution* (7th edn, 2007), chap. 26.

means of providing Mr Cobbe with a remedy,[48] but the proposition is not one that requires or depends upon any estoppel.

16 It is relevant to notice that the amendments to Mr Cobbe's pleaded prayer for relief, made when the specific performance and damages for breach of contract claims were abandoned, include the following:

> '(4) Alternatively, a declaration that [the defendant company and Mrs Lisle-Mainwaring] are estopped from denying that [Mr Cobbe] has such interest in the property and/or the proceeds of sale thereof as the court thinks fit.'

This is the only pleaded formulation of the estoppel relied on by Mr Cobbe and, with respect to the pleader, is both meaningless and pointless. Etherton J concluded, in para. 85 of his judgment, that the facts of the case 'gave rise to a proprietary estoppel equity in favour of Mr Cobbe', but nowhere identified the content of the estoppel. Mummery LJ agreed (paras 60 and 61 of his judgment, concurred in by Dyson LJ (para. 120) and Sir Martin Nourse (para. 141)), but he, too, did not address the content of the estoppel. Both Etherton J and Mummery LJ regarded the proprietary estoppel conclusion as justified by the unconscionability of Mrs Lisle-Mainwaring's conduct. My Lords, unconscionability of conduct may well lead to a remedy but, in my opinion, proprietary estoppel cannot be the route to it unless the ingredients for a proprietary estoppel are present. These ingredients should include, in principle, a proprietary claim made by a claimant and an answer to that claim based on some fact, or some point of mixed fact and law, that the person against whom the claim is made can be estopped from asserting. To treat a 'proprietary estoppel equity' as requiring neither a proprietary claim by the claimant nor an estoppel against the defendant but simply unconscionable behaviour is, in my respectful opinion, a recipe for confusion.

17 Deane J, in *Muschinski v Dodds* (1985) 160 CLR 583, in a judgment concurred in by Mason J, drew attention to the nature and function of constructive trusts in the common law. His remarks, at pp 612–616, repay careful reading but I would respectfully draw particular attention to a passage, at pp 615–616, relevant not only to constructive trusts but equally, in my opinion, to proprietary estoppel. He said:

> 'The fact that the constructive trust remains predominantly remedial does not, however, mean that it represents a medium for the indulgence of idiosyncratic notions of fairness and justice. As an equitable remedy, it is available only when warranted by established equitable principles or by the legitimate processes of legal reasoning, by analogy, induction and deduction, from the starting point of a proper understanding of the conceptual foundations of such principles... Under the law of this country—as, I venture to think, under the present law of England... proprietary rights fall to be governed by principles of law and not by some mix of judicial discretion, subjective views about which party "ought to win"... and "the formless void" of individual moral opinion...'

A finding of proprietary estoppel, based on the unconscionability of the behaviour of the person against whom the finding was made but without any coherent formulation of the content of the estoppel or of the proprietary interest that the estoppel was designed to protect invites, in my opinion, criticism of the sort directed by Deane J in the passage cited. However, Mr Ivory, counsel for Mr Cobbe both in the Court of Appeal and before your Lordships, has relied on authority and to that I must now turn.

---

[48] Lord Scott rejected the claim to a constructive trust, which was made on the basis of *Pallant v Morgan* [1953] Ch 43; see p. 583, n. 63, above.

18   Oliver J stated the requirements of proprietary estoppel in a 'common expectation' class of case in a well known and often cited passage in *Taylors Fashions Ltd v Liverpool Victoria Trustees Co Ltd (Note)* [1982] QB 133, 144:

> 'if A under an expectation created or encouraged by B that A shall have a certain interest in land, thereafter, on the faith of such expectation and with the knowledge of B and without objection by him, acts to his detriment in connection with such land, a court of equity will compel B to give effect to such expectation.'

Note the reference to 'a certain interest in land'. *Taylors Fashions* [p. 1012, above] was a case where the 'certain interest' was an option to renew a lease. There was no lack of certainty; the terms of the new lease were spelled out in the option and the lessees' expectation was that on the exercise of the option the new lease would be granted. The problem was that the option had not been registered under the Land Charges Act 1925 and the question was whether the freeholders, successors in title to the original lessors who had granted the option, could be estopped from denying the right of the lessees to exercise the option. But what is the comparable expectation and the comparable 'certain interest' in the present case? Mr Cobbe's expectation, encouraged by Mrs Lisle-Mainwaring, was that upon the grant of planning permission there would be a successful negotiation of the outstanding terms of a contract for the sale of the property to him, or to some company of his, and that a formal contract, which would include the already agreed core terms of the second agreement as well as the additional new terms agreed upon, would be prepared and entered into. An expectation dependent upon the conclusion of a successful negotiation is not an expectation of an interest having any comparable certainty to the certainty of the terms of the lessees' interest under the *Taylors Fashions* option. In the *Taylors Fashions* case both the content of the estoppel, i.e. an estoppel barring the new freeholders from asserting that the option was unenforceable for want of registration, and the interest the estoppel was intended to protect, i.e. the option to have a renewal of the lease, were clear and certain. Not so here. The present case is one in which an unformulated estoppel is being asserted in order to protect Mr Cobbe's interest under an oral agreement for the purchase of land that lacked both the requisite statutory formalities (section 2 of the 1989 Act [p. 18, above]) and was, in a contractual sense, incomplete.

19   A reference to the expectation of 'a certain interest in land' had appeared in the speech of Lord Kingsdown in *Ramsden v Dyson* (1866) LR 1 HL 129, 170 [p. 1008, above]...

20   Lord Kingsdown's requirement that there be an expectation of 'a certain interest in land', repeated in the same words by Oliver J in the *Taylors Fashions* case, presents a problem for Mr Cobbe's proprietary estoppel claim. The problem is that when he made the planning application his expectation was, for proprietary estoppel purposes, the wrong sort of expectation. It was not an expectation that he would, if the planning application succeeded, become entitled to 'a certain interest in land'. His expectation was that he and Mrs Lisle-Mainwaring, or their respective legal advisers, would sit down and agree the outstanding contractual terms to be incorporated into the formal written agreement, which he justifiably believed would include the already agreed core financial terms, and that his purchase, and subsequently his development of the property, in accordance with that written agreement would follow. This is not, in my opinion, the sort of expectation of 'a certain interest in land' that Oliver J in the *Taylors Fashions* case or Lord Kingsdown in *Ramsden v Dyson* had in mind.

21   Mr Ivory cited, also, a number of other authorities in support of his proprietary estoppel case.

His Lordship referred to *Plimmer v Wellington Corpn* (1884) 9 App Cas 699, p. 1065, below; *Inwards v Baker* [1965] 2 QB 29, p. 1049, below; *Crabb v Arun District Council* [1976] Ch 179, p. 1051, below; *Laird v Birkenhead Railway Co* (1859) John 500; *Holiday Inns Inc v Broadhead* (1974) 232 EG 951; *Attorney-General of Hong Kong v Humphreys Estate (Queen's Gardens) Ltd* [1987] AC 114, p. 27, above, and continued:

26   Both Etherton J and Mummery LJ in the Court of Appeal recognised that, in cases where negotiations had been made expressly subject to contract and a contract had not in the end been forthcoming, it would be very difficult for a disappointed purchaser to establish an arguable case for a proprietary estoppel. Etherton J, having referred to the relevant authorities, accepted the improbability that in a subject-to-contract case a proprietary estoppel might arise (paras 119 and 120), but distinguished the present case on the footing that Mrs Lisle-Mainwaring had encouraged Mr Cobbe to believe that if he succeeded in obtaining planning permission the second agreement would be honoured even though not legally binding (para. 123) and, also, I think, that nothing equivalent to a subject-to-contract reservation had ever been expressed (para. 119) and that no issue likely to cause any difficulty had been raised in the negotiations that culminated in the second agreement: para. 122. In the Court of Appeal Mummery LJ dealt with the subject-to-contract point at [2006] 1 WLR 2964, paras 53–57. The second agreement, he said, at para. 57, 'was never expressly stated to be "subject to contract" either by use of that well known expression or by other language to the same effect'. He agreed with Etherton J, at para. 56, that

> 'proprietary estoppel could be established even where the parties anticipated that a legal binding contract would not come into existence until after planning permission had been obtained, further terms discussed and agreed and formal written contracts exchanged.'

27   My Lords, I can easily accept that a subject-to-contract reservation made in the course of negotiations for a contract relating to the acquisition of an interest in land could be withdrawn, whether expressly or by inference from conduct. But debate about subject-to-contract reservations has only a peripheral relevance in the present case, for such a reservation is pointless in the context of oral negotiations relating to the acquisition of an interest in land. It would be an unusually unsophisticated negotiator who was not well aware that oral agreements relating to such an acquisition are by statute unenforceable and that no express reservation to make them so is needed. Mr Cobbe was an experienced property developer and Mrs Lisle-Mainwaring gives every impression of knowing her way around the negotiating table. Mr Cobbe did not spend his money and time on the planning application in the mistaken belief that the agreement was legally enforceable. He spent his money and time well aware that it was not. Mrs Lisle-Mainwaring did not encourage in him a belief that the second agreement was enforceable. She encouraged in him a belief that she would abide by it although it was not. Mr Cobbe's belief, or expectation, was always speculative. He knew she was not legally bound. He regarded her as bound 'in honour' but that is an acknowledgement that she was not legally bound.

28   The reality of this case, in my opinion, is that Etherton J and the Court of Appeal regarded their finding that Mrs Lisle-Mainwaring's behaviour in repudiating, and seeking an improvement on, the core financial terms of the second agreement was unconscionable, an evaluation from which I do not in the least dissent, as sufficient to justify the creation of a 'proprietary estoppel equity'. As Etherton J said, at para. 123, she took unconscionable advantage

of Mr Cobbe. The advantage taken was the benefit of his services, his time and his money in obtaining planning permission for the property. The advantage was unconscionable because immediately following the grant of planning permission she repudiated the financial terms on which Mr Cobbe had been expecting to be able to purchase the property. But to leap from there to a conclusion that a proprietary estoppel case was made out was not, in my opinion, justified. Let it be supposed that Mrs Lisle-Mainwaring were to be held estopped from denying that the core financial terms of the second agreement were the financial terms on which Mr Cobbe was entitled to purchase the property. How would that help Mr Cobbe? He still would not have a complete agreement. Suppose Mrs Lisle-Mainwaring had simply said she had changed her mind and did not want the property to be sold after all. What would she be estopped from denying? Proprietary estoppel requires, in my opinion, clarity as to what it is that the object of the estoppel is to be estopped from denying, or asserting, and clarity as to the interest in the property in question that that denial, or assertion, would otherwise defeat. If these requirements are not recognised, proprietary estoppel will lose contact with its roots and risk becoming unprincipled and therefore unpredictable, if it has not already become so. This is not, in my opinion, a case in which a remedy can be granted to Mr Cobbe on the basis of proprietary estoppel.

29 There is one further point regarding proprietary estoppel to which I should refer. Section 2 of the 1989 Act declares to be void any agreement for the acquisition of an interest in land that does not comply with the requisite formalities prescribed by the section. Subsection (5) expressly makes an exception for resulting, implied or constructive trusts. These may validly come into existence without compliance with the prescribed formalities. Proprietary estoppel does not have the benefit of this exception. The question arises, therefore, whether a complete agreement for the acquisition of an interest in land that does not comply with the section 2 prescribed formalities, but would be specifically enforceable if it did can become enforceable via the route of proprietary estoppel. It is not necessary in the present case to answer this question, for the second agreement was not a complete agreement and, for that reason, would not have been specifically enforceable so long as it remained incomplete. My present view, however, is that proprietary estoppel cannot be prayed in aid in order to render enforceable an agreement that statute has declared to be void. The proposition that an owner of land can be estopped from asserting that an agreement is void for want of compliance with the requirements of section 2 is, in my opinion, unacceptable. The assertion is no more than the statute provides. Equity can surely not contradict the statute.[49]

Lord Walker of Gestingthorpe:

87 The informal bargain made in this case was unusually complex, as both courts below acknowledged. When a claim based on equitable estoppel is made in a domestic setting the informal bargain or understanding is typically on the following lines: if you live here as my carer/companion/lover you will have a home for life. The expectation is of acquiring and keeping an interest in an identified property. In this case, by contrast, Mr Cobbe was expecting to get a contract....

---

[49] Followed by Peter Smith J in *Hutchison v B & DF Ltd* [2008] EWHC 2286 (Ch), [2008] All ER(D) 41 (Oct) at [68]. See, however, *Herbert v Doyle* [2008] EWHC 1950 (Ch), [2008] All ER(D) 40 (Aug) at [15], per Herbert QC: 'Lord Scott's statement of his present view was avowedly obiter, and in my view it remains the case that, if all the requirements are otherwise satisfied for a claim based on proprietary estoppel to succeed, the claim will not fail solely because it also consists of an agreement which falls foul of section 2. The analysis of such a case may be that the court gives effect to the proprietary estoppel by recognising or imposing a constructive trust, and it is this which enables section 2(5) to apply'.

91 Mr Cobbe's case seems to me to fail on the simple but fundamental point that, as persons experienced in the property world, both parties knew that there was no legally binding contract, and that either was therefore free to discontinue the negotiations without legal liability—that is, liability in equity as well as at law, to echo the words of Lord Cranworth LC in *Ramsden v Dyson* (1866) LR 1 HL 129, 145–146. Mr Cobbe was therefore running a risk, but he stood to make a handsome profit if the deal went ahead, and the market stayed favourable. He may have thought that any attempt to get Mrs Lisle-Mainwaring to enter into a written contract before the grant of planning permission would be counter-productive. Whatever his reasons for doing so, the fact is that he ran a commercial risk, with his eyes open, and the outcome has proved unfortunate for him. It is true that he did not expressly state, at the time, that he was relying solely on Mrs Lisle-Mainwaring's sense of honour, but to draw that sort of distinction in a commercial context would be as unrealistic, in my opinion, as to draw a firm distinction depending on whether the formula 'subject to contract' had or had not actually been used.

92 Mr Dowding devoted a separate section of his printed case to arguing that even if the elements for an estoppel were in other respects present, it would not in any event be unconscionable for Mrs Lisle-Mainwaring to insist on her legal rights. That argument raises the question whether 'unconscionability' is a separate element in making out a case of estoppel, or whether to regard it as a separate element would be what Professor Peter Birks once called 'a fifth wheel on the coach': Birks & Pretto (eds), *Breach of Trust* (2002), p. 226. But Birks was there criticising the use of 'unconscionable' to describe a *state of mind* (*Bank of Credit and Commerce International (Overseas) Ltd v Akindele* [2001] Ch 437, 455). Here it is being used (as in my opinion it should always be used) as an objective value judgment on *behaviour* (regardless of the state of mind of the individual in question). As such it does in my opinion play a very important part in the doctrine of equitable estoppel, in unifying and confirming, as it were, the other elements. If the other elements appear to be present but the result does not shock the conscience of the court, the analysis needs to be looked at again. In this case Mrs Lisle-Mainwaring's conduct was unattractive. She chose to stand on her rights rather than respecting her non-binding assurances, while Mr Cobbe continued to spend time and effort, between Christmas 2003 and March 2004, in obtaining planning permission. But Mr Cobbe knew that she was bound in honour only, and so in the eyes of equity her conduct, although unattractive, was not unconscionable.

(iii) Proprietary estoppel in the House of Lords: right granted

Thorner v Major

[2009] 1 WLR 776 (HL, **Lords Hoffmann, Scott of Foscote, Rodger of Earlsferry, Walker of Gestingthorpe** and **Neuberger of Abbotsbury**)[50]

Lord Hoffmann:

1 My Lords, the claimant, David Thorner, is a Somerset farmer who, for nearly 30 years, did substantial work without pay on the farm of his father's cousin, Peter Thorner. The judge found that from 1990 until his death in 2005 Peter encouraged David to believe that he would inherit

---

[50] [2009] 16 EG 136 (G. Featherstonhaugh). *Re Basham* [1986] 1 WLR 1498; [1987] Conv 211 (J. E. Martin); [1987] CLJ 215 (D. Hayton); *Gillett v Holt* [2001] Ch 210; [2000] CLJ 453 (M. Dixon), [2000] All ER Rev 244 (P. J. Clarke), 370 (C. H. Sherrin); [2001] Conv 78 (M. P. Thompson). See also Sir Christopher Slade's Child & Co Oxford Lecture 1984 on the *Informal Creation of Interests in Land* at p. 12.

the farm and that David acted in reliance upon this assurance. In the event, however, Peter left no will. In these proceedings, David claims that by reason of the assurance and reliance, Peter's estate is estopped from denying that he has acquired the beneficial interest in the farm. The judge [2008] WTLR 155 found the case proved but the Court of Appeal [2008] WTLR 1289 reversed him.

2 Such a claim, under the principle known as proprietary estoppel, requires the claimant to prove a promise or assurance that he will acquire a proprietary interest in specified property. A distinctive feature of this case, as Lloyd LJ remarked in the Court of Appeal, at para. 65, was that the representation was never made expressly but was 'a matter of impli-cation and inference from indirect statements and conduct'. It consisted of such matters as handing over to David in 1990 an insurance policy bonus notice with the words 'that's for my death duties' and other oblique remarks on subsequent occasions which indicated that Peter intended David to inherit the farm. As Lloyd LJ observed, at para 67, such conduct and language might have been consistent with a current intention rather than a definite assur-ance. But the judge found as a fact that these words and acts were reasonably understood by David as an assurance that he would inherit the farm and that Peter intended them to be so understood.

3 The Court of Appeal said, correctly, that the fact that Peter had actually intended David to inherit the farm was irrelevant. The question was whether his words and acts would reasonably have conveyed to David an assurance that he would do so. But Lloyd LJ accepted, at para. 66, that the finding as to what Peter would reasonably have been understood to mean by his words and acts was a finding of fact which was not open to challenge. That must be right. The fact that he spoke in oblique and allusive terms does not matter if it was reasonable for David, given his knowledge of Peter and the background circumstances, to have understood him to mean not merely that his present intention was to leave David the farm but that he definitely would do so.

4 However, the Court of Appeal allowed the appeal on the ground that the judge had not found that the assurance was intended to be relied upon and that there was no material upon which he could have made such a finding. The judge had found that David had relied upon the assurance by not pursuing other opportunities but not, said Lloyd LJ, that Peter had known about these opportunities or intended to discourage David from pursuing them.

5 At that point, it seems to me, the Court of Appeal departed from their previously objective examination of the meaning which Peter's words and acts would reasonably have conveyed and required proof of his subjective understanding of the effect which those words would have upon David. In my opinion it did not matter whether Peter knew of any specific alternatives which David might be contemplating. It was enough that the meaning he conveyed would reasonably have been understood as intended to be taken seriously as an assurance which could be relied upon. If David did then rely upon it to his detriment,[51] the necessary element of the estoppel is in my opinion established. It is not necessary that Peter should have known or foreseen the particular act of reliance.

6 The judge found, at para. 98, not only that it was reasonable for David to have understood Peter's words and acts to mean that 'he would be Peter's successor to [the farm]' but that it was reasonable for him to rely upon them. These findings of fact were in my opinion sufficient to support the judge's decision.

---

[51] For detrimental reliance, see pp. 1036–1038, below.

7 The judge held that the equity in David's favour created by the proprietary estoppel required a declaration that Peter's personal representatives held the farm with its chattels, live and dead stock and cash at bank on trust for David absolutely. The personal representatives object on two grounds. First, they say although the judge placed reliance on the incident of the handing over of the insurance policy in 1990, the assurance was not unequivocal until affirmed by later words and conduct, after which the detriment suffered by David was a good deal less than if one took the whole period from 1990 until Peter's death and therefore did not justify an award of the whole farm.

8 I do not think that the judge was trying to pinpoint the date at which the assurance became unequivocal and I think it would be unrealistic in a case like this to try to do so. There was a close and ongoing daily relationship between the parties. Past events provide context and background for the interpretation of subsequent events and subsequent events throw retrospective light upon the meaning of past events. The owl of Minerva spreads its wings only with the falling of the dusk. The finding was that David reasonably relied upon the assurance from 1990, even if it required later events to confirm that it was reasonable for him to have done so.

9 The second ground of objection is that the farm when Peter died in 2005 was not the same as it was in 1990. In between, he had sold some land and bought other land. I agree with my noble and learned friends, Lord Walker of Gestingthorpe and Lord Neuberger of Abbotsbury, that changes in the character or extent of the property in question are relevant to the relief which equity will provide but do not exclude such a remedy when there is still an identifiable property. In the present case, I see no reason to question the judge's decision that David was entitled to the beneficial interest in the farm and the farming business as they were at Peter's death.

10 I would therefore allow the appeal and restore the decision of the judge.

Lord Scott of Foscote:

14 One of the features of the type of cases of which the present case is an example is the extent to which proprietary estoppel and constructive trust have been treated as providing alternative and overlapping remedies and, while in no way disagreeing with my noble and learned friends' conclusion that David can establish his equity in Steart Farm via proprietary estoppel, I find it easier and more comfortable to regard David's equity as established via a remedial constructive trust. I will return to this later.

18 As to the requirement that a representation, if it is to found a claim based on proprietary estoppel, must be clear and unequivocal, a requirement that I certainly accept, there seem to me to be two respects in which Peter's representation to David that on Peter's death David would inherit Steart Farm might be thought to be lacking in the requisite certainty. First, there is the question as to the identity of Steart Farm. A contract for the sale of Steart Farm, if in writing, signed by the parties and stating the price, would not lack contractual certainty provided that evidence were available to identify as at the date of the contract the agricultural unit that constituted Steart Farm. A representation by Peter that David would, on Peter's death, inherit Steart Farm cannot, at the time the representation was made, be accorded a comparable certainty. Farm boundaries are not immutable. They change, with purchases of additional fields and/or sales of fields that were part of the farm. Steart Farm, excluding land of which Peter was merely the tenant, ranged from 350 acres in 1976 to 460 acres in 2005 when Peter died. It could not be supposed that in, say, 1990 when perhaps the most important of the representations that David would inherit Steart Farm was made by Peter, Peter was representing also that he would not alienate any part of Steart Farm. And, indeed, in the period

between 1990 and his death in 2005, Peter both sold land (for development), which thereupon ceased to be part of Steart Farm, and acquired land which was incorporated into and became part of Steart Farm. Peter's representation that David would inherit Steart Farm speaks, at least where Peter remained the owner of an agricultural entity known as Steart Farm, as from his death and if, at that time, evidence were available to identify Steart Farm with certainty, David's claim to be entitled in equity to Steart Farm cannot, in my opinion, be rejected for want of certainty of subject matter. What the position would have been, and what right could have been claimed by David, if, in say 2004, Peter had decided to give up farming and to sell the whole of Steart Farm does not arise and need not be decided. It may well be, however, that in that event, David would succeed in establishing a proprietary claim in equity and to consequential relief (cf *Gillett v Holt* [2001] Ch 210).

19 The second 'certainty' problem about a representation that David would inherit Steart Farm, a problem inherent in every case in which a representation about inheritance prospects is the basis of a proprietary estoppel claim, is that the expected fruits of the representation lie in the future, on the death of the representor, and, in the meantime, the circumstances of the representor or of his or her relationship with the representee, or both, may change and bring about a change of intentions on the part of the representor. *Gillett v Holt* was such a case. If, for example, Peter had become, before his death, in need of full-time nursing care, so that he could not continue to live at Steart Farm or continue as a farmer and needed to sell Steart Farm or some part of it in order to fund the costs of necessary medical treatment and care, it seems to me questionable whether David's equity in Steart Farm, bred from the representations and conduct in evidence in this case, would have been held by a court to bar the realisation of Steart Farm, or some sufficient part of it, for those purposes. I do not, of course, imagine for a moment that, in the circumstances I am postulating, David would have raised any objection. However, the conceptual possibility of a dispute arising in the circumstances postulated has to be borne in mind. Would it really be the case that the representations made by Peter, relied on and acted on by David as they were, would have barred the use of Steart Farm as a source of funding for the needs of Peter in a decrepit old age? For my part, I doubt it. But it is an odd sort of estoppel that is produced by representations that are, in a sense, conditional.

20 These reflections invite some thought about the relationship between proprietary estoppel and constructive trust and their respective roles in providing remedies where representations about future property interests have been made and relied on. There are many cases in which the representations relied on relate to the acquisition by the representee of an immediate, or more or less immediate, interest in the property in question. In these cases a proprietary estoppel is the obvious remedy. The representor is estopped from denying that the representee has the proprietary interest that was promised by the representation in question. *Crabb v Arun District Council* [1976] Ch 179 [p. 1051, below] seems to me a clear example of such a case. The council had represented that Mr Crabb would be entitled to have access to the private road at gateway B and had confirmed that representation by erecting gateposts and a gate across the gateway. Once Mr Crabb, in reliance on that representation, had acted to his detriment in selling off a portion of his land so that his only means of access to and egress from his retained land was via gateway B, it was too late for the council to change its mind. The council was estopped from denying that Mr Crabb had the necessary access rights. *Ramsden v Dyson* (1866) LR 1 HL 129 is another case, straightforward if viewed through the spectacles of the jurisprudence that has emerged since, of proprietary estoppel. In cases where the owner of land stands by and allows a neighbour to build over the mutual boundary, representing either expressly or

impliedly that the building owner is entitled to do so, the owner may be estopped from subsequently asserting his title to the encroached upon land. This, too, seems to me straightforward proprietary estoppel. There are many other examples of decided cases where representations acted on by the representee have led to the representor being estopped from denying that the representee had the proprietary interest in the representor's land that the representation had suggested. Constructive trust, in my opinion, has nothing to offer to cases of this sort. But cases where the relevant representation has related to inheritance prospects seem to me difficult, for the reasons I have given, to square with the principles of proprietary estoppel established by the *Ramsden v Dyson* and *Crabb v Arun District Council* line of cases and, for my part, I find them made easier to understand as constructive trust cases. The possibility of a remedial constructive trust over property, created by the common intention or understanding of the parties regarding the property on the basis of which the claimant has acted to his detriment, has been recognised at least since *Gissing v Gissing* [1971] AC 886: see particularly Lord Diplock, at p. 905. The 'inheritance' cases, of which *Gillett v Holt*; *Re Basham* [1986] 1 WLR 1498 and *Walton v Walton* (unreported) 14 April 1994; [1994] CA Transcript No 479 and, of course, the present case, are good examples, are, to my mind, more comfortably viewed as constructive trust cases. Indeed I think Mr Edward Nugee QC, sitting as a High Court judge in *Re Basham*, was of the same opinion. After stating the proprietary estoppel principle, at p. 1503, he went on, at p. 1504:

'But in my judgment, at all events where the belief is that A is going to be given a right in the future, it is properly to be regarded as giving rise to a species of constructive trust, which is the concept employed by a court of equity to prevent a person from relying on his legal rights where it would be unconscionable for him to do so.'

And, at p. 1505e, he referred to the detriment 'that the plaintiff must prove in order to raise a constructive trust in a case of proprietary estoppel'. For my part I would prefer to keep proprietary estoppel and constructive trust as distinct and separate remedies, to confine proprietary estoppel to cases where the representation, whether express or implied, on which the claimant has acted is unconditional and to address the cases where the representations are of future benefits, and subject to qualification on account of unforeseen future events, via the principles of remedial constructive trusts.

21 I am satisfied, however, that this case would, on the factual findings made by the judge and accepted by the Court of Appeal have justified a remedial constructive trust under which David would have obtained the relief awarded him by the judge. I would allow the appeal.

Lord Rodger of Earlsferry also allowed the appeal.

Lord Walker of Gestingthorpe:

30 This appeal raises two issues. The first and main issue concerns the character or quality of the representation or assurance made to the claimant. The other (which could be regarded as a subsidiary part of the main issue, but was argued before your Lordships as a separate point) is whether, if the other elements for proprietary estoppel are established, the claimant must fail if the land to which the assurance relates has been inadequately identified, or has undergone a change (in its situation or extent) during the period between the giving of the assurance and its eventual repudiation.

31 I should say at once that the defendants to the appeal did not contend that this House's decision in *Cobbe v Yeoman's Row Management Ltd* [2008] 1 WLR 1752 has severely curtailed,

or even virtually extinguished, the doctrine of proprietary estoppel (a rather apocalyptic view that has been suggested by some commentators: see for instance Ben McFarlane and Professor Andrew Robertson, 'The Death of Proprietary Estoppel' [2008] LMCLQ 449 and Sir Terence Etherton's extrajudicial observations to the Chancery Bar Association 2009 Conference, paras 27ff[52]). But *Cobbe's* case is certainly relevant to the second issue. The defendants' case is that in *Cobbe's* case this House reaffirmed the need for certainty of interest which has, it is argued, been part of the law since *Ramsden v Dyson* (1866) LR 1 HL 129. The defendants argue that *Re Basham* was wrongly decided so far as it extended, not just to the deceased's cottage, but to the whole of his residuary estate.

His Lordship considered the facts and the proceedings below, and held that there was insufficient reason for the Court of Appeal to reverse the trial judge's careful findings and conclusion that Peter's assurances, objectively assessed, were intended to be taken seriously and to be relied on. He continued:

61 In my opinion it is a necessary element of proprietary estoppel that the assurances given to the claimant (expressly or impliedly, or, in standing-by cases, tacitly) should relate to identified property owned (or, perhaps, about to be owned) by the defendant. That is one of the main distinguishing features between the two varieties of equitable estoppel, that is promissory estoppel and proprietary estoppel. The former must be based on an existing legal *relationship* (usually a contract, but not necessarily a contract relating to land). The latter need not be based on an existing legal relationship, but it must relate to *identified property* (usually land) owned (or, perhaps, about to be owned) by the defendant. It is the relation to identified land of the defendant that has enabled proprietary estoppel to develop as a sword, and not merely a shield: see Lord Denning MR in *Crabb v Arun District Council* [1976] Ch 179, 187.

62 In this case the deputy judge made a clear finding of an assurance by Peter that David would become entitled to Steart Farm.... Both Peter and David knew that the extent of the farm was liable to fluctuate (as development opportunities arose, and tenancies came and went). There is no reason to doubt that their common understanding was that Peter's assurance related to whatever the farm consisted of at Peter's death (as it would have done, barring any restrictive language, under section 24 of the Wills Act 1837, had Peter made a specific devise of Steart Farm). This fits in with the retrospective aspect of proprietary estoppel noted in *Walton v Walton* [1994] CA Transcript No 479.

63 The situation is to my mind quite different from a case like *Layton v Martin* [1986] 2 FLR 227, in which the deceased made an unspecific promise of 'financial security'.[53] It is also different (so far as concerns the award of the whole of the deceased's residuary estate) from *Re Basham* [1986] 1 WLR 1498. Your Lordships do not need to decide whether *Re Basham* was correctly decided, so far as it extended to the residuary estate, and I would prefer to express

---

[52] Published in an extended version at [2009] Conv 104.

[53] On the content of the promise, see also *Orgee v Orgee* [1997] EGCS 152 (claim to agricultural tenancy on basis of estoppel refused in the absence of details as to crucial terms on which tenancy was expected to be based, for example, provisions for repairs and rent and rent review regime); cf *JT Developments Ltd v Quinn* (1990) 62 P & CR 33; (1998) 114 LQR 351 (M. Pawlowski). See also *Parker v Parker* [2003] EWHC 1846 (Ch), [2003] NPC 94 (expectation too vague and indefinite): [2004] Conv 516 (M. P. Thompson); *Keelwalk Properties Ltd v Waller* [2002] 3 EGLR 79 (landlord's long practice of renewing leases did not found estoppel); *Sutcliffe v Lloyd* [2007] 2 EGLR 13 at [38] (promisor need not make clear that promise is irrevocable).

no decided view. But on this point the deputy judge in *Re Basham* relied largely on authorities about mutual wills, which are arguably a special case.

64 Mr Simmonds relied on some observations by my noble and learned friend, Lord Scott of Foscote, in *Cobbe's* case [2008] 1 WLR 1752, paras 18–21, pointing out that in *Ramsden v Dyson* LR 1 HL 129, 170, Lord Kingsdown referred to 'a *certain* interest in land' (emphasis supplied). But, as Lord Scott noted, Lord Kingsdown immediately went on to refer to a case where there was uncertainty as to the terms of the contract (or, as it may be better to say, in the assurance) and to point out that relief would be available in that case also. All the 'great judges' to whom Lord Kingsdown referred, at p. 171, thought that even where there was some uncertainty an equity could arise and could be satisfied, either by an interest in land or in some other way.

65 In any event, for the reasons already mentioned, I do not perceive any real uncertainty in the position here. It is possible to imagine all sorts of events which might have happened between 1990 and 2005. If Peter had decided to sell another field or two, whether because of an advantageous development opportunity or because the business was pressed for cash, David would have known of it, and would no doubt have accepted it without question (just as he made no claim to the savings account which held that part of the proceeds of the 1990 sale which Peter did not roll over into land). If Peter had decided in 2000 to sell half the farm in order to build himself a retirement home elsewhere (an unlikely hypothesis) David might well have accepted that too (as the claimant in *Gillett v Holt* [2001] Ch 210 might have accepted a reduction in his expectations, had he been asked to do so rather than being abruptly and humiliatingly dismissed: see p. 229). But it is unprofitable, in view of the retrospective nature of the assessment which the doctrine of proprietary estoppel requires, to speculate on what might have been.

66 Apart from his principled attack based on uncertainty, Mr Simmonds, realistically, did not criticise the deputy judge's decision to award David the whole farm and the whole of the farming assets. There is no ground on which to challenge the judge's discretion in determining the remedy. I would allow the appeal and restore the judge's order.

67 I wish to add a brief postscript as to *Cobbe's* case. It will be apparent from this opinion that I have some difficulty with Lord Scott's observation (in para. 14 of his opinion in that case) that proprietary estoppel is a sub-species of promissory estoppel. But the terminology and tax-onomy of this part of the law are, I acknowledge, far from uniform. The index to the first (1923) edition of George Spencer Bower's *Law relating to Estoppel by Representation* contains in its index the entry '"Equitable estoppel", a meaningless expression', a view which is developed at length in the text, with Lord Selborne LC attracting particular criticism, at p. 14, that 'a jurist so nice and discriminating in his phraseology' should have used the expression in *Citizens' Bank of Louisiana v First National Bank of New Orleans* (1873) LR 6 HL 352, 360. At the other extreme one of the leading 20th century cases, *Crabb v Arun District Council* [1976] Ch 179, shows a 'virtual equation of promissory estoppel and proprietary estoppel', as Oliver J noted in *Taylors Fashions Ltd v Liverpool Victoria Trustees Co Ltd* [1982] QB 133, 153. But this is not the place for any prolonged discussion of terminology or taxonomy.

Lord Neuberger of Abbotsbury:

84 It should be emphasised that I am not seeking to cast doubt on the proposition ... that there must be some sort of an assurance which is 'clear and unequivocal' before it can be relied on to found an estoppel. However, that proposition must be read as subject to three

qualifications. First, it does not detract from the normal principle, so well articulated in this case by Lord Walker, that the effect of words or actions must be assessed in their context. Just as a sentence can have one meaning in one context and a very different meaning in another context, so can a sentence, which would be ambiguous or unclear in one context, be a clear and unambiguous assurance in another context. Indeed, as Lord Walker says, the point is under-lined by the fact that perhaps the classic example of proprietary estoppel is based on silence and inaction, rather than any statement or action: see per Lord Eldon LC ('knowingly, though but passively') in *Dann v Spurrier* (1802) 7 Ves 231, 235–236 and per Lord Kingsdown ('with the knowledge ... and without objection') in *Ramsden v Dyson* (1866) LR 1 HL 129, 170.

85 Secondly, it would be quite wrong to be unrealistically rigorous when applying the 'clear and unambiguous' test. The court should not search for ambiguity or uncertainty, but should assess the question of clarity and certainty practically and sensibly, as well as contextually. Again, this point is underlined by the authorities ... which support the proposition that, at least normally, it is sufficient for the person invoking the estoppel to establish that he reasonably understood the statement or action to be an assurance on which he could rely.

86 Thirdly, as pointed out in argument by my noble and learned friend, Lord Rodger of Earlsferry, there may be cases where the statement relied on to found an estoppel could amount to an assurance which could reasonably be understood as having more than one possible mean-ing. In such a case, if the facts otherwise satisfy all the requirements of an estoppel, it seems to me that, at least normally, the ambiguity should not deprive a person who reasonably relied on the assurance of all relief: it may well be right, however, that he should be accorded relief on the basis of the interpretation least beneficial to him.

90 Based on the reasoning of my noble and learned friend, Lord Scott of Foscote, in *Cobbe v Yeoman's Row Management Ltd*, paras 18–20, 28, the defendants contend that the identity of the property the subject of the assurance or statement relied on to found a proprietary estoppel must be 'certain'. Accordingly, they argue, even if David would otherwise make good his pro-prietary estoppel claim, it must fail because the property the subject of the alleged estoppel in this case is not certain enough.

91 So far as the relevant facts of this case are concerned, the extent of the land owned and farmed by Peter varied. When he inherited Steart Farm in 1976, it comprised about 350 acres of freehold low-lying pasture and rough grazing. In 1990, he sold a large field for development, and used the proceeds to buy more land, so that, by 1992, he owned 463 acres, and the farm included another 120 acres which Peter rented. By 1998, he was farming only some 160 acres of that land himself, having let out the remainder on farm business tenancies. As at the date of his death, Peter was in the process of negotiating a sale of some six acres to developers.

92 In *Cobbe's* case, Mr Cobbe devoted considerable time, effort, and expertise to obtaining planning permission for land owned by Yeoman's Row. Although they reached an oral 'agree-ment in principle', the parties had decided not to enter into a contract, but Mr Cobbe went ahead on the basis, as appreciated by Yeoman's Row, that he expected them to do so once planning permission was obtained. Initially, this was also the intention of Yeoman's Row, but their inten-tion changed about three months before planning permission was obtained, although they did not tell Mr Cobbe until afterwards. Mr Cobbe's estoppel claim failed (although he was entitled to a quantum meruit payment). As I see it, Mr Cobbe's claim failed because he was effectively seeking to invoke proprietary estoppel to give effect to a contract which the parties had inten-tionally and consciously not entered into, and because he was simply seeking a remedy for the unconscionable behaviour of Yeoman's Row.

93 In the context of a case such as *Cobbe's* case, it is readily understandable why Lord Scott considered the question of certainty was so significant. The parties had intentionally not entered into any legally binding arrangement while Mr Cobbe sought to obtain planning permission: they had left matters on a speculative basis, each knowing full well that neither was legally bound—see para. 27. There was not even an agreement to agree (which would have been unenforceable), but, as Lord Scott pointed out, merely an expectation that there would be negotiations. And, as he said, at para. 18, an 'expectation dependent upon the conclusion of a successful negotiation is not an expectation of an interest having [sufficient] certainty'.

94 There are two fundamental differences between that case and this case. First, the nature of the uncertainty in the two cases is entirely different. It is well encapsulated by Lord Walker's distinction between 'intangible legal rights' and 'the tangible property which he or she expects to get', in *Cobbe's* case, para. 68. In that case, there was no doubt about the physical identity of the property. However, there was total uncertainty as to the nature or terms of any benefit (property interest, contractual right, or money), and, if a property interest, as to the nature of that interest (freehold, leasehold, or charge), to be accorded to Mr Cobbe.

95 In this case, the extent of the farm might change, but, on the deputy judge's analysis, there is, as I see it, no doubt as to what was the subject of the assurance, namely the farm as it existed from time to time. Accordingly, the nature of the interest to be received by David was clear: it was the farm as it existed on Peter's death. As in the case of a very different equitable concept, namely a floating charge, the property the subject of the equity could be conceptually identified from the moment the equity came into existence, but its precise extent fell to be determined when the equity crystallised, namely on Peter's death.

96 Secondly, the analysis of the law in *Cobbe's* case was against the background of very different facts. The relationship between the parties in that case was entirely arm's length and commercial, and the person raising the estoppel was a highly experienced businessman. The circumstances were such that the parties could well have been expected to enter into a contract, however, although they discussed contractual terms, they had consciously chosen not to do so. They had intentionally left their legal relationship to be negotiated, and each of them knew that neither of them was legally bound. What Mr Cobbe then relied on was 'an unformulated estoppel... asserted in order to protect [his] interest under an oral agreement for the purchase of land that lacked both the requisite statutory formalities... and was, in a contractual sense, incomplete': para. 18.

97 In this case, by contrast, the relationship between Peter and David was familial and personal, and neither of them, least of all David, had much commercial experience. Further, at no time had either of them even started to contemplate entering into a formal contract as to the ownership of the farm after Peter's death. Nor could such a contract have been reasonably expected even to be discussed between them. On the deputy judge's findings, it was a relatively straightforward case: Peter made what were, in the circumstances, clear and unambiguous assurances that he would leave his farm to David, and David reasonably relied on, and reasonably acted to his detriment on the basis of those assurances, over a long period.

98 In these circumstances, I see nothing in the reasoning of Lord Scott in *Cobbe's* case which assists the defendants in this case. It would represent a regrettable and substantial emasculation of the beneficial principle of proprietary estoppel if it were artificially fettered so as to require the precise extent of the property the subject of the alleged estoppel to be strictly defined in every case. Concentrating on the perceived morality of the parties' behaviour can lead to an unacceptable degree of uncertainty of outcome, and hence I welcome the decision in

Cobbe's case. However, it is equally true that focusing on technicalities can lead to a degree of strictness inconsistent with the fundamental aims of equity.

99 The notion that much of the reasoning in *Cobbe's* case was directed to the unusual facts of that case is supported by the discussion, at para. 29, relating to section 2 of the Law of Property (Miscellaneous Provisions) Act 1989. Section 2 may have presented Mr Cobbe with a problem, as he was seeking to invoke an estoppel to protect a right which was, in a sense, contractual in nature (see the passage quoted at the end of para. 96 above), and section 2 lays down formalities which are required for a valid 'agreement' relating to land. However, at least as at present advised, I do not consider that section 2 has any impact on a claim such as the present, which is a straightforward estoppel claim without any contractual connection. It was no doubt for that reason that the defendants, rightly in my view, eschewed any argument based on section 2.

104 Accordingly, in agreement with all your Lordships, I would allow this appeal.

QUESTION

Compare *Cobbe v Yeoman's Row Management Ltd* [2008] 1 WLR 1752, p. 1021, above, and *Thorner v Major* [2009] 1 WLR 776, above. How do you account for the difference in outcome of the two cases?

(iv) *Detrimental reliance*

In **Greasley v Cooke** [1980] 1 WLR 1306[54] Doris Cooke aged 16 went as a maid servant in 1938 to help in the house of a widower Arthur Greasley and was paid 10 shillings a week. From 1946 she cohabited with one of his sons until the son died in 1975. She was paid wages until Arthur's death in 1948, and thereafter continued, without wages, to live in the house and to look after it and the family, including a mentally ill daughter. After Arthur's death, members of the family led Doris to believe that she could regard the property as her home for the rest of her life and accordingly did not ask for any payment.

The Court of Appeal held that Doris was entitled to occupy the house rent-free so long as she wished to stay there. Lord DENNING MR said at 1311:

The first point is on the burden of proof. Mr Weeks referred us to many cases, such as *Reynell v Sprye* (1852) 1 De GM & G 660, 708; *Smith v Chadwick* (1882) 20 ChD 27, 44 and *Brikom Investments Ltd v Carr* [1979] QB 467, 481–483 where I said that when a person makes a representation intending that another should act on it:

'It is no answer for the maker to say: "You would have gone on with the transaction anyway." That must be mere speculation. No one can be sure what he would, or would not, have done in a hypothetical

---

[54] [1981] Conv 154 (R. E. Annand); 44 MLR 461 (G. Woodman); 125 NLJ 539 (M. P. Thompson). Detriment was required by CA in *Christian v Christian* (1981) 131 NLJ 43. See also *Watkins v Emslie* (1981) 261 EG 1192; *Dann v Spurrier* (1802) 7 Ves 231 at 235–236, per Lord Eldon LC, cited in *Taylors Fashions Ltd v Liverpool Victoria Trustees Co Ltd* [1982] QB 133n at 156; *Watts v Story* [1983] CA Transcript 319, (1983) 134 NLJ 631, p. 1036, below; Pawlowski, *The Doctrine of Proprietary Estoppel*, pp. 43–71.

state of affairs which never took place.... Once it is shown that a representation was calculated to influence the judgment of a reasonable man, the presumption is that he was so influenced.'[55]

So here. These statements to Miss Cooke were calculated to influence her—so as to put her mind at rest—so that she should not worry about being turned out. No one can say what she would have done if Kenneth and Hedley had not made those statements. It is quite possible that she would have said to herself:

'I am not married to Kenneth. I am on my own. What will happen to me if anything happens to him? I had better look out for another job now: rather than stay here where I have no security'.

So, instead of looking for another job, she stayed on in the house looking after Kenneth and Clarice. There is a presumption that she did so, relying on the assurances given to her by Kenneth and Hedley. The burden is not on her, but on them, to prove that she did not rely on their assurances. They did not prove it, nor did their representatives. So she is presumed to have relied on them. So on the burden of proof it seems to me that the judge was in error.

The second point is about the need for some expenditure of money—some detriment—before a person can acquire any interest in a house or any right to stay in it as long as he wishes. It so happens that in many of these cases of proprietary estoppel there has been expenditure of money. But that is not a necessary element. I see that in *Snell's Principles of Equity,* 27th edn (1973) p. 565, it is said: 'A must have incurred expenditure or otherwise have prejudiced himself.' But I do not think that that is necessary. It is sufficient if the party, to whom the assurance is given, acts on the faith of it—in such circumstances that it would be unjust and inequitable for the party making the assurance to go back on it: see *Moorgate Mercantile Co Ltd v Twitchings* [1976] QB 225 and *Crabb v Arun District Council* [1976] Ch 179, 188. Applying those principles here it can be seen that the assurances given by Kenneth and Hedley to Doris Cooke—leading her to believe that she would be allowed to stay in the house as long as she wished—raised an equity in her favour. There was no need for her to prove that she acted on the faith of those assurances. It is to be presumed that she did so. There is no need for her to prove that she acted to her detriment or to her prejudice. Suffice it that she stayed on in the house—looking after Kenneth and Clarice—when otherwise she might have left and got a job elsewhere. The equity having thus been raised in her favour, it is for the courts of equity to decide in what way that equity should be satisfied. In this case it should be by allowing her to stay on in the house as long as she wishes.

Dunn LJ said at 1313:

There is no doubt that for proprietary estoppel to arise the person claiming must have incurred expenditure or otherwise have prejudiced himself or acted to his detriment. The only question before us is as to the burden of proof of the detriment. The judge thought that the onus lay on the claimant to prove it. I agree that in that he fell into error for the reasons given by Lord Denning MR, and I also would allow this appeal.

In **Watts v Story** [1983] CA Transcript 319, (1983) 134 NLJ 631, the Court of Appeal (Dunn and Slade LJJ) held that an action for possession succeeded against a grandson aged 30 who had not shown 'that when the benefits derived by him from his rent free

---

[55] Similarly for the requirement of reliance where there is a material representation to another to induce him to enter into a contract: *Redgrave v Hurd* (1881) 20 ChD 1 at 21, per Jessel MR.

occupation of Apple House, Woodborough, Nottingham (owned by his grandmother whose mind was "as sharp as a razor") are set against any detriments suffered by him as a result of making the move from his Rent Act protected flat in Leeds, he has on balance suffered any detriment in financial or material terms.'

DUNN LJ said:

There was some discussion at the Bar as to what Lord Denning MR meant in the passage which I have cited from *Greasley v Cooke* [1980] 1 WLR 1306. In that case there was no doubt on the evidence that Miss Cooke had been given assurances by the Greasley family that she could regard the property as her home for the rest of her life. Equally, there was no doubt on the facts that she had suffered a detriment, because she had devoted her life to looking after the Greasley family without payment instead of getting a paid job. The only question in the case was whether that admitted detriment was caused by the assurances, or whether she would have continued to look after the family anyway because she was fond of Kenneth Greasley. The judge held that the onus was on her to prove that the detriment was caused by the assurances and that she had failed to discharge the burden of proof. That is clear from, in particular, the judgment of Waller LJ at 1312. It is in that context that the words of Lord Denning cited by the judge in this case should be read. . . .

Lord Denning was not saying that there was no need for detriment in order to establish proprietary estoppel. On the facts of the case detriment spoke for itself, and was admitted. All that Lord Denning was saying was that, the assurances having been established, there was no need for Doris Cooke to prove that the obvious detriment had resulted from them.

The law is well stated in *Snell's Principles of Equity* (28th edn) at page 561 in the following passage: 'Once it is shown that O gave assurances or other encouragement to A, and A suffers detriment, it will readily be inferred that the detriment was suffered as a result of the encouragement; the burden of proof is on O to show that A's conduct was not induced by the assurances.'

Nor, if that passage from Lord Denning's judgment is read as a whole, was he stating any new proposition of law. As the judge said, it matters not whether one talks in terms of detriment or whether one talks in terms of it being unjust or inequitable for the party giving the assurance to go back on it. It is difficult to envisage circumstances in which it would be inequitable for the party giving an assurance alleged to give rise to a proprietary estoppel, i.e., an estoppel concerned with the positive acquisitions of rights and interests in the land of another, unless the person to whom the assurance was given had suffered some prejudice or detriment.[56]

---

[56] *Coombes v Smith* [1986] 1 WLR 808 at 821 (no detriment where wife left husband and went to live with lover and their child); [1986] CLJ 394 (D. J. Hayton); *Hammersmith and Fulham London Borough Council v Top Shop Centres Ltd* [1990] Ch 237 (failure to negotiate for grant of new lease or to apply for relief against forfeiture held to be detriment; reliance presumed); *Wayling v Jones* (1993) 69 P & CR 170; [1994] LS 15 (M. Halliwell) (requirement of promise and 'conduct of such a nature that inducement may be inferred' per Balcombe LJ at 175); (1995) 111 LQR 389 (E. Cooke); [1995] Conv 409 (C. J. Davis); [1996] 16 LS 218 (A. Lawson); *Walton v Bell* [1994] NPC 55A (working long hours for low wages held to give rise to inference that it was induced by the promise being made and reliance on it); *Matharu v Matharu* (1994) 68 P & CR 93 (son's expenditure in improving property held to be detrimental reliance on part of his wife); [1995] 7 CFLQ 59 (G. Battersby); [1995] Conv 61 (M. Welstead); *Durant v Heritage* [1994] EGCS 134 (legal owner must be unable to prove that claimant, in relying on the belief, did not rely on it to his prejudice or detriment); *Gan v Wood* [1998] EGCS 77 (expenditure amounting to minor detriment held

C. SATISFYING THE EQUITY. THE REMEDY

(i) Discretionary nature of remedy. Proportionality

In **Gillett v Holt** [2001] Ch 210, ROBERT WALKER LJ said at 235:

Since Mr Gillett has established his claim to equitable relief, this court must decide what is the most appropriate form for the relief to take. The aim is, as Sir Arthur Hobhouse said in *Plimmer v Wellington Corporation* (1884) 9 App Cas 699, 714, to 'look at the circumstances in each case to decide in what way the equity can be satisfied'. The court approaches this task in a cautious way, in order to achieve what Scarman LJ, in *Crabb v Arun District Council* [1976] Ch 179, 198 called 'the minimum equity to do justice to the plaintiff'. The wide range of possible relief appears from *Snell's Equity,* 30th edn (2000), pp. 641–643 [now 31st edn, 2005, paras 10–23 to 10–27; p. 1047, below].

And in **Jennings v Rice** [2003] 1 P & CR 8, below, p. 1040, ALDOUS LJ said at p. 111, para. 36:

There is a clear line of authority from at least *Crabb* to the present day which establishes that once the elements of proprietary estoppel are established an equity arises. The value of that equity will depend upon all the circumstances including the expectation and the detriment. The task of the court is to do justice. The most essential requirement is that there must be proportionality between the expectation and the detriment.[57]

S. Gardner, 'The Remedial Discretion in Proprietary Estoppel' (1999) 115 LQR 438 at pp. 442, 444, 446, 452, 461, 468[58]

Below are set out four hypotheses. They identify a variety of ways in which the law may, in proprietary estoppel claims, make the issue of a certain remedy depend at least partly on the judge taking a certain view. They are arranged as a series, in ascending order of the extent to which they diverge from a simple proposition that the only possible remedy is expectation relief *in specie.*

---

not to suffice); *Brinnand v Ewens* [1987] 2 EGLR 67 (expenditure incurred on work done 'to make the home more comfortable'): 'The acting to the detriment must have taken place in the belief either that the claimant owned a sufficient interest in the property to justify the expenditure or that he would obtain such an interest' per Nourse LJ at 68; *Century (UK) Ltd SA v Clibbery* [2004] EWHC 1870 (Ch), [2004] All ER (D) 541 (Jul) (household chores of answering telephone calls and video-recording programmes not sufficient detriment); *Holmes v South Yorkshire Police Authority* [2008] HLR 33 (police constable occupying job-related accommodation had not acted in reliance on being able to stay there); *Powell v Benney* [2008] 1 P & CR DG12 (no causal link between assurance and detriment, but court did not consider burden of proof: [2008] Conv 253 (M. Pawlowski)). See also *Downderry Construction Ltd v Secretary of State for Transport, Local Government and the Regions* [2002] EWHC 2 (Admin), (2002) 152 NLJ 108 (reliance need not be reasonable: estoppel by representation).

[57] *Sledmore v Dalby* (1996) 72 P & CR 196, p. 1045, below; *Campbell v Griffin* [2001] EWCA Civ 990, (2001) 82 P & CR DG23, p. 1045, n. 62, below.

[58] See further (2006) 122 LQR 492 (S. Gardner).

Hypothesis 1. The approach is to vindicate the plaintiff's expectations in specie, care being taken to achieve the best match between the details of the plaintiff's expectations and the possible legal responses

Hypothesis 2. The approach is:

— to vindicate the plaintiff's expectations (care being taken to achieve the best match between the details of the plaintiff's expectations and the possible legal responses);

— to vindicate those expectations in specie if practicable, but otherwise in a monetary form; but

— to resort to some other quantum, not more generous than the expectation measure, if it is impracticable to give relief in the expectation measure

Hypothesis 3. The approach is:

— to vindicate the plaintiff's expectations (care being taken to achieve the best match between the details of the plaintiff's expectations and the possible legal responses);

— to vindicate those expectations in specie if practicable, but otherwise in a monetary form; but

— to resort to some other quantum, not more generous than the expectation measure, if it is impracticable to give relief in the expectation measure; and

— to resort to some other quantum, with no ceiling at the expectation measure, in the presence of another factor from a limited range recognised as meriting a departure from expectation relief

Hypothesis 4. The approach is for the court to adopt whatever style and measure of relief it thinks fit, for whatever reason it thinks fit

In the end…hypothesis 3 probably offers the most accurate and supportable account of the law as it stands, but it is neither a perfect match for the material to be described nor likely to be immune from challenge.

Jennings v Rice
[2003] 1 P & CR 8 (CA, **Aldous**, **Mantell** and **Robert Walker LJJ**)[59]

Mrs Royle, a childless widow, died in 1997 aged 93. She lived at Lawn House, Shapwick, Somerset. Her estate was valued at some £1.3 million net, including her house and furniture valued at £435,000. Mr Jennings, who was born in 1939, was a self-employed bricklayer. In 1970 he began to work for Mrs Royle as a part-time gardener for 30 pence an hour. He gradually did more for her, including taking her shopping and running errands. In the late 1980s Mrs Royle stopped paying Mr Jennings but told him that he did not need to be worried about not being paid, since 'he would be alright' and she would 'see to it'.

At about the same time, Mrs Royle was keen that Mr Jennings would continue to live in the neighbourhood and provided the deposit of £2,000 which enabled him and his wife to buy a house locally. She became more dependent on him, especially after

---

[59] [2003] Conv 225 (M. P. Thompson); (2002) 118 LQR 319 (M. Pawlowski); (2006) 122 LQR 492 (S. Gardner). See also *Powell v Benney* [2008] 1 P & CR DG12; [2008] Conv 253 (M. Pawslowski) (claimants' expectations to receive properties worth £280,000 were out of all proportion to the detriment which they suffered).

a burglary in 1993. From 1994 until she died in 1997 he spent almost every night on a sofa in a sitting room at Lawn House. He also collected her prescriptions, helped her to dress and go to the toilet, made sure that she had food and drink available and continued to work in the garden.

Mr Jennings claimed that under the doctrine of proprietary estoppel he should receive the whole of Mrs Royle's estate, or alternatively the value of her house and furniture, since that was his expectation. At first instance Mr Jennings was awarded £200,000. 'The judge reminded himself that the house was valued at £420,000 and was not a suitable house for Mr Jennings to reside in on his own and he took into account that Mrs Royle had no special obligations to her family. He said that to reward an employee on the scale of £420,000 was excessive. He also compared the cost of full-time nursing care, which he estimated at £200,000, with the value of the house. He reasoned that Mr Jennings would probably need £150,000 to buy a house. He concluded: "I do not think that he could complain that he had been unfairly treated if he had been left £200,000 in Mrs Royle's will. Most people would say that she would, at least, then have performed her promise to see him all right. The quality of her assurance affects not only questions of belief, encouragement, reliance and detriment, but also unconscionability and the extent of the equity. In my judgment the minimum necessary to satisfy the equity in the present case is the sum of £200,000"' (per Aldous LJ at p. 104, para. 15).

Held. Award affirmed.

Robert Walker LJ:

42 This court was referred to two recent articles which contain a full and illuminating discussion of this area: *Estoppel and the Protection of Expectations* by Elizabeth Cooke [1997] 17 LS 258 and *The Remedial Discretion in Proprietary Estoppel* by Simon Gardner (1999) 115 LQR 438. Those articles could with advantage have been cited in *Gillett v Holt* [2001] Ch 210. Both are concerned with whether the fundamental aim of this form of estoppel is to fulfil the claimant's expectations, or to compensate him for his detrimental reliance on the defendant's non-contractual assurances, or is some intermediate objective; and (following on from the identification of the correct principle) the nature of the discretion which the court exercises in granting a remedy to the claimant. The articles amply demonstrate that the range of English authorities provides some support for both theories and for a variety of intermediate positions; and that recent Australian authority (especially the decision of the High Court in *Commonwealth v Verwaycn* (1990) 160 CLR 394) has moved in favour of the reliance loss theory.

43 It cannot be doubted that in this as in every other area of the law, the court must take a principled approach, and cannot exercise a completely unfettered discretion according to the individual judge's notion of what is fair in any particular case. Dr Gardner's fourth hypothesis[60] ('the approach is for the court to adopt whatever style and measure of relief it thinks fit, for whatever reason it thinks fit') cannot be right. I do not think that the judgment of Hobhouse LJ in *Sledmore v Dalby* (1996) 72 P & CR 196 [p. 1045, below] (to which I shall return) can possibly be regarded as adopting or advocating an unfettered judicial discretion.

---

[60] The hypotheses are set out at p. 1040, above.

44 The need to search for the right principles cannot be avoided. But it is unlikely to be a short or simple search, because (as appears from both the English and the Australian authorities) proprietary estoppel can apply in a wide variety of factual situations, and any summary formula is likely to prove to be an over simplification. The cases show a wide range of variation in both of the main elements, that is the quality of the assurances which give rise to the claimant's expectations and the extent of the claimant's detrimental reliance on the assurances. The doctrine applies only if these elements, in combination, make it unconscionable for the person giving the assurances (whom I will call the benefactor, although that may not always be an appropriate label) to go back on them.

45 Sometimes the assurances, and the claimant's reliance on them, have a consensual character falling not far short of an enforceable contract (if the only bar to the formation of a contract is non-compliance with s. 2 of the Law of Property (Miscellaneous Provisions) Act 1989, the proprietary estoppel may become indistinguishable from a constructive trust: *Yaxley v Gotts* [2000] Ch 162 [p. 22, above]). In a case of that sort both the claimant's expectations and the element of detriment to the claimant will have been defined with reasonable clarity. A typical case would be an elderly benefactor who reaches a clear understanding with the claimant (who may be a relative, a friend, or a remunerated companion or carer) that if the claimant resides with and cares for the benefactor, the claimant will inherit the benefactor's house (or will have a home for life). In a case like that the consensual element of what has happened suggests that the claimant and the benefactor probably regarded the expected benefit and the accepted detriment as being (in a general, imprecise way) equivalent, or at any rate not obviously disproportionate. Cases of that sort, if free from other complications, fit fairly comfortably into Dr Gardner's first or second hypothesis (both of which aim to vindicate the claimant's expectations as far as possible, and if possible by providing the claimant with the specific property which the benefactor has promised).

46 However, the claimant's expectations may not be focused on any specific property. In *Re Basham* [1986] 1 WLR 1489, the deputy judge (Mr Edward Nugee QC) rejected the submission that there must be some clearly identified piece of property, and that decision has been approved more than once in this court. Moreover (as the judge's findings in this case vividly illustrate), the claimant's expectations may have been formed on the basis of vague and inconsistent assurances. The judge said of Mrs Royle that she:

'...was prone to saying different things at different times and, perhaps deliberately, couched her promises in non-specific terms.'

He made that observation in relation to the failure of the contract claim, but it is relevant to the estoppel claim also.

47 If the claimant's expectations are uncertain (as will be the case with many honest claimants) then their specific vindication cannot be the appropriate test. A similar problem arises if the court, although satisfied that the claimant has a genuine claim, is not satisfied that the high level of the claimant's expectations is fairly derived from his deceased patron's assurances, which may have justified only a lower level of expectation. In such cases the court may still take the claimant's expectations (or the upper end of any range of expectations) as a starting point, but unless constrained by authority I would regard it as no more than a starting point.

48 I do not see that approach as being inconsistent with authority. On the contrary, I think it is supported by a substantial body of English authority. Scarman LJ's well-known reference to 'the minimum equity to do justice to the plaintiff (*Crabb v Arun District Council* [1976] Ch 179, 198, [p. 1054, below]) must no doubt be read in the context of the rather unusual facts of that

case, but it does not stand alone. As Scarman LJ recognised, the line of authority goes back to nineteenth-century cases such as *Duke of Beaufort v Patrick* (1853) 17 Beav 60 and *Plimmer v Wellington Corporation* (1884) 9 App Cas 699 [p. 1065, below]. A passage in the opinion of the Privy Council (delivered by Sir Arthur Hobhouse) in *Plimmer's* case at pp. 713–714 is particularly instructive. The conclusion of the passage is that:

'In fact the court must look at the circumstances in each case to decide in what way the equity can be satisfied.'

Scarman LJ's reference to the minimum does not require the court to be constitutionally parsimonious, but it does implicitly recognise that the court must also do justice to the defendant.

49 It is no coincidence that these statements of principle refer to satisfying the equity (rather than satisfying, or vindicating, the claimant's expectations). The equity arises not from the claimant's expectations alone, but from the combination of expectations, detrimental reliance, and the unconscionableness of allowing the benefactor (or the deceased benefactor's estate) to go back on the assurances. There is a faint parallel with the old equitable doctrine of part performance, of which Lord Selborne said in *Maddison v Alderson* (1883) 8 App Cas 467, 475.

'In a suit founded on such part performance, the defendant is really "charged" upon the equities resulting from the acts done in execution of the contract, and not (within the meaning of the statute) upon the contract itself.'

So with proprietary estoppel the defendant is charged with satisfying the equity which has arisen from the whole sequence of events. But the parallel is only faint since in the case of estoppel there is no contract and the nexus between the benefactor's assurances and the resulting equity is less direct; the assurances are only half the story. In *Dillwyn v Llewelyn* (1862) 4 De GF & J 517, 522 Lord Westbury expressed the point in terms which anticipated Lord Selborne:

'The equity of the donee and the estate to be claimed by virtue of it depend on the transaction, that is, on the acts done, and not on the language of the memorandum [which amounted to an imperfect gift].'

50 To recapitulate: there is a category of case in which the benefactor and the claimant have reached a mutual understanding which is in reasonably clear terms but does not amount to a contract. I have already referred to the typical case of a carer who has the expectation of coming into the benefactor's house, either outright or for life. In such a case the court's natural response is to fulfil the claimant's expectations. But if the claimant's expectations are uncertain, or extravagant, or out of all proportion to the detriment which the claimant has suffered, the court can and should recognise that the claimant's equity should be satisfied in another (and generally more limited) way.

51 But that does not mean that the court should in such a case abandon expectations completely, and look to the detriment suffered by the claimant as defining the appropriate measure of relief. Indeed in many cases the detriment may be even more difficult to quantify, in financial terms, than the claimant's expectations. Detriment can be quantified with reasonable precision if it consists solely of expenditure on improvements to another person's house, and in some cases of that sort an equitable charge for the expenditure may be sufficient to satisfy the equity (see *Snell's Equity*, 30th edn, para. 39–21 and the authorities mentioned in that paragraph). But the detriment of an ever-increasing burden of care for an elderly person, and of having to be subservient to his or her moods and wishes, is very difficult to quantify in money terms.

Moreover the claimant may not be motivated solely by reliance on the benefactor's assurances, and may receive some countervailing benefits (such as free bed and board). In such circumstances the court has to exercise a wide judgmental discretion.

52 It would be unwise to attempt any comprehensive enumeration of the factors relevant to the exercise of the court's discretion, or to suggest any hierarchy of factors. In my view they include, but are not limited to, the factors mentioned in Dr Gardner's third hypothesis (misconduct of the claimant as in *J. Willis & Sons v Willis* [1979] Ch 261 or particularly oppressive conduct on the part of the defendant, as in *Crabb v Arun District Council* or *Pascoe v Turner* [1979] 1 WLR 421 [p. 1056, below]). To these can safely be added the court's recognition that it cannot compel people who have fallen out to live peaceably together, so that there may be a need for a clean break; alterations in the benefactor's assets and circumstances, especially where the benefactor's assurances have been given, and the claimant's detriment has been suffered, over a long period of years; the likely effect of taxation; and (to a limited degree) the other claims (legal or moral) on the benefactor or his or her estate. No doubt there are many other factors which it may be right for the court to take into account in particular factual situations.

53 The judge did in this case consider, although not in detail, what Mr Jennings might reasonably have earned in the way of arm's length remuneration for his services. He also considered what professional nursing care might have cost during the last eight years of Mrs Royle's life. A detailed computational approach was adopted (but with a different outcome, limited to compensation of reliance loss) by the Supreme Court of Tasmania in *Public Trustee v Wadley* [1997] 7 Tas. LR 35, in which the court discussed the appropriate hourly rate and the total number of hours of housework undertaken by a daughter who (as it was put in the dissenting judgment of Wright J):

> 'had subordinated her own life to that of her father and [whose] attentive and affectionate service, often no doubt at considerable inconvenience to herself, put her assistance on a higher plane than that of a domestic servant'.

54 That illustrates the Australian preference for compensating the reliance loss only. Under English law that approach may sometimes be appropriate (see paragraph 51 above) but only where, on the facts, a higher measure would amount to overcompensation. In my view it would rarely if ever be appropriate to go into detailed inquiries as to hours and hourly rates where the claim was based on proprietary estoppel (rather than a restitutionary claim for services which were not gratuitous). But the going rate for live-in carers can provide a useful cross check in the exercise of the court's discretion.

55 I have made some references to the general trend of Australian jurisprudence in this area. It is unnecessary to attempt any detailed study of the different views expressed by the High Court in the *Verwayen* case (which was concerned with estoppel in the very different context of litigation arising out of personal injuries suffered in a collision between two warships) or of Australian cases since then.

56 However, I respectfully agree with the view expressed by Hobhouse LJ in *Sledmore v Dalby* (1996) 72 P & CR 196 [below], that the principle of proportionality (between remedy and detriment), emphasised by Mason CJ in *Verwayen*, is relevant in England also.[61] As Hobhouse LJ observed at p. 209, to recognise the need for proportionality:

---

[61] See also at para. 30, per Aldous LJ: 'I do not believe it is necessary to examine any of the Australian authorities which appear to lean towards the view that the award should compensate the detriment. In so far

'... is to say little more than that the end result must be a just one having regard to the assumption made by the party asserting the estoppel and the detriment which he has experienced.'

The essence of the doctrine of proprietary estoppel is to do what is necessary to avoid an unconscionable result, and a disproportionate remedy cannot be the right way of going about that. Cases on interim injunctive relief have recognised the importance of proportionality in the granting of equitable remedies: see for instance *Lock International v Beswick* [1989] 1 WLR 1268, 1281. Where the court is granting final relief after investigating all the facts proportionality is even more important.

57 I do not consider that the judge made any error of law in his approach to the exercise of his discretion, or that it was otherwise flawed. He did make an error in his reference to the quantum of the relief granted in *Gillett v Holt* (the claimant was awarded a farmhouse and 42 hectares of land as well as £100,000). But every case depends on its own facts and that slip cannot in my view have played a significant part in the judge's disposal of the case.

58 I would therefore dismiss this appeal.[62]

In **Sledmore v Dalby** (1996) 72 P & CR 196,[63] Mr and Mrs Sledmore jointly purchased 15A The Green, Acomb, York. In 1965 their daughter married Mr Dalby and they moved into the house as tenants of the Sledmores. In 1976, when the daughter became ill and Mr Dalby became unemployed, the Sledmores refused to accept any more rent, but the Dalbys continued to pay the rates and maintain the house.

Between 1976 and 1979 Mr Dalby carried out substantial improvements to it, with the encouragement of Mr Sledmore. In 1979 Mr Sledmore conveyed his share to his wife, and she changed her will to ensure that her daughter inherited it to the exclusion of Mr Dalby. Mr Sledmore died in 1980 and Mrs Dalby died in 1983, and Mr Dalby continued to occupy the house rent free. He spent only a few nights a week in it, and the rest of the week in his new partner's house. He was in employment. One of his two daughters still lived at the house and she was now aged 27 and in employment. Mrs Sledmore's house was in need of repair and she was in serious financial difficulty; she was on income support and her mortgage interest, which was in arrears, was being paid by the Department of Health and Social Security.

Mrs Sledmore sought possession of 15A. In rejecting Mr Dalby's claim based on proprietary estoppel, HOBHOUSE LJ said at 208:

The judgment of Mason CJ [in *Commonwealth of Australia v Verwayen* (1990) 95 ALR 321, 331] contains a discussion of the law of estoppel which is of particular value. I will cite three passages which are relevant to what I have said and to the correct approach to the present case.

---

as they differ from the law stated by Mason CJ in *Verwayen*, which was cited by Hobhouse LJ in *Sledmore*, they do not reflect the law of this country.' For a comparison of English and Australian cases, see [2008] Conv 295 (A. Robertson).

[62] *Campbell v Griffin* [2001] EWCA 990, (2001) 82 P & CR DG23 a family carer in a similar situation was awarded £35,000 charged on the property, but had to give up vacant possession to enable the house to be sold. His rent-free occupation did not extinguish his equity; [2002] Conv 519 (M. Pawlowski); [2003] Conv 157 (M. P. Thompson).

[63] [1997] CLJ 34 (P. Milne); [1997] Conv 458 (J. E. Adams); *Ottey v Grundy* [2003] EWCA Civ 1176, [2003] All ER(D) 05 (Aug); [2004] Conv 137 (M. P. Thompson); *Murphy v Burrows* [2005] 1 P & CR DG 3 (lack of proportionality).

'In conformity with the fundamental purpose of all estoppels to afford protection against the detriment which would flow from a party's change of position if the assumption that led to it were deserted, these developments have brought a grater underlying unity to the various categories of estoppel. Indeed, the consistent trend in the modern decisions points inexorably towards the emergence of one overarching doctrine of estoppel rather than a series of independent rules': (1990) 95 ALR 321 at 330. 'The element which both attracts the jurisdiction of a Court of Equity and shapes the remedy to be given is unconscionable conduct on the part of the person bound by the equity, and the remedy required to satisfy an equity varies according to the circumstances of the case. As Robert Goff J said in *Amalgamated Property Co v Texas Bank* [1982] QB 84 at 103: "Of all doctrines, equitable estoppel is surely one of the most flexible" ... However, in moulding its decree, the court, as a court of conscience, goes no further than is necessary to prevent unconscionable conduct': (1990) 95 ALR 321 at 332, quoting Brennan J at 152 CLR 419.

'... it should be accepted that there is but one doctrine of estoppel, which provides that a court of Common Law or Equity may do what is required, but not more, to prevent a person who has relied upon an assumption as to a present, past or future state of affairs (including a legal state of affairs), which assumption the party estoped has induced him to hold, from suffering detriment in reliance upon the assumption as a result of the denial of its correctness. A central element of that doctrine is that there must be a proportionality between the remedy and the detriment which is its purpose to avoid. It would be wholly inequitable and unjust to insist upon a disproportionate making good of the relevant assumption': (1990) 95 ALR 321 at 333.

There are similarly illuminating passages in the judgment of Deane J, at pp. 346 et seq.

It is thus always necessary to ask what is the assumption made by the party asserting the estoppel for which the party affected is to be treated as responsible. In the present case it was no more than the assumption that the mother, Mrs Sledmore, would leave number 15A to her daughter Jacqueline Dalby. That was the assumption which the defendant recognised was capable of encompassing and fulfilling his legitimate expectation. That assumption was never falsified. The disappointment of the defendant was that his wife sadly died and did so before his mother-in-law; further, 20 years later, his mother-in-law is still alive. Therefore there is no assumption in the relevant sense which was ever falsified. The assumption upon which the defendant was entitled to say that he incurred the expenditure was in fact fulfilled.

The other aspect clearly illustrated by the quotations which I have made from Mason CJ is the need for proportionality. This is to say little more than that the end result must be a just one having regard to the assumption made by the party asserting the estoppel and the detriment which he has experienced. Here is it unreal to suggest that the conclusion of the County Court judge is proportionate to what happened over 15 years earlier. Similarly, it is unreal to say that the Defendant has suffered any injustice. He expended money in 1976 to 1978 upon his then family home and he and his family fully enjoyed the benefits of such expenditure. He has also enjoyed within the same framework over a period of over 15 years the rent-free occupation of the property. By the same token it cannot be properly said that there was anything unconscionable in Mrs Sledmore seeking the possession of number 15A in 1990.

In my judgment there is no estoppel operating against the plaintiff. Her claim in this action falsifies no legitimate assumption or expectation. The effect of any equity that may at any earlier time have existed has long since been exhausted and no injustice has been done to the defendant. The plaintiff is entitled to an order for possession and the defendant's counter-claim must be dismissed. This appeal should be allowed accordingly.

(ii) The range of available remedies

Snell's Equity (31st edn, 2005), paras 10.23 to 10.27

If the equity is established and the extent of it identified, effect is given to it in whatever is the most appropriate way taking into account all relevant circumstances including the conduct of the parties.[64] The court adopts a cautious approach looking for the minimum equity to do justice.[65] Often it suffices merely to dismiss an action brought by O to enforce his legal rights. Thus a claim for possession may be dismissed[66] or a claim to enforce a mortgage may be restrained.[67] Similarly, where O and A are trustees for sale, O's application to have the trust executed may be refused.[68] In such cases the equity is given effect as a defence like any other estoppel. Often, however, more positive action is required.[69]

(1) INJUNCTIONS. O may be restrained by injunction from interfering with possession of land,[70] or from exercising a right to cut down trees and so destroy the beauty of improvements made by A in which he has acquiesced,[71] or from obstructing ancient lights altered by A with O's acquiescence.[72] Further, the injunction may be granted subject to an undertaking by A, e.g. to exercise compulsory powers of acquisition.[73]

(2) CHARGE FOR EXPENDITURE. A may be given an equitable lien on the property for his expenditure,[74] or for the value of his improvements,[75] and in such a case he or she will be treated as a mortgagee in possession.[76] Alternatively, an order for possession against A may be made conditionally upon O repaying the cost of improvements effected by A[77] or it may appear that A has already had 'sufficient satisfaction' for his expenditure, and so is entitled to no relief.[78]

---

[64] *Burrows & Burrows v Sharp* (1991) 23 HLR 82. See also *Lord Cawdor v Lewis* (1835) 1 Y & C Ex 427 at 433; and *Plimmer v Mayor of Wellington* (1884) 9 App Cas 699 at 713, 714.

[65] *Baker v Baker* (1993) 25 HLR 408 and *Gillett v Holt* [2001] Ch 210 at 235E-F (cited by Aldous LJ in *Jennings v Rice* [2002] EWCA Civ 159 at [32]-[35]).

[66] *Forbes v Ralli* (1925) LR 52 Ind App 178; *Inwards v Baker* [1965] 2 QB 29 [p. 1049, below]; *Williams v Staite* [1979] Ch 291; and *Powell v Thomas* (1848) 6 Hare 300 (injunction restraining action for ejectment).

[67] *Steed v Whitaker* (1740) Barn Ch 220.

[68] *Jones v Jones* [1977] 1 WLR 438.

[69] *Quaere* why in *Cullen v Cullen* [1962] IR 268 the equity was held to give no more than a defence.

[70] *Duke of Devonshire v Eglin* (1851) 14 Beav 530 (obstruction of water course) and *Maharaj v Chand* [1986] AC 898 (occupation of home).

[71] *Jackson v Cator* (1800) 5 Ves 688.

[72] *Cotching v Bassett* (1862) 32 Beav 101.

[73] *Somersetshire Coal Canal Co v Harcourt* (1858) 2 De G & J 596.

[74] *Neesom v Clarksom* (1845) 4 Hare 97 (form of account); *Unity Joint Stock Mutual Banking Association v King* (1858) 25 Beav 72 (land) (discussed in Cooke *Estoppel and the protection of expectations* (1997) 17 LS 258, 271–272 in the context of a reliance based remedy); *Re Foster* [1938] 3 All ER 357 (life insurance policy); *Veitch v Caldicott* (1945) 173 LT 30; *Taylor v Taylor* [1956] NZLR 99; *Hussey v Palmer* [1972] 1 WLR 1286 (trust interest proportionate to expenditure discussed in (1973) 89 LQR 2); and *Campbell v Griffin* [2001] EWCA Civ 990 (charge over the relevant property until sold). See now *Jennings v Rice* [2002] EWCA Civ 159 at [51] (citing this paragraph in the 30th edition): 'Detriment can be quantified with reasonable precision if it consists of expenditure on improvements to another person's house, and in some cases of that sort an equitable charge for the expenditure may be sufficient to satisfy the equity.'

[75] *Raffaele v Raffaele* [1962] WAR 29, discussed by D. E. Allan (1963) 79 LQR 238.

[76] *Neesom v Clarkson* (1845) 4 Hare 97.

[77] *Dodsworth v Dodsworth* (1973) 228 EG 1115 [p. 1068, below] and *Baker v Baker* (1993) 25 HLR 408.

[78] See *A-G v Balliol College, Oxford* (1744) 9 Mod Rep 407 at 412, per Lord Hardwicke LC (expenditure by lessee); *Fontana NV v Mautner* (1980) 254 EG 199 (tenant holding over for substantial period of time

(3) CONFERMENT OF TITLE. In many cases justice cannot be done by the mere use of the doctrine by way of defence, or by the recoupment of expenditure[79] but A must be granted some right. Thus if O has made an imperfect gift of the land to A, as by merely signing an informal memorandum[80] or uttering words of abandonment,[81] the court may compel O to perfect the gift by conveying the land to A.[82] In such cases the court may act by analogy with the specific performance of contracts: where A's expenditure with O's knowledge plays the part both of valuable consideration and of part performance.[83] If the circumstances do not suggest a gift, O may be compelled to convey the land on being paid its unimproved value,[84] or to hold the land on trust of land (and to hold the proceeds after discharge of the respective expenditure of A and O to divide the residue between them)[85] or to hold the land under a constructive trust.[86] The circumstances may indicate that A is to have a lease,[87] specific performance of an option to grant a lease,[88] a perpetual easement,[89] a life interest under the Settled Land Act 1925,[90] a perpetual licence[91] or a licence as long as he desires to use the premises as his home[92] or a licence to remain until a loan is repaid,[93] and a lessor may be compelled to grant a licence to assign or estopped from asserting that consent to assignment has been granted.[94] Again, if O has encouraged A to move to or acquire other land, O may be compelled to purchase A's original land.[95]

(4) COMPENSATION. In *Plimmer v Mayor of Wellington*[96] the court held that A was entitled to a perpetual licence but granted compensation because it had been acquired by compulsory

---

although the case also failed on grounds of reliance); and *Sledmore v Dalby* (1996) 72 P & CR 196 [p. 1045, above] (where A had already enjoyed 20 years' rent free occupation and O was in some hardship).

[79] See *Pascoe v Turner* [1979] 1 WLR 431 at 438 [p. 1056, below].

[80] *Dillwyn v Llewelyn*, (1862) 4 De GF & J 517.

[81] *Thomas v Thomas* [1956] NZLR 785 (husband and wife).

[82] *Pascoe v Turner* [1979] 1 WLR 431; *Voyce v Voyce* (1991) 62 P & CR 290; and *Lim Teng Huan v Ang Swee Chuan* [1992] 1 WLR 113.

[83] See *Dillwyn v Llewelyn*, above, at 521, 522. In this context note Lord Russell of Killowen's unduly restrictive interpretation of *Ramsden v Dyson* (below) in *Ariff v Jadunath Majundar* (1931) LR 58 Ind App 91 at 102, 103.

[84] *Duke of Beaufort v Patrick* (1853) 17 Beav 60.

[85] *Holiday Inns Inc v Broadhead* (1974) 232 EG 951 (proposed joint venture to build and operate hotel on O's land) and *Wayling v Jones* (1993) 69 P & CR 170 (share of the proceeds of sale awarded in quasi-matrimonial case).

[86] *Yaxley v Gotts* [2000] Ch 162 (discussed in para. 10–20 above).

[87] *Stiles v Cowper* (1748) 3 Atk 692; *Siew Soon Wah v Yong Tong Hong* [1973] AC 836; *Griffiths v Williams* (1977) 248 EG 947 [p. 1061, below]. See also *Gregory v Mighell* (1811) 18 Ves 328 (an early part performance case) and *Ramsden v Dyson* (1866) LR 1 HL 129 (where the claim to a long lease of course failed).

[88] *Taylors Fashions Ltd v Liverpool Victoria Trustees Co Ltd* [1982] QB 133n, [p. 1012, above].

[89] *Ward v Kirkland* [1967] Ch 194; *ER Ives Investment Ltd v High* [1967] 2 QB 379 [p. 1074, below] (equitable easement) and *Crabb v Arun District Council* [1976] Ch 179 [p. 1051, below] (legal easement where payment was considered but not imposed in the circumstances).

[90] *Ungurian v Lesnoff* [1990] Ch 206.

[91] *Plimmer v Wellington Corpn* (1884) 9 App Cas 699 [p. 1065, below] (where the effect of the perpetual licence was to enable A to obtain compensation on compulsory acquisition).

[92] *Inwards v Baker* [1965] 2 QB 29 [p. 1049, below] (son builds a bungalow on father's land); *Maharaj v Chand* [1986] AC 898; and *Matharu v Matharu* [1994] 2 FLR 597.

[93] *Re Sharpe* [1980] 1 WLR 219 [p. 1109, below].

[94] See *Willmott v Barber* (1880) 15 Ch D 96 (where the claim failed) and *Rose v Stavrou* [2000] L & TR 133 (where the claim succeeded).

[95] *Salvation Army Trustee Co Ltd v West Yorkshire Metropolitan County Council* (1980) 41 P & CR 179.

[96] (1884) 9 App Cas 699 [p. 1065, below].

acquisition. There is a long history of awarding compensation in satisfaction of the equity because of the particular circumstances of the case[97] but the court is now moving towards a separate remedy of compensation.[98] The requirement that the court be satisfied that the remedy is proportionate to the detriment suffered may encourage the court to award compensation assessed by reference to a reliance based measure more regularly.[99] But there is no reason why the court should not also award compensation to A based on an expectation measure where this is appropriate.[100]

(a) Negative protection[101]

Inwards v Baker[102]
[1965] 2 QB 29 (CA, Lord Denning MR, Danckwerts and Salmon LJJ)

In 1931, the younger Mr Baker wished to build a bungalow for himself on land which he hoped to purchase, but the project was beyond his means. His father said 'Why not put the bungalow on my land and make the bungalow a little bigger?' The son did so, building the bungalow largely through his own labour and expense. He lived there continuously until his father's death in 1951, and also from his father's death until the proceedings began.

The land was left elsewhere in a will dated 1922, and in 1963 the trustees for sale of the land brought proceedings for possession.

Held. The son could not be disturbed.

---

[97] See *Dodsworth v Dodsworth* (1973) 228 EG 1115 [p. 1068, below] (A awarded £700 compensation for improvements but granted a licence until it was paid); *Tanner v Tanner* [1975] 1 WLR 1346 (A had already vacated); *Burrows v Burrows & Sharp* (1991) 23 HLR 82 (relationship broken down); *Baker v Baker* (1993) 25 HLR 408 (relationship broken down); *Wayling v Jones* (1993) 69 P & CR 170 (O had disposed of the land); and *Clough v Kelly* (1996) 72 P & CR D22.

[98] See *Gillett v Holt* [2001] Ch 210 at 237H–238C (where the court awarded the freehold of part of the property and £100,000 'to compensate for the exclusion of Mr Gillett from all the rest of the farming business'); *Campbell v Griffin* [2001] EWCA Civ 990 (A awarded approximately 25% of the value of the property); *Jennings v Rice* [2002] EWCA Civ 159 at [37] [p. 1040, above] (where the court awarded £200,000 out of the estate); and *Grundy v Ottey* [2003] EWCA Civ 1176 (£50,000 out of the estate and a flat or an additional £50,000). See also *Giumelli v Giumelli* (1999) 196 CLR 101.

[99] *Hussey v Palmer* and *Dodsworth v Dodsworth* (above) are examples of the court adopting a reliance based measure of damage. The 'cross-check' suggested by Robert Walker LJ in *Jennings v Rice* also points towards a reliance based measure. But they are not the norm: see Gardner *Remedial Discretion in Proprietary Estoppel* (1999) 115 LQR 438 [p. 1039, above] for the range of factors which the court has taken into account in assessing compensation. See, in particular, his Hypothesis 3, at 452–460.

[100] See *Giumelli v Giumelli* (1999) 196 CLR 101 where the court rejected an argument that it was bound to award a reliance based measure following *Commonwealth of Australia v Verwayen* (1990) 170 CLR 394. The court awarded compensation based on the value of A's expected interest in the relevant property after taking into account a number of broad factors. For the approach taken by Australian courts more generally see Robertson, 'Satisfying the Minimum Equity: Equitable Estoppel Remedies after Verwayen' (1996) 20 MULR 805 and 'Reliance and Expectation in Estoppel Remedies' (1998) 18 LS 360.

[101] (1976) 40 Conv (NS) 416 (A. M. Everton). See also *Jones v Jones* [1977] 1 WLR 438 (but it is not clear whether the case fits best into this category or (b) acquisition of proprietary interest); *Matharu v Matharu* (1994) 68 P & CR 93 (licence to occupy for life, protected against claim for possession; but defendant did not acquire any beneficial interest in the property by virtue of the estoppel).

[102] (1965) 81 LQR (R. H. Maudsley); *Ward v Kirkland* [1967] Ch 194 at 235–243; *ER Ives Investment Ltd v High* [1967] 2 QB 379; *Siew Soon Wah v Yong Tong Hong* [1973] AC 836; *Maharaj v Chand* [1986] AC 898.

Lord Denning MR: The trustees say that at the most Jack Baker had a licence to be in the bungalow but that it had been revoked and he had no right to stay. The judge has held in their favour. He was referred to *Errington v Errington and Woods* [1952] 1 KB 290 [p. 1099, below] but the judge held that that decision only protected a contractual licensee. He thought that, in order to be protected, the licensee must have a contract or promise by which he is entitled to be there. The judge said: 'I can find no promise made by the father to the son that he should remain in the property at all—no contractual arrangement between them. True the father said that the son could live in the property, expressly or impliedly, but there is no evidence that this was arrived at as the result of a contract or promise—merely an arrangement made casually because of the relationship which existed and knowledge that the son wished to erect a bunga- low for residence.' Thereupon, the judge, with much reluctance, thought the case was not within *Errington's* case, and said the son must go.

The son appeals to this court. We have had the advantage of cases which were not cited to the county court judge—cases in the last century, notably *Dillwyn v Llewelyn* (1862) 4 De GF & J 517, and *Plimmer v Wellington Corpn* (1884) 9 App Cas 699 [p. 1065, below]. This latter was a decision of the Privy Council which expressly affirmed and approved the statement of the law made by Lord Kingsdown in *Ramsden v Dyson* (1866) LR 1 HL 129, 170 [p. 1008, above]. It is quite plain from those authorities that if the owner of land requests another, or indeed allows another, to expend money on the land under an expectation created or encouraged by the landlord that he will be able to remain there, that raises an equity in the licensee such as to entitle him to stay. He has a licence coupled with an equity. Mr Goodhart urged before us that the licensee could not stay indefinitely. The principle only applied, he said, when there was an expectation of some precise legal term. But it seems to me, from *Plimmer's* case in particular, at 713–714, that the equity arising from the expenditure on land need not fail 'merely on the ground that the interest to be secured has not been expressly indicated...the court must look at the circumstances in each case to decide in what way the equity can be satisfied.'

So in this case, even though there is no binding contract to grant any particular interest to the licensee, nevertheless the court can look at the circumstances and see whether there is an equity arising out of the expenditure of money. All that is necessary is that the licensee should, at the request or with the encouragement of the landlord, have spent the money in the expectation of being allowed to stay there. If so, the court will not allow that expectation to be defeated where it would be inequitable so to do. In this case it is quite plain that the father allowed an expectation to be created in the son's mind that this bungalow was to be his home. It was to be his home for his life or, at all events, his home as long as he wished it to remain his home. It seems to me, in the light of that equity, that the father could not in 1932 have turned to his son and said: 'You are to go. It is my land and my house.' Nor could he at any time thereafter so long as the son wanted it as his home.

Mr Goodhart put the case of a purchaser. He suggested that the father could sell the land to a purchaser who could get the son out. But I think that any purchaser who took with notice would clearly be bound by the equity. So here, too, the present plaintiffs, the successors in title of the father, are clearly themselves bound by this equity. It is an equity well recognised in law. It arises from the expenditure of money by a person in actual occupation of land when he is led to believe that, as the result of that expenditure, he will be allowed to remain there. It is for the court to say in what way the equity can be satisfied. I am quite clear in this case it can be satisfied by holding that the defendant can remain there as long as he desires to as his home.

I would allow the appeal accordingly and enter judgment for the defendant.

Danckwerts LJ: I agree and I will add only a few words. It seems to me the claim of the defendant in respect of this property is amply covered by *Errington v Errington and Woods, Dillwyn v Llewelyn,* and *Plimmer v Wellington Corpn.* Further, it seems to me to be supported by the observations of Lord Kingsdown in *Ramsden v Dyson.* It is true that in that case Lord Kingsdown reached a result on the facts of the case which differed from that reached by the other members of the House of Lords, but Lord Kingsdown's observations which are relevant in the present case have received support since that case was decided; and, in particular, I would like to refer to the observations in the judgment of the Privy Council in *Plimmer v Wellington Corpn.* It is said there (1884) 9 App Cas 699 at 713: 'Their Lordships consider that this case falls within the principle stated by Lord Kingsdown as to expectations created or encouraged by the landlord, with the addition that in this case the landlord did more than encourage the expenditure, for he took the initiative in requesting it.'

There are similar circumstances in the present case. The defendant was induced to give up his project of building a bungalow on land belonging to somebody else other than his father, in which case he would have become the owner or tenant of the land in question and thus have his own home. His father induced him to build on his, the father's, land and expenditure was made by the defendant for the purpose of the creation of the bungalow.

In my view the case comes plainly within the proposition stated in the cases. It is not necessary, I think, to imply a promise. It seems to me that this is one of the cases of an equity created by estoppel, or equitable estoppel, as it is sometimes called, by which the person who has made the expenditure is induced by the expectation of obtaining protection, and equity protects him so that an injustice may not be perpetrated.

I am clearly of opinion that the appeal should be allowed and judgment should be entered for the defendant.

(b) Acquisition of proprietary interest

1. Easement[103]

Crabb v Arun District Council
[1976] Ch 179 (CA, **Lord Denning MR, Lawton** and **Scarman LJJ**)[104]

The plaintiff owned two acres of land. The outlet to the road was through a point of access (point A) to a lane owned by the defendants, and by a right of way over that lane in a northerly direction to the road.

He decided to divide his land into two parts, and to sell them separately. This would require another point of access to the South, together with an additional right of way over the lane, to serve the Southern part. This was negotiated with the defendants at a meeting in July 1967, at which there was an oral agreement in principle that the

---

[103] See also *E R Ives Investment Ltd v High* [1967] 2 QB 379, p. 1074, below; *Bexley LBC v Maison Maurice Ltd* [2007] 1 EGLR 19 (local authority estopped from denying permanent means of access to highway; although estoppel cannot fetter authority's statutory discretion, nor validate what would otherwise be an *ultra vires* act, the Council had power to grant the means of access under Highways Act 1980 or by licence).

[104] (1976) 40 Conv (NS) 156 (F. R. Crane); (1976) 92 LQR 174 (P. S. Atiyah); 342 (P. J. Millett); (1995) 58 MLR 637 at p. 640 (G. Battersby).

plaintiff should have another access at point B; but no formal agreement was signed. The defendants, in accordance with the terms of the informal agreement, fenced the boundary between their land and the plaintiff's, leaving gaps at A and B, and erected gates at these points, the gateposts being set in concrete.

The plaintiff sold the Northern part, together with the right of way and access from point A. Differences arose between the plaintiff and defendants. The defendants uprooted the gatepost at point B, continued the fence to cover the gateway, and left the Southern part of the plaintiff's land landlocked. They offered access at point B and right of way for £3,000. The action was for a declaration and injunction, claiming that the defendants were estopped by their conduct from denying the plaintiff a right of access at point B and a right of way.

Held. Rights of access and way awarded to the plaintiff without payment.[105]

Scarman LJ: I agree that the appeal should be allowed. The plaintiff and the defendants are adjoining landowners. The plaintiff asserts that he has a right of way over the defendant's land giving access from his land to the public highway. Without this access his land is in fact landlocked, but, for reasons which clearly appear from the narration of the facts already given by my Lords, the plaintiff cannot claim a right of way by necessity. The plaintiff has no grant. He has the benefit of no enforceable contract. He has no prescriptive right. His case has to be that the defendants are estopped by their conduct from denying him a right of access over their land to the public highway. If the plaintiff has any right, it is an equity arising out of the conduct and relationship of the parties. In such a case I think it is now well settled law that the court, having analysed and assessed the conduct and relationship of the parties, has to answer three questions. First, is there an equity established? Secondly, what is the extent of the equity, if one is established? And, thirdly, what is the relief appropriate to satisfy the equity? See *Duke of Beaufort v Patrick* (1853) 17 Beav 60; *Plimmer v Wellington Corpn* (1884) 9 App Cas 699 [p. 1065, below] and *Inwards v Baker* [1965] 2 QB 29 [p. 1049, above], a decision of this court, and particularly the observations of Lord Denning MR at 37. Such therefore I believe to be the nature of the inquiry that the courts have to conduct in a case of this sort. In pursuit of that inquiry I do not find helpful the distinction between promissory and proprietary estoppel. This distinction may indeed be valuable to those who have to teach or expound the law; but I do not think that, in solving the particular problem raised by a particular case, putting the law into categories is of the slightest assistance....

I come now to consider the first of the three questions which I think in a case such as this the court have to consider. What is needed to establish an equity?

His Lordship discussed Lord Kingsdown's speech in *Ramsden v Dyson* (1886) LR 1 HL 129, 170, and the 'five probanda' set out by Fry J in *Willmott v Barber* (1880) 15 ChD 96, 105–106: see p. 1009, above, and continued:

Mr Lightman, in the course of an interesting and vigorous submission, drew the attention of the court to the necessity of finding something akin to fraud before the equity sought by the plaintiff

---

[105] See *Crabb v Arun District Council (No 2)* (1976) 121 SJ 86 where Crabb was refused an enquiry as to damages. See also *Salvation Army Trustee Co Ltd v West Yorkshire Metropolitan County Council* (1980) 41 P & CR 179 (where proprietary estoppel was extended to the *disposal* of an interest in land where the disposal was closely linked by an arrangement that also involved the acquisition of an interest in land); discussed in *A-G of Hong Kong v Humphreys Estate (Queen's Gardens) Ltd* [1987] AC 114 at 126, 127.

could be established. 'Fraud' was a word often in the mouths of those robust judges who adorned the bench in the 19th century. It is less often in the mouths of the more wary judicial spirits today who sit upon the bench. But it is clear that whether one uses the word 'fraud' or not, the plaintiff has to establish as a fact that the defendant, by setting up his right, is taking advantage of him in a way which is unconscionable, inequitable or unjust. It is to be observed from the passage that I have quoted from the judgment of Fry J that the fraud or injustice alleged does not take place during the course of negotiation, but only when the defendant decides to refuse to allow the plaintiff to set up his claim against the defendants' undoubted right. The fraud, if it be such, arises after the event, when the defendant seeks by relying on his right to defeat the expectation which he by his conduct encouraged the plaintiff to have. There need not be anything fraudulent or unjust in the conduct of the actual negotiations—the conduct of the transaction by the defendants.

The court therefore cannot find an equity established unless it is prepared to go as far as to say that it would be unconscionable and unjust to allow the defendants to set up their undoubted rights against the claim being made by the plaintiff. In order to reach a conclusion upon that matter the court does have to consider the history of the negotiations under the five headings to which Fry J referred. I need not at this stage weary anyone with an elaborate statement of the facts. I have no doubt upon the facts of this case that the first four elements referred to by Fry J exist. The question before the judge and now in this court in whether the fifth element is present: have the defendants, as possessor of the legal right, encouraged the plaintiff in the expenditure of money or in the other acts which he has done, either directly or by abstaining from asserting their legal rights? The first matter to be considered is the meeting on site of 26 July 1967. Pennycuick V-C made a finding of fact about the meeting; and for myself I am not prepared to dissent from his finding. But the substance of the finding of fact has to be regarded; not its phrasing. One must not be misled by words or phrases into misconstruing the nature of the finding. Pennycuick V-C found there was no definite assurance given by the defendants' representative to the plaintiff and his architect.

His Lordship summarised the evidence and continued:

That was a finding that there was acceptance in principle that there should be access and a right of way over the defendants' land at point B; and I am content to go no further and to base my judgment on what I believe to be that finding of Pennycuick V-C. Clearly the plaintiff and Mr Alford came away from that meeting in the confident expectation that a right would in due course be accorded to the plaintiff. Mr Alford did foresee 'further processes.' Of course, there would be further processes. The nature of the legal right to be granted had to be determined. It might be given by way of licence. It might be granted by way of easement. Conditions might be imposed. Payment of a sum of money might be required. But those two men, the plaintiff and his architect, came away from the meeting in the confident expectation that such a right would be granted upon reasonable conditions. What happened? By August—a month or less, after the meeting—posts for a fence were already on the ground, though not erected. There was already an indication, at about that time, I think—if not then, certainly soon after—of the presence of a gap at point B, that being the point of access agreed in principle. During the later months of 1967 nothing relevant transpired in the conduct of the negotiations between the plaintiff and the defendants. I accept Mr Lightman's submission that relationship as well as conduct is relevant: but during this period their relationship did not develop at all. They remained adjoining landowners, one of whom had agreed in principle at a meeting upon the site that there should be a right of way from point B over his land to the public road. Yet, things were happening. In the later months of 1967 the defendants, who were the local authority, were busy developing on neighbouring land, which the plaintiff's predecessor in title had sold them, a council housing estate. Lorries were being used for carting building materials, removing debris and so forth; and these lorries were in fact going upon the land of the plaintiff. Unfortunately materials on the land, the property of the plaintiff, were being pilfered. And so there came a meeting in January 1968, the point of which was to draw the attention of the defendants' officers to the situation which was developing. By the time the meeting took place the fence, which the defendants were obliged under the conveyance of their estate to erect between their land and the plaintiff's land, was substantially in position with gaps at point A, the access to the northern land, and at point B, the access in dispute. Nobody on behalf of the defendants gave the slightest indication to the plaintiff and his representatives at that meeting that there was going to be any difficulty or was likely to be any difficulty about access at point B. The confident expectation with which the plaintiff and Mr Alford left the meeting in July remained remarkably undisturbed by the meeting of January 1968. Indeed it was reinforced because there on the ground, plain for all to see, was a fence with gaps which accorded exactly with the agreement in principle reached in the previous July. Ten days later the defendants ordered gates, and by March the gates were installed. I ask myself: as at March 1968 had these defendants encouraged the plaintiff to think that he had or was going to be given a right? To use the language of Fry J, had they done it directly or had they done it by abstaining from asserting a legal right? Their encouragement of the belief in the mind of the plaintiff and Mr Alford was both direct and indirect. It was direct because of what they had done on the ground. It was indirect because ever since the July meeting they had abstained from giving the plaintiff or his architect any indication that they were standing on their rights, or had it in mind to go back, as, of course, they were entitled at that stage to go back, upon the agreement in principle reached at that meeting. And so matters proceeded until September 1968. By now, be it observed, over a year had passed since that first meeting when there was agreement in principle. Nothing had been done to disabuse the minds of the plaintiff and Mr Alford of the expectation reasonably induced by what the defendants' engineer then said: and there had been the direct encouragement of the gates. In September 1968, without telling the defendants or giving them any notice, so far as I am aware, the plaintiff entered into a contract to sell the northern piece of land without reservation over that land of any right of way. This was the act which was detrimental to the interests of the plaintiff. He did it in the belief that he had or could enforce a right of way and access at point B in the southern land.

One of the points taken by Mr Lightman is that the defendants had no notice of the sale, and therefore no opportunity to correct what on his case was a false belief in the mind of the plaintiff. Mr Millett in the course of his submissions conceded that he had not found in the books any case in which the sort of estoppel which we are here considering had arisen when the fact known to the defendants was an intention and not the realisation of that intention. That is, of course, what differentiates this case from one such as *E R Ives Investment Ltd v High* [1967] 2 QB 379 [p. 1074, below]. There the party who was found to be estopped did have notice of what the other party was doing at the time he was doing it. Therefore I think Mr Lightman rightly invites us to face this question: Does the fact that the defendants had no notice of the sale of the northern land before it was completed destroy the equity? Mr Lightman will concede, as I understand this part of his argument, no more than this: that the plaintiff might have been able to establish an equity if he had referred to the defendants before binding himself to the purchaser of the northern land: for that would have given the defendants an opportunity of disabusing the mind of the plaintiff before he acted to his detriment. The point is worthy of careful consideration. I reject it because, in my judgment, in this sort of proceedings, the court must be careful to avoid generalisation. I can conceive of cases in which it would be absolutely appropriate for a defendant to say: 'But you should not have acted to your detriment until you had had a word with me and I could have put you right.' But there are cases in which it is far too late for a defendant to get himself out of his pickle by putting upon the plaintiff that sort of duty; and this, in my judgment, is one of those cases. If immediately following the July meeting the clerk to the defendant authority had written saying: 'I have had a report of the meeting with the assistant engineer and I must inform you that whether or not there is to be an easement or a licence is a matter which can only be decided by the council,' the plaintiff would not now establish his equity: in selling the northern land without reservation of a right of way, he would have acted at his own risk. But one has to look at the whole conduct of the parties and the developing relationship between them. By September 1968, 13½ months after the initial meeting, the plaintiff must really and reasonably have been attaching importance to the abstention of the defendants from declaring to him in correspondence, or by telephone to his agent, their true position, namely, that there would be no acceptance in principle of a right until the matter had been considered by the authority itself. By that time there had been, as well, the laying out of the fence and the installing of the gates. It is for those reasons—the passage of time, the abstention and the gates—that I think the defendants cannot rely upon the fact that the plaintiff acted, without referring to the defendants, on his intention—an intention of which they had had notice ever since their agent was informed of it at the meeting in July 1967. I think therefore an equity is established.

I turn now to the other two questions—the extent of the equity and the relief needed to satisfy it. There being no grant, no enforceable contract, no licence, I would analyse the minimum equity to do justice to the plaintiff as a right either to an easement or to a licence upon terms to be agreed.[106] I do not think it is necessary to go further than that. Of course, going that far would support the equitable remedy of injunction which is sought in this action. If there is no agreement as to terms, if agreement fails to be obtained, the court can, in my judgment, and must, determine in these proceedings upon what terms the plaintiff should be put to enable him to have the benefit of the equitable right which he is held to have. It is interesting that there has been some doubt amongst distinguished lawyers in the past as to whether the court can so proceed. Lord Kingsdown refers in fact to those doubts in a passage, which I need not quote, in *Ramsden v Dyson* (1866) LR 1 HL 129, 171. Lord Thurlow clearly thought that the court did have this power. Other lawyers of that time did not. But there can be no doubt that since *Ramsden v Dyson* the courts have acted upon the basis that they have to determine not only the extent of the equity, but also the conditions necessary to satisfy it, and they have done so in a great number and variety of cases, I need refer only to the interesting collection of cases enumerated in *Snell's Principles of Equity*, 27th edn (1973), at pp. 567–568, para. 2(b).[107]

In the present case the court does have to consider what is necessary now in order to satisfy the plaintiff's equity. Had matters taken a different turn, I would without hesitation have said that the plaintiff should be put upon terms to be agreed if possible with the defendants, and, if not agreed, settled by the court. But, as already mentioned by Lord Denning MR and Lawton LJ, there has been a history of delay, and indeed high-handedness, which it

---

[106] Lord Denning MR at 190 (with whom Lawton LJ agreed at 192) declared that the plaintiff had an easement.

[107] See now 31st edn (2005), paras 10–23 to 10–27, p. 1047, above.

is impossible to disregard. In January 1969 the defendants, for reasons which no doubt they thought good at the time, without consulting the plaintiff, locked up his land. They removed not only the padlocks which he had put on the gates at point B, but the gates themselves. In their place they put a fence—rendering access impossible save by breaking down the fence. I am not disposed to consider whether or not the defendants are to be blamed in moral terms for what they did. I just do not know. But the effect of their action has been to sterilise the plaintiff's land; and for the reasons which I have endeavoured to give, such action was an infringement of an equitable right possessed by the plaintiff. It has involved him in loss, which has not been measured; but, since it amounted to sterilisation of an industrial estate for a very considerable period of time, it must surpass any sort of sum of money which the plaintiff ought reasonably, before it was done, to have paid the defendants in order to obtain an enforceable legal right. I think therefore that nothing should now be paid by the plaintiff and that he should receive at the hands of the court the belated protection of the equity that he has established. Reasonable terms, other than money payment, should be agreed: or, if not agreed, determined by the court.

For those reasons I also would allow the appeal.

2. Fee simple estate

(1) Without compensation

Pascoe v Turner[108]
[1979] 1 WLR 431 (CA, **Orr, Lawton** and **Cumming-Bruce LJJ**)

The plaintiff and defendant lived together in the plaintiff's home. Later, the plaintiff purchased another house and they moved in. He told the defendant that the house was hers, and everything in it. In reliance on this gratuitous promise, she expended, to the plaintiff's knowledge, her own money on repairs, improvements and redecoration; and also on furniture.

Later, when the relationship ended, the plaintiff gave to the defendant two months' notice to determine the licence.

Held. The defendant occupied the house as a licensee. There was a gift of the contents, but no valid gift or declaration of trust of the house. But an estoppel operated in her favour, and this could most properly be satisfied by a conveyance of the house to the defendant.

Cumming-Bruce LJ (giving the judgment of the court):

The issues

The appeal raises three issues about the house: (a) Did the defendant prove the trust found by the judge? (b) Did she prove such facts as prevented the plaintiff by estoppel from asserting his legal title? (c) If the answer to that question is yes, what is the equitable relief to which she is entitled? In respect of the contents of the house, did the defendant prove that they were given to her by the plaintiff's voluntary gift? ...

---

[108] [1979] Conv 379 (F. R. Crane); (1979) 42 MLR 574 (B. Sufrin); (1995) 58 MLR 637 at p. 642 (G. Battersby). Cf. *Dillwyn v Llewelyn* (1862) 4 De GF & J 517; *Voyce v Voyce* (1991) 62 P & CR 290 (donee of farm and cottage from licensor ordered to convey fee simple to licensee); *Durant v Heritage* [1994] EGCS 134.

The judge found that the plaintiff had made a gift to her of the contents of the house. I have no doubt that he was right about that. She was already in possession of them as a bailee when he declared the gift. Counsel for the plaintiff submitted that there was no gift because it was uncertain what he was giving her. He pointed to a safe and to the defendant's evidence that she had sent round an orange bedroom suite to the plaintiff so that he should have a bed to sleep on. The answer is that he gave her everything in the house, but later, recognising his need, she gave back some bits and pieces to him. So much for the contents.

Her rights in the realty are not quite so simply disposed of because of section 53 and section 54 of the Law of Property Act 1925. There was nothing in writing. The judge considered the plaintiff's declarations, and decided that they were not enough to found an express trust. We agree. But he went on to hold that the beneficial interest in the house had passed under a constructive trust inferred from words and conduct of the parties. He relied on the passage in *Snell's Principles of Equity,* 27th edn (1973), p. 185, in which the editors suggest a possible definition of a constructive trust. But there are difficulties in the way. The long and short of events in 1973 is that the plaintiff made an imperfect gift of the house. There is nothing in the facts from which an inference of a constructive trust can be drawn. If it had not been for section 53 of the Law of Property Act 1925 the gift of the house would have been a perfect gift, just as the gift of the contents was a perfect gift. In the event it remained an imperfect gift and, as Turner LJ said in *Milroy v Lord* (1862) 4 De GF & J 264, 274: 'there is no equity in this court to perfect an imperfect gift.' So matters stood in 1973, and if the facts had stopped there the defendant would have remained a licensee at will of the plaintiff.

But the facts did not stop there. On the judge's findings the defendant, having been told that the house was hers, set about improving it within and without. Outside she did not do much: a little work on the roof and an improvement which covered the way from the outside toilet to the rest of the house, putting in a new door there, and Snowcem to protect the toilet. Inside she did a good deal more. She installed gas in the kitchen with a cooker, improved the plumbing in the kitchen and put in a new sink. She got new gas fires, putting a gas fire in the lounge. She redecorated four rooms. The fitted carpets she put in the bedrooms, the stair carpeting, and the curtains and the furniture that she bought are not part of the realty, and it is not clear how much she spent for those items. But they are part of the whole circumstances. There she was, on her own after he left her in 1973. She had £1,000 left of her capital, and a pension of some kind. Having as she thought been given the house, she set about it as described. On the repairs and improvement to the realty and its fixtures she spent about £230. She had £300 of her capital left by the date of the trial, but she did not establish in evidence how much had been expended on refurbishing the house with carpets, curtains and furniture. We would describe the work done in and about the house as substantial in the sense that that adjective is used in the context of estoppel. All the while the plaintiff not only stood by and watched but encouraged and advised, without a word to suggest that she was putting her money and her personal labour into his house. What is the effect in equity?

The cases relied upon by the plaintiff are relevant for the purpose of showing that the judge fell into error in deciding that on the facts a constructive trust could be inferred. They are the cases which deal with the intention of the parties when a house is acquired. But of those cases only *Inwards v Baker* [1965] 2 QB 29 [p. 1049, above] is in point here. For this is a case of estoppel arising from the encouragement and acquiescence of the plaintiff between 1973 and 1976 when, in reliance upon his declaration that he was giving and, later, that he had given the house to her, she spent a substantial part of her small capital upon repairs and improvements to the house. The relevant principle is expounded in *Snell's Principles of Equity,* 27th edn, p. 565 in the passage under the heading 'Proprietary Estoppel,' and is elaborated in Spencer Bower and Turner, *Estoppel by Representation,* 3rd edn (1977), chapter 12 entitled 'Encouragement and Acquiescence.'

The cases in point illustrating that principle in relation to real property are *Dillwyn v Llewelyn* (1862) 4 De GF & J 517; *Ramsden v Dyson* (1866) LR 1 HL 129 and *Plimmer v Wellington Corpn* (1884) 9 App Cas 699. One distinction between this class of case and the doctrine which has come to be known as 'promissory estoppel' is that where estoppel by encouragement or acquiescence is found on the facts, those facts give rise to a cause of action. They may be relied upon as a sword, not merely as a shield. In *Ramsden v Dyson* the plaintiff failed on the facts, and the dissent of Lord Kingsdown was upon the inferences to be drawn from the facts. On the principle, however, the House was agreed, and it is stated by Lord Cranworth LC and by Lord Wensleydale as well as by Lord Kingsdown. Likewise in *Plimmer's* case the plaintiff was granted a declaration that he had a perpetual right of occupation.

The final question that arises is: to what relief is the defendant entitled upon her counterclaim? In *Dillwyn v Llewelyn* there was an imperfect gift of land by a father who encouraged his son to build a house on it for £14,000. Lord Westbury LC said, at 521:

> 'About the rules of the court there can be no controversy. A voluntary agreement will not be completed or assisted by a court of equity, in cases of mere gift. If anything be wanting to complete the title of the donee, a court of equity will not assist him in obtaining it; for a mere donee can have no right to claim more than he has received. But the subsequent acts of the donor may give the donee that right or ground of claim which he did not acquire from the original gift. Thus, if A gives a house to B, but makes no formal conveyance, and the house is afterwards, on the marriage of B, included, with the knowledge of A, in the marriage settlement of B, A would be bound to complete the title of the parties claiming under that settlement. So if A puts B in possession of a piece of land, and tells him, "I give it to you that you may build a house on it," and B on the strength of that promise, with the knowledge of A, expends a large sum of money in building a house accordingly, I cannot doubt that the donee acquires a right from the subsequent transaction to call on the donor to perform that contract and complete the imperfect donation which was made.'

In *Plimmer's* case the Privy Council pose the question, how should the equity be satisfied? (See pp. 713, 714.) And the Board declare that on the facts a licence revocable at will became irrevocable as a consequence of the subsequent transactions. So in *Thomas v Thomas* [1956] NZLR 785 the Supreme Court of New Zealand ordered the defendant to execute a proper transfer of the property.

In *Crabb v Arun District Council* [1976] Ch 179 [p. 1051, above], this court had to consider the principles upon which the court should give effect to the equity: see Lord Denning MR at 189. Lawton and Scarman LJJ agreed with the remedy proposed by Lord Denning MR. On the facts of that case Scarman LJ expressed himself thus at 198–199:

His Lordship quoted the paragraph set out on p. 1055, above, beginning 'I turn now to...' and continued:

So the principle to be applied is that the court should consider all the circumstances, and the counterclaimant having at law no perfected gift or licence other than a licence revocable at will, the court must decide what is the minimum equity to do justice to her having regard to the way in which she changed her position for the worse by reason of the acquiescence and encouragement of the legal owner. The defendant submits that the only appropriate way in which the equity can here be satisfied is by perfecting the imperfect gift as was done in *Dillwyn v Llewelyn*.

Counsel for the plaintiff on instructions has throughout submitted that the plaintiff is entitled to possession. The only concession that he made was that the period of notice given in the letter of 9 April 1976 was too short. He made no submission upon the way the equity, if there was an equity, should be satisfied save to submit that the court should not in any view grant a remedy more beneficial to the defendant than a licence to occupy the house for her lifetime.

We are satisfied that the problem of remedy on the facts resolves itself into a choice between two alternatives: should the equity be satisfied by a licence to the defendant to occupy the house for her lifetime, or should there be a transfer to her of the fee simple?

The main consideration pointing to a licence for her lifetime is that she did not by her case at the hearing seek to establish that she had spent more money or done more work on the house than she would have done had she believed that she had only a licence to live there for her lifetime. But the court must be cautious about drawing any inference from what she did not give in evidence as the hypothesis put is one that manifestly never occurred to her. Then it may reasonably be held that her expenditure and effort can hardly be regarded as comparable to the change of position of those who have constructed buildings on land over which they had no legal rights.

This court appreciates that the moneys laid out by the defendant were much less than in some of the cases in the books. But the court has to look at all the circumstances. When the plaintiff left her she was, we were told, a widow in her middle fifties. During the period that she lived with the plaintiff her capital was reduced from £4,500 to £1,000. Save for her invalidity pension that was all that she had in the world. In reliance upon the plaintiff's declaration of gift, encouragement and acquiescence she arranged her affairs on the basis that the house and contents belonged to her. So relying, she devoted a quarter of her remaining capital and her personal effort upon the house and its fixtures. In addition she bought carpets, curtains and furniture for it, with the result that by the date of the trial she had only £300 left. Compared to her, on the evidence the plaintiff is a rich man. He might not regard an expenditure of a few hundred pounds as a very grave loss. But the court has to regard her change of position over the years 1973 to 1976.

We take the view that the equity cannot here be satisfied without granting a remedy which assures to the defendant security of tenure, quiet enjoyment, and freedom of action in respect of repairs and improvements without interference from the plaintiff. The history of the conduct of the plaintiff since 9 April 1976 in relation to these proceedings leads to an irresistible inference that he is determined to pursue his purpose of evicting her from the house by any legal means at his disposal with a ruthless disregard of the obligations binding upon conscience. The court must grant a remedy effective to protect her against the future manifestations of his ruthlessness. It was conceded that if she is granted a licence, such a licence cannot be registered as a land change, so that she may find herself ousted by a purchaser for value without notice. If she has in the future to do further and more expensive repairs she may only be able to finance them by a loan, but as a licensee she cannot charge the house. The plaintiff as legal owner may well find excuses for entry in order to do what he may plausibly represent as necessary works and so contrive to derogate from her enjoyment of the licence in ways that make it difficult or impossible for the court to give her effective protection.

Weighing such considerations this court concludes that the equity to which the facts in this case give rise can only be satisfied by compelling the plaintiff to give effect to his promise and her expectations. He has so acted that he must now perfect the gift.

(2) With compensation

In **Lim Teng Huan v Ang Swee Chuan**[109] [1992] 1 WLR 113, A built a house on land which he jointly owned with L. A and L entered into a contract, under which L acknowledged that he had no title to the house and agreed to exchange his half share in the land for unspecified land which he expected to obtain from the Government of Brunei. The contract was void for uncertainty. L claimed that he was the sole beneficial owner of A's share.

In rejecting L's claim, the Privy Council held that L was estopped from denying A's title to the whole of the land, and that he was entitled to compensation representing a half-share in the present value of the land without the house; on payment L should convey his half-share in the land to A. Lord BROWNE-WILKINSON said at 117:

The decision in *Taylors Fashions* showed that, in order to found a proprietary estoppel, it is not essential that the representor should have been guilty of unconscionable conduct in permitting the representee to assume that he could act as he did: it is enough if, in all the circumstances, it is unconscionable for the representor to go back on the assumption which he permitted the representee to make. The Court of Appeal therefore held that, upon payment of compensation, the defendant was entitled to a declaration of ownership of the plaintiff's share and to the injunction which he sought on the counterclaim....

Before their Lordships' Board, two main points were in issue. First, were the Court of Appeal right in holding that the plaintiff was perpetually estopped from claiming title to his one half share of the land? Second, were the Court of Appeal justified in assessing the compensation payable by the defendant in the way that they did?

As to the first question, their Lordships have no hesitation in agreeing with the conclusions and reasoning of the Court of Appeal....

Sir Michael Ogden submitted that in any event the right way to give effect to the estoppel was not to vest the whole of the land in the defendant absolutely but to confer on him a status of irremovability, i.e. the defendant should be entitled to live free in the house so long as he wished but if the house and land were sold in the future the plaintiff should be entitled to his half share. Sir Michael Ogden was not able to elucidate how long this status of irremovability was to endure: for example, on the defendant's death would those succeeding his estate also be irremovable? Moreover such an estoppel would not give effect to the manifest common intention of the parties, viz. that the land should belong outright to the defendant and that the plaintiff should be entitled to compensation for giving up his half share. Their Lordships agree with the decision of the Court of Appeal.

As to the second point there is no disagreement on the general principle: the plaintiff should receive, by way of compensation, the value of the land as a site excluding such part of its value as is attributable to the preparatory works carried out in 1982.

---

[109] [1993] Conv 173 (S. K. Goo); *Price v Hartwell* [1996] EGCS 98 (joint owner licensee permitted to remain on premises so long as she made mortgage repayments, but must refund payments made by licensor after his severance of joint tenancy).

3. Grant of lease

Griffiths v Williams

(1977) 248 EG 947; [1978] EGD 919 (CA, **Megaw, Orr** and **Goff LJJ**)

No. 1 Gordon Villa, in Hereford, was owned by Mrs Cole, who was the mother of Mrs Williams, who was the mother of Mrs Griffiths. Mrs Williams was a school teacher, who had lived most of her life at the house.

Mrs Cole had always indicated her intention of leaving Mrs Williams a life interest in the house, and made a will to that effect in 1971. But in 1974, she changed her will, and left the house absolutely to Mrs Griffiths.

Mrs Williams looked after Mrs Cole in her latter years, and expended her money on repairs and improvements to the house. She did so primarily for the care of her mother, but also in the belief that she would be entitled to live in the house for the rest of her life.

Held. Mrs Williams was protected under the doctrine of estoppel. The award of a life interest was not appropriate, because that might create a settlement under the Settled Land Act 1925.[110] Mrs Williams should receive (with all the parties' agreement) a lease determinable upon death, with no power to assign, and at a nominal rent which did not exceed two thirds of the rateable value.

Goff LJ: [The] equity is said to arise because the grandmother had repeatedly assured Mrs Williams that she would be allowed to live in the house for the whole of her life, and because, on the faith of those assurances, Mrs Williams had expended money upon the property which otherwise she would not have done. It emerged at the trial that she had spent in all, out of her own moneys, a sum of £2,000. Part of that was spent upon improvements to the property which consisted of putting in a bathroom and an indoors toilet, rewiring for electricity, concreting the yard, and repairs to one of the walls; but part of it had been spent in paying outgoings. In so far as the expenditure was of the latter character, I doubt whether it would raise an equity in Mrs Williams' favour, because it could be regarded simply as current payment for the benefits which she was enjoying by being allowed to live in the house. But in so far as money was spent upon permanent improvements such as I have mentioned, it would be capable of creating what is known as promissory estoppel.[111] It seems that a grant in aid towards the improvements was obtained from the local authority; but, even so, as I read the evidence Mrs Williams did incur expenditure out of her own money on improvements. But the evidence does not show how the £2,000 should be broken down between expenditure of that character and expenditure on current repairs.

In these circumstances, in my judgment, we have to determine three questions, which were propounded by Scarman LJ in his judgment in the case of *Crabb v Arun District Council* [1976] Ch 179 [p. 1051, above] the relevant passage being at 193. I will read them from another case where they were cited, namely, *Jones v Jones* [1977] 1 WLR 438, because there Roskill LJ answered those questions—of course, on the facts of the case before him, but the answers

---

[110] For the problems of finding a SLA settlement in this context, see the discussion in this case, below; and further discussions in *Dodsworth v Dodsworth* (1973) 228 EG 1115, p. 1068, below, and *Binions v Evans* [1972] Ch 359, p. 1102, below. After 1996 no further settlements can be created under SLA 1925: TLATA 1996, s. 2(1); p. 516, above.

[111] Presumably proprietary estoppel is intended.

I think throw light on the nature of the questions and what the approach to answering them should be. I cite from the judgment of Roskill LJ at 443, where his Lordship said:

'As for the rest, Lord Denning MR has referred to the decision of this court, consisting of himself and Lawton and Scarman LJJ, in *Crabb v Arun District Council*. I would refer to the three questions, posed by Scarman LJ at the beginning of his judgment, which the court has to ask in relation to the now well-settled law of estoppel, at 193. "First, is there an equity established?" The answer here is unquestionably Yes. "Secondly, what is the extent of the equity, if one is established?"—and the answer, shortly is that the equity is of a possessory nature entitling the defendant to remain in this house—'

and then (though not relevant for present purposes)

'but it would not, in my judgment, extend to the defendant's wife. "And, thirdly, what is the relief appropriate to satisfy the equity?"'

Then he went on to answer that question, saying:

'All the members of the court in *Crabb v Arun District Council* thought that in some circumstances a court might impose the making of payment of some form or another as a condition of giving effect to the equity, but in the present case it seems to me that it would be wrong to impose as a condition of protecting the equity that the defendant should pay rent to the plaintiff for the following reasons....'

which he then set out.

That indicates to my mind that the third question is one upon which the court has to exercise a discretion. If it finds that there is an equity, then it must determine the nature of it, and then, guided by that nature and exercising discretion in all the circumstances, it has to determine what is the fair order to make between the parties for the protection of the claimant.

So I direct my mind to the first question: Was there here an equity? Mr McCarthy says that there was not, because the defendant failed to prove, and the learned judge did not find, that the grandmother at the time the improvements were effected knew that Mrs Williams was making a mistake as to her position. He relied on the passage in *Snell's Equity*, 27th edn at p. 566, where it is said:

'Knowledge of the mistake makes it dishonest for him to remain wilfully passive in order afterwards to profit by the mistake he might have prevented. The knowledge must accordingly be proved by "strong and cogent evidence."'

He also points to the learned judge's judgment, where he said:

'It was clear that Mrs Williams—and I think this would apply to most sensitive people in her position—was reluctant to admit, even to herself, that in spending her own money on housekeeping and house improvement, she was thinking predominantly of her own inheritance rather than the care and comfort of her mother. What she did say, however, was that had it occurred to her that her enjoyment and benefit of these improvements, or rather of the house as improved (a house that she had always regarded as her home) would be limited to her mother's life span, she would have had to think whether she was not obliged to look more closely to her own future.... It was equally clear, however, that none of this occurred to her at the time, or perhaps even not until it was put to her in this court.'

In so far as it is necessary to prove that Mrs Williams made a mistake, I think the mistake is to be found in her belief that she would be allowed to live in the house for the whole of her life.

But I do not myself think that it really depends upon mistake. The equity is based upon the fact that where one has made a representation on the faith of which another party has expended his money, then the man who made the representation will not, to the prejudice of the other, be allowed to go back on it and assert his strict legal rights if to do so would be unconscionable. I cite this passage from the judgment of Lord Denning MR in *Inwards v Baker* [1965] 2 QB 29 at 37:

His Lordship quoted the paragraph set out on p. 1050, above, beginning 'So in this case…', and continued:

The facts in that case were different, but the principle appears to me to apply precisely to the facts of the present case. Mrs Williams' evidence, which the learned judge preferred to that of Mrs Griffiths, was as follows: 'Whenever the question arose in any discussion Mrs Williams had always been assured that the house was her home of life. That was always what was said and she never expected more than a life interest.' That does not read as if it was the lady giving evidence, but the notes of the evidence appear throughout in that form, and this was obviously a record which the learned judge was making of the evidence which had been given before him. Then Mr Hedley Williams, whose evidence the learned judge also accepted, said—or the effect of his evidence is recorded—as follows: 'He had always understood that the house was his mother's for life, and this had been said to, or in front of, him over many years by both his grandmother and his mother'; and, again, 'As to the improvements etc. there was no objection by the grandmother and he had never heard any mention (prior to his grandmother's death) of his mother leaving, or being asked to leave.' So when the learned judge speaks of what Mrs Williams would have thought had it occurred to her, it is clear that it would have occurred to her but for the fact that Mrs Cole, the testatrix, was throughout repeatedly assuring Mrs Williams that she could live in the house for the rest of her life. It seems to me, on this evidence, clear that Mrs Williams expended her money on the faith of those repeated assurances, and it is, I think, an irresistible inference that Mrs Cole knew that Mrs Williams was relying on the assurances which she herself was repeatedly making to her daughter. In my judgment, therefore, there is no doubt at all in this case but that an equity is made out.

I therefore pass to the second question, and that is: What is the equity? That must be an equity to have made good, so far as may fairly be done between the parties, the representation that Mrs Williams should be entitled to live in the house rent-free for the rest of her life.

So I come to the third question, which is really the one which gives rise to such difficulties as there are in this case. In *Dodsworth v Dodsworth* (1973) 228 EG 1115 [p. 1068, below] this court unanimously decided that if an equity of this nature were implemented by giving the claimant the right to occupy the house (as it was in that case) for his life, the result would be to create a tenancy for life within the meaning of the Settled Land Act, and so the party setting up the equity would get more than it was ever represented that he should have, because he would get all the statutory powers of a tenant for life under the Act: he could sell the property and take the income of the proceeds for his life, or he could grant a long lease. In that case the court does not seem to have considered what may in such cases be a difficult problem, namely, what is the 'settlement?' I think there are many authorities which establish that a right to occupy property for one's life is the equivalent of a tenancy for life under the Act. But the Act defines 'settlement' in section 1 in these terms:

'Any deed, will, agreement for a settlement or other agreement, Act of Parliament, or other instrument, or any number of instruments, whether made or passed before or after, or partly before and partly after, the commencement of this Act, under or by virtue of which instrument or instruments any land, after the commencement of this Act, stands for the time being....'

and then follow the various limitations which make it settled land.

Where the interest arises under a contract or other agreement, of course, there is no difficulty, because that falls fairly and squarely within the words of subsection (1) of section 1. But where what is set up is an equity arising from acting upon a representation, it is not obvious how that can be brought within the terms of section 1(1). There are two other cases in which this type of problem was considered by this court, namely, *Binions v Evans* [1972] Ch 359 [p. 1102, below] and *Bannister v Bannister* [1948] 2 All ER 133 [p. 1101, below]. In *Binions v Evans* the Master of the Rolls thought that such an equity would not in any event create a settlement; but, with all respect, I think his reasoning leads to difficulties, because at 367 he reached the conclusion that it created an equitable interest, and once that is established then the ground on which he said (at 366) there was no settlement appears to me to be undermined. The other two Lord Justices who heard that case, Megaw LJ and Stephenson LJ, felt that they were bound by the earlier decision in *Bannister v Bannister* to hold that there was a settlement; but they did not direct themselves to any question under section 1; nor, I think, need they have done so, because in *Binions v Evans* and the earlier case of *Bannister v Bannister* there was actually an agreement. So that the difficulty which in my view arises, on the case of *Dodsworth v Dodsworth* and upon the present case, of seeing whether there can be a settlement when you have an interest which appears to give you a tenancy for life but there does not obviously appear to be anything which is a 'settlement' within the Act, did not arise in those two earlier cases. If it were necessary, we would have to decide what is, I think, a serious problem—whether *Dodsworth v Dodsworth* is binding upon us or whether it was decided strictly *per incuriam* because the learned Lord Justices who heard it did not advert to section 1 of the Settled Land Act, and, if it be not binding upon us, whether in truth it be right, and if so, what is the answer to the conundrum posed by subsection (1) of section 1. It may be that in such a case there is a settlement, and it is the order of the court declaring the equity, which is an 'instrument' and, therefore, the 'settlement' within the meaning of that subsection.

Happily, by the good sense of the parties in accepting a solution of the problem which I propounded for their consideration, it is unnecessary for this court to resolve those problems. In *Dodsworth v Dodsworth,* having decided that a right of occupation for the whole life of the claimant would be a wrong way of giving effect to the equity because it would create a settlement under the Settled Land Act and give the claimant too much, the court then adopted an alternative suggestion of compensation by recouping the claimant his expenditure (I think with interest) and giving him possession until payment. They recognised that that really went too far the other way; and certainly it would not be appropriate in this case—if for no other reason, because of the difficulty of quantification. But it seems to me that *Dodsworth v Dodsworth* proceeded upon the basis which I have spelt out of *Crabb's* case—that the third problem is one of discretion: the court ought to see, having regard to all the circumstances, what is the best and fairest way to secure protection for the person who has been misled by the representations made to him and subsequently repudiated.

In the present case, it seemed to me, and I suggested to the parties, that the fairest way of dealing with the matter would be to direct the plaintiffs to grant Mrs Williams a long lease, determinable upon her death, at a nominal rent, since that would give her the right of occupation for her whole life and could not in any event give her the statutory powers under the Settled Land Act. The nominal rent would be an obligation not contemplated when the representations were made to her, but perfect equity is seldom possible.

There appeared to be only two objections to this course. One was that she might assign the lease; but that can be dealt with by including in the lease an absolute covenant not to assign, and by her giving an undertaking to this court, which I understand she is prepared to do, not to assign. The other difficulty was that, if she were to marry again, her husband might be able to claim a protected tenancy under the Rent Acts. I know that to Mrs Williams that appears a flight of fantasy; but we have to take precautions to see that what we propose is something which will not go wrong in an event which is not impossible and could happen. Counsel have made inquiries and they assured us that the husband would not be entitled to protection under the Rent Acts if the rent did not exceed two-thirds of the rateable value at the relevant date; and they have ascertained that that rateable value is £46 per annum. Therefore, if we direct the lease to be at a rent of £30 per annum we will have served the two ends of keeping it below two-thirds of the rateable value and making it nominal; and that is what I would propose. I took the precaution of making it clear to counsel, and they have made it clear to the parties, that, while we might order that as a term after deciding whether or not a life interest would be a 'settlement' within the meaning of the Act, if we were to decide that it was not a settlement within the Act Mrs Williams would be entitled to claim a full life interest without reservation of any rent, and therefore we could only adopt this course of a long lease at this stage if the parties consented to it, otherwise we must first determine the problem which I have mentioned and then consider what it would be right to order in the light of that determination. Counsel, having withdrawn and consulted with their clients and taken instructions, say that they are content that we should adopt the solution proposed by me.

I would therefore allow the appeal, discharge the order of the learned deputy circuit judge, and direct the plaintiffs to grant to Mrs Williams the lease which I have indicated.

The award of a life interest would now be an interest under a trust of land: Trusts of Land and Appointment of Trustees Act 1996, p. 515, above. In **Campbell v Griffin** [2001] EWCA 990, (2001) 82 P & CR DG23 at para. 34, ROBERT WALKER LJ said that this:

would be administratively inconvenient. It would...probably involve disproportionate legal expenses (including trustees' remuneration) and might well lead to further disputes (especially in relation to Mr Campbell's keeping the property in good repair and condition).

(c) Perpetual licence

Plimmer v Wellington Corporation[112]
(1884) 9 App Cas 699 (PC, **Lord Watson, Sir Barnes Peacock, Sir Robert P. Collier, Sir Richard Couch** and **Sir Arthur Hobhouse**)

Plimmer moored an old hulk on the foreshore of Wellington Bay and used it as a wharf and store by permission of the Crown. An earthquake raised the level of the land and necessitated the building of a jetty, which Plimmer built. Between 1856 and 1861, at the instance of the Provincial Government, Plimmer extended the jetty. Subsequently the Government took possession of the jetty under statutory powers, and Plimmer

---

[112] Cf. *DHN Food Distributors Ltd v Tower Hamlets London Borough Council* [1976] 1 WLR 852, p. 1096, below (a case of a contractual licence). See also *Pennine Raceway Ltd v Kirklees Metropolitan Council* [1983] QB 382, where a licensee of land was held entitled to compensation under TPCA 1971, s. 164 as a person 'interested in the land' on withdrawal of planning permission; [1982] All ER Rev 173 (P. J. Clarke).

and another claimed compensation under the Public Works Loans Act 1882 under which any person who 'had any estate or interest in, to or out of the lands...vested in the Corporation...shall be entitled to...compensation'.

Held. The equitable right so acquired was an 'estate or interest in, to or out of land' within the meaning of the Act of 1882.

Sir Arthur Hobhouse: The law relating to cases of this kind may be taken as stated by Lord Kingsdown in the case of *Ramsden v Dyson* (1866) LR 1 HL 129. The passage is at 170:

> 'If a man, under a verbal agreement with a landlord for a certain interest in land, or, what amounts to the same thing, under an expectation created or encouraged by the landlord that he shall have a certain interest, takes possession of such land with the consent of the landlord, and upon the faith of such promise or expectation, with the knowledge of the landlord and without objection by him, lays out money upon land, a Court of Equity will compel the landlord to give effect to such promise or expectation. This was the principle of the decision in *Gregory v Mighell* (1811) 18 Ves 328, and, as I conceive, is open to no doubt. If at the hearing of the cause there appears to be such uncertainty as to the particular terms of the contract as might prevent a Court of Equity from giving relief if the contract had been in writing but there had been no expenditure, a Court of Equity will nevertheless, in the case which is above stated, interfere in order to prevent fraud, though there has been a difference of opinion amongst great judges as to the nature of the relief to be granted. Lord Thurlow seems to have thought that the Court would ascertain the terms by reference to the Master, and if they could not be ascertained would itself fix reasonable terms. Lord Alvanley and Lord Redesdale, and perhaps Lord Eldon, thought this was going too far; but I do not understand any doubt to have been entertained by any of them that, either in the form of a specific interest in the land, or in the shape of compensation for the expenditure, a Court of Equity would give relief, and protect in the meantime the possession of the tenant. If, on the other hand, a tenant being in possession of land, and knowing the nature and extent of his interest, lays out money upon it in the hope or expectation of an extended term or an allowance for expenditure, then, if such hope or expectation had not been created or encouraged by the landlord, the tenant has no claim which any Court of Law or Equity can enforce. This was the principle of the decision in *Pilling v Armitage* (1805) 12 Ves 78, and, like the decision in *Gregory v Mighell*, seems founded on plain rules of reason and justice...'

In the present case, the equity is not claimed because the landowner has stood by in silence while his tenant has spent money on his land. This is a case in which the landowner has, for his own purposes, requested the tenant to make the improvements. The Government were engaged in the important work of introducing immigrants into the colony. For some reason, not now apparent, they were not prepared to make landing-places of their own, and in fact they did not do so until the year 1863. So they applied to John Plimmer to make his landing-place more commodious by a substantial extension of his jetty and the erection of a warehouse for baggage. Is it to be said that, when he had incurred the expense of doing the work asked for, the Government could turn round and revoke his licence at their will? Could they in July, 1856, have deprived him summarily of the use of the jetty? It would be in a high degree unjust that they should do so, and that the parties should have intended such a result is, in the absence of evidence, incredible....

Their Lordships will not be the first to hold, and no authority has been cited to them to shew that after such a landowner has requested such a tenant to incur expense on his land for his benefit, he can without more and at his own will take away the property so improved. Their Lordships consider that this case falls within the principle stated by Lord Kingsdown as to expectations created or encouraged by the landlord, with the addition that in this case the land-lord did more than encourage the expenditure, for he took the initiative in requesting it....

The question still remains as to the extent of interest which Plimmer acquired by his expenditure in 1856. Referring again to the passage quoted from Lord Kingsdown's judgment, there is good authority for saying what appears to their Lordships to be quite sound in principle, that the equity arising from expenditure on land need not fail merely on the ground that the interest to be secured has not been expressly indicated.

In such a case as *Ramsden v Dyson* the evidence (according to Lord Kingsdown's view) shewed that the tenant expected a particular kind of lease, which Vice-Chancellor Stuart decreed to him, though it does not appear what form of relief Lord Kingsdown himself would have given. In such a case as the *Duke of Beaufort v Patrick* (1853) 17 Beav 60, nothing but perpetual retention of the land would satisfy the equity raised in favour of those who spent their money on it, and it was secured to them at a valuation. In such a case as *Dillwyn v Llewlyn* (1862) 4 De GF & J 517, nothing but a grant of the fee simple would satisfy the equity which the Lord Chancellor held to have been raised by the son's expenditure on his father's land. In such a case as that of the *Unity Joint-Stock Mutual Banking Association v King* (1858) 25 Beav 72, the Master of the Rolls, holding that the father did not intend to part with his land to his sons who built upon it, considered that their equity would be satisfied by recouping their expenditure to them. In fact, the Court must look at the circumstances in each case to decide in what way the equity can be satisfied.

In this case their Lordships feel no great difficulty. In their view, the licence given by the Government to John Plimmer, which was indefinite in point of duration but was revocable at will, became irrevocable by the transactions of 1856, because those transactions were sufficient to create in his mind a reasonable expectation that his occupation would not be disturbed, and because they and the subsequent dealings of the parties cannot be reasonably explained on any other supposition. Nothing was done to limit the use of the jetty in point of duration. The consequence is that Plimmer acquired an indefinite, that is practically a perpetual, right to the jetty for the purposes of the original licence, and if the ground was afterwards wanted for public purposes, it could only be taken from him by the legislature.

An analogy to this process may be found in such cases as *Winter v Brockwell* (1807) 8 East 308 and *Liggins v Inge* (1831) 7 Bing 682. These cases shew that where a landowner permits his neighbour to execute works on his (the neighbour's land), and the licence is executed, it cannot be revoked at will by the licensor. If indefinite duration, it becomes perpetual. Their Lordships think that the same consequence must follow where the licence is to execute works on the land of the licensor, and owing to some supervening equity the licence has become irrevocable.

There are perhaps purposes for which such a licence would not be held to be an interest in land. But their Lordships are construing a statute which takes away private property for compensation, and in such statutes the expression 'estate or interest in, to or out of land' should receive a wide meaning. Indeed the statute itself directs that, in ascertaining the title of anybody to compensation, the Court shall not be bound to regard strict legal rights only, but shall do what is reasonable and just. Their Lordships have no difficulty in deciding that the equitable right acquired by John Plimmer is an interest in land carrying compensation under the Acts of 1880 and 1882.[113]

---

[113] Cf. *Canadian Pacific Rly Co v R* [1931] AC 414 at 428–429; *Lee-Parker v Izzet (No 2)* [1972] 1 WLR 775 at 780–781.

(d) Licence to occupy until expenditure reimbursed, or other monetary award[114]

In **Dodsworth v Dodsworth** (1973) 228 EG 1115, [1973] EGD 233, giving the judgment of the court, RUSSELL LJ said:

In this case the plaintiff, aged over 70, owned in 1967 a bungalow near Boston, Lincolnshire, and lived there alone. Her younger brother and his wife—the two defendants—returned to England from Australia and were looking for a house to acquire as their home. The plaintiff persuaded them to join her in her bungalow. The judge held on the evidence that the defendants spent a sum of over £700 on improvements to the plaintiff's bungalow in the expectation, encouraged and induced by the plaintiff, that the defendants and the survivor of them would be able to remain in the bungalow as their home—sharing of course with the plaintiff while she lived—for as long as they wished to do so, in circumstances that raised an equity in favour of the defendants on the footing of principles exemplified in a passage from Lord Kingsdown's speech in *Ramsden v Dyson* (1866) LR 1 HL 129, and in other cases since then. The judge, however, held on the evidence that the parties did not intend to create a legal relationship. Not many months after the defendants moved into the bungalow, the plaintiff repented of her invitation for reasons, or alleged reasons, which need not be rehearsed. She started proceedings for possession: the defendants counterclaimed to assert an equity. The plaintiff did not appear at the hearing, and her claim for possession was non-suited. The question on the counterclaim was whether the proper way in which the equity should be satisfied would be to make some order which would assure the defendants in their occupation of the bungalow as their home for as long as they wished, or on the other hand to declare in effect that possession could only be obtained against them by the plaintiff if they were repaid their outlay on improvements to the bungalow.

The judge decided upon the latter as the appropriate course. His main ground was this. The plaintiff was anxious to sell the bungalow and buy a smaller and less expensive one for herself. She could not do this, having no other capital asset, if the defendants were entitled to stay rent free. She would therefore have to continue sharing her home for the rest of her life with the defendants, with whom she was, or thought she was, at loggerheads. Against this the defendants would, on leaving, recover and have available towards another home the expenditure which they laid out in the expectation, albeit encouraged by the plaintiff, of ability to stay there as their home. We think that the judge in balancing these considerations was entitled, and right, to come to that decision. We do not accept that the judge was wrong on the ground submitted to us that where the extent of the expectations was defined, though without intention to create a legal relationship, between the parties, compensation for outlay could not be an appropriate satisfaction of the equity. On the appeal, the plaintiff having died intestate after notice of appeal, leave was given to the respondents, who are her administrators under a grant of letters of administration, to be joined as parties to the appeal. They do not contend that there was not an equity. They support the view, in the changed circumstances, of the judge that it was proper to satisfy the defendants' equity by protecting their occupation unless and until their expenditure was reimbursed.

---

[114] The claimant cannot be compensated for losses that do not flow from the reliance on the representation: *Wormall v Wormall* [2004] EWCA Civ 1643, (2004) Times, 1 December (representation that daughter could occupy property as long as it continued to be family farm; disturbance costs of moving earlier than expected could not be compensated because the relocation 'was always on the cards': at [39], per Jonathan Parker LJ).

Now it is clear that the ground upon which the judge mainly decided upon the appropriate remedy has, by the plaintiff's death, disappeared. But what is the situation now? Apart from the equity, the situation is this. The estate vested in the legal personal representatives consists only of the bungalow. This is subject to a standing mortgage of some £200 to £300. Its value free of any occupation rights in the defendants might be £5,000. Under the Administration of Estates Act 1925 the administrators hold the bungalow on trust for sale and to pay out of the proceeds of sale debts, duties, if any, and administration expenses (which must include their costs of this appeal), and then to divide among ten stirpes of beneficiaries, the first defendant in fact being one stirps. The immediate problem seems to be this. If immediate and direct effect is given to the expectations of the defendants, to take effect in priority to the respondents' entitlement and statutory duties, we cannot see but that it will lead, by virtue of the provisions of the Settled Land Act, to a greater and more extensive interest than was ever contemplated by the plaintiff and the defendants.[115] The defendants would necessarily become joint tenants for life. As such they could sell the property, or quit and let it. In the one case, they would be entitled to the income of the invested proceeds of sale for life and the life of the survivor: in the other, they would be entitled to the net rents. None of these possibilities could conceivably have been embodied in the expectations giving rise to the equity in question, and we do not think that it can be right to satisfy such an equity by conferring upon the defendants a greater interest in the property than was envisaged by the parties. This, we should say, is a point which appears to have been overlooked in *Inwards v Baker* [1965] 2 QB 29 [p. 1048, above].

Is it possible in the present case to give effect to the expectation without falling foul of the impact of the Settled Land Act? ... Yes it was. In short therefore we do not see how we can sensibly, and without awarding to the defendants a greater interest in law than was within the induced expectation, satisfy this equity save by securing their occupation until this expenditure has been reimbursed, which was the effect of the judge's order or declaration.[116]

(e) No remedy

In **Appleby v Cowley** (1982) Times, 14 April,[117] a claim was based on proprietary estoppel, that the plaintiffs were entitled to occupy a building in Nottingham indefinitely and use it as barristers' chambers subject to indemnifying the defendant,

---

[115] For the problems of finding a SLA settlement in this context, see p. 1061, n. 110, above.

[116] *Burrows v Sharp* (1991) 23 HLR 82 (clean break only proper and fair solution in view of breakdown between parties; compensation in return for loss of accommodation); [1992] Conv 54 (J. E. Martin); *Baker v Baker* (1993) 25 HLR 408 (granny flat); *McGuane v Welch* [2008] 2 P & CR 24 (agreement to transfer lease: equity satisfied by charge on the lease to compensate for expenditure incurred in reliance; the detriment was quantifiable in financial terms and could be completely reversed; 'to order the transfer of the lease ... would enforce the performance of a transaction, which was not a binding contract for sale, at a price that was at a substantial undervalue and in respect of which the transferor had received no independent advice': per Mummery LJ at [44]); *Clarke v Swaby* [2007] 2 P & CR 2 at [18], per Lord Walker of Gestingthorpe ('often the equity can best be satisfied by a monetary award').

[117] The extract is taken from the Bar Library Transcript. A claim based on fiduciary or confidential relationship was also rejected. One reason was 'the nature of the alleged beneficiaries. I do not think that practising barristers are in consimili casu with children, wards, patients, clients and the like. As a class they are not immature, weak, credulous creatures, easily persuaded and ready to yield their powers of decision to others.'

See also *Sledmore v Dalby* (1996) 72 P & CR 196, p. 1045, above, at 209, per Hobhouse LJ ('The effect of any equity that may at any earlier time have existed has long since been exhausted'); *Clarke v Swaby* [2007] 2 P & CR 2 at [18].

Mr Cowley, for the costs of providing it. In holding that the claim failed, MEGARRY V-C said:

That leaves the fourth head of expenditure, the repairs and renovations to the roof and exterior walls in 1973 at a cost of some £7,700.... As the law has developed, it may be that in cases in which a claim based on proprietary estoppel is made, the real question comes down simply to whether or not the assertion of strict legal rights would be unconscionable, without any detailed conditions or criteria being specified: see *Taylors Fashions Ltd v Liverpool Victoria Trustees Co Ltd* [1982] QB 133n at 151–154 and *Amalgamated Investment and Property Co Ltd v Texas Commerce International Bank Ltd* [1982] QB 84 at 103–104. In the present case, would it be unconscionable for the company to take the benefit of these remedial works to its building?

I think that there are circumstances in which the answer would be Yes. If soon after the works had been done the company had evicted all the members of chambers, or had required them to make payments equal to the full rental value of the chambers, then the company might well be said to be reaping the fruits of the expenditure unfairly. However, that is not what has happened. When the work was being done the rental value of the premises for which some £1,500 a year had been paid for some 10 years was about £4,300; and as events have turned out, Mr Cowley is making no claim for use and occupation at a rate grater than £1,500 a year until 30th November 1976 onwards. In those circumstances I think Mr Cowley may echo the phrase of Lord Hardwicke LC in *A-G v Balliol College, Oxford* (1744) 9 Mod Rep 407 at 412, when directing an inquiry in chambers, and say that the plaintiffs have had 'sufficient satisfaction' for their expenditure. Certainly I do not think that Mr Cowley is acting unconscionably. It may be a nice academic point whether the result is that no case of proprietary estoppel has been established, or whether it is that such a case has been established but no remedy should be granted. I shall not debate that. All I need do is to say that the claim on proprietary estoppel fails. Certainly I can see nothing which comes within measurable distance of establishing any sort of a case that because of the expenditure the plaintiffs are beneficially entitled to the building, subject to indemnifying Mr Cowley.

In **Savva v Costa** [1980] CA Transcript 723, (1981) 131 NLJ 1114 (Buckley, Shaw and Oliver LJJ), the plaintiff, a Cypriot seamstress, and the defendant had lived together from 1967 to 1968. Thereafter the defendant assumed responsibility for the maintenance and education of their two children who lived with the plaintiff. In early 1977 the defendant suggested to the plaintiff that she should move with the children and live in a house which he owned. The plaintiff's expenditure on work carried out to the house was substantial; the defendant was aware that the work was going on, although he claimed that he had protested that some of it was extravagant and unnecessary.

In May 1977, the defendant indicated his intention to transfer the house to trustees for the two children, on terms that the plaintiff would be permitted to reside there with them. The plaintiff claimed a beneficial half share in the property, or, alternatively, a lien on the property for the amount which she had expended.

In rejecting both claims, OLIVER LJ said:

Mr Goodenday has drawn our attention to a line of authorities, starting with the well-known dictum of Lord Kingsdown in *Ramsden v Dyson* and applied in *Plimmer v Wellington Corpn* (1884) 9 App Cas 699 [p. 1065, above]; *Inwards v Baker* [1965] 2 QB 29 [p. 1049, above]; *Ward v Kirkland* [1967] Ch 194 and other cases. These relate to what is known as a proprietary estoppel. The effect can be summarised by saying that where A under an expectation created or encouraged by B that A shall have a certain interest in land, expends money on B's land on the faith of such expectation and to the knowledge of B, a court of equity will not allow B to take the benefit of such expenditure without giving effect to the expectation so created or encouraged. The expenditure in such circumstances gives rise to an equity to which the court will give effect in such way as may be appropriate in the circumstances of the individual case. It may be by injunction, it may be by declaring a trust of the beneficial interest or it may be by a declaration of lien for monies expended. This line of cases Mr Goodenday has conveniently referred to as 'the representation cases'; but he accepts that, in the light of the learned deputy judge's findings of fact in the instant case, he cannot bring himself directly within them. What he submits is that the representation cases do not exhaust the category of cases in which equities of this type can arise. There are, he suggests, two other categories of case, under either of which he is entitled to succeed in the claim which he makes for a beneficial interest in the property.

The first category of case represents, as he submits, an extension of the *Ramsden v Dyson* principle to a situation in which there is no representation or expectation, but merely an expenditure of money with the consent of the landowner. If I have his submission aright, Mr Goodenday expresses the principle thus: Where a person expends money on the land of another with the knowledge and consent of that other but without any sort of representation, this gives rise to an equity in the person making the expenditure to have either an interest in the land commensurate with his expenditure or at least a lien for the amount expended.

In support of this Mr Goodenday relies upon two authorities.

His Lordship referred to *Unity Joint Stock Mutual Banking Association v King* (1858) 25 Beav 72, and *Hussey v Palmer* [1972] 1 WLR 1286, and continued:

Now these cases do not, in my judgment at any rate, support any such broad principle as that for which Mr Goodenday contends. Mr Reid submits, and for my part I accept the submission, that on analysis they are not extensions of the *Ramsden v Dyson* principle, but merely examples of its application, and they do not support the broad proposition relied upon by Mr Goodenday that mere expenditure with the consent of the landowner is sufficient to raise an equity without any representation or expectation created by the landowner. The *Unity Joint Stock Banking* case was so treated in *Chalmers v Pardoe* [1963] 1 WLR 677, itself a representation case, and it is clear that in *Hussey v Palmer,* the common expectation was that the plaintiff would continue to live in the house, an expectation which was not realised in the event, but on the strength of which the expenditure was made.

In my judgment these cases cannot be prayed in aid to demonstrate that the mere expenditure by A on improvements to B's land with B's knowledge without more, gives rise to some equity in the payer....

In the instant case, on the facts as found by the learned deputy judge, there was no agreement and there was no request on the part of the defendant. The plaintiff was aware that the house belonged to the defendant and if she believed that she was to get any interest in it, there is nothing to indicate that the defendant knew that that was her belief. The most that can be inferred in these circumstances is that she expended monies in improvements in the expectation that, as in fact was and is the case, she would be permitted to live there with the children.

His Lordship rejected a claim based on 'a resulting trust which arises by the establishment by evidence of conduct of a common intention on the acquisition of the property, that the beneficial interest shall be shared in some way': *Gissing v Gissing* [1971] AC 886, and continued:

I should perhaps add this. As the learned deputy judge pointed out, his decision in no way determined the question of the plaintiff's right to continue in occupation of the property. That was not in issue before him and it is not in issue before this court. It may very well be that, although Mr Goodenday has felt unable to rely upon the principle of *Ramsden v Dyson* to establish the equitable interest claimed by the plaintiff in this action, the plaintiff would be entitled, if her enjoyment of the property is terminated in the future, to invoke that principle in support of a claim to an irrevocable licence—an equity to which, if it is established, the court might then give effect by a declaration of lien as suggested in *Hussey v Palmer,* if the circumstances and the duration or terms of the licence were thought to render that course appropriate. That is something about which I think it safer and wiser to express no view. It was not argued below and, understandably, there are no findings by the learned deputy judge as to the terms or duration of any such licence—matters which it would be essential, as I see it, to determine before the court could give any relief. The plaintiff's occupation has not in fact been disturbed and Mr Reid, on instructions, disclaims any present intention on his client's part to disturb it. I agree with the learned deputy judge, therefore, that it would be premature for the court to intervene now, and indeed it does not, as I think, have before it the material to enable it to do so. I mention the matter only to make clear that the present appeal, which I would dismiss, is in no way determinative of such rights of occupation as the plaintiff may have, or be entitled to, or of the course which the court might think it appropriate to take if such occupation were to be disturbed in the future.

SHAW LJ said:

I only append a footnote. The questions raised and to be decided on this appeal are of course confined to the issues with which the learned deputy judge had to deal, and to his findings of fact in regard to them. It may be that there remain outside the context of the present proceedings, prospective potential rights which will accrue to Miss Savva in certain eventualities; the existence and nature of those rights may have to be determined in the future; they are not within the ambit of this appeal.

I would therefore echo Lord Justice Oliver's indication as to what the position in law might be if Miss Savva were at any time to be denied the advantage of residing in No 6 Windermere Road, having regard to the considerable expenditure by her on the improvement of the property....

If at some time it should be sought to turn Miss Savva out, there would arise a serious question as to the protection of an interest in the property on her behalf commensurate with the money she has spent on improving its condition so as to provide a proper degree of amenity for the accommodation of the children, who are intended to be the ultimate proprietors of the property.[118]

D. PROPRIETARY ESTOPPEL AS AN INTEREST IN LAND

Most cases of proprietary estoppel have involved the original parties—that is, a claim by the person who was led to believe that he had, or would acquire, an interest in the

---

[118] See also *Bristol and West Building Society v Henning* [1985] 1 WLR 778, p. 215, n. 297, above.

land against the person who made the representation to the claimant or acquiesced in the claimant's mistake about his rights in the land. In such cases no question normally arises as to whether the nature of the equity, before the time when court has adjudicated upon the claim and granted a remedy, is proprietary. If, however, the land in respect of which the equity has arisen is transferred to a third party before the remedy is granted, the question arises as to whether the transferee of the land is bound by the equity.

Law Commission Consultative Document: Land Registration for the Twenty-First Century 1998 (Law Com No. 254), paras 3.35 and 3.36

3.35 It will be apparent from this that the doctrine of proprietary estoppel involves two stages. First, the circumstances must occur which generate the 'equity' in B's favour. Secondly, the court may give effect to that equity in proceedings brought for that purpose or in which it is in issue. Clearly, once the court has declared how the equity should be satisfied there is little difficulty. If B is held entitled to a property right, that right can then be recorded in the usual manner on the register.[119] In such circumstances the register can be amended to give effect to the order of the court.[120] The difficulty arises in the interim period between the equity arising and effect being given to it. There is some controversy as to the status of the equity in this interim period. Because the court may not grant B any proprietary rights over A's land, but only, say, a sum of compensation, some commentators have tended to regard B's equity as a purely personal right.[121] If that is so, it cannot be protected against third parties either as a minor interest, or by B's actual occupation of the land affected, as an overriding interest.[122] Against this however, there are good reasons for regarding the inchoate equity as a property right.[123] There is indeed some authority that, where title to the land is unregistered, the equity is binding on both a purchaser of the land affected who has notice of B's rights[124] and a donee regardless of notice.[125] Furthermore, where the title is registered, not only has it been accepted that an equity arising by estoppel coupled with actual occupation could be an overriding interest,[126]

---

[119] See Graham Battersby, 'Informal Transactions in Land, Estoppel and Registration' (1995) 58 MLR 637, 641, 642.

[120] See Land Registration Act 1925, s. 82(1)(a).

[121] See D. J. Hayton, 'Developing the Law of Trusts for the Twenty-First Century' (1990) 106 LQR 87, 97, n. 26.

[122] Under the Land Registration Act 1925, s. 70(1)(g).

[123] See in particular Graham Battersby, 'Contractual and Estoppel Licences as Proprietary Interests in Land' [1991] Conv 36, 45; Simon Baughen, 'Estoppels Over Land and Third Parties: An Open Question' (1994) 14 LS 147, 154; Graham Battersby, 'Informal Transactions in Land, Estoppel and Registration' (1995) 58 MLR 637, 642.

[124] Duke of Beaufort v Patrick (1853) 17 Beav 60, 78; Inwards v Baker [1965] 2 QB 29, 37; E R Ives Investment Ltd v High [1967] 2 QB 379. In Lloyds Bank Plc v Carrick [1996] 4 All ER 630, 642, Morritt LJ commented that '[i]n the circumstances it is unnecessary to consider further the submission... to the effect that a proprietary estoppel cannot give rise to an interest in land capable of binding successors in title. This interesting argument will have to await another day, though it is hard to see how in this court it can surmount the hurdle constituted by the decision of this court in Ives v High'.

[125] Voyce v Voyce (1991) 62 P & CR 290, 294, 296.

[126] Lee-Parker v Izzet (No 2) [1972] 1 WLR 775, 780, obiter. Cf. Habermann v Koehler (1996) 73 P & CR 515, where the Court of Appeal remitted a case for a retrial to determine inter alia whether an equity arising by estoppel could bind a purchaser as an overriding interest under Land Registration Act 1925, s. 70(1)(g).

but it is already the practice of the Land Registry to allow such an equity to be registered as a minor interest.[127]

3.36 In view of the increasing importance of estoppel as a mechanism for the informal creation of rights over land, it is obviously desirable to clarify in relation to registered land the status of an equity arising by estoppel before effect has been given to it by a court order. We therefore provisionally recommend that an equity arising by estoppel or acquiescence in relation to registered land should be regarded as an interest from the time at which it arises.[128] This will make clear that such an equity is a minor interest and that it may also exist as an overriding interest where the person having the benefit of it is in actual occupation.

(i) Unregistered land

E R Ives Investment Ltd v High[129]
[1967] 2 QB 379 (CA, Lord Denning MR, Danckwerts and Winn LJJ)

In 1946, the defendant, High, began to build a house on a plot of land. Soon after, Westgate, his neighbour, started to erect a block of flats in such a way that their foundations encroached by about one foot upon the defendant's land. The defendant and Westgate agreed that the foundation could remain, and that the defendant should have a right of way for his car across Westgate's yard. The agreement for the right of way was never registered.

Westgate sold the block to Flt.-Lt. and Mrs Wright who knew of the agreement, and also knew that in 1959 the defendant erected a garage so sited that it could only be approached across the yard. In 1960, the defendant contributed to the surfacing of the yard.

In 1962 the Wrights sold the flats to the plaintiffs, expressly subject to the right of way. The plaintiffs sued the defendant for trespass to the yard, claiming that the defendant had no legal right of way, and that if he was entitled to an equitable easement, it was void against them because it was not registered.

Held. The defendant was entitled to use the way across the yard.

---

[127] Under the Land Registration Act 1925, ss. 49(1)(f) (notice); 54(1) (caution). See Ruoff & Roper, *Registered Conveyancing*, 8–02; 35–33; 36–13.

[128] It has not been definitively settled when an equity arises. At the very latest it will be when the circumstances make it unconscionable for the land owner, A, to go back on the expectation which he has created by representation or conduct: *Lim v Ang* [1992] 1 WLR 113, 118. In most cases that will be when the other party, B, has acted to his detriment in reliance upon the expectation. That moment will not always be easy to define.

[This was also recommended in the Law Commission Report on Land Registration for the Twenty-First Century 2001 (Law Com No. 271), paras 5.29–5.31, and was enacted as LRA 2002, s. 116(a); p. 1077, below.]

[129] (1967) 31 Conv (NS) 332 (F.R. Crane). See also *Montague v Long* (1972) 24 P & CR 240; *Lloyds Bank plc v Carrick* [1996] 4 All ER 630, 642, per Morritt LJ ('In the circumstances it is unnecessary to consider further the submission…to the effect that a proprietary estoppel cannot give rise to an interest in land capable of binding successors in title. This interesting argument will have to await another day, though it is hard to see how in this court it can surmount the hurdle constituted by the decision of this court in *Ives v High*'); *Voyce v Voyce* (1991) 62 P & CR 290 at 296 (donee in no better position than predecessor who was estopped: per Dillon LJ); *Sen v Headley* [1991] Ch 425 at 440.

Lord Denning MR: One thing is quite clear. Apart from this point about the Land Charges Act 1925, Mr High would have in equity a good right of way across the yard. This right arises in two ways:

1. Mutual benefit and burden.

The right arises out of the agreement of November 2, 1949, and the subsequent action taken on it: on the principle that 'he who takes the benefit must accept the burden.' When adjoining owners of land make an agreement to secure continuing rights and benefits for each of them in or over the land of the other, neither of them can take the benefit of the agreement and throw over the burden of it. This applies not only to the original parties, but also their successors. The successor who takes the continuing benefit must take it subject to the continuing burden. This principle has been applied to neighbours who send their water into a common drainage system: see *Hopgood v Brown* [1955] 1 WLR 213; and to purchasers of houses on a building estate who had the benefit of using the roads and were subject to the burden of contributing to the upkeep: see *Halsall v Brizell* [1957] Ch 169 [p. 748, above]. The principle clearly applies in the present case. The owners of the block of flats have the benefit of having their foundations in Mr High's land. So long as they take that benefit, they must shoulder the burden. They must observe the condition on which the benefit was granted, namely, they must allow Mr High and his successors to have access over their yard: cf. *May v Belleville* [1905] 2 Ch 605. Conversely, so long as Mr High takes the benefit of the access, he must permit the block of flats to keep their foundations in his land.

2. Equity arising out of acquiescence.

The right arises out of the expense incurred by Mr High in building his garage, as it is now, with access only over the yard: and the Wrights standing by and acquiescing in it, knowing that he believed he had a right of way over the yard. By so doing the Wrights created in Mr High's mind reasonable expectation that his access over the yard would not be disturbed. That gives rise to an 'equity arising out of acquiescence.' It is available not only against the Wrights but also their successors in title. The court will not allow that expectation to be defeated when it would be inequitable so to do. It is for the court in each case to decide in what way the equity can be satisfied: see *Inwards v Baker* [1965] 2 QB 29 [p. 1049, above]; *Ward v Kirkland* [1967] Ch 194 and the cases cited therein. In this case it could only be satisfied by allowing Mr High and his successors to have access over the yard so long as the block of flats has its foundations in his land.

The next question is this: was that right a land charge such as to need registration under the Land Charges Act 1925? For if it was a land charge, it was never registered and would be void as against any purchaser: see section 13 of the Act.[130] It would, therefore, be void against the plaintiffs, even though they took with the most express knowledge and notice of the right.

It was suggested that the agreement of November 2, 1949, was 'an estate contract' within Class C(iv). I do not think so. There was no contract by Mr Westgate to convey a legal estate of any kind.

It was next suggested that the right was an 'equitable easement' within Class D(iii). This class is defined as 'any easement right or privilege over or affecting land created or arising after the commencement of this Act, and being merely an equitable interest'. Those words are almost identical with section 2(3)(iii) of the Law of Property Act 1925, and should be given the same

---

[130] Now LCA 1972, s. 2(5); p. 67, above.

meaning. They must be read in conjunction with sections 1(2)(*a*), 1(3) and 4(1) of the Law of Property Act 1925. It then appears that an 'equitable easement' is a proprietary interest in land such as would before 1926 have been recognised as capable of being conveyed or created *at law,* but which since 1926 only takes effect as an equitable interest. An instance of such a proprietary interest is a profit à prendre for life. It does not include a right to possession by a requisitioning authority: see *Lewisham Borough Council v Maloney* [1948] 1 KB 50. Nor does it include a right, liberty or privilege arising in equity by reason of 'mutual benefit and burden,' or arising out of 'acquiescence,' or by reason of a contractual licence: because none of those before 1926 were proprietary interests such as were capable of being conveyed or created *at law.* They only subsisted *in equity.* They do not need to be registered as land charges, so as to bind successors, but take effect in equity without registration: see an article by Mr C. V. Davidge on 'Equitable Easements' in (1937) 53 Law Quarterly Review, p. 259 and by Professor H. W. R. Wade in [1956] Cambridge Law Journal, pp. 225–226.

The right of Mr High to cross this yard was not a right such as could ever have been created or conveyed at law. It subsisted only in equity. It therefore still subsists in equity without being registered. Any other view would enable the owners of the flats to perpetrate the grossest injustice. They could block up Mr High's access to the garage, whilst keeping their foundations in his land. That cannot be right.

I am confirmed in this construction of the statute when I remember that there are many houses adjoining one another which have drainage systems in common, with mutual benefits and burdens. The statute cannot have required all these to be registered as land charges.

I know that this greatly restricts the scope of Class D(iii) but this is not disturbing.[131] A special committee has already suggested that Class D(iii) should be abolished altogether: see the report of the Committee on Land Charges ((1956) Command Paper 9825, para. 16).[132]

Winn LJ: During the 12 years from 1950 to 1962 purchasers from Mr Westgate of his plot of land, a Flt. Lt. Wright and his wife, managed and from time to time resided in Francis Court. They not only licensed Mr High, as had Mr Westgate, to pass over the yard, probably motivated by their knowledge that their footings protruded, but allowed and even encouraged him when he proposed to build himself a garage on his eastern boundary so that, after he first bought a car in about 1960, he could drive it in and across their yard; they also accepted a contribution from him to the cost of resurfacing that yard. Thus they represented to him that he had a right so to do. A very clear equity and also an estoppel thus arose against them preventing them from denying Mr. High use of the right of way: cf. per Upjohn J in *Halsall v Brizell* [1957] Ch 169, 182. It is, however, to be observed that that case related more specifically to benefits and burdens arising under a deed and held that such benefits could not be taken without assuming also the burdens: cf. also *Inwards v Baker* [1965] 2 QB 29, a case of standing by with knowledge that expenditure was being incurred in reliance upon conduct of the party against whom an equity was therefore held to arise. Notice of this equity, which amounted to an equitable easement, was given in paragraph 9 of the particulars of the auction at which the plaintiffs bought Francis Court, and the land on which it stood, and by the draft of the conveyance of the property.

---

[131] See *Shiloh Spinners Ltd v Harding* [1973] AC 691 at 719–721, p. 68, above.
[132] P. 648, n. 87, above.

In my opinion the plaintiffs as successors in title are bound by that estoppel. I do not regard myself as thereby saying anything contradictory of the proposition submitted to the court that the said equity or equitable easement, as distinct from the estoppel, was rendered void as against the plaintiffs by the statutes to which I have referred. Estoppels arising from representations made by owners of land that rights exist affecting their land will, unless in form they are limited to the duration of the interest of the representor, bind successors to his title.

(ii) Registered land

In registered land an equity by estoppel, like a 'mere equity'[133] is given the same priority as an equitable interest, and will therefore bind a transferee of the land except a disponee for valuable consideration where the equity has not been protected, either by entry of a notice in the register, or as an overriding interest by the beneficiary being in discoverable actual occupation of the land.

Land Registration Act 2002

116 Proprietary estoppel and mere equities[134]

It is hereby declared for the avoidance of doubt[135] that, in relation to registered land . . . —

(a) an equity by estoppel . . .

has effect from the time the equity arises as an interest capable of binding successors in title (subject to the rules about the effect of dispositions on priority[136]).

(iii) Overreaching

Cheshire and Burn's Modern Law of Real Property (17th edn, 2006), p. 845

A further question, however, arises which is critical to the analysis of the licensee's rights against the purchaser. Even if the equity by estoppel is recognized as having a sufficiently proprietary quality to bind the purchaser, can the purchaser overreach it by paying the purchase money to two trustees[137] and thereby transfer the burden of the equity to the purchase money? It has been said that the equity cannot be overreached.[138] However, in a case where the equity

---

[133] P. 1006, above.

[134] Law Commission Consultative Document: Land Registration in the Twenty-First Century (Law Com No. 254), paras 3.33–3.36; [2003] CLJ 661 (B. McFarlane).

[135] For the position under LRA 1925, see *Brocket Hall (Jersey) Ltd v Clague* [1998] CLY 4367; *Habermann v Koehler (No 2)* (2000) Times, 22 November; *Lloyd v Dugdale* [2002] 2 P & CR 167; (2002) 146 SJ 90 (M. Pawlowski).

[136] For the rules governing priority of interests on disposition of the land, see LRA 2002, ss. 28–30 and Sch. 3; pp. 170–220, above.

[137] Or a trust corporation: LPA 1925, s. 2 [p. 548, above].

[138] *Shiloh Spinners Ltd v Harding* [1973] AC 691 at 720–721, per Lord Wilberforce, approving the approach of CA in *ER Ives Investment Ltd v High* [1967] 2 QB 379 (unregistered land); *Sweet v Sommer* [2005] EWCA Civ 227, [2005] All ER (D) 162 (Mar) at [26], per Morritt VC (registered land).

is to be satisfied with the grant of an interest which would itself be overreachable, it has been suggested that the equity arising by estoppel should also be overreachable.[139] This only adds to the controversy as to the nature of the equity before it is satisfied.

E. RELATIONSHIP BETWEEN PROPRIETARY ESTOPPEL AND CONSTRUCTIVE TRUST[140]

Cheshire and Burn's Modern Law of Real Property (17th edn, 2006), pp. 907–908

The close relationship between the doctrines of proprietary estoppel and constructive trust has been discussed by judges in a number of cases;[141] and some cases arise on facts which might equally well be analysed as a constructive trust based on the common intention of the parties, or proprietary estoppel.[142] Some recent developments might appear to have brought these doctrines even closer together. We have seen that the Court of Appeal in *Oxley v Hiscock*[143] has emphasised the court's discretion in deciding the value of the parties' respective interests under a constructive trust based on their common intention to share property; and *Jennings v Rice*[144] has also emphasised the courts' discretion in deciding on the remedy to be awarded in a case of proprietary estoppel. However, this similarity can be deceptive.[145] The court in *Oxley v Hiscock* described the discretion only in a case in which the parties had agreed to share but had not agreed on the value of their respective shares. In a case of constructive trust, the courts appear to assume that if there is an agreement as to the value, that agreement will be given effect. In a case of proprietary estoppel, however, the court in *Jennings v Rice* made clear that, even it there is a clearly evidenced representation as to the interest to be conferred, the court will not necessarily order it; the remedy is still at the discretion of the court. This emphasises that the nature of the claimant's right under the equity arising by estoppel is more uncertain,

---

[139]   *Birmingham Midshires Mortgage Services Ltd v Sabherwal* (2000) 80 P & CR 256 at [24], per Robert Walker LJ.

[140]   Gray, paras 9.2.118–9.2.122; M & W, paras 11.032, 16.036.

[141]   Sir Nicolas Browne-Wilkinson VC in *Grant v Edwards* [1986] Ch 638 at 656–7; Lord Bridge of Harwich in *Lloyds Bank plc v Rosset* [1991] 1 AC 107 at 132 [p. 576, above]; Robert Walker LJ in *Birmingham Midshires Mortgage Services Ltd v Sabherwal* (2000) 80 P & CR 256 at [24], *Yaxley v Gotts* [2000] Ch 162 at 176–177 and *Jennings v Rice* [2003] 1 P & CR 8 at [45]. See also Sir Christopher Slade, *The Informal Creation of Interests in Land* (1984) Child & Co Oxford Lecture. [See now, however, Lord Walker of Gestingthorpe in *Stack v Dowden* [2007] 2 AC 432 at [37], below; Lord Scott of Foscote in *Cobbe v Yeoman's Row Management Ltd* [2008] 1 WLR 1752 (p. 1021, above) at [29] 'Section 2 of the [LP(MP) A 1989] declares to be void any agreement for the acquisition of an interest in land that does not comply with the requisite formalities prescribed by the section. Subsection (5) expressly makes an exception for resulting, implied or constructive trusts. These may validly come into existence without compliance with the prescribed formalities. Proprietary estoppel does not have the benefit of this exception'. See also *Thorner v Major* [2009] 1 WLR 776 at [20] (Lord Scott of Foscote), p. 1030, above.]

[142]   See, e.g., *Jennings v Rice*, above, at [45], per Robert Walker LJ, discussing *Yaxley v Gotts* [2000] Ch 162; *Kinane v Mackie-Conteh* [2005] EWCA Civ 45, [2005] 2 P & CR DG 3. The requirement of reliance by the claimant on the parties' common intention to share—which resonates with the language of estoppel—reinforces this analogy.

[143]   [2005] Fam 211. [P. 578, above. See now also *Stack v Dowden* [2007] 2 AC 432; p. 580, above.]

[144]   [2003] 1 P & CR 8.

[145]   (2004) 120 LQR 541 at 545–546 (S. Gardner); [2004] Conv 496 (M. P. Thompson).

more precarious than that arising under a constructive trust which gives effect to the parties' common intention. It also shows that, in the case of such a constructive trust, the right is from the beginning an interest in land—a beneficial interest in the land itself, albeit to a share which the court may not yet have quantified, if the parties did not agree it. However, in the case of proprietary estoppel, the right is only an 'equity'—the right to seek a remedy; but it is not yet a full interest in the land. Indeed, it may never be, if the court does not order a property interest as the remedy.

In **Stack v Dowden** [2007] 2 AC 432, p. 580, above, at p. 448, para. 37, LORD WALKER OF GESTINGTHORPE said:[146]

I add a brief comment as to proprietary estoppel. In paras 70 and 71 of his judgment in *Oxley v Hiscock* [2005] Fam 211 Chadwick LJ considered the conceptual basis of the developing law in this area, and briefly discussed proprietary estoppel, a suggestion first put forward by Sir Nicolas Browne-Wilkinson V-C in *Grant v Edwards* [1986] Ch 638, 656. I have myself given some encouragement to this approach (*Yaxley v Gotts* [2000] Ch 162, 177) but I have to say that I am now rather less enthusiastic about the notion that proprietary estoppel and 'common interest' constructive trusts can or should be completely assimilated. Proprietary estoppel typically consists of asserting an equitable claim against the conscience of the 'true' owner. The claim is a 'mere equity'. It is to be satisfied by the minimum award necessary to do justice (*Crabb v Arun District Council* [1976] Ch 179, 198), which may sometimes lead to no more than a monetary award. A 'common intention' constructive trust, by contrast, is identifying the true beneficial owner or owners, and the size of their beneficial interests.

QUESTIONS

1. How would you reformulate the principle of *Ramsden v Dyson?* Consider, in particular whether
   (*a*) there is, or should be, any difference between estoppel by acquiescence or silence, estoppel by encouragement and promissory estoppel;
   (*b*) the principle should be confined to land or other property.

2. Is the requirement of unconscionability referable to the establishment of the equity, or to its satisfaction, or to both?

3. Do the courts apply the same criteria when considering whether an equity is established in the case of
   (*a*) a claim to a proprietary interest; and
   (*b*) a defence to an action for possession?
   See *Pascoe v Turner* [1979] 1 WLR 431, p. 1056, above; *Savva v Costa* [1980] CA Transcript 723, p. 1071, above; *Bristol and West Building Society v Henning* [1985] 1 WLR 778.

4. Should proprietary estoppel be regarded as a species of constructive trust? See *Re Basham* [1986] 1 WLR 1498 at 1503; *Thorner v Major* [2009] 1 WLR 776 at [20], p. 1030, above; and section E, p. 1078, above.

---

[146] [2008] Conv 401 at 414–415 (H. Delaney and D Ryan).

5. If the transferee of land is bound by an equity arising by proprietary estoppel, what is the nature of the interest by which he is bound, given that the court has not yet exercised its discretion to determine the claimant's interest (if any) in the land? Is the interest choate, or inchoate? Will the circumstances of the transferee be relevant in determining the claimant's remedy? (1995) 58 MLR 640–643 (G. Battersby); Pawlowski, *The Doctrine of Proprietary Estoppel*, chap. 7; C & B, pp. 826–827. And will the original representor remain personally liable after disposal of the land? [2005] Conv 14 (S. Bright and B. McFarlane).

6. Consider the position of the defendant in *Inwards v Baker* [1965] 2 QB 29, p. 1049, above, if he had remained in possession for 13 years: [1991] Conv 280 (M. Welstead).

7. What criteria have emerged to guide the courts in 'satisfying the equity' which arises for proprietary estoppel?

8. How would you solve

   (*a*) *Inwards v Baker* [1965] 2 QB 29, p. 1049, above and

   (*b*) *E R Ives Investment Ltd v High* [1967] 2 QB 379, p. 1074, above,

   if the title of the land were registered?

9. An aged relative asks his adult child to move into his house and look after him for the rest of his days. In return the relative makes an oral promise to leave the house by will to the child or to the child and his or her spouse. The child moves in, but the aged relative fails to leave the house by will. Consider the possible legal analyses and solutions, and in particular

   (*a*) in property, as a licence;

   (*b*) in trust, as an express or constructive trust (or a resulting trust if the child makes any financial contribution);

   (*c*) in succession, under the Inheritance (Provision for Family and Dependants) Act 1975.

   See generally [1982] CLJ 290 (S. J. Burridge); *Thorner v Major* [2008] 2 FCR 435 at [68] and in HL at [2009] 1 WLR 776, p. 1027, above.

IV. LICENCES[147]

In its simplest form, a licence is a permission to enter upon land. It makes lawful what would otherwise be a trespass;[148] and, in the absence of special circumstances, is revocable at the will of the licensor. It is not a proprietary interest, and is not the

[147] C & B, chap. 23; Gray, parts 10.2–10.5; M & W, chap. 34; MM, chap. 12; Smith, chap. 22; H & M, chap. 27; Dawson and Pearce, *Licences Relating to the Occupation or Use of Land* (1979); (1954) 70 LQR 326 (Lord Evershed).
[148] Vaughan CJ in *Thomas v Sorrell* (1673) Vaugh 330 at 351.

subject matter of a grant. But there are many ways in which a licence has progressed from this simplistic form. After the Judicature Acts 1873–1875, equitable remedies became available to protect a licensee in suitable cases. The years since World War II have seen a rapid development of their use, and this development is even now not fully worked out. The earlier cases focused on the question whether the licensee was to be protected against the licensor, by an injunction restraining the licensor from revoking the licence. Protection of the licensee against the licensor inevitably gave rise to the next question; whether the licensee was also to be protected against third parties, who would usually be the successors in title of the licensor. Protection against third parties further gave rise to the question whether such a licence had acquired proprietary characteristics. It may be that a licence which protects the licensee against third parties should be regarded as 'proprietary' in nature, or it may be that an interest should only be regarded as proprietary[149] if it is capable of being assigned, bought and sold, and of passing through the estate of a deceased person. There have not yet been cases in which a protected licensee has purported to 'sell' his licence. But there are cases in which licensees have been held to be entitled to an order transferring to them an easement, or a life interest, or a fee simple in the land;[150] or have been held, even in the absence of such order, to be entitled to compensation, in their capacity as licensees, under statutory provisions authorising the payment of compensation to persons having interests in the land.[151]

However, in all such cases it is not the licence itself which confers on the licensee the right to an injunction restraining the licensor from revoking the licence, or the right to an interest in the land. There is something beyond the licence—a contract; or a constructive trust; or an equity arising by way of estoppel (proprietary estoppel). In other words, a licensee does not, *qua* licensee, have more than a simple personal permission to be on the land. But the licence may be *protected* by the terms of a contract, or by the licensee having an interest arising under a constructive trust or proprietary estoppel.[152] And the strength of protection which this offers to the licensee depends upon the nature of the right which is conferred by contract, constructive trust or proprietary estoppel. Each of these will be looked at in turn; but it will be useful, first of all, to lay down some of the basic propositions of the common law relating to licences. The modern development has been by way of the application of equitable principles and remedies to that situation.

---

[149] *National Provincial Bank Ltd v Ainsworth* [1965] AC 1175 at 1247–1248.
[150] P. 1051, above.   [151] P. 1065, above.
[152] Dawson and Pearce, *Licences Relating to the Occupation or Use of Land*, use nine categories of licence: Bare Licences; Contractual Licences; Licences by Estoppel; Licences arising under the doctrine of benefit and burden; Licences arising under the doctrine against derogation from grant; Licences and s. 62 LPA 1925; Licences arising by operation of law; Licences coupled with an interest; Licences as interests under a constructive trust.

A. THE COMMON LAW RULES[153]

(i) A bare and gratuitous licence is revocable at the will of the licensor

The licensee here avoids being a trespasser only because of the licensor's permission to enter. Such is the position of a guest at dinner, or of a picnic party in a friend's garden. The licensee then becomes a trespasser, but is first allowed a reasonable time in which to collect his goods, if any, and to leave the land.[154]

(ii) Entry upon a licence does not make it irrevocable

There was a doctrine[155] of long standing, but little relied on, to the effect that, if a licence has been acted upon, it is no longer revocable. Such an argument would prove too much, for it disregards the many cases in which licensees are permitted to be evicted after entry;[156] and also disregards the reasoning in other cases in which the licensee has been protected on other grounds. *Tayler v Waters* (1816) 7 Taunt 374, one of the leading cases in support of this theory, was disapproved in *Wood v Leadbitter* and described as being 'to the last degree unsatisfactory' (1845) 13 M & W 838 at 852, p. 1082, below. If the principle of *Tayler v Waters* had developed, it 'would go close to reversing the general rule of the revocability of licences'.[157] The cases have been explained as illustrations of the principle of estoppel, discussed below.[158] But there is no indication that the judges in the cases so thought, and no express reference to that principle. A related but distinct concept appears in modern law in the rule formulated

---

[153] C & B, pp. 832–833; Gray, part 10.2; M & W, paras 34.001–34.003, 34.005–34.006; MM, pp. 427–429; Smith, pp. 455–456; Dawson and Pearce, pp. 22–24, 68–73.

[154] [2002] CLJ 89 (J. Hill); *Minister of Health v Bellotti* [1944] 1 All ER 238; *Canadian Pacific Rly Co v R* [1931] AC 414; *Australian Blue Metal Ltd v Hughes* [1963] AC 74; *Wallshire Ltd v Advertising Sites Ltd* [1988] 2 EGLR 167; *Express Newspapers plc v Silverstone Circuits Ltd* (1989) Times, 20 June (right to place advertisements on bridge at Woodcote Corner); *Governing Body of Henrietta Barnett School v Hampstead Garden Suburb Institute* (1995) Times, 13 April (nine months' notice given to school 'for all purposes from four to four score' held to be inadequate 'by any standards of reasonableness'; public nature of licensee's function, known to the licensor, taken into account); [1996] CLJ 229 (T. Kerbal).

For a possession action under RSC Ord 113 (now CPR Part 55) by a licensee against a trespasser on the land which the licensee occupies, even though not in de facto occupation of it, see *Manchester Airport plc v Dutton* [2000] QB 133; [1999] Conv. 535 (E. Paton and G. Seabourne) cf. *Countryside Residential (North Thames) Ltd v Tugwell* [2000] 2 EGLR 59.

For the abandonment of a licence, see *Bone v Bone* [1992] EGCS 81 (no formalities are necessary: 'it is enough that the parties have so conducted themselves that it ought to be inferred that they have mutually agreed to bring the contract to an end').

[155] *Webb v Paternoster* (1619) Palm 71; *Wood v Lake* (1751) Say 3; *Winter v Brockwell* (1807) 8 East 308; *Tayler v Waters* (1816) 7 Taunt 374; *Wallis v Harrison* (1838) 4 M & W 538 at 544; *Feltham v Cartwright* (1839) 5 Bing NC 569; *Wood v Manley* (1839) 11 Ad & El 34 where, however, the licence was coupled with an interest, for the licensee was the owner of the hay; *Bendall v McWhirter* [1952] 2 QB 466 at 479, per Denning LJ; *Armstrong v Sheppard and Short Ltd* [1959] 2 QB 384; *Hounslow London Borough Council v Twickenham Garden Developments Ltd* [1971] Ch 233 at 255; (1965) 29 Conv (NS) 19 (M. C. Cullity).

[156] E.g. *Winter Garden Theatre (London) Ltd v Millennium Productions Ltd* [1948] AC 173, p. 1088, below.

[157] (1965) 29 Conv (NS) 19 at p. 31.   [158] See Dawson and Pearce, p. 31.

by Lord EVERSHED in *Armstrong v Sheppard and Short Ltd* [1959] 2 QB 384 at 399: 'If A gives authority to B for the doing of an act on A's land, and the act is done and completed, then, whatever be the strict description of the authority... it is, generally speaking at any rate, too late for A... to complain of it.'[159]

(iii) A licence is not the subject matter of a grant

This and the following proposition are closely related, and are both based upon the elementary rule that a grant of property is not revocable. A conveyance transfers to the grantee the subject matter of the grant, and it is beyond the grantor's power to recall.

But, of course, to be effective, the conveyance must have concerned something which the law recognises as being the subject matter of a grant and capable of being conveyed. A licensee, as stated above, is merely 'not a trespasser'. A licence is not a piece of property. But a licence may be coupled with a grant of an interest in property, real or personal, and, as shown in (iv) below, it will then be irrevocable.

In **Wood v Leadbitter** (1845) 13 M & W 838, 153 ER 351,[160] the plaintiff bought a ticket entitling him to enter the grandstand at Doncaster racecourse. On account of alleged malpractices on a previous occasion, he was ordered by the defendant, who was the servant of Lord Eglintoun, the steward of the course, to leave the racecourse. On his refusal, he was physically removed, no more force being used than was reasonably necessary. His action for assault and false imprisonment failed. He was a licensee only; and not a grantee of an interest in land. ALDERSON B, delivering the judgment of the Court of Exchequer, said at 845, at 354:

It may further be observed, that a license under seal (provided it be a mere license) is as revocable as a license by parol; and, on the other hand, a license by parol, coupled with a grant, is as irrevocable as a license by deed, provided only that the grant is of a nature capable of being made by parol. But where there is a license by parol, coupled with a parol grant, or pretended grant, of something which is incapable of being granted otherwise than by deed, there the license is a mere license; it is not an incident to a valid grant, and it is therefore revocable.

This may be logical; but hardly satisfactory. Where a licensee has paid to enter premises for a period of time, and he observes the terms and conditions of the licence, is it right that the licensor should be allowed to break the contract and turn the licensee into a trespasser?

In **Hurst v Picture Theatres Ltd** [1915] 1 KB 1, the plaintiff bought a ticket for 6d. to watch a cinema show at a theatre of the defendants. During the performance, the plaintiff was requested to leave on the ground, as the defendants incorrectly believed, that he had not paid for his ticket. He refused, and was ejected forcibly, but without the

---

[159] See *Hounslow London Borough Council v Twickenham Garden Developments Ltd* [1971] Ch 233 at 255.
[160] On the background to the case, see (1993) 14 Journal of Legal History 28 (P. Polden).

use of unnecessary violence. His action for assault and false imprisonment succeeded by a majority of 2 to 1. The majority (BUCKLEY and KENNEDY LJJ) found that he had an interest in the land. Since the Judicature Act, an interest in land could be granted without a deed. A contract for valuable consideration of which equity would decree specific performance would suffice.

The fallacy of this reasoning was shown by PHILLIMORE LJ, dissenting. The doctrine of *Walsh v Lonsdale* (1882) 21 Ch D 9, p. 30, above, he said, is that a man 'has the estate which equity thinks he ought to have. That has no bearing on the question if there is no estate, and no interest in land given by the document relied on'.

In short, contractual licences are not grants. They are contracts, and should be treated as such.

In **Cowell v Rosehill Racecourse Co Ltd** (1937) 56 CLR 605, LATHAM CJ said at 615:

The doctrine of *Wood v Leadbitter* is clear and coherent. If a man creates a proprietary right in another and gives him a licence to go upon certain land in order that he may use or enjoy that right, the grantor cannot divest the grantee of his proprietary right and revest it in the grantor, or simply determine it, by breaking the agreement under which the licence was given. The grantee owns the property to which the licence is incident, and this ownership, with its incidental licence, is unaffected by what purports to be a revocation of the licence. The revocation of the licence is ineffectual. Easements and *profits à prendre* supply examples of interests to which licences to enter and remain upon land may be incidental.

The majority judgment in *Hurst's* case modified, if it did not reject, the law of *Wood v Leadbitter* by holding that a 'right to see' a spectacle was an interest which could be granted so that a licence to go into a theatre or a racecourse to see a play or to witness races was, when given for value, irrevocable because it was a licence coupled with an interest. Further, the majority judgment held that, in so far as *Wood v Leadbitter* rested upon the rule that no incorporeal hereditament affecting land can be created or transferred otherwise than by deed, the Judicature Act had radically changed the position. The court was now bound to give effect to equitable doctrines and would therefore ignore the absence of a seal and would (as in *Frogley v Earl of Lovelace* (1859) John 333) grant an injunction to protect the right granted.

The first ground of the decision, in my opinion, ignores the distinction between a proprietary right and a contractual right. In *Wood v Leadbitter* there was obviously a contractual 'interest' in a sense quite different from that in which the word was used in *Wood v Leadbitter*. The learned judge said that there was a grant of a right to come to see a spectacle. The licence is described as 'only something granted to him for the purpose of enabling him to have that which had been granted to him, namely, the right to see.' The 'right to see' is treated as the 'interest' which has been 'granted.'

It is clear that the learned judge used the word 'grant' in a sense very different from that in which it was used in *Wood v Leadbitter*. It was there used in relation to interests in land which were, if they existed at all, clearly proprietary interests. The right to see a spectacle cannot, in the ordinary sense of legal language, be regarded as a proprietary interest. Fifty thousand people who pay to see a football match do not obtain fifty thousand interests in the football ground.

The second ground of the decision in *Hurst's* case is based upon the opinion that the plaintiff in *Wood v Leadbitter* failed because he did not have a grant under seal of the right which he claimed. It is true that the absence of a seal was a complete reply, in an action at law, to the contention of the plaintiff that he had an interest in the land upon which a race meeting was being held. But in fact the presence of a seal would not have assisted the plaintiff to establish the impossible proposition that he had an easement in gross. It is true that, as the majority judgments in *Hurst's* case state, a grant of an interest in land need not, in order to be effective in a court of equity, be made by deed, and that, since the Judicature Act, this rule is enforced in all divisions of the High Court in England: *Walsh v Lonsdale* (1882) 21 ChD 9, [p. 30, above]. But this proposition does not justify the assertion that interests in land can, since the Judicature Act, be created by simple contract even though, before that Act, they were of such a character that they could not be created by deed as interests in land. Buckley LJ applies to the facts of *Hurst's* case the statement of Parker J in *James Jones & Sons Ltd v Earl of Tankerville* [1909] 2 Ch 440 at 443 that an injunction restraining the revocation of a licence 'merely prevents' the defendant 'from breaking his contract, and protects a right in equity which but for the absence of a seal would be a right at law, and since the *Judicature Act* it may well be doubted whether the absence of a seal in such a case can be relied on in any court.' This statement was made with respect to a proprietary right (a *profit à prendre*) and it is a begging of the question to apply it to a case in which the matter in dispute is whether the alleged interest is such that it can be an interest in land, whether created by deed or not. *Frogley v Earl of Lovelace,* which is relied upon in *Hurst's* case, was a case of an agreement for a *profit à prendre,* an incorporeal hereditament. Thus the second ground for the majority judgments in *Hurst's* case cannot, in my opinion, be supported. I regard the dissenting judgment of Phillimore LJ as a convincing statement of the true position both at law and in equity.

(iv) A licence coupled with a grant (or an interest) is irrevocable

It is an anciently established rule that a licence coupled with a proprietary interest (in land or in a chattel) is irrevocable.[161] The interest must, of course, have been correctly granted. In the grant of incorporeal hereditaments in realty at common law, a deed was needed; but, since the Judicature Act, a specifically enforceable contract to grant an interest suffices to create in equity the equivalent interest.[162]

In the case of licences coupled with a chattel interest, that interest must again be properly granted, usually by gift or sale. Thus, where the occupier gives or sells a stack of coal on the land to a purchaser, the donee or purchaser is entitled to enter the land to take away the coal, and the donor or seller cannot deny him the right.[163] And a contract to cut and carry away timber on the Earl of Tankerville's Estate[164] created a chattel interest in the cut timber and a realty interest in the growing trees.

---

[161] *Webb v Paternoster* (1619) Palm 71; *Wood v Manley* (1839) 11 Ad & El 34; *James Jones & Sons Ltd v Earl of Tankerville* [1909] 2 Ch 440.

[162] *Walsh v Lonsdale* (1882) 21 ChD 9, p. 30, above.

[163] *Wood v Manley* (1839) 11 Ad & El 34.

[164] *James Jones & Sons Ltd v Earl of Tankerville* [1909] 2 Ch 440.

B. LICENCES FOR CONSIDERATION:
CONTRACTUAL LICENCES[165]

(i) The contract

Before a licensee can seek a remedy by virtue of the contract he must show that the revocation of the licence was in breach of contract. This means, in the first place, showing that there was a contract, which is not always straightforward in a domestic context where there is generally a presumption against a contract based on the absence of an intention to create legal relations.[166] In the second place, the licensee must show that there is a breach: that is, that the terms of licence, under the express or implied terms of the contract, were such that the licensor's purported revocation is wrongful. The crucial question in considering the revocability of contractual licences is whether the licence is revocable according to the proper construction of the contract.[167] Express provision will often be made. In its absence, the right to revoke will depend upon the intention of the parties as gathered from all the surrounding circumstances. There is no presumption one way or the other;[168] but it will presumably be more difficult to establish the non-revocability of a licence unlimited in time than it would be in the case of a licence for a specific period. The court may find that the licensor has a right to revoke upon giving reasonable notice, and will determine what that period is.

(ii) Damages for breach of contract

It has been seen that much confusion has been caused by the inability of the common law to give protection to a contractual licensee unless he has a proprietary interest in the land or chattels upon it. This position, based upon *Wood v Leadbitter*, meant that the licensor could, without giving any reason, turn out at will any watchers of a cinema show, horse race or football match.[169] The only difference between a contractual and

---

[165] C & B, pp. 834–839; Gray, part 10.3; M & W, paras 34.004, 34.008–34.011, 34.016–34.019; MM, pp. 477–482; Smith, pp. 456–464; Dawson and Pearce, pp. 24–38, 73–97, 133–144, 153–161, 167. See Megarry J's summary in *Hounslow London Borough Council v Twickenham Garden Developments Ltd* [1971] Ch 233 at 254; *Chandler v Kerley* [1978] 1 WLR 693, p. 1090, below.

[166] CFF, chap. 5. In *Tanner v Tanner* [1975] 1 WLR 1346 Lord Denning MR said that 'the court should imply a contract by [the licensor, the father of the licensee's children]—or, if need be, impose the equivalent of a contract by him'. See also *Chandler v Kerley* [1978] 1 WLR 693, p. 1090, below. No contract was implied in similar circumstances in *Horrocks v Forray* [1976] 1 WLR 230 (described in (1976) 40 Conv (NS) 362 (M. Richards) as '*Tanner v Tanner* in a middle class setting'); *Coombes v Smith* [1986] 1 WLR 808 (no contract implied that man would provide mistress with house for rest of her life).

[167] In *Winter Garden Theatre (London) Ltd v Millennium Productions Ltd* [1948] AC 173, p. 1088, below, HL construed the licence as being revocable by the licensor; CA, however, had construed it as irrevocable.

[168] Ibid at 203, per Lord Macdermott. Lord Porter said at 195 that a licence was prima facie revocable. See also *Re Spenborough UDC's Agreement* [1968] Ch 139; *Beverley Corpn v Richard Hodgson & Sons Ltd* (1972) 225 EG 799.

[169] Per Phillimore LJ in *Hurst v Picture Theatres Ltd* [1915] 1 KB 1, p. 1083, above; *Cowell v Rosehill Racecourse Co Ltd* (1937) 56 CLR 605, p. 1084, above.

a gratuitous licence was that, in the former, the licensor must pay damages.[170] These were commonly assumed to be the price which the licensee had paid to enter. But there seems to be no reason why the damages should not reflect the loss of the licensee's expectation under the contract, or the sum which the licensor might reasonably have been expected to pay to the licensor for the surrender of the licence.[171]

(iii) Injunction to restrain breach of contract

The more realistic question, however, is whether a licensee may obtain a remedy to prevent the revocation of the licence. The plain fact is that the common law had no appropriate remedy; and this may explain the development of the tenuous and unsatisfactory common law doctrine that a licence, once entered upon, was irrevocable.[172]

After the Judicature Act 1873, equitable remedies became available.[173] We saw that, in *Hurst's* case,[174] the Court of Appeal found that the licensee should be protected; but only by reasoning the weakness of which is shown in the dissenting judgment of Phillimore LJ, and in the judgment of Latham CJ in *Cowell v Rosehill Racecourse Co Ltd* (1937) 56 CLR 605, p. 1084, above. The availability of equitable rights and remedies is vital in this situation. If, on a proper construction of the contract, the licensor has no right to revoke, the question is whether the case is one in which it is appropriate to protect the licensee by an injunction restraining the licensor from breaking the contract, or whether the licensee should be left to his remedy in damages. The normal way of protecting a contractual licensee against wrongful revocation is by issuing an injunction to restrain the breach by the licensor. And, as we shall see, the Court of Appeal has held that a contractual licence may also be enforceable by a decree of specific performance.[175]

A licensee who is himself in breach of the terms of the contractual licence will not be protected;[176] nor presumably if the effect of the injunction would be to compel people to live together in intolerable circumstances.[177] And it has been held that a

---

[170] *Kerrison v Smith* [1897] 2 QB 445 was the first case to decide that an action will lie for damages revoking a licence.

[171] *Tanner v Tanner* [1975] 1 WLR 1346 at 1352, per Brightman LJ. This is similar to the measure of damages for breach of a restrictive covenant under *Wrotham Park Estate Co v Parkside Homes Ltd* [1974] 1 WLR 798, p. 750, n. 52, above.

[172] P. 1082, above.

[173] And, in case of conflict with the common law, equity prevails: p. 31, n. 84, above.

[174] [1915] 1 KB 1, p. 1083, above. The plaintiff received £150 as damages for assault and false imprisonment.

[175] *Verrall v Great Yarmouth Borough Council* [1981] QB 202, p. 1094, below.

[176] *Thompson v Park* [1944] KB 408, where the defendant had 'been guilty at least of riot, affray, wilful damage, forcible entry, and, perhaps, conspiracy', per Goddard LJ at 409. The defendant was a preparatory school master who had moved, with his pupils, to the plaintiff's school when the defendant's premises were unavailable because of the war.

[177] Ibid, per Goddard LJ at 409.

licensee, whose occupation of premises was dependent upon his employment, was not protected where he was dismissed in breach of contract.[178]

In **Winter Garden Theatre (London) Ltd v Millennium Productions Ltd** [1948] AC 173, the appellants granted to the respondents a licence to use and present plays in the Winter Garden Theatre in Drury Lane for a period of six months, from 6 July 1942, with an option to renew for a further six months at an increased payment. The licence provided that on the expiration of these periods the respondents should have the option to continue the licence for an unstated period, terminable by them at a month's notice. No provision was made for termination by the appellants. The options were duly exercised. The appellants retained possession of the bars and cloakrooms. After three years the appellants wished to terminate the licence, and on 11 September 1945 served a notice requiring the respondents to vacate the theatre on 13 October 1945. The respondents refused to leave and brought an action for a declaration that the licence was not revocable; or, alternatively, if it was, that a reasonable period after the service of the notice had not expired.

The House of Lords held that, on the proper construction of the contract, the licence was terminable on giving reasonable notice, and that the notice given was reasonable. The question of wrongful revocation did not arise. But, on that subject, Lord UTHWATT said at 202:

My view as to the construction of the agreement renders it unnecessary to consider whether *Hurst v Picture Theatres Ltd* [1915] 1 KB 1 [p. 1083, above] was rightly decided, or to express any concluded opinion on the question of the remedies now open in every court to a bare licensee who claims that the licensor has in breach of his bargain affected to revoke it. I merely confess my present inability to see any answer to the propositions of law stated by the Master of the Rolls in his judgment in the case under appeal.[179] The settled practice of the courts of equity is to do what they can by an injunction to preserve the sanctity of a bargain. To my mind, as at present advised, a licensee who has refused to accept the wrongful repudiation of the bargain which is involved in an unauthorised revocation of the licence is as much entitled to the protection of an injunction as a licensee who has not received any notice of revocation; and, if the remedy of injunction is properly available in the latter case against unauthorised interference by the licensor, it is also available in the former case. In a court of equity, wrongful acts are no passport to favour.

The Court of Appeal in this case had been faced with the question of the proper solution to the problem of the protection of a contractual licensee under a contract which was construed as irrevocable; it had taken a different view from the House of

---

[178] *Ivory v Palmer* [1975] ICR 340. For a consideration of the question of the circumstances in which misbehaviour by a licensee whose licence is protected by proprietary estoppel will allow his licence to be terminated, see *Williams v Staite* [1979] Ch 291; *Brynowen Estates Ltd v Bourne* (1981) 131 NLJ 1212; *Willis & Sons v Willis* [1986] 1 EGLR 62; *Manton Securities Ltd v Nazam* [2008] EWCA Civ 805, [2008] 2 P & CR DG19.

[179] Below.

Lords of the construction of the contract. The statement of the law by Lord GREENE MR, referred to by Lord Uthwatt is as follows [1946] 1 All ER 678 at 684:

The next question which I must mention is this. The respondents[180] have purported to determine the licence. If I have correctly construed the contract their doing so was a breach of contract. It may well be that, in the old days, that would only have given rise to a right to sue for damages. The licence would have stood revoked, but after the expiration of what was the appropriate period of grace the licensees would have been trespassers and could have been expelled, and their right would have been to sue for damages for breach of contract, as was said in *Kerrison v Smith* [1897] 2 QB 445. But the matter requires to be considered further, because the power of equity to grant an injunction to restrain a breach of contract is, of course, a power exercisable in any court. The general rule is that, before equity will grant such an injunction, there must be, on the construction of the contract, a negative clause express or implied. In the present case it seems to me that the grant of an option which, if I am right, is an irrevocable option, must imply a negative undertaking by the licensor not to revoke it. That being so, in my opinion, such a contract could be enforced in equity by an injunction. Then the question would arise, at what time can equity interfere? If the licensor were threatening to revoke, equity, I apprehend, would grant an injunction to restrain him from carrying out that threat. But supposing he has in fact purported to revoke, is equity then to say: 'We are now powerless. We cannot stop you from doing anything to carry into effect your wrongful revocation?' I apprehend not. I apprehend equity would say: 'You have revoked and the licensee had no opportunity of stopping you doing so by an injunction; but what the court of equity can do is to prevent you from carrying that revocation into effect and restrain you from doing anything under it.' In the present case, nothing has been done. The appellants are still there. I can see no reason at all why, on general principles, equity should not interfere to restrain the licensors from acting upon the purported revocation, that revocation being, as I consider, a breach of contract.

Looking at it in that rather simple way, one is not concerned with the difficulties which are suggested to arise from the decision of this court in *Hurst v Picture Theatres Ltd* [1915] 1 KB 1, p. 1083, above. Counsel for the respondents agreed that in this court he could not ask us to take a different view to the view there taken. It is a decision which has not satisfied everybody, but, quite apart from that decision, the simple propositions which I have just enunciated, which I cannot help thinking are right, would appear to me to get round any difficulties which might be felt as to the reasoning in *Hurst v Picture Theatres Ltd*. We are not concerned here with a licence coupled with a grant. Nothing of that kind is suggested. It is not suggested that that type of licence is in question here. It is a pure licence and nothing else, and the breach of the licence contract by the licensor could be restrained by a court of equity, and a court of equity would interfere to prevent the licensor taking steps pursuant to this wrongful revocation. That seems to me to put the matter right so far as this case is concerned.[181]

---

[180] I.e., *Winter Garden Theatre (London) Ltd* who became the appellants in the House of Lords.

[181] See also *Hounslow London Borough Council v Twickenham Garden Developments Ltd* [1971] Ch 233 at 254, where Megarry J summarised the law relating to contractual licences; (1971) 87 LQR 309; *Mayfield Holdings Ltd v Moana Reef Ltd* [1973] 1 NZLR 309.

Chandler v Kerley
[1978] 1 WLR 693 (CA, **Lord Scarman, Megaw** and **Roskill LJJ**)[182]

Lord Scarman: This appeal is concerned with the right to occupy a dwelling-house, 30 Salisbury Road, Testwood, Totton, in Hampshire. The plaintiff owns it: the defendant, with her two children, occupies it. She will not leave, because she says the plaintiff has agreed that she may stay there as long as she pleases. The plaintiff went to the Southampton County Court with a claim for possession, alleging that the defendant was a trespasser, her licence having been terminated. The defendant not only resisted the claim, but also counterclaimed for a declaration that she is a tenant for life, alternatively that 'she is the beneficiary under a trust... upon terms that she is entitled to remain therein with her children for as long as she wishes.' In this court the defendant was allowed, the plaintiff not opposing, to amend her counterclaim by adding in the further alternative that she is a licensee for life, or for so long as her children remain in her custody and the younger is of school age and so long as she does not remarry, or for a period terminable only by reasonable notice.

On 26 May 1977, Judge McCreery dismissed the plaintiff's claim and gave judgment for the defendant on the counterclaim, declaring that the defendant is a beneficiary under a trust upon terms that she is entitled to occupy the house for her life or for so long as she pleases. The plaintiff now appeals.

The facts are unusual. The plaintiff, Mr Chandler, acquired the house from the defendant, Mrs Kerley, and her husband in the following circumstances. In 1972 Mr and Mrs Kerley jointly bought the house for £11,000, intending it to be their family home. The purchase was partly financed by a building society mortgage for £5,800. Mr Kerley paid the mortgage instalments. They have two children, both of whom are now living with their mother. In 1974 the marriage broke down. In May of that year Mr Kerley left home, not to return. However, he continued to pay the building society instalments. The defendant and the children continued to live in the house.

At about the time Mr Kerley left home, the defendant met the plaintiff. They became friends: sexual intercourse followed, and the defendant became the plaintiff's mistress. This relationship continued until January 1976, when it ended.

Early in 1975 Mr Kerley stopped paying the building society: he said he could not afford it. He and his wife put the house on the market for £14,950, but failed to find a buyer—even when in the autumn they reduced the asking price to £14,300. Meanwhile the building society was threatening to foreclose. The defendant naturally told the plaintiff of her anxieties. He wanted to help, and said he could afford £10,000, but no more. Finally, it was agreed that the Kerleys should sell the house to the plaintiff for that figure, and the house was sold to him in December 1975. The net proceeds of sale, after they had paid off the debt to the building society, were divided—£1,000 to the defendant and £1,800 to Mr Kerley. The defendant accepted less than her half-share because she understood that the plaintiff was going to let her live in the house.

The arrangement between the plaintiff and the defendant which made all this possible was, according to the judge's findings, the following. The plaintiff agreed to buy the house for £10,000 (a figure substantially less than the asking price) upon the understanding that the

---

[182] *Roach v Johannes* [1976] CLY 1549 (licence of 'paying guest' terminable on giving reasonable notice, which in the circumstances was not less than 21 days); *Piguet v Tyler* [1978] CLY 119 (irrevocable licence for life of defendants, who had, by arrangement with plaintiff, surrendered protected tenancy to look after plaintiff's aged mother).

defendant would continue to live in it indefinitely till he moved in. For at this time, 1975, they contemplated living together in the house as man and wife once they were free to do so, that is to say, after a divorce between Mr and Mrs Kerley. The defendant, very sensibly, did ask the plaintiff what would happen if they parted: he replied that he could not put her out.

Within six weeks of the purchase of the house, the plaintiff had brought their relationship to an end. It was not suggested, however, that he did so in order to get the defendant out of the house. Nevertheless he did purport in 1976 to serve a notice terminating her licence. It was given by solicitors' letter dated April 29 requiring the lady to quit on May 28.

The judge found that the plaintiff had granted the defendant an express licence and that the notice was not effectual to terminate it. There is now no challenge to these findings. The defendant is, therefore, a licensee, whose right to occupy has not yet been terminated. In so far, therefore, as the appeal is against the dismissal of the plaintiff's claim for possession, it must fail. The true dispute, however, between the parties arises on the counterclaim. There are two substantial issues: (1) the terms of the licence; and (2) whether the defendant has an equitable interest arising under a constructive trust; and, if so, what is the extent of the interest.

The judge's findings as to the terms of the licence are obscure. He rejected the submission made on behalf of the defendant that she had an implied licence to remain in the house all her life: yet he also held (and I quote from the notes of judgment) 'that there was an express agreement between the two and, as a result, there was a constructive trust with Mr Chandler as trustee and Mrs Kerley being the beneficiary.' It is possible, though certainly not clear to me, that the judge is here finding an express agreement that she may remain for life: for he certainly granted her a declaration that she had an equity to that effect. But, whatever the finding as to the terms of the agreement, the reasoning of the judge in this passage is, in my judgment, unsound. If the defendant can establish a licence for life, there is neither room nor need for an equitable interest. Since the fusion of law and equity, such a legal right can be protected by injunction: see *Hurst v Picture Theatres Ltd* [1915] 1 KB 1 [p. 1083, above], *Winter Garden Theatre (London) Ltd v Millennium Productions Ltd* [1948] AC 173 [p. 1088, above] and *Foster v Robinson* [1951] 1 KB 149 per Lord Evershed MR, at 156. If she cannot establish such a licence (express or implied), she cannot establish an equity: for no question of estoppel arises in this case. It is simply a case of what the parties envisaged by their arrangement: see *Dodsworth v Dodsworth* (1973) 228 EG 1115 [p. 1068, below], where the Court of Appeal considered it not right to confer upon the defendants a greater interest than was envisaged by the parties. In the present case the parties certainly intended that the arrangement between them should have legal consequences. If, therefore, they agreed upon a right of occupation for life, there is a binding contract to that effect: if they did not so agree, there is nothing to give rise to an equity to that effect.

In a case such as the present, the role of equity is supportive and supplementary. Where the parties have contracted for a licence, equity will today provide an equitable remedy to protect the legal right, for example by injunction, which may be by interlocutory order, if the court considers it just and convenient: see section 45, Supreme Court of Judicature (Consolidation) Act 1925.[183] If, however, the legal relationship between the parties is such that the true arrangement envisaged by the parties will be frustrated if the parties are left to their rights and duties at law, an equity will arise which the courts can satisfy by appropriate equitable relief. An old illustration of equity at work in this way was given by Parker J in *Jones v Earl of Tankerville*

---

[183] Now Supreme Court Act 1981, s. 37.

[1909] 2 Ch 440, 443 (quoted in *Hurst's* case [1915] 1 KB 1, 9). Likewise in another old case, *Frogley v Earl of Lovelace* (1859) John 333, Page Wood V-C granted an injunction to restrain the defendant from interfering with the plaintiff shooting over his land 'until the defendant shall have executed a proper legal grant of the right claimed by the plaintiff.'

The judge in the present case believed he was constrained by the decision in *Bannister v Bannister* [1948] 2 All ER 133 [p. 1101, below] to declare the existence of a right of occupation for life, even though he had rejected an implied contractual right to that effect. But, when analysed, *Bannister v Bannister is* no more than an illustration of the supportive and supplementary role of equity. It was a case in which the plaintiff gave an oral undertaking that the defendant would be allowed to live in the cottage rent-free for as long as she desired. The defendant could not show a legal right: but she did establish the existence of an understanding or arrangement with the plaintiff which, though giving rise to no legal right, brought into existence an equity which the court thought it just to satisfy by declaring the defendant had an equitable life interest in the cottage with the plaintiff as her trustee. The court treated this life interest as the equivalent to a tenancy for life under the Settled Land Act 1925.[184]

Errington v Errington and Woods [1952] 1 KB 290 [p. 1099, below] is a decision which follows the same pattern. The arrangement in that case was oral. The father bought a house, put his son and daughter-in-law into occupation and promised them that if they paid the instalments on the mortgage the house would be theirs when the last instalment was paid. The Court of Appeal held that the arrangement conferred upon the daughter-in-law (father having died, son having left his wife and she continuing to pay the instalments) a contractual right of occupation which carried with it an equity which on payment of the last instalment would give her a good equitable title to the house. The case may be said to be a classic illustration of equity supplementing a contractual right so as to give effect to the intention of the parties to the arrangement. *Binions v Evans* [1972] Ch 359 [p. 1102, below] is to the same effect.

The defendant in this appeal, however, relied strongly on *Bannister v Bannister* to support a submission that she has a tenancy for life. Like Megaw LJ in *Binions v Evans* at 370, I find great difficulty in understanding how the court in *Bannister's* case came to conclude that there was in that case a tenancy for life under the Act. It was, however, a matter which depended upon the particular facts of the case.

As Russell LJ commented in *Dodsworth v Dodsworth* (1973) 228 EG 1115 [p. 1068, above], there is a risk that such an inference may fall foul of the Settled Land Act 1925, which confers a power of sale and of leasing upon the tenant—powers which cannot, for instance, have been in the minds of the parties in the present case. The present is *not*, in my judgment, a case of life tenancy: and in this respect *Bannister v Bannister* is a decision to be treated as turning on the particular facts of that case.

The most recent case to which we were referred is the decision of the Court of Appeal in *Tanner v Tanner* [1975] 1 WLR 1346. It is close on its facts to the present case, in that the defendant was found to have no proprietary interest in the house but did have a contractual right to live in it until her two children, of whom the plaintiff was the father, were no longer of school age. The defendant had been the mistress of the plaintiff, who had bought the house (when she had been a tenant protected by the Rent Act) to provide accommodation for her and their two children. The court held it to be a case of contractual licence, Lord Denning MR saying at 1350:

---

[184] For the problems of finding a SLA settlement in this context, see p. 1061, n. 110, above.

'It was a contractual licence of the kind which is specifically enforceable on her behalf: and which he can be restrained from breaking: and he could not sell the house over her head so as to get her out in that way.'

It is yet another case of a contractual licence supported by equity so far, and only so far, as is necessary to give effect to the expectations of the parties when making their arrangement.

Accordingly, the task in this case is to determine what were the terms of the arrangement, express and implied, between the parties. I agree with the judge that it is not possible to imply a licence to the defendant to occupy the house for her life. The plaintiff had invested £10,000 in the house and, in the absence of express stipulation, cannot be supposed in the circumstances to have frozen his capital for as long as the defendant pleased or for the duration of her life. On the other hand, the plaintiff was well aware that the defendant wanted the house as a home for her children as well as for herself. It would be wrong, however, to infer, in the absence of an express promise, that the plaintiff was assuming the burden of housing another man's wife and children indefinitely, and long after his relationship with them had ended. The balance of these factors leads me to the conclusion that the defendant's contractual licence was terminable upon reasonable notice, and that the notice must be such as to give the defendant ample opportunity to re-house herself and her children without disruption. In my judgment 12 calendar months' notice is reasonable in the circumstances.

For these reasons I do not think this is a case in which it is necessary to invoke the support of any equitable doctrine. The defendant is entitled to 12 months' notice. It follows that the appeal against the dismissal of the claim to possession fails in my judgment, the licence not yet having been determined. The order upon the counterclaim should, in my judgment, be varied so as to substitute for the declaration granted by the judge a declaration that the defendant's licence is terminable upon reasonable notice and that reasonable notice is one of 12 calendar months from its service.

In **Hardwick v Johnson** [1978] 1 WLR 683 a mother purchased a house for occupation by her son and daughter-in-law as their home. Rent of £7 per week was payable, but it ceased to be paid after a month or two, and the mother did not demand it. Within a year the marriage was collapsing, and the son was about to leave his wife. The mother sued for possession and arrears of rent. The daughter-in-law gave birth to a child, and claimed to be entitled to remain in possession on paying £7 a week. The Court of Appeal held that the licence was irrevocable. The daughter-in-law was not in breach in respect of the arrears because the mother had indicated no desire to claim the rent. ROSKILL LJ said at 690:

When one looks at the correspondence before action brought and indeed at the pleadings, one sees an ever increasing number of legal arguments being found upon a perfectly simple family arrangement; but in my judgment this case can be decided upon one very short ground. It is plain, as the deputy judge said, that there was here never any tenancy. It is equally plain, in my judgment, that there was here a licence; and for my part, with respect to Lord Denning MR, I prefer to call it a contractual licence rather than an equitable licence.

The only question we have to decide is what was the nature of that contractual licence. Was it a licence to both the son and his future wife as joint licensees or was it a licence to the son alone? Nobody contemplated the possibility that this marriage would break down as soon as it did. Nobody contemplated that the son would within a couple of years or so go off and have an affair with another woman, abandoning his wife with the child of the marriage who remained in the house. What the parties would have agreed upon if they had thought of that possibility in March 1973 no one can tell; but the court, as Lord Denning MR has said and as has been said many times before (and Lord Diplock also said it in *Pettitt v Pettitt* [1970] AC 777, 821–823), has in those circumstances to impute to the parties a common intention to make some arrangement in the events which have occurred, albeit unexpectedly. I cannot, for my part, think that anybody would impute to these parties an intention that if the marriage broke down as soon as it did and the husband went off with another woman the wife would be liable to be ejected from the home together with the child of the marriage. It seems to me that the arrangement was perfectly straightforward: it was a joint contractual licence to the husband and wife to live there. It was not conditional upon the marriage succeeding. It was not conditional upon a number of other possibilities.

I am disinclined to express any opinion on what if any events that licence is now determinable. Suffice it to say that in my judgment it is not determinable in the event which has occurred, namely, that the husband has left the wife—no divorce proceedings are pending, as Lord Denning MR has said—since that licence was not given only to the husband. It seems to me that no event has yet taken place which justifies the bringing to an end of this contractual licence; and therefore, for that reason, I think the deputy circuit judge reached the right conclusion in a careful and closely reasoned judgment.

Lord Denning said that the licence was a personal equitable licence. Browne LJ delivered a judgment agreeing with Roskill LJ.

(iv) Specific performance

Verrall v Great Yarmouth Borough Council
[1981] QB 202 (CA, **Lord Denning MR, Roskill** and **Cumming-Bruce LJJ**)

The Conservative council of Great Yarmouth agreed in April 1979 to a two-day hiring of the Wellington Pier Pavilion by the National Front for its annual conference in October. In May 1979 the council, following a change in its political control to Labour, purported to repudiate the contract. An action was brought on behalf of the National Front for specific performance.

Held. Specific performance granted.

Lord Denning MR: Since the *Winter Garden* case, it is clear that once a man has entered under his contract of licence, he cannot be turned out. An injunction can be obtained against the licensor to prevent his being turned out. On principle it is the same if it happens before he enters. If he has a contractual right to enter, and the licensor refuses to let him come in, then he can come to the court and in a proper case get an order for specific performance to allow him to come in. An illustration was taken in the course of the argument. Supposing one of the great political parties—say, the Conservative Party—had booked its hall at Brighton for its conference in September of this year: it had made all its arrangements accordingly: it had all its delegates coming: it had booked its hotels, and so on. Would it be open to the local council to repudiate that agreement, and say that the Conservative Party could not go there? Would the only remedy be damages? Clearly not. The court would order the council in such a case to perform its contracts. It would be the same in the case of the Labour Party, or whoever it may be. When arrangements are made for a licence of this kind of such importance and magnitude affecting many people, the licensors cannot be allowed to repudiate it and simply pay damages. It must be open to the court to grant specific performance in such cases....

The newly constituted council is bound by what the old constituted council did. The newly constituted council must honour the contract. I see no sufficient reason for not holding the council to their contract. In the interests of our fundamental freedoms—freedom of speech, freedom of assembly, and the importance of holding people to their contracts—we ought to grant specific performance in this case, as the judge did.

(v) Enforcement of contractual licences against third parties

The next question is whether a contractual licence, which is irrevocable by the licensor, is binding on a third party. On the one hand, it is well settled that, subject to few exceptions, contractual rights are binding on the parties to the contract only.[185] On the other hand, the protection given to the licensee may be of little use if a transfer of the land to a third party leaves that third party free to claim possession, and leaves the licensee to his remedy in damages against the original licensor. Further, it might be argued[186] that a licensee's right to protection by injunction against the licensor gives him some sort of equity, and it is arguable that such an equity should give him protection against all but bona fide purchasers for value without notice.

Whether or not contractual licences should be held to be binding on third parties is ultimately a policy question. So it has been in other areas of the law. Contractual restrictions on the use of chattels have been held not to be binding on third parties even though they have express notice of the restriction.[187] By contrast, the great case of *Tulk v Moxhay*[188] decided that a covenant restricting the user of land was binding on successors in title of the covenantor taking with notice. It was soon found that so wide a doctrine would create burdens on land for which there was no justification, and the basis of the doctrine was later changed so as to limit the running of the burden to cases in which the continuation of the covenant was necessary to protect land capable of benefiting; more like a negative equitable easement.[189] The point is that the whole

---

[185] The doctrine of privity of contract provides at common law that only the parties to a contract can sue on it, or be sued under it: *Tweddle v Atkinson* (1861) 1 B & S 393; *Dunlop Pneumatic Tyre Co Ltd v Selfridge & Co Ltd* [1915] AC 847; *Beswick v Beswick* [1968] AC 58; *Woodar Investment Development Ltd v Wimpey Construction (UK) Ltd* [1980] 1 WLR 277; CFF, chap. 14; Treitel, chap. 14. An important exception to the privity rule was made by the Contracts (Third Rights of Third Parties) Act 1999, p. 771, above; but this only allows a third party in defined circumstances to take the *benefit* of a contract, and does not allow a contract to *burden* a third party.

[186] *Errington v Errington and Woods* [1952] 1 KB 290 at 298–299, quoted and criticised by Fox LJ in *Ashburn Anstalt v Anstalt* [1989] Ch 1 at 16–17; p. 1097, below.

[187] *De Mattos v Gibson* (1858) 4 De G & J 276; *Lord Strathcona Steamship Co Ltd v Dominion Coal Ltd* [1926] AC 108; *Port Line Ltd v Ben Line Steamers Ltd* [1958] 2 QB 146. See however, *Swiss Bank Corpn v Lloyds Bank Ltd* [1979] Ch 548 at 569–575; revsd. on different grounds [1982] AC 584; (1982) 98 LQR 279 (S. Gardner).

[188] (1848) 2 Ph 774, p. 754, above.   [189] Pp. 751–753, above.

question whether an equity enforceable against one contracting party is enforceable against third parties is determined, not by a rule of thumb, but by an examination of the policy questions applicable to the particular situation.

On this basis, it would seem clear that contractual licences should not, in the ordinary case, be binding on third parties. Otherwise, thousands of minor personal arrangements, like hotel bookings, contracts for lodgings, car parking contracts, and a host of other minor non-proprietary arrangements would in effect come on to the title; with no effective way of determining the question whether or not the third party had notice. After all, the contractual licensee has his remedy in damages.

Authority is to the same effect.[190] In spite of the privity of contract rule, however, a contractual licensee may be able to enforce a right against a third party, if the facts give rise to some other legal relationship outside the sphere of contract, i.e. under the doctrine of proprietary estoppel or of the constructive trust. In both these spheres, which require different criteria of proof and give rise to different remedies, the licensee acquires either an equity as a licensee protected by proprietary estoppel or an equitable interest as a beneficiary under a trust, which is capable of being enforced against a third party. *Errington v Errington* [1952] 1 KB 290, p. 1099, below is generally accepted as being a case of a contractual licence. But there is clearly an estoppel situation also. In *Binions v Evans* [1972] Ch 359, p. 1102, below, the conveyance was made expressly subject to the contractual right of the licensee; and this was held to create a constructive trust. In *Ashburn Anstalt v Arnold* [1989] Ch 1, p. 1097, below, however, the Court of Appeal took the view that the mere fact that land is expressed to be conveyed 'subject to' a contract does not necessarily imply that the grantee is to be under an obligation, not otherwise existing, to give effect to the provisions of the contract. In *DHN Food Distributors Ltd v Tower Hamlets London Borough Council* [1976] 1 WLR 852[191] an irrevocable contractual licence was said, as one of three rationes in the case, to give rise to a constructive trust, and to 'give to DHN a sufficient interest in the land to qualify them for compensation for disturbance' upon compulsory purchase by the local authority. In *Re Sharpe* [1980] 1 WLR 219, p. 1109, below, an irrevocable licence to occupy a house until a loan was repaid, 'whether it be called a contractual licence or an equitable licence or an interest under a constructive trust', was held to be binding on the trustee in bankruptcy of the licensor.

It will be obvious that this possibility of the multiple characterisation of the right gives to the court the powers which it needs to reach a just solution.[192]

---

[190] *Clore v Theatrical Properties Ltd and Westby & Co Ltd* [1936] 3 All ER 483; *King v David Allen & Sons, Billposting Ltd* [1916] 2 AC 54, below; *Ashburn Anstalt v Arnold* [1989] Ch 1, p. 1097, below. See also *Midland Bank Ltd v Farm Pride Hatcheries Ltd* (1980) 260 EG 493, p. 62, above, where the issue of the binding effect of a contractual licence on a third party was not raised; *Lloyd v Dugdale* [2002] 2 P & CR 167, per Sir Christopher Slade, p. 1106, below.

[191] (1977) 93 LQR 170 (D. Sugarman and F. Webb); (1977) 41 Conv (NS) 73; p. 1111, below.

[192] For the multiple characterisation of the rights of the licensee see p. 1109, below.

King v David Allen and Sons, Billposting Ltd
[1916] 2 AC 54 (HL, **Lord Buckmaster LC,**
Earl Loreburn and **Lord Atkinson**)

By an agreement of 1 July 1913, the appellant gave to the respondents an exclusive permission to affix advertisements for a stated period to the walls of a cinema which was to be built.

In September 1913 the appellant executed a lease of the property to the cinema company, but the lease, disregarding arrangements previously made, contained no reference to the agreement of 1 July. The company refused to allow the advertisement to be posted and the respondents brought an action against the appellant King, for breach of the agreement of 1 July.

Held. The appellant (the licensor) was liable in damages.

Earl Loreburn: My Lords, I agree in the opinion expressed by the Lord Chancellor, and with him I greatly regret the position in which Mr King has been placed, which seems to me to be hard upon him. He has behaved perfectly honestly in the whole business, and one cannot help regretting the expense to which he has been put.

I have very little to add to what has been said, but I look at the case in this way. The plaintiffs say that Mr King promised them for four years the use of a certain wall for advertising purposes by the agreement of July 1, 1913, and they say that after that Mr King demised that land, and that Mr King's lessees refused to make good the promise in regard to advertisement. Well, if the agreement of July 1, which purports to be on the face of it a licence, was equivalent to creating an incorporeal hereditament or a sufficient interest in land, Mr King did not break his contract in making the lease, and would not be responsible for any trespasses that were committed by his licensees. But we must look at the document itself, and it seems to me that it does not create any interest in land at all; it merely amounts to a promise on the part of Mr King that he would allow the other party to the contract to use the wall for advertising purposes, and there was an implied undertaking that he would not disable himself from carrying out his contract. Now Mr King has altered his legal position in respect of his control of this land. Those to whom he granted the lease have disregarded his wishes and refused to allow his bargain to be carried out, and they have been practically enabled to do so by reason of the demise that he executed. In these circumstances it seems to me that there has been a breach in law of the contract of July 1, and Mr King has disabled himself from giving effect to it as intended by parting with his right to present possession. That is enough to establish a case for damages against Mr King. There may be a remedy over against the lessees. I say nothing of that, because they are not here, and I do not wish either to encourage or to discourage any further proceedings; but this I think is clear: that the existence of such a remedy, if remedy there be, does not release Mr King from his liability to answer for breaking the contract which he made.

In **Ashburn Anstalt v Arnold** [1989] Ch 1,[193] prior to 28 February 1973, Mr Arnold held the head lease, and Arnold & Co the sublease of shop premises in Gloucester Road, Kensington, forming part of registered land owned by Cavendish Land Co Ltd.

---

[193] [1988] CLJ 353 (A. J. Oakley); 104 LQR 175 (P. Sparkes); 51 MLR 226 (J. Hill); Conv 201 (M. P. Thompson); All ER Rev 176 (P. J. Clarke). The Appeal Committee dismissed a petition for leave to appeal [1989] Ch 32.

By agreements on 28 February, Mr Arnold sold the headlease to Matlodge Ltd and Arnold & Co the sublease also to Matlodge Ltd. On the same day the benefit of these agreements was assigned by Matlodge Ltd to Cavendish Land Co Ltd, the headlease and the sublease thereby merging with the freehold.

Clause 5 of the agreement between Arnold & Co and Matlodge Ltd provided that from the date of completion the vendors would 'be entitled as licensees to remain at the property and trade therefrom' until 29 September, without payment of rent, and from that date to remain there until it received notice from the purchaser that he was ready to demolish and redevelop the property, whereupon it would give up possession and in due course be granted a lease of shop premises on the redeveloped site.

Cavendish Land Co Ltd transferred the freehold to the Legal and General Assurance Society Ltd, who then sold it to Ashburn Anstalt, the plaintiff, subject to the 1973 agreement between Arnold & Co and Matlodge Ltd. The plaintiff claimed possession from the defendants who had been in actual occupation throughout.

In dismissing the plaintiff's claim, the Court of Appeal held (1) that Clause 5 of the agreement created a lease which was binding on the plaintiff as an overriding interest under section 70(1)(g) of the Land Registration Act 1925.[194]

(2) obiter, that, on the assumption that clause 5 created a contractual licence, it would not be enforceable against the plaintiff. It did not create an interest in land, nor did it give rise to a constructive trust.[195]

Fox LJ said at 13:

If, as we have concluded, Arnold & Co. is a tenant, it follows that the plaintiff holds the land subject to the tenancy. That is sufficient to dispose of the claim, as the action is for possession. Since, however, we have heard full argument on the case, we will consider the position on the basis that we are wrong, and no tenancy was created.

It is Arnold & Co.'s case that even if the 1973 agreement created no tenancy after 28 February 1973, so that its occupancy thereafter is that of a contractual licensee only, its rights are nevertheless binding upon a purchaser for value with notice of the licence....

Until comparatively recently it would, we think, have been rejected. As long ago as 1674, in *Thomas v Sorrell* (1674) Vaugh 330, 351, Vaughan CJ said:

'A dispensation or licence properly passeth no interest, nor alters or transfers property in any thing, but only makes an action lawful, which without it had been unlawful.'

A number of cases in this century support that view....

His Lordship referred to *Daly v Edwardes* (1900) 83 LT 548; affd sub nom *Edwardes v Barrington* (1901) 85 LT 650; *Frank Warr & Co Ltd v London County Council* [1904] 1 KB 713; *King v David Allen & Sons (Billposting) Ltd* [1916] 2 AC 54, p. 1097, above; *Clore v Theatrical Properties Ltd* [1936] 3 All ER 483 and continued:

Down to this point we do not think that there is any serious doubt as to the law. A mere contractual licence to occupy land is not binding on a purchaser of the land even though he has notice of the licence.

---

[194] P. 183, above; now LRA 2002, Sch. 3, para. 2, p. 196, above.   [195] P. 1104, below.

We come now to a case which is of central importance on the present issue. That is *Errington v Errington and Woods* [1952] 1 KB 290. A father, wishing to provide a home for his son who had recently married, bought a house with the help of a building society mortgage. He paid a lump sum towards the purchase price, the remainder of which was provided by the building society's loan. The loan was repayable by instalments. He retained the conveyance in his own name and paid the rates, but he promised that if the son and daughter-in-law continued in occupation and duly paid all the instalments, he would then transfer the property to them. The father died and by his will left the house to his widow. Up to that time the son and his wife had lived in the house and paid the instalments. The son then separated from his wife and left the house. The daughter-in-law continued to pay the mortgage instalments. The widow then sought possession of the house from the daughter-in-law. The county court judge dismissed the action. He held that the daughter-in-law was a tenant at will and that the claim against her was statute-barred. That reasoning was rejected by the Court of Appeal, though the actual decision of the judge was upheld. Denning LJ, whose reasons for dismissing the appeal were concurred in by Somervell LJ, said, at 298–299:

'it seems to me that, although the couple had exclusive possession of the house, there was clearly no relationship of landlord and tenant. They were not tenants at will but licensees. They had a mere personal privilege to remain there, with no right to assign or sub-let. They were, however, not bare licensees. They were licensees with a contractual right to remain. As such they have no right at law to remain, but only in equity, and equitable rights now prevail. I confess, however, that it has taken the courts some time to reach this position. At common law a licence was always revocable at will, notwithstanding a contract to the contrary: *Wood v Leadbitter* (1845) 13 M & W 838. The remedy for a breach of the contract was only in damages. That was the view generally held until a few years ago: see, for instance, what was said in *Book v Palmer* [1942] 2 All ER 674, 677 and *Thompson v Park* [1944] KB 408, 410. The rule has, however, been altered owing to the interposition of equity. Law and equity have been fused for nearly 80 years, and since 1948 it has been clear that, as a result of the fusion, a licensor will not be permitted to eject a licensee in breach of a contract to allow him to remain: see *Winter Garden Theatre (London) Ltd v Millennium Productions Ltd* [1946] 1 All ER 678, 680, per Lord Greene, and in the House of Lords per Lord Simon; nor in breach of a promise on which the licensee has acted, even though he gave no value for it: see *Foster v Robinson* [1951] 1 KB 149, 156, where Sir Raymond Evershed MR said that as a result of the oral arrangement to let the man stay, he was entitled as licensee to occupy the premises without any payment of rent for the rest of his days. This infusion of equity means that contractual licences now have a force and validity of their own and cannot be revoked in breach of the contract. Neither the licensor nor anyone who claims through him can disregard the contract except a purchaser for value, without notice.'

It is not in doubt that the actual decision was correct. It could be justified on one of three grounds. (i) There was a contract to convey the house on completion of the payments giving rise to an equitable interest in the form of an estate contract which would be binding on the widow: see Megarry & Wade, *The Law of Real Property* 5th edn (1984), p. 806. The widow was not a purchaser for value. (ii) The daughter-in-law had changed her position in reliance upon a representation binding on the widow as a privy of the representor: see Spencer Bower and Turner, *Estoppel by Representation,* 3rd edn (1977), p. 123. (iii) The payment of the instalments by the son or the daughter-in-law gave rise to direct proprietary interests by way of constructive trust, though it is true that, until *Gissing v Gissing* [1971] AC 886, the law relating to constructive trusts in this field was not much considered.

Accordingly, it does not appear to have been necessary, in order to produce a just result, to have accepted the broad principle stated, at p. 299, in the passage which we have quoted, that 'Neither the licensor nor anyone who claims through him can disregard the contract except a purchaser for value without notice.' That statement itself is not supported by any citation of authority, and indeed we do not think it could have been supported on the authorities. None of the cases prior to *Errington v Errington and Woods* to which we have referred, except *Thomas v Sorrell,* is mentioned in the judgments and it does not appear that any was cited.

His Lordship referred to *Winter Gardens Theatre (London) Ltd v Millennium Productions Ltd* [1948] AC 173; *National Provincial Bank Ltd v Ainsworth* [1965] AC 1175; *Re Solomon* [1967] Ch 573 and continued:

It must, we think, be very doubtful whether this court's decision in *Errington v Errington and Woods* is consistent with its earlier decisions in *Daly v Edwardes* 83 LT 548; *Frank Warr & Co v London County Council* [1904] 1 KB 713 and *Clore v Theatrical Properties Ltd* [1936] 3 All ER 483. That decision cannot be said to be in conflict with any later decision of the House of Lords, because the House expressly left the effect of a contractual licence open in the *Hastings Car Mart* case. But there must be very real doubts whether *Errington* can be reconciled with the earlier decisions of the House of Lords in *Edwardes v Barrington* 85 LT 650, and *King v David Allen & Sons (Billposting) Ltd* [1916] 2 AC 54. It would seem that we must follow those cases or choose between the two lines of authority. It is not, however, necessary to consider those alternative courses in detail, since in our judgment the House of Lords cases, whether or not as a matter of strict precedent they conclude this question, state the correct principle which we should follow.

Our reasons for reaching this conclusion are based upon essentially the same reasons as those given by Russell LJ in the *Hastings Car Mart* case [1964] Ch 665, 697, and by Professor Wade in the article, 'Licences and Third Parties' (1952) 68 LQR 337, to which Russell LJ refers. Before *Errington* the law appears to have been clear and well understood. It rested on an important and intelligible distinction between contractual obligations which gave rise to no estate or interest in the land and proprietary rights which, by definition, did. The far-reaching statement of principle in *Errington* was not supported by authority, not necessary for the decision of the case and per incuriam in the sense that it was made without reference to authorities which, if they would not have compelled, would surely have persuaded the court to adopt a different ratio. Of course, the law must be free to develop. But as a response to problems which had arisen, the *Errington* rule (without more) was neither practically necessary nor theoretically convincing. By contrast, the finding on appropriate facts of a constructive trust may well be regarded as a beneficial adaptation of old rules to new situations.[196]

QUESTION

Should contractual licences be interests in land? See (1953) 16 MLR 1 (G. C. Cheshire); (1952) 16 Conv (NS) 323 (F. R. Crane); (1953) 17 Conv (NS) 440 (L. A. Sheridan); (1984) 100 LQR 376 (S. Moriarty) and articles on p. 1097, n. 193; Dawson and Pearce, chap. 11; Smith, pp. 461–464.

---

196 P. 1102, below.

C. LICENCE PROTECTED BY CONSTRUCTIVE TRUST[197]

In a few cases the licensee's occupation of the land has been protected through an application of the doctrine of the constructive trust. Such a trust arises in various circumstances by operation of law when the court is of opinion that it is in the interests of justice or for the prevention of unjust enrichment that such a trust should be found. In the present context, the finding of a constructive trust in favour of the licensee creates an equitable interest in the land in his favour.[198] This solution has sometimes been too readily applied, without appreciating the conveyancing problems which follow. This development stems back to *Bannister v Bannister* [1948] 2 All ER 133, where the facts provided a compelling situation for the protection of an old lady who had no proprietary interest in the premises. This was before the modern development of the doctrine of proprietary estoppel which can now be invoked to protect licensees. The advantage of an estoppel theory is that the court has available to it a much wider choice of remedy.[199] *Bannister v Bannister* would probably be so treated at the present day.[200]

(i) Purchaser taking subject to licensee's right

Bannister v Bannister
[1948] 2 All ER 133 (CA, **Scott and Asquith LJJ** and **Jenkins J**)

The defendant was the owner of two cottages, Nos. 30 and 31. In 1943, she sold them to the plaintiff, her brother-in-law, for £250 (£150 below the market price) under an oral arrangement by which the brother-in-law would 'let you stay [in No. 30] as long as you like, rent free'. No mention of this arrangement was made in the conveyance. The defendant lived in the cottage until 1945 when she gave up possession of all except one downstairs room. In 1947, the plaintiff claimed possession of that, on the ground that she was a tenant at will only.

Held. The defendant was entitled to a life interest determinable upon her ceasing to reside in the cottage under a constructive trust created by the oral agreement.

Scott LJ: It is, we think, clearly a mistake to suppose that the equitable principle on which a constructive trust is raised against a person who insists on the absolute character of a conveyance to himself for the purpose of defeating a beneficial interest, which, according to the true bargain,

---

[197] C & B, pp. 839–841; Smith, pp. 464–466. On constructive trusts generally, see H & M, chap. 12; Underhill and Hayton, *Law of Trusts and Trustees* (17th edn, 2006), chap. 8; Maudsley & Burn, *Trusts & Trustees* (7th edn), chaps 7, 8; Oakley, *Constructive Trusts* (3rd edn, 1997), chap. 11; Elias, *Explaining Constructive Trusts*.

[198] For the view that a constructive trust in this situation creates a personal right, rather than an interest in the property, see (2004) 120 LQR 667 (B. McFarlane).

[199] Pp. 1047–1072, above; p. 1107, below.

[200] (1977) 93 LQR 561 (J. A. Hornby); [1980] Conv 250; *Binions v Evans* [1972] Ch 359, p. 1102, below; *DHN Food Distributors Ltd v Tower Hamlets London Borough Council* [1976] 1 WLR 852, p. 1111, below; *Re Sharpe* [1980] 1 WLR 219, p. 1109, below.

was to belong to another, is confined to cases in which the conveyance itself was fraudulently obtained. The fraud which brings the principle into play arises as soon as the absolute character of the conveyance is set up for the purpose of defeating the beneficial interest, and that is the fraud to cover which the Statute of Frauds or the corresponding provisions of the Law of Property Act, 1925, cannot be called in aid in cases in which no written evidence of the real bargain is available. Nor is it, in our opinion, necessary that the bargain on which the absolute conveyance is made should include any express stipulation that the grantee is in so many words to hold as trustee. It is enough that the bargain should have included a stipulation under which some sufficiently defined beneficial interest in the property was to be taken by another. The above propositions are, we think, clearly borne out by the cases to which we were referred of *Booth v Turle* (1873) LR 16 Eq 182, *Chattock v Muller* (1878) 8 ChD 177, *Re Duke of Marlborough* [1894] 2 Ch 133, and *Rochefoucauld v Boustead* [1897] 1 Ch 196. We see no distinction in principle between a case in which property is conveyed to a purchaser on terms that the entire beneficial interest in some part of it is to be retained by the vendor (as in *Booth v Turle*) and a case, like the present, in which property is conveyed to a purchaser on terms that a limited beneficial interest in some part of it is to be retained by the vendor. We are, accordingly, of opinion that the third ground of objection to the learned county court judge's conclusion also fails. His finding that there was no fraud in the case cannot be taken as meaning that it was not fraudulent in the plaintiff to insist on the absolute character of the conveyance for the purpose of defeating the beneficial interest which he had agreed the defendant should retain. The conclusion that the plaintiff was fraudulent, in this sense, necessarily follows from the facts found, and, as indicated above, the fact that he may have been innocent of any fraudulent intent in taking the conveyance in absolute form is for this purpose immaterial.... The plaintiff holds No. 30 in trust during the life of the defendant to per- mit the defendant to occupy the same for so long as she may desire to do so, and subject thereto in trust for the plaintiff. A trust in this form has the effect of making the beneficiary a tenant for life within the meaning of the Settled Land Act, 1925.[201]

(ii) *Third parties taking expressly subject to licensee's right*

Binions v Evans[202]
[1972] Ch 359 (CA, **Lord Denning MR, Megaw** and **Stephenson LJJ**)

The trustees of the Tredegar Estate in Monmouthshire and South Wales entered into an agreement with Mrs Evans, the 79 year old widow of an employee of the Estate. The trustees agreed to permit her to reside in and occupy a cottage on the estate for the remainder of her life as tenant at will rent free. She agreed to keep it in a proper manner and 'personally occupy and live in it as a private residence only and not assign, sub-let or part with the possession' of it. Two years later the trustees sold the cottage to the plaintiffs expressly subject to Mrs Evans's tenancy agreement, a copy of which was handed to the purchasers. Six months later the plaintiffs gave Mrs Evans notice to quit as a mere tenant at will and claimed possession of the cottage.

---

[201] See now TLATA 1996, s. 2, p. 516, above. For the problems arising upon the finding that the trust constituted a settlement under SLA 1925, see p. 1061, n. 110, above.

[202] (1972) 88 LQR 336 (P.V.B.); (1972) 36 Conv (NS) 266 (J. Martin); 277 (D. J. Hayton); [1973] CLJ 123 (R. J. Smith); (1973) 117 SJ 23 (B. W. Harvey); (1977) 93 LQR 561 (J. A. Hornby).

Held. Order for possession refused. Per Megaw and Stephenson LJJ: Mrs Evans was tenant for life under the Settled Land Act 1925.[203]

Lord Denning MR (having held that Mrs. Evans was not a tenant at will, nor a lessee nor a tenant for life under the Settled Land Act):

Suppose, however, that the defendant did not have an equitable interest at the outset,[204] nevertheless it is quite plain that she obtained one afterwards when the Tredegar Estate sold the cottage. They stipulated with the plaintiffs that they were to take the house 'subject to' the defendant's rights under the agreement. They supplied the plaintiffs with a copy of the contract: and the plaintiffs paid less because of her right to stay there. In these circumstances, this court will impose on the plaintiffs a constructive trust for her benefit: for the simple reason that it would be utterly inequitable for the plaintiffs to turn the defendant out contrary to the stipulation subject to which they took the premises. That seems to me clear from the important decision of *Bannister v Bannister* [1948] 2 All ER 133 [p. 1101, above] which was applied by the judge, and which I gladly follow.

The imposing of a constructive trust is entirely in accord with the precepts of equity. As Cardozo J once put it: 'A constructive trust is the formula through which the conscience of equity finds expression,' see *Beatty v Guggenheim Exploration Co* (1919) 225 NY 380, 386: or, as Lord Diplock put it quite recently in *Gissing v Gissing* [1971] AC 886, 905, a constructive trust is created 'whenever the trustee has so conducted himself that it would be inequitable to allow him to deny to the cestui que trust a beneficial interest in the land acquired'.

I know that there are some who have doubted whether a contractual licensee has any protection against a purchaser, even one who takes with full notice. We were referred in this connection to Professor Wade's article Licences and Third Parties in (1952) 68 LQR 337, and to the judgment of Goff J in *Re Solomon* [1967] Ch 573. None of these doubts can prevail, however, when the situation gives rise to a constructive trust. Whenever the owner sells the land to a purchaser, and at the same time stipulates that he shall take it 'subject to' a contractual licence, I think it plain that a court of equity will impose on the purchaser a constructive trust in favour of the beneficiary....

In my opinion the defendant, by virtue of the agreement, had an equitable interest in the cottage which the court would protect by granting an injunction against the landlords restraining them from turning her out. When the landlords sold the cottage to a purchaser 'subject to' her rights under the agreement, the purchaser took the cottage on a constructive trust to permit the defendant to reside there during her life, or as long as she might desire. The courts will not

---

[203] For the problems of finding a SLA settlement in this context, see p. 1061, n. 110, above. The defendant in such a case might now be able to enforce the term in the contract of sale of the cottage by which the purchasers agreed to allow her to stay, as long as the parties expressly or impliedly intended her to have the right to enforce it: Contracts (Rights of Third Parties) Act 1999, s. 1; p. 772, above. The licensee is not thereby enforcing her (existing) licence against the purchaser, but taking the benefit of the purchaser's (new) contractual undertaking.

[204] Lord Denning's first analysis (at pp. 367–368) was to the effect that Mrs Evans was a contractual licensee, and that such a licence gives the licensee, from the outset, an equitable interest in the land: 'the courts of equity will not allow the landlord to turn the occupier out in breach of the contract: see *Foster v Robinson* [1951] 1 KB 149, 156; nor will they allow a purchaser to turn her out if he bought with knowledge of her right—*Errington v Errington and Woods* [1952] 1 KB 290, 299.' This analysis of contractual licences was disapproved by CA in *Ashburn Anstalt v Arnold* [1989] Ch 1, p. 1097, above.

allow the purchaser to go back on that trust. I entirely agree with the judgment of Judge Bulger. I would dismiss this appeal.

Stephenson LJ: Apart from authority, I would not have thought that such an interest could be understood to amount to a tenancy for life within the meaning of the Settled Land Act 1925, and I would have thought that the other terms of her tenancy (as I think it ought properly to be called) are inconsistent with a power to ask for the legal estate to be settled on her or to sell the cottage. But *Bannister v Bannister* is a clear decision of this court that such words as have been used in this agreement (excepting, I must concede, the words 'as tenant at will of them') create a life interest determinable (apart from the special considerations introduced by the Settled Land Act 1925) on the beneficiary ceasing to occupy the premises and the landlords hold the cottage on trust to permit her to occupy it 'during her life or as long as she lives,' as Judge Bulger held, and subject thereto in trust for them.

I therefore find it unnecessary to consider or decide the vexed questions (1) whether this agreement is or creates an irrevocable contractual licence to occupy, and (2) whether such a licence has been elevated to a status equivalent to an estate or interest in land by decisions of this court such as *Errington v Errington and Woods* [1952] 1 KB 290 or *Foster v Robinson* [1951] 1 KB 149 or still awaits legislation before it can so achieve transmissibility to subsequent purchasers with notice: see the rival views set out by Goff J in *Re Solomon* [1967] Ch 573. 582–586.[205]

In **Ashburn Anstalt v Arnold** [1989] Ch 1, p. 1097, above. Fox LJ said at 22:

The constructive trust principle, to which we now turn, has been long established and has proved to be highly flexible in practice. It covers a wide variety of cases from that of a trustee who makes a profit out of his trust or a stranger who knowingly deals with trust properties, to the many cases where the courts have held that a person who directly or indirectly contributes to the acquisition of a dwelling house purchased in the name of and conveyed to another has some beneficial interest in the property. The test, for the present purposes, is whether the owner of the property has so conducted himself that it would be inequitable to allow him to deny the claimant an interest in the property: see *Gissing v Gissing* [1971] AC 886, 905, per Lord Diplock.

His Lordship referred to *Bannister v Bannister* [1948] 2 All ER 133, p. 1101, above; *Re Schebsman* [1944] Ch 83 and *Binions v Evans* [1972] Ch 359, p. 1102, above, and continued:

[In *Binions v Evans* Lord Denning MR] held that the plaintiffs took the property subject to a constructive trust for the defendant's benefit. In our view that is a legitimate application of the doctrine of constructive trusts. The estate would certainly have allowed the defendant to live in the house during her life in accordance with their agreement with her. They provided the plaintiffs with a copy of the agreement they made. The agreement for sale was subject to the agreement, and they accepted a lower purchase price in consequence. In the circumstances it was a proper inference that on the sale to the plaintiffs, the intention of the estate and the plaintiffs was that the plaintiffs should give effect to the tenancy agreement. If they had failed to do so, the estate would have been liable in damages to the defendant.

His Lordship referred to *DHN Food Distributors Ltd v Tower Hamlets Borough Council* [1976] 1 WLR 852; *Re Sharpe* [1980] 1 WLR 219, p. 1109, below; *Lyus v Prowsa Developments Ltd* [1982] 1 WLR 1044, p. 223, above, and continued:

---

[205] Megaw LJ also suggested at 371 that the plaintiffs would be guilty of the tort of interference with existing contractual rights if they were to evict the defendant; (1977) 41 Conv (NS) 318 (R. J. Smith).

We come to the present case. It is said that when a person sells land and stipulates that the sale should be 'subject to' a contractual licence, the court will impose a constructive trust upon the purchaser to give effect to the licence: see *Binions v Evans* [1972] Ch 359, 368, per Lord Denning MR. We do not feel able to accept that as a general proposition. We agree with the observations of Dillon J in *Lyus v Prowsa Developments Ltd* [1982] 1 WLR 1044, 1051.

> 'By contrast, there are many cases in which land is expressly conveyed subject to possible incumbrances when there is no thought at all of conferring any fresh rights on third parties who may be entitled to the benefit of the incumbrances. The land is expressed to be sold subject to incumbrances to satisfy the vendor's duty to disclose all possible incumbrances known to him, and to protect the vendor against any possible claim by the purchaser... So, for instance, land may be contracted to be sold and may be expressed to be conveyed subject to the restrictive covenants contained in a conveyance some 60 or 90 years old. No one would suggest that by accepting such a form of contract or conveyance a purchaser is assuming a new liability in favour of third parties to observe the covenants if there was for any reason before the contract or conveyance no one who could make out a title as against the purchaser to the benefit of the covenants.

The court will not impose a constructive trust unless it is satisfied that the conscience of the estate owner is affected. The mere fact that that land is expressed to be conveyed 'subject to' a contract does not necessarily imply that the grantee is to be under an obligation, not otherwise existing, to give effect to the provisions of the contract. The fact that the conveyance is expressed to be subject to the contract may often, for the reasons indicated by Dillon J, be at least as consistent with an intention merely to protect the grantor against claims by the grantee as an intention to impose an obligation on the grantee. The words 'subject to' will, of course, impose notice. But notice is not enough to impose on somebody an obligation to give effect to a contract into which he did not enter. Thus, mere notice of a restrictive covenant is not enough to impose upon the estate owner an obligation or equity to give effect to it: *London County Council v Allen* [1914] 3 KB 642 [p. 755, above].

The material facts in the present case are as follows. (i) There is no finding that the plaintiff paid a lower price in consequence of the provision that the sale was subject to the 1973 agreement. (ii) The 1973 agreement was not contractually enforceable against Legal & General, which was not, therefore, exposed to the risk of any contractual claim for damages if the agreement was not complied with. The 1973 agreement was enforceable against Cavendish and it seems that in 1973 Cavendish was owned by Legal & General. There is no finding as to the relationship between Cavendish and Legal & General in August 1985, when Legal & General sold to the plaintiff. And there is no evidence before the deputy judge as to the circumstances or the arrangements attending the transfer by Cavendish to Legal & General. (iii) Whilst the letter of 7 February 1985 is not precisely worded, it seems that Legal & General was itself prepared to give effect to the 1973 agreement.

In matters relating to the title to land, certainty is of prime importance. We do not think it desirable that constructive trusts of land should be imposed in reliance on inferences from slender materials. In our opinion the available evidence in the present case is insufficient. The deputy judge, while he did not have to decide the matter, was not disposed to infer a constructive trust, and we agree with him.[206]

---

[206] *Sparkes v Smart* [1990] 2 EGLR 245 (collusive transaction between purchaser of freehold farm and ageing tenant, purchaser's father-in-law, with object of destroying youngest son's tenancy; CA held obiter constructive trust in favour of the son).

In **IDC Group Ltd v Clark** [1992] 1 EGLR 187,[207] Sir Nicolas BROWNE-WILKINSON V-C, in holding that an agreement for the provision of a fire-escape route through a door in a party wall into the interior of an adjacent flat was not enforceable against a third party, said at 189:

[In *Ashburn Anstalt v Arnold* [1989] Ch 1, pp. 1097, 1104, above] the Court of Appeal put what I hope is the *quietus* to the heresy that a mere licence creates an interest in land. They also put the *quietus* to the heresy that parties to a contractual licence necessarily become constructive trustees. They also held (at p. 25 D-E) that the mere fact that property is sold subject to a contractual licence is not sufficient to create a constructive trust. They held (at p. 26A) that the mere fact that somebody has purchased with notice of a claim does not give rise to a constructive trust....

The result, as it seems to me, is that in the normal case a conveyance of land subject to or with notice of prior incumbrances or prior interests will not operate so as to make enforceable under a constructive trust such prior incumbrances or interests which would otherwise be unenforceable. However, in certain circumstances equity raises a constructive trust because it is unconscionable for the person having received such property not to give effect to the terms on which he received it. As the Court of Appeal said, and with respect I would agree, at p. 26E:

'In matters relating to the title to land certainty is of prime importance. We do not think it desirable that constructive trusts of land should be imposed in reliance on inferences from slender materials.'

It is important always to bear in mind that it is of the greatest importance that the title to land should be capable of being ascertained in accordance with well-known procedures. To raise constructive trusts which do not fit into the conveyancing machinery currently operating, thereby giving rise to liabilities of which purchasers might otherwise not be aware, is a dangerous course to pursue.

In my judgment, the decision in *Ashburn Anstalt* does not warrant the creation of a constructive trust unless there are very special circumstances showing that the transferee of the property undertook a new liability to give effect to provisions for the benefit of third parties. It is the conscience of the transferee which has to be affected and it has to be affected in a way which gives rise to an obligation to meet the legitimate expectations of the third party.

In **Lloyd v Dugdale** [2002] 2 P & CR 13, SIR CHRISTOPHER SLADE summarised the law at p. 182, para. 52:

The relevant principles to be extracted from the authorities may for present purposes be summarised as follows:

(1) Even in a case where, on a sale of land, the vendor has stipulated that the sale shall be subject to stated possible incumbrances or prior interests, there is no general rule that the court will impose a constructive trust on the purchaser to give effect to them. In *Ashburn Anstalt v Arnold* at page 25E, Fox LJ, delivering the judgment of the Court, expressed agreement with the following observations of Dillon J in *Lyus v Prowsa Development Ltd* at page 1051:

'By contrast, there are many cases in which land is expressly conveyed subject to possible incumbrances when there is no thought at all of conferring any fresh rights on third parties who may be

---

[207] The decision was upheld by CA [1992] 2 EGLR 184.

entitled to the benefit of the incumbrances. The land is expressed to be sold subject to incumbrances to satisfy the vendor's duty to disclose all possible incumbrances known to him, and to protect the vendor against any possible claim by the purchaser...So, for instance, land may be contracted to be sold and may be expressed to be conveyed subject to the restrictive covenants contained in a conveyance some 60 or 90 years old. No one would suggest that by accepting such a form of contract or conveyance a purchaser is assuming a new liability in favour of third parties to observe the covenants if there was for any reason before the contract or conveyance no one who could make out a title as against the purchaser to the benefit of the covenants.'

(2) The court will not impose a constructive trust in such circumstances unless it is satisfied that the conscience of the estate owner is affected so that it would be inequitable to allow him to deny the claimant an interest in the property: (see *Ashburn Anstalt v Arnold* at pages 22E-F and 25H).

(3) In deciding whether or not the conscience of the new estate owner is affected in such circumstances, the crucially important question is whether he has undertaken a new obligation, not otherwise existing, to give effect to the relevant incumbrance or prior interest. If, but only if, he has undertaken such a new obligation will a constructive trust be imposed. The importance of this point was repeatedly stressed in *Ashburn Anstalt v Arnold*: see, for example, at pages 23G, 25A–26A, and 27B. See also *Lyus v Prowsa Development Ltd* at page 1051; *IDC Group Ltd v Clark* (1992) 1 EGLR at page 190B–C; *Melbury Road Properties 1995 Ltd v Kreidi* [1999] 3 EGLR 108 at page 110G.

(4) Notwithstanding some previous authority suggesting the contrary, a contractual licence is not to be treated as creating a proprietary interest in land so as to bind third parties who acquire the land with notice of it, on this account alone: see *Ashburn Anstalt v Arnold (supra)* at pages 15H and 24D.

(5) Proof that the purchase price by a transferee has been reduced upon the footing that he would give effect to the relevant incumbrance or prior interest may provide some indication that the transferee has undertaken a new obligation to give effect to it: see *Ashburn Anstalt v Arnold (supra)* at page 23F-G. However, since in matters relating to the title to land certainty is of prime importance, it is not desirable that constructive trusts of land should be imposed in reliance on inferences from 'slender materials'; *ibid.*, at page 26E.'

D. LICENCE PROTECTED BY PROPRIETARY ESTOPPEL[208]

The doctrine of proprietary estoppel has already been discussed in detail.[209] It has played a significant part in the modern development of the law of licences. As we have

[208] C & B, pp. 841–849; Gray, part 9.2; M & W, chap. 16, paras 34.013, 34.020; MM, pp. 69, 483–489; Smith, pp. 466–471; Dawson and Pearce, pp. 29–36, 97–99, 144–145, 161–163; [1981] Conv 347 (P. N. Todd); [1982] Conv 118 at pp. 125–132 (A. R. Everton); (1984) 100 LQR 376 (S. Moriarty); [1986] 49 MLR 741 (J. Dewar); [1991] Conv 36 (G. Battersby). See also, on general aspects of proprietary estoppel, further articles cited at p. 1007, n. 31, above.

On the relationship between contractual licences and licences protected by estoppel, see the controversy between [1981] Conv 212; [1983] Conv 285 (A. Briggs) and [1983] Conv 50, 471 (M. P. Thompson). On the relationship between proprietary estoppel and constructive trusts, see p. 1076, above. For the multiple characterisation of a licensee's rights, see p. 1109, below.

[209] Pp. 1007–1078, above.

seen, the doctrine deals with the equities arising out of a situation in which one party (A) makes a representation or promise to another party (B) to the effect that B has or shall have an interest in, or right over, A's property, or acquiesces in B's mistaken belief that he has or shall have such an interest or right. If A intends B to act in reliance to his detriment on the representation, promise or mistaken belief, and B does so act in reliance, an equity is said to arise, which may prevent (estop) A from asserting his own strict legal rights to his property. B will have the right to seek a remedy from the court to protect this equity, and the remedy may sometimes even give effect to B's expectations by granting him the interest in A's land which A led him to believe he had or would acquire.

This doctrine has been applied to many cases involving licences, where B is in occupation of A's land in the belief that he has or is to acquire an interest in it or a right over it. The licence may be gratuitous or contractual. The categories of licences may therefore overlap.[210] If the licence is contractual, the licensee may be protected under the doctrines relating to contractual licences, discussed above; and it may be unnecessary to invoke the doctrine of estoppel.[211] Where, however, the licensee is seeking protection against a third party, proprietary estoppel is more effective. It will be seen that the courts appear to have these factors in mind in categorising licences.

Decisions to protect licensees of all kinds raise a number of difficulties. Some of these have been seen in the context of contractual licences. With licences protected by estoppel, the courts recognise their power and duty in these cases as being to 'look at the circumstances in each case to decide in what way the equity can be satisfied';[212] and in recent years the courts have emphasised the role of proportionality in their decision as to the remedy to be awarded.[213] Whilst this provides flexibility in finding a solution to protect the licensee, it necessarily also generates uncertainty as to the nature and scope of the licensee's rights, beyond the simple licence, until the court has adjudicated on a claim relating to the licence.[214]

The range of remedies which the court has at its disposal has been set out already.[215] Negative protection—typically, an injunction restraining the licensor from interfering with the licensee's occupation under the terms of the licence—has advantages in situations where the time is not yet ripe for a final settlement, and the licensee seeks simply to resist any disturbance to his occupation, as where a son builds a bungalow on his father's land in the expectation of being allowed to stay there for the rest of his life.[216] In

---

[210] In *Hardwick v Johnson* [1978] 1 WLR 683, p. 1093, above, the Court of Appeal divided 2–1 on the question of the type of licence. But that made no difference to the result. See also *Re Sharpe* [1980] 1 WLR 219, p. 1109, below.

[211] *Tanner v Tanner* [1975] 1 WLR 1346.

[212] *Plimmer v Wellington Corpn* (1884) 9 App Cas 699, p. 1065, above, at 714; *Chalmers v Pardoe* [1963] 1 WLR 677 at 682; *Inwards v Baker* [1965] 2 QB 29, p. 1048, above, at 37; *ER Ives Investment Ltd v High* [1967] 2 QB 379, p. 1074, above at 395; *Crabb v Arun District Council* [1976] Ch 179, p. 1051, above, at 188.

[213] Pp. 1039–1046, above.   [214] P. 1114, below. And see question 5 on p. 1080, above.

[215] Pp. 1047–1072, above.

[216] *Inwards v Baker* [1965] 2 QB 29, p. 1049, above. The son claimed only that he had been promised a licence for life, and did not pursue a claim that he had been promised or given the fee simple: [1965] 2 QB 29 at 30–31. Cf. *Dillwyn v Llewelyn*, n. 218, below.

several cases, the court, applying the doctrine of proprietary estoppel, has found it best to declare that some interest is to be vested in the licensee, as where a mistress was given possession of a house and told that it was hers but the formalities necessary for the conveyance of the legal title had not been complied with;[217] or where a daughter had lived in her mother's house in order to look after her in the belief that she would be entitled to live there for the rest of her life.[218] The court has also ordered that a licensee's licence should be perpetual—which gave the licensee a sufficient right to the land to found a claim for compensation for compulsory purchase.[219] On the other hand, the court has sometimes awarded only a licence to occupy pending reimbursement by the licensor of expenditure incurred by the licensee in respect of the land,[220] or a licence which is time-limited,[221] or no remedy at all—either because the licensee's claim to a remedy was premature and the licensor was not seeking to disturb the licensee's occupation of the land,[222] or because any equity which might found a claim to a proprietary remedy had been exhausted by the time the claim came before the court.[223]

E. MULTIPLE CHARACTERISATION OF LICENSEE'S RIGHT. CONVEYANCING DIFFICULTIES

Re Sharpe
[1980] 1 WLR 219 (Browne-Wilkinson J)[224]

An aunt lent £12,000 to her nephew to enable him to purchase a property in Hampstead for £17,000. She also spent over £2,000 on its decorations and fittings, and paid off some of the nephew's debts in order to stave off his bankruptcy. The understanding

217 *Pascoe v Turner* [1979] 1 WLR 431, p. 1056, above (order for conveyance of fee simple). See also *Dillwyn v Llewelyn* (1862) 4 De GF & J 517 (father had signed an unexecuted and gratuitous memorandum of conveyance in favour of his son, and the son had spent no less than £14,000 in building himself a home, with his father's knowledge and approval. HL ordered conveyance of the land without payment); *Voyce v Voyce* (1991) 62 P & CR 290 (gift of land and cottage on condition that donee 'did it up').

218 *Griffiths v Williams* (1977) 248 EG 947, p. 1061, above (consent order for grant of lease determinable on licensee's death).

219 *Plimmer v Wellington Corpn* (1884) 9 App Cas 699, p. 1065, above.

220 *Dodsworth v Dodsworth* (1973) 228 EG 1115, p. 1068, above; *Burrows v Sharp* (1991) 23 HLR 82 (clean break; compensation in return for loss of accommodation); *Campbell v Griffin* [2001] EWCA Civ 990, (2001) 82 P & CR DG23 (family carer ordered to vacate property to enable it to be sold, but granted a charge over the property to secure the interest (£35,000) he was held to have by way of proprietary estoppel); [2002] Conv 519 (M. Pawkowski); [2003] Conv 157 (M. P. Thompson).

221 *Clark v Clark* [2006] 1 FCR 421 at [43]-[45] (company to be allowed to use accessway for purpose of business, but not for an indefinite period: it would no longer be unconscionable for landowner to claim back his land if company ceased to carry on same business, or ceased to provide a living for landowner and his brother, its sole and equal shareholders).

222 *Savva v Costa* [1980] CA Transcript 723, (1981) 131 NLJ 1114, p. 1070, above.

223 *Appleby v Cowley* (1982) Times, 14 April, p. 1069, above; *Sledmore v Dalby* (1996) 72 P & CR 196, p. 1045, above.

224 [1980] Conv 207 (J. Martin), suggesting proprietary estoppel as a preferable basis for the decision; (1980) 96 LQR 336 (G. Woodman).

was that the aunt should live there and be looked after by the nephew and his wife. The aunt moved in, the nephew finally went bankrupt, and his trustee in bankruptcy made a contract to sell the property with vacant possession for £17,000.

Held. The circumstances gave rise to a constructive trust in the aunt's favour, which conferred on her an interest binding on the trustee in bankruptcy

Browne-Wilkinson J: I turn then to the alternative claim that Mrs Johnson is entitled to something less than an aliquot share of the equity in the premises, namely, the right to stay on the premises until the money she provided indirectly to acquire them has been repaid. This right is based upon the line of recent Court of Appeal decisions which has spelt out irrevocable licences from informal family arrangements, and in some cases characterised such licences as conferring some equity or equitable interest under a constructive trust. I do not think that the principles lying behind these decisions have yet been fully explored and on occasion it seems that such rights are found to exist simply on the ground that to hold otherwise would be a hardship to the plaintiff. It appears that the principle is one akin to or an extension of a proprietary estoppel stemming from Lord Kingsdown's well-known statement of the law in *Ramsden v Dyson* (1866) LR 1 HL 129, 170 [p. 1008, above]. In a strict case of proprietary estoppel the plaintiff has expended his own money on the defendant's property in an expectation encouraged by or known to the defendant that the plaintiff either owns the property or is to have some interest conferred on him. Recent authorities have extended this doctrine and, in my judgment, it is now established that, if the parties have proceeded on a common assumption that the plaintiff is to enjoy a right to reside in a particular property and in reliance on that assumption the plaintiff has expended money or otherwise acted to his detriment, the defendant will not be allowed to go back on that common assumption and the court will imply an irrevocable licence or trust which will give effect to that common assumption. Thus in *Errington v Errington and Woods* [1952] 1 KB 290 [p. 1099, above], Denning LJ held that the son, who had paid the instalments under the mortgage in the expectation that the property would eventually become his, had an equitable right to stay in occupation until the mortgage was paid off. In *Tanner v Tanner* [1975] 1 WLR 1346, the plaintiff was held entitled to a licence to occupy a house bought in contemplation of it being a home for herself and her children, there being no express contract to that effect. In *Hardwick v Johnson* [1978] 1 WLR 683 [p. 1093, above], where the plaintiff's house had been occupied by the plaintiff's son and his first wife under an informal family arrangement, the Court of Appeal imputed an intention to grant an irrevocable licence to the wife on payment by her of a weekly sum.

Applying those principles to the present case, I have little doubt that as between the debtor on the one hand and Mrs Johnston on the other, the circumstances in which she provided the money by way of loan in order to enable the premises to be bought do give rise to some right in Mrs Johnson. It is clear that she only loaned the money as part of a wider scheme, an essential feature of which was that she was to make her home in the property to be acquired with the money loaned. Say that immediately after the property had been bought the debtor had tried to evict Mrs Johnson without repaying the loan; can it be supposed that the court would have made an order for possession against her? In my judgment, whether it be called a contractual licence or an equitable licence or an interest under a constructive trust, Mrs Johnson would be entitled as against the debtor to stay in the house. *Dodsworth v Dodsworth* (1973) 228 EG 1115 [p. 1068, above] shows that there are great practical difficulties in finding that she is entitled to a full life interest: but there is no reason why one should not imply an intention that she should have the right to live there until her loan is repaid, which was the result reached in *Dodsworth v Dodsworth.*

Unfortunately, this case does not arise for decision simply between Mrs Johnson on the one hand and the debtor on the other. She has to show some right good against the trustee in bankruptcy and the purchaser from the trustee in bankruptcy. Due to an unfortunate procedural position, the purchaser is not a party to this application and nothing I can say can, or is intended to, bind him. As an antidote to the over-indulgence of sympathy which everyone must feel for Mrs Johnson, I put on record that the purchaser's plight is little better. He apparently had no reason to suspect that there was any flaw in the trustee's right to sell with vacant possession. As a result of the trustee's inability to complete the sale he cannot open the business he intended and he and his wife and two children are being forced to live in a small motorised caravan parked in various places on or near Hampstead Heath.

Is then Mrs Johnson's right against the debtor binding on the trustee in bankruptcy? This is an important and difficult point and, were it not for the urgency of the matter and the late stage of the term, I would like to have given it longer consideration. In general the trustee in bankruptcy steps into the shoes of the debtor and takes the debtor's property subject to all rights and equities affecting it: see Halsbury's *Laws of England,* 4th edn, vol. 3 (1973), para. 594. However, the trustee in bankruptcy is free to break any merely contractual obligation of the debtor, leaving the other party to his remedy in damages, which damages will only give rise to a right to prove in the bankruptcy.

Are rights of the kind spelt out in the cases I have referred to merely contractual licences or do they fetter the property and create some right over it? On the authorities as they stand, I think I am bound to hold that the rights under such an irrevocable licence bind the property itself in the hands of the trustee in bankruptcy. Lord Denning MR has, on a number of occasions, said that these licences arise under a constructive trust and are binding on the third party's acquiring with notice. These statements are for the most part obiter dicta with which other members of the court have not associated themselves, preferring to rest their decision on there being a contractual licence. But in *Binions v Evans* [1972] Ch 359 [p. 1102, above], a third party taking with notice of, and expressly subject to, such a licence was held bound by it. In that case the liability could not have depended merely on contract. Closer to the present case is a decision which was not referred to in argument and therefore any comments on it must be treated with some reserve. In *DHN Food Distributors Ltd v Tower Hamlets London Borough Council* [1976] 1 WLR 852, certain premises were legally owned by one company (Bronze) but occupied by an associated company (DHN) under an informal arrangement between them. The premises were compulsorily acquired and the question was whether any compensation for disturbance was payable, it being said that Bronze had not been disturbed. The Court of Appeal held that DHN had an irrevocable licence to remain in the premises indefinitely and this gave DHN a compensatable interest in the land. Lord Denning MR said, at 859.

'It was equivalent to a contract between the two companies whereby Bronze granted an irrevocable licence to DHN to carry on their business on the premises. In this situation Mr Dobry cited to us *Binions v Evans* [1972] Ch 359, to which I would add *Bannister v Bannister* [1948] 2 All ER 133 and *Siew Soon Wah v Yong Tong Hong* [1973] AC 836. Those cases show that a contractual licence (under which a person has the right to occupy premises indefinitely) gives rise to a constructive trust, under which the legal owner is not allowed to turn out the licensee. So, here. This irrevocable licence gave to DHN a sufficient interest in the land to qualify them for compensation for disturbance.'

Goff LJ also made this a ground of his decision: see pp. 860 to 861.

It seems to me that this is a decision that such contractual or equitable licence does confer some interest in the property under a constructive trust. Accordingly, in my judgment, it follows that the trustee in bankruptcy takes the property subject to Mrs Johnson's right to live there until she is repaid the moneys she provided to acquire it.

Mr Moss, for the trustee in bankruptcy, argued that this was the wrong approach. He said that the species of constructive trust which Lord Denning MR was considering in the cases was different from the traditional constructive trust known to equity lawyers. It is not, Mr Moss says, a substantive right but an equitable remedy: see per Lord Denning MR in *Hussey v Palmer* [1972] 1 WLR 1286, 1290, and in *Binions v Evans* [1972] Ch 359, 368. Then, says Mr Moss, the time to decide whether to grant such a remedy is when the matter comes before the court in the light of the then known circumstances. In the present case those circumstances are that the debtor is a bankrupt and Mrs Johnson has failed to put forward her claim until after the trustee has contracted to sell the property to an innocent third party, notwithstanding two inquiries as to whether she had a claim. Accordingly, he says, it would not be equitable to grant her an interest under a constructive trust at this time.

I cannot accept that argument in that form. Even if it be right to say that the courts can impose a constructive trust as a remedy in certain cases—which to my mind is a novel concept in English law—in order to provide a remedy the court must first find a right which has been infringed. So far as land is concerned an oral agreement to create an interest in it must be evidenced in writing: see section 40 of the Law of Property Act 1925.[225] Therefore if these irrevocable licences create an interest in land, the rights cannot rest simply on an oral contract. The introduction of an interest under a constructive trust is an essential ingredient if the plaintiff has any right at all.[226] Therefore in cases such as this, it cannot be that the interest in property arises for the first time when the court declares it to exist. The right must have arisen at the time of the transaction in order for the plaintiff to have any right the breach of which can be remedied. Again, I think the *DHN Food Distributors Ltd* case shows that the equity predates any order of the court. The right to compensation in that case depended on substantive rights at the date of compulsory acquisition, not on what remedy the court subsequently chose to grant in the subsequent litigation.

Accordingly, if I am right in holding that as between the debtor and Mrs Johnson she had an irrevocable licence to remain in the property, authority compels me to hold that that gave her an interest in the property before the bankruptcy and the trustee takes the property subject to that interest. In my judgment the mere intervention of the bankruptcy by itself cannot alter Mrs Johnson's property interest. If she is to be deprived of her interest as against the trustee in bankruptcy, it must be because of some conduct of hers which precludes her from enforcing her rights, that is to say, the ordinary principles of acquiescence and laches which apply to all beneficiaries seeking to enforce their rights apply to this case.

I am in no way criticising the trustee in bankruptcy's conduct; he tried to find out if she made any claim relating to the £12,000 before he contracted to sell the property. But I do not think that on ordinary equitable principles Mrs Johnson should be prevented from asserting her rights even at this late stage. She is very old and in bad health. No one had ever advised

[225] See now LP(MP)A 1989, s. 2, under which the contract must be in writing (not merely evidenced in writing): p. 18, above.

[226] See Sir Christopher Slade's Child & Co Oxford Lecture 1984 on *The Informal Creation of Interests in Land* at p. 12.

her that she might have rights to live in the property. As soon as she appreciated that she was to be evicted she at once took legal advice and asserted her claim. This, in my judgment, is far removed from conduct which precludes enforcement by a beneficiary of his rights due to his acquiescence, the first requirement of acquiescence being that the beneficiary knows his or her rights and does not assert them.

Accordingly, I hold that Mrs Johnson is entitled as against the trustee in bankruptcy to remain in the property until she is repaid the sums she advanced. I reach this conclusion with some hesitation since I find the present state of the law very confused and difficult to fit in with established equitable principles. I express the hope that in the near future the whole question can receive full consideration in the Court of Appeal, so that, in order to do justice to the many thousands of people who never come into court at all but who wish to know with certainty what their proprietary rights are, the extent to which these irrevocable licences bind third parties may be defined with certainty. Doing justice to the litigant who actually appears in the court by the invention of new principles of law ought not to involve injustice to the other persons who are not litigants before the court but whose rights are fundamentally affected by the new principles.

Finally, I must reiterate that I am in no way deciding what are the rights of the purchaser from the trustee as against Mrs Johnson. It may be that as a purchaser without express notice in an action for specific performance of the contract his rights will prevail over Mrs Johnson's. As to that, I have heard no argument and express no view. I do, however, express my sympathy for him in the predicament in which he finds himself.

I therefore dismiss the trustee's application for possession against Mrs Johnson.[227]

Cheshire and Burn's Modern Law of Real Property (17th edn, 2006), pp. 847–849

In the 1950s there grew up the concept of the deserted wife's licence. A husband who deserted his wife could not turn her out of the home, even though he owned it. And this protection was extended through a series of cases[228] to protect the deserted wife against third parties to whom the home might be transferred. This situation created conveyancing complications, and the doctrine was disapproved by the House of Lords in *National Provincial Bank Ltd v Ainsworth* in 1965,[229] on the ground that the wife held no proprietary interest recognized by the law. The deserted wife was thus left unprotected against third parties. The criticism which followed led to the registration of a deserted wife's 'right of occupation' under the Matrimonial Homes Act 1967 (now Family Law Act 1996).[230]

---

[227] See *Bristol & West Building Society v Henning* [1985] 1 WLR 778 at 783, where Browne-Wilkinson LJ said: 'Nothing in this judgment should be taken as expressing any view on the questions… whether the decision in *Re Sharpe* was correct.'

[228] *Bendall v McWhirter* [1952] 2 QB 466; *Ferris v Weaven* [1952] 2 All ER 233; *Street v Denham* [1954] 1 WLR 624; *Lee v Lee* [1952] 2 QB 489n; *Jess B Woodcock & Son Ltd v Hobbs* [1955] 1 WLR 152; *Westminster Bank Ltd v Lee* [1956] Ch 7; *Miles v Bull* [1969] 1 QB 258.

[229] [1965] AC 1175 [p. 1002, above]. See also *Hall v King* [1987] 2 EGLR 121 where Sir John Donaldson MR said at 122: 'A wife's right to occupy the matrimonial home is of a very special nature, depending upon her status as a wife and not upon any leave or licence of her husband… This accords with common sense and experience. Whoever heard of a husband expressly or impliedly saying to his wife "Do come and stay with me in the matrimonial home, dear".'

[230] [P. 602, above.]

The problem presented in *National Provincial Bank Ltd v Ainsworth* is a very real one in the context of the conveyancing system, and is relevant throughout the law of licences. One basic principle of the 1925 legislation was to provide for the documentation of all dealings with the legal estate and for equities and equitable interests to be either overreachable or registrable. The principle is all the more obvious with registered land, when the intention is to record everything except overriding interests. From a conveyancer's point of view, these are good principles, but the system has not remained intact either in the case of unregistered land,[231] or in the case of registered land because of the wide provision for the protection of overriding interests of a person in actual occupation of the land.[232] A very significant inroad into these principles of conveyancing is found in the modern development of licences. If the licence has a sufficiently proprietary quality that it can bind a third party, then, even where only negative protection is given to the licensee,[233] a purchaser is faced with the interest of the licensee as a blot on his title. The licensee may be in possession, and the purchaser may thus have what would be considered to be constructive notice under the pre-1926 cases.[234] But these rules are now taken over by provisions for registration, and licences are not registrable under the Land Charges Act 1925. Indeed, it would be a disaster for the licensee if they were; for many of the licence situations arise in connection with personal family affairs, without legal advice, and as a matter of practice would hardly ever be registered; and, further, if they were registrable and not registered, they would in unregistered land be void even against a purchaser who actually knew of the licence.

The difficulties are even greater where the licensee receives an award of an undocumented proprietary interest or estate. Once the case has been determined, the proper documentation can be prepared, but the licensee's protection cannot depend upon the trial of the action. The protection is given in equity, and not by the court's decision; and, as we have seen,[235] it has been recognised that an equity arising by estoppel has a sufficiently proprietary quality to bind the purchaser before the court's decision if (in unregistered land) he has notice of it or (in registered land) it is protected by notice or as an overriding interest. And it is not at all clear whether the purchaser can overreach the equity.[236] Before 1997 there was a particular danger attached to the court's decision to award the licensee a life interest, since it was arguable that the licensee would thereby become a tenant for life under the Settled Land Act 1925. The point was first noticed by Scott LJ in *Bannister v Bannister*,[237] a case decided on the theory of constructive trust. The point was overlooked in many of the licence cases.[238] The view has been expressed that the Settled Land Act 1925 would not apply.[239] Russell LJ,

---

[231] *E R Ives Investment Ltd v High* [1967] 2 QB 379 (proprietary estoppel) [p. 1074, above]; *Poster v Slough Estates Ltd* [1969] 1 Ch 495 (right of entry to remove a fixture on termination of lease); *Caunce v Caunce* [1969] 1 WLR 286; *Kingsnorth Finance Co Ltd v Tizard* [1986] 1 WLR 783 [p. 216, above] (beneficial interest of wife who had contributed towards purchase price); *Shiloh Spinners Ltd v Harding* [1973] AC 691 [p. 68, above] (equitable right of entry on breach of covenant).

[232] LRA 1925, s. 70(1)(*g*); *Hodgson v Marks* [1971] Ch 892; *Williams and Glyn's Bank Ltd v Boland* [1981] AC 487 [p. 203, above]; LRA 2002, s. 29, Sch. 3, para. 2; s. 116.

[233] *Inwards v Baker* [1965] 2 QB 29.   [234] *Hunt v Luck* [1901] 1 Ch 45.

[235] [Pp. 1072–1077, above.]

[236] [P. 1077, above.]

[237] [1948] 2 All ER 133 [p. 1101, above].

[238] Cf. *Inwards v Baker*, above.

[239] *Binions v Evans* [1972] Ch 359 at 366, per Lord Denning MR (unintended settlement) [p. 1102, above]. See also *Ivory v Palmer* [1975] ICR 340 at 347, where Cairns LJ said '*Binions v Evans* stretched to the very limit the application of the Settled Land Act'. See (1977) 93 LQR 561 (J. A. Hornby).

on the other hand, noted in *Dodsworth v Dodsworth*,[240] that the award of a life interest would 'lead, by virtue of the provisions of the Settled Land Act, to a greater and more extensive interest than was ever contemplated by the plaintiff and the defendants'. Since the Trusts of Land and Appointment of Trustees Act 1996 came into force on 1 January 1997,[241] however, settlements can no longer be created under the Settled Land Act 1925, and so the award of a life interest no longer gives the licensee a statutory fee simple and the wide powers of a tenant for life. However, an even more serious problem arises for the purchaser where a fee simple is awarded to the licensee, as in *Pascoe v Turner*.[242] The licensor holds the legal estate, and the licensee has an equity entitling him to the fee simple: he is the equitable owner.[243] In registered land the licensee in actual occupation who had not protected his interest by a notice in the register would be held to have an overriding interest,[244] and therefore the purchaser is bound by the equity and liable to be deprived of his title—and without any way of having been able to determine with certainty at the time of his purchase what rights were held by the licensee, given the inchoate nature of the equity before the court order. In unregistered land the old principle of notice presumably applies;[245] and its application must be particularly difficult where, as in *Pascoe v Turner*, the licensee had not the slightest idea that she was entitled to a fee simple.

QUESTIONS

1. Is a licence protected by proprietary estoppel an interest in land? Can it be sold? Does it pass with the land? Is it assignable? See *Hamilton v Geraghty* (1901) 1 SR NSW Eq 81; *Lands Comr v Hussein* [1968] EA 585; (1969) ASCL 354 (E. H. Burn); *ER Ives Ltd v High* [1967] 2 QB 379 at 395; *Cameron v Murdoch* [1983] WAR 321 at 360; affd (1986) 63 ALR 575 at 595.

2. Consider the solutions reached in the various cases in Section D (proprietary estoppel), and compare them with those reached in Sections B (contractual licences) and C (constructive trust).

3. To what extent is a licensee's right to protection affected by his conduct (*a*) before and (*b*) after his licence is established? Why are contractual licences and licences protected by estoppel treated differently? See *Thompson v Park* [1944] KB 408; *Ivory v Palmer* [1975] ICR 340; *Williams v Staite* [1979] Ch 291; [1986] Conv 405 (M. P. Thompson); *Brynowen Estates Ltd v Bourne* (1981) 131 NLJ 1212; *Willis & Son v Willis* [1986] 1 EGLR 62; *Gonthier v Orange Contract Scaffolding Ltd* [2003] All ER (D) 331 (Jun); *Manton Securities Ltd v Nazam* [2008] EWCA Civ 805, [2008] 2 P & CR DG19; Dawson and Pearce, pp. 223–224.

---

[240] (1973) 228 EG 1115 [p. 1068, above].

[241] [Chap. 6, above.]

[242] [1979] 1 WLR 431; p. 1056, above.

[243] *Voyce v Voyce* (1991) 62 P & CR 290 at 294, per Dillon LJ.

[244] LRA 2002, s. 30, Sch. 3, para. 2, replacing LRA 1925, s. 70(1)(g) [pp. 183, 196, above].

[245] *E R Ives Investment Ltd v High* [1967] 2 QB 379 [p. 1074, above].

4. Before the Trusts of Land and Appointment of Trustees Act 1996 the courts were reluctant to allow an estoppel licence to create a settlement: *Dodsworth v Dodsworth* (1973) 228 EG 1115, p. 1068, above; *Griffiths v Williams* (1997) 248 EG 947, p. 1061, above. Even though no new strict settlements can be created after 1996 (p. 516, above), are there circumstances in which the courts might still be reluctant to satisfy an equity in favour of a licensee by granting a licence for life? *Matharu v Matharu* (1994) 68 P & CR 93; *Dent v Dent* [1996] 1 WLR 683; [1996] All ER Rev 258 (P. J. Clarke).

5. Do you think that Parliament should intervene to give protection to a licensee for life? See the statutory protection given in Ireland: Republic of Ireland Registration of Title Act 1964, s. 81; Northern Ireland Land Registration Act 1970, s. 47; (1970) 21 NILQ 389 (B. W. Harvey); Wylie, *Irish Land Law* (2nd edn, 1986) paras 20.15–20.19; Law Commission Working Paper No. 94 on Trusts of Land (1985), paras 16.6–16.18.

INDEX